CASTLES OF STEEL

BY THE SAME AUTHOR

Nicholas and Alexandra

Peter the Great

Dreadnought

The Romanovs

Journey (coauthor)

CASTLES OF STEEL

Britain, Germany, and the Winning of the Great War at Sea

ROBERT K. MASSIE

Jonathan Cape
London

Published by Jonathan Cape 2004

6 8 10 9 7 5

First published in Great Britain in 2004 by
Jonathan Cape
Random House, 20 Vauxhall Bridge Road, London SW1V 2SA

Random House Australia (Pty) Limited
20 Alfred Street, Milsons Point, Sydney,
New South Wales 2061, Australia

Random House New Zealand Limited
18 Poland Road, Glenfield,
Auckland 10, New Zealand

Random House South Africa (Pty) Limited
Endulini, 5A Jubilee Road, Parktown 2193, South Africa

The Random House Group Limited Reg. No. 954009
www.randomhouse.co.uk

Book design by J. K. Lambert
Map illustrations by David Lindroth

A CIP catalogue record for this book is available from the British Library

ISBN 0-224-04092-8

Papers used by Random House are natural, recyclable products made from wood grown in sustainable forests; the manufacturing processes conform to the environmental regulations of the country of origin

Printed and bound in Great Britain by
Clays Ltd, St Ives PLC

For Deborah, Christopher, Sophia, and Nora

All nations want peace,

but they want a peace that suits them.

ADMIRAL SIR JOHN FISHER

Contents

Maps

CASTLES OF STEEL

CHAPTER 1

July 1914

On an afternoon in early July 1914, a middle-aged man with restless, bright blue eyes and curly, iron-gray hair boarded his yacht in the German Baltic harbor of Kiel, and the following morning departed on his annual summer cruise to the fjords of Norway. Two unusual and striking features marked the vacationing traveler: one of these he was eager to display; the other he was even more anxious to conceal. The first was his famous brushy mustache with its extended, upturned points, the creation of a skillful barber who worked on it every morning with a can of wax. The other, hidden from sight, but all the more noticeable for that, was his left arm, three inches shorter than the right. This misfortune was the result of an extraordinarily difficult breech delivery performed without anesthesia on his eighteen-year-old mother, Princess Victoria of England. He was unable to raise his left arm, and the fingers on his left hand were paralyzed. Every doctor had been consulted, every treatment attempted; nothing worked. Now, the useless hand was gloved and carried in his pocket, or placed at rest on the hilt of a sword or a dagger. At meals, a special one-piece knife-and-fork set was always placed next to his plate. To compensate for the helplessness of his left arm, he had developed the right to an unusual degree. He always wore large jeweled rings on his right hand; sometimes, grasping a welcoming hand so hard that the rings bit and the owner winced, the hand shaker said merrily, "Ha ha! The mailed fist! What!"

There were two sides to the traveler's behavior. He was a man of wide reading, impressive although shallow knowledge, a remarkable memory for facts, and, when he wished, amiability and charm. He had a strong, clear voice and spoke equally well in German and English although his English had the slightest trace of an accent and when he resorted to English slang, which he liked to do, he frequently got it wrong. He "talks with great energy," said an Englishwoman who saw him often, "and has a habit of thrusting his face forward and wagging his finger when he wishes to be emphatic." "If he laughs," said an English statesman who knew him, "which he is sure to do a good many times, he will laugh with absolute abandonment, throwing back his head, opening his mouth to the fullest extent possible, shaking his whole body and often stamping with one foot to show his excessive enjoyment of any joke." His moods changed quickly. He could be expansive and cheery one day, irritable and strident the next. His sensitivity to suspected slights was acute, and rejection turned him quickly to arrogance and menace. Remarkably, he could switch between personalities like an actor. He had complete control of his facial expressions. In public, he tightened his features into a glowering mask and presented himself as the lofty, monarchical figure his rank proclaimed. Other times, he allowed his face to relax and a softer, milder expression appeared, one indicating courtesy and affability—sometimes even gentleness.

This complicated, difficult, and afflicted person was Kaiser William II, the German emperor and Supreme War Lord of the most powerful military and industrial state in Europe.

The imperious side of William II's character was the handiwork of Otto von Bismarck, the Iron Chancellor and creator of the German empire, who inflamed the young prince in his youth with the glory of monarchy. Astride a white horse, wearing the white cuirassier uniform of the Imperial Guard and a shining brass helmet crested with a golden Hohenzollern eagle, William saw himself as an embodiment of the divine right of kings. "We Hohenzollerns derive our crowns from Heaven alone and we are answerable only to Heaven," he announced, adding that God was "our old ally who has taken so much trouble over our homeland and dynasty." *Ich und Gott* were the two rulers of Germany, he declared, sometimes forgetting who was answerable to whom. "You have sworn loyalty to Me," he once told a group of new army recruits. "That means, children of My guard, that you . . . have given yourself to Me, body and soul. . . . It may come to pass that I shall command you to shoot your own relatives, brothers, yes, parents—which God forbid—but even then you must follow My command without a murmur." He drew surprising historical analogies. In 1900, sending a contingent of German troops to China at the time of the Boxer Rebellion, he shouted to the departing soldiers, "There will be no quarter, no prisoners will be taken! As a thousand years ago, the Huns under King Attila gained for themselves a name which still stands for terror in tradition and story, so may the name of German be impressed by you for a thousand years on China."

—

Englishman and German, yachtsman and medieval warlord, bumptious vulgarian and representative of the Deity: William never quite determined who he was. He changed his mind with bewildering frequency, but, in the opinion of his former chancellor, Bernhard von Bülow, the kaiser was "not false but fickle. He was a weathercock whose direction at any given moment very largely depended on the people with whom he happened to associate." Albert Ballin, who built the Hamburg-America Line into the largest steamship company in the world, would always say, "Whenever I have to go and see the emperor, I always try and find out whom he's just been with, because then I know exactly what he's thinking."

—

Despite her gold and white paintwork ("gleaming swan plumage," one passenger called it), the top-heavy *Hohenzollern,* with her ram bow and bell-mouthed funnels, was the unloveliest royal yacht in Europe. Her navigation officer, Erich Raeder,* described her as a "lumbering monstrosity . . . [that] rolled in rough weather to a point uncomfortable even for old sailors. Her watertight integrity would not have met the safety requirements of even an ordinary passenger ship." None of this troubled the kaiser, who used her only in the Baltic, the North Sea, and the Mediterranean, never in the heavier seas of the North Atlantic. In any case, his cruises to Norway were spent mostly at anchor in a spectacular fjord. There, surrounded by sparkling blue water, granite cliffs and dark green forests, plunging waterfalls wreathed in mist, and patches of sloping meadow dotted with farmhouses, William felt completely at ease. Some rules were always observed—no one ever spoke to the kaiser unless he had spoken first—but now, at fifty-five, he was more mature and composed than the youthful Prince Hal of a quarter century before. When he embarked on the first of his all-male yachting trips to Norway, taking with him a dozen friends whom he referred to as his "brother officers," the atmosphere resembled that of a rowdy junior officers' mess. By 1914, the atmosphere had become more correct, but the guest list remained all male. William's wife, Empress Augusta, whom he called Dona, remained in Berlin. "I don't care for women," he said. "Women should stay home and look after their children."

The kaiser's day on the yacht was rigidly scheduled: mild exercises before breakfast; in good weather, an hour in his small sailboat; in the afternoons, shore excursions or rowing contests between the crews of the *Hohenzollern* and the escorting cruiser *Rostock*. These activities, however, were not allowed to interfere with the kaiser's afternoon nap. To get the most from this hour and a half of rest, William always removed all of his clothing and got into

*Raeder would become a Grand Admiral and Commander-in-Chief of the German navy in World War II.

bed. "There's nothing like getting in between two clean, cold sheets," he declared. At seven, the company sat down to dinner, where the kaiser drank only orange juice sipped from a silver goblet. Every evening after dinner, the party gathered in the smoking room. This summer, along with songs and card games, William and his guests listened to lectures on the American Civil War.

—

William's love of yachting—like his decision to build a powerful navy—had roots in his English heritage. His mother, who had married the Prussian Crown Prince Friedrich, was Queen Victoria's eldest daughter; William was the queen's eldest grandchild. He considered the British royal family to be *his* family; when he was angry at his British relatives, he described them as "the damned family." He always held his grandmother in awe; Uncle Bertie, the Prince of Wales and future King Edward VII, stirred mixed feelings. William sensed—correctly—that Bertie saw him as bothersome and looked down on him as a parvenu. This duality in William's life—Prussia versus England, Bismarck versus Queen Victoria—warred within him constantly and affected the face he turned toward the public. Indeed, the split personality of Imperial Germany was almost perfectly mirrored by the personality of the kaiser: one moment, warm, sentimental, and outgoing; the next, blustering, threatening, and vengeful.

William measured culture, sophistication, and fashion by English yardsticks. His highest approbation was reserved for the Royal Navy. In his memoirs, he wrote, "I had a peculiar passion for the navy. It sprang to no small extent from my English blood." For William, the appeal of Osborne House, Queen Victoria's seaside palace on the Isle of Wight, was that Portsmouth, the premier base of the Royal Navy, was only five miles away across the Solent. "When as a little boy I was allowed to visit Portsmouth and Plymouth hand in hand with kind aunts and friendly admirals, I admired the proud English ships in those two superb harbors. Then there awoke in me the wish to build ships of my own like these someday and when I was grown up to possess as fine a navy as the English." When he was ten, William boarded the new Prussian armored frigate *König Wilhelm.*

> Heavy on the water lay the ironclad hull of this colossus from whose gun ports a row of massive guns looked menacingly forth. I gazed speechless on this mighty ship towering far above us. Suddenly shrill whistles resounded from her and immediately hundreds of sailors swarmed up the sky-high rigging. Three cheers greeted my father [Crown Prince Friedrich, heir to the Prussian throne]. . . . The tour of the ship . . . revealed to me an entirely new world . . . massive rigging . . . the long tier of guns with their heavy polished muzzles . . . tea and all sorts of rich cakes in the admiral's cabin.

Once he became kaiser and long before he had a significant navy of his own, William took up yachting. Every August between 1889 and 1895, he appeared at Cowes on the Isle of Wight for Regatta Week, for which hundreds of large sailing yachts gathered from all over the world. Moored before the esplanade of the Royal Yacht Squadron, they stretched into the distance, their varnished masts gleaming in the sunlight. William loved the elegance and excitement he found at Cowes. When his own steam yacht entered the harbor, Royal Navy vessels offered a twenty-one-gun salute, and hundreds of private yachts and other anchored craft dipped their pennants. The queen always gave a banquet at Osborne House; the Prince of Wales entertained at the Royal Yacht Club. William began to race, commissioning one after another huge sailing yachts all named *Meteor,* the later versions specifically designed to defeat Uncle Bertie's *Britannia*. When they succeeded and their owner loudly trumpeted his victories, the Prince of Wales abandoned the sport. "The Regatta used to be a pleasant relaxation for me," he told a German diplomat in London, "but now, since the kaiser takes command, it is a vexation." Sadly, whatever William said or did to make himself agreeable in England, Britons from the top down instinctively disliked him. William was aware of the low esteem in which he was held; once, when the South African empire builder Cecil Rhodes was visiting Berlin, William said to him, "Now, Rhodes, tell me why is it that I am not popular in England? What can I do to make myself popular?" Rhodes replied, "Suppose you just try doing nothing." The kaiser frowned, then burst out laughing and slapped Rhodes on the back.

William had outlived two British monarchs: his grandmother and his uncle. His attitude toward their successor, his younger cousin King George V, was patronizing. "[George] is a very nice boy and a thorough Englishman who hates all foreigners," he said to Theodore Roosevelt. "But I don't mind as long as he does not hate Germans worse than other foreigners." Toward George's look-alike cousin, Tsar Nicholas II, the kaiser's patronizing took on a domineering tone. William liked to remind Nicholas that it had been "my good fortune to be able to help you secure that charming angel who is your wife." (Empress Alexandra of Russia was born in the Rhineland grand duchy of Hesse-Darmstadt.) The kaiser addressed his letters to "Dearest Nicky," closing them "Your affectionate Willy." Behind Nicholas's back, the kaiser was writing that "the tsar is only fit to live in a country house and grow turnips."

—

For most of its history, the military kingdom of Prussia had shown no interest in the sea. It possessed no major commercial harbor, and most of its seacoast was a stretch of shallow bays and dunes on the Baltic. This deficiency was partially rectified in 1854, when Prussia persuaded the Grand Duke of Oldenburg to sell a five-square-mile plot on Jade Bay; there, over the next fifteen years, the North Sea naval base of Wilhelmshaven was constructed. In 1869, the Prussian navy acquired the 9,700-ton ironclad *König Wilhelm,* then one of the largest warships in the world. This ship, built in England at the Thames Iron Works, remained Prussia's and Germany's largest warship for twenty-five years. During the Franco-Prussian War, however, the *König Wilhelm,* along with Germany's other three ironclads, remained at anchor, forbidden to fight against the overwhelming strength of the French naval squadrons blockading the German coast. Even so, French supremacy at sea did nothing to save France and Napoleon III from swift defeat by the Prussian army. The fact that sea power had made no difference confirmed a traditional belief of the German General Staff; therefore, during the first sixteen years of Bismarck's newly proclaimed German empire, the German navy was commanded by generals who considered warships useful only for coastal defense.

From the beginning of his reign, William II was determined that this would change and that Germany would have a navy commensurate with its new military and industrial power. Beginning in the 1890s, the German population and industrial base exploded upward. Between 1891 and 1914, the Reich's population soared from 49 million to 67 million. In 1890, German coal production was half of Britain's; by 1913, the two were equal. In 1890, German steel production was two-thirds of Britain's; in 1896, it first exceeded Britain's; in 1914, Germany produced more than twice as much steel as Great Britain. It was the same in almost every field. Rapid urbanization; the growth of railways; the proliferation of blast furnaces, rolling mills, and factory chimneys; the development of chemical, electrical, and textile industries; the rise of the world's second largest merchant fleet; and booming foreign trade and overseas investments—these combined to create a state that economically as well as militarily dominated the European continent. William was not content. He was embarrassed by the mediocrity of Germany's small, scattered colonial empire; he wanted to expand German influence around the globe, to achieve world power, *Weltmacht.* For this purpose, he needed a navy—not just a few ships to defend Germany's coast, but a world navy. "Our future is on the seas," he told his people. "We must seize the trident." This was William's obsession, but it took him nine years to find the man who could give him what he wanted.

In time, the massive figure of Grand Admiral Alfred von Tirpitz, with his bald, domed head and his famous forked beard, became instantly recognizable in Germany. The creator of the German navy, Tirpitz was its state secretary (cabinet minister) for twenty years; after Bismarck, he was the most influential government official in Imperial Germany. Like William II, he admired and envied the Royal Navy. During his years as a cadet, Prussia's small fleet had spent as much time in Britain as at home. "Between 1864 and 1870," Tirpitz wrote, "our real supply base was Plymouth. Here we felt ourselves almost more at home than in peaceful and idyllic Kiel. In the Navy Hotel at Plymouth we were treated like British midshipmen. We preferred to get our supplies from England and in those days we could not imagine that German guns could be equal to British." Tirpitz's admiration extended to English education and the English language. He spoke English, read English newspapers and English novels, and enrolled his two daughters at Cheltenham Ladies' College.

Tirpitz believed that sea power was a critical factor in national prosperity and greatness. In this, he was a disciple of the American naval officer Alfred Thayer Mahan, who, in *The Influence of Sea Power upon History,* published in 1890, had traced the rise and fall of maritime powers in the past and demonstrated that in every case, the state that controlled the seas controlled its own fate; states deficient in naval power were doomed to decline. Britain now had a world empire because she was the preeminent sea power; the lesson for Tirpitz was that if Germany wished to pursue *Weltmacht,* only possession of a powerful navy, with a strong force of battleships at its core, could make it possible. When the kaiser appointed Tirpitz state secretary in 1897, "the German navy," the admiral wrote later, "was a collection of experiments in shipbuilding surpassed in exoticism only by the Russian Navy." He worked quickly; on March 26, 1898, the Reichstag passed the First Navy Bill, authorizing construction of nineteen battleships and eight armored cruisers. On June 14, 1901, the Second Navy Bill was approved, doubling the projected size of the fleet to thirty-eight battleships and twenty armored cruisers. This achievement so delighted the kaiser that he raised the state secretary into the hereditary Prussian nobility: Alfred Tirpitz became Alfred von Tirpitz. Subsequent amendments to the Navy Laws increased the planned size of the fleet to forty-one battleships.

As the new German battleships slid down the ways, and his fleet became the second largest in the world, William's pride soared. He had always loved uniforms; now he had a closet filled only with naval uniforms. When his grandmother made him an honorary admiral in the Royal Navy, his delight was transcendent. "Fancy wearing the same uniform as St. Vincent and Nelson," he burbled to the British ambassador, and to the queen he wrote, "I now am able to feel and take an interest in your fleet as if it were my own and with keenest sympathy shall I watch every phase of its further development." By 1914, he had become not only a Grand Admiral of the Imperial German Navy, but also an admiral in the Imperial Russian Navy, in the British Royal Navy, and in the royal navies of Sweden, Norway, and Denmark. Once he received the British ambassador in the uniform of an English Admiral of the Fleet; another time, he attended a performance of *The Flying Dutchman* in his uniform as an admiral. Frivolous, even ludicrous, as these episodes seem, they provide a key to the purpose of the building of the German navy. It was designed not only to project German power and influence overseas, but also to reinforce William's confidence and ego in the presence of his English relatives. "It never even occurred to William II to go to war against England," said Bernhard von Bülow, who was chancellor of Germany for nine years of William's reign.

> What William II most desired and imagined for the future was to see himself, at the head of a glorious German fleet, starting out on a peaceful visit to England. The English sovereign, with his fleet, would meet the German kaiser in Portsmouth. The two fleets would file past each other; the two monarchs, each wearing the naval uniform of the other's country, would then stand on the bridges of their flagships. Then, after they had embraced in the prescribed manner, a gala dinner with lovely speeches would be held in Cowes.

This was not how the new German navy was seen in Great Britain. To Britons, sea power was life and death. When the world's strongest military power began building a battle fleet rivaling that of the greatest sea power, the British government and people asked themselves the reason. Arthur Balfour, a former prime minister, writing for German readers, tried to explain: "Without a superior fleet, Britain would no longer count as a power. Without any fleet at all, Germany would remain the greatest power in Europe." His words made no difference and, with more and more German dreadnoughts accumulating every year and a formidable German fleet now concentrated only a few hours' steaming time from England's North Sea coast, the British government began to shift away from a century of "Splendid Isolation." As the apparent danger across the North Sea mounted, old enmities and rivalries were composed, old frictions smoothed, and new arrangements made. Between 1904 and 1908, Britain became, if not a full-fledged ally, at least a partner of her erstwhile enemies France and Russia. And with the birth of the Entente, the kaiser and Tirpitz discovered that they had achieved the opposite of what they had intended. Instead of expanding German power, the rise of the new navy had pushed Great Britain into the camp of Germany's antagonists. Germany had a shaky partner in Italy, a member of the creaking Triple Alliance (which also included Austria), but this did not prevent the kaiser from complaining that the fatherland was encircled by enemies. To face this threat, he believed, Germany could count on only a single loyal ally.

—

Loyal, but on the verge of disintegration. The Dual Monarchy of Austria-Hungary, a multiethnic empire ruled by Austrians and Hungarians but whose population was three-fifths Slav, was crumbling. The emperor Franz Josef was too old to arrest this decomposition; a bald little gentleman with bushy muttonchop whiskers, he was eighty-four in 1914 and already had sat on the Hapsburg throne for sixty-eight years. During that time, his wife, Empress Elizabeth, had been assassinated; his brother, Emperor Maximilian of Mexico, had been executed by a firing squad; his only son, Crown Prince Rudolf, had committed suicide; and now his nephew, Archduke Franz Ferdinand, the new heir to the throne, had also been assassinated. Politically, the most flagrant cause of his current troubles was the small, independent Slav kingdom of Serbia, which acted as a magnet on the restless populations of Austria's South Slav provinces. Many in the Austrian government and army believed that the polyglot empire could save itself only by crushing the "dangerous little Serbian viper." But a preventive war against Slav Orthodox Serbia meant confronting Serbia's protector and ally, Slav Orthodox Russia. And Austria, in 1914, was too weak to confront Russia without German support.

Fortunately for Vienna, by 1914 the German government considered the continued existence of the creaking Hapsburg empire vital to Germany's position. Not every German was convinced; as late as May 1914, Heinrich von Tschirschky, the kaiser's ambassador in Vienna, cried out, "I constantly wonder whether it really pays to bind ourselves so tightly to this phantasm of a state which is cracking in every direction." But then the specter of encirclement rose up: if Austria disintegrated, Germany would face France and Russia alone. This mutual dependence—of Austria on Germany and Germany on Austria—was well understood in Vienna, and the Hapsburg monarchy was thoroughly prepared to exploit the German predicament. In fact, Vienna was not required to beg for German support. For months, the kaiser, at his strutting, bellicose worst, had encouraged Austria to take action against Serbia. "The Slavs were born to serve and not to rule," William told the Austrian foreign minister during a visit to Vienna in October 1913. "If His Majesty the Emperor Franz Joseph makes a demand, the Serbian government must obey. If not, Belgrade must be bombarded and occupied until his will is fulfilled. And you may rest assured that I stand behind you and am ready to draw the sword." As he spoke, the kaiser placed his right hand on the hilt of his sword.

The assassination in Sarajevo of Franz Ferdinand and his wife by a Bosnian Serb provided the pretext Austria needed. The assassin belonged to a secret Serb organization, the Black Hand, whose objective was to detach Bosnia and other Slav provinces from the Hapsburg empire and incorporate them into a Greater Serbia. The Serbian government was not involved, but the assassin had connections with Serbian police officials and his revolver had come from the Serbian State Arsenal. Sympathy for Austria was universal in Europe. "Terrible shock for the dear old emperor," King George V wrote in his diary. Everyone expected some form of reckoning; Austria's purpose was to enlarge the punishment into the demolition of the Serbian state. But behind Serbia stood Russia. Accordingly, an Austrian decision for war was contingent on a German promise to bar Russian intervention. On July 5, the Austrian ambassador in Berlin officially asked the kaiser what Germany's position would be in the event of an Austrian-Serbian war. William understood the underlying question and replied that he did not believe that Russia would enter; he doubted that the tsar would place himself on the side of "a savage, regicide state." Nevertheless, he said that Germany would stand by Vienna whatever decision was made. "Should a war between Austria-Hungary and Russia be unavoidable," the ambassador reported the kaiser as saying, "we might be convinced that Germany, our old faithful ally, would stand at our side." This statement was the famous "blank check" by which the Supreme War Lord of the German empire gave his ally permission to strike down Serbia. If Russia interfered, there would be a German war against Russia. And, if that happened, the German war plan dictated that Germany also fight Russia's ally France. That Britain might become involved seemed so unlikely, so unthinkable, that it was never discussed. Meanwhile, holding the "blank check," Austrian diplomats began drafting an ultimatum to Belgrade so severe in its demands that "the possibility of its acceptance is practically excluded."

—

William, before leaving on his vacation, had asked whether, in view of the crisis, he should postpone or even cancel his cruise to the Norwegian fjords. For the same reason, he suggested that perhaps the High Seas Fleet should give up its summer exercises in the North Sea. The chancellor, Theobald von Bethmann-Hollweg, was adamant; both the kaiser and the fleet should proceed; sudden cancellations would only alarm an already nervous Europe. The politicians and the army saw no risk of trouble with Britain, but the Naval Staff believed that to send the fleet out of German waters at a time of international tension was risky. During the Norwegian cruise, the fleet would sometimes be divided, with separate squadrons visiting different ports. This scattering would leave the fleet vulnerable to a surprise British attack; German naval officers had never forgotten that a sudden peacetime attack on the German fleet to destroy it before it was fully developed had been publicly advocated in England by no less a figure than Admiral Sir John Fisher, the builder of the modern British navy. And, the Naval Staff noted, just when the German fleet was in Norway, the British fleet, mobilized and concentrated for a review by the king, would be unusually well prepared for such an attack. These concerns were overruled by the chancellor and on July 10, three days after the kaiser's departure, the German High Seas Fleet sailed to conduct exercises in the Skagerrak and off the coast of Norway.

Aboard the *Hohenzollern,* the first two weeks of the cruise passed in a holiday mood while the Balkan crisis remained in the background. On July 14, William sent a generalized well-wishing message to Emperor Franz Josef, assuring the old monarch that he was ready to fulfill his "joyful duty" by supporting Austria against the Serbs. The kaiser was sharper with his own Foreign Office, counseling it to be firm because Serbia was not "a nation in the European sense, but only a band of robbers that must be seized for its crimes." On July 23, the day the Austrian ultimatum was delivered in Belgrade, there was tension on the yacht. The Naval Staff ordered Admiral Friedrich von Ingenohl, Commander-in-Chief of the High Seas Fleet, to bring his battle squadrons into Sogne Fjord where the *Hohenzollern* was anchored. The following day, Ingenohl recommended bringing the fleet home from Norway, but again, the chancellor overruled him, protesting that the fleet's recall would aggravate the crisis. On the afternoon of the twenty-fourth, William carried out his schedule, leading an excursion ashore to the village of Wik to visit its famous old wooden church. That day, no news regarding the reception of the ultimatum in Belgrade reached the *Hohenzollern.* Then, in the evening in the smoking room, the kaiser received a telegram that brought a flush to his cheeks. He laid it aside and continued to play cards.

The following day, July 25, the Norddeutsch wireless news service published the text of the Austrian ultimatum. After breakfast, the kaiser arrived on deck and said to Admiral Georg von Müller, Chief of the Naval Cabinet, who was holding the Norddeutsch message in his hand, "That's a pretty strong note." "It certainly is," Müller replied, "and it means war." William advised Müller not to worry, saying that Serbia would never risk a war. After his morning sail, the kaiser was handed a news agency bulletin reporting consternation in Belgrade and a Russian declaration that she could not remain disinterested. Amid excitement on the yacht, the kaiser gave orders to the High Seas Fleet, now coaling in Norwegian harbors, to prepare to sail for home. At ten a.m., the massive dreadnought *Friedrich der Grosse,* flagship of the High Seas Fleet, steamed into Sogne Fjord and anchored near the *Hohenzollern.* Admiral Ingenohl came on board the yacht where he found himself receiving an "operational briefing" by the Supreme War Lord. If war with Russia came, Ingenohl was to take the fleet to the Baltic and bombard and destroy the Russian Baltic ports of Reval and Libau. The admiral remained calm, knowing that if war came, the High Seas Fleet would not be used in the Baltic. "I received verbal orders from the kaiser," Ingenohl said later, "to take the fleet to the Baltic . . . to be able to strike the first blow against Russia in event of war. When I pointed out the danger of England taking part in the war, and the consequent necessity of having the battleships in the North Sea, the kaiser answered emphatically that there was no question whatever of England's intervention. In spite of repeated representations, I could only succeed in obtaining permission to send the various units to their home ports, thus enabling the larger proportion of the heavy ships and scouting craft to enter the North Sea."

Meanwhile, Müller and General Moritz Lyncker, Adjutant General to the kaiser and Chief of the Military Cabinet, agreed that William should break off the cruise. At 3:00 p.m., Müller on his own initiative ordered the captain of the yacht to get up steam. William was taking his usual afternoon nap and had asked to be called at 4:30, but Müller went to see him early and spoke to him while he was still in bed. "I explained the latest telegram from Belgrade, mentioned Lyncker's opinion, and advised him to sail for home at 6 o'clock. He reflected for a moment and replied, 'Very well. I agree. Can I go ashore for half an hour?' I said I had no objection to this and while the kaiser paid farewell visits, I settled details of the homeward voyage of the fleet which was arranged for the following evening."

At 6:00 p.m., the *Hohenzollern* weighed anchor. It was a calm, clear summer evening and, as the yacht sailed out of the Sogne Fjord, the kaiser stood on the bridge for a long time enjoying the tranquil picture of mountains and forests. Müller was with him. At one point, William insisted that there would be no war; that at the last moment the leaders of all states would shrink from that appalling responsibility. Serbia, he said, would accept the Austrian terms, and Vienna would be satisfied. Next morning, July 26, when the yacht reached the open sea, a heavy swell obliged closing all the hatches and forbidding passengers from going on deck. A telegram arrived from the chancellor, discreetly reproaching the kaiser for returning early and for ordering the fleet to return merely on the strength of a news agency report. William reacted angrily. "My fleet has orders to sail for Kiel," he said, "and to Kiel it is going to sail." After the war, the ex-kaiser remembered in his memoirs: "While I was on my summer vacation trip, I received but meager news from the Foreign Office and was obliged to rely principally on the Norwegian newspapers from which I received the impression that the situation was growing worse. I telegraphed repeatedly to the chancellor and the Foreign Office that I considered it advisable to return home but was asked each time not to interrupt my journey. When I learned from the Norwegian newspapers—*not from Berlin*—of the Austrian ultimatum to Serbia and immediately after the Serbian reply to Austria, I started upon my journey home without further ado."

On July 27, the *Hohenzollern* arrived at Kiel; a deeply tanned William stepped ashore and boarded his train for Potsdam. The next morning, he read the text of the Serbian reply to the Austrian ultimatum. Serbia had agreed to surrender almost every vestige of national sovereignty. So abject was the Serbian surrender that the kaiser declared that Austria had been given all she wanted. "A brilliant achievement at forty-eight hours' notice," he declared. "This is more than anyone could have expected. A great moral victory for Vienna . . . it [has] removed any reason for war." That afternoon, he received what seemed to be more good news from his younger brother, Prince Henry of Prussia. Two days before—on the twenty-sixth—Henry had come up to London from the yachting races at Cowes and had called on his cousin King George V at Buckingham Palace. "The news is very bad," the king had said. "It looks like war in Europe. You had better go back to Germany at once." Henry said he would go that evening and asked, "What will England do?" According to the king's notes, he said, "I don't know what we shall do. We have no quarrel with anyone and I hope we shall remain neutral. But if Germany declares war on Russia, and France joins Russia, then I am afraid we shall be dragged into it." Henry's version of George's answer was different: "We shall try all we can to keep out of this and shall remain neutral." Both men were honest. No doubt Henry heard what he wanted to hear—that Britain hoped to remain neutral—and did not attend to George's fear that, despite these hopes, Britain might become involved. "Well," said Prince Henry on leaving, "if our two countries will be fighting on opposite sides, I trust it will not affect our own personal friendship." Once he reached Berlin, Henry reported this conversation to his brother, who, in turn, seized on it as George V's promise to remain neutral. During the next few days, when men around the kaiser, most persistently Tirpitz, warned that England might come in, William—although fully aware that England was a constitutional monarchy, ruled by Parliament—said loftily, "I have the word of a king."

Meanwhile, on July 27, the High Seas Fleet returned to Kiel. On July 31, the German dreadnoughts were moving again, this time west through the Kiel Canal to the naval bases on the North Sea. The Naval Staff, concerned about England, had decided that the oldest German battleships and armored cruisers would be sufficient to deal with the Russians, who had lost most of their navy ten years before in the Russo-Japanese War. On August 1, Germany ordered general naval mobilization, but the kaiser and the chancellor still were certain that Britain would remain neutral.

—

For many years, summer maneuvers in the waters around the British Isles had been a regular feature of the Royal Navy's annual routine. In the summer of 1914, however, these maneuvers were canceled and replaced by a test mobilization of the British reserve fleet. This decision had nothing to do with the developing European crisis and stemmed from a conversation in October 1913 between Winston Churchill, the First Lord of the Admiralty, and Prince Louis of Battenberg, the First Sea Lord, in which the two men were discussing the need to save money. Churchill was under constant pressure from David Lloyd George, the Chancellor of the Exchequer, and other colleagues in the Liberal Cabinet to pare the enormous sums being spent on building dreadnoughts. The amount allotted to the navy in 1914, over £50 million, would be the largest disbursement of this kind in British history. One economizing measure—only a gesture, admittedly—would be to substitute a test mobilization of the Third Fleet, the reserve fleet, for the annual summer maneuvers. Cancellation of the maneuvers would save only a pittance—£100,000 worth of coal and oil burned—but at least the Admiralty would have made the gesture toward the Exchequer.

In March 1914, therefore, when Churchill presented the House of Commons with the yearly Naval Estimates (the Admiralty's annual budget request), he announced the change. The plan was to call back from civilian life twenty thousand men of the fleet reserve, man the Third Fleet's two squadrons of the navy's oldest predreadnought battleships, and place every vessel in the Royal Navy on a war footing. Once this was done, King George V would review the entire British fleet at Spithead; afterward, the ships would carry out brief exercises at sea and then disperse.

The fleets and ships involved varied greatly in power and readiness. The First Fleet, the core of British naval power, was built around three battle squadrons of modern dreadnoughts manned by regular navy crews and always ready for action. The Second Fleet, two battle squadrons of relatively recent predreadnought battleships with attendant smaller craft, needed only to collect its regular navy personnel from various naval training schools ashore. The Third Fleet's old ships, whose capabilities and readiness the mobilization was designed to test, were more or less permanently moored in quiet harbors and tended by skeleton maintenance crews. To make them ready for sea and turn them into fighting machines, thousands of naval reservists were now to be called up and brought aboard.

It was coincidence that the Royal Navy's test mobilization, determined as a matter of budgetary economy, occurred at a time of crisis in the Balkans. On July 10, as the Austrian Foreign Ministry was drafting its ultimatum to Serbia, thousands of British naval reservists began arriving at manning depots, where they were issued uniforms and boarded their assigned ships. By July 16, the Second and Third Fleets had sailed from their home ports to join the First Fleet for the royal review at Spithead, between Portsmouth and the Isle of Wight. On July 17, King George arrived and the First Lord, bursting with pride, presented the monarch with a fleet that Churchill declared to be "incomparably the greatest assemblage of naval power ever witnessed in the history of the world."

On Monday morning, July 20, the armada put to sea for exercises. Every ship was decked with flags, with bands playing and sailors and marines lining the rails. The fleet took six hours to pass the royal yacht, even steaming at fifteen knots. The next three days were spent in tactical exercises in the Channel. On July 23, the three fleets parted company. The ships of the Third Fleet began returning to their home ports to discharge their crews and lapse again into tranquillity. The First and Second Fleets moved to Portland harbor, where they were to remain until Monday morning, July 27. By noon that day, however, the harbor would be empty, the separate battle squadrons dispersed, some to begin gunnery exercises, others to release their crews on midsummer leave. The Second Fleet would return to its home ports to send its crews back to gunnery schools, torpedo schools, and other training establishments ashore. By Friday, some of the ships would be in dry dock for overhaul, others tied to quays for lesser repairs.

There seemed no reason not to return the fleet to peacetime status. Despite the tragedy at Sarajevo, Europe appeared calm. The kaiser had departed on his annual summer cruise in the Norwegian fjords. The president of France had departed on July 13 to visit St. Petersburg, the capital of France's principal ally, Russia. Accordingly, on July 23, at the conclusion of the naval exercises, Admiral Sir George Callaghan, Commander-in-Chief of the First Fleet, informed the Admiralty that he was ready to break up the fleet. The Admiralty replied: "First Fleet squadrons all disperse on Monday July 27 in accordance with your approved program."

But on Thursday, July 23, 1914, Austria handed her ultimatum to Serbia. Early on Friday, July 24, the British foreign secretary, Sir Edward Grey, received the text at the Foreign Office; he described it as "the most formidable document ever addressed from one state to another." Along with demands that would practically strip Serbia of its national sovereignty, it contained a forty-eight-hour time limit for Serbian acceptance. That afternoon, when Grey informed the British Cabinet, members listened dutifully but to most the crisis seemed far away. "Happily," Prime Minister H. H. Asquith wrote the king that evening, "there seems to be no reason why we should be anything more than spectators." Churchill decided to let the Royal Navy continue to stand down from its war footing and return the older ships to peacetime status.

Nevertheless, Admiral Callaghan was worried. When no steps had been taken on Saturday the twenty-fifth to halt the demobilization process, he reminded the Admiralty that if nothing was done, his fleet would be broken up on Monday. That Saturday morning, however, the crisis appeared to have eased, perhaps even passed, for word reached London that Serbia had accepted most of the Austrian terms. Asquith and members of the Cabinet promptly left the capital for the weekend. Churchill had rented a small holiday house, Pear Tree Cottage, at Cromer on the Norfolk coast for his wife and young children, who were already there. Leaving the First Sea Lord to keep watch at the Admiralty, Churchill reached his family on the one o'clock train. Prince Louis did not approve of the general exodus, complaining that "ministers with their weekend holidays are incorrigible." The next morning, Sunday the twenty-sixth, Churchill said, "I went down to the beach and played with the children. We dammed the little rivulets which trickled down to the sea as the tide went out. It was a very beautiful day. The North Sea shone and sparkled on the horizon." Twice that morning, at nine o'clock and again at noon, Churchill left the beach to walk to the house of a neighbor who owned a telephone. He called Prince Louis and learned in the first call that there were rumors that Austria might not accept Serbia's submission; at noon the First Sea Lord told him that Vienna had declared the Serbian response unsatisfactory, had severed diplomatic relations, and had ordered mobilization of the Austrian army. Emperor William was reported to be returning to Berlin, and the High Seas Fleet to be concentrating off the Norwegian coast. In this context, dispersing and demobilizing squadrons of the British navy seemed a grandly wrongheaded decision. Within hours, the naval reservists would have scattered; to mobilize them again would take time. But to arrest their discharge would be politically provocative. Churchill decided to return to London immediately. In the meantime he told Prince Louis that, as the man on the spot, he should "do whatever was necessary." By the time Churchill appeared at the Admiralty that evening, Prince Louis, on his own initiative, had signaled Callaghan: "No ships of the First Fleet or flotillas are to leave Portland until further orders." Ships of the Second Fleet were to remain at their home ports, in proximity to the men in their crews who were in schools. Churchill immediately approved everything the First Sea Lord had done.

For Admiral Callaghan, the order came at the eleventh hour. The core of his fleet, the dreadnought battle squadrons, was to disperse the following morning. Already, the dreadnought *Bellerophon* of the 4th Battle Squadron had been detached and was on her way to Gibraltar to refit in the dry dock there. Six of his cruisers, most of his destroyers, and all of his minesweepers were at their home ports with half their crews away on leave. Still, he was able to halt the dispersal before it went any further, and he began immediately to reassemble his fleet. From London, Captain Wilhelm Widenmann, the German naval attaché, who was closely monitoring these activities, telegraphed a report to Berlin:

> The British fleet is preparing for all eventualities. First Fleet is assembled at Portland. The ships of the Second Fleet are fully manned. The schools on shore have not reopened. Ships of the Second and Third Fleets have coaled, completed with ammunition and supplies. In consequence of the training of reservists, just completed, the latter can be manned more quickly than usual. The destroyer and patrol flotillas and the submarines are either at or en route to their stations. No leave is being granted; officers and men already on leave have been recalled. In the naval bases and dockyards, great activity reigns. Special measures of precaution have been adopted: all dockyards, magazines, oil tanks, etc., being put under guard. Repairs of ships in dockyard hands are being speeded up. A great deal of night work is being done. Outwardly, complete calm is preserved in order not to cause anxiety by alarming reports about the fleet. Movements of ships, which are gen-

erally published daily by the Admiralty, have been withheld since yesterday.*

Churchill and the navy were preparing for war, but most members of the British Cabinet still saw no great urgency. Tuesday, July 28, brought the danger closer. Austria categorically rejected the Serbian note, refused to negotiate, and declared war. In St. Petersburg, the Russian General Staff urged the tsar to mobilize the entire Russian army, but Nicholas II agreed to mobilize only the military districts on the border with Austria-Hungary. Churchill decided not to wait. The First Fleet must be moved to a place of safety; the Admiralty had only a vague idea of the whereabouts of the High Seas Fleet and worried about the vulnerability of the mass of ships in Portland harbor to surprise torpedo attack by German destroyers. Churchill's larger purpose was to ensure that the First Fleet (soon to be designated the Grand Fleet) should sail and be at its war station before Germany could know whether Britain would become an enemy "and therefore if possible before we had decided ourselves. . . . At 10 o'clock on Tuesday morning, I proposed this step to the First Sea Lord and Chief of Staff and found them whole-heartedly in favour of it. We decided that the fleet should leave Portland at such an hour on the morning of the 29th as to pass the Straits of Dover during the hours of darkness . . . at high speed, and without lights . . . and proceed to Scapa Flow." At 5:00 that evening, the order flashed from the radio masts atop the Admiralty to the signal mast of *Iron Duke:* "Tomorrow, Wednesday [July 29], the First Fleet is to leave Portland for Scapa Flow. Destination is to be kept secret except to flag and commanding officers." Callaghan was to send the fleet north under his second in command, Vice Admiral Sir George Warrender, so that he could travel himself to London in order to consult at the Admiralty. Even as Sir George Callaghan boarded a train for London, his dreadnoughts were moving out of Portland harbor, not to return for more than four years. No one has written a better description of this scene than Churchill himself:

> We may now picture this great fleet with its flotillas of cruisers steaming slowly out of Portland harbor, squadron by squadron, scores of gi-

*Widenmann's extensive information came from a network of minor spies, mostly British in German pay, operating in and around British naval bases. Their existence had been discovered three years earlier but, in a classic counterintelligence procedure, they were allowed to continue because, as Churchill realistically put it, "others of whom we might not have known would have taken their place. Left at large," Churchill continued, "we read their communications which we [then] regularly forwarded to their paymasters in Berlin. Up to this point, we had no objection to the German government knowing that exceptional precautions were being taken by the navy. But the moment had now come to draw down the curtain. . . . On a word from me, the Home Secretary laid by the heels all these petty traitors who for a few pounds a month were seeking to sell their country."

> gantic castles of steel wending their way across the misty, shining sea, like giants bowed in anxious thought. We may picture them again as darkness fell, eighteen miles of warships running at high speed and in absolute darkness through the narrow Straits, bearing with them into the broad waters of the North the safeguard of considerable affairs. The strategic concentration of the fleet had been accomplished with its transfer to Scottish waters. We were now in a position, whatever happened, to control events and it was not easy to see how this advantage could be taken from us. A surprise torpedo attack, before or simultaneous with a declaration of war, was at any rate one nightmare gone forever. If war should come, no one would know where to look for the British fleet. Somewhere in that enormous waste of waters to the north of our islands, cruising now this way, now that, shrouded in storms and mists, dwelt this mighty organization. Yet from the Admiralty building we could speak to them at any moment if need arose. The king's ships were at sea.

To dispatch the British fleet to its war station would send a dramatic diplomatic signal; for this reason, Churchill decided to keep the movement a secret not only from the Germans but also from the British Cabinet. Knowing that many members abhorred the idea of Britain becoming involved in what they considered a continental war, he later explained, "I feared to bring this matter before the Cabinet lest it should mistakenly be considered a provocative action likely to damage the chances of peace." His further argument was disingenuous: "It would be unusual to bring movements of the British fleet in home waters from one British port to another before the Cabinet. I only therefore informed the prime minister who at once gave his approval." In another account of the same meeting, Churchill wrote: "He [Asquith] looked at me with a hard stare and gave a sort of grunt. I did not require anything else."

By Thursday morning the deed was done and Churchill, pleased with himself, was able to share his pleasure. "We looked at each other with much satisfaction when on Thursday morning the 30th the flagship reported herself and the whole fleet well out in the center of the North Sea." Later that day, Churchill learned that Jacky Fisher had come into the Admiralty; he immediately invited the old admiral into his office. "I told him what we had done and his delight was wonderful to see," Churchill reported. The German ambassador, learning that the fleet had slipped away, lost no time in complaining to the Foreign Office. Coolly, Grey told him that "the movements of the fleet are free of all offensive character and the fleet will not approach German waters."

Even now, no one, including the British Cabinet and public, believed that Britain would become involved. The factor that did most to mislead the Continent was England's imperturbable calm. Bernhard von Bülow had noticed this serene detachment some years before, when he accompanied the kaiser on a visit to England:

> Many [British politicians] do not know much more of continental conditions than we do of the condition in Peru or Siam. They are also rather naive in their artless egoism. They find difficulty believing in really evil intentions in others; they are very calm, very phlegmatic, very optimistic. The country exudes wealth, comfort, content and confidence in its own power and future. The people simply cannot believe that things could ever go really wrong, either at home or abroad. With the exception of a few leading men, they work little and leave themselves time for everything.

Now England was enjoying the most beautiful August weather in many years. The holiday season had begun and the coming weekend would be prolonged by a bank holiday on Monday. Even as Russia, Austria, France, and Germany were mobilizing, English vacationers were flocking to the railway stations and the beaches. It was not surprising that foreign observers—the Germans hopefully and the French anxiously—concluded that Great Britain had determined to stand aside from the war about to engulf Europe.

—

Winston Churchill was confident that by sending the Grand Fleet into "the enormous waste of water to the north of our islands" he had guarded it against surprise attack; he worried, nonetheless, about its strength relative to that of the High Seas Fleet. On paper, the ratio of dreadnoughts—twenty-four to seventeen—looked reassuring. But for the First Lord, it was not enough. "There was not much margin here," he wrote later, "for mischance nor for the percentage of mechanical defects which in so large a fleet had to be expected." Providentially, the margin could be enlarged at a single decisive stroke. For years, British shipyards had been building warships for foreign navies. Sometimes, depending on the specifications required by the various admiralties, these ships were more powerful than vessels the same shipyard was building for Britain. In 1913, for example, Vickers completed *Kongo,* then the finest battle cruiser in the world, for Japan. Mounting ten 14-inch guns, lavishly armored, and capable of 27 knots, she was superior in almost every respect to the latest British battle cruiser, *Tiger,* still, in July 1914, undelivered to the Royal Navy. When *Kongo* sailed for home, she left behind, under construction in British shipyards, four other foreign superdreadnoughts, all equal to Britain's best. Two were being built for Turkey and two for Chile. Now, in the summer of 1914, as the European crisis worsened, the Turkish ships—*Reshadieh,* modeled on the *Iron Duke* class, and *Sultan*

Osman I, carrying fourteen 12-inch guns, were nearing completion and preparing to sail for the Bosporus. At this point, the First Lord insisted that the Turks must not be permitted to take physical possession of their ships.

The first of the Turkish vessels, the 23,000-ton dreadnought *Reshadieh,* was similar to *King George V,* carrying ten 13.5-inch guns. The second, larger, battleship eventually would earn a unique place in the history of naval construction for, within a single year, it was owned by three different governments. For a decade, the three principal South American powers, Argentina, Brazil, and Chile, had been conducting their own dreadnought-building race, draining each country of a quarter of its annual national income. Brazil began by ordering from British yards a pair of 21,000-ton dreadnoughts each carrying twelve 12-inch guns. Argentina responded by ordering two 28,000-ton battleships with twelve 12-inch guns—one ship from the New York Ship Building Company, the other from the Fore River Shipyard in Quincy, Massachusetts. Brazil, alarmed by the larger size of the new Argentine vessels, returned to Britain in 1911 to order a third new battleship. This vessel was to be a phenomenon: the longest dreadnought in the world, with the unequaled armament of fourteen 12-inch guns set in seven turrets. Laid down in September 1911 at Armstrong's Elswick yard in Newcastle upon Tyne, she was launched in January 1913 as *Rio de Janeiro.* By October, however, cheap rubber from Malaya had undermined the market value of Brazil's rubber exports; the Brazilian government, unable to pay for the new ship, put the unfinished dreadnought up for sale. Turkey stepped forward, and on December 28, 1913, *Rio de Janeiro* became *Sultan Osman I.* Meanwhile, Chile had ordered two new 28,000-ton British-built dreadnoughts, each designed to carry ten 14-inch guns, but in July 1914 both were a year from completion.

It was on the two Turkish battleships, therefore, that the Admiralty focused its attention. Although a clause in the building contracts permitted the British government to buy back the ships in a national emergency, the Turks were unlikely to sell them willingly. The two vessels had cost the impoverished nation almost £6 million. Some of the money had been borrowed from bankers in Paris and some came from taxes—on sheep and wool, on tobacco, and on bread. In January 1914, all December salaries of civil servants, none yet paid, were diverted to pay for the ships. But still more money was needed. Every Turkish town and village contributed; women sold their hair to raise money; collection boxes were placed on the bridges across the Golden Horn and on ferryboats plying the Bosporus. Purchase of the two dreadnoughts became a unifying national cause.

Meanwhile, at the Elswick yard, British workers were altering the ship to meet the needs of her new owners. Nameplates in Portuguese carrying instructions and locations were unscrewed and replaced. The admiral's stateroom and dining room were fitted with seasoned mahogany paneling, Ottoman carpets, silk lampshades, and a pink-tiled bath. Belowdecks, the crew was given more space by eliminating numerous watertight bulkheads. Lavatory arrangements appropriate to European or Brazilian usage were altered as toilet bowls were ripped out and replaced by rows of conical holes in the deck, suitable for the Turkish practice of squatting.

The Ottoman navy waited anxiously. With Russia constructing a new fleet on the Black Sea and Greece building a dreadnought in Germany and negotiating to buy two predreadnoughts from the United States, Turkey urgently needed a modern navy. Her ships were hopelessly out-of-date; one old battleship mounted wooden guns, which her officers hoped would seem real to a viewer on shore. By July 1914, the Turks were impatient to bring the new ships home and parade them to the nation off the Golden Horn. *Rashadieh* was ready in early July, but the British Admiralty advised that she remain in England until the two ships could sail for Turkey together. Meanwhile, hints from Whitehall to Armstrong and Vickers suggested that there was no need to hurry delivery of the two vessels. Pressure on the Admiralty increased when, on July 27, a shabby Turkish passenger ship, carrying 500 Turkish sailors to man the *Sultan Osman I,* arrived in the Tyne and berthed across the narrow river from the new battleship. The official delivery date was set for August 2. On the morning of August 1, the thirteenth 12-inch gun was hoisted on board and placed in its turret. The final and fourteenth gun was expected later that day. But still no ammunition had been delivered.

On Friday, July 31, with European war impending, Churchill made his decision. "In view of present circumstances," the First Lord informed the builders, "the Government cannot permit the ship to be handed over to a Foreign Power." The following morning, Armstrong, fearing that the Turkish captain and his sailors waiting across the river might try to board the new battleship and hoist the Turkish flag, placed armed guards at the dockyard gates. On August 2, a company of British army Sherwood Foresters with fixed bayonets marched on board. Stunned, the Turks could do nothing.

Churchill never apologized. "The Turkish battleships were vital to us," he said later. "With a margin of only seven dreadnoughts we could not afford to do without these two fine ships." He attempted to patch up the damage by offering that at the end of the war Turkey should receive either the two "requisitioned" dreadnoughts, fully repaired, or else their full value; he added that, in any case, Britain would pay Turkey a thousand pounds a day for every day she kept them. The offer would stand so long as Turkey remained neutral.

Sultan Osman I, renamed *Agincourt,* steamed into Scapa Flow on August 26. Some British officers feared that the firing of her first full broadside would break her back, but when it happened the simultaneous blast of fourteen 12-inch guns broke only her crockery. *Reshadieh,* renamed *Erin,* reached the British fleet soon after. The North Sea dreadnought ratio now rose to twenty-six British against seventeen German. This still did not sufficiently calm the First Lord; in September 1914, *Almirante Latorre,* the first of the unfinished 28,000-ton Chilean dreadnoughts, was "requisitioned" by the Admiralty. A year later, she joined the Grand Fleet as HMS *Canada.* The other Chilean battleship was also "requisitioned," and was completed in 1918 as the aircraft carrier *Eagle.*

—

On Wednesday, July 29, even as the British fleet was steaming toward Scapa Flow, the Austrian bombardment of Belgrade began. Russia immediately began mobilizing her southern forces. Germany announced that unless Russia ended her mobilization against Austria, Germany would mobilize and declare war. The Russians continued. On Friday, July 31, Germany sent an ultimatum to St. Petersburg demanding Russian demobilization within twelve hours. At noon the next day, Saturday, August 1, the ultimatum expired and Germany declared war on Russia.

For the next three days, Great Britain remained neutral. The factor that ultimately unified British thinking was Belgium, across whose territory the German General Staff meant to send 700,000 men to strike the French army on its weak left wing. A British treaty with Belgium guaranteed that country's neutrality. On Saturday, August 1, Britain asked both France and Germany for assurances that, in the event of war, Belgian territory would not be violated. France immediately gave full assurances; Germany refused to reply. Thereupon the German ambassador in London was given formal notice that if Belgium was invaded, Britain might take action. Early that afternoon, the British ambassador in Berlin reported that British ships were being detained in German ports. Learning this, the Admiralty decided to mobilize the Royal Navy. All patrol and local defense flotillas were ordered to remain out at night, and the same naval reserves who had been discharged after the test mobilization were ordered back to their ships. On Sunday, August 2, Germany delivered an ultimatum to Belgium demanding that the German army be allowed uncontested passage across Belgian territory. On Monday, August 3, Germany declared war on France. The Royal Navy commissioned nine ocean liners as armed merchant cruisers, including *Lusitania, Aquitania, Caronia,* and *Mauretania.* Soon, *Lusitania, Aquitania,* and *Mauretania* were released, the cost of their fuel being judged out of proportion to their usefulness. At 6:00 a.m. on Tuesday, August 4, news came that the German army intended to cross the Belgian frontier at four o'clock that afternoon. At 9:30 a.m., the Foreign Office protested to Berlin. At noon came a German reply which assured that no Belgian territory would be annexed, but also stated that Germany could not leave Belgian territory unoccupied to be used by the French as an avenue for attacking Germany. No doubts remained; at 5:50 p.m., the Admiralty informed the navy that Berlin had been sent a formal British ultimatum, which would expire at midnight Berlin time.

Unless an acceptable reply was received by then, war would begin. "In view of our ultimatum," the message said, "they may decide to open fire at any moment. You must be ready for this,"

At eleven o'clock in London—midnight, Berlin time—on Tuesday, August 4, the British ultimatum expired, unanswered. From the Admiralty, the war telegram flashed to all ships and stations under the White Ensign around the world. "Commence hostilities against Germany." The old battleship *Prince of Wales* was coaling in Portland harbor when a bugle sounded. "The collier's winches suddenly stopped," recalled one of the ship's officers, "and the bosun's mate passed the word: 'Hostilities will commence against Germany at midnight.' The loud cheers which followed were soon silenced by the renewed clatter of the winches and the thud of the coal bags as they came in with increased speed."

CHAPTER 2

"*Goeben* Is Your Objective"

While Britain decided whether to go to war, France, which had no choice, prepared for the German blow. General Joseph Joffre, commanding the armies of France, urgently required the presence at the front of the XIX Army Corps, totaling 80,000 men. On the eve of war, these men were in North Africa and it became the imperative task of the French Mediterranean fleet to convoy them across the sea to Marseilles. To escort the troopships, one French dreadnought, six predreadnoughts, six armored cruisers, and twenty-four destroyers were available. Two other new French dreadnoughts, which might better have served France in the Mediterranean that month, were far away to the north on a mission of national *gloire,* escorting the president of the Republic on a state visit to St. Petersburg. Their absence created a potential danger: if the prewar Triple Alliance of Germany, Austria, and Italy held firm, the combined fleets of these three powers would be superior to the French Mediterranean fleet and the safe passage of the XIX Corps would be in jeopardy.

The war plan of the Triple Alliance called for the three fleets to assemble on the outbreak of hostilities at the port of Messina in Sicily. From there, they were to steam out and wrest control of the Mediterranean from France. By August 1914, the Austrian navy, based at Pola, at the head of the Adriatic, possessed two dreadnoughts, along with three older battleships and a handful of cruisers and destroyers. The Italian fleet also had three new dreadnoughts, but only one was ready for war. Germany, with no naval base of its own in the Mediterranean, maintained just two warships in the inland sea. One of these, however, was the battle cruiser *Goeben,* a ruggedly constructed vessel of 23,000 tons whose ten 11-inch guns and design speed of

28 knots made her the most powerful fast warship in the Mediterranean. The other German vessel was *Breslau,* a new light cruiser of 4,500 tons, with a speed of 27 knots and twelve 4.1-inch guns. *Goeben* worried Britain's First Lord, who had no doubt that war was coming and that Britain would become involved. *Goeben,* Churchill grimly predicted, "would easily be able to avoid the French . . . [battleships] and brushing aside or outstripping their cruisers, break in upon the transports and sink one after another of these vessels crammed with soldiers."

To bar the passage of the French troopships was one of the purposes for which *Goeben* had been sent to the Mediterranean in 1912. A second mission, especially congenial to the kaiser, was to remind the people of the Mediterranean of the glory and long arm of the German emperor. When the big gray ship arrived in the Mediterranean, her ten 11-inch guns jutting from five turrets, her twelve 6-inch guns bristling from casements, her plain wardroom, with neither sofas, nor armchairs, nor pictures on the walls—all suggested a ship ready for war. But in reality, by the summer of 1914, *Goeben* was below peak efficiency. Two years of constant steaming without drydocking had taken a toll. The ship's bottom was fouled and her engines were plagued by worn-out, leaking boiler tubes, which reduced steam pressure and, therefore, speed. Even so, the two German ships constituted a formidable force. Their commander, Rear Admiral Wilhelm Souchon, was a short, dark-haired man, fifty years old, who sometimes wore and sometimes shaved off a thick black mustache. Of French Huguenot ancestry and, like many officers in the Imperial Navy, lacking the ennobling "von," he appeared on first acquaintance a curious kind of sea dog. "A droop-jawed, determined little man in an ill-fitting frock coat, looking more like a parson than an admiral": so an American diplomat in Constantinople described him.

Souchon and *Goeben* were visiting Haifa, in the eastern Mediterranean, when the the news of Sarajevo arrived. The assassination, the admiral knew, would agitate Europe; this quickly led him to worry about *Goeben*'s leaking boiler tubes. He telegraphed Berlin, asking that new tubes be sent to the Austrian base at Pola, then sailed from Haifa for the Adriatic. The ship arrived on July 10; for the next eighteen days, the crew worked to locate and replace defective tubes. The work was done while the sun burned down from a cloudless sky, creating almost unbearable heat inside the steel hull. The battle cruiser had twenty-four boilers; from them, 4,000 defective tubes had to be extracted and replaced. The work was still unfinished when a signal from Berlin warned that war was imminent.

While the crew cheered the news, waved their caps, and tapped their feet to marching music by the ship's band, Souchon pondered his next move. Neither Austria nor Italy seemed ready for naval war, and Souchon rejected the thought of remaining in the Adriatic, subordinate to an Austrian admiral not inclined to fight Britain and France. Assuming that he was alone in the

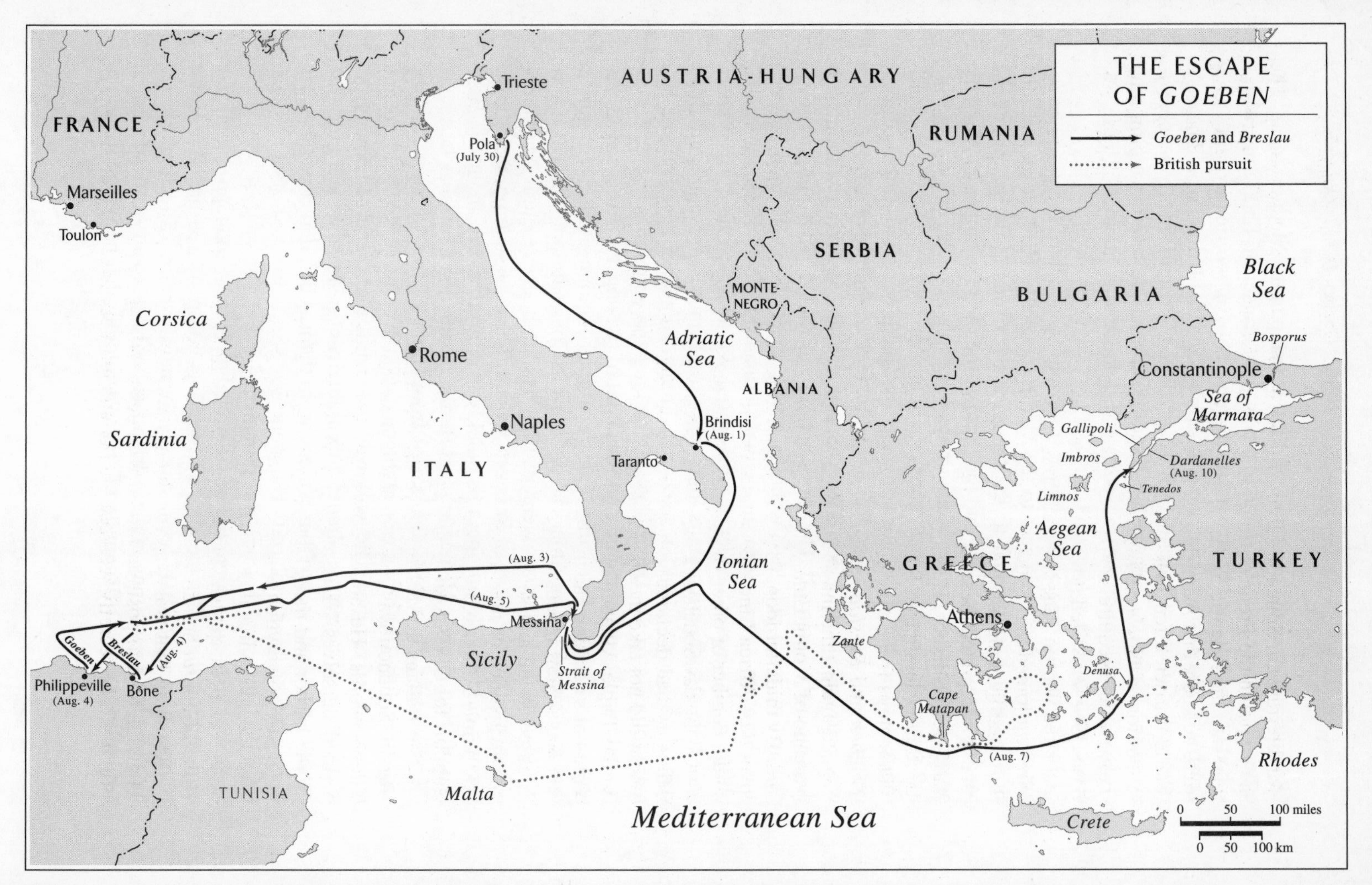
THE ESCAPE OF GOEBEN
Goeben and Breslau
British pursuit
AUSTRIA-HUNGARY
FRANCE
RUMANIA
SERBIA
BULGARIA
MONTE-NEGRO
ALBANIA
ITALY
GREECE
TURKEY
TUNISIA
Black Sea
Bosporus
Constantinople
Sea of Marmara
Gallipoli
Imbros
Dardanelles (Aug. 10)
Tenedos
Limnos
Aegean Sea
Athens
Denusa
Cape Matapan
(Aug. 7)
Rhodes
Crete
Zante
Ionian Sea
Adriatic Sea
Trieste
Pola (July 30)
Marseilles
Toulon
Corsica
Sardinia
Rome
Naples
Brindisi (Aug. 1)
Taranto
(Aug. 3)
(Aug. 5)
Messina
Strait of Messina
Sicily
Goeben
Breslau
(Aug. 4)
Philippeville (Aug. 4)
Bône
Malta
Mediterranean Sea
0 50 100 miles
0 50 100 km

Mediterranean, Souchon considered steaming west, inflicting what damage he could on the French troop transports, then forcing his way past Gibraltar and into the Atlantic to attack Allied trade. If he could make it to the North Sea, he knew that Admiral Franz Hipper, commander of the High Seas Fleet battle cruiser force, would welcome his powerful ship. But the uncertain condition of *Goeben*'s boilers prohibited the sustained high speed that this move would require. By July 29, Souchon had made up his mind. Leaving Pola, *Goeben* sailed down the Adriatic, and on August 1—the day Germany declared war on Russia—anchored off Brindisi, on the heel of Italy. There, *Breslau* joined her. Souchon's ships needed coal, but the Italians refused to bring colliers alongside, saying that the sea was too rough. Souchon accurately interpreted these excuses as evidence that Italy was about to renounce the Triple Alliance. He moved on to Taranto and then, his need for coal now acute, to Messina, in Sicily, where he could rendezvous with German merchant ships from which coal could be commandeered. During the morning, *Goeben* and *Breslau* steamed past the rugged cliffs of the Calabrian coast, jagged against the intense blue of the sky. At noon, they passed beneath the volcano of Mount Etna, its perpetual plume of smoke issuing from the summit. By midafternoon, they had anchored in Messina harbor, where the German East Africa Line passenger steamer *General,* bound for Dar es Salaam, and a number of other German merchant ships awaited them.

On the day Souchon reached Messina, Italy declared her neutrality. Austria-Hungary had declared war on Serbia on July 28 without consulting Rome, and it did not take the Italians long to remember that they had agreed to join in the Triple Alliance as a strictly defensive arrangement. The Italian government's decision had the wholehearted support of the Italian navy; the Italian Naval Staff repeatedly had warned that the fleet could not protect Italy's long coastline and seaboard cities from the French and British fleets. The news, justified or not, was a blow for Souchon. Italy's neutrality eliminated the Triple Alliance, the naval assembly at Messina, and the prospect of any support for *Goeben* and *Breslau.*

The Italians at Messina were prompt to implement their new neutrality. Again, Souchon was refused coal. "Shameless" and "treachery" were Souchon's words. He added defiantly, "We did not plead much. We simply helped ourselves." His method was to order alongside all German ships in the harbor and then, "in the twinkling of an eye," use axes and crowbars to destroy everything—decks, bulkheads, cabins, passageways—that obstructed the removal of their coal. This procedure produced two thousand tons—of poor quality, but it was better than none. Souchon also requisitioned *General* herself for use as an auxiliary naval tender.

Knowing that war was imminent, but lacking orders from Berlin, Souchon decided to position his ships to deliver the first blow. At midnight on August 2, he secretly weighed anchor and left Messina by the northern exit, which led to the Algerian coast. He hoped to catch the French troopships at sea; if not, he could at least attack the embarkation ports of the XIX Corps and make "the African coast . . . echo to the thunder of German guns." The port of Bône was assigned to *Breslau,* the harbor of Philippeville to *Goeben.* Steaming west, Souchon learned the next day from his wireless that Germany was at war with France.

—

In August 1914, three dreadnought battle cruisers—*Inflexible, Indomitable,* and *Indefatigable*—were the core of the British Mediterranean Fleet. These early ships of Jacky Fisher's revolutionary fast dreadnought design averaged 18,000 tons and a speed of 25 knots. They were inferior to Vice Admiral Sir David Beatty's more modern British battle cruisers in the North Sea; they were also 5,000 tons lighter and several knots slower than *Goeben.* But with eight 12-inch guns apiece to the German ship's ten 11-inchers, they were more heavily armed. And there were three of them, making the margin of battle cruiser heavy guns in the Mediterranean twenty-four British against ten German. Wishing to enhance this margin, on July 28 Churchill had suggested sending a fourth older battle cruiser, *New Zealand,* from the North Sea, but Prince Louis had refused to further diminish Beatty's strength. The British Mediterranean Fleet also included four large armored cruisers—*Defence, Warrior, Black Prince,* and *Duke of Edinburgh*—all relatively new but already obsolete, made so intentionally by Fisher, who had decreed that in wartime, his faster, more powerful battle cruisers would gobble up armored cruisers "like an armadillo let loose on an ant-hill." Four modern British light cruisers and a flotilla of sixteen destroyers made up the balance of the Mediterranean Fleet.

While the British government struggled with issues of war and peace, Admiral Sir Archibald Berkeley Milne, the Commander-in-Chief of the Mediterranean Fleet, awaited orders at Malta, his principal base. In the days just before the war, he had been given no clear instructions. War came to Europe in convulsive spasms: first Austria against Serbia, then Russia against Austria, then Germany against Russia, then Germany against France, and finally Germany against Great Britain. Military and naval planning was complicated by the fact that, on any given day, no one knew which nations were in the war, which were not, and which might or might not come in tomorrow. This was especially true of any consideration involving Great Britain, which did not itself know whether it was going to war until the day it did so. Amid this confusion, Winston Churchill, wielding the power of the the Cabinet at the Admiralty, personally drafted operational telegrams to Royal Navy admirals and ships. On Thursday, July 30, he told Admiral Milne that his primary mission would be to assist the French in covering the North African troopships. But the First Lord, his fertile imagination brimming with possibilities, embellished his message with further instructions, and the result was to swamp the conventional mind of Admiral Milne. This was the message Milne received:

> Your first task should be to aid the French in transportation of their African army corps by covering and if possible bringing to action individual fast German ships, particularly *Goeben,* which may interfere with that transportation. . . . Except in combination with the French as part of a general battle, do not at this stage be brought to action against superior forces. The speed of your squadrons is sufficient to enable you to choose your moment. You must husband your force at the outset and we shall hope later to reinforce the Mediterranean.

Later, Churchill explained that the phrases "superior forces," "the speed of your squadrons," and "husband your forces" were meant to guide Milne in dealing with the Austrian fleet. But Churchill also could not take his eyes away from *Goeben,* and he had convinced himself that its destruction and Milne's other assignments largely overlapped. The extent to which the German battle cruiser affected his thinking was displayed in subsequent signals flowing to Milne from the Admiralty. Following the original July 30 message, Churchill signaled again on August 2: "*Goeben* must be shadowed by two battle cruisers." And on August 3: "Watch on mouth of Adriatic should be maintained but *Goeben* is your objective. Follow her and shadow her wherever she goes, and be ready to act on declaration of war which appears probable and imminent." Again, on August 4, when informed that the British battle cruisers *Indomitable* and *Indefatigable* had *Goeben* in sight: "Very good. Hold her. War imminent."

Milne did his best to obey this stream of orders. On August 1, after receiving Churchill's first message, he concentrated his fleet beneath the sand-colored limestone ramparts of the ancient fortress of Valletta at Malta. Early on August 2, when he received the Admiralty order saying that "*Goeben* must be shadowed by two battle cruisers" and the Adriatic "watched," Milne dispatched his second in command, Rear Admiral Ernest Troubridge, with *Indomitable* and *Indefatigable,* the four armored cruisers, the light cruiser *Gloucester,* and eight destroyers to guard the mouth of the Adriatic. But Admiral Souchon had already left the Adriatic. On August 2, *Goeben* and *Breslau* had been seen at Taranto by the British consul, who urgently reported the sighting to the Admiralty. Suddenly, a thought troubled Churchill and his colleagues in London. Told that the two German ships had left Taranto, they decided that Souchon was headed into the Atlantic to attack British trade. To counter this threat, Admiral Troubridge's two battle cruisers were ordered to detach from his command and proceed westward at high speed "to prevent *Goeben* leaving Mediterranean." At nine o'clock that night, *Indomitable* and *Indefatigable* left, heading for Gibraltar at 22 knots.

Milne had now been assigned four tasks: he was to support the French in protecting the troop convoys in the western Mediterranean; he was to observe and bottle up the Austrians in the Adriatic; he was to find and sink *Goeben* wherever she was; and he was to prevent the German battle cruiser from breaking out past Gibraltar. Unfortunately, on the high seas, these objectives did not fit together with the same seamlessness they achieved in the mind of the First Lord. And the Churchillian stream of overlapping, frequently contradictory instructions was enough to bewilder a man far more astute than Admiral Milne.

—

Sir Archibald Berkeley Milne, known to the service as Arky-Barky, was a short, dapper fifty-nine-year-old bachelor who wore a white beard and a black mustache. He was descended from two admirals, his father and his grandfather. His own career had been fashionable; during long service on the royal yachts, he had won the friendship of the Prince and Princess of Wales, later King Edward VII and Queen Alexandra. Milne, wreathed in smiles and heavy with gold braid, was always available to pose on deck for the queen, snapping away with her Brownie camera. He shot, fished, and collected rare orchids, and he had become a rear admiral by 1903. In 1912, Winston Churchill, the new First Lord, gave pleasure to the new king, George V, by recommending the king's friend Arky-Barky as Commander-in-Chief of the Mediterranean Fleet.

Learning of the appointment, Jacky Fisher erupted. Milne had served under Fisher's archenemy, Admiral Lord Charles Beresford, and once had offered to testify against Fisher in an Admiralty proceeding. Milne, Fisher raged, was a "backstairs cad," a "sneak," a "serpent of the lowest type," and "Sir Berkeley Mean who buys his *Times* second-hand for a penny." Milne had won his new post through social connections, Fisher roared. Milne "went to Balmoral and crawled. . . . Winston has sacrificed the country to the court. . . . Winston, alas! (as I have had to tell him) feared for his wife the social ostracism of the Court and succumbed to [Milne's] appointment—a wicked wrong. . . . The mischief is done. Milne, an utterly useless commander . . . is now the senior admiral afloat." Fisher's wrath was so great that he broke temporarily with Churchill: "I fear this must be my last communication with you. . . . I am sorry for it, but I consider you have betrayed the navy . . . and what the pressure could have been to induce you to betray your trust is beyond my comprehension. You are aware that Sir Berkeley Milne is unfitted to be the senior admiral afloat, as you have now made him. . . . I can't believe that you foresee all the consequences. [This will be] IRREPARABLE, IRREMEDIABLE, ETERNAL!"

Milne was neither wicked nor incompetent; he was ordinary. And he was far from solely responsible for the debacle that followed. The underlying cause of his flawed strategy and faulty dispositions was Britain's unwillingness to commit absolutely to France. French uncertainty as to Britain's role in the coming war continued right up to the afternoon of August 4, when, after the British ultimatum had been sent to Berlin, Churchill finally received a group of French admirals at the Admiralty. There, the First Lord, employing his broadly Anglicized French, declared in a burst of good fellowship, "Use Malta as if it were Toulon [the main French naval base in the Mediterranean]." Two days later, Prince Louis concluded an agreement that gave France, in the person of Vice Admiral Augustin Boue de Lapeyrère, general direction of naval operations in the Mediterranean.

None of this helped Admiral Milne. The two admiralties might be talking, but no arrangements had been made for communication between French and British commanders at sea. At 4:00 a.m. on August 3, Admiral de Lapeyrère put to sea with the entire French Mediterranean fleet, steaming south toward Algeria to provide protection for the troop transports of the French North African army corps. His battleships and cruisers, organized in three squadrons, were in sufficient strength, he believed, to deal with *Goeben* and *Breslau.* However, to make certain that the two fast German ships did not, as Churchill feared, "break in upon the transports . . . crammed with soldiers," de Lapeyrère postponed for several days the date of the troopships' sailing from Africa. Admiral Milne did not know this. Ordered by Churchill to give priority to the protection of the French transports, he focused diligently on that assignment, even though the French fleet itself was there to protect them and the transports themselves were not yet at sea. Not until August 2 was Milne given authority to communicate with the French. When he tried to do so, Milne could not raise the French admiral by wireless and was eventually obliged to send a light cruiser to Bizerte "in quest of his colleague," de Lapeyrère.

Lack of communication with the French caused difficulties, but Milne's situation was made worse by the fact that communication between his flagship and the First Lord at the Admiralty was all too rapid. This was the first naval war in which admiralties could intervene directly to control ship movements by means of cable and wireless radio. This new technology, enabling orders to be dispatched from London night and day, offered a powerful temptation to the restless First Lord. Frequently ignoring the First Sea Lord, whose proper role was the operational control of warships, Churchill began sending orders directly to admirals and ships at sea. Milne was merely the first to feel this forceful and articulate presence looming over his shoulder.

—

Milne guessed correctly that, after Taranto, *Goeben* might call at Messina, and he sent the light cruiser *Chatham* from Malta to investigate. *Chatham* passed through the strait at 7:00 a.m. on August 3, examining the anchorage. She found nothing; *Goeben* and *Breslau* had sailed six hours earlier. All through Sunday the third, the German ships steamed westward, avoiding normal shipping lanes and showing no lights at night. At 2:35 a.m. on August 4, as Souchon was nearing the Algerian coast, an unexpected signal arrived from the Naval Staff in Berlin: Souchon was to reverse course and make for Constantinople. On August 2, Germany and Turkey had signed a defensive alliance against Russia. The Turks were reluctant, however, to take the actual step into war and the German embassy in Constantinople was recommending application of pressure on the grand vizier and his Cabinet. The sight of *Goeben* anchored off the Golden Horn was thought likely to offer formidable persuasion.

Souchon, then approaching the climactic moment of firing live ammunition at an enemy, ignored the order. "The idea of turning about, so short a time before that moment so ardently desired by us all, before opening fire—my heart could not accept that," he later wrote. He continued west; soon the jagged contours of the Algerian coast, tinted red by the rising sun, came into view. Slowly, Souchon approached the harbor at Philippeville, first running up the Russian flag to deceive his enemies. As he came closer, a watchman waved from the harbor lighthouse, and vendors in boats loaded with bananas, pineapples, and coconuts put out from shore. Suddenly, the Russian flag came down, the German war flag ran up, and *Goeben*'s 5.9-inch guns lashed out, "sowing death and panic," in Souchon's words. After ten minutes, during which only fifteen shells were fired, the Germans withdrew. They had hit neither troops nor troopships, but had managed to damage the railway station, blow up a magazine, and knock over the hospitable lighthouse. "Our trick succeeded brilliantly," said a member of the crew.

It was a token bombardment, but Souchon was satisfied. The admiral now intended to obey his orders to go to Constantinople, twelve hundred miles to the east. First, however, he needed more coal, which meant a return to Messina. By midmorning, the two German ships were steaming east. A splendid Mediterranean day, with the sky arching overhead "like a giant azure bell and a gently ruffled sea, glittering to the horizon," added to the cheerfulness of the German sailors.

—

Until German shells began exploding in Philippeville, Admiral Milne at Malta had no idea where *Goeben* was. Thirty-six hours earlier—that is, at 12:50 a.m. on August 3, just as Souchon was leaving Messina to raid the African coast—a message from the First Lord had brought Milne the instruction to find *Goeben* "and shadow her wherever she goes." That evening, *Indomitable* and *Indefatigable* had been stripped away from Troubridge and ordered westward. The result, on August 3, was that the German battle cruiser, steaming west from Messina to bombard the Algerian ports, was being followed by two powerful British ships. On the morning of the fourth, after the bombardment of Philippeville, they found her.

At 10:34 a.m., Captain Francis Kennedy of *Indomitable,* the senior officer of the two British battle cruisers, sighted *Goeben* 17,000 yards ahead, coming east in his direction at 20 knots. His own speed was 22 knots, which meant that the British and German ships were rushing toward each other at an effective speed of almost 50 miles per hour. Although, because the two nations were still at peace, *Goeben*'s main turret guns—like his own—were trained fore and aft, Kennedy observed that the German crew—like his own—was at action stations. On opposite courses 8,000 yards apart, the warships passed one another in silence.

Officers on *Goeben*'s bridge had sighted the columns of smoke directly ahead, then seen them evolve into the shapes of two broad-beamed "giant grey monsters" moving toward them at high speed. Even from a distance, Souchon himself immediately recognized that these were "not French ships with a big freeboard, but English tripod mast capital ships of the *Indomitable* class. . . . I don't dare to open fire as I don't know whether England is our enemy. I am astonished that they don't fire." The British ships, once past *Goeben,* grew smaller in the German battle cruiser's wake. Then, to their dismay, Souchon and his officers saw *Indomitable* and *Indefatigable* turning. With thick black smoke pouring from their stacks, Kennedy's ships began to follow, 10,000 yards astern. By urgent wireless, Kennedy informed Milne, and Milne informed the Admiralty.

Souchon, aware that war might come at any moment and worried that the British ships might get the news before he did, ordered full speed. Gradually, the shadowing exercise escalated into a chase and *Goeben*'s speed climbed to 24 knots. In the engine rooms of the German battle cruiser, the heat became excruciating. "The overheated air affected lungs and heart," said a crew member. "We worked in air forced down by ventilators. . . . The artificial draft roared and hissed . . . [and] drove into open furnace doors, fanning the glowing coal, and swept roaring up the smokestacks. In the engine room, there was the whir of the turbines, revolving at ever increasing speed; the whole ship trembled and quaked [and] the long grey hull shot through the glistening, foaming waters." White spray rolling back from her bow, black smoke staining the sky for miles astern, *Goeben* raced eastward; slowly but perceptibly, the distance between the pursuers and their prey increased. The *Indomitable* class had been designed for 25 knots, and six years earlier *Indomitable* herself had surpassed 26 in trials; but after long overseas service, the hulls of both British battle cruisers were fouled. Their engines needed overhaul and the ships were short of wartime crew, particularly the stokers required to feed the boiler furnaces by shoveling coal. Nevertheless, for six hours, Kennedy kept station astern, determined to stay within range.

Meanwhile, even as the Admiralty was learning that *Goeben* had been found and that two battle cruisers were shadowing her, the British Cabinet was deciding whether to send an ultimatum to Berlin. Churchill, exultant at the news that the *Goeben* was in sight, sent his message "Very good. Hold her. War imminent." But because Milne had forgotten to mention in which direction the German ships were going, Churchill wrongly assumed that Souchon was still steaming west to attack the French transports. On this basis, he sent an urgent memorandum to the prime minister and the foreign secretary: "*Goeben* . . . is evidently going to interfere with the French transports which are crossing today." He asked that he be permitted to add to his signal to Milne and Kennedy the following: "If *Goeben* attacks French transports, you should at once engage her." Asquith and Grey agreed, but the prime minister suggested that first the matter should be put before the Cabinet, which was about to meet. Churchill, his blood high, ignored the prime minister and sent off the authorization to attack before going to meet his fellow ministers. At the meeting, Asquith scribbled to Venetia Stanley, "Winston with all his war paint on is longing for a sea fight to sink the *Goeben*."* The Cabinet, however, refused to allow the Royal Navy to start sinking ships before the war had begun; at 2:05 p.m. Churchill was forced to send to Milne and Kennedy a retraction. The ultimatum to Germany had been sent and would expire at midnight, he said, and "no act of war should be committed before that hour. . . . This cancels the authorization to *Indomitable* and *Indefatigable* to engage *Goeben* if she attacks French transports."

For the remainder of the afternoon, Churchill and the War Staff, waiting at the Admiralty, "suffered the tortures of Tantalus. . . . At any moment, the *Goeben* could have been smitten at under ten thousand yards range by sixteen 12-inch guns firing nearly treble her own weight of metal. At about five o'clock, Prince Louis observed that there was still time to sink *Goeben* before dark." Churchill, bound by the Cabinet decision, was silent and sulky, "unable to utter a word. . . . We hoped to sink her the next day," he wrote. "Where could she go? Pola seemed her only refuge. According to international law, nothing but internment awaited her elsewhere."

During the afternoon, the weather in the central Mediterranean turned hazy, and the deep blue of the sea changed to gray. At 3:00 p.m., the two British battle cruisers were joined in the chase by the light cruiser *Dublin,* which Kennedy posted out of gun range on *Goeben*'s starboard beam. Kennedy then attempted to increase speed in order to keep *Goeben* within range; for a few minutes, he appeared to be overtaking her. This effort notwithstanding, however, certain British institutions were not be trifled with: "Sent hands to tea at 3:30 with *Indefatigable* to go to tea after us,"

*Between 1912 and 1915, H. H. Asquith, the British prime minister, was passionately in love with a young woman named Venetia Stanley. In August 1914, when Asquith was sixty-two and Venetia was twenty-seven, she dominated his thoughts. He wrote to her two or three times a day, often while Cabinet meetings were in progress around him. To Venetia, he not only expressed his intense desire for her company and approval, but he also divulged the most secret British diplomatic and military information. Curiously, the relationship always remained platonic.

Kennedy recorded in his action report. By 3:45 p.m., *Goeben* and *Breslau* were pulling away into a misty haze; at 4:00, *Goeben* was only just in sight against the horizon. *Dublin* held on, but at 7:37 p.m. the light cruiser signaled, "*Goeben* out of sight now, can only see smoke; still daylight." By nine o'clock, the smoke had disappeared, daylight was gone, and *Goeben* and *Breslau* had vanished. At 9:52 p.m., on Milne's instructions, *Dublin* gave up the chase. At 1:15 a.m., a signal from Malta informed the Mediterranean Fleet that war had begun.

—

Souchon, having outrun the British battle cruisers, returned to Messina at dawn on August 5 with his crew exhausted. Even in port, however, there could be no question of rest. His enemies, the German admiral assumed, would be coming up and waiting for him just outside Italian territorial waters. Nor could *Goeben* stay for long without risking internment. Indeed, before the end of the day, a group of the same Italian naval officers whom Souchon had counted on to be his allies came aboard to grant him permission to coal "for the last time" and to tell him that he was allowed to remain in their neutral port no longer than the twenty-four hours permitted under international law. Souchon replied that he would reckon the twenty-four hours from the time they had given him their message.

The morning went by with the two German warships lying motionless in the heat. Souchon had ordered coal from Italian suppliers, but by midday no coal had appeared. Early in the afternoon, he began collecting coal from German merchant ships in the harbor. Then, toward evening, the first collier sent by the Italian government arrived; others followed, and soon the long gray hull of *Goeben* was surrounded: colliers on one side, the liner *General* on the other. Not only the navy crews shoveled coal: Souchon enlisted four hundred German civilian volunteers from the merchant ships. Through the night, sacks of coal were swung across to the warships and clattered down on the steel deck, where shovels began to ply. In the heat, the men began to falter. Souchon tried beer, coffee, lemonade, band music, exhortation, and the example of officers who stripped off their shirts and worked beside the crew. Nothing could keep the men on their feet. In groups they were sent off to sleep in passenger bunks on board *General,* where, black with grime and sweat, they passed out on snow-white sheets.

By noon of her second day at Messina, *Goeben* had loaded 1,500 tons of coal and her crew was exhausted; men lay collapsed on deck, shovels still gripped in their blistered hands. "With a heavy heart, for there was still much coal to be transferred," Souchon halted the coaling—"It was essential," he said, "to have at least some rest before preparing for battle"—and gave the order to raise steam for departure at five o'clock. Meanwhile, everyone in Messina knew that the German battle cruiser was preparing to meet its doom. "Numerous Sicilians, avid for sensation, besieged us night and day," Souchon recorded.

> People in rags offered to sell fruit, tidbits, postcards, and keepsakes of every kind; singers with mandolins, mouth organs and castanettes; policemen, girls, monks, soldiers, . . . [nuns] and even some well-dressed people, tried untiringly to grapple with our half-naked, coal-blackened men, to steal everything that was not riveted or nailed down, from their jumper buttons to shovel handles, in memory of "those about to die." The noise of coaling, the whistle of steam, the din of windlasses, the grinding of shovels mingled with the dust, the smell of oil and sweat, and finally the cries of paper sellers with special posters: "Into the Jaws of Death" . . . "The Last Departure" . . . "Disgrace or Death" . . . "The Perilous Leap to the Peak of Glory" . . . "All Day to Die" . . . "Shame or Defeat" . . . "Voyage to Death or Glory."

In his cabin, amid the noise of the coal scuttles, Souchon considered what to do. A defensive alliance had been concluded between Germany and Turkey, and he had been ordered to proceed to Constantinople. But in the three days since that order arrived, a diplomatic hitch had developed, making the earlier message from Berlin premature. Passage of the German battle cruiser through the Dardanelles would violate the neutrality that Turkey was still attempting to maintain. A majority of the Turkish Cabinet was insisting that permission for *Goeben* to enter the Dardanelles must be withdrawn, and the grand vizier had not yet made up his mind. This resulted in a new wireless from the German Naval Staff, which Souchon received at Messina at 11:00 on the morning of August 6: "At present time your call Constantinople not yet possible for various reasons."

The same message from Berlin bore the additional bad news that Austria had refused to give Souchon active naval assistance. There were several reasons. First, Austria, although Germany's ally against Russia, was not yet at war with France. Second, Admiral Anton Haus, the Austro-Hungarian naval commander, considered his new, untried fleet inferior to France's and did not wish to do battle without help from the Italians. Once Italy had declared its neutrality, Haus decided that it would be foolhardy to rush out of the Adriatic to Souchon's rescue, exposing his ships to the French fleet. In addition, the Austrian government was anxious to avoid conflict with Great Britain and had told Haus that it did not want his ships engaging British warships. As a result, Souchon was informed that the Austrian fleet would not be coming south to support him.

Under these circumstances, Berlin authorized Souchon himself to decide where he should go. The admiral chose Constantinople, despite previous orders. "It was impossible for me to remain in the Mediterranean in face of the crushing superiority of the enemy and total lack of means of subsistence," he said. "I did not want to enter the Adriatic and be dependent on the Austrians. Thus, I firmly decided to enter the Dardanelles, if necessary against the will of the Turks, to carry the war into the Black Sea. I hope to carry the Turks with me in a war against their traditional enemy, the Muscovites."

His decision made, Souchon gave orders: *Goeben* would weigh anchor at five o'clock that afternoon. *Breslau* would follow 10,000 yards behind. If there was no battle outside the harbor, he would steer north toward the Adriatic. After dark, he would make a wide, surreptitious turn to the southeast, hoping to elude pursuers, and then make for the Aegean Sea, where a chartered Greek collier had been ordered to meet him. Success, Souchon reckoned, depended on the enemy's uncertainty as to his destination, on their ignorance of his damaged boilers and reduced capacity for speed, and on his own ability to shake off pursuit and meet the collier. But success was far from certain: before departing, Souchon wrote his will and sent it ashore. Then, at five o'clock on the afternoon of August 6, *Goeben* and *Breslau* steamed out the southern exit of the Messina Strait. The ship was cleared for action, the men were at the guns, and on deck the band was playing.

—

Admiral Milne was not waiting outside the harbor. Once *Goeben* had outrun *Indomitable* and *Indefatigable* and gone into Messina, Milne had fallen back on what he understood to be his primary mission: protecting the French transports. To achieve this, he positioned his force to block any attempt by *Goeben* to break westward toward the north-south sea-lanes between France and North Africa. Now aware that *Goeben* was capable of bursts of speed superior to his own fastest ships, Milne considered that the only sure way to accomplish his mission was to concentrate his battle cruisers west of Sicily. There, given sufficient warning of the enemy's approach, he could intercept and confront *Goeben* with his more numerous heavy guns. Accordingly, Milne waited with *Inflexible* and *Indefatigable* (*Indomitable,* which had burned most of her coal in the chase, had gone into Bizerte to refill her bunkers) for *Goeben* to come out the northern exit to the Messina Strait and head to the west. The light cruiser *Gloucester* was assigned to patrol the southern exit, which was the path to the east. The Admiralty, informed of these arrangements, approved.

Milne had learned on the morning of August 6 that *Goeben* and *Breslau* were at Messina. At that point, a different admiral—a Nelson at Copenhagen, or a Cunningham at Mers el-Kébir—might simply have ignored Italian neutrality and gone in after the German ships. But this would have meant flouting specific Admiralty orders. At 6:00 p.m. on August 4, even as *Goeben* was outdistancing her two pursuers and before Great Britain officially went to war, Milne had been told that the "Italian government have declared neutrality. You are to respect this neutrality rigidly and not allow any of His Majesty's ships to come within six miles of Italian coast." The policy had originated in the Foreign Office; at this delicate moment, with Italy backing away from the Triple Alliance, Sir Edward Grey did not wish to affront Italian sensibilities. The sinking of a single enemy ship, even the most powerful ship in the Mediterranean, could not take precedence. After the war, Churchill regretted the refusal to authorize British warships to follow *Goeben* into the Messina Strait. He did not mention Grey; rather, he said that neither Prince Louis nor Vice Admiral Frederick Sturdee, the Chief of the Admiralty War Staff, had mentioned the matter to him. "Had it been put to me, I should at once have consented. The prize was well worth the risk of vexing the Italians."

But if Milne was not to pry them out, why did he not simply bottle them up? He might have abandoned his distant deployment west of Sicily, posted a strong force including a battle cruiser at either end of the strait, and simply waited for *Goeben* to emerge. This would have been thoroughly in accord with Churchill's August 3 instructions: "*Goeben* is your objective. Follow her and shadow her wherever she goes and be ready to act on declaration of war." Churchill himself later declared that this was what Milne should have done: "Certainly, if . . . [Milne] had in reliance on these dominant and reiterated instructions, managed to put one battle cruiser [on] each side of the Straits of Messina, instead of all on one side, and in consequence had brought *Goeben* to action as would have been inevitable, and if he had thus protected the French transports in the most effectual manner by fighting *Goeben,* no one could have found fault with him on the score that he had exceeded his orders."

The question of Austria's role added to Milne's troubles and responsibilities. Britain was at war with Germany, but what about Germany's ally? "Is Austria neutral power?" the admiral asked the Admiralty on August 5. The reply, like almost every message coming from London, was ambiguous: "Austria has not declared war against France or England. Continue watching Adriatic for double purpose of preventing Austrians from emerging unobserved and preventing Germans entering." This message created further confusion. Having first advised that *Goeben* would attack the French transports, then having supposed that she might make a dash for the Atlantic, the Admiralty now speculated that Souchon could, after all, be thinking of returning to the Adriatic to link up with the Austrians. Milne, still focusing on the French transports, kept his fleet divided: the three battle cruisers remained with him off Sicily in the west, while Admiral Troubridge and his four armored cruisers continued to guard the Adriatic. Milne at this point specifically warned Troubridge not to take on the entire Austrian fleet: "First Cruiser Squadron and *Gloucester* . . . are not to get seriously engaged with superior force."

—

Under a rich blue afternoon sky, *Goeben* and *Breslau* left Messina on August 6 and steamed south over a gently rolling sea. Increasing speed to 17 knots, the two ships were scarcely out of neutral waters when the smoke and masts of the waiting *Gloucester* appeared. At a discreet interval, the British light cruiser fell in behind, trailing her quarry along the coast of Calabria through the twilight and into a bright, moonlit night. From his bridge, Souchon watched *Gloucester* take up her shadowing role, but did not interfere. Had he done so, the contest would have been over quickly: *Gloucester* possessed two 6-inch guns, which outmatched *Breslau,* but stood no chance against *Goeben,* which could destroy her with a single salvo of 11-inch shells. Aware of this, Captain Howard Kelly of *Gloucester* hung back, keeping the Germans in sight and regularly reporting their position, course, and speed. Brilliant light from an enormous moon hanging over the sleeping Calabrian mountains both aided and threatened Kelly: he could keep watch easily, but the clear visibility would speed his doom if *Goeben* chose to turn on him. Through the night, despite *Goeben*'s efforts to jam his transmitter, Kelly's radioman continued to tap out signals to Milne and Troubridge.

At first, Souchon was content with this arrangement. Then, after five hours of this game of the mouse chasing the cat, and unwilling to take the time to turn and devour his enemy, the admiral decided that he must stop pretending that he was headed for the Adriatic. Observed or not, if he was to reach the Aegean on the coal in his bunkers, he must change direction. At 10:46 p.m., *Gloucester* signaled Milne and Troubridge: "*Goeben* altering course to southward." Just before midnight, *Goeben* and *Breslau* altered course again, this time to the southeast. Troubridge then signaled Milne, "*Goeben* is going towards Matapan." Beyond Cape Matapan lay the Aegean, the Dardanelles, and Constantinople.

At this point, Admiral Troubridge, patrolling south of Corfu at the entrance to the Adriatic, commanded the only British force that might interrupt *Goeben*'s voyage. Individually, the armored cruisers *Defence, Warrior, Duke of Edinburgh,* and *Black Prince* were smaller, slower, and weaker than the German battle cruiser, but there were four of them, they averaged 14,000 tons, and, in combination, their twenty-two 9.2-inch guns fired a heavy broadside. Troubridge also had eight destroyers armed with torpedoes. Thanks to *Gloucester*'s reporting, Troubridge knew Souchon's course and speed. Informed at first that *Goeben* was headed north for the Adriatic, Troubridge had placed himself in a position to fight her in darkness and relatively confined waters, where his weaker ships would have a chance to get in close and neutralize the German advantage in range and gun caliber. After midnight, when it became clear that Souchon was heading away from the Adriatic,

Troubridge realized that if he steamed south at once, he still might be able to intercept *Goeben.* Unable to contact Milne, he decided on his own to attempt to do this. For four hours in the bright moonlight, the quartet of big British armored cruisers steamed south at 19 knots, their maximum speed, with the prospect of action at daybreak. No one in the Royal Navy who knew Troubridge, the man and the admiral, could doubt that this decision would lead to a rewarding display of professional skill and courage.

—

Ernest C. T. Troubridge was a genial, rugged, fifty-two-year-old seaman whose thick mane of white hair had earned him the sailors' nickname the Silver King. His navy pedigree, like Milne's, was impeccable: his great-grandfather, a comrade of Nelson's, had been at the Battle of the Nile. Troubridge himself had become a close friend of Prince George, later King George V, when the two were young lieutenants and when Troubridge was known as "the handsomest officer in the navy." As an observer with the Japanese fleet during the Russo-Japanese War, he had seen from Admiral Togo's bridge the devastating effectiveness of long-range, heavy-caliber naval guns. Fisher liked Troubridge and, writing to the younger officer, said that he had "met Mrs. Troubridge in the Abbey and lost my heart." In 1911, he became Winston Churchill's private naval secretary; in 1912, the First Lord appointed him chief of staff of the newly created Naval War Staff. When Troubridge came to the Mediterranean to take over the armored cruisers and serve as deputy to Admiral Milne, his relationship with the Commander-in-Chief was correct but not warm. By August 1914, Troubridge already had been designated to command the British Mediterranean Fleet once Admiral de Lapeyrère had assumed the supreme Allied naval command and Milne, his tour of duty concluded, had returned to England.

Despite his reputation, Troubridge worried as his ships steamed south. Before he left Malta, Milne had shown him Churchill's July 30 message declaring "you must husband your force at the outset" to avoid "being brought to action against superior forces." These instructions, Troubridge knew, had been addressed to Milne and referred to any possible engagement between the three British battle cruisers and the twelve slower but more heavily armored Austrian battleships. But the fact that Milne had shown Churchill's message to Troubridge gave it application to him, too. After this meeting and before sailing on August 2, Troubridge had called his captains together and warned them that "they must not be surprised if they saw me with the squadron run away." In addition, Milne had specifically warned him not to seriously engage a superior force. Here, again, Milne was referring to the Austrian fleet—but, again, Troubridge applied the admonition more generally. He had no doubt that in daylight *Goeben,* with her speed and the size and range of her guns, was a force superior to his own and that therefore his instructions not to engage applied. He also had to consider that his destroyers were seriously short of coal and had been falling behind the squadron; by daylight, only three of the original eight would still be in company. Nevertheless, he still believed that he might succeed if he could meet and attack *Goeben* at dawn, when poor light might partially nullify the advantage of the greater range of the German vessel's guns.

These thoughts were turning in Troubridge's mind when, at 2:45 a.m., he found himself confronted in the flagship chart room by *Defence*'s captain, Fawcett Wray.

"Are you going to fight, sir?" asked Wray, who, as Flag Captain, was also Troubridge's second in command. "Because, if so, the squadron ought to know."

"Yes," Troubridge replied. "I know it is wrong, but I cannot have the name of the whole Mediterranean Squadron stink." Troubridge then signaled his ships: "I am endeavoring to cross the bows of *Goeben* by 6 a.m. and intend to engage her if possible. . . . If we have not cut him off . . . [I intend] to avoid a long-range action."

Wray, a gunnery expert, went away disturbed by this answer. Forty-five minutes later, he came back determined to express his opinion. He found Troubridge lying on his bunk in his cabin. The lights were out but the admiral was awake. "I don't like it, Sir," said Wray. "Neither do I, but why?" asked Troubridge.

Wray knew that Troubridge had orders not to engage "a superior force," and he shared Troubridge's opinion that, at a range greater than 16,000 yards, *Goeben* was such a force. Wray explained to the admiral how *Goeben,* using her superior speed, could circle the squadron "at some range outside sixteen thousand yards which her guns would carry and your guns will not. It seems likely to be the suicide of your squadron."

Troubridge asked whether Wray was certain that the cruisers could not get in close before *Goeben* opened fire. Wray said that he was convinced of this, but that he would ask for confirmation from his ship's navigator. Before Wray left to find this officer, Troubridge said, "I cannot turn away now. Think of my pride." Wray replied, "Has your pride got anything to do with this, Sir? It is your country's welfare which is at stake."

When *Defence*'s navigator appeared, Troubridge asked whether, on its present course and speed, the squadron would have any chance of bringing *Goeben* within range of the British 9.2-inch guns before daylight. The navigator replied that there was no chance. A few minutes after 4:00 a.m., Troubridge called off the interception. When Wray went back to see him, he said, "Admiral, that's the bravest thing you have done in your life." Later, Wray added, "I think he was in tears."

At 4:05 a.m., Troubridge signaled Milne: "Being only able to meet *Goeben* outside the range of our guns and inside his, I have abandoned the chase with my squadron. *Goeben* evidently going to Eastern Mediterranean. I had hoped to meet her before daylight." He asked for instructions, giving Milne a chance to overrule him and order battle at all costs. For six hours, according to Troubridge, he received no reply. Then Milne signaled, "Why did you not continue to cut off *Goeben*? She's only going seventeen knots." (Milne knew this from *Gloucester*'s reports.) By then, however, Troubridge had turned back; at 10:00 a.m., he entered the port of Zante to coal his destroyers before returning to watch the Adriatic.

Later that morning in a long message to Milne, Troubridge attempted to explain his decision: "With visibility at the time, I could have been sighted from 20 to 25 miles away and could never have got nearer unless *Goeben* wished to bring me to action which she could have done under circumstances most advantageous to her. . . . I had hoped to have engaged her at 3.30 in the morning in dim light. . . . In view of the immense importance of victory or defeat at such an early stage of a war, I would consider it a great imprudence to place a squadron in such a position to be picked off at leisure and sunk while unable to effectively reply."

—

Meanwhile, unaware that a battle with four British armored cruisers had been in the offing and had been called off, Souchon continued eastward. When the red ball of the sun rose out of the sea—about the time the British cruisers might have opened fire—the blue Ionian Sea was empty. Then, far astern, a column of smoke appeared. It was *Gloucester.* Souchon, of course, was unaware that the three British battle cruisers, the only antagonists whose speed and power truly menaced his force, were far away to the west; for all he knew they were just behind *Gloucester,* straining to overtake. Once again, every spare man in *Goeben*'s crew went below to the coal bunkers and boiler rooms. Inside these steel compartments, where the temperature was 125 degrees Fahrenheit, half-naked men, sweat streaming down their bodies, flung coal into the furnaces. Black coal dust penetrated their noses, clogged their throats, inflamed their eyes. Every two hours, the men were rotated up to the relative paradise of the open deck, where they lay insensible until summoned to return below. As the day progressed, it grew worse. The ship's boiler tubes began to burst and spouts of steam and boiling water spurted onto bare bodies. Four men were scalded to death.

On his bridge, Souchon paced. He was afraid to turn and engage *Gloucester,* as, for all he knew, British battle cruisers might be just over the horizon. At the same time, he could not meet his collier and coal with *Gloucester* in view. Desperate to rid himself of this shadow, he signaled *Breslau* to scare her away by pretending to lay mines in her path.

On his own bridge, Captain Howard Kelly of the *Gloucester* was equally anxious to delay *Goeben* until—as he assumed was imminent—Milne arrived. All day, Kelly had been ignoring Milne's command to "gradually . . . drop astern to avoid capture." When *Breslau* turned back, Kelly decided to attack her and thereby force the battle cruiser also to turn and deal with him. At 1:35 p.m., *Gloucester*'s forward 6-inch gun opened fire at a range of 11,500 yards. Splashes rose in the sea astern of *Breslau.* The German light cruiser immediately replied, first with ranging shots, then with rapid, accurate salvos, one grouping landing only thirty yards from the British ship. Kelly responded by increasing speed, closing the range to 10,000 yards, and turning sufficiently to fire his full broadside.

This scuffle finally provoked Souchon. From *Gloucester*'s bridge, *Goeben,* a distant smudge in the haze over the bow, was seen to turn. Bright glows marked the flash of her guns; seconds later, tall white columns of water, produced by 11-inch shells, appeared in the sea. Kelly, having achieved his purpose of forcing the battle cruiser to arrest her progress, broke off and fell back. Souchon, who could not afford to spend precious coal chasing a light cruiser, resumed his course. *Gloucester* resumed shadowing. At 2:45 p.m., Kelly signaled Milne: "Have engaged at long range with *Breslau* and retreated when *Goeben* turned. I am now following again." *Gloucester,* firing eighteen rounds of 6-inch and fourteen rounds of 4-inch, had hit *Breslau* at the waterline, but this inflicted no casualties and failed to affect her speed. For another three hours, Kelly trailed his enemies. Then, at 4:40 in the afternoon, when the mountains of Cape Matapan, the central southern promontory of the Peloponnesian Peninsula, appeared on his port bow, with his coal nearly exhausted and with stern orders from Milne forbidding him to go beyond Matapan, Kelly broke off. He had done his best, had hung on tenaciously and only relinquished the chase under explicit orders. Free at last, *Goeben* and *Breslau* rounded the cape and entered the Aegean Sea.

—

Through the long day during which *Gloucester* with her two 6-inch guns and ten 4-inch guns had pursued *Goeben* and attacked her consort, Admiral Milne had kept his three battle cruisers with their combined total of twenty-four 12-inch and forty-eight 4-inch guns at Malta. When the Commander-in-Chief finally cleared Valletta harbor at 1:00 a.m. on August 8, he set an easterly course for Cape Matapan, where the German force had last been seen by *Gloucester* eight hours before. Milne's speed was a leisurely 12 knots; still convinced that Souchon's course was an elaborate feint and that eventually *Goeben* would turn back for the western Mediterranean, the British admiral was saving his coal for battle. At 2:30 the next afternoon, an urgent signal from the Admiralty upset this stately progress: "Commence hostilities at once against Austria." Milne's original war orders dictated that in the event of war with Austria, he should concentrate near Malta and keep watch on the Adriatic. Obediently, he turned north to merge his three battle cruisers with Troubridge's four armored cruisers and to prepare to engage the Austrian fleet. *Goeben* was forgotten.

In fact, war between Britain and Austria did not come for another four days. The erroneous war telegram was a product of the misplaced initiative of an Admiralty clerk who, discovering a draft of the contingency coded war message lying in a tray on a colleague's desk and wishing to be helpful, sent it off. Four hours later, the mistake was corrected and Milne was told by an embarrassed Admiralty, "Negative my telegram hostilities against Austria." Nevertheless, for nearly twenty-four hours, Milne kept his fleet concentrated; then, leaving Troubridge to guard the Adriatic, he again turned to the east. Still in no hurry, still waiting for *Goeben* to turn, he reduced his speed to 10 knots. *Goeben* had gone into the Aegean? Splendid! Now to devise a plan to keep her bottled up. If all went as Milne planned, the German battle cruiser would never come near the French transports.

—

Souchon, at last free of surveillance, still needed coal. He signaled his collier, coming from Piraeus, to meet him at Denusa, a remote, sparsely inhabited island on the far side of the Aegean. Through the daylight hours of August 8, *Goeben* cruised furtively among the Greek islands and, at dawn on the morning of August 9, slid quietly into the bay of Denusa, which was deserted except for a few fishermen. While the sun rose higher and heat radiated from the sheer rock walls of the surrounding cliffs, *Goeben* and *Breslau* coaled simultaneously, one warship made fast to each side of the collier. Both ships were cleared for action and prepared to get under way in thirty minutes. Coaling continued through the night by candlelight; the searchlights normally used to illuminate the decks remained switched off lest beams or glow be seen far out to sea. Day and night, lookouts posted on the summit of a cliff swept their binoculars across the horizon. The first signs of danger, however, were reported from *Goeben*'s wireless room: beginning at nine on the evening of the ninth, the ship's radio operators began picking up signals from British warships. The signals grew louder. At 3:00 a.m. on August 10, Milne and three battle cruisers entered the Aegean.

While his men shoveled coal, Souchon thought about what he should do. It was essential to communicate with Constantinople; despite his earlier bravado, he had come to believe that an attempt to enter the Dardanelles without Turkish permission risked naval and diplomatic disaster. To avoid revealing his whereabouts by using *Goeben*'s radio, he sent the liner *General,* now in the Aegean operating under his orders, to the island of Smyrna to forward a message to the German embassy in Constantinople: "Indispensable military necessity requires attack on enemy in the Black Sea. Go to any lengths to arrange for me to pass through the Straits at once with permission of Turkish government if possible; without formal approval if necessary." The hours passed and Souchon waited for an answer. The sun set and the moon rose, but there was no reply. At 3:00 a.m. on August 10, learning that the British had entered the Aegean, he decided that, with an answer or without one, he must leave at dawn for the Dardanelles; there he would enter or fight whoever he had to: British or Turkish. Finally, he received an ambiguous message forwarded from Constantinople by *General:* "Enter. Demand surrender of forts." Souchon did not know whether he was being told to force his way into the passage or was being requested to save face for the Turks by staging a charade of battle. Not knowing, he still had to sail.

At first light on August 10, clouds of black smoke poured from *Goeben*'s funnels, anchor chains rattled in, and *Goeben* followed by *Breslau* glided out of the harbor. Across a flat, silvery sea, the two ships steamed north at 18 knots toward the Dardanelles. By noon, stifling heat crushed down from a white sky; the only animation came from blue water foaming back from the ships' bows and washing along the gray steel sides. At five that afternoon, when the sun was lower and the western sky blazed in fiery splendor, watchers on *Goeben*'s bridge could see the island of Imbros and the plains of ancient Troy. Coming closer, they observed the coast of Asia Minor dividing itself from the narrow tongue of the Gallipoli peninsula with the gleaming water of the Dardanelles, the fabled Hellespont, in between. Off Cape Helles at the mouth of the Dardanelles, *Goeben* and *Breslau* halted. The German officers stared at the the water flowing smoothly out of the Narrows and looked up at the brown heights on both sides of the entrance. They could see clearly the outer forts of Kum Kale on the Asiatic side and those of Sedd el Bahr on the European side. Behind, farther up the historic passageway, lay the massive fortress of Chanak with its heavy guns. Over all of these fortifications, the green crescent flag waved in the evening breeze. Motionless, the two ships lay before the entrance. An uncanny hush filled the air. Then came the signal "Action Stations." Slowly, *Goeben*'s turrets swung around until the muzzles of the 11-inch guns were trained on the forts. The 5.9-inch guns in their casements also swiveled into position. There was a responding movement in the forts, and the long, menacing barrels of the coastal guns were trained on the two German ships.

Souchon had to make a decision. Should he attempt to fight his way through? He knew that the British were coming up behind; already his lookouts reported distant columns of smoke behind him on the horizon. From the signal bridge, he signaled Cape Helles: "Request pilot." Two dark shapes emerged from the small harbor at Cape Helles; they were Turkish destroyers coming at full speed. Uncertain of their mission, *Goeben*'s secondary guns trained on the approaching ships. Then the Turkish leader hoisted flags signaling, "Please follow me." The delay had been caused by uncertainty in Constantinople. The commander of the Chanak fortress had reported that the German warships had requested permission to enter the Straits. Enver Pasha, the Ottoman war minister, who controlled the forts and the minefields, pondered the risks to Turkey and to himself and then declared, "They are to allow them to enter." Asked whether the British warships following the Germans should be fired on, Enver paused and then said, "Yes."

Goeben and *Breslau* moved slowly into the Narrows, passing a shoreline, now hilly, now flat, lined with villages and vineyards. Along the way, the Germans could see numerous fortifications, many of them obsolete, lying half concealed beneath the heights. Twilight came as they glided past Chanak, the old, rust-colored fortified castle, and turned into a little creek where they anchored peacefully. Supper arrived with the crews still standing by the guns. Later that night, Souchon was told, a British warship had appeared off the entrance to the Dardanelles and had been refused permission to enter.

For three days, *Goeben* lay quietly at anchor. Then the battle cruiser and her consort steamed out into the Sea of Marmara, with the green coastline shimmering in the distance across a light blue sea. A few hours later, the German sailors saw at last the imperial city of Constantinople glittering in the sunlight. Before their eyes lay its chain of hills, its giant domes and soaring minarets, the ancient castles, the white palaces and villas, the massive, crumbling city walls, the rows of dark cypresses, the flowering gardens along the water. Their voyage was over.

—

Ironically, the *Goeben*'s arrival at the Dardanelles brought great satisfaction in Britain. *Goeben,* apparently so quickly hounded out of the Mediterranean into what seemed ignominious internment, was depicted as a hunted animal scurrying for cover; her escape became part of a glorious "sweeping of the seas" by the Royal Navy. Asquith wrote to Venetia Stanley that the news was "interesting," but that "as we shall insist that the *Goeben* should be manned by a Turkish instead of a German crew, it doesn't matter much. . . . The Turkish sailors cannot navigate her—except onto rocks or mines."

The Turks were unsure whether to be pleased or frightened by this turn of events. A nervous proposal that the Germans disarm *Goeben* and *Breslau,* "temporarily and superficially only," was scornfully rejected by Souchon. No one knew what to do next, until the German ambassador suggested that perhaps the ships could be "sold" to Turkey. This would not only solve the immediate problem but also serve as retribution on the British for their "requisition" of the two Turkish battleships. The idea was quickly accepted by both countries. On August 16, a solemn ceremony took place off the Golden Horn. The crews were mustered on deck and informed that their ships had been bought by Turkey. The German flag was lowered, the crescent was raised, and the Turkish naval minister officially received the *Jawus Sultan Selim* (the former *Goeben*) and the *Midilli* (the former *Breslau*) into the Ottoman navy. The following morning, fezzes were brought out to the ships and distributed to the men. The day of worship aboard the two ships was advanced from Sunday to Friday. At about this time, the pro-Allied Turkish minister of finance met a distinguished Belgian to inform him sadly that the Germans had captured Brussels. The Belgian pointed to *Goeben* lying at anchor off the Golden Horn and said, "I have even more terrible news for you. The Germans have captured Turkey."

When the British ambassador protested what had happened, he was informed that *Goeben* and *Breslau* were now Turkish ships. If so, the ambassador contended, the German crews should immediately disembark and be repatriated to Germany. Ah! but they were no longer Germans, Enver told him; they were Turks: they wore fezzes and worshiped on Fridays. In any case, Enver pointed out, the best native Turkish sailors were still in England, waiting to man the two British-built dreadnoughts; nothing could be done until these men returned. Churchill, who had explained the confiscation of the Turkish battleships by saying, "We could not afford to do without these two fine ships," now rumbled that Turkey's behavior in the acquisition of the *Goeben* and *Breslau* was "insolent," "defiant," and "openly fraudulent."

On September 23, Admiral Souchon was appointed Commander-in-Chief of the Ottoman navy, but Turkey remained at peace. She did not close the Dardanelles to Russian trade or take any other action violating her own neutrality. In the German embassy and in Berlin, consternation grew; it began to seem that the Ottoman empire might never actually enter the war as an ally. From Turkey's perspective, there seemed to be no need to go to war: no one had attacked her; no one, neither the Russians nor the British, even posed a serious threat. Indeed, the unexpected entry into the war of Great Britain, whose fleet and diplomacy had always been a buttress of Ottoman power, raised serious doubts and hesitations in Constantinople. While trying to sort out the situation and calculate who might win this war, Turkey's ministers smiled and prevaricated.

This state of affairs continued for ten weeks. Ultimately, Admiral Souchon saw his duty: it was to precipitate war. On October 27, with Enver's collaboration, he took his fleet—*Goeben, Breslau,* a Turkish cruiser, and four Turkish destroyers—into the Black Sea for "maneuvers." Once at sea, he steamed to the Russian coast and, on the morning of October 29, with no declaration of war and no warning, bombarded Odessa, Sevastopol, and Novorossisk. Russian civilians were killed, oil tanks were set on fire, and a Russian gunboat, a minelayer, and six merchant ships were sunk. "I have thrown the Turks into the powder keg and kindled war between Russia and Turkey," Souchon wrote to his wife.

The rest happened quickly. The grand vizier, protesting that he not been consulted, threatened to resign, and a majority of the Cabinet wished to disavow the violent act, but Enver prevailed. He had only to point to *Goeben,* with her German crew—fezzes notwithstanding—and her 11-inch guns, lying off the

Golden Horn. On October 30, the British ambassador presented an ultimatum to Turkey, demanding that the German crews be removed within twelve hours. There was no response. The British still hoped to prod the Turks back from the brink by a demonstration of sea power; on November 3, *Indomitable* and *Indefatigable* with two French battleships bombarded the forts at the entrance to the Dardanelles. The British ships fired forty-six 12-inch shells at Fort Sedd el Bahr on the tip of the Gallipoli peninsula, blew up a magazine, and raised huge clouds of dust. Still the Turks did not respond. On November 4, Russia declared war on the Ottoman empire, and the following day Britain and France followed suit.

Thereafter, the iron gates of geography closed on Russia. With access barred, first to the Baltic, and now to the Black Sea, the tsar's empire was left dependent for imports and exports on the White Sea port of Archangel, ice-bound for many months. Ninety percent of Russia's grain exports had come out through the Bosporus and the Dardanelles. The closure of that passage-way had an even greater choking effect on imports; now cannons, rifles, shells, and other essentials of war had no route by which to travel from Western arsenals to Russian armies. In time, this would contribute to Russia's collapse. Turkey's entry into the war also critically affected Britain's strategy, leading to the bloody failure of the Gallipoli campaign and the diversion of manpower into the campaigns of the Middle East and Mesopotamia. Ultimately, Turkey paid for her choice with the breakup of the Ottoman empire. After the war, Winston Churchill himself wrote a grim epitaph to this historical episode. When *Goeben* arrived at the Dardanelles, he said, she brought with her "more slaughter, more misery and ruin than has ever before been borne within the compass of a ship."

—

At the Admiralty, early satisfaction that the Mediterranean had been "cleansed" quickly soured into mortification that *Goeben* had been allowed to escape. Admiral Milne was recalled on August 18, came home, and retired. Sensitive to criticism, he argued that he had successfully carried out his primary orders to defend the French troopships. Battenberg backed Milne on this point; indeed, no one could argue that the transports had been attacked. As for *Goeben,* Milne declared accurately that the Admiralty had given him no hint that Turkey was a possible destination for the German ship. Why should he, a sea officer with his own pressing naval concerns, have been expected to fathom a secret diplomatic arrangement of which the Foreign Office, the Cabinet, and the Admiralty had no knowledge? Milne put the blame for *Goeben*'s escape equally on the Admiralty's failure to give him guidance and on Troubridge for his failure to intercept. On August 30, a Court of Inquiry announced that after "careful examination" of Milne's behavior and decisions, "their Lordships approved the measures taken by him in all respects."

Troubridge's career at first seemed unaffected. On September 8, once Admiral de Lapeyrère's French battleships had taken over responsibility for containing the Austrians in the Adriatic, Troubridge's force, again buttressed by *Indomitable* and *Indefatigable,* was posted at the entrance to the Dardanelles. "Your sole duty," Churchill told him, "is to sink *Goeben* and *Breslau,* under whatever flag, if they come out of the Dardanelles." But there was much talk in the navy about the failure to fight *Goeben,* and someone—if not Milne, then someone else—had to be held responsible. Troubridge was chosen. Surprisingly, the most vehement of his critics was the normally mild-mannered First Sea Lord, Prince Louis of Battenberg. Troubridge was guilty of "amazing misconduct," Battenberg wrote to Milne. Troubridge, Prince Louis continued elsewhere, had "signally failed in carrying out the task assigned to him. . . . Not one of the excuses which Admiral Troubridge gives can be accepted for one moment. . . . The escape of *Goeben* must forever remain a shameful episode in this war. The flag officer . . . responsible . . . cannot be trusted with any further command afloat and his continuance in such command constitutes a danger to the state."

Troubridge returned to England to face a Court of Inquiry. The court judged that he had "had a very fair chance of at least delaying *Goeben* by materially damaging her," and passed the case up to a court-martial convened on board the battleship *Bulwark* at Portland on November 5. The Admiralty did not dare charge Troubridge with cowardice; his reputation for physical courage was too high. Rather, the charge was brought that Troubridge "did, from negligence or through other default, forbear to pursue the chase of His Imperial German Majesty's ship *Goeben,* being an enemy then flying." Troubridge based his defense on the instructions from the Admiralty and from Milne not to engage a superior enemy force. Churchill's July 30 message to Milne, shown to Troubridge at Malta, was exhibited: "Do not be brought to action against superior force." Troubridge also cited Milne's signal to him on August 5: "First Cruiser Squadron and *Gloucester* . . . are not to get seriously engaged with superior force." The Admiralty prosecutor responded that the term "superior force" in both messages clearly referred to the Austrian fleet; Troubridge argued that under certain conditions the term also applied to *Goeben.* For a number of years, he told the court, it had been his "fixed and unalterable opinion that the advent of battle cruisers had killed the armored cruiser." Milne, he contended, was thoroughly familiar with his opinion; in 1913, the Commander-in-Chief had asked him to lecture on the subject to officers of the Mediterranean Fleet. Indeed, according to Troubridge, their most recent discussion had come during the interview between Milne and himself at Malta on August 2:

Troubridge: "You know, sir, that I consider a battle cruiser a superior force to a cruiser squadron, unless they can get within range of her."

Milne: "That question won't arise as you will have *Indomitable* and *Indefatigable* with you."

When Troubridge sailed that evening, of course, *Indomitable* and *Indefatigable* sailed with him. But on the following day, on Admiralty orders, Milne had stripped away the two battle cruisers and sent them charging toward Gibraltar, leaving Troubridge with only his armored cruisers. The Court of Inquiry had expressed regret that Troubridge had not made it clear to Milne that "he had no intention to engage *Goeben* in open water in daylight with his squadron unless supported by a battle cruiser." In fact, Troubridge had done so repeatedly.

Troubridge also claimed that at the same Malta interview, Milne had conceded that the man on the spot must be the final arbiter as to what constituted a "superior enemy" (in court, Milne reluctantly conceded that he had said this). Once the battle cruisers were taken away, Troubridge contended, his squadron was obviously inferior in gun power and speed: his armored cruisers had never registered hits at over 8,000 yards; their best speed in company was 17 knots. These factors left him—as the man on the spot—in no doubt that *Goeben* constituted a superior force, which he was forbidden to engage. "All I could gain [by engaging]," he said, "would be the reputation of having attempted something which, though predestined to be ineffective, would be indicative of the boldness of our spirit. I felt that more than that was expected of an admiral entrusted by Their Lordships with great responsibilities."

Milne, who was present throughout the Troubridge proceedings, was consistently hostile to his former subordinate. Addressing the Court of Inquiry, Milne had declared that he had expected Troubridge to fight *Goeben* and that in such an action it would have been difficult for *Goeben* to engage four ships at once; in practice, most single ships had all they could do to aim and fire at two enemy ships. For this reason, Milne said, he did not approve of Admiral Troubridge's abandonment of the chase. Troubridge, regarding Milne, limited himself to expressing his "deep conviction . . . that *Goeben* had no right to be escaping at all and that if she had been sealed up in the Strait of Messina by the battle cruisers, as I thought she ought to have been, she would never have escaped."

Ultimately, the judgment of the court-martial, like Troubridge's decision in the early hours of August 7, came down to a calculation of the relative strength of four armored cruisers as against one battle cruiser. Troubridge claimed that his first decision to attack was "a desperate one" made in the face of clear orders by his immediate superior *not* to engage "a superior force." "But I made it and for a time I stuck with it," he said. "Gradually, however, it forced itself more and more upon my mind that though my decision might be natural, might be heroic, it was certainly wrong and certainly in the teeth of my orders. . . . It was at this psychological moment . . . that my Flag Captain came back to me. . . . It was his duty . . . and, as a matter of fact, I did in reality completely agree with [him]. After he left me I thought it over a little further and then I made my decision."

Many British naval officers simply did not agree with Troubridge that in daylight *Goeben* constituted a force superior to his four armored cruisers. Battenberg emphatically declared that the twenty-two British 9.2-inch guns and fourteen 7.5-inch guns would have nullified and overpowered *Goeben*'s ten 11-inch guns. The Admiralty prosecutor argued that Troubridge had "assumed too readily" that all was well with *Goeben;* that she could steam at full speed and had plenty of coal and no worry about using up her ammunition. Churchill declared after the war that "the limited ammunition of *Goeben* would have had to have been wonderfully employed to have sunk all four British armored cruisers one after another at this long range." Churchill also pointed out that at the Battle of the Falkland Islands a few months later, *two* British battle cruisers were to use up nearly three-quarters of their ammunition sinking only *two* German armored cruisers.

Captain Fawcett Wray of *Defence* supported Troubridge, restating the opinion he had expressed to the admiral in his ship's chart room: "Up to the range of sixteen thousand yards, *Goeben* must be a superior force to one *Defence* or four *Defences*. . . . For four ships to try to attack her is . . . impossible because you could not get . . . [within] sixteen thousand yards unless she wanted you to, but if you did get within sixteen thousand or twenty thousand yards . . . it . . . [would be] suicidal."

Oddly, the court-martial devoted no time to a consideration of comparative armor. Nor had Troubridge apparently ever asked himself whether his cruisers' 9.2-inch or 7.5-inch shells would penetrate *Goeben*'s heavy 11-inch armor. An answer was provided at Jutland, when the German battle cruiser *Seydlitz,* similar in construction to *Goeben,* survived twenty-two hits from 12-inch, 13.5-inch, and 15-inch British shells, each with many times the penetrating and destructive power of Troubridge's 9.2-inch shells. Nor did Troubridge's defenders mention the vulnerability of his own thinly armored ships to 11-inch shellfire. Jutland made it painfully clear that armored cruisers were spectacularly vulnerable to heavy shells fired by battleships or battle cruisers; that day, four of the ships that had pursued the *Goeben*—the battle cruiser *Indefatigable* and the armored cruisers *Defence, Black Prince,* and *Warrior*—blew up and sank because heavy German shells penetrated their inadequate armor.

The verdict of the court-martial was handed down on November 9. The court accepted Troubridge's judgment that, under the circumstances of weather, time, and position at the time the two sides would have met—6:00 a.m. in full daylight on the open sea—*Goeben* constituted a "superior force." The court acknowledged that Troubridge's instructions, passed to him from the Admiralty by Milne and repeated to him again by Milne, ordered him not to engage a "superior force." Admiral Troubridge, therefore, was "fully and honourably" acquitted.

In the larger sense, however, neither Milne nor Troubridge ever received full acquittal. Troubridge afterward was given various commands on shore, but he never again served at sea. Milne remained on half pay for the rest of the war. Fisher continued to blame the "serpent" Milne for *Goeben*'s escape. "Personally, I should have shot Sir Berkeley Milne," Fisher wrote to a friend. He changed the prewar "Sir Berkeley Mean" to "Sir Berkeley Goeben," adding that "this most disastrous event . . . [a] lamentable blow to British naval prestige, would never have occurred had Sir B. Milne had been off Messina with the three battle cruisers . . . as if international law mattered a damn." Many historians agreed that Milne's failure to blockade Messina was the key. When Sir Julian Corbett, the official navy historian, criticized Milne for not guarding both entrances to the Straits of Messina with his battle cruisers, Milne raged at the presumption of "an amateur on shore" daring to criticize a senior naval officer. Arthur Marder, the American naval historian, closed his account of the episode by citing Milne's remark "They pay me to be an admiral. They don't pay me to think."

Within the navy, the court-martial left a basic issue unresolved: when an officer finds himself confronting a possibly superior force, should he ignore the odds, summon raw courage, and attack, or should he retreat and await a better day? Nelson's dictum "No captain can do very wrong if he places his ship alongside that of an enemy" had become holy writ in the Royal Navy, but Nelson had said it at Trafalgar, when his fleet of sailing ships had physical parity and psychological superiority over the enemy. In the modern era, no British destroyer captain was expected to invoke Nelson and lay his ship alongside—or even singlehandedly attack—a German dreadnought. The navy expected the exercise of judgment along with a display of courage; this was the verdict and lesson of the Troubridge court-martial. And, in fact, the subsequent battles of Coronel, the Falkland Islands, and Jutland strongly supported Troubridge's belief that bigger ships firing heavier guns could destroy smaller, weaker ships with relative ease, especially when the smaller ships could not—or did not choose to—run away.

Nevertheless, the Troubridge court-martial left a bad taste in the mouths of British sailors for many years. Twenty-five years later in the South Atlantic, a situation arose somewhat similar to the one faced by Troubridge. In December 1939, early in World War II, the German pocket battleship *Graf Spee,* a formidable ship armed with six 11-inch and eight 5.9-inch guns, encountered three smaller British cruisers, which among them carried six 8-inch and sixteen 6-inch guns. The British commodore Henry Harwood did not hesitate to engage. *Graf Spee,* concentrating her heavy gunfire on the largest British ship, the heavy cruiser *Exeter,* put this enemy out of action, but she did not seriously harm or shake off the two light cruisers, *Ajax* and *Achilles,* which continued to pepper her with gunfire and threaten her with torpedoes. After an all-day battle, the damaged *Graf Spee* retreated into the neutral harbor of Montevideo, Uruguay, claiming the legal seventy-two-hour respite to make repairs. During this span, the two small British cruisers waited outside territorial waters while British reinforcements, including a battle cruiser and an aircraft carrier, hurried toward the scene. In the end, *Graf Spee* emerged, steamed into shallow offshore water, and scuttled herself. Then her captain, Hans Langsdorff, went to a hotel room and shot himself. In the aftermath, Britain's First Sea Lord, Admiral Sir Dudley Pound, wrote to Harwood, "Even if all our ships had been sunk you would have done the right thing. . . . Your action has reversed the finding of the Troubridge court martial and shows how wrong it was."

CHAPTER 3

Jellicoe

John Rushworth Jellicoe, Winston Churchill once said, was "the only man on either side who could lose the war in an afternoon." In appearance, the new Commander-in-Chief of the Grand Fleet seemed an implausible bearer of this immense responsibility. A small, quiet man, fifty-five years old when he took command in 1914, Jellicoe had never been known to raise his voice. Those in the navy who knew him said that this was because he never had to; John Jellicoe was obeyed instinctively. From a distance, he looked nondescript. He was only five and a half feet tall.* His brown eyes were set deep in a wrinkled, weathered face. His prominent nose, jutting from under a small, old-fashioned navy cap, made his profile distinctive, but far from handsome. Then, coming closer, people saw the feature that distinguished John Jellicoe: the light in his eyes, which simultaneously shone with bright intelligence and radiated patience, calm, and kindliness.

Jellicoe commanded the Grand Fleet in August 1914 because Jacky Fisher had insisted that no one else would do. Over many years, Fisher, the irrepressible founder of the modern Royal Navy, rushing through life from one volcanic controversy to the next, had steered this, his most promising protégé, from one assignment to the next, each leading to Fisher's eventual goal: to have Jellicoe in command of the British fleet when war with Germany began. "Jellicoe to be Admiralissimo on October 21, 1914, when the battle of Armageddon comes along," Fisher wrote in 1911. A year later, he

*This is not as short as it may sound today. Like Jellicoe, King George V was five foot six; Winston Churchill was five foot six and a half, and Jellicoe's famous colleague Admiral David Beatty was five foot seven.

added, "If war comes before 1914, Jellicoe will be Nelson at the Battle of St. Vincent [where Nelson served brilliantly under Admiral Sir John Jervis]. If it comes in 1914, Jellicoe will be Nelson at Trafalgar." Now Admiralissimo of the armada Fisher had built, Jellicoe was ready. Twenty-two months of skirmishing would follow and then, on May 31, 1916, he would lead the most powerful British fleet ever sent to sea into the climactic naval battle of the war, the greatest clash of armored ships the world had ever seen.

Jellicoe's strength was his thorough professionalism, his cool, analytical mind, and his iron self-control. He was neat, polite, and methodical. He believed in naval traditions, procedures, and decorum, among which were loyalty, scrupulous fairness, and genuine concern for the personal affairs of his officers and men. The fleet responded to Jellicoe's transparent sincerity and obvious selflessness by giving him unreserved affection and trust. He was, said one of his Grand Fleet captains, "our beloved Commander-in-Chief, the finest character that ever was."

Jellicoe's professional experience and powers of concentration and organization were exceptional. He brought to his command an almost unparalleled technical knowledge and a lifelong, deeply ingrained confidence in himself. Beyond this, Jellicoe possessed something else rare among the hundreds of conventional officers on the Navy List: he had an original mind. It was not the mind of a dreamer and genius like Fisher, whose ideas ranged across the whole spectrum of naval affairs. Jellicoe's was the practical, realistic mind of an engineer. Fisher asked Why? and Why not? Jellicoe asked How? and How much? When he found the answers, he understood, better than anyone else in the British navy, the difficulties the navy faced. He was aware of the technical achievements and rapid progress of the German navy. He knew that German ships were superior in armor protection and that German shells, torpedoes, and mines were more reliable than British. He was familiar with German skill in gunnery, in which he was himself an expert. As he warned Churchill on the eve of war, it was highly dangerous to assume, as Churchill did, that British ships were superior to German as fighting machines.

Jellicoe was not without weaknesses. Sometimes, loyalty to old friends blinded him to their limitations and made him slow to relieve them of command. A more serious flaw was his tendency to do everything for himself—his difficulty in delegating responsibility. Because of his own immense capacity for work and extensive grasp of technical detail, he often dealt with matters that might have been left to subordinates. During his rise to the top, one of his superiors noted that he "really does too much. He must learn to work his captains and staff more and himself less. At present he puts himself in the position of, say, a glorified gunnery lieutenant. This will not do when he gets with a big fleet. He must trust his staff and captains and if they don't fit, he must kick them out!"

This advice did not change Jellicoe's nature. As he rose higher and his responsibilities grew greater, his reluctance to delegate never left him. He had what he considered a powerful reason: knowing better than anyone else the strengths and weaknesses of his fleet, he did not want a subordinate's monumental mistake to place that fleet in jeopardy. In sum, he did not want the war to be "lost in an afternoon" by somebody else. As supreme commander, with a consuming sense of the vital importance of the Grand Fleet to Great Britain, he remained fundamentally cautious. Accordingly, his knowledge of the flaws hidden within his ships produced a careful, undramatic strategy. No temptation, however glittering, was to be allowed to place the supremacy of the British Grand Fleet at risk. While John Jellicoe was Commander-in-Chief, the war would not be lost in an afternoon.

—

John Jellicoe, whose family and friends always called him Jack, was born into an English middle-class family in Southampton on December 5, 1859. His father, a captain in the Royal Mail Steam Packet Service, rose to become marine superintendent of the line and, eventually, commodore and a company director. Jack, the second of four sons, grew up in a harbor world where the primary events were the comings and goings of ships. Unsurprisingly, at twelve, in the summer of 1872, he joined the Royal Navy training ship *Britannia* as a cadet. He was small, almost diminutive, at four feet six inches, but he did well from the beginning; the head of the school called him "one of the cleverest cadets we have ever had." When he left as a midshipman two years later, Jellicoe was first in his class of thirty-eight and had also managed to grow two inches. Outside the classroom, he was courteous, friendly, unassuming, and enthusiastic at sports: a model young man. These qualities earned him a rare prize, described by Commodore James Goldrick, a present-day historian who is also a serving officer in the Royal Australian Navy: "Jellicoe was admired not only by his seniors and subordinates, but also by his contemporaries, that most critical of audiences." Yet Jellicoe never forgot his ultimate objective. On the flyleaf of one of his *Britannia* notebooks, a childish hand proclaims the book to be the "Property of Admiral Sir John Jellicoe."

Britannia was the beginning of a lifetime of "Firsts" in seamanship, navigation, gunnery, and torpedoes. Jellicoe went to sea in sailing ships and coal-burning vessels; he sailed around the world, and in a single year, at the age of sixteen, he grew another five inches—up to five foot one. By 1886, the year he turned twenty-seven, he was five foot six—as tall as he would ever be. As a lieutenant on the battleship *Colossus* anchored at Spithead, he showed his strength, quick reflexes, and instinctive bravery when, in a high wind and with a strong tide running, a seaman fell overboard and was swept astern. Jellicoe saw what was happening and immediately jumped in. *Colos-*

sus's captain was watching: Jellicoe "swam with extraordinary vigor . . . [and] succeeded in reaching the man before he sank and in keeping him afloat until a boat picked them up. The bluejacket was brought aboard insensible but soon recovered. Lieutenant Jellicoe smilingly received my congratulations and walked quietly to his cabin to put on dry clothes."

Jellicoe's close connection with Jacky Fisher began in 1884, when Jellicoe was on the staff at HMS *Excellent* Gunnery School at Portsmouth, of which Fisher was captain. Thereafter, Jellicoe adopted Fisher's beliefs in reform, efficiency, and readiness; in technological change, personnel management, and the importance of big guns and gunnery. In addition, from that time on, Jellicoe swam in the "Fishpond"—the pool of junior officers whom Fisher considered promising, whom he worked to promote, and who, like Jellicoe, would go on to higher command and fame. Fisher's sponsorship sometimes carried penalties as well as rewards, but Jellicoe's qualities were always so obvious that he managed to avoid the charge that his rise was due to favoritism. In September 1889, when Fisher became Director of Naval Ordnance, he brought Lieutenant Jellicoe along as his assistant. When Fisher went home at night, Jellicoe would still be at his desk, working sometimes until eleven p.m.

In 1891, Jellicoe, at thirty-one, was promoted to commander and sent to the Mediterranean Fleet as second in command of the battleship *Victoria,* flagship of Admiral Sir George Tryon. It was an assignment he was lucky to survive. When, on the afternoon of June 22, 1893, Tryon made an inexplicable blunder that sent *Victoria* into a fatal collision with *Camperdown,* Jellicoe was lying in his cabin with a fever of 103 degrees; he had been there a week, ill with dysentery. "I felt the shock," he wrote to his mother,

> and put on a pair of trousers and a coat and went on deck to superintend the launching of boats. I found the *Camperdown* had cut right into us and although we closed all the watertight doors, we seemed to be sinking fast. I had hardly started before the ship heeled right over, capsized, and went down eight minutes from the collision. As she went over, I climbed down the side and after being sucked down some way came to the top again. Any amount of men were killed by the propellers which kept on working as the ship went over as they fell onto them. It must have been an awful sight from the other ships. I was picked up. The curious thing is that my temperature today is normal so the ducking did me good.

Victoria went down with 358 of her 649 officers and men, including Tryon. Jellicoe was one of 291 survivors.

Returned to England and promoted to captain, Jellicoe again was working with naval ordnance when he happened to meet Sir Charles Cayzer, a self-made, wealthy shipowner. At Cayzer's house, the guest was introduced to the host's second daughter, Gwendoline. The navy captain was thirty-nine; the young woman was nineteen. There was an attraction, but Jellicoe's career intruded. In 1897, Jellicoe was invited by Vice Admiral Sir Edward Seymour, Commander-in-Chief of the China Station, to serve as Seymour's Flag Captain on the battleship *Centurion.* For three years, the assignment was routine. In Hong Kong and other Far Eastern ports, Jellicoe met and became friendly with the kaiser's brother, Prince Henry of Prussia, then in command of the German East Asia Squadron, and with Captain Henning von Holtzendorff, later Commander-in-Chief of the High Seas Fleet and Chief of the German Naval Staff, and with other German officers. A closer bond between the British and German squadrons was forged in the summer of 1900 during the dramatic international effort to relieve the besieged Western legations in Peking. When the legations, surrounded and threatened by thousands of Boxer rebels, appealed for help, an international naval landing force of more than two thousand men was hastily assembled. Seymour, the senior Western naval officer, took command of the relief column and named Jellicoe his Chief of Staff. Setting off by train to reach Peking, seventy miles away, the force was blocked and attacked by thousands of Chinese. Jellicoe commanded troops under fire until one day he was hit by a bullet on the left side of his chest. The impact spun him around and left him spitting blood. A doctor, injecting morphine, told him that the wound was probably mortal, whereupon Jellicoe wrote his will in six lines, leaving everything to his mother.

While he lay stretched out in the bottom of a river sampan, heavily bandaged, his place as Seymour's chief aide was taken by Captain Guido von Usedom, commander of the 500-man German contingent. Somehow, even in this unpromising place, Jellicoe's medical prospects began to improve. The prospects for the international column, now in retreat, were not as bright. At one point, an English journalist tried to cheer him by concocting good news. Later the journalist wrote, "I don't think I shall ever forget the contemptuous flash of the eyes Jellicoe turned on me or the impatient remark, 'Tell me the truth. Don't lie.' " Jellicoe recovered, but for the rest of his life, he carried the Chinese bullet in his lung.

Home in England after an absence of four years, Jellicoe found Gwendoline Cayzer waiting. He was forty-two; she was twenty years younger; they married in July 1902. Their age difference followed a pattern established by many career officers of the Victorian British army and navy. Some did not marry at all; Kitchener and Admiral of the Fleet Arthur Knyvet Wilson were examples. Others first established their careers up to the level of colonel or captain, then came home in their forties to marry much younger women and begin a family. In Jellicoe's case, marriage was a pleasant and entirely conventional buttress to his career. His wife's money from her father enabled them to live in a larger house than his navy pay could provide. In time, five daughters were born and eventually, when Jellicoe was fifty-nine and had retired from the navy, a son.

In October 1904, when Jacky Fisher became First Sea Lord, he summoned Jellicoe, as "one of the five best brains in the navy," to help design Britain's revolutionary all-big-gun battleship HMS *Dreadnought,* the ship that made all existing battleships obsolete and gave her name—dreadnought—to all subsequent battleships. This achieved, Jellicoe embarked on a steady climb up the ladder of promotion and responsibility, alternating between duty at sea and assignments at the Admiralty. For two years, he was Director of Naval Ordnance, responsible for the design and supply of all guns and ammunition for the navy. In 1907, he was promoted to rear admiral, knighted, and sent to sea as second in command of the Atlantic Fleet, based at Gibraltar. In 1908, Jellicoe returned to the Admiralty for two years as Third Sea Lord and Controller, where his task was the design, building, fitting out, and repairing of all ships of the Royal Navy. During these years, first at Naval Ordnance and then as Controller, Jellicoe's growing knowledge of the technology of shipbuilding raised in him a concern about the Royal Navy's weaknesses as well as its strengths. With Germany building the High Seas Fleet, he studied the comparative designs and capabilities of British and German warships and realized that in many respects his friends across the North Sea were building better ships. One German advantage, he wrote, "was that of far greater protection both in the way of armor above and below water, and in more complete water-tight subdivision below water as protection against torpedo or mine attack." By extension, he realized that the superior hull subdivision in German capital ships was made possible by their greater beam. "Our vessels," he said glumly, were "being limited in beam by the width of existing docks and the difficulty of persuading our government to construct newer and wider docks."

Jellicoe also worried about the effectiveness of British heavy-gun shells fired at long ranges. To test his fears, he arranged trials, which demonstrated that the standard British naval shell was effective when fired at close range across a flat trajectory and hitting armor at a 90-degree angle. But when these same shells were fired at long range and struck armor at oblique angles, they often failed to penetrate and thus also failed to burst in the vitals of the target ship. Concerned, Jellicoe requested the Ordnance Board to design and produce a new armor-piercing shell effective at the ranges at which future sea battles were likely to be fought. Before the matter was resolved, he departed, and subsequent Controllers allowed it to drop.

Jellicoe's desire to renew ties with some of the German naval officers he had known in China led him to accept an invitation to visit Germany in the summer of 1910. "I had a decided admiration and considerable liking for German naval officers and men," he later wrote. "I knew personally a great many of the senior officers and I felt a great respect for the efficiency of the

German navy." Persuaded to come to the Kiel Regatta by his old comrade in arms Guido von Usedom, now an admiral in command of the naval base at Kiel, Jellicoe also saw Prince Henry, the kaiser's brother, as well as William himself, who asked Jellicoe to race with him on his sailing yacht *Meteor.* The Royal Navy benefited from this German visit when Jellicoe subsequently obtained Admiralty approval for construction of two wide floating dry docks capable of lifting the largest battleships out of the water. "On my way to Kiel," he later explained, "I passed through Hamburg where several large floating docks were in use for commercial liners. I visited the largest of these and discussed their use with Germans." Besides their greater size, these docks had an additional significance, which became apparent during the war. "All our existing dock accommodation was in vicinity of the English Channel and the south of England," Jellicoe explained. With no naval base on the North Sea where the Grand Fleet was based, he, as Commander-in-Chief of the Grand Fleet, arranged for one of these floating docks to be towed to Cromarty Firth, where it was used seventy times by battleships and battle cruisers, saving them the longer voyage and the need for a destroyer escort passing back and forth to the permanent docks at Plymouth and Portsmouth.

It was as controller at the Admiralty that Jellicoe had his first unpleasant experience with a politician. The Welsh firebrand and Chancellor of the Exchequer, David Lloyd George, struggling to limit government spending on armaments, vehemently opposed the allotment of large sums to the Royal Navy to counter the growth of the German fleet. In February 1909, Jellicoe pointed out that in the construction of gun mountings, a key factor in the time required to turn out completed battleships, the Germans had recently become more proficient; therefore, prudence demanded that Britain increase naval spending even more. At a meeting at which Jellicoe was present, the chancellor walked up and down, venting his anger. "I think it shows an extraordinary neglect on the part of the Admiralty that all this should not have been found out," he said. "I don't think much of any of you admirals and I should like to see Lord Charles Beresford at the Admiralty, the sooner the better." Reginald McKenna, who was then First Lord, reacted quickly. "You knew perfectly well," he said to Lloyd George, "that these facts [increased German skill in making gun mountings] were communicated to the Cabinet at the time and your remark was, 'It's all contractors' gossip'—or words to that effect."

In December 1910, Jellicoe left the Admiralty to become Commander-in-Chief of the Atlantic Fleet. He was at sea when he learned by wireless that his five-year-old daughter, Betty, had died of a mastoid infection; she had come to the dock perfectly healthy a few weeks before to see him off. In 1911, he became second in command of the Home Fleet and in 1912 was promoted to vice admiral and returned to the Admiralty as Second Sea Lord. By this time, few in the navy questioned Fisher's wisdom in grooming Jellicoe for supreme command. Captain Wilhelm Widenmann, the German naval attaché in London, informed Tirpitz on January 11, 1912, "If one asks English naval officers which admiral would have the best chances for a brilliant career on the basis of his capability, one almost always receives the same answer: besides Prince Louis of Battenberg, unquestionably Sir John Jellicoe. Sir John possesses the absolute confidence of his superiors as well as his subordinates."

During his two years as Second Sea Lord, Jellicoe and his family lived in a large, comfortable house in Sussex Square. Every morning, he walked two miles to the Admiralty, and every evening the two miles back. At the Admiralty, he found the new First Lord, Winston Churchill, fifteen years younger than himself, to be brilliant, assertive, and, he thought, dangerously self-confident. "It did not take me very long," Jellicoe wrote later,

> to find out that Mr. Churchill was very apt to express strong opinions upon purely technical matters. Moreover, not being satisfied with expressing opinions, he tried to force his views upon the Board. His fatal error was his entire inability to realize his own limitations as a civilian. I admired very much his wonderful argumentative powers. He surpassed the ablest of lawyers and would make a weak case appear exceedingly strong. While this gift was of great use to the Admiralty when we wanted the naval case put well before the government, it became a positive danger when the First Lord started to exercise his powers of argument on his colleagues on the Board. Naval officers are not brought up to argue a case and few of them can make a good show in this direction.

In May 1913, Sir John and Lady Jellicoe were invited to Berlin on the occasion of the marriage of William II's only daughter. The guests included King George V of England and Tsar Nicholas II of Russia; the ceremony became the last meeting of prewar European monarchs before the outbreak of hostilities fifteen months later. Jellicoe, a minor figure among the royalty, nevertheless had a busy schedule. He was given a two-hour ride in a zeppelin; he was invited to lunch by the German chancellor, Theobald von Bethmann-Hollweg, and then to dinner by the kaiser. After dinner with William, Jellicoe had a long conversation with the emperor and Tirpitz about the different methods used to select naval cadets in the two countries. Tirpitz, charmed by the Jellicoes, invited them to tea to meet his daughter, who had just returned from two years at Cheltenham Ladies' College. Before leaving, Jellicoe asked the founder of the German navy to return the visit by coming to England and staying at his own house. "He thanked me," Jellicoe said, "but said that he would certainly be murdered if he were to visit England, as the British objected so strongly to his naval policy." While in Berlin, Jellicoe attended the annual dinner of the German naval officers who had served in China and, in the course of conversation, asked who were the rising men of the German navy. He was told that "certainly one of the future leaders" was an admiral named Reinhard Scheer.

In July 1913, Jellicoe's term as Second Sea Lord was interrupted by a special assignment. In war games involving 350 warships, Jellicoe commanded the "Red Fleet," representing a German naval force convoying an invading German army to England. The "army" was only a token force—three battalions of infantry and a battalion of marines—but Jellicoe managed to completely outmaneuver the defending "Blue Fleet," commanded by Britain's senior naval officer afloat, Sir George Callaghan, Commander-in-Chief of the Home Fleet. Avoiding Callaghan, Jellicoe successfully landed the invading troops at the mouths of the Humber and the Tyne. In fact, Jellicoe had done too well: Churchill, observing the exercises from Jellicoe's flagship, *Thunderer,* hurriedly ended the maneuvers lest they tell the Germans how the thing might actually be done. There was a further consequence. Churchill was dazzled by Jellicoe's "brilliant and daring" performance (he wrote to Jellicoe that "the results leave your naval reputation second to none"), and he was convinced that Fisher was right: here was the man to command the British fleet at the Battle of Armageddon.

—

On a London midsummer evening, Jellicoe sat alone in a first-class compartment on a train departing Kings Cross station for the north of Scotland. In his hand, he held a wax-sealed envelope containing a letter delivered to him by an Admiralty messenger a few moments before the train left the station. He was not to break the seal until instructed to do so by specific Admiralty order, but, to his consternation, he knew what the letter inside would say. The contents would make him Commander-in-Chief of the British Grand Fleet, the gray armada that would serve as the shield of the British empire and the sword of British naval supremacy. Once opened and read, the letter would bestow on him the greatest responsibility the navy could offer. Distractedly tapping the envelope on his knee, then turning to look out the window at England rushing past in the twilight, Jellicoe hoped that the order to open the letter would not come. The day was Friday, July 31, 1914.

Alone in his compartment through the night, Jellicoe had time to think about the events of the preceding three days and, especially, of that afternoon. On Tuesday, the twenty-eighth, Vice Admiral Jellicoe, the Second Sea Lord at the Admiralty, had gone to a dinner given by Lord Morley at which the other guests included Churchill; the Lord Chancellor, Richard Burdon Haldane; Field Marshal Earl Kitchener of Khartoum; and Lord Bryce, just returned from a long tour as British ambassador to the United States. When Jellicoe remarked conversationally to Bryce that the European horizon "looked to be very clouded," Bryce asked what he meant. Jellicoe said it seemed as though England might soon be at war with Germany. "War with Germany?" Bryce exclaimed. "Absurd! Why, any British government that did such a thing would be thrown out of office immediately." Twenty-four hours later, Churchill, who shared Jellicoe's opinion, took the precautionary step of ordering the British First Fleet to proceed to the remote northern fastness of Scapa Flow.

With the fleet at its war station, Churchill and his colleague Prince Louis of Battenberg, the First Sea Lord, confronted another decision. For nearly three years, the First Fleet—soon to be renamed the Grand Fleet—had been under the command of Admiral Sir George Callaghan, a capable, popular sailor who was sixty-two years old. Callaghan had done well. The fleet had improved in readiness and in December 1913 the admiral's two-year appointment had been extended for a third year. The succession thereafter was already arranged: in December 1914, Jellicoe would step into Callaghan's shoes. Both men had accepted this turnover as a routine rotation of senior naval officers. The First Lord of the Admiralty, however, was not a naval officer, and famously had no special respect for naval routines and traditions. And Churchill, increasingly, had come to believe that, as a wartime commander, Callaghan would not do.

On Wednesday, July 29, as his fleet steamed north, Admiral Callaghan was not with his ships, but at the Admiralty in discussion with Churchill and Battenberg. During these face-to-face talks, Churchill's doubts about Callaghan intensified. To some, sixty-two years might not seem old, but to the exuberant thirty-nine-year-old First Lord, it appeared to be the threshold of senescence. He worried that the admiral might fail under the mental and physical strains that war would put upon him. Jellicoe, on the other hand, was seven years younger, talented, experienced, and already in line to command the fleet as Callaghan's successor.

During his meeting with Callaghan, Churchill resolved to accelerate the forthcoming change. He did not reveal this intention to Callaghan, and his first move was only a half step: he told Callaghan that, in order to relieve him of some of his burdens as Commander-in-Chief, he was sending Jellicoe immediately to the Grand Fleet as second in command. The First Lord then summoned Jellicoe and gave him his new assignment. Callaghan appeared to welcome the arrangement and, before leaving London to join the fleet, arranged with his new assistant that the dreadnought *Centurion* should be Jellicoe's flagship. But Churchill, although he said no more to either man on the twenty-ninth, did not intend that Jellicoe continue long as assistant. On Friday afternoon, the thirty-first, Jellicoe had a long conversation with the First Lord and the First Sea Lord. At this meeting, it became clear to Jellicoe that, "in certain circumstances," he might abruptly be appointed Commander-in-Chief in succession to Callaghan; Jellicoe understood that "certain circumstances" had to do with the imminence of war. Still, nothing was settled. When Jellicoe boarded his train that night for Scotland, he understood that the final decision had not been made and that when the Admiralty decided, he would know because he would be instructed to open the envelope he held in his hand.

Jellicoe was a calm, orderly man, self-confident and ambitious, but always within the established framework of naval traditions. Given his respect for the decorum and hierarchy of the service, Jellicoe found the sequence of events orchestrated by Churchill distressing, even repugnant. He and Callaghan were brother officers and personal friends. "I had the most profound respect and admiration for him," Jellicoe said. They had served together in China during the Boxer Rebellion and, when Callaghan became Commander-in-Chief of the First Fleet in 1911, Jellicoe had commanded the best of his battle squadrons. Now, after three years, Callaghan knew his fleet and its senior officers and ships intimately. Under these circumstances, the plan to push Sir George aside seemed outrageous, almost unthinkable. The Commander-in-Chief, Jellicoe knew, had no idea that he was about to be summarily replaced. Might he not regard Jellicoe's participation—albeit involuntary and unwilling—as a personal betrayal?

Equally, Jellicoe worried "that the fleet might conclude that I had been in some measure responsible for the change." The navy was an intensely loyal service and the fleet trusted and admired its Commander-in-Chief. A change of command would come as a shock and would be certain to breed resentment. None of this would be helpful to a new commander at the beginning of a war. Already, there was opposition in the fleet to Jellicoe's coming even as second in command. Callaghan, on returning from the Admiralty to Scapa Flow, had told Vice Admiral Sir Lewis Bayly, commander of the 1st Battle Squadron, that Jellicoe would be coming as his assistant. Bayly had declared that the assignment of an assistant was an insult and said that if he had been the Commander-in-Chief he would have hauled down his flag in protest.

Jellicoe might be worried about what others would think, but his reluctance to succeed Callaghan had nothing to do with lack of personal confidence that he could do the job. At fifty-four, after a forty-two-year navy career, he knew that professionally, mentally, and physically he was ready to command the Grand Fleet. He was younger than Callaghan and had more recent experience with modern weapons. He knew that he was a better fleet commander than Callaghan. This had been made clear the previous year, in those naval maneuvers during which Jellicoe's attacking Red Fleet had thoroughly outmaneuvered the defending Blue, led by Callaghan.

While Jellicoe worried how Callaghan and others would perceive his promotion, Churchill was hurrying to make it a fact. To remove Callaghan, a close friend of King George V, Churchill needed the king's approval. On July 31, the day Jellicoe left for Scotland, the First Lord wrote to the king to warn him that should war come he would submit the name of Sir John Jellicoe for supreme command. Regretfully, Churchill said, he had come to the conclusion that Callaghan was too old. "These are not times," he urged the monarch, "when personal feelings can be considered unduly. We must have a younger man. Your Majesty knows well the purely physical exertion which the command of a great fleet demands."

The following day—Saturday, August 1—as Germany and Russia went to war, Churchill decided that Jellicoe's appointment must be immediate. He wrote again to the king, asking "respectfully and most earnestly" for approval of the change. Confident that approval would come, the First Lord also wrote to Lady Jellicoe, saying of her husband, "We have absolute confidence in his services and devotion. We shall back him through thick and thin. Thank God we have him at hand."

Meanwhile, that Saturday morning, Jellicoe reached the small Scottish North Sea port of Wick, where the light cruiser *Boadicea* was waiting to take him across the Pentland Firth to Scapa Flow. When he arrived, however, the town and harbor were enveloped in fog and the short voyage had to be delayed. While he waited, Jellicoe telegraphed to Churchill the first of a series of extraordinary messages pleading that the change of command not take place or, at the very least, be postponed. The first of these was sent at 10:30 p.m. on August 1:

> PERSONAL: DETAINED WICK BY FOG. AM FIRMLY CONVINCED AFTER CONSIDERATION THAT THE STEP YOU MENTIONED TO ME IS FRAUGHT WITH THE GRAVEST DANGER AT THIS JUNCTURE AND MIGHT EASILY BE DISASTROUS OWING TO EXTREME DIFFICULTY OF GETTING IN TOUCH WITH EVERYTHING AT SHORT NOTICE.
>
> THE TRANSFER EVEN IF CARRIED OUT CANNOT SAFELY BE ACCOMPLISHED FOR SOME TIME.
>
> I BEG MOST EARNESTLY THAT YOU WILL GIVE MATTER FURTHER CONSIDERATION WITH FIRST SEA LORD BEFORE YOU TAKE THIS STEP.
>
> JELLICOE

Believing that a career naval officer would better understand his position than the civilian First Lord, Jellicoe sent a copy of the telegram to Prince Louis, adding a sentence:

> YOU WILL UNDERSTAND MY MOTIVE IN WIRING IS TO DO MY BEST FOR COUNTRY, NOT PERSONAL CONSIDERATIONS.

On Sunday morning, the second, still waiting at Wick for the fog to lift, Jellicoe sent another telegram, this one addressed to both the First Lord and the First Sea Lord:

> REFERENCE MY PERSONAL TELEGRAM LAST NIGHT. AM MORE THAN EVER CONVINCED OF VITAL IMPORTANCE OF MAKING NO CHANGE. PERSONAL FEELINGS ARE ENTIRELY IGNORED IN REACHING THIS CONCLUSION.

Late in the morning, the fog thinned and *Boadicea* left Wick with Jellicoe on board. He arrived at Scapa Flow early in the afternoon and went on board *Iron Duke* to report to Callaghan. Jellicoe found his situation extremely awkward: "When I reported myself to the Commander-in-Chief, the knowledge of the event which was apparently impending made the interview both embarrassing and painful, as I could see that he had no knowledge of the possibility of his leaving the fleet, and obviously I could not tell him."

While Jellicoe was with Callaghan aboard the flagship, a telegram came in to *Centurion.* The First Lord was tiring of Jellicoe's protests:

> I CAN GIVE YOU 48 HOURS AFTER JOINING. YOU MUST BE READY THEN.

But Jellicoe, just back from his painful interview with Callaghan, was not ready. From *Centurion,* he signaled at 11:30 p.m. on August 2:

> PERSONAL TO THE FIRST LORD AND THE FIRST SEA LORD:
>
> YOURS OF SECOND. CAN ONLY REPLY AM CERTAIN STEP CONTEMPLATED IS MOST DANGEROUS. BEG THAT IT MAY NOT BE CARRIED OUT. AM PERFECTLY WILLING TO ACT ON BOARD FLEET FLAGSHIP AS ASSISTANT IF REQUIRED TO BE IN DIRECT COMMUNICATION. HARD TO BELIEVE IT IS REALIZED WHAT GRAVE DIFFICULTIES CHANGE COMMANDER-IN-CHIEF INVOLVES AT THIS MOMENT. DO NOT FORGET LONG EXPERIENCE OF COMMANDER-IN-CHIEF.

Jellicoe slept poorly on Sunday night. On Monday morning, August 3, he tried again to reverse Churchill's decision:

> QUITE IMPOSSIBLE TO BE READY AT SUCH SHORT NOTICE. FEEL IT IS MY DUTY TO WARN YOU EMPHATICALLY THAT YOU COURT DISASTER IF YOU CARRY OUT INTENTION OF CHANGING BEFORE I HAVE THOROUGH GRIP OF FLEET AND SITUATION.

Jellicoe's telegrams now stood somewhere between insubordination and farce, but he still refused to give up. At 11:30 the same morning, he made his final appeal:

> ADD TO LAST MESSAGE. FLEET IS IMBUED WITH FEELINGS OF EXTREME ADMIRATION AND LOYALTY FOR COMMANDER-IN-CHIEF. THIS IS VERY STRONG FACTOR.

Winston Churchill had had enough. He was not only the First Lord of the Admiralty; he was also a member of a Cabinet and government making the ultimate decision for war or peace. Germany, Austria, France, and Russia already were at war and the German government had just presented a twenty-four-hour ultimatum to Belgium. Despite Britain's treaty obligations to Belgium, four members of the Asquith Cabinet, opposed to British participation in any continental war, had resigned. Others were wavering. Churchill's patience was exhausted and he had no further time for a fidgety admiral, even a prospective Commander-in-Chief. The First Lord's final message, sent off on the afternoon of the third, allowed for no rebuttal:

> I AM TELEGRAPHING COMMANDER-IN-CHIEF [CALLAGHAN] DIRECTING HIM TO TRANSFER COMMAND TO YOU AT EARLIEST MOMENT SUITABLE TO THE INTEREST OF THE SERVICE. I RELY ON YOU AND HIM TO EFFECT THIS CHANGE QUICKLY AND SMOOTHLY, PERSONAL FEELINGS CANNOT COUNT NOW ONLY WHAT IS BEST FOR US ALL. YOU SHOULD CONSULT HIM [CALLAGHAN] FRANKLY.
>
> FIRST LORD

At four a.m. on Tuesday, August 4, Jellicoe received the signal to break the seal on his Admiralty envelope. As he knew it would, the letter inside contained his appointment as Commander-in-Chief of the Grand Fleet. Now obliged to act, he proceeded at once to board *Iron Duke,* where he found Callaghan already in possession of his own Admiralty signal:

> THEIR LORDSHIPS HAVE DETERMINED UPON, AND H.M. THE KING HAS APPROVED, THE APPOINTMENT OF SIR JOHN JELLICOE AS COMMANDER-IN-CHIEF. YOU ARE TO STRIKE YOUR FLAG FORTHWITH, EMBARK IN THE *SAPPHO* OR OTHER CRUISER, AND COME ASHORE AT QUEENSFERRY, REPORTING YOURSELF AT THE ADMIRALTY THEREAFTER AT YOUR EARLIEST CONVENIENCE. THESE ORDERS ARE IMPERATIVE.

Callaghan's emotions were under control. He had known that eventually Jellicoe would be his successor, but not that his own appointment was to be cut short. At the Admiralty conference only a week before, Churchill and Battenberg had given him no intimation that they were contemplating a change. Nevertheless, Callaghan behaved, Jellicoe said later, "as always, as a most gallant officer and gentleman, and his one desire was to make the position easy for me, in entire disregard of his own feelings." The two admirals agreed that Jellicoe should take command the following day, August 5. Even as they were talking, however, another signal came in from the Admiralty ordering the fleet to sea that very morning. Callaghan decided to give up command immediately. At 8:30 a.m. on August 4, as the Grand Fleet was leaving the harbor, he hauled down his flag and left Scapa Flow.

The fleet watched him go with dismay and indignation. Most officers felt that it was grossly unfair that the man who prepared them for war should be so abruptly dismissed on the eve of battle. Two senior vice admirals commanding Grand Fleet battle squadrons, Warrender and Bayly, signed a joint telegram to the Admiralty asking that the decision be "reconsidered." Beatty, commanding the battle cruisers, telegraphed extravagantly to Churchill and Battenberg that the change "would cause unprecedented disaster. . . . Moral effect upon the fleet at such a moment would be worse than a defeat at sea. It creates impossible problems for successor."* The Admiralty replied that their lordships understood these requests, but that they ought not to have been sent. Churchill—who later admitted that what had been done to Callaghan was "cruel"—telegraphed Jellicoe: "Your feelings do you credit and we understand them. But the responsibility rests with us and we have taken our decision. Take up your great task in buoyancy and hope. We are sure that all will be well."

The fleet's indignation was short-lived, and Jellicoe, quickly shouldering the burden of wartime command, soon gained universal respect. Nevertheless, two officers—the two most concerned—were slow to recover from the trauma. "I hope I never have to live through such a time as I had from Friday to Tuesday," Jellicoe wrote on August 7 to Hamilton, his successor as Second Sea Lord. "My position was horrible. I did my best but could not stop what I believe is a grave error. I trust sincerely it won't prove to be so. Of course, each day I get more into the saddle. But the tragedy of the news to the Commander-in-C was past belief, and it was almost worse for me." To his mother Jellicoe wrote, "I felt quite ill and could not sleep at all. It was so utterly repugnant to my feelings. But the Admiralty insisted and four hours before the fleet left, I was ordered to transfer my flag as acting Admiral to the flagship and poor Sir George Callaghan left her utterly broken down. It was a cruel and most unwise step." Fortunately for Jellicoe, his feelings on the matter had been transparent and it soon became clear that Callaghan had understood them. On August 21, the former Commander-in-Chief wrote to his successor:

> My dear Jellicoe:
>
> My disappointment has been made much easier to bear by the very kind letters I have been receiving these last few days.

*Writing to his wife, Beatty was more judicious: "We received the terrible news that the Commander-in-Chief has been relieved by Jellicoe. I fear he must have been taken ill. It is a terrible handicap to start a war by losing our Commander-in-Chief and it will break his heart. Jellicoe is undoubtedly the better man and in the end it will be for the best, but he hasn't the fleet at his fingertips at present."

Yours of the 13th which has just reached me is one of them and I am indeed grateful to you for all you say. It was a hard time, but we will forget it as we doubtless will both have many more shocks before it is all over.

The King was most kind and did a great deal to put me right with myself.

Good luck, old Chap

Three and a half years later, when Jellicoe's only son, George, was born, Cosmo Lang, the Archbishop of Canterbury, came to the Isle of Wight to christen the child. Crossing the Solent on the same boat, Admiral Sir George Callaghan told the archbishop that all the admirals who had served with Jellicoe in the Grand Fleet had subscribed to purchase a gold christening cup, which he would present to Jellicoe. After the dinner following the service, Jellicoe took Callaghan aside and said to him, "Look here, old chap, I have long waited to have a chance of showing you some papers to prove that I did everything I could to avoid that painful episode which neither of us can forget. Here they are." Instantly, Callaghan replied, "Damn your papers, my dear fellow, I don't want to see them. I have never had any doubt about it."

—

Burdened by the suddenness of his appointment and the pain it had inflicted, Jellicoe took up his immense responsibilities. With the great weapon placed in his hands, he had not only to shield the coasts of Britain from invasion, to guard the exits from the North Sea, and to foil the purposes of the German High Seas Fleet; he had to do more. The nation, the navy, the Admiralty, and the ebullient First Lord expected far more. All believed in Britain's invincibility at sea and all looked to this small man to bring them victory. And it was not just victory they demanded, but the absolute, annihilating triumph at sea bestowed upon England a century before by another small British admiral: Horatio Nelson.

CHAPTER 4

First Days

Jellicoe would have been happy to give England the glorious victory for which it yearned; the problem was to arrange that victory and persuade the Germans to cooperate. For more than a century after Trafalgar, the British navy possessed no detailed, carefully worked out war plan. Instead, British naval officers universally assumed that when war broke out, the fleet would immediately take the offensive. In 1871, when Vice Admiral Sir Spencer Robinson was asked how the navy would be employed in wartime, he replied, "The only description I could give is that wherever it is known that the enemy is, our ships would go and endeavour to destroy him. If you saw a fleet assembling at a stated port, you would send your fleet to that port to attack it. That is my view of the way in which war should be carried out." This virile opinion was shared by successive Boards of the Admiralty; they restated it in writing on July 1, 1908, when the Sea Lords instructed the Commander-in-Chief of the Channel Fleet that "the principal object is to bring the main German fleet to decisive action and all other operations are subsidiary to this end." The theme of the instant, all-out assault was drummed into the British public. Nelson had won at Trafalgar, *The Spectator* declared on October 29, 1910, "because our fleet, inspired by a great tradition and a great man, recognised that to win you must attack—go far, fall upon, fly at the throat of, hammer, pulverise, destroy, annihilate—your enemy."

But what if the enemy refused to cooperate? Suppose, in this new war, the Germans, despite possessing the second largest navy in the world, held their ships out of reach inside heavily fortified harbors, awaiting their own moment to strike? Until 1912, when Churchill came to the Admiralty, the Royal Navy had planned to deal with this possibility just as Nelson had dealt with

Napoleon's navy before Trafalgar: with a close, inshore blockade, monitoring every action of the enemy fleet and bringing it to battle if and when it came out. This time, a close British blockade of the German North Sea coast would be established with destroyers and other light forces constantly patrolling a few miles offshore, ready to report any German sortie before falling back on the British battleships cruising nearby. Fisher was the first to recognize that the submarine, the torpedo, and the mine had tossed this policy of close blockade on the scrapheap. No British admiral would be allowed to keep a fleet of battleships cruising back and forth in the Heligoland Bight in the close and constant presence of German submarines, destroyers, and minefields. This would mean, the Admiralty explained to the Committee of Imperial Defence in 1913, "a steady and serious wastage of valuable ships." In addition, there was the problem of fuel. Sailing ships in Nelson's day required only the wind; steel warships needed coal and oil. Destroyers patrolling the entrance to Heligoland Bight would have to return to port every three or four days to refuel; with a third of the force always absent, a close blockade would require twice as many modern destroyers as the Royal Navy possessed.

By 1913, the British navy had accepted these realities, abandoned close blockade, and adopted a new policy of distant blockade. In essence, this meant that rather than blockading the German coast, the British navy would close off the entire North Sea. Here, geography lent a powerful helping hand. As the naval historian Arthur Marder put it, "In a war with Germany, Britain started with the crucial geographic advantage of stretching like a gigantic breakwater across the approaches to Germany"; Mahan had said the same thing: "Great Britain cannot help commanding the approaches to Germany." The existence of the British Isles, stretching over 700 miles from Lands End to the northern tip of the Shetlands, left only two maritime exits from the North Sea into the Atlantic. The first was the Straits of Dover, twenty miles wide at their narrowest point. Here, the new technology of undersea weaponry came down in Britain's favor. "Owing to recent developments in mines, torpedoes, torpedo craft and submarines," declared a Committee of Imperial Defence paper on December 6, 1912, "the passage of the Straits of Dover and the English Channel by ships of a power at war with Great Britain would be attended with such risks that, for practical purposes, the North Sea may be regarded as having only one exit, the northern one." This "northern one" was the 200-mile-wide gap at the top of the North Sea, between northern Scotland and the southern coast of Norway. In these stormy waters, the blockade would be enforced by cruiser patrols supported by the dominating presence of the Grand Fleet at Scapa Flow. With these two exits barred, then, in the words of the naval writer Geoffrey Callender, "so long as Admiral Jellicoe and the Dover patrol held firm, the German fleet in all its tremendous strength was literally locked out of the world. The Hohenzollern dread-

Shetland Islands
Fair I.
Scapa Flow
Orkney Islands
Pentland Firth
Cromarty Firth
Invergordon
Peterhead
Lough Ewe
Aberdeen
SCOTLAND
May I.
Firth of Forth
Rosyth
Glasgow
Edinburgh
Lough Swilly
Tory I.
Newcastle
R. Tyne
Belfast
Hartlepool
Whitby
Scarborough
R. Tees
GREAT BRITAIN
IRELAND
Liverpool
R. Humber
Dublin
ENGLAND
Yarmouth
Gorleston-
Lowestoft
Cork
Berehaven
Queenstown
WALES
Harwich
London
Sheerness
Chatham
Portsmouth
C. Gris Nez
Devonport
Plymouth
Portland
Spithead
English Channel
Le Havre
THE NORTH SEA THEATER
FRANCE

NORWAY
SWEDEN
Skudesnaeshavn
North Sea
The Skaw
Skagerrak
Kattegat
ttle of Jutland
1916
JUTLAND
DENMARK
Battle of
Dogger Bank
1915
Horns
Reef
ogger
ank
Baltic
Sea
Amrun Bank
Kiel Canal
Heligoland
Battle of
Heligoland Bight
1914
Keil
Heligoland Bight
Brunsbüttel
Cuxhaven
Hamburg
Borkum
Wilhelmshaven
Emden
Jade
bay
Bremen
R. Weser
R. Ems
HOLLAND
R. Elbe
GERMANY
eebrugge
Ostend
nkirk
Antwerp
R. Rhine
Brussels
BELGIUM
LUXEMBOURG
ris
0
50
100 miles
0
50
100 km

noughts could not place themselves on a single trade route, could not touch a single overseas dominion, [and] could not interfere with the imports on which the British Isles depended." Distant blockade did not mean that British ships and sailors would simply sit as watchmen at the ocean gates and surrender the North Sea to the Germans. A new Admiralty war plan defined the Grand Fleet's new role: "As it is at present impracticable to maintain a perpetual close watch off the enemy's ports, the maritime domination of the North Sea . . . will be established as far as practicable by occasional driving or sweeping movements carried out by the Grand Fleet . . . in superior force. The movements should be sufficiently frequent and sufficiently advanced to impress upon the enemy that he cannot at any time venture far from his home ports without such serious risk of encountering an overwhelming force that no enterprise is likely to reach its destination." This was a practical strategy to contain the threat of the German fleet, the best that could be devised with the resources available. Unhappily for British jingoists, in uniform and out, it was not a strategy that guaranteed an immediate, annihilating victory over the High Seas Fleet.

—

Britain's abandonment of close blockade came as a blow to the German Naval Staff, which had planned to turn the Royal Navy's traditional offensive exuberance to its own purposes. Most German naval officers had expected that the British navy would begin the war with an immediate effort to destroy the High Seas Fleet. "Before the war," wrote Captain Otto Groos, the official German naval historian, "the whole training of our fleet and to some extent even our shipbuilding policy and even certain constructional details (for instance a small radius of action of a large number of our destroyers) was based on the assumption that the British would organize a blockade of the Heligoland Bight with their superior fleet." A major attack, the Germans believed, was coming. "There was only one opinion among us, from the Commander-in-Chief down to the latest recruit, about the attitude of the English fleet," said Reinhard Scheer, commander of the German fleet at Jutland. "We were convinced that it would seek out and attack our fleet the minute it showed itself and wherever it was." The battle, close to German ports, might go either way, the Germans thought, but damaged German ships could be expected to limp or be towed home; damaged British ships retreating across the North Sea would be subject to further German attacks—as well as the perils of bad weather, engine failure, or rising water inside their hulls. Because of this, English losses were expected to be greater; this would help create the "equalization of forces" that the German navy urgently desired. Thus it was that when the expected British onslaught into the Bight failed to materialize, the premise on which the Germans had based their strategy was overturned. And when the British navy failed to establish even a semblance of a close blockade, German U-boats and torpedo-carrying destroyers were deprived of any ability to harass and diminish the blockading fleet.

The war had scarcely begun when Germany's admirals and captains, robbed of their intended wartime strategy, finding the exits to the North Sea barred and the lower and middle North Sea turned into a watery no-man's-land, discovered that they did not know what to do.

—

Because each side was waiting for the other to act, nothing so dramatic as the British pursuit of *Goeben* occurred in the North Sea during the first weeks of the naval war. The Grand Fleet went to sea under Jellicoe, spreading its battle squadrons and flotillas for miles across the gray waves. They saw nothing. On August 6, Jellicoe dispatched his light cruisers to search the coastal waters of Norway. They found nothing. At dawn on the morning of August 7, the fleet returned to Scapa Flow to coal; by twilight, it was back at sea. This routine, exhausting for men and wearing for ships, became the normal life of the Grand Fleet for the next fifty-two months.

The war's first blow in home waters was struck, not by this enormous fleet, but by a single, humble vessel. In the misty dawn of August 5, when the war was only five hours old, the British cable ship *Teleconia* dragged her grappling irons along the muddy bottom of the southern North Sea. Five German overseas cables, snaking down the Channel from the port city of Emden, on the Dutch frontier, were her quarry: one to Brest, in France, another to Vigo, in Spain, a third to Tenerife, in North Africa, and two to New York. One by one, *Teleconia* fished up and cut all five of the heavy, slime-covered cables. That same day, a British cruiser severed two German overseas cables near the Azores. Thus, from the war's first day, Germany was cut off from direct cable communication with the world beyond Europe.

Meanwhile, as Jellicoe's armada cruised in the north, the light forces based at Harwich sank their first German ship—and suffered Britain's first loss. At dawn on the fifth, Commodore Reginald Tyrwhitt of the Harwich Force took his two destroyer flotillas to sea in a sweep toward the coast of Holland. At 10:15 a.m., this sortie produced a result: a British fishing trawler informed the destroyer *Laurel* that a vessel in its vicinity was "dropping things overboard, presumably mines." Two destroyers investigated; at 11:00 a.m., through rain squalls, they sighted a steamer ten miles away. The vessel resembled one of the Hook of Holland steamers providing peacetime ferry service for the Great Eastern Railway between Harwich and the Netherlands. Captain H. C. Fox, commanding the 3rd Destroyer Flotilla from the light cruiser *Amphion,* joined the chase and soon the destroyer *Lance* fired "the first British shot in the war."

The target was the 1,800-ton Hamburg-America Line excursion steamer *Königin Luise,* whose peacetime work was ferrying passengers back and forth from Hamburg to Heligoland. On the eve of war, she had been moved into a dockyard, repainted in the colors of British Great Eastern Railway steamers plying between Harwich and the Hook of Holland, and loaded with 180 mines. On the evening of August 4, while the British ultimatum still waited unanswered in Berlin, *Königin Luise* slipped out to sea with a patchwork crew of peacetime sailors and navy regulars. Her mission was to use her disguise to sow mines in the shipping lanes off the mouth of the Thames.

Königin Luise's first mine went over the side at dawn, and others followed through the morning. Then *Amphion,* coming up behind her own destroyers, opened fire and by noon, *Königin Luise* was lying on her port side in the water. Fifty-six of a crew of 130 were rescued by *Amphion.* Half of these prisoners were incarcerated in a compartment in the light cruiser's bow, for the grim reason that "if we go up on a mine, they might as well go first."

Returning to Harwich and attempting to avoid the area in which he thought *Königin Luise*'s mines might be floating, Fox sighted another suspicious steamer. This vessel, like the *Königin Luise,* wore the colors of the Great Eastern Railway, but unlike the ship Fox had just sunk, it was flying a large German flag. Seeing this, the flotilla opened fire. The steamer quickly hauled down the German flag and hoisted the Red Ensign of the British merchant marine. Eventually, it became clear that the vessel was a genuine Great Eastern Railway steamer, *St. Petersburg,* flying German colors because she was carrying the German ambassador to Great Britain, Prince Karl Max Lichnowsky, and his wife and staff from Harwich to the neutral Netherlands for repatriation to Germany. The German flag had been raised to give her immunity from attack by any German ships she might encounter. Her identity and mission established, she was permitted to steam away toward Holland. Fox continued toward Harwich.

Suddenly, a mine exploded against *Amphion*'s bow. The explosion killed and wounded many British seamen and, among the German prisoners in the bow, only one survived. With his ship ablaze and sinking, Fox gave the order to abandon ship. Just as he did, a second explosion occurred. "The foremost half of the ship seemed to rise out of the water," Fox said later. "Masses of material were thrown into the air to a great height, and I personally saw one of the 4-inch guns and a man turning head over heels about 150 feet up." The cause of the second explosion was never established, although Fox believed that it was another mine. Within fifteen minutes, his ship went down. One hundred and thirty-two British seamen were killed or wounded along with twenty-seven men from the *Königin Luise.* Twenty-eight German prisoners were brought back to England. When Fox reached Harwich on a destroyer, his friend Commodore Roger Keyes rushed aboard and was shocked to see Fox "stagger out of the chart house horribly burnt and disfigured."

Four days later, at the northern end of the North Sea, the next encounter occurred. Near noon on August 8, south of Fair Island, between the Orkneys and the Shetlands, the British dreadnought *Monarch,* conducting gunnery practice with her sisters *Ajax* and *Audacious,* was attacked by a submarine torpedo, which missed. Then, at dawn the next day, August 9, the light cruiser *Birmingham* sighted a submarine lying motionless on the surface in a thick fog. The U-boat was stationary, and *Birmingham*'s crew could hear hammering inside. The cruiser immediately opened fire and the submarine, *U-15,* slowly got under way. *Birmingham,* her wake boiling, turned and at high speed rammed *U-15* amidships, slicing her in half. The wreckage sank quickly, carrying down all twenty-three men of the crew and leaving behind on the surface only "the strong odor of petroleum and . . . rising air bubbles." It was the first U-boat kill of the war. *Birmingham,* suffering only superficial damage, was able to continue with the fleet. The triumph pleased the Admiralty, but the fact that a U-boat was operating so far north alarmed Jellicoe, who suggested that he withdraw the fleet from Scapa Flow to bases farther west. The Admiralty replied that this was impossible; for the next eight days, the Grand Fleet's presence was needed to safeguard the passage of the British Expeditionary Force to France. On the morning of August 8, Churchill had signaled Jellicoe: "Tomorrow, Sunday, the Expeditionary Force begins to cross the Channel. During that week the Germans have the strongest incentives to action."

—

During the period from August 9 to August 22, when 80,000 British infantrymen and 12,000 cavalrymen—with their horses—were crossing to Le Havre and other French ports, the Admiralty did not know what to expect: a surface attack by German destroyers into the Channel to savage the transports; a concentrated submarine assault on the vessels crowded with soldiers; or a massive challenge to the Grand Fleet by the dreadnoughts of the High Seas Fleet. On August 12, the bulk of the expeditionary force began to cross. During the days of the heaviest transportation—August 15, 16, and 17—Heligoland Bight was closely blockaded by British submarines and destroyers, supported by the Grand Fleet in the central North Sea. On August 18, the last day of heavy traffic, thirty-four transports crossed in twenty-four hours. During this time, the German navy did not appear. No ship was molested or sunk; not a man, soldier or sailor, was drowned. The concentration of the British Expeditionary Force in France was completed three days earlier than anticipated in the prewar plan and, on the evening of August 21, British cavalry patrols made contact with the Germans in Belgium. Three days later, the British army was heavily engaged near Mons.

—

The cause of this German inactivity was not known in Britain, and the stillness created fears that something terrible might be in store. These fears centered on the nightmare of a German invasion, or, more likely, a series of amphibious raids on England's east coast. (Churchill estimated that up to

10,000 Germans might be landed.) In fact, at no time during the Great War did either the General Staff of the German army or the German Naval Staff ever seriously discuss or plan an invasion of England on any scale, large or small. The passivity of the German fleet while the BEF was crossing stemmed from other causes. Despite the kaiser's cries of betrayal by his English cousins and Bethmann-Hollweg's hand-wringing over "a scrap of paper," officers in the German army were neither surprised nor troubled by Britain's entry into the war. The Army General Staff had expected the British to come in. "In the years immediately preceding the war, we had no doubt whatever of the rapid arrival of the British Expeditionary Force on the French coast," testified General Hermann von Kuhl, a General Staff officer. The staff calculated that the BEF would be mobilized by the tenth day after a British declaration of war, gather at the embarkation points on the eleventh, begin embarkation on the twelfth, and complete the transfer to France by the fourteenth day. This estimate proved relatively accurate. More important, the Germans did not much care what the British army did. Confident of a quick victory on the Western Front, they felt that measures taken to prevent the passage of the BEF would be superfluous. The kaiser had described the British as a "contemptible little army," and Helmuth von Moltke had told Tirpitz, "The more English, the better," meaning the more British soldiers who landed on the Continent, the more who would be quickly gobbled up by the German army.

The Imperial Navy thought differently, and once the passage of the expeditionary force began, many in the German fleet were anxious to contest it. The Naval Staff was surprised that the BEF was under way so early; they had not expected the cross-Channel movement to begin until August 16. This, added to its surprise at Britain's institution of a distant rather than a close blockade, created an atmosphere of uncertainty in the German navy, which militated against acts of sudden boldness. In fact, despite the heavy protection given the Channel transports, a bold approach might have produced favorable results for the Germans. During the crossing of the expeditionary force, the Grand Fleet moved south and kept to sea as much as possible, but Jellicoe's destroyers were constantly returning to base for fuel. A strong German attack, with destroyers dashing into the Channel to torpedo the transports, could have been attempted against the comparatively light British forces based in southern waters, with the attackers returning to Germany before Jellicoe could intervene. But without the support of heavy ships, Ingenohl believed, the German destroyer force would be massacred, and he held it back. As for submarines, ten U-boats already had gone to sea in an effort to find the British blockade line and locate the Grand Fleet. Ordered out on August 6, they were beyond wireless communication and thus could not be summoned to attack in the Channel. The German navy, therefore, did nothing.

—

Once the main body of the BEF was safely across the Channel, the Admiralty turned its attention to the wider seas. The threats there, besides *Goeben* and *Breslau,* were the two powerful armored cruisers of the German East Asia Squadron, and seven widely scattered light cruisers. One effective antidote to the German light cruisers would have been Britain's fast new light cruisers, but at the outbreak of war the Royal Navy still had too few of these. "We grudged every light cruiser removed from home waters," said Churchill, who believed that "the fleet would be tactically incomplete without its sea cavalry." The Admiralty had to make do with other ships, older, slower, less capable. Many of Britain's numerous predreadnought battleships were dispatched around the globe—*Glory* to Halifax, *Canopus* to Cape Verde, *Albion* to Gibraltar, *Ocean* to Queenstown—to serve as rallying points in case German armored cruisers broke out of the North Sea onto the oceans. Elderly British armored cruisers, some only a few months from the scrap yard, were mobilized and sent to sea. Twenty-four commercial ocean liners were armed and commissioned as auxiliary merchant cruisers.

In addition, there were troopships to be convoyed across the oceans. Two British regular army infantry divisions, broken into separate battalions and scattered on garrison duty around the globe from Bermuda to Hong Kong, had to be collected and brought home. Thirty-nine regular army infantry battalions from the British Indian army were to be gathered up and formed into the 27th, 28th, and 29th Divisions. They, in turn—to preserve order in India and the prestige of the Raj—were to be replaced in India by three undertrained Territorial divisions brought out from England. To the military mind, all this shuffling and exchanging, designed to place in France the best-trained soldiers Britain possessed, made excellent sense. To the navy, required to transport and convoy these thousands of men in different directions, the task was complicated, burdensome, and dangerous. Nevertheless, it was done. During September, two British Indian divisions and additional cavalry—50,000 men—were crossing the Indian Ocean bound for Europe. The Australian politician Andrew Fisher, soon to become prime minister, had declared that Australia would support "the mother country to the last man and the last shilling," and volunteers had swarmed into recruiting depots. A New Zealand contingent waited to be escorted across 1,000 miles of South Pacific Ocean to Australia, where it would be added to 25,000 Australians and with them be convoyed to Europe. The threat of German surface raiders on the sea-lanes forced a delay in the sailing of the Australian convoy, but on November 1, the convoy carrying the Australian and New Zealand Army Corps sailed from Perth for the Red Sea and the Suez Canal.

Meanwhile, two Canadian divisions were escorted across the Atlantic. The Canadian convoy sailed from the St. Lawrence on October 3 with more than 25,000 enthusiastic volunteers embarked in thirty-one ships. Detailed, uncensored stories in Canadian newspapers had followed the enlistment and training of these men, their boarding of the transports, the nature of the convoy, and its escort. With all this information freely available, the Canadian government belatedly became apprehensive for the convoy's safety. The original close escort, a squadron of old British cruisers under Rear Admiral Rosslyn Wester Wemyss, had seemed inadequate to the Canadian government, whereupon the Admiralty added the old battleships *Glory* and *Majestic.* In addition, the Grand Fleet battle cruiser *Princess Royal* was secretly dispatched from Scapa Flow to rendezvous with the convoy in the mid-Atlantic and protect it against any German battle cruiser that might slip out of the North Sea. The movements of the *Princess Royal* were extraordinarily stealthy and her presence was concealed even from the Canadian government. Had the ship's involvement been known, the Canadians would have been reassured, but Jellicoe insisted that the fact be revealed to no one. He had permitted the vessel to go because he understood the political disaster that would accompany any harm coming to the convoy. Nevertheless, he could not bear the German Naval Staff and the High Seas Fleet commander knowing that his battle cruiser force had been diminished by this major unit. And so it was that in the middle of the Atlantic, Rear Admiral Wemyss was astonished one day to see looming nearby the massive gray shape of *Princess Royal.*

Ten days later, as the convoy approached the English Channel, a U-boat was reported off the Isle of Wight. The army's wish had been to come up the Channel and disembark the troops at Portsmouth, near the British army's main training camps. Nevertheless, within an hour of the submarine report, the Admiralty asserted its paramount responsibility for the safety of the convoy and the transports were ordered into Plymouth, at the western end of the Channel. There, on October 14, the first Canadians came ashore in England.

With the navy's help, the equivalent of five British regular army divisions had been carried to Europe and replaced in the Indian subcontinent by three divisions of Territorial troops from England. Two Canadian divisions had crossed the Atlantic, and, although this was not concluded until December, two divisions were to be convoyed from Australia and New Zealand to Egypt. The effect of this concentration was to add five British regular army divisions to the six divisions with which Great Britain had begun the war. By the end of November, the British army in France had been raised from five to approximately thirteen divisions of regular, highly trained troops. This did not count the Canadian and Australian divisions training in England and Egypt, the ten Territorial Army divisions which remained for the moment in England, or the twenty-four divisions of new volunteers that Lord Kitchener was raising. For the Admiralty and the navy, the important thing was that all these vast, complicated movements at sea had been completed "without the loss of a single ship or a single life."

CHAPTER 5

Beatty

During the Great War, Britain's best-known admiral was not John Jellicoe. It was David Beatty. The youngest British admiral since Nelson, the commander of the famous Battle Cruiser Squadron, and then, succeeding Jellicoe, the Commander-in-Chief of the Grand Fleet, Beatty personified the Royal Navy to the British public. He was everything they liked to imagine in a naval hero: brave, impetuous, eager to attack, driving his ships toward the enemy at maximum speed—and then demanding that they go even faster. Beatty possessed the charisma that the calm and cautious Jellicoe lacked, and throughout the war the younger man—Beatty was twelve years younger than Jellicoe—was the darling of the popular press. It was Beatty's postcard photo, not Jellicoe's, that placarded every newsagent's window and sold in the millions.

Beatty's aura radiated in part from his genuine accomplishments and in part from successful exhibitionism. He was short and trim, easy to miss in a crowd, until he made himself instantly recognizable on board ship and in photographs by turning himself into a seagoing dandy. He tilted his famous extra-wide-brimmed cap over his eyes at a jaunty, devil-may-care angle; he stuck his thumbs rakishly into the pockets of his blue uniform jacket, which his tailor had been instructed to make with six brass buttons instead of the regulation eight. Like other flamboyantly egotistical and successful warriors—George S. Patton, who wore pearl-handled revolvers and high riding boots while commanding tanks, or Douglas MacArthur sloshing ashore (toward an army cameraman) on a newly captured Pacific island, wearing sunglasses and his self-designed, gold-braided hat, his trademark corncob pipe clenched between his teeth—Beatty used visual imagery to capture popular fancy.

Behind the imagery in Beatty's case lay a brilliant, frequently controversial career—and a life of private pain. A hero of colonial wars in the Sudan and China, twice promoted far ahead of other men his age, Beatty had attempted to mesh his naval career with marriage to a wealthy woman and, at her insistence, to present himself as a man of fashion in hunting circles and London society. Over the years, this effort took a heavy toll. Sometimes on the bridge of his flagship, Beatty would release his inner tension by making faces. "For no apparent reason," said an officer who served with him, "he would screw his face into a fearsome grimace and hold it quite unconsciously for a minute or two." Another peculiarity was his addiction to fortune-tellers: a Mrs. Robinson, a Madame Dubois, and, in Edinburgh when he commanded the Grand Fleet, a "Josephine."

David Beatty's wartime fame was fully justified. He was an audacious sea commander, a fighting admiral who gave his country significant victories and who also made significant mistakes. What the man in the street, the popular press, and even many of his colleagues in the navy did not know was how Beatty managed to do this and at what cost. Only a few could look behind the facade and "observe the private unhappiness and uncertainty in that hollow pose."

—

David Beatty was born on January 17, 1871, in a country house in Cheshire, but his roots lay in the Anglo-Irish squirearchy of County Wexford. Beatty's family heritage revolved around the army and the stables. For forty years, his grandfather was Master of the Wexford Hounds. David's father had served in the British cavalry in India, then left the army and moved from Ireland to Cheshire, where his four sons and a daughter were born. Curiously, this father was six feet four inches tall and had long arms and big hands and feet, whereas his two older sons, Charles and David, were short and had small hands and feet. Life at home was tumultuous; their father was eccentric, irascible, and tyrannical and became a heavy drinker; their mother, famous in her youth for her long, golden hair, died an alcoholic. Nevertheless, everyone in the family excelled on horseback, taking risks to the point of recklessness. David's parents both rode Irish hunters in pursuit of foxes and then came home to a tame fox kept in the house. David's three brothers followed their father into the army; his older brother, Charles, fought in the Boer War, earning a DSO, and then became a well-known gentleman jockey and steeplechase rider. During the Great War, Charles rejoined the army and died of wounds suffered in France. David's younger brother William became an owner and trainer of horses at Newmarket, and his youngest brother, George, like their father, became famous as a gentleman jockey, polo player, and steeplechase rider. David, the second son, shared the family passion for riding, but unlike his father and brothers, he decided to go to sea.

This is the surface history of David Beatty's early life. There is a deeper layer, rigidly suppressed while Beatty was alive, which helps explain the character and behavior of the famous admiral. He and his brother Charles were born out of wedlock. Their father had stolen the wife of another man and together he and she had produced two illegitimate sons within twelve months. At that time in Britain, legitimacy had as much to do with preservation of landed property as with morality. "Natural children" or "bastards" were banned from inheriting landed estates, which passed from father to the eldest legitimate son. When Charles and David were born—Charles in 1870; David in 1871—their mother was married to a Mr. Chaine. Six months after David's arrival, Mr. Chaine belatedly divorced his wife, who then married Captain Beatty. After the parents married, two other sons and a daughter, all legitimate, were born; legally, the two later sons became possible heirs as Charles and David were not. From the time the older brothers discovered the facts of their birth, they faced a lifelong apprehension that somebody else would discover the relevant birth and marriage certificates. As his fame grew larger, David, in particular, had to live with the possibility that the secret might come out. As it happened, no one learned the truth, and Charles inherited the family estate, eventually passing it along to his own eldest son.

In 1884, at thirteen, David Beatty left this turbulent, complicated family behind and entered *Britannia.* His record as a cadet was mediocre; he left eighteenth in a class of thirty-three. When he was a midshipman, influence gained him a three-year appointment to *Alexandra,* flagship of the Duke of Edinburgh, Queen Victoria's second son and Commander-in-Chief of the Mediterranean Fleet. Unsurprisingly, Beatty's interest outside the navy was riding and he often rode as a jockey on the racetrack and polo grounds at Malta, mounted on horses and ponies belonging to other officers. When he returned to England to take naval courses at Greenwich, his performance continued to be mediocre; the explanation perhaps had something to do with the fact that his cabin at Greenwich was filled with warmly inscribed photographs of London actresses. Thereafter, he served on the royal yacht, in the West Indies, and again in the Mediterranean, where he joined the battleship *Camperdown* a few months after she rammed and sank *Victoria* with Jellicoe on board.

In 1896, when Beatty was a twenty-five-year-old navy lieutenant of no particular distinction, he was sent to command a gunboat on the Upper Nile during Kitchener's march to reconquer the Sudan. Here, in the first major turning point in his career, Beatty's quick reflexes and instinctive bravery thrust him forward. When a shell struck his gunboat and came to rest unexploded, Beatty, under fire for the first time, calmly picked it up and threw it overboard. In the spring of 1898, Beatty commanded the shallow-draft gunboat *Fateh,* assigned to provide gunfire support for the army's advance up the Nile. Following Kitchener's famous victory at the Battle of Omdurman on September 2, Beatty and his gunboat carried the victorious general 400 miles farther up the Nile to Fashoda, where Britain, in the person of Kitchener, met France, represented by Captain Marchand. Beatty was praised by Kitchener—"I cannot speak too highly of this officer's behavior"—and was awarded a DSO. More important to Beatty, at twenty-seven he was promoted to commander over the heads of 400 lieutenants senior to him. The usual time served as a lieutenant before promotion to commander was eleven or twelve years. Beatty had done it in six.

On returning from Egypt to England, Beatty had four months' leave, which he devoted to foxhunting. It was in the country, on horseback, that he met a married American woman living in England, Ethel Tree, the only daughter of the enormously wealthy Chicago department-store owner Marshall Field. Riding sidesaddle, wearing a top hat and veil, slim and graceful with a long neck, high cheekbones, and dark hair, Ethel Tree was sophisticated, widely traveled, and, said Beatty's nephew and biographer Charles Beatty, "free ranging in her affections." Her fearless riding immediately appealed to Beatty, who noticed not only her beauty and horsemanship, but, being a second son with no inheritance whose naval pay amounted to a few hundred pounds a year, the money behind her. He quickly discovered that her marriage to Arthur Tree was unhappy and that she had a three-year-old son, Ronald. Despite her encumbrances, a strong attraction—perhaps more—sprang up between David and Ethel. For both, the relationship was risky. In Queen Victoria's reign, a divorced woman could not be received in society; above all, no divorced person could be presented at court. As for Beatty, an officer known to be the lover of a married woman or who married a divorced woman exposed himself to social ostracism and placed his naval career in jeopardy. As it happened, these considerations became moot in April 1899, when Beatty was appointed commander of the battleship *Barfleur* on the China Station. To Ethel, this separation was shocking; no man she liked had ever walked away from her before.

Beatty was not with the international expedition sent to relieve the besieged legations in Peking, but he was ashore in China, having landed with 150 men from *Barfleur* to bolster the defense of the beleaguered river port of Tientsin. Nine days after landing, Beatty was wounded twice within twenty minutes, first in the left arm below the shoulder, and then in the left wrist. He emerged from a local hospital with his arm in a sling and was ordered home for surgery to preserve the use of his arm. After the campaign, Beatty was one of four navy commanders who fought in China raised to the rank of captain. He was twenty-nine. The average age for promotion to captain was forty-two, and he had been promoted over the heads of 218 other Royal Navy commanders.

Beatty returned to England a hero, and Ethel Tree moved quickly to reengage his attention. When he first left for China, they had exchanged letters, but during his two years in the Far East, rumors reached him that she was constantly being seen in the company of another man, although she remained married to Tree. Nevertheless, when he arrived in Portsmouth, he received a letter and telegram from her suggesting that they resume their relationship. His first response was to air his grievances: "Some months ago all letters from you ceased absolutely and entirely. And letters came from other people telling me that you and 'X' were never seen apart and continually in each other's pockets and this by people who did not even know what you are to me so what was I to think? . . . I am not easy going and have an awful temper and I landed from China with my heart full of rage and swore I did not care if I ever saw you again." Then he about-faced and accepted her offer: "So great is the joy at seeing you, to me, the sweetest creature on God's earth, but you admit you are an awful flirt. . . . Unfortunately I shall go on loving you to the bitter end, and now if this operation does not go right what use to you is a one-armed individual?"

The operation to restore full use of his left arm took place in September 1900. It was mostly successful, but Beatty was left with two permanently crippled fingers. Meanwhile, Ethel had forced her husband to file for divorce in America. "Dear Arthur," she wrote him, "I have thought over your suggestion that we should live together again and I can never consent to it. There is no use discussing our differences. I shall never live with you again. Yours truly, Ethel F. Tree." To speed the action, she accepted the charge of desertion, thereby losing custody of her child. On May 12, 1901, the divorce was granted. Ethel's son Ronald Tree later condemned his "wilful and beautiful mother" for deserting him and his father, and said that the "divorce crushed my father's spirit . . . he dropped out of the world."* Ten days after the divorce, David and Ethel were married in the London registrar's office. Beatty was thirty; she was twenty-seven.

No one knows how much this couple knew about each other before they married. Beatty had been given a glimpse, but he could not have fully recognized the nature of his new wife. Keenly aware of the power of her beauty and wealth to attract men, accustomed to their constant, devoted attention, she always acted as she pleased and expected to get what she wanted. Beatty's nephew, on the other hand, is certain that Ethel never knew about her husband's illegitimacy; had she known, he says, the fact would have placed a formidable weapon in her hands. Even so, their wedding marked the start of a long battle between Ethel and the navy, with Beatty struggling in the middle. She resented the separations that were part of service life and refused

*In 1914, when her former husband was dying at the age of fifty-two, Ethel, who had not seen her son Ronald for ten years, sent a woman to the hospital to tell the sixteen-year-old boy, "Your mother has sent me to take you away." Appalled, Ronald sent the messenger away and returned to his father's bedside. Arthur Tree died the next day.

to be left behind like an ordinary navy wife when her husband went to sea. What he saw as attention to duty, she saw as deliberate neglect and selfish dismissal of her needs. Recrimination was constant. A pattern evolved: first a storm of rage, then tears, then, on both sides, an orgy of apology. Beatty's affection for his wife was greater than hers for him, which equipped her with the greater power to hurt. In his constant effort to placate her, his letters became pleading, pitiable, sometimes almost childish.

At first, these problems were submerged in the early joys of marriage, aided by the fact that David remained ashore. Two years passed between his being wounded in China and an Admiralty medical board passing him as fit for duty at sea. During these years, he learned to live as she preferred him: a gay, extravagant man of fashion in hunting circles and London society, posing next to his wife. Nevertheless, the reckoning came; once certified fit for sea duty, he was posted to three years in the Mediterranean Fleet. At first he tried to confront his wife's anger. She was staying at the Bristol Hotel in Paris when he wrote, "You have done a great deal of grumbling in your letters of late. Of course you have been brought up differently and like all American wives do not understand why their husbands should be anywhere else but with them." Then, succumbing to his own ambition, he turned to her for help, making a distasteful appeal that she use her charms to help him advance his career. "My darling Tata," he wrote,

> I had hoped that by going to Dunrobin you would have made a friend of the old Duke and that therefore in the future, should I ever require any outside assistance, he would be more likely to take an interest in someone he knew than someone he knew little about, and therefore might be of the utmost assistance to me. One has to think of these things when one lives a public life and if one wants to get on and not throw a chance away and no one can afford to let slip opportunities of making friends with those who can assist you.

Eventually Ethel followed him to Malta, where the Mediterranean Fleet was based, and there, in 1905, their first son, David, was born. Their relationship seemed close; when he was with her, he indulged her whims; when he was away, they wrote or telegraphed every day. He always wanted more. "Well, love, you might be a little more communicative," he wrote to her. "It's only twopence a word. Give me a shilling's worth and say how the weather is. It brightens me up." Most of his letters pleaded for signs of attention and affection; he asked endless questions about her feelings and activities. Her letters to him were less frequent, less intimate, more gossipy, and filled with tart, derogatory opinions of the navy and navy people. Professionally, he always did well: he commanded the cruisers *Juno, Arrogant,* and *Suffolk;* he was a strict, forceful, efficient captain, not overly popular, but his ships routinely won prizes in weapons competitions. Among his fellow captains and other officers, however, his youth and wealth stirred jealousy; and Ethel's behavior sometimes caused embarrassment. She never completely lost her Chicago accent, and her habit of shouting for her husband in a piercing voice—"J-aaack!"(her nickname for him)—grated on English ears. Once when Beatty drove *Suffolk* too hard returning to Malta, thereby damaging her engines, there were rumors of disciplinary action. A story passed around the fleet that Ethel had said, "What? Court Martial my David? I'll buy them a new ship." She never gave up urging him to leave the navy. Even in 1905, while she was making an effort to please him, she wrote, "I have thought for a long time that your abilities where you are, are wasted. I am sure you would succeed in another trade and would, I am sure, satisfy your ambition quite as much, if not more, and our life would certainly be much happier. Sometimes I feel as if I really could not stand the strain of these terrible partings very much more."

As the years went by, Beatty struggled to balance his ambition and the burden of his unusual marriage. He had made an almost Faustian bargain: Ethel's wealth had brought him mansions in London, halls in Leicestershire and Scotland for shooting, and a private yacht. She helped his career by enabling him to enter higher political and social circles—although still not the court circle—but she often reduced him to private despair. Shane Leslie, a Beatty biographer, who knew both Beattys well, wrote that she was "beautiful, opulent, ambitious and unhinged by her hereditary fortune and by an insane streak. She brought him many gifts; great beauty, a passionate and jealous love, sons, wealth, houses, and a personality he could not conquer, for against him was arrayed a distraught spirit which brought their home life to utter misery." Beatty told Leslie that he was "the most unhappy man in the world": "I have paid terribly for my millions," he said.

At the end of 1905, he returned to London, where, to Ethel's delight, he settled down for three years as Naval Adviser to the Army Council. In December 1908, he went back to sea as captain of the predreadnought battleship *Queen,* in the Atlantic Fleet, which was commanded by Prince Louis of Battenberg. In his letters to Ethel, he attempted to please her by belittling the officers around him: "We have eight admirals and there is not one among them, unless it be Prince Louis (who is lazy and has other disadvantages) who impresses one that he is capable of great effort." Ethel was scarcely interested. The Atlantic Fleet was based at Gibraltar, a socially barren place. When the fleet spent Christmas week in that harbor, she did not come to join him. Instead, chagrined by his absence, she began seeing other men. These relationships, she insisted, were innocent: "As you know, 'Lion' and I were a great deal together and I became very fond of him . . . although not the way I care for you, dear. I honestly say I like the companionship of other men but that is because most women bore me." In reply, Beatty blamed himself: "I felt as if I was an ogre dragging you to some fearful place that you dreaded. You see, dear, your happiness is the one thing I have to live for and if only you are happy and contented, so am I. But I fear I am making a hash of it somehow." Nevertheless, he went on, "If you have come to the decision that you want to go your own way without interference from me, as apparently is the fashion nowadays, would it not be fairer to say so? I have many faults. No one can see them more than you. Won't you in kindness point out where I fail and in what I upset you, as it would appear I do at times?"

His marriage wobbled, but Beatty's career continued to prosper and by the end of 1909, he had reached the top of the list of captains. But because of the periods spent ashore, first when he was recovering from wounds and later when he served on the Army Council, he had not served the time at sea required for promotion to admiral. Jacky Fisher intervened and, on his recommendation, an exception was made. On January 1, 1910, by a special Order in Council, David Beatty became, at thirty-eight, the youngest British admiral since Nelson. "Rear Admiral Beatty," *The Times* pointed out, "will not only be the youngest officer on the flag list, but will be younger than over ninety percent of the officers now on the captains' list."

None of this gave Ethel what she really wanted. Her husband's spectacular success and the presence of her two sons were not much good to her as long as she was barred from the summit of society.* Her wealth had opened many doors, but her status as a divorced woman had kept the highest door firmly closed. Now Ethel fixed on this new objective: she was determined to be presented at court; if she was not, her husband would quit the navy. As Beatty explained his situation to another officer, "My little lady likes the good things of this world including the gay side of it. She has a nice house in town and is sufficiently supplied with the necessary to be able to live in

*On April 2, 1910, a few months after Beatty became an admiral, a second son, Peter, was born. In his infancy, Peter's eyelids stuck together when he slept, a condition called ophthalmia neonatorum. This condition, probably acquired from his mother during the process of birth, suggested meningitis. Treated by frequent eye irrigation, the infection cleared up, but, according to Beatty's nephew, complications over the years indicate that the problem may have been of venereal origin. An even more surprising statement by Charles Beatty is that "David must have known that he could not have been the boy's father. This was generally accepted in later years and I was told who the other man was: [he came from] a well-known family of the British aristocracy."

As a mother to David Junior and Peter, Ethel was little better than she had been to the abandoned Ronald. When Peter was two, Ethel left him and went to gamble in Monte Carlo. Beatty, remaining with the boys in London, wrote her that Peter kept saying, over and over, "Mum, Mum, come!" As he grew older, Peter became practically blind, and "meningeal symptoms made it difficult for him to control the nerve reflexes of his head and neck, making him slobber and appear uncouth." He lived into adulthood, but Ethel, says Charles, "made no secret of her embarrassment at his conspicuous disability in company and in private she often ignored or even mocked him."

London and enjoy the entertaining and being entertained that a season produces. And it has undoubtedly struck her that my being in the service precludes her from participating in what to her provides something of the joy of life." Their friends saw the situation more baldly. "David was threatening to leave the Navy," said Eugenie Godfrey-Fausset. "Ethel was putting on one of her hysterical acts . . . she would force David to leave the Navy unless she was received at Court." In 1911, Eugenie's husband, the naval aide-de-camp and close friend to the new monarch, George V, arranged that Ethel Beatty, formerly Ethel Tree, be formally presented to the King of England.

Even as Ethel triumphed without forcing her husband to leave the navy, Beatty was risking his career on his own. He already had imperiled it by marrying a divorced woman; now he risked it again by refusing a major sea command. In 1911, as a new rear admiral, he was offered the respectable assignment of second in command of the Atlantic Fleet, a command that Jellicoe before him had automatically accepted as a necessary rung on the ladder of promotion. Beatty turned it down. The Atlantic Fleet was based at Gibraltar; Beatty had asked for the Home Fleet, which was more likely to be involved in any coming war with Germany—and which was based closer to home and to Ethel. His refusal, once known, stirred bitterness. Sea commands were scarce; to turn one down seemed almost unthinkable. Many officers senior to him also preferred the Home Fleet and were waiting in line for an appointment. The Sea Lords were shocked by Beatty's effrontery and Captain Ernest Troubridge, the First Lord's naval secretary, wrote to him, "The fact is that the Admiralty view is that officers should serve where the Admiralty wish and *not* where they themselves wish."

Beatty's friends thought his behavior foolishness, a reckless gamble with his whole future; others described it as insufferable arrogance. Despite his physical courage in the Sudan and China, Beatty's rapid promotions had not endeared him to his seniors and contemporaries. Many dismissed him as merely a dashing officer suddenly endowed with great wealth whose heart was not in the service. It was said that he had too many interests ashore—a millionaire wife, a place at society dinner tables, polo and foxhunting. Everyone was aware that, without his wife's money, he could never have challenged the Admiralty. Now, despite his record, he appeared to have gone too far; it was rumored that Beatty would never be offered another assignment. Indeed, for almost two years after his early promotion to admiral, Beatty remained unemployed.

Then, once again, Fortune handed him a prodigious gift. In 1911, when he refused the Atlantic Fleet appointment, Reginald McKenna was First Lord of the Admiralty. In October of that year, Asquith reshuffled his Cabinet, McKenna moved on, and Winston Churchill arrived at the Admiralty. Beatty still had no assignment when Battenberg suggested to the new First Lord that the prickly young admiral had talent and might be useful. Churchill had heard the prevailing gossip that Beatty preferred the life of a wealthy socialite to service in the navy. But the new First Lord was familiar with Beatty's exploits and navy record and invited the rebellious admiral in to see him. According to Churchill, this was not their first meeting. In his book *My Early Life,* he recalled that fifteen years before, on the eve of the Battle of Omdurman and his own extravagantly self-publicized charge with the 21st Lancers, he was strolling along the west bank of the Nile when he was hailed from a white gunboat anchored twenty or thirty feet from the shore. "The vessel was commanded by a junior naval lieutenant named Beatty. We had a jolly talk across the water while the sun sank. Then came the question, 'How are you fixed for drinks? Can you catch?' And a large bottle of champagne was thrown from the gunboat falling into the river near the shore. Happily, a gracious Providence decreed the water to be shallow and the bottom soft." Churchill promptly "nipped into the water up to my knees and bore the precious gift in triumph back to our Mess."

Beatty did not remember the episode, but before their late 1911 meeting at the Admiralty, he had no high opinion of Winston Churchill, whom he considered a flamboyant, irresponsible political maverick. In 1902 he had written to Ethel: "You are quite right, Winston Churchill is not nice; in fact, he is what is generally described as a fraud." His point of view had not changed in December 1909 when it seemed that Churchill might be named to lead the Admiralty: "I see in the papers that Winston Churchill will become First Lord of the Admiralty. No greater blow could possibly be delivered to the British Navy." Now, at their meeting in Churchill's office, the thirty-seven-year-old politician and the forty-year-old admiral appealed to each other. (There is an apocryphal story that when Beatty entered his office, Churchill looked up and said, "You seem very young to be an admiral." Whereupon Beatty is said to have replied, "And you seem very young to be First Lord of the Admiralty.") In any case, Churchill immediately set aside the Sea Lords' opinions of Beatty. "My first meeting with the Admiral," he said, "induced me immediately to disregard their unfortunate advice. He became at once my Naval Secretary." Privately, Beatty still regarded Winston as an enthusiastic amateur. Writing to Ethel, he said, "I had two hours solid conversation with W.C. . . . I think he had rather a shock at first but in the end he saw things with my eyes." In April 1913, he wrote, "I hope to be able to squeeze some sense into him."

Beatty's new position gave him plenty of opportunity to influence Churchill. By tradition, the First Lord had at his disposal the Admiralty yacht *Enchantress,* a 4,000-ton miniature ocean liner with an exceptional wine cellar, which allowed the political head of the navy to act as seagoing host to any persons he chose. During a Mediterranean cruise in May 1912, Churchill's guests included Asquith, Asquith's daughter Violet, Prince Louis of Battenberg, Kitchener, Jacky Fisher, and other senior politicians and military officers on board to participate in decisions about Britain's strategy in the Mediterranean. Beatty, with unparalleled access to the political and military chieftains of the British empire, nevertheless wrote to Ethel,

> Oh dear, I am so tired and bored. Winston talks about nothing but the sea and the Navy. Old Asquith spends his time immersed in a Baedeker Guide and reading extracts to an admiring audience. Prince Louis is, of course, charming but not terribly exciting . . . that old rascal Fisher never stopped talking and has been closeted with Winston. . . . I find this wretched party on board getting duller and duller. Mrs Winston is a perfect fool. Old Asquith is a regular common old tourist. . . . On shore it makes one ashamed to have to introduce him as the Prime Minister of Great Britain.

Churchill, of course, did not know what Beatty was writing to his wife, and over the next fifteen months, the young First Lord decided that Beatty "viewed naval strategy and tactics in a different light from the average naval officer; he approached them, it seemed to me, much more as a soldier would. His war experiences on land had illuminated the facts he had acquired in his naval training. His mind had been rendered quick and supple by the situations of polo and the hunting field." In addition to winning Churchill's favor, Beatty's work positioned him splendidly to help himself. It was his duty—as it had been Troubridge's—to keep track of appointments, to know what posts were becoming vacant, and to supply the First Lord with suggestions in assigning flag officers. From this vantage, a naval secretary could virtually arrange his own next post. In the spring of 1913, command of the Battle Cruiser Squadron, the most coveted appointment possible for a rear admiral, became available, and everything fell into place. "I had no doubts whatever," Churchill wrote of Beatty later, "in appointing him over the heads of all to this incomparable command, the nucleus as it proved to be of the famous Battle Cruiser Fleet—that supreme combination of speed and power, the strategic cavalry of the Royal Navy." On March 1, 1913, David Beatty hoisted his admiral's flag in *Lion,* flagship of the 1st Battle Cruiser Squadron.

Command of these fast, powerful ships perfectly suited David Beatty; he led them with the dash and flair that characterized him in the saddle. In war, his tactic was to attack; in peacetime, he burned his restless energy in riding, hunting, or tennis—he played until darkness made the ball invisible. His Flag Captain—the captain of his flagship—Ernle Chatfield, described him as having "a love of doing everything at high pressure and high speed." His ships and squadron began exercising at 24 knots rather than the usual 14, and firing at 16,000 yards rather than the customary 9,000. His tactics, pushing the offensive and courting risk, differed greatly from those of the Home Fleet commander, Sir George Callaghan, whom Beatty described to Ethel as "a nice old thing, full of sound common sense." Nor did Beatty wish to keep the image of himself and his squadron hidden from the public. Less than two months after taking command, he invited a well-known naval journalist, Filson Young, to visit *Lion* and observe the battle cruisers exercising at sea. Young took a long walk with Beatty over the Scottish hills, dined with the five captains of Beatty's force, watched the battle cruisers firing at long range, and was given plenty of time to observe the admiral controlling everything from the flagship's bridge.

Ethel, whatever the distinction of her husband's new command, did not change. She continued trying to adjust his schedule to accommodate her own. At one point, Beatty discovered that she was suggesting to the First Lord and to Admiralty officials whom she met in society that the battle cruisers be shuttled from one place to another to suit her own convenience. This time, Beatty's letter was sharp: "You must not bother Prince Louis or Winston by asking them where we are going and to send them here or there because you want to spend Whitsuntide with me. It won't do. The Admiralty have a good deal to do without having to consider which port will suit the wives best."

Nevertheless, Ethel was very much a part of David Beatty's greatest social triumph when together in St. Petersburg they acted as host and hostess to the Emperor and Empress of Russia. At the end of May 1914, the Admiralty decided to display British naval power in the home waters of the German and Russian empires. In June, Vice Admiral Sir George Warrender led four new dreadnought battleships, *King George V, Ajax, Audacious,* and *Centurion,* into Kiel at the time of the annual yacht races attended by the kaiser. At the same time, Beatty took the 1st Battle Cruiser Squadron, including *Lion, Princess Royal, Queen Mary,* and *New Zealand,* farther up the Baltic, to St. Petersburg. Because the head of the Gulf of Finland was too shallow to permit the big ships to come up to the city, they moored in the naval harbor of Kronstadt, twenty miles from the mouth of the Neva River. And no sooner were the four giant ships swinging on their moorings than a smaller vessel, a 200-ton yacht, appeared and dropped her anchor within shouting distance of *Lion.* It was Ethel's yacht *Sheelah.* During ten days of ceremonial lunches and banquets and visits to the theater, opera, and ballet, Ethel never left David's side. When Nicholas II, his wife, Alexandra, and their four daughters came to lunch on *Lion,* the tsar was shown through the gun turrets and magazines while his daughters were escorted around the deck by four British midshipmen. When Beatty and his captains lunched with the imperial family at the country palace at Tsarskoe Selo, Ethel accompanied them. His own hospitality, Beatty decided, had been too meager, so he invited 2,000 Russian guests to a ball on board the British warships. As this number of guests was beyond the capacity of *Lion*'s broad quarterdeck to accommodate, *New Zealand* was made fast alongside. Her deck provided space for dancing, while the flagship's deck, covered by red-and-white-striped awnings, was set with 200 circular supper tables. Covered gangways joined the two ships, which were hung with bunting and colored lights. With the help of the British embassy in St. Petersburg, 1,200 bottles of champagne were wrested from diplomatic cellars all over the city. Twenty whole salmon weighing twenty pounds apiece were set in blocks of ice on the serving tables. For Ethel, it was a culmination: here was Ethel Field Tree Beatty of Chicago acting as hostess to the representatives of a 300-year-old imperial dynasty. Nor was this the last of Beatty's successes that summer. On returning from Russia, he was knighted and on August 2, with war imminent, he was promoted to the rank of acting vice admiral.

—

Jellicoe and Beatty presented such immense contrasts in temperament, dress, style of life, professional experience, and command behavior that it is difficult to imagine them working together. Jellicoe was a consummate professional, calm, deliberate, and meticulous, with a thorough mastery of his ships and guns acquired over a long career afloat and ashore. As a result, he was always greatly admired in the navy. He had come up the traditional way, and in his steady upward progress there was never any question that he was bound for the top. As for Beatty, the navy was not so sure. In many ways, Beatty was the antithesis of Jellicoe. He was brave, high-strung, impatient for action. His career had advanced in fits and starts. Brilliant performance under fire had led to rapid promotions, leapfrogging him over his contemporaries—but then he had held himself back by his own unorthodox and, many thought, arrogant behavior. Jellicoe had been at the top of every class; Beatty had scraped through with Second and Third Class certificates. Beatty's meteoric career was due to forceful, almost instinctive action in moments of crisis; seizing these opportunities, he had bounded up the ladder of promotion. A commander at twenty-seven and a captain at twenty-nine, he was promoted so quickly that he outstripped his technical education and had performed no particularly distinguished service to the navy on shore or in routine assignments at sea. The difficult technical issues and decisions that dominated Jellicoe's naval career never much interested Beatty, and he never became deeply involved in any particular branch of his profession. He lacked Jellicoe's knowledge of the vulnerability of British ships to enemy weapons; indeed, this information burst on Beatty suddenly at Jutland when two of his six giant battle cruisers blew up under German shellfire, each explosion killing a thousand men. Beatty's response was "There seems to be something wrong with our bloody ships today."

In intellectual ability and professional knowledge, Jellicoe stood far above Beatty. The naval journalist Bennet Copplestone made the point that Jellicoe would have risen to the top in peace or war, whereas Beatty's success was likely only in wartime; his qualities needed battle to bring them out. Nevertheless, war came, and when it did Beatty, like Jellicoe—both placed in their respective commands by Winston Churchill—seemed to be in the right place. After the war, Admiral Sir William Goodenough, whose light cruisers fought every battle alongside the battle cruisers, said of David Beatty:

> I have often been asked what it was that made him so preeminent. It was not great brains. . . . I don't know that it was great professional knowledge, certainly not expert knowledge of gun or torpedo. It was his spirit, combined with comprehension of really big issues. The gift of distinguishing between essentials and not wasting time on non-essentials. The spirit of resolute, at times it would seem almost careless, advance (I don't mean without taking care; I mean without care of consequence) was foremost in his mind on every occasion.

CHAPTER 6

The Battle of the Bight

During the first three weeks of war, while the Grand Fleet was constantly at sea and the strain on ships and men was heavy, most vessels of the High Seas Fleet remained tied to their quays in Wilhelmshaven and other naval harbors. The British, unable either to reach their enemies deep inside the Heligoland Bight or tempt them out into the North Sea, were frustrated. "We are still wandering about the face of the ocean . . . entirely in the hands of our friends the Germans as to when they will come out and be whacked," Beatty wrote to Ethel on August 24. "For thirty years I have been waiting for this day, and have as fine a command as one could wish for and can do nothing. Three weeks of war and haven't seen the enemy." The press and the public shared the navy's frustration. The BEF was retreating in France and the German advance on Paris seemed irresistible, but land war was one thing, naval war another. At sea, Britons expected another Trafalgar the day after war was declared. When this did not happen, the cry arose, "What is the Navy doing?" In response, and in keeping with his own aggressive nature, Winston Churchill constantly demanded "offensive measures" from the Admiralty.

The First Lord's impatience was shared by two high-spirited second-level naval officers, Commodore Reginald Tyrwhitt of the Harwich destroyer flotillas and Commodore Roger Keyes, who commanded the long-range submarines, also based at Harwich. The two commodores were close friends, and their shared eager belligerence endeared them to their subordinates and to the youthful First Lord, but not often to senior admirals. Tyrwhitt and Keyes believed that it was not enough to patrol outside the Bight, hoping the Germans would come out; they wanted their Harwich forces to go in. "When are we going to make war?" Keyes demanded. The British fleet, he declared, possessed "absolute confidence" that "when the enemy come out we will fall on them and smash them." What Keyes wanted was to implant this same belief in the Germans: that "when we go out, those damned Englanders will fall on us and smash us."

Keyes was the British naval officer most familiar with what was happening inside the Heligoland Bight. Since the war's first hours, his submarines had been patrolling these waters and their captains thus acquired extensive knowledge of the enemy's movements and habits. They had learned, for example, that every evening German light cruisers escorted destroyers to a point twenty miles northwest of Heligoland; from that point the destroyers fanned out farther north to patrol against British submarines and minelayers. Returning at daylight, the German destroyers were met by light cruisers and escorted home. Keyes believed that this information could be put to use. His plan, which Tyrwhitt enthusiastically endorsed, was described by Churchill as "simple and daring": as the German destroyers returned to their dawn rendezvous, a superior force of British cruisers and destroyers, coming down in darkness from the north, would sweep in behind them from east to west across the Bight and catch them in a trap. The plan would involve the thirty-one destroyers of Tyrwhitt's two flotillas and nine of Keyes's long-range submarines. Three British submarines were to be employed as bait, showing themselves on the surface west of Heligoland, then turning and running before submerging; if they were successful, the pursuing German destroyers would be drawn out to sea, where Tyrwhitt would intercept them. Other British submarines would lie close off Heligoland to attack any German cruisers or capital ships coming out of the Jade to assist their destroyers.

When Keyes first took his plan to the Admiralty, he found the War Staff "too fully occupied with the daily task to give the matter much attention." Undaunted, the young commodore asked for an interview with the First Lord, who saw him on August 23.* The meeting, Keyes said, "gave me an opportunity of bursting into flame . . . which fired the First Lord." The following morning, Churchill presided over a conference at the Admiralty, attended by Prince Louis, Sturdee, Tyrwhitt, and Keyes. Here Keyes's plan was approved, with modifications. Instead of reaching the German rendezvous point at dawn and attempting to catch the returning German night destroyer patrols, the operation would begin later, at eight in the morning, when the night patrols were back in port and the German day destroyers were coming out to take station. As in the original plan, these would be lured out to sea by three surfaced British submarines, *E-6, E-7,* and *E-8*. And then Tyrwhitt's destroyers, sweeping between the Germans and their base, would

*Keyes was "young" relative to the admirals, not to the First Lord. In 1914, Keyes was forty-two, Churchill thirty-nine.

intercept, trap, and devour them. The plan involved risk: it meant exposing almost fifty British warships within a few miles of Germany's principal naval base. For this reason, the Admiralty insisted that the operation be conducted rapidly and the ships withdrawn before the High Seas Fleet could raise steam, emerge into the Bight, and, in their turn, entrap and destroy the British light forces. To provide insurance, Keyes and Tyrwhitt suggested that the Grand Fleet be brought down from Scapa Flow. And to add strength to the destroyer sweep, they asked that the six modern light cruisers of Commodore William Goodenough's 1st Light Cruiser Squadron be available as close support. Sturdee vetoed both of these requests; neither Churchill nor Prince Louis chose to overrule the Chief of Staff. In place of the massive support for which Keyes and Tyrwhitt were hoping, Sturdee approved only the positioning of the battle cruisers *New Zealand* and *Invincible* forty miles northwest of Heligoland and the stationing of four old *Bacchante*-class armored cruisers a hundred miles to the west. The operation was scheduled for August 28. Keyes's submarines were to leave Harwich on the twenty-sixth, and Keyes himself would follow in the destroyer *Lurcher* to coordinate the operations of his undersea craft. Tyrwhitt's destroyers would sail at dawn on August 27.

On August 26, the day before he was to leave Harwich, Tyrwhitt had taken possession of a new flagship, the recently commissioned light cruiser *Arethusa.* For some time, Tyrwhitt had been complaining about his previous flagship, the light cruiser *Amethyst,* commissioned in 1904. The older ship was "damned slow," he had grumbled, pointing out that it was impossible to lead and coordinate flotillas of 30-knot destroyers from a flagship with a maximum speed of 18 knots. Now, to his delight, he had transferred "from the oldest and slowest to the newest and fastest light cruiser." As designed, *Arethusa* had a speed of 29 knots and two 6-inch and six 4-inch guns; supposedly, she could outrun and outfight any German light cruiser in the High Seas Fleet. In fact, on August 26, 1914, the new ship was scarcely in condition to fight at all. She had been in commission only fifteen days; her new crew was untested; her highest speed in trials had been only 25 knots; her 4-inch guns frequently jammed when fired. Tyrwhitt boarded his new flagship at 9:00 a.m. on August 26 and immediately took her to sea for firing practice. When the 4-inch guns jammed, firing was discontinued. Nevertheless, at 5:00 on the morning of the twenty-seventh, Tyrwhitt sailed on *Arethusa,* leading the 3rd Flotilla of sixteen modern *L*-class destroyers. His subordinate, Captain Wilfred Blunt, followed in the older light cruiser *Fearless,* leading the 1st Flotilla of fifteen slightly older destroyers.

The unreadiness of *Arethusa* was the first of many flaws in the execution of Keyes's plan. A second, more serious error threatened the entire success of this first British naval offensive of the war. The plan conceived by the two Harwich commodores had been approved by the First Lord, the First Sea

Lord, and the Chief of Staff, but not until August 26, two days after the Admiralty conference, did anyone inform the Commander-in-Chief of the Grand Fleet. Even then, Jellicoe was told only that "a destroyer sweep of First and Third Flotillas with submarines suitably placed is in orders for Friday from East to West, commencing between Horns Reef and Heligoland, with battle cruisers in support." Jellicoe was immediately alarmed. He was certain that the force assigned was too weak to operate so close to the enemy's base—that if the light forces became entangled and were unable to withdraw, and if the High Seas Fleet came out, two British battle cruisers and a quartet of elderly armored cruisers would be unable to deal with the German dreadnoughts. Less than two hours after receiving Sturdee's signal, Jellicoe responded to the Admiralty: "Propose to cooperate on sweep on Friday moving Grand Fleet cruisers and destroyers to suitable positions with Battle Fleet near. Request I may be given full details of proposed operations by land-wire tonight. I am leaving at 6 a.m. tomorrow." After he had sent this signal, Jellicoe continued to worry. Why, he wondered, would the Admiralty keep the Commander-in-Chief in ignorance of so large and risky an operation? At 6:00 that evening, he signaled again: "Until I know the plan of operations, I am unable to suggest the best method of cooperation but the breadth of sweep appears to be very great for two flotillas. I could send a third [destroyer] flotilla, holding a fourth in reserve, and can support by light cruisers. What officers will be in command of operations and in what ships so that I can communicate with them? What is the direction of the sweep and [the] northern limits, and what ships will take part?" Sturdee's reply was brief and surly: "Cooperation by battle fleet not required. Battle cruisers can support if convenient." Given qualified permission, Jellicoe immediately ordered three of Beatty's battle cruisers, *Lion, Queen Mary,* and *Princess Royal,* to sail from Scapa Flow at 5:00 the following morning, August 27, to join *New Zealand* and *Invincible.* He also ordered Goodenough's six modern light cruisers, *Southampton, Birmingham, Nottingham, Lowestoft, Falmouth,* and *Liverpool,* to accompany Beatty from Scapa Flow. Ultimately, it was this action by Jellicoe—adding Beatty's battle cruisers, plus Goodenough's light cruisers, to the forces approved by the Admiralty—that saved the day. And once Beatty and Goodenough had sailed, Jellicoe himself followed them to sea with the four battle squadrons of the Grand Fleet. Only when all of his ships and squadrons were at sea did Jellicoe inform the Admiralty of what he had done.

When Beatty left Scapa Flow, he, too, had only a vague idea of the nature of the next day's operation. At 8:00 a.m., he signaled his battle cruisers and light cruisers, "We are to rendezvous with *Invincible* and *New Zealand* at . . . 5:00 a.m. [August 28] to support destroyers and submarines. . . . Operation consisting of a sweep . . . Heligoland to westward. . . . Know very little, shall hope to learn more as we go along." By noon, the Admiralty had given

Beatty the position from which Tyrwhitt's destroyers would begin their sweep and the course they would follow; he was never supplied with the assigned positions of British submarines. Beatty was asked how he proposed to support the operation. He replied that Goodenough's light cruisers would follow Tyrwhitt's destroyers ten miles astern and that he and the battle cruisers would remain thirty miles to the northwest.

Soon, these Admiralty errors were compounded. Just after 1:00 p.m. on the twenty-seventh, a message from the Admiralty informing Keyes and Tyrwhitt that the operation had been reinforced by Beatty and Goodenough was sent to Harwich for transmission to the two commodores, who were already at sea. But the wireless signal and the information it contained never reached Keyes or Tyrwhitt, because when the Admiralty message arrived at Harwich, it was mistakenly placed on a desk to await their return. Accordingly, Tyrwhitt and Keyes began the battle wholly unaware that Beatty's battle cruisers and Goodenough's light cruisers were on their way. Ironically, the greatest threat posed by this ignorance was to the British battle cruisers and light cruisers. Before sailing, the captains of Tyrwhitt's destroyers and Keyes's submarines had been told that *Arethusa* and *Fearless* were the only British ships larger than destroyers that would be present in the Bight. If other big ships appeared, Tyrwhitt's destroyers and Keyes's submarines were to assume that they were German, and they were to attempt to torpedo them.

Before dawn on August 28, such an encounter almost occurred. Tyrwhitt's ships, moving south toward Heligoland, sighted the blurred shapes of three four-funneled light cruisers. Tyrwhitt flashed the designated challenge and to his enormous relief received the proper reply; they were a part of Goodenough's squadron. Then, perplexed, Tyrwhitt asked, "Are you taking part in the operation?" "Yes," Goodenough replied. "I know your course and will support you. Beatty is behind us." Thus, Tyrwhitt knew and could inform his destroyer captains that six additional light cruisers, as well as Beatty's battle cruisers, might make an appearance. But Keyes, on board *Lurcher,* and the captains of his submarines, beneath the surface, remained ignorant.

—

Keyes's information regarding German defensive arrangements in the Bight was accurate. In these early weeks of the war, the German navy believed that the "heavily superior" British fleet would attack and provoke a battle off Heligoland. Meanwhile, says the German naval history, "our task was to keep the Heligoland Bight and the river mouths clear of British submarines and mines . . . [so as not to find] ourselves blocked in." The Germans considered using defensive minefields for this purpose, "but senior commanders feared that minefields would hamper too much the movement of our own [surface] forces . . . in the battle they felt sure was coming." In lieu of minefields, the

Germans substituted—as Keyes's submarine captains had told him—elaborate and extensive patrols by destroyers, light cruisers, and U-boats. "We overworked our destroyers and light cruisers in this effort," says the German naval history, "especially the personnel, the boilers and the engines of the destroyers. On patrol duty we had no less than four light cruisers and two destroyer flotillas by day and five light cruisers and three destroyers flotillas at night." Dawn on August 28 found these arrangements functioning routinely.

—

At 5:00 a.m. that day, Tyrwhitt in *Arethusa* was steering for the eight o'clock rendezvous twelve miles northwest of Heligoland. Behind him steamed the sixteen destroyers of the 3rd Flotilla and, two miles behind them, *Fearless* with her fifteen destroyers. Eight miles astern of *Fearless* were Commodore Goodenough's six light cruisers. As the sky began to lighten, the sea was calm and the weather clear, although, toward land, a misty haze hung over the water. Visibility was about 6,000 yards—three miles. At daybreak, Keyes's submarines, *E-6, E-7,* and *E-8*—the designated bait—surfaced and advanced toward Heligoland. As they approached the island, visibility dropped to 5,000 yards, which meant that, in order to be spotted, the submarines would have to go in closer.

First contact between British and German surface ships came at 7:00 a.m., when *Arethusa* sighted the German destroyer *G-194* three miles ahead on her port bow. The German ship immediately turned and ran south for Heligoland, and Tyrwhitt detached four British destroyers to pursue. *G-194* radioed, "Attacked by enemy cruisers," to Rear Admiral Leberecht Maass, commander of High Seas Fleet destroyers, whose flagship was the light cruiser *Köln.* Maass, in turn, signaled Rear Admiral Franz Hipper, who, besides commanding the High Seas Fleet battle cruisers, was responsible for the defense of the Bight. This morning, the patrolling destroyers had been assigned three German light cruisers, *Stettin, Frauenlob,* and *Ariadne,* as support. *Stettin,* 3,494 tons and capable of 25 knots, was anchored at half steam in the lee of Heligoland; *Frauenlob* was nearby. *Ariadne* remained in Jade Bay. These ships, each carrying ten 4.1-inch guns, were strong enough to overpower destroyers, but none would stand a chance against the 6-inch guns of Goodenough's modern *Southampton*s. Another German light cruiser, *Mainz,* lay at a mooring in the river Ems, and *Köln, Strassburg, Rostock,* and *Kolberg* were in Wilhelmshaven. *Danzig* and *Münchou* lay at Brunsbüttelkoog at the western end of the Kiel Canal. In Wilhemshaven, too, lay Hipper's battle cruisers, *Seydlitz, Moltke,* and *Von der Tann,* although *Seydlitz* was partially disabled with condensor troubles. But because of the tide, neither the battle cruisers nor the battleships of the High Seas Fleet could steam out into the Bight until noon. Low water in the Jade on August 28 was at 9:33 a.m., when the depth over the bar would be only twenty-five feet, too shallow for German dreadnoughts.

Hipper, receiving news of the first contact, never imagined that his battle cruisers would be needed. Assuming that his destroyers were being attacked only by British destroyers, he ordered the German light cruisers already on station, *Stettin* and *Frauenlob,* to "hunt [British] destroyers," and instructed his light cruisers still in harbor to raise steam. One by one, as they were ready, eight German light cruisers put to sea: *Mainz* from the Ems River, *Strassburg, Köln, Ariadne, Stralsund,* and *Kolberg* at intervals from the Jade; *Danzig* and *München* were to move down the Elbe estuary from Brunsbüttelkoog. Long before any of these German light cruisers arrived, however, the German patrol destroyers, hearing reports of British submarines on the surface, were steaming north at 21 knots. Suddenly, the sound of gunfire—the four British destroyers were chasing and firing at the German destroyer *G-194*—told them that a surface action was under way. Unprepared for this, they started to turn to the south, but before their turns were complete, they saw through the mist the high bow waves of many British destroyers steaming directly toward them. When the British opened fire, the German destroyer *V-1,* lagging behind, was hit. As the British destroyers were coming within range of the 8-inch guns of the Heligoland shore defense batteries, the German destroyer *G-9* signaled urgently for covering fire. But the shore artillerymen, hampered by the thick mist, were unable to identify the ships by nationality and held their fire. A German destroyer-minesweeper, *D-8,* was struck by a British shell, which hit the bridge, killing her captain. *T-33,* another destroyer-minesweeper, also was hit. For these small German ships, salvation could come only if the German light cruisers quickly intervened.

Tyrwhitt, meanwhile, had lost sight of his four detached destroyers. Then, hearing the sound of gunfire to the east and worrying that these ships might be under attack by a superior German force, he temporarily abandoned the planned westward sweep and, at 7:26 a.m., swung his whole flotilla east, toward Heligoland, to rescue his missing ships. Before long, he sighted ten German destroyers and settled down to a full-speed chase with *Fearless* and her flotilla following. The mist was thickening, and although Tyrwhitt could see the enemy destroyers on both his port and starboard bows, he was unable to gain on them. For half an hour this running battle continued, heading straight toward Heligoland, until suddenly, out of the mist, the island's 200-foot-high red cliffs loomed up over the bows of his ships. He turned away.

At 7:58 a.m., *Frauenlob* and *Stettin* arrived to cover their own retreating destroyers. The presence of these two ships reversed the tactical situation: now Tyrwhitt's destroyers had to deal not simply with German destroyers, but with German light cruisers. Following doctrine, the British destroyers immediately broke off pursuit and fell back on their own light cruisers, *Arethusa* and *Fearless.* A light cruiser battle, the first of the day, began and, almost immediately, so many British shells were hitting the sea near *Stettin* that it looked as if the ship "were in boiling water." Having achieved her purpose in covering the flight of the German destroyers, *Stettin* turned back toward Heligoland. Her captain wished to bring his boilers to full steam before returning to the fight.

Meanwhile, *Arethusa* was left alone with *Frauenlob.* Nominally superior to the German ship, *Arethusa* now displayed the effects of her too-recent commissioning. Two of her 4-inch guns were jammed and useless and a third was eliminated by a German shell; only her forward 6-inch gun was behaving reliably. Her wireless and searchlights were inoperable and water was filling her engine room. *Frauenlob*'s gunnery was excellent; Tyrwhitt later reported fifteen direct hits on the port side alone. Surprisingly, *Arethusa* lost only eleven men killed and sixteen wounded, although one of the dead was Tyrwhitt's young signal officer, who had been standing on the bridge next to the commodore. *Arethusa* fought back and, with the single gun she had in action, managed to hit *Frauenlob* ten times. One of these shells struck the bridge, killing or wounding thirty-seven men including the captain and forcing *Frauenlob* to sheer off and head for the protection of the Heligoland batteries. For a while, her survival was uncertain, but she reached Heligoland and then went on to Wilhemshaven. The first phase of the battle was over. *Arethusa* had been seriously damaged, *Frauenlob* was out of action, and a German destroyer and two destroyer-minesweepers had been badly hurt.

It was 8:12 a.m. With the Germans withdrawing and Heligoland close at hand, Tyrwhitt signaled his force to re-form and recommence the planned sweep to the west. Almost immediately another skirmish developed. Tyrwhitt's turn brought his flotillas across the path of another group of six German destroyers of the outer patrol, now returning to Heligoland. In the mist, five of these destroyers escaped around the flanks of Tyrwhitt's force, but their leader, *V-187,* was not so lucky. At 6,000 yards, Tyrwhitt's ships opened fire on this German ship fleeing south. The German destroyer was moving at high speed and seemed likely to get away when, to the astonishment of the British pursuers, she made a high-speed turn and headed straight back toward them. The cause of this unexpected event was that Goodenough, coming down from the northwest, had detached and sent ahead two of his light cruisers, *Nottingham* and *Lowestoft. V-187,* fleeing the British destroyers, suddenly and to her horror saw these two British Town-class cruisers ahead in her path. To escape, the German commander risked everything and doubled back. Initially, his unorthodox tactic succeeded: he sped unharmed past the first line of pursuing British destroyers. Then he ran into the second line. Immediately, *V-187* was surrounded by eight British destroyers, who circled their crippled opponent, firing point blank at 600 yards. Her flag still flying, *V-187* stopped firing. The British destroyers also ceased fire; they stopped their engines and began lowering boats to rescue survivors. Some of the Germans misinterpreted this action. Because their own flag still was flying, they believed that the boats in the water must be carrying boarding parties coming to seize their ship. To make clear that the battle was not over, a

German officer aimed and fired a gun at the British destroyer *Goshawk* 200 yards away, hitting her in the wardroom. The British ships reopened fire. At the same time, scuttling charges exploded in the German destroyer's hull; at 9:10 a.m., *V-187* sank, her colors still flying.

Boats from the five British destroyers were in the water and British seamen had just started pulling German sailors out of the sea when fountains of water from plunging German shells appeared around them. Through the mist, the light-gray hull and three funnels of a German light cruiser appeared. It was *Stettin,* her boilers now at full power, returning to action. When she opened fire, four of the British destroyers managed to get their boats back alongside, pick up the boat crews, and hurry away. The empty boats were left adrift. One destroyer, *Defender,* had put in the water two boats that, during the rescue operation, had wandered some distance. When *Stettin* opened fire, *Defender*'s captain made a quick decision to save his ship by leaving his boats behind. One British officer and nine seamen along with twenty-eight German prisoners were in the boats. The British sailors, abandoned in the middle of the Bight, believed themselves lost when an apparent miracle occurred. The surface battle had been observed through his periscope by the captain of the British submarine *E-4.* When *Stettin* arrived, he fired a torpedo at her, but the cruiser avoided it and attempted to ram. *E-4* escaped by diving. Twenty minutes later, when the captain put his periscope back up, there were no ships in sight, but the boats were still there, filled with Germans, some of them wounded, whom the British boat crews were helping as well as they could by tearing up their own clothes to make bandages. Suddenly, to the amazement of everyone in the boats, a submarine rose beside them from out of the sea. *E-4* took on board all the British sailors and three Germans—the commodore, a petty officer, and a seaman—"as a sample." The captain had no room on his small craft for the rest of the Germans, but before submerging, he gave those left behind water, biscuits, a compass, and the course to Heligoland, fourteen miles away.

There followed on the British side a sequence of events that can only be seen as farce. The cause lay in the Admiralty's failure to inform all British forces involved in the operation that other friendly forces were present. At 8:10 a.m., Goodenough had intercepted *Arethusa*'s signal that she was in action, and had detached two of his six light cruisers, *Lowestoft* and *Nottingham,* to go to Tyrwhitt's assistance. At 8:30 a.m., Goodenough and his four remaining light cruisers were steaming toward a position twenty miles southwest of Heligoland; from this position they meant to support Tyrwhitt's westward sweep. Keyes, supervising his submarines from *Lurcher,* however, had no reason to know or suspect that any four-funneled British light cruisers were in the vicinity. When, therefore, at 8:15 a.m., he made out two four-funneled cruisers (*Lowestoft* and *Nottingham*) steaming on the same course as himself, he signaled *Invincible* that he was in touch with two enemy cruisers. They had not attacked him, Keyes said, and with only his two destroyers, he was too weak to attack them; accordingly, for the moment he would shadow them. Goodenough intercepted Keyes's signal and, wholly unaware that the ships Keyes was reporting were his own two detached vessels, decided to take his four remaining light cruisers to Keyes's assistance.

By 8:53 a.m., Goodenough on *Southampton* had *Lurcher* in sight. This meeting compounded the confusion. Keyes, still uninformed that *any* British cruisers were in area, and now seeing four new light cruisers, assumed he was in the presence of four *additional* German cruisers. Believing himself overwhelmingly outgunned, he steered his two small destroyers toward *Invincible* and *New Zealand,* signaling that he was being chased by four hostile cruisers and that he was leading them toward the battle cruisers. This ludicrous but perilous situation was made even worse when Tyrwhitt, hearing Keyes's message, tried to help his friend by also signaling to Goodenough: "Please chase westward. . . . Commodore (S) [Keyes] is being chased by four light cruisers." Inadvertently, of course, Tyrwhitt was asking Goodenough for help against Goodenough himself. The episode ended harmlessly when Keyes finally saw and recognized the silhouette of *Southampton* and signaled, "Cruisers are our cruisers [of] whose presence in this area I was not informed."

This mystery cleared up, Goodenough turned west to follow Tyrwhitt's sweep. This led to further danger, because it brought his light cruisers over the line of British submarines of whose presence he was unaware. Nor could Keyes, who now knew that the four cruisers were British, communicate with his submarines beneath the surface. Alarmed, Keyes signaled to Goodenough: "I was not informed you were coming into this area; you run great risk from our submarines. . . . Your unexpected appearance has upset all our plans. There are submarines off Ems." Goodenough's reply was tart: "I came under detailed orders. I am astonished that you were not told. I have signaled to *Lion* that we should withdraw. *Nottingham* and *Lowestoft* are somewhere in the vicinity." In fact, an incident of a British submarine and a British cruiser attacking each other had already occurred. A little before 9:30 a.m., the *Southampton* had sighted a periscope at 500 yards. It belonged to *E-6,* which fired two torpedoes at the light cruiser; both missed. *Southampton,* steaming at high speed, swerved to ram, and the submarine escaped only by crash-diving. Goodenough signaled to *Nottingham* and *Lowestoft* to rejoin, but the two separated ships failed to get his signal and wandered off out of action for the rest of the day.

The final misunderstanding caused by British Admiralty blunders occurred at 9:45 a.m., when Tyrwhitt heard Keyes's signal that *Lurcher* was being chased by four enemy cruisers. Following his appeal to Goodenough to rescue Keyes, Tyrwhitt bravely turned his own damaged *Arethusa* back to the east to do what he could to help. Almost at once, he sighted a three-funneled cruiser, this one a genuine enemy, *Stettin;* with his destroyers, Tyrwhitt pursued her into the mist. Then, at about 10:10 a.m., he encountered the eight destroyers of the *Fearless* flotilla returning from sinking the German destroyer *V-187.* Fearing that he was again getting too close to Heligoland, and aware that other German light cruisers would be emerging from the river mouths, Tyrwhitt broke off the chase, reversed course, and once again headed west.

By this time, *Arethusa* could steam no faster than 10 knots. In the engagement with *Frauenlob,* her feed tank had been holed, her torpedo tubes demolished, all her guns except the forward 6-inch put out of action. As Tyrwhitt's two destroyer flotillas were now concentrated around her and no enemy was in sight, it seemed a favorable moment for making repairs. Accordingly, at 10:17 a.m. Tyrwhitt signaled the 1st Flotilla to cover his crippled ship and told Blunt in *Fearless* to come alongside. For the next twenty minutes, both British light cruisers lay dead in the water, their engines stopped, while the *Arethusa*'s engine-room crew and repair parties worked frantically. By 10:40 a.m., the hole in the feed line was plugged, the ship was able to resume at 20 knots and all but two of her 4-inch guns were unjammed and ready for action.

It was approaching 11:00 a.m. British forces had been in the inner Bight for four hours and it was certain that a vigorous enemy counterattack would be coming. Indeed, it was on the way. *Stettin* was prowling about, emerging from and disappearing into the haze, and three more German light cruisers, *Köln, Strassburg,* and *Ariadne,* were approaching from Wilhelmshaven. Admiral Maass, commander of High Seas Fleet destroyers, who was on board *Köln,* did not know whether the battle was continuing, but he hoped at least to be able to pick off some British cripples or stragglers. Meanwhile, Hipper had ordered a fifth light cruiser, *Mainz,* to attack Tyrwhitt's destroyers from the rear. *Mainz* sailed north from the Ems at 10:00 "to cut off the retreat of the hostile ships," as her executive officer put it. In Wilhelmshaven, the German battle cruisers were raising steam and at 8:50 a.m., Hipper had requested permission from Ingenohl to send out *Moltke* and *Von der Tann* at the first opportunity. The Commander-in-Chief had approved, but because of the tide, the heavy ships could not yet cross the Jade bar.

Thus, as *Arethusa* was restarting her engines, three German light cruisers were about to join *Stettin* on the scene. Fortunately for Tyrwhitt, Admiral Maass was so eager to fall upon and annihilate the intruding British destroyers that he did not take time to concentrate his force. Maass never imagined that Goodenough and Beatty were anywhere near. One by one, the German cruisers arrived and attacked. *Strassburg* appeared first and opened fire on *Arethusa.* "We received a very severe and most accurate fire from this cruiser," Tyrwhitt wrote in his report. "Salvo after salvo was falling between twenty and thirty yards short, but not a single shell struck. Two torpedoes were also fired at us, being well-aimed, but short." Outgunned in a crippled ship, Tyrwhitt ordered twelve destroyers to attack *Strassburg* with torpedoes. One torpedo passed near *Strassburg*'s bow, another under her stern, and the German ship turned away. Tyrwhitt, ever more anxious to get away to the west, gathered his destroyers to turn again in that direction. But as he did so, *Köln,* with Admiral Maass on board, appeared from the southeast. The weary British ships turned to engage her and Tyrwhitt, mistaking *Köln* for a powerful *Roon*-class armored cruiser, urgently signaled Beatty: "Am attacked by large cruiser. . . . Respectfully request that I may be supported. Am hard pressed." Beatty responded by ordering Goodenough to send two more of his light cruisers to assist *Arethusa.* Instead, Goodenough came himself with his entire squadron at high speed. Tyrwhitt, meanwhile, had gained another respite: *Köln* liked facing the massed torpedo tubes of the Harwich destroyers no more than *Strassburg* had, and she also retreated into the mist. For a fourth time, Tyrwhitt's force turned west.

—

At 11:00 a.m., when Tyrwhitt was entangled in what he described as "a hornet's nest," Beatty and his five battle cruisers were still marking time forty miles to the northwest. Around 10:00 a.m., the admiral had broken radio silence to give his position and to tell all British ships that for the time being he would remain where he was. Through the morning, he had been "intercepting various signals [from Tyrwhitt, Keyes, and Goodenough] which contained no information on which I could act." He had understood that Keyes had mistaken Goodenough's cruiser squadron for the enemy and subsequently that Tyrwhitt's force was heavily engaged and in distress. But why was Tyrwhitt still so close to Heligoland? Why had he made so little progress to the west? During the four hours since the fighting began, Tyrwhitt had advanced barely fifteen miles. Now, the British light forces, hotly engaged only twenty miles west of Heligoland, were still within easy reach of Wilhelmshaven. Beatty possessed a copy of the German coastal tide tables and knew that soon after noon, Hipper and Ingenohl would be able to send their dreadnoughts to sea. Already, Beatty had ordered Goodenough's light cruisers to hurry to Tyrwhitt's assistance, but he realized that against at least four, and possibly as many as six, German cruisers—including perhaps one large armored cruiser—this might be insufficient. With every minute, the possibility grew that the British light cruisers and destroyers would be overwhelmed.

Beatty, pacing on *Lion*'s bridge, understood that the responsibility was his. As vice admiral commanding the Battle Cruiser Squadron, he far outranked the three commodores, Goodenough, Tyrwhitt, and Keyes. The decisions he faced were not easy ones. If he went forward, he exposed his ships to enemy mines and submarines—and to British submarines, ignorant of his presence. In addition, there was the strong possibility that within a short time, German battle cruisers and perhaps battleships would be coming out. The mist to the east was thickening and for his battle cruisers to be surprised by the sudden appearance of German dreadnoughts could mean catastrophe. One of these dangers—submarines—Beatty felt he could ignore. The sea was glassy calm, which made periscopes easy to detect, so no submarine could close in without danger of being rammed. Besides, his ships traveling at high speed could rush past a submerged submarine before it reached a position to fire.

Still, for a moment, Beatty hesitated. "What do you think we should do?" he asked Captain Ernle Chatfield of *Lion,* standing beside him on the battle cruiser's bridge. "I ought to go forward and support Tyrwhitt, but if I lose one of these valuable ships, the country will not forgive me." Chatfield, admitting later that he was "unburdened by responsibility and eager for excitement," replied, "Surely we must go." Beatty nodded, and at 11:35 a.m., counting on high speed and surprise to see him through, he swung *Lion, Queen Mary, Princess Royal, Invincible,* and *New Zealand* around to the southeast and steamed in a single line at 26 knots into the Bight. Ten minutes later, he increased speed to 27 knots and signaled to Tyrwhitt and Blunt, "Am proceeding to your support."

Even at 27 knots, Beatty was still an hour away from the embattled Harwich force. Meanwhile, Tyrwhitt faced another new antagonist, the German light cruiser *Mainz,* which had sailed independently from the Ems estuary. About 11:30 a.m., British destroyers steaming west six miles ahead of *Arethusa* sighted *Mainz.* Both sides opened fire. *Mainz* had better aim, frequently straddling although not hitting the destroyers. Eleven British destroyers fired torpedoes; all missed. This action continued for twenty minutes when, to the astonishment of the British, their German antagonist abruptly reversed course. This strange behavior was subsequently explained by the fact that *Mainz,* racing north and battling the destroyers, had suddenly seen "heavy smoke clouds . . . to the northwest and a few minutes later three cruisers of the Town class emerged from them." These were Goodenough's light cruisers coming south at full speed to the aid of *Arethusa. Southampton* and her consorts opened fire at 6,000 yards and *Mainz,* wrote one of *Southampton*'s officers, "very wisely fled like a stag." "Even in the act of turning," said one of *Mainz*'s officers, "the enemy's first salvos were falling close to us and very soon afterwards we were hit in the battery and the waist." It was an unequal contest: *Mainz* was under fire from fifteen 6-inch guns to which she could reply only with her two after 4.1-inch guns. The German light cruiser, hit at least twice, disappeared into the mist, hoping to escape. She did not. Fleeing south at 25 knots with Goodenough in pursuit, *Mainz* suddenly found herself running directly across the bows of *Arethusa* and the Harwich destroyers. Tyrwhitt, not knowing that the British light cruisers were in hot pursuit, immediately ordered twenty British destroyers to attack *Mainz* with torpedoes. The destroyers charged at close range, some approaching within 1,000 yards of the German ship. *Mainz* fought desperately and her fire was remarkably accurate. The destroyer *Laurel* fired two torpedoes, but was herself hit three times and crippled. *Liberty,* the destroyer next astern, was hit on the bridge, and her captain was killed. *Lysander,* the third destroyer in line, was not hit, but *Laertes,* the fourth, was struck by all four shells of a single German salvo and, temporarily, came to a standstill. Thirty-three British torpedoes had been fired; one observer described the sea as "furrowed" by the tracks of whitened, bubbling water.

But *Mainz* was receiving as well as dealing blows. Her rudder was jammed to starboard, she was on fire, her port engine was dead, and she was slowly turning in the direction of Goodenough's arriving cruisers. Worse was to come. Suddenly, a torpedo from the British destroyer *Lydiard* hit her. "The ship reared," wrote one of *Mainz*'s surviving officers, "bent perceptibly from end to end, and continued to pitch for some time. The emergency lights went out. We had to find our way about with electric torches." Stricken, *Mainz* turned west, straight into the arms of Goodenough's four cruisers, now only 6,000 yards away. "We closed down on her," wrote one of *Southampton*'s officers, "hitting with every salvo. She was a mass of yellow flame and smoke. . . . Her two after-funnels collapsed. Red glows, indicating internal fires, showed through her gaping wounds in her sides." One of her guns still fired spasmodically, but within ten minutes she lay a blazing wreck, sinking by the bow. Then, the mainmast slowly leaned forward and, "like a great tree, gradually lay down along the deck." "*Mainz* was incredibly brave, immensely gallant," wrote another British officer. "The last I saw of her [she was] absolutely wrecked . . . her whole midships a fuming inferno. She had one gun forward and one aft still spitting forth fury and defiance like a wild cat mad with wounds." A surviving German seaman added grim details: "The state of *Mainz* at this time was indescribable. . . . Gun crews, voice-pipe men, and ammunition supply parties were blown to pieces. The upper deck was a chaos of ruin, flame, scorching heat and corpses, and everything was streaked with the green and yellow residue of the explosives which produced suffocating gases." At 12:20, the captain ordered, "Sink [that is, scuttle] the ship. All hands [put on] life jackets." Then he stepped outside the conning tower and was immediately killed by a shell burst. At 12:25 p.m., Goodenough signaled, "Cease Fire," and at 12:50 p.m. he ordered the light cruiser *Liverpool* to lower boats and pick up the men swimming in the water.

At this point, Commodore Keyes with *Lurcher* and *Firedrake* arrived. Seeing *Mainz*'s smoking decks littered with men wounded and unable to move, he took *Lurcher* alongside, the steel plates of the two ships grinding with the movement of the sea. By this action, Keyes was able to evacuate and save 220 men. One man refused. "A young German officer [who] had been very active in directing the transport of the wounded" now stood motionless on the deck of his doomed ship. Keyes, anxious to push off before the cruiser capsized and guessing what was in this young man's mind, shouted to him that "he had done splendidly, we must clear out, he must come at once, there was nothing more he could do, and I held out my hand to help him jump on board." But the young man scorned to leave his ship as long as she remained afloat. "He drew himself up stiffly, saluted, and said, 'Thank you. No.' " A few minutes later, *Mainz* rolled over, lay on her side for ten minutes, then turned bottom up and sank. Happily, the young officer who had refused Keyes's offer was found in the water and rescued; another survivor was Lieutenant Wolf von Tirpitz, a son of the German Grand Admiral.

Tyrwhitt still was not out of danger. One German light cruiser had been sunk and another damaged, but eight more were converging on his battered force. *Stettin* and *Strassburg* were still about; *Köln,* with Rear Admiral Maass, *Stralsund, Kolberg, Ariadne, München,* and *Danzig* were on the way; and still another, *Niobe,* was hastily coaling at Wilhelmshaven. Meanwhile, *Arethusa, Laurel, Laertes,* and *Liberty* were badly damaged and would have to be withdrawn from the Bight in the face of attacks by the German light cruisers. Fortunately for the British, the actions of the German ships remained uncoordinated. All were careening about, looking for smaller British ships to attack, fleeing when confronted by larger British warships. The British, at least, were attempting to exercise tactical control; for the Germans it was a confused barroom brawl. The ability to identify an antagonist depended on factors such as the number of funnels and the shape of the bows, characteristics difficult to make out in that day's weather.

As shells from *Strassburg* and then from *Köln* began to fall near *Arethusa,* Tyrwhitt began to wonder whether he and his ships would be overwhelmed. "I really was beginning to feel a bit blue," he wrote after the battle. Then, suddenly, out of the haze to westward, the shadowy form of a large ship loomed up. She was coming at high speed, black smoke was pouring from her funnels, and a huge white wave was rolling back from her bow. Alarm and dismay were followed by relief and joy when the oncoming giant was identified as HMS *Lion.* One by one, out of the mist astern of the leader, four more huge shapes came into view. "Following in each other's wake, they emerged . . . and flashed past us like express trains," said an officer aboard *Southampton.* "Not a man could be seen on their decks; volumes of smoke poured from their funnels; their turret guns, trained expectantly on the port bow, seemed eager for battle." A young lieutenant serving on one of Tyrwhitt's crippled destroyers described the same moment: "There straight ahead of us in lovely procession, like elephants walking through a pack of . . . dogs came *Lion, Queen Mary, Princess Royal, Invincible* and *New Zealand.* Great and grim and uncouth as some antediluvian monsters, how solid they looked, how utterly earthquaking. We pointed out our latest aggressor to them . . . and we went west while they went east . . . and just a little later we heard the thunder of their guns."

For *Arethusa* and her flock, the battle was over. For *Lion* and her sisters, it was beginning.

—

Aboard the British battle cruisers, excitement was at a peak: "As we approached," said Captain Chatfield of *Lion*,

> everyone was at action stations, the guns loaded, the range-finders manned, the control alert, the signal men's binoculars and telescopes scouring the misty horizon . . . one could hardly see two miles. Suddenly the report of guns was heard . . . [and] on our port bow, we saw . . . the flash of guns through the mist. Were they friendly or hostile? No shell could be seen falling. Beatty stood on the bridge by the compass, his glasses scanning the scene. At length we made out the hulk of a cruiser—indeed, she was little more than a hulk—[this was *Mainz*] her funnel had fallen and her foremast had been shot away, a fire raged on her upper deck. She . . . had been engaged by all four ships of Goodenough's squadron. We swung around ninety degrees to port. "Leave her to them," said Beatty. "Don't fire!"

At 12:37 p.m., *Lion* approached *Arethusa* and her destroyers, which were under attack by *Strassburg* and *Köln. Strassburg* turned and fled. *Köln,* however, was doomed. As Beatty steered to cut her off from Heligoland, the German light cruiser remained for seven minutes in clear sight on *Lion*'s bow. "The turrets swung around . . . [and] our guns opened fire, followed by those of the squadron," said Chatfield. "In a few moments, the German was hit many times by heavy shells; she bravely returned our fire with her little four inch guns aiming at our conning tower. One felt the tiny four-inch shell spatter against the conning tower armor, and the pieces 'sizz' over it. In a few minutes, the *Köln* was . . . a hulk."

Even so, Rear Admiral Maass's flagship did not sink; indeed, she received a brief reprieve. Just at that moment, a small, two-funneled German light cruiser appeared, steaming east, directly across *Lion*'s path. Beatty immediately abandoned the shattered *Köln* and led his ships in pursuit of this new prey. Although by this time *Invincible* (which could make no better than 25 knots) and *New Zealand* (not much faster) were lagging behind the three modern Cats (as the London press had eagerly described the *Lion*-class battle cruisers), which were traveling at 28 knots, Beatty did not detach either of the two to sink *Köln.* Aware that he was close to the enemy's base and that German dreadnoughts could appear at any moment, he wished to keep his squadron concentrated. Chatfield described what happened next: "A small German ship, a mile on [*sic*] the starboard bow . . . made off at right-angles, zig-zagging. Pointing her out to . . . [the gunnery officer] I told him to cease firing at *Köln* and to engage . . . [the new enemy ship] before she could torpedo us. He rapidly swung the 13.5-inch turrets round from port to starboard and re-opened fire. Three salvos were enough and the German disappeared from sight; an explosion was seen and a mass of flame."

The victim was the old light cruiser *Ariadne,* which had followed *Köln* from Wilhelmshaven through the mists out onto the battlefield. When Beatty, leaving the crippled *Köln,* turned his attention to *Ariadne,* the range was under 6,000 yards. *Ariadne* had no chance. She ran for it, but, said one of her officers, "the first salvo fell about three hundred and thirty yards short, but the second pitched so close to our boat that the towering columns of water broke over our forecastle and flooded it." *Lion*'s third salvo struck home and, as *Princess Royal* joined the assault, *Ariadne* staggered away, "completely enveloped in flames," and helpless. Beatty left her behind. *Ariadne,* like *Köln,* remained afloat, but the heat and smoke made it impossible for her crew to remain on board. The men assembled on the forecastle, gave three cheers for the kaiser, sang "Deutschland über Alles," and awaited rescue. Shortly after two o'clock the German light cruiser *Danzig* appeared and lowered boats. For a while, the fires on *Ariadne* were dying down and her captain, hoping to save his ship, asked *Stralsund* to take her in tow. It was too late: at 3:10 p.m., she rolled over and went to the bottom, her colors still flying.

Despite his success, Beatty was nervous about his proximity to Heligoland and Wilhelmshaven; from one of his ships, an officer could see chimneys along the German coast. He knew that the water over the Jade bar was deepening and that the German dreadnoughts would probably be coming out. And one of his destroyers reported the presence of floating mines. For these reasons and because it was now his primary duty to cover the withdrawal of Tyrwhitt's damaged ships, it was time to go. At 1:10 p.m., only forty minutes after he arrived on the scene, Beatty turned *Lion* and her sisters to the northwest and made a general signal to all British forces in the Bight: "Retire." On this arc of retreat, he sighted, a mile and a half away, the crippled *Köln,* still afloat, still flying her flag. "The Admiral told me to sink her," Chatfield said. "We put two salvos from the two foremost turrets into her; she sank beneath the waves stern first." Beatty ordered his four accompanying destroyers to pick up survivors. They had begun to search when a submarine was reported and they departed. Two days later a German destroyer discovered a single stoker, Adolf Neumann, still alive and "drifting among corpses [held up] in lifejackets." According to Neumann, "About 250 men" jumped into the sea before *Köln* went down. "On the next day I saw close around me 60 men apparently still living. One after another, they fell prey to the sea." The rest of *Köln*'s company of more than 500 men, along with Rear Admiral Maass, had perished.

Up to this point, four German cruisers—*Frauenlob, Mainz, Köln,* and *Ariadne*—had been sunk or damaged, but four more—*Stettin, Stralsund, Strassburg,* and *Danzig*—were still prowling in the fog. These four ships were saved by the mist; on a clear day, Beatty's heavy guns could have reached out and smashed them all. As it was, *Strassburg* had a close encounter. She sighted the British battle cruisers, then busy dispatching *Köln,* before they sighted her. Momentarily, the British were confused: *Strassburg* had four funnels, while most German cruisers had only three. The German captain realized that he might be mistaken for one of the *Southamptons* and boldly held on course rather than turning and running. The ploy succeeded: by the time the British issued a challenge, *Strassburg* had vanished into the haze.

Meanwhile, help for the Germans was on the way. *Moltke* and *Von der Tann* crossed the Jade bar at 2:10 p.m., and Hipper signaled all German light cruisers to fall back on the two battle cruisers. Ingenohl was cautious. Hipper's battle cruisers were told "not to engage the [enemy] battle cruiser squadron"; Hipper himself, an hour astern in *Seydlitz,* did not want to make the same mistake the German light cruisers had made by attacking piecemeal; he refused to risk his two battle cruisers in the absence of his powerful flagship. At 2:25 p.m., *Moltke* and *Von der Tann* rendezvoused with the German light cruisers. Hipper himself arrived in *Seydlitz* at 3:10 p.m., just in time to watch *Ariadne* sink. The German admiral then began a wary reconnaissance with three light cruisers ahead of his three battle cruisers, searching for the missing light cruisers *Mainz* and *Köln,* from whom there had been no word for over three hours. By four o'clock, Hipper was ready to give up and turn his ships in order to be back in the Jade before low water. "At 8:23 p.m.," says the German naval history, "*Seydlitz* anchored in Wilhelmshaven roads and Rear Admiral Hipper reported to the fleet commander [Ingenohl] and verbally gave him an account."

—

As Beatty's battle cruisers turned toward home, sailors on board *Lion* rushed up on deck to cheer their admiral. Beatty was not ready to celebrate. *Arethusa,* despite her temporary repairs, was crawling along at 6 knots, protectively surrounded by twenty-three destroyers. Beatty found this speed too slow and, at 9:30 p.m., ordered the old armored cruiser *Hogue* to take *Arethusa* in tow. In this fashion, at the end of a rope, Tyrwhitt's flagship arrived back at the Nore at 5:00 p.m. on the following day, August 29. From there, she raised enough steam to move up to Chatham under her own power.

While the retreat and towing operations were under way, Beatty remained nearby. Once all British ships were out of danger, he spread Goodenough's light cruisers before him and swept off to the north, toward Scapa Flow. Two days after the battle, on August 30, the 1st Battle Cruiser Squadron and the 1st Light Cruiser Squadron entered the Flow on a calm summer evening when the sky was streaked with light and cloud. As *Lion* and her sisters steamed down the lines of anchored Grand Fleet battleships, the crews lined the decks and cheered. Beatty was embarrassed. He felt that, given the superiority of his force, his success was unexceptional. Unfortunately, just as *Lion* glided to a halt, her anchor chain jammed in the chocks. She had to go back and make a second approach, which meant coming down the line again. Again, she was cheered. This time, Beatty was seriously annoyed, thinking that his flagship's second passage would be seen as exhibitionism. He was reassured when another admiral signaled, "It seems your anchor was rammed home as hard as your attack." A more practical sign of respect for the ships that had fought the battle came from the battleship *Orion,* whose crew volunteered to help the men of *Southampton* with the hard, dirty work of coaling. Twelve hours later, Jellicoe came into the Flow aboard *Iron Duke* and Beatty went on board the flagship to report. Both men were relieved; both knew the risks Beatty had run. As Beatty later told Arthur Balfour, "The end justified the means, but if I had lost a battle cruiser, I should have been hanged, drawn, and quartered. Yet it was necessary to run the risk to save two of our light cruisers and a large force of destroyers which otherwise would most certainly have been lost."

The action was Britain's first naval victory of the war. Besides the three German light cruisers, a destroyer, *V-187,* had been sunk; *Frauenlob* had been severely damaged; and two more light cruisers, *Strassburg* and *Stettin,* had also been damaged. German casualties totaled 1,242, including 712 men killed (one of whom was Rear Admiral Maass), and 336 prisoners of war. On the British side, the light cruiser *Arethusa* and three destroyers had been heavily damaged, but all had come home. There were surprisingly few British casualties: 35 men were killed and 40 wounded in all ships. *Arethusa,* the ship most severely punished, suffered 11 killed and 16 wounded.

Overnight, news that British warships had penetrated the Bight to within sight of the red cliffs of Heligoland swept across Britain. "We had a great reception all the way from the Nore to Chatham," Tyrwhitt reported from *Arethusa.* "Every ship and everybody cheered like mad. When *Arethusa* came past Sheerness to dock at Chatham, crowds gathered from every direction and cheers rose to skies. . . . Winston met us at Sheerness and came up to Chatham and fairly slobbered over me. Offered me any ship I liked and all the rest of it." The *Daily Express* headlined its story, "We've Gone to Heligoland and Back! Please God, We'll Go Again!"

The public hero was Beatty; Jellicoe commended the vice admiral for taking "the only action which was possible." If Beatty and Goodenough had not been sent by Jellicoe or had not arrived in time, two British light cruisers and thirty-one British destroyers might have been massacred by the eight German light cruisers. Justifiably pleased with himself, Beatty wrote to Ethel, "It was good work to be able to do it within twenty miles of . . . Heligoland, with the whole of the High Seas Fleet listening to the boom of our guns." He praised the Germans: "Poor devils, they fought their ships like men and went down with colours flying like seamen against overwhelming odds. . . . Whatever their faults, they are gallant . . . and indeed are worthy foemen." Beatty was miffed, however, when he received no immediate praise from the Admiralty. "I had thought I should have received an expression of appreciation from Their Lordships," he wrote to Ethel four days after the battle, "but have been disappointed, or rather not so much disappointed as disgusted, and my real opinion has been confirmed that they would have hung me if there had been a disaster, as there very nearly was, owing to the extraordinary neglect of the most ordinary precautions on their part. However, all's well that ends well, and they haven't had the opportunity of hanging me yet and they won't get it."

Tyrwhitt also became a hero, and his picture was sold on London streets. "It really was awfully fine and not half so unpleasant as I expected," he wrote to his wife and sister. "I can only wonder that everyone on the upper deck was not killed. . . . My signal officer was the only man killed on the bridge, such a nice boy. He was talking to me at the time and had just pointed out that we were on fire."

Not everyone on the British side was pleased. Many officers saw not so much a victory won as a catastrophe narrowly escaped. The Admiralty had failed to inform the Grand Fleet commander what ships were to be present. Until Beatty disclosed his presence, no one knew who was in overall command. British light cruisers had been sighted by British destroyers and reported as enemies to the very ships they had just spotted. British submarines had attacked British surface ships. To the extent that one man was responsible, it was Sturdee. As Chief of Staff, he had taken it upon himself not to inform Jellicoe of the operation until the last minute and then had rejected Jellicoe's suggestion that he bring out the Grand Fleet in support. If Jellicoe on his own initiative had not sent Beatty and Goodenough to sea, the result might have been a disaster.

Keyes was thoroughly disgusted; instead of victory he saw wasted opportunity. "I think an absurd fuss was made over that small affair," he wrote to Goodenough on September 5. "It makes me sick . . . to think what a complete success it might have been. . . . We begged for light cruisers to support us and deal with the enemy's light cruisers which we knew would come out . . . but were told none were available. If you had only known what we were aiming at [and had] had an opportunity of discussing it with

Tyrwhitt and me . . . we might have sunk at least six cruisers and had a 'scoop' indeed."*

Jellicoe's faith in the Admiralty's judgment was diminished, but he had been Commander-in-Chief for only three weeks and his protest was muted. He was dismayed by poor tactical control during the battle and by the fact that captains had communicated without reporting their own position, course, and speed or that of the enemy.† Actually, in this first major battle, fought on a typical hazy North Sea day in August, and made worse by the clouds of black smoke pouring from the funnels of many ships, both sides learned much about the difference between peacetime maneuvers and real war. Considering that large numbers of ships were traveling at high speed in restricted waters, that nobody knew who else was present, and that poor visibility made communication difficult, the British record was creditable. Both Tyrwhitt and Blunt retained control over their destroyer flotillas. Goodenough, although two of his cruisers wandered off early in the day, kept his remaining four cruisers together throughout the action. Beatty did best, holding his five battle cruisers in tight formation, refusing to detach a single ship to finish off the crippled *Köln.*

The British were lucky. *Arethusa* never should have been at sea. To take her out, as Tyrwhitt did—a new ship with a new crew unfamiliar with the

*In the aftermath of the battle, Keyes had another matter to settle with Goodenough. While *Liverpool,* one of Goodenough's light cruisers, was standing by to pick up survivors of the sinking *Mainz,* Keyes arrived in *Lurcher* and, as the ranking officer, took charge of the rescue operation. "I think it right to tell you," Goodenough subsequently wrote to Keyes, "that the officer of the *Liverpool*'s cutter was terribly upset at someone on board one of the destroyers calling him . . . a coward—apparently for not coming closer to pick up more. As a matter of fact, I consider that I went beyond my duty in leaving a ship to pick up anyone when the place was sown with mines and submarines and I do not intend to do it again. Please remember me to your wife."

As Keyes knew very well, Goodenough was aware that the guilty party was Keyes himself. He quickly admitted this to Goodenough: "I ought not to have used the word 'coward.' And I much regret it. I only did so under great feeling and after repeated appeals to the officer to close and save life, which he ignored. There were men within 50 yards of him at least 100 yards from *Mainz,* but he would do nothing. . . . When she . . . slowly sank, instead of closing, he pulled away hard . . . probably prompted by excessive prudence . . . and an ignorant fear of suction. In this case there was none. I felt sick and ashamed, and do still, to think that a British officer should have behaved in such a manner."

Goodenough accepted this explanation and in subsequent letters between "Roger" and "Bill," they spoke no more about it.

†Stephen King-Hall, a lieutenant aboard *Southampton,* later pointed out that after two or three days at sea without seeing a landmark or lightship of any sort, a ship had to rely on sights of the sun or stars to fix her position. When the weather was bad, these were often not available. In that case, the captain was forced to rely on dead reckoning—that is to say, on plotting his course and speed since leaving harbor, with estimates of the effect of winds, currents, and tides. In the middle of a battle, with constant changes of course and speed, to fix an exact position by this method was almost impossible.

ship, and new guns tested only enough to know that they frequently jammed—was foolhardy. Submarines had little effect, although concern that they might be present had led Beatty to conduct his charge at the highest possible speed. British destroyers fired a large number of torpedoes but scored only a single hit, on the cruiser *Mainz*. After the battle, the Admiralty complained about the expenditure of shells by the battle cruisers and torpedoes, saying that the lavish usage was unjustified in relation to the number of German ships sunk. Unfortunately, in the next North Sea action, off the Dogger Bank, Beatty's captains adhered to this warning and fired too carefully. Chatfield of *Lion* later complained that with "a greater expenditure of ammunition in the early stages of Dogger Bank, more complete results might have been obtained."

Despite these failings, disaster had been avoided and victory achieved. "The battle was of immense moral, if of slight material, importance, in its effect upon the two fleets," said the *New Statesman*. Chatfield declared: "It was no great naval feat, but carried out under the nose of the German Commander-in-Chief, it actually meant a good deal both to Germany and England. We had shown our sea ascendancy."

—

If the British were disappointed that their victory was not greater, the Germans were horrified by their material losses and shamed by the blow to their pride. Like the British, the Germans were guilty of poor intelligence and planning. The German naval history declares that it was a fatal error for the Naval Staff to assume that British light forces would attack in German home waters without the support of heavy ships. It was on this assumption that the German light cruisers had emerged one by one and entered the battle piecemeal. Much of the German mishandling of the battle was due to the weather. The hanging morning mists made it difficult for the German destroyer and light cruiser captains to see their enemies and to learn how many and what types of British ships were present. To make the confusion worse, no captain reported the poor visibility to the admirals in Wilhelmshaven—where the weather was absolutely clear. Hearing no bad news, Hipper and Ingenohl assumed that their light cruisers actually had battlefield superiority; it was on this optimistic note that *Mainz* was dispatched from the Ems to attack the retreating British destroyers from the rear. This disastrous German misunderstanding of what was happening was not corrected until 2:35, when *Strassburg* suddenly signaled, "Enemy battle cruiser squadron, course southwest." Thereafter, it was the tardiness of the German command in sending out its own battle cruisers to support its hard-pressed light cruisers—even once the tide over the Jade bar permitted—that enabled Beatty to get his lame ducks out of the Bight. Had Hipper wished to pursue and engage Beatty, he might have been able to catch up. On Ingenohl's orders, he did not try.

In addition, there was no tactical coordination of the German light forces.

The British commodores at least kept their cruisers and destroyers under a semblance of control; the Germans had none. Their light cruisers came rushing out individually to devour the British destroyers—and were themselves devoured. Even before Beatty appeared, Maass and Hipper had failed to concentrate before going out to attack; on a number of occasions, British destroyers were able to repel the attack of a single German light cruiser. A coordinated attack by a group of German light cruisers would have inflicted far greater damage on the British and might have saved *Mainz* even after Goodenough appeared. Against battle cruisers, though, light cruisers had no hope. There were other lessons. German light cruiser and destroyer armament was proven inferior. British light cruisers armed with 6-inch guns were more than a match for German light cruisers with 4.1-inch guns. The German guns could fire faster, but the impact of a 6-inch shell was far more deadly. A similar comparison favored British destroyers: they were heavier, faster, and better armed than their German counterparts.

Nevertheless, for the German navy there were bright spots. German gunnery had been rapid and accurate. Had the two sides been evenly matched, then, in the conditions of haze, in which ships appeared and suddenly vanished, the Germans should have prevailed. The English admired the way in which the German salvos were bunched even when they did not hit. German ships displayed physical proof of Tirpitz's long-prescribed adage that a warship's primary responsibility is to remain afloat; the destroyer *V-187* and the three light cruisers absorbed enormous damage before they finally sank. Most of all, the Germans could take pride in the courage of their captains, officers, and men. In reporting the defeat to the kaiser, Ingenohl slathered his officers and men with praise. He spoke of "the long-suppressed battle ardor and the indomitable will of your Majesty's ships to get at the enemy." "However heavy the losses," he said, "this first collision with the enemy gave proof of the eagerness to do battle." The men's "confidence in their own ability," he assured William, "has not been shaken but has grown." No Briton would argue; after the Battle of the Bight, no British sailor ever belittled German bravery.

Despite these bright spots, depression afflicted the German fleet. Officers and men were humiliated at having allowed more than fifty British warships, including five capital ships, to penetrate so close to the shore of the fatherland. Hipper, particularly, felt the defeat; he privately placed the blame on the division of command in the High Seas Fleet. Hipper had always wanted to keep at least one battle cruiser on patrol in the Bight, but the Commander-in-Chief had refused to expose the battle cruisers in this defensive role. In Hipper's view, therefore, Ingenohl was ultimately responsible for leaving the German destroyer patrols vulnerable to attack whenever the tide over the Jade bar was low. At Hipper's request, a change in the defensive arrangements for the Bight was made, and beginning in September extensive defensive minefields were laid. With the end of the need for destroyer and light cruiser patrols, "the larger part of the light surface forces became available for other tasks." In addition, an important change in tactical doctrine was made: there would be no more piecemeal arrivals by German warships. If the British came back, full squadrons would respond, or nobody would.

In the long run, the most significant result of the battle was its effect on the kaiser. Exhilarated by news of the German army's constant success on the Western Front, William suddenly was forced to confront the fact that the British fleet had stormed into German home waters and sunk a number of his "darlings." This bold stroke was confirmation that the near adulation that William had always felt for the Royal Navy was not misplaced; the spirit of Nelson, one of William's heroes, was still alive. The German fleet, for which Britain's friendship had been squandered, seemed now at risk from the bold actions of Nelson's heirs. To preserve his ships, the kaiser determined that the fleet must "hold itself back and avoid actions which can lead to greater losses." The main body of the High Seas Fleet was ordered not to fight outside the Bight, and not even inside the Bight against superior forces. Admiral Pohl, Chief of the German Naval Staff, wired Ingenohl that "in his anxiety to preserve the fleet [William] . . . wished you to wire for his consent before entering a decisive action."

Tirpitz was appalled by the kaiser's decision. It was the beginning of a struggle between the Grand Admiral and the monarch. Tirpitz insisted that the High Seas Fleet should be used for what it was: a weapon of war. Restricting it to a defensive role, he believed, was madness. "August 28 [was] a day fateful both in after-effects and in incidental results for the work of our navy," Tirpitz wrote after the war. What Tirpitz wanted was that

> on the approach of the English, the order . . . [be] instantly given "the whole fleet to sea with every vessel we have." If there were larger elements of the British fleet in the Bight, there could be nothing better than to come to battle so near to our own ports. . . . But the reverse course was followed. The Emperor did not wish for losses of this sort. . . . Orders [were] issued by the Emperor . . . after an audience with Pohl, to which I as usual was not summoned, to restrict the initiative of the Commander-in-Chief of the North Sea Fleet. The loss of ships was to be avoided; fleet sallies and any greater undertakings must be approved by His Majesty in advance. I took the first opportunity to explain to the Emperor the fundamental error of such a muzzling policy. This step had no success, but on the contrary there sprang up from that day forth an estrangement between the Emperor and myself which steadily increased.

The kaiser prevailed and the High Seas Fleet was tethered. The British, on the other hand, were eager to try again. On September 9, a well-planned repetition of the Bight operation—coordinated by Jellicoe this time—was carried out in the hope of drawing out the German fleet. Beatty with six battle cruisers (*Inflexible* had joined him from the Mediterranean) supported the light forces, and the whole Grand Fleet lay over the horizon 100 miles north of Heligoland. The Harwich flotillas penetrated to within twelve miles of Heligoland, but saw no German ships. Beatty told Ethel, "They knew we were coming and not a soul was in sight. I fear the rascals will never come out, but will only send out minelayers and submarines. They seem . . . wanting in initiative and dash with their battle cruisers. . . . It looks as if we should go through the war without ever coming to grips with them. Such a thought is more than I can bear." On September 28, Keyes and Tyrwhitt tried to arrange still another penetration, but reports of vast new German minefields led to cancellation. [We] could not go messing about there any more," said Tyrwhitt, adding dejectedly, "We, the Navy, are not doing much, but if the Germans won't come out, what can we do?"

After the war, Churchill gilded this victory, plucked from near catastrophe, with the glow of Destiny: "The Germans knew nothing of our defective staff work and of the risks we had run," he wrote.

> All they saw was that the British did not hesitate to hazard their greatest vessels as well as their light craft in the most daring offensive action and had escaped apparently unscathed. They felt as we should have felt had German destroyers broken into the Solent and their battle cruisers penetrated as far as the Nab. The results of this action were far-reaching. Henceforward, the weight of British naval prestige lay heavy across all German sea enterprise. . . . The German Navy was indeed "muzzled." Except for furtive movements by individual submarines and minelayers, not a dog stirred from August till November.

CHAPTER 7

Submarines and Mines: "Fisher's Toys"

Jacky Fisher's British navy was built to carry massive guns firing heavy shells with enormous penetrating power over long range. To this purpose, the dreadnought battle fleet had been equipped, first with 12-inch, then with 13.5-inch, and ultimately with 15-inch guns. But even as the size and destructive power of naval guns increased, other weapons, less visible and often more dangerous, were being developed to destroy ships. These were torpedoes and mines, designed to explode below the waterline against the hull of an enemy ship. The advantage, as John Keegan has succinctly put it, is that "water conducts shock far more efficiently than air."

Submarines, torpedoes, and mines all predated the Great War. Mines had been used in the American Civil War, where they were called torpedoes ("Damn the torpedoes," said Rear Admiral David Farragut as he led his Union squadron over a Confederate minefield in Mobile Bay). But after the Battle of Tsushima in 1905, where the Russian navy was annihilated by Japanese heavy naval guns, it was the big gun, not the torpedo or mine, that was believed to be the decisive weapon. The submarine, however, possessed a unique advantage over the massive, armored ship equipped with great guns: it could make itself invisible. Approaching underwater, it could attack without revealing its presence except for the few chosen moments when it pushed its periscope above the surface. In the 1890s, the world's most advanced submarines were being built in America by John Philip Holland, an Irish nationalist who, after immigrating to the United States, devoted himself to designing and building weapons that could sink British warships. On the surface, a 160-horsepower gasoline engine gave Holland's boat a speed of 7½ knots; beneath the surface, it made 6½ knots on power from an electric battery. Holland's employer, the Electric Boat Company in New London,

Connecticut, was a private enterprise and the navies of the world soon beat a path to its door. The Royal Navy purchased a single Holland submarine in 1900 and, impressed by its potential, then built five undersea craft under license. The French navy began with experiments of its own but later came around to Holland's designs. By the summer of 1914, 400 submarines, most of them evolutionary progressions from Holland's original design, existed in sixteen navies.

Fisher had been one of the first to see the potential of the submarine. In 1903, he announced their power to revolutionize war at sea: "Death near—momentarily—sudden—awful—invisible—unavoidable! Nothing conceivably more demoralizing!" In 1904, before the *Dreadnought* was designed, he wrote, "I don't think it is even faintly realized—the immense impending revolution which the submarine will effect as offensive weapons of war." The submarine, he repeated constantly, was "the battleship of the future," and the torpedo the naval weapon of the future. The problem was how to deliver the torpedo to the target. In 1903, the effective range of torpedoes was 1,000 yards. By equipping battleships with quick-firing guns and screening them with anti-torpedo-boat vessels (Fisher named them destroyers), navies could make it hazardous for an enemy surface vessel to come close enough to launch its torpedoes. But a submarine, Fisher realized, was an ideal means of bringing torpedo-launching tubes within range of major enemy warships in daylight.

When Fisher first became interested, submarines were far from the deadly weapons they were to become in two world wars. Slow, limited in radius of action and in time submerged, afflicted with restricted vision in daylight and total blindness at night, they seemed relatively harmless—to some, even ridiculous. Admiral Lord Charles Beresford dismissed them as "playthings" and "Fisher's toys." Then, as the potential of the undersea craft became more apparent, scorn was mingled with indignation and fear. Submarines, British admirals grumbled, were unethical and "un-English . . . the weapon of cowards who refused to fight like men on the surface." Admiral Sir Arthur Wilson, Commander-in-Chief of the Channel Fleet, so despised this "underhanded method of attack" that he wanted the Admiralty to announce publicly that all submarine crews captured in wartime would be hanged as pirates. Fisher thought differently. His objective was to send enemy warships to the bottom of the sea. He did not care whether the weapons that sent them there were cowardly, underhanded, or un-English; he only cared that they worked. If submarines could torpedo and sink enemy warships, Britain should have submarines, and the more the better. To overcome opposition, Fisher looked for allies. He guided King Edward VII through the submarine *A-1* when she was in dry dock and took the Prince of Wales (later King George V) with him in the same submarine when she submerged off Portsmouth. (The Princess of Wales, watching from an observation ship, was heard to say quietly, "I shall be very disappointed if George doesn't come up.")

As First Sea Lord, Fisher worked with Captain Reginald Bacon, whom he described as "the cleverest officer in the navy" and later appointed as the first captain of the revolutionary battleship *Dreadnought.* In 1904, Bacon commanded the navy's entire submarine force, consisting of six small boats. His officers and crews considered themselves an elite corps and, in fleet maneuvers in March 1904, they made a name for themselves. Their enemy was the Home Fleet and they hit Sir Arthur Wilson's battleships so many times with unarmed torpedoes that umpires reluctantly ruled two of the battleships "sunk." Unfortunately, the submarine *A-1* was rammed and actually sunk by a passing merchant vessel, which had not been warned that an undersea craft might be passing beneath its bow. The real lesson of the maneuvers, Bacon reported, was that the presence of submarines "exercised an extraordinary influence on the operations" of a battle fleet: for safety, battleships now must always be accompanied by a large screen of destroyers. A decade later, Jellicoe was putting this lesson into practice in the North Sea.

By the time Roger Keyes was appointed Inspecting Captain of Submarines in 1910, the British submarine force had climbed to sixty-one boats: twelve ancient *A*'s, eleven elderly *B*'s, thirty-seven *C*'s, the new *D-1,* and eight more *D*'s under construction. When war broke out four years later, Britain had seventy-four submarines, more than any other naval power in the world, but this number was grossly misleading. Most of the boats were old coastal vessels of the *A, B,* and *C* classes whose average underwater speed (about 8 knots) and endurance (about twelve hours) were too limited to allow them to accompany a friendly surface fleet or to seek and attack an enemy fleet. They rarely remained at sea for more than a few days and never ventured any great distance from the British coast. In 1907, Britain first began to develop the *D* class, oceangoing vessels of 500 tons, diesel powered, with a surface speed close to 15 knots. The *E*-class boats that followed grew to a length of 178 feet and a displacement of 660 tons; they could achieve a surface speed of 15½ knots and an underwater speed of 9½ knots, and they could dive safely to 200 feet (the depth at which pressure from the sea would crush the boat was around 350 feet). These submarines were equipped with torpedoes with an extreme range of 11,000 yards and that had gyroscopes enabling the torpedoes to maintain an accurate course.

The appointment of Keyes in 1910 was a surprise. Keyes was a destroyer captain with no experience as a submariner, and his new assignment was not only to command and train the existing force but also to oversee all submarine construction. Keyes made enemies by looking abroad for experimental vessels and periscopes better than those produced at home.* Nevertheless, he attracted a number of bold, sometimes eccentric young officers. Enthusi-

*The British firm of Vickers was now building submarines under license from Holland and Electric Boat.

asm was high and clothing irregular; his men, Keyes said, "dressed like North Sea fishermen." The rest of the navy looked upon them and their vessels as "almost a service apart."

Fisher, in retirement after 1910, never abandoned his passionate advocacy of submarines. Ten years after his warning vision of "death near—momentarily—sudden—awful," he was vigorously pressing the new First Lord, Winston Churchill, to "build more submarines!" On December 13, 1913, he wrote, "I note by examining the Navy list there have been no less than 21 removals of submarines since I was First Sea Lord and only 12 additions. *Do you think this is satisfactory??* And the remainder of *A* and *B* classes are now approaching 10 years of age and there are 19 of them which figure in our totals. *We are falling behind Germany in large submarines!*"

When war came, the eight boats of the *D* and nine of the new *E* class were assigned to carry the offensive into German waters. Based at Harwich and commanded by Keyes, they were under the direct control of the Admiralty and not of Jellicoe; as a result, like Tyrwhitt's destroyer flotillas, they led a somewhat freewheeling life of their own. To help overcome a submarine's inherently restricted range of vision even in clear weather, Keyes acquired two modern destroyers to scout ahead of his flotillas. Flying his commodore's pennant in *Lurcher,* Keyes personally led a number of early scouting operations deep into Heligoland Bight. Duty aboard these "overseas" submarines was arduous and frustrating. There were no big targets. The German battleships rarely came out and the men remained cramped below because, as Keyes reported, "the notoriously short, steep seas which accompany westerly gales in the Heligoland Bight . . . make it difficult to open the conning tower hatches and vision is limited to about 200 yards. There was no rest to be obtained on the bottom . . . even when cruising at a depth of sixty feet, the submarines were rolling and moving vertically twenty feet."

On September 13, one of Keyes's submarines scored the flotilla's first major success. *E-9,* commanded by Lieutenant Commander Max Horton, had spent the previous night lying on the bottom six miles south of Heligoland. At daybreak, the submarine surfaced and at once sighted a light cruiser less than two miles away. Horton fired two torpedoes at a range of 600 yards and, as *E-9* dived, one explosion was heard. Rising again, Horton could see that the cruiser had stopped, but shots from an unseen vessel splashed nearby and *E-9* dived again. When Horton came back to the surface an hour later, he saw nothing but trawlers searching for survivors. His victim had been the eighteen-year-old, 2,000-ton German light cruiser *Hela.* Three weeks later, on October 6, patrolling off the Ems, Horton torpedoed and sank the German destroyer *S-126.*

An earlier encounter involving one of Keyes's boats may have been the first of its kind. On September 10, *D-8* saw a surfaced enemy submarine, *U-28,* and fired a torpedo. The German, seeing the torpedo coming, quickly submerged and, as a British staff monograph remarked, "Under the circumstances, stalemate was practically inevitable for neither boat knew what to do with the other; and after an hour and a quarter during which the two boats simultaneously rose and simultaneously dived again, the German retired." On October 18, however, the British submarine *E-3,* patrolling off the Ems, was stalked, cornered, torpedoed, and sunk in a coastal bay by a German submarine. This event, too, was a first of its kind.

—

Originally, Alfred von Tirpitz, founder of the Imperial German Navy, had scorned submarines. When the subject came up in the Reichstag in 1901, Tirpitz announced, "We have no money to waste on experimental vessels. We must leave such luxuries to wealthier states like France and England." Every pfennig was to go into the massive battleship-building program designed to challenge the Royal Navy. By the time of the 1905 estimates, Tirpitz had given ground and Krupp was told to build one *Unterseeboot* (abbreviated in German as *U-boot* and in English as "U-boat"), "for experiments connected with submarines." Germany thereby became the last major naval power to possess a submarine. When *U-1* completed her sea trials in 1907, she was pronounced satisfactory for coastal operations, but it was warned that "her employment on the high seas is attended with danger." Gradually, however, Tirpitz released more money, and between 1908 and 1910, fourteen more U-boats were ordered. All were powered on the surface by kerosene engines and underwater by an electric battery. In 1910, German builders switched to diesels for surface propulsion; again, Germany was the last major naval power to make this shift. At the outbreak of war, Germany had twenty-four U-boats in commission, with fifteen under construction. She now ranked fifth in the world in number of submarines—behind Britain, France, Russia, and the United States. But, because Germany had started later, she had as many modern submarines as anyone else.

Nevertheless, Tirpitz and the Naval Staff had little faith in the capabilities of U-boats, and the initial role assigned to German undersea craft was defensive. This stemmed in part from the Naval Staff's obsessive belief that in the event of war, the British navy would charge into the Bight in an attempt to engage and destroy the High Seas Fleet. In accordance with this fixation, all U-boats were based on Heligoland, where the submarines were integrated into the defensive arrangements of the Bight. By day, an outer observation line made up of a destroyer flotilla patrolled on a concentric arc thirty miles northwest of Heligoland. The U-boats, usually a half-flotilla of seven, formed a static line, riding on the surface at mooring buoys, twenty miles out. The plan called for the outer-line destroyers to retreat, drawing approaching enemy forces over this line of U-boats, which was to submerge and launch torpedo attacks. In conjunction with massed torpedo attacks by

German destroyers, the Naval Staff hoped that the U-boats would be able to whittle away at the numerical superiority of the attacking British squadrons before the High Seas Fleet sortied from the Jade.

On the eve of war, when the main body of the High Seas Fleet returned from the Norwegian coast to assemble in the Elbe and the Jade, the U-boat flotillas awaited orders at Heligoland. The orders came quickly: Commander Hermann Bauer, chief of the U-boat flotillas, was ordered to reconnoiter the North Sea, discover the whereabouts of the Grand Fleet, and establish the location of any British patrol or blockade lines. On the second day of the war, August 6, at 4:20 a.m. in thick, rainy weather, ten older submarines from the 1st Flotilla—*U-5, U-7, U-8, U-9,* and *U-13* through *U-18,* selected because their captains were the more experienced commanders—sailed from Heligoland. Reaching a position near the Dogger Bank, they spread out on a sixty-mile front—seven miles between boats—and began a surface sweep northwest up the North Sea. Their goal was the latitude of the Orkneys.

Throughout their 350-mile outward voyage, the nine U-boats (one had engine trouble and returned home) failed to sight even one enemy warship. Then on August 9, between the Orkneys and the Shetlands, *U-15* had her fatal encounter with the light cruiser *Birmingham.* On August 12, seven of the original ten submarines returned to Heligoland. One had returned earlier, *U-15* had been sunk, and nothing was ever heard from *U-13;* it was speculated that she had struck a German mine in one of the defensive minefields laid in the Bight. The results of this pioneering operation did little to vindicate the U-boat in the eyes of the German Naval Staff. Ten U-boats had failed to damage, let alone sink, an enemy warship, yet two of their number had been lost. "Our submarine fleet was as good as any in the world—but not very good," said one German officer. Although the U-boats brought back the first evidence that there was no close blockade, they had been unable to establish the location of a blockade line. The Naval Staff did not know that *U-15* had reached the Orkneys and concluded that the Grand Fleet was so far away from Germany that it was beyond the capacities of U-boats to find it.

A few U-boats continued to sail, and one of these sorties led to revenge for the sinking of the *U-15.* Certain that major British warships were based at the Firth of Forth, Bauer persuaded his superiors to let him post a regular patrol of two U-boats off the estuary. On August 30, 1914, *U-20* and *U-21,* the only two submarines available for offensive operations, were ordered to attempt an attack inside the Firth. On September 5, *U-20* came up the estuary almost as far as the Forth Bridge, but seeing nothing and unaware that Beatty's battle cruisers were anchored a few hundred yards above the bridge, turned back. Meanwhile, out to sea, Captain Otto Hersing, in *U-21,* spotted the 3,000-ton light cruiser *Pathfinder* on patrol off Abs Head, ten miles southeast of May Island. Although his submarine was pitching and rolling in a stormy sea, Hersing maneuvered until he was within 1,500 yards—just short of a mile—and fired one torpedo. The torpedo hit and the explosion detonated the ship's forward magazine. Four minutes later, *Pathfinder* plunged to the bottom, taking with her more than half her crew of 360. *U-21* escaped, having achieved the war's first sinking of a British warship by a German submarine.

Pathfinder was a ten-year-old ship of marginal value, but her loss had a strong impact on Jellicoe. The torpedoing confirmed the Commander-in-Chief in his belief that the southern and central North Sea were dangerous for large warships, and thereafter he held the Grand Fleet as far to the north as the Admiralty would permit. Some British officers found Jellicoe's fears exaggerated, and in other parts of the navy operating orders and tactical routines relating to submarines were more relaxed. The result was a spectacular disaster. Only three and a half weeks after Beatty's triumph in the Bight, the Royal Navy lost more men in ninety minutes than the Germans had lost in the all-day battle around Heligoland. The weapon responsible for this British defeat was one small German submarine.

—

At the beginning of the war, the Royal Navy possessed a multitude of elderly surface warships that Fisher had wanted to scrap, but which remained afloat, requiring crews whose numbers were out of all proportion to the vessels' fighting value. Among these were the six 12,000-ton armored cruisers of the *Bacchante* class, laid down in 1898 and 1899, and now thoroughly worn out. Their engines, designed to make 21 knots, could scarcely produce 15. Nevertheless, rather than scrapping them outright, the Admiralty had placed the *Bacchante*s in Reserve Fleet limbo; no money was to be spent repairing them, but they were to be kept in the inventory until they were utterly useless. In the summer of 1914, they were tied up, rusting peacefully, at Medway on the Thames estuary.

The outbreak of war brought these old ships back to life. Each cruiser carried two 9.2-inch guns and eight 6-inch guns, which might be used to punch holes in any German light cruisers or destroyers their shells managed to hit. For this reason, a coat of fresh, gray war paint was applied, ammunition and supplies were hoisted in, and more than 700 officers and men marched aboard each ship. The seamen came from the Royal Navy Reserves and the Fleet Reserves, a pool of navy pensioners, many of them middle-aged family men. Like many reserve ships in the Royal Navy, the old *Bacchante*s were local ships; most men in the crews came from nearby towns and villages, which took pride in their men now going to sea. To compensate for the inexperience of the crews, the old armored cruisers were assigned regular navy captains and officers. In addition, each ship was alloted nine young cadets from the Royal Naval College at Dartmouth, most of them boys under fifteen.

Because the cruisers were old and slow and their crews were new, there was never a thought that they should operate with the Grand Fleet. Instead, they were assigned to patrol the "Broad Fourteens," a patch of the southern North Sea off the Dutch coast named for its latitude. Five of the ships, *Bacchante, Aboukir, Hogue, Cressy,* and *Euryalus,* were based at Harwich, where their mission was to support Tyrwhitt's destroyers and Keyes's submarines in blocking any German surface force attempting to attack the transports carrying the BEF to the continent. Frequent bad weather had altered this arrangment, however, and instead of acting in support of the smaller ships, the old cruisers, better able to cope with the rough seas, became the front line. Back and forth, day after day, the cruisers patrolled their beat, remaining at sea without rest, taking turns going in to coal. As the autumn advanced and the seas rose higher, the accompanying destroyers frequently returned to port. Meanwhile, the cruisers had fallen into bad habits. It was intended that they maintain 15 knots, with occasional zigzagging. Fifteen knots proved impossible, as the ships' aging engines suffered repeated breakdowns; Rear Admiral Arthur Christian considered himself fortunate if he had three of his five cruisers available at any time. At over 13 knots, the *Bacchante*s gobbled up coal; accordingly, they usually plodded at 12 knots, which often slipped to 9. None of the British cruisers zigzagged, because none had ever sighted a periscope.

The danger attached to this disposition had been noticed elsewhere. From Harwich, Tyrwhitt and Keyes insisted that the old ships were museum pieces that never should have been sent to sea. On August 21, Keyes wrote to Rear Admiral Sir Arthur Leveson, director of the Admiralty's Operations Division: "Think of . . . [what will happen if] two or three well-trained German cruisers . . . fall in with those *Bacchantes.* How can they be expected to shoot straight or have any confidence in themselves when they know that they are untrained and can't shoot? Why give the Germans the smallest chance of a cheap victory and an improved morale [?] . . . For Heaven's sake, take those *Bacchantes* away! . . . The Germans must know they are about and if they send out a suitable force, God help them . . ." In giving these warnings, all were thinking of a sudden attack by fast, modern surface ships; no one—not even Keyes, who was Commodore for Submarines—worried about a threat from German submarines.

On September 17, Keyes's warnings reached the navy's highest level. Churchill and Sturdee were aboard a train traveling north to confer with Jellicoe on board the *Iron Duke* at Loch Ewe. Tyrwhitt and Keyes, although relatively junior in this company, had been included in the meeting because Churchill admired their initiative. Aboard the train, the First Lord encouraged both commodores to speak up. Keyes mentioned that the Grand Fleet referred to the elderly *Bacchante*s as "the 'live bait' squadron." Throughout Winston Churchill's life, there was no better way to attract his attention than to use graphic language. On this occasion, caught by the arresting phrase, he demanded to know what it meant. Keyes explained.

Aboard *Iron Duke,* Churchill brought up the matter of the *Bacchante*s and recommended that they be withdrawn. Jellicoe agreed. Sturdee objected, attempting to squash Keyes: "My dear fellow, you don't know your history. We've always maintained a squadron on the Broad Fourteens." Nevertheless, the following day Churchill sent a memo to Battenberg, who had not been present at Loch Ewe: "The *Bacchantes* ought not to continue on this beat. The risk to such ships is not justified by the services they render. The narrow seas, being the nearest point to the enemy, should be kept by a small number of good, modern ships." Prince Louis agreed and told Sturdee to issue the necessary orders. Churchill, assuming that orders given would be obeyed, thereupon dismissed the subject from his mind. Sturdee, however, continued to focus on the danger of a German surface attack on the cross-Channel lifeline. He admitted that the *Bacchante*s were too slow for tactical work with destroyers capable of more than twice their speed and he agreed that the old armored cruisers should be relieved as soon as possible by the new light cruisers of the *Arethusa* class beginning to come from the builders' yards. But of eight *Arethusa*s under construction, only one had actually been delivered to the navy. In the meantime, Sturdee argued, the *Bacchante*s were better than nothing; in heavy weather, when the destroyers had to be withdrawn, the old cruisers provided essential early warning and a first line of defense for the Channel. Battenberg allowed himself to be persuaded and on September 19 approved an order to the *Bacchante*s to remain on patrol in the Broad Fourteens. Battenberg did not tell Churchill. Later, Prince Louis admitted, "I should not have given in."

—

On the night of September 17, the weather in the Broad Fourteens became so rough that the destroyers screening the old armored cruisers were sent back to Harwich. The 12,000-ton ships remained on patrol at 10 knots, their captains not thinking of zigzagging because they had been told that seas impossible for a destroyer would be equally impossible for submarines. At 6:00 a.m. on September 20, the patrol was reduced from four cruisers to three when *Euryalus* returned to Harwich to coal. Rear Admiral Christian, who normally would have remained with the squadron at sea, was prevented by the high waves from transferring by boat to *Aboukir* and so went into harbor with his flagship. Command of the squadron passed to the senior captain, John Drummond of *Aboukir.*

For two days, September 20 and 21, the three remaining cruisers continued on their beat, pitching and rolling over the Broad Fourteens. By sunset on the twenty-first, Drummond signaled Christian in Harwich, "Still rather rough, but going down." During the night, the wind dropped almost completely. To the west off Harwich, however, it continued blowing, and Tyrwhitt waited until 5:00 a.m. on the twenty-second to leave there with a light cruiser and eight destroyers bound for the Broad Fourteens. Their journey would take four hours.

At six o'clock that morning on the Broad Fourteens, with the eastern horizon fading from black to gray, *Aboukir, Hogue,* and *Cressy* were two miles apart, riding easily at 10 knots through a moderate sea. Because Admiral Christian had left no specific instructions about submarines and Drummond had issued none, the ships were not zigzagging, although all had posted lookouts for periscopes and one gun on each side of each ship was manned. At 6:30 a.m. this tranquil scene was shattered by an explosion on *Aboukir*'s starboard side.

—

To Admiral von Tirpitz, submarine attacks on warships at sea seemed an unpromising form of warfare, and to most German naval officers, these vessels appeared too small and fragile even for coastal work. It was, therefore, with a certain compassionate reluctance that the Naval Staff ordered the fleet's handful of early U-boats to cast off their moorings and set out into the North Sea on August 6. Among these craft was *U-9,* one of the fourteen kerosene-burning submarines built between 1910 and 1911. One hundred and eighty-eight feet long, displacing 493 tons, this undersea boat had a crew of four officers and twenty-four men. Two torpedo tubes were mounted in the bow and two in the stern, and the submarine sailed with all tubes loaded. Two reserve torpedoes were carried on rails in a forward compartment from where they could be slid into the bow tubes once their predecessors had been fired. On the surface, burning kerosene, the boat could reach 14 knots; beneath the surface, switching to electric batteries, she could manage 8. Cramped space and foul air had given the submarine service a reputation for unhealthfulness as well as danger, and only recently had crews been permitted to sleep on board in port. In December 1912, as an experiment, six U-boats with crews aboard had remained on the surface anchored to buoys for six days in Heligoland Bight; this was considered an astonishing endurance achievement. Diving was always considered risky, and in rough weather, tactical procedure called for attacks to be made with the conning tower above the surface. Nevertheless, because kerosene motors smoked heavily, a U-boat on the surface sailed with a pillar of black smoke towering overhead. This made detection easy for enemy destroyers: of the fourteen kerosene burners with which Germany began the war, twelve were lost.

The captain of *U-9* was Otto Weddigen, a slight, blond, thirty-two-year-old Saxon, known for his courteous manner but also as a wrestler, a runner, and a swimmer. Weddigen disdained the common perception that submarines were scarcely more than iron coffins. In January 1911, he survived an episode during a routine training exercise in which *U-3* sank to the bottom of Kiel harbor because someone accidentally had left open one of the ventilators. Under thirty feet of water, the boat was filling with water and chlorine gas created by the chemical reaction of salt water with the acid in the battery cells of the electric motors. Nevertheless, the crew managed to close the open ventilator and then use high-pressure air to expel water from the U-boat's forward buoyancy tanks, raising the bow to the surface. One after another, twenty-eight men escaped through a twenty-eight-foot-long, 17.7-inch wide torpedo tube. Weddigen also was famous for leaping into the North Sea and rescuing a seaman who slipped off the narrow deck of a surfaced U-boat. When the waves hurled him against the steel hull of the boat, Weddigen's arm was broken. Two weeks later, the base commandant found Weddigen conducting a sailors' gymnastics class and asked whether, with his bad arm, the exercise was not difficult. "Oh, no," Weddingen replied. "I have only broken one arm."

By 1914, Weddigen commanded his own submarine, *U-9.* He chose his crew carefully and trained it first on land, in dummy submarines. When his men were ready, Weddigen began testing *U-9*'s limits. Fifty feet down was the normal operating depth, but Weddigen dove deeper. He remained at sea in heavy weather, running his boat through high seas, both awash and submerged. He regularly practiced reloading torpedo tubes at sea, trundling forward the two reserve torpedoes hanging from overhead rails and sliding them into the empty bow tubes. Before long, Weddigen's men considered themselves one of the elite units of the German navy. When they went to sea, they—and all submariners—were granted special privileges: gramophone players and records, sausages, smoked eels, chocolate, tobacco, coffee, jam, marmalade, and sugar. There was one exception: no beer was allowed on submarines. Weddigen was also practical about life in wartime; on August 14, he was married at the military chapel in Wilhemshaven.

Weddigen's first wartime assignment was to patrol the stretch of the southern North Sea west of the low, sandy Frisian Islands between Borkum and Heligoland. *U-9* sailed from Wilhelmshaven on August 6, but engine trouble forced her to return and kept the submarine in the dockyard for the next six weeks. On September 16, the Naval Staff ordered the Commander-in-Chief of the High Seas Fleet to send a U-boat to attack British transports landing troops at Ostend. *U-9* was ready, but a three-day gale postponed the mission; the storm was so severe that on the island of Borkum, a German aircraft shed with two seaplanes inside was washed into the sea. Finally, at 5:00 on the morning of September 20, Weddigen was able to leave harbor, but the weather failed to improve. A rising northwest wind and heavy swells made the submarine's gyrocompass useless and Weddigen fell back on one of the mariner's age-old methods: navigating by soundings. Battered by ten-foot waves, he rode out the storm on the surface with his engines turning only enough to keep the bow into the sea. Uncertain of his position, he gave up the attempt to reach the Channel off Ostend and, hoping to get a bearing from a point on land, turned south toward the coast of Holland, a place notorious for shoals. On September 21, he located himself not far from the Dutch seaside resort of Scheveningen; he was fifty miles off course. Stopping his electric motors to conserve their batteries, and hoping to rest his weary crew, he took the submarine down to fifty feet where, still pitching and rolling, *U-9* spent the night.

At dawn on September 22, *U-9* started her electric motors and rose to the surface. Weddigen had traveled 200 miles on this patrol so far and was ready to turn back for home. Before leaving, he decided to take a last look at his surroundings. When her periscope broke the surface, Weddigen and his First Officer, Johann Spiess, got an agreeable surprise: "Light streamed from the eastern horizon and spread over a cloudless sky," Spiess wrote after the war. "The wind was a whisper and the sea was calm save for a long, low swell. Visibility was excellent. The horizon was a clear, sharp line where sea met sky. . . . A few Dutch fishing boats lay shadowed against the sunrise as if in some vividly colored print." There was nothing else. The submarine rose and lay on the surface, and Weddigen went down for breakfast. While the captain was below, Spiess in the conning tower spotted smoke and a mast on the horizon. He immediately turned off the kerosene motors to eliminate the column of smoke overhead and summoned the captain. Weddigen hurried up the ladder, took a look, and ordered the U-boat to dive.

At periscope depth, Weddigen, glued to his eyepiece, watched the mast grow into a ship, then two ships, then three. They were warships steaming parallel, 4,000 yards apart. He thought at first that they must be a screen for a fleet, but, seeing no larger ships behind, he made preparations to attack. Steering in their direction, alternately raising and lowering his periscope, he reported, "three cruisers, each with four funnels." "I could see their gray-black sides riding high out of the water." Weddigen steered for the middle ship of the three. Approaching on his target's port bow, he moved in close "to make my aim sure." At 6:20 a.m., he fired a torpedo from bow tube number 2 and ordered a dive to fifty feet. As the submarine slid down, the crew listened. At a range of 550 yards, the time required for the torpedo to travel to the target and for the sound of an explosion to travel back would be thirty-one seconds. Thirty-one seconds later, the submariners heard "a dull thud, followed by a shrill-toned crash." Cheers broke out on *U-9,* and Weddigen and Spiess forgot formality and slapped each other on the back.

—

The torpedo hit *Aboukir* amidships on the starboard side below the waterline. Water flooded into the engine and boiler rooms, bringing the cruiser to a stop and causing a list to port. On the bridge, Captain Drummond, seeing no sign of a submarine, assumed that his ship had hit a mine. He hoisted the mine warning signal and ordered the other two cruisers to come closer so that he could transfer his wounded men. As *Aboukir*'s list increased to twenty degrees, he tried to right her by flooding compartments on the opposite side. The list increased and it became obvious that the ship would sink, but when "Abandon ship" was sounded, only a single boat was available. The others had been smashed in the explosion or could not be swung out and lowered for lack of steam to power the winches. Twenty-five minutes after she was hit, *Aboukir* capsized. She floated, her red-painted bottom up, for five minutes, tempting a few seamen to scramble up her slimy bottom and cling to her keel. When she sank, the clingers went with her.

As *Hogue* and *Cressy* approached to help, Captain Wilmot Nicholson of *Hogue* realized that he was dealing with a submarine and signaled *Cressy* to look out for a periscope. Even so, Nicholson steamed slowly among the men in the water while his crew threw overboard mess tables, chairs, anything that would float, and then stopped and lowered all his boats. His men—those who had a moment to look—were transfixed by a sight none of them had ever seen: a big ship rolling over in her death agony. One young officer remembered seeing "the sun shining on pink, naked men walking down her sides, inch by inch, as she heeled over, some standing, others sitting down and sliding into the water, which was soon dotted with heads." At 6:55 a.m., as *Aboukir* was giving her final lurch, *Hogue,* nearby, was struck by two torpedoes, five seconds apart. There was "a terrific crash . . ." recalled an officer, "the ship lifted up, quivering all over . . . a second later, another, duller crash and a great cloud of smoke followed by a torrent of water."

—

After firing a single torpedo at *Aboukir* and going deep, Weddigen cautiously brought *U-9* back near the surface and raised his periscope. Watching the stricken *Aboukir,* he saw white steam blowing out of the ship's four funnels as the cruiser heeled over and was impressed by the "brave sailors," remaining at their gun stations. He also saw *Hogue* and *Cressy* creeping through the water, lowering boats. He now knew that his target had not been a light cruiser, as he had originally believed, but a large armored cruiser. And before his eyes were two identical sisters. Weddigen reloaded his empty torpedo tube and selected his second target, *Hogue.* Through his periscope, he saw the big, gray, four-funneled ship, her White Ensign waving in the morning breeze, her colored signal flags fluttering from their halyards. The ship was stationary, only 300 yards away. Taking no chances, Weddigen fired both bow tubes. As the two torpedoes leaped from the tubes, the shift in weight distribution affected the submarine's balance and her bow rose and suddenly broke the surface. *Hogue*'s gunners immediately opened fire. Weddigen struggled to regain ballast, succeeded, and took the U-boat down again to fifty feet. A few seconds later he heard two explosions.

—

Hogue's gunners continued to fire even after the two torpedoes exploded against her side. Captain Nicholson ordered all watertight doors closed, but within five minutes the quarterdeck was awash and the cruiser rolled over to starboard. An explosion sounded deep inside and Nicholson repeated the order given by Captain Drummond: "Abandon ship." Ten minutes after she was struck, *Hogue* capsized. When she sank, at 7:15 a.m., her boats were just returning with the survivors of *Aboukir.*

—

Weddigen, advised by his chief engineer that his electric batteries were running low, nevertheless decided to continue his attack. Two torpedoes remained in *U-9*'s stern tubes and he had one reserve for a bow tube. Coming back up to periscope depth, he and Spiess looked and saw the water "littered with wreckage, crowded lifeboats, and drowning men." The third cruiser had stopped to rescue survivors. Weddigen maneuvered so that his stern was aimed at this immobile ship and at 7:20 a.m., one hour after his first shot, he fired both stern torpedoes. "This time we were so bold that we did not dive below periscope depth but watched," Spiess said. "The range was a thousand yards. We waited and then a dull crash came. We waited for the second. But it never came. The second torpedo had missed." Weddigen had one torpedo left. He brought the U-boat around again, aimed the bow at the enemy, moved in to 550 yards, and fired his last torpedo.

—

When a periscope was reported on *Cressy*'s port bow 300 yards away, Captain Robert Johnson opened fire and put his engines to full speed, intending to ram. He saw and hit nothing and *Cressy* slowed, stopped, and lowered her boats. While his crew attempted to rescue the men in the water, Johnson began sending wireless signals to the Admiralty: "*Aboukir* and *Hogue* sinking! . . ." The message and position were constantly repeated. About five minutes later, a periscope was seen on the starboard quarter and the track of a torpedo at a range of 500 yards was plainly visible. "Full speed ahead, both," Johnson ordered, but he was too late. Before *Cressy* could gather momentum, she was hit forward on the starboard side. Those already in the water saw "a sudden explosion and a great column of smoke, black as ink." The cruiser heeled about ten degrees to starboard, then momentarily righted herself. A second torpedo passed behind her stern, but at 7:30, about a quarter of an hour after the first hit, a third torpedo struck the ship on the port beam, rupturing the tanks in a boiler room and smothering the men there in scalding steam. On deck, Captain Johnson walked around saying, "Keep cool, my lads. Pick up a spar and put it under your arm. That'll keep you afloat until the destroyers pick you up." *Cressy* rolled over to starboard and lay on her side. She paused, then continued to roll until she was floating bottom up with her starboard propeller out of the water. She remained in this position for another twenty minutes and then, at 7:55 a.m., she too went down. *Cressy*'s distress signal was picked up by Tyrwhitt at 7:07 a.m. The first message gave no account of what had happened or where they were, but Tyrwhitt said, "Knowing where they were supposed to be, I dashed off at full speed and a few minutes later we received their position from *Cressy* and part of a signal which ended abruptly and then there was no more."

—

Cressy's survivors suffered even more than the crews of her sisters. All of *Cressy*'s boats had been away, picking up survivors of *Hogue* and *Aboukir;* these now returned crowded with men from the other ships. Survivors struggled to climb over the gunwales; as many as five men clung to a single life jacket and a dozen to a single plank. There were Dutch fishing trawlers nearby, but having seen three big ships explode, capsize, and go down before their eyes, they hesitated to approach. Not until 8:30 a.m. did a small Dutch steamship, *Flora,* out of Rotterdam, arrive, and, regardless of danger, rescue 286 men. "It was very difficult," said the captain of *Flora.* "The survivors were exhausted and we were rolling heavily. All were practically naked and some were so exhausted that they had to be hauled aboard with tackle." Another small Dutch steamer, the *Titan,* rescued 147 men. Then two British trawlers arrived and pulled more men from the sea. Commodore Tyrwhitt with his eight destroyers came up at 10:45 a.m. Tyrwhitt steamed alongside an English trawler loaded with men and later recalled, "They looked just like rows and rows of swallows on telegraph lines, all huddled together to keep themselves warm; they were all naked or nearly so." Four of the destroyers began to take aboard survivors from the trawler, while the other four began to hunt for the U-boat. Of those aboard the three old armored cruisers, 837 were disembarked at Harwich, shoeless, wrapped in blankets, their hair and bodies soaked in oil. Sixty-two officers and 1,397 men had drowned.

—

Weddigen watched his last torpedo hit *Cressy*'s side, producing a white cloud of smoke and steam. As the stricken cruiser slowly rolled over to port, "men climbed like ants over her side and then, as she turned turtle completely, they ran about on her broad flat keel until a few minutes later, she slid beneath waves." The U-boat captain was filled with admiration for the British sailors. "She careened far over but all the while the men of the *Cressy* . . . stayed at their guns looking for their invisible foes. They were brave and true to their country's sea traditions." Then, jubilant, Weddigen set a course for Wilhelmshaven, knowing that in the relatively calm sea, British destroyers soon would be coming. His electric power was almost exhausted and he could not remain submerged. On the surface, he saw that the weather was radiant and the swell of the ocean had subsided even more. There was no sign of destroyers, but it could not be long, and *U-9* was vulnerable. She could not outrun them; with her plume of kerosene smoke, she could not hide; lacking electrical power, she could not submerge for long. Accordingly, he steered for the Dutch coast, deciding to risk grounding on the shoals in an effort to lose the silhouette of his conning tower against the outline of the shore. At noon, he caught sight of Tyrwhitt's pursuing destroyers coming up fast, each throwing an enormous bow wave, but fortunately, they did not detect the small U-boat. That night, he again sank to the bottom to wait. At dawn the following day, Weddigen rose to find another clear morning and an empty ocean. As he approached the lightship at the mouth of the Ems, he signaled, "On 22 September between six and nine a.m., *U-9* sank three British warships . . . with six torpedoes."

—

Rumors of the victory had reached Germany the previous night, following the arrival of *Flora* and *Titan* in Holland. On the twenty-fourth, *U-9* arrived in Wilhelmshaven to receive an enthusiastic reception from the ships of the High Seas Fleet. Thereafter, all Germany rose in ovation at Weddigen's achievement. The kaiser awarded Weddigen the Iron Cross, First Class. The Iron Cross, Second Class went to every member of *U-9*'s crew. Weddigen became Germany's first naval hero of the war. With a 493-ton boat and twenty-eight men, he had sunk 36,000 tons of British warships and killed nearly 1,400 British seamen. The effect was enormous in neutral countries where, although the prowess of the German army was taken for granted, the supremacy of the British navy had never been doubted.

In Great Britain, the shock was profound. No one believed the German announcement that the catastrophe had been the work of a single U-boat; it was assumed that as many as five or six submarines must have been involved. "It is well-known that German submarines operate in flotillas of six boats," declared *The Times* on September 25. "If it is true that only one, *U-9,* returned to harbor, we may assume that the others are lost." Practically speaking, the loss of the three old ships scarcely affected the overwhelming superiority of the Royal Navy. The three cruisers, said Churchill, were "of no great value; they were among . . . [our] oldest cruisers and contributed in no appreciable way to our vital margins." It was the loss of life and the blow to Britain's naval prestige that stunned the nation. The number of men who died was small compared to the casualties the army was suffering in France, but the suddenness and totality of the loss at sea struck hard. From within the navy came harsh criticism. Beatty, once a lieutenant on *Aboukir,* wrote to his wife, "We heard *Aboukir* crying out yesterday morning . . . over 400 miles away, but never contemplated it was a disaster of . . . [this] magnitude. . . . It was bound to happen. Our cruisers had no conceivable right to be where they were . . . sooner or later they would surely be caught by submarines or battle cruisers. . . . It was inevitable and faulty strategy on the part of the Admiralty." From retirement, Fisher wrote angrily, "It was pure murder sending those big armoured ships in the North Sea."

A wave of public criticism rolled over the First Lord. Later, Churchill himself ironically summarized his opponent's arguments: "The disaster . . . followed from the interference of a civilian minister in naval operations and the over-riding of the judgement of skilful and experienced admirals." In fact, of course, the dispositions were the responsibility of the First Sea Lord and the Chief of Staff, while the faulty tactics were the fault of the admiral and captains on the scene. These, Churchill did not spare: "One would expect senior officers in command of cruiser squadrons to judge for themselves the danger of their task and especially of its constant repetition; and while obeying orders, [they] should have spoken up, rather than going on day after day and week after week, until superior authority intervened or something lamentable happened. . . . Moreover, although the impulse which prompted the *Hogue* and *Cressy* to go to the rescue of their comrades in the sinking of the *Aboukir* was one of generous humanity, they could hardly have done anything more unwise or more likely to add to the loss of life. They should at once have steamed away in opposite directions, lowering boats at the first opportunity."

Officially, a naval Court of Inquiry, employing hindsight, declared that "a cruiser patrol established in a limited area at so short a distance from an enemy's submarine base was certain to be attacked by submarines, and the withdrawal of the destroyers increased the chance of a successful attack, while diminishing those of saving life." On October 2, Admiral Christian was removed from command and placed on half pay. Battenberg later exonerated him and also made allowances for the three ship captains, who "were placed in a cruel position, once they found themselves in waters swarming with drowning men." Captain Drummond was criticized for not zigzagging and for not ordering out destroyers on the night of the twenty-first as the weather began to moderate, but praised for his conduct once his ship had been hit. Battenberg did not feel that a court-martial for Drummond was justified, but he remained on half pay and did not command again at sea. When Fisher arrived at the Admiralty two months later, he observed "that most of the officers concerned were on half pay, that they had better remain there, and that no useful purpose could be served by further action."

The sinking of the three ships stimulated immediate changes. The two surviving sisters, *Euryalus* and *Bacchante,* were banished from the North Sea and sent to duty at Gibraltar, beyond the range of U-boats. Zigzagging at 13 knots was made mandatory for all large warships in submarine waters. The Admiralty sent a grim command to the navy: "If one ship is torpedoed or strikes a mine, the disabled ship must be left to her fate, and other large ships clear out of the dangerous area, calling up minor vessels to render assistance." Never again, either in Parliament or the press or at one of his London clubs, did Admiral Lord Charles Beresford describe submarines as "playthings" or "toys."

—

Three weeks later, Otto Weddigen was back at sea and, because British captains were still ignoring both the lesson of the *Bacchante*s and Admiralty orders, he sank a fourth British armored cruiser, this time off Aberdeen on the coast of Scotland. Six ancient ships of the 10th Cruiser Squadron, including the twenty-three-year-old, 7,350-ton *Hawke,* were patrolling off Aberdeen. On the morning of October 15, these vessels were spread in patrol formation at ten-mile intervals. At 9:30 a.m., *Hawke* and her sister *Endymion* stopped dead in the water for fifteen minutes to permit *Hawke* to send a boat to pick up mail. By 10:30, *Endymion* had moved out of sight and *Hawke,* her boat rehoisted, was proceeding at 13 knots but without zigzagging. Suddenly, there was an explosion under her forward funnel, she began to list, and there was time only to lower two boats before she capsized and sank. Because the squadron had steamed over the horizon, none of this was known until, at 1:20 p.m., another ship in the squadron reported a submarine attack. Immediately, the flagship signaled all ships to steam northwest at full speed. All ships replied, except *Hawke.* A destroyer, sent to search, found a boat holding twenty-one men; a day later a Norwegian steamer picked up another forty-nine survivors from a second boat. The rest of the crew, nearly 500 men, was lost.

—

Thirty-six hours after Jellicoe learned that *Hawke* had been torpedoed, he received a report that a U-boat was *inside* the Grand Fleet base at Scapa Flow. Convinced now that neither the North Sea nor Scapa Flow was safe for the Grand Fleet, the Commander-in-Chief asked permission to withdraw it still farther to the west. Reluctantly, the Admiralty authorized the temporary transfer of two battle squadrons to two new harbors, Loch-na-Keal, on the Isle of Mull on the Scottish west coast, and Lough Swilly, on the east coast of northern Ireland. Both harbors had narrow, easily defended entrances, and Lough Swilly also had a shallow bottom which would make entry difficult for a submerged submarine. Ironically, Jellicoe's search for security by shifting his battle squadrons led to the Grand Fleet's first major loss. Having preserved his dreadnought fleet intact for the first three months of the war, he suddenly was stripped of one of his most powerful ships when the new 23,000-ton dreadnought *Audacious,* carrying ten 13.5-inch guns, was sunk—not by gunfire or a torpedo, but by a German mine.

—

Because a mine cannot distinguish the nationality of a ship that runs into it, the Hague Convention of 1907 had agreed to keep the open seas free of these lethal weapons floating beneath the ocean's surface. Belligerents were permitted to lay offensive minefields only in hostile territorial waters; that is, within three miles of an enemy's coast. Nevertheless, because the North Sea is generally shallow and therefore particularly suitable for moored contact mines, the German navy, preparing for war, began accumulating a large stock with the intention of using them aggressively. Beginning on the war's first day, when the converted steamer *Königin Luise* laid her mines off the Suffolk coast, German ships and submarines placed over 25,000 mines in the North Sea, most of them in defiance of the Hague Convention. Commodore Tyrwhitt was appalled by this "indiscriminate and distinctly barbarian mining." Expecting a short war, he noted that "it will be months before the North Sea is safe for yachting."

When war came, the British navy was wholly unprepared for large-scale mining, offensive or defensive. Mines had been effectively used in the Russo-Japanese War; Lord Fisher, always open to new weapons and new tactics, had been impressed. But the navy in general considered the mine, like the submarine, a "cowardly weapon," "the weapon of the weak," "a weapon no chivalrous nation should use." Britain, accordingly, possessed few mines and no offensive mining strategy or equipment. In the first ten days of October, a small defensive minefield was laid in an attempt to seal off the northern approaches to the Channel, but the enterprise failed. British mines, poorly designed and constructed, sometimes blew up under the sterns of the minelayers. And within a few weeks, the anchored mines began to break loose from their moorings and drift down the Channel, making passage dangerous for British cross-Channel traffic. Equipment for dealing with German mines was equally inadequate. Before the war, only fourteen elderly British destroyers had been converted into minesweepers. When Jellicoe took command, the Grand Fleet was assigned a total of six.

Lacking minesweepers, the Admiralty discovered that the most effective method of dealing with German mines was to sink the minelayers. Success in this effort was rare. One notable moment came on October 17, when the light cruiser *Undaunted* and four destroyers of Tyrwhitt's Harwich Force patrolling off the Dutch coast encountered four old German destroyers steaming west across the southern North Sea. The ships, *S-115, S-117, S-118,* and *S-119,* each carrying twelve mines, had left the Ems at 3:30 a.m. Their mission was to lay their mines at the mouth of the Thames, but when they met *Undaunted* and her squadron at 1:30 p.m., they turned and ran for home. The top speed of the German ships was 20 knots—that of the British, 30; by midafternoon, two Germans had been sunk and the other two, turning back to help, also went to the bottom. Thirty German officers and men from the four ships survived.

Eleven days later, on October 28, the Germans struck back. In mid-October, the fast, 17,000-ton North German Lloyd liner *Berlin,* armed as a cruiser and equipped with a large number of mines, passed through the North Sea into the Atlantic with orders to mine the approaches to Glasgow on the river Clyde. Off the northern Irish coast, however, *Berlin*'s captain decided to alter his plan and lay his mines off Tory Island, northwest of Lough Swilly, then serving as a Grand Fleet anchorage. The German captain was unaware of the Grand Fleet's presence; he chose the site because it lay across the main trade route from Liverpool to America. On the night of October 22, *Berlin* laid 200 mines across the entrance to the channel used by most shipping in and out of Liverpool. *Berlin* then sailed north to attack trade with Archangel, but was damaged in autumn gales and forced to seek shelter in Trondheim, where she was promptly interned by the government of Norway. Meanwhile, on October 26, the Tory Island minefield claimed its first victim when the British merchantman *Manchester Commerce* struck a mine and sank. For several days, word of this loss reached neither the Admiralty nor Jellicoe aboard *Iron Duke* at Lough Swilly.

Believing that the fleet was safe, Jellicoe ordered Vice Admiral Sir George Warrender to take his battle squadron—the eight newest and most powerful dreadnoughts in the Grand Fleet—to sea for gunnery practice. At 9:00 a.m. on the morning of October 28, the squadron, with *Audacious* steaming third in line, was just turning onto the gunnery range when a violent explosion occurred under the port side aft of *Audacious.* The port and center engine rooms began to flood and the vessel began to settle by the stern. No one knew the cause of the explosion, but as a minefield so far to the west seemed implausible, a torpedo appeared the likely culprit. Following Admiralty orders issued after the sinking of *Cressy* and her sisters, Warrender hurriedly asked Lough Swilly to send help, then gathered up the rest of his squadron and sailed away.

At first, Captain Cecil Dampier of *Audacious* believed that she was sinking so fast he must abandon her. Presently, as the escorting light cruiser *Liverpool* circled the dreadnought at high speed, the settling slowed and Dampier found that the battleship still could make 9 knots on her starboard engine. He decided that if he could make the twenty-five miles to Lough Swilly, he might be able to beach her there before she sank. Jellicoe, meanwhile, ordered every available vessel—destroyer, tug, and trawler—out from Lough Swilly and Loch-na-Keal to assist *Audacious* and to prevent the submarine—if one was present—from attacking again. Until he was certain that no U-boat was present, Jellicoe did not dare send a battleship to attempt a tow, but the old predreadnought *Exmouth* was put on short notice to be ready to go. Meanwhile, Vice Admiral Sir Lewis Bayly, commander of the other battle squadron still at anchor in Lough Swilly, offered to go to *Audacious* by destroyer and take command of the salvage effort. Jellicoe agreed.

For two hours, *Audacious* struggled under her own power, moving fifteen miles nearer Lough Swilly, with the water rising steadily inside her hull. At 10:50 a.m., the remaining engine room was swamped and the vessel came to a halt. Dampier brought her bow around to the sea, and began sending away his crew in boats to the surrounding smaller craft. Because the captain still believed he had a chance to save his ship he and 250 volunteers remained on board as a working party. Nevertheless, *Audacious* continued inexorably to settle. Then, at 1:30 p.m., the 45,000-ton White Star liner *Olympic,* sister of the iceberg-destroyed *Titanic,* on the last day of a voyage from New York to Liverpool, appeared. Responding to distress signals, *Olympic*'s captain, H. J. Haddock, volunteered to help. Dampier asked Haddock to take his ship in tow and Haddock, ignoring the threat of submarines or mines, attempted to comply. Destroyers carried hawsers from *Audacious* to the liner, but although Haddock managed to make a little headway with the battleship in tow, the heavy seas and the weight of the sinking dreadnought quickly made the task impossible; *Audacious,* shearing into the wind, repeatedly snapped the hawsers.

In the early afternoon, a report of the sinking of the *Manchester Commerce* the night before by a mine in the same vicinity reached Jellicoe. At 4:40 p.m., the admiral also learned that a four-masted sailing vessel had struck a mine the previous night in the same area. At 5:00 p.m., Jellicoe, now certain that *Audacious* had been mined, not torpedoed, ordered *Exmouth* to sail from Lough Swilly and attempt to tow in the sinking ship. But by the time *Exmouth* arrived, it was too late. Admiral Bayly, Captain Dampier, and the few officers and men still on board were taken off and the waterlogged ship was abandoned. *Liverpool* was ordered to stand by through the night, but at 9:00 p.m., after a twelve-hour struggle, *Audacious* suddenly capsized and, a few seconds later, blew up. Ironically, this explosion in the empty vessel was responsible for the only casualty in the sinking of the battleship. A piece of debris, flying 800 yards, landed on the deck of *Liverpool,* where it killed a watching petty officer.

Jellicoe, dismayed by this loss of a dreadnought, was desperately anxious that the sinking be kept a secret. That night, when *Olympic* reached Lough Swilly, the admiral prohibited any communication between ship and shore. Then he signaled the Admiralty, urging that the news be suppressed. The Grand Fleet's margin in numbers over the High Seas Fleet was so slight—Jellicoe reckoned that he now had seventeen serviceable dreadnoughts to Ingenohl's fifteen—that knowledge of this loss might bring the Germans out at the wrong time. Jellicoe realized that, owing to the presence of *Olympic,* the loss probably could not be concealed for long, but any time he could gain would help. Churchill and his colleagues agreed, but because concealment of naval losses was so contrary to British and Royal Navy tradition, the Admiralty could not issue this order on its own. The decision went up to the Cabinet.

The Cabinet decided to withhold the news, but its decision was based less on the situation in the North Sea than on the situation in the eastern Mediterranean. In Constantinople, by October 28 and 29, the Germans, aided by the presence of *Goeben,* were on the brink of persuading Turkey to enter the war. Most Turks, the British ambassador warned London, now expected the Germans to win, and news of a dramatic German victory in the form of the sinking of a modern dreadnought might tip the scale. Accordingly, the Cabinet granted Jellicoe's request. This did no good with regard to Turkish neutrality. Two days later, Admiral Souchon took his battle cruiser and other ships into the Black Sea to bombard Russian ports, and Turkey entered the war.

Even so, for several days, *Olympic* was detained at Lough Swilly. A number of American passengers were on board, many of whom had lined the rails, snapping their Brownie cameras while the liner attempted to tow the sinking battleship.* On November 14, the *Philadelphia Public Ledger* published a photograph of *Audacious* sinking. Nevertheless, news of the loss was officially suppressed and the Admiralty announced only that the ship had been damaged. Her crew was instructed to keep the loss a secret and the men were quietly reassigned to other ships. Thereafter until the end of the war, *Audacious* remained on all lists of ships and fleet movements.† Her sinking was announced on November 13, 1918, two days after the armistice that ended the war. By then, the ship had achieved another distinction: of the forty-one British dreadnought battleships that fought in the Great War, *Audacious* was the only one lost to enemy action.

—

Four days after the sinking of *Audacious,* Jellicoe traveled to London to confer with Churchill and the new First Sea Lord, Jacky Fisher. In preparation for this meeting, the Commander-in-Chief wrote a letter to the Admiralty, dated October 30, explaining his concerns about the dangers to his fleet from submarines and mines. Prewar estimates as to the capabilities of German

*One of these passengers was Charles M. Schwab, chairman of the Bethlehem Steel Company. Detained on board *Olympic* in Lough Swilly, Schwab got word to Jellicoe that he had crossed the Atlantic to discuss important War Office contracts and wished to proceed to London as soon as possible. Jellicoe immediately had a conversation with Schwab during which he asked the American to call on Lord Fisher, who had just returned to the Admiralty. In London, Schwab saw the new First Sea Lord; he returned to America with a contract to build submarines for the Royal Navy.

†Admiral Scheer, commenting on this episode after the war, said, "We can only approve . . . not revealing a weakness to the enemy."

U-boats had been found to be too low: the sighting of U-boats as far north as the Orkneys on the fourth day of the war had convinced Jellicoe that his heavy ships were threatened no matter where they were in the North Sea. His reaction was to move his fleet ever farther away. Already, on September 30, he had written to Churchill, "It is suicidal to forgo our advantageous position in the big ships by risking them in waters infested with submarines. The result might quite easily be such a weakening of our battle fleet and battle cruiser strength as seriously to jeopardize the future of the country by giving over to the Germans the command of the open seas." Until the threat could be dealt with, Jellicoe suggested, he should operate the battle fleet at a latitude of 60 degrees north—above the Orkneys—with a line of cruisers spread 120 miles to the south to continue the blockade. The Admiralty did not approve, and recurring sweeps by the fleet in the northern half of the North Sea continued.

In his October 30 letter, Jellicoe formally restated his intended battle tactics. The Germans, he said, "rely to a great extent on submarines, mines, and torpedoes and . . . will endeavour to make the fullest use of them [in a naval battle. However, they] cannot rely on having all of their submarines and minelayers available unless the battle is fought in the southern North Sea. My object will therefore be to fight in the northern North Sea." At some point, Jellicoe continued, he expected the two main fleets to meet. When this happened, he would seek a long-range, heavy-gun action; the Germans probably would attempt to involve submarines as well as surface ships. If U-boats accompanied the High Seas Fleet, Jellicoe advised the Admiralty, he would be cautious before rushing into battle.

"This may and probably will involve a refusal to move in the invited direction," he continued.

> If, for instance, the enemy battle fleet were to turn away from our advancing fleet, I should assume the intention was to lead us over mines and submarines and decline to be so drawn. I desire particularly to draw the attention of their Lordships to this point since it may be deemed a refusal of battle and might possibly result in failure to bring the enemy to action as soon as it is expected. Such a result would be absolutely repugnant to the feelings of all British naval officers and men, but with new, untried methods of warfare, new tactics must be devised. . . . [These,] if not understood, may bring odium upon me, but so long as I have the confidence of their Lordships, I intend to pursue the proper course to defeat and annihilate the enemy's battle fleet, without regard to uninstructed opinion or criticism.
>
> The situation is a difficult one: it is quite possible that half our battle fleet might be disabled by underwater attack before the guns opened fire at all. . . . The safeguard against submarines will consist in moving

> the battle fleet at very high speed to a flank before the gun action commences. This will take us off the ground on which the enemy desires to fight. . . . [But] if the battle fleets remain in sight of one another . . . the limited submerged radius of action and speed of submarines will prevent them from following . . . [the surface ships] and I feel that, after an interval of high-speed maneuvering, I could safely close.

This cautious attitude was to dominate Jellicoe's handling of the Grand Fleet during his years as Commander-in-Chief. The primary purpose of the navy, Jellicoe believed, was not destruction of the enemy fleet, but command of the sea with the accompanying ability to maintain the blockade. He was entrusted with the safety of the dreadnought fleet; his greatest fear was that, by chance or a trap, he might find himself in a situation where torpedoes or mines would suddenly devastate his fleet and critically alter the balance of naval strength. The truth was, Jellicoe believed that however agreeable it might be to defeat the High Seas Fleet, doing so was not an absolute prerequisite to winning the war at sea. He therefore had little interest in a pell-mell, winner-take-all attack, wherever and whenever the enemy battle fleet might appear. Such caution might not be in the tradition of Nelson, but no previous British admiral had confronted invisible weapons such as submarines and mines.

To put such a proposal in October 1914 before an Admiralty about to court-martial Admiral Troubridge for his failure to hurl his squadron at *Goeben* required unassailable self-confidence and an iron sense of purpose. But on November 7, the new Admiralty Board approved the Commander-in-Chief's letter and assured him of its "full confidence in your contemplated conduct of the fleet in action." Jellicoe, cautious as always, sent a copy of his letter and the original of the Admiralty reply to his bankers for safekeeping.

CHAPTER 8

"Shall We Be Here in the Morning?"

The dangers to the fleet at sea from submarines and mines were hazards posed by powerful, new weapons used with increasing skill by a resourceful, determined enemy. Unfortunately, another peril was inflicted on the British Grand Fleet by its own government and Admiralty. No safe harbor awaited Jellicoe and his ships when they returned from the sea. Arriving at Scapa Flow on August 2, the future Commander-in-Chief found the main war anchorage of the Grand Fleet wholly undefended against surface attack—for example, a sudden violent inrush of enemy destroyers launching torpedoes at the lines of anchored dreadnoughts. There were no man-made barriers to prevent silent, invisible penetration by submerged submarines. The fleet's other northern bases, Rosyth on the Firth of Forth and Cromarty Firth, near Inverness, were scarcely better protected. As a result, during the war's early months, Jellicoe always felt more secure when his ships were at sea, despite the U-boats and mines that might be in their path. Thus, between August and December 1914, the Grand Fleet steamed 16,800 miles. During this time, Jellicoe's *Iron Duke* burned over 14,000 tons of coal, more than half its own weight. The flagship was in harbor for only one day in August 1914, and for six complete days in September. Inevitably, this constant movement meant wear on the ships' machinery and strain on the men. Postponed maintenance led to increased breakdowns. Gradually, as more and more ships were detached for repairs, the size of the Grand Fleet battle line began to shrink.

Churchill described the situation: "The Grand Fleet was uneasy. She could not find a resting place except at sea. Conceive it, the *ne plus ultra,* the one ultimate sanction of our existence, the supreme engine which no one had then were reembarked. In 1913, proposals were made to install twenty-two permanent guns and a number of searchlights in concrete emplacements. Nothing was done. In November 1913, Churchill announced that Cromarty had been chosen as a major base over Scapa Flow. "Having to choose between the two," Churchill informed Battenberg, "we deliberately chose Cromarty as the vital place to be fortified." And now that this decision was made, Churchill told the First Sea Lord, he wanted no further debate over the relative merits of the two bases: "The Admiralty have been so frequently charged with changeableness in its views that the greatest care must be taken to avoid any [further] accusation. . . . Unjust disparagement of Cromarty would have the worst effects. . . . It ought to be possible to make the case for some light armament for Scapa Flow without reflecting on Admiralty policy regarding Cromarty." Nine months later when the war began, therefore, Jellicoe and the Grand Fleet confronted this situation: the work at Rosyth, officially described as the fleet's principal North Sea base, was still unfinished; at Cromarty, the only entrance to the base was comparatively narrow and well defended by gun emplacements, but there were no obstructions against submarines; and Scapa Flow remained naked.

—

On July 29, 1914, as the British fleet sailed north from Portland, the Orkney Territorials were called out and small groups of men drawn from the Orkney Royal Garrison Artillery made their way to their war stations. Normally, these guard parties consisted of ten men, but the detachment at Rackwick in Hoy numbered twenty, for this was where the all-important telegraphic cable from the Admiralty in London emerged from the Pentland Firth and came ashore. Colliers and tankers had been arriving for several days; the first warships to arrive in the Flow were destroyers of the 4th Flotilla, which had been patrolling the Irish Sea during the Home Rule crisis. The arrival of the dreadnought fleet on July 31 was largely hidden by a summer fog, but for hours battleships, cruisers, and destroyers slipped quietly through Hoxa Sound; that night, over a hundred warships lay in the Flow.

From the first day of August, the great fleet lay at anchor, stretched out in lines off Scapa Pier on the north side of the Flow. The Grand Fleet itself then numbered ninety-six ships, including three battle squadrons comprising in all twenty-one dreadnoughts, eight predreadnoughts, and four battle cruisers. Attached were eight armored cruisers, four light cruisers, nine other cruisers, and forty-two destroyers. On arrival, the ships finished clearing for war. Wooden fittings and anything else likely to burn were wrenched away and taken ashore or dumped over the side. Soon, the shores of the Flow were strewn with mahogany and teak fittings while boats piled high with chests of drawers, chairs, and an occasional wardroom piano made their way to the pier. Surplus ships' boats were sent ashore and hauled up on the beaches while elegant steam pinnaces, gleaming with brass brightly polished for the naval review only the previous week, were permanently moored in sheltered bays.

The first official indication that the Flow had achieved the status of a war harbor came on August 2 with the posting of notices that harbor navigation lights might soon be extinguished. The remainder of the Orkney Territorials were called out on August 2 to join marines from the ships preparing emergency gun positions. Shadows of an enemy presence flickered with the news that the German liner *Prinz Friedrich Wilhelm* with 500 passengers had been anchored in Kirkwell Bay only eight days before war began. The German cruise ship *Kronprinzessin Cecilie,* a regular visitor to the Orkneys in prewar days, was reported to have passed through Stronsay Firth only twenty-four hours before the expiration of the British ultimatum. And then on August 5, the first day of war, the first German prisoners were landed at Scapa pier. They were thirteen unlucky members of a fishing-boat crew caught at sea by the coming of the war.

Inside the anchorage, a small fleet headquarters was established at Scapa Bay on the northeastern shore of the Flow. This consisted of a few auxiliary vessels, mostly drifters (small fishing boats), and two seagoing repair ships, *Cyclops* and *Assistance,* anchored off Scapa pier. *Cyclops* was connected to a shore telegraph cable that ran to Kirkwell Post Office, thence across the Pentland Firth to Scotland, London, and the Admiralty. Because the harbor was essentially undefended, Jellicoe's predecessor, Sir George Callaghan, did what he could to improvise. Field artillery pieces and Royal Marines were landed from the fleet and small guns were mounted at entrances to the anchorages. There were, however, no searchlights, so the artillery was of little value at night and the guns' caliber was too small to be effective even against unarmored ships. In addition, Callaghan stationed destroyers and light cruisers at the main harbor entrances and set patrols at sea to the east of Pentland Firth.

These emergency measures were designed to guard against the threat that, in the first days, most worried Callaghan and, subsequently, Jellicoe: a surprise attack on the anchored British fleet by German destroyers. "I often wondered," Jellicoe said later, "why the Germans did not make greater efforts to reduce our strength in capital ships by destroyer . . . attacks on our bases in those early days. . . . In August 1914, Germany had ninety-six destroyers . . . with a speed of at least thirty knots. . . . They could not have put them to better use than in an attack on Scapa Flow." But German destroyers did not come, perhaps because of the risk of interception by a superior force during the 900-mile round-trip passage across the North Sea. Another reason, however, was that the German Naval Staff, with its professional approach to war, never imagined that their powerful maritime enemy could have left the defense of its primary wartime base to nothing more than rocks, tides, and weather. This was Jellicoe's view. "I can only imagine that the Germans credited us with possessing harbor defenses and obstructions which were non-existent," he said. "It may have seemed impossible to the German mind that we should place our fleet, on which the empire depended for its very existence, in . . . [this] position."

Nor, in turn, did the British ever attack German harbors. Jellicoe later explained that when the war began Britain was critically short of the fast, modern destroyers and submarines needed to carry out such an operation. In the autumn of 1914, Britain had in home waters only seventy-six destroyers; of these, forty were allotted to the Grand Fleet, where they were desperately overworked; the remaining thirty-six were based at Harwich. Britain's older destroyers, although numerous, had limited fuel capacity and were used only for patrolling outside east coast harbors or in the Straits of Dover. Jellicoe and the Admiralty, aware of the powerful modern artillery and extensive minefields that defended the German naval bases, decided that to throw Britain's limited modern destroyer force against these defenses would have been grossly irresponsible. Jellicoe also argued against a submarine effort to penetrate the German bases. Owing to the shallowness of German rivers, British submarines could not enter in a submerged condition. "It appeared to me," Jellicoe concluded, "that an attack on their ships in harbor would meet with no success and that we could not afford to expend any of our exceedingly limited number of destroyers or submarines in making an attack . . . [probably] foredoomed to failure."

Despite this assessment, Jellicoe soon realized that a far greater danger than German destroyers menaced his fleet when it lay at anchor: German submarines. Before the war, no one had imagined that such a thing was possible. Because British submarines had never been able to remain at sea long enough to reach Heligoland from Scapa Flow, the Admiralty had been convinced that Scapa was beyond the range of U-boats from Germany. This belief was short-lived: the ramming of *U-15* by *Birmingham* off Fair Island in the first week of the war gave Jellicoe early evidence that German submarines were already operating in the northern North Sea. Even so, the Admiralty at first did not believe the submarines were coming from Germany; instead, it imagined that the Germans must have a secret base somewhere on the coast of Norway.

Distance was expected to provide an outer shield for Scapa Flow, but the main defense of the anchorage was believed to have been generously provided by other elements of nature. There were simply too many natural obstacles—tides, currents, rocks—to permit navigation by a submerged submarine. The approaches to Hoxa Sound, the only wide and deep entrance, lay through the Pentland Firth, a race of fiercely turbulent tidal streams flowing around the northern tip of Scotland at a rate of 8 to 10 knots. Churchill accepted the conventional belief that these factors made the Flow impenetrable: "No one, we believed, could take a submarine submerged through the intricate and swirling channels." Jellicoe, on the other hand, believed that a submarine "could master the currents by proceeding on the surface at night, or submerged with a periscope showing by day," especially if the effort was made at slack water. Experienced British submarine officers shared Jellicoe's opinion and believed that passage through the lesser channels would be difficult, but that the main Hoxa Channel, if otherwise undefended, could be penetrated by a determined submarine commander.

—

On Monday, September 1, Jellicoe's fears appeared to have been realized: a submarine was reported *inside* Scapa Flow. The episode, which came to be known as the First Battle of Scapa Flow, began on a quiet evening when the anchorage was shrouded in rain showers and driving mist. Twelve dreadnoughts, armored and light cruisers, and the 4th Destroyer Flotilla were anchored off Scapa pier engaged in coaling, taking on stores and ammunition, and cleaning boilers. Those battleships equipped with antitorpedo nets had spread them out. About 6:00 p.m., as dusk was deepening, the light cruiser *Falmouth,* anchored near the northeastern entrance to the Flow, suddenly opened fire on what she reported as a submarine periscope. Other "sightings" followed: the dreadnought *Vanguard* fired on an object reported as a periscope; a destroyer on patrol near the Hoxa entrance opened fire; the armored cruiser *Drake* signaled that she had sighted a submarine. Who knew what had been seen? The sky was darkening in rain and mist and the eyes of the lookouts were reddened by strain. Jellicoe, taking no chances, ordered the fleet to raise steam and "prepare for torpedo attack." The light cruisers and destroyers weighed anchor and began signaling and racing about. More guns boomed as ships fired at new "sightings," and shells landed and exploded on farms and fields on the surrounding islands. Picket boats, trawlers, and other small craft cruised up and down the lines of big ships to confuse the "submarine," to force it to keep its periscope down, and, if it was sighted, to ram it. Searchlights played back and forth across the water. Colliers and store ships were ordered alongside battleships lacking antitorpedo nets to take the blows of attacking torpedoes. By 9:30 p.m., with black funnel smoke adding to the thickening murk, the dreadnoughts began to feel their way out to the Pentland Firth. It required seamanship, with no navigational lights and visibility dropping at times to less than a hundred yards. Nevertheless, by 11:00 p.m. the fleet had cleared not only the Flow but the Pentland Firth, and the admiral could breathe more easily. By midnight, the vast anchorage was empty except for *Cyclops* with her vital telephone line and the destroyers left behind thrashing the Flow in search of a U-boat.

Later, Jellicoe reported of this "battle": "No trace of a submarine was discovered and subsequent investigation showed that the alarm may have been false, the evidence not being conclusive either way." The Commander-in-Chief maintained, however, that the only possible action when such an alarm was raised was to take the fleet to sea despite the dangers of haste, fog, or stormy weather. The incident also convinced Jellicoe that "the fleet could not remain at a base that was so open to this form of attack as Scapa Flow." From that moment on, the insecurity of his naval bases haunted Jellicoe; on any night, he feared, submarines might come into the anchorage and send his fleet to the bottom. Feeding his nightmare was the torpedoing of *Pathfinder* on September 5 off the entrance to the Firth of Forth, and the dramatic loss of the three *Bacchante*s on September 22. "I long for a submarine defense at Scapa," he wrote to Churchill on September 30. "It would give such a feeling of confidence. I can't sleep half so well inside as when outside, mainly because I feel we are risking such a mass of valuable ships in a place where, if a submarine did get in, she practically has the British dreadnought fleet at her mercy up to the number of her torpedoes."

There were other episodes when U-boats were believed to be inside British anchorages. Jellicoe's "First Battle of Scapa" was followed in mid-October by Beatty's "Battle of Jemimaville." As Beatty's battle cruisers steamed slowly into Cromarty Firth, the bow wave of a destroyer was misidentified as the wake of a U-boat periscope. A 4-inch gun opened fire, causing damage to a roof and chimney in the nearby village of Jemimaville. A baby lying in a cradle was slightly injured; the parents were soothed when a fleet doctor told them that at least two submarines had been sunk. Then, on October 16, one day after the cruiser *Hawke* was sunk with a loss of 500 lives, Jellicoe again was told that a U-boat was inside Scapa Flow. Once more the waters of the Flow were churned by propellers as the fleet put to sea. Although Jellicoe reported the next day that he believed the report was false, he also told the Admiralty that he could not continue using Scapa Flow until an effective submarine defense was in place. He took the fleet and retreated west to the remote bases of Loch-na-Keal, on the Isle of Mull in western Scotland, and Lough Swilly, on the north coast of Ireland. He did not return to Scapa Flow until November 9. Even then, when Admiral Sir Percy Scott, the Royal Navy's premier gunnery expert, spent a night on board *Iron Duke* at Scapa Flow, Scott asked before retiring, "Shall we be here in the morning?" "I wonder," Jellicoe replied.

The Commander-in-Chief was not the only British admiral alarmed by the vulnerability of the Grand Fleet's bases. On October 17, Beatty took the unorthodox step of writing directly to the First Lord, sending his letter by hand with an officer going to London. Beatty had been the First Lord's naval secretary, knew Churchill well, and thus emboldened, skipped the official chain of command—including Jellicoe.

"I think it is right that you should know how things generally affect the fleet," he told the First Lord.

> At present we feel that we are working up for a catastrophe of a very large character. The feeling is gradually possessing the fleet that all is not right somewhere. The menace of mines and submarines is proving larger every day and adequate means to meet or combat them are not forthcoming and we are gradually being pushed out of the North Sea and off our own particular perch. How does this arise? By the very apparent fact that we have no base where we can with *any* degree of safety lie for coaling, replenishing, refitting and repairing, after two and a half months of war. . . .
>
> As it is, we have no place to lay our heads. We are at Loch-na-Keal, Isle of Mull. My picket boats are at the entrance, the nets are out and the men are at the guns, waiting for coal which has run low, but ready to move at a moment's notice. Other squadrons are in the same plight. We have been running now hard since 28th July; small defects are creeping up which we haven't time to take in hand. Forty-eight hours is our spell in harbor with steam ready to move at four hours' notice, coaling on an average of 1,400 tons a time; night defence stations. The men can stand it, but the machine can't and we must have a place where we can stop for from four or five days every now and then to give the engineers a chance. Such a place does not exist, so the questions arises, how long can we go on? . . . The remedy is to fix upon a base and make it impervious to submarine attack. . . .
>
> I think you know me well enough to know that I do not shout without cause. . . . I would not write thus if I did not know that you with your quick grasp of detail and imagination would make something out of it.

Beatty's letter helped to galvanize Churchill. On October 23, the First Lord wrote to Jellicoe, "Every effort will be made to secure you rest and safety in Scapa and adjacent anchorages. Net defence hastened utmost and strengthened. . . . I wish to make absolute sanctuary for you there. . . . Ask for anything you want in men, money, or material. You must have a safe resting place; tell me how I can help you." On November 2, two days after Fisher returned as First Sea Lord, specific reinforcements were ordered: forty-eight armed trawlers were to go to Scapa Flow; rafts and barges were to be fitted with antisubmarine nets and sent north; twelve additional destroyers would join the Grand Fleet immediately; another light cruiser squadron was to be formed for North Sea patrol work; heavy booms and electrically operated mines for the anchorages were to be supplied without delay.

—

When the war had been won and the answers mattered less, questions finally were asked: Why did the Grand Fleet begin the war without a North Sea base? Why had it taken so long to choose among the various alternative sites? Why, in varying degrees, had they been left undefended? Who was responsible? Jellicoe, the man who had been most immediately affected by the lack of a protected base, pointed no finger at any individual. In his book *The Grand Fleet,* published in 1919, he employed his usual measured language: "In pre-war days, though it had been decided that the use of northern bases would be necessary in the event of a war with Germany, the bases had not been prepared to meet the new situation. . . . In fact, the situation was that, whilst we had shifted our fleet to the north, all the conveniences for the maintenance of that fleet were still in the Channel ports." Specifically, as to Scapa Flow, he continued, the question of providing shore-based defenses had been discussed "on more than one occasion," but nothing had been done because of lack of funds.

Churchill took some passages in Jellicoe's book as criticism of himself. When the former First Lord's own five-volume work about the war, *The World Crisis,* began to appear in 1923, he defended himself by placing responsibility in part on Jellicoe. In 1923, as in 1914, Churchill believed that Jellicoe's anxiety concerning submarines had been excessive:

> No one seriously contemplated hostile submarines in time of war entering the war harbors of either side and attacking the ships at anchor. To achieve this the submarine would have to face all the immense difficulties of making its way up an estuary or inlet amid shoal water and intricate navigation, submerged all the time and with only an occasional glimpse through the periscope; secondly, while doing this, avoiding all the patrolling craft which for many miles kept watch . . . thirdly, to brave the unknown and unknowable terrors of mines and obstructions of all sorts, with which it must be assumed the channels would become increasingly infested. It was thought these deterrents would prove effectual. Looking back, we can see now that this assumption was correct. There is no recorded instance of a German submarine having penetrated into any British war harbor.

Nevertheless, Churchill continued, "all of a sudden, the Grand Fleet began to see submarines in Scapa Flow. . . . Guns were fired, destroyers thrashed the waters, and the whole gigantic armada put to sea in haste and dudgeon. . . . Of course, there never was a submarine in Scapa Flow. None during the whole war achieved the terrors of the passage . . . none ever penetrated the lair of the Grand Fleet."

Then the former First Lord turned to defend himself:

> Reproach has been levelled at the Admiralty for not having accurately measured this danger before the war and taken proper precautions

> against it. It would have been a matter of enormous expense to create a vast system of booms with deep nets and other obstructions for the defense of all our northern harbors. I should have had the very greatest difficulty in coming to the Cabinet and Parliament with such a demand during 1913 and 1914. Not only was every penny of naval expenditure challenged, but this particular expenditure would have been clearly of a most alarmist character. . . . Still, if the Sea Lords and the Naval Staff had recommended solidly and as a matter of prime importance the provision of these great obstructive works at the Forth, at Cromarty, and at Scapa, it would have been my duty to go forward. But no such recommendation was made to me in the years preceding the war. . . . It certainly does not lie with anyone who was a member of the then Board of Admiralty to level such reproaches. [Jellicoe then had been Second Sea Lord.] Sir John Jellicoe's book, although no doubt not intended for such a purpose, has been made a foundation for several reflections upon our pre-war arrangements. . . . He recounts the dangers to which his fleet was subjected; but had he, either as Controller or Second Sea Lord, foreseen these dangers, he would of course have warned his colleagues and his chief. It is clear therefore that if the Admiralty is to be criticized in this respect, it would be unfair to cite him as an authority.

Churchill's defense was well constructed. When he says that as First Lord he acted (or failed to act) in accordance with the professional advice he received, his position appears reasonable. But, elsewhere in *The World Crisis,* we read Winston Churchill's description of his own role in the administration of the Admiralty: "I interpreted my duty in the following way: I accepted full responsibility for bringing about successful results and in that spirit I exercised a close general supervision over everything that was done or proposed. Further, I claimed and exercised an unlimited power of suggestion and initiative over the whole field, subject only to the approval and agreement of the First Sea Lord on operational matters. Right or wrong, that is what I did, and it is on that basis that I wish to be judged."

—

Once Churchill concentrated his mind on Jellicoe's needs, the work was accelerated. By the end of October, the defenses of Rosyth were completed and the entrance to Cromarty was secure. By the end of November, the land defense of Scapa Flow had been reinforced by heavy guns. The ancient battleship *Hannibal,* carrying four 12-inch guns, had been anchored to cover the Hoy entrance while her sister *Magnificent* guarded the Hoxa entrance. More 6-inch and 4-inch guns, manned by Orkney Territorials and Royal Marine reservists, were mounted in shore batteries. Antisubmarine obstructions multiplied. The first of these were simply buoys moored across the channels with herring nets strung between them. As autumn turned to winter, the weather and tides tore them to pieces. Stronger steel nets were laid, and double lines of drifters moored to nets were stationed in strings across Hoxa, Switha, and Hoy Sounds. Fifty trawlers, fitted with guns and explosive sweeps that could be detonated from the towing ship, patrolled the entrances. Electric contact mines were laid and booms constructed of miscellaneous rafts and barges carried torpedo nets. These obstructions were maintained by trawlers moored in positions in which they were exposed to the whole fury of winter gales; in many cases they were within a few yards of a rocky coast with heavy seas breaking over them and bringing on board tons of water. The trawler captains knew that, for the safety of the fleet, they had to remain where they were and maintain the barriers.

Also during November, the first block ships, elderly but still serviceable merchant ships, were sunk across the eastern channels. These sacrifices were only partly successful. The block ships were brought up to the Flow light, with no cement ballast. Ideally, they were to be sunk quickly by blowing their bottoms out, but it was difficult to make them go down in just the right spot with 8- and 9-knot tides pushing against their hulls. It could be done only during the brief intervals of slack water when the tide was turning. And, once in position, there was danger of winter gales shifting them or even breaking them up. Still, they were better than nothing. By the end of 1914, sunken ships had been placed across all of the narrower channels. In time, these rusting, reddish-brown hulls and superstructures would become part of the Orkneys scenery. Particularly conspicuous for many years in Kirk Sound was the rusty but still graceful *Thames,* with her three masts, two funnels, and clipper bow with its bowsprit rising above the surface. This left the three main entrances of Hoxa, Switha, and Hoy sounds to be closed by buoys and drifters with steel nets and booms with "gates" to permit the entry and exit of friendly ships.

Scapa Flow was so large that high winds and bad weather created dangerous conditions even inside the harbor. At the end of October 1914, the exposed nature of Scapa Bay and its pier on the northern side of the harbor dictated removal of the fleet anchorage and base across the Flow to the southwestern side. The dreadnought battle squadrons now lay north of Flotta Island, and the destroyer flotillas, fleet auxiliaries, and base ships for administration, communications, repairs, ship maintenance, ordnance, hospital ships, and supply ships were placed in rows up and down Longhope, Gutter, and Weddell Sounds, and along the Hoy shore. Even so, conditions worsened in winter. Darkness set in at 3:30 p.m. The wind howled continuously and winter gales sometimes reached a hundred miles an hour. Even inside the Flow, heavy seas damaged large ships, immobilized destroyers, and made it impossible to lower boats. The first of these winter storms came on November 11 when most of the Grand Fleet was present. All work on harbor defense stopped and all ships kept up steam for sea. Again, at the beginning of December, Scapa Flow was struck by a three-day gale. Every ship had two anchors down, yet several battleships still dragged their anchors and four seamen were washed overboard and drowned.

From November to February, bad weather, the short hours of winter daylight, and delays in the supply of necessary materials held up the work. The first line of permanent obstructions in the Hoxa entrance was completed only on December 29, 1914, the first line in Switha Sound on January 12, 1915, and that in Hoy Sound on February 19, 1915. All the while, Jellicoe bombarded Churchill and Fisher. "It seems to be impossible to get the departments at the Admiralty to realize that this is a base and the most important one in the country [and] that the fleet here is enormous," he wrote to Fisher in January. Defensive minefields were laid in the principal entrances to the Flow in February 1915; by the end of May, a second line of submarine obstructions had been completed. Thereafter, when the Grand Fleet lay at Scapa Flow, its Commander-in-Chief began to feel secure.

There was a moment following the German battle cruiser raids on the English east coast when Churchill and the Admiralty argued that Scapa Flow was too remote to permit the Grand Fleet to intercept the raiders. They favored bringing the fleet down to the Firth of Forth. Jellicoe disagreed. The Forth, he pointed out, with its single exit, could be closed by mines or bad weather while the Flow, with its several exits, was less vulnerable to these factors. Moreover, the fleet could reach the open sea more quickly from the Flow. In addition, Scapa had the advantage of being so large that ships could train without leaving the harbor. In the great stretch of water between its sheltering ring of islands, there was ample space for exercise grounds and, beginning in November 1914, gunnery and torpedo practice took place inside the Flow itself. Guns of up to 6-inch caliber were used in both day and night firing; this continued for the rest of the war. In this argument, Jellicoe had his way and, for as long as he remained Commander-in-Chief, Scapa Flow remained the primary base of the Grand Fleet.

—

During the fifty-two months of the Great War, only two German U-boats actually attempted to penetrate the anchorage at Scapa Flow. The first of these efforts occurred on the morning of November 23, 1914. The previous night, Captain Heinrich von Hennig, commanding *U-18,* was passing eastward off the Orkneys when he saw that the Pentland Skerries navigation light was lit and decided to make the attempt. He used the light as a guide to cruise on the surface as far as the Skerries where, his batteries fully charged, he dived. By 11:00 a.m. on the morning of the twenty-fourth, *U-18* was moving up Hoxa Sound. There, however, her periscope was sighted by a patrolling trawler, which promptly rammed the intruder. The wounded submarine managed to crawl away to the east, but Hennig was finally forced to scuttle his craft near the Pentland Skerries. He and his crew were rescued by British destroyers.

Four years later, on October 25, 1918, *UB-116* sailed from Heligoland. Technology had advanced enormously since Jellicoe's anxious days in the autumn of 1914. Hoxa Sound, which the submarine's captain intended to enter, was defended by hydrophones that picked up the sound of all approaching ships, by seabed cables that caused the needle of a galvanometer to flick when an electric current was induced by the magnetic field of any crossing vessel, and by mines that could be detonated electrically from the shore. The hydrophones gave first warning of *UB-116* approaching Scapa Flow after nightfall on October 28. No friendly ship was expected. The minefield was activated and searchlights swept and probed the waters. The submarine's captain, apparently believing that as long as he remained submerged he could not be detected, continued forward. He was not actually sighted until 11:30 p.m., when he came up to periscope depth, probably to check his position. He was seen near the boom entrance heading straight for it. Two minutes later the submarine's magnetic field activated the needles on shore. A button was pressed. The mines detonated and *UB-116* was instantly destroyed, leaving oil on the surface and a mass of crushed, twisted metal on the seabed. There were no survivors. *UB-116* was the only submarine destroyed by a shore-controlled minefield during the Great War, and the last U-boat sunk during that war.

—

Twenty-five years passed and, in a new war between Great Britain and Germany, the main British fleet once again was based at Scapa Flow. Winston Churchill had returned to the Admiralty as First Lord. And, once again, a German submarine attempted to penetrate the great anchorage. The operation was carefully planned by the supreme German submarine commander, Admiral Karl Doenitz, who selected *U-47,* commanded by Captain Gunther Prien, to perform the mission.

At 7:00 p.m. on October 13, 1939, Prien surfaced near Scapa Flow. High tide that night on the eastern side of the Flow was at 11:38 p.m. At 12:27 on the morning of October 14, *U-47* entered Kirk Sound. The tide was unusually high, but it required all of Prien's skill to maneuver the 100-foot-long *U-47* through the swirling waters and past the old block ships in the sound. On the surface and hugging the northern shore, he edged the submarine past the sleeping village of St. Mary's. No one saw him, although the shore was close and a man on a bicycle was seen pedaling home along the coast road. Prien rounded a point and suddenly he was in the open Flow. There, against the land to the north, he could see the huge shadow of a battleship with its tall mast rising above it. Just before 1:00 a.m., remaining on the surface, he closed to 4,000 yards and fired three torpedoes from his bow tubes. No result was seen from *U-47,* but on board *Royal Oak,* people heard a muffled explosion near the bow. So incredible did it seem to the admiral and captain on board that a torpedo could have struck them, safe in Scapa Flow, that they attributed the explosion to some internal cause, possibly in one of the forward storage rooms. Twenty minutes passed while *U-47* reloaded her tubes; then she fired a second salvo. Three torpedoes, striking in quick succession amidships on the starboard side, ripped the bottom out of *Royal Oak.* At 1:30 a.m. the battleship rolled over and went to the bottom, taking with her more than 800 men of her crew of 1,400. *U-47* crept away. Running on the high tide, Prien successfully navigated the unblocked channel on the south side of Kirk Sound, almost scraping the side of the sunken block ship *Thames.* An hour later, he was out of the Flow, heading for Germany.

The impossible had happened: a battleship of the Royal Navy had been torpedoed and sunk inside its main war harbor. Churchill, who years before had boasted that no German submarine "ever penetrated the lair of the Grand Fleet," was not held responsible this time; he had been in office only six weeks, and he survived to become prime minister. Immediately after the sinking, he ordered all smaller entrances to Scapa Flow permanently barricaded with massive concrete blocks dropped from overhead wires running on pulleys across the channels. Now these tumbled-together "Churchill Barriers" are a permanent part of the Orkneys landscape. So also is a large buoy marking the position in Scapa Bay where *Royal Oak* rests on the bottom.

CHAPTER 9

Prince Louis Departs

By early October, many people in Britain believed that something was wrong with the navy. August had provided the bright moment of victory in the Bight, but also the escape of *Goeben.* September had produced the loss of the three *Bacchante*s. The navy's positive contributions—the passage of the BEF, the establishment of the North Sea blockade, and the throttling of German overseas commerce—were either unglamorous or unrecorded. Even within the navy, officers were disgusted with the defensive strategy of the distant blockade. "We are only playing at war," groaned Beatty. "We are as nervous as cats, afraid of losing lives, losing ships, and running risks. Until we risk something, we shall never gain anything."

Someone at the Admiralty must be guilty, the British public decided. Churchill was the obvious target. He was young, brash, flamboyant, famous, hated by some, mistrusted by many. It was said that the First Lord was a brilliant but erratic amateur, whose energy and arrogance had led him to interfere in technical and strategic matters beyond his competence. Even Beatty, who had been the First Lord's naval secretary and who owed to Churchill his leapfrog promotion to command the Battle Cruiser Squadron, repeatedly criticized Churchill in letters to his wife: "Winston, I hear, does practically everything and some more besides." "If he would either leave matters entirely alone at the Admiralty which would be the best thing to do, or give it his entire and complete attention, we might get forward, but this flying about and putting his fingers into pies which do not concern him is bound to lead to disaster." "If we only had a Kitchener at the Admiralty we could have done so much more and the present state of chaos in naval affairs would never have existed. It is inconceivable the mistakes and blunders we have made and are making."

For those already disparaging Churchill's performance at the Admiralty, his October adventure in Antwerp provided fresh ammunition. When the German army swept through Belgium and northern France, it left the great port of Antwerp far behind. As a port and a symbol, Antwerp, the last remaining stronghold of the Belgian nation, had great significance. Positioned on the far left flank of the Allied front in the west, it might—if it could be held—become a sally port from which the Allies could thrust into the flank of the German army in France.

British responsibility for helping in the defense of Antwerp lay with the War Office, and Churchill's involvement came on Kitchener's initiative. On the night of October 2, the First Lord left London for a weekend visit to Dunkirk, where a squadron of British naval airplanes was based. At 11:00 p.m., with London twenty miles behind, Churchill's special train to Dover was suddenly halted and returned to the city. A car rushed the First Lord to Kitchener's house in Carlton Gardens, where he found the war secretary, Sir Edward Grey, and Prince Louis of Battenberg, the First Sea Lord. (Asquith was in Wales making a speech.) Churchill was told that the Belgian government intended to evacuate Antwerp the following day; the fall of the city, which must follow, would pose a threat to the French Channel ports and to cross-Channel communications. Bound for the Continent in any case, the First Lord offered to go to Antwerp to survey the situation. Kitchener accepted. Churchill returned to Victoria Station and arrived in Antwerp the following afternoon. That morning, the British Cabinet had met and approved the dispatch of the Royal Marine Brigade to bolster the city's Belgian garrison. Encouraged by this evidence of British support, the Belgian government postponed its evacuation and Churchill threw himself into the city's defense. The Royal Marine Brigade arrived in Antwerp on October 4; the following day, the First Lord summoned as additional reinforcement the raw reservists of the First and Second Naval Brigades; combined, the three British infantry brigades were combined into the new, 10,000-strong Royal Naval Division. Awaiting their arrival, Churchill commandeered an open Rolls-Royce and toured the front lines. The mammoth German siege howitzers that had destroyed the fortress of Liège had now been trundled up before Antwerp and were belching one-ton shells at the Antwerp forts, which were being pulverized one by one. As pieces of shrapnel screamed across the flat, boggy countryside, Churchill, wearing a broad smile, and "waving his stick . . . would walk a few steps and stare towards the enemy's direction." By October 5, Churchill had convinced himself that Antwerp's continued resistance depended on his remaining in the city. That morning, he took the extraordinary step of telegraphing Asquith, suggesting that he resign from the Admiralty and the Cabinet in order to "undertake command of the [British] relieving and defensive forces assigned to Antwerp. . . . I feel it my duty to offer my services." Churchill's telegram, read aloud to the Cabinet by the prime minister, brought a roar of incredulous laughter. Kitchener, however, did not think Churchill's offer risible; he was ready to commission the former lieutenant of hussars as a lieutenant general in the British army and give him command of British troops in Antwerp. Asquith, annoyed, declared that Churchill could not be spared from the Admiralty and telegraphed him to return immediately. The First Lord was back in London on October 7.

The British force in Antwerp helped to delay the fall of the city, but could not prevent its capitulation on October 10. Churchill later argued that the British effort had given the Allies time to secure the channel ports of Dunkirk and Calais, but many regarded the Antwerp expedition as a fiasco and blamed the First Lord for romantic vainglory. "What we desire chiefly to enforce upon Mr. Churchill," said the *Morning Post,* "is that he is not a Napoleon, but a Minister of the Crown with no time to organize or lead armies in the field. . . . To be photographed and cinematographed under fire at Antwerp is an entirely unnecessary addition . . . to his proper duties." Asquith was furious at the sending of the two naval brigades partly made up of raw recruits, one of whom was his own son, Arthur. "I can't tell you what I feel of the wicked folly of it all," he wrote to Venetia Stanley. The navy condemned the First Lord for wasting the untrained men of the Royal Naval Division, 1,500 of whom retreated into the Netherlands and were interned there. Beatty fumed that Churchill had made "such a darned fool of himself over the Antwerp debacle. The man must have been mad to have thought he could relieve . . . [Antwerp] by putting 8,000 half-trained troops into it."

The Antwerp episode eroded Churchill's position in the government. Nevertheless, because Asquith could think of no one to replace him at the Admiralty, Churchill survived. But if the mercurial First Lord was not to be held responsible for the navy's problems, who could be? There was, in fact, another figure at the Admiralty, a man older, more dignified, less visible, who, because of his name and background, was even more vulnerable than Churchill. This was the most senior officer in the Royal Navy, the First Sea Lord, Prince Louis of Battenberg.

—

The origins of the House of Battenberg, an unkind chronicler once wrote, are lost in the mists of the nineteenth century. It is true that most of Prince Louis's names and titles were concocted and attached to him during his lifetime. When he was born in Graz, Austria, in 1854, his family name was Hesse. His father, Prince Alexander of Hesse, was one of the legion of younger sons of great European houses who swarmed through aristocratic parlors—splendidly connected but, once of age, forced to cast about for an occupation and an income. Prince Alexander's nineteen-year-old sister Marie mightily advanced her brother's fortunes by marrying the future Tsar Alexander II of Russia; soon thereafter, twenty-year-old Prince Alexander was appointed a major general in the Russian army. He lost this rank when he eloped with one of his sister's ladies-in-waiting, a Polish woman of German, French, and Hungarian blood, at which point an infuriated tsar withdrew both imperial favor and the army commission. Alexander offered himself to the Austrian army, again became a general, and in Graz fathered Louis, the future First Sea Lord. When Prince Alexander retired to Hesse, his older brother, now the Grand Duke of Hesse, found names, titles, and a homestead for the itinerant general and his family. The marriage was recognized morganatically: Alexander was to remain a royal highness and a prince; his wife would have the lesser title of countess. The children would be princes and princesses, but they were to be serene—not royal—highnesses and would have no right of succession to the Hessian throne. Ten miles south of Darmstadt, the grand duke found his brother a village called Battenberg where a small castle sat on a mountain bluff above the river Eder. Here, the boy Louis, now titled His Serene Highness, Prince Louis of Battenberg, grew up speaking German, French, Italian, Russian, and English.

Another frequent visitor to Hesse was Queen Victoria's second son, Alfred, Duke of Edinburgh, known in the family as Affie. An officer in the Royal Navy catapulted to the rank of captain at the age of twenty-three, Affie liked visiting his sister Alice, now the wife of the grand duke. He also liked wearing his uniform, which young Louis much admired. Gratified, Affie suggested that this young relative by marriage enter the British navy and join him on a cruise around the world. Louis was eager, his parents approved, and, in October 1868, he crossed the Channel, took the oath of allegiance to the queen, and became a British subject. An obstacle arose: all naval cadets were required to pass a physical examination. Louis's eyesight was mediocre, but ingenuity saw him through. Told that he would be asked to read the time from a clock on the dockyard tower, he set his watch by the clock before going into the exam. When the question was asked, he managed a furtive peek at his watch and answered correctly.

From the start, Louis's path in the navy diverged from that of an ordinary cadet. A month after his entry, still scarcely knowing port from starboard, he was assigned to accompany the Prince and Princess of Wales on a five-month cruise that took them up the Nile and then through the Dardanelles to Constantinople. Bertie, the twenty-seven-year-old heir to the throne, decided that fourteen-year-old Louis was "a remarkably nice boy." When, on account of his heavy German-English accent, young Louis was so harassed on ship by other boys that he wanted to quit the navy, the Prince of Wales, whose accent had similar inflections, advised him to "stick it out a bit longer." Thereafter, when Louis was on leave in England, he stayed with the prince and princess at Sandringham in Norfolk or at Marlborough House in London, where a permanent bedroom was kept for him. In 1875, he accompanied Bertie to India, where he hunted tigers, stuck pigs, and broke his collarbone falling from a horse.

During these years, the demands of a naval career often rubbed against the delights and temptations of high society. The tall young officer with blue eyes, a black beard, and a gentle manner played the piano and the flute; he danced, rode, and shot; he was a prince and he was often in the company of the Marlborough House set surrounding the Prince of Wales. In this society in 1880, Louis met Lillie Langtry, said to be the most alluring woman in England. The Prince of Wales had been Lillie's admirer, but, now ready to move on, he affably passed her along to Louis. Louis fell in love. He wished Lillie to divorce the hapless, off-stage Mr. Langtry and marry him. Lillie, inconveniently, became pregnant. Louis's parents, appalled at the prospect of another morganatic stain on the Battenberg credentials, reacted promptly. Louis was assigned to a warship headed around the world while an agent was dispatched to Lillie to arrange a financial settlement. On March 8, 1881, behind a heavy curtain of discretion, Lillie's daughter, Jeanne-Marie, was born. For twenty years, she did not know the name of her real father.

In 1884, Louis married his cousin Princess Victoria of Hesse, a granddaughter of Queen Victoria. Here, the circumstances of Louis's relationship with Mrs. Langtry were reversed; this time a member of the morganatic, nonroyal branch of the Hessian family was marrying up. Queen Victoria, always partial to the Hessian children of her dead daughter Alice, approved and attended her granddaughter's wedding.* Now Louis knew or was related to everybody. His younger brother Alexander, known as Sandro, became the ruling prince of Bulgaria. Another brother, Henry, called Liko, married Queen Victoria's youngest daughter, Beatrice. To the future King George V, Louis could write chummily, "My dearest Georgie," and sign himself, "Goodbye, my dear, old boy, Ever your affectionate shipmate, Louis." Before long, Prince Louis was connected through his wife's sister to the Hohenzollern dynasty; then, through another of his wife's sisters, to the Romanovs. Victoria's sister Irene of Hesse married Prince Henry of Prussia, the younger brother of Kaiser William II. Then Victoria's youngest sister, Alix of Hesse, became engaged to Nicholas, the Russian tsarevich. Two years later, Captain Prince Louis of Battenberg, RN, and his wife attended the coronation of the Emperor Nicholas II and his wife, Empress Alexandra.

Louis never quite knew the extent to which this far-reaching network of family relationships helped or hurt his career. He liked to think that he had advanced on his own abilities. "I hate the idea of getting anything, as regards naval work, at the hands of the king, my uncle. [In fact, King Edward VII was his wife's uncle.] I want to get it on my own merits, if I have any," he wrote. For the most part, he seems to have succeeded. Year by year, he climbed the

*Louis and Victoria's first child, also named Alice, eventually married Prince Andrew of Greece and became the mother of Prince Philip, Duke of Edinburgh, consort of Queen Elizabeth II. As a result, when Prince Louis's great-grandson Prince Charles becomes King of England, a descendant of the morganatic Battenbergs will—at last—occupy a royal throne.

ladder, but there was no leaping ahead of others as Affie had done. Yet as much as Louis hated remarks that he was a "German princeling" or a "court favorite," hard as he tried to adapt himself to the hearty "band of brothers" atmosphere of Victorian navy wardrooms, he *was* a princeling, born a German, and there *was* favoritism. He was married to one of Queen Victoria's favorite granddaughters, and the sovereign was fond of him. "I am sure you must miss dear Ludwig, one of the kindest and best of husbands," the queen wrote to Princess Victoria in 1887, using the German form of Louis's name, a practice she often applied within the family. In 1891, the queen intervened directly to boost thirty-seven-year-old Louis up the ladder. Writing to the First Lord of the Admiralty, she declared, "She hopes and expects that Prince Louis of Battenberg, to whose merits everyone who knows the service well can testify, will get his promotion at the end of the year. . . . There is a belief that the Admiralty are afraid of promoting officers who are princes on account of the radical attacks of low newspapers and scurrilous ones, but the Queen cannot credit this. . . . She trusts there will be no further delay in giving him what he deserves." Three months later, Louis was promoted.

Sometimes, Louis resisted royal wishes. In 1895, both the queen and the Prince of Wales urged him to accept the captaincy of the royal yacht. The queen had asked for this because she wanted to see more of her great-grandchildren, Bertie because he liked Louis's company. Prince Louis, fearing that the appointment would mean the end of his regular navy career, gently refused.

In the mid-nineties, he became captain of a cruiser and then of two battleships. He was the Director of Naval Intelligence and, in 1904, was promoted to rear admiral and given command of a cruiser squadron.

Even across the Atlantic, Prince Louis attracted special attention. In 1906, Louis brought his squadron up Chesapeake Bay to Annapolis and was invited by Theodore Roosevelt to dinner at the White House. In New York, he stayed with Colonel John Jacob Astor. But Louis was a professional sailor, and he turned his voyage back across the Atlantic into a feat of seamanship. For seven days, seven hours, and ten minutes, Battenberg's six coal-burning armored cruisers raced side by side 3,327 miles from Sandy Hook, New Jersey, to Gibraltar. The average speed of the squadron was an unprecedented 18½ knots and Battenberg's flagship won by 300 yards. He became a vice admiral in 1907 and second in command of the Mediterranean Fleet, then Commander-in-Chief of the Atlantic Fleet. His reputation was bright; his ships and squadrons won cups for gunnery and smartness; his skills as a tactician and fleet commander were widely recognized. Ernle Chatfield, the wartime captain of the battle cruiser *Lion* and himself a future First Sea Lord, described Battenberg as "perhaps the outstanding officer on the flag list. He had a brilliant career at sea and was a great tactician and fleet handler. He was severe, but just." A senior navy captain added, "There are literally hundreds of naval officers who would be quite ready to believe black was white if he issued a memo to that effect." Lord Selbourne, a former First Lord, said simply, "He is the ablest officer the Navy possesses."

Louis did not conceal his ultimate ambition and when, in December 1912, Churchill made him First Sea Lord, the appointment was widely praised. Fisher called him "more English than the English" and "the most capable administrator on the Admiral's list, *by a long way.*" Lord Selbourne declared that "if his name had been Smith he would ere now have filled various high offices to the great advantage of the country, from which he has been excluded owing to what I must characterize as a stupid timidity. He has in fact nearly had his naval career maimed because he is a prince and because of his foreign relationships . . . a better Englishman does not exist or one whom I would more freely trust in any post in any emergency." Churchill said simply to Asquith, "There is no one else suitable for the post."

Personally, Winston Churchill and Louis Battenberg possessed similarities of background. Both were blue-blooded sons of younger sons of aristocratic houses: Louis descended from the Grand Dukes of Hesse, Churchill from the Dukes of Marlborough. Both were welcome and comfortable in society; both had risen to the top largely on merit. There the similarities faded. Churchill was only thirty-nine in 1914; Battenberg was sixty. Churchill had taken greater risks, broken rules, challenged the established order, and leaped ahead of his contemporaries. Battenberg had followed the rules in his steady climb up the promotion ladder. Nevertheless, Churchill respected Battenberg's record and intelligence, while Prince Louis believed that he could advise and guide the mercurial politician, steering him away from trouble within and outside the navy.

For twenty prewar months, Battenberg and Churchill worked together. Prince Louis had an orderly mind and, unlike many British admirals, he understood the meaning of sea power; indeed, he had talked with Mahan. Churchill, on coming to the Admiralty, had—as instructed by Asquith and the Cabinet—created a War Staff, but it was a purely advisory body with no executive authority. As First Sea Lord, Battenberg attempted to nurture and enhance its role, appointing a series of intelligent, talented officers. Prince Louis also worked hard to define the mutually supporting roles of the British and French fleets, even though the two navies were bound merely by an "understanding." Within the Admiralty, Battenberg never challenged Churchill's supremacy. A constant flow of initiatives sprang from the fertile mind of the First Lord, and Battenberg settled into the role of adviser, judge, mediator, and facilitator. Rather than opposing Churchill directly, Battenberg tried to channel the First Lord's thinking into paths of compromise, moderation, and conciliation. There were moments when he had to restrain Churchill from trampling too hard on naval tradition. One such instance involved the naming of new dreadnoughts in 1912. Traditionally, the First Lord proposed names and the king usually agreed. In 1913, Churchill proposed *Oliver Cromwell* for one of the five new 15-inch-gun superdreadnoughts being laid down that year. The king reacted violently to the suggestion that one of his ships should be named for the man who had cut off the head of his ancestor King Charles I. Churchill pushed hard until Battenberg cautioned the First Lord, "All my experience at the Admiralty and close intercourse with three sovereigns leads me to this: from all times the sovereign's decisions as to names for H.M. ships [have] been accepted as final by all First Lords." If Churchill persisted, he concluded, "the service as a whole would go against you." Churchill backed down, and the new dreadnought became HMS *Valiant.**

Once the war began, however, Churchill cast advice and restraint aside. As the supreme political authority at the Admiralty, he saw himself as solely responsible to the prime minister, the Cabinet, Parliament, and the country for the war at sea; the First Sea Lord, the Admiralty War Staff, and the admirals in the fleet were there to carry out his orders. His imagination was often brilliant and his energy was phenomenal; somehow, his capacity for work actually increased under the pressures of war. Conduct of the war was centralized in a tiny ad hoc Admiralty War Group run by Churchill and including the First Sea Lord, the chief of the War Staff, and the naval secretary. Churchill himself described its working: "We met every day and sometimes twice a day, read the whole position and arrived at a united decision on every matter of consequence. . . . Besides our regular meetings, the First Sea Lord and I consulted together constantly at all hours." Nevertheless, Churchill admitted, he often acted on his own: "It happened in a large number of cases that, seeing what ought to be done and confident of the agreement of the First Sea Lord, I myself drafted the telegrams and decisions and took them personally to the First Sea Lord for his concurrence before dispatch." Further, Churchill said, "I accepted full responsibility . . . and exercised a close general supervision over everything that was done or proposed. Further, I claimed and exercised an unlimited power of suggestion and initiative, subject only to the approval and agreement of the First Sea Lord on all operative matters."

The trouble was that Churchill's concept of his role, added to his constant demand for haste, eliminated normal staff procedure in presenting alternative views. Often, orders were written and issued quickly, without the advantage of staff analysis, and subordinates were effectively eliminated from any role in decision making. Admiralty messages had flair, but because they

*King George V blocked another Churchill battleship name proposal the following year. The First Lord had suggested *Pitt,* to honor the two great prime ministers, father and son. The king rejected the name on an intuition derived from his own many years as a naval officer. Sailors, he knew, tended to find obscene or scatological nicknames for warships; *Pitt* was too easy and would have an inevitable result. Churchill bowed, not without grumbling that this thought was "unworthy of the royal mind."

were written by an amateur, their language was often ambiguous. The advent of modern wireless communications added to the complication. Now, the Admiralty could communicate directly with the admirals and ships at sea, who began receiving messages straight from the desk and hand of the First Lord. Constitutionally, Churchill was entitled to do this, but it created confusion at the Admiralty and in the fleet. Already, in the episode of the *Goeben*'s escape, the confusion of orders emanating from Churchill's pen had befuddled Admiral Milne and confused Admiral Troubridge.

Nowhere was the effect of this erosion of professional authority greater than in the office of the First Sea Lord. Traditionally, the naval officer filling this role was responsible for the worldwide conduct of naval operations; Battenberg, however, had all but ceded this role to the First Lord. Prince Louis was responsible for keeping the fleet mobilized in the week before the war, but as time passed, and the whirlwind activity of the First Lord increased, Prince Louis's authority and self-confidence deteriorated. During the first three months of war, the First Sea Lord wrote few minutes and memoranda. Churchill wrote the cables to Milne regarding *Goeben;* it was the First Lord who wrote on September 18, four days before the *Bacchante*s were sunk: "These cruisers ought not to continue on this beat." Battenberg's original response had been "Concur." Soon, Prince Louis's nickname around the Admiralty was "Quite Concur."

—

It was in this context of losses at sea and restlessness in the fleet that public discussion over Louis's German birth began. The accusation that he was something less than a full-fledged Englishman, like the charge that he was a "court favorite," had been heard throughout his career. Most officers in the navy respected and admired Battenberg, but not all. Some were jealous of his court connections. Others knew that he was a Fisher man and they, being Fisher's enemies, became Battenberg's, too. At the time Prince Louis was promoted to rear admiral, several senior officers mounted a campaign against him. Prince Louis was aware of their sentiments; on July 24, 1906, he wrote to Fisher, "I heard by chance what the reasons were which [Admirals] Beresford and Lambton and all that tribe gave out *urbi et orbi* against my becoming Second [Sea] Lord or any other Lord and fleet command; that I was a damned German who had no business in the British Navy and that the Service for that reason did not trust me. I know the latter to be a foul lie. . . . It was however such a blow to me that I seriously contemplated resigning my command there and then." Complaints were heard again when it became known that he was to be made an acting vice admiral and second in command of the Mediterranean Fleet. King Edward heard about the complaints and asked Fisher about them. Fisher replied, "I have never known more malignant rancour and jealousy as manifested by Lord Charles Beresford and

Hedworth Lambton as against Prince Louis and I regret to say Lord Tweedmouth [then First Lord] is frightened of what these two can do in exciting the Service against the avowed intention of making Prince Louis an acting Vice Admiral." This resentful antagonism never died out; indeed, it spread to the press. In 1911, when Louis was appointed Second Sea Lord, Horatio Bottomley, editor of the weekly *John Bull,* protested, "Should a German boss our navy? Bulldog breed or Dachshund? It would be a crime against our empire to trust our secrets of national defence to any alien-born official. It is a heavy strain to put upon any German to make him a ruler of our navy and give him the key to our defences." The *Daily Mail* wrote: "It is a curious stroke of fortune by which one brother-in-law directs the operations of the British navy . . . and the other in person commands the German fleets at sea." (Prince Henry of Prussia then commanded the High Seas Fleet.)

Unfortunately and unwittingly, the Battenbergs contributed to popular misperceptions. In an era of a naval armaments race with Germany, they kept their home in Germany and made frequent and widely reported visits to their relatives in Darmstadt. There was an advantage—which Churchill recognized—in having a First Sea Lord who knew the German navy and many of its senior officers and who was related by marriage to Prince Henry of Prussia and the kaiser. But these connections aroused suspicions. No one understood this better than Queen Victoria, who had counseled the Battenbergs "to live more in England" and "embrace English life." Even in the active navy, officers who admired Battenberg saw an irritating German side to his personality. Prince Louis, said his biographer Richard Hough,

> never understood, through all his long service life . . . why his peculiarly German manner of being right, and always right, of not being ashamed of showing he had brains, rubbed his fellow officers the wrong way. "These are the kind of administrative blunders which are never made in Germany," he once wrote . . . [to a friend]. Louis could no more cure this tendency than he could completely refine and Anglicize his faint German accent which ruffled feelings further when declaiming about the efficiency of German ways.

In fact, there was little affection between the Hohenzollerns, who were disdainful of the impoverished, morganatic Battenbergs, and the Rhineland Hessian Battenbergs, who shuddered at the behavior of the Prussian Hohenzollerns. Prince Louis once tartly rebuffed a German admiral who had reproached him as a man born in Germany for serving in the British navy. "Sir," said Prince Louis, "when I joined the Royal Navy in the year 1868, the German empire did not exist." By 1914, he had been a British subject for forty-six years and most of his male relatives had served or were serving the British crown. Louis's brother Henry had married Queen Victoria's daughter, then gone to Africa with the British army for the Ashanti campaign, where he caught fever and died. Henry's son, and Louis's nephew, Prince Maurice of Battenberg, was an infantry lieutenant with the King's Royal Rifles in France. Prince Louis's two sons, George and Louis, were in the Royal Navy. That he might have to fight against Germany was a source of anguish for Prince Louis, but he had seen the possibility for years and had no doubts about his own loyalty to Great Britain and the Royal Navy. The problem was that once the Royal Navy began to suffer unexpected wartime reverses, the First Sea Lord became an easy target for blame.

Jingoistic nationalism in Britain in the early weeks of the Great War resulted in the smashing of windows of shops owned by German immigrants, the stoning of dachshunds, and public insulting of people with foreign names. Hysteria fanned by the popular press left no one immune. Violet Asquith, the prime minister's daughter, was asked "whether it was true that my father drank the kaiser's health after dinner." In this predjudiced context, the holding of the navy's highest post by a German-born prince at the beginning of a war with Germany became a focus of grievance. Louis was called a Germhun, a term coined by Horatio Bottomley. There were rumors that the First Sea Lord was secretly dealing with the Germans, that he had deliberately engineered the loss of the three armored cruisers, and that he had been imprisoned in the Tower on the orders of the king. Stories about Prince Louis reached the Naval School at Osborne, where his thirteen-year-old son, Louis (known as Dickie), was a cadet. "The latest rumor . . . here," he wrote to his mother, Princess Victoria, is "that Papa has turned out to be a German spy and has been discreetly marched off to the Tower where he is guarded by Beefeaters. Apparently the rumor started . . . by the fact that an admiral has been recalled from the Mediterranean to find out about the *Goeben* and *Breslau* escaping. People apparently think he let the German cruiser escape as he was a spy or an agent. . . . I got rather a rotten time of it for about three days as little fools . . . insisted on calling me a German spy and kept on heckling me."

Rumors of this kind reverberated not just among the boys at Osborne but in Belgravia drawing rooms and the clubs of St. James, where Louis's old enemies, a group of elderly retired admirals, gathered. This "syndicate of discontent," as Fisher called it, had always been envious of Battenberg's relations with the court and hostile to his advancement to the navy's highest post. The most bigoted was Beresford, enraged that Fisher, a middle-class nobody, and now Louis, a German prince, had both become First Sea Lord, an office he never had reached. At one point in his vendetta, Beresford wrote an article belittling Louis's record as a naval officer and demanding that he be expelled from the navy because of his German birth. He sent this to the editor of every London newspaper, asking that it be published anonymously. No one agreed.

Before the war, this cabal had limited itself to spasmodic attacks, expecting that Batttenberg would resign from the Admiralty if war were declared. When Prince Louis did not do so, his enemies became choleric. On the evening of August 28, a group of members of the Carlton Club, among them Beresford and Arthur Lee, a onetime Civil Lord of the Admiralty and a future First Lord, was standing in a hallway. According to Lee, "the conversation having turned upon German spies, Lord Charles Beresford expressed the opinion that all Germans, including highly placed ones, ought to leave the country as they were in touch with Germans abroad. Louis' name was not mentioned, but soon after . . . Beresford said that 'good taste' should lead Louis to voluntarily resign his position. However good an officer he might be, 'nothing could alter the fact that he is a German, and as such should not be occupying his present position. He keeps German servants and has property in Germany.' "

Lee protested and praised Louis. "I admit all that," said Beresford, "but none the less he is a German and he entered the Navy for his own advantage, not ours. Feeling is very strong in the service about his being First Sea Lord—it is strongly resented." When Lee expressed surprise at this statement, Beresford continued, "I am entitled to speak for the service. I know the opinion of my brother officers on the subject. It is very strong." Lee referred the matter to Churchill, who immediately took it up with Beresford: "In time of war, spreading of reports likely to cause mistrust or despondency is certainly a military offence." Beresford at first denied Lee's story and then told Churchill that what went on in London clubs was private and that Lee had no right to draw attention to the conversation. Whereupon Churchill replied:

> Dear Lord Charles Beresford:
>
> I am clearly of the opinion that the safety of the state overrides all questions of club etiquette and that personal ties must give way to public requirements at a time like this. Free expressions of opinion which are legitimate in time of peace, cannot be permitted now. Everyone has to uphold confidence or be silent. . . . We have an absolute right to your aid and influence in this and I hope it is on this footing that I may continue to address you. Yours sincerely.

This closed the incident but did not end the malevolent gossip. Horatio Bottomley, scenting the kill, stepped up his campaign. Scurrilous letters to Louis began to appear in the Admiralty mail. Others came to newspaper offices. The First Sea Lord was pinioned and increasingly helpless. He knew about the calumnies uttered at the Carlton Club and about the vicious letters arriving at the Admiralty; he saw the constant erosion of his role at the Admiralty; he knew that he was losing the confidence of the First Lord, the

Cabinet, and his fellow officers. Gout, from which he had suffered for years, chose this moment to strike him down.* To Churchill, it became obvious that Battenberg often was trying to hide his pain. Demoralized, realizing that his health and capacity for work were failing, Prince Louis sank into depression. Decisions became difficult. Officers entering his room at the Admiralty were shocked to see the First Sea Lord sitting alone, quietly reading *The Times.*

Meanwhile, Churchill knew that if the clamoring public was to be given a head from the Admiralty, that head would be his or Battenberg's. The Lord Chancellor and former war minister Richard Burdon Haldane, eventually to be forced out of office himself because he had been to a German university and admired German culture, wrote to Churchill on October 19, 1914, that, whatever else happened, "you must not ever consider leaving the Admiralty at this period of crisis. You are unique and invaluable to the nation. . . . Do not pay the least attention to the fools who write and talk in the press." Haldane suggested another remedy: "I should like to see Fisher and Wilson brought in, and Prince Louis kept with them as Second Sea Lord." Churchill grasped this suggestion and, on October 20, first spoke to Fisher about returning to the Admiralty. The next day he discussed the idea with the prime minister. "Winston has been pouring out his woes in my ear," Asquith wrote to Venetia Stanley. "I think Battenberg will have soon to make as graceful a bow as he can to the British public."

The press campaign against the Admiralty intensified. On October 21, the *Morning Post* assaulted Churchill, declaring that "grave doubt is expressed on every hand . . . there is a First Lord who is a civilian and cannot be expected to have any grasp of the principles and practice of naval warfare . . . [but who] now seeks to guide the operations of war." Unless Churchill departed, the paper said, "further mistakes and further disasters" could lead to "the destruction of the empire." Bottomley resumed his cannonade against Battenberg: "Blood is said to be thicker than water; and we doubt whether all the water in the North Sea could obliterate the blood ties between the Battenbergs and the Hohenzollerns when it comes to a question of a life and death struggle between Germany and ourselves. We shall further repeat our demand that Prince Louis of Battenberg be relieved."

On October 27, the navy suffered its heaviest material loss of the war to that point, the sinking of the dreadnought *Audacious.* The tension at the Admiralty was extreme. Churchill walked to 10 Downing Street and, later in the day, Asquith wrote to Venetia Stanley, "Winston came here before lunch in a rather sombre mood. He has quite made up his mind that the time has come

*"Prince Louis was a big man and had a big appetite," said his colleague the Director of Naval Intelligence, Rear Admiral Henry Oliver. "At breakfast, he had porridge, fish, eggs, bacon, a large plate of cold ham, hot muffins or crumpets, then a lot of toast and butter and jam, and finished on fruit. His meal was enough to have fed an officer's mess."

for a drastic change in his [Admiralty] Board; our poor blue-eyed German will have to go and (as W. says) he will be reinforced by two 'well-plucked chickens.' " The reference was to the retired former First Sea Lords Fisher and Wilson. From Downing Street, Churchill went to the palace and informed the king that he and the prime minister wished to replace Prince Louis. Reluctantly, the king consented and informed his uncle, the Duke of Connaught, of "poor Louis B's resignation." The last of Churchill's interviews was with Prince Louis himself; it was made the more painful because that morning Louis had learned that his twenty-three-year-old nephew, Prince Maurice of Battenberg, had died of his wounds in France. Churchill told Louis that he and the prime minister requested the First Sea Lord's resignation. "Louis behaved with great dignity & public spirit and will resign at once," Asquith told Venetia.

Prince Louis resigned on October 28. "Dear Mr Churchill," he wrote, "I have lately been driven to the painful conclusion that at this juncture my birth and parentage have the effect of impairing in some respects my usefulness on the Board of Admiralty. In these circumstances, I feel it to be my duty, as a loyal subject of His Majesty, to resign the office of First Sea Lord, hoping thereby to facilitate the task of the administration of the great service to which I have devoted my life, and to ease the burden on H.M. Ministers." Privately, Louis wrote to Churchill: "I beg you to release me. I am on the verge of breaking down and cannot use my brain for anything." The following day Prince Louis went to the palace to say good-bye to the king. "There is no more loyal man in the country," George V wrote that night in his diary. Leaving the king, Louis returned to the Admiralty and did a remarkable thing: he sent a personal message asking his daughter to come to see him. In his last hour at the Admiralty, Prince Louis of Battenberg met his daughter Jeanne-Marie Langtry for the first time.

The resignation provoked another storm, this time in support of Prince Louis. Jellicoe telegraphed his "profound sorrow" and "deepest possible regret." J. H. Thomas, a prominent Labour MP, wrote to *The Times* that the campaign against the First Sea Lord was "the most mean and contemptible slander I have ever known." Lord Selbourne declared "that anyone should have been found to insinuate suspicions against . . . [Prince Louis] is nothing less than a national humiliation." Louis himself, assessing the event, blamed the government's weakness. To a friend, Battenberg admitted, "It was an awful wrench, but I had no choice from the moment it was made clear to me that the Government did not feel themselves strong enough to support me by some public pronouncement." To Jellicoe, he wrote that Churchill "up to the end stood by me and, at first, the prime minister too, but the pressure from without became at last too strong—at least the Cabinet did not feel themselves to be strong enough to protect one of their principal servants. The moment this was made clear to me I walked out of the building and gave those in charge to understand that they would neither see nor hear from me until Peace was signed."

Battenberg's departure did not snuff out anti-German feeling in Great Britain or put an end to its toll of prominent men. Of these, Haldane was the most significant. His famous 1912 mission to Berlin, attempting to negotiate an end to the dreadnought-building competition, was characterized in the press as treason; he was accused of being in secret correspondence with the German government; he was charged with having delayed mobilization of the army and the dispatch of the BEF; he was said to have a German wife and to be the illegitimate brother of the kaiser. "On one day," Haldane wrote, "in response to an appeal in the *Daily Express,* there arrived at the House of Lords 2,600 letters of protest against my supposed disloyalty to the interests of the nation. These letters were sent over to my house in sacks, and I entrusted the opening and disposal of the contents to the kitchen maid." Haldane resigned from the government in May 1915 and "before the war ended was threatened with assault in the street and was on some occasions in some danger of being shot at." Nor did the rising xenophobia threaten only admirals and Cabinet ministers. In June 1917, when King George V heard that people were saying he was pro-German because his family had German names, "he started and grew pale." Hurriedly, English names were proposed: Plantagenet, York, Lancaster, and England. Eventually, by royal proclamation, the new family name of the dynasty became Windsor. Soon after, Prince Louis wrote to his daughter Louise, who became Queen of Sweden: "George Rex . . . wished to see me. . . . I was closeted with him a long time. . . . [He was] being attacked as being Half-German and surrounding himself by relatives with German names. . . . [His conclusion] was that he must ask us Holsteins, Tecks, and Battenbergs to give up using in England our German titles and to assume English surnames. . . . [He] suggested we turn our name into English: viz Battenhill or Mountbatten." Prince Louis of Battenberg's metamorphosis into Louis Mountbatten, Marquis of Milford Haven, was finalized while he was visiting a country house. He noted the change by writing in the guest book, "Arrived Prince Hyde. Departed Lord Jekyll."

Two weeks after the armistice, a gratuitous act of official cruelty was inflicted on the new Marquis. The First Sea Lord, Rosslyn Wester Wemyss, a protégé of Beresford, sent Louis a letter telling him that he would not be employed again and suggesting that he might wish to retire from the service to make room for younger men. Louis retired at once, writing Wemyss that he had remained on the active list when he left the Admiralty only because Churchill and the government had promised him another active assignment once the war was over. In 1921, this hostile attitude was reversed when First Lord Arthur Lee proposed that "to right a great wrong," the Marquis of Milford Haven be promoted to Admiral of the Fleet, only the second time in history this had been done for a retired officer. King George agreed at once and Louis was promoted. Five weeks later, he died.

Louis's son, who with the change of name became Lord Louis Mountbatten, never forgot what had happened to his father. He made the navy his career, resolving to reach the same office from which his father had been forced to resign. Along the way, Mountbatten served in the Second World War as Supreme Allied Commander in Southeast Asia, as the last British Viceroy of India, and as the first Governor General of independent India. Known as Earl Mountbatten of Burma, he became an Admiral of the Fleet and First Sea Lord and then rose higher to serve for six years as Britain's first interservice Chief of the Defence Staff.

—

Prince Louis's resignation as First Sea Lord on October 28, 1914, spared him from having to deal with what would have been still another cause of accusation. On November 1, 1914, three days after Louis left the Admiralty, Vice Admiral Maximilian von Spee inflicted on the Royal Navy its worst defeat in over a century.

CHAPTER 10

Admiral von Spee's Voyage

Framed by ancient hills and cooled by fresh breezes from the sea, the German town of Tsingtao on the north China coast prepared for summer. At the beginning of June 1914, the gardens were in bloom and all was in order in this distant outpost of the German empire. Constructed in only seventeen years, the European town seemed older and more settled than that. The broad roads were shaded by acacias, the brick houses had red-tiled roofs reminiscent of Central Europe, the modern Prinz Heinrich and Strand hotels were filled with visitors from Germany, England, and America. There was an impressive library, an observatory, a grammar school where Chinese children learned German, a high school where they would be taught trades, the yellow brick German-Asiatic Bank, and the famous Tsingtao brewery, then—and still today—producing exceptional beer. Above the trees rose the towers of Christ Church and of the station of the Shantung Railway, which communicated with the rich German-administered coal mines in the interior. Europeans could stroll on the Kaiser Wilhelm Embankment, go to the racecourse, or swim from the pebbly bathing beach on Empress Augusta-Victoria Bay. Hills with green meadows, pine woods, mountain streams, bamboo groves, and plantations of mulberry trees where silkworms were raised encircled the town. In the hills, too, a new Chinese quarter had been built, "to keep the native population as far as possible away" from the Europeans.

This German colony on the Yellow Sea, 6,000 miles from Berlin, had been created by an investment of 50 million marks for a single purpose: to serve as the base of a cruiser squadron of the Imperial Navy. The site had been selected by the founder of the navy himself, Grand Admiral Alfred von Tirpitz, during his brief tour of command at sea before Kaiser William II summoned him home to manage the building of the High Seas Fleet. In the spring of 1896, Tirpitz had cruised up and down the China coast and had selected this harbor on the Shantung peninsula. The German government offered to buy the territory, but the Chinese, although militarily impotent following their defeat by Japan in 1895, refused. Then, by one of those happy coincidences that sometimes assist in overcoming obstacles to imperial ambition, two German Catholic missionaries were murdered in the province on November 1, 1897. "We must take advantage of this excellent opportunity," announced the kaiser in Berlin, "before another great power either dismembers China or comes to her aid! Now or never!" The German East Asia Squadron appeared in the bay, German marines were landed, and, on March 6, 1899, Germany was granted a ninety-nine-year lease on the port and its hinterland. "Thousands of German Christians will breathe again when they see the ships of the German navy in their vicinity," the kaiser exulted. "Hundreds of German merchants will shout with joy in the knowledge that the German empire has at long last set foot firmly in Asia. Hundreds of thousands of Chinese will shiver if they feel the iron fist of the German empire lying firmly on their neck. I am determined to show once and for all that the German emperor is a bad person with whom to take liberties or have as an enemy."

Now, in early June 1914, four German warships, painted white against the Pacific sun, lay in the Tsingtao roadstead. The mission of these vessels, the armored and light cruisers of the East Asia Squadron of the Imperial Navy, was to police the kaiser's possessions scattered across the expanse of the Pacific Ocean. In the central Pacific, there were the Marianas, the Carolines, the Marshall Islands, and Samoa, some annexed outright, some purchased in 1899 from an impoverished Spain after the naval disaster at Manila Bay had rendered the Spaniards powerless in the Pacific. To the south lay other German colonies: the Bismarck Archipelago, the Solomon Islands, German New Guinea, Neu Pommern (which British maps called New Britain), and Neu Mecklenberg (formerly New Ireland). The guarding of these territories—a collection of volcanic islands, coral atolls, and swatches of jungle—was the responsibility of the East Asia Squadron. If war broke out against France or Russia, the East Asia Squadron was expected to do well. If war came with Japan—routinely described by the kaiser as the land of "yellow monkeys," or the "Yellow Peril"—little success was anticipated against the powerful Japanese fleet. Against Great Britain, war was not contemplated.

The two largest warships moored in Tsingtao harbor, *Scharnhorst* and *Gneisenau,* made up the core of the German squadron. These armored cruisers were sisters: seven years old, 11,400 tons, capable of 22 knots, and carrying eight 8.2-inch guns and six 5.9-inch guns. In firing exercises, *Scharnhorst* and *Gneisenau* had twice won the Kaiser's Cup as the best gunnery ships in the German navy. There were good reasons for this: the ships of the East

Asia Squadron were manned by special, long-service crews and Admiral von Spee, the squadron commander, was a gunnery expert. According to the admiral, these two ships could fire three salvos in one minute. Three modern light cruisers, *Emden, Leipzig,* and *Nürnberg,* were also under Spee's command. Roughly similar, all completed between 1906 and 1908, they were around 3,500 tons, reached speeds approaching 25 knots, and carried ten 4.1-inch guns. At the beginning of June 1914, *Emden* and *Leipzig* were at Tsingtao, while *Nürnberg* was off the west coast of Mexico. On June 7, *Leipzig* sailed from Tsingtao on a transpacific voyage to relieve *Nürnberg.*

The admiral commanding the East Asia Squadron was, in many ways, unusual in the Imperial Navy. An aristocrat in a fleet primarily officered by men from the middle class, a devout Catholic whose peers were largely Protestant, Vice Admiral Count Maximilian von Spee was sufficiently learned in the natural sciences to have made of them almost a second career. His appearance was conspicuous. He was tall—the tallest man in the squadron—and broad-shouldered and had a back as straight "as if he had swallowed a broom handle." He had blue eyes, a straight nose, bushy gray eyebrows, and a white clipped beard. Energetic, resolute, patient, and calm, he had a single vice: an addiction to bridge.

Spee was born in Copenhagen on June 22, 1861, the fifth son of a Danish mother and a Prussian father, Count Rudolf, whose roots went back to 1166. The family's Catholic religion was unusual, Prussia and Denmark both being strongholds of Protestantism; nevertheless, this faith was long-standing. One sixteenth-century von Spee had been a Jesuit poet. Maximilian had been privately tutored in a family castle and then in Switzerland before he entered the navy at sixteen. As a junior officer serving off the coast of the German colony of Cameroon in Africa, he contracted rheumatic fever, which left him with permanent rheumatism. He married and had two sons, Otto and Heinrich, and a daughter, Huberta. His service in predreadnought battleships and cruisers brought him his reputation as a gunnery specialist, and he became captain of the battleship *Wittelsbach,* Chief of Staff to the Admiral, North Sea Station, and second in command of the Scouting Groups of the High Seas Fleet. In November 1913, he was promoted to vice admiral and sent to command the East Asia Squadron. Otto and Heinrich, both naval officers, came to the Far East to serve with him, Otto as a lieutenant on *Nürnberg,* Heinrich on board *Gneisenau.*

During the months before war broke out, Spee led his squadron from port to port, steeling himself against an endless sequence of receptions, lawn parties, banquets, and balls. European life in the colonies did not suit him. "The women seemed a simple, unsophisticated lot," he wrote to his wife after a reception in Batavia. "Only one seemed to have any pretensions to sophistication, a Mrs. M., an American, I believe." At Singapore, "the English officers and their wives were quite wild, doing the newest American dances . . . they are almost indecent." At Manila, the tango, performed by Americans, was performed "almost indecently. It needs supervision." Worst of all were German diplomatic receptions where, as one of the hosts, he was required to stand and receive guests. "To my shame," he confessed to his wife, "I lied at least eight hundred times last night. You say, 'It is my greatest pleasure to meet you,' while you are thinking how much better it would have been if they had stayed at home." Aboard ship, Spee's rank condemned him to a certain isolation, but he would sometimes smoke a cigar in the wardroom and was always happy to join in a game of bridge. As a commander, he inspired loyalty as well as respect. He was willing to ask for advice, but having made a decision, he expected obedience. If his decision was wrong, he would admit it—later.

—

This summer, there was a sense of anticipation in the harbor and colony of Tsingtao. It was the custom before the war for German and British warships on foreign stations to work together and assist one another. The Royal Navy allowed the German East Asia Squadron to dry-dock ships at its Hong Kong base, and an annual exchange of ceremonial and social visits had become routine. In 1913, when the German squadron had been at Hong Kong, German officers were entertained aboard the British armored cruiser *Monmouth.* Now, in June 1914, the hosts were to become the guests and the armored cruiser *Minotaur,* flagship of the British Far Eastern Squadron, carrying the squadron's commander, Vice Admiral Sir Thomas Martyn Jerram, were coming to visit Tsingtao. The German squadron looked forward to seeing this British warship. *Minotaur* and her two sisters, *Defence* and *Shannon,* each 3,000 tons heavier than *Scharnhorst* and *Gneisenau,* had been built in specific response to the construction of the two German ships. As it was, they were the last armored cruisers ever built. Within a year of their completion, Fisher's faster and more powerful dreadnought battle cruisers were going to sea.

On June 12, *Minotaur,* dark gray and bristling with twelve gun turrets, was welcomed in Tsingtao harbor. Her officers dined on *Scharnhorst* and danced with German women on the deck of *Gneisenau.* The deck was trimmed with bunting, plants, and electric lights; the dance floor, set beneath the elevated muzzles of the after turret guns, was shielded from the night air by heavy canvas curtains; platters of meats, cakes, bread, and butter, and glasses of wine and beer, were spread on the wardroom tables. Ashore, British sailors competed with Germans in relay races, boxing matches, soccer (the British won, 5–2), and a tug-of-war (won by the Germans). British officers were escorted on automobile excursions into the countryside to visit Buddhist temples and hilltop summer houses. The "brotherhood of the sea" was invoked in speeches and toasts. Even so, *Gneisenau*'s second in command noted, "I do not think we were far wrong in the belief that they desired a little glimpse at our readiness for war." And after *Minotaur* sailed, it was widely reported that one English officer had admired the town and harbor and then, smiling at his host, declared, "Very nice place, indeed! Two years more and we have it."

In Tsingtao, the British visit was a preliminary to the month's most significant event: the German East Asia Squadron's departure on a three-month cruise through the central and southwestern Pacific. The voyage was to proceed along a chain of volcanic islands and coral atolls in the Marianas, the Carolines, and the Marshalls to the easternmost point of the cruise, German Samoa. From there, the ships would turn southwest to Fiji, Bougainville, the Bismarck Archipelago, and New Guinea. The return to Tsingtao was scheduled for September 20, whereupon many officers would return home across Russia on the Trans-Siberian Railway and, after two years of China service, be home in Germany in time for Christmas. Admiral von Spee particularly looked forward to the Pacific voyage; he was an amateur naturalist and an ingrained collector, and the cruise would be his first opportunity to observe many varieties of plants and species of birds and fish. He was also especially happy that the cruise would reunite him with his friend Captain Julius Maerker, the new captain of *Gneisenau.* Not only was Maerker a naturalist, he also was devoted to bridge.

Gneisenau left Tsingtao first, sailing in bright sunshine on the morning of June 20; *Scharnhorst* would follow three days later. *Gneisenau* paused in Nagasaki to coal; the officers bought silk to carry home for Christmas. From Japan, the ship steamed south, crossing the Tropic of Cancer and entering the tropics on June 26. Daily, the sun was higher at noon and the temperature rose. Awnings were spread over sections of the deck and the crew was issued straw hats and warned about sunburn. The tropical nights came quickly and, under a multitude of stars, officers and men sat on deck, enjoying the cooler air and talking quietly. On the twenty-ninth, still in wireless touch with Tsingtao, the crew of *Gneisenau* learned of the assassination of Archduke Franz Ferdinand.

From Pagan Island at the northern end of the Marianas chain, *Gneisenau* moved on to Saipan, the capital of the German Marianas, and then to Rota, where some officers went ashore to shoot goats beneath the coconut trees. Leaving Rota, *Gneisenau* steamed past Guam, which "alone of the Marianas has a good natural harbor and belongs to the Americans," noted a German officer. On July 6, the ship entered the vast Truk atoll in the mid-Carolines. Here, behind a wall of white spray created by ocean waves thundering against the encircling reef of coral, lay an immense turquoise lagoon sprinkled with volcanic islands with peaks rising to a thousand feet. *Scharnhorst* was already there and together the two ships began to coal. The work, impossible in the noonday heat, was done at night, creating surreal effects as the white steam rising from the hoisting cranes mixed with clouds of black coal dust, swirled in the searchlights of the warships and slowly drifted across the calm water. Every day, decorated native canoes surrounded the anchored ships offering fruits, native fabrics, and handmade artifacts. Sometimes dancers, gleaming with palm oil and covered with flowers, came on board to pound their feet, clap their hands, and slap their thighs in rhythm, while from the turret tops, upper works, and masts, German sailors looked down and grinned.

Admiral von Spee found Truk a naturalist's wonderland. Exploring the islands and the shallow waters of the lagoon, he studied the structure of the coral and admired the rare mammals and fishes, the brightly colored birds, the butterflies, the flowers and other tropical plants. It was a delicious distraction, but the temporary naturalist remained an admiral. At Truk, Spee received a stream of messages from Berlin. On July 7, the Naval Staff warned him that "the political situation is not entirely satisfactory." Understanding that his Pacific cruise would have to be modified, the admiral decided to await developments at Ponape, 400 miles east of Truk. He also ordered *Emden,* still at Tsingtao, to postpone her scheduled cruise up the Yangtze. The two armored cruisers left Truk on July 15 and, at noon on July 17, approaching Ponape from the southwest, the *Gneisenau*'s second in command saw "a glorious sight . . . the massive mountains of Ponape bathed in brightest sunshine and all around us as far as the eye could reach, the sea was covered with chains of mountainous waves, keeping pace with our course. . . . The green and brown masses of the mountain gradually dissolved into forest and rock, encircled by a single white wreath. This was the outer reef against which break[s] ceaselessly the foaming spray of the huge waves of the Pacific Ocean. . . . Through the roar of the swell, we came into calmer waters." The two ships spent two weeks at Ponape, anchored off villages where the German flag floated above the palm trees. On shore, the sailors discovered pools of fresh water for bathing and washing clothes. Officers climbing Nankjob peak looked down on the cobalt-shaded ocean stretching to the horizon, the foam-flecked reef of coral enclosing the blue-green water of the lagoon, the brown huts with red roofs dotted between mangroves and palms, the natives fishing from canoes. White clouds sailing across a limitless blue sky suddenly gave way to fierce tropical squalls. Strong winds howled, the clouds turned black, and water fell in dense, thick columns.

On July 27, while Spee was at Ponape, the Naval Staff informed him of Austria's ultimatum to Serbia. "Strained relations between Dual Alliance and Triple Entente. . . . Samoan cruise will probably have to be abandoned. *Nürnberg* has been ordered to Tsingtao. Everything else is left to you." The admiral, realizing that it was wrong to send *Nürnberg,* then at Honolulu, to Tsingtao, which the British and possibly the Japanese were likely to attack, countermanded Berlin's order and told *Nürnberg* to meet him at Ponape. Meanwhile, at Tsingtao, his supply ships were being loaded. *Emden,* assigned to escort them, sailed on July 31 with the large, elegantly furnished North German Lloyd liner *Yorck,* the armed merchant cruiser *Prinz Eitel Friedrich,* and eight colliers.

On the night of August 1, the message "threatened state of war" reached Spee at Ponape. The navy's procedure on receipt of this signal was the same whether a ship was at Kiel or in the mid-Pacific; the vessel was stripped for battle and all peacetime and nonessential belongings were sent ashore. On *Scharnhorst* and *Gneisenau,* wood paneling and tapestries were torn from the wardroom walls, and sofas, stuffed armchairs, carpets, and sideboards were taken ashore. Two items were allowed to remain in *Gneisenau*'s wardroom: a piano and a picture of the kaiser hanging on the wall. The admiral's dining room was denuded of silverware, pictures, chairs, and carpets. Each officer was permitted to keep only a writing table and a chair. Trunks were packed with formal dress coats, brocaded jackets, and gold-striped breeches for ceremonial occasions, and all sports clothing and equipment. From each small cabin came the collected gifts and souvenirs: bronze and porcelain vases, Japanese temple lanterns, ivory carvings, silks, bows, arrows, spears. "The whole beautiful world through which we had passed . . . flashed before us as we packed away all these treasures," said an officer. On Sunday, August 2, a message came that Germany was at war with Russia and on the night of the fifth, the squadron heard that "the British had elected to side with our enemies. Against France and Russia it would have been a merry war for which we were perfectly ready," said *Gneisenau*'s second in command, but Britain's action was a "piece of treachery . . . a perfidy . . . unleashed against us."

At dawn on August 6, Spee's last day at Ponape, *Nürnberg* appeared at the entrance to the lagoon. During the morning, men from other ships helped the light cruiser to coal, and a herd of pigs was slaughtered onshore and meat and fresh water were ferried out. At noon, the admiral and his two sons went ashore to offer confession to the Catholic Apostolic Vicar of the Marianas and Carolines. At 5:00 p.m., *Scharnhorst* and *Gneisenau* passed out through the reef into the long ocean swell and headed northwest. In order to rendezvous with the supply ships coming down from Tsingtao, Spee had decided to retrace his steps to Pagan Island, a thousand miles to the north.

The German ships now observed wartime routine. The crews were divided into two watches, with the off-duty watch always sleeping fully dressed. Lookouts posted in the crow's nests scanned the horizon; some of the guns were constantly manned. The heat was intense; at midday, the sun beat down so fiercely that it was impossible to place a hand on any exposed iron part of the ship. Two hours every afternoon were devoted to weapons drill, followed by a break for coffee, then a meal; then half the crew went to sleep. "The monotonous noise of the screws churning the water went on interminably, the ship rose and fell on the billows . . . in this way, day after day passed during our long traverse of the Pacific Ocean and time and space seemed to us illimitable," wrote an officer on *Gneisenau.* At dawn on August 11, the two volcanoes of Pagan Island rose out of the sea, and that morning they anchored. Later that day, the armored cruisers were joined by *Emden, Prinz Eitel Friedrich,* the colliers from Tsingtao, and a flock of chartered coastal steamers bringing fresh water, live cattle and pigs, mountains of potatoes, fresh vegetables, flour, beer, wine, and tobacco.

While his ships coaled and provisioned at Pagan, Admiral von Spee pondered how and where they should be used. There were many possibilities. The vastness of the Pacific offered the shelter of space; once he had vanished no one could say where he was or where he might reappear. There were, of course, constraints on his actions. He was cut off from Tsingtao, his only base; he had no place to dry-dock his ships or to make more than temporary repairs; he could depend only on his own resources. In Winston Churchill's simile, "Von Spee was a cut flower in a vase; fair to see, yet bound to die." His most pressing and permanent problem was coal. German agents in ports around the rim of the Pacific were already working to buy coal and charter colliers to rendezvous with him, but the worldwide network of the British Admiralty kept watch on every port, every ton of coal, and every likely collier.

Admiral von Spee, in choosing his theater of operations, had to consider where he could hurt the enemy most and where he could survive the longest. He had two tactical alternatives. He could break up the squadron and scatter his ships so that each could wage individual trade warfare and commerce destruction. Or he could keep his ships together and embark on squadron warfare against the enemy navy. It would be difficult to do both; an attempt to combine squadron war with trade war would inhibit, and might well doom, both. It was the inclusion in the squadron of *Scharnhorst* and *Gneisenau* that made trade warfare almost impossible. The essential element of a lone raider was speed, not size. Spee's three fast light cruisers were superbly equipped for trade warfare: they could catch and sink any merchantman in the world and they could outrun almost any enemy warship. But the big, powerful armored cruisers, each more than three times as heavy and with a crew over twice as large as that of a light cruiser, burned too much coal. Had the Naval Staff intended the East Asia Squadron for trade warfare, six additional light cruisers would have been far more useful than two armored cruisers. A further consideration was that if the admiral scattered his ships, they might do considerable damage, but ultimately each raider would be hunted down by a superior enemy. The advantage in keeping his squadron together was that, in combination, his ships had a better chance of survival. The weakness was that, operating together, they might achieve nothing at all.

But the German Naval Staff had not structured the East Asia Squadron to make war on commercial trade. Its mission had been to represent Imperial

Germany in the Far East. Display, visual impact, respect, and prestige were qualities associated with big ships and heavy guns, not with light cruisers, however fast. Further, Maximilian von Spee, a proud man, a vice admiral in the Imperial Navy, the commander of the only remaining overseas squadron of the German fleet, had no thought of wasting *Scharnhorst* and *Gneisenau* as lone commerce raiders. Already, Spee had indicated his poor opinion of the value of trade warfare by summoning *Leipzig, Nürnberg,* and *Emden* to join him in the central Pacific, thereby concentrating rather than scattering the combat power of his squadron.

The Naval Staff in Berlin had realized that once war broke out it would be difficult to communicate with German warships overseas; flag officers and captains, therefore, were instructed to use their own initiative. "In event of a war against Great Britain," read the Imperial Navy War Orders, "ships abroad are to carry on cruiser warfare unless otherwise ordered. . . . The aim . . . is to damage enemy trade; this must be effected by engaging equal or inferior enemy forces, if necessary." To this general instruction, the kaiser had added personal advice and exhortation. From the moment war breaks out, he said, each captain "must make his own decisions. . . . Above all things, the officer must bear in mind that his chief duty is to damage the enemy as severely as possible. If he succeeds in winning an honorable place for his ship in the history of the German Fleet, I assure him of my imperial favor." A few weeks later, when the Naval Staff in Berlin was as much in the dark as to Spee's whereabouts as the British Admiralty in London, a German staff appreciation reasserted the independence of commanders at sea: "It is impossible to judge from here . . . it is useless to issue any orders . . . we are ignorant of the Commander-in-Chief's [Spee's] dispositions . . . any interference on our part might be disastrous. The Commander-in-Chief must have complete liberty of action."

Nürnberg, arriving at Ponape from Honolulu on August 5, reported that the British China Squadron had concentrated at Hong Kong. Admiral Jerram's squadron was by no means superior to Spee's, but Jerram was not the only potential enemy to the west. Even before Britain's ally Japan declared war on August 23, it was clear to Spee that, if he returned north to Tsingtao, he might have to face the Japanese fleet. Accordingly, he rejected going west, to China. He could go south to the German base at Rabaul in the Bismarck Archipelago, and beyond toward Australia. But somewhere to the south also was the dreadnought battle cruiser *Australia* carrying eight 12-inch guns, and Spee had no desire to fight this fast, powerful ship. And even if he did not meet the battle cruiser, there was little he could do in the south. Australia's principal harbors and cities were too heavily defended to be bombarded, and to waste ammunition dueling with shore batteries would be foolish. He could fire on open towns and embarrass the Dominion and British governments, but this would produce no military results. And in the south

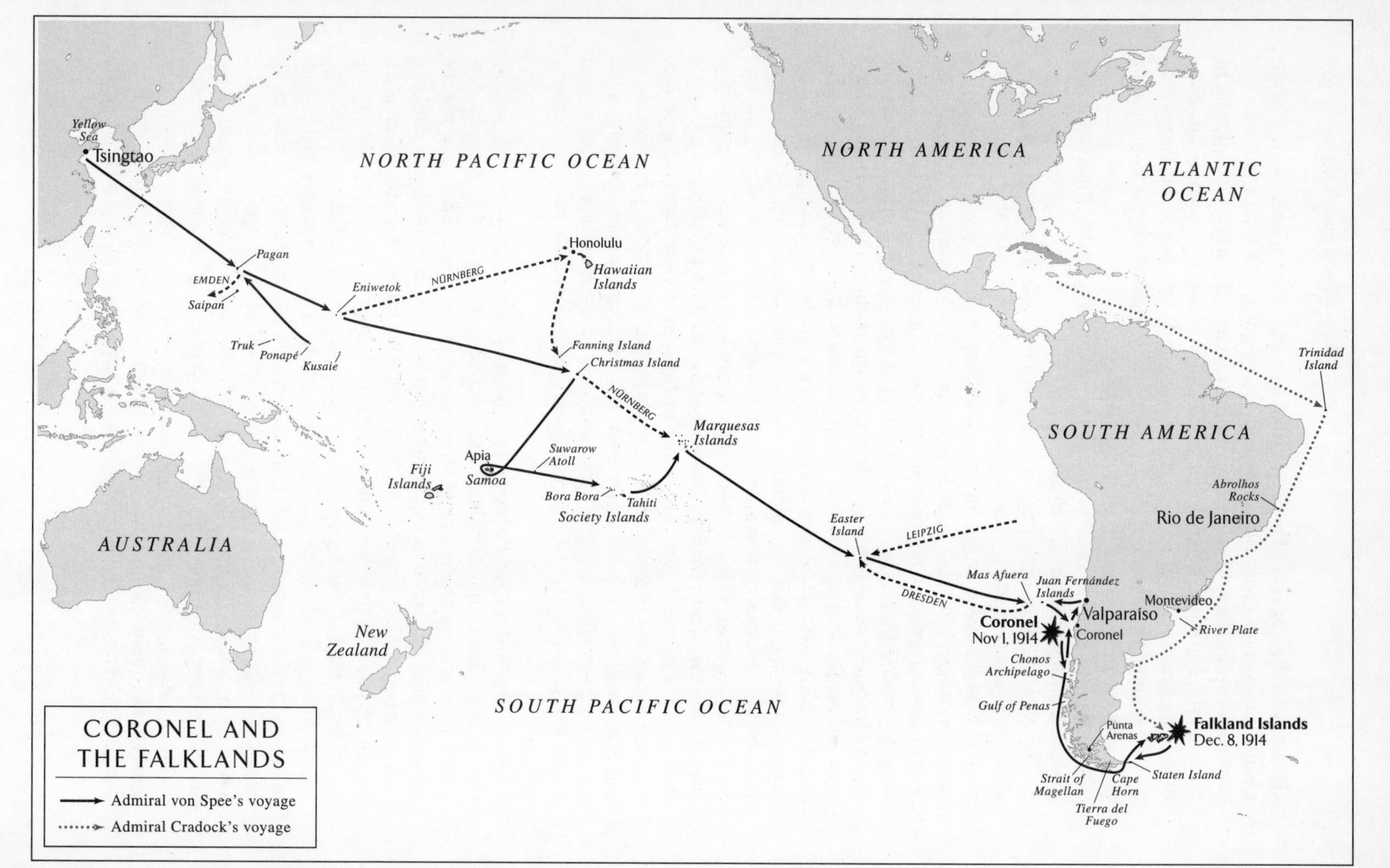
CORONEL AND
THE FALKLANDS
Admiral von Spee's voyage
Admiral Cradock's voyage
NORTH PACIFIC OCEAN
NORTH AMERICA
ATLANTIC
OCEAN
SOUTH AMERICA
SOUTH PACIFIC OCEAN
AUSTRALIA
New
Zealand
Yellow
Sea
Tsingtao
Pagan
EMDEN
Saipan
Truk
Ponapé
Kusaie
Eniwetok
NÜRNBERG
Honolulu
Hawaiian
Islands
Fanning Island
Christmas Island
NÜRNBERG
Marquesas
Islands
Fiji
Islands
Apia
Samoa
Suwarow
Atoll
Bora Bora
Tahiti
Society Islands
Easter
Island
LEIPZIG
DRESDEN
Mas Afuera
Juan Fernández
Islands
Valparaíso
Coronel
Coronel
Nov 1, 1914
Chonos
Archipelago
Gulf of Penas
Punta
Arenas
Strait of
Magellan
Cape
Horn
Tierra del
Fuego
Staten Island
Falkland Islands
Dec. 8, 1914
Montevideo
River Plate
Rio de Janeiro
Abrolhos
Rocks
Trinidad
Island

he would be able to obtain coal only from whatever ships he might chance upon—too precarious a source for a squadron the size of his.

Another possibility was the Bay of Bengal and the Indian Ocean, where he could attack busy trade routes. He might commit slaughter on the Australian and New Zealand troop convoys moving toward the Red Sea, the Suez Canal, and Europe, but he did not know their schedules or the strength of the naval forces that would be escorting them. And here, too, he would have difficulty finding coal. To supply his entire squadron from prizes would be impossible and the prospect of *Scharnhorst* and *Gneisenau* drifting helplessly, their coal bunkers empty and their boilers cold, had no appeal. Admiral von Spee ruled out going west.

The east remained. In the distant east, across the Pacific, on the coast of South America, there was British trade to be disrupted. Here, there was no Japanese fleet and no British squadron to oppose him. The coast of the Americas, North and South, presented an 8,000-mile stretch of neutral nations from the southern Canadian border down to Cape Horn. Many of these nations would sell him coal. Further, if he continued east around the Horn into the South Atlantic, the important South American trade routes to Europe lay open to attack. And once out in the Atlantic Ocean, he might even find his own way home to the North Sea.

The prospect of finding help in the coastal towns of South America was especially attractive. Chile, with its large German population, had many German businesses and commercial houses. In every Chilean port, German merchant ships were anchored, unable to leave, but fitted with wireless facilities and available for use as supply ships, colliers, or communications relay points for the German East Asia Squadron. In Chile, the German ships, business enterprises, consulates, and embassies and their network of communication facilities and intelligence operations surpassed even those of the well-organized British. Above all—and this was the overriding factor—in Chile, Spee would find it easy to obtain coal. *Scharnhorst* and *Gneisenau* each had a capacity of 2,000 tons of coal. At 10 knots, each ship burned a hundred tons a day and could steam for twenty days. At 20 knots, the figures were 500 tons a day and four days. No captain, however, wished his bunkers to get too low; it was a general rule in all navies to keep the bunkers at least half full at all times. This dictated to Spee a coaling stop every eight or nine days. He already had ruled out the Indian Ocean because, as he wrote in his war diary, "we have no coaling bases in the Indian Ocean and no agents whom we can get in touch with. If we proceed towards the American coast, we shall have both at our disposal."

August 13, 1914, was Maximilian von Spee's fifty-third birthday. That morning, he summoned his captains on board *Scharnhorst* and, standing before a large map of the Pacific, told them what he planned to do. The squadron would remain together, he said. Given the likelihood of Japan's entry into the war, it would not return to Tsingtao. Instead, they would go to the west coast of South America where, owing to German influence, they would enjoy better facilities for supply and communication with home. On the American coast, they would face no enemy warships and, if the war lasted long enough, they would have a chance from there of breaking through for home.

Typically, Admiral von Spee asked his captains for their opinions. Karl von Müller of *Emden* suggested an amendment to the admiral's plan: "If coaling the whole squadron in East Asian, Australian and Indian waters presents too great difficulties, I asked might we consider the dispatch of at least one light cruiser to the Indian Ocean." Müller proposed his own ship, *Emden,* the squadron's most modern and fastest. Spee thought about it and agreed; a single light cruiser could coal from captured steamships, a squadron could not. That evening, the East Asia Squadron sailed from Pagan for the coral atoll of Eniwetok in the Marshall Islands. Early the next morning, with rain falling, seamen on the other ships were surprised to see *Emden* and one of the colliers suddenly turn out of the formation. The signal "We wish you success" ran up *Scharnhorst*'s halyard, and Müller replied, "I thank Your Excellency for the confidence placed in me." Once the light cruiser had disappeared to the south, the squadron learned that *Emden* was bound for the Indian Ocean.

Scharnhorst, Gneisenau, Nürnberg, the armed merchant cruiser *Prinz Eitel Friedrich,* the liner *Yorck,* and eight supply ships moved slowly eastward toward Eniwetok, traveling at the 7- to 10-knot speed of the supply ships. Even so, on one ship carrying livestock, the animals were so hurled about in the swell that many bones were broken and, bellowing and bleating, they were pushed into the sea. The ships held frequent battle drill, loading and reloading the guns, *Scharnhorst* and *Gneisenau* aiming at each other as targets. At the end of the day, the officers watched the sunset and then retreated to the wardroom to gather around the piano, while the men sang or smoked in the moonlight.

At noon on August 19, the German squadron approached Eniwetok, a green fringe of palms and sun-baked beach between the sky and the water. Behind lay an immense coral atoll and a vast lagoon sufficient to shelter an immense number of ships. Here Spee remained for three days, relatively secure in the knowledge, gained from intercepted wireless traffic, that the nearest enemy force, an Australian squadron, was far to the southwest. But he had no other news; on August 11, the German wireless station on Yap in the western Carolines had been destroyed by the British cruiser *Minotaur.* In order to maintain a tenuous contact with Berlin, Spee sent *Nürnberg* back to Honolulu to pick up newspapers and mail and to advise the Naval Staff by cable, "I shall proceed to Chile . . . arriving at Juan Fernández on October 15." Meanwhile, his caravan of ships departed Eniwetok on August 22 and continued its progress across "the seemingly limitless desert of the Pacific Ocean." The crews were baked by the equatorial sun; the thermometer often recorded 104 degrees Fahrenheit in the shade. The nights were worse. "In the evening," wrote Captain Maerker of *Gneisenau,* "the portholes have to be closed and blacked out so that the heat becomes unbearable. Then of course there is nothing to do but think and that's bad."

The squadron's next stop was Majuor, an atoll at the southeastern edge of the Marshall Islands. This was another spacious lagoon, another expanse of shallow turquoise water distinguished from the dark blue of the outside ocean, another beach of hot sand with palm trees stirring in the hot wind. Here, on August 26, Spee learned of Japan's declaration of war. Here, too, he was joined two days later by the armed merchant cruiser *Cormoran,* which had escaped from Tsingtao, escorting two cargo steamers and two other store ships. In all, the admiral now had 16,593 tons of coal and 3,000 tons of water in reserve. When he sailed for Christmas Island on August 29, the German cruisers carried coal in sacks on their decks.

Admiral von Spee continued slowly east across the wide, empty ocean, his progress marked only by the long trails of black smoke pouring from his funnels. On September 1, the squadron crossed the 180th meridian, adding a calendar day, which permitted one *Gneisenau* officer to celebrate his birthday twice. On the seventh, they reached Christmas Island—on the equator, a British possession intermittently visited by gatherers of copra. Here, *Nürnberg* rejoined them, having paused at Fanning Island to cut the British cable running from the Fiji Islands to Hawaii. From Honolulu, *Nürnberg* brought news. She had learned that on August 30, Apia, the capital of German Samoa, had been occupied by New Zealand troops. Von Spee summoned another council of captains and proposed a surprise descent on Samoa in hopes of catching British vessels anchored in the harbor.

The squadron left Christmas Island on September 9 and crossed the equator the next day. Samoa, their destination, was a range of volcanic islands, some of the peaks rising 4,000 feet out of the sea. A strait separates the two large islands of Samoa; the eastern island was American, the western had been German. With luck, a surprise attack by Spee's squadron might catch in the bay several steamers engaged in supplying provisions for the newly arrived New Zealand garrison. With even better luck, the battle cruiser *Australia* might be found at anchor; if so, Spee planned to attack her with torpedoes. But when he reached Apia before dawn on September 14, the anchorage was deserted except for a three-masted American schooner and a smaller sailing vessel. To send sailor landing parties ashore and attempt to recapture the island would have been too costly in casualties and ammunition; the Germans steamed away without firing a shot. When Spee heard the Apia wireless station, out of range of his guns, broadcasting his position, he decided on the simplest of naval ruses: he first turned and steamed to the northwest; then once out of sight of land, he again headed east. The success of this deception was to have terrible consequences for the British navy.

Admiral von Spee's next stopping point was the isolated, British-owned Suvorov Island, 500 miles east of Samoa, but finding that a huge ocean swell prevented coaling, he continued another 700 miles to Bora-Bora, an island of the Tahiti group in the lush French Society Islands. Bora-Bora, with its volcanic mountains, dense foliage, and settled population, was a welcome change from the flat, sun-baked, deserted coral atolls they had left behind. *Scharnhorst* and *Gneisenau* anchored off Bora-Bora, displaying no national flag. The French authorities, believing the visitors were English, sent out a police officer in a boat flying the tricolor and offered to help "the British admiral." The policeman met only German officers who spoke English or French, and the subterfuge continued as other representatives of the local government came on board to present a huge bouquet of flowers, pass along war news, and, in response to gentle questioning, describe the defenses of Papeete. The Germans paid with gold for coal, pigs, poultry, eggs, fruit, vegetables, and several oxen, slaughtered immediately. In the afternoon, as the cruisers weighed anchor, a large French flag was hoisted in a farewell salute from the shore. In reply, the Germans politely raised the German naval ensign.

From Bora-Bora, Spee continued on to Papeete, the port and capital of Tahiti. Papeete, its harbor and town lying in the shadow of 7,000-foot volcanic peaks, was known to be defended; as the German squadron approached on the morning of September 22, the cruisers prepared to lower boats for an armed landing. But the French had been warned from Bora-Bora: all navigation aids in the harbor had been removed; the town's inhabitants had fled to the hills; all supplies of coal that Spee might use had been set afire, and a huge black cloud was spreading over the harbor. Spee fired briefly at the anchored French gunboat *Zélée,* which capsized and sank. From the hills, French artillery fired back, their white puffs of smoke showing amidst the trees until Spee's gunners silenced them. Afterward, the French sent a steamer to Samoa to report the attack, but not until September 30 did the news reach London.

From Tahiti, Spee took his squadron 850 miles farther east, to the French Marquesas. Arriving off the island of Nuku Hiva on September 26, he remained for seven days, coaling and stocking fresh provisions. The crews went ashore to bathe in fresh water and the admiral paid a courtesy visit on the Catholic mission and collected more specimens of tropical plants.

On October 2, when Spee left the Marquesas, sailing southeast, he was leaving behind the sunny climate and lush, flowering landscapes of the tropics. Now, angling down toward the coast of South America, the crews found the temperature cooler and they ceased going barefoot on deck. The length of the voyage was beginning to tell: sand mixed with soda was used instead of soap; dysentery and beriberi began to appear. Spee's objective was Easter

Island, a solitary, volcanic, treeless speck of land lying off all trade routes. On the way, *Scharnhorst*'s wireless room picked up a signal from the German light cruiser *Dresden,* 3,000 miles away. *Dresden* had come around the southern tip of South America from the Atlantic and now was off the west coast of Chile; she signaled that she was probably being followed into the Pacific by the British armored cruisers *Good Hope* and *Monmouth.* On October 4, Spee signaled *Dresden* to join him at Easter Island. Other ears, however, could pick up wireless signals: this message from *Scharnhorst* was intercepted by a British wireless station at Suva in the Fiji Islands. Passed to London, it provided the Admiralty not only with the East Asia Squadron's position but also with its destination. Spee, unaware, believed that his long voyage was approaching a successful conclusion. On October 11, writing in his diary at sea, he noted that 5,000 tons of coal were due at Easter Island, to be brought by colliers from San Francisco escorted by the light cruiser *Leipzig.* "If no enemy ship approaches Easter Island," he wrote, "we can, with fresh coal, continue [to the coast of Chile] via Juan Fernández."

Dresden arrived at Easter Island first, during the night of October 11. Admiral von Spee's squadron arrived the following day, anchoring in Angaroa, also known as Cook's Bay, on the island's deserted east coast, away from the little colony. The supply ships *Yorck* and *Göttingen* came alongside the armored cruisers, but the long, southwesterly swell rolled the ships day and night, slamming them against each other, impeding coaling and the hoisting out and launching of boats. On October 14, *Leipzig* rounded the northern point of the island, bringing with her three colliers from San Francisco with 3,000 additional tons of coal.* Spee's reinforced squadron was now up to full strength: two armored and three light cruisers.

Easter Island, a possession of Chile, lies 2,200 miles west of South America. Seven miles across at its widest point and thirty-four miles in circumference, the island and its rough grass then supported 250 Polynesian inhabitants, 12,000 sheep, and 2,000 head of cattle. The administrator and nominal governor of the island was the manager of the sheep and cattle ranch, a British subject named Percy Edmonds. The island had no contact with the world other than that provided by a Chilean sailing vessel, which ar-

**Leipzig*'s cruise had been relatively uneventful. At the beginning of August 1914, she was at Mazatlán Bay on the west coast of Mexico in company with a British sloop and an American warship. Before hostilities began, Captain Johannes Haun sailed north and ten days later was off the entrance to the Straits of San Juan de Fuca, the gateway to Vancouver and Seattle. On August 11, he coaled at San Francisco and then lay off the Golden Gate for five days, keeping Allied shipping in port. On September 3, the Naval Staff signaled Haun to "transfer cruiser warfare to southwest America and the Atlantic." Moving south, he operated with little success between the coast of Peru and the Galápagos Islands until October 1, when he received orders from Berlin to rendezvous with *Dresden.* On October 3, *Dresden* signaled that she was on her way to Easter Island to join Spee and, accordingly, *Leipzig* also steered for Easter Island.

rived twice a year to carry its beef and wool to market. Without wireless, the islanders knew nothing of the world war; Edmonds, accordingly, was happy to supply Von Spee with fresh meat and vegetables. Cattle were lassoed and slaughtered on the beach, and boatloads of beef and mutton went out to the ships. The Germans also bought livestock for the future, and *Gneisenau* departed Easter Island with eleven lambs and a calf penned on her steel deck. Edmonds accepted payment in checks payable by a German bank in Valparaíso, which subsequently and "vastly to his astonishment and relief" were honored.

One morning, the admiral and his elder son, Otto, from *Nürnberg,* went ashore to look at the mysterious statues for which Easter Island is famous. There were scores of these giant, monolithic figures, between twenty and thirty feet high and wearing conical brimmed hats. Most were lying prostrate when the two German visitors saw them, but once they stood in rows on terraces at the water's edge. Curiously, all originally were looking, not out to sea as commonly imagined, but inland. The largest weighed up to fifty tons. How had they been transported from the mountain quarries? Whom did the faces represent? Gods whom the carvers wished to propitiate? Chiefs who wished to leave an image of themselves behind?* At the other end of the island, these questions were of such consuming interest to a group of visiting Britons, the members of an archaeological expedition headed by the husband-and-wife team of Scoresby and Katherine Routledge, that they did not bother to cross the island to look at the German ships. Mrs. Routledge, hard at work, declared that she had no intention of riding for four hours "to gaze at the outside of German men of war." Her concern, rather, was that the visiting officers would come to visit their site, "and being intelligent Germans, would photograph our excavations. We therefore . . . covered up our best things."

Spee rested at Easter Island for six days. At five p.m. on October 18, with his coal bunkers full and his storage lockers replenished, with lambs and calves penned on his decks, he left for Más Afuera, one of the Juan Fernández group of volcanic islands, 450 miles from the Chilean coast. *Leipzig,* sent ahead to reconnoiter, reported that Más Afuera was clear. Eight days and 1,500 miles later, on the morning of October 26, the German squadron reached Más Afuera. On the island's northwest side, a sheer wall of rock rose 3,000 feet straight from the sea. At the base of this gigantic cliff lay the

*Sadly, the statues offered the inhabitants little protection against the perils of this world. An early-eighteenth-century population of 4,000 had plunged to 175 by the end of the nineteenth; internecine warfare, Peruvian slavers, and smallpox were responsible. In 1888, when Chile annexed the island, the survivors were confined to a single village and given 5,000 acres to farm for their subsistence. The remaining 30,000 acres of grasslands were assigned to the grazing of cattle and sheep.

island's best anchorage, a little underwater ledge no deeper than twenty-five or thirty fathoms beyond which the bottom plunged thousands of feet to the ocean floor. Here, the ships cautiously took soundings and anchored. From their decks, the seamen looked up at the volcanic cliff, the steep, thickly wooded slopes cut by zigzag paths, and the thousands of goats nibbling the dry grass. Because Más Afuera was inhabited only by fishermen and their families, Von Spee ignored its Chilean nationality. One afternoon while the squadron was coaling in the damp air and heavy swell, the admiral went ashore to observe the island's seabirds and bring back some of its early-blooming spring plants.

Admiral von Spee remained at Más Afuera for three days and two nights. Then, in bright moonlight on the night of October 28, the Germans steamed away, leaving behind the massive figure of the rock cliff, which for a long time was visible across the water. A day and a half later, when the ships were forty miles west of the port of Valparaíso, "in glorious sunlight, we saw the snow-capped summit of Aconcagua, the highest mountain of the Andes, rising above the haze of the coast." The Pacific voyage of the East Asia Squadron was over.

—

Admiral von Spee had crossed the great ocean, but up to this point, his achievement—beyond the worry he had caused the British Admiralty—had been minimal. He had done no military damage and, because there was no British trade in the regions he had traversed, he had taken no prizes. His voyage had been a technical success; his ships had steamed 12,000 miles through tropical heat without engine trouble; he had kept them supplied, and the morale of his men remained excellent. But, in three months of war, he had done little to contribute to the German cause. From this failure, however, one ship of the East Asia Squadron was excluded. This was *Emden.*

The light cruiser *Emden* was the most successful German commerce raider of the Great War. Her forty-one-year-old captain, Karl von Müller, demonstrated what could be done by a fast, modern ship commanded by a man of outstanding ability. Tall and blond, with delicate features and a quiet manner, Müller displayed the qualities Britons liked to associate with their own naval officers: daring, skill, courage, and chivalry. For almost three months after its detachment from Spee's squadron—that is, from August 14 until November 9—this 3,500-ton ship, operating in the Bay of Bengal and the Indian Ocean, ravaged Allied shipping and paralyzed trade along the east coast of India. A single light cruiser compelled the Admiralty to keep ships in ports and provide strong escorts for Anzac troop convoys. During these seventy days, Müller intercepted twenty-nine Allied and neutral merchantmen, sinking sixteen British merchant ships, a Russian cruiser, and a French destroyer. He was ingenious: *Emden* had three funnels; Müller quickly made a fourth out of canvas, disguising his ship as an English four-funneled light cruiser. He was scrupulously courteous, even courtly, to his prisoners. No seaman taken from the ships he sank was harmed; all were sent into port on another intercepted ship at the first opportunity. When the captain of one British merchant ship about to be sunk with explosives asked whether he could bring his harmonium to safety, Müller obliged, although the German sailors assigned the task grumbled about "furniture removal." Two French sailors killed in action against *Emden* were wrapped in tricolor flags and buried at sea with military honors and a gun salute. Müller presided and made a speech about fallen heroes.

Emden began her marauding career in the Bay of Bengal and between September 10 and September 14 sank eight steamers on the approaches to Calcutta before the Admiralty realized that the ship had left the Pacific. Müller's enterprise flourished so magnificently that at one point, said one of his officers, "we had five or six vessels collected at one spot. You could just see the tops of the funnels of one, the next was under the water right up to her decks, the next was still fairly normal, just rolling from side to side as she filled with water." All vessels trading in the bay were immediately held in port. In darkness on the night of September 22, Müller approached to within 3,000 yards of the port city of Madras, switched on his searchlights, and during half an hour fired 125 shells at the Burmah Company's oil tanks, destroying nearly half a million gallons of kerosene. On October 28, he entered Penang roads at dawn and torpedoed and sank an anchored Russian cruiser. The following day in the open sea, he sank a French destroyer by gunfire.

The British public, seeing that a few German cruisers were apparently doing whatever they chose on the oceans and sinking British merchantmen day after day, was astonished and indignant. Total losses of British tonnage were infinitesimal relative to the nation's huge maritime resources—*Emden* and *Karlsruhe,* the other successful raider, between them sank 39 merchant ships out of 4,000 vessels at sea, 176,000 tons out of 16 million—but the public demanded to know why, given British naval supremacy, this was happening at all. "The *Emden*'s company have proved their gallantry," wrote the London *Daily Chronicle.* "We admire the sportsmanship of their exploits as much as we heartily wish that the ship may soon be taken." The Admiralty offered a variety of excuses but, as the naval historian Arthur Marder has written, "the chief reason is that the sea is very large and afforded ample opportunities, with its many archipelagos, for the game of hide and seek."

And then, at last, *Emden* was caught. On November 9, Müller approached the Cocos Islands, where the operators of the cable station saw him coming and sounded an alarm. A large Australian troop convoy bound for the Red Sea and Egypt happened to be passing fifty-five miles to the north and heard the signal. The escorting Australian light cruiser *Sydney,* 3 knots faster, 2,000 tons heavier, and with bigger guns than the *Emden,* was dispatched, and within two and a half hours, the *Emden,* burning and wrecked, was driven onto a reef, where Müller surrendered. He and his officers were allowed to keep their swords and were sent to Malta as prisoners for the rest of the war. Once her raiding career was over, public anxiety in Britain metamorphosed into admiration greater than that accorded to any other German warship in the Great War. "It is almost in our heart to regret that the *Emden* has been captured or destroyed," said the *Daily Telegraph.* "The war on the sea will lose something of its piquancy, its humour and its interest now that the *Emden* is gone."

CHAPTER 11

Admiral Cradock's Voyage

Once *Goeben* and *Breslau* had disappeared into the Dardanelles, Admiral von Spee and his squadron became the dominant overseas preoccupation of the British Admiralty. The threat was shadowy but ominous: a powerful force of enemy warships had vanished into the immensity of the Pacific Ocean. With Spee at large, many of Britain's distant possessions and overseas trade routes were at risk, and it was impossible to tell where the German admiral would strike. "The map of the world in the Admiralty War Room measured nearly twenty feet by thirty," Winston Churchill wrote after the war. "Being a seaman's map, its center was filled by the greatest mass of water on the globe: the enormous areas of the Pacific filling upwards of three hundred square feet. On this map the head of a pin represented the full view to be obtained from the masts of a ship on a clear day." At all possible danger points, Britain must be ready, but as Churchill explained, "we could not be strong enough every day, everywhere, to meet him." Therefore, he said, "as the days succeeded one another and grew into weeks, taking the Caroline Islands as the center, we could draw daily widening circles, touching ever more numerous points where they might suddenly spring into action." But the circles remained empty.

One solution would have been to take the offensive, to give priority to locating the East Asia Squadron, to assemble a force that would hunt through every archipelago until it found Spee and completed his destruction. This course was not chosen. Oddly, it was not that the Admiralty did not have sufficient ships of sufficient strength for this purpose. The German East Asia Squadron was recognized in Whitehall as an efficient and powerful unit with excellent morale, led by an experienced and skilled commander. Even so, the forces available to the British Admiralty were superior and, properly deployed, should have had success. In the Pacific, Great Britain, her empire, and her allies could call upon a modern dreadnought battle cruiser, two small battleships, a dozen armored cruisers, five modern light cruisers, and numerous other ships.

At the outbreak of war, these ships were deployed in three squadrons. The China Squadron, based at Hong Kong under Vice Admiral Sir Thomas Martyn Jerram, consisted of the armored cruisers *Minotaur* and *Hampshire,* two light cruisers, and the predreadnought battleship *Triumph. Minotaur,* Jerram's flagship, just back from visiting Admiral von Spee at Tsingtao, was newer, bigger, and faster than *Scharnhorst* and *Gneisenau* and carried heavier guns. The armored cruiser *Hampshire* was older and less strong, but the light cruisers *Newcastle* and *Yarmouth* were far superior in size, speed, and gun power to *Emden* and *Nürnberg. Triumph* was a curiosity. Originally built for Chile, she was smaller than *Minotaur* and, at 18 knots, slower than *Scharnhorst* and *Gneisenau.* Her value lay in her four 10-inch and fourteen 7.5-inch guns. As war approached, *Triumph* lay demobilized in a Hong Kong dockyard. An urgent message from the First Lord brought her back to life, but a crew could not easily be found. Jerram quickly demobilized four Yangtze River gunboats, snatching the officers and men from their decks and placing them on the battleship, but this was not enough. An effort to recruit Chinese stokers produced not a single man. In the end, volunteers were solicited from Hong Kong's military garrison and two officers and 106 men of the Duke of Cornwall's Light Infantry boarded the battleship and were incorporated into the crew. On the East Indies Station at Singapore, Rear Admiral Sir Richard Peirse commanded the battleship *Swiftsure,* a sister of *Triumph,* and two light cruisers. His main responsibilities lay westward, toward the Bay of Bengal and the Indian Ocean. In addition, at the outbreak of war the French Admiralty placed the armored cruisers *Montcalm* and *Dupleix* under British command and the Russians did the same with their old light cruisers *Askold* and *Zhemchug.*

These British squadrons were hodgepodges of ships, mixing old and new, big and little, fast and slow, strong and weak; this was the result of Admiralty uncertainties and compromises as to what could be spared from home waters and who the enemy in the Pacific was likely to be. The squadrons thus were very different from Spee's homogeneous force; neither the China nor the East Indies Squadron alone could have brought the German admiral to action if he chose to avoid it, or have been certain of defeating him if he chose to fight. But these squadrons were not all that was available to the Admiralty. The strongest naval force in the Pacific (aside from the fleet of Japan, which was neutral when war began) belonged to the Dominion of Australia. And the Australian squadron based at Sydney and commanded by Rear Admiral Sir George Patey included the dreadnought battle cruiser *Australia,* an *Indefatigable*-class vessel constructed in Britain. *Australia,* with her eight 12-inch guns and 26 knots of speed, might by herself defeat

Scharnhorst and *Gneisenau*—although simply by separating and steaming in opposite directions, one of the German ships could have escaped. Two modern 5,600-ton, 26-knot light cruisers, *Sydney* and *Melbourne,* each carrying eight 6-inch guns, and two older light cruisers completed Patey's squadron. In combination, these three British empire squadrons heavily outnumbered Spee's force, and if they had been ordered to hunt down and destroy the East Asia Squadron, its life surely would have been short.

But British warships and admirals in the Pacific had been given conflicting responsibilities during August and early September 1914. The paramount concern of the British government in the first weeks of the war was to help stem the onslaught of the German army rushing down on Paris. Everything Britain could do to assist the French had to be done. Most of the British regular army was hurried to the Continent. Within a few weeks, tens of thousands of Dominion troops had been offered by Canada, Australia, and New Zealand, and every effort had to be made to bring them to Europe. But, with German surface raiders on the oceans, these troops had to move in convoys escorted by warships. The East Indies Squadron, for example, was immediately assigned to escorting troops westward from India and none of its ships were free to help seek out and destroy Admiral von Spee. In addition, the Admiralty and government, encouraged by the Australian and New Zealand governments, were busy playing the old imperial game of colony-grabbing, endeavoring to occupy as much of Germany's overseas territory as possible. In part, this was an effort to reward the Dominions for their loyalty to the mother country. But there was more to it. Well in advance, the British Admiralty had planned—in the case of war with Germany—to dismantle the German colonial empire. Months before war came, the Admiralty had invited Australia and New Zealand to be prepared to send expeditions to New Guinea, Yap, Nauru, and Samoa, knowing that these expeditions would have to be escorted by naval forces. Thus stimulated, New Zealand's eye fell on the German islands to her northeast, particularly German Samoa, lying on her trade route to the west coast of America. Australia wished to snap up the whole of German New Guinea and other possessions administered from Rabaul, including the Bismarck Archipelago and the Solomon Islands. Both governments saw these acquisitions as a means of rallying public support for the dispatch of the Anzac expeditionary forces to Europe, and they were quick in insisting on these projects: on August 8, the New Zealand government informed the Admiralty that if a naval escort could be furnished, the expedition to attack Samoa could start on August 11. Churchill assented. Simultaneously, an expedition organized by the Australian government was forming to invade and seize German New Guinea. Admiral Patey's force, including *Australia,* was assigned to escort these two seaborne expeditions. Locating Spee's armored cruisers, therefore, was given third priority, behind convoying troops to Europe and plucking ripe colonial plums.

On August 30, Patey, with *Australia, Melbourne,* and *Montcalm,* arrived off Apia, the capital of German Samoa, where, without resistance, he put ashore an occupying force of New Zealand troops. On September 15, he landed the Australian expedition at Rabaul. Thereafter, Patey was told, he was to escort the Australian troop convoy to Europe, at least as far as Aden on the Red Sea. But on September 14, *Scharnhorst* was reported at Samoa, and on September 24, *Australia* and *Montcalm* were released to hunt for Admiral von Spee. They had proceeded only 200 miles toward the Marshalls and Carolines when they learned that on September 22, *Scharnhorst* and *Gneisenau* had bombarded Papeete. Tahiti was 5,000 miles away; to coal and provision for a voyage of this length, Patey returned again to Rabaul. On October 2, he finally sailed for the Fiji Islands. Arriving there on October 12, but forbidden to go farther east, Patey spent the next three weeks defensively patrolling the Fiji–New Zealand trade route. Apparently, the Admiralty did not consider that if Spee was headed for South America, it might be useful to put *Australia* on his trail. Patey himself never agreed with the Admiralty's priorities. Long before September 15, when Spee was first located at Samoa, he was certain that the East Asia Squadron's most likely destination was South America. Jerram, too, had wished to begin the war by seeking out Spee. As early as August 17, he had signaled the Admiralty: "Probably *Scharnhorst, Gneisenau . . . Nürnberg* are now together. . . . Possible objective of German squadron . . . Pacific coast of America."

There was another, even more powerful Allied naval force in the Pacific: the Japanese fleet. Japan entered the war on August 23, 1914, with a navy of three dreadnoughts, including *Kongo,* and fifteen other battleships. Until the Japanese came in, the Admiralty had thought it possible that Admiral von Spee might return to Tsingtao, but once Japan declared war, this idea evaporated. And by the time the Japanese had joined the search for Spee, he had vanished. Japan's priority, in any case, was different from Britain's. On August 15, Tokyo gave Berlin an ultimatum to surrender Tsingtao within seven days. The Germans refused, Japan declared war, and a siege of the port began. From Berlin, the kaiser ordered the garrison to fight to the end, thinking to strengthen its courage by telegramming: "God be with you in the difficult struggle. I think of you." Meanwhile, Japanese squadrons proceeded to occupy German possessions in the Marshalls and Carolines. Only late in October, when these other assignments had been completed and Tsingtao was about to fall, were Japanese ships specifically ordered to join the hunt for Admiral von Spee. By then, he was on the other side of the Pacific.

—

Far more important to the Admiralty and the British war effort than anything that could happen on the west coast of South America—indeed, anywhere in the Pacific Ocean—was the protection of British trade in the North and

South Atlantic. Across this ocean moved a larger volume of shipping than anywhere else in the world. The critical nature of trade with the United States and Canada was obvious, but the importance of securing the wide avenue of commerce from Buenos Aires and Montevideo on the river Plate to Europe was almost equal. At the outbreak of war, the threat to Britain's trade in the western Atlantic amounted to two fast German light cruisers, *Dresden* and *Karlsruhe,* supplemented by the possibility that some of the fast German civilian liners that had taken refuge in harbors in the United States might emerge as armed merchant cruisers. For the British and the German navies, the sudden coming of war had meant a rapid reshuffling of relationships. In peacetime, the two had displayed in the western Atlantic the same unusual blend of comradeship and wariness seen on the coast of China. During the 1914 revolution in Mexico, *Dresden* had patrolled in concert with warships of the Royal Navy for the protection of European citizens and property. A light cruiser of 3,200 tons with an armament of ten 4.1-inch guns and two torpedo tubes, *Dresden* was the only German warship in the western Atlantic at that time. But she was due for relief; on July 25, she met her replacement, the new light cruiser *Karlsruhe* of 4,800 tons and twelve 4.1-inch guns, at Port-au-Prince. As a result, when war was declared, Germany had two light cruisers in the western Atlantic. Both ships received orders to attack British trade.

To meet this threat, Rear Admiral Sir Christopher Cradock, commander of the British navy's North American and West Indies Station, had been given four old County-class armored cruisers: *Suffolk, Berwick, Essex,* and *Lancaster,* plus the modern light cruiser *Bristol.* Soon after mobilization, these ships were reinforced by five more cruisers from England. Four were old armored cruisers: *Carnarvon, Cornwall, Cumberland,* and *Monmouth,* commissioned from the Reserve Fleet and sent overseas without opportunity to evolve into efficient fighting units. Still another obsolescent cruiser, *Good Hope,* was detached from the Grand Fleet at Scapa Flow and sent to Cradock, who made her his flagship.

In the first month of war, Admiral Cradock reached several conclusions about his assignment. He realized from observation and intelligence that the German liners were not coming out of New York. And he learned that both German light cruisers were operating far to the south of his normal station: *Karlsruhe* was reported at Curaçao and *Dresden* off the mouth of the Amazon, where her presence was raising anxiety among shippers and traders down the coast of South America. The Admiralty agreed that the threat in the North Atlantic was diminished; accordingly, on September 3 a new South American Station was created, with Cradock in command. His assignment was to move down the coast of South America to protect merchant shipping in the South Atlantic and to find and sink *Dresden.* Protection of the West Indies and the upper South Atlantic and responsibility for dealing with the threat of *Karlsruhe* were transferred to Rear Admiral A. C. Stoddart, who was to have *Carnarvon, Cumberland,* and *Cornwall.*

The force with which Cradock was to carry out his South Atlantic mission was thoroughly ragtag. *Good Hope,* his flagship, was twelve years old and displaced 14,100 tons. When she was new and first put to sea, she had several distinctions. "She was the fastest cruiser afloat, having done over 24 knots on trial," said her gunnery officer, Lieutenant Ernle Chatfield, later captain of the battle cruiser *Lion.* And "we were the first new ship to be painted grey all over." Even so, considering the large size of her hull, *Good Hope* was laughably undergunned, with two 9.2-inch and sixteen 6-inch guns, half of the latter mounted in broadside batteries so close to the water that they could not be fired in a heavy sea. When Fisher became First Sea Lord, he complained that "the guns . . . on the main deck are practically useless. We know this from experience. Half the time they cannot see the . . . [target] for want of view and the other half they are flooded out by the sea." Not yet old, *Good Hope* was, in fact, already obsolete. She had been made so not only by the advent of battle cruisers but by the appearance of more modern armored cruisers only a few years younger, for example, *Scharnhorst* and *Gneisenau. Good Hope* had been consigned to the Third Fleet with other old armored cruisers of her era, then suddenly was recommissioned on mobilization with a crew of whom 90 percent were reservists. When she steamed out of Portsmouth on August 2, a Salvation Army band played "Nearer, My God, to Thee." In the three months that followed, her untrained crew carried out only one full-caliber shoot. "It certainly is the limit," a regular navy gunnery officer wrote later, "taking a ship like that off the dockyard wall, giving her four rounds [per gun] of practice, and then putting her up against a ship like *Scharnhorst.*"

Good Hope at least carried two heavy 9.2-inch guns, but Cradock's other armored cruiser, *Monmouth,* an eleven-year-old, 10,000-ton County-class armored cruiser, carried no heavy guns at all. Here, Fisher's bitter comment was "Sir William White designed the County class but forgot the guns." In fact, *Monmouth* carried fourteen 6-inch guns, but they were old and had no greater range than the 4.1-inch guns of the modern German light cruisers. Worse, many of *Monmouth*'s guns were sheltered behind gun-port doors only a few feet above the water; in a heavy sea, the doors had to remain shut or the waves would come in. Not infrequently at night, the men on the starboard forward main deck gun would ask permission to shut the gun port, normally kept open for night defense stations, because they were being washed out by the sea. Like many other ships, *Monmouth* was a victim of haste and improvisation in the Admiralty's mobilization. About to be scrapped, she was hurriedly recommissioned on August 4, crewed with naval reservists, coast guardsmen, boy seamen, and naval cadets and dispatched to the South Atlantic. When *Monmouth* met the new light cruiser

Glasgow at sea on August 20, *Glasgow*'s officers were appalled. "Sighted *Monmouth* at eleven a.m.," wrote one *Glasgow* officer. "She had been practically condemned as unfit for further service, but was hauled off the dockyard wall commissioned with a scratch of coast guardsmen and boys. There are also twelve little naval cadets who are keen as mustard. She left England on August 4, she is only half equipped and is not in a condition to come six thousand miles from any dockyard as she is kept going only by superhuman efforts." Still another vessel added to Cradock's polyglot squadron was the 12,000-ton converted Orient Lines liner *Otranto,* sent off to war with six 4.7-inch guns. *Otranto*'s mission was to hunt down converted German merchant ships of her own kind; no one intended that she should fight enemy warships.

When Admiral Cradock's improvised squadron steamed into the South Atlantic, *Glasgow* was already there. The only modern British warship on the western side of the Atlantic Ocean, the three-year-old *Glasgow* was a Town-class light cruiser of 4,800 tons, a sister of *Gloucester,* which had dogged *Goeben.* Designed for 25 knots, she had gone faster when her turbine engines burned coal that had been sprayed with oil. Her armament of two 6-inch and ten 4-inch guns made her more than a match for any German light cruiser, and her regular navy crew was as well trained and efficient as any in the German fleet. Beyond this, *Glasgow* had an exceptional captain in John Luce. For two years, he and his ship had been showing the flag and single-handedly guarding British interests along the east coast of South America, his beat extending from the mouth of the Amazon down to the Straits of Magellan. Under his protection were the vital trade routes supplying Britain with meat and grain from the river Plate, nitrates from Chile, and coffee from Brazil; on any given day in peacetime, hundreds of British and German merchantmen would be moving along these routes. At the end of July 1914, *Glasgow* was in Rio, expecting shortly to return to England. Believing they would soon be home, members of the crew had bought Brazilian parrots to take back with them; sixty birds were housed in cages on deck in the warm South Atlantic air. When the Admiralty telegram warning of war arrived, the crew began stripping away superfluous woodwork and sending armchairs, books, and other personal possessions ashore. The men could not bear to give up their parrots, however, and Luce agreed that the birds could stay. Officers' civilian clothing received no exemption; only Lieutenant Hirst, the intelligence officer, was allowed to keep his plain clothes. "Later on," he said, "when leave could be taken, it was amusing to see my whole range of suits going ashore in the officers' boat, worn by messmates of varying sizes."

Luce's primary concern, once war began, was lack of a coaling base. South America during the Great War was a neutral continent except for the colonies of British Guinea on the northeast coast and the British Falkland Islands, 2,000 miles to the south. In peacetime, *Glasgow* could buy coal anywhere. But once hostilities commenced, under international rules of war, a warship could coal and provision only once every three months in any given neutral country; admiralties and captains on both sides preferred to reserve this privilege for emergencies. Even in wartime, there was no difficulty obtaining coal; it could be bought from British firms or through British agents in foreign ports. But *Glasgow*'s operations—and those of other British warships coming south—were certain to be hampered by the lack of a safe harbor where the coal could be transferred from colliers into warships. During the two years Luce had served on the station, he had located two places that, in an emergency, might serve. One was Abrolhos Rocks, a group of rocky islets, surrounded by reefs, fifteen miles off the Brazilian coast, north of Rio and near the main trade route between the Plate and the North Atlantic. The islets, the largest of them three-quarters of a mile long, were uninhabited except for the keeper of a lighthouse, but they belonged to Brazil. However, three miles out to sea from the lighthouse—and thus outside Brazilian territorial waters—an anchorage of sorts had been formed by reefs above or just below the surface. The site was exposed to the southeast trade winds and the prevailing southeasterly swell caused ships alongside each other for coaling to grind together, denting side plates and starting leaks, but there was no alternative. Luce's other temporary coaling site, also in international waters, lay in an area in the broad, shallow estuary of the Plate itself, seven miles off the coast of Uruguay, where ships could anchor in forty- or fifty-foot water. Beyond that, the British navy had only the harbor of Port Stanley in the Falkland Islands.

—

As Cradock's squadron steamed down the east coast of South America, the admiral spread his net for *Dresden.* The net came up empty in respect to the fugitive light cruiser but did produce another result. At the end of August, the 19,000-ton Cunard armed merchant liner *Carmania* arrived in the South Atlantic from England, bringing Cradock's ships a cargo of coal, provisions, and a large quantity of frozen meat. These supplies delivered, *Carmania,* which had been equipped with eight 4.7-inch guns, remained with Cradock. It was in this capacity that the ship was detached from the main force and ordered to reconnoiter Trinidad Island, which the Admiralty suspected was being used as a secret German coaling base. This island, not to be confused with the British island colony of Trinidad in the West Indies, lies about 600 miles east of South America on the same latitude as Rio, and belonged to Brazil. Far from any trade route, it was no more than a mid-ocean group of sharp coral rocks inhabited by seabirds and scuttling land crabs.

Shortly after 11:00 a.m. on September 14, as the ocean was ruffled by a moderate breeze, *Carmania,* coming down from the northeast, sighted three German steamships at anchor in a bay at the western end of the island. One was a large liner, and the others were colliers, their derricks busy transferring coal to the bigger vessel. On seeing *Carmania,* the three ships immediately separated and made off in different directions. The large ship was the new Hamburg–South America Line liner *Cap Trafalgar,* 18,710 tons and 590 feet long, whose wartime assignment was to prey on British trade in the South Atlantic. At the outbreak of war, *Cap Trafalgar* had been at Buenos Aires, where she installed heavy lumber to buttress her decks for gun mountings and painted two funnels to resemble the markings of a British Union Castle liner. On September 2, *Cap Trafalgar* had rendezvoused at Trinidad Island with the German gunboat *Eber,* where she mounted two 4.1-inch guns and eight machine guns, and took aboard most of *Eber*'s navy crew of 392 officers and men. Lieutenant Wirth of the Imperial Navy became the liner's new captain. Thereafter, *Cap Trafalgar* had cruised for ten days looking for British merchantmen, but the air was so filled with British naval wireless signals that Wirth became more concerned about the safety of his ship than with attacking enemy vessels. Now he was back at Trinidad Island to coal.

When *Carmania* appeared, *Cap Trafalgar* decided to run for it and soon was making 18 knots. *Carmania,* designed for 18 knots, could make only 16. Then, for unknown reasons, Wirth changed his mind and decided to fight, and turned *Cap Trafalgar* onto a converging course. At noon, when the distance between the two ships was down to 8,000 yards, *Carmania* opened fire. *Cap Trafalgar* fired back, and the world's first battle between ocean liners began. *Carmania* had overwhelming superiority in guns, but battle between ships of this size and design was awkward. Neither ship had any kind of coordinated fire control; each gun crew simply fired whenever a target appeared in its sights. On both big liners, the upper deck where the guns were mounted was seventy feet above the hold where the ammunition was stored. As there were no ammunition hoists, the shells had to be carried to the guns by hand.

The range continued to fall. At 4,500 yards, *Carmania* began firing salvos from her port guns and two of these broadsides struck *Cap Trafalgar* on the starboard waterline. The German ship replied as well as she could, but most of her shells went high and *Carmania* was hit mostly in her masts, funnels, derricks, and ventilators. When the range came down to 3,000 yards, the German machine-gunners opened fire and the bullets hammered noisily but harmlessly against the steel sides of *Carmania.* When the barrels of *Carmania*'s port-side 4.7-inch guns—all of them over twenty years old—became red-hot, her captain, Noel Grant, solved the problem by turning his ship around to bring her starboard guns into action.

Within half an hour, *Cap Trafalgar* was on fire forward and was listing to starboard. *Carmania* was also in trouble. A German shell had passed through the captain's cabin under the forebridge and started a fire; the fire main was cut, so no water was available. With the flames out of control, *Carmania*'s foredeck was abandoned and, in order to steer the ship, orders were relayed through megaphones to a rudder station at the stern. Meanwhile, flames and smoke sucked down the ventilators set the engine-room crews to gasping and choking. Nevertheless, *Carmania* had begun to prevail when Wirth decided to attempt a second escape. *Cap Trafalgar* still had the higher speed and *Carmania,* in pursuit, continued firing until, beyond her maximum range of 9,000 yards, her adversary was out of reach. By 1:30 p.m., the British believed that *Cap Trafalgar* had escaped. The reality was different: Captain Wirth had been killed, the fires burning fore and aft had made the German decks untenable, the ship's list was increasing. Then, suddenly, the great vessel heeled over, resting her funnels on the surface of the water. At 1:50 p.m., *Cap Trafalgar* sank, first lifting her stern high in the air. Five boatloads of men pulled away.

Carmania's precarious condition after the battle made it impossible for her to stop and pick up the German seamen. The fire raging in the fore part of his ship forced the British captain to steer *Carmania* before the wind so that the flames would be blown out over her bow rather than down his decks. In this situation, he could not steer in the direction of the German lifeboats. In addition, *Carmania* had five holes at the waterline, and the forebridge with all its steering and navigational instruments and its communications to the engine rooms had been destroyed. Beyond that, smoke had been seen on the northern horizon and Captain Grant feared the possible arrival of a German warship, which he believed that *Cap Trafalgar* had been continually signaling during the action. In fact, the smoke rose from one of the German colliers, now flying an American flag in hope of misleading *Carmania* and being allowed to collect the survivors. *Carmania* did not interfere; the collier took its surviving compatriots into Buenos Aires.

The wounded British liner limped away to the Abrolhos Rocks and eventually to Gibraltar for repairs. The ship had been hit seventy-nine times; five men had been killed, four died of wounds, and twenty-two were injured. Most of the casualties occurred among the men on deck, for the most part among the gun crews and ammunition-supply parties. No one below was harmed except by smoke inhalation.

—

By September 18, when Cradock and his squadron reached the river Plate, *Dresden* already was around Cape Horn and in the Pacific. From the moment this light cruiser had sailed from St. Thomas in the Virgin Islands, her captain, Fritz Lüdecke, had displayed little interest in trade warfare. He had stopped and sunk one British freighter in the South Atlantic and let others go, destroying only their wireless equipment. Otherwise, his objective was to reach Cape Horn; he stopped only to coal. On September 5, he arrived at Orange Bay in Tierra del Fuego, on an uninhabited stretch of coastline just east of Cape Horn. Here, hidden against the desolate shore and a backdrop of the snow-topped mountains of Hoste Island, *Dresden* met a collier and remained for eleven days to rest and adjust her engines. While she was there, she received, by way of Punta Arenas, a message from Berlin: "It is advisable to operate with *Leipzig.*" On September 16, Lüdecke departed Orange Bay and, accompanied by a pair of supply vessels, passed slowly around the Horn. Believing himself now out of danger, he eased down to a speed of 8 knots to help his collier manage the heavy sea. He continued north up the Chilean coast, coaling in Bahia San Quintin in the Gulf of Penas, then cruising off the small port of Coronel. On September 30, Lüdecke left the South American coast for remote Más Afuera and from there his wireless room established contact with *Scharnhorst.* On October 4, he sailed for the rendezvous at Easter Island, arriving on the afternoon of October 12.

—

Cradock, steaming south and already looking beyond his own area of responsibility, wondered aloud whether Spee might be coming across the Pacific. "*Gniesenau* and *Scharnhorst* reported Caroline Islands . . . 8 August," he signaled the Admiralty on September 5. "Is there any later information as to movements? Several German colliers said to be in vicinity of Magellan Straits." The Admiralty could tell him only, "No certain information of these ships since 8 August. . . . Magellan Straits and its vicinity quite possible. Falkland Island anchorages might be used by them." On September 14—the same day that *Carmania* sank *Cap Trafalgar,* and while Cradock was in the river Plate—the Admiralty took a stronger position. Whitehall still had no definite news of Spee's whereabouts, but the repeated warnings of Patey and Jerram had created concern, and a telegram to Cradock, forwarded by the British minister in Rio, contained a multitude of new orders: "There is a strong probability of *Scharnhorst* and *Gneisenau* arriving in the Magellan Straits or on the west coast of South America [where] the Germans have begun to carry on trade. . . . Leave sufficient force [in the Atlantic] to deal with *Dresden* and *Karlsruhe.* Concentrate a squadron strong enough to meet *Scharnhorst* and *Gneisenau,* making Falkland Islands your coaling base. *Canopus* is now en route to Abrolhos; *Defence* is joining you from Mediterranean. Until *Defence* joins, keep at least *Canopus* and one 'County' class cruiser with your flagship. As soon as you have superior force, search Magellan Straits with squadron, being ready to return and cover the River Plate, or, according to information, search north as far as Valaparaiso. Break up the German trade and destroy the German cruisers."

This telegram, lengthy, complicated, and sometimes contradictory, bore heavy responsibility for what happened later. Cradock, reading the message, understood that Spee might be coming toward him. To meet this threat, he was ordered to concentrate a squadron strong enough to meet and "destroy the German cruisers." He was to move his primary base south to the Falklands. The southeastern Pacific, it was implied, would be added to his theater of operations, but, simultaneously, he was to leave behind in the Atlantic sufficient ships to deal with *Dresden* and *Karlsruhe.* He was assured that reinforcements were on the way: the old battleship *Canopus* was en route and, more important, the modern armored cruiser *Defence* would join him from the Mediterranean. Until *Defence* arrived, *Good Hope* and *Monmouth* should stick close to *Canopus* for mutual protection. He was to search the Magellan Straits, but he was also to be ready either to double back to the Plate or to proceed up to Valparaíso to harass German trade, "according to information."

Evaluating the strengths of the two ships being sent to reinforce his squadron, Cradock could think of little use for *Canopus,* and for the next seven weeks he would continue to wonder how to employ this lumbering predreadnought. Completed in 1899, *Canopus,* at 12,950 tons, was lighter than Cradock's flagship, the 14,000-ton armored cruiser *Good Hope.* To please nineteenth-century admirals, *Canopus* had been built with a ram, a weapon dating back to Phoenician and Roman galleys and designed to pierce the hull of an enemy vessel that somehow came too close. It was true that the old battleship carried four 12-inch guns, but they were of an early design and their maximum range of 13,000 yards was no greater than that of Von Spee's sixteen 8.1-inch guns. In any case, by 1912 the ship's general deterioration had forced the Admiralty to place her and her five sisters in the Reserve Fleet, with scrapping scheduled for 1915. For over two years, *Canopus* had been moored at Milford Haven with only a maintenance party aboard. In July 1914, she was granted a last reprieve to swell the numbers at the Spithead Review and then, when war came, her temporary recommission was extended. Manned by a crew of partially trained reservists, she spent several weeks escorting the BEF across the Channel and then was ordered to the Cape Verde Islands, and then to the Falklands. Her speed was unreliable: "Few [ships of the *Canopus* class] can steam well now except for short spurts," said a contemporary naval annual. In preparation for the Spithead Review, her old engines were coaxed to push her through the water at 16 knots, but all knew that this figure was illusory; Churchill credited her with an actual speed of 15 knots; Jellicoe qualified this by saying, "If she did not break down."

The modern armored cruiser *Defence,* on the other hand, was precisely what Cradock needed. This was a ship of 14,600 tons with four 9.2-inch guns and ten 7.5-inch guns and a speed of 23 knots. *Defence* was one of the last three British armored cruisers ever built. Completed in 1908 after the launch of the battle cruiser *Invincible,* she was faster and more powerfully armed than Spee's two armored cruisers; indeed, she and her sisters, *Minotaur* and *Shannon,* had been laid down in reply to the building of *Scharnhorst* and *Gneisenau.* Cradock's older armored cruisers, *Good*

Hope and *Monmouth,* were weaker than Von Spee's ships but just as fast; now, bolstered by *Defence,* he should be able to meet the Germans on equal terms.

Even promised reinforcement of his squadron, Cradock could make little sense of the Admiralty's September 14 signal. He might have sufficient strength to fight Admiral von Spee, but he did not have enough ships to do everything he had been told to do. At best, he would need to rely on guesswork and luck, shuttling ships back and forth to the place of greatest danger. The confusion of overlapping orders recalls the instructions to Milne at the outbreak of war: to destroy *Goeben,* cover the French transports, and keep the Austrian fleet from leaving the Adriatic. The originator of both sets of orders was Churchill (once again, the language is unmistakable) and, again, the First Lord's strategy was approved by Prince Louis and Sturdee.

Reading the September 14 message, Cradock doubtless wondered why *Canopus* was being sent. The background to this decision reveals something of how things were working at the Admiralty. At the first suggestion that Spee might appear on the coast of South America, a War Staff memorandum of September 7 had recommended reinforcing Cradock with three armored cruisers and a light cruiser from the Mediterranean. Prince Louis and Sturdee had gone further, advocating the dispatch of two battle cruisers from the Grand Fleet to the South Atlantic. But Jellicoe objected to this weakening of Beatty's force and Churchill refused to overrule the Grand Fleet Commander-in-Chief. Ultimately, the Admiralty decided that only *Defence* could be spared. Battenberg, however, insisted that something more be done for Cradock. *Canopus,* ram and all, then serving no purpose at the Cape Verde Islands, was that something more.

Meanwhile, another event upset all of these arrangements. On September 14, Admiral von Spee suddenly appeared off Samoa, hoping to find the New Zealand troop transports at anchor. Samoa was 2,500 miles farther east than the German squadron's last known position, so Churchill and his colleagues, once they began drawing fresh circles on their maps, would normally have been left in little doubt that Spee was headed for South America. Then, presumably, the Admiralty would have confirmed and perhaps even increased its reinforcement of Cradock. But Spee, finding nothing at Apia, steamed away to the northwest—a false course—before doubling back to the east. The Admiralty was deceived by this elementary ruse used by sea captains for centuries. Spee, London now assumed, was returning to the Far East. And if he was not making for South America, there was no need to reinforce Cradock. *Defence,* which on September 14 had been summoned from the Dardanelles, had traveled as far as Malta. On September 18, these orders were canceled and *Defence* was ordered back to the Dardanelles. Essentially, Cradock was told that he no longer need worry about the German East Asia Squadron. The fatal signal read: "Situation changed . . . *Gneisenau* appeared off Samoa on 14th and left steering NW. German trade on west coast of America is to be attacked at once. Cruisers need not be concentrated. Two cruisers and an armed liner appear sufficient for Magellan Straits and west coast. Report what you propose about *Canopus.*" In this message, there was no mention of the cancellation of *Defence*'s sailing orders. For weeks, Cradock continued to expect this powerful ship; he calculated that if she had left the Mediterranean shortly after receiving the September 14 telegram and was steaming toward him at 15 knots, she would arrive at the river Plate early in October.

Cradock, with *Good Hope, Monmouth, Glasgow,* and *Otranto,* was in the river Plate when the Admiralty's September 18 message arrived. Told that Spee was no longer coming east, Cradock decided that two cruisers—*Glasgow* and *Monmouth*—and his armed liner *Otranto* would suffice to search the Magellan Straits and go up the South American west coast to disrupt the activities of German merchant ships. He had no use for *Canopus* and proposed to leave her as a guard ship at the river Plate. Once *Defence* arrived, he would have her "coal and await orders" with *Canopus.*

Cradock's departure from the Plate was delayed by a gale, but on September 22, he left for the Straits of Magellan. At this point, he understood that the only enemy ship the Admiralty thought he was likely to meet was *Dresden.* Privately, however, he still suspected that Spee's East Asia Squadron might be making for South America. Before leaving Montevideo, he wrote a personal letter to King George V, whom he had known during the monarch's naval career. "I have a feeling that the two [German] heavy cruisers from China are making for the Straits of Magellan and am just off there to 'search and see,' " he said. A memorandum Cradock left at the British consulate in Montevideo underlined this suspicion. It emphasized the "urgent importance that any and all information of movements of . . . *Gneisenau* and *Scharnhorst* and other China cruisers should reach Rear Admiral [Cradock] . . . without delay." Before leaving it behind, Cradock had deleted from the message a line that revealed the depth of his concern: "Delay may entail loss of H.M. ships."

Steaming south, Cradock encountered a merchant ship on September 25 that told him that *Dresden* had passed into the Pacific a week before. On the twenty-eighth, the British squadron arrived at the Chilean port of Punta Arenas, in the Magellan Straits, where the British consul reported that *Dresden* had been at Orange Bay on the southern coast of Tierra del Fuego. Hoping that the German ship still might be there and that he could catch her by surprise, Cradock left Punta Arenas after midnight—without lights, to conceal his departure from the town's large German colony. On September 29, in thick weather and falling snow, the British squadron threaded the narrow, uncharted Cockburn Channel where high, snow-covered mountains and glaciers came down to the water on either side. The Cape Horn weather was freakish: gusts of wind roared down the mountains, whipping calm seas into foam; then the ships would round a bend and find the water still as glass.

Leaving the channel, the squadron rounded Cape Horn west to east and charged into Orange Bay. They found it empty, although a landing party discovered a tablet left by *Dresden,* saying that she had been there September 8, 9, and 10. The following day, Cradock sent *Otranto* to Punta Arenas and took the rest of his squadron to the Falklands to coal. At Punta Arenas, *Otranto* intercepted a German wireless signal suggesting that *Dresden* had returned to Orange Bay. Cradock left the Falklands at high speed and made another descent on the remote anchorage. Arriving on the night of October 6, he again found the bay empty. Thereupon, he ordered Captain Luce of *Glasgow* to take his light cruiser with *Monmouth* and *Otranto* to search up the Chilean coast as far as Valparaíso. *Good Hope,* with Cradock aboard, would return to the Falklands to coal, to remain in closer wireless touch with Montevideo and London, and to guard against the possibility that *Dresden* might double back and return to the South Atlantic.

Glasgow, Monmouth, and *Otranto* made a memorable westward passage around Cape Horn. A gale piled up mountainous seas and "it blew, snowed, hailed and sleeted as hard as it is possible to do these things," wrote one of the squadron officers. "I thought the ship would dive under altogether at times. . . . *Monmouth* was rolling 35 degrees at times . . . the ship was practically a submarine." On *Otranto,* another officer said, "We finally got past caring what might happen, what with the strain, the weather, and the extreme cold." On October 12, Luce's three ships reached a temporary coaling base established at Vallenar roads, among the Chilean fjords in the Chonos Archipelago. The water and the scenery in the shadow of Mount Isquiliac reminded British sailors of a Scottish loch on a summer day: a blue lagoon surrounded by green islands with mountains rising to 5,000 and 6,000 feet and, in the distance, the snowcapped higher Andes. Explorers from the ships had difficulty penetrating past the fringe of beach; beyond lay an almost impenetrable forest, dense with boulders, fallen tree trunks, thick scrub, and bog pitted with deep holes filled with wet, slippery moss.

Having coaled, Luce left *Otranto* behind, and with *Glasgow* and *Monmouth* steamed north up the Chilean coast. Admiral von Spee's squadron was much on his mind. "It seemed to both the captain of *Monmouth* and myself," Luce said later, "that we were running a considerable risk without much object, and I should personally have preferred to go alone in *Glasgow* which I knew to be faster than any of the Germans, and unless caught against the land, would be able to avoid a superior force. *Monmouth,* which had been long due for a refit, was at the best only equal in speed to the Germans and her fighting value would not avail against the enemy's superior armored cruisers. I was therefore very anxious to complete my mission before Von Spee appeared on the coast." On October 14, Luce reached Coronel, a small coaling harbor lined by white sand beaches and forests of fir and eucalyptus, 275 miles south of Valparaíso. The next day, *Glasgow* arrived at Valparaíso and anchored among a number of German merchant vessels that had sought refuge in the harbor. While his ship loaded provisions, Hirst went ashore to the English club "for a good square meal." He found it "an extraordinary place; nobody spoke a word to me, although I was in uniform; simply stared at me as though I were a wild beast." *Glasgow* remained only a few hours and then returned to Vallenar. On October 18, the entire British squadron was back at sea off Valparaíso. Rolling uncomfortably in the big Pacific swells, *Glasgow*'s officers envied their comrades on the *Good Hope* "snug as a bug at Port Stanley . . . her men breaking up the pubs—*our* pubs." On October 21, *Monmouth* reported additional boiler defects and announced that she would be completely out of action by January. "She has already been condemned twice," Hirst noted.

Meanwhile, at Port Stanley in the Falklands, Admiral Cradock had been waiting for two weeks for instructions and reinforcements. On the evening of October 7, he received an Admiralty signal sent from London on October 5, which once more entirely changed his situation. On the night of October 4, a British radio station at Suva in the Fiji Islands had intercepted a message from *Scharnhorst* declaring that the German squadron was steaming east from the Marquesas toward Easter Island. As Easter Island lies halfway between Tahiti and the South American coast, the news left little doubt as to Von Spee's destination. There was yet time for the Admiralty to reinforce Cradock. It did not do so. "It appears that *Scharnhorst* and *Gneisenau* are working across to South America," the Admiralty signaled Cradock on October 5. "You must be prepared to meet them. . . . *Canopus* should accompany *Glasgow, Monmouth* and *Otranto,* the ships to search and protect trade in combination. . . . If you propose *Good Hope* to go [to the west coast], leave *Monmouth* on east coast." The Admiralty, in other words, was telling Cradock to be ready to meet Spee, but also to split his force; if he decided to take *Good Hope* into the Pacific, he was to leave *Monmouth* behind to protect trade in the South Atlantic. Notably, the Admiralty did not mention *Defence.*

Cradock replied the next day, October 8, but because of delays in transmission, his signal was not received in London until October 11. He began by questioning the Admiralty's assumption that Spee's two armored cruisers would be accompanied by only a single light cruiser. His own visits to Orange Bay clearly indicated that the *Dresden* was in the Pacific where, he assumed, she would join *Nürnberg* and *Leipzig,* giving Spee three light cruisers. He asked specifically, "Does *Defence* join my command?" He also asked whether "regulations of the Panama Canal Company permit passage of belligerent ships."* Cradock's question about *Defence* was prompted by

*Cradock's question about the Panama Canal arose from the possibility that von Spee might take that route between the Pacific and the Atlantic and thus avoid South America and the South Atlantic. The great interocean waterway had been formally opened on August 16, 1914. Since that day, the British Foreign Office had been pressing to discover what rules the

the Admiralty's continuing failure to keep him informed as to her whereabouts. In fact, despite Whitehall's new assessment that Spee probably was approaching South America, there had been no renewal of orders for *Defence* to join Cradock. Yet no one had told Cradock that the powerful, modern armored cruiser on which he was counting would not be coming. By not mentioning *Defence* in any of its messages to Cradock, the Admiralty now appeared to assume that four ill-matched vessels—a stumbling, elderly battleship, an old armored cruiser, a fast, modern light cruiser, and an armed merchant liner—would be enough to deal with Spee if the German squadron turned up.

The Admiralty had not answered Cradock's October 8 signal when, on October 11, he sent another. In this message, the admiral made a sound suggestion of benefit to the navy's overall strategic deployment, but one that ultimately damaged his own situation. He pointed out the risks of a single British squadron attempting to cover both the east and west coasts of South America. If Spee was indeed on his way to South American waters, and if the only available British squadron was concentrated on the west coast off Chile, the Germans might manage to evade this squadron and slip around Cape Horn into the South Atlantic. Once there, they could destroy all British coaling bases—the Falklands, the river Plate, and the Abrolhos—and ravage British trade all the way up to the West Indies. To guard against this eventuality, he suggested that a new backup squadron of additional ships be formed on the east coast. In retrospect, it seems probable that when Cradock spoke of forming a new squadron, he assumed that he would control the operations of both the east and west coast squadrons. The bulk of his present squadron—*Glasgow, Monmouth,* and *Otranto*—was already on the west coast. The new east coast squadron he had in mind would consist of a grouping of *Good Hope* (now at the Falklands), *Canopus* (on the way), *Defence* (which he believed was on the way), and *Cornwall* (brought down from the mid-Atlantic).

The Admiralty decided to follow Cradock's suggestion. The admiral obviously was right in saying that if he took his present squadron up the Chilean coast and Spee went around him into the South Atlantic, the Germans could create havoc on the river Plate. The Admiralty's decision, transmitted on October 14, was to form a strong, new east coast squadron, as Cradock had recommended. This new squadron would include the old armored cruisers *Carnarvon* and *Cornwall,* the new light cruiser *Bristol* (a sister of *Glasgow*), two armed merchant cruisers, and *Defence,* which now was

---

Americans would impose on the traffic of belligerent warships. The U.S. State Department refused to give a straightforward answer, although it seemed that the Americans would agree to a maximum of three of a belligerent power's ships at one time, enough for *Scharnhorst, Gneisenau,* and one other ship—a light cruiser or a collier—to pass through.

once again summoned from the Mediterranean. The new squadron would be based at the river Plate, not at the Falklands, and it would be commanded by another rear admiral, not by Cradock.

Had Cradock been left to decide whether, where, and when the two squadrons should be concentrated, he might have beaten the enemy. But with no additional ships and no single commander to determine how the available ships should be deployed, the plan was inadequate. Luce was to write:

> It always appeared to me that we fell between two stools. There was not force available at the moment to form two squadrons of sufficient strength and speed and we should not have advanced into the Pacific until this was forthcoming, but [should] have concentrated in the Straits using the Falklands as a base. The [British] trade on the west coast was not of vital importance and could have been kept in harbor until von Spee's position was revealed—which was bound to happen if he was to do anything. Cradock seems to have thought, however, that the Admiralty were pressing him to attack and his ardent fighting spirit could not brook anything in the nature of defensive strategy.

Much of the confusion in London and the Falklands can be blamed on the lack of clarity in the signals passing between the two points. Churchill, forwarding Cradock's October 11 message to Prince Louis, clearly did not understand Cradock's thinking: he minuted his copy to the First Sea Lord, "It would be best for the British ships to keep within supporting distance of one another, whether in the Straits or near the Falklands, and to postpone the cruise along the west coast until the present uncertainty about *Scharnhorst-Gneisenau* is cleared up. They and not the trade are our quarry for the moment. Above all, we must not miss them." Battenberg, satisfied that Cradock knew this, replied to Churchill's note with the single word, "Settled." Nevertheless, from this memorandum, it is obvious that Churchill was unaware that three of Cradock's four ships were already far up the Chilean coast. Then two days later, Churchill and Battenberg again discussed the situation and the First Lord subsequently minuted to the First Sea Lord:

> I understand from our conversation that the dispositions you proposed for the South Pacific and South Atlantic were as follows: 1) Cradock to concentrate at the Falklands *Canopus, Monmouth, Good Hope* and *Otranto.* 2) To send *Glasgow* to look for *Leipzig* and attack and protect trade on west coast of South America as far north as Valparaiso. 3) *Defence* to join *Carnarvon* in forming a new combat squadron on the trade route from Rio. . . . These arrangements have my full approval. I presume Cradock is aware of the possibility of *Scharnhorst* and *Gneisenau* arriving on or after the 17th in his neighborhood and that if

not strong enough to attack he will do his utmost to shadow them, pending the arrival of reinforcements.

There was much in these two memoranda that would have confused and upset Admiral Cradock had he been able to read them. He had never been told merely to "shadow" *Scharnhorst* and *Gneisenau;* on the contrary, on September 14, he had been given an order, never countermanded, to "destroy the German cruisers." Churchill spoke to Battenberg of "pending . . . reinforcements"; Cradock long ago had asked for reinforcement and *Defence* had been promised, then, without his knowledge, withdrawn. The memorandum makes clear that the Admiralty now believed that *Canopus* was sufficient reinforcement.

The Admiralty's October 14 signal reached Cradock at Port Stanley on October 15. *Defence,* he now learned, was to join Stoddart, not him, but at least *Defence* was coming to the South Atlantic. As Stoddart was junior to him on the Navy List, he still might order Stoddart to send *Defence* to join him at the Falklands. And with *Defence* in mind, Cradock had not yet begun to protest against the Admiralty's exaggerated opinion of the value of *Canopus.* It was *Canopus*'s four 12-inch guns that encouraged Churchill to believe that Cradock would have superiority over Spee's two armored cruisers. All other considerations—her age, her tired boilers and machinery, her raw crew—were set aside. In fact, *Canopus*'s 12-inch shells certainly would have harmed the German armored cruisers—if they had hit them. Many doubted their ability to do that. The battleship's two 12-inch turrets were in the charge of Royal Navy Reserve lieutenants who, before the war, had never stepped inside a battleship gun turret. Nevertheless, Churchill, in sending *Canopus* to Cradock, colorfully described the old battleship as "a citadel around which all our cruisers in those waters could find absolute security." With *Canopus* in company, the First Lord proclaimed, Admiral Cradock's squadron was safe; *Scharnhorst* and *Gneisenau* would never dare venture within range of those 12-inch guns. Lieutenant Hirst of *Glasgow* held "entirely a contrary opinion. . . . [*Canopus*] was seventeen years old. Her antique 12-inch guns . . . had a maximum range of . . . three hundred yards less than those of the German heavy cruisers, and they were difficult to load and lay on the heavy sea way prevalent in the South Pacific."

The Admiralty had told Admiral Cradock on September 14 that he was to "break up German trade and destroy the German cruisers." On October 5, he was instructed, "You must be prepared to meet them [*Scharnhorst* and *Gneisenau*] in company . . . *Canopus* to accompany *Glasgow, Monmouth* and *Otranto.*" But how could he accomplish this with a squadron tied to *Canopus*? The old battleship's best official speed was 16 knots; the speed of the German armored cruisers was over 20. Then came the discovery that *Canopus* could not make even 16 knots. The Admiralty had calculated that

Canopus would reach the Falklands on October 15, but she did not leave the river Plate until October 17. The following day, her captain, Heathcoat Grant, signaled Cradock at Port Stanley that he hoped to arrive on the twenty-second and that his ship's best speed was 12 knots.* Dismayed, Cradock passed this news to the Admiralty on October 18, advising, "I trust circumstances will enable me to force an action, but fear that strategically, owing to *Canopus,* the speed of my squadron cannot exceed twelve knots."

Cradock may have assumed that the absurdity implicit in the idea of a 12-knot British squadron attempting to intercept and "force an action" with a 20-knot German squadron was so obvious that someone at the Admiralty would grasp it. Then, either London would issue a new set of orders, assigning him a different mission, or send him immediate reinforcements, instructing him to await their arrival before accepting action. Unfortunately, the Admiralty simply took Cradock at his word, interpreting his message to mean that the admiral intended to keep *Canopus* with him as he had been told to do and that he would travel at her best speed. Churchill confirmed this after the war, writing, "It is clear that up to this date the admiral fully intended to keep concentrated on the *Canopus,* even though his squadron speed should be reduced to twelve knots." Cradock thus faced a painful choice: he could obey Admiralty instructions and operate in company with *Canopus,* thereby forfeiting any chance of bringing the Germans to action; or he could fight without *Canopus* and face the probability of defeat. Churchill considered the second alternative—fighting without presence of *Canopus*—illogical and disobedient; Cradock considered the first—letting the Germans slip by unmolested—cowardly and unthinkable.

When *Canopus* finally appeared at Port Stanley on October 22, Captain Grant confirmed to Cradock that his old battleship's best speed was 12 knots. Worse, Grant reported that he could not leave port at any speed until he re-

*Soon after sending this signal to Cradock, Grant discovered that his engineer officer was a sick man whose health had been so undermined by the strain of maintaining the battleship's ancient machinery with a scratch crew that he had deliberately exaggerated her mechanical difficulties. This engineer commander, William Denbow, who for two years had been responsible for *Canopus*'s engines while she was laid up in Care and Maintenance, was unwillingly sent off to war along with the old ship and her old engines. When he found himself bound on a long voyage for the South Atlantic, his nerves failed. During the voyage, he never left his cabin, never inspected the engines, and never spoke to his subordinates. Captain Grant, apparently, knew nothing of this. Not until after Cradock had been told that the ship's engines were suffering from faulty condensers and could produce no more than 12 knots did a junior officer find the courage to tell the captain that Denbow "lived in his cabin. The day before we reached Port Stanley, I sent to the Captain . . . a written report about the Engineer Commander's strange behavior." By the time Grant knew, Cradock had sailed from Port Stanley, and Grant decided not to pass along the story. Denbow was placed under medical surveillance and, at Vallenar on the Chilean coast, he was transferred to a supply ship, to be invalided out of the navy.

paired his leaking condensers and cleaned his boilers; even then, he would be restricted to 12 knots. Disgusted, Cradock ordered *Canopus* to remain at Port Stanley until she was ready and then to follow him—he would pause to allow her to catch up—and escort his colliers around to the west coast. That afternoon, Cradock himself sailed in *Good Hope* to join the rest of his squadron. The time for Spee's appearance was already past; he felt that he could not leave his detached ships—*Glasgow, Monmouth,* and *Otranto*—exposed any longer on the Chilean coast without the support of *Good Hope.* Before leaving, he sent a simple report to London: "*Good Hope* left [Port Stanley] 22 October via Cape Horn. *Canopus* following on 23rd via Magellan Straits with three colliers for west coast of South America."

—

At fifty-two, Rear Admiral Sir Christopher Cradock was a small, immaculately dressed bachelor with wide-set eyes and a neatly trimmed, pointed beard; a diplomat's wife in Mexico described him as "shining with that special, well-groomed English look." He lived alone except for his dog, who accompanied him everywhere, but he thrived on human society. Often on board *Good Hope,* he left his admiral's quarters and joined the ship's officers for a drink in the wardroom. An aide to the governor of the Falklands remembered that while Cradock was at Port Stanley, he and his dog "would come wandering up to Government House every day for a yarn and a meal or else the Governor would go off to *Good Hope.* He was a dear old bloke and keen as a terrier."

Kit Cradock had joined the navy at thirteen and had served afloat and ashore for forty years. In 1900, as an officer in the China Squadron, Cradock was playing polo in Hong Kong with his friends Beatty and Keyes when the Boxer Rebellion broke out. He went ashore with the British naval brigade to capture the Taku forts and, under heavy fire, led a company of British, German, and Japanese sailors across a sunbaked mud flat to storm the west gate of a fort. For this, the kaiser gave him the Prussian Order of the Crown with Swords. In 1910, Fisher, as First Sea Lord, announced that Captain Cradock is "one of our very best officers." He was promoted to rear admiral and knighted, and in February 1913 took command of the prestigious North American and West Indies Station.

The navy was Cradock's life. The majesty and invincibility of the Royal Navy formed the bedrock of empire and the cornerstone of his beliefs. For him, said the contemporary naval writer Sir Archibald Hurd, "the navy was not a mere collection of ships, but a community of men with high purpose"; in this brotherhood, tradition, courage, honor, and discipline counted more than ships, boiler power, and gun calibers. In his leisure, Cradock wrote three books about the navy, including *Whispers from the Fleet,* a volume of avuncular advice for young officers. Among topics considered, Cradock counseled on burials at sea: "When a hammock is being used as a shroud, the last stitch of the sailmaker's needle is neatly popped through the tip of the nose. Then there can be no mistake."

Cradock was known in the fleet as a man who "fought hard, played hard, and did not suffer fools gladly." His favorite signal was said to be "Engage the enemy more closely." Home from the sea in his native Yorkshire, he hunted with near recklessness and he told a friend and fellow admiral that he hoped when his time came it would be in action at sea or by breaking his neck on the hunting field. By 1914 when he went to war, Cradock was one of the Royal Navy's most decorated admirals. Among the three rows of ribbons on the left breast of his jacket, however, one was stained with ink. "That ribbon," he told the governor's aide at Port Stanley, "belongs to the First Class Order of the Blue Ape, or something, that the kaiser gave me. I couldn't tear it out without ruining all the others; so I got an ink bottle and made it look as unpleasant as possible."

According to Luce, Cradock knew when he left Port Stanley that he was going to his doom. Sir William Allardyce, the governor of the Falklands, later told Luce that "Cradock thought his chances were small and that he had been let down by the Admiralty especially when his request for *Defence* had been denied." Bidding Allardyce farewell, Cradock said that he would never see him again and gave him a large sealed packet to be sent home to the Admiralty as soon as his death was confirmed. The packet contained a letter to his friend Admiral Hedworth Meux, to be forwarded "only in case . . . my squadron disappears—and me too—completely. I have no intention, after forty years at sea, of being an unheard victim." To Meux he vowed, "I will take care I do not suffer the fate of poor Troubridge." The governor's aide at the Falklands had a similar recollection of Cradock's mood: "The admiral was a very brave old man; he knew that he was going to almost certain death in fighting these new and powerful ships and it seemed to be quite all right as far as he was concerned. . . . He knew what he was up against and asked for a fast cruiser with big guns to be added to his squadron for he had nothing very powerful and nothing very fast, but the Admiralty said he'd have to go without. So old Cradock said, 'All right; we'll do without,' and he slipped off quietly early one morning and left *Canopus* to look after the colliers and transports and picked up *Glasgow* and *Monmouth* and set off to look for these crack Germans."

—

On October 26, as *Good Hope* was steaming north up the coast of Chile, Cradock signaled his intentions to the Admiralty. He confirmed his determination to find and to fight Spee, but he also made clear his distaste for *Canopus* and his desire for *Defence:* "With reference to orders to search for the enemy and our great desire for early success, I consider it impractical on account of *Canopus*['s] slow speed to find and destroy enemy squadron. Have therefore ordered *Defence* to join me after calling for orders at Montevideo. *Canopus* will be employed in necessary work of convoying colliers." This message arrived on October 27, at a time of turmoil at the Admiralty. Battenberg was about to resign and, on October 30, Churchill recalled Fisher. Thus it was that on the days when *Glasgow* was off Coronel, *Good Hope, Monmouth,* and *Otranto* were steaming north to join her, and *Canopus* was laboring up from the Magellan Straits, Churchill was, in his own words, "gravely preoccupied." He passed Cradock's signal to the War Staff with the minute, "This telegram is very obscure and I do not understand what Cradock intends or wishes." In fact, Cradock's message angered the First Lord. The admiral appeared either to have obtusely misunderstood or to be deliberately thwarting Admiralty orders. Cradock was saying that *Canopus,* the "citadel" around which he had been told to concentrate his squadron, was useless to him and that he was relegating this "citadel" to convoy work. Further, Cradock was telling Stoddart to send him *Defence,* the ship around which the new east coast squadron was to be built. Indeed, Stoddart immediately protested that if *Defence* was taken from him, he must immediately be sent two additional fast cruisers to replace her. On the evening of October 28, Churchill abruptly countermanded Cradock's orders to Stoddart to send him *Defence:* "*Defence* is to remain on east coast under orders of Stoddart," decreed the Admiralty. "This will leave sufficient force on each side in case the hostile cruisers appear there on the trade route." Regarding Cradock's decision to relegate *Canopus* to convoy work, the Admiralty made no comment.

The words "sufficient force" emphasized that the Admiralty did not consider that Cradock required any addition to his squadron in order to fulfill his mission. But had *Defence* been present at Coronel, the outcome might have been different. Her guns matched those of *Scharnhorst* and *Gneisenau* and her presence would have given Cradock a second regular Royal Navy ship and a second fully trained Royal Navy crew. It still would been two professionally manned British ships against five Germans, but with *Good Hope* and *Monmouth* adding their guns, the scale might have been balanced. This was Cradock's view.*

The Admiralty's message probably reached the admiral around one p.m. on November 1, when *Glasgow* brought it out to the flagship from Coronel. If he read it, the signal would explain his subsequent behavior. His decision to leave *Canopus* behind apparently had been approved for the Admiralty had made no comment. *Defence* had again been denied him. And he had been as-

*In the end, *Defence* was an unlucky ship. As Troubridge's flagship in the Mediterranean, she had played an unheroic role in the *Goeben* fiasco. Now as Cradock went to meet Spee, *Defence* remained idle at the river Plate. Eighteen months later, she blew up and sank at Jutland.

sured that, without these two ships, his squadron still constituted a "sufficient force."

Thus, five ships, of which only one—the smallest—was ready to fight a modern, well-trained foe, represented the Royal Navy off the west coast of South America on November 1, 1914. "The words 'sufficient force' must have seared the soul of a fearless and experienced officer whose impetuous character was well-known at the Admiralty," Hirst wrote later. Churchill was to argue that the "sufficient force" signal never reached Cradock, who was therefore not influenced by it in reaching his bold and suicidal decision. But Hirst said it reached *Glasgow* during her visit to Coronel, that his ship brought it out to *Good Hope* just before the action, and that he was certain that Cradock read it. Thereafter, "tired of protesting his inferiority, the receipt of this telegram would be sufficient to spur Cradock to hoist, as he did half an hour later, his signal, 'Spread fifteen miles apart and look for the enemy.' " Three hours later he met the East Asia Squadron. Cradock's last signal, wirelessed to *Canopus,* was a proper epitaph for a man who had always hoped he would break his neck on the hunting field or be killed in battle: "I am going to attack the enemy now."

Churchill later admitted that, had he not been distracted by the Admiralty upheaval over Battenberg's departure and Fisher's arrival, "I am sure I should have reacted much more violently to the ominous sentence 'shall employ *Canopus* convoying colliers.' " October 30 was Fisher's first day back in office as First Sea Lord and Churchill gave the old admiral a two-hour briefing on the worldwide deployment of the Royal Navy. "The critical point," Churchill recalled, was in South American waters. "Speaking of Admiral Cradock's position, I said, 'You don't suppose he would try to fight them without the *Canopus*?' He did not give any decided reply."

—

On the morning of October 27, *Good Hope* joined *Glasgow, Monmouth,* and *Otranto* in the remote fjord of Vallenar roads, where Cradock was beyond wireless contact with the Admiralty. Still hoping to receive further clarification or modification of his orders by way of Montevideo, he dispatched *Glasgow* back to Coronel to collect any waiting messages that might have come over land wire. Before *Glasgow* left, she sent a boat around the anchorage to collect outgoing mail from the other ships. Visiting in the wardrooms of the armored cruisers, Hirst found most officers expecting a battle and fatalistic about their prospects. "Two of the lieutenant commanders in *Monmouth,* both old shipmates, took me aside to give me farewell messages to their wives," he said. "*Glasgow* has got the speed," they told him, "so she can get away; but we are for it." When the light cruiser departed at 6:30 p.m., she carried Cradock's last signal to the Admiralty: "*Monmouth, Good Hope* and *Otranto* coaling at Vallenar. *Glasgow* patrolling vicinity of Coronel to intercept German shipping, joining flag later on. I intend to proceed northward secretly with squadron after coaling and keep out of sight of land." *Canopus,* then plowing through the Straits of Magellan, was not mentioned.

Two days later, as Cradock and his squadron were leaving Vallenar, *Canopus* and her two colliers appeared in the fjord. The old battleship, her captain reported, could go no farther without spending another twenty-four hours repairing her high-pressure piston glands. Cradock told Captain Grant to anchor, do the work, and follow as soon as possible. Grant, however, never reported to Cradock that his ship's potential speed now was higher than 12 knots. Later, he explained that, knowing the admiral's opinion of his ship, he doubted the squadron would wait for him to catch up. Whether Cradock, knowing the truth about *Canopus*'s marginally higher speed, would have waited and fought the battle in her company will never be known.

Meanwhile, *Glasgow* was steaming north, "alone this time, much to my satisfaction," said Luce. On the afternoon of the twenty-ninth, the wireless office began to intercept heavy traffic in German code, indicating that a warship—the signals indicated *Leipzig*—was not far away. The signals were so strong, Luce said, "that we expected to sight the enemy at any moment." As a result, Luce hesitated to take his ship into Coronel. He worried that if he entered the neutral port, he might be trapped in a place where his ship's greater speed would be useless. He signaled Cradock, who gave permission to delay entering the harbor. Accordingly, for two days, *Glasgow* waited outside Coronel. On the night of the thirtieth, Luce again heard *Leipzig*'s call sign broadcast from no more than 150 miles away, but at daybreak the ocean was empty.

At twilight on October 31, *Glasgow* entered Coronel harbor and Hirst, the intelligence officer, went ashore to collect and send messages and mail. In handing over papers, the worried British consul stressed to Hirst the existence of both a strongly German and pro-German minority along the Chilean coast, and the consequent probability that the light cruiser's presence already had been reported. That night, in full view of the anchored *Glasgow,* the German consulate and the German merchant ships in the harbor blazed with light. One of these vessels was *Göttingen,* a supply ship that Spee had sent into Coronel, which promptly signaled her admiral: "British light cruiser anchored in Coronel Roads at 7:00 p.m. on 31 October." At 2:00 a.m., *Glasgow*'s wireless room was listening to almost continuous, high-pitched Telefunken signal notes that indicated the presence of enemy ships in the vicinity. The number of wireless messages convinced Luce that the German squadron was approaching, and he decided to sail at nine o'clock the next morning. Cradock, sweeping up from the south and hoping to catch *Leipzig,* ordered Luce to rendezvous with the squadron forty miles west of Coronel at noon the next day, November 1.

—

Admiral von Spee, leaving Más Afuera on October 27, had been informed by a German port agent at Punta Arenas that a "British Queen class battleship" had been seen that day headed west through the Straits of Magellan.* He also knew from other German agents that ships of Admiral Cradock's squadron had appeared farther up the Chilean coast. Accordingly, soon after his men saw the peaks of the Andes, he ordered his two armored cruisers to remain out of sight of the coast and instructed that all wireless communications between warships be preceded by *Leipzig*'s call sign. Spee realized that the presence of this light cruiser was known and he hoped that this duplicity would keep the presence of his other ships a secret. On October 30, he began sending his supply ships into Valparaíso and Coronel to take on supplies and coal. On the thirty-first, the admiral himself was at sea in *Scharnhorst* fifty miles off Valparaíso when he learned from *Göttingen* that *Glasgow* had slipped into Coronel. As the British ship could not remain in port for more than twenty-four hours without violating Chilean neutrality, Spee decided to trap and destroy this relatively small enemy. If *Glasgow* used all of her twenty-four hours, she would sail by the end of the afternoon on November 1; accordingly, Spee planned to arrive off Coronel before five p.m. *Nürnberg* was assigned to steam past the harbor entrance to see whether the British cruiser was there; the remaining ships were to spread in an arc outside with *Scharnhorst* to the north and *Gneisenau* to the south. Both admirals, thus, suffered from the same misunderstanding; each believed himself to be pursuing a single enemy light cruiser and neither was aware of the presence of other, larger enemy ships.

Sunday, November 1, was All Saints' Day, and Spee's seamen, coming down from Valparaíso toward Coronel, rejoiced in a clear early-spring morning. The sea was dark green and the strong wind from the south tipped the crests of the waves with white foam that sparkled in the sunlight. At 10:30 a.m., the crew of *Gneisenau* went to church service on deck, but the hymn *"Ein' feste Burg ist unser Gott"* ("A Mighty Fortress Is Our God") was muffled by the sound of the wind howling in the rigging and sending bursts of spray back from the foredeck. The midday meal included special allowances of cocoa and bread spread with marmalade. By noon, the wind, moving around to the southwest, had reached Force Seven—28 to 33 knots, or 31 to 37 miles, per hour—and the ships, plunging south at 14 knots through the heavy swell, began to pitch and roll. The squadron was strung out; *Scharnhorst, Gneisenau,* and *Leipzig* were in front and the other two light

*In fact, the ship was *Canopus*. It was an understandable mistake; the two classes had similar profiles and similar armament. But the *Queen*s were five years younger and the 2,000 additional tons they carried had gone into armor and engines.

cruisers behind. Toward noon, when *Nürnberg* stopped to examine two Chilean ships, she fell back twenty-five miles astern of the flagship. At 4:00 p.m., when British wireless signals became very loud, *Nürnberg* was ordered to rejoin. At 4:17 *Leipzig* sighted smoke and masts across the stormy seas far to starboard and at 4:20, a drum thundered the order "Clear the decks for action." Coming closer, the Germans could see the funnels and then the hulls of the British light cruiser *Glasgow* and the armed merchant cruiser *Otranto.*

—

The morning of November 1 dawned bright on board *Glasgow* in Coronel harbor. Patches of fog lingering on the hilltops around the bay blew away in a strong wind that tempered the warmth of a spring day. At 9:15 a.m., having collected messages and mail for the admiral and the squadron, *Glasgow* carefully slipped out of the harbor. Out in the open sea, Luce saw nothing. He took his ship north until he was out of sight of land, then turned southwest. As the light cruiser's bow plunged into the rising sea, green water swept the foredeck, and spray whipped over the bridge. Four hours later, forty miles west of Coronel Bay, Luce sighted *Good Hope, Monmouth,* and *Otranto,* coming north at 15 knots. The flagship and *Monmouth* were already rolling like barrels and *Otranto,* with the sail area of her tall side broadside to the wind, was even worse. At the rendezvous point, the strong wind and heavy sea made it impossible for any ship to lower a boat. In order to transfer to Cradock the messages and intelligence he had brought out from Coronel, Luce placed the papers in a 6-inch cartridge case, which *Glasgow* towed slowly across the bows of the flagship, which had come to a halt. Using a grapnel, *Good Hope*'s crew plucked the case from the sea, an effort that earned both ships Cradock's signal "Maneuver well executed."

Meanwhile, strong wireless signals indicated that *Leipzig* was not far to the north. Having heard nothing from the German armored cruisers, Cradock assumed that they were not nearby. At 1:50 p.m., the admiral signaled his squadron to form a line of search spreading fanwise, east to west, fifteen miles between ships, and to head north at 10 knots. Nearest the coast was *Glasgow,* with her professional, regular navy crew; next to her was *Monmouth,* with a reserve crew and twelve young naval cadets; beyond, the thin-skinned *Otranto* looming like a haystack out of the sea; and farthest west, carrying the only two heavy guns in the British squadron, *Good Hope.* On board the flagship, as his squadron swept north over the tumultuous seas, Cradock went to his cabin to study his messages and go through his mail.

CHAPTER 12

The Battle of Coronel

Leipzig was not alone off Coronel that afternoon. Vice Admiral Count Maximilian von Spee was there with the whole strength of the German East Asia Sqaudron. Once *Glasgow* was sighted to the southwest, Spee moved to intercept her. He ordered all boilers lighted, summoned his two lagging light cruisers, *Dresden* and *Nürnberg,* and, without waiting for them, began to chase. Black smoke belched from *Scharnhorst*'s funnels; "In a quarter of an hour," Spee wrote later, "we were steaming at twenty knots against a heavy sea, throwing up clouds of spray which soaked to the bones the men in the forward turret and the magazine below." Meanwhile, *Leipzig* had also seen *Monmouth* and *Otranto* and had informed the admiral.

The chase phase of the action continued for ninety minutes. Once the British had reversed direction, the two squadrons were steaming south on almost parallel courses separated by 15,000 yards. Spee, aware that he had the superior force, made his preparations calmly. "Does my smoke disturb you?" he signaled to *Gneisenau* and made adjustments to *Scharnhorst*'s course to give her sister a clear view of the targets. "When the sun was sufficiently low on the horizon not to dazzle the gunners," wrote an officer on board the *Gneisenau,* "and the enemy ships were sharply outlined against the blaze of the setting sun, while the lofty Chilean coast, dark and cloud-capped, formed our background . . . [we], on signal from *Scharnhorst,* moved . . . towards the enemy. The distance, then about 13,500 yards, began to diminish more rapidly. The eyes of the range-finders were glued to the rubber eyelets of their long-range field glasses, through which they perceived the enemy magnified ten times." Spee opened fire at 7:04 p.m., at 11,000 yards. Each German ship was instructed to fire at the corresponding ship in the enemy line: *Scharnhorst* at *Good Hope, Gneisenau* at *Monmouth, Leipzig* at *Glasgow,* and *Dresden* at *Otranto.* After the first salvo, *Scharnhorst* fired three salvos a minute, and at 7:09 p.m. observed her first hit on *Good Hope.* Soon afterward, Cradock's ships began to fire back.

—

The sun was sinking in the western sky at 4:20 p.m., when Luce, heading north, saw smoke on his starboard bow, toward the coast. *Otranto,* then only two miles west of *Glasgow,* signaled that she, too, had seen the smoke on the horizon. Luce reported this to Cradock, fifty miles away in *Good Hope,* then rang for full speed and turned to investigate. The smoke cloud expanded as he approached; soon, from a distance of twelve miles (24,000 yards), he identified a three-funneled light cruiser and then, farther off, two four-funneled armored cruisers. Luce knew instantly what they were: "We had in sight the two German armored cruisers." Until that moment, *Scharnhorst* and *Gneisenau* were not positively known to be on the Chilean coast. "But when we saw those damned four funnels," said another *Glasgow* officer, "we knew there was the devil to pay."

Luce steamed closer to establish Spee's course. "Enemy steering between southeast and south," he signaled, and then turned away to gather up *Monmouth* and *Otranto* and join *Good Hope,* still out of sight to the west. Cradock, who had learned of *Leipzig*'s presence about the same time that Spee was informed of *Glasgow*'s, immediately turned toward the enemy. For a few minutes, when the two squadrons first made contact, both admirals were surprised, each believing that he had been closing in on a solitary enemy light cruiser. This impression was sustained by the coincidence that *Leipzig,* the single German light cruiser that Cradock expected to find, was the first to be sighted by the British force, while *Glasgow,* the light cruiser that Spee had hoped to trap in Coronel, was the first to be seen by the German squadron.

Before Cradock, steaming north, turned toward the enemy, he had the entire Pacific Ocean on his port bow, with ample sea room to escape. *Good Hope, Monmouth,* and *Glasgow* all could make more than 20 knots and thus were faster than Von Spee's two armored cruisers, but *Otranto*'s best speed that afternoon was 16 knots, inferior to all of the German ships. Thus, while Cradock with his three warships might have run for protection back to the 12-inch guns of *Canopus,* he could have done so only by leaving *Otranto* behind. Later, critics asked why *Otranto* was present at all with the British squadron at Coronel. The answer is that Cradock had not expected to meet the East Asia Squadron that afternoon. He was hunting one light cruiser, and in this effort, *Otranto,* by extending his search line, had a useful part to play. Once *Scharnhorst* and *Gneisenau* appeared, however, *Otranto* became a heavy liability: if Cradock slowed down to her speed, he surrendered 6 or

7 knots; if he left her behind she could fall prey to any one of the German ships. "We all thought he would leave *Otranto,*" wrote *Glasgow*'s gunnery officer, "[but] he did not like leaving [her] to look after herself. . . . She is such an enormous hulk she can be seen for miles on the darkest night." Cradock made his choice, signaling his squadron, "I cannot go down and engage the enemy at present leaving *Otranto.*"

Cradock now knew that the long anticipated encounter with Spee was at hand. At 5:10 p.m., he signaled all ships to head toward *Glasgow,* the ship nearest the enemy. Having decided to fight and because Royal Navy ships were not trained for battle at night, he decided to force an action while daylight remained. He formed his ships into a single line—*Good Hope* leading, then *Monmouth, Glasgow,* and *Otranto*—on a southeasterly course at 16 knots, the highest speed of which *Otranto* was capable. His intention was to bring the Germans within range of his squadron's numerous 6-inch guns; unfortunately, this course also headed the ships diagonally across a heavy sea on the side toward the enemy. Here, the waves rolling up against the closed casements of *Good Hope*'s and *Monmouth*'s lower port gun batteries rendered these guns useless. With these gun ports closed and because of the shorter range of all of the British 6-inch guns, Spee's sixteen 8.2-inch guns were opposed at this stage only by the two 9.2-inch guns of *Good Hope.*

Thereafter for almost an hour, the two lines of ships swept south on a roughly parallel course, 14,000 yards apart. To British sailors looking across the water, the German squadron gave an intimidating impression of confidence and power. *Scharnhorst* and *Gneisenau,* their red, gold, and black battle flags stiff in the wind, black smoke billowing from their funnels, the waves racing along their towering white sides, seemed to ride irresistibly over the seas. To the west, the British line presented a hodgepodge assembly, wallowing and plunging through the swells, green water breaking over their bows, their main deck guns awash, their telescopes and gun sights drenched by icy spray and encrusted with salt.

Nevertheless, Cradock believed that he had a chance. His position to the west of Spee offered a great advantage in terms of light. The British squadron was between the enemy and the setting sun, putting the low afternoon rays directly into the Germans' eyes. As the British closed the range, the sun would blind the German gun layers while at the same time lighting up the German ships as targets. Conversely, Cradock realized, after the sun went down, this advantage would be reversed. Rather than having the setting sun in their eyes, the enemy gunners would be looking—for at least half an hour after sunset—at the black shapes of his ships starkly silhouetted against the afterglow in the western sky. The Germans, meanwhile, would be lost in the gray obscurity of the inshore twilight. Cradock decided to force an immediate action, To have a chance, he knew that he must come close enough to effectively use his armored cruisers' seventeen 6-inch guns. At 6:18 p.m., he increased speed to 16 knots, hoisted the signal "Follow in the admiral's wake," and turned closer toward the enemy. At the same moment, he wirelessed *Canopus,* laboring up the coast 250 miles to the south, "I am going to attack the enemy now."

Admiral von Spee refused to have it so. He realized as well as Cradock the danger of having his gun layers blinded by glare from the setting sun, and he had no intention of letting his enemy come within range until the sun had set. His squadron speed was now 20 knots, giving him the power to dictate time and range, and he deliberately refused immediate action. Edging away to port, keeping himself between Cradock and the coast, he established a new range of 18,000 yards. Thwarted, Cradock turned back to a parallel southerly course. Then, as the sun slid into the sea and evening crept over the sky, the German ships became indistinct against the background of gathering darkness. To the west, the four British ships, steaming in a neat line one behind the other, were sharp-etched in black silhouette against the red-gold panorama of the afterglow.

At 6:50 p.m., the sun sank beneath the horizon. "And now began the saddest naval action in the war," Winston Churchill wrote. "Of the officers and men in both the squadrons that faced each other in these stormy seas so far from home, nine out of ten were doomed to perish. The British were to die that night; the Germans a month later." Once the advantage of light had abandoned Cradock, Spee immediately altered course and brought his ships to within 12,300 yards of the British squadron. At 7:04 p.m., he hoisted the signal to open fire, and orange flashes blossomed from *Scharnhorst* and *Gneisenau.* Soon gray-white mushrooms, beautifully grouped, rose from the sea 500 yards short of the British flagship. From the beginning, despite the fact that the ships on both sides were rolling, the shooting of the two German armored cruisers was not merely superior; it was remarkable. It was as if they were at peacetime gunnery practice; *Scharnhorst*'s first salvo landed 500 yards short; her second was 500 yards over; then, with an awful inevitability, the third salvo smashed into the British flagship. Within five minutes, Spee had achieved decisive hits on both British armored cruisers. *Scharnhorst*'s third salvo struck *Good Hope*'s forward 9.2-inch gun turret, and her foredeck exploded in flames. Thus, even before he fired his first shot, Cradock was deprived of one of his squadron's two big guns. Meanwhile, *Gneisenau* fired rapid salvos at *Monmouth,* striking her forecastle. As *Good Hope* and *Monmouth* steamed through a forest of water spouts, men on *Glasgow* observed the curious effect of sheets of flame continuously bathing the sides of both ships with the heavy sea sliding along the sides seeming to have no effect.

Cradock decided to move in closer. And with every minute, the tactical disadvantage of the British ships increased. The Germans now were almost invisible. Heavy seas pounding against their ships were sending bursts of spray into the faces of the British gunners, telescopes were blurred, and in the growing darkness, spotters could not mark the fall of shots. There was nothing at which to aim except the flashes of the German guns, while Spee's gun layers continued to hit their well-defined targets with salvos fired three a minute. The battle quickly became, in the words of one British survivor, "the most rotten show imaginable." Two relatively new German cruisers, winners of competitive gunnery tests in the German navy and manned by 2,200 trained German sailors, were pitted against two obsolete ships manned by scratch crews of Britons, the vast majority of whom had been happily pursuing civilian lives less than six months before. The lower deck guns of the German armored cruisers were able to fire, but the main deck casements of *Good Hope* and *Monmouth* had to be kept closed lest the guns be smothered by the sea. Not that the German ships faced no difficulties. "The waves rose high in the strong wind," said one German officer. "Water foamed up over the cruisers' forecastles and then flowed streaming over the upper decks. The crews and ammunition carriers found it difficult to keep their feet." An English 6-inch shell penetrated on the starboard side of *Gneisenau* into the officers' wardroom where it burst. Water poured in rapidly, but the ship's carpenters, up to their necks in water, stopped the leak. A British shell hit the after turret between the guns and temporarily jammed the mechanism that enabled the turret to rotate. It was repaired and the guns reopened fire. But for the British, it was infinitely worse. *Glasgow* never observed any gunfire at all from the lower gun casements of the two British armored cruisers. That meant that sixteen German 8.2-inch guns were opposed by only one 9.2-inch gun and a few 6-inch guns. The German salvos thundered rhythmically at twenty-second intervals, whereas, Spee reported, the British gunners fired only one salvo to his three.

Otranto played no active part in the battle. *Dresden* had fired briefly at the armed merchant cruiser and *Otranto*'s Captain Edwards, seeing that his ship could do nothing useful, signaled Cradock to ask if he should keep out of range. Cradock's reply was garbled and provided no clear orders. Then *Gneisenau* put two shells over Edwards's bridge and a column of water spouted up fifty yards off his starboard bow. Unable to reply with his 4-inch guns, Edwards prudently drew out of line onto *Glasgow*'s starboard quarter. Even here, owing to her huge bulk and the short range of her guns, *Otranto* could serve no purpose except as a looming target, which the enemy could use to determine the range to the British line. Realizing this, Captain Edwards took her away to the west as fast as she would go.

The main action lasted only fifty-two minutes. With the early loss of *Good Hope*'s forward 9.2-inch gun, Cradock's chances of harming the enemy at anything but 6-inch-gun range had been cut in half. Even his smaller guns had little effect: *Monmouth*'s 6-inch gunfire was at first very rapid, but because *Gneisenau* was out of range the British shells landed in the sea. And once *Gneisenau* turned her full attention on *Monmouth,* the British shooting quickly became ragged. Her gun crews fought their guns, but the foredeck was burning and black smoke billowed along her exposed port side. Outranged by the German guns that were straddling the British line along its length, and with his own 6-inch guns having difficulty reaching the enemy, Cradock had a single thought: to come still closer. As he led his squadron across the shell-torn seas to bring his 6-inch guns to bear, he was punished fiercely and *Good Hope*'s masthead and foretop repeatedly glowed red as shells from *Scharnhorst* burst against them. By 7:23 p.m., the range was down to 6,600 yards and still Cradock came on. Spee, fearing that this was a torpedo attack, edged away to the east. At 7:35 p.m., Cradock still plunged toward the German line 5,500 yards away. "The enemy had the range perfectly and all their salvos straddled our lines. The scene was appalling," said a *Glasgow* officer.

As the British kept coming, *Gneisenau*'s guns shortened the range and the execution became terrible. One shell struck *Monmouth*'s fore 6-inch turret and blew off the roof. As flames licked up out of the steel shell, a second, larger explosion shattered the entire forward part of the ship; when the flames subsided, the forward turret had completely disappeared. Still *Gneisenau*'s shells crashed through her decks; heavy seas were flooding into her gaping bows and she began heeling to port. Then, as though beaten out of line by sheer weight of metal, *Monmouth* began to lose speed and yaw away to starboard. For a while, it seemed to those watching from *Glasgow* that she was having some success in overcoming her fires, but she never rejoined the line and gradually her guns lapsed into silence.

Darkness settled, the moon came up behind the clouds, and the Germans, except for the relentless flashes of their guns, were invisible to their enemies. Not so *Good Hope* and *Monmouth,* which flared like twin beacons. Frequently, both ships, already bright with flames, flashed into vivid orange as another shell detonated against their superstructures. In the dark, the German gun layers used the fires in the British ships as aiming points. "As the two big enemy ships were in flames," noted one German officer, "we were able to economize [on use of] our searchlights."

Good Hope was in forlorn condition. Although the single 9.2-inch gun on her stern continued to fire once a minute, the shells crashing into the flagship had ripped away her upper works and decks and the smoke pouring from her funnels was an incandescent red. Still, she pushed stubbornly ahead, her upper port 6-inch battery defiant. At 7:42 p.m., *Good Hope,* as though in a final desperate effort to sell her life dearly, gathered all her remaining strength, turned directly toward her tormentors, and charged them, trailing fiery clouds of flame behind her. Spee ordered his ships out of her path and then, at a range of less than 5,000 yards, poured in rapid-fire broadsides from both *Scharnhorst* and *Gneisenau.* His salvos blanketed *Good Hope;* she staggered under the rain of blows and came to a halt with her upper deck a sea of flame.

It was now quite dark, with the moon intermittently obscured by clouds and occasional rain squalls. By 7:50 p.m., the stricken British flagship, which had absorbed at least thirty-five direct hits from *Scharnhorst,* could be seen, silent and burning, close to the enemy. A *Glasgow* midshipman, watching *Good Hope,* saw "her funnels illuminated by a fire burning near the bridge. A moment later, there was a tremendous detonation . . . and the whole of her forepart shot up in a fan-shaped sheet of flame." A broad column of flame rose from amidships where it illuminated a cloud of debris flung still higher in the air. "She looked," said Spee, "like a splendid firework display against a dark sky. The glowing white flames, mingled with bright green stars, shot up to a great height." Then the column of fire broke and fell, to wash along the decks and cover the hull with waves of flame. Debris crashed into the sea and the forward section of the ship silently detached itself and slid down into oblivion. Incredibly, two 6-inch guns of the after port battery each fired twice more into the darkness. Then her fire ceased and she lay drifting, a low, dark, gutted hull, illuminated by a red glare. After this, all was black and, despite her proximity, she was never seen again. Ironically, so close had *Good Hope* been to the German line that for a moment *Glasgow*'s gunners thought it was the German flagship, not their own, that had exploded.

—

In contrast to the horrors that descended on *Good Hope* and *Monmouth, Glasgow* bore a charmed existence. At 7:05, she had begun firing her two 6-inch guns over 10,000 yards, first at *Leipzig* and then at *Dresden. Glasgow*'s gun layers, firing from a rolling platform only eight feet above the waterline, could hardly see their targets, and the smoke of *Scharnhorst* and *Gneisenau,* driven by the wind, made them even more difficult to see. Nevertheless, *Glasgow* continued firing while her gunnery officer searched in the darkness for signs of the fall of shot. The effort was fruitless and *Glasgow* hit neither *Leipzig* nor *Dresden.*

Meanwhile, the two German light cruisers were firing back. *Leipzig*'s initial salvo fell short of *Glasgow* and her fire remained ineffective until 7:15 p.m., when the British cruiser came within range of the German 4.1-inch guns. From that point on, Luce's ship was engaging both German light cruisers, and, at times, also *Gneisenau.* All this time, *Glasgow* could see the two bigger British ships being cruelly punished. No one on board *Glasgow* actually saw *Good Hope* founder, but everyone knew that she could not have survived. Once the British flagship was gone, *Scharnhorst* switched her fire to *Monmouth,* and *Gneisenau* to *Glasgow;* huge splashes began erupting around the unarmored British light cruiser. Moonlight gave *Glasgow* an occasional glimpse of the enemy ships and, shifting fire from *Leipzig* to *Gneisenau,* she scored at least one hit with her forward 6-inch gun on *Gneisenau*'s after turret. For a few minutes the turret could not be trained, but the armor was not pierced and soon the German guns returned to action.

By eight o'clock, Luce knew that he was tempting fate by continuing the action. For an hour, his ship had been exposed to the fire of both *Leipzig* and *Dresden* and for ten minutes he was the target of the 8.2-inch shells of *Gneisenau.* His own guns could do little against this adversary and his gunnery officer was unable even to see the splashes of his shells in order to correct ranges. "The moon was rising behind the enemy, dimly showing him up at times while he could no longer see us, and they only fired when they could see the flash of our guns," Luce said. "We kept up our fire a little longer until I realized that each time we fired we brought on ourselves the combined fire of the whole [German] squadron." Accordingly, at 8:05, Luce ordered his ship to cease fire.

Luce's ship had been extraordinarily lucky. In part, this was due to the difficulties *Dresden* and *Leipzig* had faced in fighting their guns while pitching and rolling in the heavy seas. Together, the two German light cruisers had fired more than 600 shells at *Glasgow,* but had hit her only five times. Three shells had lodged harmlessly in coal bunkers, where the lumps of coal had squelched their explosive force; one broke up, without bursting, against a conning tower support. The only significant hit came from a 4.1-inch shell from *Leipzig* that burst aft on the waterline just above the port outer propeller and tore a large hole about six feet square. One compartment was flooded but there was no spreading or damage to the adjacent compartments and the ship's speed was not affected. *Glasgow* was still able to steam away at 24 knots and cover 5,000 miles before she was repaired. Remarkably, not a single man of *Glasgow*'s crew was killed or severely wounded. Four slightly wounded seamen returned to duty within a few days.

Glasgow's parrots were not as lucky. As the ship went into action, it was decided that it would be unkind to leave the birds in their cages and, although the vessel was fifty miles from the coast, the parrots were released. For a while, each time the guns were fired, they rose, flew about, then settled back on *Glasgow*'s upper deck. As the battle wore on, the parrots became dazed and perched apathetically about the ship. Hirst saw two perched on a gun barrel just before it fired; others lined up on the funnel stays and the edges of boats. Only ten parrots survived the battle.

Once Luce ceased firing, he turned to see what he could do for the stricken *Monmouth.* At 8:15 p.m., he found the battered armored cruiser, listing and down by the bow. The fires on her deck had been put out and she was trying to turn to the north, to get her undamaged stern into the large waves rolling up from the south. By the time *Glasgow* arrived, the moon in the east had risen above the clouds to light up the sea and reveal four enemy ships approaching in line abreast; soon they would sight the British ships. "Are you all right?" Luce signaled by flashing light. *Monmouth*'s captain, Frank Brandt, replied, "I want to get stern to sea. I am making water badly forward." "Can you steer northwest?" Luce asked, hoping that the *Monmouth* could limp to the Chilean coast. "The enemy are following us astern," he added.

For almost ten minutes, *Glasgow* hung off *Monmouth*'s port quarter, but there was nothing Luce could do. The enemy was near, the area was flooded with moonlight, and Luce had to decide whether to share *Monmouth*'s fate without being able to render any real assistance, or to attempt to escape. "I felt that I could not help her but must be destroyed with her if we remained," Luce said later. "With great reluctance, I therefore turned to the northwest and increased to full speed." Before leaving, *Glasgow* passed under the *Monmouth*'s stern. As the light cruiser went by for the last time, the crew of the stricken ship was heard cheering and, amid the voices of men, some thought they heard the higher notes of a boy.

Two of *Glasgow*'s officers later justified Luce's decision: "It was obvious that *Monmouth* could neither fight nor fly," said one. "It was essential that there should be a survivor of the action to turn *Canopus* which was hurrying at her best speed to join up and, if surprised alone by four or five ships . . . must have shared the fate of the other ships. *Monmouth* was therefore reluctantly left to her fate." Another officer agreed. "It was awful having to leave," he said, "but I don't see what else the skipper could have done."

Glasgow headed west at full speed, losing sight of *Monmouth* astern at 8:50 p.m., and then turned south toward *Canopus*. Throughout the action, the Germans had ceaselessly jammed British wireless transmissions, and *Glasgow* had been unable to get any messages through. Now, as she raced south, the jamming effect declined and her wireless was able to tell *Canopus* the dreadful story. At first, as *Glasgow* rushed south at 24 knots, there was hope that *Monmouth* might have eluded the enemy and be limping to safety. Then, half an hour later, the men on *Glasgow*'s decks saw a searchlight beam flickering on the northern horizon. Distant firing broke out again and seventy-five gun flashes were counted. Then, silence. *Glasgow* knew that the Germans had found *Monmouth*. Later, one *Glasgow* officer remembered that "utterly dispirited and sick at heart . . . I went down to my cabin to snatch a few hours of sleep. . . . I threw myself onto my bunk, wet clothes and all. . . . We were humiliated to the very depths of our beings. We hardly spoke to one another for the first twenty-four hours. We felt so bitterly ashamed of ourselves for we had let down the King; we had let down the Admiralty; we had let down England. What would the British public think of the Royal Navy?"

By 8:15 p.m., with the ocean shining under bright moonlight broken by clouds and scattered rain squalls, Admiral von Spee had lost contact with his enemies. *Scharnhorst* slowed, and with his flagship lying athwart the sea and rolling heavily, Spee signaled his light cruisers: "Both British armored cruisers severely damaged. One light cruiser apparently fairly intact. [German] light cruisers to pursue and attack with torpedoes." Upon receiving this order, *Leipzig* turned at 18 knots toward a glare visible to the northwest that Captain Johannes Haun supposed might be a burning ship. By the time he reached the position, he could see nothing from his bridge, but members of his crew who were on the main deck throwing cartridge cases overboard observed lifeless bodies amid a mass of floating debris. They failed to report this to Haun, who therefore did not pass the information along to Spee; the admiral remained ignorant that he had sunk the British flagship. A few minutes later, *Dresden* stumbled upon *Leipzig* and, believing her to be *Glasgow,* prepared to fire a torpedo. Recognition came just in time.

Meanwhile, *Nürnberg,* which had been twenty-five miles behind the squadron when the firing began, believed that she had missed the battle. Receiving Spee's torpedo order, Captain Karl von Schönberg turned his ship in the direction from which he had last heard gunfire. At 8:35 p.m., a lookout reported a column of smoke on the starboard bow and Schönberg steered for it at 21 knots, but it disappeared into the darkness (this was *Glasgow,* which had just left *Monmouth* to her fate). Schönberg then observed another, larger ship about two miles farther away on his starboard beam. Here, he found a heavily damaged British armored cruiser, listing 10 degrees to port, but still under way, her guns silent. As *Nürnberg* approached, the crippled vessel heeled still more so that the guns on her port side were useless. Schönberg closed in, switched on his searchlight, and recognized *Monmouth,* lacking her forward 6-inch turret. The searchlight also picked out the White Ensign, still flying, and repair parties moving about the shattered decks. *Monmouth*'s propellers still threshed under her stern, and her steering appeared undamaged. Schönberg waited, his searchlight pointedly illuminating the White Ensign 600 yards away. *Monmouth* did not fire, but there was no movement to lower the flag. At 9:20, Schönberg opened fire, deliberately aiming high; still the White Ensign was not struck. *Nürnberg* next fired a torpedo, which missed. Schönberg ceased fire, switched off his searchlights, and waited. Then, *Monmouth* began to gather speed and turn toward *Nürnberg,* possibly, the German believed, intending to ram or to bring her starboard guns to bear. As *Monmouth* turned, *Nürnberg* circled and passed under *Monmouth*'s stern, now rising high out of the sea. At point-blank range, Schönberg fired. No shot could miss; the shells ripped open the unprotected part of the hull. *Monmouth* shuddered and heeled farther until the sea rolled over the port deck rail and lapped around the funnels. Soon, the ship was lying on her side, her ensigns drooping toward the water, her red keel rising. At 8:58 p.m., *Monmouth* capsized and went down. Schönberg made no attempt to rescue; the seas were too heavy and his lookouts reported smoke from approaching, unidentified four-funneled ships. Eventually, as the ships came closer, they were recognized as *Scharnhorst* and *Gneisenau.*

Later, Captain Schönberg wrote: "I fired until the *Monmouth* had completely capsized, which . . . proceeded very slowly and majestically, the brave fellows went under with flags flying, an indescribable and unforgettable moment as the masts with the great top flags sank slowly into the water. Unfortunately, there could be no thought of saving the poor fellows. First, I believed that I had an enemy before me, secondly the sea was so high that hardly a boat could have lived in it. Moreover, all my ship's boats were secured before the action." Even so, after the battle, many of *Nürnberg*'s officers were ill at ease about their slaughter of a helpless enemy. "It was terrible to have to fire on poor fellows who were no longer able to defend themselves," said Lieutenant Otto von Spee, the admiral's son. "But their colors were still flying and when we ceased fire for several minutes they did not haul them down."

The battle was over. *Nürnberg* signaled the flagship, "Have sunk enemy cruiser," and Spee replied, "Bravo, *Nürnberg*!" There were no survivors from *Monmouth* or *Good Hope.* Sixteen hundred British seamen had died. Christopher Cradock, his wish fulfilled, was one of them.

—

By 10:15 p.m., Spee decided that *Good Hope, Glasgow,* and *Otranto* had escaped. The last two were of little concern, and he believed that *Good Hope* was so heavily damaged that she would either sink or make for Valparaíso for repairs, in which case he hoped to persuade the Chilean government to disarm and intern her. But there remained the British battleship sighted off Punta Arenas; from signals intercepted by *Scharnhorst* he knew that the battleship was coming north. Deciding not to risk an encounter with this ship, Von Spee himself turned north at 10:20 p.m.

On Monday morning, November 2, the day after the battle, the sun was shining, the wind had dropped, the sea was calm, and the ships of the East Asia Squadron, steaming at 10 knots, gently rose and fell in the following swell. In the clear air, the Germans could see the distant coastline of Chile and, more important, far and wide an empty ocean. When Spee ordered a diligent search for the shattered hulk of *Good Hope* or any evidence of her sinking, the observations made by *Leipzig*'s crew finally reached him. Admiral von Spee now knew that he had command of the sea in the southeast Pacific. To acknowledge the victory, he gave his ships the opportunity to close his flagship and cheer him, responding, "With God's help, a glorious victory. I express my thanks and congratulations to the crews." Assessing the damage to his squadron, Spee found that *Scharnhorst* had been hit only twice and that both shells had failed to explode. One British 6-inch shell had hit forward on the starboard side above the armored belt, making a hole three feet square and penetrating to a storeroom—but it did not explode. "The creature just lay there," wrote Spee, "as a kind of greeting." A second shell hit a funnel without doing serious damage. The four shells that struck *Gneisenau* had not seriously harmed her. The three German light cruisers had not been hit. Not a single German officer or seaman had been killed; three men from *Gneisenau* had been slightly wounded. For Spee, the most serious consequence of the battle was that he had expended half of his ammunition. At Coronel, *Scharnhorst* had fired 422 8.2-inch shells and had only 350 left; *Gneisenau* had fired 244 and had 528 left. The ammunition had been well spent; even in the heavy sea, the gunnery of the armored cruisers had been superb. *Scharnhorst,* for example, scored at least thirty-five direct hits on *Good Hope.* But the fact was that there were no more projectiles to feed to the guns, short of Wilhelmshaven or Kiel.

In a private letter written the day after the action, Spee analyzed his victory:

> *Good Hope,* though bigger than *Scharnhorst,* was not so well armed. She mounted heavy guns, but only two, while *Monmouth* succumbed to *Gneisenau* because she had only 6-inch guns. The English have another ship like *Monmouth* hereabouts and in addition, it seems, a battleship of the *Queen* class carrying 12-inch guns. Against the latter we can hardly do anything. Had they kept their force together, we should probably have got the worst of it. You can hardly imagine the joy which reigns among us. We have at least contributed something to the glory of our arms—although it might not mean much on the whole in view of the enormous number of English ships.

At dawn on Tuesday, November 3, *Scharnhorst, Gneisenau,* and *Nürnberg* entered the bay of Valparaíso. As international law prohibited more than three warships of a belligerent nation visiting a neutral port at the same time, *Leipzig* and *Dresden* remained at sea, escorting colliers to Más Afuera. Entering the roadstead in the morning sunshine, the German sailors saw the town spread around the bay, the hills behind, and, in the distance, the high mountains. The harbor was filled with ships, thirty-two of them German merchant vessels driven to seek refuge by the war. News of the victory spread quickly and the large German population of Valparaíso was enthusiastic. The German ambassador to Chile, Dr. Eckart, and the consul general, Dr. Gumprecht, boarded *Scharnhorst,* followed by officers of the German merchant ships, who crowded the decks. Hundreds of men from the merchant ships offered themselves for enrollment in the squadron, even as stokers. One hundred and twenty-seven were accepted.

Many of the squadron's officers went ashore, where they visited German bookstores and cafés and admired the "pretty, black-eyed women." Admiral von Spee did not share in the general enthusiasm. "When I went ashore to call on the local admirals, there were crowds at the landing place," he said. "Cameras clicked and people cheered. The local Germans wanted to celebrate, but I positively refused." Nevertheless, he yielded to Gumprecht's pressure and walked with thirty of his officers to the city's German Club. This solid yellow building was an outpost of dark wood and German respectability whose hallways and paneled dining rooms were hung with full-length portraits of Kaiser William I, Chancellor Otto von Bismarck, and Field Marshal Moltke, the victor of the Franco-Prussian War. Spee and his officers dutifully signed the guest book, then mounted the grand staircase to find themselves confronting a large bust of Kaiser William II, mustache bristling. Under a grand chandelier in the reception hall, the admiral was polite for over an hour until a "drunken, mindless idiot raised a glass and said, 'Damnation to the British Navy!' " Spee gave him a cold stare and declared that neither he nor his officers would drink to such a toast. Instead, he said, "I drink to the memory of a gallant and honorable foe," put down his glass, picked up his cocked hat, and walked to the door. Outside, in the bright sunlight, a woman stepped forward to present him with a bouquet of flowers. "They will do nicely for my grave," he said, refusing them. That night, although the masts and decks of the German warships were brilliantly illuminated as in peacetime, Spee did not sleep. He had no illusions as to what was coming. "I am quite homeless," he confided to an old friend, a retired naval doctor who lived in Valparaíso. "I cannot reach Germany; we possess no other secure harbor; I must plough the seas of the world doing as much mischief as I can until my ammunition is exhausted or a foe far superior in power succeeds in catching me."

—

The British consul at Valparaíso learned of Spee's presence off the Chilean coast on November 2, but he did not know then that a battle had taken place the day before. The consul's telegram reporting the appearance of the German squadron reached London on November 3, whereupon Fisher, now First Sea Lord, urgently prodded his colleagues to improve the precarious position in which he supposed Cradock to be. That evening, the Admiralty finally sent the orders for which Cradock had waited so long: "*Defence* has been ordered to join your flag with all dispatch. *Glasgow* should keep in touch with the enemy. You should keep in touch with *Glasgow* concentrating the rest of your squadron including *Canopus*. It is important that you should effect your junction with *Defence* at earliest possible moment." In light of the Admiralty's previous signals to Cradock and of what now had happened, this message offered grim humor. "All dispatch . . . earliest possible moment"—Montevideo is 4,000 miles by sea from Valparaíso; at a constant speed of 15 knots and allowing for coaling stops, it would have taken the *Defence* two weeks to join Cradock. As Churchill later confessed, "We were already talking to the void."

The first news of the battle arrived at the Admiralty on the morning of November 4, in the form of sparse accounts from German sources. The following day, the Admiralty issued a preliminary public statement, which was published in that evening's newspapers: "The Admiralty have no official confirmation [of the news from Germany]. The Admiralty cannot accept these facts as accurate at the present time for the battleship *Canopus,* which had been specially sent to strengthen Admiral Cradock's squadron and would have given him a decided superiority, is not mentioned in them." The next day, the sixth, the Admiralty amplified its disclosure, saying that reports received by the Foreign Office from Valparaíso "state that a belligerent warship is ashore on the Chilean coast and it is possible that this may prove to be the *Monmouth.* . . . The action appears . . . to have been most gallantly contested, but in the absence of the *Canopus,* the enemy's preponderance of force was considerable." Already, the Admiralty was establishing its line of defense: had the *Canopus* been present, the disaster would not have occurred.

When more complete accounts arrived and were published, the British public was shocked. Some newspapers blamed Cradock: Why, with an obviously inferior force, had he given battle? Where *was Canopus*? Other papers and voices asked why the Admiralty had assigned and permitted Cradock to fight a powerful squadron with an inadequate force. This, overwhelmingly, was the navy's view. "Can you imagine anyone sending such a mixed and unsuitable mob down for the job?" asked *Glasgow*'s gunnery officer. In the navy, the defeat at Coronel was reckoned in terms of human life and diminished naval prestige rather than as a serious strategic blow. The sinking of two obsolete, second-rate cruisers amounted to a tiny reduction of British naval strength, but 1,600 men including the admiral had died; in exchange, three Germans had been wounded. And Coronel came only six weeks after the loss of *Aboukir, Hogue,* and *Cressy.* In the two disasters, 3,000 British sailors had died.

Professionally, the question became not Why was the battle lost? but Why was it fought? Who blundered, the admiral or the Admiralty? Captain William Sims, an Anglophile American naval officer who, when his country entered the war twenty-nine months later, would become the senior U.S. naval officer in Europe, declared that "the British have allowed their . . . old cruisers to be caught in the presence of a much more powerful enemy and have suffered the penalty. They have committed the grave mistake of despising the enemy." Beatty had no doubt as to where responsibility lay: "Poor old Kit Cradock has gone, poor old chap," he wrote to Ethel. "He had a glorious death, but if only it had been in victory instead of defeat. . . . His death and the loss of his ships and the gallant lives in them can be laid to the door of the incompetency of the Admiralty. They have . . . broken over and over again the first principles of strategy."

The worst that could be said of Cradock was that he was impetuous, a trait for which, along with courage, he was well known. Luce of *Glasgow* said, "He had no clear plan or doctrine in his head, but was always inclined to act on the impulse of the moment. . . . Cradock was constitutionally incapable of refusing or even postponing action if there was the smallest chance of success." Beatty, Cradock's friend of many years, added ruefully, "I fear he saw red and did not wait for his proper reinforcement, the *Canopus*." Churchill's explanation to Jellicoe was that Cradock had "let himself be caught or has engaged recklessly with only *Good Hope* and *Monmouth*." This became the official Admiralty version, which Churchill presented to the Cabinet. It was adopted by that body at its November 4 meeting, and Asquith subsequently reported it to the king. Indeed, the condemnation went further: Cradock was declared to have been acting in disobedience of express orders to concentrate his whole squadron including *Canopus* and to run no risk of being caught by a superior force.

The principal exponent of this position was Winston Churchill, who, even after the war, rejected all criticism of his role in the Coronel disaster. "I cannot accept for the Admiralty any share of the responsibility for what followed," the former First Lord declared. "The first rule of war is to concentrate superior strength for decisive action and to avoid division of forces or engaging in detail. . . . With *Canopus*, Admiral Cradock's squadron was safe. *Scharnhorst* and *Gneisenau* would never have ventured to come within range of her four 12-inch guns. To do so would have been to subject themselves to very serious damage without any prospect of success. The old battleship, with her heavy armor and artillery, was in fact a citadel around which all our cruisers in those waters could find absolute security." In the view of the former First Lord, the whole responsibility for what happened at Coronel rested on Cradock, who, he insisted, had been expressly instructed to operate in company with *Canopus*. Churchill bore down hard on this point: "It ought not to be necessary to tell an experienced admiral to keep concentrated and not to be brought to action in circumstances of great disadvantage by superior forces. Still, in telegram after telegram, the importance of not being separated from *Canopus*, especially sent him for his protection, was emphasized." In fact, however, this command was not emphasized—indeed, it was not even mentioned—in the Admiralty's October 28 signal to Cradock, which came in response to the admiral's announcement that he had relegated *Canopus* to convoy duty. Later, Churchill conceded that with *Canopus* holding them back it would have been impossible for Cradock's cruisers to catch the Germans, but he argued that at least the presence of the battleship would have prevented the Germans from catching and killing the British ships. From within the shelter of this floating fortress, Churchill declared, Cradock could have raised the alarm. Then, once the Admiralty had been informed of Spee's whereabouts, "we could instantly concentrate upon them from many quarters." Logical in retrospect, this was neither the substance nor the tenor of the orders sent to Cradock in the weeks preceding Coronel.

Cradock, of course, did not see *Canopus* as a citadel or a place of shelter; he saw her as an incubus. From his point of view, it was not the old battleship's guns that mattered; it was her speed. He had been told that she could make no more than 12 knots. That her engineer commander was deranged and that, aided by a following sea and a gale wind, she made 15 knots in a frantic effort to reach the battle area, are immaterial; Cradock was never to know. What he did know was that if he followed the tactics prescribed by the Admiralty—drawing the Germans south to fight a battle involving *Canopus*—he might well find himself placed in the dreadful position of watching the enemy circle around him and steam unmolested around the Horn. There, naked, lay the main British coaling station in the South Atlantic, the Falkland Islands. Nor was that all. For if Spee, arriving in the South Atlantic, could announce to the world that he had come simply by steaming around a Royal Navy squadron too cowardly to fight, the shame would be unbearable. It would never be forgotten that a Royal Navy squadron had refused battle—or that the officer in command was Christopher Cradock.

Cradock, in short, was not the man to seek "absolute security" in the shelter of a "citadel." He had been told that he had a "sufficient force" to deal with Spee. Because *Canopus* could not keep up, he had informed the Admiralty that he was leaving her behind. Apparently aware of this, the Admiralty had not revoked its order to search and fight. Perhaps if Cradock had received the Admiralty's November 3 telegram in time, he would have understood that his mission had been changed from searching and fighting to shadowing and reporting. In that case, he might have ordered the speedy *Glasgow* to investigate the smoke off the Chilean coast that afternoon while he himself fell back on *Canopus*. And then—perhaps—sheltered beneath the guns of the old battleship, he might have been content merely to signal that Spee's squadron had been located. But this Admiralty telegram was dispatched from London forty-eight hours after the battle and Cradock's death. The admiral knew that afternoon that the odds were against him, but he believed that he had no choice. "The *Defence* had been refused him and he was as good as told that he was skulking at Port Stanley," said a *Glasgow* officer. "What else was there for him to do except go and be sunk? He was a very brave man and they were practically calling him a coward. If we hadn't attacked that night, we might never have seen them again and then the Admiralty would have blamed him for not fighting." This was Cradock's meaning when he wrote to Meux, "I will take care I do not suffer the fate of poor Troubridge."

The tragedy can be blamed, in part, on a failure of clarity in language.

Cradock never put his requirements and apprehensions clearly before a busy War Staff. He was candid when he told the governor before leaving the Falklands that with such a weak force he had no hope of success, but his protests to the Admiralty were in the form of hints rather than declarations. Cradock should have understood that London had failed to comprehend his situation, but admirals of his generation had not been brought up to question orders, particularly if the questions seemed to suggest the admiral's concern for his own personal safety. Cradock had protested as much as a British admiral could.

In defeat, Cradock became a hero. Confronting this new situation, Churchill, ever resourceful with language, found a way simultaneously to honor and praise the hero, deplore his judgment, and shroud Admiralty responsibility. In anticipation of a parliamentary question after the battle, Churchill prepared a statement declaring that Cradock had consciously and bravely sacrificed his squadron in a vain effort to cripple Spee. "We are of the opinion," Churchill wrote, "that feeling he could not bring the enemy immediately to action as long as he kept with *Canopus,* he decided to attack them with his fast ships alone, in the belief that even if he himself were destroyed . . . he would inflict damage on them which . . . would lead to their certain subsequent destruction. . . . Though the Admiralty have no responsibility for this decision, they considered it was inspired by the highest devotion."

This explanation of Cradock's behavior was clothed in further eloquence by Arthur Balfour, the former prime minister and Churchill's successor as First Lord. At the 1916 dedication of the Cradock memorial at York Minster, Balfour asked:

> Why did . . . [Cradock] attack, deliberately, a force which he could not have reasonably hoped either to destroy or put to flight? Remember what the circumstances of the German squadron were. The German admiral in the Pacific was far from any port where he could have refitted. If he therefore suffered damage, even though he inflicted far greater damage than he received, his power might be utterly destroyed. If Admiral Cradock judged that his squadron, that he himself and those under him, were well sacrificed if they destroyed the power of this hostile fleet, then I say that there is no man, sailor or civilian, but would say that such a judgement showed . . . only the highest courage . . . in the interests of his country. If I am right there never was a nobler act. We shall never know the thoughts of Admiral Cradock when it became evident that, outgunned and outranged, success was an impossibility. He must have realized that his hopes were dashed forever. . . . His body is separated from us by half the world and he and his gallant comrades lie far from the pleasant homes of England. Yet they have their reward . . . theirs is an immortal place in the great roll of naval heroes.

When the first volume of *The World Crisis* appeared in 1923, Churchill was severely criticized by many retired officers for acquitting the Admiralty of all blame for Coronel. Churchill responded, attempting to justify himself in the *Morning Post,* but so unconvincing were his arguments that an editorial declared that "by attacking the memory of an heroic martyr to his duty and his orders" the former First Lord cast the blame "upon the principal victim of his own error of judgment. . . . He would have been wiser to have left the reputation of the dead sailor alone."

—

Two British ships were sunk at Coronel, but three escaped. *Canopus* picked up *Glasgow*'s message at 2:00 a.m. on November 2 and immediately reversed course. Heading south for the Magellan Straits, she soon slowed to 9 knots as she exchanged a following sea under her stern for heavy seas over her bow. *Otranto* eluded her enemies by steaming 200 miles west into the Pacific, then turning south and east and rounding Cape Horn. *Glasgow* on the morning after the battle was running south at 20 knots with green water over the forecastle while carpenters worked in the stern to shore up damage. On November 4, three days after the battle, *Glasgow* entered the Magellan Straits and that night, without stopping, passed Punta Arenas. At the eastern end of the Straits, she anchored and awaited *Canopus,* which appeared on the sixth. Then, together, the old battleship and the light cruiser sailed for the Falkland Islands, 300 miles away. For the crew of the damaged *Glasgow,* the sight of the old *Canopus* wallowing behind was reassuring. Not everyone aboard the light cruiser knew that the old battleship twice had signaled, "Not under control."

At dawn on Sunday, November 8, seven days after the battle, the two ships anchored at Port Stanley. At that moment, the outlook for the Falklands, no longer protected by the guns of Cradock's squadron, was bleak. The 200 barren islands, with their rugged, indented coastlines, dozens of remote harbors, and treeless brown moors, made up one of the loneliest outposts of the British empire. The little town of Port Stanley, on the south side of East Falkland, consisted of two streets of houses constructed of timber and corrugated iron. The town's population was a little over a thousand and another thousand farmers and shepherds were scattered through the remainder of the islands, living on the moors or in tiny villages. On this rugged terrain, swept by rain and wind throughout the year, the inhabitants, mostly of Scottish ancestry, raised sheep. During breeding season, millions of penguins, seals, and sea lions congregated on the rocky shores. Despite the economic insignificance of the islands, their defense was crucial to Britain; no other protected harbor and coaling station was available to the British navy in the South Atlantic. As soon as *Canopus* and *Glasgow* arrived, seventy islander volunteers, sheep farmers or fishermen, came out to help with coaling.

From the population, a rifle militia of 300 men had been formed. Women and children had been sent to the hills, valuables were buried, and an earth rampart had been raised around the wireless station. *Glasgow* contributed to the defense by sending ashore a small field gun with ammunition. Then, having taken aboard enough coal to reach the river Plate, the two ships sailed at 6:00 p.m. During the night, however, Grant signaled that *Canopus* was again near breakdown and that he must have five days to repair his engines. In London, Fisher realized that this "citadel" would be useless in a sea battle. He ordered her to return to Port Stanley, where she was to run herself aground on the mud flats at the eastern end of the inner harbor and transform herself into a stationary steel fort to protect the harbor and the town.

Lame old *Canopus* now became an immobile, unsinkable gun platform. From where she lay, behind the low peninsula of rocks and sand that separates Port Stanley from the South Atlantic, she was almost invisible from the sea. To further blend her into the landscape, the crew took down her topmasts and splashed brown and green camouflage paint across her funnels and upper works. A line of crude mines made from empty oil barrels and filled with explosives to be detonated by electric wires from the shore was strung across the entrance to the outer harbor. Seventy Royal Marines from the battleship landed with small artillery pieces and constructed beach defenses at three possible landing sites. A lookout station was established on Sapper Hill, a 400-foot hill two miles south of the village with a sweeping view of the sea to the south and east. On a smaller promontory nearer the harbor, a fire control station was manned by ship's officers. Telephone lines were strung from both of these observation points to the battleship. Thus the Falklands and *Canopus* awaited Admiral von Spee.

Meanwhile on November 11, *Glasgow* reached the river Plate where she found *Defence,* whose crew lined the rails and cheered. On the twelfth, *Glasgow* and *Defence* left the Plate together for Abrolhos Rocks, in accordance with an Admiralty decision to withdraw all British naval forces from the South Atlantic until reinforcements could arrive. On November 14, a sunny warm day, with the nightmare of Coronel two weeks behind them, *Glasgow*'s crew appeared on deck wearing white summer uniforms.

CHAPTER 13

"Very Well, Luce, We'll Sail Tomorrow"

In London at seven o'clock on the morning of November 4, the Admiralty received the first news of the disaster at Coronel. The First Lord reacted immediately, asking the whereabouts of the battle cruisers *Australia* and *Invincible* and the armored cruisers *Defence, Carnarvon, Cornwall,* and *Kent,* and how long it would take each of them to reach Abrolhos Rocks, Rio, and Punta Arenas. An urgent signal was sent to Stoddart: "*Carnarvon, Cornwall* should join *Defence* off Montevideo. *Canopus, Glasgow, Otranto* ordered if possible to join you there. *Kent* will come from Sierra Leone. Enemy will most likely come on to the Rio trade routes. Reinforcements will meet you shortly from England."

Stoddart, whose flagship was *Carnarvon,* now commanded all British warships in the South Atlantic. It was another heterogeneous collection: four armored cruisers of different classes and capabilities, two modern light cruisers (one under repair), the armed merchant cruiser *Macedonia,* and the obsolete battleship *Canopus,* about to be grounded on the Port Stanley mudflats. Stoddart mustered his squadron at Abrolhos Rocks. All the armored cruisers were present by November 17 and, a few days later, *Glasgow,* repaired, came in from Rio.

Four armored cruisers was a considerable force and the inclusion of *Defence,* denied to Cradock, would give Stoddart a fair chance against Admiral von Spee. Stoddart would have two 9.2-inch, fourteen 7.5-inch, twenty-two 6-inch, and ten 4-inch guns against the Germans' sixteen 8.2-inch, twelve 5.9-inch, and thirty-two 4.1-inch guns. The critical question was the range at which Stoddart should engage. Because Spee's sixteen 8.2-inch guns had a longer reach than all but the *Defence*'s two 9.2-inch guns, the British, once again, would have to come closer. There was no doubt that German gunnery would be superior, but the British would have the advantage in speed. The odds, in sum, were roughly even, but after Coronel, the Admiralty did not wish to sponsor a fair fight. From the moment Churchill heard about Cradock's defeat, he wished to send the battle cruiser *Invincible.* "But I found Lord Fisher in a bolder mood," Churchill wrote of the old admiral he had just appointed as First Sea Lord. "He would take two battle cruisers from the Grand Fleet for the South American station." Within six hours of receiving a first report of Coronel, the First Lord and the First Sea Lord signaled Jellicoe at Scapa Flow: "Order *Invincible* and *Inflexible* to fill up with coal at once and proceed to . . . [Devonport] with all dispatch. They are urgently needed for foreign service."

Churchill gave Fisher credit for this bold decision. The hunting down and destruction of enemy armored cruisers was the purpose for which Fisher had designed and built battle cruisers. Combining high speed and big guns, they were his beloved "greyhounds" and the dispatch of two of them to the South Atlantic was meant to ensure not merely Spee's defeat, but his annihilation. "Sir John Jellicoe rose to the occasion and parted with his two battle cruisers without a word," said Churchill—but, in fact, neither Jellicoe nor Beatty was pleased to be giving up two battle cruisers to hunt down two armored cruisers on the far side of the world. Five days later, when Fisher persuaded Churchill to strip away a third battle cruiser, this time *Princess Royal,* one of Beatty's beloved Cats, and send it to the West Indies to guard against Spee coming through the Panama Canal, Jellicoe protested vehemently. It is "important not to weaken the Grand Fleet just now," the Commander-in-Chief wrote to Fisher. "I will of course do the best I can with the force at my disposal, but much is expected of the Grand Fleet if the opportunity arises, and I hope I shall not be held responsible if the force is unequal to the task devolving upon it." The Admiralty attempted to mollify Jellicoe by pointing out that the newest British battle cruiser, *Tiger,* then doing gunnery and torpedo exercises in southern Ireland, was about to join Beatty, and that three new dreadnought battleships, *Benbow, Emperor of India,* and *Queen Elizabeth,* were nearly ready. Jellicoe remained unpacified. The four new ships were not yet part of his fleet, he said, and when they arrived they would be raw. He also grumbled that if a third battle cruiser had to go, Fisher should have taken the older, 12-inch-gun *New Zealand* instead of the 13.5-inch-gun *Princess Royal* because *New Zealand* was adequate to deal with Spee and more economical in her consumption of coal.

To appease the angry sea admirals, Fisher, uncharacteristically apologetic, wrote to Beatty, who had supported Jellicoe's complaint about the taking of *Princess Royal.* "I admit the force of all your arguments," Fisher said. "We have nought else . . . [to meet] the eventuality (not yet improbable) of the '*Scharnhorst* and Co.' coming through the Panama Canal to New York to release the mass of armed German liners ready there to emerge into the Atlantic. Why the *Vaterland* [the 52,000-ton queen of German transatlantic liners, interned in New York with its German crew on board] has not 'nipped out' already is beyond me. . . . As I told Jellicoe, had I known of the *New Zealand* having more coal endurance, I would have taken her. I'm in the position of a chess player coming into a game after some damned bad moves have been made in the opening of the game by a pedantic ass. . . . It's very difficult to retrieve a game badly begun."

The two battle cruisers first assigned, *Invincible* and *Inflexible,* belonged to the first generation of Jacky Fisher's dreadnoughts. Completed in 1908, they weighed 17,250 tons, carried eight 12-inch guns, and could make at least 25 knots. To achieve such heavy armament and high speed within their tonnage, they had sacrificed armor and were no better protected than an armored cruiser. Already, both had participated in the war: *Inflexible* had pursued *Goeben,* and *Invincible* had been with Beatty in the Battle of the Bight. On Thursday morning, November 5, both battle cruisers were moored in Cromarty Firth. That evening, with *Invincible* leading, they steamed out into the North Sea and, at 17 knots, went north and west through Pentland Firth, then south through the Irish Channel. They were off the Eddystone Light at the western end of the Channel at 5:00 a.m. on November 8. A thick fog covered Plymouth Sound and *Invincible* grounded briefly on a sandbar; the tide rose and by 2:00 p.m., she was resting in a dry dock. *Inflexible* followed into a second dry dock. The ships were to have their bottoms cleaned and machinery repaired, and then embark coal, ammunition, and supplies, not only for themselves, but for other ships in the South Atlantic. Nevertheless, as Churchill observed, "Once ships fall into dockyard hands, a hundred needs manifest themselves." Next morning, Admiral Edgerton, the head of the Devonport dockyard, wired the Admiralty: "The earliest possible date of completion of repairs to *Invincible* and *Inflexible* is midnight November 13. Repairs to boilers of *Invincible* cannot be finished before." A hurricane blew through the Admiralty. "Friday the thirteenth! What a day to choose!" Fisher exclaimed. "Shall I give him a prog?" Churchill asked. Fisher wanted more than a prog, and the message to Edgerton, drafted by Churchill, was peremptory: "*Invincible* and *Inflexible* are needed for War Service and are to sail Wednesday, November 11. Dockyard arrangements must be made to conform. You are held responsible for the speedy dispatch of these ships in a thoroughly efficient condition. If necessary dockyard men should be sent away in the ships, to return as opportunity offers."

On Monday, November 9, although the ship was still in dry dock, *Invincible*'s decks were stacked with stores and provisions. That night, the battle cruiser was moved out of dry dock to a coaling jetty. Her crew began coaling just before midnight and continued until 11:30 the next morning with a break for cocoa at 3:00 a.m. and another for breakfast at 7:30. The repairs were never finished; when she sailed, *Invincible* had several dozen workmen still on board.

Meanwhile, the Admiralty had appointed an officer to command the force. It was not to be Rear Admiral Stoddart. Command of two battle cruisers and numerous armored cruisers called for a vice admiral and, as it happened, an officer of this rank was immediately available from the inner circle of the Admiralty itself. The appointment, however, was not conceived in thoughtful discussion, but in rancor and compromise. The rancor was Fisher's; the compromise, Churchill's. On returning to the Admiralty as First Sea Lord, Fisher had brought with him a fierce resentment against the Chief of Staff, Vice Admiral Sir Frederick Doveton Sturdee. This feeling stemmed from an old feud. Ten years before, during his first appointment as First Sea Lord, Fisher had assigned Sturdee as Chief of Staff to Lord Charles Beresford, then Commander-in-Chief of the Mediterranean Fleet. According to Sturdee, before he took up his post, Fisher asked him "to keep an eye on Charlie as he was inclined to be rather rash and rather wild on Service matters. He asked me to write to him privately about my chief. This request I never complied with. Such a disloyal act was so obvious it did not require a second thought." Subsequently, during the long, bitter vendetta waged by Beresford against Fisher that resulted in both resigning in 1910, Sturdee sided with Beresford. Fisher, with all the power of his volcanic personality, detested Sturdee. When news of Coronel reached Whitehall, and Fisher persuaded Churchill to send out two battle cruisers, the new First Sea Lord walked into Sturdee's room to give him this information. Sturdee could not restrain himself from pointing out that he himself had suggested just such a move before Coronel but had been overruled. Fisher, believing that his initiative was being challenged, flushed and left the room. He went straight to Churchill to announce that he would not tolerate "that damned fool at the Admiralty for one day longer."

Frederick Doveton Sturdee, then fifty-five, was a short, bulldog-shaped man with a Roman nose, a heavy lower jaw, and flourishing eyebrows. He had entered the navy at twelve, specialized in gunnery and torpedoes, and developed a reputation as a tactician. After serving under Beresford in the Mediterranean and Channel Fleets, he was promoted to rear admiral in 1910 and knighted in 1913. Appointed to the Admiralty in May 1914, he quickly made himself disliked. It was said that he was rigid, pedantic, conceited, and surly. Wanting to do everything himself, he refused to listen to advice from subordinates. When his dispositions of the fleet were criticized, he became obstinate; even after the loss of the three *Bacchante*s, Sturdee continued to press for regular cruiser patrols on the Broad Fourteens. Opinions about him split along old fault lines: Beresford described him as "one of the most brilliant, if not the most brilliant, officer of my acquaintance"; Fisher called him a "pedantic ass . . . is, has been, and always will be." Fisher blamed Sturdee for the assignment of ships and squadrons in the weeks preceding Coronel: "Never such utter rot as perpetrated by Sturdee in his world-wide dispersal of weak units! Strong nowhere, weak everywhere!"

Nevertheless, Churchill trusted Sturdee. Fisher's anger had to be assuaged, but the First Lord refused to make the Chief of Staff the scapegoat for Coronel. Suddenly, a solution presented itself: two battle cruisers were about to leave England on an important mission; a commander for this force was needed; Sturdee could be removed from the Admiralty and Fisher would be pleased. The First Lord summoned Sturdee and told him, "The destruction of the German [Spee's] Squadron is an object of high and immediate importance. I propose to entrust this duty to you." Sturdee immediately accepted, turned over his duties as Chief of Staff to Rear Admiral Sir Henry Oliver, and departed by train for Devonport. On Wednesday the eleventh, Sturdee boarded *Invincible* and hoisted his vice admiral's flag. By midmorning, the captains of both battle cruisers reported their ships ready for sea. "Very well," Sturdee said laconically, "we sail at four p.m." At noon, Lady Sturdee and their daughter came aboard for a farewell meal. Sturdee brought with him the new title of Commander-in-Chief, South Atlantic and Pacific. "Your main and most important duty," his orders read, "is to search for the German armored cruisers . . . and bring them to action. All other considerations are to be subordinate to this end." All British ships and naval officers, including Stoddart, in all the oceans where von Spee might appear, were placed under Sturdee's command.

—

The battle cruisers steamed west and south, through the Bay of Biscay, around the tip of Spain, past Portugal, past Madeira with sunrise lighting its 6,000-foot peak. Daily, the weather grew warmer and the sea shaded to deeper blues. The sea routine of the naval service set in: the officers breakfasted on porridge, fish patties, eggs, and bacon, lunched on bread, butter, jam, and cakes, and for dinner had soup, salt beef, macaroni, cheese, dessert, and coffee. Tea at 4:00 p.m. was followed by officers' deck hockey. On Sunday mornings, the captains inspected their ships at 10:00 and church services on deck followed at 11:00. Once the weather was warm, a swimming pool was rigged by stretching a canvas between the two forward 12-inch guns; the officers used it between seven and eight a.m.; the men in the evening. On November 17, officers and men changed from their winter blue uniforms into summer white. On deck in bright sunshine, they watched groups of flying fish, like "small flocks of birds," breaking the surface, flying, plunging, reappearing, soaring.

Six days out from England, the battle cruisers anchored in the wide, semicircular bay of Porto Grande on St. Vincent, one of the Portuguese Cape Verde Islands, off the coast of Africa. As they approached, the British sailors saw an 8,000-foot volcanic mountain, its peak wreathed in clouds, rising straight from the sea. The harbor itself was crowded with ships, including eight German steamers sheltering in the neutral port. As soon as their anchors splashed, the battle cruisers were surrounded by brightly colored boats with green oranges, bananas, and coral necklaces for sale. Colliers came alongside, and coaling continued through the night. A tragedy marred this procedure. In the middle of the night, a sixteen-year-old boy attending a cable motor on board *Invincible* dropped off to sleep. His hand, resting on the rolling cable, was caught and the boy was dragged completely around the cable drum. He died instantly. The following day, *Invincible,* under way, halted in mid-ocean and the boy was buried at sea.

Sturdee proceeded south at a constant, economical 10 knots, his speed, like Spee's in the Pacific, dictated by coal. His ships' appetites were huge and the distances immense: 2,500 miles from Devonport to the Cape Verde Islands; 2,300 miles from Cape Verde to the Abrolhos Rocks; 2,200 from the Abrolhos Rocks to the Falklands. The admiral wanted his approach unknown. His ships maintained radio silence and although it took Sturdee twenty-six days to travel from Devonport to the Falklands, the information that he was coming never reached Spee. This was less a success of British security than a failure of German intelligence. At Devonport, it was widely known that the two battle cruisers were off to deal with Spee. News of the voyage also became known in Rio and Montevideo, thanks to talkative radio operators, German and British, at Cape Verde. On November 17 at a club in Rio, Lieutenant Hirst of *Glasgow* overheard two Englishmen discussing the imminent arrival of the two battle cruisers. The Germans had a good cable connection with Chile, but when they did learn about Sturdee's coming, either it was too late to reach Spee by wireless at sea or they simply did not realize the urgent nature of the news.

At dawn on November 26, Sturdee reached Abrolhos to find Stoddart's cruiser squadron and nine colliers riding at anchor. Soon, the sea was filled with small boats going from ship to ship. *Invincible* had brought fifty-four bags of mail from England and *Inflexible* distributed a month's provisions—including beer, which Stoddart's men had not tasted for weeks. Then, under a merciless sun, in temperatures of 100 degrees, the battle cruisers coaled. The armored cruiser *Defence,* no longer needed to confront Spee, was dispatched to bolster the squadron at Capetown. At a conference of captains on the morning of November 27, Sturdee declared that Spee could not reach the river Plate before he did and that even if the Germans came into the South Atlantic, they probably would steam slowly up the middle of the ocean. He admitted that Spee might attack the Falklands, and arrangements were made for Port Stanley to send a daily wireless signal so that silence could be interpreted as the loss of that colony. Sturdee's plan was that if he arrived at the Falklands before Spee came around the Horn, he would use the islands as a coaling base and then set his fast light cruisers, *Glasgow* and *Bristol,* to ferreting the harbors in Tierra del Fuego and the fjords of the Chilean archipelago. Once the prey was located, the battle cruisers were to come at high speed. The squadron, he announced, would sail from Abrolhos on the twenty-ninth. Captain Luce of *Glasgow* was surprised to hear that Sturdee intended to remain at Abrolhos for another two days. Luce, who had been at the Falklands and was aware of the deep anxiety of the inhabitants, felt that this was unjustifiable; in addition, the tactical urgency of Sturdee reaching the Falklands before Spee seemed obvious. "In some trepidation," he wrote later, he went back to the flagship after the conference. "I hope you don't mind me coming over, sir," he said to Sturdee, "and please don't imagine I am questioning your orders, but thinking it over, I do feel we should sail as soon as possible."

"But, dammit, Luce," Sturdee replied, "we're sailing the day after tomorrow. Isn't that good enough for you?" Luce persisted and Sturdee relented: "Very well, Luce, we'll sail tomorrow."

At 10:00 on the morning of November 28, Sturdee led his force to sea. Sweeping south in bright sunshine, the ships spread in a fanlike search pattern, each ship at the maximum distance—twelve miles in good weather—that permitted visual communication by signal light. Two days later, with the sea still calm and visibility excellent, Sturdee ordered firing practice. *Carnarvon* towed a target for *Kent,* which fired 144 rounds of 6-inch ammunition; then *Kent* towed for *Carnarvon.* The battle cruisers fired their 12-inch guns at 12,000 yards, the range at which Sturdee intended to engage. *Invincible* fired thirty-two shells, four from each gun, at a target towed by *Inflexible.* Only one hit was obtained, but the near misses were declared satisfactory. *Inflexible* then fired thirty-two rounds at an *Invincible* target and scored three hits. While *Invincible* was hauling in her target, the wire cable wrapped itself around the starboard outboard propeller. Sturdee halted the entire squadron for twelve hours in mid-ocean while divers went down and attempted to clear the fouled propeller. They failed, but to avoid wasting more time, the squadron got under way with *Invincible* steaming on only three propellers.

As the ships steamed farther south, the air grew colder, the sea changed from deep blue to green and gray, and the swells were flecked with whitecaps. Spouting whales and an albatross were seen and the crews changed from summer white uniforms back into winter blue. The Falkland Islands first appeared through rain squalls at around 9:00 on Monday morning, December 7. Twenty-seven days and 7,000 miles after leaving England, the battle cruisers passed the Cape Pembroke lighthouse, marking the entrance to Port Stanley harbor, and carefully made their way through the string of improvised mines strung across the harbor mouth. Along the shore on each side as they glided into the anchorage, the crews saw seals and penguin rookeries. Port Stanley harbor is divided by a narrow channel into two bays: Port William, the outer, deeper anchorage, and Port Stanley, the inner harbor and site of the small settlement. In Port William, the two battle cruisers and the armored cruisers dropped anchor. *Bristol* and *Glasgow,* being of shallower draft, proceeded through the narrow channel into the inner harbor, where the little settlement spread itself along the shore. Five minutes after anchoring, divers went down to clear the tightly wound cable from *Invincible*'s propeller. Before morning, the propeller was free. The squadron needed coal, but because only two colliers were available, the warships had to take turns. *Cornwall* was given permission to put out fires in order to clean her boilers and *Bristol* was allowed to dismantle an engine for repair. The armed merchant cruiser *Macedonia* was assigned to patrol the harbor entrance and the armored cruiser *Kent,* keeping steam up inside the anchorage, was instructed to relieve *Macedonia* at 8:00 the following morning.

Then Sturdee summoned his captains on board *Invincible.* There were reports of German colliers at Dawson Island in Tierra del Fuego, which suggested that Spee might soon be coming around Cape Horn. Sturdee, wishing to get around the Horn before the Germans, declared that the British squadron would remain at the Falklands for only forty-eight hours; they would sail, he said, on Wednesday, the ninth. Meanwhile that day, the officers of *Invincible* and *Inflexible* were to have five hours' shore leave; the officers of the armored and light cruisers would have their turn the following day. Proceeding ashore in their ships' boats, the battle cruiser officers saw *Canopus* dressed in her strange colors, sitting on her mudbank. They were welcomed at the small town pier by the rector of Christ Church, who invited them to afternoon tea. Returning to their ships at six o'clock, they looked at the barren hills to the west and bundled their coats tighter against the cold wind coming up from Antarctica.

—

After his victory, Admiral von Spee remained in Valparaíso harbor for less than the twenty-four hours permitted and sailed on November 4. A day and a half later, he was back at Más Afuera, 400 miles out in the Pacific. *Leipzig* was already there, small against the towering cliff, and had brought with her a prize, a French four-masted bark loaded with 3,600 tons of Cardiff coal. The vessel and her cargo were both welcome; the coal was stowed and the bark's canvas sails were cut up and resewn into 300 useful coal sacks.

For nine days, the East Asia Squadron remained in the shadow of the cliff. There, the German sailors learned that Tsingtao had fallen and that *Emden*'s voyage had come to an end. *Leipzig* and *Dresden* took their turn going into Valparaíso for receiving and sending messages, while aboard the anchored *Scharnhorst,* Spee considered his next move. Oddly, he seemed in no hurry. He must have known that Britain would react aggressively to Cradock's defeat and that it was to his advantage to reach the South Atlantic before the

Admiralty in London could send out reinforcements. Still, he dawdled. Why? Spee's lethargy had several possible causes. Undoubtedly, he was fatigued; six months of relentless daily responsibility during a 15,000-mile voyage across the Pacific, climaxing in a violent naval battle, were sufficient reason for that. But there was more than weariness in Spee's procrastination. He was an aggressive, skilled commander in battle, but when he considered the strength of his squadron in opposition to the overwhelming, worldwide power of the British navy, he tended to gloom and fatalism. Imbued since youth with respect for the Royal Navy, he felt that whatever he did, in whatever direction he went, it scarcely mattered; his small squadron inevitably must encounter the avenging power of his enemies. These forebodings explain his advice to his admirer in Valparaíso that she keep her flowers for his grave.

Spee also faced a number of practical difficulties. Cradock had inflicted little material damage on the German ships, but he had significantly weakened their fighting power by depleting their magazines. Another battle in the Southern Ocean would empty the magazines and leave the armored cruisers impotent in any attempt to break through the British North Sea blockade. As always, Spee worried about coal, and this consideration led him to reaffirm at Más Afuera the decision he had made at Pagan Island: he ruled against commerce raiding, which still appealed to the captains of his light cruisers. The squadron, he declared, would remain together.

The East Asia Squadron left Más Afuera on November 15, headed for the tip of South America and the South Atlantic. Four days later, the ships entered the Gulf of Penas on the coast of Chile, 300 miles north of the Straits of Magellan, and anchored in Bahía San Quintín, beneath the peaks of the Cordilleras, crowned in that region by Cerro San Valentín, 13,000 feet high and capped with snow. Not far away, two glaciers, the San Rafael and the San Quintín, reach down to the water. From their decks, the German seamen stared at the sunlight shining on the mountain peaks, the glowing, prismatic colors of the glacier ice, and the luxuriant green virgin forests along the water's edge. Boats launched in water still as glass made their way back and forth between floating pieces of blue-green ice broken off from the glacier.

Surrounded by the natural silence of this uninhabited place, the German ships coaled again and the admiral conducted a ceremony. The kaiser, exultant, had signaled that he was personally awarding Spee the Iron Cross, First Class and the Iron Cross, Second Class. In addition, the admiral was ordered to select from among his officers and men 300 others to receive the Iron Cross, Second Class. Spee chose his captains, gunnery officers, engineer officers, wireless officers, chief engineers, and his own staff; the rest of the awards were left to the individual ship captains to parcel out. The admiral went from ship to ship, naming and congratulating the recipients (although the medals themselves waited in Germany for the squadron's return) and outbursts of cheering echoed through the low mists hanging over the water.

In Bahía San Quintín, Spee received a message from Berlin, written before the Battle of Coronel and brought to him from Valparaíso by *Dresden* and *Leipzig*. In most respects, the signal, containing general Naval Staff guidelines, conformed to Spee's own thinking and decisions:

> 1. Little result can be expected from war against commerce in the Pacific. In the Atlantic, in view of the strict watch kept by the enemy on the principal trade routes, commerce raiding is possible only with ships operating in groups [large enough to] have nothing to fear from enemy naval forces.
>
> 2. On the other hand, the coal supply for ships operating in groups will become more difficult because, owing to British pressure, neutral states continually extend their prohibitions on exports. Even supplies . . . [from] New York can hardly be counted upon. Coal taken from captured ships will hardly suffice for cruisers operating in groups.
>
> 3. [Therefore], it is left to your discretion to break off cruiser warfare against trade as soon as you think it advisable and to attempt to break through to Germany with all the ships you can concentrate.
>
> 4. You may succeed if your careful preparations are accompanied by good luck. One of the conditions necessary for success is to take in enough coal in South America to reach the Canaries or at any rate the Cape Verde islands. . . . It may be necessary to secure the cooperation of the High Seas Fleet in breaking through the enemy blockade in the North Sea; therefore, your intentions should be communicated early. . . .
>
> 7. Relations with Argentina and Brazil are not friendly. Portugal is hesitating about joining our enemies. . . . Spain is neutral. . . . If Portugal declares war against us, it might be possible to take coal by force from the Portuguese islands of Cape Verde, the Azores, and Madeira.

This memorandum provided no recent intelligence or orders, but it made clear that the Naval Staff agreed that using the cruiser squadron to attack Allied trade would be unwise. Admiral von Tirpitz had strongly advocated that Spee drop everything else and attempt to break through for home. When Spee's telegram announcing the Coronel victory arrived, Tirpitz had "proposed to put him [von Spee] free . . . to run up the center of the Atlantic. . . . The ammunition left after the heavy expenditure of the engagement seemed to me insufficient for a second battle. I therefore proposed that we should place von Spee, with whom we could communicate via Valparaiso, at liberty to avoid the east coast of South America, making the northward voyage in the middle of the Atlantic or nearer the African coast. . . . [We should] tell Spee that we did not expect any further active operations from him and that . . . his task was now to make his way home . . . through the vast tracts of the Atlantic. . . . The prestige of Coronel would have been established." Tirpitz, however, did not have operational command of the navy. And Admiral Hugo von Pohl, the Chief of the Naval Staff, was unwilling "to encroach in any way on the freedom of action of the Count [von Spee]." Tirpitz could not overrule Pohl and the order to sail directly home was never sent. A message from Pohl, sent after Coronel, reached Valparaíso on November 16, and also was passed to Spee by *Leipzig:* "What are your intentions? How much ammunition do you have?" Spee replied that the two armored cruisers had about half their ammunition and the light cruisers rather more. As to his intentions, Spee replied: "The cruiser squadron intends to break through for home."

Coal, as always, remained the determinant. Spee had promises, estimates, and advice, none of which he could burn in his furnaces. Besides, the promises were blurred: the Naval Staff had said that 40,000 tons of coal could be delivered from New York by neutral steamers already chartered; then, in the same message, he was told that these supplies could not be counted upon. Fourteen thousand tons awaited Spee in the Canary Islands—unless Portugal became a belligerent on the Allied side. Before going into Bahía San Quintín, Spee himself had sent messages to Montevideo and New York, asking that steamers—"German if possible"—meet him at Puerto Santa Elena on the South Atlantic coast of Argentina with 10,000 tons of coal. Meanwhile, in Bahía San Quintín, his ships, preparing to sail, were gorging themselves on coal, cramming their bunkers and then piling more on the decks.

Spee had also to consider the deployment of the British navy. He now knew that both *Monmouth* and *Good Hope* had been destroyed and that *Glasgow* had escaped. He had been told that the armored cruisers *Defence, Cornwall,* and *Carnarvon* were in the river Plate; the whereabouts of *Canopus*—the "*Queen*-class battleship"—were unknown. From a collier, joining him from Punta Arenas, he learned that on November 15 a British steamship had arrived in Punta Arenas from Port Stanley and reported that there were no British warships in the Falkland Islands; obviously, the steamer had departed Port Stanley before *Canopus* returned on November 12. Later, German agents at Rio learned that *Canopus* was present at Port Stanley. This information reached Montevideo on November 20, but by then both Montevideo and Valparaíso were out of wireless touch with the German squadron. Spee therefore believed that the Falklands were undefended and that the thousand-mile stretch of ocean from Tierra del Fuego north to the river Plate was empty.

The East Asia Squadron put to sea from the Gulf of Penas on the afternoon of November 26. Steaming out into the ocean, the ships were caught up in a heavy southwest swell. The wind rose steadily and by late evening the sea was piling up in large rollers with spray driving off the crests. At first, the size and power of the armored cruisers kept them riding over the waves, but the smaller ships, top-heavy with coal on deck, rose, swayed, and plunged. Then, with the wind rising higher, the bows of *Scharnhorst* and *Gneisenau* lifted toward the crests of the waves, breached them, and sent tons of water thundering and foaming down on the decks before running out the scuppers. As the day wore on, the smaller ships were practically submerged in the mountainous seas.

The worst day of the passage was November 29, off the western entrance to the Magellan Straits. Between peaks and valleys of water, *Gneisenau* and *Scharnhorst* often disappeared from each other's view. Rope lines were stretched for safety on decks and even in the officers' wardrooms. Worried about the safety of their ships, the captains of *Leipzig* and *Dresden* ordered their crews to jettison their deck cargos of coal. "The seas were huge," said a *Leipzig* officer, "at one minute level with the deck, next forty feet below you. . . . We sheered out of line. Heavy seas had shifted the deck cargo . . . [and the] scuppers were stopped with coal, so that with three feet of water on deck and we were in danger of capsizing. We turned up into the wind to have our bows into the sea . . . while all hands turned out to shovel coal overboard. Men were standing waist deep in icy water."

By the following morning, the wind had dropped, and although rain and hail still pelted the ships, squadron speed was raised to 10 knots. At noon on December 1, the German sailors saw Cape Horn, the southern extremity of the American continent. "Rain clouds hung over the jagged peak rising sheer out of the water, the rock which mounts guard between the Atlantic and Pacific Oceans," said a *Gneisenau* officer. The next day, an iceberg, 200 feet high and 650 yards long, pale blue in the sunlight, was sighted. East of the Horn, the squadron encountered and seized a three-masted English sailing ship carrying 2,800 tons of Cardiff coal. The next morning, prize in hand, they reached sheltered waters at the eastern end of the Beagle Channel and anchored off Picton Island. The *Dresden,* short of coal, had informed the admiral that she now had too little to make Santa Elena on the Argentine coast. With prospects for fuel in the South Atlantic uncertain, Spee decided to take the time to parcel out the newly acquired English coal. While the men were coaling, parties of officers landed on the desolate shore beneath the black mountains of Tierra del Fuego to shoot ducks and bring back branches with red berries to decorate their cabins for Christmas. Spee visited *Gneisenau* to see his son Heinrich and to play bridge with Maerker. Another three days went by. And still, Spee displayed no sense of urgency.

On the morning of December 6, the admiral summoned his captains on board *Scharnhorst* and proposed an attack on the Falkland Islands, which he believed were undefended. He wished to destroy the wireless station at Port Stanley, the key to British communications in the South Atlantic, to burn any stocks of coal (his bunkers were full), and to capture the British governor in reprisal for the British seizure of the German governor of Samoa. At this meeting, only two officers—his Chief of Staff and Captain Schönberg of *Nürnberg*—favored this plan; the other captains wished to avoid the Falklands and proceed directly north to attack Allied trade in the estuary of the river Plate. Consultation is one thing, command another, and Spee, finding the image of a defenseless Port Stanley too great a temptation, overruled the majority. As a precaution, he decided that only *Gneisenau* and *Nürnberg* would carry out the attack; the rest of the squadron would wait over the horizon. He instructed Captain Maerker to draw up an operational plan.

Maerker's plan was this: once detached from the squadron, *Gneisenau* and *Nürnberg* would proceed at 14 knots to a point five miles east of the Cape Pembroke lighthouse, arriving by 8:30 a.m. From this point, they would look into the harbor and, if it was clear of enemy ships, *Gneisenau* would move to the entrance to Port William and lower boats, which would sweep the entrance clear of mines. Then *Nürnberg* would steam all the way into the inner Port Stanley harbor while *Gneisenau* would follow as far as the channel connecting Port William with Port Stanley. There, the big armored cruiser would anchor and send landing parties in armed cutters to the town. Covered by the 4.1-inch guns of *Nürnberg,* they would destroy the wireless station and the coal stocks and try to bring the governor back to the ship. When their work was done, the two ships would leave the harbor and rejoin the squadron not later than 7:30 p.m.

The meeting ended at noon and the captains returned to their ships. That afternoon in clear weather, the East Asia Squadron steamed eastward along the south coast of Tierra del Fuego. The next day, Monday, December 7, Admiral von Spee and his ships turned northeast toward the Falkland Islands.

CHAPTER 14

The Battle of the Falkland Islands

The night was clear and the visibility exceptional even at two in the morning when officers on *Scharnhorst*'s bridge first made out the dark masses of the Falkland Islands on the northern horizon. The early summer dawn three hours later promised a rare, cloudless day, the first in weeks. At 5:30 a.m., Admiral von Spee signaled *Gneisenau* and *Nürnberg* to leave the squadron and proceed to reconnoiter Port Stanley. The admiral, with *Scharnhorst, Dresden,* and *Leipzig,* would remain to the south, while his three colliers waited off Port Pleasant, a bay twenty miles southwest of Port Stanley. As the sun came up, Captain Maerker and Commander Hans Pochhammer of *Gneisenau* got a better look at the coast, whose capes, bays, and hills they identified with the aid of compass, binoculars, and maps. On deck, a landing party was assembling; Pochhammer looked down from the bridge at the men in white gaiters carrying rifles, one oddly bringing his gas mask. As promised, the summer morning was near perfect: the sea was calm, with only a slight breeze from the northwest gently rippling the surface; the sky was high, clear, and azure. Port Stanley was hidden from the south by a range of low hills, but by seven o'clock, as they came closer, Maerker and Pochhammer could see their first target, the radio mast on Hooker's Point. They also noticed, near the place where the Cape Pembroke lighthouse stood at the tip of a sandy, rock-strewn peninsula, a thin column of smoke. It appeared to rise from the funnel of a ship.

The British squadron began to coal early that summer morning. By 4:30 a.m., the collier *Trelawny* was secured to the port side of *Invincible* and at 5:30 a.m. all hands had been summoned to begin coaling. By two hours later, when the crew was piped to breakfast, 400 tons had been taken aboard. Coaling never resumed that day. Just after 7:30 a.m., a civilian lookout in the observation post on Sapper Hill saw two columns of smoke on the southwestern horizon. He raised his telescope, then picked up his telephone and reported to *Canopus:* "A four-funnel and a two-funnel man of war in sight steering northwards." (*Nürnberg* had three funnels, but because of the angle of the approaching ship, the spotter missed one.)

At 7:45 a.m., *Canopus* received the Sapper Hill message. Because there was no land line between the grounded *Canopus* and Sturdee's flagship in the outer harbor, Captain Grant could not pass along the message by telephone. And because *Invincible* was out of sight, hidden from him by intervening hills, he could not signal visually. *Glasgow,* however, was anchored in a place from which she could see both *Canopus* and *Invincible.* Accordingly, *Canopus* hoisted the signal "Enemy in sight." *Glasgow* saw it and, at 7:56 a.m., Luce raised the same flags on his own mast. There was no response from *Invincible,* busy coaling and surrounded by a haze of coal dust. Impatiently, Luce, still in his pajamas, snapped at his signal officer, "Well, for God's sake, do something. Fire a gun, send a boat, don't stand there like a stuffed dummy." The firing of a saluting gun and its report echoing through the harbor attracted attention. By training a powerful searchlight on *Invincible*'s bridge, *Glasgow* passed the message. Meanwhile, Luce said to his intelligence officer, " 'Mr. Hirst, go to the masthead and identify those ships.' Halfway up," Hirst said, "I was able to report, '*Scharnhorst* or *Gneisenau* with a light cruiser.' "

Spee had achieved complete surprise. Sturdee, not imagining the possibility of any threat to his squadron, had made minimal arrangements for its security. The armed merchant cruiser *Macedonia* was slowly patrolling outside the mouth of the harbor. The armored cruiser *Kent,* assigned to relieve *Macedonia* and the only warship that could get up full steam at less than two hours' notice, was anchored in Port William. *Invincible, Inflexible, Carnarvon,* and *Cornwall* also were anchored in Port William; *Bristol* and *Glasgow* were in the inner harbor where *Canopus* was grounded. By eight o'clock, only *Carnarvon* and *Glasgow* had completed coaling and *Carnarvon*'s decks still were stacked with sacks of coal. *Kent, Cornwall, Bristol,* and *Macedonia* had not yet begun to replenish their bunkers; they would fight that day with what remained from Abrolhos. *Bristol* had closed down her fires for boiler cleaning and opened up both engines for repairs, and *Cornwall* had one engine under repair. In *Cornwall*'s wardroom, her officers, many already in civilian clothes, were breakfasting on kippers, marmalade, toast, and tea and making plans for a day of shooting hares and partridges on the moors behind the town.

The sound of *Glasgow*'s gun found Admiral Sturdee in the act of shaving. An officer raced to the admiral's quarters, burst in, and announced that the Germans had arrived. Later, Sturdee was reported to have replied, "Send the men to breakfast." After the war, Sturdee gave his own version of the moment: "He [Spee] came at a very convenient hour because I had just finished dressing and was able to give orders to raise steam at full speed and go down to a good breakfast." It was said of Sturdee that "no man ever saw him rattled." Nevertheless, while the admiral may have been pleased by the luck that had brought the enemy so obligingly to his doorstep, he may also have wondered whether perhaps the greater luck was on Spee's side. The situation of the British squadron was awkward; *Kent* was the only warship ready to fight. It was possible that Spee might boldly approach Port Stanley harbor with his entire squadron and unleash a storm of 8.2-inch shells into the crowd of ships at anchor. In the confined space of the harbor, some British ships would mask the fire of others and Sturdee would be unable to bring more than a fraction of his superior armament to bear. Accurate salvos from *Scharnhorst* and *Gneisenau* might damage, even cripple, the battle cruisers. Even once the British ships raised steam, Spee still might stand off the harbor entrance and subject each vessel to a hail of shells or a volley of torpedoes as it emerged. With these apprehensions in every mind, all eyes were on the flagship to learn what steps Sturdee intended to take.

At 8:10, signal flags soared up *Invincible*'s halyards. *Kent,* the duty guard ship, was ordered to weigh anchor immediately and proceed out through the mine barrier to protect *Macedonia* and keep the enemy under observation. The battle cruisers were told to cast off their colliers so as to leave themselves freer to fire even while they were still at anchor. All ships were ordered to raise steam and report when they were ready to proceed at 12 knots. *Carnarvon* was to clear for action, to sail as soon as possible, and to "engage the enemy as they come around the corner" of Cape Pembroke. *Canopus* was to open fire as soon as *Gneisenau* and *Nürnberg* were within range. *Macedonia,* unfit for battle against warships, was ordered to return to harbor. Having issued his orders, Sturdee went to breakfast.

At 8:20 a.m., the observation station on Sapper Hill reported more smoke on the southwestern horizon. At 8:47, *Canopus*'s fire control station reported that the first two ships observed were now only eight miles off and that the new smoke appeared to be coming from three additional ships about twenty miles off. Meanwhile, bugles on all the ships in the harbor were sounding "Action," the crews were busy casting off the colliers, smoke was pouring from many funnels, and the anchorage was covered with black haze. The engine room staffs aboard *Cornwall* and *Bristol* hurried to reassemble their dismantled machinery.

Sturdee's breakfast was short. He was on deck at 8:45 a.m. to see *Kent* moving down the harbor to take up station beyond the lighthouse. "As we got near the harbor entrance," said one of *Kent*'s officers, "I could see the smoke from two ships on our starboard over a low-lying ridge of sand." It would be another hour before the battle cruisers and *Carnarvon* could weigh anchor, and still longer before *Cornwall* and *Bristol* were ready.

—

At the Admiralty, few details were known and the worst was feared. At 5:00 p.m. London time, Churchill was working in his room when Admiral Oliver, now Chief of Staff, entered with a message from the governor of the Falkland Islands: "Admiral Spee arrived at daylight this morning with all his ships and is now in action with Admiral Sturdee's whole fleet which was coaling." "These last three words sent a shiver up my spine," said Churchill. "Had we been taken by surprise and, in spite of our superiority, mauled, unready, at anchor? 'Can it mean that?' I said to the Chief of Staff. 'I hope not,' was all he said."

—

"As we approached," said the commander of *Gneisenau,* "signs of life began to appear. Here and there behind the dunes, columns of dark yellow smoke began to ascend . . . as if stores [of coal] were being burned to prevent them falling into our hands. In any case, we had been seen, for among the mastheads which could be distinguished here and there through the smoke, two now broke away and proceeded slowly east towards the lighthouse. . . . There was no longer any doubt that warships were hidden behind the land. . . . We thought we could make out first two, then four, then six ships . . . and we wirelessed this news to *Scharnhorst.*"

The Germans, up to this point, had little premonition of serious danger. Then *Gneisenau*'s gunnery officer, Lieutenant Commander Johann Busche, staring through his binoculars from the spotting top on the foremast, believed that he saw something ominous: tripod masts. When he reported this to the bridge, Captain Maerker curtly dismissed the observation. Tripod masts meant dreadnoughts, Busche was told, and there were no dreadnoughts in the South Atlantic. Maerker continued to take *Gneisenau* and *Nürnberg* closer to their initial bombardment position four miles southwest of Cape Pembroke. He did not bother to pass Busche's report along to Admiral von Spee.

As *Gneisenau* and *Nürnberg* drew closer, the 12-inch guns of *Canopus,* invisible to the German ships, were being elevated and trained on them by guidance from the shore observation post. When Maerker's two ships were near Wolf's Rock, six miles short of Cape Pembroke, they slowed their engines, turned, and glided to the northeast, swinging around to present their port broadsides to the wireless station. But *Canopus,* sitting on her mudbank, spoke first. As soon as her gunnery officer, ashore in the observation post, judged the range to be down to 11,000 yards, he gave the signal. At 9:20 a.m., both 12-inch guns in the battleship's forward turret fired. The reverberating roar shook the town and the harbor and produced shrill cries from circling flocks of seabirds. The shots fell short, but the Germans hoisted their battle flags, turned, and made away to the southeast. As they did so, *Canopus* tried again with another salvo at 12,000 yards. Again the shots were short, but this time by less, and some observers believed that one of the shells ricocheted, sending fragments into the base of a funnel on *Gneisenau.* With the Germans moving out of range, *Canopus* had played her part. She had saved the wireless station, the anchored ships, and the town from bombardment, and had provided Sturdee's squadron with time to leave the harbor. Captain Grant ordered a cease-fire.

—

Captain Maerker had just signaled Spee that *Gneisenau* was about to open fire when he received a shock. Without warning, two gigantic mushrooms of water, each 150 feet high, rose out of the sea a thousand yards to port. This was heavy-caliber gunfire, although the guns themselves could not be seen. Immediately, Maerker hoisted his battle ensigns and turned away, but not before a second salvo spouted up 800 yards short of his ship. Before abandoning his mission, Maerker considered a final attempt to harm the enemy. The first British cruiser coming out of the harbor was recognized as a County-class ship (it was *Kent*) and Maerker, believing that she was trying to escape, increased speed to cut her off outside the entrance to Port William. Scarcely had he settled on a closing course, however, when he received a signal from *Scharnhorst.* This was not the unopposed landing Spee had planned. He had no wish to engage British armored cruisers or old battleships with 12-inch guns and he ordered Maerker to suspend operations and rejoin the flagship: "Do not accept action. Concentrate on course east by south. Proceed at full speed." Spee retreated because, although he now knew that a 12-inch-gun ship or ships were present, he was certain that they were old battleships that his squadron could easily outrun. Maerker turned and made off at high speed toward the flagship twelve miles away.

—

By 9:45 a.m., *Glasgow* had come out of the harbor and joined *Kent.* The light cruiser's captain, John Luce, carrying memories of Coronel, was eager to attack the Germans by himself, but he was ordered to remain out of range, trail the enemy, and keep Admiral Sturdee informed. At 9:50 a.m., the rest of the squadron weighed anchor and proceeded down the harbor. First came *Carnarvon* with Stoddart aboard, then *Inflexible, Invincible,* and *Cornwall;* only *Bristol,* still reassembling her engines, and *Macedonia* were left behind. At 10:30 a.m., as the last of the line of British ships cleared the Cape Pembroke lighthouse, five retreating plumes of smoke could be seen on the southwestern horizon. Three hours had passed since the enemy first came in sight, and Sturdee could be thankful for the fine weather. Had there been fog or mist, he might have had less than half an hour's notice of Spee's arrival.

Instead, the sun was shining from a blue, cloudless sky, and a light northwesterly breeze scarcely ruffled the sea: ideal conditions for a long-range action. Everyone on both sides who survived the battle recalled the extraordinary weather: "The visibility of the fresh, calm atmosphere surpassed everything in the experience of sailors," recalled Pochhammer of *Gneisenau.* "It was a perfect day," wrote an officer on *Inflexible,* "very rare in these latitudes and it was a beautiful sight . . . when the British ships came around the point and all flags (we had five ensigns flying to make sure not all should be shot away) with the sun on them." Aboard *Invincible,* a sublieutenant was "struck by the magnificent weather conditions and, seizing my camera, climbed up the mast into the main top. The air was biting cold as I . . . stood and watched the enemy . . . away to the southwest, five triangles of smoke on the horizon. It was a brilliant sunny day, visibility at its very maximum. And there they were, the squadron that we thought would keep us hunting the seas for many weary months . . . providentially delivered into our hands."

The battle cruisers, their speed climbing to 25 knots, crept inexorably to the head of the line, passing *Carnarvon,* overtaking *Kent,* then alone with only *Glasgow* before them. From the flagship's bridge, Sturdee, watching the smoke from the five fleeing ships, knew that, barring some wholly unforeseen circumstance, Spee was at his mercy. His force was superior; *Invincible* and *Inflexible,* just out of dry dock, could steam at 25 knots; Spee's armored cruisers, after five months at sea, would be fortunate to manage 20. Thus, Sturdee could bring Spee's armored cruisers within range of his 12-inch guns in less than three hours and then would have six hours before sunset to complete their destruction. The weather was beyond his control, but so far there was nothing to indicate any change in the prevailing near perfect conditions. Up *Invincible*'s halyard soared the signal "General Chase."

Lieutenant Hirst of *Glasgow* afterward recalled: "No more glorious moment in the war do I remember than when the flagship hoisted the signal 'General Chase.' . . . Fifteen miles to the eastward lay the same ships which we had fought at Coronel and which had sent brave Admiral Cradock and our comrades to their death." *Glasgow,* out in front and off to the side, had a splendid view of the British battle cruisers as they charged ahead, their bows cleaving the calm, blue sea with white bow waves curling away, their sterns buried under the water boiling in their wakes, their 12-inch-gun turrets training on the enemy with the barrels raised to maximum elevation. Above, on the masts and yards, Royal Navy battle ensigns stood out stiffly, the white color of the flags in stark contrast to the black smoke pouring from the funnels. There was no hurry; the admiral had a clear, empty ocean in front of him. Just as Spee at Coronel had been able to use his advantage of greater speed and heavier guns to destroy Cradock, so Sturdee would be able to use his own greater power and speed to destroy Spee. Each British battle cruiser carried eight 12-inch guns, firing shells weighing 850 pounds. The German armored cruisers carried eight 8.2-inch guns, each firing a shell of 275 pounds. Sturdee could use his speed to set the range; then, keeping his distance, use his big guns to pound Spee to pieces.

According to Commander Pochhammer of *Gneisenau,* it was not until the chase was under way that the Germans were certain of the identity of the two big ships that had emerged from the harbor. "Two vessels soon detached themselves from the number of our pursuers; they seemed much faster and bigger than the others as their smoke was thicker, wider, more massive," Pochhammer said. "All glasses were turned upon their hulls." It was not long before the spacing of the three funnels and the unmistakable tripod masts forced the German seamen to confront "the possibility, even probability, that we were being chased by English battle cruisers . . . this was a very bitter pill for us to swallow. We choked a little . . . the throat contracted and stiffened, for it meant a life and death struggle, or rather a fight ending in honorable death."

Meanwhile, Sturdee calmly set about making his tactical arrangements. He had difficulty seeing the enemy because of the volume of smoke belching from the battle cruisers' funnels, but *Glasgow* reported the Germans twelve miles ahead, making 18 to 20 knots. Knowing that Spee could not escape, Sturdee decided to postpone an immediate engagement. He ordered *Inflexible* to haul out on *Invincible*'s starboard quarter, stationed *Glasgow* three miles ahead of *Invincible* on the port bow, and instructed *Kent* to drop back to his port beam. Soon, with the battle cruisers and *Glasgow* making 25 knots, he found that he was leaving his own armored cruisers behind. At eleven o'clock, the admiral signaled *Carnarvon* and *Cornwall,* five miles behind the battle cruisers, asking what their maximum speed was. *Carnarvon* replied 20 knots (actually, it was 18) and *Cornwall* 22. Not wanting his squadron scattered too widely, Sturdee reduced the speed of the battle cruisers from 25 to 24 knots and then to 20 knots to allow the squadron to come closer. These changes, in effect, nullified the signal for General Chase. Nevertheless, so confident of the day's outcome was Sturdee that, at 11:32 a.m., he signaled, "Ships' companies have time for next meal." Men who had begun the day shifting sacks of coal and were covered with grime now had an opportunity to wash and change clothes. "Picnic lunch in the wardroom," wrote one of *Invincible*'s officers. "Tongue, bread, butter, and jam." No one remained below, however, and soon the upper decks were lined with officers and men, sandwiches in hand, watching the five German ships on the horizon.*

*Meanwhile, around 11:00 a.m., just as the British light cruiser *Bristol* came out of the harbor, the signal station on Mount Pleasant reported sighting three new ships—"transports or colliers"—about thirty miles to the south. There had been unfounded rumors that German

Aboard the German ships, the mood was somber. "Towards noon, the two battle cruisers . . . were about 18,500 yards away. Four other cruisers were observed," said Pochhammer. "We took our meal at the usual time, eleven forty-five, but it passed off more quietly than usual, everybody being absorbed in his own thoughts." As the meal finished, the thunder of heavy guns sounded across the water. "Drums and bugles summoned us to our battle stations. A brief handshake here and there, a farewell between particularly close friends, and the mess room emptied." Soon after noon, Sturdee became impatient. It was evident that Stoddart's flagship, *Carnarvon,* still six miles astern and unable to force more than 18 knots out of her engines, could not catch up. As *Cornwall* could manage 22, she was ordered to leave *Carnarvon* and come on ahead. Even this seemed too slow and Sturdee decided to begin his attack with the two battle cruisers. At 12:20 p.m., Captain Richard Phillimore came aft on *Inflexible* and told his men that the admiral had decided "to get along with the work." The crew cheered and the battle cruisers again moved up to 25 knots.

Admiral von Spee, less than ten miles ahead, was heading southeast at 20 knots. *Gneisenau* and *Nürnberg* were 2,000 yards ahead of *Scharnhorst, Dresden* was on the flagship's port beam, and *Leipzig* lagged behind. Gradually, this speed increased to 21 knots, except for *Leipzig,* which continued to fall behind. By 12:47 p.m., Sturdee had closed the range to *Leipzig* to 17,500 yards, and he hoisted the signal "Engage the enemy."

At 12:55 p.m., there was flash, thunder, and smoke. The first shot was claimed by Captain Phillimore of *Inflexible* (known in the service as Fidgety Phill), who had opened fire at *Leipzig* with his A turret, a two-gun salvo at the range of 16,500 yards. This was 4,000 yards farther than any British dreadnought had ever fired at a live target, and from his post high in *Inflexible*'s foretop, her gunnery officer, Lieutenant Commander Rudolf Verner, saw the shells fall 3,000 yards astern of the German squadron. Again *Inflexible* fired and Verner experienced "the roar from the forward turret guns and heavy masses of dark, chocolate-colored cordite smoke tumbling over the bow; a long wait and tall white 'stalagmites' growing out of the sea behind the distant enemy." Soon after, *Invincible* opened fire with a two-gun salvo from her A turret, and high fountains of water rose from the sea a thousand yards short of the target. Within fifteen minutes, however, when the range was down to 13,000 yards, the tall splashes began straddling *Leipzig.* One

---

nationals were gathering at South American ports to occupy and garrison the Falklands, and Sturdee ordered *Bristol* and *Macedonia* to intercept and destroy these ships. Two of the ships, which turned out to be the colliers *Baden* and *Santa Isabel,* were overtaken; their crews were taken off and both vessels were sunk by gunfire. Later, once the German squadron for which the coal had been intended had been sunk, the British regretted having destroyed such valuable cargo. The third German ship, the collier *Seydlitz,* escaped and was interned in Argentina.

salvo raised towering columns of water so close to the small ship that both sides lost sight of her and thought she had been hit.

Leipzig's plight forced Spee to make a decision. Looking back, he could see the high bow waves of the battle cruisers, the clouds of black smoke pouring from their funnels, the jets of orange flame shooting out through smoke, and, after an agonizing wait, the towers of water rising soundlessly alongside the hapless light cruiser. The admiral made his choice. At 1:20 p.m., *Invincible* observed the German squadron splitting up: the three light cruisers were turning to starboard, to the southwest, while *Scharnhorst* and *Gneisenau* were turning to port, east-northeast, directly into the path of the onrushing battle cruisers. Spee had realized that the British combination of 12-inch guns and higher speed gave his squadron no chance in a prolonged chase and that it was only a matter of minutes before the lagging *Leipzig* received a crippling blow. In order to give his three light cruisers a chance to escape, he chose to hurl his armored cruisers against the British battle cruisers. "*Gneisenau* will accept action. Light cruisers part company and try to escape," the admiral signaled. The German light cruisers immediately turned to starboard, their wakes curling away from *Scharnhorst.*

Sturdee had foreseen that the German squadron might do this. In three typewritten pages of instructions issued at Abrolhos Rocks, he had instructed that if, in an action, the East Asia Squadron divided itself, the British battle cruisers would see to the destruction of the German armored cruisers, while the British armored cruisers dealt with the German light cruisers. Therefore, as soon as Luce in *Glasgow* saw the German light cruisers turn away, and without any signal from Sturdee, he immediately left his position ahead of the battle cruisers and made for the fleeing German ships. *Kent* and *Cornwall* followed Luce in this new chase while *Carnarvon,* now ten miles astern and too slow to have any chance of overtaking the enemy light cruisers, continued in the wake of the battle cruisers.

As his light cruisers swung away to the southwest, Spee led *Scharnhorst* and *Gneisenau* around hard to port, to the northeast toward *Invincible* and *Inflexible.* The main action between the battle cruisers and the armored cruisers now began with the two admirals jockeying for position. Spee's hope was to get as close to the enemy as he could with his shorter-range guns, just as Cradock had tried to do with *Good Hope* and *Monmouth* at Coronel. Sturdee understood this maneuver and, four minutes after Spee had turned toward him, he deliberately turned 90 degrees to port, parallel with the enemy. Sturdee was resolved to fight at his own range, beyond the reach of the German 8.2-inch guns (13,500 yards), but within range of his own 12-inch (16,400 yards). He meant to use against Spee the same tactics that Spee had used against Cradock.

The two squadrons now were running parallel toward the northeast, with *Invincible* training on *Scharnhorst,* and *Inflexible* on *Gneisenau.* At 1:30 p.m., the German cruisers, their guns elevated to achieve maximum range, opened fire. Their first salvos were short; then, with the range diminishing to 12,000 yards, the third salvo straddled *Invincible* and five columns of water shot up around her. Soon, all four ships were firing broadsides, which included their rear turrets. "The German firing was magnificent to watch," said an officer on *Invincible,* "perfect ripple salvos all along their sides. A brown-colored puff with a center of flame marking each gun as it fired. . . . They straddled us time after time." *Scharnhorst,* especially, lived up to her reputation as a crack gunnery ship, and at 1:44 p.m., she hit *Invincible.* The shell burst against the battle cruiser's side armor, causing a heavy concussion but failing to penetrate.

From the beginning, Sturdee's intention to fight at a range beyond the reach of Spee's guns had been frustrated by the Germans' having the lee position. The dense smoke from the battle cruisers' funnels was blowing toward the enemy, obscuring the British gun layers' view of their targets. In addition, the discrepancy between the range of the British 12-inch and the German 8.2-inch guns was only about 3,000 yards, a narrow margin for Sturdee to find and maintain. For a few moments when the range dropped below 12,000 yards, the Germans fired rapidly and effectively. Then, at two o'clock, to ensure that a lucky German shot did not cripple one of his battle cruisers, Sturdee edged his ships away to port and opened the range to 16,000 yards, where Spee could not reach him. At the same time, he reduced speed to 22 knots to lessen the effects of funnel smoke. For the next fifteen minutes, there was a lull in the action and the two squadrons gradually drew apart.

In this first phase, despite the disparity in strength, the battle had been far from one-sided. In contrast to the rapidity and accuracy of German fire, British gunnery had been an embarrassment. During the first thirty minutes of action, the two battle cruisers fired a total of 210 rounds of 12-inch ammunition. *Inflexible* had scored three hits on *Gneisenau,* one below the waterline and another temporarily putting an 8.2-inch gun out of action, while *Invincible* could claim only one probable hit on *Scharnhorst.* At this rate the battle cruisers would empty their magazines without sinking the enemy. The primary cause of this bad shooting was smoke. The wind blowing from the northwest carried dense funnel smoke and clouds of cordite gas belching from the gun muzzles down toward the enemy, almost completely blinding *Invincible*'s gunners in the midships and stern turrets. The only clear views were those over the bow from A turret and that of the gunnery officer high in the foretop. *Inflexible*'s situation was even worse: she was smothered and blinded not only by her own smoke but also by *Invincible*'s smoke blowing across her line of vision. This excuse notwithstanding, the performance of the battle cruisers caused deep misgivings. "It is certainly damned bad shooting," a friend said to Lieutenant Harold Hickling of *Glasgow.* "We were all dismayed at the battle cruisers' gunnery, the large spread, the slow and ragged fire," Hickling added later. "An occasional shot would fall close to the target while others would be far short or over." An officer in *Invincible*'s P turret was alarmed to observe that "we did not seem to be hitting the *Scharnhorst* at all." Said Hickling, "At this rate, it looks as if Sturdee, not von Spee, is going to be sunk."

Excessive smoke was not the only cause of the slow, inaccurate gunfire of the battle cruisers. A British officer in the spotting top of *Invincible,* Lieutenant Commander Hubert Dannreuther, who happened to be a godson of the composer Richard Wagner, found that his excellent, German-made stereoscopic rangefinder was rendered useless not only by smoke, but also by the vibration caused by the ship's high speed, and by the violent shaking of the mast whenever A turret fired. In *Invincible*'s P turret, conditions were impossible. The gun layers could see nothing except enemy gun flashes through enveloping clouds of smoke, and every time Q turret, across the deck, fired over them, everyone in P turret was deafened and dazed by the blast. On *Inflexible,* Lieutenant Commander Rudolf Verner in the battle cruiser's foretop was almost the only man aboard his ship who could judge the location of the enemy, and he, handicapped by the smoke from the flagship ahead, had great difficulty observing what damage his gunners were causing.

From afar, however, the battle appeared as a dramatic tableau. "With the sun still shining on them, the German ships looked as if they had been painted for the occasion," said an officer on *Kent,* coming up astern. "I have never seen heavy guns fired with such rapidity and yet such control. Flash after flash traveled down their sides from head to stern, all their 5.9-inch and 8.2-inch guns firing every salvo. Of the British battle cruisers, less could be seen as their smoke drifted across their range. Their shells were hitting the German ships. . . . Four or five times, the white puff of a bursting shell could be seen on *Gneisenau.* . . . By some trick of the wind, the sounds were inaudible and the view was of silent combat, the two lines of ships steaming away to the east."

In fact, the few large British shells that managed to hit were inflicting serious damage. "A shell grazed the third funnel and exploded on the upper deck above . . . ," said *Gneisenau*'s Commander Pochhammer. "Large pieces of shrapnel ripped down and reached the coal bunkers, killing a stoker. A deck officer had both his forearms torn off. A second shell exploded on the main deck, destroying the ship's boats. Fragments smashed into the officers' mess and wounded the officers' little pet black pig. Another hit aft entered the ship on the waterline, pierced the armored deck and lodged in an ammunition chamber . . . [which] was flooded to prevent further damage. . . . These three hits killed or wounded fifty men."

Suddenly, Spee made another move: he turned and made off to the south, hoping that the pall of smoke over the British ships would obscure his flight and that in that direction he might find a cloud bank, a rain squall, a bank of fog. Said Pochhammer: "Every minute we gained before nightfall might decide our fate. The engines were still intact and were doing their best." Because of the smoke surrounding their ship, it took a few minutes for *Invincible*'s officers to realize what was happening; by then, Spee had opened the distance to 17,000 yards. Once Sturdee understood, he swung his battle cruisers around and chased at 24 knots. He still had sufficient time and the afternoon remained bright. This second pursuit lasted forty minutes, during which the range was reduced to 15,000 yards; then the battle cruisers turned to port to free their broadsides. At 2:45 p.m., the British battle cruisers recommenced the cannonade.

Eight minutes after Sturdee opened fire, Spee abandoned his southerly flight, and for the second time took his two armored cruisers around to the east to accept battle. The German ships turned in unison and once again broadside salvos of 12-inch and 8.2-inch shells thundered from the opposing lines. Spee now was trying to come closer. The British were within range of his 8.2-inch guns, but he was maneuvering to close to 10,000 yards, where his secondary armament of 5.9-inch guns could come into play. Gradually, the two lines drew nearer; by 3:00 p.m., the range had diminished to just over 10,000 yards and, at extreme elevation, the port German 5.9-inch batteries opened fire. *Invincible* suffered more heavily as German gunners concentrated on her; for the next fifteen minutes, Sturdee's flagship was hit repeatedly by both 8.2-inch and 5.9-inch shells. One 8.2-inch shell plunged through two decks and burst in the sick bay, which was empty. Somehow, on the British ships, this kind of luck seemed to hold; the ship was pummeled, but there were almost no casualties. When the canteen was wrecked, crew members cheerfully gathered up the cigarettes, cigars, chocolate, and tins of pineapple scattered across the deck. Not all the German shells exploded. One 8.2-inch shell cut the muzzle of a forward 4-inch gun, descended two decks, and came to rest unexploded in the admiral's storeroom, nestling between his jams and a Gorgonzola cheese. An unexploded 5.9-inch shell passed through the chaplain's quarters, entered the paymaster's cabin, where it tumbled dozens of gold sovereigns from his money chest over the deck, and then passed harmlessly out the ship's side.

The action was now at its most intense. The fire of the battle cruisers had become more accurate and both *Scharnhorst* and *Gneisenau* were blanketed by huge waterspouts. Now German spotters, like the British, were greatly hampered and could not see whether they were hitting. "The thick clouds of smoke from the British funnels and guns obscured our targets so that, apart from masts, only the sterns were visible," said Pochhammer. "Again we tried to shorten the distance but this time the enemy was careful not to let us approach and we knew that we were in for a battle of extermination." Time after time, *Scharnhorst* shuddered as 12-inch shells pierced her deck armor and exploded in her mess decks and casements. One 12-inch shell hit a 5.9-inch gun, exploded, and tumbled gun and gun crew into the sea. *Gneisenau* was also suffering. A huge explosion smashed the starboard engine room; water flooded in and, when the pumps became unworkable, the compartment was abandoned. Splashes from 12-inch shells landing in the sea nearby were throwing huge volumes of water over the decks, sometimes extinguishing fires set by previous, more accurate shells.

By 3:15 p.m., the action had been under way for two and a quarter hours. From the spotting tops, the scene remained the same: a cloudless sky, a calm surface ruffled by a breeze, and, from the two groups of ships, clouds of black smoke punctured by the orange flashes of guns. On *Invincible*'s bridge, Sturdee sensed that time was passing, the afternoon waning, the matter dragging out. The smoke interference plaguing his gun layers was now so intolerable that the admiral led his battle cruisers around to port, back across their own wakes, navigating an arc from which they emerged at 3:30 p.m. on a southwesterly course with *Inflexible* leading. This placed the battle cruisers on the windward side of the German ships and for the first time they had a clear view of their targets. With *Inflexible* now in front, Verner was at last able to observe the enemy and the effects of his own ship's gunnery. By 3:35 p.m., he said, "for the first time I experienced the luxury of complete immunity from every form of interference. . . . I was now in a position to enjoy the control officer's paradise: a good target, no alterations of course, and no 'next-aheads' or own smoke to worry one." During the turn, two of *Scharnhorst*'s 8.2-inch shells struck *Invincible*'s stern, wrecking the electric store and the paint shop, and a 5.9-inch shell exploded on the front plate of A turret between the two guns, which dented, but did not pierce, the armor. These hits on the British battle cruisers did nothing to reduce their fighting value.

Spee countered Sturdee's turn by suddenly turning again himself, this time back to starboard, heading northwest as if to parry Sturdee by crossing his bows. In fact, Spee's reason for swinging his ships was that so many guns on the *Scharnhorst*'s port side were out of action that he wished to bring his other broadside to bear. And, indeed, once the turn freed her disengaged side, the fresh starboard batteries opened a brisk fire. *Gneisenau,* not nearly so badly damaged and still firing all of her 8.2-inch guns, followed the flagship around and engaged *Invincible.* British shells crashed into the sea near the German ship and drove torrents of seawater across the ruins of her upper deck. Fire parties found themselves struggling to keep their feet in this surging flood. Worse, a hit on *Gneisenau* below the waterline flooded two boiler rooms, reducing her speed to 16 knots and giving her a list to port that made her port 5.9-inch guns unusable.

At this moment, when the two squadrons were trading blow for blow, an apparition appeared four miles to the east. A white-hulled, full-rigged, three-masted sailing ship, flying the Norwegian flag and bound for the Horn with all canvas spread, was, in the words of a British officer, "a truly lovely sight . . . as she ran free in the light breeze, for all the world like a herald of peace."

Scharnhorst, still plunging ahead through a forest of waterspouts, now had been struck by at least forty heavy shells. And there was no respite; with implacable regularity, orange flames glowed from *Invincible*'s turrets and a few minutes later more 850-pound shells burst on *Scharnhorst*'s deck or plunged through to the compartments below. What surprised the British was the volume of fire still coming back from a ship as badly battered as *Scharnhorst.* Her upper works were a jungle of torn and twisted steel; her masts and her third funnel were gone and the first and second funnels were leaning against each other; her bridge and her boats were wrecked; clouds of white steam billowed up from the decks; an enormous rent was torn in her side plating near the stern; red and orange flames could be seen in her interior; and she was down three feet at the waterline. Yet still her battle ensign fluttered from a jury mast above the after control station and still her starboard batteries fired. From *Invincible*'s spotting top, Dannreuther reported, "She was being torn apart and was blazing and it seemed impossible that anyone could still be alive." On *Inflexible,* Verner, astounded by the continuing salvos from the German armored cruisers, ordered his crews to fire "rapid independent," with the result that at one point, P turret had three shells in the air at the same time, all of which were seen to land on or near the target. Yet the German fire continued. "We were most obviously hitting [*Scharnhorst,*] but I could not stop her firing. . . . I remember asking my rate operator, 'What the devil can we do?' "

At about this time, a shell splinter cut the halyard of Spee's personal flag on *Scharnhorst* and Captain Maerker on *Gneisenau* noticed that the admiral's flag no longer flew from the flagship's peak. If Spee was dead, Maerker would be in command of the squadron. He signaled: "Why is the admiral's flag at half mast? Is the admiral dead?"

Spee replied, "No, I am all right so far. Have you hit anything?"

"The smoke prevents all observation," Maerker said.

Spee's last signal was characteristically generous and fatalistic. "You were right after all," he said to Maerker, who had opposed the attack on the Falklands.

Nevertheless, for another half hour, *Scharnhorst*'s starboard batteries boomed out. Then, just before four o'clock, she stopped firing. Sturdee signaled her to surrender, but there was no reply. Instead, slowly and painfully, the German cruiser's bows came around. Listing to port, with three of her four funnels and both her masts shot away, her bow so low that waves were washing over the forecastle, *Scharnhorst* staggered across the water toward her enemy. As she did so, Spee sent his last signal to *Gneisenau:* "Endeavor to escape if your engines are still intact." At just that moment, *Carnarvon* arrived on the scene and opened fire with her 7.5-inch and 6-inch guns. These blows were gratuitous. With water pouring into her bow, *Scharnhorst* rolled over on her side. Then, at 4:17 p.m., her flag still flying, her propellers turning in the air, the armored cruiser went down, leaving behind a cloud of steam and smoke. Every one of the 800 men on board, including Admiral von Spee, went down with her. Sturdee's battle cruisers, still under fire from *Gneisenau,* did not stop to look for survivors, and fifteen minutes later, when *Carnarvon* passed over the spot, her crew saw nothing in the water except wreckage.

Once her sister was gone, *Gneisenau* was subjected to an hour and a half of target practice by the two British battle cruisers. Salvos of 12-inch and smaller shells smashed into the ship, shattering her funnels, masts, and superstructure and flooding a boiler room and an engine room. The Germans still fired back, aiming mainly at *Invincible* and hitting the British flagship three times in fifteen minutes. One of these hits struck and bent the armored belt at the waterline; the result was the flooding of one of the battle cruiser's compartments. But this success could not reverse the conclusion. The British ships, steaming in a single ragged line, were firing at a range of 10,000 yards, but so dense was the smoke that they still had difficulty in observing their own gunfire. At 4:45 p.m., no longer able to contain his frustration, *Inflexible*'s Phillimore abruptly turned out of line, reversed himself to port, and ran through the smoke clouds out into the sunlight. *Gneisenau* lay 11,000 yards away on his starboard beam. Now with a clear and slow-moving target at relatively close range, *Inflexible* opened a devastating fire. Phillimore had no order from Sturdee to make this turn, but the admiral understood and later approved. Nevertheless, a few minutes later, Sturdee ordered reforming of the original battle line with his flagship leading. Much to Verner's disgust, he found himself once again blinded by *Invincible*'s smoke.

For the Germans, there was no chance of escape; Maerker faced a choice between surrender and annihilation. He made his choice and held his ship on a convergence course with *Invincible,* ordering stokers from the wrecked boiler and engine rooms to fill out the ammunition parties feeding the starboard batteries. Even at the end, according to the gunnery officer, "the men with their powder-blackened faces and arms, [were] calmly doing their duty in a cloud of smoke that grew ever denser as the firing continued; the rattling of the guns running backwards and forwards; the cries of encouragement from the officers, the monotonous sound of the order transmitters, and the tinkle of the salvo bells. Unrecognizable corpses were thrust aside; on the walls were splashes of blood and brains." Below, seawater was pouring into an engine room, a boiler room, and a dynamo room and over the sucking and swirling sounds of water came the cries of trapped and drowning men. Dense clouds of smoke and steam swirled through total darkness. As the dead and wounded grew in number, the size of the ammunition parties dwindled. The wireless station was destroyed and the wireless officer's head blown off. In the medical dressing station, the ship's doctor and the ship's chaplain were killed.

It was time to end it. Sturdee brought his ships in and pounded *Gneisenau* from 4,000 yards. The vessel was a place of carnage. Her bridge and foremast were shot away, her upper deck a mass of twisted steel, half her crew dead or wounded. One of *Carnarvon*'s shots had buckled *Gneisenau*'s armored deck, jamming it against the steering gear and forcing the ship into a slow, involuntary turn to starboard. Yet despite this devastation, the armored cruiser's port guns and fore turret continued to fire spasmodically. At 4:47 p.m., she ceased firing and no colors were seen, but it was uncertain whether she had struck—several times her colors had been shot away, and each time they had been hoisted again. At 5:08 p.m., her forward funnel crashed over the side. By 5:15 p.m., *Gneisenau* had been silent long enough for Sturdee to order "Cease Fire," but before the signal could be hoisted, a jammed ammunition hoist on *Gneisenau* came free, shells again reached the cruiser's fore turret, and a final, solitary shot was fired at *Invincible.* Grimly, the battle cruisers returned to work. A last British salvo was fired and she halted, rocking in the swell, water flooding in through the lower starboard gun ports. At 5:50, Sturdee repeated his signal to "Cease Fire." Still, the German cruiser's flag remained flying.

At 5:40 p.m., Maerker had given orders to scuttle the ship. The stern torpedoes were fired and the submerged tubes left open to the sea while explosive charges were fired in the main and starboard engine rooms. With thick smoke clinging to her decks and water gurgling and gushing through the hull, the ship rolled slowly over onto her starboard side. *Gneisenau* went down differently from *Scharnhorst,* submerging so slowly that men on deck were able to muster and climb down the ship's sides as she heeled over. Survivors estimated that about 300 men were still alive at that time. Emerging on deck, the men, coal blackened from the bunkers and the engine rooms, carried the wounded with them and began putting on life belts. As the ship slowly heeled over, Captain Maerker ordered three cheers for the kaiser and there was a thin chorus of *"Deutschland, Deutschland über alles."* When the order "All men overboard" came, the men slid down the side and jumped into the water. At 6:00 p.m., *Gneisenau* sank and British seamen, watching from *Inflexible,* began to cheer until the captain ordered silence and commanded his men to stand at silent attention as their enemy went down.

When their ship went down, between 200 and 300 survivors were left struggling in the water. A misty, drizzling rain was falling, the sea was beginning to roughen, there was a biting wind, and the temperature of the water was 39 degrees Fahrenheit. The British battle cruisers, 4,000 yards away, carefully closed in on the survivors, attempting to repair and launch their own damaged boats, steaming slowly, lowering boats, and throwing ropes. All around the ships, rising and falling on the swell, men floated, some on hammocks, some on spars, some dead, some still alive and struggling, then drowning before a boat could reach them. A few German sailors were able by their own efforts to swim to the high steel sides of a British ship and be pulled in by ropes. Some were so numbed by the shock of cold water that they could not hold on to anything and drowned within sight of the rescuing boats and ships. Some were alive but too weak and, before they could be brought in, drifted helplessly away into the dark. The wind brought awful cries from the men in the water. "We cast overboard every rope end we had . . . ," said a young English midshipman, "trying to throw to some poor wretch feebly struggling within a few yards of the ship's side. If we missed him, the swell would carry him out of reach. We could do nothing but try for another man. . . . Some of the Germans floated away, calling for help. It was shocking to see the look on their faces as they drifted away and we could do nothing to save them." Every effort was made; when *Carnarvon* with Stoddart on board reacted slowly in joining the rescue work, Sturdee dropped his mask of imperturbability. "Lower all your boats at once," he signaled imperatively, and *Carnarvon* lowered three boats, which picked up twenty Germans. By 7:30 p.m., the rescue work was completed. Of *Gneisenau*'s complement of 850 men, *Invincible* had brought aboard 108, fourteen of whom were found to be dead after being lifted on deck. *Inflexible* picked up sixty-two, and *Carnarvon* twenty. Heinrich von Spee, the admiral's son, did not survive.

One of those saved was Commander Pochhammer, second in command of *Gneisenau.* After the war, he recalled:

> The ship inclined more and more. I had to hold tight to the wall of the bridge to avoid sliding . . . then *Gneisenau* pitched violently and the process of capsizing began. . . . I felt the ship giving way under me. I heard the roaring and surging of the water come nearer. . . . The sea invaded a corner of the bridge and caught me. . . . I was caught in a whirlpool and dragged into an abyss. The water eddied and murmured around me and droned in my ears. . . . I opened my eyes and noticed it was brighter. . . . I came to the surface. The sea was heaving. . . . I saw . . . [our ship] a hundred yards away, her keel in the air[;] the red paint on her bottom glistened in the sunset. In the water around me were men who gradually formed large and small groups. . . . Albatrosses with three to four yards wingspan surveyed the field of the dead and avidly sought prey. . . . It was a consoling though mournful sight to see the first of the English ships approaching . . . to see her brought to a standstill as near to us as appeared possible, her silent crew ranged along the side, throwing spars to help support us and making ready to launch boats. One boat was put in the water, then re-hoisted because obviously it was damaged and leaked. . . . The wind and the swell were slowly driving the English away from us. Eventually, two boats were

> launched . . . a smaller one . . . [came] in our direction, a sort of dinghy, four men were rowing . . . a young midshipman in the bow. A long life line was thrown to me . . . [but] I lacked strength to climb into the boat. The boat was half full of water. Eventually, the little boat bobbed alongside the giant, whose flanks had a dirty, yellow color. . . . I was quite unable to climb the rope ladder offered to me. A slip knot was passed under my arms . . . and then, all dripping, I found myself on a ship of His Britannic Majesty. From the hat bands I saw it was the *Inflexible.*

Wrapped in blankets, given a hot-water bottle and brandy, and placed in a bunk in the admiral's quarters, Pochhammer was treated as a guest of honor. Even in the cabin, the German officer was cold; British warships, he discovered, were not heated by steam but by small electric stoves. Captain Phillimore came to see him and invited him to dinner in the officers' wardroom. There, Pochhammer, who spoke English, was offered ham, eggs, sherry, and port. Gradually, other rescued German officers appeared. That evening, as the senior surviving officer of the East Asia Squadron, he was handed a message from Admiral Sturdee: "Flag to *Inflexible.* Please convey to Commander of *Gneisenau:* The Commander-in-Chief is very gratified that your life has been spared and we all feel that the *Gneisenau* fought in a most plucky manner to the end. We much admire the good gunnery of both ships. We sympathize with you in the loss of your admiral and so many officers and men. Unfortunately the two countries are at war. The officers of both navies who can count friends in the other have to carry out their country's duty, which your admiral, captain and officers worthily maintained to the end." Commander Pochhammer replied to Sturdee: "In the name of all our officers and men I thank Your Excellency very much for your kind words. We regret, as you, the course of the fight as we have learned to know during peacetime the English Navy and her officers. We are all most thankful for our good reception." That night, falling asleep, Pochhammer felt the vibrations as *Inflexible* moved at high speed through the South Atlantic.

—

The pursuit of the German light cruisers continued through the afternoon into darkness. For over two hours, from 1:25 p.m. to 3:45 p.m., in a straightforward stern chase, *Glasgow, Kent,* and *Cornwall* raced south after *Leipzig, Dresden,* and *Nürnberg.* The pursuing British ships—two armored cruisers and a light cruiser—were overwhelmingly superior in armament: *Kent* and *Cornwall* each carried fourteen 6-inch guns and *Glasgow* had two 6-inch and ten 4-inch; if the British could catch the Germans, the outcome was certain. In this situation, however, success depended more on speed than on guns and, except in the case of *Glasgow,* the margin of speed was narrow.

When the three German light cruisers broke away to the south, they were ten to twelve miles ahead of their pursuers. Had their design speed still been applicable—*Nürnberg*'s and *Dresden*'s were over 24 knots, *Leipzig*'s 23—their chance of escape would have been excellent. Nominally, *Glasgow,* designed to reach 26½ knots, could catch them, but one ship could not possibly have overtaken and overwhelmed three. Here, however, design speeds did not apply. The German ships had been at sea for four months with no opportunity to clean their hulls, boilers, and condensers. Beyond decreased efficiency and slower speeds, any attempt to force these propulsion systems to generate sustained high speeds could actually pose a threat. Under the extreme pressures reached in a high-speed run, boilers and condenser tubes contaminated by the processing of millions of gallons of salt water might leak, rupture, even explode.

Glasgow quickly developed 27 knots and drew ahead of *Cornwall* and *Kent.* By 2:45 p.m., Luce, who was the senior officer on the three British cruisers, found himself nearly four miles ahead of his own two armored cruisers and within 12,000 yards of *Leipzig.* He opened fire with his bow 6-inch gun. One shell hit *Leipzig,* provoking her to turn sharply to port to reply with a 4.1-inch broadside. The first German salvo straddled *Glasgow* and when the next salvo scored two hits, Luce pulled back out of range. This reciprocal maneuver was repeated several times, but each time *Leipzig* turned to fire, she lost ground, giving the two slower British armored cruisers opportunity to creep up.

At 3:45 p.m., the German light cruiser force divided. *Dresden,* in the lead, turned to the southwest, *Nürnberg* turned east, and *Leipzig* continued south. Luce had to make a choice. For over an hour, his *Glasgow,* in front of *Kent* and *Cornwall,* had been firing at *Leipzig,* the rearmost of the German ships. The leading German ship, *Dresden,* already had a start on him of sixteen miles. The sky was clouding over; rain squalls were in the offing; at the earliest, if he pursued the distant *Dresden,* Luce could not come up within range until 5:30 p.m. He therefore decided to make sure of the two nearer, slower German ships and to let *Dresden* go. As the sky became overcast, then turned to mist and drizzle, *Dresden* grew fainter in the distance and eventually faded from sight.

The three pursuing British ships now followed two Germans: *Glasgow* and *Cornwall* pursued *Leipzig* to the south, while *Kent* went after *Nürnberg* to the east. *Cornwall* began hitting *Leipzig* with her fourteen 6-inch guns, while *Leipzig* gamely hit back at *Cornwall* with her ten 4.1-inch guns. *Cornwall,* shielded by her armor, thrust on without hesitation to give and take punishment. Using Sturdee's tactics, she closed the enemy at full speed, firing her forward guns, then, as soon as *Leipzig* began to hit back, turned sharply to starboard to bring her broadside to bear. And while *Cornwall* was drawing *Leipzig*'s fire, *Glasgow* closed in from a different direction to hammer the enemy with her own 6-inch and 4-inch batteries. For nearly an hour, these tactics continued. *Leipzig,* hit time after time, was doomed, but her gunfire remained expert. She fired rapidly, hitting *Glasgow* three times and *Cornwall* ten.

At 6:00 p.m., with the range down to 7,000 yards, *Cornwall* began firing special high-explosive shells. The effect was immediate. A large fire broke out forward on *Leipzig* and her gunfire became sporadic. Nevertheless, the German light cruiser continued to fire back until 7:05 p.m., by which point her mainmast and two of her funnels were gone and she had become an inferno of flashes and dark smoke. At this point, *Cornwall* ceased fire, expecting the enemy to strike her colors. *Leipzig* did not strike. Accordingly, *Cornwall* closed to 5,000 yards and fired more salvos. When the two British cruisers drew in to see whether she had struck, she was seen to be a wreck, but her flag was still flying on the remains of her foremast. Luce waited. He was about to signal, "Am anxious to save life. Do you surrender?" when *Leipzig* fired another—and as it turned out, final—shot.

What happened next was the result of a grim misunderstanding. *Leipzig* had fired her last shot. Captain Haun was ready to abandon and scuttle his ship; her seacocks had been opened and Haun had ordered all hands on deck with their lifesaving gear. A hundred and fifty men gathered amidships, hoping to be saved. But the German ensign was flying. Luce, for his part, was ready to accept *Leipzig*'s surrender, but with the flag still flying she was considered an active enemy. The difficulty was that the fires burning around the base of the mast where the flag was flying prevented anyone from lowering it. Haun already had told his men, "If anyone can reach the ensign, they can haul it down, for we shall sink now"; one sailor had made a dash through the inferno and collapsed, burning, before he reached the mast. The British waited for a reply that did not come, and at 7:25 p.m., Luce ordered both *Glasgow* and *Cornwall* to resume firing. The effect on the groups of men gathered on *Leipzig*'s open deck was appalling. The shells burst in the middle of the groups; a few minutes earlier, when the light cruiser had fired its last shot, there had been 150 men left. Now fifty remained.

At 8:12 p.m., *Leipzig,* listing and seeming about to capsize, fired two green distress lights. Luce took these as a signal of surrender, ordered another cease-fire, and cautiously approached within 500 yards. At 8:45 p.m., Luce ordered boats put in the water. *Glasgow* and *Cornwall* each lowered two boats as fast as they could be made seaworthy. Among those still alive on *Leipzig* was Captain Haun, who, when the British again stopped firing, sat calmly sharing his cigarettes. When he saw the rescue boats approaching, Haun ordered the survivors into the water. Then, still smoking, he walked forward and disappeared. The boats were within forty yards of the stricken ship and the boat crews saw German seamen jumping into the water when *Leipzig* sank. Heeling over to port, a mass of flames and smoke, she disappeared at 9:23 p.m., eighty miles from the point where *Gneisenau* had gone down. *Glasgow*'s boats picked up seven officers and ten men; *Cornwall,* one man. The high proportion of officers saved was due to the whistles they carried for use in the water.

Leipzig had hit *Cornwall* eighteen times, but because of her armor plate, the British cruiser had not lost a single gun or man. *Glasgow* was hit twice; one man was killed and four wounded. Because *Glasgow*'s magazines were empty of 6-inch shells, the two British ships returned to Port Stanley.

—

At 4:15 that afternoon, *Kent* had just begun firing at *Leipzig* when *Nürnberg* left her sisters and steamed away to the east. *Kent* followed *Nürnberg.* The two ships were different in almost every way. *Kent* was an armored cruiser with heavier guns, but she was old and had been recommissioned only sixty-seven days before. Three-fifths of her crew were from the naval reserve. When she left Portsmouth for the South Atlantic on October 12, half her crew became seasick in the Bay of Biscay. By November 13, the ship's doctor was writing in his diary, "We are a crippled old ship, rushed out before our engine room was really efficient. We are now unable to condense water quickly enough and cannot steam more than ten knots. So we crawl south." *Kent* joined Stoddart's squadron at the Abrolhos Rocks before Sturdee's arrival and went out to fire her 6-inch guns at a target 5,000 yards away. "Our shooting was rotten," her doctor summarized. *Nürnberg,* on the other hand, was a modern light cruiser with a professional crew. Her armament was inferior but her shooting was excellent. On paper, both ships were listed as capable of 23 knots, but *Kent,* having repaired her old engines and by some nautical miracle, would actually exceed that. By 11:00 on the morning of the Falklands battle, she reached 23 knots; by 4:00 p.m. she was moving at 24, partly because she was light, having loaded no coal since Abrolhos. *Kent*'s speed also owed something to the frenzied efforts of the crew, who, to make up for the shortage of coal, fed everything made of wood aboard the ship into the furnaces: gunnery targets, ship's ladders and doors, the officers' wardroom furniture, the crew's mess tables, benches, the chaplain's lectern and the paymaster's desk; at the end, timbers were being ripped from the decks.

As the afternoon wore on, the weather turned to mist and drizzle. Nevertheless, the race went on and *Kent* began to catch up. At 5:00 p.m., when *Kent* was 11,000 yards astern, *Nürnberg* opened fire. Nine minutes later, *Kent* fired back with her bow 6-inch gun. For some time no apparent damage was done to either ship. Then, at 5:35, just as *Kent* had begun to despair of a decisive action before dark, *Nürnberg* abruptly slowed to 19 knots. Two of her careworn, salt-contaminated boilers had burst and, although outwardly she still appeared undamaged, she was unable to flee. With the range reduced to

4,000 yards, Captain von Schönberg took his ship around for her last fight, broadside to broadside. *Kent,* willing to accept hits on her armor, bored in, using her heavier guns. Most of *Nürnberg*'s 4.1-inch shells failed to penetrate, exploding against the armored sides of *Kent.* One shell, however, burst in a gun position, killing or wounding most of its crew. Shortly before 6:00 p.m., another hit wrecked *Kent*'s wireless room; thereafter, the ship could receive wireless messages, but could not transmit.

Meanwhile, *Nürnberg* was on fire, her funnels were torn and twisted, her mainmast was gone, and only two guns on the port side were firing. Still, she refused to surrender. By 6:25 p.m., she was dead in the water; after 6:35, she fired no more shots. *Kent* then ceased fire and stood off awaiting surrender, but the German colors remained flying. The British fired again and at 6:57 p.m., the colors were hauled down. *Nürnberg,* now a burning wreck, lowered wounded men into her one surviving boat, which promptly sank. *Kent* closed in through the mist and saw the flames dancing above the light cruiser's deck and shooting out from portholes and jagged holes in the hull. The rain pattering on the decks and hissing into the fires had little effect because it was accompanied by gusts of wind that fanned the flames more than the rain quenched them. As *Kent* launched two hurriedly patched boats, *Nürnberg*'s captain gathered the survivors, thanked them, called for three cheers for the fatherland, then marched to his conning tower to await the end. With *Nürnberg* settling by the bow, *Kent*'s searchlight picked up a German seaman, standing high in the air on her upraised stern, waving a German ensign lashed to a pole. At 7:27 p.m., *Nürnberg* turned on her side and sank. Those on *Kent*'s deck heard faint cries from the water and the British ship steamed slowly toward them, throwing ropes over the side and using searchlights to assist the searching boat crews. The sea was growing rougher, the water was intensely cold, and albatrosses arrived to attack the living and dead floating in their life jackets. Nevertheless, until 9:00 p.m. *Kent*'s boats continued to search. Of 400 men in *Nürnberg*'s crew, twelve were picked up alive; five of these later died. Otto von Spee was never found and became the third member of his family to die that day.

Kent had been hit thirty-seven times by 4.1-inch shells, but her armor had not been pierced. Her casualties were four killed and twelve wounded. That night, *Kent*'s officers ate boiled ham and went to bed. Next morning, they found their ship surrounded by deep fog and their captain uncertain as to where he was. The ship was critically short of coal and with her radio out of action, they could hear other ships calling " *'Kent! Kent!'* . . . but we could not transmit"; the result was that for twenty-four hours, Admiral Sturdee and the rest of the British squadron remained ignorant of her fate. The following afternoon, *Kent* limped into Port Stanley.

—

Sturdee, hearing nothing from *Kent* and fearing the worst, had taken *Invincible, Inflexible,* and *Bristol* to the southwest at 18 knots, making for *Kent*'s last known position. She might be sunk; her men still might be alive in the sea. He found nothing; the following afternoon a message from *Macedonia* announced that *Kent* was making for Port Stanley and that she had sunk *Nürnberg.* Sturdee still wanted *Dresden,* but by 10:30 a.m. on December 10, when he was within fifty miles of Staten Island at the eastern end of Tierra del Fuego, the fog was so thick that continuing the search was useless. With his battle cruisers short of coal, Sturdee abandoned the hunt and returned to the Falklands, arriving in Port William at 6:30 a.m. on the eleventh. There, with a strong west wind chopping the waters of the bay, he found the other ships of his squadron anchored and coaling. As soon as her anchor was dropped, *Invincible*'s divers went down and found a hole in her hull six feet by seven feet.

That night, Commander Pochhammer of *Gneisenau* was invited by Sturdee to a dinner party aboard the flagship. As the guest of honor, he was placed at the British admiral's right hand and, during the meal, responded to questions about the battle. At the end of the dinner, glasses of port were passed around and Sturdee informed his guest that he was about to propose the traditional toast of "The King" but that he would understand if Pochhammer preferred not to drink. The German commander replied that, having accepted Sturdee's invitation to dinner, he would conform to the Royal Navy's established custom, which he knew well from prewar days. Back in Germany after the war, however, Pochhammer gave a different version of the incident. When Sturdee proposed the toast, he said later, he considered it "outrageous" and had "an overwhelming desire to throw my glass of port on the deck. My glass almost shivered in my hand, so angry did I feel. For a moment, I meditated throwing the contents in the face of this high personage [Sturdee]." Eventually, in fact, Pochhammer placed the glass back on the table without raising it. An awkward silence followed until Phillimore of *Inflexible* resumed conversation. In general, British hospitality was extended to all German officers. What particularly impressed Verner was the German officers' "emphatic and unanimous statement that when they received the news that Great Britain had allied herself with France, they could hardly believe their senses. In their own words it was to them 'absolutely incredible' that Englishmen could ever become the Allies of so degenerate a race as the French." From *Macedonia,* which left Port William with the German prisoners on board on December 14, a German lieutenant wrote home, "There is nothing at all to show that we are prisoners of war."

At 3:00 a.m. on the thirteenth, Sturdee was awakened and handed a report from the Admiralty: the British consul in Punta Arenas had reported that *Dresden* had arrived in that harbor on the afternoon of the twelfth and was coaling. The original message had been sent thirty-six hours before and only

Bristol was ready for sea, but at 4:00 a.m. she sailed. At 8:30 a.m., *Inflexible* and *Glasgow* followed. *Bristol* arrived at Punta Arenas on the afternoon of the fourteenth to find that *Dresden* had departed at 10:00 the night before. *Invincible* remained at Port William for three days, making temporary repairs. She had been hit twenty-two times; twelve of these hits were by 8.2-inch shells. Two bow compartments were flooded. Most serious was the nasty hole on the waterline, which flooded a coal bunker alongside P turret, giving the ship a 15-degree list to port. This hole was beyond the capacity of the ship's company to repair so the bunker was left flooded and all surrounding bulkheads were shored up. Remarkably, despite the physical damage to the ship, not one of *Invincible*'s crew of 950 had been killed and only two were slightly wounded. *Inflexible,* obscured so long by the flagship's smoke, had received only three hits. Splinters had killed one man and wounded three others.

On December 15, *Invincible,* with Sturdee on board, steamed out of Port Stanley. On the twentieth, she anchored in the river Plate to coal, then coaled again at Abrolhos on December 26. On January 11, the battle cruiser reached Gibraltar and went into dry dock. Sturdee and his staff departed from there for England on January 28 on board the liner *India.* Leaving *Invincible,* the admiral shook hands with all the officers while the crew, lining the rails, gave him three cheers. Sturdee was enormously pleased with himself. The night after the battle, he had turned to *Invincible*'s captain and said, "Well, Beamish, we were sacked from the Admiralty, but we've done pretty well."

—

How well, in fact, had he done? Sturdee's assignment had been to destroy a far weaker enemy, one who had neither the strength to defeat him nor the speed to escape. Why had it taken so long—three and a half hours to sink *Scharnhorst* and five to sink *Gneisenau*? The two battle cruisers had fired as many as 600 shells apiece, the greater part of their 12-inch ammunition, to sink the two armored cruisers. There were many reasons for what at first sight seemed inefficient ship handling and inept gunnery in the British squadron. Before the war, few British naval officers had appreciated the inherent inaccuracy of naval guns at long range. The only time that Lieutenant Commander Dannreuther, the gunnery officer of *Invincible,* had been allowed to fire at ranges in excess of 6,000 yards was during the practice authorized by Sturdee on the way south to the Falklands—and he had been gunnery officer of the battle cruiser since 1912. Nor had peacetime practice disclosed the difficulties of shooting accurately from a rapidly moving platform at a rapidly moving target. Further, no one had considered that when ships were traveling at high speed, the intense vibration created by engines and propellers might rattle and blur the gun layers' and trainers' telescopes. Nor had prewar maneuvers revealed the obscuring effects of billowing funnel smoke at high speed. As the war went on, the expected rate of shells fired to hits achieved became 5 percent. That was approximately the ratio in the Falklands, but at this early time in the war, everyone expected better and therefore it seemed a failure.

Nevertheless, Sturdee had in large part fulfilled the task entrusted to him. His achievement, within four weeks of leaving the Admiralty, was hailed, not least by the inhabitants of the Falklands. "It really is a spanking victory," wrote the governor's aide-de-camp. "Last night His Excellency had all the Volunteers and most of the so-called leading people of Port Stanley up to Government House for a drink to the King and the Royal Navy." The king himself sent congratulations and, on December 11, Sturdee received signals from Jellicoe on behalf of the Grand Fleet and from the French and Russian admiralties. Beatty, tired of constant criticism of the navy, said, "It has done us all a tremendous amount of good. . . . I hope it will put a stop to a lot of the unpleasant remarks . . . that the British Navy has been an expensive luxury and is not doing its job." Beresford sent his "warm congratulations on the splendid achievement of my old friend and chief of staff . . . how clever of him to find out the enemy so quickly."*

Fisher was overjoyed at the victory, but not at all pleased with Sturdee. The triumph was, in fact, Fisher's greatest of the entire war and praise was heaped on the First Sea Lord, because of the victory and because it vindicated his conception of the battle cruiser. This was what battle cruisers had been designed to do: to hunt down enemy armored cruisers "like an armadillo and lap them up." Gleefully, he called the battle "the only substantial victory of ours in the war (and as Nelson wished, it was not a victory, it was annihilation). . . . And the above accomplished under the sole direction of a septuagenarian First Sea Lord who was thought mad for denuding the Grand Fleet of our fastest battle cruisers to send them 14,000 miles on a supposed wild goose chase . . . and how I was execrated for inventing the battle cruisers." On December 10, Fisher wrote to Churchill, "We cannot but be overjoyed at the *Monmouth* and *Good Hope* being avenged! But let us be self-restrained—*not too exultant—till we know details! Perhaps their guns never reached us!* (We had so few casualties!) We know THEIR gunnery was excellent! Their THIRD salvo murdered Cradock! So it may have been like shooting pheasants: the pheasants not shooting back! Not too much glory for us, only great satisfaction. . . . Let us wait and hear before we crow! Then again, it may be a wonder why the cruisers escaped—if they have escaped—I

*On the matter of promptitude, Sturdee subsequently gave no credit to Luce for the timely arrival of the British squadron at Port Stanley. Indeed, when Luce reminded him of their discussion at Abrolhos Rocks, Sturdee reacted coldly. Yet if Luce had not persuaded the admiral to leave Abrolhos a day before he meant to, Spee would have reached the Falklands first. What might have happened then, no one can say.

hope not. . . . *How Glasgow must have enjoyed it!*" Churchill wrote back: "This was your show and your luck. I should have only sent one greyhound [battle cruiser] and *Defence.* This would have done the trick. But it was a niggling coup. Your flair was quite true. Let us have some more victories together and confound all our foes abroad—and (don't forget) at home." Delighted, Fisher replied, "Your letter pleasant. . . . It is all too sweet for words. . . . It is palpably transparent."

—

Despite these glowing words, the First Lord and the First Sea Lord soon found themselves in acute disagreement. The subject was Sturdee. Fisher was furious that *Dresden* had not been destroyed and, in a vindictive spasm, declared that Sturdee should not leave South American waters until the fugitive light cruiser had been hunted down. As *Invincible* and *Inflexible* had to come home, this would have meant transferring Sturdee to *Carnarvon,* an inferior command for a vice admiral and a public slap on the heels of his recent triumph. When Churchill vetoed this proposal, Fisher went into a sulk. *Dresden*'s escape, the First Sea Lord said, was "criminal ineptitude." After the battle, Fisher complained, Sturdee had swept a limited area for only a single day, then abandoned the search. Fisher felt that it must have been obvious where *Dresden* was headed and that immediately after the action, Sturdee should have sent at least one ship to Punta Arenas. On December 13, when Sturdee was informed that *Dresden* was back at Punta Arenas intending to coal, the Admiralty ordered him to destroy her before she could be interned by the Chilean government. Once again, *Dresden* escaped before Sturdee's cruisers could arrive. On all these counts, Fisher's wrath boiled high. In three blunt messages, he asked Sturdee to "report fully reason for course you have followed since action." Highly irritated, Sturdee retorted, "Their Lordships selected me as Commander-in-Chief to destroy the two hostile armored cruisers and I endeavoured to the best of my ability to carry out their orders. I submit that my being called upon in three separate telegrams to give reasons for my subsequent action was unexpected." Fisher would have none of this. "Last paragraph of . . . your signal . . . is improper and such observations must not be repeated," he thundered, adding, "Their Lordships await your written report and dispatches before coming to any conclusion."

In Fisher's view, he himself was primarily responsible for the Falklands victory and Sturdee was simply lucky. Fisher, as First Sea Lord, had designed the ships and had sent them out on time. Now here was Sturdee, praised in every newspaper, returning to London to receive public acclaim for an easy victory won with Fisher's greyhounds. Here, too, was Sturdee, offered command of the eight dreadnoughts of the 4th Battle Squadron of the Grand Fleet. And eventually, in the 1916 honors list, Sturdee was to be named a baronet, the first promotion to an hereditary knighthood for a naval officer since Trafalgar. Jealous and infuriated, Fisher continued to characterize Sturdee's tactics as "dilatory and theatrical." After the battle, when Sturdee passed through London and reported to the Admiralty on his way to Scapa Flow, he was kept waiting for several hours before the First Sea Lord would see him. The interview lasted five minutes, during which, according to Sturdee, Fisher displayed no interest in the battle except to criticize his failure to sink *Dresden.*

Captain Herbert Richmond, a staff officer who disliked Sturdee, agreed wholeheartedly with Fisher. It was "an irony," he said, "that Sturdee, the man who more than anyone else is responsible for the loss of Cradock's squadron, should be . . . made a national hero. . . . The enemy . . . [ran] into his arms and [saved] him the trouble of searching for them. He puts to sea with his . . . greatly superior force and has only to steer after them and sink them which he not unnaturally does. If he didn't he would indeed be a duffer. Yet for this simple piece of service, he is acclaimed as a marvelous strategist and tactician. So are reputations made!" Fisher, whose hates were inscribed on granite, never forgave. "No one in history was ever kicked on to a pedestal like Sturdee," he wrote in 1919. "If he had been allowed to pack all the shirts he wanted to take, and if Edgerton . . . [the port admiral at] Plymouth had not been given that peremptory order, Sturdee would have been looking for von Spee still."

Meanwhile, *Dresden* had disappeared. After the battle, she had rounded Cape Horn, passed through the Cockburn Channel, and anchored at Scholl Bay in the wildest region of Tierra del Fuego. On December 11, with her coal bunkers empty, she made her way sixty miles north to Punta Arenas, where she was allowed to coal and from where her presence was reported to Sturdee at Port Stanley. Captain Lüdecke's next refuge was in lonely Hewett Bay, 130 miles down the Barbara Channel, which offered many avenues of escape into the Pacific Ocean. Thereafter, the fugitive ship spent weeks hiding in the maze of channels and bays that divided the desolate islands on the south coast of Tierra del Fuego.

The British began a methodical search. There were dozens of possible hiding places and *Glasgow* and *Bristol* looked into most of them, searching the Magellan Straits and the islands and channels around Cape Horn, ferreting through uninhabited bays, sounds, and inlets. *Inflexible* steamed up the coast of Chile, into the Gulf of Penas and Bahía San Quintín, where Spee had coaled before rounding the Horn. *Glasgow* and *Bristol* passed through the Darwin Channel and into Puerto Montt, searching the Chilean coastal fjords along the way, then rendezvoused with *Inflexible* off Cape Tres Montes. On December 19, *Inflexible,* having gone up the coast as far as

Coronel, was withdrawn from the search and ordered home to England. She returned, ultimately, not to the North Sea, but to the Dardanelles.

All summer—this was the southern hemisphere—*Kent* and *Glasgow* continued hunting *Dresden* through narrow channels lined by mountains, glaciers, and forests. "Occasionally," wrote *Glasgow*'s Hirst, "at the head of some magnificent gorge, the lower slopes of a glacier show pale green shades against the snow. . . . The water has all the glassy calm of a Scottish loch, but a tide line of streaky bubbles shows on either side and occasionally we meet twisted tree trunks. . . . The majestic silence leaves a deep impression unrelieved by any cheering signs of human habitation. As night closes in and the vault darkens, the ship seems proceeding slowly up the aisle of a cathedral . . . deep bays become transepts and choir and a fringe of low islands ahead lining the channel draped in snow are the surpliced priests. Solitude reigns eternal in this abyss of waters." But solitude did not mean peace for the British crews. Approaching an unknown headland, the men were at action stations, their guns training slowly, as the ship steamed cautiously around bare rock cliffs, the far side of which they could not see. They were playing hide-and-seek and the enemy might pounce on them from behind any headland with guns firing at point-blank range and torpedoes in the water. They found only uninhabited landscapes, flocks of aquatic birds, and myriads of fish and other sea creatures.

In mid-February, *Dresden* began moving north up the coast of Chile, keeping 200 miles out to sea to avoid detection. Her luck was waning, however, and on March 8, an afternoon fog burned off and *Kent* and *Dresden* suddenly sighted each other, 11,000 yards apart. For five hours, *Kent* struggled to get within range: at one point flames thirty feet high were coming out of her funnels; at another, most of the crew was ordered aft to sit over the propeller to make it "bite" harder. It was not enough: once again, *Dresden* drew off and disappeared. During the chase, however, *Kent* intercepted a signal from *Dresden* telling a collier to meet her at Más á Tierra in the Juan Fernández Islands. The following day, *Dresden* arrived in Cumberland Bay on Más á Tierra and anchored 500 yards from shore. Twenty-four hours passed and the Chilean government declared that, in accordance with international law, the German ship must consider herself interned. Captain Lüdecke argued that his engines were disabled and that international law permitted him to stay eight days for repairs. As the island had no wireless communication with the mainland, the governor could do nothing except to send a lobster boat to inform his government. *Dresden,* of course, down to forty tons of coal, was waiting for her collier.

On the basis of the intercepted message, *Kent* summoned *Glasgow* and together the two ships steamed toward Más á Tierra. At dawn on March 14, the two British cruisers rounded Cumberland Point. There at last, half hidden against the volcanic walls rising 3,000 feet behind her, they saw *Dresden.*

She was at anchor, her flag flying, smoke wisping up from her funnels. As *Glasgow* approached, *Dresden* trained her guns. Luce, deciding that this was not the behavior of an interned ship and justifying his own action by *Dresden*'s repeated violations of Chilean neutrality, opened fire. The Germans fired back. At this point, the Chilean governor, who was in a small boat headed out to meet the British ships, found himself on a battlefield with shells falling near his boat. He hurried to safety. Within four minutes, the battle was over and *Dresden,* on fire and with a hole at her waterline, hoisted a white flag. A steamboat flying a parley flag from *Dresden* brought Lieutenant Wilhelm Canaris to complain that the German light cruiser was in Chilean territorial waters and therefore under Chilean protection.* Luce called out to him that the question of neutrality could be settled by diplomats and that meanwhile, unless *Dresden* surrendered, he would blow her out of the water. During this time, Captain Lüdecke had been busy with preparations to scuttle his ship and when the parley boat returned, *Dresden*'s company, many of them still half dressed, scrambled into their boats and made for the shore. The sea valves were opened and the German crew gathered on the beach to watch their ship sink. For twenty minutes, they were anxious as the vessel showed no signs of going down. Then, suddenly, she rolled over to port, water pouring down her funnels, and sank. On shore, the Germans sang their national anthem.

One midshipman and eight sailors from *Dresden* had been killed and three officers and twelve men were wounded. The ships' doctors from *Glasgow* and *Kent* went ashore and amputated the right leg of *Dresden*'s second in command. One British doctor, feeling that Lüdecke, the captain, was rude, retaliated by writing in his journal that Lüdecke had a "villainous-looking face" and "a great pendulous nose." Now that *Dresden* had disappeared, the Chilean governor switched his protest of violated neutrality to the British, who, he said, had caused property damage: two British shells had come ashore without exploding and other shell fragments had ricocheted. Luce resolved the matter by taking ashore a bag of gold sovereigns and asking the inhabitants to line up and make their claims. The wrecking of a lobster shed was settled for £60. A claim on behalf of a cow, said to be so frightened by a falling shell that she might never again produce milk, was liquidated for £15. The governor then gave Luce a certificate declaring that all claims against the British navy had been settled.

Dresden was the last survivor of the German overseas cruisers scattered around the world at the outbreak of war. She had traveled farthest—19,000 miles—and survived longest, yet she had done the least damage. Over seven

*Canaris later became an admiral and chief of Hitler's military intelligence. In 1944, he was involved in an anti-Hitler conspiracy, for which, in the final weeks of World War II, he was hanged by the Gestapo.

and a half months, she sank only four British merchant ships, totaling 13,000 tons. From the time of her escape from the Falklands on December 8 until she was destroyed on March 15, *Dresden* sank two sailing ships. Of the five German captains who reached the Falklands with Admiral von Spee, only Lüdecke survived the battle and the war.

It was only a matter of weeks before the oceans were entirely clear. Early in March, the armed merchant cruiser *Prinz Eitel Friedrich,* which had captured ten vessels in the preceding two months, arrived at Newport News, Virginia, with a number of prisoners to put ashore. The ship claimed the right of refit and engine repairs, but while she was in port it became public knowledge that one of her victims had been an American vessel. The American government interned her. This left only the German armed merchant cruiser *Kronprinz Wilhelm* still at large. She gave up in April and voluntarily came in to Newport News to be interned.

During the search for *Dresden,* the British were also hunting for *Karlsruhe,* last reported in October off the coast of Brazil. In her raids along the South Atlantic trade route, *Karlsruhe* sank sixteen British ships before she met a sudden end off the coast of Barbados. Her fate was shrouded in mystery until March 1915. The first clue came when some of her wreckage washed ashore 500 miles away. Her survivors eventually found their way back to Germany and reported that on November 4, 1914, she had suffered an internal explosion and foundered with the loss of 261 officers and men. This German disaster occurred three days after Coronel, but for the next four months, the British Admiralty did not know.

CHAPTER 15

Fisher Returns to the Admiralty

The extended infatuation between Jacky Fisher and Winston Churchill originated in April 1907, in Biarritz, where both were staying as guests of a mutual friend. Fisher, a shining eccentric of sixty-six, was First Sea Lord and at the height of his power; Churchill, although a blue blood and the maverick grandson of a duke, was then merely the thirty-two-year-old under secretary for the colonies. But that Churchill would go far—unless he self-destructed—no one doubted. "He is a wonderful creature," said H. H. Asquith, the prime minister, "with a curious clash of schoolboy simplicity and what someone said of genius: 'a zigzag streak of lightning in the brain.' " From the beginning, Fisher and Churchill recognized each other's qualities. "We talked all day and far into the nights," Churchill remembered. "He told me wonderful stories of the navy and of his plans—all about dreadnoughts, all about submarines . . . about big guns and splendid admirals and foolish, miserable ones and Nelson and the Bible. . . . I remembered it all. I reflected on it often." Fisher, for his part, "fell desperately in love" with Churchill and was "perhaps the first to be told" of the young Cabinet minister's engagement a few weeks later to Clementine Hozier.

In April 1908, when Asquith succeeded the failing Henry Campbell-Bannerman as Liberal prime minister and was reshuffling the Cabinet, Fisher hoped that Churchill would become First Lord of the Admiralty. Churchill, however, accepted the presidency of the Board of Trade, which he felt offered more scope for exercising independent authority. By 1910, Churchill was ready to move and requested Asquith to give him either the Admiralty or the Home Office; Asquith chose to make him home secretary. Fisher retired on his sixty-ninth birthday, January 25, 1910. Nevertheless, neither the old admiral nor the rising politician forgot their Biarritz conversations and in March Fisher wrote to Churchill, "My dear Winston: Now that I am absolutely free of the Admiralty I suppose I may venture to ask to be welcomed once more into your arms unless in the meantime you've got to hate me." Churchill's reply came the next day: "My dear Fisher: I am truly delighted to get your letter. I stretched out several feeble paws of amity—but in vain. I like you very much indeed. . . . I have deeply regretted since that I did not press for the Admiralty in 1908." Thereafter, their correspondence became frequent. Fisher's letters were couched in his flamboyantly affectionate style, usually beginning "My beloved Winston" and concluding with "Yours to a cinder," or "Yours till Hell freezes," or "Yours till charcoal sprouts." Churchill's replies were more respectfully sedate. On October 25, 1911, he finally went to the Admiralty and that morning, before leaving the Home Office, he wrote: "My dear Lord Fisher: I want to see you very much. When am I to have that pleasure? You have but to indicate your convenience and I will await you at the Admiralty." Three days later, they met at a country house and again talked far into the night. "I plied him with questions and he poured out his ideas," said Churchill. "It was always a joy to me to talk to him on these great matters, but most of all he was stimulating in all that related to the design of ships. He also talked brilliantly about admirals, but here one had to make a heavy discount on account of the feuds. My intention was to hold the balance even and, while adopting in the main the Fisher policy, to insist upon an absolute cessation of the vendetta." During these days, the new First Lord began to think about bringing the former First Sea Lord back to the Admiralty. "I began our conversations with no thought of Fisher's recall," Churchill said later. "But by Sunday night, the power of the man was deeply borne in upon me and I had almost made up my mind to do what I did three years later and place him again at the head of the Naval Service. . . . All the way up to London the next morning I was on the brink of saying, 'Come and help me.' " But Churchill was deterred by Fisher's age and by his fear that the pernicious intraservice feuding would resume. Even so, Fisher was pleased. "I think Winston Churchill will do all I've suggested to him," he wrote to his son. "He's very affectionate and cordial."

Over the next three years Fisher remained in retirement, but he had Churchill's ear and much of what Churchill did at the peacetime Admiralty was on Fisher's advice. It was Fisher's encouragement that spurred Churchill to the adoption of 15-inch guns for the five *Queen Elizabeth*–class dreadnoughts. Fisher's old animosities surfaced when Churchill appointed Admirals Sir Hedworth Meux and Sir Berkeley Milne to high commands and he lashed out that Churchill had "betrayed the navy." This storm quickly passed and Churchill next persuaded Fisher to take control of a matter critical to the navy: the conversion to fuel oil. Fisher had long been obsessed by the idea of using fuel oil for turbine propulsion; oil was cleaner, safer, and more efficient than coal; it would drive the new 15-inch-gun battleships at 25 knots. Churchill now wished to turn this obsession into reality. "My dear Fisher," he wrote, "The liquid [oil] fuel problem has got to be solved. . . . No one else can do it so well. Perhaps no one else can do it at all. You have got to find the oil; to show how it can be stored cheaply; how it can be purchased regularly and cheaply in peace and with absolute certainty in war. Then . . . develop its application in the best possible way to existing and prospective ships." Churchill argued that Fisher must do it for his own sake, not just the navy's. "You need a plough to draw. Your propellers are racing in the air." Fisher agreed and become chairman of the oil commission.

For three years, the honeymoon continued. Churchill and Fisher both enjoyed and profited from their relationship. On January 1, 1914, Churchill wrote to Fisher, "Contact with you is like breathing ozone to me." On February 24, the First Lord's private secretary wrote to Fisher, "Winston is quite cross with you for not coming to see him. He says he wants to talk to you badly about many things." On July 15, Winston wrote to Clementine, "Tomorrow old Fisher comes down to the yacht with me. This always has a salutary effect." Once war began, Fisher came often to see Churchill at the Admiralty. As Prince Louis's health deteriorated and he retreated to the seclusion of his room, Churchill yearned for Fisher's sparkling, irreverent dynamism. During these weeks, Churchill studied the seventy-three-year-old admiral,

> [watching] him narrowly to judge his physical strength and mental alertness. There seemed no doubt about either. On one occasion, when inveighing against someone whom he thought obstructive, he became so convulsed with fury that it seemed that every nerve and blood vessel in his body would be ruptured. However, they stood the strain magnificently and he left me with the impression of a terrific engine of mental and physical power burning and throbbing in that aged frame. . . . I therefore sounded him [about returning] in conversation without committing myself and found that he was fiercely eager to lay his grasp on power.

On October 19, when the Cabinet knew that a change at the Admiralty was necessary, Haldane suggested to Churchill that the restoration of Fisher would "make our country feel that our old spirit of the navy was alive and come back." The following day, Churchill went to Asquith and asked for approval to bring Fisher back, declaring "that I could work with no one else. I was well aware that there would be strong, natural and legitimate opposition in many quarters to Fisher's appointment, but, having formed my own conviction, I was determined not to remain at the Admiralty unless I could do justice to it. So in the end, for good or for ill, I had my way."

Not without opposition from the highest in the land. Churchill went to see the king on October 27 to warn him of what was coming and to inform him that he proposed to nominate Fisher as Battenberg's replacement. King George had long detested Fisher (who for his part disliked the monarch) and mistrusted many of the reforms the admiral had initiated. He argued that Fisher was too old and too untrustworthy and that his return to the Admiralty would reopen old wounds. The king preferred almost anyone to Fisher and, during the interview, suggested alternatives. He proposed Sir Hedworth Meux; Churchill declared that Meux lacked the necessary technical expertise. The king suggested Sir Henry Jackson; Churchill conceded Jackson's scientific and intellectual attainments but said that he was colorless and lacked the energy to do the work. The king mentioned Sturdee; Churchill shook his head. Jellicoe, whom both men liked, was irreplaceable in the Grand Fleet. The interview broke up with the king and the First Lord in complete disagreement; Churchill went back to Asquith to say that if he did not get Fisher he would resign.

Unable to persuade Churchill, the king appealed to the prime minister. Asquith came to the palace on the afternoon of October 29 and fully supported his First Lord: Meux would not inspire confidence in the navy, Jackson lacked personality, Sturdee was more suited to command a fleet than to remain in Whitehall. Then Asquith warned the king that if Fisher were not brought back, Churchill, whose knowledge of the navy was unique and whose services could not be dispensed with, would resign. Faced with this threat, George V had no choice. Constitutionally, he could not oppose his ministers, but he felt it his duty to record his protest. He would approve Fisher's appointment, he wrote to Asquith after the meeting, but he did so "with some reluctance and misgivings. . . . I hope that my fears may prove to be groundless." The following morning, the thirtieth, the new First Sea Lord spent an hour in audience with the king at Buckingham Palace. The visit was a success and King George, who had not seen Fisher for six years, confessed to his diary, "He seems as young as ever." The monarch and the admiral agreed to meet once a week and, when Fisher returned to Whitehall, Churchill wrote jubilantly to Asquith, "He is already a Court Favourite!"

The public hailed Fisher's return, reacting as it had three months earlier to the appointment of Kitchener when it found comfort and reassurance in the presence of a legendary British hero. Fisher's age was overlooked, as were his cantankerous moods and the methods that had roiled and divided the navy. The press gave a cautious blessing: "Undoubtedly the country will benefit," said the *Times,* expecting that Fisher would restore public confidence in the navy through a more aggressive strategy while at the same time restraining Churchill's impetuosity. From the navy, the response was mixed. "They have resurrected old Fisher," Beatty wrote to his wife on November 2. "Well, I think he is the best they could have done, but I wish he was ten years younger. He still has fine zeal, energy and determination, coupled with low cunning which is eminently desirable just now. He also has courage and will take any responsibility. He will rule the Admiralty and Winston with a heavy hand." A few admirals expressed dismay: Rear Admiral Rosslyn Wester Wemyss called it a "horrible appointment" and predicted a falling-out between Fisher and Churchill. "They will be thick as thieves at first until they differ on some subject, probably as to who is to be No. 1 when they will begin to intrigue against each other."

Fisher, on returning to the Admiralty, assumed that he had come to take command of the great naval weapon he had forged during his previous dramatic term as First Sea Lord. At once, he swung into action. "Everything began to move. Inertia disappeared. The huge machine creaked and groaned. . . . He was known, feared, loved, and obeyed," wrote his friend, protégé, and biographer, Admiral Reginald Bacon. Fisher's first task was to reinvigorate the Admiralty itself. He made new appointments; he swept away deadwood. Churchill had followed up on Haldane's suggestion and asked a retired former First Sea Lord, Admiral of the Fleet Sir Arthur Wilson, to return to the Admiralty as Chief of Staff. Wilson had refused to accept any official position, since he did not relish having to side with either Fisher or Churchill against the other should they disagree. But he agreed to come back in an unofficial and unpaid capacity, giving advice when asked and being available to work on a variety of special tasks. Sturdee, the incumbent Chief of Staff, had to go. Fisher, it may be remembered, detested Sturdee, a prominent member of Beresford's camp, and Fisher also suspected him of being responsible for the flawed dispositions that had brought about the Coronel disaster. Churchill, who knew that the faulty dispositions were as much his doing as Sturdee's, was unwilling to sack him and, instead, sent him to the South Atlantic to find and destroy Admiral von Spee.

The workaholic Henry Oliver was appointed Chief of Staff in Sturdee's place. Oliver had been Director of Naval Intelligence before the war, supplying the First Lord and the Admiralty with facts and numbers related to comparative British and German naval strength. On October 14 he became naval secretary to the First Lord. Now, only a few weeks later, Fisher proposed that he be made Chief of Staff with the rank of acting vice admiral. Thereafter, Oliver, dedicated, unruffled, and inexhaustible, worked fourteen hours a day, Sundays included, and never took leave. He had broad common sense and sufficient self-confidence to stand up to both Churchill and Fisher. His method was simple: if he could not get either to see his point of view, he would agree with them and then quietly go away and do as he thought best. If he was found out, he was rarely overruled. In the months ahead, this combination of Churchill, Fisher, Wilson, and Oliver, known as the War Group or the Cabal, met at least once a day—often many times in a day.

The key relationship, of course, was that between Churchill and Fisher, "a genius without a doubt" and "a veritable dynamo," as they described each other. Even apart from the thirty-four-year age difference, they made a curious pair. Churchill enjoyed the company of the clever, wily, irascible, ruthless old man; he warmed to the quips and quotations, the uncompromising judgments, the feeling of movement and accomplishment. For all Churchill's vanity, he was too clever not to allow himself to be guided by someone with Fisher's weight of experience. Yet the First Lord always knew where ultimate authority lay. "I was never in the least afraid of working with him," said Churchill, "and I thought I knew him so well and had held an equal relationship and superior constitutional authority so long, that we could come through any difficulty together." Churchill's appreciation of Fisher at this stage of the admiral's life was heartfelt and eloquent:

> Lord Fisher was the most distinguished British naval officer since Nelson. The originality of his mind and the spontaneity of his nature freed him from conventionalities of all kinds. His genius was deep and true. Above all, he was in harmony with the vast size of events. Like them, he was built upon a titanic scale. But he was seventy-three years of age. As in a great castle which has long contended with time, the mighty central mass of the donjon towered up intact and seemingly everlasting. But the outworks and the battlements had fallen away, and its imperious ruler dwelt only in the special apartments and corridors with which he had a life-long familiarity.

Fisher's age and the enormous weight of his new responsibilities forced him to parcel out his energy carefully. Their new working relationship also required Churchill to alter his own routine. Fisher usually awoke before 4:00 a.m. in his room at Admiralty House, had a cup of tea, and was in his office by 5:00. He worked diligently during the morning, ate a spartan lunch, and returned to his desk in the afternoon. By this time, Churchill later remembered, "the formidable energy of the morning gradually declined and with the shades of night, the admiral's giant strength was often visibly exhausted." He went home to an early supper and bed. Once, when Lady Randolph Churchill, the First Lord's mother, invited him to dinner, Fisher excused himself, saying, "I can't dine out—I go to bed at 9:30 and get up at 3:30—I don't go anywhere. Winston is quite enough dissipation for me. I want no more!"*

*Fisher was seventy-three, but few men of any age could stand up to Churchill's formidable persuasive powers. Rear Admiral Reginald Hall, the wartime Director of Naval Intelligence, explained how, on one occasion, he managed it:

> Once, I remember, I was sent for by Mr. Churchill very late at night. He wished to discuss some point or other with me—at once. To be candid, I have not the slightest recollection what it was; I only know that his views and mine were diametrically opposed.

Lady Randolph's son lived rather differently. He awoke at 8:00 a.m., had breakfast in bed, and, still in bed, began his work. One astonished admiral, a witness to this "extraordinary spectacle," described the First Lord "perched up in a huge bed, and the whole of the bedspread littered with dispatch boxes, red and all colors, and a stenographer sitting at the foot—Mr. Churchill himself with an enormous Corona Corona in his mouth, a glass of warm water on the table by his side and a writing pad on his knee." The First Lord then arrived at the Admiralty, spent a few hours, departed for a leisurely luncheon, enjoyed an extended nap, and worked until dinner. He was always invited out and, after several stimulating hours of talk, he would return to the Admiralty, work through until one or two in the morning, and then retire to bed. Four hours later, Lord Fisher would arrive to begin his day. On this basis, the Admiralty kept what Churchill called "an almost unsleeping watch through the day and night." To coordinate this dual control, Churchill said, "we made an agreement between ourselves that neither of us should take any important action without consulting the other, unless previous accord had been reached." Even the color of their respective notations and comments on Admiralty documents was coordinated: Churchill habitually used a pen with red ink; Fisher used a green pencil. "Port and starboard lights," Fisher called this system. And for a while the system worked.

—

Fisher returned to the Admiralty during days of crisis. He succeeded Prince Louis on Thursday, October 29. On Sunday, November 1, the Battle of Coronel was fought. On Tuesday, November 3, German battle cruisers appeared off Yarmouth on the English east coast. The very next day, Wednesday, the fourth, reports of the disaster at Coronel reached London, and that afternoon Fisher persuaded Churchill to detach *Invincible* and *Inflexible* from the

---

We argued at some length. I *knew* I was right, but Mr. Churchill was determined to bring me round to his point of view and he continued his argument in the most brilliant fashion. It was long after midnight and I was dreadfully tired, but nothing seemed to tire the First Lord. He continued to talk and I distinctly recall the odd feeling that, although it would be wholly against my will, I should in a very short while be agreeing with everything he said. But a bit of me still rebelled and recalling the incident of the broken shard in Kipling's *Kim,* I began to mutter to myself: "My name is Hall, my name is Hall. . . ."

Suddenly, he broke off to look frowningly at me. "What's that you're muttering to yourself?" he demanded.

"I'm saying," I told him, "that my name is Hall because if I listen to you much longer I shall be convinced that it's Brown."

"Then you don't agree with what I've been saying?" He was laughing heartily.

"First Lord," I said, "I don't agree with one word of it, but I can't argue with you. I've not had the training."

So the matter dropped and I went to bed.

Grand Fleet to deal with Spee. Meanwhile, on Tuesday, in the midst of these other events, Fisher convened a conference of Admiralty officials and principal British shipbuilders to launch the largest emergency shipbuilding effort in the history of the Royal Navy: eventually 606 new vessels flying the White Ensign were to go to sea. At the outbreak of war, the Admiralty had ordered accelerated work on all warships building in British shipyards, with priority to be given to vessels that could be finished in six months. Three months later, when it was apparent that the war would be longer, the policy was changed to "everything that can be finished in 1915 and nothing that can't." But only twelve new destroyers and twelve new submarines had been ordered. Fisher considered this grossly inadequate and convened the November 3 meeting to change course. His most urgent concern was the construction of submarines; that same day he placed orders with British shipbuilders for an additional twenty. Then, staring at the Admiralty Director of Contracts, he threatened to "make his wife a widow and his house a dunghill if he brought paper work or red tape into the picture; he wanted submarines, not contracts. . . . If he did not get them within eight months, he would commit *hara-kiri.*" At this, Keyes, who was present, made the mistake of laughing. Fisher then turned on Keyes "with a ferocious glare, and said, 'If anyone thwarts me he had better commit *hara-kiri* too.' " Later that day, Fisher saw the American steel magnate Charles Schwab, who as a passenger on *Olympic* had witnessed the sinking of *Audacious.* Schwab took home orders for another twenty submarines to be built by Bethlehem Steel in the United States and Canada. They were delivered within six months.

From submarines, Fisher passed to other types of ships. Five half-finished dreadnought battleships of the *Royal Sovereign* class, originally designed to burn coal, were reconfigured to burn oil. Two new British battleships, *Repulse* and *Renown,* funded but not yet laid down, each originally intended to carry eight 15-inch guns in four turrets, had been allowed to languish on drawing boards because so much time would be required for their completion. On December 19, following the dramatic vindication of the battle cruiser design at the Falkland Islands, Fisher demanded that the two battleships be radically redesigned and built quickly as fast battle cruisers. They were needed, he declared, to catch the newest German battle cruiser, *Lützow,* which had a design speed of 28 knots. In the two new British ships, 32-knot speed would be obtained by sacrificing one heavy turret with its two 15-inch guns and putting the weight thus saved into more powerful propulsion machinery. Armor also suffered; instead of the shielding that protected dreadnought battleships, the new battle cruisers carried only the armor of the early *Indefatigable*s. Both keels were laid down on Fisher's seventy-fourth birthday, January 25, 1915. He insisted that they be completed within fifteen months; in fact, *Repulse* required nineteen and *Renown* twenty.

With these two big battle cruisers under construction, Fisher went further and ordered three fast 19,000-ton ships, *Courageous, Glorious,* and *Furious. Courageous* and *Glorious* carried four 15-inch guns and *Furious,* as originally designed, two 18-inch. Because Parliament had not approved more large armored ships, but had sanctioned additional light cruisers, Fisher designated these vessels "large light cruisers" and had them built under conditions of extraordinary secrecy. All were designed with 32-knot speed, a draft of only 22 feet—five feet less than any other British capital ship—and armor so thin that the Grand Fleet, which dubbed them *Outrageous, Uproarious,* and *Spurious,* could find almost no use for them. "They were an old man's children," said Churchill. "Nevertheless, their parent loved them dearly and always rallied with the utmost vehemence when any slur was cast upon their qualities." Eventually, all three were converted into aircraft carriers.

Fisher's immense shipbuilding program also included new light cruisers and destroyers, and thirty-seven inshore monitors: 6,000- or 7,000-ton ships with slow speed and no special armor, but carrying two 12-inch or 14-inch guns. Useless in a sea battle, they were meant only to bombard enemy positions onshore. The First Sea Lord also ordered 200 steel-plated, oil-powered motor barges for landing troops upon hostile beaches. These early amphibious landing craft, forerunners of the flotillas vital to Allied operations in the Atlantic and Pacific in the Second World War, were designed to carry 500 infantrymen at a speed of 5 knots and were fitted with extended landing bridges that could be lowered from their bows onto a beach. Their appearance earned them the name of Beetles; soon, their purpose—along with the purpose of the new monitors and battle cruisers—would be revealed.

Churchill rejoiced in his new First Sea Lord's burst of energy. "Lord Fisher hurled himself into this business with explosive energy," he was to write, "and in four or five glorious days, every minute of which was pure delight to him, he presented me with schemes for far greater construction of submarines, destroyers, and small craft than I or any of my advisers had ever deemed possible. . . . Probably never in his long life had Fisher had a more joyous experience than this great effort of new construction. Shipbuilding had been the greatest passion of his life . . . [and] here were all the yards of Britain at his disposal and every Treasury barrier broken." No one was allowed to stand in his way. The army, still entirely made up of volunteers, had been recruiting in the shipyards, a practice that infuriated Fisher. To stop it, he went directly to Lord Kitchener and demanded an immediate "order to his subordinates to cease enticing away men from our shipyards. I told him that [if he did not], I would resign that day at 6 p.m. my post as First Sea Lord and give my reasons in the House of Lords. . . . [Kitchener] wrote the order there and then, without hesitation." To all this activity, Churchill gave a green light: "I backed him up all I could. He was far more often right than wrong, and his drive and life-force made the Admiralty quiver like one of his great ships at its highest speed."

—

The grand purpose for which Fisher ordered the construction of three shallow-draft "large light cruisers," dozens of inshore monitors, and scores of large landing craft was an operation that the new First Sea Lord was convinced would win the war: an invasion of the Baltic Sea by the British fleet and the subsequent landing of an army on the north German coast. Fisher had always believed that the British army's greatest effectiveness lay in amphibious operations—as "a projectile to be fired by the navy." He never liked the idea of sending the army to France to act as an extension of the French left wing; "criminal folly," he had called it. As early as the 1905 Moroccan Crisis, Fisher—certain that Britain's enemy in the next war would be Germany—was thinking of an amphibious operation to seize control of the Baltic. Since his visit to Russia with King Edward VII in 1908, he had nursed the idea of substituting "a million Russian soldiers" for British troops in a proposed landing on the Pomeranian coast "within eighty-two miles of Berlin." This force would be disembarked "on that 14 miles of sandy beach, impossible of defence against a Battle Fleet sweeping with devastating shells the flat country for miles, like a mower's scythe—no fortifications able to withstand projectiles of 1,450 lbs.!"

Fisher had no difficulty infusing his enthusiasm into Churchill. As early as August 19, 1914, the First Lord had sounded out the Russian Commander-in-Chief, Grand Duke Nicholas, on the possibility of a combined Baltic operation. Churchill offered to send the British fleet through the Belts, the channel between Denmark and Sweden. This could not be done, he cautioned, until either a decisive naval battle had been won against the High Seas Fleet or the Kiel Canal had been blocked so that the German fleet could not shift rapidly between the North Sea and the Baltic. But once established in the Baltic, Churchill continued, the British fleet could "convoy and land" a Russian army on the German coast to take Berlin. The Russian reply was tentatively favorable. "We gratefully accept in principle the First Lord's offer," the grand duke wrote, adding that "the suggested landing operations would be quite feasible and fully expedient should the British Fleet gain command of the Baltic Sea."

Fisher's return to the Admiralty temporarily linked the two powerful advocates of a Baltic naval offensive. When Churchill showed Fisher his correspondence with the Russian government, the admiral's eyes shone with enthusiasm. The new First Sea Lord's huge naval building program, begun during Fisher's first week in office and launched with the First Lord's endorsement, was filled with shallow-draft vessels designed to work in the shallow waters of the Baltic. But beyond their agreement on the grand objective of entering the Baltic, the two men differed. Fisher favored an immediate, direct naval attack on the Baltic without any preliminary effort to defeat the High Seas Fleet in battle; the German navy, he said, could be locked up inside Heligoland Bight by the laying of extensive minefields. Churchill remained dedicated to action in the Baltic, but he had reluctantly accepted that the British navy could not pass through the Belts without preliminary action to neutralize the High Seas Fleet—and that this action would have to consist of something stronger than laying minefields. Churchill's idea was to "storm and seize" an island close to the German coast; this, he believed, would provoke the Germans to a major sea battle in the island's defense; if it did not, capture of the island would provide a base to help blockade the High Seas Fleet. Three islands loomed largest in these plans: Borkum, off the Ems River; Sylt, off the coast of Schleswig-Holstein; and Heligoland itself. Unfortunately for Churchill, all of his island-seizing proposals were declared impracticable by Admiralty staff experts; it was one thing, they said, to seize an island, but quite another to hold it and keep it supplied at a considerable distance from England and a very short distance from the enemy. (One exception to the naysayers was Admiral Sir Arthur Wilson, who vehemently advocated the seizure of Heligoland, although it was bristling with artillery, surrounded by minefields, and lay only thirty miles from Wilhelmshaven, the main base of the High Seas Fleet.) Even in the face of overwhelming professional disapproval—"a palpable reluctance . . . manifested by lethargy," the First Lord called it—Churchill refused to give up. Oliver recalled that "Churchill would often look in on his way to bed to tell me how he would capture Borkum or Sylt. If I did not interrupt or ask questions, he would capture Borkum in twenty minutes."

Ultimately, the issue narrowed to a disagreement between Churchill and Fisher. "I am wholly with you about the Baltic," Churchill wrote to Fisher on December 22. "But you must close up this side first. You must take an island and block them in; or you must break the canal or the locks, or you must cripple their fleet in a general action. No scattering of mines will be any substitute for these alternatives." After the war, Churchill took a harsher view of Fisher's views: "Although the First Sea Lord's strategic conceptions were centered in the entry of the Baltic . . . I do not think he ever saw his way clearly through the great decisive and hazardous steps which were necessary for the success of the operation. . . . He talked in general terms about making the North Sea impassable by sowing mines and thus preventing the Germans from entering it while the main strength of the British fleet was in the Baltic. I could not feel any conviction that this would give us the necessary security."

While the two principal proponents of the Baltic plan continued arguing over means, an opportunity appeared at the Dardanelles, and the Baltic project faded away. This outcome came as a huge relief to the man who commanded the Grand Fleet and whose duty—had he been so ordered—would have been to lead his ships into the Baltic. Jellicoe's general reluctance to risk his fleet was coupled with a specific condemnation of Churchill's Borkum scheme. He could not understand, Jellicoe wrote, "how an attack on Borkum could possibly assist fleet operations in the Baltic or lead to the German fleet being driven altogether from the North Sea." As for Sir Arthur Wilson's idea of seizing Heligoland, Jellicoe wrote simply, "We one and all doubted Sir A.'s sanity."

—

During their first weeks together at the Admiralty and before the Baltic project began to divide them, a continuing, prolific, and mellow exchange of letters, notes, and memoranda flowed between the First Lord and the new First Sea Lord. Their relationship worked because, in addition to a shared fierce determination to defeat the enemy, each knew how to speak to the other, assuaging ego with compliments while still making the desired point. Churchill deferred to the old sea dog whenever he could, and Fisher responded in avuncular kind. On December 8, he offered Churchill advice when the First Lord returned from one of his numerous, much-criticized visits to France. "Welcome back!" Fisher wrote. "I don't hold with these 'outings' of yours! I know how you enjoy them! Nor am I afraid of responsibility while you're away! But I think it's too venturesome! Also, it gives your enemies cause to blaspheme!" Despite these warm feelings, it was not long before signs of friction appeared at the summit of the Admiralty. Fisher's ego had much to do with it. It was not easy for a First Sea Lord who had ruled and revolutionized the navy to see operational signals going out to the fleet, sent by the First Lord with the notation "First Sea Lord to see after action." In addition, Fisher's volcanic energy often overflowed established channels, and his huge outpourings on naval matters were combined with a limitless, incautious correspondence with people outside the service. Before long, his extreme language, his triple underlinings in green pencil, his capitalizations, his exclamation points, and his frequent threats of resignation were alarming as much as assisting the First Lord.

Essentially, the two men were competing for control of Britain's sea power. On this matter, both had miscalculated. The First Lord's determination to restore Fisher had rested on the assumption that he could control and use the old admiral. Paradoxically, Fisher and others had agreed to his restoration on the grounds that he alone would be capable of controlling Churchill. When this failed to happen, the admiral began to complain. "My beloved Jellicoe," he wrote to the Commander-in-Chief on December 20, "Winston has so monopolized all initiative in the Admiralty and fires off such a multitude of purely departmental memos *(his power of work is absolutely amazing!)* that my colleagues are no longer *'superintending Lords'* but only *the First Lord's registry!* I told Winston this yesterday and he did not like it at all, *but it is* true! and the consequence is that the Sea Lords are atrophied and their departments run really by the Private Office, and I find it a Herculean task to get back to the right procedure, and quite possibly I may have to clear out." Beatty had caught a whiff of this discord. "The situation is very curious," he wrote to Ethel on December 4, 1914. "Two very strong and clever men, one old, wily, and of vast experience; one young, self-assertive with a great self-satisfaction but unstable. They cannot work together. They cannot both run the show."

Long afterward, when because of the collision between the admiral and the politician, both men had been stripped of power, Violet Asquith, the prime minister's daughter and a close friend of Churchill's, asked him whether he had had any

> inkling that he was on the edge of a volcano in his relations with Fisher. He said "No," they had always got on well, differed on no principle, he had always supposed him to be perfectly loyal, etc. Poor darling Winston. . . . He is quite impervious to the climatic conditions of other people. He makes his own climate and lives in it and those who love him share it. In an odd way, there was something like love between him and Fisher, a kind of magnetic attraction which often went in reverse. Theirs was a curiously emotional relationship, but, as in many such, they could neither live with, nor without, each other.

CHAPTER 16

"The Requirements of the Commander-in-Chief Were Hard to Meet"

Historically, the Royal Navy never seriously concerned itself with numbers when it went into battle. Against the Armada, Howard and Drake brought ninety ships to face Medina Sidonia's 130. At the Battle of St. Vincent, Jervis had fifteen line-of-battle ships against Spain's twenty-seven; at Trafalgar, Nelson's twenty-seven annihilated Villeneuve's thirty-three. In 1914, however, Admiral Sir John Jellicoe, already concerned about the threat of submarines and mines and about his lack of a secure harbor, worried about the comparative strength of the Grand Fleet and the German High Seas Fleet. Throughout his two and a quarter years of command, Jellicoe kept a jealous watch over his ships; any attempt by anybody to remove a vessel, for whatever reason, was fiercely resented and likely to provoke a storm of protest. In the months ahead, Jellicoe was to begrudge even the taking of navy machine guns for the Dardanelles campaign as "weakening the Grand Fleet in principle."

Now, in the course of a fortnight in late October and early November, the fleet had been dramatically weakened. First came the sudden loss of *Audacious,* then the withdrawal of three of Beatty's battle cruisers to hunt Spee. Of these reductions in strength, it was the dispatch to the western Atlantic of the modern 13.5-inch *Princess Royal* that most upset Jellicoe. He argued that, instead of taking *Princess Royal,* Fisher should send the older, slower *New Zealand,* which, he believed, would suffice to deal with Spee's armored cruisers. Enabled by bad weather to delay by one day *Princess Royal*'s departure from Cromarty, he boldly questioned the First Sea Lord, "Is *Princess Royal* to go? . . . strongly urge *New Zealand* instead." "*Princess Royal*'s coal expenditure is not far from double that of *New Zealand,*" he explained. Jellicoe was Fisher's protégé, his own carefully selected and nurtured choice as Grand Fleet commander, but this bit of insubordination did not sit well with the crusty First Sea Lord. "*Princess Royal* should have proceeded at once on Admiralty orders," he signaled the Commander-in-Chief.

Beatty fully supported Jellicoe's effort to prevent the taking of one of his powerful Cats. Although, on November 6, his squadron was reinforced by the arrival of the new battle cruiser *Tiger,* Beatty refused to agree that this new ship was a substitute for *Princess Royal.* "The *Tiger* is absolutely unfit to fight," he wrote to Fisher. "Three out of her four dynamos are out of action for an indefinite period and her training is impeded by bad weather which might continue for many weeks at this time of year. . . . At present she is quite unprepared and inefficient." In this state, Jellicoe chimed in, "she would simply be a present for the Germans." Stripped of *Invincible, Inflexible,* and *Princess Royal,* Beatty was left with four battle cruisers—*Lion, Queen Mary, Tiger,* and *New Zealand*—to face Hipper's four battle cruisers—*Seydlitz, Moltke, Derfflinger,* and *Von der Tann.* In a letter to Jellicoe, Beatty pointed out that the change in relative strength of the two squadrons might perhaps dictate new battle tactics. He had always assumed that his duty was to engage Hipper's battle cruisers when and where he could find them. However, now that his own force lacked its previous clear predominance, he asked for a ruling as to what he should do if he encountered the German squadron. Jellicoe forwarded Beatty's letter to the Admiralty, covering it with one of his own:

> We cannot rely on much if any superiority in gunnery in my opinion. The German fleet has shown itself to be highly efficient and their gunnery . . . has been markedly excellent. I can only repeat once more my request for the *Princess Royal.* . . . I can only inform Sir David Beatty . . . that he must do the best he can with the force at his disposal . . . but I hold a very strong opinion that we are running the greatest risk of losing an opportunity of inflicting a severe defeat on the enemy . . . by not adhering to the principle of concentration in the decisive theater.

The Admiralty's reply to Jellicoe was austere: "The inferiority of the 1st Battle Cruiser Squadron to the German [Battle] Cruiser Squadron . . . is so slight that it should not make any difference in the Vice Admiral's duty to engage the latter if opportunity offers." Nevertheless, Fisher, recognizing his own words and beliefs in Jellicoe's language, attempted to make amends. He summoned the battle cruiser *Indomitable* from the Mediterranean to join Beatty, and two armored cruisers to join Jellicoe. On November 28, he wrote Beatty a remarkably conciliatory letter: "I admit the force of all your arguments. . . . The eventuality (not yet improbable) has still to be faced of the

Scharnhorst and Company coming through the Panama Canal to New York to release the mass of armed German liners ready to emerge into the Atlantic. Why the *Vaterland* has not 'nipped out' already is beyond me! Remember, the last new German battle cruiser, *Derfflinger* . . . is even later commissioned than the *Tiger,* and we know has had very little gunnery practice. . . . As I told Jellicoe, had I known of the *New Zealand* having more coal endurance, I would have taken her. I am in the position of a chess player coming into the game after some damned bad moves have been made in the opening of the game. . . . It's very difficult to retrieve a game badly begun."

As November progressed, Jellicoe's anxieties grew. He worried about the three absent battle cruisers and he worried even more about his day-to-day strength in the basic unit of naval supremacy, dreadnought battleships. On paper, which was where Churchill viewed and compared numbers, the Grand Fleet had a comfortable superiority over the High Seas Fleet. On August 2, when Jellicoe took command, the Grand Fleet had nineteen dreadnought battleships and four dreadnought battle cruisers.* Since then, the former Turkish battleships now named *Erin* and *Agincourt* had come to the fleet and *Iron Duke*'s sisters, *Emperor of India* and *Benbow,* were coming in December. Meanwhile, the German High Seas Fleet, which had begun the war with thirteen dreadnought battleships and four battle cruisers, had received or was about to receive three new dreadnought battleships. Each fleet had been augmented by one new battle cruiser, the British *Tiger* and the German *Derfflinger.*

On paper, this arithmetic—nineteen battleships to thirteen in August; twenty-three to sixteen in December–January—was always favorable to Jellicoe. These were the numbers the First Lord saw and they satisfied him that all was well. But numbers on paper told only part of the story. During the war's first months, the Grand Fleet, lacking a secure base, was constantly at sea moving at high speed to thwart the U-boats. By November, continual high-speed steaming had taken a toll on condensers and other propulsion machinery. Breakdowns were occurring and Jellicoe was compelled to establish a regular repair schedule, sending ships, one from each battle squadron at a time, down to their home ports on the south coast for refits. Sadly, these ailments most affected the newest 13.5-inch-gun dreadnoughts, including Jellicoe's own flagship, *Iron Duke.* Thus, during one two-week period, *Iron Duke* and *Ajax* both had leaking condenser tubes, which affected their speed, *Orion* had gone to Glasgow for examination of her main turbine supports, *Superb* had turbine trouble with stripped blades, *Conqueror* was refitting at Devonport, and *New Zealand* was in dry dock at Cromarty. At

*Six other British battle cruisers were scattered around the world: *Inflexible, Indomitable,* and *Indefatigable* in the Mediterranean, hunting *Goeben; Invincible* at Queenstown in southern Ireland, guarding the Atlantic trade route; *Australia* in the Pacific; and *Tiger* in training.

best, the result was the permanent absence from the Grand Fleet of two or three of its most important vessels as well as perhaps one battle cruiser, one or two armored cruisers, a light cruiser, and six destroyers. Recalculating relative strength on the basis of these additional factors, Jellicoe's arithmetic differed from Churchill's. He reckoned that, allowing for breakdowns and refits, he had nineteen dreadnoughts against sixteen German dreadnoughts. And since the competent but uninspired Admiral von Ingenohl could always choose a day to come out when all sixteen of his dreadnought battleships and four battle cruisers were available, the effective strength of the Grand Fleet was no more than that of the High Seas Fleet. On this point, no one at the Admiralty disputed Jellicoe. Indeed, Churchill himself had offered the maxim that "We must always be ready to meet at our average moment anything that . . . [the] enemy might hurl against us at his selected moment."

Jellicoe's pessimistic arithmetic and cautious hoarding were subject to criticism during and after the war. But he refused to give way, knowing that the gray ships stretched out in lines at Scapa Flow were the primary defense of the nation. Nor was this all. Jellicoe knew or suspected something that Churchill did not know and that Jacky Fisher would never admit: vessel for vessel, German ships were better constructed than British ships. It was Jellicoe's conviction, derived from years at the Admiralty and considerable experience with the German navy, that in matters such as armor plating, underwater protection, watertight subdivision of compartments, gunnery control, and some types of shells, the British fleet was inferior to the German. If so, the Grand Fleet was not the overwhelmingly superior weapon the country, Churchill, and many in the navy believed it to be.

Churchill found Jellicoe's constant complaints hard to bear. He believed that Jellicoe always magnified his own disadvantages and credited the enemy with more ships than he actually possessed. Not having a naval background, Churchill tended to compare ships solely by the size of their guns and he could not understand Jellicoe's insistence that until her crew was properly trained and her machinery thoroughly tested, a ship was virtually useless. When the Admiralty sent the Grand Fleet a new ship, the First Lord counted it; until the ship was ready, Jellicoe did not. A tone of exasperation crept into the First Lord's relationship and correspondence with Jellicoe: "The requirements of the Commander-in-Chief were hard to meet," Churchill wrote after the war.

> If at any time two or three [capital] ships were absent from the Grand Fleet for a week or two, the Commander-in-Chief drew severe comparisons between the High Seas Fleet and his own. He was a master of this kind of argument. From his own side he deducted any ship which had any defect, however temporary, however small—even defects which would not have prevented her from taking her place in the line

> in an emergency. He sometimes also deducted two or three of the most powerful battleships in the world because they were not trained up to the full level of efficiency of the others, and these were absolutely blotted out as if they were of no value whatever. The enemy he always credited with several more ships than we now know they had or were then thought likely to have. . . . Unable to deny that the British line of battle could fire a broadside double in weight to that of the Germans, he developed a skilful argument to prove that this advantage was more than counteracted by other disadvantages. . . . He dwelt on this even at a period when his fleet had been reinforced by seven or eight additional units of enormous power without any corresponding accession to the enemy's strength.

Jellicoe's argument with the Admiralty extended beyond dreadnoughts to include the eight predreadnought battleships of the *King Edward* class, each of which carried four 12-inch guns. Jellicoe wanted them stationed as far north as possible in order to bring thirty-two additional heavy guns to bear on the High Seas Fleet when Ingenohl came out to fight; the Admiralty wanted to keep them farther south to help defend the east coast from raids or invasion. On November 13, Churchill attempted a general mollification of the Commander-in-Chief: "Since war began you have gained two dreadnoughts on balance and will by 20th have twenty-seven superior units to twenty. We intend *Princess Royal* to join you as soon as *Scharnhorst* is dealt with. During the next month you should suspend sending ships away for refit, doing the best you can at Scapa. . . . If . . . you still feel need for further reinforcement, we propose stationing *King Edwards* at Rosyth, where they can join you for general action or repelling invasion. . . . If you agree, the eight *King Edwards* will be ordered to sail tonight."

But Jellicoe did not want the *King Edward*s at Rosyth; he wanted them farther north—at Scapa Flow or Cromarty. Further, he replied, the twenty-seven dreadnoughts cited by the Admiralty included two ships that had never fired a gun and a third whose crew was only partially trained. The Admiralty, however, refused to change its orders. "We cannot reinforce you at present, nor alter our dispositions," Churchill wrote on November 17. Taking these positions, Churchill had the support of Fisher and Sir Arthur Wilson. "I think we have to stand fast," Fisher had written to Churchill regarding Jellicoe's request to move the *King Edward*s north. "The Tyrwhitt mob and our overseas submarines are our sole aggressive force in the South." But Fisher did not blame Jellicoe for requesting reinforcements. Writing to Churchill, he noted, "As A. K. Wilson observed a moment ago, both he and I would probably have written exactly the same letter as Jellicoe, trying to get all we could! Yours till death, F."

The Admiralty, having told Jellicoe that it was sending the *King Edward*s to Rosyth, then inflicted fresh pain by insisting that he surrender some of his Grand Fleet destroyers to screen the old battleships. Churchill's letter had a defensive tone: "The coast has been so denuded of destroyers for sake of strengthening the force with you (amounting now to seventy-one) that there is only a skeleton force between the Naze [Harwich] and St. Abbs Head [Rosyth], a distance of 300 miles. . . . You should detach half a flotilla [that is, ten destroyers] of the seventy-one destroyers at Scapa to act with . . . [the *King Edwards*]. . . . We are sending a comparative table of your fleet and German High Seas Fleet which makes it quite clear that, without the *King Edwards,* you have such a preponderance of gun power that with equal gunnery efficiency, a successful result is ensured." To soothe, Churchill added, "The Admiralty have in mind the importance of getting back the *Princess Royal* as soon as the situation admits."

Jellicoe reacted with controlled anger. He declared that the seventy-one destroyers mentioned by the Admiralty included ten that were absent from his fleet, refitting. He pointed out that the forty destroyers of the Harwich flotillas had been omitted from Churchill's mention of the "skeleton force" between the Naze and St. Abbs Head. "I regret to appear importunate," he continued, "but must beg for reconsideration of the order detaching a half flotilla" to join the *King Edwards* at Rosyth. Without these ten destroyers, he said, the safety of the dreadnought battle fleet was endangered. A U-boat attack on Scapa Flow was quite feasible and "as I am directed to use this base, I trust I shall not be held responsible for any disaster that may occur." As for a major fleet action, Jellicoe did not take the Harwich Force destroyers into account as he felt that they could not be counted on to join the Grand Fleet at the moment the Germans chose to come out. "I know perfectly well," he wrote to Fisher on December 4, "that the Harwich flotillas will not join me in time." Jellicoe also knew that the Germans had eight flotillas comprising eighty-eight destroyers assigned to the High Seas Fleet and that every one would certainly be there on the day Ingenohl chose to come out. The German destroyers "have five torpedoes each—total four hundred forty torpedoes," he continued. He himself might arrive for this battle bringing as few as thirty-two or even twenty-eight destroyers. The result, he warned the First Sea Lord, might be retreat. "You know the difficulty and objections to turning away from the enemy in a fleet action, but with such a menace, I am bound to do it unless my own destroyers can stop or neutralize the [enemy's] movement." "I cannot but feel," he concluded, "that with my present weakness in destroyers, I am greatly handicapped in obtaining the crushing victory over the High Seas Fleet that is expected of me." In reply to this argument, the Admiralty gave little ground, declaring only that eight, not ten, of Jellicoe's destroyers must leave Scapa Flow for Rosyth.

Overall, Churchill found these discussions "wearing," but, counseled by Fisher, he never considered making a change in command. "No one can blame the Commander-in-Chief for endeavouring to keep his command up to the highest level of strength," he wrote of Jellicoe after the war. "I always tried to sustain him in every possible way. He bore with constancy the many troubles and perplexities of the early months. . . . Even when I did not share his outlook, I sympathised with his trials."

—

If Jellicoe objected to the Admiralty taking three battle cruisers from the North Sea to deal with Spee, and stripping away Grand Fleet destroyers to meet other needs, he was certainly not mollified when Churchill began sending him "battleships" and "battle cruisers" that he had not asked for and did not want. These were not real warships, but dummies—old merchant ships transformed into likenesses of dreadnoughts, intended to deceive the enemy as to where the real battleships and battle cruisers might be. The idea—to create a make-believe battle squadron that could pass itself off at sea as real—was entirely Churchill's. On October 21, he wrote to Prince Louis, then still First Sea Lord:

> It is necessary to construct without delay a dummy fleet; ten merchant vessels . . . mocked up to represent battleships. . . . The actual size need not correspond exactly, as it is notoriously difficult to judge the size of vessels at sea, and frequently even destroyers are mistaken for cruisers. We are bearing in mind particularly aerial and periscope observations where deception is much more easy. It is not necessary that the structures be strong enough to stand rough weather. Very little metal would be required and practically the whole work should be executed in wood and canvas. . . . Even when the enemy knows we have such a fleet . . . he will always be in doubt as to which is the real and which is the dummy fleet. . . .
>
> The matter is urgent. . . . The utmost secrecy must be observed and special measures must be taken to banish all foreigners from the districts where the mocking up is being done. I should hope to receive the list of ships which are selected for conversion tomorrow. . . . I should expect in a fortnight, or at the outside in three weeks, that ten vessels will actually be at our disposal.

Admiral Sir Percy Scott, the famous gunnery expert, was called from retirement to supervise this structural chicanery and, before the end of the month, steamships were commandeered and brought to the Harland and Wolff shipyard in Belfast. The first ten vessels selected were elderly liners, the oldest being thirty-four years old. To determine how each transformation was to be accomplished, an Admiralty draftsman made a tracing of the steamer and placed it over a battleship design on the same scale. "The next day," according to Scott, "Messrs. Harland & Wolff had about two thousand men cutting . . . fine merchant ships to pieces." Within a week, wood and canvas structures were reproducing guns, turrets, boats, tripod masts, and bridges. Because a liner rises higher out of the water than a battleship, the merchantmen were filled with thousands of tons of ballast to push the hulls lower. The shapes of bows and sterns were altered. False funnels were added and were equipped with fireplaces to burn combustible materials that would emit thick clouds of smoke. Navy anchors were made of wood or were simply painted on the bows. Once these vessels were ready, they came under the command of Captain H. J. Haddock of the White Star Line, now himself transformed into a commodore in the Royal Navy Reserve. Only two weeks before, Haddock had been master of the 52,000-ton transatlantic liner *Olympic;* his seamanship in the attempt to tow the sinking dreadnought *Audacious* had attracted the admiring attention of the Admiralty.

Only five weeks after Scott took charge, the first dummies put to sea. On December 7, the Grand Fleet at Scapa Flow looked on with amusement as two 7,000-ton dummies, the thirty-two-year-old former *City of Oxford* and the twenty-seven-year-old former *Michigan,* masquerading as 25,000-ton *St. Vincent*–class dreadnoughts, arrived in the anchorage. Other dummies followed. As they came in—*Montezuma, Ruthenia, Tyrolia, Oruba, Mount Royal, Montcalm, Perthshire*—they were officially referred to by their warship names—*"Iron Duke," "King George V," "Orion," "Marlborough,"* and *"Vanguard."* No one was fooled. Real battleship squadrons were usually made up of generally homogeneous ships. But when the dummies came together, some were twice the size of the others. Their speeds varied greatly. Some could make 15 knots, others 10, others only 7, and, as a squadron's speed must be that of the slowest member, 7 knots became the speed at which the dummies could steam together. A 7-knot squadron could not operate with the 20-knot Grand Fleet. "The ships," said Jellicoe, "could not accompany the fleet to sea and it was very difficult to find a use for them in home waters." The suggestion that they be used as bait was rejected. An encounter with the enemy would have led to massacre.

Despite Churchill's insistence on secrecy, the existence of the dummy squadron quickly became known in Germany, prompting the German Naval Staff to wonder about its purpose. Toward the middle of January 1915, Ingenohl convinced himself that a British naval offensive was imminent and that the dummy warships were part of a plan for running block ships into Heligoland Bight and sinking them in the mouths of the Elbe, the Weser, and the Jade. This idea had not occurred at the Admiralty.

Finding no way to use them, the Admiralty sent the finished dummies from Scapa Flow to Loch Ewe where, as new units were commissioned, Commodore Haddock's collection continued to grow. Four more steamers were commandeered and turned into battle cruisers: *"Queen Mary"* (formerly

Cevic), *"Tiger"* (formerly *Merion*), *"Indomitable"* (formerly *Manipur*), and *"Invincible"* (formerly *Patrician*). By January, fourteen imitation battleships and battle cruisers were ready for sea, still without purpose, but absorbing the services of a number of valuable officers and seamen. At the end of April, the dummy *Queen Mary* was sent to patrol off New York City as a message to the German liners interned in the harbor that, if they violated their internment and tried to break out, a British battle cruiser was waiting to gobble them up. The assault on the Dardanelles suggested another use; the dummy battle cruisers *Indomitable* and *Tiger* departed Loch Ewe on February 19. To avoid being seen, they passed through the Strait of Gibraltar at midnight, and they were forbidden to enter the harbors of Gibraltar or Malta where they could be studied close up. The dummy *Invincible* followed six weeks later. Churchill hoped that by sending them to the Mediterranean, where they might be seen at a distance, they might "mislead the Germans as to the margin of British strength in home waters" and tempt the enemy to come out and do battle in the North Sea. The Turks did misidentify the dummy *Tiger* and reported her to a German submarine. On May 30, she was hit and sunk by torpedo and four British seamen drowned. A British midshipman with the Dardanelles fleet found grim humor in the event, imagining the U-boat captain "astonished to see the surviving crew clinging to the floating wooden turrets."

Thereafter, the curtain came down on the theatrical. Once Churchill left the Admiralty, the dummy fleet, which had cost Britain £1 million and four lives and Germany a single torpedo, quickly disappeared. One dummy, representing *Orion,* was temporarily retained and, in August 1915, she was sent from Scapa to Rosyth with a heavy list to suggest a disabled battleship going south for repairs. Escorted by destroyers, she hoped to attract German submarines, which the destroyers would then sink. The effort failed. Eventually, all of the dummy dreadnoughts were returned to reality and reverted to mundane roles as oilers, water ships, block ships, a torpedo depot ship, and a troop transport.

CHAPTER 17

The Yarmouth Raid and Room 40

At dawn, HMS *Halcyon,* a small, twenty-year-old minesweeping gunboat, nosed out of the port of Yarmouth into the drifting mist off the Norfolk coast to take up her daily duty: hunting for drifting mines in the coastal shipping channel. Two elderly destroyers, *Lively* and *Leopard,* followed *Halcyon* to begin their own routine offshore patrols. It was November 3, 1914, and these three ships along with four other old destroyers constituted Yarmouth's defense. There were no land fortifications. Before the war, a territorial battery of mobile 6-inch guns had been stationed nearby, but when the army had gone to France, the guns went too. Since the sinking of the three *Bacchante*s on the Broad Fourteens, no heavy ships were anywhere nearer than the old predreadnoughts at Sheerness, a hundred miles away. Beatty's fast battle cruisers were 300 miles to the north, at Cromarty, and most of Jellicoe's battleships were twice that distance away, at Lough Swilly in northern Ireland.

In the early light, *Halcyon* made her way northeast through calm water toward the Cross Sand light vessel. *Lively* and *Leopard* were two miles astern. Suddenly, two unknown ships, both four-funneled light cruisers, appeared five miles to the north. *Halcyon* signaled a challenge. This was greeted with nearby splashes from shells fired by small-caliber naval guns, followed by towering waterspouts created by 11-inch shells. In the mist, *Halcyon* could not make out the identity of her assailants, but in fact she was confronting three German battle cruisers, a large armored cruiser, and four light cruisers. Rear Admiral Franz Hipper and the battle cruiser squadron of the High Seas Fleet were conducting the German navy's first major offensive into British home waters.

—

One month earlier, on October 3, Admiral von Pohl, Chief of the Naval Staff, and Admiral von Ingenohl, Commander-in-Chief of the High Seas Fleet, had met on board *Friedrich der Grosse* to discuss the kaiser's decision to keep the fleet on the defensive in the North Sea. The imperial decision, however, did not preclude offensive minelaying off the British coast; the first result was an effort on October 17 by four German destroyers to lay mines off the Thames. When all four destroyers were sunk before laying a single mine, Ingenohl decided to retaliate, taking advantage of William's ruling that "the battle fleet must avoid heavy losses, but there is nothing to be said against the battle cruisers trying to damage the enemy." If they were fortunate, battle cruiser raids would draw units of the Grand Fleet south onto German-laid minefields and across a line of U-boats. Besides, attacks on English coastal towns promised a strong morale effect: positive in Germany, negative in Britain. Hipper was eager to undertake the mission.

Final authorization for a raid on the Norfolk coast came on October 29. Light cruisers were assigned to lay mines off Yarmouth and Lowestoft in order to disrupt coastal shipping lanes and fishing traffic while Hipper's battle cruisers bombarded Yarmouth. Typically cautious, Ingenohl had not admitted to the kaiser that a bombardment was planned; in his telegram requesting permission for the raid, he merely mentioned that battle cruisers would "escort the [mine-laying] cruisers."

At 4:30 on the afternoon of November 2, Hipper's flagship, *Seydlitz,* along with *Moltke, Von der Tann,* and *Blücher,* departed the Jade with four light cruisers, *Strassburg, Graudenz, Kolberg,* and *Stralsund;* the latter was to lay the mines. At 6:00 p.m., two dreadnought battle squadrons of the High Seas Fleet followed them into the Bight to provide support. The battle cruisers swung north in an arc past Heligoland to avoid patrolling British submarines and then, out in the North Sea, Hipper altered course to the west and increased speed to 18 knots. On the bridge of *Seydlitz,* the admiral's excitement was obvious; for the first time in the war, a major German naval force was about to enter enemy waters. Not much concerned about British surface opposition because he expected to surprise the enemy, he worried mainly about mines. "I don't want to go to the bottom so ingloriously," he said. "To run on mines and sink off the English coast is hardly what I'm out for!" At midnight, the advancing squadron encountered clusters of fishing trawlers. Hipper feared that some might have wireless sets that could be used to report his presence and he tried to avoid them, but the small vessels were too numerous.

Approaching England in darkness at high speed, Hipper's captains found themselves uncertain of their exact position. (At the outbreak of war, the British Admiralty had removed most North Sea navigation buoys and lights.)

Then, at 6:30 a.m., *Seydlitz* spotted a buoy marked "Smith's Knoll Watch." Now that he knew where he was, Hipper steamed south across Yarmouth Bay, preparing to bombard the town. Almost immediately, however, the Germans noticed a small warship five miles away on the port beam and *Strassburg* and *Graudenz* quickly opened fire. Hipper, afraid that the two light cruisers were too close to the British minefields, ordered them to cease and instructed *Seydlitz* alone to fire from a distance on the little *Halcyon.* Nevertheless, the other German battle cruisers immediately joined in. The eagerness of the German gun crews was responsible: this was their first sight of an enemy vessel in wartime. The result was that so many large shell splashes smothered the small target that accurate spotting was impossible. Drenched and lucky, *Halcyon* escaped.

—

When the German guns began firing, the destroyer *Lively* hurried up and, seeing *Halcyon*'s acute danger, laid down a smoke screen between her and the enemy. For a quarter of an hour, the two small ships were under heavy fire. *Halcyon* was struck on the bridge, her radio room was damaged, and three men were wounded; *Lively* was not hit. At 7:40 a.m., Hipper realized that he was wasting time fighting these small ships and that a further pursuit to the south would take his force into a known minefield. He ceased fire and turned his battle cruisers back to sea. As they departed, the battle cruisers flung a few scattered shells toward Yarmouth, but the projectiles hit only the beach. Meanwhile as the light improved, *Stralsund* finished laying a line of mines five miles long in the Smith's Knoll passage.

Once out of danger, *Halcyon* repaired her radio and began broadcasting a general warning. *Leopard* also was signaling: "Two battle cruisers and two armored cruisers open fire on *Lively* and myself." Local British forces began to move. The destroyer *Success* joined *Lively* and *Leopard* in following Hipper eastward out to sea. The three "off-duty" destroyers of the Yarmouth patrol began raising steam. The submarines *E-10, D-5,* and *D-3,* lying in Yarmouth harbor, put to sea. Coming out on the surface, *D-5* struck a mine—whether one of *Stralsund*'s or a drifting British mine, no one ever knew—and in less than a minute the submarine went down. Two officers and two men in the conning tower were saved; the rest of the crew was drowned. None of the other submarines saw anything of Hipper's squadron.

Through all this, the Admiralty was silent. Normally, shells falling on an English beach would have triggered an instant signal: "Send the navy!" Nevertheless, since 7:00 a.m., the Admiralty had been monitoring wireless signals but doing nothing; no warnings went out, no orders flashed that ships and squadrons were to get under way. In fact, the Admiralty and the British navy were in temporary disarray. It was a difficult time: the new First Sea Lord, Jacky Fisher, had been in office only three days and, at 3:10 that morning, the first word had come of the disaster in the South Pacific at Coronel. In addition, for the first time in the war, the Commander-in-Chief of the Grand Fleet was absent from his fleet. Jellicoe had been summoned to London for an Admiralty conference on November 2, and on November 3 he was returning by train to Scotland.

At 8:30, *Halcyon* reached Yarmouth and was able to send a more accurate report: the enemy force had included four battle cruisers and four light cruisers and was last seen twelve miles off Lowestoft. Owing to the time necessary for decoding, there was further delay before the Admiralty received this information. Then, for another ninety minutes, the Admiralty remained silent, intercepting and recording signals but taking no action. By 9:55 a.m., when the Admiralty, coming to life, ordered Beatty south with his battle cruisers and summoned Jellicoe's battle squadrons—without Jellicoe, who was still in transit—from their Irish anchorages, Hipper had left the coast of England fifty miles behind.

Later, Winston Churchill made the case for delay:

> Early in the morning of November 3 . . . heavy shells were reported to be bursting in the water and on the beach near Yarmouth. The First Sea Lord and I reached the War Room from our bedrooms in a few minutes. The question was What did it mean? It seemed quite certain that German battle cruisers would not be sent only to throw a few shells at an open town like Yarmouth. Obviously, this was a demonstration to divert the British Fleet from something else which was going to happen—was perhaps already happening. . . . We had no means of judging. The last thing it seemed possible to believe was that first-class units of the German fleet would have been sent across the North Sea simply in order to disturb the fisher-folk of Yarmouth. If the German demonstration off Yarmouth was the prelude or concomitant to a serious attempt to break into the Channel, the very greatest naval events would follow. Meanwhile, nothing to be done but put everyone on guard. . . . Several hours of tension passed; and then gradually it became clear that the German battle cruisers were returning home at full speed and that nothing else was apparently happening; and the incredible conclusion forced itself upon us that the German Admiralty had had no other purpose than this silly demonstration off Yarmouth beach.

—

Before the affair was concluded, however, the German navy suffered a serious loss. On the night of November 3, the returning fleet found the river mouths covered by dense fog, and Ingenohl ordered all ships to anchor overnight in Schillig roads. At dawn the next day, although the fog was still so thick that it was impossible for one ship to see another, the 9,350-ton armored cruiser *Yorck* received permission to proceed into Wilhelmshaven for repairs to her fresh-water tanks. To do this, the ship had to pass through a small gap in the double row of mines that guarded the southern side of Schillig roads. In the murk, *Yorck* lost her way. A change of current carried her to the wrong side of the moored mine-warfare vessel marking the entrance to the swept channel. Turning hard to correct her error, the cruiser was carried south by the current and struck broadside against a mine. A minute later, she hit another mine, capsized, and sank. Many in the crew saved themselves by clinging to the keel, now protruding above the shallow water. Others, numbing in the icy sea, attempted to swim to safety. Two hundred and thirty-five men drowned.

The Imperial Navy's first major surface offensive into the North Sea had been an embarrassment. Weak British forces in the Yarmouth area had been surprised, but largely undamaged. The shore bombardment had churned only sand and water. The one success the Germans could claim was that their newly laid minefield had destroyed one British submarine and three fishing trawlers. The German Naval Staff was disappointed and Hipper, in a temporary fit of depression, refused to pin on the Iron Cross the kaiser had awarded him after the raid. "I won't wear it," he declared, "until I've done something." And, as it happened, most German officers were eager to try again. Ingenohl continued to be averse to risk, but, as he admitted after the war, "It appeared that the risk [in such a raid] was not as [great as] it seemed. If the battle cruisers suddenly appeared on the spot at daybreak, remained there for an hour or an hour and a half, and then retreated at high speed, it would be a very unfortunate coincidence indeed if, just at this time of the year, when the days were so short, superior enemy forces were met before dark. For so much time would have elapsed before the enemy forces could get up steam and put to sea . . . that our ships would already have a considerable lead."

In this hopeful forecast, Ingenohl left out two factors, one of which he ought to have considered, the other about which he could not have known. The first was bluntly spelled out later in a critical paragraph of the official German naval history: "One could not assume so great a factor of safety in the superior speed of our battle cruisers as it might appear here [in Ingenohl's argument]. A single casualty by mine or submarine or any other accident—for example a machinery failure or an unlucky hit by enemy guns on a single ship—could suddenly decrease the speed of the battle cruiser squadron so that the assistance of the [High Seas] fleet, all too far astern, would come too late." As it happened, Hipper's raids continued, and eventually just such a scenario became a reality.

The other danger to German ships engaged in raids on the British coast—a danger that Ingenohl did not know or even imagine—was that soon the British would know in advance when his ships were putting to sea and where they were going.

—

Wireless telegraphy was used by all warships and many merchantmen in 1914 and already, through the foresight of Rear Admiral Henry Oliver, the prewar Director of Naval Intelligence, the British navy had constructed radio directional stations along the east and southeast coasts of Britain. By taking cross bearings, these stations enabled listeners to establish the position—and from successive positions, the course—of any enemy ship sending wireless signals. But once hostilities began and British wireless stations began picking up German messages, establishing only the positions and courses of ships seemed insufficient. The intercepted German wireless signals were in code, and the Admiralty wanted to know what the coded messages contained. While the messages, forwarded to the Admiralty, piled up on his desk, Oliver moved to create an organization that could discover exactly what the Germans were saying to one another—an organization, that is, which could break the German codes. To tackle this job, Oliver turned to a friend, the former Director of Naval Education, Sir Alfred Ewing. Described by his son as a "short, thick-set man with keen blue eyes overshadowed by ill-kept, shaggy eyebrows," Ewing invariably wore a gray suit, "a mauve shirt, a white butterfly collar, and a dark blue bow tie with white spots." He had been a professor of engineering in Tokyo, had held chairs at Dundee and Cambridge Universities, where he had done pioneering studies of Japanese earthquakes, and was married to an American whose great-great-uncle was George Washington. Ewing agreed to Oliver's request and immediately went off to the library of the British Museum to study its collection of old codebooks. Then, gathering around him a small group of German scholars and university dons, he established a secret Admiralty department, which began working in his own cramped office. In their first weeks, they sorted and filed intercepts and learned to identify call stations and to distinguish naval messages from military ones, but they made no progress in deciphering German naval messages. And then—twice from German captains' shipboard safes and once from the bottom of the sea—the Admiralty was handed the solutions to these mysteries. The German navy began the war with three principal codes. Within four months, the British navy was in possession of all three.

The first German naval codebook fell into Allied hands in the first week of the war when, on August 11, the German steamship *Hobart* was seized off Melbourne by a boarding party of Australians. The German captain attempted to destroy his confidential documents; he was seen in the act and the papers were confiscated. They included a copy of the "Handelsverkehrsbuch" (HVB), a codebook originally intended for communication between German warships and merchantmen, but expanded for use by naval shore commands, coastal stations, and, eventually, U-boats and zeppelins. Its importance was not realized in Melbourne until September 9, when the Naval Board there belatedly informed the British Admiralty of its prize. A copy was dispatched by steamer to England, but it was not until October that the HVB code finally reached London. By then, the Admiralty had acquired a second and even more secret German code contained in the "Signalbuch der Kaiserlichen Marine" (SKM).

The book, six inches thick, fifteen inches long, twelve inches wide, and bound in blue leather, was a gift from the Russians. This is what happened: just after midnight August 26, the German light cruisers *Augsburg* and *Magdeburg* and three destroyers were moving through dense fog along the Russian Estonian coast in the upper Baltic. Unable to see the other ships, *Magdeburg* became separated and went aground 400 yards off the northwestern tip of Odensholm, a small, sandy island with a lighthouse and a signal station, at the entrance to the Gulf of Finland. *Magdeburg*'s captain tried desperately to free his ship, running the engines forward and backward at full speed, throwing overboard anchors, anchor chains, coal, ammunition, minelaying rails, bulkhead doors, and most of the vessel's fresh drinking water. *Magdeburg* refused to move. At 8:30 a.m., the fog lifted and the German destroyer *V-26* arrived. Her effort to tow *Magdeburg* into deeper water failed. Soon, *Magdeburg*'s radio room was reporting signals from approaching Russian ships. Captain Richard Habenicht, realizing that his situation was hopeless, decided that his duty was to blow up his ship. Explosive charges were placed, and *V-26* came alongside to take off the crew. Suddenly, there came a shout: "The fuses are lit." This was premature; the crew was not ready and now the vessel would blow up in four and a half minutes.

Besides wishing to save his crew, Habenicht was urgently concerned that the cruiser's secret documents not fall into Russian hands. On board were four copies of the principal German navy codebook, the SKM, one on the bridge, one in the chart house, one in the radio room, and one hidden in a locker in the captain's cabin. The radio officer had already taken one of the copies to the engine room and burned it. In the confusion following the cry that the fuses had been lit, he directed his men to carry the codebooks from the bridge and the radio room to the *V-26*. At this moment, the ship's First Officer, unable to find the captain, ordered "Abandon Ship!" Hearing this, the signalman carrying the bridge copy of the codebook threw it over the side and then jumped overboard himself. When the explosive charge detonated, pieces of the ship splashed down on the men in the water. The radioman carrying the codebook from the radio room disappeared, along with the codebook he was carrying. *V-26* picked up some of the men, struggling to swim, but for fear of being destroyed by a second explosion, the destroyer backed away and left the stricken ship. Soon afterward, the Russian light cruisers *Palladia* and *Bogatyr* appeared and sent a boarding party to *Magdeburg*, which, being aground, could not sink. Searching the wreck, a Russian naval lieutenant broke open the locker in Habenicht's cabin. Inside, he found the fourth copy of the SKM, forgotten in the excitement. Later, Russian divers inspecting the seabed around the stranded vessel found two more codebooks; the bridge copy that had been thrown overboard and the other lost by the vanished radioman.

The Russians now were in possession of one of the deepest secrets of the German navy. Recognizing its value, they notified their ally and set aside for the British the undamaged SKM, the one found in Habenicht's locker, which bore the serial number 151. They kept the waterlogged codebooks for themselves. As Churchill told the story later, "[When] the German light cruiser *Magdeburg* was wrecked in the Baltic, the body of a drowned German under-officer was picked up by the Russians a few hours later, and clasped in his bosom by arms rigid with death, were the cypher and signal books of the German Navy. . . . On September 6, the Russian Naval Attaché came to see me. He had received a message from Petrograd that . . . the Russians felt that, as the leading naval Power, the British Admiralty ought to have these books and charts. If we would send a vessel . . . the Russian officers in charge of the books would bring them to England. We lost no time in sending a ship and, late on an October afternoon, Prince Louis and I received from the hands of our loyal allies these sea-stained, priceless documents."*

The codebook went immediately to the Admiralty's new codebreaking agency. Ewing's codebreakers were still struggling to unscramble it when they received from Australia the copy of the Handelsverkehrsbuch, or HVB, taken from the German merchant ship off Melbourne. Together, the SKM and HVB codes gave Ewing's handful of cryptanalysts plenty to do. More experts were recruited and a new, larger workplace—Room 40 of the Old Building of the Admiralty—was found. On the same corridor as the First Sea Lord's office, the room was twenty-four feet by seventeen feet, looked out on an inner courtyard, and was quiet and remote from the rest of the Admiralty. Eventually, as work and personnel expanded, more space was needed and nearby rooms were commandeered. But, to the few people who knew of its existence, "Room 40" became and remained the unofficial name for the codebreaking office.

The work was complex, but during November the British began to succeed in translating portions of German naval messages. Mostly, they were of a routine naval housekeeping character, but, increasingly, collection of these scraps provided a body of information from which the enemy's arrange-

*The facts were not quite as luridly dramatic as this. No codebooks were taken from "arms rigid with death," nor was the copy the Admiralty received "sea-stained." In fact, the fat blue volume, Number 151 of the SKM, now in the Public Record Office in London, shows no sign of immersion in salt water: it came from the thoroughly dry interior of Captain Habenicht's safe.

ments in the Heligoland Bight could be understood. Then, early in December, Room 40 had another stroke of luck when a third major German navy codebook arrived in Ewing's office. It came as a result of the battle on October 17 when a British squadron had sunk four German minelaying destroyers off the Dutch coast. Before *S-119* went down, the destroyer's captain had properly dropped his secret papers overboard in a lead-lined chest. They remained on the seabed for six weeks until, on November 30, a British fishing trawler happened to haul up the chest as part of its daily catch. Inside were secret charts of the North Sea marked with the German operational grid used to plot the location of friendly and enemy warships. The chest also contained a codebook new to the British, the Verkehrsbuch (VB), intended primarily for cable communication with warships overseas or with naval attachés or embassies, and sometimes, with special reciphering, used by senior naval officers at sea. By December 3, the book and the charts were "drying before Ewing's fire." The new book was immediately useful. "Some days earlier"—the story is told by David Kahn, the preeminent contemporary historian of codes and codebreaking—"the British had intercepted two almost identical German naval messages. One was encoded entirely in the *Magdeburg* codebook and so could be read by Room 40. A small part of the second was encoded in the newly found code. . . . [Thus] the *Signalbuch* gave meaning to the coded portion of the *Verkehrsbuch* message. . . . Comparison . . . revealed the formula for conversion." Now virtually any wireless signal made by the German navy and intercepted by the British could be read by the Admiralty.

Once deciphered by Room 40, intercepted signals were placed in a red envelope and rushed by messenger to Admiral Sir Arthur Wilson, who personally carried the most critical messages to the First Lord, the First Sea Lord, and the Admiralty War Group. From there, the information—although never the source—was disseminated to those who needed to know. For months, the existence of Room 40 was kept secret from everyone in the fleet except Jellicoe and Beatty. Churchill was even more convinced that this policy was correct when Jellicoe, complaining that too much time was lost having messages decoded in London before being sent to him, pleaded to have intercepted coded messages sent directly to a decoding staff aboard his flagship. This request from the Commander-in-Chief arrived at the Admiralty in a lower-level British navy code. Churchill, who feared precisely that low-level leaks would inform the Germans that their code had been broken, was furious.

The German Naval Staff was determined not to believe that its secret codes had been compromised. Immediately after the loss of *Magdeburg,* the admiral commanding the German squadron dutifully reported, "*SKM* key not known to have been destroyed." The Naval Staff replied, "No fears of dangerous consequences are entertained here through the possible loss of the signal book." Subsequently, Prince Henry of Prussia, the kaiser's brother, and, at that time, Commander-in-Chief of the Baltic Fleet, declared it to be a "virtual certainty" that the Russians had acquired the grid naval charts from the wreck of *Magdeburg* and a probability that they also had recovered an SKM. The Naval Staff refused to act on this warning, and although the reciphering keys were changed—at first every three months, then as often as every week—the basic SKM remained in service until May 1917, two years and nine months after *Magdeburg* was sunk. When, with the passage of time, the appearance of British ships directly in the path of German surface squadrons or U-boats could no longer be ascribed to coincidence, the Naval Staff and the Commander-in-Chief of the High Seas Fleet looked frantically for explanations. Traitors inside the German navy, spies in the ports and dockyards, secret radio messages from British and neutral fishing trawlers: all were suspected. The one explanation the German navy flatly refused to believe was that the enemy was decoding German wireless messages.

The Germans contributed to their intelligence defeat not only by this exaggerated belief in the security of their codes, but also by excessive use of wireless transmissions. Ironically, they fell into this trap partly because of the excellence of their transmitters. The radio tower at Nauen, near Berlin, for example, could broadcast to the Mediterranean, the Americas, southern Africa, and even China. All German warships carried excellent radio equipment and could transmit signals over hundreds of miles; thus equipped, captains and radio operators tended to be garrulous. With this unintended assistance, British interception of German wireless traffic increased rapidly; by 1917, all messages from the Bight were being intercepted; by the end of the war, signals between German ships in port were routinely picked up. Eventually, 20,000 German naval wireless messages passed through Room 40 and were decoded. Without the breaking of the German codes, the battles of Dogger Bank and Jutland would not have been fought. Nor, later, would the U-boats have been defeated.

CHAPTER 18

The Scarborough Raid: "Within Our Claws"

Before the Great War, Scarborough, on the Yorkshire coast, was known as the Queen of Watering Places in the north of England. The town's reputation owed much to its magnificent site: rolling green moors ended abruptly in a sweeping curve of high cliffs overlooking wide beaches of brown, tidal sand. Two broad bays, north and south, are divided by a headland rising 300 feet from the sea; the headland is crowned by a ruined medieval castle with walls eighty feet high and twelve feet thick. Towering over the surf at its base, the great castle on the high rock rears up like a symbol of a defiant, unconquerable England.

The fine sea bathing brought vacationers to Scarborough; once there, they were offered other diversions. The South Cliff promenade provided a panoramic view of the broad sands, the castle, the bay, and the North Sea. Footpaths, crisscrossing down the cliffside, allowed strollers to pass through gardens, rest on gazebo benches, and eventually emerge at a handsome spa on the water's edge. The town had two theaters, a music hall, an aquarium, and a museum, all permanently booked or heavily patronized. In the summers, Scarborough's population swelled from a winter low of 40,000 to a high of 200,000, and the large hotels along the clifftop esplanades had no rooms to let. The largest of these, the Grand Hotel, an immense Victorian pile of red and orange brick, was famous throughout Europe. The architect had invoked a chronological theme: four corner towers represented the seasons of the year, twelve stories represented the months, fifty-two chimneys the weeks, and 365 rooms the days. Ultimately, not all of the chimneys or rooms were built, but when it opened in 1867, a journalist reported that in its "greatness, vastness of enterprise, magnificence of appearance and sensational result," the Grand Hotel "reflected the tastes and tendencies of the present age."

In winter, the bathers and strollers departed and a northern austerity settled over the town. As sea and sky turned gray, the fishermen still came and went with the tide, but the rest of the permanent population retired into semi-hibernation. The war did not change this behavior. Scarborough had no harbor, only a small stone-walled tidal basin, beneath the castle rock, which gave refuge to North Sea herring boats. The town had no industry, no military significance, and no defense.

On Wednesday, December 16, 1914, a heavy mist hanging over the sea and harbor made early morning even darker than usual. At eight o'clock, some townspeople were still in bed; others were getting up; others were having breakfast by gaslight. Suddenly, over the drowsy town, there burst a series of explosions. Hotel guests with rooms on the sea stumbled to their windows. Through the mist they saw and heard stabbing spurts of flame, followed by loud, reverberating booms. "I could see in the mist the outline of a ship only about a mile and a half from the shore, north of the castle headland," said one hotel guest. "It was steaming slowly south across the bay, discharging salvos." Fay Lonsdale, a well-known actress, was appearing at a theater in town and staying at the Grand Hotel. "Just before eight o'clock, I heard a tremendous noise and got out of bed," she said. "I looked out the window and saw a huge flame and cloud of smoke. . . . Then, near the front of my room, a shell struck and the room shook. I got under the table, still partly dressed. Someone shouted, 'Come downstairs.' I joined the other residents and maids in the cellar."

There was more than one ship off Scarborough and the sound of guns merged into a continuing roll of thunder. The flames flashed in the fog; there followed a brief pause, then the boom of the guns, another pause, then the rumble of explosions somewhere in the town. Again and again, the townspeople heard the whistling shriek of incoming shells. When the projectiles came close, the shriek was cut short by a tremendous crash, the shattering of glass, the rumbling of collapsing roofs, and the sudden upward boil of a column of dirty smoke.

The townspeople understood that they were under bombardment. Some remained calm: Sir George Sitwell, father of Edith, Osbert, and Sacheverell, went down to the cellar, but his wife, Lady Ida, remained "resolutely in bed." Most people, some still in nightclothes, ran into the streets. Men tended to run to the cliffs or the seawall to see what was happening; women grabbed their children and rushed away from the sea, looking for a cellar or some other place of shelter. Soon, thousands of people were streaming through the streets, making their way to the railway station, where they crowded into every railway car standing there, even those not attached to engines. Others jammed the main road, which led up onto the moors behind the town.

Not everyone escaped. At eight o'clock, a postman named Alfred Beal was delivering mail in Filey Road. Margaret Griggs, a maidservant, had just opened the door and Beal was handing her letters when a shell burst against the side of the house. Beal and Griggs both died instantly. John Hall, a member of the town council, was dressing in his bedroom when a shell broke his leg and arm and pierced his chest. When his daughter ran into the room, he told her that he "was killed." He died on the way to the hospital.

Scarborough Castle, the town's most prominent landmark, became a target. The high walls of the keep and the outer southern wall were hit and an old yeomanry barracks was demolished. The Grand Hotel, perched on a cliff above the South Bay beach, was another target. Shells punched three large holes in the seaside façade. A glass-fronted restaurant café running along the seafront was wrecked. The following morning a reporter found a welter of bricks and plaster, smashed tables and chairs, and shattered glass. In the middle of the room, he was surprised to discover an unharmed table on which stood a decanter of red wine, untouched.

The town had become a landscape of gaping holes, roofless houses, smashed timbers, scattered bricks, stones, and broken glass. The top half of a severed telegraph pole dangled from its own lines. Live wires from broken tram lines whipped on the pavement. Every hotel window facing the sea on the South Cliff was broken. Three churches were hit. One was St. Mary's, in whose churchyard Anne Brontë, the younger sister of Charlotte and Emily, was buried. Anne, who had come to Scarborough hoping to cure, or at least stave off, her tuberculosis, died in 1849 at the age of twenty-eight. Sixty-five years later, a German shell passed over her grave and smashed in the western door of the ancient church.

At 8:30 a.m., the guns stopped firing and the ships disappeared into the mist. Seventeen people were dead and ninety-nine had been wounded, all civilians.

—

Whitby was next. A fishing village twenty-one miles north of Scarborough at the mouth of the river Esk, Whitby possessed an architectural treasure in its twelfth-century abbey standing on a cliff above the town. At nine o'clock that morning, two warships approached from the south. About a mile from shore, they opened fire at their primary target, a coast guard signal station on the cliff near the abbey. The first shell exploded against the cliff just below the station. Frederick Randall, a thirty-year-old coast guard boatman who happened to be walking out of the station, was decapitated by a flying splinter. Another shell struck the brown sandstone ruins of Whitby Abbey a few hundred yards away. Still others burst amid the red-tile-roofed houses of the town below. William Tunmore, a sixty-one-year-old railway cartman, was trying to calm his horse at a rail crossing when a shell burst nearby. He died with a splinter in his chest. Ten minutes after the bombardment had begun, it ceased. The warships departed, leaving behind two dead and two wounded.

—

Hartlepool, north of the river Tees and about sixty miles up the Yorkshire coast from Scarborough, was a shipbuilding and manufacturing town with a population of 90,000. In 1914, it possessed two tidal basins and six docks covering 850 acres, a boiler and engineering works, iron and brass foundries, steam-saw and timber-planing mills, paint and paper factories, and a soap works. In peacetime and even in wartime, Hartlepool exported machinery, ships, coal, iron ore, woolens, and cottons. For this reason, according to the rules of war, the town was a legitimate target for naval bombardment. Hartlepool's military defense consisted of three nineteen-year-old 6-inch guns, mounted on the seafront, and a battalion of the Territorial Army's Durham Light Infantry. In the harbor, the navy had stationed two obsolete light cruisers, four small destroyers, and one submarine.

The army at Hartlepool had been warned that something might happen. At midnight the night before, a War Office telegram had instructed that "a special lookout be kept all along east coast at dawn tomorrow." Accordingly, eleven officers and 155 men of the Durham Light Infantry were aroused at 4:30 a.m. Each soldier was issued 250 rounds of ammunition and a can of tea. If nothing had happened by 11:30 a.m., the men were told, they would have the rest of the day off. Then the detachment marched off to previously dug trenches north of the town and prepared, the men assumed, to repel invasion. All three of Hartlepool's coast artillery guns were sited in Old Hartlepool, a peninsula jutting out to sea. Two of these guns, side by side, formed the Heugh Battery; the other gun was a hundred yards away, near an old lighthouse. At 6:30 a.m., the gun crews reported themselves ready. They were not kept waiting long. At 7:46 a.m., their commander received a report that dreadnoughts had been sighted at the mouth of the Tees not far away; a few minutes later, he was told that three large ships were coming in at high speed.

The navy at Hartlepool was not specifically warned; in wartime, the navy was supposed always to be ready. Besides, standing Admiralty orders instructed that all coastal patrol vessels were to be at sea before dawn. But on the two previous days, the weather had been so poor that Rear Admiral G. A. Ballard, commanding all coastal defense vessels along the British east coast, had modified this instruction, instructing his captains to put to sea only when individually ordered to do so. Consequently, on December 16, Captain Alan C. Bruce, of the light cruiser *Patrol,* who was also the senior naval officer in Hartlepool, had dispatched only his four small, elderly destroyers to sea, holding his two light cruisers and his submarine in port. Hartlepool was a tidal harbor with a narrow channel; the tide was so low that morning, and the swell outside so high, that he judged an attempt to cross the bar with the cruisers and submarine to be unnecessarily hazardous.

At 7:45 a.m., *Doon, Test, Waveny,* and *Moy* were steaming on routine patrol five miles northeast of Hartlepool when men on the bridge of the division leader, *Doon,* became aware of three large vessels approaching from the southeast. The mist was too thick for *Doon*'s captain to make out the nature or nationality of the vessels, so he signaled his ships to increase speed and investigate. Five minutes later, the strange ships suddenly opened fire; simultaneously, two were recognized as German battle cruisers. Salvos began to straddle the destroyers and, as the German shells burst on contact with the water, the British ships were showered with splinters. Destroyers could harm big ships only with torpedoes and, as the British ships were beyond effective torpedo range, all but *Doon* turned away. *Doon* continued to advance; at 5,000 yards she launched a single torpedo, which missed; then she retreated with one man dead and eleven wounded.

The bombardment of the Hartlepools, beginning at 8:10 a.m., came as a shock even to the forewarned shore artillerymen. When the unfamiliar ships first appeared offshore, the waiting British gunners watched them with admiration; they seemed so large, so close, and so powerful that they could not possibly be anything but British. A group of men belonging to the Durham Light Infantry was standing together near the Heugh Battery, treating the affair as if it were a holiday display, when a shell exploded in their midst, killing seven men and wounding fourteen. Both guns of the Heugh Battery immediately fired at the leading ship. The lighthouse gun engaged the third ship in line, which was smaller than the first two. The three enemy ships were firing 11-inch, 8.2-inch, and 5.9-inch shells at the British batteries. That the batteries were not annihilated was due to a fluke: the ships were firing at such short—almost point-blank—range that there was insufficient time to permit the operation of their delayed-action fuses. Also, many of the shells were passing over the battery and hitting houses or falling onto the docks and the town behind. Other shells landing near the British guns ricocheted, bouncing along intact, before exploding.

Meanwhile, inside the harbor, Captain Bruce was trying to get *Patrol* out to sea. The light cruiser proceeded past the breakwater, but by the time she reached the channel to the open sea, the water around her was boiling with shell bursts. Captain Bruce ordered full speed to make a dash for it, but as *Patrol* came into clear view of the nearest enemy ship, now identified as an armored cruiser, two 8.2-inch shells smashed into her, killing four men, wounding seven, and forcing Bruce to steer her aground. There she remained. The other British light cruiser, *Forward,* spent the entire engagement in the harbor trying to raise steam. By the time she emerged, the Germans had vanished.

The submarine *C-9* followed *Patrol* in her dash toward the sea, and the salvos that damaged *Patrol* splashed all around *C-9*. To save herself, *C-9* submerged although it was near low tide and only eighteen feet of water covered the bar. She instantly grounded and took so long to pull herself out of the mud that by the time she was clear, the enemy was gone. After the raid, Roger Keyes, the Commodore of Submarine, found it "deplorable" that *C-9,* "which was stationed in Hartlepool solely to meet the situation which arose," had not been out on morning patrol. With the attacking battle cruisers steaming slowly back and forth and with the armored cruiser having come to a complete halt in the middle of Tees Bay, the German ships would have made ideal targets for a submerged submarine.

The Royal Navy had failed at Hartlepool, but the British shore batteries continued their duel with the enemy ships. Poor visibility caused by mist and swirling dust from the collapse of houses immediately behind them hampered the British gunners, but they managed to track the two battle cruisers, now about 1,000 yards apart, steaming slowly northward. The two guns of the Heugh Battery aimed at the leading ship, concentrating their fire on the masts and superstructure because their 6-inch shells were exploding without much effect against the armored sides and turrets. About 8:25 a.m., both Heugh guns switched to the second ship. A few hundred yards away, the lighthouse gun was firing at and hitting the armored cruiser. Unfortunately, as the cruiser moved north, the lighthouse gun was forced to cease firing because it could no longer shoot without hitting the lighthouse. At 8:52 a.m., when the last round had been fired and the bombarding ships turned out to sea, none of the three British shore guns had been silenced.

The German naval history records that "1,150 shells of heavy, medium and light caliber had been fired at the batteries and other points of military importance in the city." The damage was severe. The attack had begun as families were having breakfast, leaving for work, getting ready for school. When flashes of light were followed by claps of what everyone took to be thunder, a guest having breakfast in one of the hotels said with a smile, "The Germans have come." The waiter serving him laughed. Shipyard workers who had picked up their tools at 7:30 a.m. were working at Grey's shipyard when there was an enormous crash and a column of black water rose inside the breakwater. Seven men in the shipyard were killed and two ships under construction collapsed on the building ways. The mate of a ship in the harbor was hit in the spine by a splinter and died.

When the two battle cruisers shifted their fire from the docks and shipyards to the center of West Hartlepool, they aimed at the steelworks, the gasworks, and the railway cargo and passenger stations. A large gas tank collapsed in flames. Two other gas tanks standing close together were struck and a large volume of gas escaped; that night, with no gas for illumination, West Hartlepool was lit by candlelight. Shell bursts and fires damaged seven churches, ten public buildings, five hotels, and more than 300 houses. In East Hartlepool, three churches and the Carnegie Library were hit. Victoria Place, just behind the lighthouse, suffered worst of all; scarcely a house remained standing. Roads and pavements were covered with broken glass and shattered masonry and the air stank acridly of explosives.

As at Scarborough, people had tried to flee to the train station or to the open country. A family named Dixon was running down a street when a shell burst over them. Fourteen-year-old George, eight-year-old Margaret, and seven-year-old Albert died; Mrs. Dixon, covered with blood, was left alive holding her baby, John, who was unhurt. One shell entered a house and killed a father, a mother, and six children, leaving only an infant alive. A boy had his foot blown off. A body lay in the middle of a street surrounded by hats which been blown out the window of a hat store. Seven-year-old Sarah Wilkinson insisted on going to school, saying, "I must get that medal, mother." She was blown to pieces in Crimdon Street. Next day, in front of a shattered house in Turnbull Street, a six-year-old boy cried out, "Look, there's my teddy bear up there. I'm sure mother's up there, too."

Eighty-six civilians died in the Hartlepools and 424 were wounded. Including the casualties at Scarborough and Whitby, the German navy had killed 105 men, women, and children and wounded 525. Eight German sailors had been killed in the operation and twelve wounded.

—

The news that German battle cruisers had bombarded North Sea towns shocked and outraged Britain. For the first time in 247 years, English blood had been spilled on English soil by foreign naval guns.* The raiding ships were branded the "assassin squadron" and "the Scarborough bandits." Winston Churchill publicly assured the mayor of Scarborough that "the stigma of the baby-killers of Scarborough will brand its officers and men while sailors sail the seas." Sir Walter Runciman, the MP for Hartlepool, wrote to his constituents describing the attack "as a colossal act of murder by ingrained scoundrels with results that will stamp them for all time as heinous polecats." The fact that two of the three towns were undefended drew particular fury. "The bombardment . . . was an infamous crime against humanity and against international law," declared the *Daily Chronicle* of London. The law in question was the Convention on Bombardments by Naval Forces, signed at The Hague on August 17, 1907, by forty-four nations including Great Britain and Germany. Article I of the convention stated: "The attack or

*On June 8, 1667, a Dutch fleet of sixty warships and troop transports under Admiral Michiel de Ruyter attacked the British naval base at Sheerness, inside the Thames estuary. The Dutch bombarded the fort, landed troops, took the fort by assault, and carried off English guns. On June 12, de Ruyter advanced unopposed up the Medway, burned four anchored English ships-of-the-line, then towed back to Holland the eighty-gun *Royal Charles,* the largest vessel in the Royal Navy. The loss and humiliation were compensated when, in the Peace of Breda signed in July 1667, England was awarded the small Dutch town and colony of New Amsterdam at the mouth of the Hudson River in North America.

bombardment by naval forces of ports, towns, villages, habitations or buildings which are not defended, is prohibited." The *Chronicle* drew a distinction between the different towns attacked: "So far as the Hartlepools are concerned, no complaint can be made of the enemy's action. The bombardment of entirely undefended watering-places like Whitby and Scarborough is another matter. Such action has never in history been taken by a civilized power before the present war."

The Germans were the primary objects of public anger, but the Royal Navy did not escape. Why had the navy failed to prevent the raid? After spending millions on dreadnoughts to ensure sea supremacy, why had English civilians died from German naval gunfire? The Admiralty, meeting the criticism, admitted that it could not provide absolute security against occasional raids and tried to put the matter into perspective. "Demonstrations of this character against unfortified towns or commercial ports, though not difficult to accomplish provided a certain amount of risk is accepted, are devoid of military significance," the Admiralty announced. "They may cause some loss of life among the civil population and some damage to private property which is much to be regretted; but they must not in any circumstances be allowed to modify the general naval policy which is being pursued." The British fleet, in short, would remain concentrated in the north.

Most newspapers stood by the Admiralty, pointing out that the raid had been of no military importance and that one of its purposes was to create public pressure to force the Admiralty to split the British fleet into defensive positions along the east coast. "The best police force," remarked *The Observer,* "can firmly preserve general order, but cannot prevent some cases of murder, arson and burglary." A *Times* editorial declared: "It would no doubt be very comforting to each cluster of dwellers on the East Coast to see a British dreadnought anchored before their front doors . . . but protection of these shores is not the primary object of the Royal Navy in War." "The purpose of the Royal Navy," *The Times* explained, "is to engage and destroy the ships of the enemy." The press in the north of England accepted this premise, but not without qualification. "We hope that the authorities will not forget that although the shelling of a town may be insignificant from a military point of view, it is significant enough to the people who live in the town," said the *Northern Daily Mail.* "No doubt the larger questions of naval strategy must take precedence over the defence of particular localities, but at the same time, we may be permitted to hope that we are not to be made a target for German ships even in the interest of higher strategy."

British justice has age-old procedures, immune to modification even in times of war. Here, British subjects had died and jury inquests in the bombarded towns attempted to describe the causes of death and identify the perpetrators. "There has been no attack on an English town by an alien enemy for hundreds of years," the Hartlepool coroner informed his jury. "Therefore

I have no precedent for the guidance of the jury." In Scarborough, the jury foreman asked, "Cannot we use the word 'murder'?" The coroner replied that if the jury returned a verdict of murder, he "would have to go through the formality of binding the police over to prosecute someone." The persons responsible, he pointed out, were the officers of the German ships, and, as the jury was bound to recognize, these persons were unavailable. Frustrated, the prosecutors terminated the proceedings.

—

Through the autumn, Franz Hipper had been eager to take his battle cruisers to sea and had constantly proposed new operational plans. On November 8, only five days after returning from his abortive raid on Yarmouth, the commander of the 1st Scouting Group had suggested a sortie against British merchant trade in the Skagerrak. The British, he argued, would have been forced by his approach to Yarmouth to bring their battle cruisers south to strengthen their east coast defenses; therefore, a raid to the north might catch them off guard. And if he began sinking British merchantmen in northern waters, the Grand Fleet, or part of it, was bound to rush to their aid. Whereupon, as Hipper planned it, the British warships would fall prey to the waiting U-boats he proposed to station off the Firth of Forth, Cromarty, and the entrances to Scapa Flow.

Ingenohl rejected Hipper's proposal, but the High Seas Fleet commander recognized that something must be done. Since the Battle of the Bight, his fleet had been fretting at the inaction imposed upon it. Morale was deteriorating. The kaiser had given the Commander-in-Chief a command to hold back the fleet in order to preserve control of the Baltic and permit the release of coast defense troops to alleviate the manpower demands of the army. But William had left a loophole: "This does not, however, prevent favorable opportunities being used to damage the enemy. . . . There is nothing to be said against an attempt of the battle cruisers in the North Sea to damage the enemy." In the language of this memorandum, Ingenohl recognized that the kaiser, eager for victories but abhorring risk, was willing to settle for smaller, even hit-and-run successes. Specifically, he was willing to expose Hipper's battle cruisers, but not the dreadnought battleships. Accordingly, on November 16, Ingenohl asked permission to send Hipper alone back to England's east coast, and on the nineteenth William consented. A submarine, *U-27*, was dispatched on the twenty-first to reconnoiter the coastal waters and locate the minefields between Scarborough and Hartlepool. The mission was secret, so much so that none of the crew were aware of its purpose; when the submarine returned, her captain reported that the shore defenses were weak, that the commercial coastal traffic was heavy, and that an area reaching out as far as twelve miles off the Yorkshire coast appeared free of mines. Planning for the operation continued. The Naval Staff insisted that all four of

Hipper's battle cruisers participate and, because *Von der Tann* was in dry dock for boiler repairs, Hipper's sortie was postponed until mid-December.

The sudden annihilation of Spee's squadron at the Battle of the Falklands was another spur to the east coast raid. The Falklands defeat had depressed the German fleet and the German people and Ingenohl believed that Hipper's sortie might provide a tonic. Practically speaking, too, it was clear that British battle cruisers had been stripped from the Grand Fleet and dispatched to the South Atlantic. Ingenohl did not know which British ships had gone, but he was confident that Beatty's force was now depleted by at least two. (The Germans never learned of the absence of *Princess Royal.*) An opportunity to attack a weakened enemy should not be ignored; Hipper must strike before these ships returned to the North Sea.

The German plan took shape: Hipper would take four battle cruisers and an armored cruiser (the British Admiralty always classified *Blücher* as a battle cruiser; the Germans, more accurately, listed her as a powerful armored cruiser), four light cruisers, and escorting destroyers to the Yorkshire coast. At daylight, his ships would bombard Scarborough and Hartlepool while one of his cruisers laid mines in the coastal shipping lanes. Ingenohl would support Hipper by taking the dreadnought battle fleet to the eastern edge of the Dogger Bank. The kaiser had forbidden Ingenohl to risk a major fleet action, and the admiral had no intention of disobeying; his hope was to lure part of the Grand Fleet over minefields, thereby harming the British without loss to himself. Ingenohl knew he was stretching his orders and he was careful to protect himself in a manner common in Imperial Germany: he did not tell the kaiser what he intended to do.

At 3:00 a.m. on December 15, Hipper's flagship, *Seydlitz,* sailed from the Jade, followed by *Moltke, Von der Tann,* the newly completed *Derfflinger, Blücher,* four light cruisers, and eighteen destroyers. One of the light cruisers, *Kolberg,* carried a hundred mines. That afternoon, Ingenohl and the main body of the High Seas Fleet followed Hipper into the North Sea. The armada under Ingenohl's command that day—eighty-five surface warships—was the most powerful German naval force ever to put to sea. And this did not count the twenty-seven ships that had gone ahead with Hipper. Ingenohl's destination was the eastern edge of the Dogger Bank, where he intended to arrive at daybreak the following morning. This position would not be far enough to the west to provide effective support if Hipper got into early trouble, but it marked the extreme limit of Ingenohl's courage.

Meanwhile, twelve hours ahead of the battle fleet, Hipper was sweeping at 15 knots across the North Sea. At first, passing Heligoland, the sea was calm and the weather hazy. At noon, a light rain began to fall. Dutch fishing trawlers were sighted and although Hipper worried that some might be acting as British spy ships, he could do nothing. Toward evening, in rising wind and heavy rain squalls, the German ships passed the Dogger Bank. Showing no lights, the destroyer flotillas closed in on the battle cruisers to provide night protection. When Hipper sighted trawlers carrying navigation lights, he altered course, hoping they would not see the big gray shapes sliding past in the darkness. As the night wore on, German radiomen began to pick up British wireless activity and Hipper worried again that one of the fishing trawlers or perhaps a British submarine had given him away. Nevertheless, emboldened by the knowledge that the main battle fleet was behind him, he steamed forward.

At midnight, one of the destroyers in Hipper's van began calling the light cruiser *Strassburg,* saying, "Have lost touch. Course, please." In reply, *Strassburg* growled, "Stop wireless." Hipper, hearing the exchange, was enraged. "Doesn't the ship [the destroyer] know where we're heading? Can't they get in touch again at daylight? The fools will give us away." Silenced, the lost destroyer, *S-33,* certain that she could not regain contact, reversed course for home. Along the way, however, she had an adventure. At 4:00 a.m., approaching the Dogger Bank from the west, *S-33* stumbled into four British destroyers. Thinking quickly, the German captain turned his ship onto a parallel course with the British, hoping to convince them in the darkness that he was one of them. Although he was only 200 yards from the nearest ship, the ruse succeeded, and for twenty minutes *S-33* steamed along in company with her enemies before slightly altering course and slipping away. Again breaking radio silence, the lost destroyer signaled Hipper the position of the four destroyers. Hipper was alarmed to learn that a British force was behind him but reasoned that the destroyers could be gobbled up in the morning by the High Seas Fleet.

An equal concern for Hipper was the rising wind and sea. *S-33* had already lost touch and his other destroyers were taking a pounding. *Strassburg,* now nearing the English coast, reported, "Bombardment off shore not possible owing to heavy sea. Lights visible ahead. Coast not distinguishable. Cannot keep course owing to heavy sea. Turning east." (The facts were worse than *Strassburg* reported. Some destroyers had rolled so heavily that they had lost their masts, their main decks were two feet under water, and their torpedo tubes, which had been unloaded, could not be reloaded.) On *Seydlitz,* Hipper paused to reflect. *Strassburg*'s Captain Retzmann was trustworthy and his reports and judgment were certain to be accurate. Hipper wondered what to do. Give up the whole enterprise just as he approached his goal? Return home again with nothing accomplished? Hold on with the battle cruisers alone? But could he dispense with the protection provided by light cruisers and destroyers if he sent these smaller ships back to the battle fleet?

Standing in *Seydlitz*'s chart room, the admiral turned to consult his first staff officer, Commander Erich Raeder. Before Raeder could answer, however, Hipper made up his mind.

"We'll put this through. I'm not going to let my command down."

"But the light forces—?" Raeder began.

"Will be sent back to the main fleet. Only the *Kolberg* will remain with us. She must get rid of her mines."

At 6:35 a.m., Hipper signaled *Strassburg, Stralsund, Graudenz,* and the seventeen destroyers remaining with him to turn back and join Ingenohl's main battle fleet.* As the light cruisers and destroyers were turning out of the wind onto an easterly course, Hipper divided the remainder of his force. Rear Admiral Tapkin with *Derfflinger, Von der Tann,* and *Kolberg* headed south for Scarborough; Hipper with *Seydlitz, Moltke,* and *Blücher* turned north, toward Hartlepool. The Southern Group under Tapkin performed its task as assigned. Initially, the battle cruisers were having trouble navigating in the thick mist along the darkened coast. Then, a brightly lighted train running south along the shore provided guidance and led the German ships to within a mile of the Scarborough headland. At 8:06 a.m., they opened fire with their secondary batteries of 5.9-inch guns. Meanwhile, *Kolberg* moved south and at 8:14 a.m. began to lay a minefield off Flamborough Head from the coast to ten miles out. The purpose was to block possible interference with the bombardment by the Humber or Harwich flotillas and, in the longer run, to disrupt British coastal trade. After firing for half an hour, *Derfflinger* and *Von der Tann* turned north for Whitby, where they bombarded the signal station and the town. They met no opposition.

The Northern Group, *Seydlitz, Moltke,* and *Blücher,* had a more difficult experience. At 7:18 a.m., when the German ships first arrived off Hartlepool, Hipper could see the streetlights of the town and the flames of factory furnaces. Hartlepool was known to be a defended port and the young captain of the submarine *U-27*, which had reconnoitered these waters, was on board the flagship, pointing out to Hipper the location of the 6-inch guns on the headland and other features of the town and harbor. Hipper's group did not achieve complete surprise. At 7:46 a.m., a signal station at the mouth of the Tees suddenly demanded recognition signals. At 7:55 a.m., four British destroyers appeared out of the mist to the northeast. The German ships opened fire with main and secondary batteries and, amid a storm of 11-inch and 5.9-inch shells, all but one of the destroyers retreated to the north. The remaining destroyer "with remarkable coolness, in spite of heavy fire, renewed the attack," according to the German naval history. It fired a torpedo and then it, too, turned back into the mist. Thereafter, the bombardment of Hartlepool began. *Seydlitz* and *Moltke,* steaming slowly northeast of the town, fired 154

*Hipper had not imagined that the main fleet no longer would be waiting at the designated rendezvous. Only with this expectation, Hipper said later in his report, had he "decided in favor of sending the [storm-battered] light forces back over a long and unprotected space of almost 100 miles."

5.9-inch shells and *Moltke* thirty-eight 11-inch shells at the Heugh Battery. *Blücher,* to the south, came to a halt in the middle of the bay and fired her 8.2-inch and 5.9-inch guns at the British gun near the lighthouse. The British batteries replied and a brisk artillery engagement ensued. The Heugh Battery hit *Seydlitz* three times and *Moltke* once. The lighthouse gun fired so accurately at *Blücher* that the German ship moved north out of the gun's arc of fire. At 8:50 a.m., when Hipper's ships turned out to sea and disappeared, none of the British guns had been silenced. *Blücher* had suffered four direct hits from 6-inch shells. The bridge and an 8.2-inch turret had been damaged, two 5.9-inch guns were out of action, and nine German seamen had been killed or wounded.

At 9:30 a.m., Hipper rendezvoused with the Scarborough-Whitby force, *Kolberg* rejoined, and Hipper signaled Ingenohl, "Operation competed. Course south south east. 23 knots." At this moment, turning for home, Hipper was about fifty miles to the rear of the storm-beleaguered light cruisers and destroyers he had dismissed three hours earlier. These small ships, even though they were now running before the sea, were still in trouble. For this reason, the light forces had split up, each flotilla or half-flotilla proceeding on its own. Hipper wondered whether he should attempt to regather them about him, but visibility was so poor that he decided to let them continue ahead of him toward the rendezvous with the High Seas Fleet. Wanting precise information as to the battle fleet's position, Hipper asked one of his officers, "Where is the main fleet?" He could scarcely believe the reply: "Running into the Jade." Hipper let out "an old-fashioned Bavarian oath," said Captain von Waldeyer-Hartz. Ingenohl had deserted Hipper; he was alone. Nor was that all. Some of his damaged light cruisers and destroyers out in front—between his battle cruisers and Germany—appeared to be encountering British warships.

—

The margin between the British and German fleets in the North Sea was narrower during the last two months of 1914 than at any other time during the war. *Audacious* had been lost. Four of Jellicoe's battleships were refitting as a result of the strain imposed by constant sea-keeping. Three of Beatty's battle cruisers had been withdrawn to deal with Spee's East Asia Squadron. Never again during the whole course of the war was the situation so favorable for a German challenge to the Grand Fleet. The three British admirals most concerned, Fisher, Jellicoe, and Beatty, worried about this margin through November. After the Yarmouth raid, Fisher had a hunch that it was a precursor of things to come. He had always recognized the likelihood of German raids involving fast ships taking advantage of the usually poor visibility in the North Sea. He was certain the Germans would come again once they knew that important capital ships were absent from home waters. In late

November, he alerted the navy to the probability of a "flying raid" or an "insult bombardment" against the east coast.

Jellicoe needed no warning. Convinced, like Fisher, that the Germans must know that *Invincible, Inflexible,* and *Princess Royal* were not in the North Sea, he pinpointed December 8 as the optimum day for a raid because the moon and tides would be favorable. Beatty, for his part, was anxious because if Hipper's battle cruisers came, it would be his responsibility to intercept and engage. The ratio of British to German strength in battle cruisers was far from Beatty's liking. On November 6, he had received the new battle cruiser *Tiger,* but this increase was more than wiped out by his loss of the three ships sent to hunt down Spee. Beatty now had four battle cruisers to Hipper's five (including *Blücher*). Even Churchill, by nature an optimist, was wary and on December 11, he warned Jellicoe: "They can never again have such a good opportunity for successful operations as at present and you will no doubt consider how best to prepare your forces."

The truth was that the Admiralty had more to go on than the First Lord's intuition. Room 40 had begun to provide useful information. When the German battle cruisers began hit-and-run raiding at Yarmouth on November 4, Room 40 was not yet fully operational, but on the evening of December 14, crucial information was intercepted for the first time. At about seven o'clock that Monday night, Sir Arthur Wilson walked into Winston Churchill's room at the Admiralty and asked for an immediate meeting with the First Sea Lord and the Chief of Staff. Fisher and Oliver quickly appeared. Wilson explained that Room 40 had pieced together the knowledge that within a few hours, the German battle cruisers and other ships would be putting to sea. There was a strong possibility that the German squadron would be off the English coast at dawn on the sixteenth. But the Room 40 codebreakers did not predict the operation in its entirety. The intercepted signals gave a clear picture of the movements of Hipper's forces, but damagingly failed to report that Ingenohl would be bringing the High Seas Fleet out as far as the Dogger Bank. Indeed, Wilson, relying on what he had learned from Room 40, told the small group in Churchill's office that the High Seas Fleet appeared *not* to be involved. Assuming this to be true, the small group in Churchill's office decided to respond with less than maximum force. British battleships, battle cruisers, cruisers, and destroyers in sufficient number to deal easily with Hipper's battle cruisers were assigned to act. At 9:30 p.m. on December 14, the Admiralty signaled Jellicoe at Scapa Flow:

> Good information just received shows that German First [Battle] Cruiser Squadron with destroyers leave Jade River on Tuesday morning early and return on Wednesday night. It is apparent from information that battleships are very unlikely to come out. The enemy force will have time to reach our coast. Send at once, leaving tonight, the

> Battle Cruiser Squadron and Light Cruiser Squadron supported by a Battle Squadron, preferably the Second. At daylight on Wednesday they should be at some point where they can make sure of intercepting the enemy during his return. Tyrwhitt, with his light cruisers and destroyers, will try to get into touch with the enemy off the British coast and shadow him, keeping the Admiral informed. From our information, First [German Battle] Cruiser Squadron consists of four battle cruisers and there will probably be three flotillas of destroyers.

Another telegram, sent to Tyrwhitt at Harwich, instructed him to have his light cruisers and destroyers under way off Harwich "before daylight tomorrow." A third telegram went to Keyes, dispatching eight submarines with their controlling destroyers, *Lurcher* and *Firedrake,* to the island of Terschelling off the Dutch coast to guard against a German move south into the Channel.

Jellicoe obeyed. The 2nd Battle Squadron, commanded by Vice Admiral Sir George Warrender, included the six newest and most powerful ships in the navy, the dreadnoughts *King George V, Ajax, Centurion, Orion, Monarch,* and *Conqueror.* The four fast, modern light cruisers of the 1st Light Cruiser Squadron, *Southampton, Birmingham, Nottingham,* and *Falmouth,* commanded by Commodore William Goodenough, had been bloodied at the Battle of the Bight. From Cromarty came Beatty's 1st Battle Cruiser Squadron, now reduced to *Lion, Queen Mary, Tiger,* and *New Zealand.* And from Harwich, Tyrwhitt was ordered to put to sea with his light cruisers, *Aurora* and *Undaunted,* and two flotillas with a combined forty-two destroyers.

The force selected was immensely powerful, but Jellicoe was worried and annoyed by this division of his fleet; the Commander-in-Chief wished to take the entire Grand Fleet to sea. Jellicoe knew that all his many battle squadrons would not be required to deal with Hipper alone. But who could tell how reliable the Admiralty's new intelligence source might be? It was Jellicoe's permanent conviction that to preserve British naval supremacy the Grand Fleet must always be concentrated. The six dreadnoughts of the 2nd Battle Squadron, points out James Goldrick, "were precisely the sort of [detached] force that the Germans dreamed of being able to isolate and destroy."* The Admiralty dispositions—it seemed to Jellicoe—"were giving them that chance." When Jellicoe protested, the Admiralty made a gesture: still forbidden to bring down the whole Grand Fleet, he was permitted to bring out as insurance Rear Admiral William Pakenham's 3rd Cruiser Squadron from Rosyth, the four armored cruisers *Antrim, Devonshire, Argyll,* and *Roxburgh.*

*Normally, there were eight ships in a British dreadnought battle squadron. But the 2nd had been reduced to six, first by the sinking of *Audacious* on October 27, and then by the sending of *Thunderer* on December 8 to Devonport for the retubing of her condensers.

Ultimately, after events had proved Jellicoe correct about bringing out the entire Grand Fleet, Churchill attempted to defend the Admiralty's bad decision: "A great deal of cruising had been imposed on the fleet owing to the unprotected state of Scapa and it was desirable to save wear and tear of machinery as much as possible. Moreover, risks of accident, submarine and mine which were incurred every time that immense organization went to sea, imposed a certain deterrent on its use except when clearly necessary. The decision was, in light of subsequent events, much regretted. But it must be remembered that the information on which the Admiralty was acting had never yet been tested, that it seemed highly speculative in character, and that for whatever it was worth, it excluded the presence at sea of the German High Seas Fleet."

Although the Admiralty determined the strength of the force, Jellicoe remained in operational command and it was he who selected the rendezvous point, twenty-five miles southeast of the Dogger Bank in the middle of the North Sea. With over 300 miles of English coastline exposed, no one could predict where Hipper would strike. Jellicoe therefore selected the position most favorable for intercepting the German battle cruisers on their return. The rendezvous point was about 180 miles west-northwest of Heligoland and 100 miles southeast of Scarborough on the English coast; the British squadrons were to be at this position at 7:30 on the morning of December 16. Unbeknownst to anyone on either side, this spot "was only thirty miles south of the dawn rendezvous point Admiral von Ingenohl had chosen for the High Seas Fleet."

For the purpose of intercepting Hipper's returning ships, the rendezvous point was the best that could have been chosen. Churchill, writing later, gives the impression that it was the Admiralty that placed the ships in position to intercept; in fact, it was Jellicoe. The important point, however, is that both the Admiralty and the Commander-in-Chief had coolly decided in advance that they would not attempt to defend English seaside towns; their intention, rather, was to intercept the raiders as they returned home. This meant that the Germans would be able to bombard largely without opposition whatever towns or targets they chose. The Admiralty, applying war's grim calculus, was prepared to accept this damage in exchange for the destruction of Hipper's scouting groups. This decision, of course, was unknown to the citizens of Scarborough, Hartlepool, or Whitby and to the British press and general public, which, in the wake of the bombardments, asked, Where was the navy? The secret, whose purpose was to withhold from the Germans the knowledge that their codes had been broken and that Britain had early knowledge of German fleet movements, remained undisclosed until after the war.

Because Jellicoe remained at Scapa Flow with most of the Grand Fleet, command of the intercepting force went to Vice Admiral Sir George Warrender, commander of the 2nd Battle Squadron and second in rank to Jellicoe in the Grand Fleet. It was Warrender who on July 29 had been entrusted to bring the fleet to Scapa Flow, when the Commander-in-Chief, Sir George Callaghan, was summoned to London. An experienced and respected officer, Warrender had made his battle squadron the fleet's most efficient in gunnery. Nevertheless, given the complexities of modern naval warfare and the rapidity with which decisions had to be made, Warrender should not have been in command. His mind worked gradually and his responses were further slowed by a growing deafness. Goodenough, the light cruiser commodore, praised Warrender as possessing "an imperturbability that no circumstances could ruffle." But a young lieutenant aboard *Southampton* put Admiral Warrender's "imperturbability" in a different context when he wrote to his father, a retired admiral, that Warrender "never spoke in peacetime because he was deaf and everyone thought he must be thinking a lot. When war came, everyone said, 'Good gracious, what was he doing the whole time?' "

—

Warrender's six battleships and four light cruisers sailed from Scapa Flow at 5:30 on the morning of December 15, a few hours after Hipper left Wilhelmshaven. High winds and heavy seas running against the strong tide of the Pentland Firth obliged Warrender to leave behind at Scapa all of the destroyers normally assigned to his battle squadron. As it was, his ships clearing the Orkneys suffered in the maelstrom of the Pentland Firth. The sea hammered the small light cruisers *Boadicea* and *Blanche* (*Boadicea*'s bridge and several members of her crew were carried overboard) so badly that both ships had to turn back to Scapa for repairs.

Beatty was at Cromarty on Monday night, December 14, when he received Jellicoe's order to join Warrender's force at sea the following morning. Soon after midnight, *Lion*'s torpedo nets came in and the boiler rooms began to raise steam. Warrender, having left his own destroyers behind, asked Beatty to bring from Cromarty the eight destroyers attached to the Battle Cruiser Squadron. Of the eight, only seven were ready for sea, but those seven sailed with Beatty at 6:00 a.m. From *Lion*'s deck, an officer watched as the battle cruisers "passed in the dark through the boom defense of Cromarty and out beyond . . . when we encountered a very heavy sea which caused even *Lion* to roll in a disquieting manner. Daylight found us out of sight of land on a south-easterly course in heavy weather." Beatty met Warrender off Moray Firth at eleven in the morning and, as Beatty had received no details of the operation or of enemy movements, Warrender used visual signals to give him what information he had. "I think raid [objective is] probably Harwich or Humber," he signaled. He ordered Beatty: "Do not get more than five miles ahead of me. . . . If you get engaged, draw enemy towards battle squadron. If . . . [Tyrwhitt] does not join us, I fear only enemy's destroyers. . . . First Light Cruiser Squadron . . . [will be] under your command to engage enemy's light cruisers and head off destroyers. . . . Warn cruisers to beware of mines floating or dropping astern. Have you any suggestions?" During the afternoon of the fifteenth, Jellicoe, concerned about Warrender's shortage of screening destroyers, asked the Admiralty to send Tyrwhitt and his flotillas to meet Warrender the following morning at the 7:30 a.m. rendezvous. The Admiralty refused, however, and when Tyrwhitt sailed from Harwich at 2:00 p.m. on the fifteenth with four light cruisers and two flotillas of destroyers, his instructions were merely to be off Yarmouth at daylight and await further orders.

Through the night of the fifteenth, Warrender's force steamed southeast for the rendezvous they were to reach at 7:30 a.m., half an hour after sunrise. The night steaming formation placed the battle cruisers five miles ahead of the battleships, with the four light cruisers five miles to starboard and the four armored cruisers one mile to port. Admiral Beatty's seven destroyers were ten miles to port of the battleships, with orders to close in at daylight and act as a screen. Worried about the threat of torpedo attack by German destroyers, Warrender—repeating Jellicoe's request—asked during the night that Tyrwhitt's destroyer flotillas be ordered to join him in the morning. Again, the Admiralty refused and Tyrwhitt's instructions remained in place: simply to be off Yarmouth at dawn.

At 5:15 on the morning of December 16, with their ships steaming at an easy speed toward the rendezvous, the officers and men of Beatty's four battle cruisers and Warrender's six battleships were ignorant of the danger they were approaching. No one on the British side had an inkling that the High Seas Fleet was at sea. And yet, several hours away, Admiral von Ingenohl was steering toward them with fourteen dreadnought battleships, eight predreadnought battleships, nine cruisers, and fifty-four destroyers. With this overwhelming preponderance, Ingenohl had only to hold his course to encounter and perhaps destroy ten British capital ships. And on December 16, 1914, these ten ships provided the margin of British naval supremacy.

CHAPTER 19

The Scarborough Raid: Hipper Escapes

The night was overcast and Beatty's seven destroyers—*Lynx, Ambuscade, Unity,* and *Hardy,* followed some distance behind by *Shark, Acasta,* and *Spitfire*—were steaming southeast, ten miles to port of Warrender's battleships. At 5:15 a.m., *Lynx,* at the head of the column, became aware of a strange destroyer 500 yards off her port bow. The unknown ship was challenged; when she replied wrongly, and turned away, *Lynx* and her sisters gave chase. Their prey was the German destroyer *V-155,* a part of the advance screen of the High Seas Fleet. Both sides opened fire and, in this encounter, German gunnery proved superior. *Lynx* was hit twice and at 5:41 had to sheer away with a jammed propeller. As she involuntarily turned 180 degrees, the destroyers behind automatically followed and *V-155* scored a hit below the waterline on *Ambuscade,* next astern. At 5:50 a.m., *Ambuscade,* with five feet of water on her mess deck, dropped out of line.

This skirmish was the beginning of a sporadic, disorderly, close-range battle between a few British destroyers and a far stronger force of German cruisers and destroyers that continued in darkness and heavy weather for the next two hours. At 5:53 a.m., *Hardy* and *Shark,* in line behind *Lynx,* sighted a light cruiser on their port beam at 700 yards. It was *Hamburg,* which with her two destroyers was also attached to the advance screen of the High Seas Fleet. *Hamburg* had hurried forward as soon as *V-155* reported herself in action. Now, sighting and challenging *Hardy,* the German cruiser switched on her searchlights and opened fire. Almost every shot struck home. Within six minutes, *Hardy*'s steering gear was disabled, the ship was on fire, the engine room telegraph was cut, and the captain was commanding the ship from the engine room hatchway. Nevertheless, *Hardy* managed to hit back, destroying

Hamburg's searchlight platform and then firing a torpedo. Some aboard the British destroyer believed that they saw an upheaval of water alongside the German light cruiser and that the torpedo had scored a hit. In fact, the torpedo had missed, but the fact that it had been launched caused *Hamburg* to turn away. Of far greater significance, *Hamburg* reported the torpedo firing to Ingenohl, the German Commander-in-Chief.

The small British destroyer force had been severely mauled. None had been sunk, but three of the original seven had been seriously damaged and were no longer able to fight. *Shark*'s division, however, was able to keep formation and continued at 25 knots to resume station on Warrender's battleships at daylight. It was now six o'clock and the first streaks of light were beginning to appear in the east. At 6:03 a.m., *Shark* sighted five destroyers to the east; although there were now only four British ships, they attacked at full speed and the German destroyers retreated. It was at about this time that destroyer captains on both sides began to sense that they were involved in something larger than a chance skirmish of light forces. To the British, it was now clear that they had run into a screen of light cruisers and destroyers and that behind it was a more serious force. At about the same time, the officers of the German light cruisers and destroyers were making a similar assessment: that the British destroyers were screening a larger force, probably including heavy ships.

—

The presence of British destroyers on the Dogger Bank had been reported to Admiral von Ingenohl as early as 4:20 a.m., when the German destroyer *S-33,* unable to find Hipper and returning home alone, saved herself by pretending that she was British. The report worried Ingenohl. Like Warrender, the German admiral feared a destroyer torpedo attack on his battleships, especially a night torpedo attack. An hour later, at 5:23 a.m., when news of the destroyer action reached his flagship, *Friedrich der Grosse,* the admiral's apprehension markedly increased. Already, he had stretched his instructions by taking his battleships so far out to sea. And now here he was in the middle of the North Sea in the darkness of a December night, seeing the flashes of guns on the horizon, with British destroyers reported in action, a British torpedo in the water, his screen retreating, the British pursuing—and an hour still remaining before daybreak. Ingenohl was convinced that the British destroyers were part of the massed flotillas that would be screening the entire Grand Fleet. In this state of alarm, the kaiser's command that the High Seas Fleet not risk action outside Heligoland Bight loomed urgently in his mind, and his courage took leave. At 5:30 a.m., he made a general signal for all squadrons to reverse course and turn southeast. The German admiral, said Sir Julian Corbett, author of the official British naval history, "fairly turned tail and made for home, leaving Hipper's raiding force in the air." *Lynx* and her small sisters little knew that their brisk offensive action had ultimately caused the great German armada to flee.

Even setting aside his abandonment of Hipper, Ingenohl's decision was wrong. The German fleet had reached the rendezvous point on the eastern edge of the Dogger Bank when *V-155*'s reports began to come in. At the moment the German Commander-in-Chief decided to retreat, the British battleships and battle cruisers were only ten miles southwest of the port wing of the High Seas Fleet. Had Ingenohl continued on course, then between eight and nine o'clock in that morning's clear weather, his scouts would have come within sight of the British battle cruisers and battleships coming down from the north. A battle would have been inevitable. A British Naval Staff monograph published later showed no doubt as to what was at stake: "Here at last were the conditions for which the Germans had been striving since the beginning of the war. A few miles away on the port bow of the High Seas Fleet, isolated and several hours' steaming from home, was the most powerful homogeneous battle squadron of the Grand Fleet, the destruction of which would at one blow have completed the process of attrition and placed the British and German fleets on a precisely even footing as regards numerical strength." Ingenohl had only to turn west again, and within twenty minutes in fine clear weather, he would have had the British Battle Cruiser Squadron and six prized battleships at his mercy. But by nine o'clock, the opportunity had slipped away. "Never again," as James Goldrick observes, "would such an opportunity to redress the balance present itself to the Imperial Navy." Most German admirals already understood this. Said Scheer, who that day commanded the German 2nd Battle Squadron, "Our premature turning onto an east-southeast course had robbed us of the opportunity of meeting certain divisions of the enemy." Tirpitz went further, proclaiming that this was the one heaven-sent, never-recurring opportunity for a battle with the odds enormously in the Germans' favor. "On December 16," he wrote, "Ingenohl had the fate of Germany in the palm of his hand. I boil with inward emotion whenever I think of it."

Churchill later rejected Tirpitz's assumption that Ingenohl would have won a crushing victory had he not turned away. Writing after the war, the former First Lord attempted to exonerate himself and the Admiralty from the charge that, by refusing Jellicoe's request to send the whole Grand Fleet, they were responsible for placing Warrender and Beatty in jeopardy. The British ships, Churchill argued, could easily have run away:

> There was . . . no compulsion upon Admirals Warrender and Beatty to fight such an action. . . . In this part of the sea and at this hour the weather was quite clear. They would have known what forces they were in the presence of before they could become seriously engaged. There would not have been any justification for trying to fight the High

> Seas Fleet of twenty-two battleships with six battleships and four battle cruisers even though these comprised our most powerful vessels. Nor was there any need. The British Second Battle Squadron could steam in company at twenty knots or could escape with forced draft at twenty-one, and only six of Von Ingenohl's ships could match that speed. As for the battle cruisers, nothing could catch them. The safety of this force, detached from the main British Fleet, was inherent in its speed. Admirals Warrender and Beatty could therefore have refused battle with the German Fleet and it would certainly have been their duty to do so.

Undoubtedly, Churchill was correct as to the sailor's duty to avoid a much superior foe and as to the higher speed of the British ships. Yet on the heels of Troubridge's court-martial for avoiding battle and Cradock's heroic, suicidal charge at Coronel, running away at high speed was not a tactic that British naval officers, particularly David Beatty, were likely to employ. Jellicoe understood this. Churchill did not.

As the German battle squadrons wheeled to port, heading southeast, the armored cruiser *Roon* and her destroyers, which had been directly ahead of the battleships, found themselves in the rear of the new formation. For forty minutes, the two fleets were steaming on almost parallel courses, the British destroyers south of the Germans, the British battle cruisers and battleships to their southwest. The screens continued to brush against each other. At 6:16 a.m., *Roon* saw and was seen by *Lynx* and *Unity,* and *Roon* turned away. Her captain recognized the destroyers as British and worried about the risk of torpedo attack. Earlier, Ingenohl had received *Hamburg*'s report of her encounter with *Hardy,* including the fact that the British destroyer had launched a torpedo. Now, from *Roon,* he heard about another destroyer contact. Confirmed in his belief that the sea was swarming with enemies, Ingenohl at 6:20 a.m. signaled a further turn to port and at high speed made directly for Germany.

—

To the north, with *Lynx* out of action, command of the small group of British destroyers had passed to Commander Loftus Jones, the captain of *Shark.* Jones now had four destroyers left, one of which, *Hardy,* had managed to repair her steering apparatus. At 6:20 a.m., Jones ordered these ships onto a southeast course, hoping to sight either Warrender's British battleships or more Germans. At 6:50 a.m., Jones saw smoke to the southeast and at 6:59, he discovered five German destroyers. What Jones was seeing was *Roon*'s group of ships, which had been a part of the advance screen of the High Seas Fleet, but had now become the German rear guard. Along with *Roon* and a number of destroyers, the group contained the light cruisers *Stuttgart* and *Hamburg.*

Unaware of the identity or number of their enemies, the British destroyers attacked at full speed. Visibility was limited in the dawn light and it was several minutes before Jones recognized the shape of a large, four-funneled cruiser looming behind the German destroyers. Jones identified the ship as *Roon.* Quickly sheering off to the northeast, he signaled Beatty at 6:50 a.m.: "Am keeping in touch with large cruiser *Roon* and five destroyers steaming east." Unfortunately, *Shark*'s effort to report was beset by problems. Initially, she had difficulty sending because of German jamming and, accordingly, the message was held up until 7:25 a.m. In addition, in the darkness and confusion of battle, Jones, *Shark*'s captain, had lost his true position and his report placed his ships fifteen miles from where they actually were. Warrender in *King George V* received the message, as did the battle cruiser *New Zealand,* assigned by Beatty to act as guard ship for transmissions to the battle cruisers by the British destroyers. But for no discernible reason other than incompetence, *New Zealand* failed to pass this information to Beatty.

Meanwhile, Jones in *Shark* continued to maintain contact with *Roon.* At 7:40 a.m., when the British destroyers were still hoping to reach a position from which to launch torpedoes, Jones suddenly discovered that he was confronting not simply *Roon,* but also *Stuttgart* and *Hamburg.* The two German light cruisers turned to pursue and Jones, his small ships in peril, hastily reversed course, increased speed to 30 knots, and signaled Beatty, "I am being chased to westward by light cruisers." The British destroyers rapidly outdistanced their pursuers, even though the patched-up *Hardy* could make no better than 26 knots. At 8:02 a.m., *Roon* signaled *Stuttgart* and *Hamburg* to give up their pursuit, reverse course, and head southeast in the wake of the retreating High Seas Fleet. Jones, running away as fast as he could and not realizing that the Germans had broken off the chase, continued to the northwest, where he was now rapidly approaching Beatty. At 8:50 a.m., Jones and his four battered British destroyers reached Goodenough's four light cruisers, which were serving as Beatty's screen.

—

Meanwhile, Warrender was trying to understand what was happening. Since 5:40 a.m., when *Lynx* had signaled that she was engaging German destroyers, he had known that a German surface force was at sea, but no one had provided him with accurate positions, courses, or speeds. As a result, Warrender decided to continue southeast for the morning rendezvous point. *Shark*'s signal that she had identified a large armored cruiser *(Roon)* did not alter his plan; if there was a German cruiser force behind him to the northeast, it would be better to let them get as far behind him as possible before he and his battleships turned north to cut off their retreat. By 7:10 a.m., Warrender could see Goodenough's light cruisers and, a few minutes later, Beatty's battle cruisers. Warrender was also expecting to see Tyrwhitt and his destroyer flotillas, but Tyrwhitt was nowhere to be seen. In fact, he was still where he had been told by the Admiralty to be: 100 miles away, inside the minefields off Yarmouth, awaiting orders. Nevertheless, at 7:30 a.m., as the British squadrons maneuvered to take up daylight steaming positions, all portents seemed favorable. Daylight was breaking with a cloud-flecked sky, a calm sea, and all the visibility that a clear winter's morning could provide. If there were German ships in this part of the North Sea, there seemed no place where they could hide.

Beatty, nevertheless, was restless. He had spent the morning pacing the bridge of *Lion* with Ernle Chatfield, *Lion*'s captain. When the British destroyers on Warrender's flank first signaled that they were in touch with the enemy and under fire from cruisers, Chatfield asked Beatty "if I might lead around to support them, but he refused. Signals came in that one or two of our destroyers were having a bad time. It seemed to me a wonderful opportunity for us to go to their support, but Beatty took the line that Warrender was in command and he had to carry out his orders and proceed to the rendezvous." This diffidence was not in Beatty's character. At the Battle of the Bight, as the senior officer present, he had charged in to aid the beleaguered British destroyers; here, as Warrender's subordinate, he held back.

The signal for "Action" sounded on *Lion* at seven o'clock. "The fine sunrise and clear sky gave promise," Chatfield wrote. But matters quickly went amiss. At 7:25 a.m., when Warrender received *Shark*'s signal about *Roon,* he assumed that Beatty had also received *Shark*'s message and that the British battle cruisers were steaming toward the position the destroyer had given. Not until 7:36 a.m. did Warrender suspect that something was wrong and signal Beatty, "Have you received message from *Lynx*?" *Lion* had not; nor did she receive this signal from *King George V.* Subsequently, when Beatty wheeled his battle cruisers into their screening position, thereby turning them directly away from *Shark* and *Roon,* Warrender knew that something was terribly wrong. At 7:55 a.m., he urgently signaled Beatty, "Are you going after *Roon*?"

Beatty was surprised. "Have heard nothing of *Roon,*" he replied. Warrender immediately forwarded the signals he had received. Just as *Lion* was reading these, *New Zealand,* after thirty minutes' delay, finally also relayed *Lynx*'s signals. Beatty acted quickly to intercept *Roon.* He reversed course and dispatched *New Zealand,* formerly at the rear of his formation and now closest to the position given by *Shark,* to head for that point at 24 knots. To make it less likely that *Roon* would escape, Beatty spread Goodenough's light cruisers two miles apart, ahead of the other three battle cruisers now following *New Zealand* at 22 knots.

This chase of *Roon* was continuing and *New Zealand,* followed by the rest of the British battle cruisers, was slowly closing the gap when a new series of signals began to arrive in *Lion*'s wireless room. At 8:42 a.m., *Lion* intercepted a signal from the light cruiser *Patrol,* leader of the Hartlepool flotilla.

Patrol, 150 miles from *Lion,* was telling the Tyne guard ship *Jupiter* that she was engaging two enemy battle cruisers. No position was given, but everyone knew that *Patrol* belonged to the 9th Destroyer Flotilla, patrolling inshore off the Yorkshire coast. For a few minutes, Beatty hesitated. Seriously troubling as the message was, he hated having to abandon the pursuit of *Roon.* The message was only an intercept; meanwhile, *New Zealand* was almost within gun range of a significant enemy ship. Ten minutes later, the issue was resolved by a second intercept, this one a message from the Admiralty to Jellicoe at Scapa Flow: "Scarborough being shelled." At nine o'clock, Beatty made his decision. Pursuit of *Roon* was abandoned, *New Zealand* was ordered to rejoin the battle cruiser squadron, and Beatty turned all of his ships directly toward Scarborough.

Warrender had intercepted the same messages and, even before Beatty reversed the battle cruisers, he had turned his battleships to the west. Believing *Patrol* to be farther south than she actually was, Warrender had first set his course for the Humber. "Scarborough being shelled," he signaled Beatty. "I am proceeding to Hull." "Are you?" Beatty replied, in effect. "I am going to Scarborough." A few minutes later, Warrender reached the conclusion that Beatty was right and also decided to steer for Scarborough. By 9:35 a.m., the British forces were steaming in two main groups: Beatty's four battle cruisers with Goodenough's four light cruisers were ten miles ahead and to the northwest of Warrender's six battleships and Pakenham's four armored cruisers. All were steering west to cut Hipper's line of retreat from the English coast.

—

The morning of December 16 found Winston Churchill, who had slept at the Admiralty, awaiting news. "I was in my bath when the door opened and an officer came hurrying in from the War Room with a naval signal which I grasped with dripping hand: 'German battle cruisers bombarding Hartlepool.' I jumped out of the bath. . . . Pulling on clothes over a damp body, I ran downstairs to the War Room. The First Sea Lord [Fisher] had just arrived from his house next door. Oliver, who invariably slept in the War Room and hardly ever left it by day, was marking the positions on the map. Telegrams from all the naval stations on the coast affected by the attack and intercepts from our ships in the vicinity speaking to each other, came pouring in, two or three to the minute."

From the perspective of naval strategy, this was news for which the Admiralty War Group had hoped: the Germans had fallen into a British trap. "The bombardment of open towns was still new to us at that time," Churchill continued.

> But, after all, what did that matter now? The war map showed the German battle cruisers within gunshot of the Yorkshire coast while a hun-

> dred and fifty miles to the eastward, between them and Germany, cutting mathematically their line of retreat, steamed in the exact positions intended, four British battle cruisers, and six of the most powerful battleships in the world. Attended and preceded by their cruiser squadrons and flotillas, this fleet of our newest and fastest ships, all armed with the heaviest guns then afloat, could in fair weather cover and watch effectively a front of nearly a hundred miles. In the positions in which dawn revealed the antagonists, only one thing could enable the Germans to escape annihilation at the hands of an overwhelmingly superior force. And while the great shells crashed into the little houses of Hartlepool and Scarborough, carrying their cruel message of pain and destruction to unsuspecting English homes, only one anxiety dominated the thoughts of the Admiralty War Room. The word "Visibility" assumed a sinister significance. At present it was quite good enough. Both Warrender and Beatty had horizons of nearly ten miles. There was nothing untoward in the weather indications. At 9 a.m. the German bombardment ceased and their ships were soon out of sight of land, no doubt on their homeward voyage. We went on tenter-hooks to breakfast. To have this tremendous prize—the German battle cruiser squadron whose loss would fatally mutilate the whole German Navy and could never be repaired—actually within our claws and to have the event all turn upon a veil of mist, was a racking ordeal.

The day before, Churchill and his Admiralty colleagues had overruled Jellicoe's request to involve the entire Grand Fleet in the trap being laid for Hipper. Now, suddenly, they decided that Warrender and Beatty must be reinforced. Jellicoe, who already had the Grand Fleet with steam up at Scapa Flow, was ordered to take his ships to sea. Bradford with the 3rd Battle Squadron (the eight predreadnought *King Edwards*) at Rosyth was told to join Warrender. (Jellicoe, as Commander-in-Chief, modified this Admiralty disposition. He wanted to concentrate the full power of the Grand Fleet; accordingly, he instructed Bradford not to join Warrender but to rendezvous with the Grand Fleet.) Tyrwhitt, still tethered off Yarmouth with his four light cruisers and two destroyer flotillas by Admiralty orders, was released to join Warrender. Tyrwhitt eagerly attempted to obey, but leading his ships out from the shoals off Yarmouth into the open sea, he soon found that his destroyers, plunging into heavy waves and gale winds, were suffering badly and he ordered them back to Yarmouth. Proceeding with his four light cruisers alone, Tyrwhitt ordered a speed of 25 knots; he found that in these seas, the ships could make barely 15. Commodore Keyes was told to move his submarines from their station off Terschelling into the Bight and to try to catch enemy ships returning to port.

—

The sea floor of the southwest shoal of the Dogger Bank was dangerously shallow for dreadnoughts, British or German. Although the bottom of the sea lay under at least forty-two feet of water, it was strewn with the wrecks of sunken ships, whose rusting masts and superstructures sometimes rose up near the surface. To avoid these submerged navigational hazards, the British squadrons steaming west to intercept Hipper divided. Beatty led his battle cruisers north of the patch; Warrender took his battleships and armored cruisers to the south. By eleven o'clock, Beatty was clear of the patch and had altered course northwest for Scarborough. But now a new obstacle loomed. Two large minefields, each thirty to forty miles long and extending ten miles out to sea, had been laid by the Germans off the Yorkshire coast earlier in the autumn. The British had located the fields and, considering them useful as a protection against raiding, had thickened and improved them by laying additional mines. Between these two minefields there was a north-south gap of clear water fifteen to twenty miles wide, which Hipper had used to approach the coast. Now, Warrender, anxious to find Hipper at any cost, signaled Beatty, "Light cruisers must go in through minefield to locate enemy." Simultaneously, Warrender asked the Admiralty for permission to take his battleships through the same mined waters.

At this point, Jellicoe, monitoring all messages to and from the Admiralty, intervened. The Commander-in-Chief was acutely aware of the location of the minefields and he believed that Hipper, attempting to escape, would steer due east through the same gap he had used coming in. At 10:04 a.m., Jellicoe signaled Warrender and Beatty the exact location of the Scarborough-Whitby gap, saying, "Enemy will in all probability come out there." At 10:55, the Admiralty replied to Warrender's question about taking his ships over the minefields: "Enemy is probably returning towards Heligoland. You should keep outside minefield and steer so as to cut him off." The British were almost in position to do this: Warrender's battleships and armored cruisers were headed for the southern end of the gap; Beatty, ten miles to the north, was headed directly for the northern end of the gap with his light cruisers spread out like a fan ahead of his battle cruisers; Trywhitt was moving up from Yarmouth to join Warrender. The trap was closing. "At eleven o'clock," Churchill wrote, "the four German battle cruisers, with their light cruisers returning independently sixty miles ahead of them, were steaming due east for Heligoland at their highest speed. At the same time all our four squadrons were steaming due west in a broad sweep directly towards them. The distance between the fleets was about a hundred miles and they were approaching each other at an aggregate speed of over forty miles an hour."

Then the weather intervened. The promise of early dawn—clear weather, good visibility, and calm sea—had been realized during most of the morning. Now, a little after eleven o'clock, with the opposing battle cruiser squadrons only a hundred miles apart and steaming directly toward each other, the weather suddenly changed. As late as 11:05 a.m., when the crew of *Southampton* was sent below to dinner, they left the deck in brilliant sunshine. Fifteen minutes later, called back to action stations, they found themselves coming up into rain and high wind. The wind blowing from the northwest was pushing the early-morning storm—the same storm that had bedeviled Hipper's small ships near the English coast—out into the middle of the North Sea. Rain squalls and heavy mists scudded over the water. Visibility plummeted, first to five miles, then to two, sometimes to one. Beatty, heading into the wind, was obliged to reduce speed to 18 knots. Within the next half hour, thick mists and driving rains from the northwest whipped the sea into white foam and sometimes blotted out the light cruisers in the screen ahead of Beatty's battle cruisers. Then, at 11:25 a.m., *Southampton,* the wing ship on the southern edge of the light cruiser screen, sighted an enemy—then many enemies—three miles ahead and steaming straight toward her. They were *Stralsund* and eight destroyers, some of the ships that Hipper had sent back because of heavy seas off the English coast.

Goodenough, commanding Beatty's light cruisers from *Southampton,* flashed recognition signals. The unidentified ships failed to reply and he prepared to engage. By this time, spray blowing off the turbulent seas was drenching *Southampton*'s bridge, where Goodenough stood. Under such conditions, it was practically impossible to fight an enemy to windward; the gun crews would be blinded. Nevertheless, Goodenough signaled Beatty, "Engaged with enemy cruisers." *Stralsund* returned *Southampton*'s fire, then turned away to the south; in the mist and heavy seas, neither cruiser scored hits. Meanwhile, even as *Birmingham, Nottingham,* and *Falmouth* were turning to support him, Goodenough perceived two additional German light cruisers, *Strassburg* and *Graudenz,* and more destroyers coming up. Wholly involved in what was happening on his spray-swept bridge, Commodore Goodenough failed to report these additions to Beatty, and that failure led to a sequence of other damaging British mistakes.

Beatty, on the bridge of *Lion* a few miles to the northwest, was aware that *Southampton* was in action; he had seen the flashes of gunfire lighting up the North Sea murk and heard the deep notes of the cannonade carried on the wind. Confirmation came with Goodenough's signal: "Engaged with enemy cruisers." Beatty was willing to have *Southampton* engaged and also willing that *Birmingham* leave his screen to join *Southampton.* But he worried that with this departure of two of the four light cruisers of his screen, his four battle cruisers would become exposed and vulnerable. Beatty's preoccupation throughout the day was to locate and destroy the German battle cruisers. Up to that moment, he had received no report of their whereabouts other than *Patrol*'s signal from Hartlepool that she was in action with two of them. Reports from the Admiralty had stated only that "dreadnoughts" were bombarding Scarborough. Eventually, these German battle cruisers had to return home. But to locate and fight them as they raced home, Beatty absolutely required an advance screen, both to give warning and to be ready to repel an attack by enemy destroyers. Warrender already had stripped away Beatty's destroyers to screen the battleships; now, it appeared to Beatty, Goodenough was taking away his light cruisers to engage an enemy to the south. With *Southampton* and *Birmingham* departed, Beatty's screen was reduced to two ships, *Nottingham* and *Falmouth.*

Suddenly, even these two ships began to leave him. With chagrin and dismay, Beatty watched from the bridge of *Lion* as his two remaining light cruisers steered across his bow on their way to join *Southampton.* He did not understand. He believed that *Southampton* and *Birmingham* were engaging a single German light cruiser. Had Goodenough signaled him that other enemy light cruisers and destroyers had appeared, Beatty might have realized that his commodore had encountered Hipper's screen. He might then have assumed that Hipper's battle cruisers would logically be following this screen, probably close astern. Given this assumption, David Beatty would almost certainly have turned not only his two remaining light cruisers but also his four battle cruisers in *Southampton*'s direction.

Beatty, however, could make none of these assumptions because Goodenough had reported only the first German ship, *Stralsund.* Therefore, at 11:50 a.m., when Beatty saw *Falmouth* and *Nottingham* leaving him to join *Southampton* and *Birmingham,* the vice admiral considered it a foolish waste of scarce resources. Irritated, he turned to his Flag Lieutenant, Ralph Seymour, and said, "Tell that light cruiser to resume station." The Flag Lieutenant was uncertain whether "that light cruiser"—now only a shadow in the mist on *Lion*'s beam—was *Nottingham* or *Birmingham;* they were sisters with identical silhouettes. To name the ship wrongly in signaling would cause confusion, so he told the signalman operating the searchlight to address her simply as "light cruiser." The signal beam was steadied on the cruiser and the signal made: "Light cruiser resume station for lookout duties. Take station ahead five miles." The signal was aimed directly at *Nottingham* and intended only for her and for *Falmouth.* As the name of the light cruiser was not included, however, *Nottingham*'s captain assumed that the signal was meant for the entire light cruiser squadron and he properly passed it along to Commodore Goodenough. *Birmingham,* astern of *Southampton* and already firing at the enemy, also saw *Lion*'s signal and also passed it along to Goodenough. On receiving it, Goodenough, although in action with the enemy, felt that he must obey. With enormous reluctance, he broke off the battle and turned his ships to return to *Lion.* As the British light cruisers headed west into heavy seas and the German light cruisers turned south into the mists, Goodenough briefly resighted *Stralsund,* by herself. He took her to be still another, as yet unreported German cruiser and signaled Beatty: "Enemy's cruisers bearing south by east."

When Beatty received this message, he realized that *Southampton* was returning to *Lion* and had abandoned her fight with the enemy. Beatty was astonished. At 12:12 p.m., he brusquely signaled Goodenough, "What have you done with enemy light cruiser?"

"They disappeared steering south when I received your signal to resume station," Goodenough replied.

Beatty was stunned that a British naval officer would break off an action. "Engage the enemy," he signaled bluntly.

Goodenough, hapless, answered, "There is no enemy in sight now."

Beatty, now enraged, let Goodenough feel the force of his fury: "When and where was the enemy last seen? When you sight enemy, engage him. Signal to resume previous station was made to *Nottingham.* I cannot understand why, under any circumstances, you did not pursue enemy."

After this sharp public criticism from his superior (Beatty's signals were visible to other ships of Goodenough's squadron), Goodenough felt terrible. In the days to come, he was made to feel worse. His excuse that he had obeyed Beatty's order was never accepted by Beatty, who knew that the idea of calling off *Southampton* and *Birmingham* had never entered his head. The only mitigation Goodenough could find was that when he turned away, the German light forces were steering southeast, heading directly into the path of Admiral Warrender's battleships and armored cruisers. Contact seemed certain.

Indeed, at 12:15 p.m., Warrender, then fifteen miles southeast of Beatty and steering for the southern edge of the minefield gap, sighted and was seen by the same German light cruisers and destroyers that had just left Goodenough. The Germans, approaching at high speed on an opposite course, saw the British first. When the captain of *Stralsund* saw Warrender's giant battleships looming up through the mist, he, with great presence of mind, flashed the recognition signal that Commodore Goodenough had made to him half an hour before. This deception earned him one minute. In the driving rain, Warrender himself, on the bridge of *King George V,* did not see the German ships. But only a few hundred yards away, Rear Admiral Sir Robert Arbuthnot in *Orion,* leading the battle squadron's 2nd Division, had a clear view. *Orion* immediately signaled to *King George V,* "Enemy in sight," and *Orion*'s captain, Frederic C. Dreyer, a gunnery expert, ordered his main turrets trained on the leading German light cruiser. Eagerly, then frantically, Dreyer begged Arbuthnot's permission to open fire. Arbuthnot refused. "No, not until the Vice Admiral [Warrender] signals 'Open fire,' " he said. The order never came. *Orion* never fired.

A few minutes later, Warrender himself sighted *Stralsund* and her sisters on the starboard bow of *King George V.* The number of German ships was difficult to tell; they could merely be seen from time to time as they ran out of one rain squall and disappeared into another. In any case, Warrender, like Arbuthnot, did not open fire; instead, he ordered Pakenham to take his four armored cruisers and chase. This pursuit was a futile exercise: the 25-knot German light cruisers and destroyers rapidly pulled away from Pakenham's 18-knot armored cruisers and disappeared into another rain cloud, never to be seen again. Afterward, Dreyer of *Orion* was desolate, saying later, "Our golden moment had been missed." Subsequently, he wrote of Arbuthnot: "He never spoke to me about it afterwards, but I am certain from his silence that he was mortified to realize that he had been too punctilious. If we had fired, the other five battleships would have done so."

Both Beatty and Warrender had now encountered and then lost the enemy light cruisers. And both knew that the German battle cruisers—the real prey they were hunting—were still to the west and coming east. But the British had no idea of Hipper's position, course, or speed. Beatty's movements now became particularly frantic. Like a pack of hunting dogs, his ships rushed this way and that, sometimes around in a circle, trying to pick up the scent. Once Goodenough's light cruisers had resumed position in front of the battle cruisers, Beatty continued to steer west toward the northern end of the gap in the minefield. He expected to arrive around 12:30 p.m., whereupon he meant to turn south and to begin patrolling back and forth. Had he followed this plan, only unimaginably bad weather could have prevented him from sighting the German battle cruisers as they emerged from the gap at around 1:00 p.m. But fate again intervened in the form of a signal sent by Warrender to Beatty at 12:25 p.m.: "Enemy cruisers and destroyers in sight." Fifteen minutes later, Warrender followed up with another signal: "Enemy's course east. No battle cruisers seen yet." From these messages, Beatty correctly inferred that this was the same force Goodenough had engaged at 11:30 a.m. and that it was a lookout screen ahead of the German battle cruisers, which must still be some distance to the west. Beatty worried that Hipper might emerge from the gap near Warrender and, because the German ships were faster, be able to slip past. Accordingly, at 12:30 p.m., Beatty made a fatefully wrong decision. Abandoning his westward course and his intended line of patrol, he reversed course and swung his ships around to the east. His presumption now was that only his squadron was fast enough to intercept Hipper; his purpose was to place his fast ships between Hipper and Germany; in order to cut them off it was important to have sea room east of the enemy now coming out through the gap. Ironically, it was this move that allowed Hipper to escape. Had the British admiral held his westward course and established his patrol line, a battle at close range must have begun around one o'clock. When *Lion, Queen Mary, Tiger,* and *New Zealand* swung around over their own wakes and headed east, *Seydlitz, Moltke, Derfflinger, Von der Tann,* and *Blücher* were only twelve miles away.

Beatty held to his new decision, steaming eastward for forty-five minutes, until it became clear that Hipper had not tried to get away past Warrender to the south. At 1:15 p.m. therefore, Beatty abandoned his easterly course and turned northward, slowing to 15 knots. He continued in this direction for about ten miles, but, finding nothing, at 1:55 p.m. he turned again to the east. Half an hour later, he was headed southeast at 25 knots on a course that converged with the line between the southern exit and Heligoland Bight.

Warrender's luck was no better. At one o'clock, he reached the southern limit of the minefield and found nothing. Realizing that Hipper was not coming in this direction, Warrender turned north at 1:24 p.m. He was too late: Hipper had turned north at 12:45, and Hipper's battle cruisers could outrun Warrender's battleships. Nevertheless, Warrender's turn to the north brought him close to contact with Hipper; *Kolberg,* heavily damaged by the sea and lagging at only 12 knots behind the German battle cruisers, sighted Warrender's funnel smoke soon after Hipper had turned northeast. But Warrender did not see *Kolberg* or know that Hipper was there.

As the afternoon progressed, Room 40 passed to the Admiralty a stream of intercepted German signals. From there, it took up to two hours for the information to reach the British commanders at sea. For the next several hours, Beatty and Warrender tried to use these tardy intercepts to predict what the Germans would do. But decoding and transmission took too long. A signal from Hipper had given his position when he turned northeast at 12:45 p.m., but this signal was not sent to Warrender and Beatty until 2:50 p.m., by which time Hipper was far away to the north.

Meanwhile, what appeared to be ominous news was coming in from Room 40. At 1:50 p.m., the Admiralty learned from an intercepted signal from *Friedrich der Grosse* to *Stralsund* that, at 12:30 p.m., the High Seas Fleet was at sea seventy to eighty miles northwest of Heligoland. The truth was that the German fleet had reached this point in its retreat, but to the Admiralty it appeared that the German dreadnoughts were coming out. This news reached the British admirals at sea at 2:25 p.m.; to this information, the Admiralty appended a stern warning to Warrender not to pursue too far. This warning, added to the realization that Hipper had escaped, brought an end to hope for any action that day. The search continued until 3:30 p.m., when it was evident that the German battle cruisers had escaped around the northern flank of the British squadrons. At 3:47 p.m., with dusk beginning to fall, Warrender signaled Beatty: "Relinquish chase. Rejoin me tomorrow."

Nevertheless, if the High Seas Fleet was at sea, hope remained for the following day. Jellicoe, bringing two additional dreadnought battle squadrons down from Scapa Flow, ordered a concentration of the entire Grand Fleet at daybreak. At dawn on December 17, Jellicoe's armada assembled and then moved southeast, feeling for the German fleet. But after moving only fifty miles toward the Bight, Jellicoe was informed by the Admiralty that the High Seas Fleet had gone back into harbor. Before returning to its own anchorages, the British fleet spent the day in battle exercises and target practice; it relieved some of the tension and disappointment when the battle cruisers and battleships finally opened fire with their heavy guns.

—

Hipper had enjoyed extraordinary luck. When he had turned for home from the English coast at 9:30 a.m., the admiral was tired, but not especially uneasy about his return voyage. The minefields presented no hazard; he knew where they were and knew the location of the gap. The weather caused greater concern. Head seas were battering his ships, and the minelaying light cruiser *Kolberg,* lagging behind the battle cruisers, had been badly damaged; her bridge and superstructure had been almost completely swept away by the heavy waves into which she was plunging. Hipper nevertheless meant to carry out the original plan: he would steer east in the wake of his own dismissed light cruisers and destroyers, rendezvous with the High Seas Fleet near the Dogger Bank, and, together with Ingenohl, return to Germany. Hipper, of course, did not then know that Ingenohl had scuttled this plan. The Commander-in-Chief had not told him that he had encountered British destroyers, that he feared that the entire Grand Fleet was out, and that he had turned tail and was running for home. Nor did Hipper know that Beatty's battle cruisers and Warrender's battleships were at sea and were blocking his path to Germany.

At 11:30 a.m. Hipper's ships were steaming east through the middle of the minefield gap, straight toward Beatty's oncoming force. Then, at 11:39 a.m., Hipper received the message from the light cruiser *Stralsund,* fifty miles ahead, that she had encountered enemy ships, adding, "Am being chased." This was the first news Hipper had received that British warships were operating in this part of the North Sea. At 11:50 a.m., the admiral, aware by then that Ingenohl and the main German battle fleet were running for home, turned his battle cruisers southeast and went at 23 knots to the aid of his embattled light forces. As he did so, *Stralsund, Strassburg, Graudenz,* and the German destroyers, attempting to shake off *Southampton* and *Birmingham,* were turning sharply to the south. At 12:17 p.m. therefore, Hipper slightly altered course to reach *Stralsund*'s new position. Admiral Beatty was less than thirty miles away.

It was at this moment that luck came down hard on Hipper's side. The German light cruisers, deflected to the south away from Goodenough and Beatty, sighted Warrender's battleships. At 12:13 p.m., *Stralsund* urgently signaled Hipper that she had seen "five enemy battleships." Hipper immediately realized that these ships were many miles south of those reported earlier and that he now confronted not one blocking force but two. Still, despite knowing that he would have to risk fighting British battleships in order to support his own light cruisers and destroyers, Hipper continued on course for another half hour. Then, at 12:44 p.m., to his immense relief, he received another message from *Stralsund:* "Enemy is out of sight." "Are you in danger?" he signaled *Stralsund.* At five minutes past one, he received the welcome reply, "No." Now free to shed responsibility for his light forces and to concentrate on getting his battle cruisers home, Hipper turned the big ships sharply to the north to clear the danger area as quickly as possible. With rain squalls and low clouds still hampering visibility, the German battle cruisers made a wide detour around the northern edge of the Dogger Bank. Sometime between 2:30 p.m. and 3:30 p.m., the German battle cruisers were observed by two British trawlers twenty-five miles north of the Dogger Bank, steering eastward at high speed. By 7:30 the next morning, December 17, Hipper's ships were home.

—

From the perspective of the War Room at the Admiralty, Winston Churchill described this day:

> Telegraph and telephone were pouring the distress of Hartlepool and Scarborough to all parts of the kingdom and by half-past ten, when the War Committee of the Cabinet met, news magnified by rumor had produced excitement. I was immdiately asked how such a thing was possible. "What was the Navy doing and what were they going to do?" In reply, I produced the chart which showed the respective positions of the British and German naval forces, and I explained that subject to moderate visibility we hoped that collision would take place about noon. These disclosures fell upon all with a sense of awe and the Committee adjourned until the afternoon.
>
> At 10.30, the Admiralty learned that the enemy was leaving our coasts and apprised Admiral Warrender. . . . But now already ominous telegrams began to arrive. . . . No contact. . . . The weather got steadily worse. It was evident that mist curtains were falling over the North Sea. 3,000 yards visibility, [then] 2,000 yards visibility, were reported by ships speaking to each other. The solemn faces of Fisher and Wilson betrayed no emotion but one felt the fire burning within. I tried to do other work but it was not much good. . . . Then, all of a sudden, we heard . . . Goodenough report that he had opened fire upon a German light cruiser. Hope flared up. The prospect of a confused battle at close range had no terrors for the Admiralty. They had only one fear—lest the enemy should escape. . . .
>
> About half past one, Sir Arthur Wilson said, "They seem to be getting away from us." But now occurred a new development of a formidable kind. At 1.50 we learned that the High Seas Fleet was at sea. . . . We instantly warned our squadrons. . . .
>
> At 3 o'clock I went over and told the War Committee what was passing; but with what a heavy heart did I cross again that Horse Guards Parade. I returned to the Admiralty. The War Group had reassembled around the octagonal table in my room. The shades of a

> winter's evening had already fallen. Sir Arthur Wilson then said in his most ordinary manner, "Well, there you are, they have got away. They must be about here by now," and he pointed to a chart on which the Chief of Staff was marking positions every fifteen minutes. It was evident that the Germans had eluded our intercepting force and that even their light cruisers with whom we had been in contact had also escaped in the mists. Said Admiral Warrender in his subsequent report, "They came out of one rainstorm and disappeared into another."

At this point, in an effort not to let the Germans get away untouched, the frustrated Admiralty War Group launched a flurry of orders. "Twenty destroyers of . . . [the Harwich] Flotillas are waiting off Gorleston [on the Norfolk coast]," they signaled Warrender. "If you think it advisable you may direct Tyrwhitt to take them to vicinity of Heligoland to attack enemy ships returning in dark hours."

Warrender rejected the idea, replying, "Certainly not advisable as there is a strong northwest wind and nasty sea." Jellicoe simply signaled Warrender, "It is too late."

A final means of intercepting the Germans remained. Roger Keyes with ten submarines and two destroyers had been posted off the coast of Holland. At 10:34 a.m., Keyes in *Lurcher* intercepted the message that the Germans were bombarding Scarborough. Anticipating that he could be useful, he took *Lurcher* and began to steam up and down to collect his submarines. Even though the submarines were on the surface, it was a difficult task. "I had a most trying day . . . ," Keyes wrote. "In the visibility prevailing, they had to dive the moment they sighted a vessel if they wished to remain unseen . . . and by dusk I had succeeded in finding only four." At 2:10 p.m., the Admiralty sent Keyes the order he had been hoping for: "The High Seas Fleet is at sea. . . . They may return after dawn tomorrow so proceed to Heligoland and intercept them. They [will] probably pass five miles west of Heligoland steering for Weser Light." When this signal arrived, Keyes had found only four of his submarines: three British and the French *Archimède.* He ordered these four into the Bight, three to the southern side of Heligoland and one to the northern, with instructions to attack whatever enemy ships came within range. Keyes, meanwhile, continued trying to locate his other submarines.

It was too late to intercept Ingenohl. By nine o'clock that night, the High Seas Fleet was back in the mouth of the Elbe, where the squadrons would wait until dawn before going into Jade Bay. Hipper, however, was still at sea. The Admiralty knew that his battle cruisers, racing for home at 23 knots, could reach Heligoland before Keyes's submarines, which at best could make 14 knots on the surface. But Keyes's two destroyers, *Lurcher* and *Firedrake,* might overtake the Germans, and both were equipped with torpedo tubes. In the Admiralty War Room it was Sir Arthur Wilson who spoke:

"There is only one chance now. Keyes with *Lurcher* and *Firedrake* . . . could probably make certain of attacking the German battle cruiser squadron as it enters the Bight tonight. He may torpedo one or even two." To Churchill, it seemed a "forlorn hope to send these two frail destoyers with their brave commodore and faithful crews far from home, close to the enemy's coast, utterly unsupported, into the jaws of this powerful German force with its protecting vessels and flotillas. There was a long silence. We all knew Keyes well. Then someone said, 'It is sending him to his death.' Someone else said, 'He would be the last man to wish us to consider that.' There was another long pause. However, Sir Arthur Wilson had already written the following message [to Keyes]: 'We think Heligoland and Amrun lights will be lit when ships are going in. Your destroyers might get a chance to attack about 2 a.m. or later. . . .' The First Sea Lord [Fisher] nodded assent. The Chief of Staff [Oliver] took the telegram, got up heavily and quitted the room."

The Admiralty sent the signal at 8:12 p.m. It should have reached Keyes within an hour. It took five hours. The Admiralty originally had sent the signal out on the wrong wavelength, the D-band, for destroyers, which had a radius of only fifty miles. Keyes had told them to use the S-band, for submarines, which had a greater radius. Not until twenty-three minutes past midnight, when Keyes was 200 miles away from Heligoland, did the Admiralty recognize its mistake and resend the message on the S-band. Through the afternoon, Keyes had considered moving into the Bight on his own responsibility. He had held back because he anticipated that Tyrwhitt might be following the German ships with his light cruisers and destroyers and making a night torpedo attack near Heligoland. If this were so, the uncoordinated appearance of *Lurcher* and *Firedrake* could create chaos. Two days later, when Keyes went to see Churchill at the Admiralty, the First Lord said, "We sent you a terrible message the other night. I hardly expected to see you alive." "It *was* terrible," Keyes replied. "I waited three hours in the hope of getting such a message." Long afterward, Keyes wrote, "Words fail me even now, after more than nineteen years, to express my feelings when I received this belated message."

One of Keyes's submarine captains, Martin Naismith of *E-11,* did get a look at the High Seas Fleet. At dawn on the morning of December 17, as the German fleet was moving from the Weser into the Jade, Naismith observed the dreadnought *Posen* and fired a torpedo at 400 yards. Because the submarine was rolling heavily, the torpedo ran too deep, passing under *Posen*'s keel. *E-11* prepared to fire at another target, but before she could do so, a third vessel turned to ram. The submarine hurriedly dived and then, having unbalanced her trim, lunged back to the surface. By then, however, the German ships were some distance away headed into the Jade.

The Scarborough Raid was over.

—

The Scarborough Raid ended in frustration and recrimination in both the British and German navies. When the British fleet returned to port, officers and men read newspaper stories about the devastation of English towns. "The more we heard," said Lieutenant Filson Young of *Lion,* "the more bitter was our disappointment. . . . The accounts of the horrible casualties to women and children in the bombarded towns were particularly affecting."* Beatty was nearly overcome by chagrin. Sitting at his desk on *Lion,* he poured out his feelings to Ethel. On December 20, he wrote again: "The happenings of the last week have left a mark which nothing can eradicate except the total destruction of the enemy's battle and other cruisers. We were within an ace of accomplishing it the other day. . . . Our advanced ships had sighted them and then !!! I can't bear to write about it! And I can think of nothing else. . . . If we had got them Wednesday, as we ought to have done, we should have finished the war from a naval point of view."

In Beatty's opinion, the officer responsible for the fiasco was Goodenough. Once the ships were back in harbor, the cruiser commodore came on board the *Lion* and Beatty unleashed his anger at this subordinate for committing the unpardonable sin of letting go of an enemy once action had begun. Afterward, he wrote to Jellicoe:

> There never was a more disappointing day. . . . We were within an ace of bringing about the complete destruction of the enemy [battle] cruiser force—and failed. There is no doubt whatever that his [Goodenough's] failure to keep in touch with and report the presence of the enemy cruisers was entirely reponsible for the failure. . . . Time after time I have impressed upon Goodenough the necessity of using his own initiative and discretion—that my orders are expressions of intentions and they are not to be obeyed too literally. The Man on the Spot is the only one who can judge certain situations. . . . [It] nearly broke my heart; the disappointment was terrific. . . . Truly, the past has been the blackest week in my life.

As a solution, Beatty suggested removing Goodenough from command of the light cruisers and replacing him with Lionel Halsey, the captain of *New Zealand.* "He knows cruiser work and battle cruiser work and the relation of one with the other," Beatty said of Halsey. The decision was Jellicoe's.

In fact, Goodenough's action had also baffled the Grand Fleet commander. On December 18, he wrote to Fisher, saying how "intensely unhappy" he was about the whole affair. He "couldn't understand Goodenough's actions at all, so entirely unlike all he had previously done since the war began." Jel-

*Young, a journalist in peacetime, was now a reserve officer attached to David Beatty's staff.

licoe's official report to the Admiralty added, "The Commodore gives as his reason for abandoning the chase of the enemy the signal made to him to resume his station. This signal was intended by the Vice Admiral for *Nottingham* and *Falmouth.* It was a most unfortunate error. Had the Commodore disobeyed the signal, it is possible that the action between the light cruisers might have resulted in bringing the battle cruisers to action." A week later, Jellicoe drew a general conclusion for future use: "Should an officer commanding a squadron or a captain of a single vessel, when in actual touch with the enemy, receive an order from a senior officer which it is evident may have been given in ignorance of the conditions of the moment and which, if obeyed, would cause touch with the enemy to be lost, such officers must exercise great discretion as to representing the real facts before obeying the order." To this admonition, the Admiralty added its own: "To break off an action which has begun against an equal force is a most serious step; and an officer so engaged should, in the absence of previous special instructions, make sure that his superior knows that he is fighting before relinquishing the action."

Jellicoe hesitated to make so drastic a move as removing Goodenough: "Beatty [is] very severe on Goodenough but forgets that it was his own badly worded signal to the cruisers that led to the German being out of touch," he noted on the back of an envelope. As time gave opportunity for reflection, naval opinion tended increasingly to take this view and sympathize with, if not wholly exonerate, Goodenough. "Goodenough was so close to Beatty that . . . for all Goodenough knew, Beatty might have some important reason for ordering the light cruisers to get ahead [and re-form the screen]," wrote Captain John Creswell. "I reckon that the fault lay entirely with Beatty and Seymour."

Naval historians have wondered why, after Scarborough, Beatty continued to have confidence in his flag lieutenant, Lieutenant Commander Ralph Seymour. "The true guilt for the ambiguous signal from *Lion* points to Beatty's flag lieutenant whose business it was to translate Beatty's intentions," concludes the British historian Richard Hough. "A flag lieutenant's job was to select the wording and then the suitable flag, wireless signal or Morse message to express it. It was Seymour who ought to have been sacked after the Scarborough Raid fiasco, not Goodenough. Instead, he was retained at immeasurable cost to the navy and the country." During the Scarborough Raid, again at the Battle of the Dogger Bank, and twice at Jutland, Seymour failed to translate Beatty's intentions into a plain signal that allowed for no misunderstanding. "He lost three battles for me," Beatty said glumly after the war.

Fisher, raging, rejected all excuses. "They were all actually in our grasp! . . . In the very jaws of death! . . . All concerned had made a hash of it:—and heads must roll," he proclaimed. Goodenough, he announced, had been *"a fool,"* and Fisher wanted the commodore relieved. But Fisher was a minority of one: Jellicoe was tepid about removing Goodenough, Beatty decided that he did not really desire a change, and Churchill was adamant that Goodenough must be saved. Goodenough therefore remained in command. Fisher's list of heads to be rolled also included Warrender's and Bradford's. Even before the raid, he had written to Jellicoe, "I suppose you must have a very high opinion of Warrender and Bradford or you would not cling to them. I have no reason for making this remark beyond that they both seem somewhat stupid! . . . I can't stand a fool however amiable and I don't believe that in war that it is anything short of criminal to keep the wrong men in any appointment high or low. 'Changing horses while crossing the stream' is an overdone saying! It's all rot (and much worse) having regard to anyone's feelings when the safety of our Empire is at stake. OLD WOMEN MUST GO!"

In the end, none of the British naval officers in command that day was relieved. Warrender retired at the end of 1915 because of ill health. Arbuthnot, who had a reputation for aggressiveness and eagerness, remained. He never explained, nor was he ever asked to explain, why he had failed to open fire on the German light cruisers, even without the permission of his senior officer. Beatty escaped all censure and reaped only praise, his failure to intercept being blamed entirely on Goodenough.

This battle cruiser engagement did not take place, but if it had—if Beatty had continued west and encountered Hipper—how might such a contest have turned out? Warrender's battleships were fifteen miles away and could not have arrived in less than forty-five minutes. It would therefore have been four British ships against five German, including *Blücher.* Hipper's four battle cruisers were a match for *Lion, Queen Mary, Tiger,* and *New Zealand.* The two opposing groups of huge ships, rushing directly at each other at forty miles an hour through the murk, would have had time to fire only a few salvos before their opponents disappeared. Already, the Germans had proved the accuracy of their gunnery. And, as the British were to learn at Jutland, German ship construction was superior to British. David Beatty had the lion's heart, but on that day, matched against Hipper, he probably had the inferior force.

Assessing the errors made before and during the raid, Jellicoe always believed that he should not have been overruled in his wish to involve the entire Grand Fleet in the attempt to intercept. Fisher agreed with Jellicoe. "Lord Fisher said that in his opinion a great mistake had been made," Maurice Hankey, the secretary of the Committee of Imperial Defence, wrote to Balfour. "He said that he had been overruled, but that the First Lord [Churchill] had afterwards confessed to him that a mistake had been made in not utilizing the whole of Jellicoe's fleet." Thereafter, Beatty never put to sea without the Grand Fleet coming out in support. If the High Seas Fleet came out to fight, it would have to fight Jellicoe.

Overall British naval strategy was unaffected by the raid. The primary base of the Grand Fleet remained at Scapa Flow, where it would keep the cork in the top of the North Sea. In response to public apprehension about the vulnerability of the coastal towns, one change in deployment was made. Through the autumn, when the fleet retreated to Loch Ewe or Loch Swilly, Beatty had fretted that he was too far away; he wanted his battle cruisers at Cromarty or Rosyth, where they would be nearer the Bight. On December 20, the Admiralty gave Beatty permission to make Rosyth on the Firth of Forth his permanent base. The next morning, the battle cruisers left Cromarty and that afternoon steamed into the Firth of Forth. Soon after, the battle cruiser *Indomitable,* which had been refitting in the south after her return from watching the Dardanelles, joined Beatty at Rosyth, bringing his battle cruiser strength to five, even without *Princess Royal, Invincible,* and *Inflexible.*

The Admiralty was bitterly disappointed by what had happened. Scarborough, Hartlepool, and Whitby had been sacrificed in order to entrap and destroy Hipper—and Hipper had gotten away. Blame was discussed, apportioned, and set aside. Only Jellicoe mentioned another possibility: "There never was such bad luck," he said. But, in fact, luck favored both sides that day. Hipper was saved by the chance encounter of his light cruisers, first with Beatty's screen, then with Warrender's battleships. Thus warned, he was able to turn north and escape under cover of wind and rain. But if the day was a disappointment to the British commanders, groping for their prey in heavy seas and blinding rain, they were unaware of how narrowly they themselves had escaped destruction. Ingenohl, by pressing forward with more determination and directing the fire of twenty-two battleships against six, could have destroyed or crippled Warrender's battle squadron. Both sides could complain and, at the same time, be grateful.

Churchill found solace in the knowledge that Room 40 had worked and therefore, presumably, would work again. "Dissatisfaction was widespread," he admitted. "However, we could not say a word in explanation. We had to bear in silence the censures of our countrymen. We could never admit, for fear of compromising our secret information, where our squadrons were, or how near the German raiding cruisers had been to their destruction. One comfort we had. The indications upon which we had acted had been confirmed by events. The sources of information upon which we relied were evidently trustworthy. Next time we might at least have average visibility. But would there be a next time? The German admiral must have known that he was very near to powerful British ships, but which they were, or where they were, or how near he was, might be a mystery. Would it not also be a mystery how they came to be there?"

—

Germany celebrated. For the first time in two centuries, England had felt the scourge of war on its own soil. It was "a regular bombardment of fortified places" and "further proof of the gallantry of our navy," declared the Berlin *Neueste Nachrichten.* The *Berliner Tageblatt* expressed regret at the damage done to Whitby Abbey but explained that "the life of a single German soldier is for us a thousand times more important than a monumental building, even when it possesses such great historical value." The *Berliner Borsenzeitung* warned that "the bombardment possibly heralds greater events to come." But while the German people hung flags from their windows, the officer corps of the German navy knew better. A golden opportunity to pare down the British fleet had been lost. Tirpitz, never in any doubt that ship for ship, the fleet he had built was superior, believed that all it needed was a chance to whittle down the greater numbers of the Grand Fleet. Here, the chance had come—and had been thrown away. Scheer, more cautiously, agreed: "It is extremely probable that if we had continued in our original direction, the courses of the two fleets would have crossed within sight of each other during the morning." Officers of Hipper's scouting groups were angry, not just because the withdrawal had left their battle cruisers unsupported, but because the potential for larger success had been missed. Captain Magnus von Levetzow of the battle cruiser *Moltke* wrote scornfully to Admiral von Holtzendorff, the former Commander-in-Chief of the High Seas Fleet, that Ingenohl had retreated "because he was afraid to face eleven British destroyers which could easily have been eliminated. . . . Under the present leadership we will accomplish nothing."

Although Hipper shared the general chagrin at the premature flight of the German battle fleet, he apparently had no misgivings about killing and wounding hundreds of civilians. He viewed it, said his biographer Captain Hugo von Waldeyer-Hartz, "entirely as a war measure and therefore as a task imposed on him by duty. It is a regrettable but obvious fact that modern war is blind: it involves both combatants and noncombatants, slaying indiscriminately. . . . The first objective is to break a nation's morale; the collapse of its physical resistance will follow." As for Ingenohl, he defended his decision to abandon Hipper by insisting that he was obeying the order not to risk the fleet. "The advance of the main fleet by day to a juncture with . . . [Hipper's force] did not coincide with the commands issued by the *All Highest* [the kaiser] as to use of the High Seas Fleet," he said in his report after the battle. On this ground, Scheer exonerated him: "The restrictions enforced on the Commander in Chief brought about the failure of the bold and promising plan." Ironically, the kaiser, the principal author of the restrictions on the fleet, also criticized Ingenohl's behavior. This time, the monarch lectured the admiral, Ingenohl had been too careful with the High Seas Fleet and had missed an opportunity to establish its supremacy in the North Sea: "The effort to preserve the fleet must under no circumstances be carried so far that favorable prospects of a success are missed owing to the prospect of possible losses." Nevertheless, William made no changes. Friedrich von Ingenohl remained Commander-in-Chief. The basic operations order was not canceled, the restrictions were not lifted, and the High Seas Fleet commander continued to be bound by regulations that put him at fault no matter whether he risked or husbanded his ships.

CHAPTER 20

The Cuxhaven Raid: "Stupid Great Things, but Very Beautiful"

The autumn of 1914 saw war at sea revolutionized by weapons scarcely imaginable a generation earlier: the dreadnought, the submarine, the airplane, and the airship. The potential combatants had already equipped themselves with a number of airplanes, which generals and admirals conceded might be useful for observing the enemy. Airships, lifted by giant bags of lighter-than-air gas strung inside a rigid metal frame, were viewed with greater suspicion. In every war, however, weapons development moves quickly and by Christmas Day, 1914, the Royal Navy was so concerned about the danger from airships—which the Germans called zeppelins—that it mounted an attack by shipborne airplanes on a German airship base on the North Sea. In response, German zeppelins and seaplanes attacked British surface ships and submarines. The Cuxhaven Raid, as it came to be called, was history's first aircraft-carrier-based air strike. It was also the first naval battle in which, on both sides, the striking forces were made up exclusively of aerial machines.

The rigid airships made famous during the Great War bore the name of their creator, Count Ferdinand von Zeppelin. Curiously, this aerial pioneer was first inspired in St. Paul, Minnesota, when, as a twenty-five-year-old German officer, on leave from his duty as an observer with the Union army in the Civil War, he was invited to go up in a tethered military observation balloon. Count Zeppelin was enthusiastic about his first ascent and began to dream about the possibilities of lighter-than-air craft. His vision was postponed for the many decades he devoted to a regular army career. Only in 1900, after retiring from the army, did he see his own first airship, lifted by hydrogen bags, actually fly. Soon after, it crashed. Three more privately financed, Zeppelin-designed airships followed, which flew but were discarded or destroyed by fire or storm. Zeppelin's manufacturing company foundered financially, but the German public, impressed by the dedicated persistence of the little pioneer and awed by the immense size of his airships, came to the rescue. Private money flowed in to support his work, and Zeppelin became a national hero. Originally, he had meant to build huge airships for passengers and cargo, but, as a former military officer, he also recognized the airship's potential as a weapon. As war approached, the German army ordered zeppelins and on Mobilization Day it possessed seven. The Imperial Navy had only one airship, because Grand Admiral von Tirpitz had resisted any diversion of funds from the building of battleships. "As a naval officer who had got to know the force of the wind and the malice of squalls on sailing ships, I never promised myself much from the airships," Tirpitz announced. Nevertheless, during the first weeks of war, the German navy, short on light cruisers for scouting, grasped that zeppelins, with their long range and endurance, might make up this deficit. Construction of airships and airship bases received priority; within four months, the German navy had four zeppelins.

Neither airships nor airplanes stirred much interest in the Royal Navy. In 1907, the Wright brothers offered patents on their newly developed flying machine to the Admiralty; Lord Tweedmouth, the First Lord, replied that airplanes "would be of no particular value to the Naval Service." Tweedmouth, however, did not speak for his First Sea Lord, and Jacky Fisher, builder of dreadnoughts and advocate of submarines, was always open to the potential of exotic new weapons. In 1909, with Tweedmouth departed, the Naval Estimates included a request for £35,000 to build one experimental rigid airship. The money was approved and construction of the airship *Mayfly* commenced. *Mayfly* was completed in September 1911, but while she was being trundled out of her hangar for her maiden voyage, a violent cross-wind squall broke her in two, a trauma sufficient to terminate rigid-airship construction in Great Britain. Some British naval officers regretted this decision: in November 1911, Jellicoe, visiting Berlin, went up in a zeppelin and came down an advocate. As Second Sea Lord in December 1912, Jellicoe, whose duties included oversight of aeronautical developments, attempted to stimulate interest in the use of airships for scouting at sea. He compared airships favorably with airplanes, whose time in the air was, at best, five hours. Airplanes could neither fly nor land at night; they might travel at seventy miles an hour, compared with an airship's fifty, but an airship rose when it was stationary, and its buoyancy increased as its fuel was consumed. The other Sea Lords and the new First Lord, Winston Churchill, rejected Jellicoe's recommendations. "I rated the zeppelin much lower as a weapon of war than anyone else," Churchill said later. "I believed this enormous bladder of combustible and explosive gas would prove to be easily destructible. I was sure the fighting airplane . . . armed with incendiary bullets would harry, rout and burn these gaseous monsters. I therefore did everything in my power in the years before the war to restrict expenditure upon airships and to concentrate our narrow and stinted resources upon airplanes."

Fisher accepted Churchill's decision and, from retirement, pressed the new First Lord: "Aviation supersedes small cruisers and intelligence vessels. You told me you would push aviation. You were right." In fact, Churchill needed no urging. Entranced by these new flying machines and despite appeals from his wife, his friends, and his cousin the Duke of Marlborough—the duke declared that his new fancy was undignified as well as dangerous—Churchill, at thirty-eight, took flying lessons and was ready to solo when his instructor was killed. With that, the First Lord ruefully abandoned the air. Nevertheless, he continued vigorously to promote airplanes, both as scouts for the fleet and as defensive weapons "for the protection of our naval harbors, oil tanks, and vulnerable points." He acquired for the navy land-based airplanes, with wheels, and sea-based hydro-airplanes—"or seaplanes as I christened them, for short"—with floats. In 1912, a wheeled navy airplane took off from a platform on the deck of the predreadnought battleship *Hibernia* while the ship was under way; subsequently, the plane landed on shore. In 1913, the old light cruiser *Hermes* was refitted to carry two seaplanes. At the outbreak of the war, Churchill announced, "I had fifty efficient naval machines, or about one third the number in possession of the army." By September 3, with the German army on the Marne, all 150 of the British army's aircraft had been sent to France. At a Cabinet meeting that day, Kitchener privately asked Churchill whether the navy could assume responsibility for the aerial defense of Great Britain. Churchill instantly agreed.

The weeks that followed made clear the division in Churchill's mind between his disdain for rigid airships as useful components of the Royal Navy and his fear of German zeppelins as deadly, bomb-carrying raiders able to sow destruction over the British Isles. The zeppelin nightmare had first horrified England in 1910, and every year magnified it. Psychologically, there was cause: from the ground, a zeppelin, the size of a dreadnought in the sky, making its serene, unchallenged progress through the heavens, created an impression of implacable power. Sensationalist stories appeared describing enemy flying battleships, each with a heavy cargo of bombs, cruising the night skies over naked, defenseless England. During the winter of 1912 and 1913, "airships on nocturnal missions of frightening import" were "witnessed" far and wide over the British Isles; over London, Sheerness, Portland, Dover, Liverpool, and Cardiff. Alarm spread beyond the tabloids; Colonel Charles A'Court Repington, the military correspondent of *The Times,* predicted attacks by fleets of German airships on British arsenals, dockyards, and industrial centers. Repington was not alone; Churchill as

First Lord warned the Committee on Imperial Defence in December 1912 that "our dockyards, machine shops, magazines and ships lying in basins are absolutely defenseless against this form of attack."

On the second day of the war, a zeppelin actually attacked a city. Furious that stubborn resistance by the Belgian forts at Liège was upsetting the timetable of the Schlieffen Plan, German officers warned that if the invaders were not permitted to pass, zeppelins would destroy the city. The Belgians refused and on August 6, the zeppelin *L-Z* arrived overhead. Thirteen bombs dropped; nine civilians died. On August 24 and September 2, zeppelins bombed Antwerp and more civilians were killed.

Suddenly, the menace to England became real. London lay within range of the zeppelin sheds at Cologne and Düsseldorf. German airships might bomb the Houses of Parliament, Buckingham Palace, the Admiralty—or, worse, the oil tanks, power houses, lock gates, and magazines at Chatham, Woolwich, or Portsmouth. Churchill, now responsible for the air defense of Great Britain, knew he could not prevent this; he had no antiaircraft guns, no searchlights, no fighter aircraft. Eventually, as the war continued, Churchill's early belief was vindicated that "airplanes were the only means by which the zeppelin menace was destroyed. However," he said, "we were not in a position at the beginning of the war to produce effective results. Airplane engines were not powerful enough to reach the great heights needed for the attack of zeppelins in the short time available. Night flying had only just been born. . . . But it was no use sitting down and waiting a year [for defensive measures to be ready. For the moment] only offensive action could help us."

Churchill understood that although at first German zeppelins were immune in the air, this immunity deserted them on the ground. It was here that Churchill proposed to hit them, "by bombing from airplanes, the zeppelin sheds wherever these gigantic structures could be found. . . . In order to strike at the zeppelin sheds in Germany, it was necessary to start from as near the enemy's line as possible." Already on September 12, Churchill had called for stationing "the largest possible force of naval aeroplanes at Calais or Dunkirk." On September 22, four ground-based Royal Naval Air Service planes, flying from Antwerp, attacked zeppelin sheds in Düsseldorf and Cologne on the Rhine. One pilot located the target, but his bombs missed. On October 8, a British naval airplane destroyed a zeppelin in its shed at Düsseldorf. On November 21, four navy planes flying from Belfort in eastern France attacked the zeppelin construction works at Friedrichshafen, on Lake Constance. They did no damage.

There were zeppelin sheds at the German naval airship bases at Cuxhaven and Hamburg. They were beyond the range of British land-based airplanes flying from Britain, France, or Belgium, but they were not beyond the reach of air attack from the North Sea. But how might such an attack be mounted? By 1914, airplanes had taken off from ships but no plane with wheels had landed back on board a ship. Accordingly, unless air attacks from the sea on the zeppelin sheds were to be one-way missions, the planes used must be seaplanes and they must be carried most of the way to the target by ships that could recover them after the raid and bring them home. Excited by this concept, Churchill commandeered four cross-Channel passenger steamers and sent them to shipyards for alterations. (*Hermes* had been abandoned as being too old and slow.) Each of these new carriers—*Empress, Riviera, Campania,* and *Engadine*—was designed to embark three seaplanes, one forward and two aft. Long booms were installed to lift the fragile aircraft out over the side of the ship and place them in the water. Steel hangars erected on the stern decks provided shelter for the seaplanes from wind and sea. The aircraft themselves were single-engine biplanes made for the Admiralty by Short Brothers, Ltd.—Type 74s, Folders, and Type 135s—all of them with floats, two seats, and wings that folded back in order to fit the ungainly machines onto the steamers' decks. The planes' maximum speed was 78 miles an hour; the distance they could fly, fully fueled, was between 300 and 400 miles. Each plane could carry, in a rack between its floats, three nineteen-pound bombs, to be released by pulling a wire in the cockpit. A single bomb, the British believed, plunging through the roof of a zeppelin shed and bursting anywhere near the thousands of cubic feet of flammable hydrogen contained in a zeppelin, should suffice. By the end of August, three of the newly created seaplane carriers had been commissioned and sent to Harwich.

—

The First Lord's eagerness to attack the Cuxhaven zeppelin base was thoroughly shared by the two Harwich commodores, Tyrwhitt and Keyes. On October 22, Tyrwhitt came to the Admiralty. "[I] arrived at 5 p.m. and was taken at once to the Holy of Holies where Prince Louis, Winston, and Sturdee were, and a long discussion followed. I produced my little plan (or rather, Roger Keyes' plan) and got through it right away. . . . They kept me a long time and suddenly in walked the Prince of Wales."* The plan was for six seaplanes to be embarked on *Engadine* and *Riviera.* The two seaplane carriers would be escorted into the Heligoland Bight by Tyrwhitt's light cruisers and destroyers, and the force would wait while the seaplanes attacked the airship base at Cuxhaven and returned to be picked up.

The raid was scheduled for October 25. A smooth sea was essential for the seaplanes to take off from open water; at dawn on October 24, when the two carriers and their escort sailed from Harwich, the sea was calm. But a heavy rain fell during the passage across the North Sea and when, at first light on the twenty-fifth, the seaplanes were hoisted over the side, a fresh cloudburst prevented four of the six from rising off the water. A fifth sea-

*Later King Edward VIII; subsequently, the Duke of Windsor.

plane managed to fly twelve miles but turned back after the engine had stopped twice because of rain. The sixth managed to fly twenty miles, but returned because there appeared to be no chance of finding its target in the storm.

Tyrwhitt was disappointed, but, returning to the Admiralty, he found Churchill still enthusiastic. "I got considerable butter over my part in the proceedings," the commodore wrote to his wife. "We are going to try again and I can't help thinking we shall succeed this time." The next attempt came on November 23. This time Jellicoe brought the Grand Fleet into the middle of the North Sea to support the carriers, but the operation was canceled by the Admiralty before the seaplanes were lifted onto the water. Explanations for this differ: Churchill blamed poor weather; Jellicoe declared that "the enemy had a force present in the Bight which would be too strong for our detached vessels." Tyrwhitt was disgusted.

Churchill did not give up. On December 21, five days after the Scarborough Raid, Keyes and Tyrwhitt were told to try a third time. On December 23, the weather forecast was promising and the Admiralty ordered the raid to be carried out at dawn on Christmas Day. Three seaplane carriers, *Engadine, Riviera,* and *Empress,* escorted by the light cruisers *Arethusa, Undaunted,* and *Aurora* and by eight destroyers, were to sail from Harwich for the Heligoland Bight. The force would be small because Tyrwhitt believed it would be easier for a few ships to penetrate the Bight undiscovered. Keyes sent out eleven submarines, positioning some around the launch point, others at the recovery position, still others off the German river mouths to intercept the High Seas Fleet should it emerge. Around the British submarines' conning towers was painted a red and white checkerboard stripe to aid in recognition by British aviators who might need to land short of the carriers. *Engadine, Riviera,* and *Empress* would be escorted to a point fifteen miles north of Heligoland, where the seaplanes would be hoisted onto the water. After attacking the zeppelin base, the pilots were to reconnoiter the German fleet anchorages at Cuxhaven and Wilhelmshaven, noting the warships present, then fly west along the German coast to the island of Norderney; there they would turn north to rejoin the carriers, which would be waiting twenty miles offshore. Again, Jellicoe would bring the Grand Fleet into the middle of the North Sea. In this way, notes R. D. Layman, a leading contemporary historian of the Cuxhaven Raid, 150 British warships were to be employed "to deliver to the German mainland exactly eighty-one and one half pounds of explosives. This was the combined weight of the bursting charges in the twenty-seven bombs to be carried by the seaplanes."

Hoping for surprise, Tyrwhitt sailed from Harwich at 5:00 a.m. on the day before Christmas without preliminary warning to anyone, leaving "stewards who had been landed . . . to obtain extras for Christmas Day . . . on the quay frantically waving turkeys and geese" at their departing ships. Entering the

Bight at 4:30 on Christmas morning, they observed four small German patrol vessels. Soon after, *Arethusa* intercepted urgent German wireless traffic to and from Heligoland. Still two hours from the launching position, Tyrwhitt considered turning back; if enemy ships were on patrol in the Bight and if his force went forward and launched its seaplanes, the carriers would risk being discovered and sunk before their aircraft could be recovered. Nevertheless, unwilling to have come so far only to give up again, Tyrwhitt went forward.

Half an hour before dawn, the British ships reached their launch position and stopped their engines. The three carriers each hoisted three seaplanes onto a calm sea. The weather was cold and there was a breeze from the east, but the growing light revealed high visibility and no hint of fog; this was ideal flying weather. The planes were fueled for three hours' flight. At 6:30 a.m., nine seaplanes were in the water, unfolding their wings and starting their engines. At 6:59 a.m., Tyrwhitt on *Arethusa* hoisted the signal for takeoff. Two planes suffering engine failure remained on the water and were hoisted back aboard the carriers. The lightness of the breeze forced the others into extended takeoff runs, but eventually, seven British seaplanes lifted into the air, passed Heligoland, and headed southeast toward Cuxhaven. Tyrwhitt signaled his ships to turn west and steam for the recovery position off Norderney.

—

The target for the seven attacking seaplanes was the Nordholz airship base, set amid fruit orchards eight miles south of the port of Cuxhaven. The base, which in October 1914 had become the headquarters of the German Naval Airship Division, consisted of a single huge shed containing two side-by-side hangars, each 597 feet long, each the home of one zeppelin. The twin-hangar structure itself was a technological marvel: the entire 4,000-ton mass, says Layman, was "mounted on a giant turntable that could swing it into any prevailing wind, a crucial consideration in the operation of airships for a wind blowing . . . across a hangar's mouth . . . could keep a ship immobilized inside for hours or even days." Another naval airship base existed near Hamburg; between them, the two bases housed all four of the German navy zeppelins then available for North Sea operations. The four airships, all constructed in 1914, were identical: 518 feet long, lifted by 794,000 cubic feet of hydrogen, powered by three motors that could drive the ship at 50 miles an hour. Each had a crew of twenty-four and a possible bomb load of several hundred pounds.

In good weather, the British pilots easily would have seen their target. From the air on a clear day, the high walls of the huge airship hangar were visible a dozen miles away and would have been recognized by the British aviators as they passed over Cuxhaven. But the weather, so clear and bright at sea, had deteriorated during the hour it took the planes to reach the German coast. As the sun rose higher, the fringe of the coastline and the river mouths remained visible, but over the inland plain, a heavy blanket of gray fog covered villages, farms, and fields. From time to time, the fog shifted, thinned, and even gave way to small patches of blue sky—at the Nordholz base at 6:30 a.m., the zeppelin *L-6* had no difficulty lifting off for patrol.

When they arrived, the British pilots and observers looked down into "a thick ground fog drifting in masses . . . which blotted out everything except what was lying immediately under the machine." One aviator descended to an altitude of 150 feet and still could not see the ground. Another set his course by a line of railway tracks and passed over villages, farms, and plowed fields. Eventually, the tracks led him to the Jade estuary where he flew over seven light cruisers, many destroyers, and a battle cruiser, all of which vigorously fired at him. Another pilot dropped his three bombs on sheds that he thought might constitute a seaplane base. One bomb scored a hit, but the sheds subsequently turned out to be structures for drying fish. Of the seven seaplanes that had taken off, only one reached the Nordholz zeppelin base. Its crew had been mistakenly briefed that the base was farther to the south and, because dense fog obscured the immense airship hangar, they failed to recognize it and contented themselves with bombing two antiaircraft guns. Only two of the seaplanes came close to harming the enemy. One dropped three bombs near the light cruisers *Stralsund* and *Graudenz;* the closest fell into the water 200 yards from *Graudenz.* Another seaplane, her engine misfiring, gave up the search for the zeppelin base, turned back, and, passing low over the Schillig roads, caused consternation among the crews of the warships anchored there. All of the ships opened fire on the small plane and some attempted to get under way.* The seaplane was hit, but the observer, Lieutenant Erskine Childers, a Royal Navy reserve officer now on active duty and the author of the popular thriller *The Riddle of the Sands,* managed to perform his mission. Childers was an expert on the German North Sea coast and river estuaries and, knowing exactly where he was and what he saw, he pinpointed the location of seven battleships and three battle cruisers in Schillig roads.

By 9:30 a.m., the raid was over. The British seaplanes had done no military harm. Ten bombs had been dropped on woods, fields, sheds, water, and sand. Six of the seven seaplanes, flying separately, had reached Norderney and were heading out to sea to find the carriers. Their fuel tanks were almost empty.

*A long-perpetuated myth was that in the confusion caused by the appearance of British seaplanes over the Jade, the battle cruiser *Von der Tann* collided with another vessel and was severely damaged. This, supposedly, was the reason that *Von der Tann* was not present a month later at the Battle of Dogger Bank. Actually, during that battle, *Von der Tann* was in dry dock undergoing routine maintenance.

—

As British seaplanes flew this way and that over German farms, fishing sheds, and naval anchorages, and while Tyrwhitt's force was steering for the recovery position, the German surface fleet remained at anchor. This was fortunate for the attackers. Once it became clear to scouting German patrol vessels, airships, and seaplanes that there were no dreadnoughts supporting Tyrwhitt's little force in the Bight, even a few German light cruisers would have sufficed to overpower the unarmed and unarmored seaplane carriers. Tyrwhitt's ships enjoyed this lucky exemption from surface attack because of a misunderstanding on the part of the German Naval Staff. The Germans had been expecting an attack on the Bight, not from the air, but on the surface. The British Admiralty had been collecting merchant vessels to convert into masquerade battleships and battle cruisers—the dummy fleet. Word of this collection process had reached Berlin. The German Naval Staff, however, did not know its purpose and believed that the assembled ships were to be brought in and sunk in the North Sea river and estuary channels, in order to block egress by the High Seas Fleet. They assumed that the raid, when it came, would be escorted by the Grand Fleet. On December 24, the Naval Staff received "dependable information" that the British were coming on Christmas Day. Expecting that the attack would be delivered by a massive British force that could be challenged only by the entire High Seas Fleet and mindful of the kaiser's injunction that the battleships must not be risked, Ingenohl assigned the defense of the Bight on Christmas Day to U-boats and airships only. Even when reports from patrolling submarines and zeppelins indicated that the attacking British force was small, Ingenohl's caution remained unshakable; Tyrwhitt's ships, he assumed, were the vanguard of a larger British force. As a result, no German surface warship moved. Four battle cruisers, *Seydlitz, Moltke, Derfflinger,* and *Von der Tann,* were in Schillig roads, torpedo nets retracted, ready to proceed to sea, but the signal never came. At 10:00 a.m., they were ordered to reextend their torpedo nets. By then, in any case, it was too late; a thick fog had spread over the estuaries. Germany's superior surface strength was useless.

—

Nevertheless, German pilots and airship crews did their best. At 7:35 a.m., the first zeppelin most British seamen had ever seen appeared in the sky ten miles south of Tyrwhitt's force. This was the *L-6,* which had been cruising above the Bight in search of the British and whose efforts were rewarded when it spotted Tyrwhitt's ships. Twenty minutes later, British lookouts saw a German seaplane on the horizon in the same direction. Meanwhile, as the ships moved west, *Empress* developed boiler difficulties and began falling behind. Soon, this circumstance made the converted former packet boat the focal point of the first air-sea battle in history. At 9:00 a.m., two German seaplanes attacked *Empress.* The first dropped seven 10-pound bombs from 1,600 feet; the bombs burst in the water 200 yards off the starboard bow. The second seaplane dropped two 22-pound bombs more accurately from 1,800 feet; they exploded only twenty and forty feet from the ship. *Empress*'s captain did his best to throw the Germans off by zigzagging while his crew enthusiastically fired rifles at the German planes. No harm was done on either side.

Meanwhile, *L-6,* drawing closer, descended from 5,000 feet to 2,000 and, approaching *Empress* from astern, attempted to reach a position directly overhead. Despite his own ship's apparent vulnerability, Captain Frederick Bowhill of *Empress* soon discovered that the airship above him could not turn quickly. Bowhill took quick advantage: "My method of defence was to watch [the zeppelin] carefully as she manoeuvred into position directly overhead. I then went hard over. [When] I could see her rudders put over to follow me, I put my helm over the other way." By repeated turns, *Empress* was able to avoid the three 110-pound bombs dropped by *L-6,* although two fell only fifty yards away. When her bomb racks were empty, *L-6* departed.

A few minutes before ten, the Harwich Force arrived at the recovery position thirty miles north of Norderney. The sea and the sky were empty. Minutes later, two British seaplanes appeared overhead, landed near *Riviera,* and were hoisted aboard. Almost simultaneously, ten miles nearer the coast, another seaplane had landed alongside the destroyer *Lurcher,* from which Keyes was supervising his submarines. The pilot taxied up to the destroyer, shouted that he had only five minutes' worth of fuel remaining, and asked the direction to the carriers. Realizing that the rendezvous was too far off, Keyes invited the pilot to come on board and took the seaplane in tow. Tyrwhitt, meanwhile, continued to wait for the remaining seaplanes. At 10:30 a.m., his ships were attacked again by two German seaplanes, which dropped seven bombs. All missed. These air attacks convinced Commodore Tyrwhitt that "given ordinary sea room, ships had nothing to fear from either seaplanes or zeppelins." Later, writing to his sister, Tyrwhitt said, "Zeppelins are not to be thought of as regards ships. Stupid great things, but very beautiful. It seemed a pity to shoot at them." Once the last attack had died away, Tyrwhitt realized that the four overdue seaplanes were far beyond their fuel endurance and must be considered lost. He signaled, "I wish all ships a Merry Christmas," and turned his force back to Harwich.

In fact, three of the four missing planes had landed in the water near Norderney and their crews had been rescued by Keyes's submarine *E-11.* At 9:30 a.m., Captain Martin Naismith in *E-11* was waiting submerged off Norderney when, through his periscope, he spotted a British seaplane in the air. He ordered his boat to surface. The pilot, seeing the red and white band around *E-11*'s conning tower, landed nearby, reported that he had only five minutes of fuel remaining, and asked for a tow to the nearest carrier. Naismith agreed. Ten minutes later, as he was getting under way with the seaplane attached, a German airship (it was *L-5*) was seen approaching from the east. Then, to complicate matters, a submarine appeared on the surface, heading directly toward his little procession. In fact, it was the British submarine *D-6,* which had seen the seaplanes land and was coming to see whether she could help. Naismith, however, assumed she was a U-boat. A minute later, *D-6* dived—she did this because of the approach of the German zeppelin—but Naismith interpreted this maneuver as that of an enemy submarine preparing to attack. Suddenly, to add to Naismith's concerns, two more of the missing British seaplanes appeared at the end of their fuel endurance and landed near *E-11.* Naismith now faced the problem of rescuing four additional airmen in the face of what appeared to be imminent attack by an approaching airship and a submerged submarine. Casting off the towline, he maneuvered so close to one of the newly arrived seaplanes that the pilot and observer were able to step directly onto the submarine's deck; he told the two airmen in the other plane to swim to his boat. By then, the zeppelin was less than a mile away, but Naismith, mindful of orders to destroy British seaplanes that could not be brought home, ordered a machine gun brought up to the conning tower and had a seaman begin firing at the floats of the three empty seaplanes. Before the planes obliged by sinking, the zeppelin was overhead and Naismith was forced to crash-dive. Two bombs from the airship tumbled down; their explosions shook but did not harm the British submarine. Naismith took *E-11* down 140 feet to rest on the seabed, decided to remain, and there the submariners and their five guests sat down to a Christmas dinner of turkey and plum pudding. *D-6* had a narrower escape. When her captain brought her back to the surface, he looked up and found *L-5* fifty feet directly over his head. With machine-gun bullets clanging against his hull, he quickly submerged and headed for home. Six seaplanes were now accounted for; the crew of the seventh was picked up by a Dutch trawler. The fishermen kept the airmen on board for a week and then returned them to Holland where they were returned to Britain as "ship-wrecked mariners." On Christmas Day in the Cuxhaven Raid, not a man was lost on either side.

But loss was to follow. Jellicoe, hoping that the seaplane raid would provoke the High Seas Fleet to make an appearance, had spent the day cruising with the Grand Fleet 100 miles north of Heligoland. At dusk, the wind and sea were rising and by 10:00 a.m., on the morning of the twenty-sixth, a gale was raging with mountainous waves. Jellicoe turned north for home. During the passage, three men from destroyers were washed overboard and one was swept off the deck of the light cruiser *Caroline.* Three badly battered destroyers had to be sent into dry dock.

There was more. In the black hours before dawn on December 27, the Grand Fleet, pitching and rolling in the huge seas of Pentland Firth, approached Scapa Flow. When the lead battle squadron, showing no lights, turned north from the Firth into Hoxa Sound, the captain of the battleship *Monarch* suddenly saw a patrol trawler dead ahead. Attempting to turn, *Monarch* slewed directly into the path of her sister *Conqueror,* following astern. The two big ships collided, with *Conqueror* driving her bow into *Monarch*'s stern; both bow and stern were fractured and partially crushed. By December 29, *Monarch* had been mended sufficiently to permit her to sail for serious repair at Devonport. But *Conqueror* could not leave Scapa until a special salvage unit had made a temporary patch to permit her bow to take the punishment of an oncoming sea. When the crippled battleship sailed on January 21, the seas were still too heavy for her tender bow and she had to turn back for more patchwork. She finally reached Cromarty Firth on January 24; there she underwent further repair in the Invergordon floating dry dock before moving on to Liverpool for a complete reconstruction of her bow.

The loss of two of his most powerful ships was a blow for Jellicoe. *Monarch* was gone for three and a half weeks and rejoined the Grand Fleet on January 20. *Conqueror* did not return until March 6. Their absence, added to the permanent loss of their sister *Audacious,* reduced the 2nd Battle Squadron, the Grand Fleet's most modern, from eight ships to five. This deficit, plus the programmed absence of other vessels for essential overhaul, brought the Grand Fleet down to its lowest point of numerical superiority over the High Seas Fleet during the war. For several weeks in January 1915, Jellicoe and Beatty each had only a one-ship advantage over their German counterparts: eighteen dreadnought battleships to seventeen; five battle cruisers to four. Here was the numerical parity the German Naval Staff and Admiral von Ingenohl had been seeking; achieved, "not by their exertions," as Layman puts it, "but by pure luck." But Ingenohl, intimidated and cautious, would not have attempted to exploit the opportunity, even had he known it existed.

—

The Cuxhaven Raid destroyed no zeppelins or zeppelin sheds, but it had taught the Admiralty and the fleet that the previously dreaded aerial monsters need not be feared by ships at sea. Tyrwhitt wrote to his wife on December 29, "They [Churchill, et al.] are awfully pleased with the raid and most complimentary. Couldn't be nicer! I was really surprised at everybody's pleasure and delight. They want more and I expect they will get it before too long." Materially, the raid cost the British more than it did the Germans. Four British seamen had been swept overboard, four seaplanes had been lost, and two dreadnought battleships and three destroyers had been disabled. The Germans suffered no casualties and lost one seaplane. But, morally, the opposite result had been achieved. Once again, a British force had steamed into the Bight, challenging the Imperial Navy. From airship and submarine reports circulating through the German fleet, everyone soon learned that no British dreadnought had been present to support the raiding force. Four German battle cruisers, a dozen light cruisers, and scores of destroyers had been poised to go to sea, but had been denied permission. The result was shame, frustration, and renewed discussion of the need to find a new Commander-in-Chief for the High Seas Fleet.

—

The First Lord of the Admiralty recognized the Christmas Day raid in practical terms as a failure to blunt the new German airship weapon. Zeppelins were no longer to be feared by ships at sea, but Churchill, now responsible for the air defense of the British Isles, remained apprehensive about the damage airships might do when attacking cities. A New Year's Day 1915 memorandum prepared for the Cabinet declared that Churchill had "information from a trustworthy source . . . that the Germans intend to make an attack on London by airships on a great scale at any early opportunity. . . . There are approximately twenty German airships which can reach London now from the Rhine, each carrying a ton of high explosives. They could traverse the English part of the journey, coming and going, in the dark hours. The weather hazards are considerable, but there is no known means of preventing the airships coming, and not much chance of punishing them on return. The un-avenged destruction of non-combatant life may therefore be very considerable."

Fisher shared Churchill's alarm. Twenty zeppelins, each carrying a ton of bombs, would be coming, Fisher asserted in a letter to Churchill on January 4, 1915. One ton "would completely wreck the Admiralty building"; twenty tons would cause a "terrible massacre." Fisher had proposed to deter such an attack by warning the Germans in advance that any captured zeppelin personnel would be shot. "As this step has not been taken, I must with great reluctance ask to be relieved of my present official position as First Sea Lord. I have allowed a whole week to elapse much against my judgement before taking this step to avoid embarrassing the government. I cannot delay any longer." Churchill's response to this threat was typical of the way he dealt with the old admiral:

> My dear Fisher:
>
> The question of aerial defense is not one upon which you have any professional experience. The question of killing prisoners in reprisal for an aerial attack is not one for the Admiralty and certainly not for you to decide. The Cabinet alone can settle such a matter. I will bring your views to their notice at our meeting tomorrow. After much reflection, I cannot support it.

> I hope I am not to take the last part of your letter seriously. I have always made up my mind never to dissuade anyone serving in the department over which I preside from resigning if they wish to do so. Business becomes impossible on any other terms.
>
> But I sympathise with your feelings of exasperation at our powerlessness to resist certain forms of attack; and I presume I may take your letter simply as an expression of those feelings.
>
> Yours very sincerely,
> Winston S. Churchill

Fisher withdrew his resignation.

Soon afterward, on January 19, the zeppelin bombardment of England began. Two German naval airships dropped twenty bombs on Great Yarmouth and on several villages along the Norfolk coast. Four civilians were killed and sixteen wounded; the zeppelins departed untouched. In time, zeppelin night raids over London became a thrilling, popular spectacle as searchlights illuminated the silver, cigar-shaped behemoths gliding majestically overhead. During the war, fifty-seven airship raids were launched against England, the most destructive coming on September 8, 1915, when twenty-two Londoners were killed and eighty-seven injured. By August 1918, when the last zeppelin raids on England took place, the airships were larger, their speed had risen to 80 miles an hour, their lifting capacity had increased to 50 tons, and their ceiling was 18,000 feet. Over four years, airship and airplane attacks killed 1,413 people in Britain and wounded 3,408. For the first two years of the war, the zeppelins were immune to harm in the sky. Then on September 3, 1916, a German airship, *SL-11,* was "clawed down in flames"—as Churchill had predicted would happen—by a British fighter plane using incendiary bullets. The young pilot, Lieutenant William Leefe Robinson, was immediately awarded the Victoria Cross.

CHAPTER 21

The Battle of the Dogger Bank: "Kingdom Come or Ten Days' Leave"

The New Year began and Franz Hipper was restless. This most offensive-minded of the German admirals disliked keeping his men and ships on alert at a high pitch of readiness while at the same time restricting them to port. This self-contradictory policy was sapping morale. Besides, the German defeat in the Bight, his own frustrated aproach to Yarmouth, and his close escape after Scarborough rankled him. One explanation for his lack of success, Hipper believed, was that the British had known in advance about his plans. How they knew, he was uncertain, but he suspected that some of the neutral fishing vessels working on the fringes of the Bight and on the Dogger Bank were actually British spy ships. The Dogger Bank, with its shallow bottom, was a rich fishing ground and thus a natural concourse for commercial trawlers, British and Dutch; it also lay on the shortest route between Heligoland and the coast of England. A message from a trawler on the Dogger Bank, Hipper postulated, would enable Beatty's battle cruiser force to intercept—if not on the way over, at least on the way back. Repeatedly, Hipper insisted that ruthless action must be taken against these fishing boats, no matter what their nationality. Already, on his instructions, German destroyers had stopped and boarded these small vessels in or near the Bight. When, as was often the case, the papers of neutral trawlers were not in perfect order, they were brought into Cuxhaven and subjected to rigorous examination. To address this worry, Hipper proposed an operation in which his force would clear the Dogger Bank of British fishing vessels and suspicious neutral craft and would also attack any light British warships patrolling the Bank. The active operation would involve only the German battle cruisers and their escorting light cruisers and destroyers, but their withdrawal would be covered by the High Seas Fleet.

Hipper's proposal, because it was limited in scope, managed to elude the kaiser's ban on High Seas Fleet activity. On January 10, William, resisting pressure for more energetic action, had reaffirmed his decree that the preservation of the fleet was his paramount consideration. "No offensive is to be carried as far as the enemy coast with the object of fighting a decisive action there," said Pohl, on behalf of the emperor. The freedom of the battle fleet, therefore, remained as restricted as before. But William again granted Ingenohl permission to make cautious sallies with the battle cruisers for the purpose of cutting off separate British formations. After the war, Admiral Reinhard Scheer explained the fleet's dilemma: "There was never any reluctance on the part of the German navy to fight. The general aim of our fleet was not to seek decisive battle with the entire English fleet but to test its strength against separate divisions. But the policy of those who controlled it was the perfectly sound one that a fleet action should not be risked until, by mine-laying or submarines, an equalization of the opposing forces in the North Sea had been brought about. But, as action of some kind was necessary for the morale of the men, the prohibition was relaxed as far as the Scouting Forces were concerned."

Meanwhile, the High Seas Fleet was growing stronger. In the five months since the beginning of the war, four new dreadnought battleships had been added—*König, Grosser Kurfürst, Markgraf,* and *Kronprinz Wilhelm*—and one new battle cruiser—*Derfflinger.* The new battleships were 25,000-ton vessels with ten 12-inch guns and better armor protection than any contemporary British battleship; they were incorporated into the 3rd Battle Squadron commanded by Scheer, the most competent of German battle squadron commanders. In mid-January, Scheer asked Ingenohl's permission to take his new ships through the Kiel Canal into the Baltic for gunnery practice, but, because of violent storms sweeping over the North Sea, Ingenohl told him to wait. For the same reason, Hipper's battle cruiser operation on the Dogger Bank was postponed. On January 21, Ingenohl gave Scheer permission to proceed through the Kiel Canal, but on reaching the Elbe, the battleship squadron found itself in a snowstorm so thick that the captains were unable to locate the river's mouth and were forced to anchor. The following morning, January 22, the weather began to clear and Scheer's dreadnoughts entered the canal, heading away from the North Sea. In Wilhelmshaven later that day, Hipper and Vice Admiral Richard Eckermann, Chief of Staff of the High Seas Fleet, saw a forecast for clear skies and immediately suggested to Ingenohl: "If the weather tomorrow remains as it was this afternoon and evening, a cruiser and destroyer advance to the Dogger Bank would, in my opinion, be very desirable. Special preparations are unnecessary; an order issued tomorrow morning to . . . [Hipper] would be sufficient. Proceeding during the night, arriving in the forenoon, returning in the evening."

Ingenohl hesitated. With Scheer's new dreadnoughts in the Baltic, the dreadnought battleship force of the High Seas Fleet was understrength. Hipper's Scouting Groups were also depleted. During the bad weather, Ingenohl had sent the battle cruiser *Von der Tann* into dry dock for a routine twelve-day overhaul; when Hipper and Eckermann urged that the Dogger Bank operation immediately be launched, it was too late for *Von der Tann* to be refloated. Several light cruisers were also unavailable, and a number of destroyers, damaged by the winter storms, were under repair. Nevertheless, because the operation was to have a limited scope, the Commander-in-Chief gave his consent. At 10:25 the following morning, January 23, he sent a coded wireless signal to Hipper: "Scouting Forces are to reconnoiter Dogger Bank. Leave tonight at twilight; return tomorrow evening at darkness." During the day, Hipper was summoned on board *Friedrich der Grosse* to meet and discuss the operation with Ingenohl. Hipper asked that the High Seas Fleet come out to support him, but the Commander-in-Chief, with the kaiser's latest command fresh in his mind, refused. Because the main fleet would not be out, Hipper promised that if there was the slightest chance of his being cut off from the Bight by a stronger British force, he would turn quickly and run for home. Returning to *Seydlitz,* Hipper summoned his captains and explained the plan: they were to set out in darkness that evening, reconnoiter the Dogger Bank at daybreak, destroy any enemy light forces discovered there, and be back the following evening. On the way out, no fishing boats would be stopped because Hipper did not want to slow the advance or detach any destroyers for this purpose. On the homeward run, however, all fishing trawlers encountered would be stopped and rigorously examined.

At 5:45 p.m. on January 23, Hipper sailed from the Jade with the battle cruisers *Seydlitz, Moltke,* and *Derfflinger,* the large armored cruiser *Blücher,* the light cruisers *Rostock, Stralsund, Kolberg,* and *Graudenz,* and two destroyer flotillas comprising nineteen ships. The mood in the Scouting Groups was confident. Even without *Von der Tann,* Hipper commanded a powerful force, although the inclusion of the armored cruiser *Blücher* diminished rather than enhanced its effective strength. *Blücher* had been designed and built in a period of technological change so rapid that she was obsolete even before she was commissioned. She had been laid down at a time (1907) when Fisher's revolutionary battle cruiser project was not fully known and understood in Germany. As a result, Tirpitz went ahead and built her at 15,500 tons, with twelve 8.2-inch guns—almost a battle cruiser, but not quite. *Blücher* would have been successful in dealing with British armored cruisers, but she could not stand up to—or keep up with—real battle cruisers. Speed was essential in Hipper's Scouting Groups; his battle cruisers, light cruisers, and destroyers could all make between 25 and 30 knots. *Blücher*'s maximum design speed was 24 knots. Ultimately, her presence was to frustrate Hipper's plan to make a lightning thrust and a high-speed withdrawal. And it would doom *Blücher.*

The greatest threat to Hipper's success was the fact that, before his ships left harbor, the British knew he was coming. For days, Room 40 had been decoding German messages. The Admiralty knew about the dry-docking of *Von der Tann.* It was aware of the dispatch of Scheer's dreadnoughts to the Baltic. It had read Ingenohl's coded wireless message, ordering the Dogger Bank raid, listing the squadrons involved, and giving the time the operation would be launched. The result was that as Hipper's ships departed the Jade, British warships were weighing anchor and heading for the Dogger Bank.

—

On Saturday, January 23, the Admiralty's day began quietly. Fisher was in bed with a heavy cold in his apartment at Archway House, adjoining the Admiralty Building. Because the First Sea Lord was too ill to move, Churchill went over to see him and the two men talked for two hours. It was noon when the First Lord returned to his room in the Admiralty. He had just sat down when the door opened and Sir Arthur Wilson walked in. "He looked at me intently and there was a glow in his eye," Churchill recalled. "Behind him came Oliver with charts and compasses.

" 'First Lord, those fellows are coming out again.'

" 'When?'

" 'Tonight. We have just got time to get Beatty there.' "

Wilson explained what he had learned from the intercepted German message. The German battle cruisers were putting to sea that evening, he said, and, although the German signal stated only that there would be a reconnaissance in force as far as the Dogger Bank, another raid on the English coast was possible. Wilson and Oliver immediately began to calculate a rendezvous point for the British squadrons to be deployed. The two admirals drew a line on the chart, which afterward proved to be almost the exact line of the German advance. The charts and the clock showed that there was just enough time for Beatty, coming from the Forth, and Tyrwhitt, coming from Harwich, to join forces at daylight near the Dogger Bank and intercept Hipper, this time *before* he could strike. The British rendezvous was set for 7:00 the following morning, January 24, at a position 180 miles west of Heligoland and thirty miles north of the Dogger Bank.* This discussion lasted an hour; then Churchill asked Wilson and Oliver to carry the decoded message and the marked chart over to Archway House to get Fisher's approval. The First Sea Lord agreed to everything and soon after 1:00 p.m. telegrams

*After the war, Oliver claimed sole credit for successfully fixing the rendezvous point. "Wilson wanted a rendezvous about thirty miles to the south of mine," he said, "but our battle cruisers had hardly time to reach it. I knew it was hopeless to argue and we had no time to spare, so I agreed and he went away and I telegraphed my rendezvous to Beatty and Tyrwhitt and they met the Germans and each other there next morning."

went to Jellicoe at Scapa Flow, Beatty at Rosyth, and Commodore Tyrwhitt at Harwich:

> FOUR GERMAN BATTLE CRUISERS, SIX LIGHT CRUISERS AND TWENTY-TWO DESTROYERS WILL SAIL THIS EVENING TO SCOUT ON DOGGER BANK, PROBABLY RETURNING TOMORROW EVENING. ALL AVAILABLE BATTLE CRUISERS, LIGHT CRUISERS AND DESTROYERS FROM ROSYTH SHOULD PROCEED TO RENDEZVOUS, ARRIVING AT 7 A.M. TOMORROW. COMMODORE T [TYRWHITT] IS TO PROCEED WITH ALL AVAILABLE DESTROYERS AND LIGHT CRUISERS FROM HARWICH TO JOIN VICE ADMIRAL *LION* [BEATTY] AT 7 A.M. AT ABOVE RENDEZVOUS. IF ENEMY IS SIGHTED BY COMMODORE T WHILE CROSSING THEIR LINE OF ADVANCE, THEY SHOULD BE ATTACKED. WIRELESS TELEGRAPHY IS NOT TO BE USED UNLESS ABSOLUTELY NECESSARY.

The Admiralty plan was set: Beatty's five battle cruisers and Goodenough's four light cruisers coming down from the north would rendezvous at dawn with Tyrwhitt's three light cruisers and thirty-five destroyers coming up from the south. The slower ships—Vice Admiral Bradford's 20-knot predreadnought *King Edward*s, popularly known as the Wobbly Eight, and Rear Admiral Pakenham's three armored cruisers—would position themselves forty miles northwest of Beatty to intercept Hipper if he turned north. Jellicoe was to bring the Grand Fleet from Scapa Flow and cruise still farther north, ready to intervene if the High Seas Fleet was discovered coming out. Keyes's submarines were to take up intercepting positions between and attempt to torpedo any German ships emerging from the Jade. Once these orders were sent, there was nothing the War Group at the Admiralty could do but wait. "Through the long hours of the afternoon and evening . . . we shared our secret with no one," Churchill wrote. "That evening I attended a dinner the French ambassador was giving. . . . One felt separated from the distinguished company . . . by a film of isolated knowledge and overwhelming inward preoccupation . . . only one thought could reign—battle at dawn! Battle for the first time in history between mighty super-dreadnought ships. And there was added a thrilling sense of a Beast of Prey moving stealthily forward hour by hour towards the Trap."

—

On Saturday, January 23, "the morning being fairly fine," Lieutenant Filson Young persuaded a friend to go ashore and spend the afternoon in Edinburgh, across the Firth of Forth from the anchorage at Rosyth. "The day was not a success," Young recorded. "I led him up and down Princes Street and we pressed our noses against the shop windows. . . . We climbed to the ramparts of . . . [Edinburgh] Castle where we shivered in the east wind and looked down under a black sky on the celebrated view of the Forth. But all my companion noticed was . . . an undue amount of smoke coming from the funnels of the battle cruisers. . . . There was a frantic commotion at the . . . [quay] where the . . . [ships'] boats were waiting and much panic on the part of individual officers lest their respective boats depart without them. In half an hour, the pier was empty and the boats were being hoisted aboard the battle cruisers. We came on board at half past five. . . . There was an orgy of ciphering and deciphering going on in the Intelligence Office. We were to sail at once."

As the battle cruisers were raising steam, a problem of protocol was resolved. Prince Louis of Battenberg, the former First Sea Lord, was on board *New Zealand,* visiting his son Prince George, one of the ship's officers. In his heart, Prince Louis wanted to sail with the battle cruisers; and both Rear Admiral Sir Archibald Moore, the squadron commander, and *New Zealand*'s Captain Halsey urged him to stay. Battenberg decided, however, that his remaining might mean protocol trouble later and he went ashore.

At six o'clock in the winter darkness, Beatty's five battle cruisers and Goodenough's four light cruisers steamed down the Forth toward the open sea. Bradford's Wobbly Eight, along with Pakenham's three armored cruisers, followed at 8:30 p.m. Meanwhile, Tyrwhitt with the light cruisers *Arethusa, Aurora,* and *Dauntless* and thirty-five destroyers had begun leaving Harwich at 5:30 p.m. Their departure was hindered by the arrival of dense fog just as Tyrwhitt was leading *Arethusa* and seven new *M*-class destroyers out of the harbor. These eight ships made it to sea, but the departure of the other thirty Harwich vessels was delayed. Tyrwhitt, determined to reach the morning rendezvous on time, decided to thrust ahead with the ships he had, leaving the bulk of his force to follow as soon as possible. Finally, at 6:30 p.m., the twenty-two dreadnought battleships of the Grand Fleet cleared Scapa Flow to rendezvous the next morning at 9:30 a.m., 150 miles northwest of Beatty.

—

Beatty, on *Lion,* was in high spirits. Hipper was coming and this time there was neither a Warrender from whom he must take orders, nor a group of 20-knot battleships to slow him down. Bradford with the Wobbly Eight was senior in rank, but the Admiralty had specifically told him not to interfere with Beatty's command. Dining with his staff, Beatty was relaxed and cheerful. He trusted his Flag Captain, Ernle Chatfield, and left to him the task of navigating the squadron through the night. Soon after dinner, Beatty went to bed. Later, Filson Young recalled:

> I had the first watch, very quiet as wireless was practically unused while we were at sea on an operation of this kind. . . . As his custom was, the admiral looked in upon his way to his windy sea cabin and

> we talked over the chart and the possibilities of tomorrow. For some curious reason, we were confident . . . in a way we had never been before. . . . There was an air of suppressed excitement which was very exhilarating. . . . The ship drove on calmly and stiffly through the dark surges. Midnight came and with it the brief commotion incident on changes of the watch; a slight aroma of cocoa was added to the other perfumes below deck, and I departed to turn in. In my cabin I stowed everything moveable and breakable, saw that the door was hooked back, that my . . . [life vest] was on the bed, looked at my watch . . . and fell asleep.

In the darkness, with a gentle northeasterly breeze and a calm sea, Beatty and Tyrwhitt converged on Hipper. In numbers and offensive power, the British had an overwhelming advantage. A significant measure was the weight of the opposing broadsides: if all the British heavy guns fired simultaneously, they would deliver 40,640 pounds of shells. A corresponding broadside by Hipper's force would deliver only 20,288 pounds. Overall, the design of the battle cruisers on each side reflected the technological convictions of the creators of the opposing fleets. The British battle cruisers embodied Fisher's belief in high speed and heavy gun power at the cost of armor protection. Their German counterparts had evolved from Tirpitz's maxim that a ship's primary mission is to remain afloat. Hipper's ships, therefore, were more lightly armed and not greatly deficient in speed, but they were shielded by superior armor.

The four big German ships at the Dogger Bank represented a steady evolution. *Blücher* was the supreme embodiment of the armored cruiser. After *Blücher,* the Germans, by then aware that Fisher was building *Invincible*s, themselves built battle cruisers. *Von der Tann,* the first German ship of this class, was completed in 1910, weighed 19,400 tons, and had eight 11-inch guns, up to 11-inch armor, and a speed of 27 knots. *Moltke,* commissioned the year after *Von der Tann* (her sister was *Goeben*), weighed 22,640 tons, carried ten 11-inch guns and 11-inch armor, and had a speed of 28 knots. *Seydlitz,* Hipper's flagship, completed in 1913, weighed 24,640 tons; she too had ten 11-inch guns and 11-inch armor. The additional 2,000 tons had gone into boiler and engine-room machinery that boosted her maximum speed to 29 knots. *Derfflinger,* Germany's newest battle cruiser, was 28,000 tons, had eight 12-inch guns and 12-inch armor, and a speed of 28 knots.

The oldest of the British battle cruisers present that day was *Indomitable,* the third of the original *Invincible* class. Completed in 1908, she displaced 17,250 tons, only 2,000 tons more than *Blücher.* She was marginally faster (26 knots), but the significant difference lay in the offensive power of her eight 12-inch guns. On the other hand, *Indomitable*'s 7-inch armor was scarcely thicker than that of an armored cruiser. *New Zealand,* completed in

1912, was an improved *Invincible*-class vessel: 18,800 tons, eight 12-inch guns, slightly thicker armor—8 inches instead of 7—and she could make 27 knots. Beatty's first two Cats, *Lion* and *Princess Royal,* both completed in 1912, commenced a new generation of battle cruisers. They were, at 26,350 tons, far bigger than the *Invincible*s. The additional 9,000 tons had gone into eight 13.5-inch guns, yet thicker armor—9 inches—and an increase in speed to 28 knots. *Tiger,* Britain's newest Cat, completed after the war began, was bigger still at 28,000 tons. She had eight 13.5-inch guns, 9 inches of armor, and 28 knots of speed. *Tiger* also possessed an improved secondary armament of 6-inch guns instead of the 4-inch of earlier British battle cruisers; this, it was hoped, would enable her to deal more effectively with charging enemy light cruisers and destroyers.

As it was, Beatty, with five battle cruisers, was understrength that day. *Queen Mary,* one of his four Cats, with 13.5-inch guns, had just sailed for Portsmouth to go into dry dock. This was particularly unlucky for Beatty because *Queen Mary* was considered the best gunnery ship in the fleet. *Tiger,* on the other hand, was one of the worst. Commissioned in October 1914, she had joined the battle cruiser force on November 6. Although she was with Beatty on December 16 during the Scarborough Raid, she received only intermittent training in late December and early January. Moreover, her crew included a number of captured deserters, and consequently morale was low. Why this newest and most formidable battle cruiser was assigned such a motley crew was a puzzle even to Beatty. "The same efficiency could not be expected from the *Tiger* as from the other ships," he wrote after the battle. "It is not time to complain but to do the best one can with the material available. I was assured that the ship's company would have been better if it had been possible to make it so."

—

At dawn, Beatty appeared on *Lion*'s bridge with Lieutenant Commander Seymour, his Flag Lieutenant and signal officer. Looking over the stern, he could make out the four darkened battle cruisers steaming in line behind his flagship: *Tiger* in *Lion*'s wake, followed by *Princess Royal, New Zealand,* and *Indomitable.* Filson Young came on the bridge: "The eastern horizon showed light . . . but it was still dark night about us. . . . At 6:45 signals were beginning to come in from the Harwich flotilla indicating that the rendezvous chosen by the Admiralty had been hit exactly. At ten minutes to seven I went down to breakfast and when I returned fifteen minutes later, the daylight was beginning to spread and the cloud banks to roll away. It promised to be an ideal morning with a light breeze from the north-northeast and a slight swell on the sea. At seven, the bugles sounded 'Action.' "

Just after 7:00 Beatty and Goodenough arrived at the rendezvous point. Ten minutes later, Beatty sighted *Arethusa,* Tyrwhitt's flagship, and the seven fast *M*-class destroyers he had brought from Harwich. The early light of a winter morning was shining on a calm, gently undulating sea. "The day was so clear," Goodenough remembered, "that only the shape of the earth prevented one from seeing everything on it." As Tyrwhitt was taking his position three miles ahead of the battle cruisers, Beatty saw gun flashes on the southeastern horizon. Almost immediately (at 7:20 a.m.), a signal from the light cruiser *Aurora,* leading one of Tyrwhitt's fog-delayed destroyer flotillas up from Harwich, announced, "Am in action with the High Seas Fleet." The men on *Lion*'s bridge smiled at the exaggeration. Beatty told Chatfield to turn in the direction of the gun flashes and the battle cruisers steamed southeast at 22 knots.

Aurora's actual antagonist was the German light cruiser *Kolberg,* the port wing ship of Hipper's cruiser screen. What had happened was this: the light cruisers *Aurora* and *Undaunted* and twenty-eight destroyers had spent the night trying to catch up with their commodore. At dawn, when Tyrwhitt met Beatty, they were still twelve miles astern. *Arethusa,* out in front with Tyrwhitt aboard, had passed ahead of the German force, sighting nothing; *Aurora,* half an hour behind, was luckier. At 7:05, against the dawn horizon to the east, *Aurora* sighted a three-funneled cruiser and four destroyers. Her captain, thinking the ship was probably *Arethusa,* closed to 8,000 yards before giving the prescribed challenge. When he did so, the unknown ship, *Kolberg,* noted the British code and then opened fire. *Aurora* was hit three times, suffered minor damage, and began to hit back. The German ship turned away. *Aurora* sent her "Am in action with the High Seas Fleet" signal to *Lion,* then continued toward the rendezvous. At about the same time, Goodenough on *Southampton,* five miles ahead of Beatty, sighted one group of ships to the south and another to the east. Those to the south were *Aurora* and the Harwich Force; Goodenough then looked harder to the east. Visibility was improving and in the distance he made out two German light cruisers, *Stralsund* and *Graudenz,* which were in the van of Hipper's force. Then, a few minutes later, at 7:30 a.m., Goodenough sighted the German battle cruisers.

—

Earlier, as streaks of light appeared on the eastern horizon, Hipper's ships were steaming northwest at a leisurely 15 knots. Their formation was spread across a wide front to facilitate the search for British fishing vessels and, if they were fortunate, light naval patrol forces. The four big ships were in a single line. The light cruisers *Stralsund* and *Graudenz* and eleven destoyers were a few miles ahead. *Kolberg* with four destroyers was ten miles out on the port wing, *Rostock* with an equal number of destroyers was equally distant on the starboard wing. Hipper, calm and alert, stood on the signal bridge of *Seydlitz.* During the night, his ships had passed numerous fishing boats, rekindling the admiral's fears that they might be reporting to the enemy and creating another nasty surprise similar to finding Warrender and Beatty across his line of retreat from Scarborough five weeks before. "I was anxious at all costs to avoid having enemy forces between me and the German Bight at daybreak," Hipper said later. Another worry was the weather: the coming day was going to be clear with high visibility. If, by mischance, British dreadnoughts were encountered, the Scouting Groups would not be concealed by mist and rain as they had been after bombarding Scarborough, Whitby, and Hartlepool.

When Hipper's port wing light cruiser, *Kolberg,* encountered *Aurora, Kolberg*'s captain reported the incident to Hipper. The Scouting Force commander immediately steered his battle cruisers south toward *Kolberg.* Here, perhaps, were the British light forces he had come to mop up. But as Hipper approached, *Kolberg* warned him that she had sighted smoke to the southwest. At almost the same moment, *Stralsund* reported from the van that she, too, was seeing thick clouds of smoke, but in the northwest. Then *Blücher,* which had a better view than *Seydlitz,* reported seeing seven British light cruisers—four *Southampton*s and three *Arethusa*s—and more than twenty British destroyers to the northwest on a parallel course, out of gun range. These ships, Hipper knew, constituted no mere patrol force; instead, the presence of so many light cruisers and destroyers strongly suggested that more powerful ships were coming up. This ominous suspicion was reinforced when *Stralsund* signaled again, reporting that she had observed "at least eight large ships" under the smoke clouds to the northwest. Simultaneously, German interceptions of the wireless call signs of British ships appeared to indicate the approach of Warrender's 2nd Battle Squadron.

Hipper began to worry; if the ships to the northwest were indeed one of the Grand Fleet battleship squadrons, where were Beatty's battle cruisers? His own force was weaker than either Beatty's or Warrender's individually; here, possibly, the two were combining to spring a trap. Hipper knew that he could expect no support from the High Seas Fleet. He had promised to take no risks. He made up his mind quickly. At 7:35 a.m., he signaled his entire force to turn southeast and run for home at 20 knots. If the large ships seen by *Stralsund* were battleships, this speed was sufficient to maintain the present gap; if necessary, he could increase speed to 23 knots, *Blücher*'s maximum.

As the German battle cruisers settled onto their new course with *Seydlitz* still in the van, followed by *Moltke, Derfflinger,* and *Blücher,* Hipper sent his outlying light cruisers and destroyers on ahead. All German captains knew that severely damaged ships would be left behind, and Hipper did not want his smaller, weaker ships in the rear where they could be crippled by overwhelming enemy gunfire. Not until 7:50 a.m., after his ships began their run for home, did Hipper himself observe the oncoming shapes beneath the clouds of smoke to the northwest and realize that his opponents were battle cruisers. "The pace at which the enemy was closing in was quite unexpected," he said later. "The enemy battle cruisers must have been doing twenty-six knots. They were emitting extraordinarily dense clouds of smoke." Hipper's first reaction was relief: he now felt confident that he was facing one group of British dreadnoughts, not two. He also was reasonably certain that, as the British battle cruisers were usually the advance guard of the Grand Fleet, no other significant British force was likely to be operating between himself and Heligoland. Nevertheless, there was an ominous factor in identifying Beatty as his pursuer. On paper, the most modern British battle cruisers were only marginally faster than his own battle cruisers. But Hipper's squadron that day included *Blücher,* which was at least 2—and perhaps 3 or 4—knots slower than Beatty's ships.

In Wilhelmshaven, Ingenohl received news of the encounter from *Seydlitz* soon after 7:50 a.m. and ordered the High Seas Fleet to prepare for sea. There was little urgency in this command and not until 9:30 a.m. was the fleet assembled in Schillig roads. Then, at 10:00 a message from Hipper declared that he was in difficulty and needed support. The German battle fleet sailed at 10:10 a.m. but could not possibly rendezvous with the Scouting Groups before 2:30 in the afternoon. Hipper, therefore, was alone. He was 150 miles from Heligoland and three hours from any real assistance. He had a fourteen-mile head start.

—

Once Hipper made his dramatic turn to the southeast toward home, Goodenough led his four light cruisers to a position on the port quarter of the German ships from where he could observe and report Hipper's movements. At 7:47 a.m., when he was 17,000 yards northwest of *Blücher,* Goodenough was able to count the number of Hipper's big ships and signaled Beatty: "Enemy sighted are four battle cruisers, speed 24 knots." Three minutes later, Beatty himself could see the German battle cruisers on his port bow, over ten miles away. Beatty and the officers standing with him on *Lion*'s bridge were exhilarated. "As day broke," Chatfield said, "we saw a distant mass of black smoke ahead of us and a report from a cruiser indicated enemy capital ships. . . . They were Hipper's squadron at least twelve or thirteen miles distant, but it was clear weather and we still might catch them." Another officer on the bridge recalled: "On the horizon ahead could be seen . . . four dark patches with a mass of smoke overhead. These four patches, each containing more than a thousand men, were our long-destined prey."

By 8:00 a.m., the chase was on, with the British pursuing on a course parallel to Hipper, not directly astern of him. In part, Beatty chose this tactic because of his concern that the retreating enemy might drop mines in his path. More important, it permitted Beatty to use the wind to his advantage. By being downwind of Hipper in the fresh northeast breeze, Beatty's battle cruisers could fire unimpeded by smoke from their own guns and funnels. Hipper, on the other hand, would be forced to shoot directly into the smoke created by his funnels and guns. As the pursuit developed, Tyrwhitt's light cruisers and destroyers joined Goodenough's light cruisers on *Lion*'s port bow, five miles northeast of the flagship. From this position, the British light forces had multiple duties: they acted as scouts to report the enemy's course and speed; they were to intercept and repel enemy torpedo attacks; they had to be ready themselves to launch a torpedo attack if ordered; and they had to do all this without masking their own heavy ships' fire with their funnel smoke. The uselessness of their guns and torpedoes against the German heavy ships was quickly demonstrated when Tyrwhitt's seven 30-knot *M*-class destroyers raced ahead to within 7,000 yards of *Blücher.* The German armored cruiser altered course slightly to bring more guns to bear, and brought down such a storm of 8.2-inch and 5.9-inch fire on the British destroyers that, although they suffered no hits, they were forced to retreat out of range. Beatty thereafter decided to destroy the enemy by long-range battle cruiser gunfire. He told his light forces simply to stay out of the way.

The action now became a straightforward stern chase in which the key to success was speed. Hipper's fourteen-mile head start put him four miles—7,000 yards—beyond the effective gun range of the British battle cruisers. "Get us within range of the enemy," Beatty said to Percy Green, *Lion*'s chief engineer. "Tell your stokers all depends on them." "They know that, sir," Green replied. A midshipman on *Indomitable* later provided a graphic picture of the effort being made in the engine and stoke rooms of the British battle cruisers:

> The furnaces devoured coal as fast as a man could feed them. Black, begrimed and sweating men working in the ship's side dug the coal out and loaded it into skids which were then dragged along the steel deck and emptied on the floor plates in front of each boiler. . . . If the ship rolled or pitched there was always a risk that a loaded skid might [slide and crush a man]. Looking down from the iron catwalk above, the scene had all the appearance of one from Dante's Inferno. . . . Watching the pressure gauges for any fall in the steam pressure, the Chief Stoker walked to and fro, encouraging his men. Now and then the telegraph from the engine room would clang and the finger on the dial move round to the section marked "More Steam." The chief would press the reply gong with an oath, "What do the bastards think we're doing? Come on boys, shake it up, get going," and the sweating men would redouble their efforts, throw open the furnace doors and shovel still more coal into the blazing inferno.

The speed of the battle cruisers constantly increased. Beatty's signals over the next forty-five minutes tell the story:

8:10: "*Lion* to Battle Cruisers: Speed 24 knots."
8:16: "*Lion* to Battle Cruisers: Speed 25 knots."
8:23: "*Lion* to Battle Cruisers: Speed 26 knots."
8:34: "*Lion* to Battle Cruisers: Speed 27 knots."
8:43: "*Lion* to Battle Cruisers: Speed 28 knots."
8:54: "*Lion* to Battle Cruisers: Speed 29 knots."

Beatty's demands reached the impossible. *New Zealand* and *Indomitable* had design speeds of 25 knots, yet at first, even *Indomitable,* the oldest of his ships, was keeping up and eventually reached a speed above 26 knots. Beatty was grateful and at 8:55 a.m. the flagship signaled: "Well done, *Indomitable.*" The message was passed quickly to *Indomitable*'s boiler rooms. Nevertheless, Beatty kept asking for more. He knew that speeds of 27 and 28 knots could be approached only by his three leading ships, *Lion, Tiger,* and *Princess Royal,* and that 29 was one knot higher than the design speed of his fastest ship, *Tiger.* He was also aware that his demand for speeds above 27 knots would stretch out his squadron; already his first three ships, the Cats, were drawing away from the two older battle cruisers, now slowly dropping astern. Before long, a second gap began to open as *Indomitable* fell behind *New Zealand.* Beatty was willing to take the risk; if necessary, he intended to overtake and fight Hipper, three ships to four.

As a result of the stokers' effort, it became apparent to the officers on *Lion*'s bridge that they were gaining on the Germans. At eight o'clock, the range from *Lion* to *Blücher,* Hipper's rearmost ship, was 25,000 yards, about twelve and a half miles. This was 3,000 yards more than the greatest effective range of *Lion*'s 13.5-inch guns. Gradually, as Beatty called for ever greater speed, and with Hipper's squadron limited to 23 knots, the distance decreased. Meanwhile, the officers on the bridges of both flagships could do nothing but wait, staring ahead or watching behind as the distance between them grew smaller.

Beatty took this opportunity to go to breakfast, and when the admiral returned to the bridge, Chatfield went below. Filson Young remained on the bridge. "We were all in high spirits," he wrote.

> As usual when the ship was in action, the decks were deserted and although during action, the navigating staff of the ship as well as the admiral and his staff are supposed to retire to the conning tower, no one had thought of going as yet. . . . Beatty, Chatfield, the Flag Commander, the Secretary, two Flag Lieutenants and myself were all on the compass platform, enjoying the sensation and prospects of the chase in that clear North Sea air. There was immense exhilaration whenever another [flag] hoist indicating a speed signal was hauled down [and we felt] the splendid ship's jump forward through the sea.

Young had an unimpeded view.

> *Lion* being our leading ship there was nothing before me but the horizon . . . the four black smudges on the port bow that only through binoculars were identifiable as big ships . . . the farther line of our light cruisers on their quarter . . . and at the apex, the smoke from the German light cruisers and destroyers. . . . Once, far ahead, appeared more smudges, a group of trawlers fishing quietly off the Bank which suddenly found themselves enveloped in the thunder of a sea battle. The German battle cruisers passed them to the northeast and we to the southwest, so that our fire was passing over their heads. We must have appeared in the eyes of the astonished Dutch fishermen who saw us thunder past in the primitive herd formation, the bulls or battle cruisers bellowing in the van, followed by the females, light cruisers with the destroyers, like the young, bringing up the rear.

As the minutes passed, the gunnery officer on *Lion*'s bridge constantly checked his prismatic range finder to acquire the distance to *Blücher.* At 22,000 yards, the outside limit at which the target might be reached, Chatfield asked this officer, "How soon should we open fire?" At 8:45 a.m., when the range finder provided a distance of 20,600 yards, the gunnery officer turned to the captain and asked, "Should we use armour-piercing or common shell?" "Armour-piercing," Chatfield replied. Then, he said, "at long last, when the range of their rear ship was reported at twenty thousand yards, I proposed to Beatty that we should open fire. He assented."

The two turrets on *Lion*'s bow were trained on *Blücher.* One 13.5-inch gun of the upper B turret was elevated and at 8:52 a.m. a single ranging shot was fired. As the cordite smoke blew back in their faces, the watchers on the bridge fixed their binoculars on the German ship. "We could see the tiny fountain of water that told us the shot was short," said Young. Gun elevation was slightly adjusted and two more sighting shells were fired. They fell over. It was sufficient; *Blücher* had been straddled. At 9:00, *Tiger,* close on *Lion*'s heels, fired her own ranging shot at *Blücher*. At 9:05 a.m., Beatty made a general signal to the squadron: "Open fire and engage the enemy." The first two British battle cruisers immediately erupted with salvos of armor-piercing shells. Soon, *Princess Royal,* 1,000 yards astern of the *Tiger,* came within range and opened fire. To the rear, *New Zealand* and *Indomitable* plowed silently ahead, their 12-inch guns not yet able to reach.

Firing at ranges of 20,000 yards was beyond anything imagined before the war. Although the extreme range of the 13.5-inch gun—by 1914, the main armament of ten British dreadnought battleships and four battle cruisers—was 22,000 yards, prewar British gunnery training still assumed a close action at moderate speed. In the spring of 1914, Churchill ordered experimental firing at 14,000 yards, and he said, "to universal astonishment, considerable accuracy was obtained." Beatty, commanding the battle cruisers and suspecting what war would be like with these fast ships and their powerful, long-range guns, went further and asked permission to conduct his own gunnery practice at towed targets 16,000 yards away with his ships steaming at 23 knots. Now, traveling at 27 knots and firing at a range of almost 20,000 yards, the British long-range guns began to score hits. As they did so, Beatty altered course slightly to starboard, placing his battle cruisers in echelon rather than single line ahead, thus enabling each ship to bring its after turrets to bear. *Lion* first hit *Blücher* at 9:09 a.m. Ten minutes later, with the range down to 18,000 yards and with both *Tiger* and *Princess Royal* also firing at *Blücher, Lion* shifted her guns to the third German ship in line, the battle cruiser *Moltke.*

At 9:15 a.m., the Germans began to fire back. From *Lion*'s bridge, Young observed this happen:

> The enemy appeared on the eastern horizon in the form of four separate wedges or triangles of smoke. . . . Suddenly, from the rear-most of those wedges [*Blücher*], came a stab of white flame. "He's opened fire," said Captain Chatfield and we waited for what seemed a long time, probably about twenty-five seconds, until a great column of water and spray rose in the sea at a distance of more than a mile from our port bow. . . . Minute by minute the ranges came down, and during each interval further flashes were observed from the enemy and further fountains of water arose between us, always creeping a little nearer, but still short.

Before long, other German battle cruisers opened fire and the sea around both opposing groups of ships was alive with tall columns of water. From *Lion,* Young could see British shells hitting German ships. The hits appeared as "a glare amid the smoke. There was no mistaking the difference between the bright sharp stab of white flame that marked the firing of the enemy's guns and this dull, glowing and fading glare which signified the bursting of one of our own shells." *Blücher,* not surprisingly, was the most severely punished. After the battle, prisoners from *Blücher* said that they had not known which of their enemies was hitting their ship, but that the third salvo had struck on the waterline and reduced her speed and that the fourth had almost carried away the after superstructure and had disabled the two after turrets.

As the guns on both sides continued to lash out, observers on *Lion* and *Southampton* saw signs of commotion in the formation of German destroyers ahead of Hipper's battle cruisers. Concerned that Hipper might order a torpedo attack as a means of relieving pressure on his beleaguered ships, Beatty countered by signaling Tyrwhitt and the Harwich Force: "Destroyers take station ahead and proceed at your utmost speed." This effort to shield

Lion and her sisters failed because of the great speed of the British battle cruisers. At 27 and 28 knots, most of Tyrwhitt's destroyers could scarcely keep up with Beatty's big ships. They lacked the additional speed necessary to pull ahead and they continued where they were, on Beatty's port beam. Only the seven new 30-knot *M*-Class destroyers were able to respond and gradually to creep out in front of their own onrushing battle cruisers. As it happened, the anticipated German attack did not take place and the long-range artillery duel continued. With *Tiger* and *Princess Royal* now pounding *Blücher, Lion* shifted first to *Moltke* and then, as they came within range, to *Derfflinger* and *Seydlitz.* Meanwhile, *Lion* herself, leading the British charge, had come under fire. German salvos were straddling the ship and, at 9:28 a.m., one of *Blücher*'s 8-inch shells struck *Lion* on her bow A turret, not penetrating the turret's armor but producing a concussive shock that disabled the left gun.

The German cannonade also broke up the little party of observers standing on *Lion*'s bridge. "Up to now," wrote Filson Young,

> there had been very little sound but the rush of wind and water, with the occasional roar of our guns, but now the noise of firing was becoming louder and louder; the enemy's shots were falling on both sides of us quite close so that the spray . . . drenched our decks. The moment had come for an adjournment to the conning tower, that small armored citadel, the mechanical brain of the ship, whence she could be steered and maneuvered and her gunfire controlled by means of a complicated mass of voice pipes, telephones and electric and hydraulic gear. As it was already overcrowded with people indispensable for all these purposes, the Admiral's staff divided.

Young and another junior officer were dispatched to a "windy eyrie in the foretop"—the small observation platform high up the mainmast, sixty feet above the deck, eighty feet above the sea. For Young, the climb to the foretop was the most dangerous and frightening part of the battle:

> As we were climbing . . . a terrific blow and a shake proclaimed that *Lion* had been hit [this was *Blücher*'s 9:28 a.m. hit on A turret]. The climb had been bad enough in ordinary circumstances. It was perfectly horrible now. We were already pretty cold from standing in the wind, we were encumbered with thick clothing, life jackets, and oilskins and the wind on the mast . . . was terrific. It shook and tore at us until I really wondered whether my hands would be able to keep their grip on the steel rungs. . . . I felt sure that the end had come when, having dragged myself up step by step to where the floor of the foretop overshadowed us, I found the steel covering of the manhole, giving en-

trance to it, was shut. . . . It would be impossible to make the man inside it hear and my companion immediately below me on the ladder was hailing me vehemently to hurry up as he could not hold on much longer. Fortunately, the Navigating Commander, who was just leaving the bridge, [looked up and] saw our dilemma and hailed the foretop with the result that the manhole was opened just in time.

Meanwhile, said Captain Chatfield,

to the conning tower [the action station of the captain] I had to go. In it were the Chief Quartermaster, the Navigator, the two telegraph able seamen, and a signalman. It was situated immediately behind B turret, noisy and wet from spray and from steaming at high speed through the vast columns of water which somehow incredibly forced its way through the lens threads of my Ross binoculars. . . . Gradually, we had been closing the enemy who were now all engaged. The salvos fired from their guns looked like the switching on momentarily of large red searchlights; one got into the habit of allowing for the forty seconds before the salvo fell. If it fell over the ship, it was unseen and unnoticed. The *Lion* being the leading ship, received almost as good a measure of the concentration of the enemy's fire as had their rear ship, *Blücher,* the early concentration of our own.

From his perch in the foretop, Young observed the rest of the battle:

It was impossible to endure the wind standing up in this square box, so we knelt on the steel floor and could just rest our elbows on the rim and keep our eyes and [field] glasses over the edge. . . .

The Admiral and his staff did not remain long in the conning tower. The only view from that protected place is through a very narrow slit at eye level, which, although it gives a view of a kind of three quarters of the horizon, was of little use to the Admiral. He was thoroughly enjoying himself and did not like to waste his day in the cramped and crowded security of the conning tower and he and the Flag Lieutenant, the Flag Commander and Secretary were soon up on the compass platform again where the view was perfect although the danger from splinters was considerable. They were flying about us all the time in the foretop. During a lull between salvos, Beatty hailed us in the foretop to ask how we were enjoying ourselves. . . . Very soon after . . . [and following another tremendous blow that shook *Lion*], I put my head out to look down and see what happened. There was a great drift of cordite smoke all round the compass platform and to my horror, instead of the four figures I had last seen standing there, there were only four tumbled

> smudges of blue on the deck. After the smoke cleared away, I saw that they were greatcoats and presently to my inexpressible relief, my four friends reappeared eating sandwiches. . . . Being very hot in the conning tower, they had taken their greatcoats off when they came up, and there being at the moment an unusual lot of splinters flying about, the Admiral, much against his will, had been persuaded to return to the conning tower. After five minutes, he broke out again, and came on the compass platform, which he occupied for the rest of the action.

By 9:35 a.m., *New Zealand* had come within range of *Blücher* and had opened fire; now only *Indomitable* remained out of action. Having four ships within range of Hipper's four, Beatty decided to give structure to the battle and signaled his squadron, "Engage the corresponding ship in the enemy's line." His intention was a ship-for-ship distribution of fire: *Lion* should take on *Seydlitz,* leading the German line; his second ship, *Tiger,* should fire at Hipper's second ship, *Moltke;* the third British ship, *Princess Royal,* would engage *Derfflinger;* and *New Zealand* would continue to hammer *Blücher.* In sending this signal, Beatty assumed that all of his captains understood that *Indomitable* still was not within range and therefore was not included in this command. Unfortunately, Captain Henry Pelly of *Tiger* misunderstood the intended alignment. Believing that *Indomitable* was already engaging *Blücher,* Pelly, in his calculations, moved every British ship one vessel forward against the German line. Therefore, as Pelly saw it, with *Indomitable* firing at *Blücher, New Zealand* would take on *Derfflinger,* and *Princess Royal* would engage *Moltke.* This left the first two British ships, *Lion* and his own *Tiger,* to concentrate on Hipper's flagship, *Seydlitz.* Pelly thought this made good sense, especially in light of a Grand Fleet Battle Order that decreed that where there were more British than enemy ships, the two leading British ships were to attempt to incapacitate and destroy the first German. The other British captains, however, knew that *Indomitable* was excluded; they had correctly understood the intended assignments, and carried out Beatty's order. But, with both *Tiger* and *Lion* firing at *Seydlitz,* nobody engaged *Moltke.* To leave an excellent gunnery ship like this German battle cruiser undisturbed was to invite disaster. Already, most of the German squadron was aiming at Beatty's flagship and now, says Arthur Marder, "the unmolested *Moltke* was able to make excellent target practice on *Lion.*" Pelly's mistake was compounded by the fact that his inexperienced gunnery and turret officers were aiming poorly and that *Tiger*'s shells were falling 3,000 yards beyond *Seydlitz.* They did not recognize this because they took *Lion*'s shells, which were straddling the German flagship, to be their own. When Commodore Goodenough, observing the battle from the bridge of *Southampton,* signaled "Salvos of three, apparently from *Tiger,* falling consistently over," *Tiger* did not receive the message.

—

By the time Hipper had correctly identified his pursuers as battle cruisers, Beatty had closed the range to 28,000 yards (fourteen miles) and it was too late for Hipper to avoid battle. "At nine a.m.," Scheer wrote in his history of the naval war, "our battle cruisers were on a southeasterly course so that all the ships could open fire from the starboard on the English battle cruisers. Our light cruisers and both the destroyer flotillas were ahead of our battle cruisers, slightly on the starboard side." At 9:08 a.m., the German battle cruisers opened fire at 20,000 yards. Aiming was difficult, even with the excellent German stereoscopic range finders, because "the view . . . from the fire control was very much hampered and partially blinded as the result of dense smoke." Despite this handicap, Hipper was pleased by the conduct of his ships and captains: "The action signals were coming through perfectly and the movements were carried through as though at maneuvers. In spite of the high speed at which the action was being fought, the formation was keeping distance [between ships] very accurately." Hipper rarely signaled during this part of the chase. Unable to push his ships to higher speeds, he simply steered a course southeast for Heligoland. "The chances of support from our own forces were greater there," he explained, "and the farther we could succeed in drawing the enemy into the Bight, the greater prospect there would be of setting destroyers on him during the ensuing night." A melee in the Heligoland Bight, at which point Beatty would have outrun *his* supporting units, might find the tables turned with the British forced to flee while *their* wounded and stragglers were picked off one by one. Meanwhile, Hipper worried about *Blücher,* the weakest and slowest of his big ships, now steaming at the rear of his force and being battered by British gunfire. But it was not *Blücher* that would suffer the first near-catastrophic blow. It was Hipper's flagship, *Seydlitz.*

By 9:43 a.m., *Lion* was straddling *Seydlitz* at 17,000 yards. Then, at 9:45 a.m., a 13.5-inch armor-piercing shell from *Lion* struck the after deck of *Seydlitz* and pierced the armor of the aftermost turret. The powder charges being brought up were ignited by the explosion and flash fires shot upward into the turret—setting fire to the charges being delivered to the gun—and downward into the magazine. The magazine crew, seared by the flames, tried to flee forward by opening the steel doors leading to the compartments of the adjacent turret. As a result the fire spread forward, setting alight the charges there, spreading to the adjacent magazine and upward to C turret. In this way, two turrets were destroyed by a single hit and the entire crews of both turrets died almost instantly. Filson Young, staring through binoculars from *Lion*'s foretop, saw "a great glowing mass of fire appear . . . on the after part of *Seydlitz.* Well do I remember seeing those flames and wondering what kind of horrors they signified." Chatfield, witnessing the same catastrophe, had a laconic, professional reaction: "A shell struck *Seydlitz* on the after turret and a sheet of flame and smoke went up about two hundred feet in the air. I hoped she was out of action."

Seydlitz now faced the danger of a final, annihilating explosion that would detonate all of the magazines and cause the ship to disintegrate. Three men saved her: Lieutenant Commander Hagedom, Chief Artificer Hering, and Gunner's Mate Müller. Making their way through searing heat to the valves for flooding the magazines, they spun the handles and drowned the threat of explosion by permitting 600 tons of seawater to flow into the magazines. Remarkably, although 165 men had been killed and two of her five turrets destroyed, *Seydlitz* not only survived but continued in action and maintained her speed. It was an extraordinary demonstration of the excellence of German warship design and the extensive watertight subdivision of her hull.

During this crisis, Admiral Hipper stood, silently chain-smoking, on the bridge. Damage reports from different parts of the ship came to the captain standing nearby: no reply could be heard from the steering room; the two rear heavy turrets were out of action; 600 tons of water had been flooded into the magazines. Hipper seemed unaffected, almost detached. After the war, he remembered looking back and seeing "the two after turrets . . . spouting huge volumes of flame. This lasted about two minutes, then ceased for a time, to leap up afresh about a minute later. It was a strange sight to see the after part of the ship fiercely ablaze, while the three forward turrets were still firing vigorously." Hipper realized that the damage to the *Seydlitz* dramatically altered the balance in favor of the British. Beatty had five battle cruisers; Hipper had three, one of which was heavily damaged. His reaction was to send an urgent signal to Ingenohl at 9:55: "Need assistance badly." The Commander-in-Chief received the signal at 10:00 a.m., and within ten minutes the order was given to sail. But Ingenohl could not possibly be in a position to support Hipper until 2:30 p.m. As a ploy to scare off the British until he could come closer, Ingenohl replied to Hipper at 10:03 in a clear, uncoded signal: "Main fleet and flotillas will come." In code, he appended the grim reality: ". . . as soon as possible."

When Hipper appealed for help, *Seydlitz* was not the only German ship in difficulty; *Blücher,* battered by one British battle cruiser after another, her steering gear damaged, was dropping behind Hipper's formation and yawing away to the north. This course brought her within range of Goodenough's light cruisers, keeping their lookout station to the north of the British battle cruisers. Despite the pounding she had taken, *Blücher*'s fighting capacity still remained formidable and she opened an accurate fire with her 8.2-inch and 5.9-inch guns, forcing Goodenough to keep away. Nevertheless, the punishment of *Blücher* by *New Zealand* continued. At 10:30 a.m., a 12-inch hit put *Blücher*'s bow turret out of action. Soon after, a serious fire broke out amidships, her speed dropped to 17 knots, and the gap between the armored cruiser and the three German battle cruisers continued to grow.

—

Implacably, the British were overtaking their enemies. *Lion* had been hit, but appeared to have shrugged off these blows. Beatty's principal concern became the straggling out of his squadron and, to rectify this, at 9:53 a.m. he slowed to 24 knots. In consequence, the range to the German squadron, which had been decreasing for an hour, temporarily remained constant. For young officers in the British fleet, the morning was providing vivid images. "It was wonderful to see our battle cruisers steaming at top speed with spits of flame and brown smoke issuing every minute or so from their bows and sides—and in the far distance the enemy's guns flashing in reply," wrote an officer on *Aurora,* one of Tyrwhitt's Harwich light cruisers. From *Indomitable,* struggling to catch up, a young turret officer observed "the *Lion, Tiger, Princess Royal* and *New Zealand* on our starboard bow, cleaving the water at full speed. . . . We slowly gained on . . . [the Germans] . . . [then] through the navy phone came, 'A turret open fire.' . . . At 10.31 the enemy altered to port and so did we and this brought my turret [Q turret, amidships] into action against *Blücher.* In and out recoiled the guns as we pounded the enemy. 'Left gun ready,' shouts someone and another 850 pounds of explosive goes hurtling towards the enemy." Not every young officer had as good a view. Inside a turret on *New Zealand,* Prince George of Battenberg grumbled, "My range finder was useless. I was soaked through to the skin by spray coming in through the slit in my hood, hitting me in the face and then trickling down outside and inside my clothes and I was frozen by the wind which came in with the spray. My eyes were extremely sore and I was blinking all the time."

The best view belonged to Filson Young, kneeling in the foretop of *Lion.*

> Many . . . details registered . . . the smell and taste of cordite smoke as the wind drove it back from the mouths of our guns . . . the silences; lulls that came at the very heat of battle when sometimes for five or ten seconds there would be no sound but the soft brushing of the wind and its harp-like harmonies in the rigging, until a salvo from our guns would split the heavens again and, like its echo, the hollow growl of the enemy's guns. . . . One could see clearly the flashes of salvos from *Seydlitz* and *Moltke,* both of which were firing at *Lion* and, timing their flight with a stopwatch, know to a second when their arrival would be signaled either by an explosion . . . or by the uprising of a group of lovely and enormous fountain blossoms, where the water slowly rose in columns two hundred feet high that mushroomed out at the top, stood for five or ten seconds, and then as gracefully subsided, deluging our decks with tons of water. . . . It was strange to think, observing those flashes and the little black second hand ticking around the dial of the watch, "I have perhaps twenty-three seconds to live; when the little

> hand reaches that mark, then—oblivion." . . . Sometimes from the foretop one could see the shell coming, a black speck in smoky atmosphere, growing larger. . . . I remember observing in the Admiral [Beatty] and the Flag Captain [Chatfield]—who enjoyed this performance more than I have ever seen anything enjoyed by anyone—a child-like blandness of demeanour which I had at no other time observed in either of them, but which had nothing of insanity in it. And . . . the officer in charge of the fore-transmitting station, who, after the explosion of a shell . . . followed by an outbreak of screams and cries, was heard to observe: "That means either Kingdom Come or ten days' leave"—the inference being that the damage was so serious that it would mean the explosion of a magazine [and the instant destruction of the ship] or a long refit.

At this stage of the action, *Lion,* the principal target of German guns, was, said Young, "very nearly smothered with fire." At 10:01 a.m., an 11-inch shell from *Seydlitz* pierced her side armor at the waterline. Water flooded in and spread to the main switchboard compartment, where it short-circuited two of the ship's dynamos and shut down the circuits for the secondary armament and the after fire control. The ship began to list to port, but still maintained a speed of 24 knots.

Then, at 10:18 a.m., *Lion* was staggered by a massive blow, "so violent," said Young, "that we thought she had been torpedoed, and the mast to which the foretop was secured, rocked and waved like a tree in a storm. . . . [He and his companions in the foretop] looked at one another and prepared to alight from our small cage into whatever part of the sea destiny might send us, but nothing happened." The shock was so great that Chatfield, the captain, also believed that "we must have been struck by torpedoes." In fact, his ship had been hit almost simultaneously on the port side below the waterline by two heavy shells from *Seydlitz* or *Derfflinger.* One of these pierced the 6-inch main belt armor on the waterline and exploded behind it. Very quickly, all the adjacent compartments were flooded up to the main deck. In addition, a shell splinter slashed a pipe leading to a feed tank containing fresh water for the port boiler condenser, allowing salt water to pass into the system. Soon, this contamination would clog the boiler pipes and close down the port engine. The second shell exploded below the waterline against the main armored belt, not penetrating it but driving in several heavy armor plates 9 inches thick and 15 feet long. The plates were forced back two feet and more seawater entered.

Lion could not keep up her speed and the admiral knew that she could not long continue to function as squadron flagship. Beatty was deeply chagrined. His guns had been firing for an hour and a half, but no decisive result had been achieved. It was true that the wounded *Blücher* was falling behind and that spectacular flames had been observed rising above the stern of *Seydlitz.* But Hipper's flagship churned steadily ahead, not losing speed. Heligoland and the Bight were always closer and there was no knowledge as to the whereabouts of the High Seas Fleet. It was imperative, Beatty believed, to force the pursuit, to close in, to bring all of his heavy guns to bear. Accordingly, at 10:35 a.m., he signaled an 11-degree turn toward the enemy. At 10:45 a.m., he ordered another 11 degrees. At 10:47, increasingly anxious, he signaled, "Close the enemy as rapidly as possible consistent with keeping all guns bearing."

Meanwhile, the German battle cruisers were concentrating on disabling the British flagship and *Lion* was under constant, heavy fire from *Seydlitz* and *Moltke.* At 10:35, she was hit, then, a minute later, hit again. At 10:41, a shell bursting against the armor of A turret caused a small fire in A turret lobby and a message was sent to the bridge that the fire had spread. "We thought our last moment had come when we got a message up the voice pipe saying that A turret magazine was on fire," said Filson Young. "We sat waiting for the last gorgeous explosion and the eternal silence that would follow it, but it did not come and after four minutes of suspense, our sentence of death was reprieved in a welcome message that the fire was out." By 10:52 a.m., the ship had received fourteen hits. Three thousand tons of water, now flooding the lower compartments, caused a 10 degree list to port. Rising water short-circuited her last remaining dynamo and deprived the ship of all electric power. *Lion* was left with no electric lights and no wireless radio. A few minutes later, the port engine failed and the ship's speed immediately sagged to 15 knots. The flagship was losing her position at the head of the squadron.

But not before a command from Beatty had sealed *Blücher*'s doom. *Blücher*'s position at the rear of the German line made her fate inevitable. Every overtaking British battle cruiser fired at her before shifting to the larger German ships farther up the line. The armored cruiser's forward 8.2-inch turret was out of action, although she continued to fire briskly from her other guns. At 10:35 a.m., two shells pierced her armored deck amidships and penetrated down through two decks to explode in an ammunition room. The inferno spread to her two port-side 8.2-inch-gun wing turrets. Both were destroyed and every man inside was killed. The concussion also damaged her engines and jammed her steering gear. *Blücher*'s speed dropped to 17 knots and she began to fall out of the German line and sheer away to port. Beatty, seeing the armored cruiser burning and listing, leaving Hipper's squadron and erratically circling off to the north, understood what was happening. At 10:48 a.m., he ordered his rearmost battle cruiser, *Indomitable,* now finally coming into action, "Attack the enemy breaking away to northward." If he scored no other success that day, at least this crippled ship would be destroyed.

As *Lion* began to drop astern, *Tiger,* next astern, drew abreast and began to pass her. And now *Tiger* became the primary German target. She was hit on the roof of Q turret, in the intelligence office—where eight men, including Beatty's fleet engineer, were killed—and in the boat stowage area between the two after funnels. The ship's boats were set on fire and the blaze produced plumes of flame that rose above the tops of the funnels. Seen from other ships in the squadron, *Tiger* looked like a roaring, open furnace. Farther away, officers on *Moltke* believed that the blaze signified *Tiger*'s final immolation and, on returning to Wilhelmshaven, they reported that she had been sunk. In fact, within fifteen minutes the fire had consumed everything that would burn and the ship's damage control parties had the flames under control. The fighting qualities of the battle cruiser remained unaffected.

Until this moment, Beatty had conducted the battle almost without error; the only serious flaw had been Pelly's failure to understand that *Moltke,* not *Seydlitz,* was his designated target. Now, however, at the moment when *Tiger, Princess Royal,* and *New Zealand* were sweeping past the crippled flagship, there occurred a series of British mistakes that were to determine the outcome of the battle. It began with an error in observation and judgment made by Beatty. "At 10.54 a.m., submarines were reported on *Lion*'s starboard bow," Beatty reported to the Admiralty after the battle, "and I personally observed the wash of a periscope . . . on our starboard bow." To avoid this danger, he ordered a 90-degree turn to port, heading his ships almost north and cutting at a right angle across the wake of the fleeing Germans. What made Beatty's signal confusing and harmful was that *Lion* hoisted the "Alter Course" flag without the "Submarine Warning" flag; the proper sequence, which would have made the situation clear, would have been the submarine warning first, then the turn signal. The explanation is that all but two of *Lion*'s signal halyards had been shot away, so that the attempt to hoist complete, coherent signals was severely hampered. At any rate, the Battle Cruiser Squadron promptly obeyed the admiral and turned sharply to port, but Beatty's captains did not understand why. Afterward, Captain Pelly of *Tiger* wrote: "*Lion* hoisted the signal, 'Alter course 8 points [approximately 90 degrees] to port.' Whilst this signal was still flying I observed the flagship developing a big list. She was evidently badly damaged. She began to drop back and from then on took no further part in the action. *Tiger* steered to pass between her and the enemy, and the Germans' fire was concentrated on her. For nearly five minutes this 'Alter course' signal remained flying and giving us all plenty of time to comment on it. I remember asking my navigating officer if he could explain the meaning of it for to my mind it seemed to be breaking off the action. He replied, 'I have no idea, unless *Lion* has better knowledge of minefields about than we have.' "

In fact, Beatty was the only officer on *Lion*'s bridge who saw a periscope, and he ordered the turn without giving any explanation. Chatfield, *Lion*'s captain, standing at Beatty's elbow, saw nothing. Plunkett, the Flag Commander, astonished by the order, turned to the admiral and said, "Good heavens, Sir, you're not going to break off the engagement?" Beatty was aware that the new course, north by east—almost at right angles to Hipper's—meant losing ground before the chase could be resumed, but he believed that he had no choice. He had seen something that looked like a periscope and he worried that he might be leading his ships into a submarine trap, set not by one submarine but by several. He knew that the laying of this kind of trap was one of the tactics by which the German Naval Command hoped to whittle down the numerical superiority of the Grand Fleet. Jellicoe had emphasized the danger of being drawn over submarines in his letter to the Admiralty of October 30, 1914, and Beatty, although less worried than the Commander-in-Chief, was familiar with these fears.

Beatty was also concerned about mines. He knew that some German destroyers and light cruisers were equipped to lay mines from rails on their sterns and he feared that, even at such high speeds, these ships might roll mines off into the path of his pursuing ships. Striking a mine, as the *Audacious* had proved, could be as catastrophic as being hit by a torpedo. He was determined, therefore, to avoid steaming directly in the wakes of the German light ships. Once clear of the track of the German destroyers, his ships could turn back to a course parallel with Hipper. Indeed, almost immediately the admiral realized that his turn had been unnecessarily wide; four minutes later, he modified it by signaling, "Course North East." This new course converged with Hipper's.

After the battle and for many years, questions were asked about whether Beatty's turn to port was necessary. Following the action, Fisher disgustedly declared that there were no German submarines within sixty miles. Later, it was suggested that the "periscope" Beatty had seen might have been a German destroyer's torpedo surfacing after its run. (The destroyer *V-5* had fired a torpedo at 10:40 a.m., which should have finished its run and come to the surface at about 10:54 a.m.) Beatty also was criticized because, even if there had been a U-boat where he thought he saw one, the submarine could not possibly have endangered his other battle cruisers, already two miles ahead of the flagship. Admiral Sir Reginald Bacon believed that "had he [Beatty] turned and steered straight for the supposed periscope and done nothing more than warn the [destroyer] flotilla commander to send one or more destroyers to search for the submarine, then our battle cruisers would have continued the chase and we should have sunk at least two of the enemy battle cruisers and probably more." Jellicoe shared this opinion: "The best course was to turn direct at the submarine not eight points [approximately 90 degrees] away. . . . I should say that Beatty himself broke off the action by his unfortunate signal to alter course to port."

In making the turn, Beatty, of course, had no intention of breaking off the action. His plan at that moment was that *Indomitable* would intercept and destroy the crippled *Blücher* while *Tiger, Princess Royal,* and *New Zealand* would overtake and annihilate the damaged *Seydlitz* and, if possible, *Moltke* and *Derfflinger.* Nothing of this kind occurred because Beatty—in Churchill's words, "the whole spirit and direction of the battle"—was about to be stripped of effective command of the battle cruisers. To make matters worse, the final signal that the admiral managed to send was mishandled by his signal staff and consequently misinterpreted by the other ships. The cause was the heavy damage inflicted on *Lion* and the consequent breakdown of the system of communication between ships. From the beginning of the battle, Beatty's ships had operated under wireless silence and had communicated first by flashing light and then, when daylight was sufficient, by signal flags. Up to this point, there had been no difficulty: for several hours, *Lion* had snapped out crisp flag signals every few minutes. But now the flagship was severely wounded. She had been struck by fifteen heavy shells, she was listing to port, and her port engines were stopped. All three of her dynamos were gone. She had no electricity and thus no electric lights, no searchlights, and no wireless. She could communicate only by flag hoist and—of critical importance—all but two of her signal halyards had been shot away. Visual signaling by flag hoist was in the ancient tradition of the Royal Navy; in the days of sailing ships, it was the primary—in daylight, the only—means of communication. But here warships steaming at up to 28 knots were placing new, previously unimagined strains on the signalmen working on the bridge. There was, in the first place, the wind. Filson Young wrote that "it was impossible to endure the wind standing up" in the foretop of the *Lion,* yet a few feet beneath him, the flagship's signalmen were working under these same conditions. Smoke was another problem. *Lion*'s funnels were pouring out thick clouds of oily, black smoke, which obscured her signal halyards from other ships. In addition, cordite fumes from the guns of the forward main turrets swept back over the signal bridge. And this exposed area was continually drenched by spray and riddled by splinters from bursting shells. Not surprisingly, the signalmen working there made mistakes.

Beatty's frustration, as he watched Hipper's three battle cruisers drawing steadily away to the southeast even as his own flagship was losing speed, was extreme. As *Lion* dropped astern, the admiral did his best to impose his will on the deteriorating situation and make clear his intentions. Ironically, this attempt did further damage. At 11:02 a.m., Beatty had ordered "Course North East" in order to countermand his previous 90-degree turn and substitute a 45-degree turn, which would bring his battle cruisers more quickly back on Hipper's trail. For Beatty, however, a simple course correction was not enough; his nature required exhortation. Thus, while the "Course North East" flags were still flying from one halyard, he ordered Seymour to hoist "Attack the rear of the enemy" on the other remaining halyard, which happened to be adjacent. Herein lay the source of the confusion that followed.

The *Lion* was now simultaneously flying two separate signals that Beatty did not intend to be connected. The other battle cruisers did not understand this. As they read the arrangement of the flags, Beatty was sending one signal, not two. The admiral, they believed, was ordering them to "attack the rear of the enemy course northeast." Lucklessly, the two signals were hauled down together and the damage was done.* *Blücher* at that moment bore less than 8,000 yards to the northeast. Within minutes, all four British battle cruisers obediently swung away from the pursuit of Hipper's big ships and steered for the single, battered, isolated ship.

Beatty, watching what was happening and lacking electric power to operate searchlights or wireless, was beside himself. Trying one last time to restore order and make his intentions clear, he asked his Flag Commander, Reginald Plunkett, to suggest a suitable signal. "What we need now is Nelson's signal: 'Engage the enemy more closely,' " said Plunkett. "Yes, certainly. Hoist it!" Beatty replied. Flag Lieutenant Ralph Seymour looked through his signal book and, to his dismay, discovered that the signal, in use since Trafalgar, had been removed from the book. The only modern alternative he could find was "Keep nearer to the enemy." With Beatty's permission, he hoisted this signal, but it was too late. *Lion* had dropped so far astern and the halyard was so obscured by smoke that none of the other battle cruisers saw the signal.

With Beatty unable to communicate and therefore no longer in control of his squadron, command passed automatically to Rear Admiral Moore in *New Zealand,* now the third ship in line. There was no precise moment at which Moore succeeded Beatty; indeed Beatty, now rendered mute by circumstance, never formally transferred authority to his second in command. There was a period of confusion when neither admiral seemed to be directing the actions of the fleet. It was amid this confusion that victory slipped away.

Sir Archibald Moore, who had been Third Sea Lord during much of Churchill's tenure at the Admiralty, had begged for a sea command and been given the 2nd Battle Cruiser Squadron. Now, with little experience, he faced a supreme challenge: command of the British battle cruiser force in action against Franz Hipper. Moore was hampered by the fact that, at first, he was not certain that he had succeeded Beatty, of whom he was in awe. And, given his deference to Beatty, he was unusually reluctant to assume control. Eventually, it was impossible for him not to know that the command had descended upon him; twenty minutes after the turn to port, *Lion* was out of sight. Moore wished to carry out Beatty's orders. But what were they? Neither Moore nor any of Beatty's captains was certain. The squadron had just

*In naval practice, the hoisting of a flag signal merely alerts all ships of the admiral's intent. Hauling down the flag is the order to execute the command immediately.

turned sharply away from Hipper's course and the range was opening fast. Moore, of course, had not sighted a periscope and was unaware of the reason that had prompted Beatty to order an abrupt turn to the north across the rear of a fleeing enemy. When he saw the two signals "Course North East" and "Attack the rear of the enemy" flown and hauled down together, he may have wondered at Beatty's reasons, but to question and countermand what he believed to be Beatty's orders was not in the nature of Sir Archibald Moore.

The problem was the Beatty legend. Already, after only six months of war, this most famous and flamboyant of British admirals, in command of the celebrated battle cruisers for over three years, had a reputation for infallible judgment as well as courage. Moore reasoned that Beatty must have had good reasons for his signals, and Moore was ready to obey. But what did Beatty mean? Where was "the rear of the enemy"? Was it *Blücher*? On what compass bearing was *Blücher* to be found? Northeast. The signal read, "Attack the rear of the enemy bearing northeast." True, it was unlike Beatty to give up pursuit of the primary prey when there was still an opportunity of catching it, but how else should the admiral's signals be interpreted? Moore now concluded that he had no choice. He was under direct orders from Beatty to attack *Blücher* and he issued no fresh orders modifying or countermanding Beatty's last signal. At 11:09 a.m., therefore, *Tiger, Princess Royal,* and *New Zealand* ceased firing at the fleeing German battle cruisers and swung around to join *Indomitable* in the final destruction of the already doomed armored cruiser *Blücher.*

Beatty's turn away from the supposed periscope and Moore's continuation of this turn in the direction of *Blücher* saved a number of German destroyers from destruction. For some time before the British battle cruisers turned away from him and toward *Blücher,* Hipper had been considering possible methods of assisting this lagging and beleaguered armored cruiser. The most effective help he could give—rushing back with his own battle cruisers—would mean bringing on the all-out, general engagement he was doing his utmost to avoid. But there was the alternative of ordering a destroyer attack; possibly, as the British vessels maneuvered to escape his destroyers' torpedoes, *Blücher* might escape.

Up to that point in the battle, the German destroyers accompanying Hipper had been a liability. As the chase began, he had placed them ahead of his own battle cruisers, as far away as possible from the guns of the British battle cruisers, where he hoped they would be out of harm's way. Even so, some of the small ships were having trouble maintaining speed. Now, sending these frail vessels to attack the onrushing British force would bring the certainty of heavy losses. To have a chance of scoring hits, the destroyers needed to get within 3,000 or 4,000 yards of their targets; to do this in daylight, charging into the concentrated gunfire of a number of British battle cruisers, light cruisers, and destroyers, would be something close to suicide. Nevertheless, to save *Blücher,* Hipper decided to try it—and even to support the destroyer attack by closing the range with his battle cruisers. At 10:58 a.m., he made a preliminary move by ordering his big ships to turn southwest into the path of the British battle cruisers. At 11:00 he signaled, "[Destroyer] flotillas stand by to attack."

It was coincidence that the decisions of the opposing commanders during this quarter of an hour so closely affected each other. Thus, just as Hipper decided to succor the lagging *Blücher,* Beatty thought he saw a periscope and gave his order to turn away. Hipper, almost simultaneously, was signaling his battle cruisers to turn toward the British battle cruisers and his destroyers to attack. Then, seeing the entire British squadron turn sharply away (because of the "periscope"), the German admiral assumed that Beatty was reacting to evade the threat of the German destroyers. In response, at 11:07 a.m., he canceled the German destroyer attack.

Even so, Hipper felt that he must do something to aid *Blücher.* His staff was watching him closely on *Seydlitz*'s bridge. "Only when he realized the full tragedy of *Blücher* did his human sympathy break through," said Captain von Waldeyer-Hartz. "There had always been a close bond of friendship and confidence between him and his captains. He was especially fond of Captain Erdmann . . . of *Blücher.* He was therefore strongly tempted to go to his friend's aid." Hipper's officers unanimously opposed this move. Captain Moritz von Egidy of *Seydlitz* declared flatly that his ship could not continue to fight. Two of the flagship's five turrets were out of action, there was 600 tons of water in her stern, and only 200 11-inch shells remained for the main battery guns. *Derfflinger* had also been hard hit and the relatively unscathed *Moltke* could not singlehandedly engage the four British battle cruisers that remained in action. Listening, Hipper realized that in attempting to save one ship, he might lose all. "I dismissed any further thought of supporting the *Blücher* . . . now that no intervention of our main fleet was to be counted on," he said.

Few in the German navy criticized Hipper's decision to abandon *Blücher.* "If Hipper's leadership at this short moment betrayed possibly a trace of indecision, it was because Hipper the man got the better of Hipper the tactician," said Waldeyer-Hartz. "The moment . . . Captain von Egidy reported that . . . the ammunition for the heavy guns was as good as used up, Hipper forced himself—it could be seen in his eyes—to look the facts squarely in the face. There can be no doubt that, had the High Seas Fleet been advancing, he would, in spite of everything, have made an attempt to rescue the *Blücher* or at least save the ship's company from death or captivity. The decision to refrain he found extraordinarily difficult. His face clouded; an expression of injured pride, grief for his comrades who had to be abandoned, was to be read in his eyes. Then suddenly, a sharp, jerky movement—a curt order with the accustomed assurance—and the squadron turned back to a southeasterly course."

This course toward Germany soon put the German ships beyond the reach of Admiral Moore. The remainder of Hipper's return went without incident, although two of his three battle cruisers were burning, encumbered with wreckage, and crowded with dead and wounded men. *Moltke* was mostly unharmed, although her captain reported that "in stern turret D, seven men of the gun crew were so exhausted that they could [no] longer carry on . . . the ventilation gear was put out of action by the vibration of the turret and this resulted in suffocation of the men."

Retreating across the North Sea, Hipper considered sending his destroyers back for a night torpedo attack, but decided against it because their fuel was low and their crews exhausted. On the voyage home, Hipper's sadness at the loss of *Blücher* was balanced by reports that the British had lost the battle cruiser *Tiger.* One report came from *Moltke,* which had observed the large fire amidships on *Tiger* and assumed that the ship could not survive. This assessment was buttressed by a signal from the captain of the zeppelin *L-5,* cruising above the battle, who declared that he could see only four British battle cruisers. In fact, the zeppelin had arrived too late to witness the departure of *Lion,* wounded and far behind, but still afloat.

At 3:30 p.m., Hipper's battle cruisers rendezvoused with the High Seas Fleet and that night anchored in the Jade River. The following morning, *Seydlitz, Derfflinger,* and *Kolberg,* all heavily damaged, limped into Wilhelmshaven. In order to reduce her draft sufficiently to go through the locks, *Seydlitz* had to pump out the 600 tons of water in her stern. In the late afternoon of January 25, Hipper's flagship finally entered the inner harbor and went into dry dock.

CHAPTER 22

The Battle of the Dogger Bank: "Why Didn't You Get the Lot?"

Blücher, abandoned, did not escape. When Beatty hoisted his final signal to the battle cruisers, "Attack the rear of the enemy," *Blücher* was engaging Commodore Goodenough's four light cruisers at a range of 12,000 yards. For over two hours, she had been under fire from one or another of five British battle cruisers. Hit repeatedly, she had lost speed and developed a list, and only two of her six 8.2-inch turrets remained in action, but still her gunfire was straddling Goodenough's ships so accurately that at 11:05 a.m. the commodore was forced to retreat to a range of 16,000 yards. Then once again he edged in toward the German ship, beginning to score hits at 14,000 yards. Meanwhile, Commodore Tyrwhitt was coming up in *Arethusa,* accompanied by four *M*-class destroyers. At 11:20 a.m., these four ships attacked *Blücher* with torpedoes. *Meteor* came close enough to launch her torpedoes, but before she could do so, she was struck by a heavy shell that put the destroyer out of action. Her three sisters managed to fire their torpedoes and believed that they had scored five hits. *Arethusa* now bored in, peppering *Blücher* with 6-inch-gun fire until the range was down to 2,500 yards, at which point Tyrwhitt's flagship turned sharply and launched two torpedoes. Both struck, all electric power on *Blücher* failed, and the ship's belowdeck spaces went dark.

Still, it was not over. The doomed German ship now became a target for four British battle cruisers. Admiral Moore, performing the duty he believed he had been given, assembled the battle cruisers in line and with sixteen 13.5-inch guns and sixteen 12-inch guns, began to conduct a massacre. *Tiger, Princess Royal, New Zealand,* and *Indomitable* began to circle their victim, firing continuously. By then, *Blücher*'s punishment was purely gratuitous. She was a wreck, out of control, shrouded in steam and smoke: the cruiser and her destruction seemed to have been become "a kind of obsession with the captains of the two British battlecruisers [*Tiger* and *Princess Royal*]." Again and again they fired, pouring shells into the helpless mass of flame and smoke. A German survivor recalled that "*Blücher* was under fire from so many ships" that it seemed

> there was one continuous explosion. . . . The ship heeled over as the broadsides struck her, then righted herself, rocking like a cradle. . . . The shells came thick and fast with a horrible droning hum. . . . The electric plant was . . . destroyed and . . . [belowdecks] you could not see your hand before your nose. . . . The shells . . . bored their way even to the stokehold. The coal in the bunkers was set on fire. . . . In the engine room, a shell licked up the oil and sprayed it around in flames of blue and green, scarring its victims. . . . The terrific air pressure resulting from explosion in a confined space . . . roars through every opening and tears . . . through every weak spot. . . . Open doors bang to and jam—and closed iron doors bend outward like tin plates and through it all the bodies of men are whirled about like dead leaves . . . to be battered to death against the iron walls. . . . As one poor wretch was passing though a trap door a shell burst near him. He was exactly half way through. The trap door closed with a terrific snap. In one of the engine rooms . . . men were picked up by that terrible air pressure and tossed to a horrible death amidst the machinery.

The British watched with horror and awe. Near the end, a witness on *Indomitable* saw a sheet of flame leaping up from *Blücher*'s bow that "stayed for about twenty seconds and I should think must have roasted them all in their fore turret." It could not continue. At 11:45 a.m., Tyrwhitt signaled Moore that *Blücher* appeared to have struck her colors, and Moore ordered a cease-fire. As *Arethusa* and her destroyers closed in to rescue survivors, Tyrwhitt observed that *Blücher* "was in a pitiable condition—all her upper works [were] wrecked and fires could be seen raging between decks through enormous holes in her sides." Goodenough's light cruisers also approached while, farther off, the battle cruisers prepared to leave. "It was a pathetic sight to see that huge ship a mere wreck lying helpless as we steamed by," said a young midshipman on *Indomitable*.

At seven minutes past noon, *Blücher* suddenly heeled over, floated for a few minutes bottom up, and then went down. *Arethusa* and her destroyers came closer, lowered boats, and began picking up survivors from the water. One of these was *Blücher*'s Captain Erdmann, who subsequently, as a result of exposure in the cold sea, died of pneumonia as a prisoner in England. Of the 1,200 men in the crew, only 234 were saved. Afterward, the Royal Navy recognized the achievement of *Blücher* and the heroism of her crew. For over three hours, during which she had been hit by seventy shells and seven torpedoes, *Blücher* never ceased to reply. In the words of the official British naval history, "As an example of discipline, courage and fighting spirit, her last hours have seldom been surpassed."

More German sailors might have been pulled from the sea had it not been for the ill-timed arrival of two German flying machines. The zeppelin *L-5,* patrolling over the North Sea, had not been summoned by Hipper to act as an aerial scout, but her captain, Lieutenant Commander Klaus Hirsch, had picked up numerous radio messages and, curious to see what was happening, had steered his airship in the direction of the battle. *Lion* saw her first. "As we turned out of action, we observed a zeppelin approaching about eighteen or twenty miles away," said Filson Young. "I confess that we felt rather helpless with both our engines stopped and had no doubt that she was coming to finish us off. Apparently, however, she did not see *Lion,* but headed instead for *Blücher.*" A few minutes later, *L-5*'s officers and men found themselves looking down on *Blücher*'s death agony. They saw "a tremendous picture although we could hear almost nothing of the thunder of the guns because of the noise of our engines," said one of the officers. "The four English battle cruisers fired at her together. She replied for as long as she could, until she was completely shrouded in smoke and apparently on fire. At 12:07 p.m., she heeled over and capsized. We didn't drop bombs on the English ships. We had no chance because the clouds were at 1,300 feet. If we had dared fly over them at this altitude we would have been shot down."

The crews of the motionless British light cruisers and destroyers, staring up at the huge cigar-shaped airship droning overhead, felt every bit as vulnerable as the German airmen. Then, quite suddenly, attention was diverted to a second German assailant, this one actually dropping bombs. A German seaplane based on Borkum had witnessed from a distance the sinking of *Blücher.* The plane misidentified the doomed vessel as British, an error explained by the fact that all British battle cruisers had tripod masts and *Blücher* was the only large ship in the German navy with a tripod mast. The pilot and observer, looking down on the rescue operation, believed they were watching British ships pulling beleaguered British seamen out of the water. Banking around, the seaplane roared down and the observer began heaving twenty-pound hand bombs out of the rear cockpit. No British ship or sailor was hit, but Commodore Goodenough, the senior officer on the immediate scene, quickly ordered a withdrawal. Afterward, Tyrwhitt speculated that some of the German bombs might have killed German sailors in the water. In any case, he was certain that, but for the seaplane attack, he could have saved many more men from the icy seas.

As *Blücher* was sinking, Rear Admiral Moore had to decide what to do next. Admiral Hipper was now a smoke cloud on the horizon between

24,000 and 30,000 yards (twelve and fifteen miles) away, making for home at 25 knots. If Moore resumed the pursuit, he would need at least two hours to get back within range; by then, he would be much too deep inside the Bight for safety. Moore's disinclination to accept this challenge was reinforced by his flagship's interception of a signal from the Admiralty to Roger Keyes, whose submarines were approaching the German coast. The message was ominous: "High Seas Fleet coming out." Unfortunately, in *New Zealand*'s radio room, the direction of the message was reversed and Moore, on *New Zealand*'s bridge, was told that it was Keyes who had informed the Admiralty that the German battle fleet was coming out, rather than the Admiralty informing Keyes. Now Moore knew what to do. No part of his duty, or even of common sense, dictated that a British admiral should lead four battle cruisers against the High Seas Fleet in German waters. He decided to retreat. His decision was reinforced by his concern over the condition of *Lion.* He had last seen her battered and listing. Because Beatty's flagship had lost all electric power and could not send messages, Moore had heard nothing from her since losing visual contact. He decided to go to her assistance. At 11:52 a.m., he formed the battle cruisers into a new line with *New Zealand* in the van and headed northwest at 20 knots toward *Lion*'s last known position. At noon, Moore informed the Admiralty: "Reports High Seas Fleet coming out. Am retiring."

At the Admiralty, Moore's report seemed to imply grim news. "Some one said, 'Moore is reporting; evidently *Lion* is knocked out,' " Churchill wrote later. "Across my mind there rose a purely irrelevant picture. I thought of the Memorial Services I had so often attended in Westminster Abbey: the crowd and the uniforms, the coffin with the Union Jack, the searching music, Beatty!"*

—

Beatty, very much alive on *Lion,* knew nothing of these events or forebodings. When his crippled flagship fell out of line, the admiral hoped that tem-

*The First Lord's vivid imagination was enormously stimulated that day: "There can be few purely mental experiences more charged with cold excitement than to follow, almost from minute to minute, the phases of a great naval battle from the silent rooms of the Admiralty," Churchill wrote. "Out on the blue water in the fighting ships amid the stunning detonations of the cannonade, fractions of the event unfold themselves to the corporeal eye. There is the sense of action at its highest; there is the wrath of battle; there is the intense, self-effacing physical and mental toil. But in Whitehall only the clock ticks, and quiet men enter with quick steps laying slips of penciled paper before other men equally silent who draw lines and scribble calculations, and point with the finger or make brief subdued comments. Telegram succeeds telegram at a few minutes' interval, often in the wrong sequence, frequently of dubious import; and out of these a picture, always flickering and changing, rises in the mind, and imagination strikes out around it at every stage flashes of hope or fear."

porary repairs might quickly restore power to the malfunctioning port engine. Instead, Chatfield gave him "the horrid news" that nothing more could be done at sea and that, in fact, both engines needed to be stopped, at least for a while. To Filson Young, high in *Lion*'s foretop, the ship's condition at that moment—dead in the water and listing to port—seemed sufficiently precarious that he and his companions climbed down the mast, leaving behind their oilskins and other cumbersome equipment that might hamper their ability to swim. The decks, Young found, were "an extraordinary spectacle, battered and littered with fragments of smashed and twisted steel, with here and there yawning gashes where heavy shells had burst or fragments penetrated. The men came up from below and swarmed over them, picking up souvenirs in the form of splinters and fragments of shells."

Beatty, however, was unwilling to give up. As Tyrwhitt's two light cruisers and twenty-five destroyers returned and closed in to provide protection for the wounded *Lion,* the admiral signaled the destroyer *Attack* to come alongside. His intention was to board the smaller ship, speed after his four still-effective battle cruisers and resume command. Coming down from *Lion*'s bridge, Beatty found the crew pressing "around him, cheering, and, in the enthusiasm of the moment, one of them clapped him on the back and shouted 'Well done, David!' " The ship's list to port made it easy for Beatty to step from *Lion*'s slanting deck onto the forecastle of the destroyer, with Seymour, the Flag Lieutenant, clutching an armful of flags and signal books, following behind. Then, standing on the deck of *Attack* as it backed away from *Lion,* Beatty waved. "The *Lion* was one huge grandstand of cheering men," Seymour said, "but she looked a rather sad sight heeled over to port with a good many holes in her side." At 11:50 a.m., "with the admiral's flag flying proudly from her mast, the little destroyer swept off into the haze."

Beatty's desperate attempt to overtake and rejoin his squadron and continue the chase was doomed. A few minutes after noon, he came in sight of the four British battle cruisers, which had left behind the wrecked and burning *Blücher* and were coming back toward him. At a loss to understand what his ships were doing, he ordered *Attack* alongside *Princess Royal,* climbed aboard, and at 12:33 p.m., hoisted his flag on *Lion*'s sister. He hoped, on reaching *Princess Royal*'s bridge, to be told that at least one, perhaps two, of Hipper's three battle cruisers had been sunk. Instead, he learned that, despite heavy damage, the German ships had all been allowed to escape. In a rage, Beatty instantly ordered his squadron to reverse course and resume the pursuit. Within a few minutes, however, he realized that this effort was pointless. Forty precious minutes had been lost, and with them probably 30,000 yards. This was irretrievable; the German ships were by now so far away that there would be no overtaking them before they reached the German coast. In addition, the Admiralty had signaled that the High Seas Fleet was coming out. Heartsick, Beatty concluded that no more could be done. At 12:45 p.m., he again reversed course and steered west to cover the retirement of the crippled *Lion.*

The Battle of the Dogger Bank was over.

—

Beatty found *Lion,* battered and listing, making for home at 10 knots on her starboard engine, surrounded by a screen of light cruisers and destroyers. Despite the appalling appearance of her decks and superstructure, casualties had been remarkably low: two men killed and eleven wounded. The critical damage to the ship was below the waterline. Here, work parties had placed collision mats and built wooden cofferdams to stop the inflow of seawater, shored up bulkheads to prevent collapse, and started the pumps. Nevertheless, the injury to the ship's propulsion system was grave. Saltwater contamination of the boiler-feed-water system already had caused the failure of the port engine and now was also affecting the starboard engine. All dynamos were out of action and, except for the light produced by lanterns and candles, the ship was dark. No stoves were working, but Beatty's steward, left behind when the admiral departed the ship, managed to produce a cold lunch of champagne and foie gras sandwiches for the members of the staff. Young and his colleagues, their faces blackened by cordite smoke and their nerves jangled by hours under shellfire, sat down and cheered themselves at this unusual picnic.

Beatty, returning to them in *Princess Royal,* wrestled with a final, aggressive impulse. He might still inflict harm on the Germans by sending a mass of destroyers into the Bight to make a night attack on Hipper and the High Seas Fleet. At 2:30 p.m. he proposed to Jellicoe that he hold back one flotilla to screen *Lion* and thrust the rest toward Heligoland. Before Jellicoe could answer, however, *Lion*'s starboard engine began to fail. Her speed dropped to 8 knots and Chatfield was told by his engineering officer that there was no guarantee that the engine would keep going through the night. At three o'clock, Chatfield passed this information to Beatty, who ordered *Indomitable* to take *Lion* in tow. Beatty chose *Indomitable,* partly because her captain, Francis Kennedy, was known as an exceptional seaman, and partly because, should the battle somehow be renewed, *Indomitable* was the least potent of the remaining British battle cruisers. Towing a huge ship, listing with thousands of tons of water inside her and the bow down by six feet, was a dangerous and delicate operation; Kennedy needed all of his experience and skill. Simply passing and establishing the tow absorbed almost two hours. First, a 5½-inch wire hawser was passed between the two ships and successfully secured, but the wire parted when the strain of moving *Lion*'s 30,000 tons of steel plus the 3,000 tons of water was applied too quickly. On the next attempt, a 6½-inch hawser was passed over and this line, tautened more gradually, got the ship moving. At 5:00, *Lion* restarted her own starboard engine and, tethered to *Indomitable,* began the 300-mile voyage home. Eventually, linked in tandem, the two ships reached a speed of 10 knots.

In midafternoon, Jellicoe arrived. He knew that Hipper had fled and he doubted that Ingenohl remained at sea, but he wished to give *Lion* maximum protection. Accordingly, he dispatched Vice Admiral Bradford's seven predreadnoughts, along with Pakenham's armored cruisers and two light cruiser squadrons, to a blocking position twenty-five miles east of *Lion* in the direction of Heligoland. At 4:30 p.m., while *Indomitable* was attempting to establish its tow to *Lion,* the Grand Fleet appeared on the horizon. Jellicoe, understanding the dangers facing the crippled ship, immediately detached from the Grand Fleet the light cruiser *Galatea* and seventeen destroyers of the 2nd Flotilla, and the light cruiser *Caroline* and eighteen destroyers of the 4th Flotilla, adding these thirty-seven ships to *Lion*'s protective cordon. In addition to Jellicoe's battleships and Beatty's battle cruisers, *Lion* now had, by James Goldrick's calculations, "an escort of thirteen light cruisers and sixty-seven destroyers, most of the Royal Navy's front-line strength in these types."

Jellicoe's decision to strip away his own destroyers and assign them to screening *Lion* was the result of an urgent message from the Admiralty sent to *Iron Duke* at 3:45 p.m.: "Germans are preparing a night attack by destroyers but the two flotillas which were out with their battle cruisers last night have not enough fuel to take part. Our destroyers should protect damaged ships." Hipper, of course, had pondered just such an attack with his own destroyers, but—as the Admiralty had predicted—he was deterred by a shortage of fuel. And the High Seas Fleet destroyers were too far away. But neither the Admiralty, Beatty, nor Jellicoe could be certain of this.

At nightfall, anxious to remove his own (now unescorted) battleships before German destroyers could appear, Jellicoe turned the Grand Fleet back for Scapa Flow. Soon after, for the same reason, Beatty accelerated northward with his three remaining battle cruisers. Behind, the wounded *Lion,* roped to *Indomitable* and surrounded by their numerous escort, made her laborious way across the North Sea. The night was anxious for those on board. Shortly after Beatty departed, *Lion*'s starboard engine broke down again and *Indomitable,* her engines now pulling more than 50,000 tons of steel and water (her own weight plus *Lion*'s) through the sea, slowed to 7 knots. If the enemy knew this, it seemed certain that he would attempt a destroyer or submarine attack, but the hours went by without interruption. At dawn, *Lion* was still over a hundred miles from the Firth of Forth. The British destroyer flotillas re-formed as a submarine screen, but still no enemy appeared. All day, *Lion* crept along, silent and helpless.

"It was a strange journey lasting all night, all the next day and through the night following . . . along the road over which we had made such an exhilarating chase in the morning," wrote Filson Young. "The wounded *Lion* in tow of her consort was surrounded by a cloud of destroyers and from her bridge that evening I watched in the calm twilight the beautiful evolutions of these craft, weaving in and out in ever changing formation. All about us as far as we could see, the divisions were zigzagging weaving their web of safety around us." At nightfall, Tyrwhitt, commanding the sixty destroyers of the escort, issued a blunt command: "Keep a good lookout for submarines at dawn. If seen, shoot and ram them regardless of your neighbors." Inside the ship, the night passed without heat or electric light—an uncomfortable novelty for Young, who was not a professional sailor. "The silence of the ship was the strangest element of all," he said.

> The absence of those buzzings and whinings that come from the innumerable dynamos, ventilating fans, refrigerating machines and motors that are never silent . . . [and which now were silent] made audible other sounds: the echo of voices through the long steel alleyways, the strange gurgling of water where no water should be. Most of us had headaches; all of us had black faces, torn clothes and jangled nerves. The ship was as cold as ice, all the electric radiators by which the cabins were warmed being out of action. Blows and hammerings echoed on the decks down below where the carpenters were at work. The sick bay, into which I looked before turning in, was a mess of blood and dirt, feebly lighted by oil lamps. . . . The remaining staff managed to have quite a cheery little dinner with Captain Chatfield whose galley and pantry were in commission. But there is nothing so cold as an unwarmed steel warship in the winter seas. The only place to get warm was in bed; and I turned in after dinner and slept like the dead.

At midnight on the second night, the crippled ship arrived off May Island at the entrance to the Firth of Forth. Here, as *Lion* dismissed her escort and transferred her tow cable to tugboats, Beatty returned to his flagship and, accompanied by his friend Tyrwhitt, stood on the bridge as the ship was pulled slowly up the estuary. With her bow drawing an extra six feet, the battle cruiser was forced to anchor below the Forth bridge while harbor craft with additional pumps came alongside and pumped out water. This done, the ragged voyage resumed. "There was a thick fog that morning," said Filson Young, "but as we approached the little island on which the central pier of the Forth bridge is founded, we could hear sounds of cheering coming faintly to us through the mist, which thinned just enough to show us the shore of the island thronged with people cheering and waving. *Lion*'s band played 'Rule, Britannia.' As we came under the bridge, we could see that the mighty span was lined with diminutive human figures, waving and cheering."

At Rosyth, examination revealed that the *Lion*'s wounds were beyond that facility's capacity to repair. Beatty and Chadwick wanted to send the ship to Plymouth where she could be dry-docked and repaired rapidly. But the Admiralty, particularly Fisher, was anxious that the extent of her damage be kept secret and directed that the battle cruiser not be brought to one of the major naval dockyards in the south. Instead, Fisher sent her to Armstrong's shipyard at Newcastle upon Tyne even though no dry dock was available there. "It was a bad decision," said Chatfield. "We spent nearly four months in the Tyne with the ship permanently heeled over while the bottom was repaired by means of a vast wooden cofferdam." Lying on her starboard side in the black mud while damaged armor plates were removed and new plates attached, the once "proud" and "noble" *Lion* appeared to Young "incredibly small and mean."

—

The Dogger Bank was a British victory, even if it was not the total annihilation of the enemy that the British navy and public so eagerly desired. The Germans had run for home, *Blücher* had been sunk, *Seydlitz* was badly damaged, and more than 1,200 German seamen had been killed, wounded, or taken prisoner.* On the British side, *Lion* had been severely punished, but only one other battle cruiser, *Tiger,* had been struck by heavy shells. *Princess Royal* and *New Zealand* had not been touched, and *Indomitable* was hit once by an 8.2-inch shell from *Blücher.* The damaged destroyer *Meteor* was towed to safety in the Humber, and no other British destroyer or light cruiser had been hit. There was immense satisfaction in the outstanding engineering performance of the new battle cruisers, which had surpassed their design speeds without the faltering of a single turbine. Ironically, in view of what was to happen at Jutland, the British were also pleased by their ships' seeming ability to withstand punishment.

The victory provided an enormous lift to British civilian morale, depressed over the long casualty lists from the Western Front. On the twenty-fifth, even as *Lion* was under tow, Beatty received a signal from the king: "I most heartily congratulate you, the officers and ships' companies of squadrons on your splendid success of yesterday. George, R. I." The British press trumpeted the German "rout" and the avenging of the previous month's Scarborough and Hartlepool bombardments. "It will be some time before

*The best estimate of German casualties is 951 killed and 78 wounded. Most of these men were from *Blücher,* although the fire that destroyed the two after turrets of *Seydlitz* killed 153 men and wounded 33. In addition, the British rescued and took prisoner 189 unwounded and 45 wounded men from *Blücher.*

British casualties totaled 15 killed and 80 wounded. *Lion,* despite the pounding she received, suffered only 2 men killed and 11 wounded, almost all by a shell that had burst in the confined space of the A turret lobby. *Tiger* lost 2 men killed along with 9 wounded. The destroyer *Meteor* had 4 dead and 2 wounded.

they go baby-killing again," chortled *The Globe.* The victory also rebutted the German claim that the British navy was skulking in port, afraid to contest the mastery of the North Sea. "After yesterday's action," declared the *Pall Mall Gazette,* "it will not be easy for the loud-mouthed boasters of Berlin to keep up the pretence that the British Fleet is hiding itself in terror." A *Daily Mail* photograph of the capsized *Blücher*—the huge ship lying on her side and her crew scrambling down into the water—gave satisfaction to millions.

The navy knew better. "For the second time, when already in the jaws of destruction, the German Battle Cruiser Squadron escaped," wrote Winston Churchill. "The disappointment of that day is more than I can bear to think of," Beatty wrote to Keyes. "Everybody thinks it was a great success, when in reality it was a terrible failure. I had made up my mind that we were going to get four, the lot, and *four* we ought to have got." Moore became the primary target of criticism. Years later, Keyes wrote, "I think the spectacle of Moore & Co. yapping around the poor tortured *Blücher* with beaten ships in sight still to be sunk is one of the most distressing episodes of the war." Moore defended himself by saying that he had obeyed explicit orders flying from *Lion*'s signal halyards: "Attack the enemy rear bearing northeast"—the bearing of the *Blücher.* Because this confusing signal had, indeed, come from his flagship, Beatty did not ask for Moore's relief. He knew that Seymour had made an unfortunate choice in selecting and hoisting the *Lion*'s signal flags and that Moore had correctly read their literal meaning as flown. Nor did Beatty blame Seymour; he knew that, to some extent, the faultiness of the signal resulted from the shooting away of all but two of *Lion*'s halyards. "I am against all charges," he wrote to Jellicoe. "It is upsetting and inclined to destroy confidence." But, "frankly, between you and me," he admitted to the Commander-in-Chief, "he [Moore] is not of the right sort of temperament for a battle cruiser squadron. . . . Moore had a chance which most fellows would have given the eyes in their head for and did nothing. . . . It is inconceivable that anybody should have thought it necessary for four battle cruisers, three of them untouched, to have turned on the *Blücher* which was obviously a defeated ship and couldn't steam, while three others, also badly hammered, should have been allowed to escape."

Fisher, chronically unable to moderate opinions or soften blows, roared that Moore's conduct had been "despicable!" "No signals (often unintentionally ambiguous in the heat of action) can ever justify the abandonment of a certain victory such as offered itself here when the *Derfflinger* and the *Seydlitz* . . . were blazing at the end of the action . . . severely damaged." Furiously, the First Sea Lord minuted Moore's report: "The Admiralty require to know WHY the *Derfflinger* and the *Seydlitz,* both heavily on fire and in a badly damaged condition, were allowed to escape, when, as Admiral Moore states in his letter, gun range with the leading ships of the Enemy could have been maintained by *Tiger* and *Princess Royal* at all events." Jellicoe put it more gently but agreed that "if, as has since been stated, two of the enemy battle cruisers were very seriously damaged and the fact was apparent at the time, there is no doubt whatever that the Rear Admiral [Moore] should have continued the action." Moore was spared court-martial, but bitterness at his failure to annihilate a crippled, fleeing enemy lifted only gradually. Early in February, Beatty wrote to Jellicoe that Churchill "wanted to have the blood of somebody" and that the First Lord and Fisher had settled on Moore. Near the end of February, Moore was quietly removed from the Grand Fleet and assigned to command a cruiser squadron in the Canary Islands where the possibility of any appearance by German surface ships was remote.

Fisher's fiercest wrath fell on Henry Pelly of *Tiger,* whom he labeled a "poltroon." It was "inexcusable that Captain Pelly should have left a ship of the enemy [*Moltke*] unfired at and so permitt[ed] her to fire unmolested at *Lion.*" Why, the First Sea Lord roared, did Pelly, whose ship was in the lead once the flagship had staggered out of line, not take the initiative and, in the absence of a countermanding order from Moore, continue to pursue the German battle cruisers? Pelly, Fisher said, "was a long way ahead, he ought to have gone on had he the slightest Nelsonic temperament in him, regardless of signals. Like Nelson at Copenhagen and St. Vincent! In war the first principle is to disobey orders. *Any fool can obey orders!*" Beatty made excuses for Pelly. "Pelly did very badly, first in not carrying out the orders to engage his opposite number which had disastrous results [the crippling of the *Lion*]," he conceded to Jellicoe. But Beatty also recalled that Pelly was commanding a new ship and that he had been given a mixed ship's company, which included a large number of apprehended deserters. It had been an uphill task, Beatty realized, for her captain to pull them together in wartime. As for Pelly himself, Beatty said, he "had done very well up to then, he had difficulties to contend with and I don't think he is likely to do the same again. But he is a little bit of the nervous, excited type." Nevertheless, Jellicoe could find no excuse for Pelly's failure to comply with Beatty's order to engage opposite numbers. "Special emphasis is laid in Grand Fleet Orders on the fact that no ship of the enemy should be left unfired at, and a consideration of this rule should have led to the *Tiger* engaging No. 2 in line." Pelly survived because Churchill preferred to close the book on the matter. "The future and the present claim all our attention" was the First Lord's verdict. Despite his ship's continued poor shooting, Pelly was to captain *Tiger* at Jutland.

Fisher was especially furious at the failure to annihilate, as "the rendezvous was given in both cases [the Scarborough Raid and the Dogger Bank battle], and the enemy appeared exactly on the spot [identified by Room 40]." Privately, he questioned Beatty's turn away from the supposed submarine and the admiral's error in not explaining his action either to others on *Lion*'s bridge or to other ships in the squadron. The only extenuation came years later from Beatty's biographer and fellow admiral W. S. Chalmers, who pointed out that the admiral's sighting of a periscope and his decision to turn were made "in a split second from the sloping bridge of a listing ship which had borne the brunt of the battle."

On Wednesday night, January 27, Beatty, still at Rosyth, received a letter from Fisher "urgently inquiring how it was that the action had been broken off." That same night, as the battle cruisers were preparing to go back to sea, Beatty wrote a quick note to the First Sea Lord, instructing Filson Young, who knew Fisher, to carry it personally to London. Young arrived in London at 6:00 on the evening of January 29 and went immediately to the Admiralty. "I was taken to Lord Fisher at his room. . . . He had aged a great deal in three months, and the yellow face looked very old and worn, but grim as ever. . . . He shook hands . . . and turning his hard, wise old eye on me, he said, 'Well, tell me about it. How was it they got away? What's the explanation? Why didn't you get the lot? And the *Derfflinger*—I counted on her being sunk, and we hear that she got back practically undamaged. I don't understand it.' " He criticized Beatty's 90-degree turn to port. "Submarines?" said Fisher. "There weren't any; we knew the position of every German submarine in the North Sea; and there wasn't a mine within fifty miles." Two days later, Fisher told Beatty himself the same thing: "We know from themselves [that is, from Room 40 intercepts] exactly where they [the U-boats] were—hours off you." Nevertheless, when all the action reports were in, Beatty retained the full confidence of Churchill, Fisher, and Jellicoe. On the last day of the month, Fisher followed his first "very hurried line" to Beatty with warmer words: "I've quite made up my mind. Your conduct was glorious. *Beatty beatus!*"*

Beatty himself remained bitterly disappointed—the annihilating, Nelsonic victory had shriveled, in Ralph Seymour's words, to "an indecisive fight in our favor"—but the admiral's prestige in the navy soared. When Churchill visited *Lion* ten days after the battle, he found Beatty's senior officers enthusiastic. "Well do I remember," Churchill wrote, "how, as I was leaving the ship, the usually imperturbable Pakenham caught me by the sleeve, 'First Lord, I wish to speak to you in private,' and the intense conviction in his voice as he said, 'Nelson has come again.' "

—

The Dogger Bank was the first sea battle between dreadnoughts whose high speed and heavy gun power dominated the action. Both the British and German Battle Cruiser Squadrons were accompanied by flocks of light cruisers and destroyers, but except in the opening moments near dawn and, at the end, in delivering the death strokes to *Blücher,* they played little part in the

*Blessed be Beatty.

fighting. Neither submarines nor mines were involved, although fear of their presence affected British tactics. The preponderance of heavy gun power favored the British: Beatty's five battle cruisers carried twenty-four 13.5-inch and sixteen 12-inch guns to Hipper's eight 12-inch and twenty 11-inch guns. During the battle, the five British battle cruisers fired a total of 1,150 13.5-inch and 12-inch shells. The Germans fired 976 12-inch and 11-inch shells. *Lion* was hit by sixteen heavy shells from the German battle cruisers and one 8.2-inch shell from *Blücher.* Six heavy shell hits were recorded on *Tiger* and none on any of the other British ships except one 8.2-inch hit on *Indomitable* by *Blücher. Seydlitz* was hit by three heavy British shells—two from *Lion* (one of these nearly destroyed her) and one from *Tiger. Derfflinger* also was hit three times, once each by *Lion, Tiger,* and *Princess Royal.* Obviously, accuracy on both sides was poor: 3½ percent of the shells fired by the German battle cruisers hit a target while on the British side the percentage achieved by the three Cats firing at the three German battle cruisers was below 2 percent.*

The dismal gunnery figures on both sides do not take into account the circumstances of the battle: high speed, long range, smoke, and the fact that no one on either side had ever fought this kind of battle before. Nevertheless, *Lion* was hit sixteen times and no German ship more than four times. Discussion of comparative gunnery began on board *Lion* even as the ship was being towed home. "My impression," said Filson Young, "was that the German gunfire was better than ours initially, and they got on the target sooner. . . . To anyone sitting, as I was, on the target surrounded by the enemy's shells, his shooting appeared to be painfully accurate; and, indeed, towards the end of the action, when two and possibly three ships were concentrating on *Lion,* she was very nearly smothered by their fire." Young believed that one cause of poor shooting was that "we had no director firing ["a device by which all the guns can be aimed and fired simultaneously and accurately from one central position, generally on the foremast well above the smoke," according to Young's footnote definition] in any ship except *Tiger.*" Yet *Tiger,* using the new system, had scored only three hits and *Lion,* which lacked it, had scored four. The result was an erosion of confidence among British naval officers in their equipment, training, and tactics. "Every one of them," said Young, "had been brought up on the theory of the big gun, the first blow, etc. We had the biggest guns and we got in the first blows, but none of the results that . . . [we] had been taught to believe as gospel had happened. . . . We had gone on hitting, and hitting, and hitting—and three of their four ships had got home. Why?"

After the battle, Young and his shipmates assumed that its results and the

*A number of shells fired by the Cats were aimed at *Blücher,* while *New Zealand* and *Indomitable* fired only at *Blücher.*

lessons learned "would immediately have been fastened upon by the . . . navy and the Admiralty. . . . Doubtless throughout the fleet there were hundreds of officers who were keen to get all the information and technical data that they could. . . . Every gunnery officer in the fleet wanted to know exactly how the great ranges, and the high speeds of the ships engaged affected the existing organization for fire control." Accordingly, immediately after their return to the Firth of Forth, the officers of the Battle Cruiser Squadron wrote detailed reports. A wealth of technical data was forwarded to the Admiralty, but, said Young, "the Admiralty, having acknowledged the receipt of the masses of material, made no further sign." After the war, Churchill himself blithely reported: "The result of the engagement confirmed and fortified my own convictions of the great strength of the British line of battle, and in particular of the ships armed with 13.5-inch guns."

Jellicoe, whose career specialty had been gunnery, was not so complacent. Battle reports indicating superior accuracy on the part of the Germans confirmed his "suspicion that the gunnery of our battle cruiser squadron was in great need of improvement, a fact which I very frequently urged upon Sir David Beatty." Beatty needed no convincing, having, from the day he took command of the battle cruisers in 1912, urged that gunnery exercises be conducted at long range and high speed. Nevertheless, despite these admonitions and good intentions, the need for excellence in gunnery was never hammered home. "We went out to sea for fleet exercises with the same totally inadequate monthly allowance of ammunition to be expended," said Young. "[After the battle] *Lion* was fitted with . . . director fire control and other improvements, but with the Grand Fleet there was no development or modification of tactics and the reliance was still on the fallacy that all was well with our [matériel] and that we had more of it than the enemy. The result was that . . . our gunnery . . . showed the same disappointing results at Jutland as it had at Dogger Bank."

If a deficiency in the ability of the British battle cruisers to deal out punishment was recognized by some and ignored by others, ominous flaws in their ability to survive punishment remained hidden. Since the building of *Invincible,* British battle cruisers had been structurally flawed by Jacky Fisher's demand that weight in armor plate be sacrificed to weight invested in larger guns and heavy propulsion machinery that could generate higher speeds. The Germans, obeying Tirpitz's dictum that a warship's first duty is to remain afloat, had taken a different course, accepting lower speed and smaller gun caliber in return for heavier protective armor. Thus, at the Dogger Bank, *Lion* had 9-inch armor over her amidships belt, *New Zealand* 8-inch, and *Indomitable* 7-inch, while *Derfflinger* was shielded in this area by 13-inch armor and *Seydlitz* and *Moltke* by 11-inch. Ironically, the Battle of the Dogger Bank failed to illuminate this design flaw; indeed, it encouraged Fisher and the Royal Navy to believe that their choice had been correct.

Lion, despite her weaker armor, had absorbed sixteen heavy hits, had suffered few casualties, and had survived, while the better-protected *Seydlitz* had been hit only three times, but had lost two turrets and 200 men. This was one fact that permitted Churchill to preen himself on the capabilities of the 13.5-inch gun.

On both sides, the vulnerability of ships to shells fired at long range in a high, arching trajectory before plunging steeply down on enemy decks had been unknown before the battle. When dreadnought battle cruisers and battleships were designed, naval tacticans and designers had assumed that battles between capital ships would be fought at ranges of around 10,000 yards. Shells, therefore, were expected to travel on flatter, more horizontal trajectories and explode against or penetrate the sides of target ships. The sides of ships, accordingly, were more heavily armored than the decks. But at the Dogger Bank, the first dreadnought action, the British battle cruisers opened fire at 18,000 yards. Despite their heavier armor, even the German vessels lacked adequate deck armor, which was why a shell lofted from 17,000 yards away had pierced *Seydlitz*'s after deck.

Another defensive design fault manifested itself in ships on both sides at the Dogger Bank. No one in Britain or Germany had realized the menace of an explosive flash fire within an enclosed gun-turret system. In *Lion, Seydlitz,* and their sisters in both fleets, shells and powder journeyed upward on hoists from the magazines, through the turret lobbies, and into the turrets to the breeches of the guns. These separate compartments remained open and unsealed. A flash fire at any point along this extended route could spread quickly to all other points, including the magazines. Such a fire had occurred in *Lion* at the Dogger Bank and might easily have destroyed her. The fire in her A turret lobby, which caused most of her casualties, could have spread downward into her ammunition handling rooms and from there into her magazines, where a cataclysmic explosion would have destroyed the ship. Fortunately, little ammunition was present in the turret lobby and the resulting fire was small and rapidly extinguished. As a result of this escape, the intrinsic danger of fire transmission went unrecognized on board the ship and at the Admiralty and no effort was made to install antiflash devices in turret trunks to prevent flames from spreading. Not until after Jutland sixteen months later, when the battle cruisers *Queen Mary, Invincible,* and *Indefatigable* blew up from this cause, were these corrections made in British ships.

After the Dogger Bank, the Royal Navy made changes in battle orders, in communications systems, signals, and fleet organization. Jellicoe issued new Grand Fleet Battle Orders regarding distribution of fire on enemy ships; he wanted no more mistakes such as Pelly's. Beatty updated his Battle Cruiser Orders, emphasizing that captains must possess, "in a marked degree, initiative, resource, determination and fearlessness of responsibility. . . . War is a perpetual conflict with the unexpected, so that it is impossible to prescribe beforehand all the circumstances that may arise." Along with director firing systems, all battle cruisers were to be equipped with an auxilary wireless set. And Nelson's flag signal, "Engage the enemy more closely," was restored to the signal book.

The admirals at sea resisted another change urged on them by Churchill and Fisher. The First Lord, concerned that the Grand Fleet's base at Scapa Flow was too remote from the potential battlefield, wanted Jellicoe to move his ships down to Rosyth. The First Sea Lord concurred, telling Beatty that because Scapa was too far away, he doubted that "Jellicoe's Battle Squadrons will be in this war." Later, writing to Jellicoe, Fisher elaborated: "The fundamental fact is that you can never be in time so long as you are at Scapa Flow and therefore there will NEVER be a battle with the German High Seas Fleet unless von Pohl [who assumed command soon after the Dogger Bank battle] goes north especially to fight you *and that he never will*!!!" Jellicoe refused, citing the thick fogs in the Firth of Forth and his fear that Beatty "would be mined in" by the Germans. The Commander-in-Chief preferred to remain at Scapa Flow, now well protected, because the huge anchorage was so large that ships could carry out gunnery practice and torpedo drills inside the Flow, free of submarine menace. When Beatty supported Jellicoe, Churchill and Fisher backed off.

Beatty's success stimulated the Admiralty to change the structure and name of the battle cruiser force. With no need now for battle cruisers anywhere in the world except in the North Sea—the one exception was *Inflexible,* now on guard at the Dardanelles against any sortie by *Goeben*—the Admiralty could now place all these ships under Beatty's command. This new force was renamed the Battle Cruiser Fleet; *Lion,* once repaired, was set apart as its flagship. Captain Osmond de Brock of *Princess Royal* was promoted to commodore and a week later to rear admiral, and given command of the 1st Battle Cruiser Squadron, comprising *Princess Royal, Queen Mary,* and *Tiger.* Admiral Pakenham, brought from the 3rd Cruiser Squadron to replace the disgraced Moore, went to the 2nd Battle Cruiser Squadron, which included *New Zealand, Australia,* and *Indefatigable.* Rear Admiral Horace Hood was given the 3rd Squadron: *Invincible, Indomitable,* and—when she could be brought home—*Inflexible.* Against Hipper's four battle cruisers, Beatty now had nine, with a tenth to come.

Despite its new name and increased strength, the Battle Cruiser Fleet remained an organic part of the Grand Fleet and Beatty remained subordinate to Jellicoe. On March 23, the Commander-in-Chief, looking ahead and imagining the opening phases of a future battle, wrote to Beatty, employing his own particular blend of fatherly praise and gentle admonition:

> I imagine the Germans will try to entrap you by using their battle cruisers as a decoy. They know that the odds are that you will be 100 miles

> away from me, and can draw you down to the Heligoland Bight without my being in effective support. This is all right if you keep your speed, but if some of your ships have their speed badly reduced in a fight with their battle cruisers, or by submarines, their loss seems inevitable if you are drawn into the High Seas Fleet with me too far off to extricate them before dark. The Germans know you very well and will try to take advantage of that quality of "not letting go when you have once got hold," which you possess, thank God. But one must concern oneself with the result to the country of a serious decrease in relative strength. If the game looks worth the candle risks can be taken! If not, one's duty is to be cautious. I believe you will see which is the proper course and pursue it vigorously.

—

German reaction in the fleet, the press, and—where it counted most—with the kaiser was greater embarrassment and deeper depression. The Dogger Bank proved that the British fleet had not evacuated the North Sea, although this boast by the German press had never been believed in the German navy. "The dominant feeling in the [German] fleet," says Arthur Marder, "was that an inept operation had met the fate it deserved." All Germans had reason to be proud of the gallant fight put up by *Blücher;* and, in general, in this first clash of dreadnoughts, the German navy had proved—as it had with *Scharnhorst* and *Gneisenau*—that its fighting abilities, discipline, and courage were superb. The ships were splendidly handled, the guns well aimed, and signaling and damage control expert. But nothing could obscure the facts that the German navy had fled the field, lost a heavy armored ship, and left behind over a thousand men.

German seamen had special reason to be proud of their gunnery. "Our own fire was very effective," Hipper reported after the battle. "Hits could be repeatedly observed on the first and second [British] ships and fire in the second." Long before they knew that they had scored twenty-two hits on *Lion* and *Tiger* to only seven received by their own three battle cruisers, the Germans had seen their shells exploding on Beatty's flagship and had watched her turn out of the line with a heavy list. Twice, they had watched Commodore Goodenough's light cruisers come within range and then retreat; they had seen *Meteor* struck and other British destroyers give up and fall back. Finally, when they witnessed the entire squadron of British battle cruisers turning away, it naturally appeared that the British had given up the fight. Admiral Scheer observed, "There seems no obvious reason why the English battle cruisers would so soon have stopped fighting after their leader fell out and when the number of our [battle] cruisers had already dwindled to three, unless it was because our guns had severely handled them." In addition, when Hipper entered the Jade, he believed that he had sunk *Tiger.* Officers on board *Moltke* declared absolutely that they had seen the second battle cruiser in the enemy line sink. *Moltke*'s log recorded: "11:52: Hits on *Tiger* aft of third funnel and fire observed. 12:23: . . . an enemy battle cruiser which did not appear to be in the line, but to have drawn off . . . disappeared after heavy explosions." The airship *L-5,* hovering overhead, bolstered this report by reporting that it witnessed only four large British ships withdrawing after the battle. "I cannot confirm the view of *Moltke* that the second ship of the enemy line sank," Hipper reported, "though I think it is possible." Hipper reported this possibility to Ingenohl, and Ingenohl reported it to the kaiser. When, in time, it became apparent that *Tiger* was still afloat, Hipper was mortified; it underlined the fact that *Blücher,* alone of all the ships in the battle, had been abandoned.

Ingenohl endorsed Hipper's conduct of the battle. Reporting to the kaiser, he said, "The tactical dispositions were in my opinion correct; the leadership during the action was irreproachable. Further, the difficult decision to leave the damaged *Blücher* to her fate must in the circumstances be approved." Some in the navy grumbled at Hipper's abandonment of *Blücher,* but these criticisms were muted. Scheer endorsed Hipper's decision, saying, "Seeing so many [British] ships assembled, he [Hipper] must have considered it extremely probable that still more forces were behind." As Captain Ludwig von Reuter of *Derfflinger* pointed out, "With the Dogger Bank only eighty sea miles from the English coast and two hundred sea miles from Wilhelmshaven . . . the stern action chosen by Admiral Hipper was tactically correct." The real fault, most German officers believed, lay in the absence of the High Seas Fleet.

Hipper's official postbattle report and those offered by *Derfflinger*'s captain and the captains of other battle cruisers sounded similar themes. A general, urgent recommendation was that when the battle cruisers went out, they be supported by the High Seas Fleet even at the risk of a major battle with the British Grand Fleet. With this in mind, Reuter recommended that no important offensive operations go forward until all German battle squadrons (he referred to the absence of the *König*s) were available. In addition, Hipper suggested the careful placement of a line of submarines able to attack before or during the battle. Reuter added that "in English waters, our forces should be accompanied by submarines which in the case of a chasing action as took place on January 24 might reap a rich harvest." Only efficient ships, Hipper believed, should take part in battle: "All ships other than the most modern must, in view of the tremendous effectiveness of modern naval artillery, fall an easy prey to the enemy." Hipper, of course, had *Blücher* in mind.

The German Naval Staff analyzed the comparative technical deficiencies in their ships in the areas of speed, firing range, and gun caliber. As Beatty was overtaking him, Hipper had greatly envied the superior engine power of the British battle cruisers. There was no cure for this until new ships were built. Similarly, although the Germans professed to be satisfied with the performance of their smaller 11-inch and 12-inch guns, new ships under construction—the battleships *Bayern* and *Baden,* and the battle cruiser *Hindenburg*—would come to sea with 15-inch guns. There was, however, one deficiency that could be corrected before new ships were completed: the fact that at the Dogger Bank British guns could fire at longer range. Long ranges depended to a large extent on the elevation of the guns in the turrets. At the Dogger Bank, the Germans could not raise the muzzles of their gun barrels as high as the British could. To elevate the guns farther meant enlarging the opening of the gun embrasures and thereby increasing the risk of shell fragments and splinters coming into the turret. The British had done this. And, after the Dogger Bank, the Germans did so, too. Another unexpected problem was reported by Captain von Egidy of *Seydlitz:* "The consumption of ammunition surpassed anything that had been previously anticipated. During the two hours' action, the ammunition in the two turrets in which fire was continuously maintained was shot away, leaving only sixty-five and twenty-five rounds respectively. The average time between salvos was 42.3 seconds. . . . The new ships will have to be provided with greatly increased space for ammunition storage."

The Germans learned one vital lesson from the battle. The near fatal damage to the *Seydlitz* turned out—despite the terrible casualties in the turret inferno—to have been a blessing, which eventually would give the German navy a huge material advantage over the British. Understanding of the flash-like qualities of an explosive fire, and the realization that a fire in the turret system must not be allowed to penetrate to the magazine, dawned quickly on those who stared at the burnt-out after turrets of *Seydlitz* lying in a Wilhelmshaven dry dock. To quote from Ingenohl's report: "The working chamber is a danger to the entire turret. In all new construction it must be eliminated. Shell and cordite hoists must be equipped with doors which close automatically after the cages have passed. The charges must be delivered to the guns in flame-proof covering. The doors connecting the magazines to adjacent turrets must be secured with padlocks to prevent premature opening, the key must be in the custody of the turret officer and the order to open only given when all the turret's ammunition has been fired." The German navy moved quickly to implement these recommendations. Multiple, elaborate "anti-flash" shutters were installed between turrets and magazines in all battle cruisers and battleships and the risk of fires spreading was reduced by limiting the amount of combustible reserve ammunition, particularly powder, held in turret handling rooms. Of these changes and the reason for them, the Royal Navy remained ignorant.

There was one mystery that the Germans failed to solve. Hipper was alarmed by the implications of once again having sailed in secret and nevertheless encountering Beatty and Tyrwhitt directly in his path. Scheer also was concerned: "The unexpected presence of English ships . . . leads to the conclusion that the encounter was not a matter of chance and that our plan in some way or another had got to the knowledge of the English." Ingenohl reported to the Naval Staff, "It must be considered a remarkable coincidence that our [battle] cruisers would encounter the enemy precisely at dawn. It appears as if the enemy had intelligence concerning the operation." The Naval Staff reply was dismissive: "Not apparent by what means," it minuted, although it recommended watchfulness against the activities of a British agent who was supposed to pass his messages through inconspicuous newspaper advertisements. No one asked how the agent could have communicated the Dogger Bank intelligence in this manner when the decision to go to sea and Hipper's sole message to his captains occurred on the day the Scouting Groups sailed. Room 40 and its work remained a secret.

The debacle demanded a culprit. Captain Hans Zenker, of the Naval Staff, had no doubt as to who this should be. "The blame . . . lies with the Commander-in-Chief [Ingenohl]," he wrote to his superior Admiral von Pohl on February 1. "Our previous advances to the English east coast have had such an effect on English public opinion that it should have been expected that strong forces would be in the North Sea. Also, from previous experience, it should have been no surprise that the enemy had warning of our sortie. Such lack of foresight and prudence is all the more astonishing and regrettable because the Commander-in-Chief had already been excused for the defeat on August 28 [the Battle of the Bight] and, in two operations against the English east coast [Yarmouth and Scarborough], only luck enabled him to avoid painful consequences. The only way to avoid further disasters from such obstinate inflexibility is to change the Commander-in-Chief."

Ingenohl attempted to defend himself by telling the kaiser that an English battle cruiser had gone to the bottom along with *Blücher.* This failed to save him. On February 2, nine days after the battle, Ingenohl was relieved of command, along with his Chief of Staff, Vice Admiral Eckermann. The new Commander-in-Chief of the High Seas Fleet was none other than Admiral Hugo von Pohl, moved over from his post as Chief of the Naval Staff. Pohl, fifty-nine, a respected former battleship squadron commander, was described by a prewar British naval attaché in Berlin as "short and square built, but slim. Has the reputation of being a good seaman. Gives impression of ability, quickness of decision and force of character. . . . He won't enthuse people at all [but he is] . . . a man . . . with a good knowledge of his profession. He does not look healthy." Pohl was a better naval tactician than Ingenohl, but it scarcely mattered; like his predecessor, he was never allowed to prove his merit in battle. The real culprit in the defeat at the Dogger Bank was Kaiser William, who continued to demand that the fleet be preserved and that its commanders avoid battle with superior force. William tightened these restrictions when he appointed Pohl. All sorties by Hipper's battle cruisers were forbidden and for over a year German capital ships did not venture into the North Sea. As Churchill wrote, "Apart from submarine warfare, a period of fifteen months halcyon calm reigned over the North Sea. The neutral world accepted . . . [this] as decisive proof of British supremacy at sea."

After the Battle of the Dogger Bank and the consequent shackling of German dreadnoughts to their harbor buoys, different paths opened before the two opposing navies. The German Naval Staff turned to U-boat warfare and initiated a submarine campaign against merchant shipping, Allied and neutral, sailing to Allied ports. In Britain, the public was temporarily satisfied with the navy. *The National Review* saw in the restriction of "the second navy in the world to the mud banks of the Elbe . . . as supreme an exhibition of superior sea power as the world has witnessed." But this was not the mood at the Admiralty, where restless spirits wanted a more vigorous and imaginative employment of the navy's resources. Even before the Battle of the Dogger Bank, discussions were under way about the use of British sea power in offensive operations far from the North Sea.

CHAPTER 23

"A Demonstration at the Dardanelles"

For three thousand years in history and legend, the Straits of the Dardanelles, flowing for forty miles like a wide river between the hills of Europe and the plains of Asia Minor, have been a stage for courage and tragedy. Four miles from the southern entrance to the Straits stood the ancient city of Troy. At the Narrows—the classical Hellespont, where the Straits are less than a mile across—Xerxes led an army across on bridges of boats.* Here the mythical Leander swam the Hellespont at night to visit his lover, the virgin princess Hero, before, eventually, both were drowned. Here, in 1810, the Romantic poet Lord Byron swam the stream in emulation of the lovers. And here, in the early years of the Great War, occurred an effort to bring to fruition that war's only truly innovative strategy: an attempt, first by sea and then by land, to pierce and break down the barriers separating Russia from her allies and in so doing possibly to shorten the war.

The Dardanelles are a water passageway from the Mediterranean Sea and the Aegean to the Sea of Marmara. The mouth of the channel at Cape Helles on the Aegean is two miles wide, but once inside the Straits, the shoreline on either side opens out to a width of four and a half miles, then gradually comes together again at the Narrows, fourteen miles upstream. Above the Narrows, the passage widens again to an average of four miles until, twenty-six miles later, it reaches the Sea of Marmara. The water in the Straits is deep, up to 300 feet at the Narrows. Steep cliffs line the northern side, the shore of the Gallipoli peninsula; across, in Asia, where the Trojan plain reaches down to the island of Tenedos, the shoreline is low and the bot-

*Herodotus implausibly estimated Xerxes' force at 5,283,320 men.

tom is shallow. There is no tide in the Dardanelles, but water flowing from the Black Sea rivers and from the melting snows of the Caucasus Mountains creates a permanent current of 2 to 4 knots.

Three connected bodies of water—the Dardanelles, the Sea of Marmara, and the Bosporus—together make up one of the most important water passageways in the world. Linked, they form the only entrance to and exit from the Black Sea; they are a highway for all trade coming from the Danube, the Dniester, the Dnieper, and the Don and the great ports of Constantinople, Odessa, and Sebastopol. In 1914, an endless flow of steamships carried nine-tenths of Russia's exported grain through the Dardanelles. Control of this channel meant control of Russia's lifeline to the sea, to the West, to her allies. Because the Dardanelles were a Turkish waterway, Germany, Turkey's ally, meant to block them and thereby to isolate and strangle the empire of the tsars.

—

Since September 21, the Allied watchdog at the Aegean end of this critical waterway had been Vice Admiral Sackville Hamilton Carden, commander of the British East Mediterranean Squadron. Carden, a gray-bearded, fifty-seven-year-old, Anglo-Irish officer, had held this responsibility since the unlucky Rear Admiral Troubridge had been summoned home to face the inquiry into his role in the escape of *Goeben.* When this happened, Carden was occupying the position of admiral superintendent of the Malta dockyard, the final, preretirement posting of an average, undistinguished career. Certainly, Carden had never expected to command at sea again, much less be confronted with challenges of the most demanding naval and military importance. Then lightning struck, Troubridge vanished, and Carden, the only British vice admiral in the Mediterranean, found himself plucked from Malta and spirited away to command the squadron bottling up *Goeben.* Logically, this assignment should have gone to Rear Admiral Henry Limpus, who, as head of the British naval mission to Turkey, was thoroughly familiar with the Turkish government, its military and naval figures, and—of greatest immediate relevance—the defenses of the Dardanelles. Limpus was not appointed because of a delicately balanced calculation by the Foreign Office. By September 9, although the German admiral Wilhelm Souchon had become commander of the Ottoman navy and the German general Otto Liman von Sanders, the head of the German military mission, was virtual commander of the Turkish army, Turkey still remained neutral. Sir Edward Grey hoped that this neutrality could be preserved. At so uncertain a moment, it seemed to Grey that the sending of a British officer who knew most of Turkey's secrets to command a squadron off the Dardanelles might sufficiently offend the Turks as to tip the scales toward war. Thus, Limpus was sent to the Malta dockyard and Carden was brought to the fleet. This minuet of admirals enraged Churchill, who called it "a chivalry which surely outstripped common sense." Writing to Grey, he complained, "It now appears that Turkey can not only injure our whole naval position by a flagrant breach of neutrality about *Goeben,* but also is to have a veto over Admiralty appointments. . . . If [Sir Louis] Mallet [the British ambassador to Turkey] thinks he is dealing with a government amenable to argument, persuasion and proof of good faith, he is dreaming. . . . Nothing appeals to the Turkish government but force." Fisher was appalled. "Who expected Carden to be in command of a big fleet?" he wrote to Jellicoe. "He was made Admiral Superintendant at Malta to shelve him." Nevertheless, Carden was appointed and given the same belligerent instructions previously issued to Troubridge: "[Your] sole duty is to sink *Goeben* and *Breslau,* no matter what flag they fly, if they come out of the Dardanelles."

To carry out his task, Carden had his flagship, the battle cruiser *Indefatigable;* her sister *Indomitable;* two old French battleships, *Suffren* and *Vérité;* the light cruisers *Dublin* and *Gloucester;* twelve destroyers; and three British and three French submarines. For a week after the new admiral's arrival, the squadron patrolled peacefully, watching over the stream of Russian merchant ships still passing in and out of the Straits. At German insistence, the Turks had laid mines across the Narrows, but a small channel had been left open and the ships, after taking on a special pilot, continued to steam through unmolested. Then, on September 27, Carden's squadron stopped and boarded a Turkish destroyer coming out of the Dardanelles. German sailors were found on board, a violation of Turkish neutrality, and the ship was turned back. Immediately, without consulting the Turks, the German colonel commanding the forts at the Narrows ordered the waterway closed. All lighthouses were darkened, large signs were erected on the cliffs announcing that the Straits were sealed, and the minefields were extended across the Straits. Thereafter, despite international treaty obligations guaranteeing free passage of the Straits by all nations not at war with Turkey, the Dardanelles were closed. British military supplies could no longer reach Russia except through Archangel on the White Sea; Russian wheat, upon which the Tsar's empire depended for most of its foreign income, could no longer be exported. Hundreds of ships from Russia, Rumania, and Bulgaria, loaded with grain, lumber, and other products, clogged the harbor at Constantinople. Unable to find docking space, they anchored, their dense forest of masts and smokestacks swinging in unison on the stream.

The flow of merchant shipping had been cut, but for another month, Carden and his squadron continued to patrol the mouth of the Straits in peace. Then, on October 29, without awaiting a declaration of war, Admiral Souchon took *Goeben* and *Breslau,* both flying the Turkish flag, across the Black Sea and bombarded southern Russian ports. Britain, responding to this attack on her ally, dispatched an ultimatum to Turkey demanding removal of all German personnel from *Goeben* and *Breslau* within twelve hours. The British ultimatum expired at noon on October 31, and that afternoon Turkey declared war. Although Britain's retaliatory declaration waited until November 5, Churchill wanted an immediate demonstration of British displeasure. On November 3, Carden's two battle cruisers and the two French battleships bombarded the outer forts, on either side of the entrance to the Dardanelles. The bombardment was not part of any well-considered plan; rather, it was simply an expression of Churchill's belief, as he expressed it to Fisher, that "it is a good thing to give a prompt blow."

The action lasted twenty minutes. *Indomitable* and *Indefatigable* fired from 13,000 yards at Fort Sedd el Bahr on the European side while the two French battleships attacked the Kum Kale forts on the Asian side. The European forts remained silent throughout the bombardment, as the British ships were out of range, but a large magazine explosion in one of the Sedd el Bahr bastions killed five officers and sixty-one men and produced a column of gray smoke that rose an impressive 500 feet in the air. The French had less success. Because their ships were older and their guns had shorter range, they were forced to come in closer to Kum Kale. They were fired upon, at first slowly and inaccurately, but before they withdrew, shells were falling close to the ships. Overall for Carden, the day's lesson seemed positive. The admiral was encouraged to believe that by repeating and prolonging the bombardment, he could methodically destroy the outer forts, then move on and apply the same treatment to the intermediate and Narrows forts. And once the Turkish forts and guns had been blasted into silence, he could—if he wished and was so instructed—lead a British fleet into the Sea of Marmara.

This brief November encounter, while encouraging Carden and the Admiralty, also served to warn the Turks and Germans that the Straits' defenses needed strengthening. No new heavy guns could be procured and installed at short notice, but the fortress batteries were linked by telephones, range finders were set up, and range buoys laid in the water for better targeting. Mobile, quick-firing howitzers were brought from Adrianople to the Dardanelles and placed in concealed positions along the European and Asian shores. The number and power of searchlights along the waterway were increased. More German artillery officers and trained gun crews arrived. And the minefield was doubled, with eleven rather than five lines of mines stretching across the waterway.

While his enemies bolstered their defenses, Admiral Carden and his squadron, following their brief November exertions, lapsed into a three-month interlude of calm. *Indomitable* and *Indefatigable* were called home to England, and *Inflexible,* returning from the Falklands, replaced her two sisters at the Dardanelles. One exception to the general apathy occurred on December 13. Carden's officers, watching the Turks at the Narrows through field glasses from the entrance, could see Turkish ships and boats moving freely. The British submarine *B-11,* manned by two officers and eleven seamen, was dispatched to make trouble. Diving to eighty feet beneath the minefields and applying her submerged speed of 4 knots against a current in the Straits of 3 knots, the submarine proceeded laboriously up the northern shore to a point just below the Narrows. There, her raised periscope revealed a two-funneled gray warship lying at anchor. This was the 10,000-ton Turkish battleship *Messudieh,* built in 1874, rebuilt in 1902, now carrying two 9.2-inch and twelve 6-inch guns, and stationed below the Narrows to help protect the minefields. The old battleship had no chance; *B-11* fired one torpedo from 600 yards, dived, and felt the shock of the powerful explosion that meant the end of *Messudieh.* Subsequently, every member of *B-11*'s crew received a medal and her captain, Lieutenant Norman Holbrook, was awarded the Victoria Cross.

—

The real impetus for the Dardanelles and Gallipoli campaigns came from a general revulsion in Britain at the carnage taking place on the Western Front. The German march on Paris had been brought to a standstill, and by December 1914 huge armies confronted each other in trenches running from the Channel to Switzerland. No breakthrough appeared possible by either side: machine guns slaughtered infantrymen as soon as they climbed out of the trenches; by the end of November, Britain and France had lost almost a million men. This grim fact did not deter Field Marshal Sir John French, the Commander-in-Chief of the BEF, who insisted that the decisive theater lay in France and that the war could be won only by continuing to hurl waves of men into enemy machine-gun fire until somewhere, someday, the German line was pierced. It was this philosophy of war that led Siegfried Sassoon, a decorated soldier, to write,

You smug-faced crowds with kindling eye
Who cheer when soldier lads march by,
Sneak home and pray you'll never know
The hell where youth and laughter go.

Sir John French's belief was shared by France's government and generals and by Lord Kitchener, who, although he personally disliked Sir John French, remained generally supportive. Nevertheless, by the end of the year, a majority in the British War Council—Asquith, Churchill, Lloyd George, and Haldane—were eager for an alternative: a place where the Allies might attack the Central Powers at a weaker point with a lower cost in blood. This was a particularly British approach to war. Always in the past when fighting great continental powers, Britain had used her sea power to mount operations in secondary theaters; over time, these campaigns had drained the enemy's power and will to fight. And the form this strategy was to take in this particular war—an attack on the Dardanelles—had a particularly personal flavor. As First Lord of the Admiralty, Winston Churchill had helped to create the mightiest sea weapon in the history of the world. Yet this huge armada seemed almost impotent; it could not strike a telling blow because its enemy would not fight. In a man of Churchill's temperament, this passive role stirred bitter frustration. The first specific mention of an attack on the Dardanelles came in a War Council meeting on November 25, 1914, in connection with reports that the Turks were preparing an overland attack on Egypt and the Suez Canal. As a countermove, Churchill suggested a combined land and sea operation against the Dardanelles and the Gallipoli peninsula. Kitchener immediately declared that, although strategically the idea had merit, no troops were available. Churchill said that while a substantial military force—40,000, 50,000, 60,000 men—might be required, the soldiers need not necessarily be British. Fisher asked whether Greece could be persuaded to land an army on the Gallipoli peninsula. Grey replied that any immediate hopes of Greek participation were illusory, and the council passed to other business. But the seed of a campaign against Turkey had been planted.

By the end of December, the prospect of an interminable war of attrition on the Western Front seemed ever more likely. All the members of the War Council agreed that France was the decisive theater, but most believed that little progress could be made there unless the Central Powers were distracted and harmed in other areas. Churchill's restlessness about the gigantic, blood-letting frontal assaults in France was barely in check. "Are there not other alternatives than sending our armies to chew barbed wire in Flanders?" he demanded of Asquith on December 29. "Cannot the power of the Navy be brought more directly to bear upon the enemy? . . . We ought not to drift." Asquith had not replied when, by extraordinary coincidence, a voice from outside—an urgent appeal from a hard-pressed ally—precipitated a dramatic change in British policy. In the early hours of January 2, the Foreign Office received a message from Grand Duke Nicholas, the Commander-in-Chief of the Russian army. The Turkish army was seriously threatening the Russian army in the Caucasus, the grand duke said. Was there anything the British army or navy could do to persuade the Turks to draw off some of their troops?

The grand duke's message arrived at a moment when concern about Russia was acute in the British government. The Allies owed Russia much: the willingness of the grand duke and of Tsar Nicholas II to hurl the unprepared Russian army at East Prussia and Berlin in the opening weeks of the war had probably saved Paris, but it also had cost Russia the shattering defeats at Tannenberg and the Masurian Lakes. Russia had lost a million men, and secret reports of gross shortages of ammunition in Russia and of 800,000 Russian soldiers waiting without rifles behind the front lines had reached the War Office. Grey sent the grand duke's appeal to Kitchener, who, more than any other British minister, dreaded the possibility of a Russian collapse and the consequent transfer of German divisions to the Western Front. The field marshal took the telegram and walked over to the Admiralty Building to discuss with Churchill what might be done. Could Britain, for instance, make a demonstration at the Dardanelles? Kitchener asked. Churchill replied that a combined naval and military assault might be possible if Lord Kitchener could find the troops. Out of the question, Kitchener replied; not a single soldier could be spared from France. The demonstration he had in mind would be a purely naval attack. Kitchener returned to the War Office and later that day wrote in a gentler, more apologetic tone to Churchill, "I do not see that we can do anything that will very seriously help the Russians in the Caucasus. . . . We have no troops to land anywhere. . . . The only place that a demonstration might have some effect . . . would be the Dardanelles. . . . [But] we [the army] shall not be ready for anything big for some months."

There, despite fears of a Russian collapse, the grand duke's appeal might have died but for Winston Churchill's presence at the Admiralty. The First Lord, however, was reluctant to reject a challenge and, on the morning of January 3, he summoned the Admiralty War Group and told them of the Russian appeal and Kitchener's statement. Only the Royal Navy remained. What would be the prospects for a purely naval attack? The admirals were not optimistic, but a consensus was reached that some kind of effort—perhaps a renewal of the bombardment of the Dardanelles forts—could be made. Accordingly that same day, the grand duke was told that a demonstration would be carried out, although it was hardly likely to lead to a significant withdrawal of Turkish troops from the Caucasus.

This telegram pledged Britain and the Admiralty to action of some kind; now Churchill and Fisher faced the question of what that action should be. Fisher, ignoring Kitchener's declaration, advocated an immediate, powerful, joint naval and military assault: "I CONSIDER THAT THE ATTACK ON TURKEY HOLDS THE FIELD," he wrote that same day to Churchill. "But ONLY if it's IMMEDIATE. However, it won't be." He proposed taking 75,000 British troops and 25,000 Indian troops from France, embarking them at Marseilles, and landing them on the southern, or Asian, side of the Dardanelles. Simultaneously, the Greeks were to land on the northern side of the Dardanelles, which was the Gallipoli peninsula, while the Bulgarians would march on Adrianople and Constantinople. As for the navy, Fisher proposed that Admiral Sturdee take a fleet of British predreadnought battleships and ram this force through the Dardanelles into the Sea of Marmara. Reading Fisher's memorandum, Churchill saw immediately that the first three of the four ingredients of the First Sea Lord's plan were illusory: neither Kitchener nor Sir John French would permit the taking of 100,000 troops from France; the Greeks were far from ready to land in Gallipoli; the Bulgarians were still waiting to determine which side was most likely to win the war. The one element of Fisher's plan that fell within the Admiralty's possible power to effect was the First Sea Lord's suggestion that the old battleships force the Straits, if necessary on their own. To this proposal, Churchill was instantly attentive.

Unfortunately, Fisher's memorandum and Churchill's early reaction to it also represented the beginning of a misunderstanding that would grow and fester until it led to career disaster for both men. Fisher, writing the memorandum in his customary florid language, never mentioned and never imagined a naval offensive that would attempt to force the Dardanelles by ships alone. But Churchill, even as he dismissed the unrealistic elements of Fisher's letter, seized on the old admiral's reference to forcing the Straits with old battleships. Eight *Canopus*es and eight *Majestic*s, all in the category of "His Majesty's less valuable ships," were due for scrapping in 1915. A purely naval assault using them would not need the permission of Lord Kitchener, or the assistance of the Greeks or the Bulgarians. The Dardanelles forts, it was believed, were armed mainly with old guns, which could be outranged by heavy naval guns; the bombarding ships need not come in close and would therefore be untouched. Once the fleet had overcome the decrepit Turkish forts, the minefields could be rapidly cleared and the battleships could sail through to the Sea of Marmara. From this vantage point, a broad and glittering strategic vista opened to the First Lord's imagination. *Goeben* would be sunk and nothing would stand between the Allied battleships and Constantinople. So wobbly was the Ottoman empire that even a threat to its capital would topple the state. And if the state did not surrender, the battleships would wreak havoc on the city: the Turkish capital was built largely of wood and the guns of the fleet could create an inferno. Turkey's only munitions factory and its principal gun and rifle factories were on the Sea of Marmara, within the range of naval gunfire; the railway lines to Europe and, on the Asian shore, into Anatolia, lay along the coast. The example of *Goeben* was also, in a way, encouraging. If the appearance before Constantinople of a single battle cruiser carrying ten 11-inch guns had been instrumental in pushing Turkey into war, surely the arrival of twelve battleships carrying forty-eight 12-inch guns should suffice to push her out. With Turkey out of the war, the sea route to Russia would be reopened, Western munitions would flow to the Russian army, and Russian wheat would come out to the West. The wavering neutral states of the Balkans—Greece, Rumania, and Bulgaria—would know which side Victory had favored and would rush to join the Allied cause. And all of this—the delivery of a masterstroke to shorten the war—would have been achieved by the great weapon Churchill held in his hand, the Royal Navy.

Churchill sought the opinion of Admiral Carden. Fisher had agreed that Carden should be consulted, but the First Sea Lord was not shown the message. In the telegram, there was no mention of British troops from France, of Greek troops, or of Bulgarian troops. Instead the First Lord asked simply: "Do you consider the forcing of the Dardanelles by ships alone a practicable operation? It is assumed older battleships fitted with mine-bumpers would be used, preceded by colliers or other merchant craft as mine-bumpers and sweepers. Importance of results would justify severe loss. Let me know your views."

Carden's answer, when it arrived on January 5, was cautious. The admiral did not like what appeared to be the Churchillian concept of "forcing" the Dardanelles using merchant ships out in front as mine bumpers: "I do not consider Dardanelles can be rushed," he said. "They might be forced by extended operations with large number of ships." This answer, although guarded, was sufficient to encourage Churchill, who read it to the War Council and then took it back to the Admiralty for discussion. Fisher saw Carden's telegram and expressed no opinion, but, Churchill wrote later, "he seemed at this time not merely to favor the enterprise, but to treat it as a matter practically decided." Accordingly, on January 6, Churchill sent another message to Carden: "Your view is agreed with by high authorities here. Please telegraph in detail what you think could be done by extended operations, what force would be needed, and how you consider it should be used."

The War Council met again on January 8. Kitchener warned that the Germans were about to begin a new offensive in France. Lloyd George appealed for a British countermove elsewhere; his preference was the Balkans, in order to bring aid to Serbia. Kitchener replied that Sir John French still believed that the German lines in France could be broken and insisted that no effort should be made in another theater "until the impossibility of breaking through . . . [in France] was proved." The war secretary then seemed to take a momentary step back from the Western Front philosophy; he added that if an offensive were to be launched in a secondary theater, "the Dardanelles appeared to be the most suitable objective. A hundred and fifty thousand men," Kitchener thought, "might be sufficient to assist the fleet in forcing the Straits and capturing Constantinople." Having offered this observation, Kitchener then reverted to his unvarying mantra: "Unfortunately, I have no troops available." No one on the War Council challenged the inconsistency of Kitchener's comments; at that time, whatever the Supreme War Lord said was accepted without question. If Kitchener believed that an attack on the Straits might succeed, then so it might. And if Kitchener said that no British troops were available for such an enterprise, none were.

On the morning of January 12, Carden's detailed operational plan arrived in London. The admiral suggested a slow progress with the application of overwhelming force, shelling and silencing the forts one by one. First, he would attack the entrance forts at long range from outside the Straits. Once the entrance forts were destroyed, he would slowly and methodically progress up the Straits. The numerous secondary batteries of the fleet would silence the concealed guns and deal with the mobile batteries. Minesweepers would sweep a channel through which he would approach the heavy guns and forts at Chanak (Çanakkale) on the Narrows. He would demolish these and then advance into the Sea of Marmara. He would not hurry or risk taking heavy losses. "Time required for operations depends greatly on morale of enemy under bombardment; garrison largely stiffened by the Germans," he noted. "Also on weather conditions. Gales now frequent. Might do it all in a month about. Expenditure of ammunition would be large." The force required, he said, should be twelve battleships, three battle cruisers—two to deal with the *Goeben* in the Sea of Marmara—three light cruisers, sixteen destroyers, six submarines, and twelve minesweepers.

The plan was discussed the same day by the Admiralty War Group, which included Fisher, Wilson, Jackson, and Oliver. No one protested. Instead, "the plan produced a great impression upon everyone who saw it," said Churchill later. "Both the First Sea Lord and the Chief of Staff [Oliver] seemed favourable to it. No one at any time threw the slightest doubt upon its technical soundness. . . . On the contrary, they all treated it as an extremely interesting and hopeful proposal." Indeed, Fisher made a proposal of great significance. He suggested sending to Carden the new battleship *Queen Elizabeth,* the first of a class of five new dreadnoughts armed with eight 15-inch guns. The vessel, at that moment the most powerful warship afloat, had been commissioned at Portsmouth on December 22, and was scheduled to depart in February for gun calibration exercises in the calm, submarine-free waters of the Mediterranean off Gibraltar. Fisher now proposed that the dreadnought should test her huge guns against the Turkish forts at the Dardanelles rather than "firing all her ammunition uselessly into the sea at Gibraltar." *Queen Elizabeth*'s guns had a range of 22,000 yards; thus she could easily stand off and fire out of range of Turkish guns. (The Admiralty placed restrictions on her use: to preserve her gun barrels from becoming worn, the dreadnought was never to fire salvos; rather she must fire slowly and deliberately, one gun, one shell at a time.) Later, Fisher went further, adding to Carden's force the two latest of the predreadnoughts, *Lord Nelson* and *Agamemnon,* both commissioned after *Dreadnought* herself.

Thus, by mid-January, Churchill and the Admiralty were close to committing the fleet to steaming forty miles up a narrow waterway defended by forts equipped with heavy guns and also by numerous batteries of mobile howitzers. Traditionally, a bombardment of forts by ships was abhorred in the Royal Navy. The idea that naval guns should be used against land-based artillery had been condemned by Nelson, who had declared that "any sailor who attacked a fort was a fool." Mahan had elaborated: "A ship can no more stand up against a fort . . . than the fort could run a race with a ship." The primary mission of warships, these authorities declared, was to control the sea by sinking enemy warships, not to attack forts, which, no matter how many times they are hit, always refuse to sink. Ships are more vulnerable than forts: a battleship 500 feet long is a large target; any part of it can be hit, sometimes with drastic consequences for the entire vessel. A fort, on the other hand, cannot be greatly harmed except by hitting the guns themselves; usually only a direct hit will put a piece of coastal artillery out of action. On this point—the inefficacy of naval bombardment—Fisher had direct experience. The First Sea Lord had participated in the British navy's most famous previous effort to subdue land forts. In July 1883, Fisher, as captain of *Inflexible,* the most powerful battleship in the world at that time, had participated in an all-day bombardment by the British Mediterranean Fleet of the Egyptian forts at Alexandria. During the day, *Inflexible,* anchored outside the breakwater, spasmodically belched eighty-eight 16-inch shells at the forts. By late afternoon, the fleet had fired 3,000 shells but only ten of forty-four Egyptian heavy guns had been silenced.

Churchill believed that the lessons of this experience, now thirty years in the past, had been modified if not invalidated by the new technology of modern warfare. He had been profoundly impressed by the success of German heavy artillery on the Western Front. The fortresses of Liège, Namur, and Antwerp had ranked among the world's strongest, yet they had been reduced within a few days, sometimes within a few hours, by German siege howitzers. Once the bombardment began, the forts had collapsed, leaving a few dazed and blackened Belgians to crawl from the ruins and surrender. If the Belgian forts were helpless against these heavy land guns, how could the old Turkish forts on the Dardanelles withstand the enormous 12-inch and 15-inch guns of battleships? Thereupon, there formed in Churchill's mind a glorious picture of *Queen Elizabeth* relentlessly blasting the Turkish defenses with tremendous shells from her monster guns.

Unfortunately, the First Lord ignored or misunderstood the differences between controlling German land artillery at close range from forward positions, and firing naval guns at targets seven or eight miles away with no means of accurately spotting the fall of shot. The German siege howitzer was a fat, short-barreled cannon that lobbed its shell high into the air so that the missile plunged down on its target. An observer close to the target observed the location of the shell's impact and then signaled the battery to correct the range until the shell fell precisely on the desired spot. Large naval guns had an entirely different design and purpose. Shells fired from a long barrel in a low trajectory over thousands of yards were designed to strike and sink enemy warships at the greatest possible range. Spotting the fall of shot at sea was made easier for ships by the eruption of a great column of water where the shell hit. By tracking these water towers through binoculars and correct-

The North Sea: Admiral John Jellicoe's view from the bridge of his flagship, the dreadnought *Iron Duke*.
[Imperial War Museum]

Admiral John Jellicoe on the eve of taking command of the Grand Fleet.
[Imperial War Museum]

Admiral David Beatty.
[Imperial War Museum]

Iron Duke, flagship of the Great Fleet.
[Imperial War Museum]

Jellicoe climbing to the bridge of *Iron Duke*.
[Imperial War Museum]

The German battle cruiser *Goeben,* whose escape to Constantinople helped push Turkey into the war (*Goeben*'s identical sister, *Moltke,* fought the war in the North Sea). *[Imperial War Museum]*

Beatty's flagship, the battle cruiser *Lion*.
[Imperial War Museum]

The German cruiser *Blücher* sinking at the battle of the Dogger Bank.
[Imperial War Museum]

Prince Louis of Battenberg.

Admiral Maximilian von Spee.

Admiral Christopher Cradock.
[Imperial War Museum]

Lord Kitchener and the most famous of all recruiting posters. In the first eighteen months of the war, one million Britons volunteered for military service. *[Imperial War Museum]*

Left to right: Commodore Roger Keyes, Admiral John de Robeck, General Ian Hamilton. *[Imperial War Museum]*

Admiral of the Fleet Lord Fisher of Kilverstone.

Winston Churchill and Jacky Fisher.
[Press Association]

Admiral Reinhard Scheer.
[Imperial War Museum]

Admiral Franz Hipper.
[Imperial War Museum]

The British battle cruiser *Invincible,* destroyed at the battle of Jutland, its bow and stern resting separately on the shallow bottom of the North Sea. From the right, the British destroyer *Badger* approaches to pick up survivors.
[Imperial War Museum]

Left to right: Hindenburg, the kaiser, and Ludendorff.
[Imperial War Museum]

Bethmann-Hollweg.

Tirpitz.

Woodrow Wilson.

The president and Colonel House.

The German dreadnought *Bayern* sinking at anchor in Scapa Flow.
[Imperial War Museum]

ing their aim, the ship's gunners hoped eventually to hit their enemy. When a ship is firing at a fort, on the other hand, the impact of a shell produces, not an easily discernible column of water, but a cloud of debris and dust that further obscures the target, giving the observer, thousands of yards away, little help in correcting his aim. In addition, warship shells fired in a flat trajectory would not plunge onto or near the target; more likely, they would pass overhead and hit many yards—even hundreds of yards—behind.

But all of this was still to be learned.

—

The meeting of the War Council on January 13, 1915, was a prolonged and exhausting session lasting all day. Not until after sunset did the council turn to the Dardanelles. Churchill explained Admiral Carden's plan, which had arrived at the Admiralty the day before. As Hankey described the scene:

> The War Council had been sitting all day. The blinds had been drawn to shut out the winter evening. The air was heavy and the table presented that rather disheveled appearance that results from a long session. . . . At this point events took a dramatic turn for Churchill suddenly revealed his well-kept secret of a naval attack on the Dardanelles! The idea caught on at once. The whole atmosphere changed. Fatigue was forgotten. The War Council turned eagerly from the dreary prospect of a "slogging match" on the Western Front to brighter prospects, as they seemed, in the Mediterranean. The navy, in whom everyone had implicit confidence and whose opportunities so far had been limited, was to come into the front line. . . . Churchill unfolded his plans with the skill that might be expected of him, lucidly, but quietly and without exaggerated optimism.

Pointing to a map, the First Lord declared that the Admiralty "believed that a plan could be made for systematically reducing all the forts within a few weeks. Once the forts were reduced, the minefields could be cleared and the fleet would proceed up to Constantinople and destroy *Goeben.*" Churchill declared that ships for the enterprise, including *Queen Elizabeth,* were available.

Churchill's argument, Lloyd George said later, was delivered "with all the inexorable force and pertinacity, together with the mastery of detail he always commands when he is really interested in a subject." So deep was the sense of frustration, so strong the apparent need that something be done, and so infectiously enthusiastic was Churchill's presentation, that most of those who heard it were captured by its novelty and simplicity. There was no opposition. Churchill's principal naval advisers, Admirals of the Fleet Fisher and Wilson, were present, but were not called upon for their opinions, nor did they offer any remarks. Their silence permitted Churchill and the other ministers to take their acquiescence for granted. Kitchener said the plan was worth trying and that "we could leave off the bombardment if it did not prove effective." During the discussion, Asquith was seen to be writing. At length the prime minister read out the conclusion he had written: "That the Admiralty should prepare for a naval expedition in February to bombard and take the Gallipoli peninsula with Constantinople as its objective." The War Council approved unanimously. Later, many of the ministers at the meeting differed as to whether any final decision had been made. Asquith himself understood that the council was pledged to nothing more than preparations. Eventually the Dardanelles Commission was to ask, How could a fleet "take" a peninsula? How could it occupy Constantinople? But these and other questions were not asked until two years later.

—

Up to mid-January, operational planning at the Admiralty seemed to be proceeding smoothly. The French government promised to place a squadron of four battleships under Carden's command. Nevertheless, even as plans for the naval attack were taking form around him, Fisher's enthusiasm was fading. As early as January 19, the First Sea Lord was complaining to Jellicoe, who he knew would provide a sympathetic ear: "The Cabinet have decided on taking the Dardanelles solely with the navy using fifteen battleships and 32 other vessels, and keeping out there three battle cruisers and a flotilla of destroyers *all urgently required at the decisive theater at home.* There is only one way out and that is to resign. But you say 'No!' which simply means I am a consenting party to what I absolutely disapprove. *I don't agree with one single step taken. . . . The way the war is conducted both ashore and afloat is chaotic! We have a new plan every week.*" Two days later, Fisher wrote again to Jellicoe, "I just abominate the Dardanelles operation, unless a great change is made and it is settled to be a military operation with 200,000 men in conjunction with the fleet. I believe Kitchener is coming now to this sane view of the matter."

Fisher was not opposed to all amphibious operations; indeed, he had always believed that the British army "is a projectile to be fired by the navy." It was the navy's job to carry soldiers from here to there, but not to fight a land campaign. He was quite prepared for a combined navy-army operation but he would have liked it somewhere other than at the Dardanelles. His own strong preference was for a large-scale Russian landing on the German Baltic coast, followed by a march to Berlin. With this in mind, his great building program, initiated within a week of his return to the Admiralty in November, had called for a large number of armor-plated landing barges capable of carrying 500 men each and equipped with ramps for rapid disembarkation. The first of these craft were now approaching completion. But now, apparently, they were to go, not to the Baltic, but to the Dardanelles.

Underlying the specific reasons Fisher gave for opposing Churchill lay deeper reasons based on personality. His motives for turning against the Dardanelles operation stemmed at least in part from the strange administrative position into which they all had drifted. In November 1914, Asquith had formed the War Council as a select committee of the Cabinet, including Asquith, Haldane, Kitchener, Lloyd George, and Grey, along with some others like Arthur Balfour, the Conservative former prime minister. There was already an imbalance at the top: the secretary of state for war was an eminent soldier and a national hero, while the First Lord of the Admiralty was a civilian with no naval and only early military experience. Churchill was keenly aware of this inequity: "I had not the same weight or authority as those two ministers [Asquith and Kitchener] nor the same power, and if they said 'This is to be done, or not be done' that settled it," said Churchill. This modest statement is not entirely convincing. Churchill possessed unparalleled powers of persuasion and argued with incomparable virtuosity. But in the first year of war Kitchener's prestige and authority were overwhelming. "All powerful, imperturbable, reserved, he dominated absolutely our counsels at this time," Churchill said of him. On specific matters of strategy and prosecution of the war, Asquith, an urbane political and parliamentary compromiser, and Churchill, a brilliantly imaginative and articulate forty-year-old, simply could not challenge this colossus.

Below this level of supreme authority stood the generals and admirals present in War Council meetings to advise if called upon. Here, a misconception had hardened into permanence. Ministers assumed that the service chiefs would freely speak their minds, without being invited to do so, but these experts did not consider that they should break in to express opinions or dissent. Asquith, who always presided, never invited the attending service chiefs to speak but rather allowed himself to be wholly guided on military and naval matters by the secretary of state for war and the First Lord of the Admiralty. Fisher rarely spoke and never protested. "I made it a rule that I would not at the War Council kick Winston Churchill's shins," he said. "He [Churchill] was my chief and it was silence or resignation." Thus, whether they agreed with the First Lord or not, the admirals sat silent; unfortunately, this silence was taken as assent. The War Council took it for granted that when Churchill spoke, he had first settled things within his department and was speaking for the entire Admiralty.

There was another imbalance that grated on Fisher. His position was entirely different from Kitchener's. Unlike Kitchener, he was not a minister; he was only a technical adviser. He could not make policy or vote, even on matters that affected the navy. Yet to the British public Admiral of the Fleet Lord Fisher of Kilverstone was something more than the incumbent First Sea Lord: he *was* the Royal Navy. His reputation was as overwhelming as the dreadnoughts he had built, and he spoke with the blast effect of their massive guns. To Fisher, sitting and listening day after day while Kitchener dominated the War Council with his opinions, it seemed that the imperial war lord was showing an inappropriate disregard—even disrespect—for what in Britain had always been the senior service.

Until mid-January, Fisher did not openly complain about the Dardanelles plan; indeed, it was he who had proposed adding *Queen Elizabeth.* But following the January 13 meeting, Fisher had deeper misgivings. He tried to fix his forebodings about the Dardanelles adventure into some logical argument that would establish his general sense of uneasiness and that he could present to Churchill, whom he enormously liked and admired. But when he tried, Churchill had no difficulty, either privately or publicly, in proving him wrong. Not only did Fisher's own cherished scheme, a naval campaign in the Baltic, now obviously have no chance—but also, as he saw it, the Grand Fleet, the central pillar of British naval supremacy and war strategy, was now being nibbled away by the devouring demands of the Dardanelles. Fisher, after all, was the First Sea Lord who, ten years earlier, had brought the British navy home and concentrated it against the growing threat from Imperial Germany. Now, returned to office, he insisted that nothing be done to permit the loss of this hard-won supremacy.

Fisher himself precipitated a crisis on January 25 when sent his views in writing to the prime minister with a copy to Churchill. "First Lord," he wrote in a cover note, "I have no desire to continue a useless resistance in the War Council to plans I cannot concur in, but I would ask that the enclosed may be printed and circulated to members [of the War Council] before the next meeting." The memorandum pointed to the folly of the whole Dardanelles scheme. "We play into Germany's hands," Fisher wrote, "if we risk fighting ships in any subsidiary operations such as coastal bombardments or the attack of fortified places without military cooperation, for we thereby increase the possibility that the Germans may be able to engage our fleet with some approach to equality of strength. . . . Even the older ships should not be risked, for they cannot be lost without losing men and they form the only reserve behind our Grand Fleet. . . . The sole justification of coastal bombardments and attacks by the fleet on fortified places, such as the contemplated bombardment of the Dardanelles forts . . . , is to force a decision at sea, and so far and no farther can they be justified." Britain, Fisher argued, should be content with maintaining the North Sea blockade of Germany. "Being already in possession of all that a powerful fleet can give a country, we should continue quietly to enjoy the advantage without dissipating our strength in operations that cannot improve the position." Although Fisher asked that this document be circulated to the War Council, Asquith, on Churchill's recommendation, refused to do so.

Instead, Churchill replied on January 27, declaring that the central argument in Fisher's paper was indisputable: the primary responsibility of the Admiralty was to maintain the Grand Fleet at a strength sufficient to ensure defeat of the German High Seas Fleet in battle. This responsibility, the First Lord argued, was being faithfully discharged. Once again, as he had in November and December, the First Lord provided a comparative list of the numerical strength of the two fleets. In addition to everything necessary to ensure victory in a climactic North Sea battle, Churchill pointed out, Britain also had twenty-one old battleships, heavily armed and armored, completely manned and supplied with their own ammunition, lying idle since they were unfit to meet modern German ships. "Not to use them where necessary because of some fear that there would be an outcry if a ship is lost would be wrong," Churchill insisted.

Meanwhile, planning for the operation continued. By the last week of January, supplies were assembled and ships were under orders. All that was needed was the final approval of the War Council. This was to be given at a meeting scheduled for 11:30 on the morning of January 28. That morning, Churchill found Fisher's resignation on his desk: "I entreat you to believe that if as I think really desirable for a complete unity of purpose in the war that I should gracefully disappear and revert to roses at Richmond," Fisher had written. "There will not be in my heart the least lingering thought of anything but regard and affection and indeed much admiration towards yourself." Knowing that Asquith had refused to circulate his memorandum and that War Council members would be unaware of his views, Fisher also wrote to the prime minister, saying that he did not wish to attend the War Council meeting that day: "I am not in accord with the First Lord and do not think it would be seemly to say so before the Council. . . . I say that the . . . Dardanelles bombardments can only be justified on naval grounds by military cooperation which would compensate for the loss in ships and irreplaceable officers and men. As purely naval operations they are unjustifiable. . . . I am very reluctant to leave the First Lord. I have a great personal affection and admiration for him, but I see no possibility of a union of ideas, and unity is essential in war so I refrain from any desire of remaining as a stumbling block. The British Empire ceases if our Grand Fleet ceases. No risks can be taken."

The withdrawal of Fisher's support on the very day that the War Council was scheduled to approve the enterprise was awkward for both Asquith and Churchill. Struggling to keep the old admiral in line, the First Lord insisted that Fisher talk to the prime minister. Arriving with Churchill in Asquith's Downing Street study a few minutes before the council meeting began, Fisher described to the prime minister his objections to a Dardanelles operation. Churchill urged that it be allowed to continue. Asquith, forced to choose, decided that the attack should go forward. Fisher received this decision in silence and both the prime minister and the First Lord assumed that he had accepted it. Together, the three men then went downstairs to the meeting of the War Council in the Cabinet Room.

Fisher attended this meeting in the belief that in their just completed conversation, Asquith had said that a final decision on the Dardanelles was not to be taken that day. The mood at the council meeting was cheerfully optimistic; Churchill's continuing enthusiasm had colored the views of his colleagues. The First Lord reported that preparations for the attack on the Dardanelles were well advanced, but that the council must understand that the expedition "undoubtedly involves risks." As soon as Churchill finished, Fisher intervened to say that "he had understood that this question would not be raised at this meeting and that the prime minister knew his views on the subject." To this, Asquith replied that "in view of the steps which already had been taken, the question could not be well left in abeyance." Fisher thereupon stood up and made for the door. Kitchener saw this and, jumping to his feet, succeeded in reaching the door first. Steering Fisher to a window, he quietly asked the admiral what he was going to do. Fisher replied that he would not go back to the table and that he intended to resign as First Sea Lord. Kitchener pointed out that Fisher was the only man present who disagreed with the proposed operation; that the prime minister had made a decision and that it was the First Sea Lord's duty to his country to accept it and continue in office. Reluctantly, Fisher went back to the table where ministers were competing in optimistic predictions. Kitchener now declared that a naval attack was vitally important; the great merit of this form of offensive action, he said, was that "if satisfactory progress could not be made, the attack could be broken off." Balfour said that "it was difficult to imagine a more hopeful operation." Grey said that "the Turks would be paralyzed with fear when they heard that the forts were being destroyed one by one"; that the neutral Balkan powers, all anxious to be on the winning side, would watch the progress of this effort, and that he hoped that success would finally settle the attitude of Bulgaria. Through all of this, Asquith noticed, Fisher maintained "an obstinate and ominous silence."

The meeting adjourned at 2:00 p.m. to resume in the late afternoon. During this interval, Churchill, who had seen Kitchener talking privately to Fisher, spoke to the old admiral in his room at the Admiralty. The conversation was "long and very friendly," in Churchill's phrase, "I am in no way concealing the great and continuous pressure which I put upon the old admiral," Churchill admitted later, and Fisher often complained to friends about his inability to withstand these tactics. "He always out-argues me," he said to one. And to another: "I am sure I am right, I am sure I am right, but he is always convincing me against my will. I hear him talk and he seems to make the difficulties vanish and when he is gone I sit down and write him a letter and say I agree. Then I go to bed and can't sleep, and his talk passes away and I know I am right. So I get up and write him another letter and say I don't agree, and so it goes on." Something of this kind happened on the afternoon of January 28. By the end of his talk with Churchill, Fisher had consented to support the Dardanelles operation.

When the War Council reconvened in the late afternoon, Churchill—accompanied by Fisher—was able to announce that everyone at the Admiralty agreed that the navy would undertake the operation. Fisher's conversion seemed, for the moment, to be complete. "When I finally decided to go in," Fisher said later, "I went the whole hog, *totus porcus.*" Indeed, Churchill had been so successful that Fisher added *Lord Nelson* and *Agamemnon* as well as *Queen Elizabeth* to the operation. "This I took as the point of final decision," Churchill wrote. "After it, I never looked back. We had left the region of discussion and consultation, of balancing and misgivings. The matter had passed into the domain of action."

Fisher, momentarily defeated, remained unconvinced. In his own mind, his position was clear: he had favored a joint attack but he fiercely opposed a purely naval attack. He had made this view clear to the First Lord, to the prime minister, and to his colleagues at the Admiralty. Under pressure, he had been persuaded to support the attack. "When the operation was undertaken, my duty from that time on was to see that the government plan was carried out as successfully as possible with the available means. I did everything I could to secure its success. I put my whole heart into it and worked like a Trojan." But in private, he never stopped expressing his personal opinion. "The more I consider the Dardanelles the less I like it," he wrote to Churchill on March 4. At the end of March, he wrote, "A failure or check in the Dardanelles would be nothing. A failure in the North Sea would be ruin." On April 5, he wrote to Churchill again, "You are just simply eaten up with the Dardanelles and cannot think of anything else. Damn the Dardanelles! They will be our grave!"

CHAPTER 24

The Minefields

The whole fourteen-mile length of the Straits from the entrance at Cape Helles up to the Narrows at Chanak was within range of different types of Turkish artillery; indeed, there was no point in this stretch of water where a hostile vessel could not be hit by direct fire. The defense was constructed in three layers. The entrance was guarded by the outer forts, old, crenellated masonry structures, built on the white cliffs of the northern or European side. The massive fort of Sedd el Bahr, built in the seventeenth century against the Venetians, housed a mixed group of guns: two 11-inch, four 10-inch, and four 6-inch guns, with ranges up to 8,000 yards; this seemed ample, as the distance across the mouth of the Straits was only 4,000 yards. Nearby, around the point, the Cape Helles fort contained two 9.4-inch guns, which could reach out to 10,000 yards. Across the Straits, on the low green banks of the southern or Asian side, the Kum Kale fort housed two 11-inch, four 10-inch, one 8-inch, and two 6-inch guns. Another fort on the Asian shore contained two 9.4-inch guns. In sum, a total of sixteen heavy and seven medium-range guns defended the entrance to the Dardanelles. Inside the entrance where the Straits widen to four and a half miles, the Turks had established an intermediate defense consisting of medium guns, mostly 6-inch, situated in five permanent batteries, one on the European side, the other four on the Asian side. After the Allied bombardment in November 1914, the Germans and Turks made additions to this intermediate defense, bringing in eight mobile 6-inch howitzer batteries of four guns each. The number of searchlight batteries covering the minefields was increased to eight.

The ultimate defense of the Dardanelles lay at the Narrows, fourteen miles upstream from the entrance. Here, where Leander supposedly swam and where Xerxes built his bridge of boats, the channel is less than a mile across. The Narrows were protected by two massive ancient fortresses, at Kilid Bahr on the European shore and Chanak Kale on the Asian. In front of each of these old citadels, just above the beach, fortifications with heavy earth parapets had recently been constructed. Here, the Turks had mounted seventy-two guns of differing ranges and calibers, ranging from 14-inch and 11-inch down to 9.2-inch. Although less than a score of these guns were of modern design and ammunition was limited, they posed a formidable obstacle. And more ominous even than the guns were the minefields laid just below the Narrows, between Kephez and Chanak. Here, 324 mines were arranged in ten lines, ninety yards apart.

To overwhelm these defenses, the Admiralty collected warships from around the world. Admiral Carden was given the new superdreadnought *Queen Elizabeth* with eight 15-inch guns, the battle cruiser *Inflexible* with eight 12-inch guns, and twelve British and four French predreadnought battleships carrying a total of fifty-six 12-inch and eight 10-inch guns. Eight of the old battleships—*Cornwallis, Irresistible, Ocean, Albion, Canopus, Vengeance, Majestic,* and *Prince George*—were scheduled for scrapping within fifteen months, but meanwhile their old 12-inch guns were to wear themselves out bombarding old Turkish forts at the Dardanelles. The Admiralty also had added *Triumph* and *Swiftsure,* the odd pair of 10-inch-gun battleships originally built for Chile, now—with Spee eliminated—free to return from the Far East. The four French battleships—*Suffren, Bouvet, Gaulois,* and *Charlemagne*—were contemporaries of the British predreadnoughts and similarly armed. Carden also had four light cruisers, fifteen British and four French destroyers, and four British and four French submarines. Lowliest, and at this time of unrecognized significance, were twenty-one British and fourteen French fishing trawlers converted into minesweepers. Two battalions of Royal Marines were assigned to serve as a temporary landing force, not to be put ashore against entrenched opposition or a superior force. Carden's deputy was Rear Admiral John de Robeck, who was happy to be transferred from the dull assignment of commanding old cruisers patrolling against unlikely German raiders off Cape Finisterre, and Carden's Chief of Staff was the indefatigable Roger Keyes, shifted from command of the long-range submarines based at Harwich on the North Sea. In 1906 and 1907, Keyes had served as naval attaché at Constantinople and often had hired a steamer in order to study the Dardanelles forts through his telescope. Now he was to serve under the three British admirals who, in sequence, commanded the fleet at the Dardanelles from January 1915 to January 1916.

Carden's rear bases were Malta and Alexandria, but his advance base was established at Mudros on the Greek island of Lemnos, sixty miles southwest of the Dardanelles. Mudros was an immense natural harbor, two or three miles across and thirty to forty-five feet deep, capable of sheltering hundreds of vessels. Greece was not at war, but the Anglophile Prime Minister, Eleuthérios Venizélos, permitted the Allies to use the island as a base against Greece's age-old enemy, Turkey. When Rear Admiral Rosslyn Wester Wemyss arrived on February 22 to serve as base commander at Mudros, the sleepy Aegean village was not remotely prepared to become a major naval or military base. It contained only a church and seventy or eighty small houses of stone, timber, or mud, inhabited by fishermen who also grew olives and grapes. The harbor had only a single small wooden pier. There were no materials for constructing larger piers, no facilities for loading or unloading ships, no shore accommodations, and not enough fresh water. When, on March 4, 5,000 Australian troops arrived from Egypt, they were forced to remain aboard their ships from where they looked out on the brilliant blue water of the harbor and, beyond, a landscape of dry grass, small gnarled trees, and bare, windswept hills.

Carden's attack on the outer forts began in radiant sunshine on the morning of February 19. The sea was calm and there was no breath of wind when Carden's flagship, the battle cruiser *Inflexible,* and five British and four French predreadnought battleships anchored in transparent blue water and began a slow, deliberate, long-range bombardment of the forts, 12,000 yards away. The Turks, their guns out of range, remained silent. At 2:00 p.m., Carden closed to 6,000 yards, where his battleships' secondary armament opened heavy fire. Still, the Turkish guns did not reply. But at 4:45 p.m., when Carden sent *Vengeance, Cornwallis,* and *Suffren* in closer still—to 3,000 and 4,000 yards—the Turkish forts on both sides of the straits erupted into a hot cannonade, showing that they had not been destroyed at all. Then, with daylight fading and some of the forts shrouded in smoke and dust, Carden ordered a cease-fire. His deputy, Rear Admiral de Robeck in *Vengeance,* requested permission to prolong the attack, but Carden refused. The results of the bombardment were inconclusive. The Allied ships had fired 139 12-inch shells. The forts had been hit many times, but the Turkish guns had continued to fire back. Ultimately, the sailors learned that it was not sufficient simply to hit the forts with heavy shells; the only way to put a gun permanently out of action was to achieve a direct hit on the gun. The artillerymen serving the guns were equally hard to hit; under bombardment, they simply retreated into shelters and waited. In this respect, the day's events had supplied a useful lesson: to be effective, it was not actually necessary to destroy individual Turkish guns with direct hits. The ships could dominate the battle simply by keeping enemy gun crews away from their guns; then the battleships could move in ever closer and eventually would be able to pulverize forts, guns, and gunners at point-blank range.

Unfortunately, the fleet had no immediate opportunity to apply this new knowledge. That night the weather changed; over the next five days, gale winds whipped up the sea and heavy rain brought lightning and thunder, changing to sleet and snow. These conditions affected available light and because Carden could not afford to waste ammunition without good visibility, the fleet retreated to Mudros. Carden signaled London on February 24, "I do not intend to commence in bad weather leaving result undecided as from experience on first day I am convinced given favorable weather conditions that the reduction of the forts at the entrance can be completed in one day."

On February 25, the storm moved away and the bombardment of the outer forts resumed. *Queen Elizabeth, Agamemnon, Irresistible,* and *Gaulois* anchored 12,000 yards from their targets and commenced deliberate fire. *Queen Elizabeth* fired eighteen 15-inch shells, one by one, into a fort at Cape Helles; two of these scored direct hits and destroyed two guns. *Irresistible* fired thirty-five 12-inch shells into the other Helles fort and destroyed another two guns. *Agamemnon* adopted a casual attitude and was punished for it. When the ship anchored, her second in command, responsible for the vessel's smart appearance, ordered men over the disengaged port side to paint the hull. The battleship was too close, however, and a Cape Helles fort fired fifty-six shells, hitting *Agamemnon* seven times, killing three men and wounding seven, before the ship could weigh anchor and move. At 2:00 p.m., Admiral de Robeck led the ships into the mouth of the Straits and engaged the forts at close range. The Turkish guns fell silent and, in the smoke and dense clouds of dust, it seemed the guns and forts must have been destroyed. By 4:00 p.m., they appeared to be deserted. (The Turkish and German gunners had been temporarily evacuated.) At the end of this day, the French commander, Vice Admiral Emile Guépratte, posted himself in a prominent position on the bridge of his flagship, *Suffren,* and led his squadron past *Inflexible* with the French band playing "God Save the King" and "Tipperary." The British sailors cheered and their ships' bands responded with the "Marseillaise."

The following day, the twenty-sixth, the battleships put Royal Marine landing parties ashore to cover navy demolition squads—typically fifty marines covering thirty sailors—which went through the forts at Helles and Kum Kale blowing up the abandoned guns with explosive charges. In the deserted forts of Sedd el Bahr and Kum Kale, nineteen heavy guns were transformed into scrap. In nearby gun emplacements, a dozen Krupp heavy howitzers were destroyed. One group of *Irresistible* marines got as far as Krithia, a village set at the foot of a hill called Achi Baba that dominated the the lower peninsula; ironically, this was the only time in the Gallipoli campaign that British troops would get as far as Krithia, four miles north of Sedd el Bahr. The cost of these land operations was nine men killed or wounded. By March 4, however, resistance was stiffening. Turkish soldiers, returning in greater strength, drove British marines and sailors from Kum Kale and Cape Helles, killing twenty-two men and wounding twenty-seven. Nevertheless, during these landings, fifty Turkish guns of significant caliber had been destroyed.

News that a combination of naval gunfire and demolition parties had overwhelmed the old stone forts and the guns commanding the entrance to the Dardanelles pleased the Admiralty and the Cabinet. The First Lord found himself surrounded by smiling faces and impressed by "the number of persons who now were in favor of the Dardanelles operations and claimed to have contributed to their initiation." To Jellicoe, Churchill wrote, "Our affairs in the Dardanelles are prospering, though we have not yet cracked the nut." On March 2, Carden informed the Admiralty that, if good weather continued, he hoped to be through to the Sea of Marmara in two weeks. At its March 10 meeting, the War Council discussed what to do after the fall of Constantinople.

The fall of the outer Dardanelles forts also impressed the neutrals. Italy, thinking of joining the Entente, was encouraged to do so more quickly. The repercussions were especially significant in the Balkans. If the British fleet was about to appear before Constantinople, and the Ottoman empire was then to collapse, none of the Balkan states wished to be absent from the feast of spoils. The Bulgarians leaned toward the Allies. On March 1, the Greek government offered three divisions—and hinted at four or five—for an attack on the Gallipoli peninsula. The Turks were pessimistic. Across from Constantinople on the Asian side of the Bosporus, two special trains stood ready on an hour's notice to carry the sultan, his harem, and his court to refuge in the depths of Asia Minor. Inside the city, the German ambassador worried that his embassy, a huge yellow building situated on a prominent hill, would become a primary target for Allied naval guns, and began depositing his personal baggage for safekeeping at the American embassy. Far away, in anticipation that Russian wheat would soon be flowing out through the Bosporus and the Dardanelles, the price of wheat fell on the Chicago Exchange. In Berlin, Admiral von Tirpitz noted that "the capsizing of one little state may fatally affect the whole course of the war. The forcing of the Dardanelles would be a severe blow to us. . . . We have no trumps left."

In London, Carden's apparent victory strengthened the conviction of the Admiralty and the War Council that the Straits could be forced by the navy alone. If, with only trifling losses, a few hundred marines and bluejackets could take almost undisputed possession of the forts on both sides of the entrance, then Lord Kitchener's plan seemed wise: soldiers need not be used to assist the fleet at the Dardanelles—although once the ships had broken through, the army would be needed to occupy Constantinople. On the scene, however, Admiral Carden had begun to discover more immediate ways in which ground troops could be useful. Fire control officers in ground observation stations ashore would enable the ships to direct their fire more accurately on the forts at the Narrows. The howitzer and field batteries lining both sides of the Straits could be located and more easily disposed of by attack from the ground. And, as the fleet progressed, soldiers could move in and take possession of the peninsula to prevent the Turks from returning. With these considerations in mind, Carden asked General Sir John Maxwell, commanding British forces in Egypt, to provide 10,000 men to be landed on the tip of the peninsula now that the outer forts had been destroyed. The answer to Carden came not from Maxwell but from the War Office in London, which sternly declared that ground troops at this stage were not an essential part of the naval operation. Indeed, Kitchener warned General Sir William Birdwood, commander of the Anzac forces, of the riskiness of placing a small force on the Gallipoli peninsula where the Turks were believed to have 40,000 men. The troops already in camp at Lemnos, Kitchener decreed, were to remain on that island until the fleet had battered the inner forts into submission; thereupon, the field marshal conceded, it might be necessary to put a few men ashore at the Bulair neck of Gallipoli to prevent supplies from reaching isolated Turkish troops on the peninsula. Carden could not argue. A few weeks before, he had told the Admiralty and the War Council that the Straits could be forced by the fleet alone. Now he had to do it.

Ironically, even as Carden's success prompted men in London to self-congratulation and spurred Balkan governments to reexamine their diplomatic alignments, the naval assault on the Dardanelles was beginning to falter. The Allied fleet now was very large, totaling ninety warships with 814 guns, including a hundred guns of the heaviest caliber. Nevertheless, from March 1 onward, the progress of Admiral Carden's attack became progressively slower. The outer forts had been silenced and ships now could freely enter the mouth of the Straits. The next stage was to proceed up the waterway, eliminating the batteries on either side, most prominently the heavy guns in the forts at the Narrows—at Chanak on the Asian side and Kilid Bahr on Gallipoli. To achieve this, Carden meant to use the tactics that had worked on the outer forts: first, long-range bombardment; then, as the Turkish guns fell silent, closer engagement to overwhelm them with shellfire. Unfortunately, local geography, which had favored Carden in his attack on the outer forts, now favored the Turks. In attacking the outer forts, the bombarding ships had been able to use a wide expanse of the Aegean Sea to maneuver while concentrating their fire on the small land area of the forts. Now the geographic advantage was reversed: the intermediate and Narrows defenses could be attacked only from inside the narrow passageway and, as the ships moved into this confined space, they could be subjected to artillery fire from every ridge and gully up and down the shores of both sides of the Straits.

On February 26, the bombardment of the inner forts began. The old battleships steamed past the silent, ruined outer forts and, firing at long range, did little damage to the Narrows forts. The forts, firing back, caused no harm to the fleet. The warships were, however, hit repeatedly by the mobile howitzer batteries positioned along both coasts. These howitzers could not hope to cripple, let alone sink, any of the battleships but a howitzer shell striking an old ship was harassing and disconcerting, and the battleships did their best to locate and eliminate these adversaries. The difficulty in this was quickly apparent: when the Turkish field batteries opened fire, the ships tried desperately to locate them, but the guns were so well concealed that they rarely succeeded. In addition, the howitzers shifted position from day to day. On those occasions when naval gunfire did become accurate, the Turkish and German gunners simply retired into their caves or shelters until the bombardment was over and then, emerging, used oxen to pull their guns to another hidden position in the scrub. A few hours later the guns reopened fire.

Queen Elizabeth, prohibited by the Admiralty from entering the Straits, tried something different. On March 5, the dreadnought anchored off the Aegean coast of Gallipoli and fired her heavy guns over the peninsula at the Narrows forts. The arrival of 15-inch shells from this unexpected angle confused the Turks, as their protection was designed against fire from vessels coming up the Straits. But, without accurate spotting, the shells hit nothing significant. At the same time, the anchored battleship was hit seventeen times by one small field gun; one shell wrecked the ship's bakery. Next day, *Queen Elizabeth* returned to continue her bombardment, but the Turks had brought up a heavy, mobile 6-inch howitzer, which proceeded to hit the dreadnought three times on the hull below the waterline, though without penetrating her armor. The ship changed position again, but it was obvious that *Queen Elizabeth* would not hit anything unless she entered the Straits and subjected the forts to direct fire. Already, some in the fleet were beginning to doubt that naval gunfire would work in any form. "We could not go on expending ammunition on these futile bombardments," said Keyes. "We had also to consider the wear and tear on the guns which had only a limited life."

Carden, meanwhile, was beginning to grapple with the acute problem that would determine the success or failure of the whole naval offensive: how to deal with the Turkish minefields. The lower half of the fourteen-mile passage up to the Narrows was free of mines; Carden's minesweepers had established this. Beyond that point, however, eight big minefields, skillfully laid and commanded by many guns, stretched across the navigable waterway. No reasonable admiral would take valuable ships through these waters until a channel through the minefields had been swept.

The Admiralty had been aware that the Turks had mined the Dardanelles and had provided Carden with a force of makeshift minesweepers. This flotilla consisted of twenty-one small North Sea fishing trawlers, newly equipped with minesweeping gear, protected by steel plating against rifle bullets and splinters, and manned by their regular peacetime crews of fishermen, now designated as naval reserve ratings. The vessels were so underpowered that, operating at a sweeping speed of 4 to 6 knots, they could make

admitted that if the War Council were to choose this course, terminating the campaign would not be difficult: "One gesture with a wand and the whole armada assembled at the Dardanelles or moving thither—battleships, cruisers, destroyers, trawlers, supply ships, transports—would melt and vanish away. Evening would close on a mighty navy engaged in a world-arresting attack. The sun would rise on empty seas and silent shores." There were many reasons, of course, that no wand was waved. National prestige had now been invested in the expedition; neither Britain nor France wished the enemy or the neutrals to witness the spectacle of the Entente powers retreating in the face of a setback. Further, Churchill himself passionately believed that the check was only temporary; that the minefields would be swept; that the fleet would force the Straits and topple the Ottoman empire. And for the moment at least, all of the First Lord's colleagues agreed with him. Oddly, even Fisher, Churchill said later, "was never more resolute in his support." The First Sea Lord, "who had a sort of feeling that the thing was rather too much for Carden," even offered to go out to take personal command of the assault, but Churchill persuaded him to abandon the idea. The Sea Lords unanimously supported continuing the attack. So did the War Council, the War Office, the Foreign Office, and the prime minister. "Everyone's blood was up," said Churchill. "There was a virile readiness to do and dare." But all of this rested on Carden; he must go forward; he must break through.

Yet even as the Allies were steeling themselves to persevere, the morale of the Turkish and German gunners at the Dardanelles was rising. About this time, the American ambassador to Turkey, Henry Morgenthau, visited the forts at Hamidieh near Chanak and at Kilid Bahr. At Hamidieh, he found that almost everyone was German and that German, not Turkish, was the language spoken on every side. Across the Narrows, at Kilid Bahr, the ambassador found a scene quite different from the quiet, workmanlike professionalism of the Germans at Hamidieh: "Everything was eagerness and activity. Evidently the Germans had been excellent instructors but there was more to it than [that] . . . for the men's faces lighted up with all that fanaticism which supplies the morale of Turkish soldiers. . . . Above the shouts of all, I could hear the singsong chant of the leader, intoning the prayer with which the Moslem had rushed to battle for thirteen centuries: 'Allah is great. There is but one God, and Mohammed is his Prophet!' "

—

The great daylight attack—the effort to overwhelm the defenses with massed battleships covering the minesweepers—was imminent when suddenly the Dardanelles campaign suffered a significant casualty: Admiral Carden became seriously ill. Six months at sea off the Straits with mounting responsibilities had destroyed his health. "My poor admiral," Keyes noted on March 13, "is very seedy." It did not help that the next morning Carden received another insistent message from Churchill: "I do not understand why minesweepers should be interfered with by firing which causes no casualties. . . . This work has to be done. . . . Time is precious." By now, everything Carden swallowed made him wince with pain. Worrying about mines, about howitzers, about the weather, about the opinion of the Admiralty, he could not sleep. Each reply to a Churchill message took him several days to write. His situation was intolerable: he had promised an all-out attack, using the fleet alone, which he no longer believed in or had the resolution or energy to command. On March 15, after another bad night, Carden told Keyes he could not conduct a preattack conference with British and French admirals and captains. Giving up command at this point would mean the end of his career, and de Robeck and Keyes both urged him to reconsider. However, the following day a Harley Street specialist, serving with the fleet aboard the hospital ship *Soudan,* examined Carden and announced that the admiral had a dangerous ulcer and was on the verge of a "complete break down; he must have 3 or 4 weeks rest and freedom from all anxiety," Keyes wrote to his wife. Carden telegraphed his resignation to the Admiralty and on March 17 departed for Malta and England on the cruiser *Minerva.*

A new commander had to be found quickly. Carden's resignation left Rear Admiral Rosslyn Wester Wemyss, the commander of the base at Mudros, as the senior British naval officer in the eastern Mediterranean and, normally, Wemyss would have succeeded Carden. But with the fleet poised for attack, Wemyss generously and sensibly offered to step aside in favor of Carden's deputy, de Robeck, who had commanded during the actual fighting in the Straits. De Robeck was a tall, heavily built seaman of phlegmatic courage and unremarkable imagination, "a real fine fellow—worth a dozen of Carden," in the opinion of General Birdwell, who had observed both admirals during his visit to Mudros. Churchill was less impressed with de Robeck: "One could not feel that his training and experience up to this period had led him to think deeply on the larger aspects of strategy and tactics." But de Robeck possessed, at that moment, an overwhelming qualification: he was on the scene. Accordingly, Churchill quickly accepted Wemyss's offer and appointed de Robeck acting vice admiral. At noon on March 17, even as Carden was leaving Mudros, de Robeck hoisted his flag on *Queen Elizabeth.* That same day, the First Lord asked the new commanding admiral for a rapid judgment: "Personal and Secret from First Lord: In entrusting to you, with great confidence, the command of the Mediterranean Detached Fleet, I presume that you consider, after separate and independent judgement, that the immediate operations are wise and practicable. If not, do not hesitate to say so. If so, execute them without delay and without further reference at the first favourable opportunity. . . . All good fortune attend you." De Robeck replied that he accepted completely Carden's plan and that if he had good weather, the attack would begin the following day.

CHAPTER 25

The Naval Attack on the Narrows

Sunrise on March 18 promised a fine Aegean morning. The sky was clear and a light, warm, southerly breeze was blowing across a sea of the deepest blue. The fleet left its overnight anchorage under the white cliffs of Tenedos and cleared for action. What followed that day was a remarkable battle involving a number of large ships in a small area of water closely confined by land. Essentially, as Alan Moorehead has written, it was "a naval attack upon an army, or at any rate upon artillery. . . . There was no element of surprise . . . and the object of the struggle was perfectly obvious to everybody from the youngest bluejacket to the simplest [Turkish] private. All hung upon that one thin strip of water scarcely a mile wide and five miles long at the Narrows: if that was lost by the Turks, then everything was lost and the battle was over."

De Robeck's armada of eighteen battleships steaming across the sunlit waters toward the Straits made one officer believe that "no human power could withstand such an array of might and power." The admiral's plan was to silence the Turkish forts and big guns at the Narrows by long-range bombardment. Once these guns were subdued, the battleships would advance up the Straits and engage the batteries protecting the minefields. As soon as the Narrows forts and the mobile batteries were suppressed, the minesweeping trawlers would advance and, in broad daylight, sweep a passage 900 yards wide. The battleships then would advance through this swept channel up to the Narrows forts and complete their destruction at close range. If, as the admiral hoped, he could batter the forts into silence by the evening of the first day, then his fleet might complete its other assignments and enter the Sea of Marmara the following day.

De Robeck planned to begin his attack with his four most powerful British ships: *Queen Elizabeth, Agamemnon, Lord Nelson,* and *Inflexible.* They were to take position side by side across the Straits at a distance of 14,000 yards from the Narrows forts and open fire at the heavy guns situated there. They would not anchor, as it had been established that an anchored ship was too easy a target for the mobile howitzers. Instead, the battleships were to head upstream, maintaining position with their engines and propellers so that they could move quickly in response to enemy fire. These four heavy-bombardment ships—which de Robeck designated Line A—were accompanied by two predreadnought battleships, *Prince George* and *Triumph,* whose mission was to engage the howitzer batteries on either shore.

Line B, steaming a mile behind Line A, was made up of the old French battleships *Gaulois, Charlemagne, Bouvet,* and *Suffren*—flanked by two more British predreadnoughts, *Majestic* and *Swiftsure.* These six ships were to wait until the Narrows' big guns had been initially suppressed; then they were to pass through Line A and close to within 10,000 yards of the Narrows, adding their own heavy fire to that of the more modern ships. As Turkish fire diminished, Line B was to advance to within 8,000 yards of the Narrows, while behind them, Line A closed to 12,000 yards. The combined firepower of these ships would bring forty heavy guns—eight 15-inch and thirty-two 12-inch—to bear on the enemy forts. A third division, Line C, made up of four old British battleships, *Vengeance, Irresistible, Albion,* and *Ocean,* was assigned to wait outside the Straits until, on de Robeck's signal, it was summoned forward to relieve Line B, bringing fresh guns and gun crews to grind down the presumably exhausted enemy artillerymen. Once this bombardment had silenced the forts, six trawlers would advance and sweep a passage along the Asian coast. The battleships would then come up this passage to approach and pulverize the Narrows forts at point-blank range. Two more old battleships, *Cornwallis* and *Canopus,* would accompany the minesweepers and assist by suppressing the mobile Turkish howitzers.

At 10:30 a.m., *Queen Elizabeth* and the other eleven battleships of Lines A and B entered the Straits in brilliant sunshine, steaming slowly forward across the sparkling water. At 11:00 a.m., Line A reached its position, 14,000 yards downstream from the Narrows, and *Queen Elizabeth* trained the long barrels of her 15-inch guns at the Chanak forts, seven miles away. At 11:25 a.m., she opened fire while *Agamemnon, Lord Nelson,* and *Inflexible* bombarded the forts at Kilid Bahr on the opposite shore. All of the forts were hit repeatedly and at 11:50 a.m. a heavy explosion rocked one of the Chanak forts. De Robeck judged that the time had come to move closer and signaled Admiral Guépratte to bring the French battleships in Line B forward through the British line. Passing up the Straits, the French ships spread out in order to give the British ships, now astern of them, a continuing clear

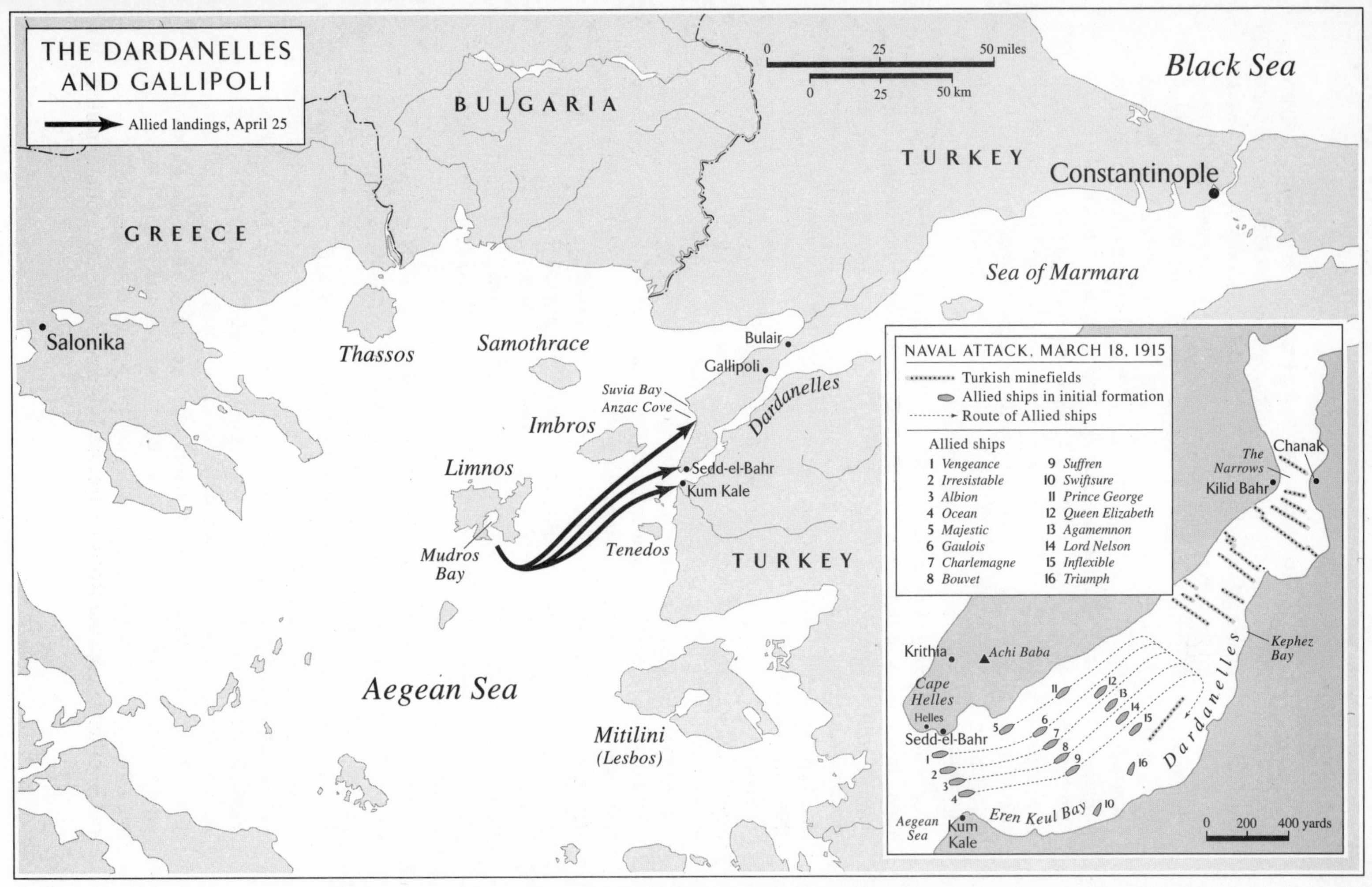

THE DARDANELLES AND GALLIPOLI
Allied landings, April 25
0 25 50 miles
0 25 50 km
Black Sea
BULGARIA
GREECE
TURKEY
Constantinople
Sea of Marmara
Salonika
Thassos
Samothrace
Bulair
Gallipoli
Dardanelles
Suvia Bay
Anzac Cove
Imbros
Limnos
Sedd-el-Bahr
Kum Kale
Mudros Bay
Tenedos
TURKEY
Aegean Sea
Mitilini (Lesbos)
NAVAL ATTACK, MARCH 18, 1915
Turkish minefields
Allied ships in initial formation
Route of Allied ships
Allied ships
1 Vengeance
2 Irresistable
3 Albion
4 Ocean
5 Majestic
6 Gaulois
7 Charlemagne
8 Bouvet
9 Suffren
10 Swiftsure
11 Prince George
12 Queen Elizabeth
13 Agamemnon
14 Lord Nelson
15 Inflexible
16 Triumph
The Narrows
Chanak
Kilid Bahr
Kephez Bay
Krithia
Achi Baba
Cape Helles
Helles
Sedd-el-Bahr
Dardanelles
Eren Keul Bay
Aegean Sea
Kum Kale
0 200 400 yards

field of fire. The forts replied vigorously and a tremendous cannonade reverberated through the Dardanelles. It was a dramatic spectacle in this confined space: the earsplitting crash and earthquake rumble of scores of heavy guns; the rows of oncoming gray ships moving through calm, blue water with towering fountains of spray rising above them; the forts obscured in clouds of smoke and dust until the pall was rent by the flash and roar of the Turkish cannons; the stabs of light from the howitzers firing from the ridges and gullies—all this under an intense blue sky flecked with white clouds. Every ship inside the Straits was subjected to determined fire from the Turkish howitzers and field guns. These shells could not be decisive against the heavy armor of hulls and turrets, but lightly protected superstructures, funnels, and upper decks suffered. At 12:30 p.m., *Gaulois* was hit by a 14-inch shell below the waterline and, leaking badly, retreated and beached herself on a small island just outside the Straits. *Agamemnon* was struck twelve times in twenty-five minutes and *Lord Nelson, Albion, Irresistible, Charlemagne, Suffren,* and *Bouvet* were also hit. These blows, however much they pierced and bent and twisted the superstructure of the ships, scarcely touched the men behind the armor: in the entire Allied fleet, there were fewer than twenty casualties.

Several of the men hit had not been shielded by armor. *Inflexible*'s fire control station, high on her forward mast, was a small platform with thin walls and a thin roof, connected by voice pipes and telephones with the bridge and the gun turrets. The gunnery officer was Commander Rudolf Verner, the same man who had watched the destruction of Admiral von Spee from this platform at the Battle of the Falkland Islands. Now, in the Dardanelles, Verner was using his binoculars to spot the effects of his ship's gunnery when a shell suddenly exploded against a signal yard just above the fire control station. Steel fragments slashed down through the station's roof and walls. Verner's right hand was partially severed, his right arm "pulped," his left arm and left leg shattered, and his skull fractured. Three seamen in the station were killed and four others, along with the assistant gunnery officer, were wounded. Verner remained conscious, saying, "Thank you, old chap," to a man who spread a mat for him to lie on. Then, remembering that he was still the officer in charge, he raised himself to the level of a voice pipe to report, "Fore-control out of action. We are all dead and dying up here. Send up some morphia." Rescue was slow in coming. The ship's bridge was in flames and the steel ladder up the mast was too hot for the ship's surgeon—who attempted the climb—to touch. A few minutes later, Verner appealed again, urgently: "For God's sake, put out the fire or we shall all be roasted." Eventually, *Inflexible*'s second in command climbed up, burning his hands severely on the ladder. Verner and the other wounded men were lowered on bamboo stretchers and taken below. *Inflexible* resumed firing.

By 2:00 p.m., according to the Turkish General Staff account, the situation of the artillerymen in the forts had become "very critical. All telephone wires [between spotters and gunners] were cut. . . . Some of the guns had been knocked out, others were half-buried, still others were out of action with jammed breech mechanisms." The gunners were demoralized and their fire grew increasingly spasmodic.

De Robeck now ordered the French squadron in Line B to withdraw and Line C, the four old British battleships waiting outside the Straits, to advance. At 1:54 p.m., *Suffren* began turning in an arc to starboard, leading her three sisters out of the action through a bay on the Asian shore. They were passing downstream, almost abreast of *Queen Elizabeth,* when *Bouvet,* the second ship in line, was rocked by a tremendous explosion. Still traveling through the water, she heeled over, capsized, and vanished—all within sixty seconds. Watchers could not believe what they had seen: at one moment the ship was there; the next, she was gone. Her captain and 639 men were drowned; sixty-six men were rescued, having saved themselves, said a *Lord Nelson* officer, by running "down her side and across her bottom as she went over, like squirrels on a wheel." As his ship rolled over, the captain's final command had been *"Sauvez-vous, mes enfants!"*

No one knew what had happened to the ship. At first, observers on both sides believed that a heavy shell had exploded her magazine and Turkish gunners redoubled their fire on other ships. The loss did not deter de Robeck and for the next two hours the bombardment continued. Two by two, *Ocean* and *Irresistible, Albion* and *Vengeance, Swiftsure* and *Majestic* approached to within 10,000 yards and fired. Some of the heavy guns at the Narrows began firing again, but by 4:00 p.m. they had stopped. Keyes called for the minesweepers. Later he said: "I did not think the fire from the concealed howitzers and field guns would ever be a decisive factor. I was wrong. The *fear* of their fire was actually the deciding factor . . . that day." Four trawlers passed *Queen Elizabeth,* heading upstream. The trawlers got their sweeps out and three mines were fished up and exploded. But then, as the trawlers came under howitzer fire, their progress wavered and, despite the attempts of their navy captains to rally the crews, they turned and ran back out of the Straits.

This embarrassment was followed by something worse. At 4:11 p.m., the battle cruiser *Inflexible,* still firing despite the damage to her foremast, suddenly struck a mine near the Asian shore. The explosion tore a hole in her bow, flooding a forward compartment and quickly drowning twenty-nine men. The tremendous shock of the explosion slammed the wounded Rudolf Verner against a bulkhead, further injuring his head. He began to bleed heavily again. As the ship was settling by the bow, Captain Phillimore ordered all men not engaged in engineering or damage control to come up to the comparative safety of the after deck. The battle cruiser then made her way slowly back down the Straits and headed for Tenedos; there she anchored in shallow water, her forward deck almost level with the sea. Verner, never losing consciousness, was moved to the hospital ship *Soudan,* where his shattered arm was taken off. "Tell my people that I played the game and stuck it out," he said to the surgeon. Two hours later, he died. Eventually, *Inflexible* was towed backward (to minimize pressure on the bow interior watertight bulkheads now keeping out the sea) to Malta, where she spent six weeks in dry dock.

Fifteen minutes after *Inflexible* limped away, *Irresistible* also struck a mine. Both engine rooms quickly flooded, leaving the ship without propulsion. The captain, not knowing what had hit his ship, ran up a green flag on his starboard yardarm, indicating that he thought his ship had been torpedoed on that side. *Irresistible* was on the extreme right of Line C, close to the Asian shore; as she drifted closer, Turkish gunners enthusiastically blasted her with shells. De Robeck promptly sent the destroyer *Wear,* which gathered more than 600 men of *Irresistible*'s crew, including eighteen dead and wounded, onto her narrow deck.

At this point, with *Bouvet* sunk, *Inflexible* creeping toward Tenedos, and *Irresistible* drifting without a crew toward the Asian shore, de Robeck decided to break off action for the day. He was appalled by what was happening to his ships, the more so as he did not know the cause. The area in which they had been operating had been swept for mines before the operation began, and just the day before, a seaplane, flying over, had reported that the water was clear. This report seemed reliable because tests near Tenedos had shown that aircraft could see mines moored as far down as eighteen feet below the surface of the clear Aegean water. What, then, was responsible? Someone on *Queen Elizabeth* suggested that perhaps the Turks were releasing mines at the Narrows and floating them down on the current.

As the fleet withdrew, Keyes was instructed to take *Wear* and, with the aid of the battleships *Ocean* and *Swiftsure,* attempt the salvage of *Irresistible.* As Keyes approached, the old ship was out of the main current, still drifting slowly toward shore. Determined to save her, he signaled *Ocean,* "The admiral directs you to take *Irresistible* in tow." The captain of *Ocean* replied that the water was too shallow for his ship to come in that close. Keyes then ordered the captain of *Wear* to ready two torpedoes to sink the derelict ship before she could go ashore and fall into Turkish hands. Before firing, however, he wanted to make certain that the water was, in fact, too shallow for *Ocean* to attempt a tow. Accordingly, *Wear* ran straight into enemy fire to take soundings. The destroyer was not hit and Keyes was able to signal *Ocean* that for half a mile inshore of *Irresistible* there was ninety feet of water. *Ocean,* steaming back and forth, "blazing away at the shore forts . . . to no purpose," did not respond to Keyes's repeated order to take the crippled ship in tow. Keyes then signaled *Ocean:* "If you do not propose to take *Irresistible* in tow, the admiral wishes you to withdraw."

Meanwhile, the situation aboard *Irresistible* had stabilized. She was down by the stern, but no lower in the water than she had been an hour before. Keyes decided that she would neither sink nor drift ashore for some time and that he would return to de Robeck and suggest that trawlers come in after dark to tow her back into the main current, which might then carry her out of the Straits. As he was leaving, he approached *Ocean* in order to repeat his order for her to withdraw. At just that moment, 6:05 p.m., *Ocean* hit a mine. There was a violent explosion and the old battleship listed to starboard. At almost the same moment, a shell hit her steering gear and she began to turn in circles. As Turkish gunners now pounded this second helpless target, destroyers raced in to remove her crew.

Bringing details of these disasters, Keyes returned to de Robeck in *Queen Elizabeth* outside the Straits. Following his report, he proposed that he go back and torpedo both of the abandoned battleships, *Irresistible* and *Ocean.* De Robeck gave permission and Keyes returned in the destroyer *Jed.* Creeping into every bay, he found nothing. Now believing that both battleships were at the bottom of the sea, Keyes went back to the flagship, where he found Admiral de Robeck enormously depressed. The day, said the admiral, had been a disaster: *Bouvet* was lost, *Gaulois* was beached, *Suffren*'s injuries were so great she had to go into dry dock; of the French squadron, only *Charlemagne* remained capable of further action. In addition, *Irresistible* and *Ocean* were gone and *Inflexible,* counted on to engage *Goeben,* needed to go to Malta for extensive repair. De Robeck was sure, he said to Keyes, that having suffered three battleships sunk and three more put out of action, he would be dismissed the following day. Keyes, who had more experience of the First Lord than de Robeck did, replied that Churchill would not be discouraged; that, instead, he would respond by sending reinforcements. Apart from the 639 men lost in *Bouvet,* casualties had been moderate: sixty-one men in the entire fleet. The three lost battleships had been due for the scrapheap, and, even with three more out of action, the fleet remained powerful. De Robeck's spirits rose and he and Keyes discussed how to deal with the minefields. The civilian trawler crews would return to England to be replaced by regular navy seamen from the lost battleships. Sweeping apparatus would be installed on destroyers. And then, when everything was ready, the navy would attack again. On this optimistic note, the admiral and his Chief of Staff ended the long day and night. Later, Keyes would write of his thoughts that night: "Except for the searchlights, there, seemed to be no sign of life [inside the Dardanelles]. I had a most indelible impression that we were in the presence of a beaten foe. I thought he was beaten at 2 p.m. I knew he was beaten at 4 p.m.—and at midnight I knew with still greater certainty that he was absolutely beaten. It only remained for us to organize a proper sweeping force and devise some means of dealing with the drifting mines to reap the fruits of our efforts. I felt that the guns of the forts and batteries and the concealed howitzers and mobile field guns were no longer a menace." De Robeck was bolstered by Keyes's optimism. "We are all getting ready for another go and are not in the least beaten or down-hearted," he declared the next day to General Sir Ian Hamilton, who had just arrived from London.

—

On the night of March 18, Chanak, in peacetime a busy commercial town of 16,000 at the Narrows, was deserted; buildings were burning, the streets were filled with rubble, the forts were pitted by huge craters. But the bombardment had put only eight big guns permanently out of action, and the Turks and Germans had suffered only 118 men killed and wounded. The explanation was that when the shellfire became intense, the artillerymen simply left their guns and retreated into earth shelters. Nevertheless, the attack had compelled the Turkish and German gunners to fire more than half of their ammunition. At 4:00 p.m. the Chanak wireless station reported that ammunition at the Hamidieh fort, the defense's strongest point, was running out. When the Allied ships withdrew, the Turkish heavy guns were left with only twenty-seven long-range high-explosive shells—seventeen at Fort Hamidieh, ten at Kilid Bahr. The howitzers protecting the minefields had fired half of their supply. What was to happen when the battle was renewed? Once the big guns exhausted the ammunition on hand, it would be simply a question of how long the howitzer batteries could keep the minesweepers away from the minefields; some thought one day, others two. Thereafter, in a matter of hours, the minesweepers would sweep a channel through to the Narrows. And beyond the Narrows, there was no defense.

One last hope remained: *Goeben.* The battle cruiser's hull had two large holes—now temporarily plugged—caused by Russian mines struck off the Bosporus. She was ordered to raise steam; if the Allied ships broke through, she was to fight to the death. At 5:00 p.m. on March 18, she sailed past the Golden Horn and the Sultan's palace, headed west toward the Dardanelles. At 6:00 p.m., a signal came that the Allied fleet was withdrawing. Through the night, *Goeben* lay in the Sea of Marmara, awaiting the renewal of the Allied attack the following day.

Meanwhile, in Constantinople, the government and the populace were convinced that the Allied fleet would break through. All Turks respected the near legendary power of the British navy; no one believed that a collection of ancient forts and guns at the Dardanelles could bar its way. Accordingly, word of the massive bombardment precipitated an exodus from the capital. The state archives were evacuated and hidden; the banks were emptied of gold; many affluent Turks already had sent their families away. The distance from Gallipoli to Constantinople was only 150 miles; most Turks expected that less than twelve hours after they entered the Sea of Marmara, British battleships would arrive off the Golden Horn.

The German and Turkish artillerymen at the Dardanelles were certain that the Allies would resume their attack in the morning. Through the night, they worked, determined to fight as long as they had ammunition. At dawn on March 19, the men were standing by their guns. When there was no sign of enemy ships, they presumed that the cause was the bad weather that had come up in the night. On the afternoon of March 19, *Goeben* was ordered to return to her base near Constantinople. Then, as the bad weather subsided, and day followed day without a sign of the Allied fleet, the defenders began to understand that they had won. They could not know, of course, of the terrible worries that had afflicted the Allied commanders because of the unexplained loss of *Bouvet, Irresistible,* and *Ocean.* The cause—as Admiral de Robeck did not know until after the war—was a single brilliant exploit: in darkness on the night of March 8, a Turkish mine expert, Lieutenant Colonel Geehl, had taken a small steamer, *Nousret,* down the Straits. Near the Asian shore, he had secretly laid a new line of twenty mines, 100 to 150 yards apart, perpendicular to the ten lines already stretching across the Straits. During the days before the massive attack of March 18, British trawler crews had never discovered these mines, nor had British airplanes spotted them from the air. For ten days, they had waited beneath the surface of the blue-green water.

—

After three hours' sleep, Roger Keyes arose on the morning of March 19 and, as he often did in times of stress, shaved with a copy of Rudyard Kipling's poem "If" propped in front of him.* He knew nothing of the plight of the gunners at the Narrows, nor of the preparations made by the Turkish government to abandon Constantinople, yet he sensed that victory was near. Even so, it was clear that the attack could not be resumed for a day or two. A strong wind was blowing, which meant heavy seas, lowered visibility, and poor gunnery. But Keyes had no thought—nor was there any thought at the Admiralty or anywhere in the Dardanelles fleet—of not continuing. A message from the Admiralty urged de Robeck to attack again. Reinforcements would be sent; the old battleships *Queen* and *Implacable* were already on their way; *London* and *Prince of Wales* would follow soon; the French admiralty was sending the battleship *Henri IV* to replace the lost *Bouvet.* A meeting of the Cabinet War Council on March 19 authorized de Robeck to "continue the naval operations against the Dardanelles if he thought fit." Keyes began organizing and equipping a new minesweeping force. On March 20,

*If you can keep your head when all about you
Are losing theirs and blaming it on you . . .

If you can meet with Triumph and Disaster
And treat those two imposters just the same . . .

two days after the attack, de Robeck reported to the Admiralty that fifty British and twelve French minesweepers, manned by volunteers from the lost battleships, would soon be available. He hoped, he said, "to be in a position to commence operations in three or four days."

—

It was not to be; March 18 marked both the climax and the termination of the purely naval assault on the Dardanelles. Thereafter, as the days passed and the anchored fleet was buffeted by high winds and driving rain, de Robeck resumed his brooding. Writing to Wemyss, he referred to the attack as "a disaster." Not only had he lost a third of his battleships, he still had no idea how this catastrophe had happened and how to prevent it from happening again. He had learned that naval guns had a much easier time dealing with ancient forts of heavy masonry than with temporary field works. He now knew that, to be fully effective, the fire of long-range guns must be accurately targeted by officers who can observe the locations and effect of bursting shells. Above all, he had learned that in restricted waters, mines protected by artillery that can intimidate minesweeping constitute a formidable defense against a fleet. But it was the loss of battleships that troubled him most. It did no good for Keyes to remind him that the battleships were old and on their way to the scrap heap. Battleships were the backbone of the Royal Navy; battleships were filled with brave men; and he, John de Robeck, had lost three. And he had no way of knowing that, if he attacked again, he would not lose another three.

On March 22, a group of senior Allied commanders gathered on board the *Queen Elizabeth* to confer about the next step. The moment the conference began, Admiral de Robeck dramatically announced that the fleet could not force the Dardanelles on its own. At this, one of the figures seated at the table nodded. General Sir Ian Hamilton, sent out by Kitchener to command the growing ground force assigned to "reap the fruits" of the navy's success, agreed with the admiral. Hamilton had arrived at the Dardanelles on March 17, just in time to witness the fleet's massive March 18 attack on the Narrows forts. He had been impressed by the mighty cannonade, but he had also seen *Inflexible* creeping away, her bridge burned out, her foretop destroyed, her bow low in the water. He had seen destroyers with decks crowded with hundreds of men from sunken or abandoned battleships. To Hamilton, it was clear that the Turkish guns, particularly the concealed howitzer batteries that were preventing British trawlers from sweeping mines, could not be completely destroyed or suppressed by naval gunfire. This, he believed, would have to be done by troops on the ground. On March 19, the day after the naval assault, he had signaled Kitchener: "I am being most reluctantly driven to the conclusion that the Straits are not likely to be forced by battleships as at one time seemed probable and that if my troops are to take part, it will not take the subsidiary form anticipated. The Army's part will be more than mere landing parties to destroy the forts; it must be a deliberate and progressive military operation carried out at full strength, so as to open a passage for the navy." Kitchener, who ten weeks before had adamantly opposed all ground operations at the Dardanelles, now replied to Hamilton, "You know my view that the Dardanelles passage must be forced, and that if large military operations on the Gallipoli peninsula by your troops are necessary to clear the way, those operations must be undertaken . . . and must be carried through."

This exchange of messages was on Hamilton's mind as he listened to de Robeck on *Queen Elizabeth.* Hamilton liked de Robeck, whom he described as "a fine-looking man with great charm of manner," and he understood the admiral's concern. Suppose the fleet, followed by the army's troopships, managed to get through the Dardanelles with the loss of another old battleship or two. With the Turks still holding both sides of the Straits, how long could the fleet remain isolated in the Sea of Marmara starved of coal and ammunition? What would happen to Hamilton's troopships and the thousands of men on board if their supply lines ran through a narrow strait dominated by enemy guns? And what about *Goeben*? With *Inflexible* damaged, de Robeck would have only the old battleships, none of which were fast enough to catch the German battle cruiser. *Queen Elizabeth* might do it, but how likely was it that the Admiralty would permit the prize superdreadnought to be exposed to the dangers involved in entering the Sea of Marmara?

Originally, Hamilton had hoped that the army would not have to land on Gallipoli and that a purely naval offensive could achieve the Allied objectives. "Constantinople must surrender within a few hours of our battleships entering the Marmara," he had written in his diary, "when her rail and sea communications were cut and a rain of shell fell upon the penned-up populace from de Robeck's terrific batteries. Given a good wind, that nest of iniquity would go up like Sodom and Gomorrah in a winding sheet of flame." But now the admiral had said that this prospect was an illusion: that his battleships could not go through without help. And de Robeck, for his part, now grasped that Hamilton had come with Kitchener's blessing to provide exactly that kind of help. The two men understood each other and no further discussion was needed. Unanimously, the conference on the *Queen Elizabeth* resolved that the naval attack should be postponed. Nothing more was to be done by the fleet until the army that Hamilton was to command was ready to act. Because the troops and their equipment were scattered across the eastern Mediterranean, they must be assembled and organized to force an opposed amphibious landing against an entrenched enemy. The general estimated that he would need about three weeks.

Keyes, busy reorganizing the minesweeping force, was absent from this March 22 meeting. When he returned to *Queen Elizabeth* and heard what had been decided, he was dismayed. "I lost no time in having it out with the admiral," he said later. He pleaded with de Robeck not to wait; the new minesweepers would be ready on April 3 or 4; they would sweep the mines and then the fleet was bound to get through. To wait for the army to return meant giving the Turks time to rebuild their defenses and bring in fresh troops and ammunition. But de Robeck's mind was made up: he would wait for Hamilton and the army; the navy would act in a supporting role. Nineteen years later, in 1934, Keyes, then an Admiral of the Fleet, wrote: "I wish to place on record that I had no doubt then, and have none now—and nothing will ever shake my opinion—that from the 4th of April onwards the fleet could have forced the Straits and, with losses trifling in comparison to those the army suffered, could have entered the Marmara. . . . This operation . . . would have led immediately to a victory decisive upon the whole course of the war."

—

On March 23, the day after the *Queen Elizabeth* conference, de Robeck broke the news to the Admiralty that he was abandoning the purely naval campaign. He proposed now to wait until April 14, when, Hamilton had told him, the army would be ready; then, together, they would conduct a combined assault against the Straits and the Gallipoli peninsula. "It appears better," de Robeck wrote, "to prepare a decisive effort about the middle of April rather than risk a great deal for what may possibly be only a partial solution." In a further signal on March 26, he added, "I do not hold the check on the 18th to be decisive, but having met General Hamilton . . . I consider a combined operation essential to obtain great results and object of campaign. . . . To attack the Narrows now with fleet would be a mistake, as it would jeopardize the execution of a better and bigger scheme."

At the Admiralty, Churchill read this telegram with "consternation." He had "regarded . . . [March 18] as only the first of several days' fighting. It never occurred to me for a moment that we should not go on within the limits of what we had decided to risk, until we had reached a decision one way or another. . . . I feared the perils of the long delay. . . . The mere process of landing an army after giving the enemy at least three more weeks' additional notice seemed to me a most terrible and formidable hazard." Immediately, the First Lord drafted a message to de Robeck, overruling the decision of the conference on *Queen Elizabeth* and commanding de Robeck "to renew the attack begun on March 18 at the first opportunity." Then, summoning Fisher and the Admiralty War Group to his room, he showed them de Robeck's telegram and his own reply and asked their approval. He met "insuperable resistance. . . . For the first time since the war began, high words were used around the octagonal table," Churchill wrote later. In the opinion of Fisher, Wilson, and Jackson, de Robeck's message had transformed the situation at the Dardanelles. They had been willing, they told the First Lord, to support an attack by the navy alone, "because it was supported and recommended by the commander on the spot." But now de Robeck had decided on something different: a joint operation by the navy and the army. De Robeck was the officer responsible; he knew the situation; to insist that he set aside his own professional judgment must not be done. Indeed, Fisher was overjoyed that at last the operation was assuming the form that he had always preferred. "What more could we want?" he asked. "The army was going to do it. They ought to have done it all along." All morning, Churchill "pressed to the very utmost the need to renew the attack. . . . I could make no headway. Nothing I could do could overcome the admirals now that they had dug their toes in." As a last resort, Churchill took the draft of his telegram to Asquith. The prime minister declared that in principle he agreed with the First Lord, but that he would not overturn the professional advice of many admirals.

At a Cabinet meeting that afternoon, Churchill announced "with grief . . . the refusal of the admiral and the Admiralty to continue the naval attack." At that point, Churchill well understood, the Cabinet's reaction might be to withdraw from the entire Dardanelles enterprise. The attack had failed and, as Kitchener had said in an earlier deliberation, "We could always withdraw if things did not go well." So far, "we had lost fewer men killed and wounded than were often incurred in a trench raid on the Western Front and no vessel of the slightest value had been sunk." But Kitchener spoke up immediately. "Confident, commanding, magnanimous . . . he assumed the burden and declared he would carry the operations through by military force." As usual, once the war lord had spoken, there was nothing more to be said. Churchill gave up and sent a message to de Robeck telling him that his new plans had been approved. Thus it was that the decision to call off the naval attack on the Dardanelles and to initiate a land campaign was made, not by a formal decision of the Cabinet or the War Council, not by the Admiralty or the War Office, but by de Robeck and Hamilton meeting one morning in the wardroom of a battleship 2,000 miles away. Thereafter, all major decisions in the campaign were made by Kitchener and Hamilton; de Robeck's role became the providing of naval gunfire support and other services when requested. The War Council, having approved the decision and the arrangements made on the battleship, never altered them, because the War Council did not meet again until May 19, eight weeks later. By then, 70,000 Allied troops were ashore at Gallipoli and a new British government, a new First Sea Lord, and a new First Lord of the Admiralty were in office.

No one can know whether, if the Allied fleet had tried again, the ships would have broken through to the Sea of Marmara. If so, what might have happened? After the war, Henry Morgenthau declared that the appearance of an Allied fleet off Constantinople in March 1915 would have toppled the Turkish government and driven that nation out of the war. "The whole Ottoman state, on that eighteenth day of March when the Allied fleet abandoned the attack, was on the brink of dissolution," Morgenthau wrote. At Constantinople, "the populace, far from opposing the arrival of the Allied fleet, would have welcomed it with joy . . . for this would emancipate them from the hated Germans, bring about peace and end their miseries. . . . Talaat [the grand vizier] had loaded two automobiles with extra tires, gasoline, and all other essentials of a protracted journey. . . . [He] stationed these automobiles on the Asiatic side of the city with chauffeurs constantly at hand. . . . But the great Allied armada never returned."

—

The first chapters of the new epic were completed. The days went by and silence settled over the Dardanelles. The weather constantly changed; mornings of warm, mirror-surface calm gave way to high winds, driving rain, storm-tossed waves, and sometimes flurries of snow. Not until the end of April, when scarlet poppies covered the fields of Gallipoli, did the tale resume its grim unfolding a few miles distant from the site of ancient Troy.

CHAPTER 26

Gallipoli: The Landings

From the beginning, the possibility of a land campaign had lurked beneath the surface of the naval attack on the Dardanelles. A plan to employ significant land forces had not emerged in the early discussions because Kitchener had declared categorically that no troops were available; this had prompted Churchill to say that the navy could force the Straits on its own. Originally, Fisher had been in the middle, believing that a Dardanelles campaign was a good idea, but only as a combined operation involving both the army and the navy. On February 23, 1915, he made this point to Lloyd George: "The Dardanelles: futile without soldiers. Somebody will have to land at Gallipoli some time or other." Thereafter, as it became clear that the navy was indeed going to try to force the Straits alone, Fisher lapsed into resentment and opposition.

By early February, however, it began to appear that Fisher was right. At the Admiralty, at the War Office, and in the War Council, realization was growing that at least some soldiers would be necessary to occupy the forts after the guns were silenced. Even Kitchener conceded this and modified his first emphatic position. "If the navy required assistance of land forces at a later stage, that assistance would be forthcoming," he informed the War Council on February 9. The fact was that, despite his statement that no troops were available, Kitchener, all along, had been hoarding in England a division of veteran soldiers, the 18,000 men of the regular army's 29th Division. On February 16, Kitchener decided to release these men and told Asquith, Churchill, and Fisher that he had assigned the division to the Aegean where it would be available "either to seize the Gallipoli peninsula after it has been evacuated [by the Turks] or to occupy Constantinople." He had also, he said, authorized the use at Gallipoli of 30,000 Australian and New Zealand troops training in Egypt.*

Word of the assignment of the 29th Division to the Mediterranean predictably infuriated Sir John French, the British Commander-in-Chief in France, who bombarded Kitchener with protests. Kitchener waffled and on February 20, four days after they were issued, the division's Mediterranean sailing orders were canceled. Kitchener's explanation to the War Council was that recent severe defeats inflicted on the Russian army might permit the Germans to transfer numerous divisions from the Eastern to the Western Front; therefore, prudence required withholding the 29th Division to shore up the Allied armies in France. Churchill, perturbed, pointed out that one division would not make the slightest difference between success and failure in France, but might have an impact in the East. He asked Asquith to overrule Kitchener and order the troops to the Aegean, but the First Lord's argument was undermined by the fact that, only a few weeks before, he himself had enthusiastically promised that the navy could force the Dardanelles alone.

Oddly, Kitchener himself kept coming back to the question of troops for the Dardanelles. After Carden's bombardment of the outer forts, the war lord grandly declared in the War Council on February 24 that "if the fleet cannot get through the Straits unaided, the army ought to see the business through. The effect of a defeat in the Orient would be very serious. There can be no going back." Nevertheless, he continued to withhold the 29th Division. Meanwhile, pressure for the involvement of ground forces continued to rise. A possibile solution was the offer on March 1 by the pro-Allied government of Eleuthérios Venizélos—impressed by Carden's destruction of the outer Dardanelles forts—to land three Greek divisions on the Gallipoli peninsula and then to advance on Constantinople. Immediately, Russia objected. The liberation of Constantinople, the restoration of the cross to the dome of the former cathedral of Santa Sophia, control of the Bosporus and the Dardanelles astride Russia's lifeline to the world's oceans—these had been objectives of Russian foreign policy for centuries. Much as the tsar's government wished to expel the hated Turk, it would not permit this expulsion to be performed by Greeks. The Russian veto snatched away the possibility of a Greek army on Gallipoli.

Still, Kitchener could not leave the problem of ground troops alone. On March 1, he had sent Lieutenant General William Birdwood, the British officer commanding the Australian and New Zealand troops in Egypt, to confer with Carden about possible use of the army. While Birdwood was at Mudros, Kitchener—still vacillating—signaled him again, cautioning that there was no intention of using troops on the Gallipoli peninsula "unless the

*The widely used abbreviation for "Australian and New Zealand Army Corps" was "Anzac." Soldiers, individually and collectively, were known as "Anzacs."

navy are convinced that they cannot silence the guns in the Straits without military cooperation on a large scale. . . . The concentration of troops at the entrance to the Dardanelles is for operations subsequently to be undertaken in the neighborhood of Constantinople." Birdwood, responding on March 6, attempted to focus his chief on reality by saying that, on the basis of what he had seen and heard, he considered Carden's estimate as to the rapid passage of the Straits "too sanguine . . . I doubt his ability to force the passage unaided." Birdwood also passed along to Kitchener his confidential opinion that Carden was "very second rate—no 'go' in him, or ideas, or initiative."

Kitchener had heard enough: on March 10, he reversed himself again. The 29th Division, he told the War Council, would go to the Aegean, although it would not sail until March 16 and could not arrive before the first week of April. In addition, he had arranged for a division of the French North African army to join the force and, with the Anzacs thrown in, there now would be 75,000 Allied soldiers available for the Dardanelles. To command this polyglot force, Kitchener turned to an old friend and protégé, General Sir Ian Hamilton, his Chief of Staff during the Boer War. On the morning of March 12, Hamilton was summoned to Kitchener's office. "Opening the door," Hamilton said, "I bade him [Kitchener] good morning and walked up to his desk where he went on writing like a graven image. After a moment, he looked up and said in a matter-of-fact tone, 'We are sending a military force to support the fleet now at the Dardanelles and you are to have command.' " Kitchener said nothing else, but resumed writing while Hamilton remained standing silently in front of his desk. Eventually, Kitchener looked up and said, "Well?" Hamilton then learned that Kitchener hoped that the fleet would get through without military help and that he contemplated Hamilton landing his troops on the shores of the Bosporus to occupy Constantinople. Once the fleet got through the Dardanelles, Kitchener declared, "Constantinople could not hold out. . . . The fleet . . . with their guns would dominate the place and if necessary, burn the place to ashes. . . . There would be a revolution at the mere sight of the smoke from the funnels of our warships." When Hamilton asked how many enemy troops were defending the Dardanelles and the names and backgrounds of the principal Turkish and German commanders, Kitchener replied that he had no idea. When Hamilton asked how many troops he himself would command, Kitchener said that the Greeks had proposed to put 150,000 men on the Gallipoli peninsula, but that in Hamilton's case "half that number will do you handsomely; the Turks are busy elsewhere; I hope you will not have to land at all; if you *do* have to land, why then the powerful fleet at your back will be the prime factor in your choice of time and place." Hamilton's troops, Kitchener decreed, were not to fight on the Asian side of the Dardanelles, because "once we began marching about continents, situations calling for heavy reinforcements would probably be created." If putting troops ashore on Gallipoli turned out to be necessary, Hamilton was not to attack until the full weight of his expeditionary force—including the 29th Division—could be thrown in. But the general was not to worry: "The peninsula is open to landing on very easy terms," he was assured. "The cross fire from the fleet . . . must sweep that stretch of flat and open country so as to render it untenable by the enemy." Hamilton was allowed one night to say good-bye to his wife and to pack his clothes. In the morning, he was back at the War Office. "I said good-bye to old K. as casually as if we were to meet again for dinner," he wrote. "He did not even wish me luck . . . but he did say, rather unexpectedly just as I was taking up my cap from the table, 'If the fleet gets through, Constantinople will fall of itself and you will have won, not a battle, but the war.' "

That afternoon, March 13, Hamilton left Charing Cross station on a special train, seen off by his friends Winston and Clementine Churchill, but not by Kitchener, who declared that he was too busy. The new commander was accompanied by a small staff of officers yanked the day before from behind their London desks. In their briefcases, they carried all the information the War Office could supply: an out-of-date map, a prewar Admiralty report on the Dardanelles defenses, an old handbook on the Ottoman army, and two tourist guidebooks to western Turkey. Whisked to France on a destroyer, then hurried south in another special train, they embarked in Marseilles on the new 30-knot light cruiser *Phaeton.* Along the way, Hamilton mused on his situation in his diary: "Only two sorts of Commanders-in-Chief could possibly find time to scribble like this on their way to take up an enterprise in many ways unprecedented—a German and a Britisher. The German because every possible contingency would have been worked out for him beforehand; the Britisher because he has nothing—literally nothing—in his portfolio except a blank check signed with those grand yet simple words 'John Bull.' "

Once *Phaeton* reached the Aegean, Hamilton, who had been born in Corfu, relished the "thyme-scented breezes . . . the crimson in the eastern sky . . . the waves of liquid opal . . . the exquisite, exquisite air . . . the sea like an undulating carpet of blue velvet outspread for Aphrodite." Reality intruded when, "at noon, passed a cruiser taking Admiral Carden invalided back to Malta."

Ian Hamilton was an exemplary British soldier of the old Victorian army, a small, professional force whose gentlemen officers lived in a clubbish, colonial world, undergirded by the plucky courage of common British soldiers. Hamilton, a delicate and romantic Scot, was a man of feverish energy. He had charm and a quick smile, he knew classical and English literature, he wrote witty letters, and he had a circle of important friends reaching far beyond the army. Most of his life, however, had been spent on the imperial frontiers in India, the Sudan, and South Africa; by 1914, he was said to have seen more active service than any other senior officer in the British army.* He had often been wounded, his left hand was paralyzed, and three times he had been recommended for the Victoria Cross. Hamilton's flaw as a commander was that, in the colonial wars that had taught him his trade, he had learned to rely on the competence of fellow British officers; they, being on the spot, were often better qualified to make decisions than the commander. He preferred to urge rather than to command and his inclination, even when things appeared to be going badly, was not to intervene. Now, in this new kind of warfare where the stakes were higher, the absence of ruthlessness in this military leader was to hurt him and his men. Nevertheless, at sixty-two, Ian Hamilton had been summoned by his old chief, the man whom he privately referred to in his diaries as Old K. He had been given an army and ordered to conduct the largest amphibious operation in the history of the world. If he succeeded, Old K. had said, he would win the war.

—

Gallipoli is a peninsula of rugged and desolate land thrusting fifty-two miles into the Aegean Sea. At its neck, the peninsula is connected to the European continent by the Bulair isthmus, three miles across. To the southwest, the peninsula broadens to twelve miles; then, continuing southwest, it tapers to a rounded tip at Cape Helles. Viewed from the sea, Gallipoli is sternly beautiful, corrugated with green and brown ridges rising to a thousand feet. To the walker or climber, the ground is rough, broken, indented with gullies, escarpments, and narrow, irregular valleys, lifting to a craggy spine of steep ridges. Six miles north of Cape Helles, the sloping hill of Achi Baba stands 590 feet above the lower peninsula; in the center of the peninsula, the crest of Chunuk Bair rises 850 feet; nearby, Sari Bair ridge, the highest point on

*When Hamilton encountered Roger Keyes off the Dardanelles, it was a family reunion of sorts. Hamilton's first overseas assignment, in 1873 when he was a twenty-year-old army subaltern, was to an Indian army unit commanded by Keyes's father, General Sir Charles Keyes. Roger Keyes's mother, wrote Hamilton, "of whom . . . [Roger] is an ugly likeness, was as high-spirited, fascinating, clever a creature as I ever saw. Camel-riding, hawking, dancing . . . she was the idol of the Punjab Frontier Force. His father . . . whose loss of several fingers from a sword cut earned him my special boyhood veneration, was really a devil of a fellow. . . . Riding together in the early morning . . . we suddenly barged into a mob of wild Waziri tribesmen who jumped out of the ditch and held us up—hand on bridle. The old general spoke Pushtu fluently and there was a parley between them. . . . Where were they going? To buy camels at Dera Ghazi Khan. How far had they come? Three days march, but they had no money. The general simulated amazement. 'You have come all that distance to buy camels without money? These are strange tales you tell me. I fear that when you pass through Dera Ismail you will have to . . . [sell] your nice pistols and knives. Oh yes, I see them quite well; they are peeping at me from under your *poshteens* [cloaks].' The Waziris laughed and took their hands off our reins. Instantly, the general shouted to me, 'Come on—gallop!' And in less than no time we were going hell for leather along the lonely frontier road. . . . 'That was a narrow squeak,' said the general, 'but you may take liberties with a Waziri if only you can make him laugh.' "

Gallipoli, is just short of a thousand feet. The shores of the peninsula are edged by sandstone cliffs, broken here and there by ravines washed out by torrential autumn and winter rains. At the mouths of some of these gullies, narrow strips of sandy or stony beach lie along the sea. For a few weeks in April and May, Gallipoli is covered with red poppies, purple lupine, large white daisies, and other flowers. Heather and wild thyme grow everywhere along with scrub: low shrubs, thick brushwood, and small clumps of stunted pine. The soil is sandy, blowing in dry weather, sticky when wet, and generally inhospitable to agriculture, although in the small villages there are fruit trees, small olive orchards, and a few vineyards. In 1914, the roads were primitive and travelers passing from one point on the peninsula to another preferred to go by boat.

This is the ground where an Allied army was to land and a Turkish army to defend in a campaign that, perhaps more than any other in the Great War, still is vividly recalled to memory by its name alone: Gallipoli.

—

Carden's destruction of the outer forts and de Robeck's assault on the Narrows had given warning. On March 24, Enver Pasha, the Turkish minister of war, had summoned Otto Liman von Sanders, the head of the German military mission, to his office and asked him to assume command of the Turkish army at the Dardanelles. Sanders, a tall, stern Prussian cavalry general, quick to make decisions, scanty with praise, and sharp in reprimand, had been sent to Turkey by the kaiser himself and viewed his position as one of extraordinary consequence. Invited to dinner at the American embassy, the general, his uniformed chest sparkling with medals, was seated next to the ambassador's daughter, to whom he boorishly refused to speak. Afterward, he bitterly complained that the personal representative of the German emperor belonged at the head of the table, not alongside an insignificant young woman. The Austrian ambassador, who had advised his American colleague on the seating arrangements, pointed out that Wagenheim was the German ambassador and that "it is not customary for an emperor to have two representatives at the same court." Sanders persisted, making himself so unpopular that all other foreign ambassadors announced that if he were ever given the kind of precedence he demanded at any function they attended, they would walk out in a body.

Despite his social pretensions, Sanders was an experienced, professional soldier and Enver had made an excellent choice. Sanders accepted the request and immediately set off for the Gallipoli peninsula, where he found himself in command of 80,000 conscript soldiers. Most were Anatolian peasants so ill clad that they passed the same vermin-infested uniforms from unit to unit in order that, on inspection, the German general would find the men before him completely dressed. Sanders noticed, however, that he often saw "shoes" made of cloth tied around the foot with a piece of string; at other times, the men simply appeared barefoot. These troops were "scattered like frontier guards" along 150 miles of seacoast on both sides of the Dardanelles; thus, an enemy on landing "would have found resistance everywhere, but no forces or reserves to make a strong and effective counterattack." Sanders corrected this deployment, pulling two divisions away from the coast and stationing them in the middle of the peninsula where they could respond to threats from several directions. He began building roads and bridges to expedite their movements. He found that the peninsula's potential landing beaches had only rudimentary fortification and he set thousands of men to digging more trenches, setting up more gun emplacements, and stringing more barbed wire, some of it out into the water in front of the beaches. Chosen men were given special training in handling machine guns and hand grenades and in sniping. "If the English will only leave me alone for eight days," he said on March 27. Later, he was to write: "The British allowed us four good weeks."

—

Hamilton defined his own instructions in their simplest form: "I have no roving commission to conquer Asia Minor. I have not come here for any other purpose whatsoever but to help the fleet through the Dardanelles. The War Office think the Gallipoli peninsula occupation is the best way to effect this purpose. So do the Admiralty and so does the admiral in executive command." To occupy Gallipoli, Hamilton now commanded 75,000 men: Englishmen, Scots, Irishmen, Australians, New Zealanders, Gurkhas, Sikhs, French Foreign Legionnaires, Senegalese, and Zouaves. These troops were scattered around the eastern Mediterranean. Some were already at Mudros, some were in Egypt, some were still in North Africa. The 29th Division was on the high seas aboard twenty-two troopships and would not arrive until the first week of April. Then, when the transports did begin to arrive, it was discovered that the ships had been loaded so rapidly and haphazardly that it was impossible to know which ones contained what equipment; wagons were in one ship, horses in another, harnesses in a third; the same chaos applied to artillery, ammunition, machine guns, tents, and supplies of food. "The slipshod manner in which the troops have been sent out from England is something awful," said Wemyss. The 29th Division, Hamilton decided, would have to be disembarked and the ships unloaded, sorted out, and repacked. This could not be done at Mudros, where there were neither docks nor cranes nor laborers. It was this situation that led Hamilton to tell de Robeck that he needed three weeks to reorganize his army in Egypt.

Hamilton's new base was at Alexandria, where his staff moved first into a large old house that had once been a brothel and had neither electricity nor running water; after dark, the staff worked by candlelight. A few days later, the army leased the Hotel Metropole for its offices. Practical information about Gallipoli was scanty. No one knew the depth of water off the beaches, the location or condition of the roads, or whether the peninsula contained any wells or fresh water springs. (Later, they were to discover that numerous springs, bubbling with fresh water, were on the ridges, where they kept the Turks plentifully supplied. Water for the Allied troops on the beaches had to be brought in barges from Egypt, 700 miles away.) There were too few small boats to carry the troops ashore, so throughout the Middle East, dozens of trawlers, lighters, and caïques were purchased for cash; in one day, British officers bought forty-two large lighters and five tugs at Piraeus. Fifteen hundred donkeys were bought or rented with their keepers and drivers. As the days passed, hundreds of ships descended on Lemnos and Mudros. The island and its little town had become the forward marshaling point for a huge naval and military operation; the immense natural harbor now was filled with battleships, cruisers, destroyers, troop transports, tramp steamers, water barges, tugs, and hospital ships.

At Alexandria and Mudros, the staff examined the question of where the army should land. Kitchener had forbidden a landing on the Asian coast, and landings on the shore inside the Dardanelles were ruled out because they would come under fire from the guns of the Narrows forts and the howitzers on the Asian shore. The peninsula's Aegean coast remained. De Robeck, trying to be helpful, suggested that Hamilton land his army at Bulair, on the peninsula's neck, thereby cutting the road to Constantinople and isolating the Turkish army on Gallipoli. Hamilton personally reconnoitered Bulair from the bridge of a British cruiser and saw that his troops would have to come ashore into a swamp, then assault a ridge of high ground honeycombed with earthwork fortifications that 10,000 Turks had been constructing for a month. With Bulair ruled out, the possible landing sites were reduced to three: Cape Helles, on the tip of the peninsula; Ari Burny, thirteen miles up the western coast of the peninsula; and Suvla Bay, a beach about a mile north of Ari Burny. Eventually Hamilton and his officers drew up their plan: the 29th Division would land on the five small beaches at the tip of the peninsula around Cape Helles. The Anzacs would go ashore at Ari Burny and, as a temporary diversion, the 16,000 troops of the French division would land at Kum Kale on the Asian side. Hamilton's hope was that by the evening of the first day, the 29th Division would seize the crest of Achi Baba, which dominated southern Gallipoli, and that the Anzacs would secure the heights of Sari Bair, astride the peninsula's middle. But Hamilton's first concern was the moment of landing itself. The troops were to be carried to Gallipoli aboard warships; a mile from the coast, the men would climb down into the ships' boats and be towed by tugs nearer the shore; close to the beaches, the boats would cast off and be rowed the final few hundred yards. In order to put a large number of men quickly ashore, an imaginative variation was proposed: the 6,000-ton collier *River Clyde* would be packed with 2,000 men, then run up on the beach, whereupon the soldiers would disembark from holes—romantically designated sally ports—cut in the ship's sides. "In my mind, the crux was to get my army ashore," Hamilton later wrote. "Once ashore, I could hardly think that Great Britain and France would not in the long run defeat Turkey."

As the landings approached, a sense of exhilaration swept through the British Mediterranean Expeditionary Force. It was assumed that the enemy was utterly inferior. Men in the ranks looked forward to "bashing Abdul" and "shoving it to Johnny Turk" while young officers, including the poet Rupert Brooke and the prime minister's son, Arthur Asquith, steeped in the classics taught in England's public schools, carried copies of the *Iliad.* "It's too wonderful for belief," Brooke wrote to Asquith's daughter, Violet. "I had not imagined Fate could be so benign. . . . Will Hero's Tower crumble under the 15-inch guns? Will the sea . . . be wine-dark? . . . Shall we be a Turning Point in History? Oh God! I've never been quite so happy in my life, I think." In England, everyone, including his friends the Asquiths, the Churchills, Bernard Shaw, and Henry James, was reading the poet's war sonnets:

Now, God be thanked Who has matched us with His hour,
And caught our youth, and wakened us from sleeping . . .

and

If I should die, think only this of me;
That there's some corner of a foreign field
That is for ever England. . . .

On the eve of the landings, the force suffered its most famous loss when Brooke, only twenty-seven, died on a hospital ship from blood poisoning. "He died at 4.46 [in the afternoon]," wrote one of his friends, "with the sun shining all round his cabin and the cool sea breeze blowing through the door and shaded windows. No one could have wished a quieter or calmer end than in that lovely bay, shielded by the mountains and fragrant with sage and thyme." His friends buried him that night on the top of a hill in a grove of olive trees.

A few hours later, the invasion fleet was off Cape Helles. Other young men would remember the moment: "Nature was so peaceful, a dead flat calm, an oily sea, a silent, beautiful rock-crowned island . . . no sound or movement in the water or air, no sign of the prodigious eruption of metal which was to greet the dawn." "On deck it is hardly light and the weather is cool. . . . There are ships everywhere . . . a whole fleet surrounds the peninsula. A light mist covers everything and white flaky clouds cling to the valleys. . . . We are now at the last lap, waiting our turn . . . not a breath of air, not a sign of movement. It is still a sheer impossibility to believe that we are at war."

Then came the opening thunderclap of the naval bombardment. The landings began at 5:30 a.m. and the men came ashore onto beaches tangled with barbed wire, swept by machine guns, and blasted by howitzers. Under a tempest of fire, boats were shattered and sank; others, filled with dead and dying, drifted away. Men clambered out of the boats, floundered up to their shoulders in the water, and were cut down, screaming. Others stepped into water too deep for them and, weighed down by their equipment, drowned unnoticed. Bodies floated out to sea or lay a few feet from shore, lapped by the wavelets. Before the sun was high, a wide crimson stain spread for a hundred feet out from the beach across the blue-green water. The *River Clyde,* with its cargo of 2,000 men packed tightly in the hold, ran in toward the beach until its propellers churned the sand near the ruined Sedd el Bahr fortress. Three hundred Turkish soldiers with machine guns waited behind a small ridge, holding their fire. The "sally ports" opened, the British infantry rushed forward, the machine guns chattered, and the gangways became choked with dead and dying men. On other beaches there was less resistance and, by nightfall, 33,000 British and Australian and 3,000 French troops were ashore. Five thousand men had been killed or wounded.

The landings failed to achieve even their first day objectives. At Cape Helles, Hamilton had hoped to seize the crown of Achi Baba before nightfall; from these heights, his artillery could range over the entire lower peninsula. From Anzac Beach, he had expected the Australians and New Zealanders to storm the crests of Chunuk Bair and Sari Bair; from these summits, they could then move down to seize the town of Maidos on the Straits and cut the peninsula in half. Instead, the British assault forces scarcely penetrated beyond the beaches. During May, three major attacks were launched on the village of Krithia, near Achi Baba, but the front advanced only a few hundred yards. When Hamilton suggested to Major General Aylmer Hunter-Weston, commander of the 29th Division, that he attack at night to cut down on casualties, Hunter-Weston replied, "Casualties? What do I care for casualties?" Hamilton, true to his nature, did not overrule his subordinate. When ground was taken, the Turks immediately counterattacked. On May 19, a mass of 30,000 Turks charged the Anzac lines; 10,000 Turks fell; the Anzacs lost 600.

The front was stalemated. The Allies could not seize the ridges; the Turks could not hurl their enemies back into the sea; and the killing ground of the Western Front was reproduced at Gallipoli. The weapons were the same: the rifle, the grenade, the machine gun, and the spade. At Anzac Beach, where the entire beachhead covered only 400 acres—less than half the size of New York City's Central Park—a labyrinth of trenches fronted by barbed wire was cut into the steep hillsides. Fire steps for snipers were set into the trench walls, with periscopes peeping over the top. To make it impossible for Allied warships to fire at the Turks without endangering their own men, Sanders ordered his soldiers to dig their trenches as close to the Allied trenches as possible; sometimes, the Allied and Turkish trenches were no more than fifteen feet apart. From the Allied front lines, hundreds of little paths ran down to the beach, worn smooth by men and animals bringing water and supplies; at one point Hamilton noted that he was unable to take the offensive because half of his men were carrying water and the other half were digging.

Hamilton soon realized that the War Office's prediction that the Turks would fiercely oppose the landings, but that once the troops were ashore, opposition would crumble, had come from a world of fantasy. Equally, he had seen that Kitchener's statement that "the cross fire from the fleet . . . must sweep that stretch of flat and open country so as to render it untenable by the enemy" bore no relation to reality at Gallipoli. As the painful and dangerous position of the army became more obvious, many men in the fleet offshore, watching with their own eyes, felt frustrated and humiliated. Keyes in particular was ashamed of the navy's inactivity. The Allied fleet now was immensely more powerful than it had been on March 18. Thirty-eight new minesweepers had been added, crewed by volunteers from the lost ships, and twenty-four destroyers had been converted for minesweeping. When de Robeck, Wemyss, and Keyes met on *Queen Elizabeth* on May 9, Keyes urged resumption of a full-scale naval attack on the Narrows. De Robeck agreed to put the suggestion before the Admiralty, but his signal to London was unenthusiastic: "From the vigour of the enemy's resistance, it is improbable that the passage of the fleet into the Marmara will be decisive, and therefore it is equally probable that the Straits will be closed behind the fleet," he wrote. "The temper of the Turkish army in the peninsula indicates that the forcing of the Dardanelles and subsequent appearance of the fleet off Constantinople would not of itself prove decisive." Keyes saw the message before it went, but, knowing the First Lord better than the admiral did, he believed that, even with the cold water thrown on it by de Robeck, this proposal would inspire Churchill to push a new attack through the Admiralty and the War Council. What Keyes did not know was the growing precariousness of the First Lord's position in London, and the strength of the forces gathering for his overthrow.

—

Week by week, Fisher's irritation with Churchill's methods of administering the Admiralty had continued to grow. He had never liked the stream of imperious memoranda that flowed from the First Lord, or Churchill's habit of sending operational messages to admirals and captains, which Fisher considered lay solely within his jurisdiction as First Sea Lord. But the greatest source of Fisher's mounting resentment was his apprehension about the Dardanelles. He feared that the Dardanelles were draining away the strength of the Grand Fleet and that he could do nothing to stop this. *"The more I consider the Dardanelles the less I like it!"* he wrote to Churchill on March 4. "No matter what happens it is impossible to send out anything more, not even a dinghy!" After the failure of the naval attack of March 18, Fisher, although relieved that the primary burden had been assumed by the army, still fought every suggestion and begrudged every instance of additional naval aid. *"We cannot send another rope yarn to de Robeck,"* he wrote to Churchill on April 2. "We have gone TO THE VERY LIMIT!!! And so they must be distinctly and most emphatically told that no further reinforcements of the fleet can be looked for! A failure or check in the Dardanelles would be nothing. *A failure in the North Sea would be ruin.*" Churchill attempted to set aside Fisher's complaints with good humor: "Seriously, my friend, are you not a little unfair in trying to spite this operation by side winds and small points when you have accepted it in principle?" Later, however, the First Lord would write that during these weeks, "every officer, every man, every ship, every round of ammunition required for the Dardanelles became a cause of friction and had to be fought for by me, not only with the First Sea Lord but to a certain extent with his naval colleagues."*

Meanwhile, the Conservative opposition was becoming aware of the increasing antagonism between the political and professional leaders of the navy. Most Conservatives disliked Winston Churchill. They remembered his famous walk across the aisle in 1904, and the label of "turncoat" had never been removed. Many Conservatives—and not a few Liberals—saw in Churchill's adventure in Antwerp, his frequent visits to France, evidence of the First Lord's immaturity and unwillingness to restrict himself to his proper sphere. Some found him personally abrasive. In particular, there no love lost between the First Lord and Andrew Bonar Law, the Canadian-born former Glasgow businessman who had replaced Balfour as leader of the Conservative party in 1911. Bonar Law believed that Churchill was too filled with quixotic, dangerous schemes, too quick to resent criticism, too obstinate to admit fallibility—in short, too irresponsible—to hold high office. Churchill, for his part, underrated Law as a fourth-rate politician and made little attempt to conceal his contempt.

De Robeck's May 9 telegram precipitated the Admiralty crisis that had

*In early May, Fisher's resentment against Churchill took a distinctly malicious turn. On May 5, the First Lord was in Paris at Asquith's request, participating in the negotiations that were to bring Italy into the war on the Allied side. Before coming home, the First Lord stopped to visit his friend Sir John French, at BEF headquarters. While her husband was away, Clementine Churchill invited Fisher to lunch. After lunch, on his way out the door, the old admiral turned to her and growled, "You are a foolish woman. All the time you think Winston's with Sir John French, he is in Paris with his mistress." Clementine, to whom Winston was faithful throughout his life, was stunned.

long been simmering. Churchill wanted to renew at least a limited attack on the Narrows forts to cover clearance of the Kephez minefield. Fisher stood fast; here was another attempt by the First Lord to hurl more men and ships into the bottomless pit of the Dardanelles. On May 11, he wrote to Churchill, "Although I have acquiesced in each stage of the operations up to the present . . . I have clearly expressed my opinion that I did not consider the original attempt to force the Dardanelles with the fleet alone was a practicable operation. . . . I cannot under any circumstances be a party to any order to Admiral de Robeck to make any attempt to pass the Dardanelles until the shores have been effectively occupied." Two days later, Fisher, attempting to buttress his position, wrote directly to the prime minister: "I honestly feel that I cannot remain where I am much longer as there is an inevitable and never-ceasing drain *daily (almost hourly)* on our resources in the decisive theatre of war. . . . We are all diverted to the Dardanelles and the unceasing activities of the First Lord, both by day and night, are engaged in ceaseless prodding of everyone in every department afloat and shore in the interests of the Dardanelles fleet." The strain between the two leaders of the Admiralty, therefore, was already acute. On May 13, it was further aggravated by the loss of another battleship at Gallipoli.

—

From the day of the landings, the sea around the Gallipoli peninsula had been unchallengeably British and French. The waters had been crowded with Allied ships: battleships, cruisers, and destroyers pounding the Turkish lines; transports, supply ships, hospital ships, and trawlers anchored off the beaches or gliding about their nautical business. This scene, which had provided the embattled soldiers with a powerful sense of security at their backs, had been taken for granted. Then came the sinking of *Goliath.*

Hugging the cliffs on the dark, moonless night of May 12, the Turkish destroyer *Muavenet,* commanded by a skillful German, crept down the European side of the Straits. Not more than a hundred yards offshore in Morto Bay lay the old battleship *Goliath,* anchored and awaiting the new bombardment assignments, which would come with morning. The destroyer, approaching the battleship through the mist, was seen and hailed—too late—by an officer on *Goliath*'s bridge. *Muavenet* surged forward and fired three torpedoes. The battleship rolled over onto her side, turned turtle, floated a few minutes upside down, then plunged to the bottom. The battleship *Majestic,* anchored nearby, switched on her searchlights. "The sea for an area of half an acre was a mass of struggling, drowning people, all drifting down towards us with the current," said a *Majestic* officer. Because the current that night was running at 4 or 5 knots, not a single man, even those in life jackets, was able to swim the short distance to shore. Five hundred and seventy men were drowned and 180 were saved. In human terms, this was the greatest loss suffered by the British navy in the Dardanelles campaign. For Turkey, it was a triumph. Every man in the destroyer's crew received a gold watch and an embroidered purse filled with gold from the sultan.

When the news reached London that afternoon, Fisher's concern about the vulnerability of *Queen Elizabeth* was violently stimulated. To calm the First Sea Lord, Churchill immediately agreed to bring the superdreadnought home and to replace her at the Dardanelles with new monitors carrying 14-inch guns. Fisher "was very much relieved at this and was grateful," the First Lord later recalled. Unfortunately, that evening the argument was rekindled. When Kitchener appeared at the Admiralty to discuss another matter, Churchill showed him the telegram he and Fisher had drafted but not yet sent regarding *Queen Elizabeth.* Kitchener, surprised, became extremely angry. He protested vehemently that the withdrawal of the principal warship at Gallipoli meant that the navy was deserting the army—and this, after the army had come to the navy's assistance when the fleet had failed to force a passage of the Dardanelles. Fisher, witnessing the field marshal's anger and listening as Churchill attempted to reassure Kitchener, flew into a rage himself: "The *Queen Elizabeth* would come home; she would come home at once; she would come home that night or he [Fisher] would walk out of the Admiralty, then and there." Kitchener rushed back to the War Office and scribbled a note to Asquith, complaining that Fisher "could not stand the fear of losing the ship. I may say that I have had to face the loss of some 15,000 men in the operations to help the navy." If the dreadnought departed, the field marshal warned, "we may have to consider . . . whether the troops had better be pulled back to Alexandria."

Nevertheless, for the moment, Fisher had won: the superdreadnought sailed for Malta and home and all thought of another naval offensive at the Dardanelles was suspended. "We think that the moment for an independent naval attempt to force the Narrows has passed," the Admiralty told de Robeck on May 14. "The army is now landed, large reinforcements are being sent. . . . Your role is therefore to support the army in its costly but sure advance and to reserve your strength to deal with the situation which will arise when the army has succeeded."

On the same day, the War Council held its first meeting since April 6. The atmosphere around the table at 10 Downing Street was, in Churchill's word, "sulphurous." *The Times* that morning had published allegations that the British army on the Western Front was scandalously short of artillery shells. Kitchener, defensive about these charges and still bitter about the withdrawal of *Queen Elizabeth,* complained that the Admiralty had let him and the army down. Fisher, unwilling to listen to charges of bad faith and near treachery directed at the navy, uncharacteristically spoke up. He had been "against the Dardanelles operations from the beginning," and "the Prime Minister and Lord Kitchener knew this fact well," he informed the council. "This remarkable interruption," Churchill said, "was received in silence." Fisher now saw himself surrounded at the War Council by his enemies and the navy's enemies. Despite the fact that de Robeck had just been told that no new naval attack was under consideration, the First Sea Lord sensed that additional diversions of ships to the Dardanelles were in the offing. His own plans were wholly ignored. "I could see that the great projects in Northern water [that is, the Baltic], which I had in view in laying down the Armada of new vessels were at an end," he told the Dardanelles Commission two years later. "If the huge commitment at the Dardanelles was to be continued, it was clearly better, in the very interests of the Dardanelles operations themselves . . . that they should be henceforth directed on the naval side by somebody who believed in them."

After the council meeting, Churchill, annoyed by Fisher's public outburst, attempted to set it in context in a letter to Asquith: "I must ask you to take note of Fisher's statement today that he was against the Dardanelles and had been all along. . . . The First Sea Lord has agreed in writing to every executive telegram on which the operation has been conducted. . . . I am attached to the old boy and it is a great pleasure to me to work with him. I think he reciprocates these feelings . . . [but] I cannot undertake to be paralyzed by the veto of a friend who, whatever the result, will certainly say 'I was always against the Dardanelles.' Someone has to take the responsibility. I will do so—provided that my decision is the one that rules." Churchill then attempted to heal the breach with Fisher. Early in the evening, he went to Fisher's office and for several hours the two men discussed the Dardanelles and what further reinforcements might be needed and could be spared. Fisher agreed to sending more monitors, which would permit bringing home more battleships. When they parted, Churchill said, "Well, good night, Fisher. We have settled everything and you must go home and have a good night's rest. Things will look brighter in the morning and we will pull the thing through together." Before leaving the Admiralty, Fisher told his secretary that the discussion had been amicable. "But," he added, "I suppose he'll soon be at me again." After Fisher's departure, Churchill remained working in his office. Going back over the list of ships to be sent to the Dardanelles, he added two new *E*-class submarines requested by de Robeck—two of the five to be completed in England that month. Churchill later said that he considered these additions a proposal, not an order, and he attached a covering note to Fisher: "I send this to you . . . in order that if any point arises we can discuss it. I hope you will agree."

At 5:00 on the following morning, Saturday, May 15, Fisher returned to the Admiralty. On his desk, he discovered the papers showing that Churchill wished to add two submarines to the list agreed on the night before. Something snapped inside Lord Fisher. At midmorning, the First Lord, hurrying toward the Admiralty across the Horse Guards Parade, was intercepted by his secretary. "Fisher has resigned and I think he means it this time," the secretary blurted. He handed Churchill a letter:

First Lord:

After further anxious reflection, I have come to the regretted conclusion that I am unable to remain any longer as your colleague. It is undesirable in the public interest to go in to details . . . but I find it increasingly difficult to adjust myself to the increasing daily requirements of the Dardanelles to meet your views. As you truly said yesterday, I am in the position of continually vetoing your proposals.

This is not fair to you besides being extremely distasteful to me.

I am off to Scotland at once, so as to avoid all questioning.

Yours truly,
Fisher

Regarding this letter of resignation as no more serious than those Fisher had written before, Churchill returned to the Admiralty to straighten things out. But the First Sea Lord was not in his office, nor in the building, nor in his living quarters. Churchill hurried back across the Horse Guards Parade to 10 Downing Street and showed Fisher's letter to Asquith. The prime minister immediately wrote to the admiral: "In the King's name, I order you to return to your post." It took several hours to locate Fisher, but eventually he was discovered at the Charing Cross Hotel. He read the prime minister's peremptory message and came to Downing Street. There, while waiting to see Asquith, he encountered Lloyd George. "A combative grimness had taken the place of his usually genial greeting," said Lloyd George. "The lower lip of his set mouth was thrust forward, and the droop at the corner was more marked than usual. His curiously Oriental features were more than ever those of a graven image in an Eastern temple with a sinister frown. 'I have resigned!' was his greeting. 'I can stand it no longer.' " Lloyd George and Asquith both urged Fisher to return to the Admiralty. Fisher refused. Asquith then asked him to remain in London and Fisher agreed. The following evening, Maurice Hankey found him at the Athenaeum Club trying "to escape from Winston."

There is something revealing about Fisher's refusal to see Churchill in these crucial days. Fisher—fierce, cunning, autocratic, and articulate within the navy—was nearly powerless against Churchill. The result was that he acquiesced in decisions that he believed to be wrong and that rose up to haunt him. In Churchill's presence, however, his confidence shriveled and he found himself unable to withstand the younger man's brimming enthusiasm and relentless logic. Part of the difficulty was that Fisher genuinely liked and admired Churchill. Aware of this, Churchill routinely exploited it, employing a combination of deference, charm, and relentless argument to overwhelm the old man's defenses. That day, for example, after seeing Asquith, the First Lord set himself to charm, wheedle, and bludgeon Fisher back into harness:

> My dear Fisher,
>
> The only thing to think of now is what is best for the country and for the brave men who are fighting. . . . I do not understand what is the specific cause which has led you to resign. If I did I might cure it. When we parted last night I thought we were in agreement. The proposals I made to you by minute were I thought in general accord with your views and in any case were for discussion between us. . . . In every way I have tried to work in the closest sympathy with you. The men you wanted in the places you wanted them, the ships you designed—every proposal you have formally made . . . I have agreed to. In order to bring you back to the Admiralty, I took my political life in my hands with the King and the Prime Minister—as you know well. You then promised to stand by me and see me through. . . . It will be a very great grief to me to part from you; and our rupture will be profoundly injurious to every public interest.

Fisher's reply reminded Churchill that his opposition to the Dardanelles campaign dated from January and that, since then, the drain on Britain's naval resources had been constant. The additional reinforcements—the two submarines—added by Churchill overnight were only the last straw. "YOU ARE BENT ON FORCING THE DARDANELLES AND NOTHING WILL TURN YOU FROM IT—NOTHING. I know you so well," Fisher wrote. "I could give no better proof of my desire to stand by you than my having remained by you in the Dardanelles business to this last moment against the strongest conviction of my life. . . . *You will remain* and I SHALL GO. It is better so. Your splendid stand on my behalf with the King and Prime Minister I can NEVER forget . . . but here is a question beyond all personal obligations." On receiving this letter, Churchill wrote one last time, claiming "in the name of friendship and in the name of duty, a personal interview." Fisher refused, saying, "Dear Winston: As usual your letter is most persuasive, but I really have considered everything. Please don't wish to see me. I could say nothing. . . . *I know I am doing right.*"

Up to this point, Fisher's resignation had been a matter primarily for Admiralty concern: a policy disagreement, which would break the professional ties between two colleagues and old friends. But the news eddied down corridors into official chambers and then out into private drawing rooms, and within hours the admiral became a focus of popular attention. "Stick to your post like Nelson," Queen Alexandra wrote to Fisher. "The nation and we all have such full confidence in you and they will not suffer you to go. You are the nation's hope." Messages poured in from the fleet. "I would far sooner lose some ships than see you leave the Admiralty," telegraphed Jellicoe. Beatty added that Fisher's departure "would be a worse calamity than a defeat at sea. . . . Please God it is NOT possible." The press had the story:

"Lord Fisher Must Not Go," blared a headline in the *Globe.* Unfortunately for himself, Fisher had not waited for this groundswell to take effect. Caught up in his first feverish indignation, he had on the day of his resignation also sent an anonymous message to Bonar Law, hinting at what he had done. Early Monday morning, May 17, Bonar Law called on Lloyd George to ask him whether, in fact, the First Sea Lord had resigned. When Lloyd George said yes, Bonar Law said, "Then the situation is impossible." He meant that once Conservative MPs learned that Lord Fisher was leaving the Admiralty and that Winston Churchill was staying, they would revolt. The unofficial party truce would end and the Conservative party would initiate a series of parliamentary debates attacking numerous aspects of the government's war policy.

Asquith quailed at this prospect. If his premiership was to survive, Bonar Law's support was critical. When Lloyd George proposed as a solution that the Liberal Cabinet that had governed Great Britain since 1906 step down in favor of a new coalition government, which would include the Conservatives, the prime minister surrendered immediately. Bonar Law's key condition for joining the government was that Winston Churchill be replaced as First Lord of the Admiralty. Asquith agreed to this. Bonar Law also demanded the sacrifice of Haldane, the Lord Chancellor, Asquith's oldest friend in politics, and Asquith agreed to this, too.

The news that he was to be replaced took Churchill by brutal surprise. The previous day, Sunday the sixteenth, the First Lord had offered Asquith his resignation, but the prime minister had said, "No, I have thought of that. I do not wish it"—and then had invited Churchill to stay for dinner. On this basis, Churchill had asked Sir Arthur Wilson to become First Sea Lord. Wilson had accepted, and the other Sea Lords had agreed to stay on. With a new Admiralty board in place, Churchill began preparing a speech for Monday afternoon in which he would report Fisher's resignation to Parliament and name Wilson as the new First Sea Lord. But events were moving too quickly. Already by Monday morning, Asquith had agreed to Bonar Law's conditions for forming a coalition. When Churchill arrived at Westminster that afternoon, assuming that he had Asquith's support, he reported to the prime minister that he had successfully reconstructed the leadership of the Admiralty. Asquith listened and then said, "No, this will not do. I have decided to form a national Government by a coalition . . . and a very much larger reconstruction will be required. . . . What are we to do for you?" At that moment, Churchill understood that he was no longer to be First Lord.

Ironically, from the beginning of the war, Churchill had urged the formation of a coalition government. The Conservative statesman to whom Churchill was closest was the erudite, aristocratic former prime minister Arthur Balfour. As an unofficial member of the War Council, Balfour had meshed smoothly into the meetings of that body. Churchill liked and trusted the elegant, articulate Balfour; he disliked, ignored, and, when contact was necessary, patronized the stolid, plain-spoken Bonar Law. Now Churchill learned that it was Bonar Law who was the arbiter of his fate and that his own removal from the Admiralty had been the sine qua non in discussions between Asquith and Bonar Law about the formation of a coalition government.

Over the next few days, as the crisis played out, both Fisher and Churchill displayed their worst qualities. Fisher's antipathy toward Churchill reached a peak in a letter to Bonar Law on the seventeenth: "W.C. MUST go at all costs! AT ONCE . . . *because a very great disaster is very near us in the Dardanelles.* . . . W.C. is a bigger danger than the Germans by a long way." At some point, this frantic assault gave birth in Fisher to a larger, extraordinarily grandiose project. He decided that he did not actually want to retreat to Scotland. His country needed him and he would serve by returning to the Admiralty as an entirely new kind of First Sea Lord, an admiralissimo, who would assume absolute control of the navy.

Unfortunately for Fisher, events were working against him. On Monday, May 17, even as Asquith was asking Churchill, "What are we to do for you?" Room 40 was decoding an intercepted German wireless message indicating that the High Seas Fleet was coming out. The First Lord hurried from the House of Commons back to the Admiralty to send the Grand Fleet to sea. At 8:00 that evening, he telegraphed Jellicoe, "It is not impossible that tomorrow may be The Day." By dawn, however, hope for a battle was fading, and by 10:00 a.m. it was clear that the German fleet was returning to its harbors. Through these alarms, the all-night vigil, and the subsequent disappointment, the First Sea Lord—still formally in office, because Asquith had not yet accepted his resignation—was absent from the Admiralty. The other Sea Lords were shocked; Churchill told the prime minister that they took "a serious view of Lord Fisher's desertion of his post in time of war for what has now amounted to six days during which serious operations have been in progress." The king, a former naval officer who did not share his mother's warm admiration of Fisher, grew red in the face when this incident was mentioned. "He should have been hanged at the yardarm for desertion of his post in the face of the enemy," George V declared. "It really was a most scandalous thing which ought to be punished with dismissal from the service and degradation."

Fisher, still rampaging around London, but never setting foot in the Admiralty, did not realize that the wind had changed. Knowing by May 19 that Churchill was doomed, he persuaded himself that this was his moment of triumph; that he was the man the government must turn to. Thus deluded, he sent Asquith a set of conditions under which he would agree to return to the Admiralty and "guarantee the successful termination of the war." Churchill must be completely excluded from the Cabinet. Balfour (who had angered him by supporting the naval attack on the Dardanelles) must not replace Churchill as First Lord. Whoever became First Lord must be restricted solely to political policy and parliamentary procedure. Sir Arthur Wilson must quit the Admiralty and a new set of Sea Lords be installed. Turning to the role he himself proposed to play, Fisher slid into megalomania: "I shall have complete professional charge of the war at sea, together with the absolute sole disposition of the fleet and the appointment of all officers of all ranks whatsoever, and absolutely untrammeled sole command of all the sea forces whatsoever. . . . I should have the sole absolute authority for all new construction and all dockyard work of whatever sort, and complete control of the whole of the Civil Establishment of the navy. These six conditions," Fisher concluded, "must be published verbatim so that the fleet may know my position." The only excuse for the breadth and tone of Fisher's demands can be that he was attempting to elevate himself to the same level of untrammeled authority already occupied by Kitchener at the War Office. But no one else saw it that way. "I am afraid that Jacky is really a little mad," said Arthur Balfour. Asquith's reaction was that the memorandum indicated "a fit of megalomania." He informed the king that "Fisher's mind is somewhat unhinged, otherwise his conduct is almost traitorous!" Privately, to Hankey, the prime minister wrote "that Fisher, strictly speaking, ought to be shot for leaving his post."

Fisher's role in the drama was over. On the afternoon of May 22, one week after he had read Churchill's proposal to send two more submarines to the Dardanelles, he boarded an afternoon train for Scotland to hide himself away at the estate of his close friend the Duchess of Hamilton. During the train's stopover at Crewe, a messenger approached and handed him an envelope. He opened it and read:

> Dear Lord Fisher,
>
> I am commanded by the king to accept your tendered resignation of the Office of First Sea Lord of the Admiralty.
>
> Yours faithfully,
> H. H. Asquith

The sixty-one-year career of Admiral of the Fleet Lord Fisher of Kilverstone, the man who created the modern Royal Navy, had come to an end.

—

Meanwhile, Churchill was struggling to save himself. He bombarded Asquith, Bonar Law, Lloyd George, and Grey, asking, eventually begging, to be kept at the Admiralty. To Lloyd George, his closest Cabinet ally before the war, he shouted, "You don't care what becomes of me. You don't care whether I am trampled under foot by my enemies. You don't care for my personal reputation." "No," Lloyd George replied, "I don't care for my own at the present moment. The only thing I care about is that we win this war." Clementine Churchill, incensed by what was happening to her husband, wrote the prime minister an angry letter: "Why do you part with Winston? . . . If you throw Winston overboard you will be committing an act of weakness and your Coalition Government will not be as formidable a war machine as your present government." Asquith did not reply, but he told Venetia Stanley that he had received "the letter of a maniac" from her cousin Clementine Churchill. To Churchill himself—who had sent him six letters in five days—Asquith finally wrote on May 21, "My dear Winston: You must take it as settled that you are not to remain at the Admiralty." The "horrible wound and mutilation"—in Churchill's private secretary's words—was confirmed. The following day, Churchill was offered and accepted a minor, essentially meaningless Cabinet post, the chancellorship of the Duchy of Lancaster. "I gather that you have been flung a bone on which there is very little meat," wrote his cousin the Duke of Marlborough. The duchy, Lloyd George wrote of this post, was an office normally given "to beginners in the Cabinet or to distinguished politicians who had reached the first stages of unmistakable decrepitude. It was a cruel and unjust degradation." May 25 was Churchill's last day at the Admiralty, and that afternoon he received a surprise visit from Lord Kitchener. "He asked what I was going to do," Churchill wrote. "I said I had no idea; nothing was settled. . . . As he got up to go, he turned and said, in the impressive and almost majestic manner which was natural to him, 'Well, there is one thing at any rate they cannot take from you. The fleet was ready.' "

Kitchener was right: the ships built by Fisher and Churchill were at sea and the men whom Fisher and Churchill had chosen were in command. It reflects poorly on Beatty, whom Churchill had saved from early retirement and promoted over a dozen admirals to command the battle cruisers, that he wrote after Churchill's fall, "The navy breathes freer now it is rid of the succubus Winston." Nor was it generous of Jellicoe, to whom Churchill gave command of the Grand Fleet on the eve of war, to write to Fisher, "We owe you a debt of gratitude for having saved the navy from a continuance in office of Mr Churchill." In the stream of newspaper articles and editorials about Churchill's departure, most were derogatory.* At that moment, the former First Lord did not know or care what any of these men were saying. Later, Clementine Churchill would say of her husband, "When he left the Admiralty, he thought he was finished. . . . I thought he would never get over the Dardanelles: I thought he would die of grief."

*Only J. L. Garvin, writing in *The Observer,* looked to the future: "He is young. He has lion-hearted courage. No number of enemies can fight down his ability and force. His hour of triumph will come."

CHAPTER 27

"Some Corner of a Foreign Field"

Ultimately, Fisher's concern about the safety of the warships at the Dardanelles had led to the reconstruction of the Admiralty and then of the government. Curiously, on May 25, just as this immense political drama was playing out and Winston Churchill was in his last hours in office, another British battleship was sunk at Gallipoli. And thirty-six hours later, when Arthur Balfour was just sitting down in Churchill's chair at the Admiralty, still another British battleship went to the bottom. Neither loss had any political impact in London, but to the navy off Gallipoli and the thousands of soldiers on the peninsula, their significance was grim.

On May 17, Admiral de Robeck had been informed that a German submarine had been sighted on the surface passing through the Straits of Gibraltar. This was *U-21,* voyaging from the Ems around the coast of Europe to the Aegean. No one at the Admiralty or in the fleet doubted that the submarine's destination was Gallipoli. On May 25, in full view of both armies on shore, the old battleship *Triumph* was torpedoed by *U-21* off Anzac Beach. As the ship began to list, a destroyer came alongside and hundreds of men stepped from the battleship's stern onto the deck of the smaller ship. Then *Triumph* turned over, floated with her keel in the air for twenty minutes, and sank, taking fifty-three men down with her. The cheers of exultant Turks, dancing in their trenches, echoed down from the hills while men in the Allied trenches watched with shock and fear. De Robeck, his fleet suddenly vulnerable, immediately ordered all large warships back to the island harbors. "I saw them in full flight, transports and battleships, the *Agamemnon* seeming to lead the van," said the British writer turned officer Compton Mackenzie. "Next morning," recorded a German officer watching from the heights, "all the ships had disappeared as if God had taken a broom and swept the sea clear."

The following day, May 26, the twenty-one-year-old *Majestic,* the oldest battleship in the Royal Navy, returned, anchored off Sedd el Bahr, spread her torpedo nets, and awaited bombardment assignments. At 6:40 on the morning of the twenty-seventh, a seaman on watch called an officer's attention to the periscope and conning tower of a submarine not far away. The officer looked and said, "Yes, and here comes the torpedo." "There was a great, muffled roar and the old ship quivered and shook in a terrible way. The masts and yards swayed as if they were coming down on top of us. . . . A huge volume of water shot up two hundred feet in the air on the port side. . . . There was only one thing to do and that was to swim for it. . . . The water was gloriously warm." The battleship rolled over and sank in shallow water, leaving her green keel protruding from the surface. There she remained for months, in full view of both armies.

—

Fisher and Churchill were gone, and three more old battleships had been sunk, but Kitchener and the new coalition War Council were not ready to give up on Gallipoli. In July, three divisions of Kitchener's New Army arrived from England on board the huge, transatlantic liners *Aquitania, Mauretania,* and *Olympic,* swelling Hamilton's force to 120,000 men. It was midsummer and the newcomers entered a landscape of Saharan desolation. Under an intense blue sky, the land and sea were covered by a suffocating haze of heat; the trenches were ovens; hot wind blew sand and white dust into eyes and mouths. For sixteen hours a day, the sun beat down so mercilessly that tinned rations of corned beef cooked in their containers. The sea, Hamilton wrote, was "like melted glass, blue-green with a dull red glow in it; the air seemed to have been boiled." To cool off, men bathed naked off the beaches, hundreds at a time, oblivious to artillery and sniper fire. (Once, a shell exploding in the water near a swimmer tore off his arm; retrieving the floating limb, the victim carried it ashore.) The flies became a plague; the ground and the walls of tents were dark with them; they swarmed in the latrines; three or four flies accompanied every forkful of food into the mouth. No one at Gallipoli escaped the torture of lice. Dysentery now affected half the army, and every day a thousand men with the disease were being evacuated from the peninsula as unfit for duty. Rank gave no immunity; both Hamilton and Wemyss were afflicted. The disease, Hamilton wrote in his diary, "fills me with a desperate longing to lie down and do nothing but rest. . . . This, I think, must be the reason the Greeks were ten long years taking Troy." Over the peninsula hung the sickening smell of death. Men who died between the two lines of trenches lay where they fell, the flies settled to feast, and the stench from corpses putrefying in the heat reached for miles out to sea.

As the months went by, both British and German officers developed great respect for the hardiness of the average Turkish soldier. Accustomed to sleeping on the ground, untroubled at being clothed in rags, happy to receive a piece of bread, some olives, and in the evening a thin soup, these peasant soldiers adapted to war and made a formidable enemy. After the war, the German influence at Gallipoli was overstated. There were never more than 500 Germans on the peninsula and although Sanders's generalship played a critical role, most German officers acted merely as advisers to Turkish commanders. Here, their usefulness was limited. "That evening, Kemal Bey assembled all his regimental commanders around him in an empty tent," wrote Hans Kannengiesser, a German colonel at Gallipoli. "They all sat in rings on the ground . . . with their legs crossed under them. . . . I at first tried to sit *a la turca,* but could not do so, so lay on the hard ground on my side. There were no chairs or tables—the Turks wrote with the paper flat on the palms of their hands. . . . Maps were not used during the discussion, of which I naturally understood no word." The strength of the army was the average soldier's willingness to accept death as unexceptional. "I do not order you to make war," Mustafa Kemal told his men. "I order you to die." Kannengiesser once saw two Turkish soldiers sitting on two corpses while eating their bread and olives. On several occasions, Allied soldiers capturing a Turkish trench confronted nightmarish horror: bodies had been embedded in the trench wall to make up part of the parapet; the trench floors were covered with the remains of separate arms, legs, and heads, all decomposing and slippery underfoot.

—

Hamilton did what he could with what he had. In mid-July, he asked Kitchener for two experienced generals to take over two of his commands. He was told that they were in France and "unavailable"; instead, elderly former officers, plucked from retirement, were sent out. He asked for a guaranteed supply of 400,000 shells a month for his artillery; the War Office replied, "It will be quite impossible to send you ammunition at this rate without stopping all operations in France. This, of course, is out of the question." Nevertheless, on August 6, Hamilton launched his final offensive. Two fresh divisions of Kitchener's New Army, just arrived from England with no experience in war, were put ashore on Suvla Beach, three miles north of Anzac Beach. To distract the Turks while the British landed, the veteran Australians and New Zealanders stormed up Lone Pine Ridge and Sari Bair from Anzac Beach. The casualties were shocking: one Australian brigade lost more than 1,700 men out of 2,900 involved; another battalion suffered 74 percent casualties; within two days, the Anzacs won six Victoria Crosses; but they failed to take the summit. Meanwhile, another column of Anzacs, British, and Gurkhas was assaulting the dominating ridge of Chunuk Bair. At dawn, the 6th Gurkha Battalion reached the top. "We bit, fisted and used rifles and pistols as clubs, blood was flying about like spray . . . and then the Turks turned and fled," said the British major commanding the Gurkhas. "I felt a very proud man: the key of the whole peninsula was ours. . . . Below I saw the Straits . . . [and] the roads leading to Achi Baba. We dashed down [pursuing the Turks] towards Maidos [on the Straits] but had only got about a hundred feet down when suddenly our own navy put six 12-inch shells into us . . . confusion . . . disaster . . . the place was a mass of blood and limbs and screams. . . . We lost about a hundred and fifty men and the regiment was withdrawn."

All of this bravery went for nought. Sir "Freddy" Stopford, commanding the troops landed at Suvla, was an amiable, doddering lieutenant general who had retired seven years earlier to battle chronic ill health. His presence at Gallipoli—indeed, in the army at all—was due to the fact that his country, beginning the war with only a small professional army, had no deep cadre of men qualified to command an army corps or even a division. Stopford, called back into service, had been given this key assignment by Kitchener even though Hamilton had named at least three other generals he thought better qualified. In any case, Stopford's landing had taken the Turks by surprise, but because his men seemed tired and thirsty, he did not push them to occupy the surrounding ridges. When Hamilton arrived a few hours later, he found 20,000 men "spread around the beaches . . . smoking and cooking, others bathing by hundreds in the bright blue bay." He discovered Stopford placidly presiding over this scene from an offshore yacht, enormously pleased that he had met so little resistance. Hamilton insisted that Stopford's men hurry to occupy the heights before the enemy arrived. "We might have the hills at the cost of walking up them today," he said. "The Lord only knows what the price of them will be tomorrow." Stopford did not disagree, but cordially excused himself from going ashore because "he had not been very fit, his knee was sore from a fall and he wanted to give it a chance to recover." The British troops remained in place and by the next morning, thousands of Turks were massed on the heights. Eventually, Stopford was relieved of command, but the opportunity, now missed, never returned. By August 21, the Suvla offensive was stalemated and Hamilton had suffered another 40,000 casualties. He told Kitchener that to attack again he would need a further reinforcement of 95,000 men.

Briefly, it seemed that he might get them. On September 2, the French made a surprise proposal to land four new divisions on the Asian side of the Dardanelles. "From bankrupt to millionaire in 24 hours! We are saved! Constantinople is doomed!" was Hamilton's gleeful reaction. But this French operation was canceled when, on October 14, Bulgaria, having observed the defeat at Suvla Bay and concluding that the Allies would never take the Dardanelles, joined the Austrian-German assault on her old foe, Serbia. A Serb defeat cleared the way for an enemy advance on Salonika, which Britain and France did not wish to lose. Accordingly, instead of gaining four new divisions, Hamilton lost two: one British and one French, taken from him and sent to defend Salonika. "We can't feed Russia with munitions through Salonika, nor can we bring back Russian wheat through Salonika," Hamilton noted bitterly.

By mid-October, the sands of the Gallipoli adventure were running out. Bulgaria's entry into the war meant the opening of a direct rail link between Germany and Constantinople with the likelihood that Turkish artillery on Gallipoli soon would have large supplies of ammunition. Already, on October 11, Kitchener had asked Hamilton for an assessment of the losses that might be incurred if Allied troops evacuated Gallipoli. Unwilling to concede defeat, Hamilton gloomily had estimated that he might lose half of his men. The reaction from London was swift: on October 16, Hamilton was relieved of command.* His replacement was a general straight from the Western Front, Sir Chârles Monro, described by Hankey as "a cheery old fellow with an odd trick of slapping you on the arm and ejaculating 'Ja!' " Monro had always believed that the Dardanelles was a foolish, hopeless "side-show" that diverted troops from France, the only theater of war where an ultimate de-

*There was another factor in Hamilton's dismissal. On September 2, an Australian journalist, Keith Arthur Murdoch, arrived at British headquarters and gave Hamilton "an elaborate explanation of why his duty to Australia could be better done with a pen than a rifle." Murdoch was permitted to visit Suvla and Anzac Beaches for a few hours; then, in breach of a signed agreement pertaining to the behavior of all war correspondents, Murdoch wrote directly to Andrew Fisher, prime minister of Australia, who passed the letter along to Asquith. In his letter, Murdoch praised the physical health, spirit, and bravery of the Australian forces and then spoke with contempt of the British troops: "You would refuse to believe that these men were really British soldiers. . . . The British physique is very much below that of the Turks. . . . They are merely a lot of child-like youths, without strength to endure or brains to improve their conditions." This was opinion, but Murdoch's worst accusation was flagrantly untrue: "The fact is that after the first day at Suvla an order had to be issued to [British] officers to shoot without mercy any [British] soldier who lagged behind or loitered in advance." Hamilton later described Murdoch's allegation as "an irresponsible statement by an ignorant man," but Asquith, inexplicably, had it reprinted on official British government stationery and circulated it to the War Council and the Committee on Imperial Defence. Neither Hamilton nor Kitchener was ever given an opportunity to respond.

Some Australians have never forgiven Britain and the British army for the loss of young Anzac lives at Gallipoli. The 1981 film *Gallipoli* also celebrated the manly beauty and heroism of the Australian soldiery, especially that of the 10th Light Horse Regiment from Western Australia. The film depicts this regiment ordered to attack again and again, repeatedly charging into Turkish rifles and machine guns and suffering 75 percent casualties at the relentless insistence of an Australian senior officer under orders to distract the Turks while the British landed at Suvla Beach. The film was mostly truthful. "The 10th went forward to meet death instantly," wrote C.E.W. Bean, in the official Australian history of the Great War, "the men running as swiftly and as straight as they could at the Turkish rifles. With that regiment went the flower of the youth of Western Australia, sons of the old pioneering families—in some cases two and three from the same home—who had flocked to Perth to enlist with their own horses and saddles."

Interestingly, Keith Murdoch's son, Rupert, was one of the film's principal financial backers.

cision could be achieved. On a single day, October 31, Monro visited the beaches at Helles, Suvla, and Anzac and then—as everyone in London knew he would—recommended immediate evacuation of the entire peninsula. He estimated that the withdrawal would cost 40,000 British casualties. Churchill's comment was bitter: "General Monro was an officer of swift decision. He came, he saw, he capitulated." On November 3, however, Kitchener rejected Monro's advice, refused to order an evacuation, and announced that he himself would go out to Gallipoli. Kitchener reached Mudros on November 9 and spent the next three days inspecting troops and positions on the peninsula. After talking with Birdwell and plodding up and down the hillsides, walking in trenches within twenty yards of the Turks, he concluded that Monro had been right: further effort was useless. He telegraphed the War Council his recommendation that Suvla and Anzac should be immediately evacuated and Helles temporarily retained. Back in London on November 30, he went straight to Downing Street and offered his resignation to the prime minister. Asquith refused to accept it.

Meanwhile, the prime minister again was trying to save his government. By early October, the Cabinet was deeply divided on the issue of Gallipoli: Bonar Law passionately favored evacuation; Churchill, fervently, and, to a lesser degree, Balfour advocated seeing the campaign through. Once Bulgaria declared war on October 18, thus establishing a direct rail link between Germany and Turkey, Bonar Law predicted that German artillery and munitions would pour into Constantinople and Gallipoli, putting Allied troops on the peninsula in extreme danger. Asquith sat on the fence. His tactic was to call for reports followed by discussions of the reports; invariably, this resulted in the passage of time and the postponement of decisions. Thus, when Hamilton was recalled and Monro sent out, everyone knew that the general would recommend evacuation. Bonar Law protested, accurately describing the mission as a waste of time. When Monro's recommendation arrived, however, so formidable was the opposition to evacuation from Churchill and others that the prime minister needed a further postponement of decision. Accordingly, Lord Kitchener was dispatched to do over again what General Monro had just done. Bonar Law, enraged, threatened to resign unless the Cabinet rescinded its decision to postpone the final decision until Kitchener made his report. On November 7, Bonar Law met Asquith and made clear to the prime minister that this conversation must be a final one between them—either evacuation or his own resignation must follow immediately. Asquith used every persuasion; Bonar Law remained firm, and, at the conclusion, the prime minister surrendered and promised that the troops would be withdrawn. Thereafter, although Kitchener did not know it, his mission became only a façade behind which the timing and sequence of the evacuation would be arranged. Luckily for Asquith, Lord Kitchener decided independently that Gallipoli should be given up and on November 23, the War

Committee duly voted for evacuation, "on the strength of Lord Kitchener's views." One man who saw what was coming did not wait for the final vote. On November 18, Winston Churchill resigned from the Cabinet and the Duchy of Lancaster and departed England to command a battalion on the Western Front. He spent his first night sleeping in a pit of Flanders mud four feet deep, containing a foot of water.

—

New horrors afflicted the men on Gallipoli. On November 26, a torrential rain followed by a two-day blizzard of sleet and snow flooded and froze the trenches. Men drowned when icy water roared down the hillsides and through the trenches; subsequently, 200 men froze to death. Eventually, over 16,000 men on the Allied side were disabled by frostbite, and 10,000 had to be evacuated. Evidence of Turkish suffering came from a stream of Turkish bodies washing down from the heights into Allied trenches.

—

Despite the lost battleships, Hamilton's removal, the gloomy visits of Monro and Kitchener, and the secret decision in London for evacuation, a countercurrent had been running through the fleet offshore. De Robeck remained opposed to a new naval attempt to force the Narrows, but Roger Keyes, his Chief of Staff, had never abandoned hope. Before Kitchener arrived, Keyes had made a new proposal: the army need only hold on to its three beachheads while the navy rushed a squadron through the Straits into the Sea of Marmara. De Robeck was a forbearing superior: "Well, Commodore," he said to Keyes, who was ten years younger, "you and I will never agree, but there is no reason we should not remain friends." Keyes had a strong ally in Rear Admiral Rosslyn Wester Wemyss, the commander at Mudros; possibly because of this, de Robeck gave his Chief of Staff permission to go to London and personally present his plan to the Admiralty. Keyes arrived in London on October 28 and called on Arthur Balfour. The new First Lord, lying back in his armchair with his knees as high as his head, listened for two hours while Keyes poured out his appeal. Then Balfour stood up, rang for tea, and said, "It is not often that when one examines a hazardous enterprise—and you will admit it has its hazards—the more one considers it the better one likes it." To the argument that de Robeck, the admiral in command, opposed the plan, Keyes replied that Wemyss, who was senior to de Robeck on the permanent Navy List and who knew the theater equally well, supported the plan and therefore should be placed in command. Balfour nodded and suggested that Keyes make a call on Kitchener who was about to depart on his visit to Gallipoli. The field marshal listened and urged Keyes to go back to the Admiralty and get a firm commitment to the naval attack. That evening, November 3, Kitchener sent a message to Birdwood, who was temporarily in command at Gallipoli:

> Most secret. Decipher yourself. . . . You know Monro's report. I leave here tomorrow night to come out to you. Have seen Commodore Keyes, and the Admiralty will, I believe, agree naval attempt to force the Straits. We must do what we can to help them, and I think as soon as ships are in the Marmara, we should seize and hold the Bulair isthmus. . . . The admiral will probably be changed and Wemyss given command to carry through the naval part of the work. . . . We must do it right this time. I absolutely refuse to sign orders for evacuation, which I think would condemn a large percentage of our men to death or imprisonment.

The morning of November 4 was the high-water mark for Keyes's mission to London and for his plan to rush the Straits. The Admiralty, temporarily moved by Keyes's enthusiasm, ordered four more old battleships, *Hibernia, Zealandia, Albemarle,* and *Russell,* plus four destroyers and twenty-four trawlers, to the Dardanelles. Balfour sent a message to de Robeck tactfully saying that the admiral probably was tired and ought to come home on leave for at least a month. That afternoon, however, the political tide began to turn. Kitchener, before leaving that night on his own visit to the Aegean, attended a meeting of the War Council where it was decided that a new naval attempt could only be authorized in support of a major new offensive by the army. As there were no fresh troops to launch such an offensive—all reinforcements for the Mediterranean were going to Salonika—the ministers decided that a naval attack by itself would be pointless. On November 7, the prime minister promised Bonar Law that the army would be evacuated. Keyes, however, was unaware of either of these decisions and returned to the Aegean believing that his plan would be approved. On November 18, however, he saw Kitchener, who by then had visited Gallipoli. "I have seen the place," he said to Keyes. "It is an awful place and you will never get through." Kitchener by then had made his own recommendation that Suvla and Anzac be evacuated and Cape Helles held.

Still, Keyes did not give up. On November 25, de Robeck departed on leave and Sir Rosslyn Wester Wemyss assumed command of the fleet in the Aegean. Thereafter, Wemyss joined Keyes in ceaseless advocacy of a renewed naval attack. On November 28, Wemyss proposed to the Admiralty that eight old battleships, four light cruisers, and ten destroyers make the attempt, followed by four battleships acting as supply vessels. Fitted with mine bumpers, the ships would enter the Straits at dark. Veiled from the searchlights by smoke screens, they would rush through the minefields and past the Narrows forts, then attack the forts from the rear. As soon as it was light, a second squadron of six more-modern battleships would attack the forts from below the minefields. The suddenness of this surprise attack, Wemyss argued, guaranteed success.

Monro, adamantly opposed to any further effort at the Dardanelles, vehemently objected. "I realised," Wemyss said later, "that in him I had an opponent to our scheme who would never deviate from his attitude of hostility towards it." Even so, for a short while, it seemed that Wemyss and Keyes might be given their chance. On December 2, Wemyss was appointed acting vice admiral, and the Admiralty asked how much time would be needed to reembark two divisions at Salonika and bring them back to Mudros. "All indications seemed pointing to fulfillment of our hopes," Wemyss said later, "when on December 8, I received a personal telegram from the Admiralty announcing that: 'in the face of unanimous military opinion, H.M. Government have decided to shorten the front by evacuating Anzac and Suvla.' " Wemyss called the decision "a disastrous mistake . . . [that] seemed to show that military opinion had prevailed and that the Western [Front] school had gained the day. . . . That naval action would have involved heavy losses is probable, but the sacrifice would have been no greater than those offered up almost daily on the Western Front with less chance of success. . . . The results of success would have been far more reaching than in any other theatre of war. Once through the Narrows: Turkey would become a negligible factor, Russia would be rejoined to the Allies, Egypt would be saved and the end of the war brought within measurable distance." Encouraged by Keyes and believing, because the government, the Admiralty, and Kitchener had so often waffled before, that this latest decision might still be reversed, Wemyss cabled Balfour: "The Navy is prepared to force the Straits and control them for an indefinite period cutting off all Turkish supplies to peninsula." He attacked Monro by name: "The 'unanimous military opinion' referred to has, I feel certain, been greatly influenced by Sir Charles Monro. . . . A few days ago General Monro remarked to me, 'If you succeed and occupy Gallipoli and even Constantinople, what then? It would not help us in France or Flanders.' I mention this to show that he has quite failed to realize the significance of the . . . Near East." Wemyss's conclusion was emphatic: "I consider evacuation disastrous, tactically and strategically. . . . I am convinced that the time is ripe for a vigorous offensive and I am confident of success."

Wemyss's telegram elicited two negative replies from London: a curt, official message from the Admiralty and a gentler, personal message from the First Lord. The official telegram said that the Admiralty was not prepared to authorize the navy singlehandedly to attempt to force the Narrows and act in the Sea of Marmara, cut off from its supplies. As reasons, the Admiralty cited the opinion of "responsible generals and the great strain thrown on naval and military resources by the operations in Greece." In any case, the Admiralty declared, "the decision of the Government to evacuate Suvla and Anzac will not be further questioned by the Admiralty." Balfour's personal message elaborated: "I view with deepest regret abandonment of Suvla and Anzac. But the military authorities are clear that those cannot be made tenable against an increased artillery fire while the Admiralty hold that the naval arguments against forcing the Straits are overwhelming. . . . Whilst success is most doubtful, very heavy losses are certain. . . . This would be represented as a heavy blow at our naval supremacy." Wemyss gave up and prepared to obey orders.

—

The evacuation of Gallipoli—in contrast to most other aspects of the campaign—was carried out with extraordinary efficiency and success. When the government's decision reached the Aegean, there were 83,000 men, 200 artillery pieces, and 5,000 horses and mules in the Anzac-Suvla beachhead. The evacuation began in secrecy on December 12 and continued nightly. To help keep the withdrawal a secret by creating the illusion of normality, empty supply boxes were ferried in during the day. By the afternoon of December 18, 40,000 men, half of the force at Anzac-Suvla, had quietly climbed into boats and disappeared over the sea. Another 20,000 were taken off on the single night of the eighteenth and the last 20,000 in a dense fog on the night of the nineteenth. In the darkness, so that the Turks would not realize that the lines were deserted, fixed rifles were rigged to fire automatically. Water dripping into a tin or candles burning through strings pulled the triggers of the abandoned rifles so that for half an hour after the troops left, shots were still being fired from the British trenches. By dawn on December 20, both Anzac and Suvla had been totally evacuated, with only one man wounded. The extent of this British talent for retreat was hailed by a German military correspondent writing in the *Vossische Zeitung:* "As long as war exists . . . [this evacuation] will stand in the eyes of students of the strategy of retreat as a masterpiece which up to now has never been attained."

Thirteen miles south of Anzac and Suvla, 35,000 Allied soldiers still remained ashore at Cape Helles. The men were withdrawn, moving in darkness and complete silence along carefully prearranged march routes marked by thick lines of chalk or white flour, while more unmanned rifles fired into the night. On the afternoon of January 7, when the garrison was down to 19,000, Sanders guessed that the Allies were leaving and ordered an attack. Turkish artillery battered the Allied trenches for four hours, but when the Turkish infantry started over the top, the British saw something they had never seen before at Gallipoli: the Turkish infantry was refusing to charge. Turkish officers shouted and struck at their men, but the soldiers, who sensed that the British were departing, would not move forward. That night and the next, the remaining Allied soldiers went down to the boats and by 4:00 a.m. on the ninth, no one remained on shore. Time-fused bombs blew up abandoned ammunition dumps and caused the only Allied casualty in the entire Gallipoli evacuation: a sailor was killed when a piece of debris fell into his boat as it was leaving the beach. When daylight came and the beaches were deserted, hordes of ragged, hungry Turks who had been living on olives and bread rushed down and threw themselves onto the piles of abandoned corned beef, biscuits, cakes, and jam. One of the final victims at Gallipoli was a Turkish soldier who died from eating too much English marmalade.

—

During the eight and a half months of the campaign, the Allied nations had landed half a million men on Gallipoli. More than half of these became casualties; 50,000 died, the rest were wounded. The 29th Division, which had arrived on the peninsula with 17,600 men, and been fed constant replacements, had suffered 34,011 casualties of whom 9,011 were killed or missing, 11,000 wounded, and 14,000 incapacitated by disease. Overall, the British, Anzac, and Indian armies endured 205,000 casualties and the French 47,000. Turkish casualties could only be estimated, even by the Turks, but the figure is between 250,000 and 350,000. Gallipoli also became a graveyard of British careers: Carden's, Hamilton's, Stopford's, Fisher's, and—so it seemed for many years—Churchill's. Kitchener survived in office, but the aura of omniscience and omnipotence had been stripped away.

Long after the campaign and the war were over, frustration still gripped the men who had advocated that the navy force the Dardanelles: Wemyss, Keyes, and Churchill. Wemyss, on returning to England, saw the First Lord and found him languidly philosophical. "Mr. Balfour," Wemyss wrote to Keyes, "was most sympathetic and assured me that he had been in sympathy with our plans from the very beginning. . . . He told me that he had been outvoted all around and ended up saying, 'Well, it is no use crying over spilt milk.' " The "spilt milk," Wemyss cried out, were "the invaluable lives and treasures squandered on this campaign. To what good were they sacrificed?" Keyes noted bitterly that the great Allied army sent to defend Salonika dug itself in and awaited an attack "which was never delivered and was probably never seriously contemplated by the enemy." Keyes also called on Balfour, who said that "he had always felt convinced that I was right about forcing the Dardanelles. . . . He said that he was a constitutional minister and had to be guided by his Sea Lords and that they had declared that we should lose twelve ships. I could not refrain from retorting that not one of his Sea Lords had any experience at the Dardanelles or had ever seen a shot fired in war." Winston Churchill carried the political scars of the Dardanelles and Gallipoli for twenty-five years, until, in 1940, he became prime minister. Nevertheless, looking back on the great adventure, he was to say, "Searching my heart, I cannot regret the effort. It was good to go as far as we did. Not to persevere—that was the crime."

CHAPTER 28

The Blockade of Germany

In the year 1915, the Great War was fought on many fronts, of which the doomed campaign at the Dardanelles and Gallipoli was only one. In the North Sea, German battle cruisers fought and lost the Battle of the Dogger Bank and then were forbidden by the kaiser to come out again. On the Western Front, armies lunged at each other in bloody offensives that despite the involvement of millions of men and, for the first time, of poison gas, left the lines of barbed wire–laced trenches essentially in place. In May, Italy declared war on Austria, her former Triple Alliance partner (Italy's declaration of war against Germany would wait until August 1916). In October, Bulgaria, emboldened by the obvious failure of the Allied armies at Gallipoli, joined the Central Powers and aided in the overrunning of Serbia. On the Eastern Front, from the Baltic to the Rumanian border, a mammoth German-Austrian offensive beginning May 1 captured Warsaw, drove the Russians out of Poland, and killed, wounded, or captured 2 million men of the Russian army. Beginning in February, German submarines began attacking merchant vessels in the waters around the British Isles. And through the year, the Allied blockade continued its silent, deadly corrosion of the German war effort.

On both sides, January of the new year had been a watershed of critical decisions. It was then that the Admiralty and the British government agreed to attack the Dardanelles. During the same weeks, the German Naval Staff, fearing the Allied blockade but forbidden to send German dreadnoughts to challenge the British fleet, proposed to employ what Admiral von Tirpitz called "the miracle weapon," the U-boat, to turn the tables and ensure that supplies to Britain would be cut off, as the British had done to Germany. Ultimately, it was by winning on these maritime battlefields—by sustaining the blockade and defeating the U-boats—that the Allies won the Great War. But it was, in a phrase used by the Duke of Wellington in describing his victory at Waterloo, "the nearest run thing you ever saw in your life."

—

The ability to blockade an enemy coast and choke off seaborne commerce has always been a potent derivative of superior sea power. Blockade was not a rapid method of waging war, however; during the Napoleonic Wars, the Royal Navy blockaded the coasts of Europe for twenty years; in the American Civil War, the Union navy had blockaded the ports of the Confederacy for more than four years. Nor was a policy of blockade free of diplomatic and military risk. The efforts of a blockading fleet to control access to enemy ports ran counter to many neutral rights as well as to the more generally espoused doctrine of freedom of the seas, which in its purest form declared that vessels of neutral nations should be able to travel on the high seas untroubled by any belligerent power. So vigorously had the new American republic supported this doctrine in 1812 that when the British stopped American merchant vessels, seized their cargoes, and then began removing American seamen and impressing them into the Royal Navy, war followed. During the American Civil War, hostilities again came close when blockading Union cruisers halted British merchant vessels bringing supplies to the South and carrying cotton back to the textile mills of England. In the American South, half a century later, memories of the Union blockade remained vivid.*

Through the eighteenth and nineteenth centuries, the rights of belligerents and neutrals regarding blockade were generally recognized. Nevertheless, before the Great War, when two Hague peace conferences attempted to codify the rules of war, it was decided that the procedures of blockade needed further clarification. Accordingly, in 1908, the British government invited the leading naval powers to a conference in London to work out specific rules of blockade and to agree on definitions of contraband. Ten nations were

*During a 1915 debate in the U.S. Senate about the potential harm posed by the British blockade, Senator Williams of Tennessee declared:

> Mr. President, we had a war over here between the States not very many years ago . . . and what did your people do to mine? Was it your army that whipped us? You know it was not. If it had not been for the women and children and men whom you starved to death, and the soldiers who could no longer wear a uniform and shoot because they had nothing to eat, I imagine we might be fighting even now. Your navy whipped us. Your sea power strangled us. Your sea power starved our population first and then starved our army afterwards. Now I am not complaining here. My forefathers did not complain; war is war, not a system of caressing, and there never was a confederate from Jeff Davis down to the humblest soldier who ever pleaded because he and his wife and children were starved by your navy.

invited: Germany, Austria, France, Russia, the Netherlands, Italy, Spain, Japan, and the United States. The conference took place between December 4, 1908, and February 26, 1909, and resulted in a draft declaration that all parties agreed was "in conformity with generally accepted principles of international law." Blockading ships, on encountering a commercial vessel approaching or leaving a blockaded port, were first to determine the nationality of the vessel. If it belonged to a hostile nation, it was fair game for seizure, the ship as well as the cargo. If the vessel was a neutral, the ship's cargo and destination became the determinants. Goods legitimately ripe for seizure were considered contraband, the simplest definition of which was "all materials useful to enemy armed forces."*

The London conference also restated the rights of neutrals. Neutral nations were empowered to prohibit belligerent blockading ships from entering their territorial waters within three miles of the coast; failure to respect this limit justified internment of the encroaching vessel for the duration of the war. Neutral nations and citizens were permitted to trade freely with belligerents, even to sell munitions to one or more belligerents. If a neutral ship was stopped, it must submit to search. If the vessel was found to be carrying munitions or other contraband, these materials would be confiscated. If the cargo consisted of conditional contraband, the ship could be detained and brought into a port of the blockading nation where the matter would be decided by a prize court. When detained cargoes were confiscated, compensation might be paid.

On February 26, 1908, the document known as the Declaration of London was signed and the delegates returned home. The document's publication, however, stirred a violent reaction in Britain, where advocates of British sea power vehemently argued that the declaration favored a neutral's right to trade over a belligerent's right to blockade, thus nullifying a major benefit of naval supremacy. Although the House of Commons supported making the declaration law, the House of Lords voted against ratification by a margin of three to one. The U.S. government, influenced by Alfred Thayer Mahan,

*There were subdivisions: "absolute contraband" covered articles unquestionably for military use only—for example, arms, munitions, and military equipment; "conditional contraband" included cargoes that could be used for either civilian or military purposes, such as fuels, railway equipment, clothing suitable for military use, gold, and silver. The "non-contraband free list" included metal ores, fertilizers, paper, copra, raw hides, raw cotton, wool, silk, flax, hemp, and, most important, all foodstuffs consigned to neutrals. Only absolute contraband could always be confiscated by a blockading power; conditional contraband could be seized only if an enemy destination could be proved; and non-contraband could not be seized at all. In the past, no lists of specific materials in these categories had been drawn up and definitions of absolute and conditional contraband had changed with the passage of time and the development of new weapons; in sailing-ship days, for example, absolute contraband included timber for ships, tar, and hemp for ropes.

an advocate of omnipotent, unfettered sea power, also refused to ratify the declaration.

—

During his term as First Sea Lord, 1910–12, Sir Arthur Wilson drafted no specific plans for a blockade of German commerce. He simply assumed that it would come about in the old-fashioned way: as a by-product of naval operations to contain an enemy fleet. The British navy would patrol aggressively inside the Heligoland Bight with strong forces of light cruisers and destroyers. No German merchant ships would pass this barrier; thus, a blockade of German merchant shipping would be an automatic, if secondary, effect of an essentially military operation. In May 1912, however, Winston Churchill's new Admiralty Board considered that if an attempt was made to execute Wilson's war plan deep inside the Bight, the British fleet would sustain heavy losses from torpedoes and mines. The new board lost no time in canceling Wilson's plan and substituting another, which called for holding the Grand Fleet on the periphery of the North Sea and snuffing out German oceanic trade by a distant blockade. "A close commercial blockade is unnecessary . . . provided that the entrances to the North Sea . . . are closed," said the Admiralty staff.

The shift to distant blockade raised legal and practical difficulties. By international law, a blockade is merely a paper or fictitious exercise unless it is rendered effective: *every* port of the blockaded country must be patrolled and blocked and all vessels must be intercepted, boarded, and their cargoes examined. Even British jurists agreed that no place could be called blockaded unless watched by a force of warships that cut all communication between the blockaded harbor and the outer oceans. In the situation Britain faced in 1914, no true, legal blockade was possible because certain German ports could not be blockaded; the British fleet did not control the Baltic and could not prevent Sweden and Denmark from trading freely with Germany.

Nevertheless, legally or otherwise, Britain had a powerful incentive to isolate a hostile Germany from world suppliers and markets. Before the war, international maritime trade played a paramount part in the German economy. Imports of foodstuffs and raw materials greatly exceeded exports, which largely consisted of manufactured goods. Germany imported about 25 percent of its food, particularly eggs, dairy products, vegetable oils, fish, and meat. One and a half million tons of wheat arrived annually from America, and 3 million tons of barley consumed by farm animals—half of Germany's annual requirement—came from Russia. Although the German empire produced 40 million tons of potatoes, sufficient for the nation's needs, German agriculture was notoriously dependent on fertilizers—potash, phosphates, and nitrates—of which 50 percent were imported from the United States, Chile, and North Africa. As for raw materials, the United

States supplied all of Germany's cotton and 60 percent of her copper. Argentina provided wool and hides. Sixty percent of these imports were carried in German vessels belonging to a German merchant marine that totaled 5.5 million tons, approximately 12 percent of the world's merchant tonnage. But from August 5, 1914, onward, Allied sea power quickly extinguished the international maritime trade of the Central Powers. Six hundred and twenty-three German and 101 Austrian merchant vessels, 1.875 million tons of shipping, took refuge in neutral harbors while Britain and her allies seized another 675,000 tons. In the first five months of war, Allied warships intercepted and captured still another 405,000 tons. Germany was left with less than 2 million tons of merchant vessels, and they were usable only in the Baltic.

Before 1914, Admiral von Tirpitz had warned that in a war with Great Britain the Royal Navy would blockade Germany, but he was confident that this could be compensated for by expanding German trade with nearby neutrals such as Holland, Denmark, Norway, and Sweden. Neutral ships, in Tirpitz's vision, would sail to Dutch or Scandinavian ports—Rotterdam or Copenhagen, for example—where their cargoes would be unloaded and subsequently transshipped to Germany by rail or coastal shipping. When war came, this machinery quickly began to operate and, within the first two weeks, the British Admiralty learned that cargoes of wheat were being unloaded in Rotterdam and sent up the Rhine on barges. Over the next several months, this trade expanded and German imports from the United States fell from a value of $32 million in December 1913 to $2 million in December 1914. In the same period, German imports from Sweden soared from $2.2 million worth to $17.7 million; from Norway, from $1.5 million to $7.2 million; from Denmark, from $3 million to $14.5 million; and from Holland, from $19 million to $27 million.

The British Cabinet moved quickly to block these channels. An order in council issued on August 20 decreed that neutral trade with Germany in conditional contraband would be regulated by the doctrine of continuous voyage. This meant that the ultimate destination of seaborne cargoes, not their initial stopping point, would become the determining factor. The British argued that if a nation at war had a right to blockade an enemy and to stop contraband from reaching him directly, then it also had a right to enforce these rights against an enemy who was supplying himself through neutral states. Contraband goods consigned to a neutral country, but destined for the blockaded country, were to be regarded as subject to seizure on the ground that the passage through the neutral country was merely part of a continuous voyage into the blockaded country. Thereafter, neither absolute nor conditional contraband intended for use by the enemy state or its armed forces could be shipped freely merely because it was consigned to a neutral receiver. "Finally, to further empower the blockade force," the order declared that "the destination . . . may be inferred from any sufficient evidence." In addition, the order in council revised the lists of absolute and conditional contraband established by the Declaration of London. The new, more comprehensive lists included many items formerly on the free list—leather for saddles, rubber for tires, copper, lead, cotton, raw wool, raw textiles, even paper, all now said to be convertible to military use. The practical effect of making conditional contraband subject to capture when it was to be discharged in a neutral port was to transform everything that had been conditional contraband into absolute contraband.

For the moment, the most controversial cargoes—food and foodstuffs—were left unaffected by the order in council. Originally, Britain did not intend to stop food supplies bound for Germany if they were to be consumed by the German civilian population. This policy was spelled out in a telegram from Foreign Secretary Sir Edward Grey to the British ambassador in Washington, Sir Cecil Spring-Rice, on September 29, 1914: "We have only two objects . . . to restrict supplies for the German army and to restrict the supply to Germany of materials essential for the making of munitions of war. We intend to attain these objectives with the minimum of interference with the United States and other neutral countries." Subsequently, the Admiralty received information that the German government had taken control of the supply and distribution of all food in the empire. Stretching a point, this could be taken to have turned virtually every German dealer in foodstuffs into a state contractor or government agent and thus, by further extension, to proclaim that all food on its way to Germany by any route was conditional or even absolute contraband. The British government reminded the United States that Article 33 of the Declaration of London had stated that "conditional contraband is liable to capture if it is shown to be destined for the use of the armed forces or of a government department of the enemy State."

Inevitably, the Allied blockade trespassed on neutral rights. By applying belligerent rights of blockade—stopping and searching ships and confiscating contraband—the Allied navies were insisting on regulating the trade of neutral nations to a degree unparalleled in history. Anticipating that this might happen, the United States on August 6, 1914, formally asked all belligerents to declare their adherence to the Declaration of London as the legal basis for naval operations connected with the blockade. Sir Edward Grey, who had just learned of the destruction of the cruiser *Amphion* in a freshly laid minefield off the English coast, replied that as the enemy evidently considered themselves at liberty to endanger neutral maritime traffic in international waters, he doubted whether the British government could undertake to observe every article in the declaration. The Admiralty, he said, must decide which rules could be followed and which must give way to "the efficient conduct of naval operations." When the August 20 order in council appeared, Americans were particularly affronted by the doctrine of continuous voyage; it seemed intolerable that the British navy be permitted to seize merchandise in transit from a neutral American port to a neutral Dutch or Scandinavian port, whatever the ultimate destination of the goods. Subsequently, in response to American complaints regarding enforcement of this doctrine, London replied that the Royal Navy's hand had been applied only lightly. From August 4, 1914, to January 3, 1915, 773 merchant vessels had sailed from America to Holland, Denmark, Norway, Sweden, and Italy. Of these, the cargoes of only forty-five had been placed in prize court, and ultimately only eight had been permanently confiscated.

Nevertheless, American complaints made Britain uneasy. As a long war seemed more and more likely, the Allies knew that they would have to draw upon the United States for food, arms, and money. To tighten and enforce the blockade of Germany while at the same time maintaining friendship with neutral America became simultaneously necessary and painfully difficult. As every added restraint on neutral shipping raised another protest from Washington, it became apparent to Britain that she might ultimately have to decide which of the two policies was the more important. If the choice had to be made, Sir Edward Grey was never in doubt as to which path he would follow. "The surest way to lose the war would be to antagonize America," he said. The British government's effort, he added, would be "to secure the maximum blockade possible that could be enforced without a rupture with the United States."

—

The daily work of the blockade was entrusted by the Admiralty to twelve obsolete cruisers, all unfit to fight modern warships. Four of these ships went to the western end of the Channel where, working with a French squadron, they patrolled the entrance from the Atlantic. Eight old cruisers of the *Edgar* class established watch over the other, wider North Sea exit, the 200-mile gap between the Shetlands and Norway. Rarely were all eight cruisers on patrol together; periodically, each vessel had to go into the Shetlands to coal. Thus, during the first four months of war, the North Sea blockade of the German empire was routinely performed by six rusty old warships, steaming ten, twenty, or thirty miles apart.

In practice, blockade duty meant an always wearying, sometimes dangerous routine. When a cargo ship was halted, a naval boarding party including two officers went across to the neutral vessel. The visitors' first task was to look at the ship's papers and establish her identity using a copy of the Lloyds registry. A more difficult task for naval officers, most of whom knew no language other than English, was to discover whether crew members and passengers calling themselves Norwegians, Swedes, Finns, Danes, or other, were, in fact, Germans. Occasionally, people were closely questioned. This examination, says A. C. Bell, the official British historian of the blockade, "was conducted with the assistance of a printed list of unusual words in every European language and with the aid of drawings of familiar objects." A German or Austrian citizen attempting to deceive the examiners "might have an exceptional knowledge of the language he professed to speak as a native, [but] it was not likely that he would, in rapid succession, [be able to] give the right word for . . . a bicycle pedal, an instep, a cheekbone, a nasturtium, or a frying pan." Halting or erroneous answers led to close inspection of the person's luggage. As for the cargo, the boarding officers would read the manifest, then descend into the hold to look about. Discovery of anything suggesting contraband, absolute or conditional, sent the vessel into port—usually Kirkwall, in the Orkneys—for a rigorous examination. There, even when the ship and its cargo were entirely cleared, several weeks might go by before the vessel was released; the natural result was neutral frustration and bitterness.

The hardships suffered by neutral seamen and shipowners were small, however, compared to those endured by the men of the blockading squadron. In normal weather in these waters, the crews, wrapped in yellow duffel suits, looked out at gray skies and rolling gray waves. When autumn gales brought winds down from the Arctic, piling the sea into short, steep ridges of water, the men on the old cruisers continued the work of the blockade. In tumultuous seas, the engines stopped, a boat was lowered, and a boarding party went down the ladder. Putting off from the tall steel side of their own vessel, the men rowed to the waiting neutral, where another ordeal awaited them. One unexpected flick of the churning sea could hurl their wooden boat against the hull, turning the craft into splinters and the boarders into floundering, drowning men.

Still, the ships gave out before the men. *Hawke,* one of the eight old cruisers, was sunk by a German torpedo on October 14. By the end of that month, *Theseus* reported bilgewater leaking into her feed tanks, *Endymion* declared urgent need for engine repairs, and *Crescent,* the flagship, developed a leaky condenser. At first, patchwork sufficed. Then, November 11 brought down on the squadron a full gale with monster waves. *Edgar,* with engine trouble, was ordered into harbor. Two ships had to heave to. *Crescent* was so battered that her admiral, Dudley de Chair, said later, "We rather feared she would go down." Once the storm had passed, half the squadron went into the Clyde for repairs. There, inspectors reported so unfavorably on the condition of the ships that, on November 20, the Admiralty ordered all of the seven remaining *Edgar*s withdrawn from service.

Replacements were available, some of them already at work. These were civilian passenger liners, of which Britain possessed more than a hundred before the war. Weighing up to 20,000 tons, with speeds from 15 to 25 knots, they had been converted into armed merchant cruisers. They were, of course, unarmored, but this was irrelevant as they were not to face enemy warships. Equipped with 6-inch and 4.7-inch guns to intimidate enemy or neutral merchant vessels, they were manned in part by the crews of the seven retired *Edgar*s. In December, Admiral de Chair gave up his 7,000-ton flagship *Crescent* for the 18,000-ton liner *Alsatian,* capable of 23 knots in pursuit, or, if maintained at a patrol speed of 13½ knots, of remaining at sea for forty-two days. By the end of December 1914, eighteen liners patrolled the blockade lines; eventually, there were to be twenty-four.

—

Germany had counted on a short war in which a blockade of its coasts would not be a factor. In Count Alfred von Schlieffen's mind when he drafted his great flanking movement for invading France through Belgium was fear of the dangers of a long war. "A campaign protracts itself," he said. "Such wars are, however, impossible when a nation's existence depends upon an unbroken movement of trade and industry." Underlying this need for haste was the basic economic structure of a powerful young empire that had existed for only forty-three years. In 1914, the German Reich was still divided into two distinct economic units. The industrial cities and manufacturing towns of the west had always been supplied with food and raw materials from overseas, imported through Rotterdam and Antwerp and thence brought up the Rhine, while the eastern agricultural areas of Germany were accustomed to sending their surplus farm products into industrial Bohemia or on to Russia. The German railway system, therefore, had never carried the food surpluses of the empire's eastern provinces to the west and now, largely diverted to military purposes, was unable to do so. Unless the flow of imports through neutral Dutch ports could be maintained, the food-consuming populations of the west were bound to suffer. It was because of this that Admiral von Tirpitz, fearing that the war would be longer than Schlieffen expected, and reviewing the potential impact of a British blockade, declared that neutrals must be used to bring supplies into Germany. Even so, German experts believed that the empire's powers of resistance would depend on early and decisive military success; overall, the conclusion was that Germany could maintain itself on its own resources for nine or ten months but no more.

Because the German government had invested so much in the Schlieffen Plan and believed so strongly in the power of the German army to deliver a quick victory, the Germany navy had been held back. The navy's war plan, in any case, had been a defensive one, which called for awaiting an expected British offensive. German planners had been aware of Admiral Wilson's earlier intention to attack Heligoland and seize islands on the German coast; anticipating this offensive, the Germans intended to turn it to their own use. The battle, the Germans hoped, would be fought in the inner Bight in the presence of their own minefields, where they could sink or cripple a significant portion of the attacking fleet. Somehow, through a failure of intelligence, the German Naval Staff remained unaware when in 1912 the Royal Navy abandoned its aggressive plan. There were suspicions that the Admiralty might adopt the strategic defensive by sealing off the North Sea at the Dover Strait and from the Orkneys to the Norwegian coast; shortly before the war, a German intelligence summary had hedged: "There is nothing certain about how Britain will wage war. A series of fleet maneuvers in previous years suggested a close blockade of our coasts; later maneuvers . . . suggest that a distant blockade had been chosen as the starting point of the British war plan." But even had they been told that the British plan had changed, most German naval officers probably would not have abandoned their belief that the full might of the Grand Fleet would come charging into the Bight in the first weeks of war. When the expected onslaught failed to materialize, the premise on which German naval strategy had been based was overturned.

Even so, the German Naval Staff still believed that the British would keep light forces within striking distance of the German bases and that these forces would be supported by heavy battle squadrons that from time to time would sweep into the Bight to flaunt their superiority. On these assumptions, the German navy continued to base its naval war plan. Because the kaiser refused to permit an early fleet action, the British fleet was to be reduced by attrition achieved by minelaying, by attack with minor vessels, including submarines, and by offensive sweeps by battle cruisers. When sufficiently large losses had been inflicted and the two battle fleets were approximately equal in strength, then the High Seas Fleet would steam out and force a major battle.

This campaign of attrition began on the war's first day when the converted steamer *Königin Luise* laid a long line of mines, one of which sank the light cruiser *Amphion.* Britain reacted quickly. The laying of mines in the open sea, beyond an enemy's three-mile coastal limit, was in violation of the Second Hague Convention. (Germany, anticipating the potential of mine warfare, had refused to accept this portion of the convention.) On August 10, the British Foreign Office sent a note to neutral powers accusing the Germans of scattering mines illegally and indiscriminately around the North Sea, endangering merchant ships of all nations. This peril, the Admiralty warned, would increase because Britain reserved the right to lay mines of its own in self-defense. Further, the note declared, the Admiralty would begin to turn back ships of all neutral flags trading with North Sea ports before they entered areas of exceptional danger. The Dutch, believing these positions a pretext for diverting the Rotterdam trade, were furious; in any case, for the moment, most neutral vessels ignored the warning.

On the night of August 25, two more German minefields were laid, off the Humber and off the Tyne. Although British minesweeping officers were convinced that the minefields had been laid by fully equipped German navy minelayers, the Admiralty concluded that the work had been done by fishing trawlers disguised as neutrals. Immediately, all east coast ports were closed to neutral fishing craft, and neutral governments were warned again about indiscriminate German mining. Near the end of October, the German Naval Staff decided to mine the approaches to a great commercial harbor; deciding on Glasgow, they dispatched the *Berlin* to the Firth of Clyde on the approaches to that city. Her captain instead mined the approaches to Tory Island where, on October 27, one of his mines sank the dreadnought *Audacious.* This shocked the British Admiralty and provided an excuse for a dramatic escalation of the war at sea. On November 2, during Jellicoe's visit to London to confer with Jacky Fisher, who had just become the First Sea Lord, the British government issued a harsh proclamation:

> During the last week, the Germans have scattered mines indiscriminately in the open sea on the main trade route from America to Liverpool via the north of Ireland. . . . These mines cannot have been laid by any German ship of war. They have been laid by some merchant vessel flying a neutral flag . . . [which is an] ordinary feature of German naval warfare. [Therefore, the Admiralty] give[s] notice that the whole of the North Sea must be considered a military area . . . [where] merchant shipping of all kinds, traders of all countries, fishing craft and all other vessels will be exposed to the gravest dangers. . . . Ships of all countries wishing to trade to and from Norway, the Baltic, Denmark, and Holland, are advised to come, if inward bound, by the English Channel and the Straits of Dover. There they will be given sailing directions which will pass them safely . . . up the east coast of England. . . . Any straying, even by a few miles from the course indicated, may be followed by fatal consequences.

This declaration, in effect saying that the whole of the North Sea was out of bounds to world shipping without the express permission of the Royal Navy, brought a storm of anger and protest. Neutral governments read the announcement as a declaration that the British government meant to sever communication between Scandinavia and America. In Germany, the decree was interpreted as an illegal declaration of economic war. Admiral Scheer, who already considered the British "lords of hypocrisy" for not having ratified the Declaration of London, was bitterly indignant. "She [Great Britain] did not consider herself bound by any international laws which would have made it possible to get food and other non-contraband articles through neutral countries into blockaded Germany," he wrote. "Thus, when the distinction between absolute and relative contraband was done away with, all German import trade by both land and sea was strangled, in particular the importation of food. . . . [Further,] neutral states were forced by England to forbid almost all export of goods to Germany in order to obtain any overseas imports for themselves. . . . Free trading of neutral merchant vessels on the North Sea was made impossible . . . because . . . all shipping was forced to pass through English waters and to submit to English control." The blockade, intended to starve Germany, Scheer said, "required time to attain its full effect. . . . Success would be achieved gradually and silently, which meant the ruin of Germany as surely as the approach of winter meant the fall of the leaves from the trees."

—

Breaking the blockade imposed by British sea power was, properly, a mission for the German navy. In the war's early months, however, the kaiser's navy had shown itself glaringly—embarrassingly—ineffective. Offensive minelaying and submarine operations against British warships had produced paltry results. The *Berlin*'s expedition had resulted in the sinking of the *Audacious,* but the Naval Staff remained convinced that the British fleet could not be significantly reduced by this means, and minelaying was discounted as a major factor in the naval war. Expectations from a U-boat campaign against the British fleet were scarcely greater. It was true that the U-boats had inflicted losses—*Pathfinder,* the *Bacchante*s, *Hawke,* and *Formidable*—but the German Naval Staff did not rate these successes highly; the torpedoed ships were old and of little combat significance. More important, submarines had proved ineffective against modern, fast-moving, escorted heavy warships. They had failed to interrupt movement across the Channel and had not sunk a single troop transport. By December 1914, most German naval officers did not believe that submarines could play a serious role in the war of attrition against the Royal Navy. Increasingly, the Naval Staff and officers in the fleet demanded a new plan, new tactics, new leadership. How could the German fleet, the second most powerful in the world, contest the command of the sea? Mine warfare and submarine attacks on warships had failed, and the emperor had forbidden his navy to force an action between the battle fleets at sea. What other possibilities existed? It was in this state of embarrassment and frustration that the German navy and government considered proposals for a submarine campaign against merchant shipping.

—

During the first months of war, when the offensive mission of German submarines was to locate and attack the British fleet and to sink British troop transports moving across the Channel, Allied merchant shipping was left mostly alone. Nevertheless, U-boat commodore Hermann Bauer, closely questioning his captains on their return to base, learned that through their periscopes these young officers were watching a heavy flow of seaborne commercial traffic moving along the English coasts. Early in October, Bauer reported these observations to his superior, Ingenohl. Stressing the deadly potential of using submarines to attack British trade, Bauer argued the uselessness of keeping the bulk of the U-boat fleet parked in defensive circles around Heligoland. Ingenohl, impressed, forwarded Bauer's recommendation to the Chief of the Naval Staff, Hugo von Pohl. "From a purely military point of view," Ingenohl wrote, "a campaign of submarines against commercial traffic on the British coasts will strike the enemy at his weakest point and will make it evident . . . that his power at sea is insufficient to protect his imports." Pohl agreed that unleashing the U-boats against merchant shipping could usefully harm Great Britain, but he hesitated; submarine warfare against commerce would be a violation of international maritime law, to which Article 112 of the German Naval Prize Regulations conformed. Further, any accidental destruction of neutral merchant vessels might provoke neutral nations into war with Germany. Accordingly, it seemed to Pohl, U-boat warfare against merchant ships could be justified only as a reprisal for some flamboyantly heinous act by the enemy. Therefore, without consulting any political leaders, Pohl decided to ignore Ingenohl's proposal.

The British Admiralty's declaration of November 2, declaring the whole of the North Sea a war zone, dramatically changed Pohl's point of view. An effort to stop shipments of conditional contraband now appeared as a gross violation of international law and the beginning of a campaign to starve the German people. Accordingly, two days after the British declaration was published, Pohl reversed himself and laid before the German chancellor a proposal for submarine warfare against commerce.

The concept of using submarines as blockading ships was technologically revolutionary and raised numerous problems. To follow the procedures of eighteenth-century sailing-ship days, the U-boat would have to surface, halt its intended prey by either a signal or a warning shot with its deck gun, send a boarding party to the vessel to establish its nationality, and, if it was an enemy, make adequate provisions for the safety of the crew and passengers before sinking it. It being patently impossible for a small, crowded U-boat to take aboard the crew and passengers of a large ship, the best that could be done was that they be allowed to enter their lifeboats before their ship was destroyed. If this happened far from land, with crew and passengers left to fend for themselves in open boats, such arrangements did not meet the requirements of international maritime law.

Ultimately, U-boat warfare was refined into one or another of two basic operational strategies: restricted and unrestricted. "Restricted" submarine warfare meant that U-boats, before torpedoing enemy merchant vessels, would surface, warn their victims, and give them time to abandon ship. All neutral ships would be spared, and passenger liners of all nations, even enemies, might be spared. "Unrestricted" U-boat warfare meant that all the old formalities of "visit and search" would be ignored and that German U-boats would torpedo without warning all merchant and passenger ships, armed or unarmed, neutral or enemy, without distinguishing between absolute and conditional contraband and without regard for the fate of crew or passengers. The argument for this seemingly barbaric method of warfare rested, ironically, on the frailty of the attacking craft: U-boats were small, slow, unarmored warships, armed only with a small deck gun and a few torpedoes; their primary defense was their ability to operate hidden underwater; once surfaced to stop and examine a merchant vessel and wait while the crew boarded lifeboats, a submarine became the most vulnerable of all warships. For this reason, most German naval officers not only endorsed Bauer's and Pohl's proposal, but wished to go immediately to unrestricted submarine warfare. "The gravity of the situation," said Admiral Scheer, "demands that we should free ourselves from all scruples which certainly no longer have any justification."

When the German chancellor, Theobald von Bethmann-Hollweg, first heard Admiral von Pohl's proposal, he was inclined to endorse it. "Viewed from the standpoint of international law, U-boat warfare is a reprisal against England's hunger blockade," he wrote to Pohl in December 1914. "When we consider the purely utilitarian rules by which the enemy regulate their conduct, [when we consider] their ruthless pressure on neutrals . . . we may conclude that we are entitled to adopt whatever measure of war is most likely to bring them to surrender." This was the pragmatic chancellor speaking, the man who a few months before had deplored Britain's entry into the war merely to uphold "a scrap of paper"—the treaty in which Great Britain had promised to defend Belgian neutrality. But while the chancellor saw nothing illegal or immoral in the proposed U-boat campaign, he argued that the decision must be made on practical grounds, involving political as well as military considerations. He feared that a U-boat blockade of Britain would provoke neutral nations and therefore could be employed only when Germany's military position on the Continent was so secure that there could be no doubt as to the ultimate outcome; once this was achieved, the navy could do as it wished because the intervention of neutral states would have no impact. Now—in December 1914—Bethmann-Hollweg told Pohl, these conditions did not exist.

The kaiser was not ready to approve a submarine campaign and he supported the chancellor. William was well aware that neutral as well as Allied ships were carrying contraband war material from America to Britain and France, and he deeply resented this fact. He feared, on the other hand, that indiscriminate sinkings by U-boats would poison relations with Holland and Scandinavia and might pitch Germany into war with the United States. William's gentler, more sentimental side also played a part. Unrestricted submarine warfare and the killing of civilians at sea conflicted with his notion of chivalry and his own self-image as a knightly figure. Wearing this mantle, he told a group of admirals in November 1914, "Gentlemen, always realize that our sword must be clean. We are not waging war against women and children. We wish to fight this war as gentlemen, no matter what the other side may do. Take note of that!"

William was reluctant to use such moderate language when speaking to Tirpitz, of whom he was somewhat afraid. The following day, he explained defensively to the Grand Admiral that while he did not object to submarine warfare in itself, he was determined to wait until it could be waged effectively. Pohl, on the other hand, was a small man who possessed little power to intimidate, but had a large talent for guile. On December 14, only three weeks after the kaiser had said no, Pohl returned with a more specific U-boat campaign proposal: planning would be completed by the end of January; a declaration would give ample cautionary notice to neutrals; U-boat operations would begin at the end of February. Again, Bethmann-Hollweg objected. Why provoke antagonism just when Britain, by its coercive blockade, was exasperating most of Europe's neutrals? At this point, Pohl received unexpected help. A month before, when Tirpitz had realized that his imperial master did not intend to risk his prized dreadnoughts, the Grand Admiral had begun to champion the idea of submarine warfare as the only alternative means by which England's power at sea might be broken. On December 21, German newspapers published an interview given by Tirpitz at the end of November to Charles von Wiegand, a German-born American journalist. The circumstances of the interview had been unusual: Tirpitz received Wiegand in his bedroom at German Supreme Headquarters at Charleville in occupied France and the Grand Admiral sat in a chair beside his unmade bed. Before speaking, he asked the reporter to submit the interview to the Foreign Ministry for clearance. Wiegand agreed, and Tirpitz plowed ahead. "America has raised no protest and has done little or nothing to stop the closing of the North Sea against all neutral shipping," he said. "Now what will America say if Germany institutes a submarine blockade of England to stop all traffic?"

Wiegand asked whether such a measure was contemplated.

"Why not, if we are driven to extremities? England is endeavoring to starve us. We can do the same, cut off England and sink every vessel that attempts to break the blockade." Once the transcription was in his notebook, Wiegand failed to submit it to the Foreign Ministry, and Tirpitz never bothered to inform the chancellor or to mention the matter to Pohl. When Wiegand published his story in a Dutch newspaper, Bethmann-Hollweg had no choice but to permit publication in Germany. Tirpitz, learning that the kaiser was irritated, breezily explained that "he wished to sound American opinion on the submarine war."

The interview reverberated through the German press. Many Germans, accepting the famous Grand Admiral as the nation's foremost authority on naval affairs, now believed that a decision was imminent to use submarines against enemy merchant shipping and that this would soon bring a victorious end to the war. A stream of articles and papers appeared, written by "eminent financiers, shipping and industrial magnates, politicians, scientists and university academics, urging [the government] not to be deterred from using a decisive weapon by false misgivings." Pohl, hoping to capitalize on this public support, came to Supreme Headquarters at Charleville on January 7, 1915, and once again presented his submarine proposals to the kaiser and the chancellor. Again, Bethmann-Hollweg opposed Pohl's plan, arguing that the uncertainty of the neutrals still made U-boat warfare too risky. Again, the kaiser supported the chancellor and opted for postponement. However, William gave indirect and unintentional backing to Pohl's proposal when, on the same day, he issued his order forbidding Admiral von Ingenohl to engage the High Seas Fleet in a major fleet action. This command confirmed U-boat warfare against commerce as Germany's only naval offensive option.

Pohl did not give up. On February 1, buttressed by the fact that he had been chosen to succeed Ingenohl as Commander-in-Chief of the High Seas Fleet, he repeated his submarine proposal to Bethmann-Hollweg for the fourth time. When the chancellor reiterated his concern that submarine warfare would antagonize America and other neutrals, Pohl replied that if the proclamation of a German war zone frightened away neutral shipping, as the naval authorities assumed it would, then, by definition, diplomatic confrontation with neutrals would not occur. Further, at this interview, Pohl deliberately lied to the chancellor: he had never set foot in a submarine at sea, but he claimed, falsely, that the U-boat captains would be able to distinguish between enemy and neutral ships and that only enemy ships would be sunk. Hearing this, Bethmann-Hollweg said he would raise no further objections. For Pohl, the rest was easy. When Admiral Gustav Bachmann relieved Pohl as Chief of the Naval Staff, he was informed by his predecessor that the launching of a German submarine campaign had been approved at the highest level and that the kaiser did not wish the matter to be raised again. The kaiser's consent, of course, had not been given, but Pohl knew how to secure it. February 4, 1915, was Pohl's last day as Chief of the Naval Staff and his first as Commander-in-Chief of the High Seas Fleet. In bright winter sunshine, the kaiser arrived in Wilhelmshaven to attend the change-of-command ceremony. As a launch carried him across the harbor to visit the battle cruiser *Seydlitz,* damaged at the Dogger Bank, Pohl, standing with the kaiser in the stern of the boat, took the submarine war order from an inner pocket and handed it to William to sign. The kaiser, excited by the presence of so many colorful uniforms against a background of giant gray warships, scribbled his name. The following morning, the declaration was published in the official *Imperial Gazette:*

> The waters surrounding Great Britain and Ireland including the whole English Channel are hereby declared to be a military area. From

> 18 February onwards, all enemy merchant ships in these waters will be destroyed, irrespective of the impossibility of avoiding in all cases danger to the passengers and crew.
>
> Neutral shipping will also be in danger in the war zone for, in view of the misuse of neutral flags ordered by the British government on 31 January and of the uncertainties of naval warfare it may not always be possible to avoid neutral vessels suffering from attacks intended for enemy ships.

The order was made public before other senior admirals were informed. Müller later damned Pohl's behavior: the declaration was unskillfully drafted; the moment had been badly chosen; the means were not sufficiently ready. "It was disloyal to Tirpitz not to have discussed the declaration," said Müller. "It was also disloyal to me. . . . [But] Pohl was anxious at all costs to get the declaration issued over his own name and February 4 was certainly the last day on which this was possible." Privately, Tirpitz raged that "Pohl, by his vanity and lack of judgement, has made a mess." Considering how few submarines were available, Tirpitz had recommended declaring a proper, effective blockade of a limited area, such as the mouth of the Thames. "Instead of which, flourish of trumpets, intimidation, and in consequence . . . England warned and given fourteen days to make preparations." Nevertheless, despite complaints, Pohl had obtained what Tirpitz and most German naval officers desired: imperial approval for striking a blow at England. If the kaiser had forbidden the use of battleships, now, at least, he would permit the U-boats to try. It was in these confused circumstances that the German submarine war on neutral merchant shipping had its beginnings.

—

For the German navy and government, the decision to unleash the U-boats was a leap into the dark. Pohl's persistence had thrust the campaign into reality, but neither he nor anyone on his staff were familiar with submarines and only Bauer and the U-boat captains themselves actually knew how the vessels could perform. Pohl knew that the number of U-boats available was grievously insufficient to enforce a submarine blockade on the whole of the British Isles. "We are not in a position to cut off England's imports to a degree that the country will suffer hunger," the Naval Staff analysts had told their chief. In fact, in May 1914, an unofficial staff study prepared at Kiel had calculated—very accurately, as experience proved—that an effective blockade of the British Isles would require at least 222 operational U-boats to maintain permanent patrols. However, Tirpitz had neglected to build submarines in peacetime; when the war zone was proclaimed in February 1915, the German navy had only thirty U-boats, only twenty of which were long-range diesel boats of the High Seas Fleet. The rest were small and obsolescent, useful only for coastal work. Again optimistically, the Naval Staff assumed that half of the diesel submarines could be at sea at any given time. And again experience proved that, allowing for the time-consuming voyage to the rich hunting grounds of the Western Approaches, the Irish Sea, and the western end of the English Channel, and the need for proper maintenance for the boats and rest for the crews, only a third of the force could be on station at a given moment.* Thus, from March to September 1915, the average number of modern U-boats on station every day was between seven and eight.

Pohl, who now commanded the High Seas Fleet submarine force, was not deterred. He intended to follow the plan recommended by Bauer. Three U-boats would operate on the Western Approaches and in the Irish Sea to interdict the main Atlantic trade routes to Liverpool and the Bristol Channel ports. One submarine would be stationed off the Thames in the English Channel, another off the Tyne, and still another off the northeast coast, covering the routes from Britain to Scandinavia. Six U-boats could not sink enough ships to halt British trade, but Pohl hoped that simply by making an appearance they would terrify merchant sailors, British and neutral. Pohl, however, was not allowed to begin the campaign without having a nervous hand placed on his sleeve. Before the U-boats sailed, the kaiser sent a telegram demanding a guarantee that within six weeks of the campaign's opening "England would be forced to modify her attitude." Tirpitz and Bachmann immediately responded that six weeks would be sufficient—"a silly question deserves a silly answer," Tirpitz noted of this exchange. On February 14, Pohl, on board *Friedrich der Grosse,* was handed another imperial telegram: "For urgent political reasons, send orders by wireless to U-boats already dispatched for the present not to attack ships flying a neutral flag, unless recognized with certainty to be enemies." Pohl was dismayed; if neutrals were promised immunity, there was no chance of frightening them away from trading with Britain. "This order makes success impossible as U-boats cannot determine the nationality of ships without exposing themselves to great danger," he telegraphed the Naval Staff. "The reputation of the navy will, in my opinion, suffer tremendously if this undertaking, publicly announced and most hopefully regarded by the people, achieves no results. Please submit my views to H.M." To this message, Pohl received no reply. Instead, the following day, still another telegram from Supreme Headquarters delayed the date fixed for the opening of the campaign: "H.M. the Emperor has commanded that the U-boat campaign to destroy commerce, as indicated in the announcement of February 4, is not to begin on February 18, but only when orders to do so are received from the All Highest."

By February 18, newly clarified instructions had been issued to U-boats:

*The Western Approaches is that part of the Atlantic Ocean extending out 300 to 400 miles from the southwestern and western coasts of the British Isles.

hostile merchant ships were to be destroyed; all ships flying neutral flags were to be spared, although neutral flags or funnel markings alone were not to be regarded as sufficient guarantees of neutral nationality. To make certain, U-boat captains were ordered to take additional evidence into account: the structure, place of registration, course, and general behavior of the intercepted vessel. Hospital ships were to be spared, as well as ships belonging to the Belgian Relief Commission, funded in America to provide food for impoverished German-occupied Belgium. On the other hand, U-boat commanders were promised that "if, in spite of the exercise of great care, mistakes should be made," they would not be held responsible. In this manner, says the official historian of the British blockade, "a handful of naval officers, most of them under thirty years of age, without political training, and isolated from the rest of the world by the nature of their duties, were . . . given a vague and indefinite instruction to give a thought to politics before they fired their torpedoes."

—

British reaction to the announcement that German submarines were about to attack Allied merchant ships was divided: some felt that the threat was ominous; others said that the Germans were posturing and that there was little danger. Arthur Balfour, long an expert on defense, warned that the threat was real. On May 6, 1913, Balfour had written to Fisher: "The question that really troubles me is not whether *our* submarines could render the enemy's position intolerable, but whether *their* submarines could render our position intolerable." Fisher had replied by reiterating his credo: that "war has no amenities" and that as far as rules were concerned, "You might as well talk of humanizing hell!" Submarines, he pointed out, had no alternative but to sink their victims and thus were indeed "a truly terrible threat for British commerce. . . . It is freely acknowledged to be an altogether barbarous method of warfare . . . [but] the essence of war is violence and moderation in war is imbecility." He added that neutral shipping could not be immune because "one flag is very like another seen against the light through a periscope." Churchill, receiving a copy of Fisher's paper, had pronounced it "brilliant," but had noted, "There were a few points on which I am not convinced. . . . Of these, the greatest is the question of the use of submarines to sink merchant vessels. I do not believe this would ever be done by a civilized power." Asquith and Prince Louis had agreed with Churchill. Even in February 1915, the Admiralty was generally satisfied that U-boats could not do much harm to Britain's enormous merchant trade. Churchill, addressing the House of Commons on February 15 on the subject of the German war zone proclamation, declared that "losses will no doubt be incurred—of that I give full warning. But we believe that no vital injury can be done if our traders put to sea regularly. . . . If they take the precautions which are proper and legitimate, we expect the losses will be confined within manageable limits, even at the outset when the enemy must be expected to make his greatest effort to produce an impression." The Foreign Office, for its part, doubted that the German government was sufficiently reckless to torpedo neutral—including American—merchant ships and concluded that the German proclamation was largely bluff.

In the end, the calculations and assumptions of both opposing belligerents—the German belief that the U-boats could terrify and drive away the neutrals, and the British estimate that the submarine war was bluff—were wrong. Bauer and Pohl had overestimated; neutral shipping did not flee in terror from the few submarines posted off British harbors. And, once the U-boats had sailed, it quickly became apparent that the diplomatic repercussions, warned of by Bethmann-Hollweg and discounted by Pohl, would be severe. On the other hand, over the years, the German submarine campaign, far from being a bluff, came close to winning the war.

—

On February 10, the U.S. government emphatically objected to the German proclamation of a war zone and warned that any harm befalling ships under the American flag, or American citizens—even if they were passengers on a belligerent vessel flying a belligerent flag—would be regarded in Washington as "an indefensible violation of neutral rights." Specifically, the American note warned that "if the commanders of German vessels of war should . . . destroy on the high seas an American vessel, or the lives of American citizens . . . the government of the United States would . . . hold the Imperial Government to a strict accountability for such acts." Italy, which was then at war with Austria but not with Germany, also spoke in strong language: if an Italian ship were sunk by a German U-boat, the Italian premier told the German ambassador, it would be *"une chose énorme."*

The unexpectedly stern language of the American protest note confronted the German chancellor with precisely the situation he had hoped to avoid. The United States was announcing that it had no intention of allowing itself to be frightened into giving up trade with Great Britain and was prepared to defend its right to freedom of maritime commerce. It was from this moment that German diplomacy toward the United States became an effort to mesh two ultimately incompatible policies: to continue to employ submarine warfare against merchant shipping while at the same time preventing America from joining the Allies. This first American note convinced Bethmann-Hollweg that he could combine these goals only by giving absolute guarantees that U-boats would not attack neutral ships. The naval command immediately protested that this limitation would make success impossible. Admiral Bachmann said flatly that if this undertaking to the Americans was given, the submarine campaign would have to be abandoned outright. Tirpitz bitterly reproached Bethmann-Hollweg for advocating any compliance with the American note. However, if, against his advice, concessions must be made, then, "in the interest of German prestige," he demanded that they should come only in return for a lifting of the British blockade on all food and raw materials and the return of all interned German cargo vessels. Hearing this, Müller, who sided with the chancellor, wrote in his diary that Tirpitz's ideas were "absolutely crazy." Müller himself believed that "the effect of submarine war on commerce was greatly exaggerated" and agreed with Bethmann-Hollweg that the American protest note could be accepted without wholesale abandonment of the U-boat offensive. William II, caught in the middle, complained that Pohl had laid this weighty question before him at a time when his mind was on other things and admitted that his consent in Wilhelmshaven harbor might have been too lightly given. Ultimately, the kaiser endorsed the chancellor's position. On February 18, on the eve of the beginning of the submarine campaign, Germany replied to the American note by saying that, while she insisted on her fundamental right to use submarine warfare against commerce and that her U-boat captains would sink British and Allied merchant ships, they would not molest American vessels, "when they are recognizable as such."

In fact, German submarines were attacking Allied merchant shipping before the war-zone proclamation was issued. The first victim was the British freighter *Glitra,* 866 tons, bound from Grangemouth to Stavanger, Norway, with a cargo of coal, oil, and iron plate. On October 20, 1914, she was halted by *U-17* fourteen miles off the Norwegian coast. A boarding party, acting in strict accordance with international law, gave the crew time to lower and enter their boats, then opened the *Glitra*'s sea cocks and sent her to the bottom. *U-17* then towed the lifeboats to within easy rowing distance of the coast. Seven days later, *U-24,* in the Channel to attack troopships, sighted the 4,590-ton French steamer *Amiral Ganteaume* off Cape Gris-Nez. The decks of the ship were crowded with figures whom the U-boat captain took to be soldiers; in fact, the vessel carried 2,500 Belgian civilian refugees. Without warning, the submarine fired a torpedo. Most of the passengers were taken off by a British steamer and the French ship, which did not sink, was towed into Boulogne, but forty people died as a result of panic. In November, *U-21* sank two small steamers, *Malachite,* 718 tons, and *Primo,* 1,366 tons, within sight of the French coast off Le Havre. Again, following the rules of prize law, the U-boat captain permitted the crews of both ships to enter their lifeboats before he sank the steamers with his deck gun. On January 30, a single U-boat, *U-21,* sank three merchant ships off Liverpool in a single afternoon. In each case, the sinkings were done under prize law rules. On February 1, the hospital ship *Asturias,* which the submarine captain genuinely mistook for a merchantman, was attacked off Le Havre but escaped. During the first six months of war—August 1914 through January 1915—ten Allied merchantmen totaling 20,000 tons had been sent to the bottom by U-boats, most of them in a gentlemanly manner and at trivial cost to the Germans who, not wishing to waste torpedoes, used bombs or shells from their deck guns.

Once the war-zone campaign began, the U-boat attack fell most heavily on the Western Approaches, through which most of Britain's essential imports passed. This vital area could be reached only by the twenty diesel boats of High Seas Fleet flotillas, leaving the older, heavy-oil-engine boats to operate in the North Sea and the Channel. At first, U-boat captains attempted to discriminate in their attacks. British and French merchant ships were sunk on sight; neutrals were stopped, the ship's papers were inspected, and, if contraband was found, the crew was allowed to take to its lifeboats and the ship was sunk by bombs or gunfire. In these cases, the papers were sent to a German prize court, which occasionally judged the neutral shipowner entitled to damages. Between February 22, when the campaign was launched, and March 28, German submarines sank twenty-five merchant ships. Sixteen of these were torpedoed without warning and fifty-two crew members were killed. Thirty-eight of these men died in a single attack, when a freighter carrying nitrates blew up. Nevertheless, on board the twenty-five ships sunk, not one passenger died and twenty of the twenty-five ships suffered no loss of life whatever. Meanwhile, every week, between 1,000 and 1,500 ships—more than 4,000 vessels a month—sailed in and out of British ports, a number that exceeded peacetime traffic in the summer of 1914.

—

At first, it seemed that there was little the Royal Navy could do to fight the U-boats. The Admiralty advised captains of British merchantmen to hoist neutral colors in the war zone, a questionable act that may have saved some vessels but also provoked a storm of protest from the neutral nations whose flags were flown. As for attacking the submarines themselves, no one knew how. Little thought had been given before the war to submarines as offensive weapons and even less to antisubmarine tactics or weaponry. The earliest British attempts to cope were primitive, even quixotic. Coastal yachts and motorboats patrolled outside British harbors, but only one in ten of these craft was armed with anything larger than a rifle. A few motor launches carried two swimmers, one armed with a black bag, the other with a hammer. If a periscope was sighted, the launch was to come as close as possible. The swimmers were to dive in and one man would attempt to place his black bag over the periscope; if he failed, the other would try to smash the glass with his hammer. Another unsuccessful scheme involved attempting to teach seagulls to defecate on periscopes. The most effective form of attack, ramming or gunfire, demanded that the submarine be caught on the surface. But as long as a submarine remained submerged, it was undetectable and invulnerable. Mines and minefields were laid down, but, being passive defenses, they had to wait for submarines to bump into them. Nevertheless, to protect the Channel from U-boats, twenty-two minefields with 7,154 mines were laid east of the Dover Strait between October and February. This mine barrier proved ineffective because British mines were of poor quality. They were visible on the surface at low tide and when struck they frequently failed to explode. Moreover, about 4,000 either sank to the bottom or drifted away. An effort to build a twenty-mile-long boom of heavy steel harbor-defense nets across the Channel from Folkestone to Cap Gris-Nez failed because the tides placed too great a strain on the mooring cables.

Not all losses at sea were British, however. During January 1915, two U-boats had been lost—one mistakenly torpedoed by a third U-boat—bringing to seven the total number destroyed in the seven months since the beginning of war. The eighteen remaining of the original twenty-five German submarines were reinforced by twelve new boats brought into service after August 1914, making a total of thirty with which to begin the new campaign. The month of March 1915 brought more German losses. On March 4, *U-8* was caught in the Dover nets and sunk by the destroyer *Ghurka.* On March 10, *U-12* was caught on the surface and rammed by the destroyer *Ariel* off the coast of Scotland. On the same day, the new *U-29,* commanded by the famous Otto Weddigen, who had sunk *Aboukir, Hogue, Cressy,* and *Hawke,* was patrolling off Scapa Flow when she encountered battle squadrons of the Grand Fleet steaming through Pentland Firth. Maneuvering to attack, Weddigen fired a torpedo at the dreadnought *Neptune* but missed. Apparently engrossed in continuing his attack, Weddigen failed to see the battleship *Dreadnought* coming up behind him. *Dreadnought,* spotting the periscope, rammed at full speed. The force of the blow threw the submarine to the surface, revealing her identity as the bow, rising high out of the water, displayed the painted number "U-29." The U-boat sank with no survivors. In all, forty-nine German U-boats were destroyed in the first twenty-eight months of war, either on the surface or, if submerged, by mines. But the British and Allied navies had neither means of detecting U-boats nor weapons other than mines to destroy them under water. Not until December 13, 1916, when *UB-29* was sunk in the English Channel, was a German submarine sunk by a British depth charge.

—

Each new, aggressive step in the naval war provoked retaliation. Britain's November 2, 1914, blockade proclamation had been presented as a response to "indiscriminate" German mining in the North Sea. In turn, the German submarine war-zone proclamation of February 4, 1915, was described as a reprisal for the British proclamation of November 2. On March 11, 1915, Britain upped the ante, announcing that, in response to the German war-zone proclamation and submarine campaign, the Allied navies would establish a total blockade of Germany. An order in council declared that by creating a war zone in which all Allied merchant ships were to be destroyed on sight without ascertaining the nature of their cargoes and the purpose or destination of their voyages, and without heed to the safety of their passengers or crews, Germany was, in effect, imposing a total blockade "with the avowed object of preventing commodities of all kinds including food for the civilian population from reaching or leaving the British Isles." In response, therefore, the Allied navies now would prevent all cargoes, contraband or not, from reaching Germany. The U.S. government protested this further restriction of the freedom of the seas, declaring that the new order conferred the rights of a blockading squadron upon British squadrons that were not blockading an enemy coast: Admiral de Chair's squadron, for example, was not patrolling off German harbors; it was strung out on a line hundreds of miles away between the Shetlands and Norway, the Faeroes and Iceland. Nevertheless, the American protest was relatively mild and a note of triumph appeared when Sir Cecil Spring-Rice, the British ambassador in Washington, wrote to Sir Edward Grey at the end of April, "I think we may say that, roughly speaking, you have achieved a very great diplomatic success in your negotiations with this government. You have asserted the rights of a belligerent in a very severe form because these rights are necessary to the existence of this country."

—

Ironically, the grounds on which Spring-Rice's message claimed and trumpeted a victory were the same—raison d'état—that the German admirals wished to invoke, but were not to be allowed to use for another two years. For the first three months of the submarine campaign, German U-boat commanders had done their best to abide by the policy of restricted submarine warfare; as a result, the U.S. government had found little about which to complain. Neutral ships had been sunk by mistake, but none were of American registry; neutral citizens had died, but none were American citizens. On March 28, this record was marred when, in the St. George's Channel, off the Irish coast, *U-28* fired a shot across the bow of the 5,000-ton British cargo and passenger liner *Falaba.* When the vessel halted, *Falaba*'s master was given ten minutes to abandon ship. While disembarkation proceeded, *Falaba* continued to send wireless messages requesting assistance; even so, *U-28* extended the disembarkation period by another ten minutes and then by still another three minutes. As time was expiring, an armed British trawler appeared, whereupon *U-28* promptly put a torpedo into *Falaba.* A hundred and four lives were lost, including that of an American passenger, Leon C.

Thrasher, a mining engineer on his way to a job in South Africa. Thrasher thereby entered history as the first U.S. citizen to be killed at sea by a German U-boat. The Woodrow Wilson administration was divided on how to react: the State Department Counselor, Robert Lansing, described the sinking as "an atrocious act of lawlessness" and argued that the Germans must be held to the threatened "strict accountability." Secretary of State William Jennings Bryan, however, insisted that American citizens who traveled on ships of belligerent powers passing through a war zone had no more right to claim immunity than they would if they were traveling across a land battlefield while a battle was being fought. President Woodrow Wilson, although disagreeing with Bryan's premise, decided that the loss of a single citizen was insufficiently grave to provoke a crisis with Germany. For the moment, Wilson merely asked the German ambassador for more information.

The month of April 1915 passed in relative calm. Then, on May 3, an American ship, the tanker *Gulflight,* carrying a cargo of oil from Port Arthur, Texas, to Rouen, was torpedoed without warning. The explosion caused only minor damage and no loss of life on board, and the ship did not sink. But two panic-stricken crew members jumped overboard and were drowned, and that night the tanker's captain died of a heart attack. Lansing characterized the attack as "wanton and indiscriminate"; again, Wilson asked for more details.

The German government may have concluded from the limited and technical nature of these enquiries that Americans and their president were inclined to acquiesce in the submarine war, but neither the American government nor its people were as indifferent as they might have seemed. If Wilson was slow to protest, it was because he was struggling to integrate the implications of this series of incidents into his personal structure of political and moral belief. Somehow, from far away, Bethmann-Hollweg sensed the deceptive quality of the apparent calm in Washington. On May 6, he wrote to Admiral Bachmann protesting "the growing number of neutral ships falling victim to submarine warfare," which may "drive the neutral powers into the camp of our enemies." Demanding once again that the safety of neutral vessels be guaranteed, the chancellor warned that he "could not be responsible for the political direction of the German empire if neutral nations were to be continually antagonized by U-boat warfare." Ironically, this letter was written one day before the nightmarish episode that the German chancellor had feared became reality. On May 7, 1915, a few miles off the Old Head of Kinsale, a rocky promontory on the southwest coast of Ireland, a U-boat torpedoed the famous Cunard transatlantic liner *Lusitania.* Among the vessel's 1,265 civilian passengers were 128 Americans.

CHAPTER 29

Lusitania and the American Reaction

When they were built seven years before the Great War, the Cunard sisters *Lusitania* and *Mauretania* were the largest, fastest, most luxurious passenger ships afloat. Each was eight decks high, 785 feet long, displaced 30,395 tons, and could carry 3,000 passengers and crew. Gold and white, glass-domed, Louis XVI dining salons and mahogany-paneled lounges and smoking rooms with huge marble mantelpieces provided a fashionable setting for first-class passengers. For those who preferred not to mingle at all with other travelers, the ships offered suites, each with a parlor with a working fireplace, two bedrooms, and a private dining room with another fireplace. Besides providing comfort, the new ships offered lofty social prestige. "Just now," said the *Philadelphia Inquirer,* "the man who came over in the *Lusitania* takes precedence of the one whose ancestors came over on the *Mayflower.*" Both vessels were powered by four turbine engines, which burned 1,000 tons of coal a day and propelled the ship at an average speed of 24 to 25 knots. The two liners were made capable of this speed for two reasons, one obvious, the other shadowy. Cunard's stated purpose was to defeat the famous "Atlantic greyhounds" of the North German Lloyd and Hamburg-America Lines and reclaim for Britain the "Blue Riband," the recognition, eventually embodied in a silver chalice, that signified the fastest passenger ship afloat. *Lusitania* achieved this triumph on her second voyage from Liverpool to New York, which took only four days, nineteen hours, and fifty-two minutes. Within a few years, the two Cunard ships (and a third sister, *Aquitania,* which entered service in 1914) were exceeded in size by the White Star liners *Olympic* and *Titanic* and then by two immense, 54,000-ton Hamburg-America liners, *Vaterland* and *Imperator,* each of which had accommodations for 5,500 passengers and crew. But for sheer speed, the Cunard ships were never overtaken.

There was another, less public reason for building great speed into the new Cunard liners. Before the war the Admiralty had no fear of submarines as a threat to Britain's maritime supply lines. Danger to British trade, the Admiralty believed, would come from fast German liners converted to armed merchant cruisers. Accordingly, the Admiralty subsidized the building of *Lusitania* and her sisters; in return, Cunard agreed to make the vessels available to the government upon request; their obvious use would be as fast British armed merchant cruisers assigned to hunt down their German equivalents. The Cunard ships, therefore, were designed to carry as many as twelve 6-inch guns; the necessary magazines, shell elevators, and revolving gun rings in the deck were installed during construction. When war broke out, *Mauretania* and *Aquitania* were requisitioned but *Lusitania* was left in Cunard service. On September 24, 1914, the Admiralty officially informed the ship line that *Lusitania*'s role would be to continue running a high-speed service between Liverpool and New York with the Admiralty having first priority on her cargo space. By May 1915, *Lusitania* was the only giant, prewar ocean greyhound from any country still carrying passengers across the Atlantic.

It was in this primary role that *Lusitania* backed away from her pier into the Hudson River just after noon on May 1, 1915, and steamed down through New York harbor to begin her 202nd voyage across the Atlantic. On board, she carried 1,265 passengers, including 129 young children and infants, the bachelor millionaire sportsman Alfred Gwynne Vanderbilt, traveling to England on business concerning racehorses, the theatrical producer Charles Frohman,* and a crew of 700; no one aboard, passenger or crew, expressed any unusual worry. Over this voyage, however, ominous portents had begun to gather. The grimmest was a black-bordered news advertisement published in forty-nine American newspapers the morning the *Lusitania* sailed:

NOTICE

> Travelers intending to embark on the Atlantic voyage are reminded that a state of war exists between Germany and her allies and Great Britain and her allies; that the zone of war includes waters adjacent to the British Isles; that in accordance with formal notice given by the Imperial German Government, vessels flying the flag of Great Britain

*Frohman, the most successful impresario of his day, was famous for his mordant show-business wit. When the celebrated English actress Mrs. Patrick Campbell reacted to criticism of her acting by saying that she was an *artiste,* Frohman assured her quickly, "Madam, your secret is safe with me."

or any of her allies are liable to destruction in those waters and that travelers sailing in the war zone on ships of Great Britain or her allies do so at their own risk.

Imperial German Embassy
Washington, D.C.

The advertisement was the work of German diplomats and sympathizers in the United States who possessed what they considered to be strong evidence that *Lusitania* was carrying contraband in the form of munitions and military supplies on her eastward voyages back to Britain. In addition, they were frustrated by frequent statements in the American press of the greater horrors of submarine warfare as compared to blockade. "The American people cannot visualize the spectacle of a hundred thousand, even a million, German children starving by slow degrees as a result of the British blockade, but they can visualize the pitiful face of a little child drowning amidst the wreckage caused by a German torpedo," said Dr. Bernhard Dernburg, the German embassy's press attaché.

If the German notice worried *Lusitania*'s passengers, it was not enough to persuade any of them to disembark. The voyage seemed safe. Since Germany's February commencement of submarine warfare against merchant ships, the liner had made four round-trip voyages unmolested. Should a U-boat spot *Lusitania* in the war zone, the liner would be flying a neutral American flag. (Colonel Edward House, President Wilson's special envoy, who traveled to Europe several times on the *Lusitania* after the war began, noted in his diary on February 5, 1915, "This afternoon, as we approached the Irish coast, the American flag was raised.") Cunard and the ship's captain both had assured the passengers that the big ship could easily outrun any submarine. Even if the worst were to happen, there would be sufficient lifeboats; after the *Titanic* disaster, Cunard had increased the number of *Lusitania*'s lifeboats from twenty-two to forty-eight.

In fact, there was reason for concern, but it was one of which *Lusitania*'s passengers were unaware. The ship's cargo space was—just as the Germans claimed—being used to carry American munitions to Britain. As *Lusitania* prepared for her last voyage, 1,248 cases of 3-inch artillery shells—four shells to a case—and 4,927 boxes of rifle ammunition—each case containing 1,000 rounds and the total weighing 173 tons, which included ten tons of explosive powder—had been placed in the liner's cargo. Whether this cargo exploded when a torpedo hit the ship has been the subject of many years of passionate, highly technical, and still unresolved debate.

The ocean voyage was serene. Captain William Turner, a short, stocky, red-faced man known as Bowler Bill for his taste in off-duty headgear, took his meals alone on the bridge to avoid sitting with passengers, whom he had once described as "a lot of bloody monkeys." As *Lusitania* approached the

German-designated war zone, he asked male passengers to help keep her dark by not lighting their cigars on deck after dinner. At 8:00 a.m. on May 7, Turner was on his bridge. Because dense fog had lowered visibility, he slowed the ship from 21 to 15 knots and began sounding the foghorn. By midmorning, when the mists were blowing away, he increased speed to 18 knots and set a course for Queenstown on the Irish coast. His plan was to pass through the St. George's Channel, between Ireland and Wales, and be off the Liverpool bar the next morning at 4:30.

—

Meanwhile, on that same morning of May 7, Captain Walther Schwieger was standing in the conning tower of *U-20* near the entrance to the St. George's Channel, staring into the fog enshrouding his submarine while he charged his electric batteries. The previous day had brought him success: using three torpedoes, he had sunk two British ships. Now, running low on fuel and with only three torpedoes left, Schwieger made a decision: if the fog had not cleared by noon, he would end his cruise and return to Wilhelmshaven. He ordered the boat to submerge and went below for breakfast. Just before noon, he heard the sound of a ship's engines coming from the surface over his head. Allowing ten minutes for the vessel to move away, Schwieger carefully rose to periscope depth and saw the British light cruiser *Juno* zigzagging away from him toward Queenstown. The fog had cleared, the sea was calm, and the sun was bright. He surfaced. And then, at 1:20 p.m., Schwieger saw a plume of smoke fourteen miles to the southwest. He waited, and the source of the smoke grew larger and took shape as a massive steamship with four tall funnels. Submerging, Schwieger set a course that would intercept this vessel at a point approximately ten miles off a rocky coastal promontory called the Old Head of Kinsale.

Two British publications, the 1914 editions of *Jane's Fighting Ships* and Brassey's *Naval Annual,* were standard issue aboard every German U-boat, and both publications placed *Lusitania* in the category of "Royal Navy Reserved Merchant Cruiser"—in effect, an armed liner. *U-20* also carried a German merchant marine officer whose duty was to help identify any merchant ship targets whose nationality was in doubt. Watching the approaching steamer through the periscope, this civilian officer became increasingly certain of what he saw: "Either the *Lusitania* or the *Mauretania,* both armed cruisers used for carrying troops," he told Schwieger. (In fact, at that moment, *Mauretania* was 150 miles away at Avonmouth, taking aboard 5,000 soldiers for the Dardanelles.) Schwieger had in his sights what he considered a legitimate target.

At 2:10 p.m., he fired a single torpedo at a range of 800 yards. The torpedo struck the starboard side of the ship just behind the bridge and slightly forward of the first funnel. No second torpedo was fired, but the detonation of the first was followed by a second, larger explosion in the same part of the ship. The forward superstructure was shattered, the bow ruptured, and fire and smoke billowed along the decks. According to Schwieger's log, *Lusitania* immediately slowed and heeled to starboard with water rising quickly over her bow. Still submerged, *U-20* came closer and made a circuit of the sinking ship. Staring through the periscope, the civilian pilot said, "Yes, by God, it's the *Lusitania.*"

—

On board *Lusitania,* some passengers were still at lunch and others were strolling on deck enjoying the spring sunshine when the torpedo struck. At first, there was concern, but no panic. Alfred Gwynne Vanderbilt devoted himself to "trying to put life jackets on women and children." Charles Frohman, smoking an after-lunch cigar, was handed a life jacket, but "soon gave it away to a woman." Together, passengers and crew members began tying other life jackets onto wicker baskets brought from the nursery, in which infants remained sleeping. When it became apparent that the ship's rapid list to starboard would make it difficult to fill and launch the lifeboats, concern turned to alarm, then terror. The lifeboats on the starboard side now hung far out over the sea, while those on the port side swung in over the rails or against the side of the ship. Several lifeboats were released at one end only; the first boat launched in this manner was filled with women and children who spilled helplessly into the water seventy feet below. Other boats, lowered too hastily and steeply, touched water bow or stern first and foundered immediately. Still others smashed inboard against the side of the vessel, crushing their passengers as the lifeboat disintegrated. At the end, as *Lusitania*'s bow plunged toward the granite seafloor 300 feet below, the liner's stern rose high in the air; at this angle, guy wires snapped and towering seventy-eight-foot funnels and even taller wireless masts toppled onto the decks. Rumbling internal explosions of steam hurled debris, bodies, and huge bubbles of water into the air. When the clouds of steam had cleared, *Lusitania* was gone. Since the torpedo struck, eighteen minutes had passed. Only six of the liner's forty-eight lifeboats floated amid the wreckage, and hundreds of men and women were struggling individually in the calm, green, sunlit sea. A ship's junior officer swimming through the wreckage found himself listening to the cries of infants floating nearby in their wicker baskets. There was nothing he could do. Gradually, the baskets sank.

—

Twelve hundred and one people drowned in the catastrophe, among them ninety-four children, of whom thirty-five were babies. Vanderbilt, Frohman, and 126 other Americans died; a total of 764 lives were saved. More would have been rescued if the cruiser *Juno,* hurrying back from Queenstown and in

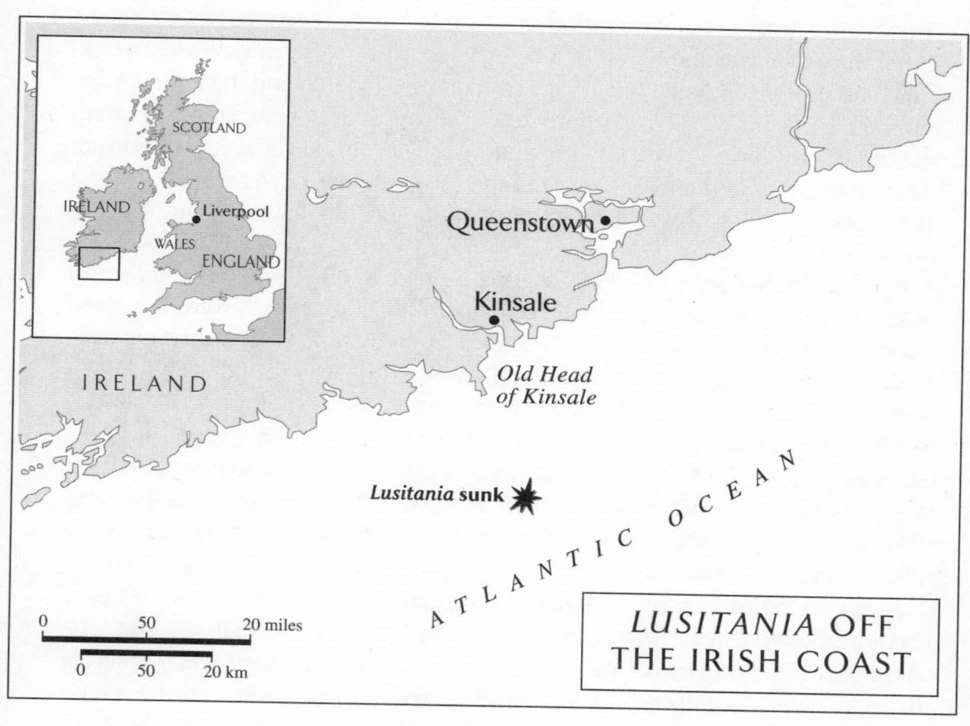
SCOTLAND
IRELAND
Liverpool
WALES
ENGLAND
Queenstown
Kinsale
Old Head
of Kinsale
IRELAND
Lusitania sunk
ATLANTIC OCEAN
0
50
20 miles
0
50
20 km
LUSITANIA OFF
THE IRISH COAST

sight of the survivors in the water, had not received a peremptory signal from the Admiralty, ordering her back into port. This command, stemming from the policy of "no live bait in the presence of submarines" laid down after the sinking of *Cressy* and her sisters, resulted in the passage of almost two hours before fishing trawlers arrived and began pulling survivors out of the sea.

Most of the world was horror-stricken. The first bodies brought in were photographed and the pictures—mostly those of dead children—were circulated in newspapers, ostensibly to help relatives identify their dead. Photographs of corpses recovered later were never seen by the public, but the American consul in Queenstown reported that "faces registered every shading of the grotesque and hideous. The lips and noses were eaten away by sea birds and the eyes gouged out . . . the trunks were bloated and distended with gases and the limbs were partially eaten away or bitten clean off so that stumps of raw bone were left protruding." The coroner's jury at Kinsale charged the submarine's officers "and the Emperor and Government of Germany, under whose orders they acted, with the crime of willful and wholesale murder."

Schwieger entered in *U-20*'s log that he had watched the calamity with mixed feelings, but his superiors and many of his countrymen were jubilant. Admiral von Pohl signaled: "My highest appreciation of commander and crew for success achieved of which High Seas Fleet is proud." The *Kolnische Volkszeitung* declared: "With joyful pride we contemplate the latest deed of our navy." Across Germany, schoolchildren were granted a holiday. A private citizen in Munich created a copper medal depicting, on one side, passengers lining up at a booth from which a skeleton was issuing tickets, and on the other side, the sinking *Lusitania,* crammed with guns, armored cars, and airplanes.*

From the point of view of American and international law, the munitions aboard *Lusitania* would have justified the stopping of the ship and—once its cargo had been identified and its passengers and crew allowed to take to lifeboats—its destruction. But the sudden, brutal torpedoing and the overwhelming loss of innocent lives made law appear irrelevant and shocked the world. Before the sinking, Americans had been angry at Great Britain because of the blockade; it was likely that, over time, this resentment would have festered and grown worse. After the sinking of *Lusitania,* American in-

*Anti-German feeling in Britain and other countries was vigorously promoted by the activity of an American citizen living in London. The German in Munich stopped when he had struck forty-four medals. One of these fell into British hands, and 300,000 copies were made in Britain and distributed around the world as evidence of German barbarism. These copies were produced by Gordon Selfridge, an American who had opened a department store in Oxford Street in 1909 and subsequently become a friend of Asquith's. In 1937, Selfridge became a naturalized British subject.

dignation and, ultimately, wrath were focused on the German submarine war, not the British blockade.

—

The critical question for Britain and Germany was how the American people, and particularly President Woodrow Wilson, would react. Two former presidents, Roosevelt and Taft, called for war. From London, the U.S. ambassador, Walter H. Page, reported that unofficial opinion in England was that the United States must fight or forfeit all respect. Colonel Edward House, the president's friend and confidential emissary and Page's guest of honor at an embassy dinner, emotionally told the others around the table that within a month the United States would be at war. In Berlin, U.S. Ambassador James W. Gerard had a similar premonition; he reserved sleeping-car accommodations on a train for Switzerland for himself and his wife.

The president of the United States had a different reaction. Thomas Woodrow Wilson, a man of iron Calvinist principles and deep Presbyterian faith, believed that his country had a special mission in the world. America had been spared the history of tyranny and corruption that had debased older societies. Coming late into being, it now stood as man's hope; its destiny was to guide, liberalize, and succor all less fortunate nations and peoples. This mission and destiny were not to be squandered by rushing heedlessly into a European war. Wilson's faith applied to all aspects of his life, political and personal. "My life would not be worth living if it were not for the driving power of religion," he once told a friend visiting the White House. At the core of his belief was the conviction of being one of God's elect, a status justified only by unremitting effort to accomplish good. Wilson's Calvinist God, as described by the president's biographer August Heckscher, "was stern, absolute in his judgements, and responsible for every event in history and in the lives of individual men and women. To him, and not to any worldly powers, the believer owed a total obedience."

Wilson acquired this creed from his father, the Reverend Joseph Ruggles Wilson, a Presbyterian minister of Scottish descent who delivered it from his pulpits in Staunton, Virginia; Augusta, Georgia; and Columbia, South Carolina. Thus imbued, eighteen-year-old Tommy Wilson, a tall, thin boy with a long face, gray eyes, sandy hair, and large ears, arrived at the College of New Jersey, eventually to be renamed Princeton University. (Later, at his mother's request, Wilson renamed himself, taking up her maiden name, Woodrow.) He received a law degree from the University of Virginia Law School and a doctorate in history from Johns Hopkins; he held professorships of history at Bryn Mawr, Wesleyan, and Princeton; he became president of Princeton, and, in 1910, governor of New Jersey. He was immediately considered a presidential possibility, but at the 1912 Democratic convention in Baltimore, he won only on the forty-sixth roll-call ballot. In the November election,

Wilson won on a plurality, receiving a million fewer popular votes than Taft and Roosevelt combined, but 435 electoral votes against 84 for Theodore Roosevelt and 8 for President William Howard Taft.

Once in office, Wilson easily dominated his administration, particularly in foreign policy. Wilson was his own secretary of state.* On important matters, he cared little about the views of members of his Cabinet, but he kept a tight finger on the pulse of public opinion. Wilson's own underlying sympathies were with Britain and the Allies and he told the British ambassador, "Everything that I love most in the world is at stake. . . . If they [the Germans] succeed, we shall be forced to take such measures of defense here as will be fatal to our form of government and to American ideals." Wilson's aversion to war and his sense of America's higher mission were, he was certain, shared by the overwhelming majority of his countrymen; Congress, he knew, had strong isolationist leanings. Accordingly, he was determined that America remain neutral. From the beginning, the effort to preserve this neutrality was arduous; ultimately, it became herculean. At bottom, the difference between Great Britain and Germany was that the injuries inflicted by the two belligerents upon America were of unequal magnitude: the British navy stopped ships and sometimes seized property; the German navy sank ships and sometimes killed people.

—

Wilson had been at lunch on Saturday, May 8, 1915, when news of the *Lusitania* sinking was brought to him. By evening, he knew that over a thousand lives, many of them American, had been lost. Quietly, he slipped out into the night and, ignoring a light rain, walked alone along Pennsylvania Avenue.

*Wilson's secretary of state, William Jennings Bryan of Nebraska, was an outsized figure in American history who occupied an awkward position in Wilson's first administration. As a leader of the free-silver movement and an opponent of the gold standard, Bryan had captured the 1896 Democratic convention in Chicago with his celebrated cry, "I shall not aid in pressing down upon the bleeding brow of labor this crown of thorns; I shall not help crucify mankind upon a cross of gold." On the spot, at the age of thirty-six, the orator was nominated for the presidency. Defeated by William McKinley, he continued as the champion of the agrarian West and South against the eastern bankers and industrialists. Nominated twice again for president—in 1900 and 1908—he did not choose to run a fourth time in 1912, but threw his support to Governor Woodrow Wilson of New Jersey. Wilson, becoming president, offered Bryan the office of secretary of state in gratitude for the Nebraskan's role at the convention and also because his friends advised him that not to do so would be "political suicide."

In Washington, Bryan quickly became the despair of foreign diplomats: "talking to Mr. Bryan is like writing on ice," said the British ambassador. When he served grape juice instead of wine to European ambassadors, he became a subject of ridicule; his relations with the press deteriorated until "by self-inflicted degrees [he] passed from the vulnerable to the absurd." Nevertheless, because of his fame, his oratorical prowess, and his thirty-year leadership of the Democratic party, Bryan, four years younger than Wilson, always seemed the older man.

Returning to the White House, he retreated into his study. Over the weekend, he consulted no one, went to church, played golf, and, on Sunday evening, sat down to write the speech he was scheduled to give in Philadelphia the following day. On Monday, he addressed 15,000 people, many of them newly naturalized citizens. America, he told them, was a peaceful nation and therefore, "the example of America must be a special example . . . the example, not merely of peace because it will not fight, but of peace because peace is the healing and elevating influence of the world and strife is not. There is such a thing as a man being too proud to fight. There is such a thing as a nation being so right that it does not need to convince others by force that it is right." In Philadelphia, Wilson's words stirred prolonged cheering; when this language reached England, mention of the word "America" was publicly booed and hissed.*

On Tuesday, May 11, the Cabinet met and Wilson read aloud the typed draft of a note he had written to Germany regarding the *Lusitania.* In the note he expressed disbelief that the German government could have sanctioned so illegal and inhumane an act and then went on to explore in moral terms the nature of submarine warfare against merchant shipping:

> The government of the United States desires to call the attention of the Imperial German Government . . . to . . . the practical impossibility of employing submarines in the destruction of commerce without disregarding those rules of fairness, reason, justice and humanity which all modern opinion regards as imperative. It is practically impossible for the officers of a submarine at sea to visit a merchantman at sea and examine her papers and cargo. It is practically impossible for them to make a prize of her; and if they cannot put a prize crew on board her, they cannot sink her without leaving her crew and all on board to the mercy of the sea in her small boats. . . . Manifestly, submarines cannot be used against merchantmen . . . without an inevitable violation of many sacred principles of justice and humanity.

Despite the careful, pedagogic tone of Wilson's language, Bryan objected that the draft was too pro-British and reiterated his opposition to Americans traveling on ships belonging to nations at war. Robert Lansing, the State Department Counselor, riposted that it was too late for that; the American

*The *Lusitania* crisis coincided with turbulent events in the president's private life. On August 6, 1914, the second day of the war in Europe, Ellen Wilson, Woodrow's wife of twenty-nine years, had died of Bright's disease in their White House bedroom. On May 4, 1915, three days before the sinking of the *Lusitania,* Wilson had declared his love to a widow named Edith Galt and had been gently rebuffed. Undeterred, Wilson wrote to her after his Philadelphia speech, "I do not know just what I said in Philadelphia . . . because my heart was in such a whirl."

government already had told American citizens that it would hold the German government to "a strict accountability" for American lives and property. The United States "has permitted in silence hundreds of American citizens to travel in British steamships crossing the war zone." Now, some of them had died. The only course, Lansing urged, was to demand an official disavowal of the attack and a guarantee that it would not happen again. Bryan disagreed and demanded that the United States treat the British and German systems of economic coercion—blockade and submarine warfare—as equally objectionable; whatever protest was sent to Berlin, he said, must be balanced by an equally vigorous protest to London. The secretary of state was overruled and the American note sent to Berlin emphasized the right of American citizens to sail wherever they wished on whatever ship they chose.*

Meanwhile, a German embassy official in Washington made a statement that made things worse. Declaring that it was certain that *Lusitania* had been armed and was transporting munitions, Dr. Dernburg declared that if Americans traveled on unarmed ships carrying no contraband they would be "as safe as if they were in a cradle." However, all armed vessels carrying contraband would be sunk on sight and Americans traveling on these vessels would be "traveling on a volcano." This message, challenging a right Americans had been encouraged to believe they inherently possessed—the right to travel freely on the high seas—stirred a fresh wave of anger. Still, Wilson remained cautious, telling both Sir Cecil Spring-Rice and the German ambassador, Count Johann von Bernstorff, that he was awaiting details.

In Germany, where Schwieger and the men of *U-20* had been proclaimed heroes, Wilson's note, arriving on May 15, provoked more bitter argument. Already, Bachmann and Tirpitz had replied to the chancellor's appeal of May 6, warning Bethmann-Hollweg that submarine operations must either be continued without modification or abandoned outright. To deal with their obstinacy, the chancellor appealed to the kaiser. The same day, May 10—after the *Lusitania*'s sinking but before receipt of Wilson's protest note—William had told Bachmann that "for the immediate future, no neutral vessel shall be sunk. This is necessary on political ground for which the chancellor is responsible. It is better that an enemy ship be allowed to pass than that a neutral shall be destroyed. A renewal of a sharper procedure is kept in view." Subsequently, Bethmann-Hollweg, assuming that this order had been circulated to the fleet, informed Washington that "the most definite instructions have repeatedly been issued to German war vessels to avoid attacks on neutral shipping." The chancellor and the kaiser, however, had been deceived.

*Naturally, German newspapers vociferously agreed with Bryan. An American passenger on a British merchant ship was called a *Schutzengel,* guardian angel, and one published caricature depicted a mate reporting to the captain of a British ship that the vessel was ready to sail. "Are you sure the American *Schutzengel* is on board?" the captain asks.

The Naval Staff, now persuaded that the war at sea could be won only by U-boats, was determined not to give up, and Bachmann deliberately did not issue the emperor's order to the fleet. Behind this disobedience lay an important change in German thinking about the ends and means of naval warfare. By the end of April 1915, the naval command realized that its original justification for beginning submarine warfare against commerce—as simple retaliation against the British blockade—no longer sufficed. The Naval Staff now believed that the war at sea could only be won by a U-boat offensive against merchant shipping. Accordingly, the U-boat campaign was represented within the navy and to the German people as an inevitable evolution in naval warfare, coming in a form perhaps unprecedented but unquestionably legitimate. Admiral Scheer expressed the widespread conviction of his fellow officers when he said, "In a comparatively short space of time, U-boat warfare against commerce has become a form of warfare which . . . is adapted to the nature of modern war and must remain a part of it. For us Germans, U-boat warfare upon commerce is a deliverance. It has put British predominance at sea in question. Being pressed by sheer necessity we must legalize this new weapon, or, to speak more accurately, accustom the world to it."

The German reply to the first American *Lusitania* note attempted to blame Great Britain for the disaster. *Lusitania,* the Germans said, was an armed auxiliary cruiser, carrying guns on its decks, that habitually carried munitions to Britain and often illegally flew the American flag. These facts, the German note continued, warranted a careful examination by the American government; until this was done, Germany would delay its response to the American demand that U-boat warfare be halted. While this note was being prepared, Ambassador Gerard spoke to the German foreign minister, Gottlieb von Jagow, and then cabled Washington: "I am myself positive that Germany will continue this form of warfare. . . . The prospect of war with America is contemplated with equanimity."

During May—in spite of the kaiser's May 10 order to stop sinking neutral vessels and despite the German government's promise to the United States that neutral shipping would be spared—Danish, Norwegian, and Swedish steamers were torpedoed without warning. Bethmann-Hollweg realized that the imperial command was being disobeyed and on May 31 convened a general meeting at which the kaiser presided. At this conference, Admiral von Müller supported the chancellor's insistence that submarine operations be moderated. Further support for moderation came from General Erich von Falkenhayn, Chief of the Army General Staff, who feared the effect a break with the United States would have on other neutrals, particularly Bulgaria. Admirals Tirpitz and Bachmann "stubbornly repeated that they could not discuss any modification of U-boat orders and were only interested to know whether or not submarine operations were to be continued." William was confronted with another of those decisions he hated to make. Personally, he supported the chancellor, yet he never wished to appear to the public as less courageous than his generals and admirals. Now, not only the military men, but also the press and the Reichstag were generating enormous pressure to unleash the submarines. William's solution was to announce that if U-boat warfare were to be abandoned, the chancellor must publicly announce that he alone was responsible. Bethmann-Hollweg accepted this burden. Accordingly, on June 1, a new imperial command was issued that repeated the order Bachmann had suppressed a few weeks before: neutral ships were to be spared; U-boats were not to attack any vessel unless they were absolutely certain that the intended victim was an enemy. And, of supreme importance, passenger liners of all nations, even enemies, were not to be touched. Tirpitz and Bachmann lamented that this was an admission that *Lusitania* had been illegally torpedoed and an abandonment of Germany's strongest weapon against England. Both declared that they could not be responsible for executing the order and asked to be relieved of their commands. The two admirals were commanded to remain at their posts and, this time, the order was circulated to the fleet. Bethmann-Hollweg had maintained a precarious ascendancy.

—

When President Wilson met with his Cabinet to consider a reply to the German note of May 28, he brought to the meeting his own typewritten draft of a message in effect setting aside the German allegations that *Lusitania* had been an auxiliary cruiser carrying munitions: "Whatever may be the facts regarding the *Lusitania,*" Wilson had written, "the principal fact is that a great steamer, primarily and chiefly a conveyance for passengers and carrying more than a thousand souls who had no part or lot in the conduct of the war, was torpedoed and sunk without so much as a challenge or a warning and that men, women and children were sent to their death in circumstances unparalleled in modern warfare." In the note's closing paragraph, Wilson reiterated an American position from which, throughout the months of controversy with Germany, the American government refused to retreat: "The United States cannot admit that the proclamation of a war zone . . . may be made to operate as in any degree an abbreviation of the rights . . . of American citizens bound on lawful errands as passengers on ships of belligerent nationality."

It was on these points—the right of Americans to travel on belligerent ships, and the larger issue of whether Germany and Britain were being treated equally—that the president and his secretary of state ultimately broke. Germany had promised that ships flying the American flag would not be attacked; the sticking point was the safety of American citizens traveling on British liners. Bryan had watched with mounting dismay the president's determination to confront Germany on this issue. A lifelong pacifist, the secretary of state had argued in favor of restrictions on the right of Americans to travel in the war zone on ships of belligerent powers. There was more to the growing breach: Bryan, three times his party's candidate for president, now felt himself ignored, even humiliated, as Wilson turned increasingly to others—the ubiquitous, backstage Colonel House and the ultralegalistic Counselor Lansing—for advice. As discussions on the second *Lusitania* note continued, Bryan decided that the language in the note was provocative and must be redrafted. One who was present at the Cabinet meeting noticed that the secretary seemed to be laboring under great strain and sat back in his chair most of the time with his eyes closed. Suddenly, Bryan leaned forward and snapped, "You people are not neutral. You are taking sides." The president, with a "steely glitter" in his eyes, responded, "Mr. Bryan, you are not warranted in making such an assertion. We all doubtless have our opinions in this matter but there are none of us who can justly be accused of being unfair." On June 5, in an emotional interview with the president, Bryan announced that he had decided to resign, and on June 7, the Great Commoner left office. Lansing was appointed his successor; the following day, the second American note, as written by the president, was sent to Berlin.

—

At one point in the argument between them, Bethmann-Hollweg asked Admiral Bachmann what concessions could safely be offered to the United States, adding that "it must be taken for granted that some concession must be made to America, for Germany, if neutral, would not tolerate that a ship with 1,500 German passengers on board should be sunk without warning." Bachmann repeated what he had said before: no concessions should be offered, and modification of existing orders to the U-boats was unthinkable. Nevertheless, even Germans who supported the chancellor resented the American claim to an inalienable right to travel on belligerent ships. In a note to America, the German government observed that "there would appear to be no compelling necessity for American citizens to travel to Europe in time of war on ships carrying an enemy flag." As a solution, Jagow proposed that U.S. citizens travel to Europe only on four specially marked passenger liners, which would travel with advance notice to the German navy and which would carry no munitions or other contraband. The American government, the proposal continued, could establish such a service by purchasing four of the German passenger liners that had sought sanctuary in New York. American newspaper reaction to the proposal was explosive: "arrogant," "preposterous," "un-heard-of," cried the editorials; "Americans [are told they] may enjoy limited neutral rights if they submit to German regulations," declared a Nebraska journal.

Wilson shared this indignation, but he also realized that the overwhelming majority of Americans remained opposed to going to war. And, in any case, the nation was in no position to threaten military action. Accordingly, he rejected the idea of special passenger steamers and continued to negotiate. At the end of July, he made a statement highly agreeable to the chancellor and his allies within the German government: "The events of the past two months have clearly indicated that it is possible and practicable to conduct such submarine operations as have characterized the activities of the Imperial German navy within the so-called war zone in substantial accord with accepted practices of regulated warfare." In other words, if the U-boat captains followed the rules laid down in the kaiser's June 1 order and behaved as they had in recent weeks, the U.S. government would tolerate German submarine warfare against merchant shipping.

—

Through the summer of 1915, while Bethmann-Hollweg was struggling to placate Wilson and find some limitation on U-boat warfare that would appease America, Admiral von Tirpitz shook with rage. He hated the chancellor, whom he considered a coward and a traitor; he despised Pohl, whom he described as "ghastly," "servile," and "a contemptible little man." Tirpitz, the founder of the German navy, who in peacetime had insisted that the building of German dreadnoughts should never be limited simply because of English concern, now seemed unperturbed at the idea that submarine warfare might bring the United States into the war. He disapproved of "kowtowing" to anyone and was indignant at the conciliatory tone of German diplomatic notes after the sinking of *Lusitania.* "America is so shamelessly, so barefacedly pro-English," he wrote on July 25, 1915, "that it is hard to credit that we shall eat humble pie. Yet in this connection I believe nothing to be impossible. . . . I, for my part, will not join in a formal renunciation of submarine warfare, whereby we should abandon the only weapon we have in our hands against England in the future." When, because of American protests, submarine warfare was restricted, Tirpitz's hatred of the chancellor intensified. In the future, he told himself, he would use all his powers of persuasion and his access to the machinery of political propaganda to remove this incubus on the German navy and empire.

—

Not long after Woodrow Wilson's offer to tolerate limited submarine warfare, another British passenger liner was sunk without warning. On August 19, off Kinsale, the captain of *U-24* stopped the English steamer *Durnsley,* permitted the crew to enter their lifeboats, and then exploded bombs in the vessel's hold. The *Durnsley* went down slowly and as she was foundering, another, larger steamer approached. Schneider realized that this new vessel was a passenger ship but, "as I had been shot at by a large steamer on the 14th, I decided to attack this one from under water." He fired a torpedo. His target was the 15,801-ton White Star liner *Arabic,* bound for New York with twenty American citizens on board. The ship sank; among the forty-four passengers who died, three were Americans. No warning had been given; the act, therefore, was in defiance not only of the kaiser's June 1 order to the Imperial Navy but of the *Lusitania* settlement President Wilson was about to accept. The American president and government, besides having to deal with fresh tragedy, had been made to look foolish.

On August 26, the German chancellor convened a conference at Pless, in Silesia, to deal with the now merged crises of the *Lusitania* and the *Arabic.* He announced at the start that it was useless to belittle the anger these incidents were provoking and that unless strong assurances were given quickly, war with the United States was probable. Further, he said that he could no longer accept sole responsibility for calling an end to the submarine campaign in the face of German popular opinion. "I cannot continue to walk on a volcano," he cried. General von Falkenhayn, the Chief of the General Staff, who still hoped that America would stay out of the war, supported Bethmann-Hollweg. Indeed, once again, everyone present was united against the two old seamen, Tirpitz and Bachmann, who stubbornly insisted that the U-boat campaign must either be abandoned outright or continued without modification. In the end, the two admirals were overridden and the kaiser authorized the chancellor to conclude a general settlement with America. Both admirals immediately asked to be relieved. Müller struck quickly, removing Bachmann as Chief of the Naval Staff and installing Admiral Henning von Holtzendorff in his place. Holtzendorff, an experienced seaman, an opponent of Tirpitz, and a personal friend of the chancellor, believed that the U-boat campaign was overvalued and that if it was to continue, it must be properly regulated. William refused to accept Tirpitz's resignation, declaring that in time of war no officer was permitted to quit his post without imperial permission. Nevertheless, weary of the admiral's habitual insubordination and bullying language, the kaiser exiled him from Supreme Headquarters.

Eventually, after an exchange of diplomatic notes lasting more than three months, the German chancellor managed to satisfy the American president. On August 28, William issued an order that no passenger ships of any nationality, enemy or neutral, large or small, were to be sunk without warning. Further, the captains of the attacking submarines were to be responsible for the safety of passengers and crew. Once the president was informed of this order, American feelings calmed and the danger of American entry into the war receded. Thus, in three crises with the United States—the first in February, occasioned by the mere announcement of submarine warfare against merchant ships; the second over the sinking of the *Lusitania* in May; and the third over the sinking of the *Arabic* in August—Bethmann-Hollweg had taken the lead in drafting Germany's notes to the United States and in influencing the kaiser's orders to the U-boats.

And then, almost immediately, another episode occurred. On September 4, Walther Schwieger, the U-boat captain who sank *Lusitania,* torpedoed the 10,920-ton British liner *Hesperian* without warning off the coast of Ireland. There were Americans on board, but none were among the thirty-two persons killed. Nevertheless, the sinking was in flagrant defiance of the promise just given to Wilson. When asked to explain, German authorities at first assured the American government that no German submarine had been operating near the spot; they suggested that the ship had struck a mine. Later, a board of American officers concluded that the liner had been torpedoed, not mined, and relations between Germany and America again deteriorated. Finally, on September 18, still fearful of alienating American opinion and to ensure compliance with the kaiser's promise, Admiral von Holtzendorff recalled all U-boats from the English Channel and the Western Approaches, where the densest concentration of U.S. shipping occurred. He sanctioned continued operations in the North Sea, but decreed that they could be carried out only in strict accord with the prize regulations. Pohl, the commander of High Seas Fleet submarines, refused to allow his vessels to operate against commerce under prize regulations procedures and, rather than obeying Holtzendorff's command, withdrew all High Seas Fleet U-boats from the North Sea, virtually suspending the U-boat campaign for the rest of the year. As a sop to German public opinion, Holtzendorff and Pohl agreed that a small-scale submarine campaign should be waged in the Mediterranean, where few U.S. merchantmen were to be found.

—

Thus, by the autumn of 1915, the American and German governments had reached an agreement that, in essence, involved an American veto on U-boat tactics. The U.S. government had pronounced the submarine campaign to be legitimate and permissible only when it was directed solely against enemy, not neutral, shipping and provided also that all passenger ships were left untouched. Overall, by September 1915, when the German government settled its differences with the United States, U-boats had sunk 790,000 tons of Allied and neutral shipping. Of this, about 570,000 tons was British. This had been done in seven months by a fleet of about thirty-five submarines, which was being increased every month by four new boats of better design. Since the campaign began in February 1915, thirty U-boats had been reinforced by thirty-five new submarines; during the same period, fifteen U-boats had been lost. Thus, in September 1915, when the first submarine campaign was abandoned, fifty operational U-boats were available. For the German admirals this was stark, infuriating evidence that the campaign had been canceled for political, not military reasons.

The German admirals also knew that, under the rules by which they had been forced to operate, the submarine campaign had failed in its essential purpose. Despite losses, neutral traders had not been intimidated. Nor had economic pressure on Great Britain reached anything like the intensity necessary to coerce the British government into lifting the North Sea blockade. Throughout 1915, monthly imports of foodstuffs and raw materials into Great Britain had exceeded in volume the imports during the corresponding months of peace in 1913. Thanks to the great number of German and Austro-Hungarian merchant ships captured, seized, or detained in the early months of the war, the total tonnage available to Britain and her allies was actually greater in the autumn of 1915 than it had been at the outbreak of war a year before. But, for Britain, there were ominous signs: new merchant-ship tonnage launched, amounting to 416,000 tons for the last quarter of 1914, fell in the first quarter of 1915 to 267,000 tons and in the last two quarters of that year to 148,000 tons and 146,000 tons respectively. The latter figure was only one-third of the tonnage sunk during that quarter. The reason was that shipyards, labor, and materials had all been diverted to other work. Skilled men from the yards had been recruited for Kitchener's New Army, while yard space and materials had been assigned to Fisher's new warship-building program. As a result, in 1915, only 650,000 tons of new merchant ships was delivered. Meanwhile, hundreds of oceangoing vessels, amounting to 20 percent of British tonnage, had been requisitioned for military purposes, transporting food, munitions, stores, and supplies. This reduction in shipping available for general trade was substantially greater than the losses inflicted by the U-boats.

Nevertheless, for Britain, the primary achievement of the war at sea in 1915 was that British diplomacy and the Royal Navy had combined to bring all import trade bound for northern Europe under British surveillance and control. During the first submarine campaign, 743 neutral ships carrying supplies to Germany had been stopped by British patrols and their cargoes either seized outright or retained with compensation; this number was three times the number of British ships sunk during the same period by U-boat attack. By December 1914, Holland, Denmark, Norway, and Sweden were importing only the supplies necessary for home consumption; thus Germany was deprived of even her usual imports of foods and raw materials from her neutral neighbors. With each successive month, the British grip on German economic life tightened; by January 1916, the German people were showing signs of hardship. Textile factories were cut off from raw materials, so collars, cuffs, napkins, and handkerchiefs were made of paper. Sheets were made of wood pulp, which could not be washed. Germans cooked without fats. Shortages stirred discontent. Scarcities were not believed to be genuine. Suspicion abounded that rich people continued to dine sumptuously: townspeople generally accused farmers of hoarding food. Looking into the future, the prospects were bleaker. Germany depended not so much on imported foods as on imported fertilizers and fodder for animals; without fertilizers, the sandy soil of northern Germany would not yield normal harvests; without fodder, the herds would diminish.

Meanwhile, even as it imposed the blockade, Britain maintained a better relationship with America than Germany was able to do. While Germany had obtained grudging American tolerance of its submarine war against shipping so long as passenger ships were not attacked and American citizens not killed, Britain had established wide American acceptance for the blockade. This stemmed, in part, from the degree to which American prosperity depended upon trade with the Allies. It was true that American shipping, industrial, and farm interests regularly protested about the blockade to Washington and that on November 5, 1915, Secretary of State Lansing had told the British government that the doctrine of continuous voyage was "ineffective, illegal and indefensible." Nevertheless, the blockade continued and no serious rupture in diplomatic relations occurred. The principal reason for this differing treatment of the two belligerents was overwhelmingly simple: the British blockade threatened American property rights, while the German submarine campaign threatened American lives. The point was made in a *New York Tribune* editorial:

> There is no parallel between our differences with Germany . . . and . . . with Great Britain. . . . No question of life divides Great Britain from us and Sir Edward Grey has neither asserted the right of murder nor has he been asked by us to give assurance against murder. Our cases against Great Britain are purely civil.

—

In January 1916, after seventeen months of war, the German army occupied 90 percent of Belgium and thousands of square miles of French and Russian territory, but victory remained beyond reach. Meanwhile, the German colonies had been stripped away, the German merchant marine, second largest in the world, had been driven from the seas, the surface fleet of the Imperial Navy was tethered to its moorings, and overseas imports of foodstuffs and raw materials had been cut off. Confronting stalemate on land and sea, General von Falkenhayn, Chief of the General Staff, invited a number of generals and admirals to the Ministry of War in Berlin on December 30, 1915, where he offered two solutions. The first, he declared, would be a massive offensive on the Western Front. In February, the German army, equipped with a great superiority in artillery, would be hurled at the French fortress complex around Verdun. To hold this vital ground, he calculated, the French would pour in many divisions. Falkenhayn's objective was not so much to capture the city of Verdun or to defeat the French army outright; rather, he hoped to turn Verdun into an abattoir where he meant to bleed the French army to death under German shellfire. This attrition, Falkenhayn was convinced, would force France out of the war by the end of 1916. Then, the general asked the admirals for help. He had previously supported moderation in U-boat warfare so as not to antagonize the neutrals; now he reversed himself and asked the naval leaders to prosecute a vigorous, unrestricted submarine campaign to complement his Verdun offensive. The object was to discourage Britain so that once France was defeated, she, too, would make peace.

—

The confidence of the German naval command in its U-boats during the winter of 1916 was extraordinarily high. The submarine force had grown in numbers and the submariners were enthusiastic. Holtzendorff, the new Chief of the Naval Staff, who three months before had doubted the value of the U-boat campaign, had changed his mind. German shipping experts had told him that, with seventy U-boats available instead of the thirty-five in service in 1915, the German navy could destroy 160,000 tons of merchant shipping per month, meaning an annual loss of almost 2 million tons. Against this loss, British shipyards could only build 650,000 tons a year. Accordingly, Holtzendorff calculated, "if all restrictions were removed . . . English resistance would be broken in at most six months." Tirpitz agreed: if submarine warfare was restarted soon and executed ruthlessly, England's difficulties would become insurmountable. With France and Britain on their knees, Germany need not fear America's entry into war; long before the United States could provide significant assistance, the Allies would have surrendered.

To document his case, Holtzendorff composed a state paper recommending to the chancellor that submarine warfare be recommenced on the Western Approaches to the British Isles; that all enemy ships, armed or not, be destroyed without warning; that surfacing to examine neutral papers be avoided as much as possible; that torpedoes become the preferred method of attack; that all passenger vessels should be left alone; and that U-boat commanders who made honest mistakes should be protected. Holtzendorff's proposal, laid before the chancellor, brought back all the familiar arguments. No one doubted that a reintensified submarine campaign, overthrowing the *Lusitania* and *Arabic* settlements of the previous autumn, would bring another confrontation with the United States. The naval authorities declared that this did not matter; the war would be over before America could react. And even if America came in and the war continued, the United States lacked the military power to harm Germany. Opponents argued with equal vigor that, even applying unrestricted warfare, the U-boats could not sink as much tonnage as the admirals claimed and thus could not cripple Britain, much less win the war. Further, they would inflame the neutrals, the United States would enter the war, the war would lengthen, and ultimately, Germany would be defeated.

A week after this paper was circulated, the chancellor convened another conference at Pless. Here, Bethmann-Hollweg flatly opposed restarting the submarine campaign. For one thing, he believed that Germany could emerge triumphant from the military stalemate simply by holding on to captured territories and using them as bargaining chips in a negotiated peace settlement. As for Holtzendorff's prediction that Britain could be forced out of the war in six months by an intensified submarine campaign, the chancellor declared that nothing certain could be predicted about submarine warfare except that it would produce a struggle of unprecedented bitterness. Whether or not it worked would be decided by British endurance, a factor that could not be calculated by simple arithmetic. Britain, he said, would redouble her efforts and spend her last farthing and last drop of blood before allowing naval supremacy to be wrested from her. He added that the campaign now contemplated by the naval leaders would be directed not just at Britain but also at America and would certainly bring the United States into the war. It was foolish to disregard this danger; it would be inviting ruin to increase Germany's enemies by so mighty an adversary. If this happened, he concluded, the result would be *Finis Germaniae.*

While Bethmann-Hollweg remained steadfast, other moderates, including the kaiser, began to waver. On January 15, 1916, Müller wrote in his diary, "His Majesty took the humane standpoint that the drowning of innocent passengers was an idea that appalled him. He also bore a responsibility before God for the manner of waging war. On the other hand . . . [he had to] ask himself: could he go against the counsel of his military advisers, and from humane considerations prolong the war at the cost of so many brave men who were defending the Fatherland?" Increasingly, Müller himself was caught in this cross fire of opinion. Bethmann-Hollweg persuaded him that if Germany embarked on unrestricted submarine warfare, the neutrals and the whole civilized world would band together and deal with her as with a "mad dog." On the other hand, Holtzendorff convinced him that the new, improved U-boats really were technologically capable of dispatching Great Britain; as the condition of Germany and its allies grew worse, it seemed criminal to abstain from using the one weapon that might mean rescue. And yet, reversing the argument again, America's entry would seal defeat. "A desperate situation!" Müller wrote in his diary on February 10, 1916.

William II, unable to rule either for or against the chancellor or the admirals, came up with another compromise. Again, he accepted the chancellor's lead and decided that as head of state he could not approve a method of war that would provoke an American declaration of war against Germany. On the other hand, William was now persuaded that U-boat warfare could be decisive within six months; he therefore endorsed Holtzendorff's proposal that the submarines be sent back to sea—with limitations. As proposed, the new campaign would observe the following rules: enemy merchant vessels in the war zone were to be destroyed without warning; enemy vessels outside the war zone were to be attacked without warning only if they were armed; enemy passenger steamers were never to be attacked, inside or outside the war zone, armed or not. Nothing was said about neutrals. Most German naval officers predicted that the new campaign would not succeed under these restrictions; either U-boat commanders would be carried away by zeal and excitement when a vessel came into their sights and would fail to inspect the target in detail, or, overanxious to stay within the rules, they would allow the enemy to escape. Timing became an issue; the kaiser wished to unleash the U-boats only after Verdun had fallen, but, as the days passed, this triumph seemed ever more distant. Ultimately, the decision was made during a series of conferences at Charleville in the first week of March. Tensions were high: during one meeting, Müller reported, Bethmann-Hollweg nervously "smoked cigarette after cigarette and kept moving from one chair to another." The kaiser's mood was scarcely better: "His Majesty's nerves are strained to the breaking point. Today for the first time . . . he said, 'One must never utter it nor shall I admit it . . . but this war will not end with a great victory.' " William gave way: on March 13, the second campaign against merchant shipping began. Tirpitz was so disgusted by the limitations that he again announced his resignation: "The grave anxiety at seeing the life work of Your Majesty and the national future of Germany on the path to ruin makes me realize that my services can be of no further use to Your Majesty." This time, Bethmann-Hollweg seized the opportunity and recommended that the kaiser accept the resignation. William agreed and on March 15, 1916, after eighteen years in office, the founder of the German navy retired. William II never saw Alfred von Tirpitz again. Tirpitz's fury, reported Princess Blücher, was "indescribable. They gave out as reason for his retirement that he had broken down and needed rest. So he walked with his wife up and down the Wilhelmstrasse for two hours to prove to the crowd that it was not true and that he was in the best of health. Next day, he took off his uniform and appeared in tall hat and frock coat to show he had been 'deprived of his uniform' and talked to his wife in a loud voice so that the crowd would be able to hear."

Meanwhile, another personal circumstance had altered the command structure of the navy. In January, Admiral von Pohl, suffering from liver cancer, had declared that he could not continue as Commander-in-Chief of the High Seas Fleet. Vice Admiral Reinhard Scheer, then commander of a dreadnought battle squadron, succeeded him. Scheer's views on naval warfare were stark and emphatic. He did not view the submarine war against commerce as a substitute for some other plan, or as a compromise between conflicting plans, or as an adjunct to the campaign on land. Scheer considered the U-boat campaign against commerce as valid an act of modern warfare as an artillery bombardment or an infantry assault in the field, and he believed that it could win the war. Tirpitz's departure, therefore, had simply replaced one passionate U-boat advocate with another.

—

By March 1916, Germany possessed fifty-two modern, operational U-boats. During March and April, they accounted for fifty-seven merchant vessels grossing 157,009 tons. During these same two months, the German navy lost four U-boats, but with thirty-eight new submarines due to be commissioned within the next five months, the Naval Staff confidently expected to sink 160,000 tons of British shipping a month, perhaps more. Then, long before the validity of Holtzendorff's calculation that the U-boats could bring Britain to her knees within six months could be thoroughly tested, an incident at sea ignited another diplomatic crisis with the United States. On March 24, the passenger liner *Sussex,* with Americans on board, was torpedoed in the Channel. Ironically, this episode had no relation to the orders agreed to by the kaiser and issued by Holtzendorff regarding the conduct of the second submarine campaign. Rather, it stemmed from an earlier, subsidiary order, which had remained in force without cancellation for four months. In November 1915, the Flanders U-boat Flotilla had been ordered to attack troop transports sailing between English and French Channel ports. For three months, German submarine captains had believed that passenger vessels carrying civilian travelers used only the Folkestone-Boulogne route and that all other vessels in the Channel could be sunk without warning without fear of breaking the promises made to the United States. Accordingly, on the afternoon of March 24, when the captain of *UB-29* saw through his periscope a vessel about to enter Dieppe whose foredeck was crowded with figures whom the captain believed to be soldiers, he gave no warning and torpedoed the ship. The vessel was, in fact, the French cross-Channel passenger steamer *Sussex* carrying 325 passengers, including twenty-five Americans. The explosion severed the entire forward section of the ship. The after part remained afloat and was towed into port, but eighty people had been killed or wounded and four of the dead were Americans. The victims also included the world-famous Spanish composer and pianist Enrique Granados and his wife, who were returning to Spain after a recital tour in the United States. Thus, for the third time, the one principle on which President Wilson and his government had insisted—the inviolability of passenger ships—had been breached.

The news reached Washington the following day. Again, President Wilson chose to wait for details. On April 11, the German government announced that the damage to the *Sussex* was not caused by the attack of a German submarine. Unfortunately for German credibility, the president already had on his desk the carefully documented reports of British, French, and American experts who had scrupulously inspected the damaged hull and concluded that the *Sussex* had been torpedoed. The act appeared to be a flagrant violation of the German promise not to attack passenger vessels of any nation. The American press vociferously accused Germany of deceit and Wilson concluded that the United States was being treated with contempt. Again, he withdrew from his advisers, retreated into his study, and sat down at his typewriter. On April 19, Wilson appeared before a special session of Congress. Calling the use of submarines against commerce "utterly incompatible with the principles of humanity and incontrovertible rights of neutrals and the sacred immunities of non-combatants," he read the ultimatum he already had sent to the German government:

> If it is still the purpose of the Imperial government to prosecute relentless and indiscriminate warfare against vessels of commerce by the use of U-boats without regard to what the Government of the United States must consider the sacred and indisputable rules of international law and universally recognized dictates of humanity, the Government of the United States is at last forced to the conclusion that there is but one course it can pursue. Unless the Imperial Government should now immediately declare and effect an abandonment of its present methods of U-boat warfare against passenger and freight carrying vessels, the Government of the United States can have no other choice but to sever diplomatic relations with the German empire altogether.

German alarm at Wilson's note was very great. Up to that point, the American president had admitted that, properly conducted, submarine attacks on commerce were legitimate acts of war. Now Wilson was threatening to sever relations; war was the next step. The issue was discussed in Berlin in its starkest terms: could Germany achieve victory by unrestricted submarine warfare even if the United States entered the war, before U.S. military forces could be organized and brought to bear? In these discussions, Bethmann-Hollweg and Jagow continued to insist on the absolute necessity of preventing a break. The chancellor repeated what he had said before: America's entry would mean *Finis Germaniae.* Falkenhayn, now needing help from the navy as his attack on Verdun was failing, pressed for intensification of the U-boat war. But now Holtzendorff again switched sides. Unwilling to provoke war with America, the Chief of the Naval Staff opposed Falkenhayn and declared that Germany was more likely to secure a good peace by not pressing on with intensified submarine warfare. Admiral Eduard von Capelle, Tirpitz's successor as minister of the navy, also advised against further provoking the American government. In addition, Capelle said that even if prize law restrictions were reimposed on submarine warfare, the toll on Allied shipping need not be much reduced; he estimated that U-boats still could sink 160,000 tons per month.

The decision fell on the kaiser. Although William fretted at Wilson's "impertinence," he sided with the chancellor and canceled intensified U-boat warfare. On April 24, he instructed Holtzendorff to issue a command that "until further orders, U-boats may only act against commerce in accordance with Prize Regulations." Once again, U-boats were ordered not to destroy any ship, even an enemy vessel, without first examining its papers and ensuring the safety of the crew. The only exception allowed would come from an attempt by a ship "to escape or offer resistance." Admiral Scheer, now the Commander-in-Chief of the High Seas Fleet, scornfully refused to accept this new strategy. Following the example set by Pohl the previous autumn, Scheer on April 25 recalled to port all High Seas Fleet U-boats. He informed the Naval Staff that he had terminated the campaign, much as he regretted "the cessation of the most effective form of attack on England's economic position . . . [which] might have had decisive effect on the war's outcome." His decision was influenced by Commodore Bauer, who in March had made a voyage in *U-67* to study conditions for himself and had concluded that it was too dangerous for U-boats to operate in the waters around England in accordance with prize law. Unfortunately, Scheer's recall signal, which ended the second submarine campaign against merchant shipping, caught three High Seas Fleet U-boats still at sea, none of which received the wireless recall message; between April 27 and May 8, they sank eight merchant vessels grossing 26,000 tons. The last of these was the 13,370-ton liner *Cymric,* bound for America and torpedoed without warning off the Irish coast with the loss of five lives. The *Cymric* was the thirty-seventh passenger liner sunk by U-boats since the loss of *Lusitania* and the fourth passenger liner sunk during the second offensive. The captain of the U-boat that sank the *Cymric* was Walther Schwieger, who had torpedoed *Lusitania* and *Hesperian.*

In recalling his submarines, Scheer had a political as well as a military purpose. Submarine warfare was overwhelmingly popular with the German people, and the admiral hoped that his action would force Bethmann-Hollweg—the principal opponent of unrestricted warfare against merchant shipping—to resign in the face of a storm of public indignation. When a popular uproar failed to arise, Scheer, disappointed, reassigned his U-boats to their role from early in the war: attacking enemy warships in order to whittle down the numerical superiority of the Grand Fleet. To help this plan succeed, Reinhard Scheer decided to risk a North Sea surface action between the dreadnoughts of the High Seas Fleet and the British Grand Fleet.

The wheel of German naval strategy had come full circle.

CHAPTER 30

The Eve of Jutland

For weeks, little Hugo von Pohl, the Commander-in-Chief of the High Seas Fleet, had been struggling with cancer of the liver, and on January 8, 1916, he was taken from his flagship, *Friedrich der Grosse,* to a hospital in Berlin. Most officers in the fleet doubted that he would return and, aside from personal considerations, were glad to see him go. Pohl's eleven months in command of the fleet had been marked by a monumental and almost unbroken passivity. Five times, the battle fleet had gone to sea, but never more than 120 miles from Wilhelmshaven and never into any situation where there was serious danger of encountering the British. Meanwhile, the ships of the German battle squadrons had followed a dreary schedule: a week on patrol inside the minefields of the Bight; another week anchored, but ready for battle in Schillig roads; then passing through the Kiel Canal to practice gunnery in Kiel Bay; and then two weeks or more tied up to Wilhelmshaven quays so that their men could walk the streets, drink beer in the saloons, and sleep in redbrick barracks ashore. Tirpitz might rage that the sharp weapon he had forged was being allowed to rust, but Pohl stoutly maintained that, as the kaiser had instructed him not to risk the fleet, he was doing his duty. On January 18, the moribund Pohl was succeeded by Vice Admiral Reinhard Scheer; on February 23, Pohl died.

Scheer's appointment delighted the navy. He was fifty-three—four years younger than Jellicoe—a man of middle height, with piercing black eyes, closely trimmed hair, high cheekbones, a black mustache, and sometimes a small, tufted goatee. His thirty-eight-year career epitomized that of the professional naval officers rising through the ranks of the young German navy. Now at the top, in supreme command of Germany's forces at sea, Scheer was alert, aggressive, and confident, a strategist and tactician who could plan a campaign and then conduct a battle. "We knew that Scheer was made up of different stuff from Pohl," said Ernst von Weizsäcker, his Flag Lieutenant at Jutland. "There were many stories of his exploits as a young lieutenant. His old friends had given him the odd nickname Bobschiess [Shooting Bob] on account . . . of his likeness to his fox terrier which he was fond of provoking to bite his friends' trousers." Now, as Commander-in-Chief, Scheer wished and intended to attack his country's enemies with every weapon at his disposal.

Reinhard Scheer rose from the same middle-class background that produced the Imperial German Navy's other Great War senior admirals: Tirpitz, Hipper, Ingenohl, Müller, and Pohl. A schoolmaster's son from Hanau, on the river Main, Scheer entered the navy at fifteen without financial support or social connections. His training began on the sailing frigate *Niobe* where, in daylight and at night, Scheer and his fellow cadets scampered up the masts and crawled out on the yards. He served on the armored frigate *Friedrich Karl* and then on the armored corvette *Hertha,* which, circling the world, introduced Scheer to Melbourne, Yokohama, Shanghai, Kobe, and Nagasaki. He had two tours of duty with the German East Africa Cruiser Squadron; during the first of these, he befriended Lieutenant Henning von Holtzendorff and, a few years later, he served under Holtzendorff in the cruiser *Prinzess Wilhelm* on a voyage to the Far East. Between his African tours, Scheer spent four years at technical schools ashore, studying torpedo technology and warfare; thereafter, during his second East Africa tour, he was torpedo officer in the light cruiser *Sophie.* Returning to Germany, he became an instructor at the Torpedo Research Command in Kiel.

Scheer's growing reputation brought him into contact with Admiral von Tirpitz, himself a former torpedo specialist. With Tirpitz's appointment to the post of state secretary of the Imperial Navy, Scheer was transferred to the Navy Office Torpedo Section. In 1900, Scheer went back to sea as commander of a destroyer flotilla and then enhanced his reputation by writing a textbook on destroyer torpedo tactics. In 1903, he became chief of the Central Division of the Navy Office, which supported the Grand Admiral's efforts to expand the fleet by amendments to the Navy Laws. Scheer's work was purely technical and he had nothing to do with politics or public relations; nevertheless, on strictly naval matters, he was supremely confident and spoke freely. By now, he was in demand both in the fleet and at the Navy Ministry, which kept him on shore by making him director of the Torpedo Inspectorate. In 1905, Scheer was promoted to captain and in 1907 he took command of the predreadnought battleship *Elsass.* On December 1, 1909, Henning von Holtzendorff, now Commander-in-Chief of the High Seas Fleet, offered Captain Scheer the position of fleet Chief of Staff; six months later, Scheer, now forty-seven, was promoted to rear admiral. He left the

High Seas Fleet in 1911 to return to work for Tirpitz as chief of the General Naval Department; then, in January 1913, he rejoined the fleet as admiral of the six predreadnought battleships of the 2nd Squadron. In December 1914, Scheer took command of the 3rd Battle Squadron of new *König*- and *Kaiser*-class dreadnoughts, the most powerful ships in the High Seas Fleet. During the thirteen months that Scheer commanded this squadron under Ingenohl and Pohl, not one of those eight enormous ships fired a gun in battle. Now, with Scheer promoted to Commander-in-Chief, this was about to change.

Scheer was greatly admired by those who worked with him and for him. Weizsacker recalled that the admiral "was of cheerful disposition, had a quick mind and was without any pretensions. His optimistic nature always recovered quickly from a setback." Captain Adolf von Trotha, Scheer's Chief of Staff, had a similar view:

> One could not find a better comrade. He never stood on ceremony with young officers. But he was impatient and always had to act quickly. He would expect his staff to have the plans and orders for an operation worked out exactly to the last detail, and then he would come on the bridge and turn everything upside down. He was a commander of instinct and instant decision who liked to have all options presented to him and then as often as not chose a course of action no one had previously considered. In action he was absolutely cool and clear. Jutland showed his great gifts and a man like that must be allowed to drive his subordinates mad.

Scheer, like Tirpitz, was a forceful advocate of unrestricted submarine warfare, but, also like Tirpitz, he believed that submarine warfare alone would not defeat Great Britain. Certain—again, like Tirpitz—that German ships were qualitatively superior to British ships and that German officers and men were equal to their British opponents, Scheer was determined to go on the offensive. In February, Scheer conferred in Berlin with Admiral von Holtzendorff and the two men agreed to attempt to break the stranglehold of the British blockade at sea. Scheer's staff in Wilhelmshaven produced a document titled "Guiding Principles for Sea Warfare in the North Sea." The first principle was acceptance of the continuing fact that the unfavorable ratio of numbers of ships ruled out a decisive, all-out battle with the Grand Fleet. The second was that, within this framework, constant pressure should be exerted on the British fleet to force it to send out some of its forces to respond to German attacks. The third was that in these offensive operations, the German navy should use every weapon available: airship and submarine operations were to be combined with operations by the High Seas Fleet in deep offensive thrusts into the North Sea.

On February 23, the kaiser, accompanied by Tirpitz, Holtzendorff, and

Prince Henry, arrived in a snowstorm in Wilhelmshaven to listen as Scheer personally presented these plans to the sovereign. In the wardroom of *Friedrich der Grosse,* Scheer described to the emperor his plans to use his battle cruisers and light forces to draw the British piecemeal out of their bases. These operations, in effect a resumption of Hipper's earlier bombardments of English coastal towns, would constitute such an insult that the British navy must respond. And when the first British squadrons came out, the High Seas Fleet would be there. William listened, overcame his qualms, and agreed.

In fact, a small, preliminary offensive operation had taken place even before the kaiser's approval had been given. On February 10, German destroyers made a night sweep beyond the Dogger Bank, where they fell upon a group of British minesweepers and sank one of them. This sortie brought additional profit when Tyrwhitt's flagship, the famous light cruiser *Arethusa,* returning to Harwich, struck a German mine, parted a line while being towed, and eventually went on a shoal and broke in half. Scheer's first major effort with the entire High Seas Fleet came three weeks later when he attempted a trap of British forces in the southern North Sea. On March 5, he took the fleet to a position off Texel at the mouth of the Zuider Zee, the farthest south the German battle fleet would venture during the war. Unfortunately, snow, hail, restricted visibility, and heavy seas forced Scheer to order the fleet home before any contact was possible.

The British then made an offensive thrust of their own. Nightly zeppelin raids on London and other cities had prodded the Admiralty to attack the airship bases. On March 25, five seaplanes flying from the carrier *Vindex,* a converted merchant ship, attempted to bomb a zeppelin shed at Hoyer on the Schleswig coast. Tyrwhitt with five light cruisers and eighteen destroyers escorted *Vindex* while Beatty cruised forty-five miles away. The weather was bitterly cold, snow was falling, and the wind was rising to gale force. The result was a British fiasco: three seaplanes, launched forty miles offshore, developed engine trouble and came down in German territory, where their crews were captured. A fourth pilot discovered that there was no zeppelin shed at Hoyer and bombed what he said was a factory. The fifth pilot discovered an actual zeppelin shed farther inland at Tondern, but when he dived to attack, his bomb-release cable jammed. Meanwhile, at sea, German destroyers arrived and in a confused fight in a snowstorm, the British destroyer *Laverock* rammed her sister *Medusa,* which later had to be abandoned. Tyrwhitt's new flagship, the light cruiser *Cleopatra,* then rammed the German destroyer *G-194,* cutting her in half, but then herself was rammed by the British light cruiser *Undaunted.* A larger British disaster was avoided only when Scheer, who had ordered his battle fleet to sea, again ran into a full gale with low visibility and mountainous seas and decided to turn back.

On April 22, another British thrust toward the Skagerrak cost Beatty and

Jellicoe even more heavily. The battle cruisers, steaming off the Danish coast, ran into a sudden bank of dense fog and *Australia* and *New Zealand,* zigzagging at 19 knots, collided and were badly damaged. Then the dreadnought *Neptune* collided with a neutral merchant ship and, later that night, three British destroyers ran into one another. On April 24, Jellicoe was back at Scapa Flow coaling his ships; at 4:00 that afternoon, he learned of the Easter Rebellion in Ireland and that the High Seas Fleet had put to sea. At dawn the next day, German battle cruisers were bombarding the English towns of Lowestoft and Yarmouth.

—

Before this happened, physical disability had temporarily removed from command the most active German North Sea admiral, Franz Hipper. As commander of the battle cruisers and other ships of the Scouting Groups and also as the officer responsible for the defense of the Heligoland Bight, Hipper was bending under the weight of his duties. Fatigue was compounded by sciatica. He had difficulty sleeping, and when he managed to doze off, every sound—a step on the deck above his cabin, the slapping of halyards in the wind—reawakened him. Hipper knew he needed a rest, but once Scheer had replaced Pohl, he decided not to ask for leave just as a new Commander-in-Chief was taking over. Two months later, on March 26, Hipper, feeling "terrible pain and exhaustion," applied for sick leave. The following day, Scheer visited him on board *Seydlitz* and approved the request.

Before leaving *Seydlitz,* Hipper summoned Erich Raeder, his Chief of Staff, and described one of his worries about turning over the command to Rear Admiral Friedrich Bödicker:

> "You know I am very fond of music, I mean good and refined music," Hipper began. "I'm particularly fond of Richard Wagner, particularly *Lohengrin*! Our band . . . is at the top of its form just now."
>
> "Indeed it is, Your Excellency. We will take the greatest care to see that it remains so—"
>
> "I certainly hope so, for music is perhaps the best form of relaxation I get on board. What's worrying me is that there might be a change for the worse during my absence—"
>
> Hipper lapsed into silence. . . . After a time Raeder ventured: "Why should there be any change?"
>
> Hipper jumped from his chair, strode up and down and blurted out: "Bödicker knows nothing about music. His taste runs to nothing but Prussian marches, treacly waltzes and bits out of *Fledermaus.* I'm sure he'll end by mucking up my whole band—mucking it up, I tell you!"
>
> . . . [But] he ended up by bursting out laughing. "After all, I'll soon get them right again. I've often had to show them myself when the fiddles were going wrong!"

Hipper took a five-week cure at Bad Neundorf, then visited a nerve specialist who listened to his complaints, examined him carefully, and announced a complete absence of any damage to Hipper's central nervous system. The admiral's symptoms, the doctor declared, were caused by stress. Relieved, Hipper returned to his new flagship, the recently commissioned *Lützow,* on May 13 and resumed command.

Meanwhile, unbeknownst to Hipper, he had survived another kind of crisis. Scheer's promotion to command had pleased him; he looked forward to the promise of more vigorous North Sea action. Nevertheless, when Hipper asked for sick leave, Scheer telephoned Holtzendorff and asked that Hipper be retired. Scheer felt that "Vice Admiral Hipper no longer possesses the qualities of robustness and elasticity which . . . [command of the Scouting Groups] demands and it is also his view that the end of the leave will not effect a complete restoration of his abilities." Holtzendorff rejected the proposal because it seemed inappropriate for Scheer to be "coming forward with such radical suggestions so soon after his assumption of command." Müller wrote on this memorandum, "I agree." There is evidence that Scheer had a certain envy of Hipper's fame and sometimes belittled him in service records, but the two men worked together for another two years—at which point Hipper succeeded Scheer as Commander-in-Chief of the High Seas Fleet and Scheer became Chief of the Naval Staff in Berlin.

—

Conceived and executed in Hipper's absence, Scheer's Lowestoft plan was to deliver a hit-and-run raid on the English southeast coast timed to coincide with the rising of the German-supported Irish nationalists on Easter Sunday. The German battle cruisers, screened by six light cruisers and two destroyer flotillas, would bombard, and then retreat before the Grand Fleet at Scapa Flow could intervene. But his own battle fleet would be at sea, and if—as he hoped—either Beatty or Tyrwhitt came out to intercept, these separate elements of the British fleet would be overwhelmed. In this operation, the German battle cruisers were to be commanded by Rear Admiral Friedrich Bödicker.

Early on the afternoon of March 24, 1915, Bödicker, sailing for England, was northwest of Norderney when *Seydlitz,* still the battle cruiser flagship, struck a British mine. An explosion on the starboard side below the waterline tore a hole in the ship's hull plating fifty feet long. Eleven men were killed, 1,400 tons of water flooded in, and the ship settled four and a half feet deeper into the water. With her speed reduced to 15 knots, the battle cruiser turned back to the Jade. Bödicker shifted his flag to the new *Lützow* and continued forward. Meanwhile, Tyrwhitt with three light cruisers and eighteen destroyers of the Harwich Force was steering to intercept this overwhelmingly superior German force. Around 4:00 a.m., with the first light in the eastern sky, he saw them: six light cruisers, many destroyers—and then four battle cruisers. Too weak to attack, he turned away to the south, hoping that the German force would follow. Bödicker, however, refused to be diverted from his objective, and a few minutes later the four German battle cruisers opened fire on Lowestoft at a range of 14,000 yards. Within nine minutes, they destroyed two 6-inch shore batteries and 200 houses, killed three civilians and wounded twelve. Then Bödicker swung north to attack Yarmouth. There, visibility was so poor that, after the first salvo from all four ships, only *Derfflinger* continued firing. At this point, the German light cruisers reported that they were in action with Tyrwhitt, and Bödicker decided to go to their support.

Tyrwhitt, seeing that he was not being followed, had turned back and found himself engaging the six German light cruisers. This ended when the four German battle cruisers suddenly loomed out of the mist and opened fire at him from 13,000 yards. Again, Tyrwhitt turned to escape to the south, but this time his flagship, *Conquest,* was hit by a 12-inch shell, which killed or wounded forty men and reduced the light cruiser's speed to 20 knots. Bödicker now had an opportunity to overtake and annihilate a weaker British force, the supposed object of Scheer's offensive. Unfortunately, he failed to grasp what was offered. Satisfied with having flung a few shells into England and chasing Tyrwhitt away, he now himself reversed course and steamed east to join Scheer, only fifty miles away. Scheer, however, had had enough; suspecting that the Grand Fleet was coming south (Neumünster Radio had warned him that the British battle squadrons had sailed from northern harbors), he turned his whole fleet around and headed for home. In fact, Jellicoe and the Grand Fleet, pushing south, were handicapped by seas so heavy that Jellicoe had been forced to leave all his destroyers behind. When Scheer turned back, Beatty was still more than 200 miles away and Jellicoe was 300. There was no chance of intercepting the German fleet; both Jellicoe and Beatty were ordered home.

Scheer was disappointed. A strong German force had failed to take advantage of its superiority over a much weaker British force. In addition, *Seydlitz* had been severely damaged and would require at least a month in dry dock. In Britain, the Admiralty moved the 3rd Battle Squadron—the seven remaining *King Edwards*—from Rosyth to the Thames, permitting First Lord Arthur Balfour to reassure the distressed mayors of Lowestoft and Yarmouth that "another raid on the coast of Norfolk will be henceforth far more perilous to the aggressors . . . and, if our enemy be wise is therefore far less likely." HMS *Dreadnought* was dispatched from Scapa Flow to the Thames to add her ten 12-inch guns to the twenty-eight 12-inch guns carried by the seven *King Edwards*. It was for this reason that the ten-year-old grandparent of all the dreadnought battleships in the world missed the Battle of Jutland.

—

On the morning of April 25, when Scheer was still at sea on *Friedrich der Grosse,* returning from the Lowestoft Raid, he received a wireless message from Holtzendorff in Berlin telling him that the German government had bowed to the American president's threat to sever diplomatic relations. Until further orders, Scheer was informed, unrestricted submarine warfare would be abandoned and U-boats were to conduct commerce warfare only in accordance with prize regulations: surfacing, visiting, and searching. Scheer was enraged. Before his flagship was back in the Jade, he decided that, under these conditions, the entire U-boat offensive against merchant shipping must be abandoned. Without consulting Berlin, he recalled all High Seas Fleet U-boats then at sea.

Scheer was angry not only because the sharp sword of unrestricted submarine warfare—which he fervently believed must be used—was being laid aside, but also because the German government had been compelled to take this step by President Wilson. In the early spring of 1916, the German people had been led to expect that the U-boats would deliver a decisive stroke against England. Now, on America's demand, this campaign had been prematurely terminated. To Scheer, and to many of his admirals and captains, this submission came as a public humiliation, inflicted not only on the German government but specifically on the German navy. Something must be done about this; some new stroke must wash away this stain and justify the faith of the German people in their naval power. Scheer's solution was obvious: the High Seas Fleet must go back to sea.

Scheer's decision to recall the submarines opened new tactical possibilities. At his disposal now were a large number of modern, efficient submarines released from commerce warfare and available for use in cooperation with the surface fleet against enemy warships. Scheer had always liked the idea of submarine ambush—of U-boats, stationed off the Grand Fleet's bases, attacking British ships as they came out. What Scheer needed was a lure sufficient to draw the British to sea. The best way to bring the British out, Scheer judged, would be a German battle cruiser raid on a place *near* a major British base. He knew that Beatty's battle cruisers and other heavy ships were based on the Firth of Forth. He also knew that *Seydlitz* was scheduled to be out of dry dock by the middle of May. Accordingly, he decided that on May 17, Hipper should bombard the town of Sunderland, near Newcastle upon Tyne, 100 miles south of the entrance to the Forth. Such a challenge directly under Beatty's nose could not fail to bring the British admiral out—and into the waiting submarine ambush that Scheer intended to prepare. As *Lion* and her sisters steamed into the crosshairs of U-boat periscopes, Scheer hoped that Beatty might lose two or three of his battle cruisers to torpedoes. Meanwhile, Scheer himself with the whole High Seas Fleet would be in the North Sea only fifty miles away, ready to meet and destroy any British battle cruisers that evaded the U-boats and were pursuing Hipper. Although he knew that the Grand Fleet would come south to Beatty's support, Scheer, unaware of Room 40, assumed that he would have six or seven hours to bring Beatty to action before Jellicoe's battle squadrons could appear.

The grim possibility that the entire Grand Fleet might intervene to disrupt Scheer's operation called forth another key element of his plan. Air reconnaissance must be available to give the High Seas Fleet ample warning of the approach and composition of any British force. Scheer had no intention of becoming involved with Jellicoe's massed dreadnoughts. To prevent any possibility of this, the operation must take place in clear weather, when zeppelins could be aloft to scout. As Hipper moved across the North Sea toward Sunderland, zeppelins would patrol the area from the Skagerrak to the Forth and along the English coast down to the Channel. But zeppelins could not leave their sheds in bad weather or high wind. Further, out over the sea, they were subject to the hindrance of mist and fog covering the surface. Calm, clear weather, therefore, was essential to the Sunderland plan.

Even before Scheer's planning was complete, the operation was postponed. On May 9, it was discovered that several of the new *König*-class battleships of the 3rd Battle Squadron had developed condenser problems and the Sunderland plan was delayed until May 23. The additional time permitted Scheer to expand the operation, embracing a larger area than simply the Firth of Forth. Now sixteen High Seas Fleet U-boats and a half-dozen boats from the Flanders Flotilla were to be stationed off a number of British harbors with orders to remain on patrol from May 23 to June 1, reporting any movements of British ships and seizing any opportunity to attack. In addition, the exits from British bases were to be mined.

With the bombardment now set for May 23, Scheer dispatched his U-boats on May 17. From this moment on, a clock was ticking: the timing of the whole operation was subject to the oil supply of the submarines. By May 30, their fuel would be almost exhausted; the surface fleet operation, therefore, must be concluded on or around that date. By May 23, the U-boats were in their positions off British harbors: seven off the Firth of Forth, waiting for Beatty; one farther north, off the coast of Scotland; two in Pentland Firth, to attack the Grand Fleet when it sortied from Scapa Flow. In addition, *UB-27* had specific orders to force her way into the Firth of Forth to attack warships there. Four minelaying submarines were sent to lay twenty-two mines each off the Firth of Forth, off Moray Firth, and to the west of Pentland Firth in the Orkneys. In addition, Flanders Flotilla U-boats sailed to attack the Harwich Force. All of these submarines had been ordered to remain on station until June 1 and to avoid being discovered prematurely. Wireless reports were to be made only in urgent situations: on sighting the enemy's main body putting to sea, and then only after all possibilities of attack had been exhausted.

On May 22, the High Seas Fleet was preparing to sail the following day when Scheer received disturbing news: *Seydlitz* still was not ready for sea. Previously, the Wilhelmshaven dockyard had reported that her repairs would be completed by May 22, but a flooding test carried out in the dock the night before had revealed that her damaged underwater broadside torpedo area still was not watertight. Unwilling to leave without *Seydlitz,* Scheer again reluctantly postponed the operation, this time until May 30. This left only two days for the Sunderland operation to take place before the fuel endurance of the submarines already at sea would be exhausted.

Meanwhile, the U-boats patrolling off British coasts were waiting. On May 22, *U-42,* stationed off Sunderland, reported everything clear for the next day's bombardment—which, of course, had been canceled. Thereafter, fog and low visibility made it difficult for the submarines to observe while, at the same time, the sea was so smooth that even the appearance of a periscope was enough to give them away. British patrol activity was intense. One submarine minelayer, *U-74,* was sunk by trawler gunfire as she was making her way into Moray Firth. Another, *U-72,* developed an oil bunker leak before laying her mines off the entrance to the Firth of Forth. A broad trail of oil on the surface made her too easy to locate and she had to return to port. A third minelayer, *UC-3,* disappeared on May 27, perhaps after hitting a British mine in the eastern Channel. On May 29, a fourth minelayer, *U-75,* operating in thick fog, laid her twenty-two mines off the Orkneys, between Marwick Head and the Brough of Birsay. This minefield had no effect on the Battle of Jutland, but on June 5, four days after the battle, one of the mines exploded to strike an immense psychological blow at the British nation.

During these days, Scheer, on board *Friedrich der Grosse,* was watching the window of opportunity closing inexorably on his Sunderland raid. First, the repairs to the battleships' condensers and then to *Seydlitz* had postponed Hipper's bombardment until May 29. That was dangerously close to June 1, the last day the U-boats manning his ambushes would have sufficient fuel to remain on patrol. Now, increasingly, this three-day window had to be considered in conjunction with another factor: the weather and its effect on zeppelin operations. Unfortunately, after the U-boats sailed for Britain, a spell of bad weather set in; day after day, the fleet airship commander reported air reconnaissance impossible.

Disappointed, Scheer was yet unwilling to give up on the operation and waste the mine and U-boat ambushes staked out. He formed an alternative plan: if the weather continued bad and the zeppelins could not fly, he would not fling his battle cruisers across the North Sea at Sunderland; instead he would send Hipper north to cruise provocatively off the Norwegian coast as though to attack British shipping in the Skagerrak. The overriding objective would be the same: to lure the British out and expose them to U-boat attack. Hipper's presence off Norway would be reported; the operation still would likely bring Beatty rushing out—over the waiting submarines. Meanwhile,

Scheer and the battle squadrons, steaming north in Hipper's wake, would be waiting for Beatty only forty miles to the south. And if the Grand Fleet should also come, these were safer waters for the German fleet. The Skagerrak was much closer to German than to British bases, and with the Danish coast protecting his starboard—eastern—flank and destroyer and light cruiser screens spread far to the west on his port flank, zeppelin reconnaissance was unnecessary; Scheer still would have sufficient warning and ample time after annihilating Beatty to retreat to the safety of the minefields in the Bight.

May 28 was the day of decision. The U-boats lying off British bases had orders to depart and return to base on the evening of June 1. Departure of the High Seas Fleet therefore was imperative if the U-boat trap was to work. The possibility of putting Scheer's original Sunderland plan into operation now hung on the availability of air reconnaissance over the next twenty-four to thirty-six hours. At that moment, strong northeasterly winds in the Bight ruled out airship reconnaissance and Scheer decided that if the wind did not moderate by May 30, he would abandon Sunderland and substitute the Skagerrak.

At midnight, May 28, all ships anchored in Jade roads were ordered to prepare to raise steam. At noon on May 29, *Seydlitz* was declared seaworthy and released from the dockyard. At 3:00 p.m. the following day, with strong northeasterly winds still blowing, the commander of the Naval Airship Division reported that no adequate zeppelin reconnaissance could be done during the next two days. Scheer immediately decided to execute his alternative plan; at 3:40 on the afternoon of May 30, a wireless signal from *Friedrich der Grosse,* "31 G. G. 2490," went out to the assembly of ships in Schillig roads. The signal meant "Carry out top secret instruction 2490 on May 31." The Skagerrak operation would commence before dawn the following morning.

—

An hour after midnight on Wednesday, May 31, the ships of the High Seas Fleet began raising their anchors. First out to sea were the battle cruisers, led by the new *Lützow,* a sister of *Derfflinger.* On her bridge, returned from sick leave and restored to self-confidence, was Franz Hipper, who predicted to the officers standing near him that by afternoon, they would be "at it hammer and tongs" with the British. Further, he thought that there would be "heavy losses of human life." "Well," he consoled himself, "it is all in God's hands." In Hipper's hands that day were forty ships: five battle cruisers, five light cruisers, and thirty destroyers.

An hour and a half later, as dawn was breaking, the main German battle fleet began to weigh anchor. Scheer was taking with him that day sixteen of Germany's eighteen dreadnought battleships; *König Albert* remained behind with continuing condenser problems and the new *Bayern,* the first German battleship carrying 15-inch guns, was considered too recently commissioned to be ready for battle. Six light cruisers and thirty-one destroyers sailed to screen the heavy ships. At 5:00 a.m., south of Heligoland, the six old pre-dreadnought battleships of the 2nd Battle Squadron, coming from their base on the Elbe, joined up astern of Scheer's sixteen modern battleships. To most High Seas Fleet officers, their presence seemed a serious mistake. Able to make only 18 knots, armed with only four 12-inch guns apiece, they were dubbed the five-minute ships, that being their anticipated survival time in action against dreadnought battleships. Scheer was thoroughly aware of these facts and gibes, having once commanded the squadron himself, and he had not originally intended to take the old ships with him. Nevertheless, as the time for departure approached, Rear Admiral Mauve, the squadron commander, begged the Commander-in-Chief not to leave the predreadnoughts behind. Sentiment prevailed and Scheer gave way. By including them, he handicapped himself by reducing the speed of the German battle line to 18 knots and awarding the British battle fleet a 2-knot advantage.

Scheer's main battle fleet now included fifty-nine ships: sixteen dreadnought battleships, six old battleships, six light cruisers, and thirty-one destroyers. Adding Hipper's force to Scheer's, a total of ninety-nine German warships were steaming north up the mine-free channel running to Horns Reef, a group of sandbanks stretching out into the North Sea from Denmark's Jutland peninsula. When the sun rose, "covering the sea with its magnificent golden rays," exulted the *Derfflinger*'s gunnery officer, men throughout the fleet looked out at the great spectacle of which they were a part: the famous battle cruisers in the van; then the huge light-gray dreadnoughts in a single column, rising and plunging in the swell, black smoke pouring from their funnels; and, all around, the light cruisers and destroyers. Today or perhaps tomorrow would be *Der Tag,* the Day, for which the German navy had worked so hard and waited so long.

As the day began, three messages were brought to Scheer on the bridge of *Friedrich der Grosse.* One of his submarines, *U-32,* on the surface 300 miles away, reported sighting two British dreadnoughts, two cruisers, and several destroyers off May Island, sixty miles east of the Firth of Forth. They were heading southeast. An hour later, a second submarine, *U-66,* reported eight British battleships attended by light cruisers and destroyers sixty miles east of Cromarty on an easterly course. About the same time, the German radio station at Neumünster reported intercepting British wireless messages indicating that two British dreadnoughts—or groups of dreadnoughts; the call signs did not make clear—had left Scapa Flow. Scheer considered these pieces of information and discarded them; they seemed too vague and disconnected to be related to his operation. The enemy forces were far apart and they seemed to represent isolated movements by separate units of the British fleet. There was no indication that the entire Grand Fleet was at sea; Scheer held to his northerly course.

In this sequence of early events lay Scheer's greatest miscalculation at the Battle of Jutland. Before the first shot was fired, his U-boats had failed. The submarine ambushes—the underlying reason for the entire operation—had been spectacularly useless. Submarines had neither provided Scheer with useful information nor reduced Jellicoe's superiority by a single vessel. Now, the full might of the Grand Fleet was at sea, coming toward him, unattacked, undiminished, and undetected.

—

The twelve months following the Dogger Bank had been difficult for the officers and men of the Grand Fleet. As long as the kaiser held his fleet in port, Great Britain exercised command of the sea. Yet Royal Navy tradition demanded more. British naval officers yearned for a new Trafalgar, although they knew that, before Trafalgar was fought, Nelson had spent two monotonous years patrolling off Toulon. Nor did they consider the slow strangulation of Germany by blockade a substitute for battle. Not only were they frustrated and bored; they were plagued by guilt. The army—their brothers, cousins, and friends—was dying in the trenches while they, cooped up in their gray ships, swung uselessly around mooring buoys in remote northern harbors.

Beatty, particularly, chafed. "I heard rumors of terrible casualties on the Western Front," he wrote to Ethel on May 15, 1915. "I don't think, dear heart, you will ever realize the effect these terrible happenings have upon me. . . . I feel we are so impotent, so incapable of doing anything for lack of opportunity, almost that we are not doing our share and bearing our portion of the burden laid upon the nation. . . . We spend days doing nothing when so many are doing so much. . . . [It] makes me feel sick at heart." Six months later, things seemed, if possible, worse. "The horrid Forth like a great ditch full of thick fog makes everything so cold," he wrote to Ethel. "There is no joy in life under such conditions. . . . My time must come." Beatty's time would come, but not before still another seven months had passed.

Jellicoe and the Admiralty shared Beatty's frustration. Correspondence between London, Scapa, and Rosyth continually discussed offensive projects that might lure or force the Germans out: Bombard Heligoland. Fill six tankers and twelve trawlers with oil, set them alight, and drive them into the middle of Heligoland dockyard. Bombard the High Seas Fleet in Schillig roads, then send destroyer flotillas in to attack with torpedoes, then have at them again with a midnight ram, gun, and torpedo suicide attack by five old battleships. Penetrate the Baltic with predreadnoughts to open a path to Russia. Jellicoe vetoed all these suggestions. The Commander-in-Chief favored action, but even more strongly, he opposed risk. Without a battle, Britain possessed command of the sea. Frustrating as it was, a new Trafalgar would have to wait.

The new Admiralty Board endorsed Jellicoe's caution. Lacking a Churchill, who had tried to thrust battleships through the Dardanelles, and a Fisher, who had wanted to storm into the Baltic, they made suggestions, but never pushed the Commander-in-Chief. The tone was set by Jackson, who once wrote wistfully to Jellicoe, "I wish we could entice them out from Heligoland to give you a chance. Have you any ideas for it? I wish I had." Jellicoe's replies—like this one on January 25, 1916—always came back to the bedrock of British naval strategy: "Until the High Seas Fleet emerges from its defences, I regret to say that I do not see that any offensive against it is possible. It may be weakened by mines and submarine attack when out for exercises, but beyond that no naval action against it seems practicable."

—

While the Grand Fleet waited, it grew. By April 1916, there were thirty-three dreadnought battleships and ten dreadnought battle cruisers in the Royal Navy; thirteen of these ships had been added since the beginning of the war. The battleships *Benbow* and *Emperor of India* had come to the fleet in December 1914. *Canada,* requisitioned from Chile in 1915, had been added to *Agincourt* and *Erin,* requisitioned from Turkey. Five *Queen Elizabeth*–class superdreadnoughts had joined the Grand Fleet: *Queen Elizabeth* herself, along with *Warspite* and *Barham* in 1915 and *Valiant* and *Malaya* early in 1916. These five, each mounting eight 15-inch guns and firing projectiles weighing 1,900 pounds, were then the finest battleships in the world. They were heavily armored and able to take severe punishment; their 25-knot speed was 4 to 5 knots greater than the designed speed of any German battleship and almost the same as that of the older British and German battle cruisers. They burned fuel oil, which permitted greater steaming endurance and saved their crews the exhausting labor of hand coaling and stoking. In addition, another five superdreadnoughts of the *Royal Sovereign* class, each carrying eight 15-inch guns, were on their way: *Royal Oak* and *Revenge* arrived in time to fight at Jutland; *Royal Sovereign* was a few days too late, and *Resolution* and *Ramillies* were still under construction. Overall, the British margin over the Germans in dreadnought battleships had increased substantially. Since August 1914, the Germans had added five dreadnoughts: four *Königs*—all of them present at Jutland—and the new 15-inch-gun *Bayern,* which was left behind at Wilhelmshaven.

From day to day, however, the numbers were never the same. On January 6, 1916, the predreadnought *King Edward VII,* proceeding from Scapa Flow to Belfast for dockyard maintenance, hit a mine, turned over, and sank off the Scottish coast. Fortunately, she went down slowly and all her crew was saved. On December 3, 1915, the superdreadnoughts *Barham* and *War-*

spite collided in heavy seas. *Barham,* the flagship, had hoisted a signal reducing squadron speed to 8 knots; *Warspite* misread the signal as 18 knots and began to overtake. Then just as *Barham*'s stern sank into a deep trough, *Warspite*'s bow, coming up behind, lifted high in the air. When the bow dropped, it came down on *Barham* with a noise described as "a horrible crunching, like a giant robot chewing crowbars." *Barham* was able to repair her damage at Cromarty, but *Warspite* had to go south to Devonport.

As for battle cruisers, Beatty now commanded ten of these fast ships. Two more were coming, *Renown* and *Repulse,* converted from battleships on the building ways during Jacky Fisher's brief second term as First Sea Lord. Meanwhile, to the four battle cruisers Hipper commanded at the Dogger Bank, only *Lützow,* a sister of *Derfflinger,* had been added. Their third sister, *Hindenburg,* was still under construction. Beatty's battle cruisers remained at Rosyth, where they had been based since December 1914. In addition to his flagship *Lion,* the vice admiral now had three squadrons of three ships each: the fast, 13.5-inch-gun Cats, which were *Lion*'s sisters: *Princess Royal, Queen Mary,* and *Tiger;* the second-generation, 12-inch-gun ships *New Zealand, Indefatigable,* and *Australia;* and finally, Britain's three oldest battle cruisers, *Invincible, Inflexible,* and *Indomitable.* Beatty never ceased trying to augment this force, and he and Jellicoe had been wrestling for possession of the new *Queen Elizabeth* superdreadnoughts, which had been coming to Jellicoe at Scapa Flow. Beatty declared that he needed these fast, powerful ships to stiffen the Battle Cruiser Fleet, as *Lützow* and *Hindenburg* were reported ready to join Hipper; Jellicoe resisted, wanting to keep maximum strength in his own command and to use the new dreadnoughts as a fast wing of the Grand Fleet battle line. Beatty, the Commander-in-Chief pointed out, already had ten battle cruisers to Hipper's four (five with *Lützow,* six with *Hindenburg*) and, he confided in Jackson, his feeling was that "the stronger I make Beatty, the greater is the temptation for him to get involved in an independent action." Twice—in February 1916, and again in the middle of March—Jellicoe had overruled Beatty's request for these new ships.

Three circumstances joined to reverse Jellicoe's decision. At the end of March, the Admiralty learned that *Lützow* had indeed joined the High Seas Fleet and become Hipper's flagship. Then, the collision on April 22 of *New Zealand* and *Australia* and the need of both for repairs reduced Beatty's strength from ten to eight. Meanwhile, both Jellicoe and Beatty were concerned about British battle cruiser gunnery. In one shoot in November 1915, both *Lion* and *Tiger* had performed abominably; Beatty had admitted to Jellicoe that it had been a "terrible disappointment." In March 1916, a group of junior officers from the light cruisers attached to Beatty's force, meeting one night in *Southampton*'s wardroom, agreed "collectively and separately . . . that the battle cruisers' shooting was rotten." One explanation was that Beatty's ships, lacking a gunnery range near the Firth of Forth, were unable to carry out sufficient practice. At a conference held at Rosyth on May 12, 1916, Jellicoe decided to rectify this problem by bringing the battle cruisers north from Rosyth to Scapa, squadron by squadron, to do heavy-caliber firing on the ranges developed near Scapa Flow. To plug the gap in Beatty's ranks while some of his battle cruisers were away, Beatty was to get what he wanted; the *Queen Elizabeth*s would join him at Rosyth. Accordingly, in the third week of May, Rear Admiral Horace Hood's 3rd Battle Cruiser Squadron—*Invincible, Inflexible,* and *Indomitable*—was detached from Beatty for three weeks of gunnery practice, while Rear Admiral Hugh Evan-Thomas's 5th Battle Squadron—the five *Queen Elizabeth*s—came south to bolster Beatty. Hood was displeased by the order. "This is a great mistake," he said. "If David [Beatty] gets these ships [the *Queen Elizabeth*s] with him, nothing will stop him from taking on the whole German fleet if he gets the chance." Once the five superdreadnoughts arrived, *Queen Elizabeth* herself went into a Rosyth dry dock, leaving Beatty with four. With the three *Invincible*s gone north and *Australia* still in dry dock, Beatty's force now consisted of six battle cruisers plus four fast battleships. This was the force he led at Jutland.

There were many flaws in Beatty's leadership during the battle, some of which can be traced to a curious failure beforehand. Having succeeded in his persistent effort to add the 5th Battle Squadron to his force, Beatty—inexplicably—did little to ensure its effective use. Ten days passed between the arrival of the *Queen Elizabeth*s at Rosyth and their sailing for Jutland. During this time, the four great battleships lay at anchor not far from *Lion* in the Firth of Forth. Not once did Beatty summon Rear Admiral Evan-Thomas on board his flagship so that the two men could sit down and Beatty could explain his tactics. Normally, such a conversation would take place with any new subordinate; here, it was especially important because Evan-Thomas was a battleship man, devoted to Jellicoe and the Grand Fleet, where all tactical maneuvers were controlled by explicit signals from the flagship. Evan-Thomas had never served under Beatty, and his squadron had never operated at sea with the battle cruisers. If he and they were now to fall in with Beatty's freer "Follow me!" style in battle, he needed to be told what was expected of him. Andrew Gordon, whose recent history of Jutland is one of the best ever written, calls Beatty's behavior "shockingly unprofessional. . . . For how long Evan-Thomas would have had to swing around a buoy a few hundred yards from *Lion* before Beatty bothered to talk to him, is unknown." In any case, Evan-Thomas sailed uninstructed.

There was another change in the array of the British fleet, of less significance for the moment, but with portent for the future. On April 12, 1916, a bulky, unusual-looking ship joined the fleet at Scapa Flow. She was the converted 18,000-ton Cunard liner *Campania,* a veteran of the North Atlantic tourist run, coming up from a Liverpool yard that had converted her into an aircraft carrier. Jellicoe was pleased to see her. From the beginning of the war, he had asked the Admiralty for aircraft-carrying vessels to counter the zeppelins that soared over his fleet, reporting its movements. He also yearned for some means of providing himself with aerial scouting of his own. Britain's small, early carriers, the 3,000-ton cross-Channel steamers *Engadine, Riviera,* and *Empress,* with their canvas shelters for three seaplanes, had remained with Tyrwhitt at Harwich while the Admiralty worked on something better for Jellicoe.

Seaplane operations in the open sea were inherently difficult: any combination of light wind, fog, and rough seas hampered takeoff. More important, the virtual uselessness of seaplanes as antizeppelin weapons had become obvious; the weight of their floats limited rate of climb, speed, altitude, and radius of action. The solution embodied in *Campania* was a flight deck, extending forward from the bridge over the bow, from which single-seat aircraft with wheels could take off into the wind. With their minimal weight, these craft could rise to the altitudes where the zeppelins flew, attack the monsters, then return and land in the sea near their ship; air bags would keep the plane afloat long enough for the pilot to be rescued. Jellicoe followed these developments closely and hoped for great things. "I'm glad to say we got one up yesterday," he wrote to Beatty on August 7, 1915, "the first that has risen from a ship underway. It is not a nice job for the pilot as he has to get up a speed of 45 miles an hour before he leaves the deck. . . . If there is any hitch, he . . . is certain to be finished." This system fulfilled one of Jellicoe's wishes—attacking the zeppelins—but not the other—providing himself with scouting information. Unfortunately, *Campania*'s new forward platform-ramp was not long enough for takeoff by the larger, heavier two-seat planes needed to carry the wireless equipment essential for reconnaissance work. Therefore, the new carrier remained a fore-and-aft hybrid: along with its forward flight deck, it retained a large afterdeck hangar for seaplanes, which, as before, had to be placed in the water for takeoff. Seven seaplanes and three fighters made up the new carrier's air group.

—

While the ships increased in number and evolved in design, the men in the fleet continued to wait. In many ways, their situation had improved. Scapa Flow now was a heavily fortified anchorage, and its minefields and the strong steel nets spread across its entrances permitted British admirals and sailors and their hundreds of vessels—battleships, battle cruisers, armored cruisers, light cruisers, destroyers, submarines, depot ships, oilers, colliers, store ships, ammunition ships, hospital ships, trawlers, and drifters—to rest in the same tranquil security enjoyed by their German counterparts in Wilhelmshaven. But safety in harbor was only one ingredient of life at Scapa Flow. There also was the bleak isolation of the base, the often fierce, always changeable weather, and the sheer, grinding boredom of the endless wait.

Jellicoe did what he could with fleet exercises to keep the men alert.

Again and again, the admiral took the fleet to sea, drilling the ships tirelessly in battle evolutions. Because the water inside the Flow was secure from torpedo attack and ships could practice there without danger, gunnery and torpedo drills were held every day except Sundays. At regular intervals, battleship squadrons went outside to the west of Pentland Firth for main battery firing at towed targets. On most days, the little bays around the Flow were occupied by ships firing at small targets towed by steam picket boats. After dark, the Flow would be lit by the gun flashes and searchlights of ships exercising in night firing. Occasionally, battleships exercised steaming in company without lights inside the Flow to give practice to their officers of the watch.

The island anchorage had no railway connection with the rest of the British Isles, so everything had to be brought by ship: coal, oil, ammunition, and food. Every month, 320 tons of meat, 800 tons of potatoes, 6,000 bags of flour (each weighing 140 pounds), 1,500 bags of sugar (each weighing 120 pounds), and 80,000 loaves of bread were delivered to the fleet. For the men, of course, the most important delivery was the daily mail, brought around to all ships every morning except when the seas were too high for the mail boat to come alongside.

The seasons at Scapa Flow offered spectacular contrasts. Winter was an elemental world of darkness, wind, and snow. Nightfall arrived between 3:30 and 4:00 p.m. and did not fade until 9:00 the next morning. Sometimes, the sun did not appear for days. In December 1915, Jellicoe noted fog or mist at Scapa on the fifteenth, twenty-second, and sixteenth, gales on the sixth, eighth, and twenty-third, snow on the third, fourth, eighth, and twelfth. The following month, January 1916, he recorded winds of up to eighty miles an hour on the fifth, sixth, seventh, eighth, twelfth, thirteenth, fourteenth, fifteenth, nineteenth, twentieth, twenty-second, twenty-third, twenty-fourth, and thirtieth: fifteen days out of thirty-one. When it blew hard, bending the stunted trees on shore to the ground, the heavy seas inside the Flow made it impossible to lower boats, leaving the men penned up on ships rolling on double anchors. On clear winter nights, the Northern Lights burned and crackled, flinging giant curtains of green and silver across the sky. Summers were gentler and often lovely. Scapa Flow became a world of airy space and seabirds, of blue skies and green fields, of towering cloud formations and red-gold sunsets. Looking at the shore from their anchored ships, the men saw low hills and moors purple with heather. In June, a man could fish at dawn from the deck of a battleship at 2:00 a.m. and then sit on the same spot and read his mail or a newspaper at 11:30 that night.

But fishing and reading were not enough. In the early months of war, when the fleet was continually at sea, the few hours spent in harbor were consumed in coaling and replenishing stores; then it was back to sea. As the months passed and the Germans failed to come out, the Grand Fleet spent more time at anchor. It became necessary to provide the officers and men—between 60,000 and 100,000 of them, many wrenched from their homes on the eve of war—with something more than "coaling, sleeping, sleeping, eating, sleeping, reading mail, writing letters, arguing about the war, eating, sleeping and then to sea." Leave was given only when a ship left the fleet to enter a yard in the south for repair and maintenance; then a week or two might be granted. Meanwhile, Kirkwell, a sleepy Orkney town of 4,000 inhabitants, offered a medieval redbrick cathedral and a single hotel. "I should not select it for a cheery weekend," said an officer of a light cruiser.

Football (Americans call it soccer) was one antidote. In the autumn of 1914, on the island of Flotta, football grounds were laid out in rectangles burned and smoothed out of the heather and used year-round, whenever the boats could bring players ashore. An eighteen-hole golf course was built, with battleships competing to construct individual holes. The winner was *Canada,* which imported turf from an established Scottish course and made its green "as smooth as a billiard table." Nevertheless, said a Grand Fleet officer, "it was, I suppose, one of the very worst golf courses in the world. There were no prepared tees, no fairway, no greens. But there was much bare rock, great tufts of coarse grass greedy for balls, wide stretches of hard, naked soil destructive of wooden clubs, and holes cut here and there of approximately the regulation size." Despite complaints, the course became so popular that alacrity in play was essential. A foursome would drive off the tee, then have to run down the course in order to be out of range of the next players, already shouting "Fore!" Tennis in its normal form was impossible owing to rain and continual wind, but two courts of gravel and ash were constructed and rarely went unused. There was fishing, boating, and even some shooting of ducks and grouse, although the four resident ducks on Flotta—Matthew, Mark, Luke, and John—were religiously protected. Officers enjoyed walking, hiking, and picnicking; on a summer's day, the 1,500-foot summit of Ward Hill on the island of Hoy offered a magnificent panorama of emerald-green islands set in sparkling blue water with the gray ships lined up in rows like children's toys. Flotta offered a pistol range for officers, a rifle range for men, and an annual Grand Fleet boxing championship, which drew 10,000 cheering spectators. Sailing and rowing matches between ships were frequent. Gardening became popular among both men and officers and, although neither soil nor climate were promising, edible vegetables were harvested. These were welcome, because the vegetables brought by sea to Scapa Flow sometimes arrived unrecognizable.

Most men on the ships remained on board. Deck hockey played with homemade sticks, throwing heavy medicine balls, and tugs-of-war were popular. Officers played billiards, the rolling of the ship even at anchor adding an element of challenge to the game. Motion pictures drew standing-room-only audiences. There were frequent lectures, with officers speaking about famous naval battles, great explorations, visits to the Western Front, and other subjects. Education was encouraged and, at Jellicoe's request, the Admiralty provided naval schoolmasters who held evening classes for boys and men.

Two service ships, both primarily storage lockers for frozen meat, played important roles in distracting the crews. *Borodino* became a nautical canteen, a sort of floating Fortnum & Mason dispensing extras and luxuries, where officers could buy salmon, trout, frozen game, pâté, fruit, nuts, and stuffed olives. *Ghourko* was the theater ship, fitted with a stage and places for an audience of 600. Amateur reviews, pantomimes, and musical comedies were presented and large sums were spent on props, musical instruments, scenery, and lighting. In addition, *Ghourko* offered church services, cinema, lectures, and boxing in a full-sized ring. Jellicoe visited *Ghourko* whenever he could. Although slightly deaf from a burst eardrum, he loved musical comedy, especially Gilbert and Sullivan. Surrounded by his staff and the admirals and captains of the fleet, he sat in a big armchair placed in the front row, smoking his after-dinner cigarette in a holder while he roared at a chorus line of bare-kneed midshipmen.

—

Jellicoe was the figure around whom everything in the Grand Fleet revolved. His staff admired him without qualification. "Jellicoe . . . worked with amazing rapidity," said one of these officers. "When the *Iron Duke* was in harbour, he sat at a tiny writing table in the middle of his cabin, reading despatches and memoranda, making pencil annotations and corrections, interrupted from time to time by the mass of matters and signals requiring immediate action. . . . Never did the writer see him out of temper or anything but cheerful. . . . His calm outlook never deserted him." In the evening when not at sea, Jellicoe dined at a round table in his cabin with six or seven officers from his staff and *Iron Duke*'s captain, Frederic Dreyer. The admiral was abstemious. "Every night," said the captain, "he would ask me: 'Will you split an apple, Dreyer?' and then cut it in halves and offer the plate to me with a charming smile."

Aware that his health and power of concentration were vital assets to the fleet, Jellicoe did everything possible to maintain his own physical fitness. He went ashore and walked furiously up hills and over moors. In the evenings, he played with the heavy medicine ball on *Iron Duke*'s upper deck. "It's splendid," he told Beatty. "I've already sprained a finger and a knee." At one point, Jellicoe was dissuaded with difficulty from trying out for *Iron Duke*'s gun room rugby team. His favorite exercise was golf, played on the Flotta course. Always allowed to play through, Jellicoe nevertheless played at the run, practically sprinting between holes. Wearying, the Bishop of London, an old friend, once cried a halt: "Look here, Jack, is this golf or a steeplechase?" At night in his cabin, Jellicoe did what he could to slough off the weight of responsibility by reading thrillers "of a particularly lurid description."

Nevertheless, "living over the shop" on *Iron Duke,* he found his health deteriorating. Telegrams flowed in; streams of people arrived. There were constant civilian visitors: the king, who could not be ignored; the prime minister, who also must be attended to; the Chancellor of the Exchequer, the Archbishop of Westminster, the Archbishop of York, forty colonial MPs, "five French gentlemen of eminence," and "a representative of the United States press." Always reluctant to delegate, Jellicoe received them all. Meanwhile, beneath his veneer of calm and hospitality, his worries—awareness of the weak points of the British navy, fear of German submarines, constant arguments with the Admiralty; above all, his sense of the unique immensity of his own responsibilities—wore him down. Inevitably, nervous strain brought physical repercussions.

By the beginning of January 1915, he was suffering severely from hemorrhoids. On January 25, he had a particularly bad attack. "I am not at all well," he wrote to Beatty. "Crocked up yesterday. Very bad attack of piles and general run down." Beatty, just back from fighting at the Dogger Bank, was concerned. "You must take the greatest care of yourself," he replied to the Commander-in-Chief. "What we should do without you, Lord knows." To a former colleague still at the Admiralty, Jellicoe wrote, "I am laid up for a bit. It is of course due to the worry of trying to get things done which ought to be done without my having to step in. I hope to be right early next week, but the doctor says at present it is dangerous to move out of bed." Late in January, he entered a hospital ashore to have an operation under the name "Mr. Jessop." Fisher sent up a specialist surgeon from London to take charge. Subsequently, the First Sea Lord wrote:

> My beloved Jellicoe:
>
> It is good news that the doctors telegraph to me that you are doing so well. Now do please take it easy, and damn Rosyth and everything else that worries you and simply play bridge. You are worth more than a hundred Rosyths or dozens of battleships so put that in your pipe and smoke it and take things easy.

A minor operation corrected the physical ailment, but it was a month before he returned to duty, "feeling really fit for work, though going a little slow at first." But before the end of the summer of 1915, his health began to deteriorate again. Beatty noticed and wrote, "Please don't overdo yourself. You are our only hope and must take care of yourself." In September, Jellicoe, suffering from rheumatism and neuralgia, sent for a specialist, who diagnosed pyorrhea and pulled two teeth. The Admiralty suggested that he go ashore to rest, which he did at Kinpurnie Castle in Forfarshire, belonging to his father-in-law. He paid several visits to an Edinburgh dentist and, after a fortnight, returned to Scapa Flow, still under medical supervision, but temporarily refreshed and declaring himself "a totally different being."

Through all of this, Jellicoe's relationship with the men in the fleet deepened in mutual respect and affection. Both officers and men sensed that, beyond the requirements of command, the admiral would do everything in his power to ease their lot. Once when Jellicoe read in a newspaper that one of his young staff officers had become a father, he sent for him. The young man was told to go to London and call at the Admiralty eight hours after arriving in order to bring back any official papers there for the Commander-in-Chief. Jellicoe paused, then added, "I expect you will know how to employ those eight hours." Somehow, Jellicoe managed to remember the names of an extraordinary number of ordinary seamen in the fleet and it was said that he knew and spoke to every member of the crew of *Iron Duke.* On these occasions, when the admiral approached and the sailor sprang to attention, Jellicoe always said, "At ease," and wanted to know what the sailor was doing. Reports of this behavior spread through the fleet. One day, a small boat carrying a victorious regatta crew back to its ship passed near the stern of *Iron Duke,* where Jellicoe was walking alone on the quarterdeck. When he saw the silver trophy in the bows of the boat, Jellicoe leaned over the rail, "smiling, clapped his hands, applauding. . . . A wild tumult of frantic cheering burst out almost like an explosion from every throat. . . . There was gratitude and passionate loyalty in the demonstration and it continued long after the figure on the quarterdeck had turned away. 'That's what I likes about 'im,' said a bearded seaman hoarsely. . . . 'E's that 'uman.' "

—

Scheer's apparent willingness to lead the High Seas Fleet to sea led to dialogue between the Admiralty and the British sea admirals. Jackson suggested further seaplane raids to draw the Germans out, but Jellicoe continued wary. "I am being pressed to plan another [air raid], the idea being that it will bring the German fleet out," he wrote to Beatty. "But if carried out at daylight and the German heavy ships do move, they won't be clear of the minefields and in a position where we could engage them before about four p.m. This is no time to start a fight in those waters. It also involves our hanging about for a whole day in a bad locality, using up fuel, especially of our destroyers. . . . Patience is the virtue we must exercise. . . . What do you think?"

Beatty, despite his eagerness to fight the Germans, agreed: "You ask me what I think? I think the German fleet will come out only on its own initiative when the right time arrives. . . . Your arguments regarding the fuel question are unanswerable (and measure the situation absolutely). We cannot amble about the North Sea for two or three days and at the end be in a condition to fight the most decisive battle of the war. . . . When the Great Day comes, it will be when the enemy takes the initiative."

Nevertheless, the staff on *Iron Duke* cudgeled its brains to devise a plan that would tempt the Germans out of harbor. By the end of May, Jellicoe was ready with a scheme he hoped would lure Scheer out to a position farther north than the High Seas Fleet had yet ventured. Beginning at dawn on June 2, eight British light cruisers would sweep down the Kattegat as far south as the Great Belt and the sound between Denmark and Sweden. The ships were meant to be seen from shore so that German agents would communicate with Scheer and provoke him to act. Behind the light cruisers, a single British battle squadron would cruise in the Skagerrak while, hovering to the northwest, the entire Grand Fleet would wait to pounce. This plan differed from previous bait offerings in that the cruisers would press deeper, suggesting that they meant to enter the Baltic to attack German communications. If the High Seas Fleet did not take the bait and come out far enough, Jellicoe still hoped that the German ships might venture far enough to pass over three Harwich submarines, which, as part of the plan, would submerge and wait for them from June 1 to June 3 just south of Horns Reef on the northern edge of the Bight.

Before this plan could be executed, however, the Admiralty began picking up signals that suggested that the German fleet might move first. Since May 17, Room 40 codebreakers had been peeking at Scheer's plans. The signals arranging the departure of the U-boats from their bases were the first to be deciphered; these messages were subsequently confirmed by the unusual number of signals coming from submarines in the northern North Sea. Strong antisubmarine patrols had been sent out. By May 28, it was clear to the Admiralty that something unusual was afoot: the numerous U-boats in the North Sea were not molesting merchant ships; the German fleet was assembling in the mouths of the Elbe and Jade. Early on Tuesday morning, May 30, Room 40 began deciphering signals from Scheer ordering his U-boats to remain at sea and telling the High Seas Fleet to assemble in the outer Jade by 7:00 p.m. Later that morning, Room 40 intercepted the German signal "31 G.G. 2490" addressed to all units of the High Seas Fleet. Although its meaning was unknown, it seemed likely to be an operational order of supreme importance. From the number 31, the cryptologists deduced that an operation by the German fleet was to begin the following day.

The Admiralty waited no longer. At noon, using the land telegraph direct to the flagships at Scapa Flow and Rosyth, Whitehall told Jellicoe and Beatty that the High Seas Fleet was assembling in the outer Jade and that there were indications the Germans were coming out. At 5:16 p.m. the Admiralty ordered the main fleet and the Battle Cruiser Fleet to raise steam. And then, at 5:40 p.m., a further message came to Jellicoe and Beatty: "Germans intend some operations commencing tomorrow morning leaving via Horns Reef. You should concentrate to eastward of Long Forties ready for eventualities."

That afternoon, the Honorable Barry Bingham, captain of the destroyer *Nestor* attached to the battle cruisers at Rosyth, was ashore playing golf with a friend near Edinburgh. "After a thoroughly enjoyable game," he wrote later, "we adjourned for tea to the little house I had rented on the side of the links, and then found our way down to Queensferry Pier at the regulation hour of 6:00 p.m. to catch a routine boat. While we stood waiting on the pier amid a throng of fellow officers, all eyes were suddenly drawn in the direction of the *Lion* from whose masthead there floated a string of flags with their message to all ships: 'Raise steam for 22 knots and report when ready.' "

—

At Scapa Flow and Cromarty as at Rosyth, signal flags snapping at the halyards of the flagships sent streams of boats scurrying from ship to shore, picking up crew members, while scores of funnels billowed black smoke showing that furnaces were raising steam. At Scapa, officers just beginning a game of deck hockey on board the new battleship *Revenge* began behaving like schoolboys, cheering, dancing, and hugging one another. That night, the sun set with a "blazing red and orange coloring caused by storm clouds . . . which seemed a foreboding of something dreadful about to happen." Twilight arrived and through the summer evening air came the shrill of boatswains' pipes as ship's boats were hoisted aboard, followed by the clank of anchor chains coming in. Ship after ship hoisted the flag signal, "Ready to proceed." At 9:30 p.m., beacons marking Hoxa Sound flashed on and the boom defense trawlers began to haul away the system of nets and flotation buoys and open the gates. In the growing darkness, the gray ships began to move, passing in procession through the harbor, down the four miles of Hoxa Sound, and out through the net defenses into the rolling swell of the open sea. There, the night was calm, with an overcast sky covering the stars and the islands receding into the heavy, wet mist. The dreadnoughts, silent and black, were seen by their neighbors only as shadowy forms except for a small, shaded light on the stern of each. On the bridges, officers stared ahead, while the crews at the guns looked out in all directions. "Inside the ships," wrote coauthors Langhorne Gibson and J.E.T. Harper, "in another world of bright electric light, and intense heat, the turbines hummed with steady drone and the stokers' shovels rasped as they fed coal into the boiler fires."

When the last vessels of Jellicoe's fleet cleared Hoxa Sound, the great anchorage was practically deserted. The admiral had left five warships behind, four of them deliberately: these were the new 15-inch-gun battleship *Royal Sovereign,* commissioned only three weeks before, and three destroyers. By mistake, the aircraft carrier *Campania,* which Jellicoe had so much wanted with him, was also left behind. Anchored in an isolated bay inside the Flow, she had somehow not received the order to sail. By the time *Campania*'s captain was told and got his ship to sea, he was far behind; unwilling to risk a large ship steaming unescorted in the North Sea, Jellicoe ordered her back to harbor. The Commander-in-Chief thereby deprived himself of a significant asset—aerial reconnaissance—he might have used the following day.

From Scapa Flow, on that eve of Jutland, Jellicoe in *Iron Duke* brought two battle squadrons (sixteen dreadnought battleships) and three battle cruisers (Hood's *Invincible*s), plus four old armored cruisers, eleven light cruisers, and thirty-six destroyers; in all, seventy warships. From Cromarty came another twenty-three ships: eight dreadnoughts, another four armored cruisers, and eleven destroyers. In the Forth, Beatty's six battle cruisers slipped silently past the waterside cottages and under the iron spans of the great railway bridge. Close behind followed the four *Queen Elizabeth*s led by Rear Admiral Hugh Evan-Thomas in *Barham.* Beatty also brought three squadrons of light cruisers—twelve ships in all—including the veteran 2nd Light Cruiser Squadron commanded by Commodore William Goodenough in *Southampton.* He had twenty-seven destroyers and the small aircraft carrier *Engadine* carrying three seaplanes: fifty ships in all. Elsewhere, other British ships and squadrons made ready for sea. The Admiralty believed that a German thrust might aim at the Channel, so the Harwich Force was ordered to raise steam. And the 3rd Battle Squadron—*Dreadnought* herself, and the seven remaining predreadnought *King Edward*s—was ordered to raise steam and to concentrate off the Thames estuary.

So it was that by 10:30 p.m. on May 30, while *Friedrich der Grosse* still lay at anchor in the Jade, the Grand Fleet was at sea in three great formations, 150 ships, all heading toward the Jutland Bank. That night Jellicoe was bringing 28 dreadnought battleships, 9 dreadnought battle cruisers, 8 armored cruisers, 26 light cruisers, 78 destroyers, a minelayer, and an aircraft carrier. The Grand Fleet's numerical superiority over the Germans was marked: 28 to 16 in dreadnought battleships; 9 to 5 in battle cruisers, 113 to 72 in lighter craft. In gun power, Jellicoe's superiority was even more pronounced. The British battle fleet carried 272 heavy naval guns against the German fleet's 200. And the guns of the British battleships were bigger: 48 15-inch, 10 14-inch, 110 13.5-inch, and 104 12-inch. The Germans brought 128 12-inch and 72 11-inch. Comparative figures for the battle cruisers were even more disparate: 32 13.5-inch and 40 12-inch British guns versus 16 12-inch and 28 11-inch German barrels. In addition to this overwhelming superiority in number of guns, caliber of guns, and weight of shell, the Grand Fleet also had a significant speed advantage over the High Seas Fleet. Beatty's four Cats could steam 3 knots faster than Hipper's battle cruisers, while, because Mauve's predreadnoughts were in company with the German battle line, Jellicoe's battle fleet was at least 2 knots faster than Scheer's.

At 7:37 p.m., before *Iron Duke* departed Scapa Flow, Jellicoe signaled Beatty his orders for the following day. The battle cruisers were to steer for a point 100 miles northwest of Horns Reef, arriving there at 2:00 p.m. At that time, the Grand Fleet would be sixty-five miles to the north. Then Jellicoe said, "If [there is] no news by 2 p.m. stand [north] towards me to get in visual touch."

—

Now, on both sides, the orders were given. Fifty-eight moving castles of gray steel—thirty-seven under one flag, twenty-one under the other, the dreadnoughts of the two greatest navies in the world—were about to collide.

CHAPTER 31

Jutland: Beatty vs. Hipper

It was a clear late spring day with a gentle, lazy wind and a light swell undulating the surface of the sea. The sun, rising higher, burned away the morning mist and left the water sparkling under a blue sky. At dawn, the separate Grand Fleet battle squadrons had merged into a single huge formation, which was further enlarged by the arrival around noon of Admiral Jerram's eight battleships and their escorts from Cromarty. Now the formation advanced in six columns abreast, four dreadnought battleships in each column, all zigzagging in unison every ten minutes for submarine defense. Eight miles ahead of the battleships, the eight old armored cruisers were spread widely to form a screen. The light cruisers and destroyers were stationed on either flank and astern. Because Jellicoe wished to conserve the limited fuel carried by his destroyers, the fleet was steaming at 15 knots.

On the ships, the crews relaxed; they had done this sort of thing many times before. A visitor to the fleet was impressed by the service of morning prayer on the battleship *St. Vincent:* "about a thousand bare-headed sailors standing erect in silence on the quarterdeck." At 11:00 a.m. the crews were called to action stations for drills, then dismissed to routine painting and cleaning. Afterward, off-duty men gathered on the decks and turret tops to bask in the sun. The midday meal came and went. Officers off watch smoked or dozed in wardroom armchairs or went to their cabins to lie down. A *Tiger* midshipman, asleep in the sun on the battle cruiser's quarterdeck, remembered later, "We did not appear to be expecting Huns, as we cruised along to the eastwards at no great speed."

Jellicoe with the battle fleet and Beatty with the battle cruisers and fast battleships were both moving eastward. At two in the afternoon they would turn toward each other and, about an hour and a half later, meet and form a single immense formation. If there was any response from the enemy before then, Beatty, seventy miles farther south and nearer to Germany, would encounter it first. But as the hours passed, the belief grew stronger in the British fleet that the Germans were not at sea and that this would be simply another routine and useless sweep. Despite warnings that German warships had been assembling in the Jade, there had been no reports of enemy activity since the previous night.

At 12:48 that afternoon, a signal to Jellicoe from the Admiralty seemed to confirm this belief. That morning, Captain Thomas Jackson, Director of the Operations Division of the Admiralty, had marched into Room 40 and asked where directional wireless stations placed the call sign "DK," used by Scheer's flagship, *Friedrich der Grosse*. When he was told, "In the Jade," he departed without saying or asking anything further. If "DK" was the flagship and the flagship had not sailed, it seemed reasonable to assume that the German battle fleet had not sailed. This was the assumption Jackson made and passed along to Oliver, who signaled Jellicoe: "No definite news of the enemy. They made all preparations for sailing early this morning. It was thought the fleet had sailed but directional wireless placed the flagship in the Jade at 11.10 a.m. GMT. Apparently they have been unable to carry out airship reconnaissance which has delayed them." Given this information, Jellicoe reasonably assumed that if the assembly in the Jade had been a precursor to anything, it would be at most a battle cruiser raid and that Scheer was remaining behind, perhaps to steam out later to cover Hipper's retreat.

A German ruse had succeeded, in large part because of the ignorance and arrogance of Captain Jackson. If, while he was in Room 40, Jackson had asked one more question, he would have learned that "DK" was the German Commander-in-Chief's *harbor* call sign and that when Scheer went to sea, he disguised the fact by transferring it from *Friedrich der Grosse* to a shore wireless station at the entrance to the Jade River. Scheer had been employing this subterfuge since he took command and had used it in the Lowestoft Raid, which was when Room 40 became aware of the practice. Unhappily for Jellicoe, the Grand Fleet, and the Royal Navy, Captain Thomas Jackson exemplified those British naval officers who scorned such modern capabilities and techniques as deciphering secret codes. He made no secret of his contempt for the gifted civilians who broke codes in Room 40 and he rejected the idea that such people could contribute anything useful to naval operations. They were, in Jackson's eyes, "a party of very clever fellows who could decipher coded signals," but must never be allowed to interpret them. "Those chaps couldn't possibly understand all the implications of intercepted signals," Jackson had said. Naturally, his feelings were obvious to the codebreakers and they and the captain had as little to do with each other as possible; Jackson's visit to Room 40 on the morning of May 31 was only

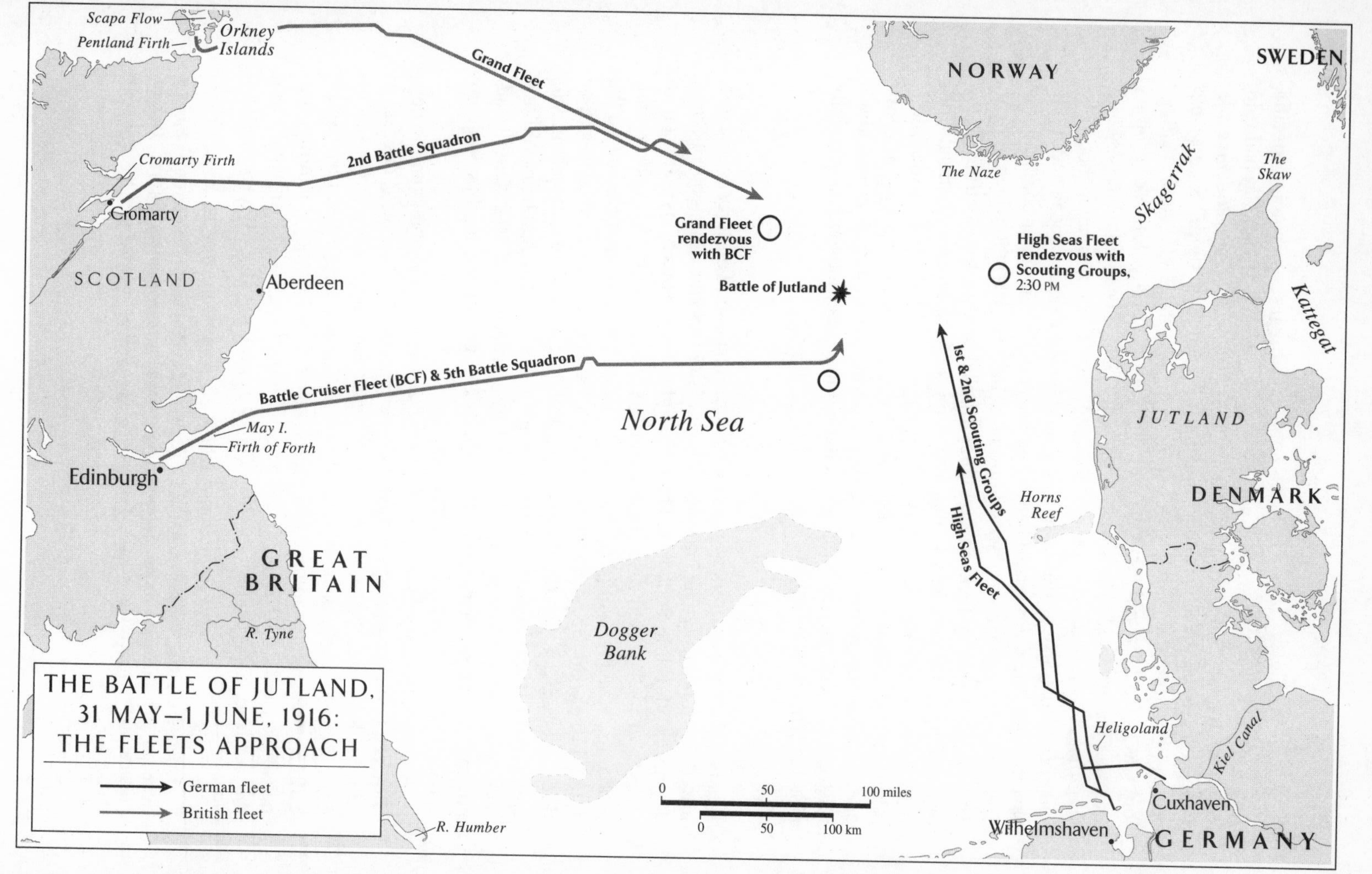

Scapa Flow
Pentland Firth
Orkney Islands
Grand Fleet
2nd Battle Squadron
Cromarty Firth
Cromarty
SCOTLAND
Aberdeen
Battle Cruiser Fleet (BCF) & 5th Battle Squadron
May I.
Firth of Forth
Edinburgh
GREAT BRITAIN
R. Tyne
R. Humber
Grand Fleet rendezvous with BCF
Battle of Jutland
North Sea
Dogger Bank
NORWAY
The Naze
Skagerrak
The Skaw
SWEDEN
High Seas Fleet rendezvous with Scouting Groups, 2:30 PM
Kattegat
JUTLAND
DENMARK
1st & 2nd Scouting Groups
High Seas Fleet
Horns Reef
Heligoland
Kiel Canal
Cuxhaven
Wilhelmshaven
GERMANY
0
50
100 miles
0
50
100 km
THE BATTLE OF JUTLAND, 31 MAY–1 JUNE, 1916: THE FLEETS APPROACH
German fleet
British fleet

his third. Therefore, when he asked the codebreakers a single, specific question, they gave him only a single, specific answer. If Jackson had told Room 40 that he wanted to know where "DK" was *so that he could pass it to Jellicoe,* they would have understood the meaning and significance of his question and told him that they were not saying that the High Seas Fleet flagship was in the Jade; only that the call sign was. Naturally, Jellicoe assumed that the Operations Division was competent and he accepted what they told him: that *Friedrich der Grosse* and the High Seas Fleet were at anchor. If he had known that Scheer was at sea, he would have increased speed and might have brought the Germans to battle two hours earlier in better conditions of light and visibility and with two additional hours of daylight in which to fight. The damage done by Jackson's bungling rippled on disastrously through the day and night.* When, at 4:40 that afternoon, Jellicoe received a signal from Beatty that he was actually in sight of the High Seas Fleet—which the Admiralty had told him was still in the Jade, 180 miles away—he lost all confidence in Admiralty messages. And that night, the Commander-in-Chief's mistrust of Admiralty information about German fleet movements painfully affected what was to happen.

—

Beatty's six battle cruisers were in two columns on a southeasterly course, followed five miles astern and northwest by the four superdreadnoughts of Evan-Thomas's 5th Battle Squadron. His three light cruiser squadrons were spread out ahead to the southeast. Beatty's orders were to hold this course until 2:00 p.m., when he would be 260 miles east of the Firth of Forth and on the Jutland Bank, off the northwestern coast of Denmark. Jellicoe then would be three hours away, but the Commander-in-Chief felt no anxiety about this gap. If Scheer and his battleships were not at sea—and he had been told that they were not—Beatty's force of six battle cruisers and four superdreadnoughts was more than adequate in speed and gun power to cope with any appearance of Hipper's battle cruisers.

At dawn, Beatty's squadrons began zigzagging; on a signal from the flagship, each column of ships turned every ten minutes in unison 22 degrees to either side of the line of advance. The signal flags used were large: rectangular flags were eleven feet by nine feet, triangular flags fifteen by eleven. Still, flag signaling had practical limits imposed by distance, visibility, funnel smoke, and wind direction. With this in mind Beatty had instructed *Tiger,* the battle cruiser nearest to *Barham,* to repeat his flag signals to Evan-

*Andrew Gordon, whose description and analysis of the Battle of Jutland are uncommonly thorough and balanced, abandons moderation when he characterizes Captain Jackson. "Ridiculous," "angry," "blustering," "insufferable," and "buffoon" are words he uses to portray this officer.

Thomas by searchlight. At 2:00 p.m., the wind remained low and the smooth sea was stirred only by the wash of bows and propellers. As far as the eye could see from *Lion*'s bridge there was no wisp of smoke or sign of ships except the British light cruiser scouting line spread eight miles ahead. At 2:10 p.m., Beatty hoisted the signal flags alerting his force to prepare to turn to the north. Five minutes later, the signal was hauled down, making the admiral's declaration of intention a command, and the battle cruisers began their turn toward the Grand Fleet. At this moment, *Lion* was fifty miles west of Hipper's flagship, *Lützow,* but the most extended flanking ships of the two cruiser screens were only sixteen miles apart.

When Beatty signaled his command to turn, not every ship in his force reacted immediately. Far to the northeast of the flagship, the British light cruiser *Galatea* on the port wing of the advanced screen had difficulty seeing *Lion*'s signal flags and so held on a few minutes before beginning her turn. During these minutes, the lookout on her starboard bridge wing suddenly called out, "Ship ahead blowing off steam." Instantly, all binoculars on the light cruiser's bridge were trained on the horizon 20 degrees off the starboard bow. There eight miles (16,000 yards) away was a stationary plume of funnel smoke against the sky. Even though Beatty's signal to turn had now been received, the light cruiser's captain decided to delay obedience and hold course to see what ship lay hove to over the horizon, and why she had stopped: one possibility was that a surfaced U-boat lay nearby and had sent a boarding party. Increasing speed, *Galatea* bore down on the smudge and soon a small merchantman appeared hull up. She was the Danish tramp steamer *N.J. Fjord,* blowing off steam from her boilers and rising and falling in the gentle roll of the sea.

Then, suddenly, the binoculars on *Galatea*'s bridge revealed something else: a low, gray shape coming out from behind the steamer's hull: a German destroyer. A few moments later, a second destroyer appeared. The bugle sounded "Action stations" and the lookout's voice came again, "Green two five [that is, 28 degrees off the starboard bow]. Cruiser . . . two cruisers." At 2:20, *Galatea* sent a flag signal to the other ships in her squadron: "Enemy in sight." Simultaneously, her wireless reported to Beatty: "Two cruisers, probably hostile, bearing east southeast, course unknown." Then at 2:28 p.m., *Galatea,* now making 28 knots, opened fire with her forward 6-inch gun. It was the first shot of the Battle of Jutland.

—

Roughly the same sequence had occurred on the German side. In bright morning sunlight, the German fleet had steered west of Heligoland, heading north. Half the gun crews were at their posts; the other half slept in hammocks slung nearby. Georg von Hase, gunnery officer of the battle cruiser *Derfflinger,* rose, shaved, had breakfast in the wardroom, and returned to his cabin to write letters. By midday dinner, excitement was rising. "Nearly everyone agreed that this time there would be an action," Hase wrote later, "but no one spoke of anything more important than fighting English light cruisers or old armored cruisers. As was always the case when we were on one of our sweeps of the North Sea, no one drank a drop of alcohol. . . . We smoked our cigars, then I went to my cabin, lay down for a siesta and watched the blue rings from my cigar." At 1:00 p.m. the drums beat the daily signal to clean the guns. Then at 2:28, alarm bells sounded, the drums beat again, and boatswains piped and shouted, "Clear for action!" This was not a drill.

By this time—2:30 p.m.—Scheer and the main body of the High Seas Fleet were well to the northwest of Horns Reef, with Hipper's battle cruisers fifty miles in advance. Spread ahead of the battle cruisers in fan formation were five light cruisers and numerous destroyers. Captain Madlung of the light cruiser *Elbing,* on the western edge of Hipper's screen, had seen the Danish freighter's smoke and sent two destroyers, *B-109* and *B-110,* to investigate. Overtaking the freighter, the destroyers signaled her to stop and each destroyer lowered a boat with a boarding party to check her papers and cargo. While the boats were in the water, the destroyers sighted smoke to the west and, soon afterward, approaching warships. Urgently recalling their boats, the destroyers broke away from the tramp steamer. When *Elbing* and her sister light cruisers hastened to their support, the battle began.

—

Beatty's mind was on other things when *Galatea*'s first contact report came in. Anticipating his scheduled rendezvous with Jellicoe, he had just signaled Evan-Thomas, "When we turn north look out for advanced cruisers of the Grand Fleet." Evan-Thomas had acknowledged the signal and *Barham* and her three sisters had just executed the turn. Nevertheless, Beatty's reaction to *Galatea*'s report was characteristically quick. At 2:32, he ordered "Action stations," increased speed to 22 knots, and turned southeast in an effort to get between the enemy ships and Horns Reef. His new course, signaled by flag hoist to his entire force, was not the one that would most rapidly bring the enemy to action; rather it was the one that would compel the Germans to action whether they wished it or not. Nor, before doing this, did Beatty wait until he ascertained the enemy's strength; remembering his experience of Hipper turning and legging it for home at the Dogger Bank, he simply turned and went at maximum speed. Indeed, he moved so quickly that he told Chatfield to put *Lion*'s helm over without waiting for his signal to be acknowledged by his other ships. The battle cruisers, their captains aware of Beatty's impetuous style, dutifully followed *Lion* around and sped away to the southeast.

But the battleship *Barham* and her three giant sisters, five miles away on

Lion's port bow, did not follow. Five miles was an extended distance to read signal flags between moving ships at sea, even with the aid of binoculars. Moreover, as Beatty's flagship continued to turn, the heavy black smoke pouring from her funnels shrouded the signal entirely. Inexplicably, *Tiger,* detailed to pass *Lion*'s signals along to *Barham* by searchlight, failed to do so. Evan-Thomas himself saw the battle cruisers turning, and *Barham*'s captain standing next to him urged the admiral to conform but Evan-Thomas had been schooled by Jellicoe strictly to obey orders. Accordingly, he waited for a specific signal from Beatty, and continued north. As Evan-Thomas said later, "The only way I could account for no signal having been received by me was that Beatty was going to signal another course to the 5th Battle Squadron, possibly to get the enemy light cruisers between us. Anyway, if he wished us to turn, the searchlight would have done it in a moment." This mischance (after the war, the word used became "failure" and Beatty and Evan-Thomas would blame each other) was compounded when *Tiger,* assigned to relay *Lion*'s signals to *Barham* by searchlight, ignored this duty. *Tiger*'s excuse was that the battle cruisers' turn had placed her in the farthest, not the nearest, position from the 5th Battle Squadron and that, under these conditions, her duty to pass along signals by searchlight must certainly have lapsed. Thus, while Beatty rushed off to the southeast, Evan-Thomas's super-dreadnoughts continued on a course almost exactly the opposite. Seven minutes later Beatty realized that the 5th Battle Squadron was not following and he repeated by searchlight the order to turn to the southeast. By the time this was accomplished, Evan-Thomas was nearly ten miles away. In this manner, Beatty's impetuous decision, coupled with the delay before *Barham* received his signal and Evan-Thomas's refusal to act without it, combined to deprive the battle cruisers of the powerful support of forty massive 15-inch guns. When Beatty went into action a few minutes later, the number of his ships had been cut from ten to six and the striking power of his guns had been cut in half. Beatty could have reunited his force by slowing his battle cruisers and letting the battleships catch up, but slowing down was not in David Beatty's nature. Obeying impulse, he charged, leaving his battleships to make their way behind. In fairness, it should be remembered that Beatty still had seen only German light cruisers; Hipper's battle cruisers were twenty-five miles away from *Lion,* and neither Beatty nor Hipper was certain of the other's presence.

—

In Beatty's force, the sounding of "Action stations" sent men running. A few were skeptical: in *New Zealand*'s wardroom several officers smiled knowingly and went out on deck to have a look. In many ships, tea was about to be served and those who had been on board any length of time thought first of food. On the light cruiser *Southampton,* Lieutenant Stephen King-Hall, dozing in the smoking room, jumped up and dashed to his cabin to set about his before-action routine: "putting on as many clothes as possible, collecting my camera, notebook, and pencils, and chocolate in case of a prolonged stay at action stations." In *Barham,* a midshipman cast a wishful glance at the tea laid out immaculately on the gun-room table and wondered when he would get a chance to eat it. On *Malaya,* where the gun-room steward was just laying the table for tea, the midshipmen on hand scuttled etiquette and began downing as much food as possible. A turret officer in *Warspite* dashed into the wardroom, grabbed as much portable food as he could, and rushed off to his station. On *Tiger,* the chaplain, awakened from a nap, went to the wardroom to find out what was happening: "All the cups and plates were on the table but the room was empty. They had evidently been called away in the middle of tea. And suddenly."

As British bugles sounded "Action stations" and German mess compartments thundered to the roll of drums, ships reverberated with swarming men and slamming hatch covers. Groups mustered at their stations where gas masks, goggles, and life preservers were issued. Damage control parties went through the ship wetting the decks and closing and dogging steel doors. In *Queen Mary,* a gunner's mate checked to make certain his turret was ready with "urinal buckets, biscuits and corned beef, drinking water and plenty of first aid dressings." Medical parties in dressing stations laid out surgical instruments, dressings, morphia, syringes, and stretchers. Fire hoses were laid out, glass windscreens on the bridges were removed, Union Jacks soared to the peaks of the mainmasts, and White Ensigns whipped from the yardarms and gaffs. Then came a stillness. Decks were deserted. No sounds came but the throb of the engines, the roar of ventilator fans, and, on deck, the splash of the sea against the hull. Most men were closed up in small steel compartments; in turret gun rooms, magazines, secondary batteries, conning towers, engine rooms, and bunkers. Out in the air on the bridges, admirals and captains, muffled in scarves and greatcoats, squinted through binoculars and walked in and out of the chart houses to study their positions on tactical compass plots. One captain wore irregular dress. *New Zealand*'s John Green had a green stone tiki pendant around his neck, and his waist was wrapped in a black-and-white flax Maori kilt called a *piu-piu,* both gifts presented to the ship by a tribal chief during the battle cruiser's visit to the Dominion in 1913. Along with the gifts came the chief's request that they be worn by the captain whenever *New Zealand* went into action; if this ritual was faithfully observed, he promised, the battle cruiser would not be seriously harmed. On this day, the news that the captain was wearing his necklace and his kilt spread reassurance among the crew. And when the Battle of Jutland was over, *New Zealand,* hit only once by a heavy shell, was the only one of Beatty's six battle cruisers to suffer no significant damage and escape all casualties.

—

Sixty-five miles to the north, on the bridge of *Iron Duke,* there was a stir as *Galatea*'s first signal came in and positions were marked on the chart. A moment later, the short, brisk figure of the Commander-in-Chief appeared and Jellicoe bent over the chart. Only light cruisers were mentioned in this report. It could mean anything, but with the Admiralty's assurance that Scheer's flagship was still at anchor in the Jade, the Germans could only be light forces, and Beatty's squadrons were more than strong enough to take care of them. Then, at 2:39, came a further signal from *Galatea*: "Have sighted large amount of smoke as though from a fleet, bearing east northeast." *Iron Duke* immediately hoisted the signal for 17 knots. A few minutes later, another message followed: "Smoke seems to be seven vessels besides cruisers and destroyers. They have turned north." Seven vessels *besides* cruisers and destroyers suggested battle cruisers. So Hipper was at sea! Jellicoe signaled for 18 knots and then for 19.

—

Galatea's report "Smoke seems to be seven vessels besides cruisers and destroyers" suggested battle cruisers to Beatty, too, and at 2:47 p.m., he ordered *Engadine* to send up a seaplane to find out exactly what lay over the horizon. Already that morning, *Engadine* had advised Beatty of the limitations imposed by that day's weather on aerial reconnaissance: "Sea suitable for getting off but not for landing. Impossible to distinguish where mist ends and water begins in coming down to sea. Will be all right if horizon clears." Now, on receiving the admiral's signal, the carrier came to a halt and a two-seat Short seaplane was pulled from her hangar and hoisted into the sea. At 3:08 p.m., only twenty-one minutes after *Engadine* received Beatty's command, Flight Lieutenant Frederick Rutland (thereafter known as Rutland of Jutland) was airborne. Low clouds forced him to remain under a thousand feet in order to see anything on the surface, and visibility varied between one and four miles. Ten minutes later, flying northeast at 900 feet, he came to within a mile and a half of the German light cruisers *Elbing, Frankfurt,* and *Pillau.* They fired at him and the seaplane was surrounded by shrapnel, some of it bursting only 200 feet away. At 3:31, Rutland's observer was able to wireless *Engadine* that he had seen enemy cruisers and several destroyers headed northwest. Then, at 3:30, while he was watching, the German force reversed course and headed southeast. Although the observer had to encode his messages before sending them, he managed to wireless *Engadine* four times over the next fifteen minutes. Three of these messages were received; *Engadine,* observing the ban on ship-to-ship wireless transmission, attempted to pass this news to Beatty and Evan-Thomas by searchlight, but failed. After a thirty-nine-minute flight, a fuel pipe ruptured and Rutland was forced to land. While sitting on the surface waiting to be picked up, the little floatplane was passed by a British light cruiser; from his back seat the observer tried desperately to semaphore the new direction in which the enemy force was steering. Soon, *Engadine* arrived, and at 4:00 p.m. the seaplane was hoisted aboard. This flight was the sum total of the part played by aerial reconnaissance on either side on the first day of Jutland.*

—

The navies of the world's first and second sea powers were now approaching collision. To the east were Hipper's battle cruisers, the modern *Lützow, Derfflinger,* and *Seydlitz,* followed by the older *Moltke* and *Von der Tann.* To the west were Beatty's four giant Cats, *Lion, Princess Royal, Queen Mary,* and *Tiger,* along with the earlier *New Zealand* and *Indefatigable.* Ten miles behind, Evan-Thomas's *Barham, Valiant, Warspite,* and *Malaya* were straining to catch up. Less than seventy miles to the north, 100 ships of the Grand Fleet accelerated their progress south while, fifty miles to the south, Scheer's main fleet, slowed by the presence of Mauve's old predreadnoughts, moved steadily north.

Hipper, aided by the position of the sun, saw his enemy first. With the sun in the west, there, starkly silhouetted against the bright blue horizon, were two columns of large dark gray ships with tripod masts: Beatty's famous battle cruisers. Meanwhile, his own pale gray ships remained indistinct against the hazy, overcast sky and misty horizon to the east. Calmly smoking his cigar, he immediately but erroneously signaled Scheer that the British battle fleet was in sight. A minute later, he correctly identified his enemy and, noting Beatty's alteration to the east, understood that the British admiral meant to cut across his wake and block his homeward path. Recalling his light cruisers from the north at 3:28 p.m., Hipper reversed onto a southerly course, slowing to 18 knots to allow the smaller ships to catch up. In fact, Hipper's intention in swinging around had a larger purpose than simply to prevent himself being cut off from his base. He meant to engage the British battle cruisers in a running fight, all the while drawing them down onto the High Seas Fleet coming up from the south. Thus, at this moment, both admirals keenly sought action: Beatty, who believed that he had caught Hipper alone and that his own six battle cruisers and four fast battleships powerfully outnumbered his enemy, meant at last to destroy this old antagonist. Hipper, believing that Beatty was alone, meant to tempt him into a running engagement, all the while drawing him down into the jaws of the High Seas

*By late morning, the wind along the German coast had moderated sufficiently to allow airships to take off, and five zeppelins had gone up. Once airborne, however, they discovered that misty weather and low cloud cover over the North Sea precluded observation. They spotted neither of the two fleets and late in the afternoon, all zeppelins were recalled.

Fleet coming up from the south. In the interim, as Beatty's 13.5-inch guns outranged Hipper's 12-inch and 11-inch, the German admiral knew that he must close the range as quickly as possible. Beatty, charging down at maximum speed with what he was certain was superior strength, seemed happy to oblige and the two lines, both steaming south at full speed, were gradually converging. In most histories of the Battle of Jutland, what happened during the next fifty-five minutes—3:45 to 4:40—is known as the Run to the South.

—

Lieutenant W. S. Chalmers on the bridge of *Lion* remembered that "it was one of those typical North Sea summer days with a thin white mist varying in intensity and having too much humidity for the sun to break up." As the two forces drew nearer, officers on both sides admired one another. In the gunnery control tower of *Derfflinger,* Georg von Hase, the ship's gunnery officer, adjusted his optical instruments to maximum power: "Suddenly my periscope revealed some big ships. Black monsters. Six tall, broad-beamed giants steaming in two columns. Even at this great distance, they looked powerful, massive. . . . How menacing they appeared, magnified fifteen times. I could now recognize them as the six most modern enemy battle cruisers. Six battle cruisers were opposed to our five. It was a stimulating, majestic spectacle as the dark grey giants approached like fate itself." To the British, their enemies revealed themselves gradually: first smoke, then masts and funnels and upper works, then stern waves, white and high; finally large, light gray hulls, pale against the gray eastern sky. On board *Tiger,* an officer remembered "how splendid the enemy battle cruisers looked . . . their last ship in particular showing up wonderfully."

At 3:45, 16,500 yards from the enemy, Beatty swung his ships into a line of battle. *Lion,* at 26 knots, was in the lead, followed at 500-yard intervals by *Princess Royal, Queen Mary, Tiger, New Zealand,* and *Indefatigable.* The four massive battleships, *Barham, Valiant, Warspite,* and *Malaya,* coming up at maximum speed, were closing the gap, down from ten to seven miles. Beatty now was certain that his own particular adversaries were going to be brought to action. His four Cats were several knots faster than Hipper's fastest ships; the two older British battle cruisers and the four *Queen Elizabeth*s—all capable of 25 knots—could almost match the older Germans. This day would be no repetition of the Dogger Bank, when Hipper began his race for home with a long head start. This time, ten fast British dreadnoughts, racing for a position to cut off Hipper from his base, could not fail to annihilate the five isolated Germans.

And yet, at that moment and afterward, even Beatty's friends wondered why he took so long to begin his work. The 13.5-inch guns of his Cats outranged Hipper's 12-inch and 11-inch guns by several thousand yards and he could have opened fire long before Hipper was able to reply. By waiting until the range had closed, Beatty denied himself a number of opening, unopposed, and possibly significant salvos. Ultimately, it was not Beatty, but his admirer Ernle Chatfield, *Lion*'s captain, who gave the order to open fire. "The enemy battle cruisers were rapidly closing us," Chatfield wrote later. "The range receiver on the bridge showed twenty thousand yards. I was on the compass platform. . . . Beatty . . . was on his own bridge below me with his staff. . . . I wanted him to come on the compass platform and sent a message . . . [to him] that the range was closing rapidly and that we ought almost at once to be opening fire. . . . But I could get no reply; the Vice Admiral was engaged in an important message to the Commander-in-Chief. Eighteen thousand yards. I told Longhurst [*Lion*'s gunnery officer] to be ready to open fire immediately. The turrets were already loaded and trained on the leading enemy ship, *Lützow.* At 3.45 p.m., the range was sixteen thousand yards. I could wait no longer and told Longhurst to open fire. At the same time the enemy did so. The firing of the ship's main armament of 13.5-inch guns was by double salvos of four guns each. . . . [Then] Beatty came on the compass platform."

Meanwhile, on the admiral's bridge of *Lützow,* Hipper stood and watched, his cigar clamped between his teeth. Commander Erich Raeder, his Chief of Staff, remembered "a moment of supreme tension as the great turrets rotated and the gray gun muzzles elevated." In their turrets and control towers, the German range takers and gun layers watched the approaching British ships, sharp and clear against the sun. "The six ships, which had been proceeding in two columns, formed a single line ahead," said Hase on *Derfflinger.* "Like a herd of prehistoric monsters, they closed on one another with slow movements, specter-like, irresistible." Hase identified *Derfflinger*'s target as the *Princess Royal,* but he could not open fire without a signal from the flagship. "At last, there was a dull roar. . . . The *Lützow* is firing her first salvo and immediately the signal 'Open fire' is hoisted. In the same second, I shout 'Salvos: Fire!' and the thunder of our first salvo crashes out."

The opposing battle cruiser squadrons, traveling on parallel southeastern courses, opened fire almost simultaneously. The Germans' firing, coming in continuous ripples down their line, won immediate admiration from their enemies. The first salvos, bunched in groups of four projectiles, were only about 200 yards short. The next straddled *Tiger,* one shot short, two hits and one over, the two hits bursting with a tremendous crash of tearing metal. The German shooting was this good despite the fact, as Hase recorded, that his gunners had to contend with "dense masses of smoke accumulated around the muzzles of the guns, growing into clouds as high as houses which stood for a second in front of us like an impenetrable wall until they were driven away by the wind." Eight miles away, Beatty's ships also were driving through continuous curtains of spray and smoke that made it difficult for their gunnery personnel to see the enemy at all, let alone get his range. Because of this, for the first ten minutes every British shell sailed far over the German line, some even as much as three miles beyond. In addition, mistaken assignments added to British difficulties. *Queen Mary* and *Tiger* had missed Beatty's signal for the distribution of fire and were shooting at the wrong ships. Correctly, *Lion* and *Princess Royal* were engaging *Lützow,* but *Queen Mary,* third in line, instead of aiming at *Derfflinger,* which was second in Hipper's line, fired at *Seydlitz,* third in the German line. The result was that for ten minutes nobody troubled *Derfflinger,* a crack gunnery ship, which steamed happily along, her guns thundering salvos every twenty seconds as if she were at target practice. Meanwhile, *Tiger* and *New Zealand* both fired at *Moltke,* while at the rear of the two lines, *Indefatigable* and *Von der Tann,* the two oldest, smallest, and slowest of the battle cruisers, carried on a private duel, undisturbed.

The Germans, who had the advantage of better light, also possessed better range finders and gun sights. "The Zeiss lenses of our periscopes were excellent," Hase reported. "At the longest distances, I could make out all details of the enemy ships; for instance, movements of turrets and individual guns which were lowered almost to the horizontal for loading." Hipper's ships found the range quickly. Four minutes after opening fire, *Lützow* hit *Lion* twice, while *Derfflinger* placed three 12-inch shells on *Princess Royal. Tiger* was hit once by *Moltke,* which then went to rapid fire and hit her again, then twice more. At the rear of the line, *Von der Tann* hammered *Indefatigable.* No one followed this more closely than Hipper on *Lützow*'s bridge. "His unruffled calm communicated itself . . . to all those on the bridge," said one of his officers. "Work was carried on exactly as it had been in peacetime maneuvers." Another officer reported that Hipper "could not be separated from the telescope. There was nothing which escaped him, nothing he forgot, and he personally issued orders even on matters of detail. Just before fire opened, the First Staff Officer and the Gunnery Officer were discussing the unfavorable fire distribution. Hipper intervened with the remark that this was *his* business. No one need worry about it." Subsequently, he interrupted a conversation about the advisability of warning the squadron about the presence of British destroyers. "Hipper left his telescope for a second or two, turned around and said somewhat sharply, 'I've seen everything, gentlemen, and will give the order when the signal is to be given.' "

War at sea was Franz Hipper's "business," and "unruffled calm" his natural state, but for a sixteen-year-old *Malaya* midshipman, at sea for only four months and now in his ship's torpedo control tower, the battle was a unique and terrible experience. A turret only a few feet away began to fire, and "from this time on, my thoughts were really more like a nightmare than the thoughts of a wide-awake human being. I don't think I felt fright, simply because what was going on around me was so unfamiliar that my brain was incapable of grasping it. Even now I can only think of the beginning of the action as through a dim haze. I remember seeing the enemy lines on the horizon with red specks coming out of them, which I tried to realize were the cause of projectiles landing around us, continually covering us with spray, but the fact refused to sink into my brain." The midshipman could see the enemy, but, with a northwesterly wind blowing their own funnel and gun smoke back into their eyes, the range finders in the British ships were having a difficult time. To add to this, two flotillas of British destroyers, which had been astern, were racing to get into their proper place ahead of the large ships, and their funnel smoke added to the murk. Nevertheless, the 13.5-inch shells of Beatty's Cats began to creep closer to their targets. "With each salvo fired by the enemy," said Hase of *Derfflinger,* "I was able to see distinctly four or five shells coming through the air. They looked like elongated black spots. Gradually, they grew bigger and then—crash—they were here! They exploded on striking the water or the ship with a terrific roar. Each salvo fired by the enemy raised colossal splashes. Some of these columns of water were of a poisonous yellow-green tinge . . . these would be lyddite shells. The columns stood up for five to ten seconds before they completely collapsed."* Eventually, at 3:55 p.m., when the range was down to 13,000 yards, *Queen Mary* scored two hits on *Seydlitz,* putting one of the waist 11-inch gun turrets permanently out of action. Four minutes later, *Lion* hit *Lützow.* Then *Derfflinger* was hit, the shell piercing a door with a glass window behind which a petty officer was standing and watching the battle. "His curiosity was severely punished," observed Hase, "the shot severing his head clean from his body."

At 4:00 p.m., *Lion* suffered a blow that might have killed her. A 12-inch shell from *Lützow* hit the British flagship on its amidships Q turret between the two 13.5-inch guns, penetrated the 11-inch armor, burst inside, and blew off the front half of the armored roof. Most of the gun-house crew was killed instantly, and both legs of the turret captain, Major Francis J. W. Harvey of the Royal Marines, were crushed. Dying, but realizing the great danger to the ship, Harvey dragged himself to the voice pipe and called down to his crew below to close the magazine doors and flood the magazine. Then he sent the only walking survivor in the gun house, a marine sergeant, to the bridge to report that the turret was out of action. Worse was to happen. The shell explosion had jarred open the breech of the elevated left-side 13.5-inch gun and the already loaded powder charge in its silk bag slid back out of the gun breech and burst open on the floor. The scattered powder instantly ignited, sending a sheet of white flame rushing down the hoist toward the magazine. Seventy officers and men were incinerated, but because the magazine doors had been closed, the flash reversed itself and vomited out through the opened turret top. The ship was saved and Harvey won a posthumous Victoria Cross.

*Lyddite is an explosive made largely of picric acid, which is yellow.

A few minutes later, the dazed, blood-stained marine sergeant in burned clothing appeared on the bridge to tell the first officer he met, "Q turret has gone, sir. All the crew were killed and we have flooded the magazines." Surprised, the officer looked back. "No further confirmation was necessary: the armored roof of Q turret had been folded back like an open sardine tin; thick yellow smoke was rolling up in clouds from the gaping hole, and the guns were cocked up in the air awkwardly. All this had happened within a few yards of where Beatty was standing and none of us on the bridge had heard the detonation."

Five minutes later, at the rear of Beatty's line, another British battle cruiser was badly hit and this time it brought catastrophe. *Von der Tann* had already fired forty-eight 11-inch shells at *Indefatigable.* Then she fired two more and the projectiles struck the British battle cruiser's after superstructure. In *New Zealand,* just ahead, the navigating officer looked back at *Indefatigable*.

> We were altering course to port at the time and it seemed as if her steering was damaged as she did not follow around in our wake but held on until she was about five hundred yards on our starboard quarter. While we were still looking at her, she was hit again by two shells, one on the forecastle and one on the fore turret. Both shells appeared to explode on impact. There was an interval of about thirty seconds and then the ship completely blew up. The main explosion started with sheets of flame, followed immediately by a dense dark smoke cloud which obscured the ship from view. All sorts of stuff was blown into the air, a fifty foot picket boat being blown up about two hundred feet, apparently intact though upside down.

Stricken, with smoke pouring from her shattered hull, *Indefatigable* rolled slowly onto her side, all the while driving through the water. Then the huge vessel turned completely over and plunged, taking with her 1,017 officers and men. Only two seamen survived, both shell-shocked and delirious when they were pulled from the sea hours later by a German destroyer. Curiously, because of the din of battle and because the *Indefatigable* was last in line, many in Beatty's squadron were unaware of what had happened. From *Lion*'s bridge, an officer looked back to admire the following ships "with their huge bow waves and flashing broadsides. Astern of the rear ship was a colossal pall of grey smoke. I gazed in amazement and at the same time realised that there were only five battle cruisers in our line. Where was the sixth? The unpleasant truth dawned on me that the cloud of smoke was all that remained of the *Indefatigable*." But the loss did not long affect the British squadron. "It happened so suddenly," said a *New Zealand* officer, "that, almost before we realized she had gone, our attention was entirely absorbed in the fierce battle now progressing. The noise of our own salvos and the shriek of enemy shells falling over or short and throwing up great sheets of spray, left one with little time to think of anything except the work at hand."

As the five remaining British battle cruisers steamed on through towering waterspouts, *Lion* took five more hits, one of which destroyed her main wireless transmitter. Beatty thereafter was able to communicate by wireless with his own ships and with Jellicoe only by passing his messages by flag or searchlight to the ship astern, *Princess Royal,* which then would relay them. Needing time to deal with the problems afflicting his squadron, Beatty eased his course to starboard, opening the range to 18,000 yards. His guns fell silent.

During this short lull, the cast in the drama changed. Since the battle began, Evan-Thomas had been pressing to catch up with Beatty, signaling his battleships that he wanted them to steam at 24½ knots. He was still eight miles behind the battle cruisers, but, as the Germans had only been making 18 to 20 knots, the superdreadnoughts were coming closer. The Germans saw him coming: "Behind the [British] battle cruiser line appeared four big ships," said Hase. "We soon identified these as of the *Queen Elizabeth* class. There had been much talk in our fleet of these ships. They carried a colossal armament of eight 15-inch guns, 28,000 tons displacement and a speed of twenty-five knots. They fired a shell more than twice as heavy as ours. They engaged at portentous ranges." Now, at 4:00 p.m., these mammoth 15-inch guns were coming within range of the rear ships of Hipper's line. Visibility remained a problem: "Although out in the open sea there was maximum visibility and a bright sun shone down warmly on a sea smooth as a pond, the eastern horizon was shrouded in sea mist and even with the aid of a telescope no movement was discernible," said a *Warspite* midshipman in the spotting top. Minutes later, two ships appeared through the haze, *Von der Tann* and *Moltke,* 19,000 yards away. It was enough to begin. The 5th Battle Squadron, meticulously schooled by Jellicoe at Scapa Flow, was one of the most accurate shooting squadrons in the Grand Fleet. After firing a few spotting rounds from the forward turrets of *Barham, Valiant,* and *Warspite,* Evan-Thomas turned 45 degrees to starboard, paralleling Hipper's course. His gun turrets swung around to port, and at 4:10 p.m., after a few ranging shots, salvos of 15-inch shells thundered down on the two German battle cruisers, landing in the water so near their targets that the German hulls "quivered and reverberated." *Von der Tann* was hit almost immediately by 1,920 pounds of steel and explosive, the shell ripping through her underwater armor, permitting 600 tons of seawater to flood into her after compartments. Then it was *Moltke*'s turn as one of these tremendous shells pierced her side armor, exploding in a coal bunker, igniting coal dust, and wrecking a 5.9-inch gun. A minute later, all four British battleships were within range. *Barham* and *Valiant* fired at *Moltke; Warspite,* adding her fire to *New Zealand*'s, shifted to

Von der Tann, joined quickly by *Malaya.* To escape this dreadful bombardment, these two rearmost German battle cruisers began to zigzag, adversely affecting their own gunnery.

Meanwhile, despite their injuries, the British battle cruisers were shooting more accurately. At 4:14 p.m., *Lion* landed a salvo on *Lützow;* at 4:17 p.m., *Queen Mary* hit *Seydlitz* again, while *New Zealand* sent a 12-inch shell into *Von der Tann*'s forward turret, putting it out of action with jammed guns and a flooded magazine. Almost simultaneously, a 15-inch shell penetrated *Von der Tann*'s armored deck aft and beat through the barbette of the rear turret, putting it out of action. Even so, *Von der Tann* hit *New Zealand* again, and *Moltke* struck back at *Tiger.* Fierce though this part of the battle was, the struggle at the head of the line was even more ferocious and punishing. Here, *Derfflinger* and *Seydlitz* together were concentrating twenty 12-inch guns on *Queen Mary.* In *Derfflinger*'s gunnery-control tower, Hase's eyes were glued on this target:

> The *Queen Mary* was firing less rapidly than we were but usually full salvos. I could see the shells coming and I had to admit that they were shooting superbly. As a rule, all eight shells fell together, but they were almost always over or short. . . . But the poor *Queen Mary* was having a bad time. In addition to *Derfflinger,* she was being engaged by *Seydlitz.* . . . At 4.26 p.m. [she] met her doom. . . . First, a vivid red flame shot up from her forepart. Then came an explosion forward, followed by a much heavier explosion amidships. Black debris flew into the air and immediately afterwards the whole ship blew up with a terrific explosion. A gigantic cloud of smoke rose, the masts collapsed inwards, the smoke cloud hid everything and rose higher and higher. Finally, nothing but a thick, black cloud of smoke remained where the ship had been. At its base, the smoke column covered only a small area, but it widened towards the summit and looked like a monstrous pine tree.

Tiger, only 500 yards astern of *Queen Mary* and moving at 25 knots, had to maneuver abruptly to avoid a collision with the doomed ship. An officer on *Tiger*'s bridge had an intimate view of what happened: "I saw one salvo straddle her. Three shells out of four hit. . . . The next salvo straddled her and two more shells hit her. As they hit, I saw a dull red glow amidships and then the ship seemed to open out like a puffball or one of those toadstool things when one squeezes it. There was another dull red glow forwards and the whole ship seemed to collapse inwards. The funnels and masts fell into the middle, the roofs of the turrets were blown a hundred feet high. *Tiger* put her helm hard-a-starboard and we just cleared the remains of *Queen Mary*'s stern by a few feet."

New Zealand, following *Tiger* at high speed, saw *Tiger* turning to starboard and immediately turned sharply to port to avoid the wreck. From *New Zealand*'s conning tower an officer reported:

> We disappeared in this dense mass of smoke and *Tiger* and ourselves passed one on either side of *Queen Mary.* We passed her about fifty yards on our port beam by which time the smoke had blown clear, revealing the stern . . . afloat, and the propellers still revolving, but the forward part had already gone under. . . . Men were crawling out of the top of the after turret and up the after hatchway. When we were abreast and only a hundred and fifty yards away, this after portion rolled over and, as it did so, blew up. The moist noticeable thing was the masses and masses of paper which were blown into the air. . . . Great masses of iron were thrown into the air and things were falling into the sea around us. Up in the air two hundred feet high [was] a boat which may have been a dinghy or a pinnace still intact but upside down. . . . Before we had passed, the *Queen Mary* had completely disappeared. This second disaster was rather stunning, but the only signal coming from the flagship was, "Battle cruisers alter course two points to port"—that is, towards the enemy.*

For those watching from *Lion*'s bridge, the horrors seemed to continue. Immediately after *Queen Mary* blew up, *Princess Royal* was straddled and disappeared into a forest of towering waterspouts. A *Lion* signalman stared in dismay and reported, "*Princess Royal* blown up, sir." Beatty, turning to Chatfield, shook his head and said, "There seems to be something wrong with our bloody ships today." Then *Princess Royal* reappeared intact from behind the massive curtains of smoke and spray.

Beatty, who had just lost a 26,000-ton battle cruiser and an 18,500-ton battle cruiser along with their crews totaling more than 2,000 men, realized that he needed help. Twelve British destroyers, led by Captain Barry Bingham in *Nestor,* had reached a point to deliver a torpedo attack on Hipper's battle cruisers, and at 4:15 p.m., Beatty signaled them to go forward. The British destroyers charged at 34 knots. From *Lützow*'s bridge, Hipper watched the attack develop; he countered by sending his light cruiser *Regensburg* with fifteen destroyers dashing out at 30 knots to meet Bingham. On both sides, the massed torpedo attacks on the enemy's capital ships quickly dissolved into numerous individual small ship battles. Churning white foam, their signal flags whipping frantically in the wind, their 4-inch guns banging incessantly, the little ships lunged at one another in the no-

*Neither the charts nor the detailed record of *Official Naval Despatches* published after Jutland include this command or alteration of course. Nevertheless, it has become a part of the Beatty legend.

man's-land between the lines of big ships. During this melee, each side launched torpedoes, but the British battle cruisers and battleships managed to avoid all eighteen torpedoes fired by the German destroyers and, by turning away, Hipper's big ships successfully evaded nineteen of the twenty torpedoes launched by the British. Somehow, one British torpedo found *Seydlitz,* exploding on her port side near the forward turret and tearing a hole forty feet long and thirteen feet wide in her side plating. Although she took in hundreds of tons of water and listed to port, the splendidly constructed German battle cruiser was able to maintain speed and hold her place in line. The tumult brought casualties to the destroyers on both sides: *Nestor* and *Nomad,* each hit in a boiler, halted under clouds of escaping steam, and later both sank. The German destroyers *V-27* and *V-29* were also sunk. At 4:43 p.m., Beatty terminated the encounter by recalling his destroyers. As the British destroyers turned back, their captains saw something incredible: Beatty and his battle cruisers were giving up their pursuit of Hipper to the southeast. They were reversing course and heading north. Apparently, Beatty was running away.

—

From his damaged flagship, Beatty now led only four battle cruisers. Exposed on *Lion*'s open compass platform, soaked by spray while shrapnel screamed around him, he seemed to his staff a heroic figure. Nevertheless, in the Run to the South, this first phase of the Battle of Jutland, Beatty was clearly the loser and Hipper the victor. The German admiral, commanding an inferior force, had sunk two British battle cruisers and two British destroyers at a cost of only two German destroyers. Hipper's position remained difficult—he had begun with five heavy ships against ten; now it was five against eight—but the German plan was succeeding and every ninety seconds brought his unsuspecting enemies one mile closer to the sixteen dreadnoughts of the High Seas Fleet. When the battle began at 3:48 p.m., Hipper and Scheer had been forty-seven miles apart; now, an hour later, Hipper at last saw in the distance ahead of him the welcome sight of Scheer's long, pale gray column. Glad as he was, Hipper now anticipated a larger victory. Beatty, hungry for battle, had impatiently taken Hipper's lure and done what the German admirals had hoped he would do: charge impetuously into a German trap. Smoothly, Franz Hipper swung his battle cruisers around 180 degrees and took up his normal battle position at the head of the northbound High Seas Fleet.

—

During the fifty-five-minute Run to the South, Beatty's three light cruiser squadrons—twelve vessels in all—which had been left behind by the admiral's turn to the southeast, had been straining to catch up and take their proper scouting positions ahead of *Lion.* In the new alignment, the veteran Commodore William Goodenough understood exactly where his place should be. "Those of us who had been in action with Sir David Beatty before knew that his general principle was to get between the enemy and his base," said Goodenough. "I therefore had no difficulty in shaping a course to the southeast." By 4:35 p.m., Goodenough's 2nd Light Cruiser Squadron was the most southerly of the three squadrons. Then, from his flagship *Southampton,* the commodore sighted farther to the southeast something no British seaman had ever seen before: the entire High Seas Fleet at sea, dozens of light gray ships, large and small, steaming against a background of gray water and gray sky, all belching black smoke and steaming in his direction.

"We saw ahead of us first smoke, then masts, then ships . . . sixteen battleships with destroyers around them on each bow," Goodenough continued. "We hung on for a few moments to make sure before confirming the message. Then my commander, efficient and cool, said, 'If you're going to make that signal, you'd better make it now, sir. You may never make another.' " Goodenough saw the reasoning and at 4:38, he flashed an electrifying wireless signal to Beatty and Jellicoe: "URGENT. PRIORITY. Have sighted enemy battle fleet, bearing approximately southeast." For Beatty, rushing toward this mighty force, and for Jellicoe pacing the bridge of *Iron Duke* fifty miles away, this signal instantly changed their perceptions of the situation. It made twaddle of the Admiralty's noon signal that the *Friedrich der Grosse* was anchored in the Jade. Instead, Scheer was here, in the North Sea, 180 miles from the Jade and only a few miles from Beatty. The British battle cruisers, already severely punished and diminished in number by Hipper, were about to face the massed guns of the High Seas Fleet.

Hipper could be pleased: he had splendidly carried out his mission. He had led Beatty's battered and diminished battle cruiser force, along with the lonely 5th Battle Squadron, into the arms of the High Seas Fleet. It seemed a moment of victory for the Imperial Navy, what the German people, the navy, and the kaiser had been awaiting for twenty years. But the real situation was not as Hipper imagined it. Standing on *Lützow*'s compass platform and watching Beatty's wounded flagship lead her remaining sisters into his "trap," the German admiral may have pictured Beatty suddenly dismayed by what was happening. In fact, Beatty had recognized the opportunity the Germans now laid before him. Here was *his* chance: with luck, he could turn and lure the High Seas Fleet into an ambush deadlier than anything the Germans might have prepared for him. Hipper and Scheer, Beatty was certain, had no idea what gigantic force lay over the northern horizon. If he turned north, seeming to flee, he could, with his superior speed, draw ahead. The 5th Battle Squadron, with its stout armor and powerful guns, would follow behind as both additional bait and a sturdy shield, keeping the Germans engaged. And then, in a little over an hour, he would rendezvous with Jellicoe. Scheer would come north confidently expecting to conduct a massacre. And a massacre would occur, but not in the form the German admirals expected.

—

Goodenough had not immediately turned after spotting and reporting the presence of the High Seas Fleet. Instead, wanting to report accurately the number, course, and speed of the enemy ships, he and his four light cruisers continued at 25 knots toward Scheer until they were only 13,000 yards away from the German battleships. Oddly, as the four light cruisers came closer, the Germans did not open fire. The reason was not visibility; Scheer himself later wrote that at 4:30 p.m., "the weather was extremely clear, the sky cloudless, a light breeze and a calm sea." Goodenough was spared because the German battleships could see the four cruisers only bow-on, a view from which one cruiser looks much like another and these ships, the Germans thought, could easily be German. Finally, at 4:48 p.m., satisfied with what he had seen, Goodenough wirelessed another URGENT PRIORITY signal to Beatty and Jellicoe: "Course of enemy's battle fleet is north, single line-ahead. Composition of van is *Kaiser* class. . . . Destroyers on both wings and ahead. Enemy's battle cruisers joining battle fleet from the north." Then, duty performed, Goodenough turned his own ships away, displaying their unmistakably British four-funneled profiles. Ten German battleships immediately opened fire. Twisting and turning between the waterspouts, the British cruisers fled. One officer estimated that forty large shells fell within seventy-five yards of *Southampton:* "I can truthfully say that I thought that each moment would be our last. . . . We seemed to bear a charmed life. . . . How we escaped amazes everyone from the Commodore downwards." In fact, the miracle was the commodore's doing. Asked later how he managed to avoid being hit, Goodenough replied, "Simply by steering straight for the splashes of the last enemy salvo!"—his thought being that, with the German gunners making constant corrections, the next salvo was unlikely to land in the same place as the one just before.

—

Beatty, after receiving Goodenough's first signal reporting the presence of the High Seas Fleet, held on to the southeast for two minutes in order to see for himself the masts of the German battleships twelve miles away. Then at 4:40 p.m., a flag hoist ran up *Lion*'s signal halyard: "Alter course in succession 16 points [180 degrees] to starboard." The flags were hauled down, the flagship's helm went over, and *Lion,* followed in turn by *Princess Royal, Tiger,* and *New Zealand,* drew a massive curve on the surface of the sea, straightening out on a reverse course, now to the northwest. By turning in succession, each on the same point, Beatty risked bringing all four of his ships one by one under the concentrated fire of the oncoming enemy battle fleet. All managed without harm, although *New Zealand,* at the tail of Beatty's line, did so by intelligently turning ahead of time on her own, before the German battleships came within range. Beatty's turrets trained around from port to starboard, and a few minutes later the duel with Hipper resumed on an opposite course, giving this phase of the battle the name of the Run to the North. Beatty was fortunate that, despite the momentum of his charge to the south, the two-minute delay to see for himself, and then his choice of a turn in succession, his squadron had pivoted just beyond the range of the leading battleships of the High Seas Fleet, Admiral Paul Behncke's elite *Königs*. Still the German dreadnoughts, now only 20,000 yards away, were steaming hard, their guns at maximum elevation, awaiting the order to fire.

—

When, at 4:40 p.m., *Lion* hoisted the flag signal for a turn to the north, Evan-Thomas on *Barham,* seven miles astern of the flagship and already firing at the rear ships in Hipper's line, missed or was once again unable to read Beatty's flags. Neither *Lion* nor *Tiger* passed the signal to *Barham* by searchlight, so the four superdreadnoughts continued steaming on course southeast, straight toward Scheer. The error or difficulty on *Barham*'s bridge was compounded by an error on *Lion*'s. Once the signal flag commanding a turn was hauled down at 4:41 p.m. and *Lion* actually began to turn, no one on the flagship's bridge noticed that the 5th Battle Squadron continued racing south. It was not until 4:48, as the southbound battleships actually passed the northbound battle cruisers a mile and a half apart on an opposite course—and with Beatty's squadron traveling at 26 knots and Evan-Thomas's at 24, they charged by each other at a combined closing speed of 60 miles an hour—that Beatty saw and understood what had happened and repeated his turn-in-succession signal—again by flag hoist—to Evan-Thomas. Then the *Lion*'s signal staff—Ralph Seymour was the officer responsible—made another, more damaging error. The flags dictating that the 5th Battle Squadron turn were hoisted at 4:48. Because Seymour forgot or was distracted, they were not hauled down until 4:54. During this six minutes while Evan-Thomas awaited his superior's command, his four dreadnoughts continued steaming toward the High Seas Fleet. By the time Seymour finally hauled down the flags, Evan-Thomas was 4,000 yards closer to Scheer, within gun range of the leading dreadnoughts of the German battle line. *Warspite*'s executive officer described the sequence:

> I suddenly saw our battle cruisers coming close by about half a mile away, going in the opposite direction and I realized that they had turned back. I noticed that *Queen Mary* and *Indefatigable* were . . . [missing] but never realized that they had been sunk. . . . "X" turret of *Lion* was askew and trained towards us [that is, away from the enemy], the guns

> at full elevation, several hits showing on her port side. . . . Then we turned . . . [180 degrees] and trained the turret around full speed. Very soon after the turn, I saw on the starboard quarter the whole of the High Seas Fleet—masts, funnels and an endless ripple of orange flashes all down the line. . . . I felt one or two very heavy shakes but it never occurred to me that we were being hit. . . . I distinctly saw two of our salvos hit the leading German battleship. Sheets of yellow flame went right over her masts and she looked red fore and aft like a burning haystack. I know we hit her hard.

When Beatty's command to turn had finally been given and received, Evan-Thomas in *Barham* led his dreadnoughts around, one after the other. As each turned on the same spot, wheeling in a semicircle 1,000 yards from a fixed point in the water, the onrushing Germans brought a concentrated fire on the British battleships. *Barham* was hit; *Valiant* was luckier and got around without being touched; *Warspite* was hit three times; and *Malaya,* the rear ship, received the concentrated fire of many German battleships. "The turning point was a very hot corner," said one of her turret officers. "It is doubtful if we, the last ship of the line, could have got through without a severe hammering if the captain had not used his initiative and turned the ship early."

After their turn to the north, Beatty's battle cruisers also continued to suffer. Soon after the turn, *Lion* and *Tiger* were hit by *Lützow* and *Seydlitz,* and Beatty steered to port to put off the enemy range finders. *Lion* found herself passing through the wide patch of oil and floating wreckage where *Queen Mary* had gone down forty minutes earlier; it seemed possible that before long she might join her sister on the bottom. Already she had been hit by thirteen heavy shells; now came two more. Nor was *Lion*'s wounding unique: *Tiger* had been hit seventeen times, *Princess Royal* almost as many. Of Beatty's four remaining battle cruisers, only *New Zealand* had escaped relatively unharmed. On the damaged battle cruisers, fires were burning, but because shell fragments had slashed fire hoses, it was difficult to bring water to the flames. Wounded men lay in the twisted wreckage until stretcher parties could pry them free and carry them to dressing stations. There, doctors sawed and stitched. In *Princess Royal,* a surgeon amputating a foot noted that the dim light of oil lanterns made "the securing of arteries particularly difficult." Nevertheless, in all four ships, the engines remained undamaged and, taking advantage of their superior speed, Beatty steered northwest at 24 knots, leaving the battle behind. Once out of range, he reduced speed and for half an hour, during which his battered ships did not fire a shot, his crews attempted to control fires, clear away wreckage, restore turrets, and transform their vessels back into warships. On *Princess Royal,* a midshipman recorded that at 5:15 there was "a lull in the action and people were going out to stretch their legs and get a little fresh air. At 5.25, the flagship signaled 'Prepare to renew the action' and at 5.43 we opened fire again." On one battle cruiser, the resumption of the battle caught the ship's paymaster by surprise. He had come on deck for some fresh air and was standing on the forward superstructure when P turret suddenly opened fire. The blast stripped off his trousers.

Meanwhile, the battle cruisers' withdrawal and time-out had left the 5th Battle Squadron to fight alone against Hipper's five battle cruisers and the four powerful dreadnoughts leading Scheer's 3rd Battle Squadron. This hour—from a few minutes before five o'clock, when the *Queen Elizabeth*s wheeled north three miles in Beatty's wake, until just after six, when they joined the Grand Fleet battle line—was their time of glory. "When we turned," said a turret officer on *Malaya,* "I saw our battle cruisers proceeding north at full speed, already seven or eight thousand yards ahead of us. I then realized that just the four of us of the 5th Battle Squadron would have to entertain the High Seas Fleet—four against perhaps twenty." Steaming at 25 knots, Evan-Thomas distributed the fire of his four ships: *Barham* and *Valiant* were to deal with the five German battle cruisers up ahead, while *Warspite* and *Malaya* took on the four *König*s coming up behind. At the head of the German battle line, Behncke and his four formidable *König*s—*König, Grosser Kurfürst, Kronprinz Wilhelm,* and *Markgraf*—pressed forward to the limit of their stokers' ability to shovel coal. All the while, their total of forty 12-inch guns lashed out. *Barham* was the first to be struck; then she was hit again; then four more times. A heavy shell wrecked her auxiliary wireless office and inflicted casualties on both wireless and medical personnel. One shell burst caused a fire in a 6-inch gun casement; a junior officer fought the fire "until swelling from burns closed his eyes." A shell fragment all but severed the leg of the ship's assistant navigator; his midshipman "did his best to tie a tourniquet, but he was much handicapped owing to the lights going out. The navigator died quickly from loss of blood." "Six, eight, nine salvos a minute" were falling around *Malaya;* between 5:20 and 5:35 p.m., the battleship was hit five times. One 12-inch shell peeled back the roof of her X turret, but inside the gun crews continued to work; another heavy shell pierced the starboard side below the waterline, admitting enough water to give the ship a starboard list. Within half an hour, *Malaya* suffered 100 casualties. "Everything was dark chaos," said one of the officers of a 6-inch gun battery. "Most of the wounded had been taken away, but several of the killed were still there . . . [and] the smell of burnt human flesh remained in the ship for weeks giving everybody a sickly nauseous feeling." In *Warspite,* the chief surgeon ordered burns to be dressed with pre-prepared picric acid gauze. "The effect was agonizing—picric acid only aggravated the burns—and the patients tore off the bandages." Thereafter, the victims lay in "restless agony . . . injections of morphine seemed to have very little effect on them." About this time, a 12-inch shell penetrated into the storage place for fresh meat and hit the armored grating over B boiler room. "On its way through the beef screen, it had carried a whole sheep with it which was wedged into the gratings. At first I thought it was a human casualty," said the ship's executive officer, moving around to inspect damage. A few compartments away, he found real human casualties: "three stokers dead, one having his head blown off and another badly smashed to pieces. Rather a horrible sight, but the burnt ones were far worse."

The human carnage and physical damage to the ships were bad enough, but for Evan-Thomas, his captains, and the crews themselves, worse was possible. The entire High Seas Fleet—Hipper's five battle cruisers and light cruisers, Scheer's sixteen dreadnoughts, six predreadnoughts, and dozens of destroyers—was rushing up behind them and if, at any moment during their 180-degree turn or their subsequent passage north, any one of the four British superdreadnoughts had been disabled, she must have shared the fate of *Blücher* at the Dogger Bank. Only one unlucky shell would have been required. It would not have been necessary to blow up the ship in a single cataclysm, as had happened with *Indefatigable* and *Queen Mary.* A more modest hit damaging the propulsion machinery or steering gear would have sufficed. And then the wounded ship would have been gobbled up. Moreover, should Evan-Thomas have decided at that point not to abandon the victim but instead to turn his squadron back to help, then perhaps all four of his ships would have been lost—although a German dreadnought or two might have been taken to the bottom with them. In any case, Scheer would have won the victory he desired, and a powerful, isolated squadron of the Grand Fleet would have been destroyed.

—

Hit after hit crashed into the four British battleships, but all the while, their thirty-two 15-inch guns roared back. During the Run to the North, Evan-Thomas's four dreadnoughts hit three of Hipper's battle cruisers and three of Behncke's battleships with 1,900-pound shells. *Barham* and *Valiant* scored hits on *Seydlitz, Lützow,* and *Derfflinger,* while *Warspite* and *Malaya* fired at *König, Grosser Kurfürst,* and *Markgraf.* Hits on *Lützow*'s main and reserve wireless stations severed these communication links to the other ships in Hipper's squadron. But, again, it was *Seydlitz* that suffered most. She was stripped of much of her fighting power, battered, listing to port, down by the bow from her torpedo wound; the question now was whether she could survive.

Briefly, at the start of the Run to the North, *Von der Tann* had made herself useful; firing at *Barham,* she had scored one hit, but then she had to give up. Her fore and aft turrets were already out of action and now her starboard waist turret, the only one that would bear on the enemy, gave out as well. The guns had become so hot that they jammed in their slides and would not return to firing positions. Captain Hans Zenker realized that his ship was no longer a fighting unit, but he kept on with Hipper to prevent concentration of enemy fire on the other ships of the squadron. At 5:30 p.m., *Lützow* and *Derfflinger* were hit again, and the fire of the German battle cruisers began to slacken. German gunners now had a setting sun glaring in their eyes, making ranging and spotting difficult.

Nevertheless, to Scheer it looked at this moment as if Beatty and Evan-Thomas were beaten. Hipper already had sunk two British battle cruisers; *Lion,* the enemy flagship, had been streaming smoke from a gaping wound for more than an hour; and Beatty's movement looked very much like flight. If Scheer could severely damage another battle cruiser or one of the *Queen Elizabeths* and then overtake and sink it, the victory he had planned would be won. Thus, Scheer vigorously urged his ships forward. At 5:20 p.m., confident that he faced no more than two isolated British squadrons and believing that a beaten opponent was escaping, he signaled "Give chase" and his whole fleet strained forward in pursuit. The four leading ships—*König, Grosser Kurfürst, Kronprinz Wilhelm,* and *Markgraf*—under Rear Admiral Paul Behncke began to draw ahead as the engine-room staffs strove for more and more speed. The slower dreadnoughts followed as well as they could, while the six predreadnoughts of the 2nd Squadron fell farther and farther astern. The long line of the High Seas Fleet straggled over twenty-five miles of sea. It did no good. Hipper's battle cruisers could not maintain more than 25 knots for any length of time, while Beatty's Cats, with their 28-knot speed, left them behind and drew out of sight.

When Beatty ended his battle cruisers' respite and signaled "Prepare to renew the action," he swung his ships from north to northeast and Hipper saw again in the mist on his port bow the distinct shapes of his old enemies. The German admiral was profoundly frustrated. *Lützow*'s wireless had been destroyed and now, when he wanted to report Beatty's reappearance, he could not; Scheer in *Friedrich der Grosse* was ten miles astern, beyond visual signal distance. The best he could do was send a man up into an exposed position to make wigwag semaphore signals to *Derfflinger* astern, to pass the news along. Meanwhile, Beatty, 14,000 yards away, was relentlessly crossing in front of him, bending back the German van to starboard. Hipper, unwilling to permit Beatty to cross his bow, had no choice but to give ground, swinging his own ships also to starboard, toward the east. This time visibility as well as firepower favored the British. "I had to work against a blinding sunset in the western sky and devastating enemy artillery," Hipper said later. "The sun stood deep and the horizon was hazy and I had to fire directly into the sun. I saw absolutely nothing of the enemy, who was behind a dense cloud of smoke—the gunnery officers could find no target although we made a superb one ourselves. There was nothing else to do but take the ships out of the battle for a while." As Hipper continually gave more ground, turning farther to the east, the whole of the German fleet now stretched out behind him in a vast, shallow curve. In the rear, more than twenty miles behind, Mauve's old predreadnoughts still steamed northwest; in the van, Hipper in *Lützow,* six miles in advance of *König,* kept swinging east as Beatty relentlessly bore down on his van.

The second round of the battle—the Run to the North—came to a close around 5:45 p.m., when one of Beatty's lookouts and then Beatty himself caught sight of the advance guard of the Grand Fleet in the distant form of the armored cruiser *Black Prince* operating on the far right wing—the southwestern edge—of Jellicoe's forward cruiser screen. Now Beatty knew that Jellicoe was close over the horizon; he knew also that Scheer, straining to catch him, was unaware of this peril. Possessing this knowledge, Beatty grimly altered course again to starboard, pressing even more heavily down on Hipper in order to deflect him from seeing the oncoming threat.

By now, the deteriorating weather had begun to exercise a dominant influence on the battle. Ironically, because of the weather, Hipper, whose mission was to scout and warn the High Seas Fleet of peril ahead, learned the next piece of dreadful news—the worst that either German admiral would hear all day—after Scheer had heard it. The smoke pouring out of funnels and gun barrels, mixing with the blowing wet mist, formed a heavy surface cloud, which moved across the battlefield creating patches of dense, sometimes nearly impenetrable haze. Hipper, steering east, was in one of these patches and therefore knew nothing of any hostile ships other than Beatty's four battle cruisers and Evan-Thomas's four superdreadnoughts. For the moment, as he swung to starboard, he and his own battle cruisers were hidden from Beatty. Three miles ahead of him to the east were Bödicker's four light cruisers; at 5:50 p.m., Hipper received a signal that they were in action with a single enemy cruiser. Five minutes later, Bödicker gave Hipper a shock: his light cruisers, he reported, now were in action with a group of British dreadnoughts to the east. Dreadnoughts? To the east? This could not be Beatty or Evan-Thomas. This was somebody else.

Moments later on *König*'s bridge, Rear Admiral Behncke, at the head of the German battleship line, suffered a shock greater than Hipper's. At 5:50 p.m., *König* and her sisters, still believing that they were in pursuit of the fleeing Beatty, raced into a large patch of thick mist. At 5:59 p.m., they emerged from it to behold a terrible sight: the Grand Fleet spread before them across the northern horizon. Twenty-four British dreadnoughts and a host of cruisers and destroyers were 16,000 yards away, racing toward them at 20 knots.

CHAPTER 32

Jutland: Jellicoe vs. Scheer

For Jellicoe, as for Scheer, the appearance of the enemy battle fleet in this part of the North Sea was a surprise. That morning, the Admiralty had advised the British Commander-in-Chief that Admiral Scheer's flagship remained anchored in the Jade. Therefore, when *Galatea*'s first contact report came in at 2:20 p.m., announcing that German ships had been sighted sixty-five miles to the south, Jellicoe supposed that there might be a skirmish brewing between opposing light cruisers and destroyers. Of course, if Beatty could come up and catch them, he would make quick work of these unlucky Germans. And if Hipper was out, Beatty, with a two-to-one advantage—six battle cruisers and four *Queen Elizabeth*s to Hipper's five battle cruisers—should manage nicely. For the Grand Fleet, however, the day probably would drag on as part of another routine, uneventful sweep. At two o'clock, most captains in the battle fleet, sharing their admiral's gloomy assessment, began sending their men to tea.

Then, contrary indications began to appear. At 2:28 p.m., *St. Vincent* reported to *Iron Duke* that she was picking up strong, nearby wireless signals from ships on the wavelength used by the High Seas Fleet. At 2:35 p.m., as Beatty was turning his battle cruisers toward Hipper and leaving Evan-Thomas behind, Jellicoe signaled the battle fleet to raise steam for full speed. Zigzagging ceased. At 2:39, *Galatea* was back, reporting a "large amount of smoke as though from a fleet." And at 2:51, another *Galatea* message arrived: "Smoke seems to be seven vessels besides destroyers and cruisers." Then *St. Vincent* signaled that she had picked up more wireless intercepts; Jellicoe increased battle fleet speed to 18 knots. At 3:00 p.m., the Commander-in-Chief ordered the Grand Fleet to prepare for action, and officers and men put down their tea cups and mugs. On *Collingwood,* Prince Albert, the future

King George VI, ill following an excessively convivial visit with friends on the battle cruiser *Invincible* two nights before, rose from his sickbed and went to his post in A turret. A midshipman in *Neptune*'s foretop noticed that "several ships were flying, instead of their customary one White Ensign, three or four ensigns from various parts of the rigging. . . . In about ten minutes the air seemed to be thick with white ensigns, large and small, silk and bunting, hoisted wherever halyards could be found." In an independent mode, the light cruiser *Blanche* flew four Union Jacks, one from each funnel.

At 3:40 p.m., Beatty reported to Jellicoe that he had sighted five German battle cruisers and many destroyers. Five minutes later, he declared that the enemy was running southeast toward home. This was followed at 3:55 p.m. by a third Beatty signal: "Am engaging enemy." Now Jellicoe knew that, forty or fifty miles to the south, Beatty and Hipper were fighting on a course that carried them directly away from him at speeds beyond the ability of his slower battleships to overtake. There was little he could do with the battle fleet except to increase speed to its maximum of 20 knots. But there was one way he might help Beatty: by sending him Hood, whose three *Invincible*s, already twenty-five miles ahead of the battle fleet, were capable of 25 knots. At 4:05 p.m., the Commander-in-Chief signaled Hood: "Proceed immediately to support Battle Cruiser Force."

Invincible, Inflexible, and *Indomitable* of Rear Admiral Horace Hood's 3rd Battle Cruiser Squadron were Britain's first battle cruisers, the eldest children of Jacky Fisher's revolution in warship design. All had performed important service: *Invincible* in the Battle of the Bight and at the Falklands; *Inflexible* and *Indomitable* had pursued *Goeben* across the Mediterranean; *Inflexible* had gone on to the Falklands and afterward returned to the Dardanelles, where she had been heavily damaged by a Turkish mine; *Indomitable* was with Beatty at the Scarborough Raid and the Dogger Bank. Now, because of the temporary switch in assignments with the five *Queen Elizabeth*s, the three old battle cruisers were with Jellicoe rather than with Beatty at Jutland. Hood's force was screened by the newly commissioned light cruisers *Chester* and *Canterbury,* and by four destroyers, *Shark, Acasta, Ophelia,* and *Christopher.*

When Beatty reported that Hipper, once sighted, had turned and bolted back to the southeast—thus beginning the Run to the South—Jellicoe signaled Hood to hurry to Beatty's support. The *Invincible*s belched black smoke and dashed away, but locating the fight turned out to be difficult; ninety minutes later, Hood was still looking. At 5:30 p.m., however, the *Invincible*s had reached a point east of the German battle cruisers, which were beginning their turn to the east. Five miles ahead of Hipper were the four light cruisers of Bödicker's 2nd Scouting Group, *Frankfurt, Wiesbaden, Pillau,* and *Elbing.* At 5:35 p.m., one British and several German ships caught sight of one another. To both sides, the dim shapes were unclear in the haze; the Germans were the first to make the correct identification. The British ship, steaming six miles west of *Invincible*'s starboard beam, was the light cruiser *Chester,* in commission less than a month and having had little opportunity for gunnery practice. Nevertheless, when her lookouts saw smoke to the west, her captain turned to investigate. Because, in the haze, Bödicker's light cruisers resembled the ships of the British 1st Light Cruiser Squadron, *Chester* came closer to take a better look. To encourage the deception, one of the German ships flashed a British identification signal, tempting *Chester* to come still closer. She was 6,000 yards away and had just recognized the three-funnel ships as hostile when the four German cruisers simultaneously opened fire. A storm of shells swept over *Chester* and within five minutes she was hit seventeen times. Her gun crews and bridge and signals personnel were ravaged, her range finder and its crew were blown overboard, all voice-pipe and electrical communications were smashed, and three of her four 6-inch guns were destroyed. But her engines remained intact and, when, a moment later, her assailants suddenly found the tables turned and themselves in terrible danger, *Chester* was able to slip away to the north.

Hood, not far away, saw the orange flashes illuminating the murk and turned toward them. He recognized *Chester* surrounded by shell splashes and then he saw the shadowy outlines of her assailants. At 25 knots, his three battle cruisers raced out of the mist, steering between *Chester* and her pursuers. Heavy battle cruiser guns opened fire at close range, catching Bödicker's surprised light cruisers in a blizzard of 12-inch shells. For *Invincible,* these were the first shells fired at an enemy since the Falklands; for *Inflexible,* since the Dardanelles. These totally unexpected main battery salvos sent the German light cruisers flying, screaming to Hipper by wireless that they were "under fire from enemy battleships." Within a few minutes, the Germans had vanished. *Elbing* escaped unhurt, but *Frankfurt* and *Pillau* had been hit and *Wiesbaden* was fatally wounded. A 12-inch shell from *Invincible* had burst in her engine room, piercing main steam pipes and putting both engines out of action. The crippled ship stopped and lay drifting in "a great cloud of steam and smoke."

To rescue the German light cruisers, Hipper sent *Regensburg* and thirty-one destroyers to charge the *Invincible*s, but before most could launch their torpedoes, they were met by a countercharge from Hood's second light cruiser, *Canterbury,* and four British destroyers. In a free-swinging brawl at close quarters, the Germans somehow got the impression that many more British ships were present than was the fact. As a result, the Germans fired only twelve torpedoes, after which the thirty-one destroyers turned back. In this action, *Shark* was hit and lay immobile in the water. *Acasta* came up and her captain asked *Shark*'s captain, Commander Loftus Jones, how he could help. Loftus Jones sent him away, saying, "Look after yourself and don't get sunk over us." *Acasta* turned and followed in *Inflexible*'s wake as she steamed north into the haze. With *Shark* sinking and many in her crew killed or wounded, Loftus Jones took a place at one gun; as he did so, "a shell took off his right leg above the knee." German destroyers were approaching and he gave the order to abandon ship. His men got him overboard onto a raft where he died just as German torpedoes were sending *Shark* to the bottom. Only six of *Shark*'s crew survived, rescued that night by a Danish steamer. Posthumously, Loftus Jones was awarded the Victoria Cross.

—

After sending Hood to join Beatty, Jellicoe received no news for thirty minutes—this was the period of Beatty's Run to the South. The Commander-in-Chief was given no details of the battle cruiser action and he learned of the loss of *Indefatigable* and *Queen Mary* only the following day. At 4:17 p.m., he asked Evan-Thomas whether the 5th Battle Squadron remained in company with Beatty. The reply was ambiguous: "Yes, I am engaging enemy." At 4:38 p.m., however, an "URGENT. PRIORITY" message came in from Goodenough in *Southampton:* "Have sighted enemy battle fleet." Scheer was coming north and, Jellicoe assumed, Beatty would fall back on the Grand Fleet, drawing the enemy after him. At 4:47 p.m., the Commander-in-Chief signaled all ships in the Grand Fleet, "Enemy's battle fleet is coming north," and the news ran through the ships like wildfire. On *Hercules,* the Russian naval attaché observed "every face radiant with enthusiasm and delight." At 4:51 p.m., Jellicoe informed the Admiralty, "Urgent. Fleet action is imminent." When the message arrived in Whitehall, Admiralty signals flowed out; ports and dockyards were to prepare to receive damaged ships; tugboats were alerted to assist cripples. In Whitehall, even the usually imperturbable First Lord, Arthur Balfour, was "in a state of very great excitement."* Tyrwhitt with the Harwich flotillas was ordered to fill his bunkers with fuel in order to be ready to supplement or relieve Grand Fleet light cruisers and destroyers that might run low.

Then, for over an hour, the Commander-in-Chief was left in ignorance. The weather was partly responsible. Patchy haze, with visibility in some directions of up to 16,000 yards and down to 2,000 yards in others, hung over the water. Throughout the afternoon, the fleets were steaming at high speed through these shrouded seas, in which not only the enemy but their own

*Balfour's presence in the Admiralty chart room during the battle did not make things easier for Oliver, the Chief of Staff. The First Lord did not actively participate in command decisions as his predecessor, Churchill, had done during the Scarborough Raid and the Battle of the Dogger Bank; rather, Balfour was an excited spectator. As Oliver described the situation: "Balfour stayed all afternoon and some of the evening . . . with his Naval Assistant and his Private Secretary, and if I went to look at a chart some of them were bound to be in the way and all the talk was distracting. When I could stand it no longer, I went to Balfour and shook his hand and said 'Good-night, Sir,' and he said good night and took his supporters away with him. It was nice of him not to be offended."

forces frequently were hidden. Often, ships appeared only as pale, shadowy silhouettes, impossible to identify, appearing and then vanishing in the murk. In this confusion, heightened by the complexity of formations and maneuvers, scouting arrangements disintegrated and detailed information became impossible to acquire or pass along. The reports, when they did come in, were as apt to be wrong as right, with no way of knowing which was which. And beyond this general problem, which affected all commanders in both fleets, Jellicoe was afflicted by something else: the failure of a subordinate to perform his duty. Beatty's primary role as a battle cruiser commander was to maintain contact with the enemy battle fleet and keep his own Commander-in-Chief informed of its strength, bearing, course, and speed. In the months before the battle, Jellicoe's instructions to Beatty had constantly stressed the need for timely information. Yet between 4:45 p.m. and 6:06 p.m., Beatty, immersed in his own battle with Hipper, had neglected or forgotten this duty and sent Jellicoe nothing. Goodenough had signaled three times—at 5:00, 5:40, and 5:50 p.m.—reporting that the enemy battle fleet was coming north, but Goodenough's descriptions of his own positions were so obviously inaccurate that Jellicoe wondered how much weight to give his information. Under enormous strain, the Commander-in-Chief reacted by attempting to tighten his tactical control of the battle fleet. Small, fidgety messages flashed from her searchlights or were signaled by semaphore. The 22-knot *Royal Oak* was reproved for slewing around astern of the 20-knot *Iron Duke:* "You must steer a steadier course in action or your shooting will be bad," Jellicoe prompted. "Keep just clear of the wake of next ahead if it helps ships to keep up," he advised the entire fleet. And to *Thunderer,* he signaled, "Can you pass *Conqueror*? If so, do so."

Meanwhile, the Grand Fleet's dark gray columns steamed forward—but toward what? Where was the enemy? Jellicoe assumed that the High Seas Fleet was pursuing Beatty to the north, but still no one was providing him with fresh, reliable information. At 5:55 p.m., he signaled *Marlborough,* leading the dreadnought column on his starboard wing: "What can you see?" Five minutes later, *Marlborough* reported that she could see "our battle cruisers bearing south southwest, steering east, *Lion* leading ship." So Beatty was nearby and, that being so, Hipper was not far away. But where was Scheer? Jellicoe heard the rumble of heavy guns on *Iron Duke*'s port bow and saw gun flashes on the southeastern horizon; these came from Hood's assault on *Wiesbaden* and her sister light cruisers. Jellicoe, who was unaware of the nature of this action, wondered whether, somehow, this could be the bearing of Scheer's battle fleet. "I wish somebody would tell me who is firing and what they are firing at," he said.

Then, just at 6:00 p.m., Jellicoe and his staff could see *Lion* for themselves; she was off his starboard bow, steaming east through the haze five miles away, driving right across the front of the battle fleet, thundering salvos to the south at an invisible foe. A long trail of smoke was pouring from a hole in her port side, the guns of her X turret were pointed up at a useless angle, and tall gray columns of water thrown up by German shells were rising between her and her sisters. A midshipman in *Benbow* also saw the British battle cruisers "suddenly burst through the mist . . . a wonderful sight, these great ships, tearing down across us, their huge funnels silhouetted against a great bank of red cordite smoke and lit up by sheets of flame as they fired salvo after salvo at the enemy whose flashes could be seen in the distance." Jellicoe had no time for admiration. Instantly, at 6:01 p.m., he flashed Beatty by searchlight: "Where is enemy's battle fleet?"

Beatty did not know the answer; he had not seen the German battleships since he had left Evan-Thomas behind in order to give his own battered ships a respite. For five minutes, therefore, as Beatty and his four surviving battle cruisers raced across the front of the British battle fleet, *Lion* did not respond to Jellicoe's question. Then, at 6:06 p.m., Beatty gave an answer of sorts by searchlight: "Enemy's battle cruisers bearing southeast." This was no help to Jellicoe. In desperation, he signaled Beatty again: "Where is enemy's battle fleet?" Again, Beatty gave no immediate answer. Seven minutes passed while Beatty searched the southern horizon with his binoculars. Then, suddenly, he saw the distinctive massive shapes of *König* and *Grosser Kurfürst.* He now knew the bearing of the enemy battle fleet and, enormously relieved, he signaled Jellicoe, "Enemy battle fleet in sight bearing south. The nearest ship is seven miles." But his signal provided neither course nor speed.

Standing on the bridge of *Iron Duke,* a small figure in a belted blue raincoat with a white scarf knotted at his neck, Jellicoe stared intently at the hazy line of sea and sky to the south. The British Commander-in-Chief was facing the most critical decision of his life: how and when to deploy the dreadnought battle fleet. The Grand Fleet had been safer from U-boat attack in cruising formation—six columns abeam, with four ships in each column—but it was impossible to fight in this formation. If the fleet was forced to open fire while still in column, only the forward guns of the leading six ships could be used. "Deployment" was the maneuver that would convert the fleet from cruising formation into a single, long battle line of twenty-four dreadnoughts, which would bring to bear all the fleet's heavy guns on the enemy. To deploy effectively, however, it was essential to know the location, formation, course, and speed of the enemy fleet; this would determine the direction of the British deployment. A battle line deployed without this knowledge—or on the basis of wrong information—might place the British fleet in the position of having its own T crossed.*

*The naval maneuver called "crossing the T" places one fleet in a line moving squarely across the leading tip of an approaching enemy fleet. From this vantage, the first fleet can bring all or most of its guns to bear in a massive broadside; the enemy can reply only with the few forward guns of its leading one or two ships. In the days of naval warfare in which the big gun was the primary weapon, to "cross an enemy's T" was every admiral's dream.

Jellicoe, staring intently into the mist ahead, attempting to pierce the haze, knew that his own eyes were not sufficient. The range of heavy naval guns in 1916 exceeded normal North Sea visibility; that was especially true on this day, May 31. Once the order to deploy was given, its execution would require at least twenty minutes. As a result, if the Commander-in-Chief waited to give the command until he himself could see the enemy, he risked having his fleet caught in the act of deployment with many of its turrets masked by his other ships. Nevertheless, Jellicoe delayed until he could be certain, holding on in column formation, considering his next move methodically as if he were working out a mathematical problem. In the next few minutes before the firing began, he must swing his six columns into a single line—east to port, or west to starboard. His decision must be the right one; once started, there was no going back. Should he deploy on the right wing—to starboard and the west? At first, Jellicoe thought so; it would bring his fleet closest to where the enemy probably was and allow him to open fire sooner and at shorter range. But with every moment, deployment on the right seemed less wise. It would bring the two fleets within immediate torpedo range of each other, and nearby German destroyers would be able to deliver a massed torpedo attack on his battleships in the act of turning. If, on the other hand, he deployed to the left, on the port wing column, the Grand Fleet battle line, heading southeast, would be 4,000 yards farther away from the enemy fleet, but would have crossed the German T. Further, he would have achieved the best possible light for gunnery; his ships, except for gun flashes, would be invisible in the eastern mists while the German ships would be silhouetted against a bright, sunset horizon to the west. "I therefore decided to deploy on the port wing," Jellicoe said later. After the war, the official German naval history endorsed Jellicoe's choice: "One must agree that . . . [a deployment on the right wing] would have been only too welcome to the German fleet."

All these calculations passed through and were resolved in Jellicoe's mind in sixty seconds. He had received Beatty's signal at 6:14 p.m. Frederic Dreyer, the captain of *Iron Duke,* was standing on his bridge when he saw *Lion*'s searchlight signaling that Scheer's battleships were to the south:

> I heard the signalman calling each word of Beatty's reply to Jellicoe's repeated demand. . . . I then heard at once the sharp, distinctive step of the Commander-in-Chief approaching—he had steel strips on his heels. He stepped quickly onto the platform around the compasses and looked in silence at the magnetic compass card for about twenty seconds. I watched his keen, brown, weather-beaten face with tremendous interest, wondering what he would do. . . . I realized as I watched him that he was as cool and unmoved as ever. Then he looked up and broke the silence with the order in his crisp, clear-cut voice to the Fleet Sig-

> nal Officer: "Hoist equal speed pendant southeast." This officer said, "Would you make it a point to port, sir, so they will know it is on the port wing column?" Jellicoe replied, "Very well, hoist equal speed pendant southeast by south." The officer then called over the bridge rail to the signal boatswain. . . . Three flags soared up *Iron Duke*'s halyards. We had not yet sighted any German vessel.

The time was 6:15 p.m.

To speed things up, while some ships were still acknowledging his flag signal, Jellicoe told his Flag Captain, "Dreyer, commence the deployment." Dreyer immediately blew two short blasts on the ship's siren—the mariner's signal for "I am turning to port"—and ordered *Iron Duke*'s helm to be put over. The admirals in adjacent columns, all watching *Iron Duke,* did the same; each blew two short blasts on his flagship's siren and put over the helm. As the six battleships leading the columns swung to port, those astern followed ship by ship, the entire line falling in line behind the port wing division led by *King George V. Iron Duke* now was the ninth ship in a single line of twenty-seven British dreadnought battleships. Sir Julian Corbett, the official historian of the Royal Navy in the Great War, calls Jellicoe's deployment decision "the supreme moment of the naval war"; Professor Arthur Marder describes it as "the peak moment of the influence of sea power upon history." Jellicoe himself was well aware of the significance of what he had just done. If his calculations were correct, his deployment would deliver the High Seas Fleet into his hands. His fleet would be in a compact line six miles long with all gunnery arcs bearing on the enemy. And it began just as he had hoped: as his battleships were turning into line, the van of Scheer's fleet loomed up to the south, first as shadowy silhouettes, then more clearly. From *Iron Duke,* the admiral himself saw three ships on the starboard beam whose shapes were those of the *König*s. Turning to the man beside him, Jellicoe said, "Dreyer, I think it is time for you to go to your station in the conning tower."

—

On either wing of this immense fleet, now transforming itself from one formation into another, the British deployment was distorted by the frantic activity of dozens of small ships: the light cruiser squadrons and destroyer flotillas attempting to reach their proper stations screening the battle fleet. As a result, on the port—the northeastern—wing, there was a mass of small ships, "as thick as the traffic in Piccadilly," weaving and dodging at full speed across the path of the dreadnoughts turning onto their new course. At the opposite—the southwestern—end of the British battlefront, where the starboard wing column was deploying, the congestion was worse. Beatty's four battle cruisers were charging across the front of the onrushing Grand

Fleet dreadnoughts, while his cruisers and destroyers were forced to pass through the area where the battleships were deploying by darting and slipping between the turning dreadnought columns. Thus, as *Galatea*'s light cruiser squadron dashed between the four battleships of the port wing column, *Galatea* herself passed close under *Agincourt*'s bow just as the dreadnought opened fire. *Agincourt* "fired a salvo over us which fairly lifted us out of the water," said one of the light cruiser's officers. "I don't know how many of her twelve 14-inch guns she fired, but I felt as if my head was blown off." There were numerous near collisions and some ships had to stop engines to avoid collision. An officer watching from *Malaya* observed "a light cruiser squadron and a destroyer flotilla gathered together in a very small area on which the enemy was concentrating all available fire. Amidst this perfect deluge of shells, the light cruisers and destroyers were twisting and turning, endeavoring to avoid each other and the big ships. . . . It will never cease to be a source of wonder to me that so few ships were hit and there were no collisions. It must have been one of the most wonderful displays of seamanship and clear-headedness that ever existed." Later, when participants looked back, the place and the moment came to be called the Windy Corner.

As the British light cruisers and destroyers scrambled to reach their new positions, another element of Jellicoe's advance screen, the large armored cruisers of Rear Admiral Sir Robert Arbuthnot's 1st Cruiser Squadron—*Defence, Warrior, Black Prince,* and *Duke of Edinburgh*—were forced by the crunch of ships to break formation and separate. But not before Arbuthnot, whose flagship, *Defence,* was steaming five miles ahead of *Iron Duke,* had spotted Bödicker's light cruisers fleeing from the three *Invincible*s and leaving behind their crippled sister *Wiesbaden.* Arbuthnot was a small, lean bantam rooster of a man, a passionate athlete who played rugby and cricket, ran in long distance races, and insisted on acting as chief referee at Grand Fleet boxing matches. His reputation at sea was as a demanding, competitive disciplinarian, but he had never forgotten—or perhaps had not been allowed to forget—that, seventeen months earlier, he had missed a golden opportunity. This was the moment when, on *Orion* during the Scarborough Raid, he had refused to open fire on German light cruisers directly under his guns, citing the need to await permission from higher authority. The next time, Arbuthnot had sworn to himself—and confided to others—he would not wait. Now, seeing *Wiesbaden* immobile and billowing smoke, he determined to send the German ship to the bottom. Only his two leading ships, *Defence* and *Warrior,* were in position to attack; *Black Prince* and *Duke of Edinburgh* had scattered when the press of British dreadnoughts had splintered his squadron. This, to Arbuthnot, was irrelevant; two armored cruisers were enough to finish *Wiesbaden,* and he turned and charged. His move attracted the admiration of an observer in *Warspite* who watched as *Defence* went by, "dressed in all her glory with her battle ensigns streaming." In his eagerness, Arbuthnot steamed directly across Beatty's course, steering *Defence* so close under

Lion's bow that the battle cruiser, firing at Hipper, was compelled to make an emergency turn to avoid ramming. Arbuthnot appeared not to care and his ships closed on *Wiesbaden,* firing 9.2-inch shells as fast as the gunners could load. But Arbuthnot and his men would pay for his impetuosity. None of the squadron commanders coming up with the Grand Fleet were informed about the enemy's position and strength and, in the poor visibility, they could not see for themselves. Arbuthnot had not asked permission to attack and no one had warned him that the High Seas Fleet was nearby. Suddenly, as he closed in on *Wiesbaden,* the massive outlines of Hipper's battle cruisers and Scheer's leading battleships loomed out of the mist only 8,000 yards away. Arbuthnot tried to turn back, but it was too late. Two German 12-inch shells struck *Defence* near her after 9.2-inch turret; the armored cruiser heeled, but righted herself and steamed on. Then, a salvo struck behind the forward turret and there was a cataclysmic explosion. A huge black cloud enveloped everything; when this smoke had cleared, the sea was empty. The 14,000-ton ship, with Admiral Arbuthnot and all 900 men of her crew, had vanished. "Twenty-four hours earlier," Gibson and Harper note, "Arbuthnot had been playing tennis at Cromarty with Lady Jellicoe."

Arbuthnot's behavior has been described as "berserk," not primarily because it led to the destruction of his own ship—he could not have foreseen the arrival of the German dreadnoughts—but because his move jeopardized the tactical situation of the entire fleet. Just when Jellicoe needed to exercise the tightest control and discipline in conducting the complex maneuver of deployment, here came Arbuthnot, charging into the middle, intent on his own affairs. In Andrew Gordon's metaphor, "while center stage should have been clearing for the leading contenders to engage, here was a supporting actor, getting in the way and babbling his own nonsensical lines."

Arbuthnot's second armored cruiser, *Warrior,* now became the focus of German attention. Heavy shells burst on this ship, smashing through her upper decks, bursting in her engine room, flinging shards of steel through boilers and steam pipes. Steam scalded many in the engine-room crew to death. Now only 8,000 yards from Scheer's battle line, *Warrior* seemed certain to share the horror of *Defence.* Curiously, it was another unscripted performance that prevented this from happening. At the moment *Warrior*'s doom seemed inevitable, a single British battleship, wholly unintentionally, intervened to save her.

—

At 6:00 p.m., Evan-Thomas's four *Queen Elizabeth*s were still doggedly following Beatty, as they had done or attempted to do throughout the afternoon. But as the British battle cruisers swung eastward, bending Hipper's line of advance and also cutting directly across the line of fire of the approaching Grand Fleet, Beatty and Evan-Thomas deliberately separated; the position of the *Queen Elizabeth*s, now that Beatty and Jellicoe had joined, was in the

Grand Fleet battle line. When an officer on *Malaya* sighted *Marlborough* leading the starboard column of the Grand Fleet, Evan-Thomas, assuming that Jellicoe would deploy to starboard and intending to place his fast battleships at the head of the entire line—their assigned place in a fleet action—began turning the 5th Battle Squadron to take station ahead of *Marlborough.* A minute later, he realized that *Marlborough* was swinging, not to starboard, but to port; that the fleet was deploying to the east, not the west, and that *Marlborough* and her 1st Battle Squadron, instead of being at the head of the deployed battle line, would be bringing up the rear. In this context, Evan-Thomas knew that his place was not in the van, but behind *Agincourt,* the last ship in Marlborough's squadron, at the very tail end of the entire British battle line. Accordingly, at 6:18 p.m., the 5th Battle Squadron began to turn to port. It was two minutes later that *Defence* blew up and *Warrior,* under heavy fire and apparently doomed, began creeping off to the northwest—toward the *Queen Elizabeth*s.

As Evan-Thomas's four battleships wheeled under fire from Scheer's advancing *Königs*, *Barham* was forced to turn sharply and reduce speed to make room for *Marlborough*'s squadron to pass ahead. Then *Warspite,* turning hard inside *Valiant* and *Malaya,* was hit near the stern by a 12-inch shell from *Kaiserin.* Finding the ship boxed in, the quartermaster "got a bit rattled and forced the helm too quick," jamming the rudder 10 degrees to starboard. The ship swerved out of line, narrowly missed a collision with *Valiant*'s stern, and continued to swing. Captain Edward Phillpotts tried to bring his ship back into line by running her engines and port and starboard propellers at different speeds to counteract the effect of the jammed rudder. He managed only to send her driving straight toward the enemy, who now concentrated on this huge target only 8,000 yards away. Still unable to bring his rudder back to port, Phillpotts decided to continue at full speed and drive his ship around in a full circle as quickly as possible. Accordingly, he made a wide turn, his ship plunging through smoke and towering shell splashes, frequently shaken by the concussion of a heavy caliber hit, but all the while still firing back with her eight 15-inch guns. The captain brought the ship around in a complete circle, but the rudder remained jammed. It being essential to present a moving target, Phillpotts took the dreadnought around again in a wider full circle, this time circling clean around the crippled *Warrior* and drawing enemy fire away from the helpless armored cruiser. Eventually, the battleship's crew managed to restore a degree of steering control to the rudder and the captain attempted to rejoin his squadron. But *Warspite* had been hit that day by a total of twenty-nine heavy German shells, thirteen of these during the two turns, and she discovered that at speeds higher than 16 knots, the sea poured in through holes in her hull armor. Leaving her sisters, she withdrew to the north and at 9:05 p.m. Evan-Thomas ordered her to return to Rosyth. *Warspite*'s misfortune, harrowing as it was, had been *Warrior*'s salvation, saving the cruiser's 900 men from the fate of *Defence.* By careening around in two full circles and drawing the enemy's fire, the battleship had effectively masked the crippled cruiser and allowed her to escape.

—

Invincible had come out of dry dock in Rosyth on the morning of May 22; that afternoon at 5:00, Hood took the battle cruiser and her sisters, *Inflexible* and *Indomitable,* north to Scapa Flow for an intensive schedule of gunnery practice. *Invincible* and her two sisters spent eight days at Scapa. On the morning of May 30, they had been out in Pentland Firth for 12-inch-gun practice; the results were reported as "highly satisfactory." By 3:45 that afternoon, they were back at anchor in the Flow, coaling and preparing for night firing scheduled to begin after dark. And on the following morning, all of Hood's ships were due to return to Rosyth. That was the afternoon, however, that Jellicoe and Beatty received the Admiralty's signal warning of a probable German sortie from the Jade. At 6:25 p.m., Jellicoe told Hood to raise steam for 22 knots, at 8:50 p.m., he ordered him to weigh anchor, and at 9:00 p.m., accompanied by the light cruisers *Chester* and *Canterbury* and four destroyers, the three battle cruisers moved down the harbor and out to sea.

—

During the Grand Fleet's deployment, Hipper won another dramatic success against the British battle cruiser force—his third of the day and, as it turned out, his last of the war. Hood, after his bludgeoning of four German light cruisers, including *Wiesbaden,* continued west in search of Beatty. He sighted the Grand Fleet approaching on his starboard bow and, at almost the same moment on his port bow, *Lion* charging eastward toward him. The normal station of Hood's three battle cruisers would have been astern of Beatty; but in maneuvering to reach it, he would have further obstructed the fire of Jellicoe's oncoming battleships. It was obvious to Hood that he should instead turn ahead of Beatty and take a position in advance of the vice admiral. Accordingly, at 6:21 p.m., Hood led his three battle cruisers around through a 180-degree turn to starboard, taking station 4,000 yards ahead of *Lion. Invincible* now found herself on a parallel course with the five German battle cruisers, visible 9,000 yards off her starboard beam. As Beatty's four battle cruisers already were engaging the three rear ships of Hipper's line, Hood's three ships, fresh from gunnery practice at Scapa Flow, trained their 12-inch guns on the two leading German ships, *Lützow* and *Derfflinger,* and immediately opened an accurate fire. "The gunnery of the 3rd Battle Cruiser Squadron was tremendous in its majestic intensity, great rippling salvos running down the line of the three ships. Hits were showing all over Hipper's battle cruisers," remembered an officer on *Tiger.* Within eight minutes, *In-*

vincible fired fifty shells at *Lützow* and hit her eight times. From *Invincible*'s bridge, Hood shouted into the voice pipe to tell the ship's gunnery officer, Lieutenant Commander Hubert Dannreuther, in the foretop: "Your firing is very good! Keep it up as quickly as you can! Every shot is telling!"

Meanwhile, *Invincible* was receiving as well as inflicting punishment. One salvo hit the battle cruiser aft, but caused no apparent damage. Then, suddenly, *Invincible* was annihilated. Commander von Hase, gunnery officer of *Derfflinger,* was watching. "At 6.29 p.m., the veil of mist in front of us split like a curtain at a theater," he said. "Clear and sharply silhouetted against the horizon, we saw a powerful ship . . . on an almost parallel course at top speed. Her guns were trained on us and immediately another salvo crashed out, straddling us completely." It was *Invincible.* Hase fired three salvos and the third fell on *Invincible*'s amidships Q turret. And then at 6:30, said Hase, "for the third time we witnessed that dreadful spectacle we had already seen in the case of *Queen Mary* and *Defence.*" When the German shells penetrated Q turret, the flash ignited the powder in the hoist and traveled down the turret trunk to the magazine, causing both Q and P turrets' magazines to explode. The whole central section—including boiler rooms, coal bunkers, and the two amidships turret systems—was ripped apart in a gigantic ball of crimson flame. Masses of coal dust spurted from the broken hull, the tall tripod masts collapsed inward, and a ball of flame mounted into the sky followed by an enormous tower of black smoke. The ship broke in half and the two severed halves sank until each rested vertically on the bottom. Then, when the smoke had cleared, a curious sight was seen. As the ship was 567 feet long and the sea was only 180 feet deep, the bow and stern were seen standing separately—a hundred feet of bow and a hundred feet of stern, each with red bottom paint and gray topside paint—rising perpendicular out of the water. There were a few survivors nearby. These men waved as *Inflexible* and *Indomitable* swept past. "I have never seen anything more splendid," said an officer in *Indomitable,* "than these few cheering as we raced by them."

When the Grand Fleet went by a few minutes later, many British seamen in the passing dreadnoughts thought the victim was a German ship. "My gun layer took her for a Hun and the crew cheered. But I could read the name *Invincible* on the stern," said an officer. It was not British naval practice for warships still in action to stop to pick up survivors, but when Beatty passed by at 6:40 p.m. and saw men in the water, he signaled the destroyer *Badger,* "Pick up survivors from wreck on starboard side." Only six men were rescued out of a crew of 1,031. One of them, Dannreuther, the gunnery officer and Wagner's godson, had been in the control top on the foremast. When he was picked up, he told his rescuers that he "had not a scratch on his entire body," and that he had merely "stepped off into the water when the foretop came down." When *Iron Duke* came by, Jellicoe asked, "Is wreck one of our own ships?" To which *Badger,* still searching for men in the sea, replied, "Yes. *Invincible.*"

—

Franz Hipper was unable to savor his third victory that afternoon over the British battle cruiser force. Three of the nine British battle cruisers that had sailed for Jutland had now been sunk, but four of Hipper's own five ships were in worse condition than the six surviving British battle cruisers. *Lützow,* Hipper's flagship, was barely afloat, with water pouring into her forward compartments, dragging her bow deep into the water. Her wireless stations had been destroyed. Facing this situation, Erich Raeder, Hipper's Chief of Staff, forced himself to confront the admiral, telling him that the ship must drop out of line and return to Wilhelmshaven as well as she could; meanwhile, Hipper must transfer to another battle cruiser. When Raeder said this, "a kind of paralysis seemed to descend on Hipper. . . . [He] issued no orders. It was the first time that he had nothing to say." Raeder tried again: "We can't lead the squadron from *Lützow* anymore, Your Excellency." "But I can't leave the flagship," Hipper protested. Raeder persisted: "We're unable to signal by wireless and anyhow our speed isn't enough." "No doubt!" said Hipper. "But my flagship!" Then Raeder spoke sharply: "The squadron needs Your Excellency," and Hipper jerked back to reality. "You're right," he said, and signaled the destroyer *G-39* to come alongside. Just before 7:00 p.m., with *Lützow* stopped and the destroyer waiting, Hipper grasped *Lützow*'s Captain Viktor Harder by the hand, saluted the officers on the bridge, and declared, "We'll come back. We won't forget you." Then, as Beatty had done at the Dogger Bank, he jumped down onto the destroyer's deck and told the captain to take him to another battle cruiser that he could use as his flagship. As Hipper departed, *Lützow,* with a huge volume of smoke pouring from her forecastle back across her bridge, turned out of line and, alone, steamed slowly off to the south. Her part in the battle was over.

For the next three hours, Hipper wandered across the battlefield in his small destroyer seeking to board another battle cruiser and make it his new flagship. He went first to *Derfflinger,* but her condition was almost as calamitous as *Lützow*'s. She had received twenty heavy-caliber shell hits; two armor plates had been torn from her bow, leaving an enormous hole open to the sea; her masts and rigging were shattered; most signal halyards were blown away or burned; her wireless apparatus was damaged so that she could receive but not send messages. And she had on board 180 dead or wounded men. Leaving *Derfflinger,* Hipper headed for *Seydlitz,* which was in even worse condition. The ship had "a hole as big as a barn door in her bow and several thousand tons of water gurgling inside her." She was listing, awash forward up to the middle deck, and also had no working wireless. *Von der Tann,* which he tried next, had no gun turrets able to fire and was valueless as a fighting unit. That left *Moltke,* still largely undamaged. Hipper's destroyer was about to come alongside *Moltke* when a new order from Scheer for the battle cruisers to attack made this impossible. As the squadron could not be controlled from the bridge of a destroyer, Hipper signaled Captain Johannes Hartog of *Derfflinger* to take temporary command until circumstances permitted *Moltke* to halt long enough to take him on board. But this did not happen until 10:00 p.m.

—

As the Grand Fleet deployed, the divisions came up to their turning points and swung into line, each ship "breaking into a ripple of flame from all her turrets" as soon as she could bring her guns to bear. Because of the haze and the interference from the funnel smoke of Beatty's ships steaming at high speed across the front of the Grand Fleet, no organized distribution of fire was possible and individual ships selected their own targets. At 6:17 p.m., *Marlborough,* leading the starboard-wing column nearest the Germans, trained on one of the *Kaiser*s at a range of 13,000 yards and fired seven 13.5-inch-gun salvos in four minutes. The other ships of her division followed: *Revenge* with eight 15-inch, then *Hercules,* then *Agincourt* with her seven turrets and fourteen 12-inch guns. At 6:23 p.m., *Iron Duke* opened fire at *Wiesbaden;* seven minutes later, she found a more suitable target in one of the *König*s and gave the German nine salvos. *Benbow, Colossus, Orion, Monarch,* and *Thunderer* joined in. Even so, for the first fifteen minutes, firing came from only about one-third of the British fleet. There were other difficulties: at 6:26 p.m., Jellicoe was forced to reduce speed to 14 knots to allow Beatty's battle cruisers to cross in front of him. This signal did not reach all ships, and there was bunching up and overlapping of battleships in the rear of the line; *Marlborough* had to reduce to 8 knots and, briefly, *St. Vincent* was forced to stop dead in the water. At 6:33 p.m., Beatty reached his new station ahead of the battle fleet's new course and Jellicoe was able to increase speed to 17 knots. By then, firing was general.

—

It was a moment of triumph for Jellicoe and of horror for Scheer. Earlier in the afternoon, the German Commander-in-Chief, in *Friedrich der Grosse,* had been optimistic about the battle's outcome. Hipper had told him that enemy light cruisers had been sighted and that the battle cruisers could handle them; in consequence, Scheer did not increase the speed of the High Seas Fleet battle squadrons. When, at 3:46 p.m., Hipper reported that six British battle cruisers were present, Scheer was delighted. The situation for which he had been hoping was developing: he had come upon a fraction of the Grand Fleet operating on its own, far from home. Scheer altered course to the northwest, toward Hipper, and his leading battleship squadron, Behncke's four

*König*s, engaged both Beatty's remaining battle cruisers and Evan-Thomas's *Queen Elizabeth*s. At maximum speed, the German dreadnoughts pressed forward, hoping to lame, and then overtake and sink, one or more of the big British vessels. Even as the Grand Fleet was preparing to deploy, Scheer was still pursuing the 5th Battle Squadron, and his battleships were firing enthusiastically at the circling *Warspite.* At 6:20 p.m., five minutes after Jellicoe's signal to deploy, the German advance continued with Scheer and his admirals wholly unaware that *König,* leading their battle line, was only 14,000 yards southeast of *Marlborough* on the Grand Fleet's starboard wing. Then, just as *Warspite* straightened out and steamed away, Rear Admiral Behncke, on *König*'s bridge, stared ahead and, to his horrified amazement, saw massed columns of battleships turning in front of him. Heavy fire began to fall on his ships and Behncke himself was wounded on his bridge. By 6:30 p.m., fifteen British battleships had come into line and, with every minute, more of Jellicoe's dreadnoughts were adding their guns to the cannonade. The Grand Fleet now was crossing the German T, punishing the head of the German line—*König, Grosser Kurfürst,* and *Markgraf.* To relieve some of the pressure, Behncke followed Hipper's battle cruisers ahead of him as they bore off to starboard; thus, without the knowledge or permission of its Commander-in-Chief, the High Seas Fleet's original course, north to the Skagerrak, was bending to the east.

Scheer, even more than Jellicoe, was hampered by lack of information. His flagship was thirteenth in line in the long German column and the admiral himself could see nothing in the haze. Scheer's Flag Lieutenant, Ernst von Weizsäcker, bluntly declared after the war that during the battle, Scheer "had but the foggiest idea of what was happening." Even as he steamed steadily toward Jellicoe, Scheer still was not convinced that the Grand Fleet was at sea; the gunfire on the horizon ahead he assumed to be coming from the battle between Beatty and Hipper. Then, five minutes after the Grand Fleet had begun its deployment and as the volume of gunfire rose and the rain of heavy shells fell thicker on his fleet, Scheer realized that something larger and more ominous than Beatty and Evan-Thomas lay across his path. "It was now obvious that we were confronted by a large portion of the English fleet," he said. "The entire arc stretching from north to east was a sea of fire. The flash from the muzzles of the guns was seen distinctly through the mist and smoke on the horizon although the ships themselves were not distinguishable." The shock to Scheer was a terrible one. And then, at 6:25 p.m., with the four *König*s in the van of his fleet immersed in a maelstrom of fire, he was handed a signal from the commander of his 5th Destroyer Flotilla; British prisoners rescued from the sunken destroyer *Nomad* had told their captors that sixty large British ships, including twenty dreadnoughts and six battle cruisers, were "in the vicinity."

What could Scheer do? He was 150 miles from home, facing a more numerous, more powerful enemy, which, thanks to the presence of Mauve's six predreadnoughts, was also superior in speed. He could not hope to win a running heavy-gun battle on a parallel course; his slower ships would certainly be lost and probably others as well. Already his punished van was beginning to lose formation. The volume of fire made it impossible to sight on and fire on any individual British ship. Worst of all, he had permitted his enemy to cross his T. Scheer was a professional and a realist; he knew that if he continued on this course, the life of his fleet could be measured in minutes.

Scheer reacted quickly. "While the battle is progressing a leader cannot obtain a really clear picture, especially at long ranges," Scheer wrote after the war. "He acts and feels according to his impressions." Scheer saw only one way out: to order a carefully rehearsed German fleet maneuver, designed for exactly this situation: when it was necessary to break away rapidly from a stronger fleet. At 6:36 p.m., Scheer signaled, *"Gefechtskehrtwendung nach Steuerbord!"* ("Battle about turn to starboard"). The maneuver called for each ship independently and simultaneously to make a 180-degree turn onto an opposite course; in this case directly away from the British fleet. The result would save time by reversing the course of the fleet without the need to follow the leader around a single point ahead. Scheer's captains had practiced the maneuver often in peacetime in the Baltic; now, when the command was given, its execution was superb. *Westfalen,* the last dreadnought in line, turned immediately. Then, together, each heeling sharply, twenty-two battleships turned in place, and, within four minutes, the entire column had vanished into the murk. To the British, watching the advancing German column suddenly fade from view, it was inexplicable.

—

Jellicoe was astonished and perplexed: the High Seas Fleet, which had been heading straight for his battle line, had suddenly vanished. And it had disappeared before Jellicoe had finished deploying all of his battleships; only at 6:40 p.m. had the last Grand Fleet division turned onto the new deployment course with *Barham, Valiant,* and *Malaya* forming astern of *Agincourt,* the last ship. And now, extraordinarily, Scheer's fleet was gone. The serious fleet action had lasted for only twenty minutes—from 6:15 to 6:35 p.m.—and even then, in the shifting banks of mist and smoke rolling toward the British line, no more than three or four enemy battleships had ever been visible from the bridge of *Iron Duke.* "I could not see his turn away from where I was on top of the chart house, nor could anyone else with me," Jellicoe said later of Admiral Scheer. "I had imagined the disappearance of the enemy to be due merely to the thickening of the mist, but after a few minutes, I realized that there must be some other reason." Only at 6:44 p.m., nine minutes after Scheer's turn and once he had finished superintending the deployment of his own fleet, did Jellicoe react. Supposing, at first, that Scheer had made only a small alteration in course, Jellicoe responded by turning the British line slightly to starboard—to the southeast. Eleven minutes later, at 6:55 p.m., Jellicoe realized that Scheer must have made a larger turn, perhaps toward the southwest, which would have been the quickest way out of the British trap. Jellicoe again altered course, this time by 45 degrees to a heading of south, still at a diverging angle from Scheer's new course to the southwest. This divergence did not concern Jellicoe; in bad visibility, he had no wish to pursue Scheer into the unknown. In addition, the new Grand Fleet course put the High Seas Fleet in ultimate peril: every mile placed Jellicoe in a better position to prevent Scheer's return to Germany.

Jellicoe's decisions before, during, and immediately after Scheer's emergency turnabout were the results of his own personal analysis and estimates; no one in the British fleet passed along any useful information to the Commander-in-Chief. Most bridge officers in the battle fleet, of course, were necessarily absorbed in their own close-quarters deployment ship-handling; Scheer's unexpected maneuver had gone virtually unobserved. But not totally unobserved: men on some British vessels—the light cruisers *Falmouth* and *Canterbury,* for example—had clearly seen Scheer's battleships turning away, but no one thought to report this fact to the flagship. *Iron Duke*'s own gunnery-control staff in the battleship's foretop witnessed the turn but failed to inform the admiral on the bridge. Throughout this critical time, therefore, Jellicoe was forced to rely solely on what he could see for himself—and he could see nothing. Even at 6:55, twenty minutes after Scheer had turned away, Jellicoe was uncertain what Scheer had done or where he had gone. Looking for help, he asked *Marlborough,* at the eastern end of the battle line, "Can you see any enemy battleships?" "No," *Marlborough* replied.

Meanwhile, more trouble was on the way: torpedoes were heading for the rear of the British line. Most of the tracks were clearly visible and easily avoided, but not all. *Revenge* felt "a heavy shock"; a torpedo had struck the side, and, failing to explode, had bounced off the underwater armor. A moment later an explosion occurred on *Marlborough*'s starboard side. A torpedo destroyed thirty feet of hull plating, killed two men, and flooded a boiler room as well as the diesel- and hydraulic-engine rooms. The battleship listed 8 degrees and her speed was reduced to 17 knots, but she managed to maintain her position in line. This, as it turned out, was the only torpedo to hit and damage a British dreadnought during the Battle of Jutland. But the hit on *Marlborough* had a powerful effect on Jellicoe, strongly reinforcing his tendency to caution. His declared policy was not to risk his battle fleet to underwater damage by following closely in the wake of a retiring enemy who might launch a destroyer torpedo attack, or sow mines in his path, or both. No one knew where the torpedo that hit the Marlborough had come from; possibly a U-boat, possibly a mine, possibly even the wreck of the immobile *Wiesbaden.* On the chance that this last possible source might be the true one, more British salvos crashed out toward that crippled vessel. Still she did not sink and, on board, thirty desperate men remained alive.

Nothing better illustrates the difficulties facing Jellicoe at Jutland than the brevity of the first clash between the two battle fleets. Despite the skill with which Jellicoe and Beatty had enmeshed the High Seas Fleet, *Iron Duke* had fired only nine salvos when Scheer turned his ships around and vanished into the mist. Even so, Jellicoe remained hopeful. He retained the superior tactical position, and when the firing stopped, he and most men in the British fleet believed this to be only a temporary hiatus in the long-awaited day of reckoning. The High Seas Fleet remained out there somewhere, and the Grand Fleet was in position to prevent Scheer from returning to the Jade. Meanwhile, as ship after ship took stock, British admirals and captains realized that the Germans had not scored a single hit on any Grand Fleet battleship. The men in the fleet were cheerfully exuberant and, during the respite, those who were able came out to take a look. Prince Albert, whose A turret in *Collingwood* had been hammering away at *Derfflinger,* emerged to sit on the turret top and escape the cordite fumes inside. Later, the king's second son wrote to his brother, the Prince of Wales, that, during the fighting, "all sense of danger and everything else goes, except the one longing of dealing death in every possible way to the enemy."

—

For twenty minutes after reversing course, Scheer retreated to the west, managing to lose Jellicoe in the mist and smoke. The turn had reversed the order of the German line: *Westfalen* now led the dreadnoughts, and *König* brought up the rear. Battle damage was severe, although not equally distributed. The battle cruisers, except for *Moltke,* were badly hurt. Behncke's battleship squadron, which had led the fleet, had been hard hit: *König* had heavy damage; *Markgraf*'s port engine was stopped and she was having trouble keeping her place in line. The other two ships of Behncke's elite division were fighting fires, plugging holes below the waterline, and shoring up bulkheads. But Scheer's other dreadnoughts were relatively unharmed, and Mauve's six old ships had not been touched. Scheer could count his superbly executed *Gefechtskehrtwendung* a brilliant success.

Then, suddenly, Scheer did something even more extraordinary. At 6:55 p.m., the same signal soared again up the halyards on *Friedrich der Grosse: "Gefechtskehrtwendung nach Steuerbord!"* The German Commander-in-Chief was calling for another simultaneous 180-degree turn. Scheer was reversing course again; he was abandoning caution, staking everything on a single throw and deliberately hurling his fleet at the center of the British battle line whose immense firepower he had already felt. For this move, no one—not even Scheer himself—ever offered a rational explanation. Certainly, the admiral was acutely aware that his fleet was still in danger, that with every mile he steamed west into the North Sea, he was farther from home. He may also have believed that Jellicoe's scouting cruisers must have seen his turn and that the whole Grand Fleet would be steering westward after him. But now, twenty minutes had passed and there was no British vessel in sight. The enemy was not following him, and Scheer wondered why. Perhaps the relative situation was better than he had thought. Perhaps he could capitalize on this. By returning to the battle he had just broken off, by attacking head-on with his entire fleet, he might surprise his enemy and throw him into confusion. And, if the Grand Fleet had moved far enough to the south, his own fleet might, in the coming darkness, be able to cross Jellicoe's rear and make for Wilhelmshaven. Along the way, he might even be able to do something for *Wiesbaden;* rescue survivors, at least.

After the battle and after the war, Scheer was asked about his decision. His answers varied. Reporting to the kaiser, he wanted William to believe that before making his extraordinary turn back to the east and exposing the kaiser's beloved fleet a second time to the crossing of its T by a superior and practically undamaged enemy battle fleet, he had carefully calculated every possibility: "If the enemy followed us," he wrote, "our action in reversing course would be classed as a retreat and if any of our rear ships were damaged, we would have to sacrifice them. Still less was it feasible to disengage, leaving it to the enemy to decide when he would meet us next morning."

> It was as yet too early to assume night cruising order. The enemy could have compelled us to fight before dark, he could have prevented our exercising our initiative, and finally he could have cut off our return to the German Bight. There was only one way of avoiding this: to inflict a second blow on the enemy by advancing again regardless of cost, and to bring all the destroyers forcibly to attack. Such a maneuver would surprise the enemy, upset his plans for the rest of the day and, if the blow fell really heavily, make easier a night escape. It also offered the possibility of a last attempt to bring help to the hard-pressed *Wiesbaden,* or at least of rescuing her crew.

After the war, Scheer, speaking candidly to friends, admitted: "The fact is, I had no definite object. . . . I advanced because I thought I should help the poor *Wiesbaden* and because the situation was entirely obscure since I had received no wireless reports. When I noticed that the British pressure had ceased and that the fleet remained intact in my hands, I turned back under the impression that the action could not end this way and that I ought to seek contact with the enemy again. And then I thought I had better throw in the battle cruisers in full strength. . . . The thing just happened—as the virgin said when she got a baby."

Some historians refuse to believe that the German Commander-in-Chief knowingly and deliberately thrust the High Seas Fleet straight into the jaws of the massive British battle line. And, if he did so, they find it incomprehensible that he placed his battle cruisers—his weakest heavy ships, with the thinnest armor, already battered and two almost sinking—in the van. Scheer himself later admitted that "if I'd done it in a peacetime exercise, I'd have lost my command." Whatever his reasons—or perhaps there was no reasoning, only impetuosity, instinct, desperation—the German admiral turned his ships around and steamed back through the same water they had just passed through.

—

Scheer's move did not, as he had hoped it would, catch Jellicoe by surprise. Once again, it was Goodenough in *Southampton* who discovered the German fleet and sounded the alarm. The commodore had faithfully and expertly followed Scheer's retreat and then, suddenly, out of the mists he saw the German dreadnoughts coming toward him. His own ship immediately came under fire, which did not prevent him from signaling Jellicoe that the High Seas Fleet was coming back. Grand Fleet officers and seamen standing on deck or sitting on turret tops tumbled back into their battle stations, and soon the giant, light gray ships—first Hipper's battle cruisers, then Behncke's battleships—appeared out of the mist. Without speculating as to his opponent's motive, Jellicoe took the offered gift.

No naval assault during the Great War was as useless as this second attack of Reinhard Scheer's. Weather and visibility were against him; as the day neared its end, his ships stood out sharply against the glowing western horizon, while to the east the Grand Fleet was shrouded in mist. Initially the resumption of British fire was sporadic, but it swiftly mounted in volume. Soon, the Grand Fleet's broadsides merged into a solid, unbroken wave of endless thunder. *Hercules* fired on *Seydlitz; Colossus* and *Revenge* on *Derfflinger; Neptune* and *St. Vincent* on *Derfflinger* and *Moltke. Marlborough,* ignoring her torpedo injury, fired fourteen salvos in six minutes and saw four of them hit. *Monarch, Iron Duke, Centurion, Royal Oak, King George V, Téméraire, Superb, Neptune*—all reported scoring hits. By 7:14 p.m., fire from the whole of the British line was sweeping the length of the German line at ranges from 10,000 to 14,000 yards. At 7:15, Beatty's battle cruisers joined in. As always, the German battle cruisers suffered most, but the cannonade also further devastated the ships in the German van. *König,* with Rear Admiral Behncke wounded on the bridge, was hit repeatedly. *Grosser Kurfürst,* next astern, was hammered seven times in two minutes by 15-inch and 13.5-inch shells from *Barham, Valiant,* and *Marlborough. Markgraf, Kaiser,* and *Helgoland* were hit. Under this torrent of heavy shells, the German column wavered; ships "bunched together"; the battleships, surrounded by towering waterspouts, found themselves overtaking and overrunning the battle cruisers. Captains ordered helmsmen to turn out of line and engine rooms to slow down, stop, and back astern. Scheer's fleet was disintegrating.

Meanwhile, the German reply to this deluge of British fire was ineffective. German gunners saw nothing but smoke and mist and, in the words of the naval historian John Irving, "an almost continuous flickering orange light right round the horizon ahead, from port to starboard." The nearly invisible British dreadnoughts could be located only by these gun flashes; German spotters desperately attempted to take ranges and fire back at the orange flashes, but they had no means of seeing the fall of shot. Only two heavy German shells hit the British battle line, both striking *Colossus.* These two 12-inch shells landed on the forward superstructure, one of them failing to explode, neither doing significant damage or inflicting casualties. A third heavy shell—an observer saw that it was bright yellow—fell short, bursting when it hit the water thirty yards from the forward turret. "Splinters penetrated . . . unarmoured parts of the ship in about 20 places," her captain reported after the battle. Two men were wounded in the foretop and three at a 4-inch-gun post. The most serious harm was done to a seaman manning a range finder on the foretop; his right arm was practically severed by a steel splinter. His life was saved by a marine captain who stopped the bleeding with a tourniquet; the arm later was amputated at the shoulder. Remarkably, these five men wounded were the only gunfire casualties suffered by Grand Fleet dreadnoughts during the Battle of Jutland.

Ten minutes of this—unanswerable salvos fired by huge guns hidden in the eastern mist—was all that Scheer could stand. He had gambled and steered a second time into the greatest concentration of naval gunfire any fleet commander had ever faced. He had lost. The attack had failed and he understood that if he persisted, his fleet would be destroyed. Now there was only one thing to do: quickly extricate as many ships as possible. The most valuable ships, the dreadnought battleships, the core of German sea power, the kaiser's glories, the cause of the naval building race with England—these must be saved, whatever the cost. To cover their retreat, the battle cruisers, already badly damaged, could, if necessary, be sacrificed. The destroyers massed on his port bow could be flung in to attack with torpedoes and lay smoke. But if it was to be done, it must be done now.

Again, Scheer acted instinctively, giving three commands intended to save his battleships. The first, hoisted on *Friedrich der Grosse* at 7:12 p.m., and left flying from the halyard for six minutes, signaled the battleships to prepare for a third emergency turnaround; this command was to be executed the moment the flags were hauled down. At 7:13 a second dramatic flag signal rose up the halyard: *"Schlachtkreuzer ran an den Feind, voll einsetzen,"* meaning "Battle cruisers, at the enemy. Give it everything!" At 7:21 p.m., the third of Scheer's orders was hoisted: a mass destroyer attack on the Grand Fleet was to cover the withdrawal of the German battleships.

The charge of the German battle cruisers has come to be called a "death ride." Although *Lützow* was out of action and the other four German battle cruisers were heavily damaged, *Derfflinger*'s Captain Hartog led the squadron at 20 knots toward the British line. Two of the ships were scarcely more than battered hulls, filled with thousands of tons of salt water, the sea rolling over their bows up to the forward turrets, more than half their guns destroyed or out of action, their compartments filled with dead and dying men. Yet they drove forward.

"We were steaming into this inferno," said *Derfflinger*'s Hase;

> the range fell from 12,000 to 8,000. . . . Salvo after salvo fell around us, hit after hit struck our ship. . . . A 15 inch shell pierced the armor of "Caesar" turret and exploded inside. The turret commander had both legs torn off and most of the gun crew was killed. The flames passed to the working chamber and then to the handling room and seventy-three of the seventy-eight men in the turret died. . . . Another 15-inch shell pierced the roof of "Dora" turret. The same horrors followed. With the exception of one man who was thrown by the concussion through the turret entrance, the whole turret crew of eighty men was killed instantly. From both after turrets, great flames were spurting, mingled with clouds of yellow smoke. . . . Then, a terrific roar, a tremendous explosion, then darkness. . . . The whole conning tower seemed to be hurled in the air. . . . Poisonous, greenish yellow gasses poured through the aperture into our control. I called out "Don gas masks" and every man put his gas mask over his face. . . . We could scarcely see anything of the enemy who were disposed in a great semi-circle around us. All we could see was the great reddish-gold flames spurting from their guns.

Derfflinger was hit fourteen times during the "death ride." *Seydlitz,* her bow already partially submerged, was hit five more times, bringing her total for the day to seventeen. *Von der Tann,* still keeping up although she could not fight, was struck again. Even *Lützow,* already hit nineteen times and now without Hipper, was seen struggling to get away. Five heavy shells in quick succession from *Monarch* and *Orion* battered the hulk again. Again, only *Moltke* escaped serious damage. The carnage ended at 7:17 p.m., when *Derfflinger* made out a new signal from *Friedrich der Grosse,* "Operate against the enemy's van." In effect, Scheer was saying that the battle cruisers had achieved their purpose and could be permitted to sheer off to starboard and draw away. Thus ended the "death ride" of the German battle cruisers, the bravest and, as it turned out, the last surface attack by dreadnoughts of the Imperial German Navy.

Scheer was able to reprieve his battle cruisers because, given a moment's respite from the Grand Fleet's overwhelming gun power, the German battleships were beginning their turn to the rear. For the third time that afternoon, the High Seas Fleet executed *"Gefechtskehrtwendung nach Steuerbord!"* This time, however, the emergency turn had none of the precision of a peacetime drill in the Baltic, none of the cool efficiency of the first course reversal forty minutes before. This time, captains turned their ships as well as they could, some to starboard, some to port, some finding their neighbors so close that collision seemed inevitable, then just missing. As they turned, the beleaguered ships fired an occasional defiant salvo from their after turrets; no shell came close to a British ship.

Nevertheless, Jellicoe soon faced another threat. The battle cruiser "death ride" had been a kamikaze charge without success, but the destroyer torpedo attack that followed helped to save the High Seas Fleet. When it came, the attack was delivered in less strength than Scheer would have wished. Only fourteen destroyers, carrying a total of fifty-eight torpedoes, were in position to obey his order, but they set out for the British line at 30 knots. They were met by a wall of fire from the 4-inch and 6-inch secondary batteries of the British battleships, by heavy shells from numerous dreadnought main battery turrets, and by the shells of British light cruisers and destroyers sent out by Jellicoe to blunt the attack. One German flotilla managed to come within 8,000 yards of the British battle line, where it launched eleven torpedoes before turning back and laying down smoke. The next flotilla, plunging into the same firestorm, launched more torpedoes, but one of its destroyers was sunk. A third wave attacked, but was out of range and fired only a single torpedo before retreating behind another smokescreen. In all, the fourteen German destroyers fired thirty-one torpedoes.

Even as the enemy destroyers were disappearing back into their own smoke, Jellicoe knew that their torpedoes were in the water. To escape this oncoming danger, the Commander-in-Chief ordered the standard Grand Fleet Battle Order response to approaching torpedoes: he turned his battleships away so that their sterns, rather than their broadsides, would be presented as targets. At 7:22 p.m., the battle fleet turned 2 points [22 degrees] away to port; then, to make sure, at 7:25, Jellicoe ordered the fleet to turn again another 2 points; in all, he now had turned a total of 44 degrees, onto a new course of southeast. Jellicoe's turn away, putting hundreds of additional yards between the launch tubes and the intended targets, may have been responsible for ten torpedoes' running out of fuel short of the Grand Fleet. Nevertheless, twenty-one torpedoes kept coming and reached the British line, forcing a number of battleships to maneuver independently to avoid them. It helped that the white torpedo tracks were visible in the water and that it was relatively easy for the men in the foretops to spot them and alert the bridges. The first torpedoes were sighted at 7:33 p.m., and separately the battleships began turning and twisting. *Marlborough,* already carrying a torpedo wound in her hull, saw and avoided another three torpedoes. She "altered course to starboard so that one track passed ahead, another passed so close astern that we should certainly have been hit if the stern had not been swinging under helm, while number three must have been running below depth because it went right under the ship." *Revenge,* next behind *Marlborough,* swung hard to port to avoid two torpedoes; one passed ten yards before her bow and the other twenty yards from her stern. *Hercules* and *Agincourt,* the third and fourth ships behind *Marlborough,* saw torpedoes and escaped by putting their helms over to port and sheering out of line. *Agincourt* then watched one torpedo pass up her port side and the other up the starboard side. A torpedo ran between *Iron Duke* and *Thunderer,* while *Colossus* eluded another. A torpedo came very close to *Collingwood*'s stern; at least four passed through the line not far from *Barham. Neptune* was pursued from dead astern with what almost appeared to be a conscious malevolence. A torpedo "following exactly in our course, but going faster than our fastest speed . . . [kept] coming closer and closer. . . . We could do nothing but wait and wait, mouths open. . . . Nothing happened." Afterward, the battleship's Action Report conjectured that the "torpedo was either deflected by the wash from *Neptune*'s propellers or ran its range out. The latter is more likely." Probably, other torpedoes went unnoticed before the danger passed. Twenty-one torpedoes had reached the British line, but none had found a victim. Meanwhile, the German battleships and battle cruisers and, now also, the destroyers had disappeared. And, for a while, the firing ceased.

Measured by his own hopes, Scheer's three desperate offensive thrusts—with his battle fleet, his battle cruisers, and his destroyers—had failed: they had cost him the remaining fighting capability of his battle cruisers, additional punishment of his battleships, the expenditure of many torpedoes, and the loss—by sinking or damage—of five destroyers. But, although Scheer could not have known this, he had managed something critically important: he had forced Jellicoe to turn away at a moment when the German fleet was in a desperate position and a little more pressure might have produced a rout. And by the time Jellicoe returned to the pursuit, Scheer and the German battle line were out of sight and out of range, ten or eleven miles distant. The fact was that for seventeen critical minutes while the fate of the High Seas Fleet hung in the balance, Scheer had been given time to disengage his battle fleet—and thereby to avoid its annihilation.

—

Turning large ships away from an oncoming torpedo attack was a tactic then approved by the British, German, French, Italian, and American navies. To protect a fleet, or even a single ship, turning away from torpedoes rather than toward them offered substantial advantages. The greatest was relative speed. The torpedoes would be approaching at 30 knots, but the ships would be steaming away from them at 20; the relative speed of the approaching missiles, therefore, would be 10 knots. By the same arithmetic, turning toward approaching torpedoes could mean that the underwater missiles were approaching at 30 knots plus 20; thus, 50 knots. Anyone could see that dealing with an enemy approaching at 10 knots was preferable to dealing with one approaching at 50 simply because the slower relative speed gave the targeted ship a better opportunity to maneuver out of the way. In addition, turning away would put more distance between the attackers' torpedo tubes and the intended victims, and this added distance might mean that some of the torpedoes would—as they did in this attack—run out of fuel before they reached their targets.

As a defensive measure against this German destroyer attack, Jellicoe's turnaway at Jutland was a complete success: no torpedo hits were scored on British dreadnoughts. But the maneuver shocked some officers in the fleet and later became the most heavily criticized British decision of the entire battle. Beatty, who at the Dogger Bank had turned away because he believed he had seen a single periscope, was privately scornful, and three of Jellicoe's squadron vice admirals had misgivings. The argument turns both on tactics and timing: at the moment Jellicoe turned away, the High Seas Fleet was beaten, in disarray, and in headlong flight. Had Jellicoe turned toward the torpedoes and pursued, rather than turning away, he might have lost some ships—so the argument goes—but he must have inflicted further heavy damage on the Germans and perhaps even brought about their total destruction. Instead, time and range were sacrificed—seventeen minutes and over 3,000 yards—and Scheer made good his escape. Jellicoe, by this decision, was said to have forsaken the Royal Navy's chance for a new Trafalgar. This view would hover over Jellicoe's reputation for the rest of his life.

Jellicoe was not left defenseless by his friends. The turn away was defended after the battle as vigorously as it was attacked. Admiral Sir Reginald Bacon, the first captain of the *Dreadnought* and eventually Jellicoe's biographer, pointed out that Jellicoe had no way of knowing how many German destroyers would attack him, how many torpedoes they would launch, or from what directions the torpedoes would come; in the event, Bacon argued, Jellicoe's turn away had saved at least six British battleships. John Irving puts this figure at "eight or even more."

But the ultimate issue, beyond questions of timing and of potential losses to the British and German fleets, was one of grand strategy. The High Seas Fleet, as it was employed by the kaiser and his admirals in the Great War, never posed a mortal threat to Britain's survival. Accordingly, the Admiralty and Jellicoe held the destruction of the German fleet to be infinitely less important than the preservation of the Grand Fleet, and thereby of overall British naval supremacy. Fervently though Royal Navy officers might yearn for a new Trafalgar, the naval status quo in May 1916 was acceptable to Great Britain; sea supremacy permitted the Allies exclusive use of the ocean highways while the blockade of Germany continued its corrosive work. Jellicoe, therefore, saw his primary duty as the preservation of the Grand Fleet. He was not afraid to risk his ships in a long-range gun battle because, as a gunnery expert, he knew the awesome weight of metal the British fleet could bring down on an enemy battle line. But he was agonizingly wary of exposing his fleet to any underwater ambush by torpedoes or mines. Jellicoe knew that Scheer was a torpedo specialist who believed that this weapon could be as decisive as the big gun and who would use it whenever he could. Moreover, he knew that the primary duty of German destroyers was to execute a massed torpedo attack; beating off enemy destroyers was their secondary duty. Finally, Jellicoe's own torpedo experts had told him that in peacetime exercises, 35 percent of torpedoes fired indiscriminately at a line of battleships would find a target. The German navy had eighty-eight destroyers; if all were present, they could launch up to 440 torpedoes. The numbers were sufficient to deprive John Jellicoe of hours of sleep.

Jellicoe, therefore, saw turning away simply as an exercise of a fundamental Grand Fleet battle tactic in use throughout his command. Long before, in his letter to the Admiralty of October 30, 1914, he had made his intentions clear. He had explained that he meant to assume the defensive against all enemy underwater weapons while attempting to conserve his ships for offensive action with their more numerous, heavier guns. If the Germans attempted to retreat or escape from a fleet action, he was determined not to pursue; if he were confronted by a concentrated torpedo attack, he would turn away. The Admiralty had approved, expressing "full confidence in your contemplated conduct of the fleet in action." On May 31, 1916, therefore, John Jellicoe simply did what he had said he intended to do.

—

For thirty minutes after Scheer's second turnabout, the guns were silent. For the first ten of these minutes, Jellicoe steered southeast, approximately 135 degrees off Scheer's course to the west. Then, feeling that the torpedo threat had evaporated, Jellicoe turned back expecting—once the dense clouds of black smoke spewed out by the retreating German destroyers had blown away—to find the High Seas Fleet where he had left it, still within gun range. But there was no sign of the Germans and, again, as with Scheer's previous turnabout, Jellicoe did not know where his enemy was. Five minutes passed and Jellicoe turned south. Still the sea was empty. At 7:40 p.m., he ordered another turn, this time to the southwest. Still nothing. Then, at 8:00 p.m., a signal from Goodenough confirmed that the Germans were heading west. Jellicoe turned farther west. By then, Scheer was fifteen miles away, out of reach. Yet the British Commander-in-Chief remained optimistic: steaming south, he was actually nearer to Germany than was Scheer.

Meanwhile, Scheer, after two encounters with Jellicoe and two emergency course reversals, found himself in an appalling situation. He now knew that he was facing the entire Grand Fleet and that this superior force lay between him and his base. He knew that he could not afford to be driven farther west and he changed course, first to the southwest. His ships now were in reverse order to that in which they had twice assaulted the British line: Mauve's old predreadnoughts were now in the van; the modern dreadnoughts were bringing up the rear. The half-demolished battle cruisers were a mile to port. Scheer's overriding purpose now was to get away: to save as much of his fleet as he could, and, above all, the dreadnought battleships. At 7:45 p.m., knowing that he must get these ships into friendly waters by daybreak, he altered course to south. The single factor now in his favor was that sundown and twilight were approaching. Perhaps night would hide him.

—

Beatty's six remaining battle cruisers, six miles ahead and to the southwest of the British battle line, had been too distant to have been affected by the German destroyer torpedo attacks that had caused Jellicoe to turn away. To Beatty at 7:45 p.m., Scheer's position was a mystery, but he was anxious to press forward and find the High Seas Fleet before daylight failed. However, he did not wish to find them by himself, without the support of at least some British battleships. The eight dreadnoughts of Jerram's squadron, now in Jellicoe's van, were 12,000 yards to his northeast and would serve admirably. On the spur of the moment—perhaps annoyed to the point of cheekiness by what he saw as the excessive caution of Jellicoe's turnaway—Beatty offered to take matters into his own hands. At 7:47 p.m., he signaled the Commander-in-Chief, "Submit van of battleships follow battle cruisers. We can then cut off whole of enemy's battle fleet." Jellicoe's supporters later described this message as typical of Beatty's "posturing"; even the modest Commander-in-Chief eventually declared, "To tell the truth, I thought it was rather insubordinate."

Beatty's signal took fourteen minutes to reach Jellicoe's hand and by this time the Commander-in-Chief saw no need for urgency. He had already turned the fleet, including Jerram's squadron, to a westerly course—nearer the enemy, in fact, than Beatty's course. Nevertheless, coming from Beatty, the signal demanded consideration. But what did the signal mean? Where was *Lion*? What could Beatty see? Jellicoe assumed that, before sending this message, Beatty must have recovered visual contact with some German ships. But what ships? The German battle fleet? The German battle cruisers? If Beatty could see Germans, Jerram, leading the van of the battle fleet in *King George V,* also must see them. Therefore, the Commander-in-Chief responded by signaling Jerram: "Follow our battle cruisers." Jerram, who received the order at 8:07 p.m. and who at that moment could see neither Beatty nor Germans, turned to the south hoping to find one or the other. By this time, however, Beatty had lost whatever contact he thought he had with the German fleet.

Then, just as the sun was setting, Beatty found the German battle cruisers only 10,000 yards away. At 8:12, all six British ships opened fire and all four German ships were hit, *Seydlitz* the hardest. A 13.5-inch shell from *Princess*

Royal exploded on her open bridge, killing half the men there and covering the navigation charts with blood. The gyrocompass was smashed; as a result, *Seydlitz,* lacking charts and compass, her steering system failing, was blind and nearly helpless. The engagement also affected Hipper, still trying to resume command of his shattered squadron. Just before Beatty opened fire, Hipper had ordered his battle cruisers to stop engines so that his destroyer could come alongside *Moltke.* He was ready to board when suddenly 13.5-inch and 12-inch British shells plunged down nearby. The boarding attempt was instantly suspended so that *Moltke* and her sisters could begin to move. Once again, Hipper was forced to watch his squadron steam away.

At 8:30 p.m., the plight of the crippled German battle cruisers attracted a group of Samaritans. Rear Admiral Mauve, seeing the helplessness of Hipper's ships, seized his chance to be useful and steered his six old battleships into the fight. Beatty's gunnery officers recognized the distinctive silhouettes of the predreadnoughts and shifted fire from the German battle cruisers to the obsolete ships. Three were hit: *Schleswig-Holstein, Pommern,* and *Schlesien; Posen,* in turn, struck *Princess Royal* with an 11-inch shell. Then, their intervention having permitted the German battle cruisers to slip away, the old "five-minute ships" turned into the gloom. Beatty did not follow.

The sun had set at 8:19 p.m. and the light was quickly fading. There was no chance of further fighting between the dreadnought fleets that day, but Jellicoe was certain that he would be able to finish the battle in the morning. That time would come soon; sunrise would arrive in five hours. Meanwhile, Scheer was trapped. The High Seas Fleet had reversed course three times and still found itself in the wrong place. Now, as darkness fell, 143 British warships lay between 93 German vessels and their safe return home.

CHAPTER 33

Jutland: Night and Morning

As darkness fell, Jellicoe was pleased with his situation. "I went back to the bridge from the conning tower at about 8:30 p.m.," said Frederic Dreyer, captain of *Iron Duke,* "and spoke to Jellicoe and [Rear Admiral Charles] Madden [the Grand Fleet Chief of Staff], both of whom expressed satisfaction at the good firing of the *Iron Duke.* I found that they agreed that everything that had happened had been according to expectation." In fact, things were far less rosy than Jellicoe supposed. The British battle cruiser force had been depleted by considerably more than the admiral actually knew; he had seen *Invincible*'s severed bow and stern sections rising from the water, but no one had informed him of the loss of *Queen Mary* and *Indefatigable. Lion* and *Princess Royal* each had one turret out of action and three turrets able to fire. Still, the British battle cruisers had served their essential purpose: they had brought Scheer to the Grand Fleet and had assisted in the reduction of their own natural enemies, Hipper's battle cruisers, to floating wreckage. *Warspite* was returning to Rosyth, but the 5th Battle Squadron still carried twenty-four 15-inch guns. *Marlborough* had been torpedoed and had lost 4 knots of speed, but was still in action. Two armored cruisers had been lost—*Defence* blown up and *Warrior* disabled—and three destroyers had been sunk, with three others damaged and out of action. Otherwise, the Grand Fleet's immense dreadnought battle line was almost untouched. Adding the three *Queen Elizabeth*s and the surviving six battle cruisers, British supremacy was even more preponderant than when the battle started.

Jellicoe's purpose now was to preserve this supremacy through the night. Keenly aware that German ships were better equipped and trained for night fighting, the Commander-in-Chief at once decided to postpone renewal of the battle until morning. A battleship night action, he believed, "must have inevitably led to our battle fleet being the object of attack by a very large German destroyer force throughout the night." To repel destroyer attacks at night required a coordinated effort by battleship searchlights and secondary armament (6-inch and 4-inch guns), aided if possible by a counterattack by friendly destroyers. The Germans were trained to do this. Searchlights and gun crews worked together: first, a thin, pencil beam would locate an enemy ship; then an iris shutter would snap aside, focusing the full beam of light on the target and, instantly, the guns would fire. Jellicoe had little confidence in the British fleet's ability to match these techniques. "It was known to me that neither our searchlights nor their control arrangements were at this time of the best type," he said. "[And] the fitting of Director Firing Gear for the guns of the secondary armament of our battleships had only just begun, although repeatedly applied for." Further, he continued, "our own destroyers would be no effective antidote at night since . . . they would certainly be taken for enemy destroyers and fired on by our own ships." In sum, Jellicoe believed that "the result of night actions between heavy ships must always be very largely a matter of chance as there is little opportunity for skill on either side. Such an action must be fought at very close range, the decision depending on the course of events in the first few minutes." Later, he put it more bluntly in a letter to the First Sea Lord: "Nothing would make me fight a night action with heavy ships in these days of destroyers and long-range torpedoes. I might well lose the fight. It would be far too fluky an affair."

Having rejected a night battle with Scheer, Jellicoe turned to the question of where he would be most likely to find the German admiral at first light. Which of several escape routes was Scheer most likely to use? Four were possible. The first, the 344-mile voyage around the northern coast of Denmark into the Baltic, Jellicoe dismissed as being too long and dangerous for the numerous ships of the High Seas Fleet he knew to be seriously damaged. That left three routes within the North Sea that would bring Scheer back safely through the minefields, British and German, in the Bight. One was southeast to the Horns Reef light vessel, then back to the Jade behind the minefields of the Amrum Bank—a reversal of the path by which Scheer had come north the previous night. Although this route was the closest to the 9:30 p.m. position of the two fleets, Jellicoe doubted that Scheer would choose it. The Grand Fleet already blocked a German passage to Horns Reef, and Scheer's fleet lacked the speed to get ahead and cut across in front of it. Was it likely that Scheer would attempt to force his way to Horns Reef through the middle of the British fleet? Jellicoe thought probably not. Twice that afternoon, Scheer had collided with the Grand Fleet battle line and both times he had immediately reversed course to get away. Jellicoe did not believe that he would try it again, even at night, and especially not when two other routes back to Germany were available. One of these lay southwest, toward the Ems, then east to Wilhelmshaven behind the German minefields; the other was due south, straight for Heligoland and the Jade Bay. Estimating that Scheer would choose one of these two, Jellicoe made his decision: "to steer south where I should be in a position . . . to intercept the enemy should he make for . . . Heligoland or towards the Ems."

Soon after nine o'clock, the British Commander-in-Chief closed up his battle fleet into night cruising formation and signaled a fleet speed of 17 knots. The dreadnoughts shifted out of their single line ahead and formed in three columns abreast, one mile apart; this was to ensure that the battleship divisions remained in sight of one another and to prevent ships mistaking one another for enemy vessels. In making these dispositions, Jellicoe did not exclude the possibility of some sort of night engagement; indeed, as Scheer was to his northwest, he expected torpedo attacks on his fleet from destroyers in that quarter. To shield his battleships from this threat, Jellicoe placed all of his own flotillas—fifty-eight destroyers—five miles astern of the battle fleet. He put them there, he said later, to "fulfill three conditions. They would be in an excellent position for attacking the enemy's fleet should it turn . . . [toward Horns Reef] during the night. They would be in a position to attack enemy destroyers should the latter search for our fleet with a view to night attack on our heavy ships. Finally, they would be clear of our own ships, and the danger of attacking our battleships in error, or of our battleships firing on them, would be reduced to a minimum."

His dispositions made, Jellicoe signaled the fleet, "No night intentions," leaving his admirals and captains to assume that they could expect four or five relatively quiet hours and a renewal of the battle at first light. The signal was welcome, although most men remained at action stations through the night. Sandwiches and tins of corned beef and salmon were handed out, along with mugs of traditional Royal Navy cocoa "made from dark slabs of rich chocolate of such a thick consistency that a spoon would stand up in it." And on *Iron Duke,* an exhausted John Jellicoe lay down fully clothed to rest for a few hours on a cot in a shelter just behind the bridge.

—

Surrounded by darkness on his own bridge, Reinhard Scheer was in a perilous situation. He was opposed by the entire Grand Fleet; he understood that if there was a battle in the morning, the Imperial Navy would be annihilated. The corollaries were plain: there must be no battle; somehow, he must escape. But there was little time; dawn would arrive at 2:00 a.m., and 3:00 would bring full daylight. Scheer knew other things about his enemy: he was aware that British warships, unlike his own, had not been trained to fight at night, and, therefore, that Jellicoe probably would prefer to postpone battle until dawn. He knew that the British battle fleet was southeast of him, somewhere between eight and twelve miles away, in a position to block his fleet from returning home by that route. In Jellicoe's course, Scheer saw his own impending doom—but also an opportunity. Jellicoe obviously had won the race to the south; if he, Scheer, continued in that direction, the British fleet would be able to deliver a terminal blow at dawn. But, Scheer conjectured, suppose he did not follow Jellicoe to the south. The nearest sanctuary, the entrance to the Horns Reef swept channel, lay to the southeast, only eighty-five miles away. Suppose, in the darkness, he were to turn southeast and somehow manage to avoid—or, if necessary, break through—the Grand Fleet and reach the Horns Reef lightship by daybreak. If this could be done, the High Seas Fleet could retreat down the Amrum Channel between the minefields and the sandbanks, and Jellicoe would be unable to follow.

Scheer decided to try. He would turn southeast for Horns Reef, keeping his battle fleet in close order, hoping to pass unnoticed in the darkness astern of the Grand Fleet, but accepting the possibility of a night action if he failed. He would maintain this course regardless of losses. Meanwhile, his own destroyer flotillas would attack the British at every opportunity, sacrificing themselves so that his dreadnoughts could escape. At 9:10 p.m., Scheer initiated this plan with a signal sent out from *Friedrich der Grosse:* "Battle fleet's course southeast by a quarter east. This course is to be maintained. Speed sixteen knots." At the same time, he sent an urgent request to the Naval Staff asking for airship reconnaissance of Horns Reef at daybreak. Repeatedly during the night, the urgent command came from the flagship: *"Durchhalten"*—"Maintain the course."

To prepare for the nocturnal breakthrough, Scheer realigned his ships. *Westfalen* and her undamaged sisters, *Nassau, Rheinland,* and *Posen,* were in the van; Scheer's flagship, *Friedrich der Grosse,* remained in the middle. Mauve's slow predreadnoughts were ordered to the rear, out of the way. For the same reason, the mangled battle cruisers also were sent to the rear. By now, *Lützow* and *Seydlitz* were incapable of renewing action. *Lützow* had received forty large-caliber hits, *Seydlitz* twenty-four shell hits and a torpedo. Steering erratically with a broken gyrocompass, she fell behind *Moltke* in the dark and was left on her own. *Derfflinger,* with 3,400 tons of water aboard and only one turret ready for action, trailed the toothless *Von der Tann.* Of Scheer's battleships, *König* had been hit by ten heavy projectiles, while *Grosser Kurfürst, Markgraf,* and *Kaiser* had received fifteen hits among them. *Wiesbaden* was sinking and four destroyers had been sunk.

—

Meanwhile, at 9:32 p.m., *Lion*—so a number of historians have written—unintentionally handed the Germans a valuable gift. Out in front of Jellicoe's battle fleet, Beatty's flagship signaled by flashing lamp to *Princess Royal,* her next astern: "Please give me challenge and reply now in force . . . as they have been lost." *Princess Royal* obediently signaled back the current identification signal. That much is certain; *Lion*'s request and her sister's compliance are both recorded in *The Battle of Jutland Official Despatches.* What, if anything, happened next is less certain. It is frequently said that because neither British battle cruiser knew that two miles away in the darkness, a sharp-eyed signalman aboard the German light cruiser *Frankfurt* was watching, the British signal was intercepted and immediately distributed to the whole German fleet: "First sign of enemy challenge is UA." If true, this would have given the Germans a second advantage: not only were their ships and crews equipped and trained to fight at night while the British were not, but they also would have been able to recognize and use the British challenge. Andrew Gordon considers German interception "implausible" for a number of technical reasons. And neither of the official naval histories of the war, British (Corbett) or German (Groos), mentions that the Germans saw this exchange of signals.

—

As Jellicoe steamed south and Scheer drove relentlessly southeast for Horns Reef, the two fleets were converging, their tracks forming the two sides of a long, narrow "V," with the British fleet, moving 1 knot faster than the German, drawing slowly ahead. Because the British battleships reached the bottom of the "V" and passed through it about fifteen minutes before Scheer's battleships arrived, "the 'V' became an 'X' . . . neither side was conscious of what was happening," and the two lines of dreadnoughts did not meet and engage. Nevertheless, with each side unaware that their pathways were crossing, spasms of sudden, ferocious violence erupted between smaller ships. The first came at 10:15 p.m. when Commodore William Goodenough and others on the bridge of the light cruiser *Southampton* became aware of the presence of unknown ships in the darkness to starboard. For a few moments, four British light cruisers and five German light cruisers steamed parallel to each other, only 800 yards apart, each side uncertain of the identity of the other. Finally, Goodenough said, "I can't help who it is. Fire!" *Dublin* fired, and almost simultaneously a dozen brilliant German searchlights illuminated the head of the British line. "Those who have not experienced it cannot possibly understand the overpowering effect of searchlights being in our face with gunfire at what was really point-blank range," said a young officer. Four German light cruisers concentrated on *Southampton,* smothering Goodenough's flagship with shell bursts and carpeting her decks with dead and wounded men. Despite this damage, the beleaguered British vessel managed to fire a torpedo, which hit the old light cruiser *Frauenlob,* a survivor of the Battle of the Bight. *Frauenlob* sank with her entire crew of 320 men.

After the war, Lieutenant Stephen King-Hall of *Southampton* gave this account of the action:

> A signalman suddenly whispered: "Five ships on the beam." The Commodore looked at them. . . . From their faint silhouettes, it was impossible to discover more than the fact that they were light cruisers. . . . We began to challenge; the Germans switched on coloured lights at their fore yardarms. A second later, a solitary gun fired from *Dublin*. . . . I saw the shell hit a ship just above the waterline 800 yards away. . . . At that moment, the Germans switched on their searchlights and we switched on ours. Before I was blinded by the lights in my eyes, I caught sight of a line of light grey ships. . . . The action lasted three and a half minutes. The four leading German ships concentrated on *Southampton*. . . . The range was amazingly close. . . . There could be no missing . . . but to load guns there must be men, flesh and blood . . . and flesh and blood cannot stand high explosives. . . . The German shots went high, just high enough to burst on the upper deck around the bridge and after superstructure. . . . Another shell burst on the searchlight just above us. . . . Fragments scoured out the insides of the gun shields of the two 6-inch guns manned by Marines. Then . . . the flash of an exploding shell ignited half a dozen rounds of powder. It became lighter than day. I looked forward. Two pillars of white flame rose aloft. One roared up the foremast, the other reached above the tops of the second and third funnels. This, then, was the end. . . . It was bad luck, but there could be no doubt; the central ammunition hoist was between those two funnels. What was it going to feel like to blow up? What ought one to do? . . . The two pillars of flame wavered and decreased in height. . . . I ran to the boat deck to get to the fire and tripped over a heap of bodies. I got up, tried not to tread on soft things, and arrived at the boat deck. The firing had ceased. . . . Everything was pitch black . . . nothing but groans from dark corners. The Germans had fled. They fled because our Torpedo Lieutenant had fired a 21-inch torpedo. At forty-one knots, the torpedo, striking the *Frauenlob,* had blown her in half.

Southampton had lost thirty-five killed and forty-one wounded, and she had also lost her wireless, the means by which Goodenough had tried to keep Jellicoe informed. In any case, this phase of the battle—in which *Southampton* was severely damaged and *Frauenlob* sunk—had occurred more or less between equals: light cruisers against light cruisers. The desperate clashes that followed would pit unequal adversaries: 900-ton British destroyers against 20,000-ton German dreadnought battleships.

—

Through the night, Room 40 continued to intercept and decode German signals and pass them along to the Admiralty Operations Staff, where ignorance and incompetence held firm. Messages, accurate and inaccurate, were sent to Jellicoe during the night; it was left to the Commander-in-Chief to sort out which was which. Worse, vital and accurate information available in London was never sent at all. At 9:55 p.m., the Admiralty supplied Jellicoe with accurate information: "Three [German] destroyer flotillas have been ordered to attack you during the night." This signal buttressed Jellicoe's view of what was likely to happen and when, as the night progressed, he heard the sounds of battle astern of his main fleet, he believed they were the result of these German destroyers trying to break through his own destroyer screen to the rear. Then, three minutes later, the Admiralty sent Jellicoe information that the Commander-in-Chief knew to be false. The German battle fleet, London advised, was ten miles southwest of *Iron Duke.* This message increased Jellicoe's already substantial distrust of Admiralty intelligence. He knew that Scheer's fleet lay northwest of him, not southwest, and, he said, "I should not for a moment have relied on Admiralty information of the enemy in preference to reports from ships which had actually sighted him to the northwest."

Meanwhile, the Admiralty had deciphered Scheer's 9:10 p.m. signal and at 10:41 p.m., Jellicoe was informed—accurately—"German battle fleet ordered home. . . . Battle cruisers in rear. Course south southeast. Speed sixteen knots." "South southeast" clearly pointed to Horns Reef. If this was true and if Scheer was to Jellicoe's northwest—as Jellicoe knew he was—the German fleet must somehow cross the track of the Grand Fleet to reach this sanctuary. By now, however, Jellicoe's confidence in intelligence coming from the Operations Division was so thoroughly shaken that he did not believe the Admiralty signal. Thus, later that night, when the sounds of heavy gunfire astern reached *Iron Duke,* the Commander-in-Chief assumed that they emanated from the expected German destroyer attacks on his screen, not from Scheer's main fleet attempting to force its way through the rear of his own huge formation. In any case, if German battleships were engaging his destroyers, he assumed that reports of battleship sightings would come pouring in to the flagship. And there were no such reports.

The crucial message that never came from the Admiralty that night was one telling Jellicoe that Room 40 had intercepted and decoded Scheer's request for zeppelin reconnaissance over Horns Reef at dawn. Coupled with the previous message giving Scheer's southeasterly course, this could have left no doubt as to the path by which the High Seas Fleet was returning home. Jellicoe said later, "The lamentable part of the whole business is that, had the Admiralty sent all the information which they acquired . . . there would have been little or no doubt in my mind as to the route by which Scheer intended to return to base. As early as 10:10, Scheer's message to the airship detachment . . . was in the possession of the Admiralty. This was practically a certain indication of his route but it was not passed to me."

Elsewhere he said, "Of course, if the Admiralty had given me this information, I should have altered in that direction during the night." As it was, assuming that he was keeping between Scheer and his base and that the British fleet would finish the battle in an all-day gunnery duel beginning at dawn, Jellicoe continued south forty miles in the wrong direction.

The message requesting airship reconnaissance was only one of *seven* German operational signals revealing Scheer's course or position between 10:43 p.m. and 1:00 a.m. that were intercepted that night by Room 40, but not forwarded to Jellicoe. Another signal containing crucial evidence was that from the commodore of all German destroyers, ordering his flotillas to assemble at Horns Reef by 2:00 a.m. This too was intercepted, but not passed to Jellicoe. Personal responsibility for this gross Admiralty failure—Arthur Marder calls it "criminal neglect"—was never officially assigned. Captain Thomas Jackson—he of the general contempt for cryptographers and signals intelligence—was not present in the War Room that night. Admiral Oliver, the Chief of Staff, charged with approving Admiralty messages sent to the Commander-in-Chief, "had left the War Room for some much-needed rest and had left in charge an officer who had no experience of German operational signals." Seeing no special significance in these decoded messages, this officer carefully placed them in an Admiralty file.

—

In the hour before midnight, when the darkness was intense and neither side knew where the other was, the leading battleships of the High Seas Fleet began to converge on the British destroyers screening the rear of the Grand Fleet. At 11:20, the lead vessels of Jellicoe's 4th Flotilla became aware of unknown ships approaching on their starboard quarter. Some appeared to be light cruisers, some larger. Believing the ships were British, *Tipperary,* the flotilla leader, waited until they were only 700 yards away and then flashed the recognition challenge. Instantly, three German battleships, *Westfalen, Nassau,* and *Rheinland,* and three light cruisers, *Hamburg, Rostock,* and *Elbing,* switched on an array of searchlights, most aimed at *Tipperary.* Then, the battleships' secondary armament burst out; within four minutes, *Westfalen* alone fired 150 5.9-inch shells. *Tipperary* burst into flames. Every new hit stoked the fires, and for several hours the misshapen but still floating mass of wreckage continued to burn.

As the British destroyers astern of *Tipperary* swerved to avoid the blazing wreck, they used their 4-inch guns to rake the superstructures of their massive opponents, hitting bridges, searchlight stations, and signal flag positions. The destroyers also launched torpedoes; one, they believed, hit *Elbing,* which nine hours earlier had fired the first shot in the battle. (Afterward, the Germans declared that the cruiser was never torpedoed.) In accordance with High Seas Fleet procedure when under torpedo attack, the German dreadnoughts turned away, from southeast to southwest. The German light cruisers, avoiding the torpedoes as well as they could, steered for the gaps in the line of their own battleships. *Elbing* misjudged and was rammed by the dreadnought *Posen.* The bow of the battleship sliced into the light cruiser, flooding both engine rooms, stripping *Elbing* of power, and leaving her adrift.

The destroyer *Spitfire,* which had been just astern of *Tipperary,* found herself confronting the dreadnought *Nassau.* Tormented by the torpedoes, *Nassau* turned at full speed to ram. The two ships collided port bow to port bow, the impact rolling the destroyer over, almost, but not quite enough, to swamp her. Then, alongside her little antagonist, *Nassau* fired her two huge forward turret guns. She was too close; the gun barrels would not depress sufficiently to hit the destroyer with shells, but even so, *Spitfire* bore the weight of *Nassau*'s rage. The concussion of muzzle blasts at close range and maximum depression swept away the destroyer's bridge, foremast, funnels, boats, and searchlight platform. Everyone on the bridge except the captain and two seamen was killed. Then, with a screech of tearing metal, the dreadnought surged down the destroyer's port side, bumping, scraping, and stripping away everything including boats and davits, "and all the time she was firing her guns just over our heads." Eventually *Nassau* cleared *Spitfire*'s stern and disappeared into the darkness, leaving twenty feet of upper deck plating on the destroyer's forecastle. *Spitfire* had lost sixty feet from the side of her hull, but remained afloat and was able to make 6 knots. Thirty-six hours later, she reached the Tyne.

Scheer was undeterred by these episodes. When the British torpedo attack forced the German battle line to turn away, the Commander-in-Chief immediately signaled *Westfalen* to resume course southeast for Horns Reef. *Nothing* must be allowed to divert the fleet from this course. Swinging back, the leading German battleships once again clashed with the 4th Flotilla. With the destruction of *Tipperary,* leadership of the flotilla had passed to the destroyer *Broke,* which almost immediately sighted a large ship on a crossing course half a mile away. Uncertain of the ship's identity despite its two funnels and a massive amidships crane—the distinctive profile of German dreadnoughts—*Broke*'s captain gave the order to challenge by searchlight. As he spoke, the stranger switched on a vertical string of colored lights, a signal unknown in the British fleet. Then the terrible sequence repeated itself and the 4th Flotilla was further dismembered: "A blaze of searchlights straight into our eyes . . . so great was the dazzling effect that it made us feel helpless," said *Broke*'s navigating officer. Then came a hurricane of shells, this time from the light cruiser *Rostock* and the dreadnoughts *Westfalen* and *Rheinland. Broke* managed to fire one torpedo before she was smashed. Everyone on her bridge was killed. The wheel was shattered, jamming the rudder to port, leaving the ship out of control and turning in a circle, still at high speed. *Sparrowhawk,* just astern, was about to fire her own torpedoes when she saw *Broke* careening toward her at 28 knots. There was no time to get out of the way; *Broke*'s bow rammed *Sparrowhawk* just in front of the bridge. The force of the blow catapulted twenty-three men from the *Sparrowhawk* across onto the forecastle of *Broke*'s embedded bow. With the two destroyers locked together and each ship believing that she was sinking, men from each ship were sent across to the other to save their lives. As *Broke* began backing astern to disengage, the destroyer *Contest* appeared out of the dark and could not avoid the entangled pair. *Sparrowhawk* was rammed again, this blow slicing off six feet of her stern. Eventually, *Broke* and *Contest* both extricated themselves and limped away. *Sparrowhawk,* now lacking both bow and stern, lay where she was, lit by the flames of the burning *Tipperary.* Around 2:00 a.m., *Tipperary,* abandoned by her crew for life rafts or the open sea, foundered and sank. Twenty-six of her survivors were taken aboard the mutilated *Sparrowhawk,* which after the failure of an attempt by the destroyer *Marksman* to tow, continued to drift until the following day she too was abandoned and sunk. The survivors of both ships were taken aboard *Marksman* and eventually reached Scotland. Meanwhile, *Broke,* with a crumpled bow, heavy shell damage, and half her crew dead or wounded, managed in *Spitfire*'s wake to creep back to the Tyne. Four of the 4th Flotilla's destroyers were out of action, but the survivors extracted revenge when a torpedo from the destroyer *Achates* hit the light cruiser *Rostock.* She limped away and, with her crew taken off by a destroyer, sank at 4:25 a.m.

A second time, Scheer's battle fleet had swung off course, and once again the stern command *"Durchhalten!"* went out from the flagship. As a result, the German line again rammed through the 4th Flotilla, or what remained of it. Again, the British destroyers used their 4-inch guns against the searchlights and superstructures of *Westfalen, Rheinland, Posen, Oldenburg,* and *Helgoland.* Every man on *Oldenburg*'s bridge was hit. Captain Hofner, bleeding heavily, staggered forward and took the wheel himself until help came.

Back on course, the ships in the German van hoped that the torpedo danger was over. It was not. *Ardent* and *Fortune,* separated from their 4th Flotilla consorts in the first attack, were searching for them. Now, *Ardent*'s captain said, they found "four big ships on a nearly parallel, but slightly converging course. They challenged several times and their challenge was not an English one. They then switched on their searchlights, picked up *Fortune* and opened fire. . . . *Fortune* was hard hit. . . . We caught a last glimpse of *Fortune* on fire and sinking but fighting still." Separated again, searching again, *Ardent* discovered "a big ship steaming on exactly the opposite course to us. I attacked at once and from a very close range our remaining torpedoes were fired, but before I could judge the effect, the enemy switched on searchlights and found us. . . . I then became aware that *Ardent* was taking on a division of German battleships. . . . Our guns were useless against such adversaries, our torpedoes were fired; we could do no more but wait in the full glare of the blinding searchlight for the shells. . . . Shell after shell hit us and our speed diminished and then stopped . . . all the lights went out. I could feel the ship was sinking." Of *Ardent*'s company, only two men, one her captain, survived. This marked the end of the 4th Flotilla's part in the battle. The twelve destroyers had done their best; now four were sunk or sinking, three others were heavily damaged, and the rest were scattered. In effect, the flotilla had ceased to exist.

—

In the harsh arithmetic of war, the loss of two light cruisers to one side and four destroyers to the other meant little. For the Germans, it was the price of success. Scheer intended to ram his battle fleet through to Horns Reef at any cost and if this could be done in exchange for two light cruisers, the bargain was an excellent one. For the British, the destruction of a destroyer flotilla might have been acceptable had its sacrifice been made useful by someone telling the Commander-in-Chief whom the destroyers were fighting. But this did not happen. Extraordinarily, as the dark horizon was lit by gun flashes and rent by the noise of the cannonade, these battles were witnessed from many British ships, but no one reported the presence of German battleships to Jellicoe. For this failure, it is easier to forgive the destroyer captains. Desperately attempting to handle their small ships so as to keep formation, avoid shellfire, and aim and launch torpedoes, they had little time to compose and send messages. But the engaged destroyers were not the only witnesses. Between 11:15 p.m. and 1:15 a.m., others could have told the Commander-in-Chief that the High Seas Fleet was crossing in his wake. Seven battleships in the rear of the British battle line were only 6,000 yards from these engagements, and three of those battleships were the most powerful dreadnoughts in the British navy.

The situation was this: by 10:00 p.m., *Marlborough,* wounded by a torpedo and no longer able to maintain the 17-knot fleet speed ordered by Jellicoe, had gradually slipped astern of the main body of the Grand Fleet. The other three dreadnoughts of her division, *Revenge, Hercules,* and *Agincourt,* remained behind with *Marlborough,* as did the three *Queen Elizabeth*s of the 5th Battle Squadron, assigned to keep station on *Marlborough.* All of these ships were within point-blank range of Scheer's battleships when they passed only three miles astern. No one had a better view than *Malaya,* the last ship in the British battle line, which saw and identified the German dreadnought *Westfalen.* According to *Malaya*'s captain: "At 11.40, [we] observed what appeared to be an attack by our destroyers on some big enemy ships steering the same way as ours. . . . The leading ship of the enemy . . . had two masts, two funnels and a conspicuous crane—apparently *Westfalen* class." All of *Malaya*'s guns trained on the enemy battleship, and the gunnery officer asked permission to open fire. Captain Algernon Boyle refused. Like Arbuthnot during the Scarborough Raid, Boyle argued that what he could see must also be visible to the flagship *Barham,* two ships ahead, and that he must await orders to fire from his rear admiral, Evan-Thomas. A few minutes later, Boyle changed his mind and reported what he had seen to Evan-Thomas. But not to *Iron Duke;* Boyle believed that a captain should respect the chain of command and pass his observations to his own rear admiral, not directly to the Commander-in-Chief.

In fact, *Barham* already had witnessed "constant attacks by torpedo craft on ships first to the west and then to the north." So had *Valiant,* the third of the three *Queen Elizabeth*s: "At 11.35 p.m., we observed heavy firing on our starboard quarter. . . . They appeared to be two German cruisers with at least two funnels and a crane amidships [the profile of German dreadnoughts] steering eastward at high speed. These cruisers then evidently sighted an unknown small number of British ships ahead of them, possibly a light cruiser and a few destroyers. . . . Both Germans switched on top searchlights and opened a very rapid and extraordinarily accurate fire on our light cruiser. She replied but was soon in flames fore and aft." Evan-Thomas, watching these attacks from *Barham*'s bridge, had seen heavy firing behind him, "which I surmised to be attacks by enemy destroyers on our light cruisers and destroyers. . . . At 10.39, heavy firing was observed . . . and destroyers appeared to be attacking the cruisers. At 11.35 p.m., a further attack was seen . . . right astern." Despite these observations, Evan-Thomas, who had twenty-four 15-inch guns at his command, did nothing. Years later, *Barham*'s captain attempted to justify his admiral's behavior. He doubted "whether the various observations of enemy ships made by ships of our battle fleet ought to have been reported to the Commander-in-Chief. I was on the bridge all night with my admiral and we came to the conclusion that the situation was known to the C.-in-C. and that the attacks were according to plan. A stream of wireless reports from ships in company with the Commander-in-Chief seemed superfluous and uncalled-for. The unnecessary use of wireless was severely discouraged as being likely to disclose our position to the enemy. . . . This may have been an error in judgement but cannot be termed 'amazing neglect.' "

—

Still another British destroyer, *Turbulent,* was sunk—blown to pieces by twenty-nine 5.9-inch shells from the dreadnought *Westfalen*—during the High Sea Fleet's continuing charge to the southeast. In all, two German light cruisers and five British destroyers were sunk during this phase of the battle, but not all of these ships went down suddenly; in most cases, the crews were taken off first by friendly vessels. This was not the case with two other warships, both large, one British and one German. Near the end of this dreadful night, two sudden, cataclysmic explosions obliterated these vessels, each with its entire crew of almost a thousand men. The first of these disasters occurred about midnight, during an intermission in the dreadnought-versus-destroyer battles. In the darkness, a solitary, large, four-funneled ship, the 13,500-ton British armored cruiser *Black Prince,* blundered smack into the center of Scheer's battle line. After the turmoil at Windy Corner near 6:00 p.m. when the 1st Cruiser Squadron was scattered and Sir Robert Arbuthnot had led two of his four ships, *Defence* and *Warrior,* into a cataract of gunfire, *Black Prince* had turned northwest, traveled too far, and lost contact. Ever since, she had steamed south through the mist, hoping to find the British fleet. At last, near midnight, she discovered a group of dreadnoughts; but they were not English. *Thüringen, Ostfriesland,* and *Friedrich der Grosse* saw and recognized her, and their gunners prepared. *Black Prince* kept coming and, less than a mile away, flashed the British recognition signal. The reply was a dazzle of searchlights and a storm of shells at point-blank range. *Black Prince*'s two central funnels were shot away, and lurid red and yellow flames rose 100 feet in the air. But her engines still worked and, roaring like a furnace, she staggered back along the length of the German line, so close, said Scheer, watching from the bridge of *Friedrich der Grosse,* "that the crew could be seen rushing backwards and forwards on the burning deck." Finally, the fire reached her magazines. She blew up with an incandescent white light and a gigantic thunderclap of noise; "a grand but terrible sight," said Scheer. Her entire crew perished, 900 men.

As dawn was breaking on the morning of June 1, this British disaster was matched by one equally dreadful for the German navy. By 1:45 a.m., Scheer's battleships, still plowing relentlessly to the southeast, had worked their way around to the port quarter of the British fleet and now were crossing the path of another—and as it happened, the last—group of British destroyers between themselves and Horns Reef, twenty-eight miles away. In the early gray light, Captain Anselan Stirling of the destroyer *Faulknor,* leading the 12th Flotilla, sighted a shadowy line of large, dark ships on his starboard beam. They were battleships, the rear of the German battle line, where, in the confusion and darkness, Behncke's battered superdreadnoughts had intermingled with Mauve's fragile predreadnoughts. When one of these ships flashed the letter "K" in Morse code—the wrong recognition signal—Stirling knew that they were German. He did not make the same mistake other British captains had made that night. He wirelessed Jellicoe. At 1:56 a.m., *Faulknor* signaled, "URGENT. PRIORITY. Enemy's battle fleet steering southeast. . . . My position ten miles astern of 1st Battle Squadron." Not only did Stirling send this message; he sent it three times: at 1:56, 2:08, and 2:13 a.m. Unfortunately, *Iron Duke* received none of these signals, perhaps because of efficient German jamming. But informing the Commander-in-Chief was only half of Stirling's duty, and he initiated the other half as well, signaling, "URGENT. I am attacking." Conditions at that hour were nearly ideal for destroyer torpedo attack: it was too light for enemy searchlights to be useful, but still sufficiently dark to make it difficult to aim at fast-moving targets. At 2:02, Stirling fired his first torpedo; two minutes later, the second; within a few minutes, he and his six destroyers had fired seventeen torpedoes at ranges of 2,000 to 3,000 yards. The torpedoes missed the big, important targets—*König, Grosser Kurfürst, Kronprinz,* and *Markgraf*—but a violent explosion shook the old predreadnought *Pommern.* "Amidships on the waterline of the *Pommern* appeared a dull, red ball of fire," said an officer of the destroyer *Obedient.* "Quicker than one can imagine, it spread fore and aft, until, reaching the foremast and mainmast, it flared up the masts in big, red tongues of flames, uniting between the mastheads in a big, black cloud of smoke and sparks. Then we saw the ends of the ship come up as if her back had been broken." *Pommern* was now in two sections; as her sister *Hannover* passed by, the stern was upside down, propellers and rudder high out of water. Part of the bow was still afloat ten minutes later, but there were no survivors. Eight hundred and forty-four men were lost.

This was the last of the Jutland night actions in which British destroyers fought German battleships and light cruisers. In these fierce, chaotic struggles, the small British ships had done the best they could and had sunk one German battleship, three light cruisers, and two German destroyers at a cost of five of their own number. What they could not do was to bar or even seriously delay the High Seas Fleet in its determined lunge to escape.

—

Through the night, the flicker of gunfire and the glare of distant searchlights were seen and heard throughout the British fleet. Some had no idea what was happening. "Every now and then out of the silence would come *bang, bang, boom,* as hard as it could go for ten minutes," said a destroyer officer whose ship was not involved. "The flash of guns lit up the whole sky for miles and miles and the noise was far more penetrating than by day. Then you could see a great burst of flame from some poor devil, the searchlights switched on and off, and then perfect silence once more." In their official reports after the battle, the captains of the dreadnoughts *Hercules, Conqueror, Colossus, Superb, Thunderer, Téméraire, Bellerophon, Vanguard,* and *Canada* all told of hearing gunfire and seeing the glare of searchlights, first to the northwest and then, as the night progressed, in an arc across the rear of the fleet. "A cruiser on fire . . . searchlight beams from her turned quite red by flames. . . . After midnight, there was intermittent firing on the port quarter, but otherwise the night passed without incident," reported *Bellerophon.* Forty-five years after Jutland, Lieutenant William Jameson of *Canada* remembered that "violent action flared up in the darkness to the northwest, passed across our wake and died away towards the east. Something tremendous was going on only a few miles away, but to our astonishment (it surprises me still) the battle fleet continued to steam south."

As the hours passed and these scenes of fire and destruction were enacted and witnessed, their significance was universally misunderstood on the large British ships. The Commander-in-Chief and his senior officers all interpreted the commotion to the north to mean that, as expected, enemy destroyers were attacking from astern and were being beaten off by the British destroyers stationed there for that purpose. Jellicoe certainly did not wish to involve his own dreadnoughts in this battle; indeed, he wanted them as far from German destroyers as possible. The irony is that the German destroyer flotillas, the element of the High Seas Fleet that Jellicoe most feared and that had loomed so large in his night dispositions, played no part in the nighttime battle. Ten German destroyers actually left the battlefield early and returned to Kiel around the northern tip of Denmark. Through the rest of the night, the remaining German destroyers searched in vain for the British battle fleet. They found nothing, suffered no losses, and might as well not have been there.

But Jellicoe did not know this. A destroyer battle to the rear of the fleet was what Jellicoe had said would happen—presumably it now was happening. And so, on board the flagship, no need to awaken the exhausted admiral to tell him that his expectation was being realized. Therefore, as his admirals and captains stood on their bridges, watching the fireworks and sipping their cocoa, the Commander-in-Chief lay resting undisturbed on his cot. And as daylight began to appear around 2:00 a.m., Reinhard Scheer completed his breakthrough across the wake of the British fleet.

—

At dawn, the sea was calm, with a heavy mist and visibility under two miles. On the bridges of German warships, still sixteen miles away from Horns Reef, binoculars swept the horizon for the British fleet. To everyone's surprise and enormous relief, it was not there. A great weight fell from Scheer's shoulders, but he and his staff remained anxious. They appeared to have succeeded, but they were not yet home; the protection of the minefields was at 2:30 a.m., still an hour's steaming away. When the head of the German battle line reached the Horns Reef light vessel, Scheer paused, waiting for *Lützow,* which had not been heard from. Then came the news that the battle cruiser had been abandoned; Scheer resumed his retreat. He had no choice. The battle cruiser squadron could no longer fight. In the 3rd Battle Squadron, three of the fleet's most powerful dreadnoughts were heavily damaged and *König,* with a hole in her bow, was drawing so much water that she could not pass through the Amrum Bank channel until high tide. Only three fast light cruisers, *Frankfurt, Pillau,* and *Regensburg,* remained available. "Owing to the bad visibility, further scouting by airship could not be counted on,"

Scheer wrote in his after-battle report. "It was therefore hopeless to try to force a regular action on the enemy. . . . The consequences of such an action would have been a matter of chance. I therefore abandoned any further operations and ordered a return to port." This was postbattle bravado. Scheer had no intention of "forcing an action" on anyone; twice he had reversed course when faced by the might of the Grand Fleet, and he had no desire to face it again. His only wish was to get away, and his exhilaration after the battle stemmed not from any feeling of triumph but from thankfulness that he had escaped. Relieved and exhausted, Scheer ordered his battle cruisers south into the swept channel, followed fifteen minutes later by the old predreadnoughts and, after another fifteen minutes, by the rest of the fleet.

On the way in, the High Seas Fleet passed safely over three British submarines lying on the bottom. The submarines, sent there as part of Jellicoe's original plan for drawing the enemy out, had left Harwich on May 30 with orders to remain submerged until June 2. No one thought of amending these instructions and, as they received no news of the battle in progress, the submarine captains knew nothing of Jutland until they returned to Harwich on June 3. Despite avoiding this danger, the German fleet did not reach home without mishap. At 5:20 a.m., the dreadnought *Ostfriesland* struck a mine five miles from Heligoland. One man was killed and ten wounded, but the torpedo bulkheads held and, after sheering out of line, the battleship managed to limp into port.

The main body of the High Seas Fleet reached the mouths of the Jade and the Elbe between 1:00 and 2:45 on the afternoon of June 1. Five battleships were left on outpost duty in Schillig roads, while damaged ships passed through the locks into the inner harbor. Already, the mood was becoming festive; as the flagship passed by, the crews of other ships lined their decks to cheer the admiral. In the flag cabin of *Friedrich der Grosse,* Scheer received reports that strongly indicated that three British battle cruisers had blown up and that *Warspite* also had been sunk. Exultant that he had inflicted these losses on a superior enemy, Scheer invited his officers to the bridge, where the tired admiral raised a glass of champagne to survival, to escape, and to what, by the following day, the German kaiser, press, and nation would be calling victory.

—

Not every vessel in the High Seas Fleet returned with Scheer. Early light on June 1 found the giant battle cruiser *Lützow* sinking into a gray sea. Battered by twenty-four heavy shells, able to make only 7 knots, she had wandered away from the fleet. By 12:30 a.m., with more than 8,000 tons of water gurgling inside her hull, her bow was so low that waves washed over the fore turret. The dynamo room was flooded, eliminating electrical power and leaving the crew to work by candlelight. An attempt to move the ship backward, stern first, in order to relieve pressure on forward internal bulkheads, had to be abandoned when, as the bow continued to sink, the stern and the propellers rose out of the sea. Fearing that his ship was about to capsize, Captain Harder called four accompanying destroyers alongside and ordered his crew of 1,040 men to board the small ships. Then, from a few hundred yards away, Harder ordered *G-38* to fire two torpedoes. *Lützow* received the blows, rolled over, and went down while the ship's company, watching from the destroyers, gave three cheers for the kaiser, three for Hipper and Scheer, and three for their ship. Then, across the empty water, they raised their voices in "Deutschland, Deutschland über Alles."

There were no cheers when *Wiesbaden* sank. Stubbornly afloat long after the Grand Fleet had passed her by, she lay rising and falling in a desolate sea. Twenty men hoping for rescue huddled together on deck in a cold northwestern wind. As the sea rose higher, the ship rolled ominously; at some time during the night, she rolled too far and went down. Everyone on board went with her except the chief stoker, who was picked up, delirious, thirty-eight hours later by a Norwegian steamer.

Seydlitz avoided *Lützow*'s fate by the narrowest of margins. With thousands of tons of water in her own damaged hull, she tried to follow *Moltke,* but lost her in the dark. Ordered to make her way independently to Horns Reef, she began a voyage filled with suspense and misery. Her charts were covered with blood and her gyrocompass was wrecked; steered by hand machinery, listing, and with her bow under water, she stumbled down the starboard side of the British battle line. *Agincourt,* with fourteen 12-inch guns, saw her. "I did not challenge her," said *Agincourt*'s captain, "so as not to give our division's position away." Passing through a gap in the British battle line, *Seydlitz* came within less than a mile of the 5th Battle Squadron. *Malaya,* with eight 15-inch guns, saw and recognized the German battle cruiser but did nothing. *Marlborough,* with ten 13.5-inch guns, identified her as "a large ship" but did not fire. "I missed the chance of a lifetime," *Marlborough*'s gunnery officer said later. "I saw the dim outline of this ship and had the main armament trained on it and put a range of 4,000 yards on the sights and asked the captain for permission to open fire. He replied 'No' as he thought it was one of our own ships. Of course what I ought to have done was to have opened fire and blown the ship out of the water and then said 'Sorry.' " *Revenge,* with eight 15-inch guns, saw *Seydlitz,* too, and her 6-inch guns were ordered to fire, but the secondary battery gun crews were out on deck watching the fireworks of the destroyer actions and by the time they were back at their guns it was too late. Thus, when a few short-range broadsides would have finished her, *Seydlitz,* already sinking, was allowed to wander safely past three British dreadnoughts.

At 1:40 a.m., *Seydlitz* reached Horns Reef—and twice ran aground on it. Twice, Captain von Egidy backed the ship off with her own engines, but by

4:40 a.m., she was down eleven feet by the bow. The light cruiser *Pillau* arrived to pilot, but in spite of this, *Seydlitz* went aground again. Again, by reversing her engines and with the aid of a rising tide, she backed off, but wind and sea also were rising and waves swept over the forward deck up to the base of the bridge. Passing through the Amrum Bank, the ship settled deeper until the keel began scraping along the bottom. The bulkheads inside the hull strained under the pressure of the sea. Men standing thigh-deep in water bailed with buckets in devastated, badly lit compartments filled with jagged fragments and, sometimes, human remains. The list reached 8 degrees and continued to grow. At 1:30 in the afternoon, *Seydlitz* turned and reversed engines to proceed stern first. *Pillau* and several minesweepers tried to tow the waterlogged ship backward, but the wire hawsers broke. Finally, at the end of the afternoon, she grounded hard on a Weser River sandbank. Tugs and two pumping ships arrived from Wilhelmshaven and she was dragged off and towed stern first to the outer Jade. There, her wounded were taken off and she was towed backward across the bar into Jade roads. She remained for four days, while, to reduce weight, the two 11-inch guns and much of the armor plate from the forward gun turret were removed. On June 6, *Seydlitz* was moved inside the harbor gates, but another week of caulking and pumping was necessary and the two 11-inch guns of the port wing gun turret were stripped out. Finally, on June 13, the ship was able to enter a floating dry dock to begin three months of repairs.

Moltke was the only relatively unharmed German battle cruiser. Hipper was on board when she became separated from the fleet, and he knew that Scheer's course was southeast toward Horns Reef. The Grand Fleet, unfortunately, was in the way. At 10:30 p.m., as *Moltke* attempted to edge through the British squadrons, Captain Johannes von Karpf suddenly saw the shadows of British dreadnoughts—the rear division of Admiral Jerram's 2nd Battle Squadron—looming up 2,000 yards away. Hoping that his ship had not been sighted, Karpf quickly put the helm hard over and the phantom ships faded silently into the darkness. In fact, *Moltke* had been seen by one of these ships, *Thunderer,* but the British captain did not open fire. "It was inadvisable to show up the battle fleet unless obvious attack was intended," he said later. A few broadsides at that range would have destroyed *Moltke,* and Hipper as well, but it was not to be. Twice more, Karpf groped eastward, trying to break through, but each time the menacing shapes of Jerram's dreadnoughts stood up against the eastern sky, and each time, Karpf altered course back to the west. After the third attempt, he gave up and with Hipper's permission ordered maximum speed to the south; at midnight *Moltke* was able to cross in front of the Grand Fleet with a clear passage home.

Two German light cruisers, *Elbing* and *Rostock,* were scuttled, like *Lützow,* by friendly hands. *Elbing,* after being rammed by *Posen,* had come to a stop with her engine rooms filled with water. At 1:00 a.m. a destroyer was ordered alongside and the crew, with the exception of a small salvage party including the captain, was taken off. When his derelict ship drifted close to a group of undamaged British destroyers, Captain Madlung gave the order for *Elbing* to be sunk with explosive charges. *Rostock* had been hit by a torpedo at 11:50 a.m. and was taken in tow. But the ship continued to settle and at 4:15 a.m., with her crew transferred, she was sunk by German torpedoes.

—

Jellicoe rose from his cot on *Iron Duke* prepared to resume the battle. His ships were ready, the crews were at action stations, the guns had remained loaded all night. The Commander-in-Chief's plan had been to turn from his southerly course and arrive off Horns Reef at daylight, but now, looking at the sea, he reconsidered. The sky was gray, visibility was less than 4,000 yards, and the fleet was disorganized and widely dispersed. Seven of his battleships—*Marlborough*'s division and the three *Queen Elizabeth*s—had dropped far astern. Beatty and the battle cruisers were nowhere in sight; missing with them were the two light cruiser squadrons Jellicoe needed for scouting. Of greatest concern, the British destroyer flotillas were scattered far and wide. Jellicoe now was in waters close to the German coast, facing the possibility of destroyer or U-boat attacks with no light forces available to screen his dreadnoughts. "These difficulties rendered it undesirable to close Horns Reef at daylight as had been my intention," he was to write in his usual laconic style. Still believing that Scheer was northwest of him rather than south or southeast, he ordered the Grand Fleet to reverse course and turn north for "the double purpose of catching Scheer and collecting the light craft which should be astern of me." At 2:30 a.m., the battle fleet swung around to the north and formed a single line ahead, accepting the danger of submarine attack in this exposed formation in order to be ready for the German surface fleet if it suddenly appeared.

At 3:15 a.m., Jellicoe sent another dreadnought home. *Marlborough,* which had been dropping steadily astern, reported that her torpedo wound would force her to reduce speed to 12 knots. Vice Admiral Cecil Burney shifted his flag from *Marlborough* to *Revenge* and, with Jellicoe's permission, ordered *Marlborough* back to the Tyne. About this same time, a zeppelin, *L-11,* appeared over the fleet and hovered four miles away. *Neptune* raised one gun of its X turret to maximum elevation and fired a 12-inch shell. The airship, said a midshipman in the battleship's foretop, "lifted its nose disdainfully to the morning breeze and disappeared to the southwest." Other British battleships fired at *L-11* with equally poor results. The significance, obvious to all in the Grand Fleet, was that now the Germans knew their exact position.

Beatty, fifteen miles southwest of Jellicoe at sunrise, was convinced that the High Seas Fleet lay to his own southwest, and, at 4:04 a.m., asked permission to sweep in that direction to find the enemy. It was too late. Five minutes earlier, an Admiralty message had been handed to Jellicoe that gave Scheer's 2:30 a.m. position as sixteen miles from Horns Reef lightship, his course as southeast, and his speed as 16 knots. Ninety minutes had passed since 2:30 and it was evident to Jellicoe that by now Scheer must have passed Horns Reef and reached safety in the protected channel. At 4:30 a.m., Beatty, unaware of this Admiralty message and not waiting for the Commander-in-Chief's reply, began exhorting his battle cruisers: "Damage yesterday was heavy on both sides. We hope today to cut off and annihilate the whole German fleet. Every man must do his utmost. *Lützow* is sinking and another German battle cruiser expected to have sunk." Ten minutes later, the author of this rhetoric received a crushing message from *Iron Duke:* "Enemy fleet has returned to harbor. Try to locate *Lützow.*"

The Battle of Jutland was over. Nothing remained for the Grand Fleet to do except to sweep north, hoping to find enemy stragglers and damaged vessels. At 4:13 a.m., Jellicoe re-formed the battle fleet into its daytime cruising order—battleship divisions of four ships each; the divisions spread abeam of one another—in order to search on a wide front and to provide better protection against U-boats. Through the morning, the fleet steamed through the desolate waters that had been the scene of the previous day's and night's battles. Flotsam of all kinds, including wooden mess stools, broken timbers, and thousands of dead fish floating belly up, killed by the detonation of shells, rolled gently in vast patches of oil. Frequently, the surface was disturbed by air bubbles rising from far below, where water had penetrated a compartment of a sunken ship. Bodies wearing the uniforms of both nations floated in life preservers; many of these men had died, not of wounds or drowning, but of exposure. Among the survivors picked up was the captain of the destroyer *Ardent,* who had watched many of his own crew die in the water during the night. "None appeared to suffer at all," he said. "They just seemed to lie back and go to sleep."

Jellicoe devoted the morning to collecting his scattered fleet and gathering information about his missing and damaged ships. By 6:00 a.m. his light cruisers had rejoined, but not until 9:00 a.m. were all British destroyers back in company. At 9:07 he signaled Beatty, "I want to ascertain if all disabled ships are on the way. Are all your light cruisers and destroyers accounted for? Where are *New Zealand* and *Indefatigable*?" Beatty replied, astonishing the Commander-in-Chief by giving the positions of the "wreck of *Queen Mary* . . . wreck of *Invincible* . . . [and] wreck of *Indefatigable.*" This first knowledge of the loss of a second and third British battle cruiser provoked a long silence between the two admirals. Then, at 11:04, Jellicoe asked Beatty, "When did *Queen Mary* and *Indefatigable* go down?" Beatty replied that it had been the previous afternoon. At 11:25, Jellicoe was back: "Was cause of sinking mines, torpedoes or gunfire?" and Beatty answered, "Do not think it was mines or torpedoes because both explosions immediately followed hits by salvos." It was in this manner that the Commander-in-Chief of the Grand Fleet learned of the sinking of two of his capital ships, nineteen hours after they went down. Heavyhearted, but with nothing more to be done, Jellicoe reported to the Admiralty that he had swept the area where the battle had been fought, found no enemy ships, and therefore was returning to base. A little after 11:00 a.m., the Grand Fleet turned northwest for Scapa Flow.

—

Meanwhile, a procession of wounded British ships was struggling homeward across the North Sea. At one point, *Marlborough* seemed to be sinking; in the hour after midnight, the dreadnought ordered the small ships in her escort to be prepared to come alongside and take off her crew; this was never necessary. Along the way, both crippled British dreadnoughts, *Marlborough* and *Warspite,* were attacked by submarines. *U-46* fired one torpedo at *Marlborough,* which missed by fifty yards; the battleship turned away and eventually made the Humber. About the same time, *Warspite,* still 100 miles from the Firth of Forth, was sighted by *U-51.* Despite a heavy sea, the submarine managed to maintain periscope depth, approach unseen to within 650 yards, and fire two torpedoes. Only one torpedo left its tube, however, because at just that moment, a large wave plunged the submarine's bow into the sea. This missile broke the surface, betraying the presence of the submarine, and *Warspite*'s captain swung his ship around, increased speed, and hurried away. Two hours later, a lookout sighted a periscope 100 yards ahead of the ship. *Warspite* attempted to ram, but *U-63,* returning with a disabled engine from its patrol off the Forth, crash-dived and escaped. At 3:30 on the afternoon of June 1, *Warspite* passed under the Forth bridge and reached Rosyth, her hull four and a half feet lower in the water than normal. Immediately, her sister *Queen Elizabeth* was moved out of dry dock so that *Warspite* could go in.

Sparrowhawk, helpless after her collision with *Broke,* drifted until dawn, when a dim shape appeared out of the mist two miles away. When the crew of *Sparrowhawk* recognized a modern German light cruiser, they readied their one remaining gun and prepared for the end. But to their astonishment, the enemy did not open fire; instead, the light cruiser rolled over, stood on her head, and sank. The stranger was the crippled ghost ship *Elbing,* abandoned by her crew.

Meanwhile, water was rising steadily in the engine rooms of the shattered armored cruiser *Warrior.* After staggering away from the battle, the cruiser had been sighted by *Engadine,* the small cross-Channel steamer converted into a seaplane carrier that had flown off a scouting seaplane early in the battle. The smaller ship's captain, seeing the big armored cruiser in trouble, had offered help. *Warrior* asked *Engadine* to remain near and when *Warrior*'s engines stopped altogether, the seaplane carrier took the waterlogged cruiser in tow. *Engadine*—a 1,600-ton ship towing a 13,500-ton ship—did her best and together they struggled along at 3 knots. During the night, however, the wind rose and *Warrior* yawed so much from side to side that *Engadine,* "bobbing about like a cork," was forced to cast off the tow. By 7:00 a.m., the armored cruiser was obviously sinking and her captain decided to abandon ship. *Engadine* tried to come along *Warrior*'s starboard side to take off her crew, but it was too difficult. The seaplane carrier backed off and tried the port side, but this attempt also failed. *Engadine* then lay off the starboard quarter—and for a while, the hundreds of men of *Warrior*'s crew believed that they would have to swim across or go down with the ship. But *Engadine* was only waiting for *Warrior*'s yawing to steady; then, once again, she came up along the starboard side. This time her approach succeeded and the two ships made fast. While their steel plates ground against each other in the heavy seas, *Warrior*'s crew mustered on deck to transfer to the other ship. The wounded went first on stretchers; then the captain ordered his crew to go by sections. Considering that the men were moving too hastily for safety, he had the bugler sound "Still." Every man fell back into ranks on deck; later, *Engadine*'s captain was to marvel at this "triumph of organization, discipline and courage." When "Carry on" sounded, the transfer resumed. Seven hundred and forty-three men were taken off, and the last to leave were the officers and the captain. At 8:00 a.m., *Warrior* was left 160 miles east of Aberdeen, never to be seen again. Thus, three of the four armored cruisers that sailed with Sir Robert Arbuthnot from Cromarty—*Defence, Black Prince,* and *Warrior*—were gone. Of the 1st Cruiser Squadron, only *Duke of Edinburgh* returned from Jutland.

—

On every British ship, men slumped and dozed wherever they were. Officers returning to their cabins and finding them wrecked and uninhabitable went to the wardroom to find every chair occupied by someone fast asleep. Admirals were no less weary. Aboard *Lion* on the afternoon of June 1, Beatty came into the chart house, "sat down on the settee and closed his eyes. Unable to hide his disappointment at the result of the battle, he repeated in a weary voice, 'There is something wrong with our ships.' Then, opening his eyes, he added, 'And something wrong with our system.' Then he fell asleep." In another part of the ship, Chatfield went down to his quarters to find his bathroom being used as an operating room. "[It was] an awful sight," he said, "[with] bits of body and arms and legs lying about." No one was more exhausted than the ships' surgeons, but their work could not end. "The wounded who could speak were very cheerful and wanted only one thing—cigarettes," remembered one officer. "The most dreadful cases were the 'burns'—but this subject cannot be written about." Nevertheless, years later, one surgeon did write about his experience at Jutland with flash burns from exploding powder: "Very rapidly, almost as one looks, the face swells up, the looser parts of the skin become enormously swollen, the eyes are invisible through the great swelling of the lids, the lips enormous jelly-like masses, in the center of which a button-like mouth appears. . . . The great cry is water. . . . They die and die very rapidly."

Not all sailors were sentimental about wounds or death. A gunner on *Warspite,* who had lost a leg, sent his friends back to look for it, hoping to recover the money he kept wrapped up in that sock. And a Cockney cook on *Chester* cheerfully told an officer "how he had found his mate lying dead with the top of his head neatly sliced off, 'just as you might slice off the top of a boiled egg, Sir.' " The tradition of the British navy required that dead men on board be buried at sea before a ship reached port and throughout the day, all across the North Sea, bodies were committed to the deep. Sail makers stitched bodies into hammocks with a hundred-pound shell at their feet, placed them on a plank, and covered them with a Union Jack. Ships slowed in heavy seas with spray sweeping the decks, chaplains with gowns blowing in the wind read prayers, bugles sounded, the planks were lifted, and the hammocks slid out from under the flags and into the water. Not all of the remains could be identified. On *Lion,* "poor charred bodies" were removed from Q turret and at noon, ninety-five mutilated forms, including six officers and eighty-nine men, were buried. *Malaya* interred many "poor, unrecognisable scraps of humanity." Afterward, on *Tiger,* "an awful smell penetrated all over the ship and we had to get busy with buckets of disinfectant and carbolic soap. Human flesh had gotten into all sorts of nooks, such as voice pipes, telephones, and ventilating shafts."

The following morning, Friday, June 2, 1916, *Lion* and the battle cruisers reached the Firth of Forth, passed under the great railway bridge, and anchored off Rosyth. At noon the same day, the Grand Fleet passed through Pentland Firth and entered Scapa Flow. During the afternoon and early evening, the battle squadrons coaled, oiled, and took on ammunition. And at 9:45 p.m., Jellicoe reported to the Admiralty that, on four hours' notice, the British fleet could go back to sea.

CHAPTER 34

Jutland: Aftermath

On Thursday afternoon, June 1, twenty-four hours before Jellicoe and the Grand Fleet returned to Scapa Flow, the High Seas Fleet reached Wilhelmshaven, and Scheer, finishing his champagne, assembled his admirals and asked for their reports. The evidence presented was impressive: they had confronted the might of the Grand Fleet; they had watched British dreadnought battle cruisers and large armored cruisers blow up before their eyes, and they had discovered their own big ships to be powerfully resistant to fatal damage from heavy-caliber British shells. Scheer telegraphed the Naval Staff in Berlin; by early evening, an official communiqué was published. The battle was announced as a German victory. Famous British ships—the battleship *Warspite,* the battle cruisers *Queen Mary* and *Indefatigable*—had been sunk (*Invincible* had been mistaken for *Warspite*). Two British armored cruisers, two light cruisers, and thirteen destroyers were described as destroyed. German losses were said to be the old battleship *Pommern* and the light cruiser *Wiesbaden; Frauenlob* and several destroyers had "not yet returned to base." Nothing was said about *Lützow, Rostock,* and *Elbing.* The victory was called the Skagerrakschlacht, the Battle of the Skagerrak, and Scheer became the Victor of the Skagerrak. The Austrian naval attaché reported to Vienna that the German fleet was "intoxicated with its victory."

The German communiqué went immediately to the news agencies of Europe and America and then to the newspapers of the world. In Germany, the presses roared with special editions. Crowds gathered at newspaper offices and around kiosks to read electrifying headlines: "Great Victory at Sea," "Many English Battleships Destroyed and Damaged." Above the entrance of *Tageszeitung,* a huge placard read, "Trafalgar Is Wiped Out." Flags appeared on Unter den Linden, then all over Berlin, then in every city and town in Germany. Schoolchildren were given a holiday. In subsequent editions, the papers spoke, not just of victory, but of "annihilation." Illustrations showed British dreadnoughts blowing up and floating upside down. Stories brimmed with contempt for the British navy; one paper described "the arrogant presumption of the British rats who have left their safe hiding places only to be trapped by German efficiency, heroism and determination." Friday, June 2, was declared a national holiday and Sunday became a day of national mourning when the dead from the fleet were buried in the naval cemetery at Wilhelmshaven. On Monday morning, the kaiser arrived in Wilhelmshaven to visit the fleet. William, described by Marder as "almost hysterical in his theatrical display of emotion," boarded the flagship, embraced Scheer, and kissed him on both cheeks. To the crew assembled on the quay beside the battleship, he shouted, "The journey I have made today means very much to me. The English were beaten. The spell of Trafalgar has been broken. You have started a new chapter in world history. I stand before you as your Highest Commander to thank you with all my heart." William then boarded other ships, kissing the captains and distributing Iron Crosses. Scheer and Hipper both were handed Germany's highest military decoration, the Ordre pour le Mérite. Scheer was promoted to admiral and Hipper to vice admiral. King Ludwig III of Bavaria then elevated Hipper, a Bavarian by birth, to the kingdom's nobility, making him Franz von Hipper. Scheer, offered a "von" by the kaiser, refused and remained simply Reinhard Scheer.

It did not take long for this public "cock-crowing," as Weizsäcker called it, to subside. The truth about the loss of *Lützow* leaked out and traveled through the country by word of mouth. On June 7, the German Naval Staff was forced to reveal its additional losses and a month later, on July 4, Scheer sent the kaiser his confidential report on the battle. The High Seas Fleet would be ready for sea by mid-August, he wrote, and he hoped to inflict serious damage on the enemy. "Nevertheless," he continued, "even the most successful outcome of a fleet action in this war will not force England to make peace." Citing "the disadvantages of our military-geographical position and the enemy's great material superiority," Scheer told the emperor that "a victorious end to the war within a reasonable time can only be achieved through the defeat of British economic life—that is, by using the U-boats against British trade."

During the morning and afternoon of Thursday, June 1, the British Admiralty waited for news from Jellicoe. London had been monitoring wireless messages between Jellicoe, Beatty, and other commanders, referring to losses, strayed ships, and their search of the battlefield; from these, it was clear that the German fleet had returned to port and that Jellicoe held command of the field. By nightfall, the Admiralty also knew that the Grand Fleet would be arriving back in its harbors the following morning. By then Jellicoe would surely report; meanwhile, the Admiralty was prepared to wait. There seemed no immediate harm in this; because of strict censorship in Britain, no one beyond a small official circle knew that the Grand Fleet had been in action.

That same Thursday evening, Reuters in Amsterdam picked up the official communiqué from Berlin and cabled it to their London bureau. The bureau sent the text to the Admiralty for the required censorship review prior to release to the British press. At the Admiralty, however, the claims in the communiqué appeared so damaging that there could be no question of revealing them to the public unless confirmed by Jellicoe. Now impatient for news, the Admiralty signaled *Iron Duke* at 9:40 p.m., summarizing the German communiqué and stressing the need for "prompt contradiction." Jellicoe did not reply. The Commander-in-Chief, passing a second night with little sleep, was preoccupied with the problems of rounding up, safeguarding, and shepherding his fleet, especially his damaged ships, back to harbor. *Warspite* and *Marlborough,* limping home, had been attacked by submarines. *Black Prince, Warrior,* and several destroyers were missing; many other destroyers were dangerously low on fuel. Further, until he had received reports from his own admirals and commodores, Jellicoe really did not know enough about what had happened during the battle to make a report. And on this day of all others, concern about an Admiralty press release was at the bottom of his list of priorities.

For these reasons, when daylight came on Friday, June 2, the Admiralty still had not heard from Jellicoe. By 8:00 a.m., ominous rumors were spreading across Britain. Some originated in Rosyth dockyard, which was preparing to receive a number of damaged ships. The arrival of other ships and the despatch of more than 6,000 uncensored messages from men coming ashore to tell loved ones they were safe spread the news that a battle had been fought. Further concealment was impossible; at 11:00 a.m., with the news from Berlin spreading around the world, the Admiralty decided to let the German communiqué be published in Britain.

To the British public, unaware even that a sea battle had taken place, it came as a bombshell. Within an hour, London newsboys were on the streets shouting, "Great naval disaster! Five British battleships lost!" Flags were lowered to half staff, stock exchanges closed, theaters darkened. Overseas, on breakfast tables in New York, Chicago, and San Francisco, the headlines read, "Britain Defeated at Sea!" "British Losses Great!" "British Fleet Almost Annihilated!" Still, the Admiralty issued no communiqué. Why not? Surely there must be another side to the story. Or had there been a spectacular defeat? Beginning that day, a tide of suspicion flooded up that would not subside for many years.

Meanwhile, at 10:35 that morning, as *Iron Duke* was entering Scapa Flow, Jellicoe signaled his first report to the Admiralty. A brief, sober summary of British losses, giving only the most conservative estimates of damage to the enemy, it seemed, taken at face value, almost to confirm the German communiqué. With the newspapers clamoring for an official statement, Balfour, Jackson, and Oliver sat down at the Admiralty during the afternoon to produce a document, which they released to the press at 7:00 p.m.:

> On the afternoon of Wednesday, May 31, a naval engagement took place off the coast of Jutland. The British ships on which the brunt of the fighting fell were the Battle Cruiser Fleet and some cruisers and light cruisers supported by four fast battleships. Among these the losses were heavy. . . . The battle cruisers *Queen Mary, Indefatigable,* and *Invincible* and the cruisers *Defence* and *Black Prince* were sunk. The *Warrior* was disabled . . . and had to be abandoned. . . . No British battleships were sunk. . . . The enemy's losses are serious. At least one battle cruiser was destroyed, one battleship was reported sunk by our destroyers during a night action; two light cruisers were disabled and probably sunk.

Balfour was the primary author of this document. The First Lord, a former prime minister, a philosopher, and a man little interested in public favor, had chosen candor: "I desired to let the people know the best and worst that I knew," he said. The communiqué, therefore, was a simple, honest recital of British losses. There was no mention of Scheer's double turnaway or of his desperate nocturnal lunge to escape. There was no explanation of the significance of British sea control after the battle.

The Admiralty's brief statement reached the public in Saturday morning newspapers on June 3. To most British readers, schooled to believe that whenever the Royal Navy encountered an enemy, the foreigners must inevitably go to the bottom, it gave a shocking impression of mishap, even disaster. The press, inherently suspicious of official pronouncements, was convinced that something was being hidden. If Jutland had been a British victory, why not say so? If it was not a British victory—and the Admiralty steadfastly refused to claim it as such—then it must have been a British defeat. Newspaper editorials struck an attitude of suspicious mourning. "The result could not be viewed with satisfaction," said the *Daily Telegraph.* "Defeat in the Jutland engagement must be admitted," agreed the *Daily News.* Newspapers in hand, Jacky Fisher, now at the Board of Invention and Research, paced up and down his office, repeating, "They've failed me, they've failed me! I have spent thirty years of my life preparing for this day and they've failed me!"

By Saturday afternoon, Jellicoe had read the British communiqué and had signaled a vigorous protest, saying that it magnified his losses, minimized Scheer's, and gave a misleading picture of the battle. The Admiralty then issued a second communiqué redistributing the balance of lost ships, but still not saying which side had won the battle. To strengthen the Admiralty's case, Balfour asked Winston Churchill, his predecessor and friend, famous for his gifted pen, to come in, examine the confidential reports of the battle, and publish his own opinion. Churchill came and was handed all dispatches from the fleet commanders. His commentary, appearing on Sunday morning, placed the battle in a larger context. He brought out the crucial fact that the High Seas Fleet had escaped destruction only by flight. He stressed that sea control depended on dreadnought battleships and that British supremacy in this respect was unimpaired. Britain had lost a first-line battle cruiser, *Queen Mary,* but the Germans had lost *Lützow,* an equivalent vessel. *Invincible* and *Indefatigable* were second-line vessels; their loss was regrettable, but far from crippling. Overall, the Royal Navy's margin of superiority continued undiminished. Churchill's essay calmed the public, but further enraged the press. Why had the Admiralty given secret information to a politician, but not to them? London journalists now were convinced that the original German communiqué had been substantially correct and that the Admiralty, in dribbling out the story, was concealing the truth.

Accordingly, a third Admiralty communiqué, appearing in the Monday morning newspapers, gave a higher estimate of German losses: two battleships, two battle cruisers, four light cruisers, and at least nine destroyers. Jellicoe, it declared, "having driven the enemy into port, returned to the main scene of action and scoured the sea in search of disabled vessels." Then, bending over backward to please, the Admiralty announced that it was lifting censorship on all official dispatches from the sea commanders concerning the battle. Learning this, Jellicoe vehemently protested that many of the details in these reports, if released to the public, would give valuable information to the enemy. Immediately on Jellicoe's telegram reaching London, censorship was reimposed—and journalistic suspicions flared higher. The Admiralty was partially vindicated the following day when the German Naval Staff admitted the loss of *Lützow* and *Rostock;* and by the end of the week, public opinion began to shift. Now there was talk of a "substantial victory"; there were reminders of the continuing blockade; there was a description of the High Seas Fleet sealed up in Wilhelmshaven while the victorious British fleet was "sweeping across the North Sea in its unchallenged supremacy." *The Naval and Military Record* announced that "the Navy's prestige stands higher today than at any period for a hundred years." The *Globe* asked: "Will the shouting, flag-wagging [German] people get any more of the copper, rubber and cotton their government so sorely needs? Not by a pound. Will meat and butter be cheaper in Berlin? Not by a *pfennig.* There is one test and only one of victory. Who held the field of battle at the end of the fight?" Arthur Balfour laconically noted, "It is not customary for a victor to run away." And a New York City newspaper told its readers: "The German fleet has assaulted its jailor, but it is still in jail."

—

The British public was just recovering from the Jutland "defeat" when newspaper headlines on Tuesday, June 6—six days after the battle—sent them reeling again. Field Marshal Lord Kitchener, the nation's military idol and the secretary of state for war, had drowned at sea aboard a British cruiser only a few miles from Scapa Flow.

The tragedy that stunned the nation came almost as a release for the hero. Kitchener, aging, tired, and fractious after twenty-two months of war, had found himself in an anomalous position: his reputation with the British public remained as high as ever, but within the Cabinet it had shrunk to a point where he was treated with almost contemptuous indifference. Lloyd George said privately that Kitchener "talked twaddle" and constantly urged Asquith to remove him from the War Office. The visible cause was the army's failure at Gallipoli; as failure at the Dardanelles had toppled Churchill and Fisher, so now failure at Gallipoli had left Kitchener tottering. Underneath lay concerns over Kitchener's remote, sometimes inexplicable behavior. One night over dinner, Balfour explained this view to his niece, who was to become his biographer:

"K. knows nothing," the First Lord said. "He does nothing right."

"He is a stupid man?" the niece asked.

"That's it; he is," Balfour replied. "He is not a great organizer, he is not a great administrator, nor a great soldier. And what is more, he knows it. He is not vain. He is only great when he has little things to accomplish."

"And yet," the niece said, "I feel as if he were rather a great man."

"You are not wrong. He is in a way. But our language has no word for the subtleties I would like to express about K. I must call his greatness *personality.* He has that in the highest sense."

Kitchener knew what his colleagues were saying, but, as he told a friend, "Rightly or wrongly—probably wrongly—the people believe in me. It is not, therefore, me the politicians are afraid of, but of what the people would say if I were to go." Early in May, an invitation from Tsar Nicholas II to visit the Russian army and confer with the Russian government on questions of military cooperation provided an excuse, as welcome to Kitchener as to his detractors, for him to leave England for three weeks. On June 4, he said good-bye to the prime minister and the king and left London from King's Cross Station for northern Scotland. From Thurso, a destroyer carried him across the Pentland Firth to *Iron Duke* in Scapa Flow. His visit was secret, but as he came up the flagship's ladder, the crew recognized the familiar figure and began to clap. Already, an unseasonable northeasterly storm had the flagship bucking at its mooring cables, and while Kitchener had lunch with Jellicoe, the weather grew worse; one officer would call it "the dirtiest night we had seen in Scapa." The Commander-in-Chief recommended that his guest postpone sailing for twenty-four hours, but the field marshal insisted that he had "a timetable and not a day to lose." Jellicoe thereupon personally changed his visitor's course out of Scapa Flow; the armored cruiser *Hampshire,* instead of taking the usual route to the east through Pentland Firth, was to take the less-used western route around the Orkneys. His intention was to give Kitchener, whose sea legs were rubbery, more comfort by putting him in the lee of the islands during the first hours of his voyage.

Just after 4:00 p.m., the towering field marshal reached out across *Iron Duke*'s spray-swept deck and clasped the hand of the small admiral. At 5:00 p.m., *Hampshire* and two escorting destroyers sailed for Archangel, turning west out of the Flow and keeping close to the sheer black cliffs of the Orkney coast. The cruiser's captain, fearing submarines, called for 18 knots, but the storm had moved from the northeast around to the northwest and the three ships, burying their noses in enormous green waves rolling in from the Atlantic, were unable to make this speed. By 6:30 p.m., the seas were so high that the destroyers had to be sent home. At 7:40 p.m., about a mile and a half off Marwick Head, *Hampshire* struck a mine, one of twenty-two laid on the night of May 27–28 by *U-75* in hopes of harming the Grand Fleet when it came out in response to Scheer's planned thrust into the Skagerrak. The cruiser heeled over and within fifteen minutes went to the bottom. No boats could be lowered in the heavy seas; and of the more than 650 men on board, only twelve survived on small float rafts to reach the base of the Orkney cliffs. Kitchener was not among them. He was last seen immediately after the explosion wearing his heavy greatcoat and heading for the bridge.*

The news reached London on the morning of June 6 and was on the street by noon. Kitchener—the blue-eyed, scarlet-faced soldier with the rampant mustache; the omnipotent war lord beckoning ("Your Country Needs You!") from recruiting posters—was gone, drowned in the care of the navy. Jellicoe, struggling to deal with the repercussions of Jutland, sank into despondency. "I feel in a measure responsible as I ordered her movements," he wrote to Jackson. "My luck is dead out for the present, I am afraid."

*Only a last-minute change of plans made at the prime minister's request prevented David Lloyd George from accompanying Kitchener on his mission to Russia and probably drowning with him. Lloyd George was minister of munitions in June 1916 and it had been arranged that he should go to see what could be done to alleviate the severe shortage of shells available to the Russian army. Then came the Easter Rebellion in Ireland and, at the end of May, Asquith asked Lloyd George to give up his Russian mission and try instead to negotiate a settlement with the Irish revolutionary leaders. Reluctantly, Lloyd George agreed, thereby saving his own life. One month later, he became war secretary; six months later, he succeeded Asquith as prime minister.

—

Beyond communiqués and headlines, who won the Battle of Jutland? Scheer and the Germans claimed victory by comparing the number of ships sunk and of seamen killed and wounded. Here, indeed, they had the advantage: Britain had lost fourteen ships (three battle cruisers, three armored cruisers, and eight destroyers), while the German navy had lost eleven (one battle cruiser, one predreadnought battleship, four light cruisers, and five destroyers). British casualties were much heavier: 6,768 men were killed or wounded, while the Imperial Navy lost 3,058. But significant footnotes must be appended to these figures. British personnel losses were higher because five large British ships suddenly blew up, each explosion destroying almost 1,000 men. Only one big German ship, *Pommern,* blew up in this manner; by contrast, the crippled battle cruiser *Lützow* sank only after her crew of more than 1,000 had been safely taken off. Further, there was the matter of proportional loss. The British had lost three battle cruisers and Germany only one, but two months after the battle Britain had seven battle cruisers ready for sea and Germany only two. The newest and best battleships of the High Seas Fleet had been heavily damaged and took weeks to repair. But of the twenty-four dreadnoughts of the British battle fleet, only one, *Marlborough,* had been sent to dry dock; of the other twenty-three, only one, *Colossus,* had been hit by two heavy German shells. The battle fleet's casualties were two men from *Marlborough* killed and the arm lost by a leading seaman on *Colossus.* Nor, aside from the loss of the men on board, did the Admiralty mourn every one of its lost ships. The armored cruisers, especially, were not missed. Slow and vulnerable, as Fisher had predicted, able neither to fight nor to run, after Jutland the remaining ships of this species were scrapped.

Besides, Jellicoe quickly made good his losses When *Warspite* went into dock at Rosyth, *Queen Elizabeth* came out. When *Malaya* went into the floating dock at Invergordon, *Emperor of India* came out. *Barham* was gone for a while, under repair at Devonport, but the dreadnought battleship *Royal Sovereign,* held back at Scapa Flow from Jutland, now was ready, and her sisters *Resolution* and *Ramillies* soon would join the fleet. *Dreadnought* herself, sent to join the Channel Fleet, could be brought back north. Among the battle cruisers, *Princess Royal* and *Tiger* went into the dockyard, but *Australia* came out. *Repulse* and *Renown* were completed in August and September. Across the North Sea, Scheer enjoyed no such quick replacement of his losses. His best three dreadnoughts, *König, Grosser Kurfürst,* and *Markgraf,* remained in dry dock for weeks; two of his four surviving battle cruisers, *Derfflinger* and *Seydlitz,* were not ready for sea until December, six months later. German light cruiser strength had been cut to six against Britain's thirty. In sum, when ships available were added up on both sides, Britain's superiority was as overwhelming as ever.

—

What caused the disparity in ship losses at Jutland? After the war, the official German naval history declared that during the battle "the superiority of German gunnery is clearly evident." Hipper's battle cruisers did shoot well in the opening stages when visibility was much in their favor, but they became less accurate once they came under fire from the 15-inch guns of the 5th Battle Squadron. The gunnery of Beatty's six battle cruisers was never more than mediocre, but when Jellicoe's battle squadrons came into action, a few minutes of their massive cannonade was sufficient to make Scheer turn and run. Even so, given a rough balance in gunnery efficiency, why did the British fleet suffer losses so much heavier? Why was it unable to sink *Seydlitz* despite twenty-two hits with heavy-caliber shells? Or *Lützow* with twenty-four? How was it that *Derfflinger* got home, having been struck twenty-two times? In short, why were German ships nearly unsinkable? And, on the other side, why did three British battle cruisers blow up?

From the beginning, Alfred von Tirpitz, who believed that "the supreme quality of a ship is that it should remain afloat," had set out to build ships that would be unsinkable. Tirpitz had been willing to accept smaller-caliber guns for his battle cruisers and battleships in order to allow more weight for armor; accordingly, *Derfflinger,* a battle cruiser, was as well protected as *Iron Duke,* a battleship, and better protected than *Tiger,* a contemporary battle cruiser. Tirpitz's approach was in direct contrast to Jacky Fisher's philosophy that dreadnoughts of all types must be built to "Hit first!" and "Hit hard!" Fisher's battle cruisers were built to overtake and destroy an enemy at long range with heavy guns. If, to achieve superior speed and striking power within a fixed tonnage, armor in British ships had to be sacrificed, so be it. And so it was: *Queen Mary,* of 27,000 tons, devoted 3,900 tons to armor, whereas *Seydlitz,* weighing 25,000 tons, carried 5,200 tons of armor. And, at Jutland, *Queen Mary* blew up while *Seydlitz* came home.

But heavier armor was only one reason damaged German warships survived at Jutland. German armor was penetrated during the battle; the vessels remained afloat because designers and builders had subdivided their hulls into an extraordinary number of small watertight compartments. Seawater entering one compartment was contained and prevented from spreading to others. *Bayern,* a new German dreadnought battleship about to join the fleet, had six engine rooms and six boiler rooms, whereas *Royal Sovereign,* a new British battleship, had three of each. The price of this honeycomb of small, watertight compartments was paid in cramped living quarters for the crew; officers were packed in four or six to a cabin, and the men lived like tinned sardines. But the ships, even when battered into wreckage, remained afloat.

Not all—or even most—of the blame for British losses at Jutland should be placed on thinner armor. There is no evidence that *Indefatigable, Queen*

Mary, and *Invincible* blew up because German 11-inch or 12-inch shells penetrated their armored hulls and burst inside their magazines. Rather, the almost certain cause of these cataclysmic explosions was that the turret systems of British battle cruisers lacked adequate flashtight arrangements and that, in each of these ships, a shell bursting inside the upper turret had ignited powder waiting to be loaded into the guns, sending a bolt of flame flashing unimpeded down the sixty-foot hoist into the powder magazines. Assuming this to be true, blame lay not with the design of British ships but with the deliberate decision by captains and gunnery officers to discard the flashproof scuttles originally built into British dreadnoughts. The Royal Navy made a cult of gunnery. To win peacetime gunnery competitions, gun crews were encouraged to fire as rapidly as possible. Quick loading and firing required a constant supply of ammunition at the breech of the gun, and thus a continuous flow of powder bags moving out of the magazines and up the hoists to the guns. Safety became secondary; gunnery officers began leaving magazine doors and scuttles open to facilitate movement; eventually, in some ships, these cumbersome barriers were removed. But for this weakness none of the three battle cruisers might have been lost.

If, before Jutland, the British Admiralty did not realize the importance of protecting magazines from powder flash, the Germans did. Both German and British turrets were penetrated by enemy shells during the battle; indeed, nine turrets on Hipper's battle cruisers were pierced by British shells. Some of these turrets burned out as a result, but there were no magazine explosions.

The Germans had profited from grim experience. At the Dogger Bank, sixteen months before Jutland, a 13.5-inch British shell had penetrated *Seydlitz*'s after turret. Powder in the turret caught fire, flashed below, and killed everyone in the two after turret systems, sending flames 200 feet above the ship. Only quick flooding of the magazines saved the ship. The Germans learned from this lesson and German warships were provided with antiflash protection for the hatches between handling room and magazines. Thus, at Jutland, powder exploded and fires wiped out turret crews on *Derfflinger* and other ships, but the flames did not penetrate to the magazines and the ships did not blow up. Belatedly, the British understood and caught up. The navy rapidly installed flashtight scuttles, which operated like revolving doors, in magazine bulkheads and turret systems throughout the fleet.

Seeking other reasons why German dreadnoughts would not go to the bottom, the British navy discovered one that was as unexpected as it was embarrassing: the ineffectiveness of its own armor-piercing shells. These heavy projectiles were designed to penetrate, but all too often at Jutland they broke up on initial impact with armor rather than piercing it and exploding inside a ship's vitals. Bad fuses were to blame: they triggered the shell into bursting prematurely, on first hitting enemy armor. The Royal Navy knew nothing about this flaw until German gossip reached it by way of a neutral naval officer two months after Jutland. In August 1916, Beatty gave a lunch party aboard *Lion* anchored at Rosyth. One of the guests was a Swedish naval officer who until recently had been attached to the Swedish embassy in Berlin. In conversation, he told Ernle Chatfield that German naval officers considered British shells "laughable"; heavy shells had not penetrated their armor but had "broken to pieces" on it. Chatfield, "hardly able to restrain myself till the guests had gone," hurried to tell Beatty. The Admiralty ordered the design of a new armor-piercing shell with a thicker head and a better fuse, which would reliably carry the bursting charges through ten and twelve inches of armor plate and then burst fifteen to twenty feet beyond. These shells, called the "green boys" for the color of their paint, doubled the power of the Grand Fleet's heavy guns, but they did not arrive in numbers until April 1918, seven months before the end of the war. None of the 12,000 eventually produced was fired at an enemy ship.

—

Suppose that Jellicoe had won the annihilating victory the nation and the navy expected. What might this have led to? The extreme assertion—that if the German fleet had been destroyed at Jutland, the war would have ended then and there—ignores, among numerous other considerations, the fact that the annihilating British victory at Trafalgar did not prevent France and Napoleon from continuing to make war for another ten years. As a practical matter, an absolute victory at Jutland in 1916 would have released thousands of British soldiers held in England by fear of a German invasion or a small-scale landing. Elimination of the High Seas Fleet might conceivably have opened the way into the Baltic, as it was the German battle fleet that barred the Kattegat to British surface ships. A British Baltic expedition probably would have suffered heavy losses to mines and submarines, but an open supply route to the hard-pressed Russians might have affected the events leading to the 1917 revolution. In addition, a British fleet in the Baltic would have tightened the blockade of Germany by preventing iron ore and other war materials from crossing from Sweden. In the North Sea and the Atlantic, annihilation of the High Seas Fleet would have deprived the U-boats of their main support; Scheer himself admitted that without the surface fleet to shield Germany's ports and coastline, the U-boats might have been mined into their own harbors.

Reversing the question, what did failure to eliminate the German surface fleet cost Great Britain and the Royal Navy? It meant that the Grand Fleet had to continue to be maintained in enormous strength, absorbing thousands of trained seamen and dozens of destroyers that otherwise could have been released to fight submarines. Without the need to build more warships, the shipyards of the Clyde and the Tyne would have been free to produce the merchant shipping essential to replace the heavy toll being extracted by U-boats. And so on, as in all of history's ifs. But the High Seas Fleet escaped.

—

In the months and years after Jutland, a curious thing happened in Britain. Because of the blurred nature of the British victory, a bitter, divisive argument arose as to which British admiral, Beatty or Jellicoe, was responsible. The Jutland Controversy, as it came to be called, began immediately after the battle, when some London journalists trumpeted that Beatty had practically won the battle before Jellicoe came up and lost it. The fact is that if any British admiral had been "defeated" at Jutland it was Beatty, who led ten capital ships into action against Hipper's five and suffered the loss of two with heavy damage to others. But for the press, Beatty could not become a scapegoat. Beatty was "Our David," the dashing, victorious admiral, the hero of the Bight and of the Dogger Bank, always willing, even eager, to welcome journalists on board his flagship. If Beatty's forces had suffered the heaviest British losses, then Beatty must have been an underdog, facing tremendous odds. He had brilliantly delivered Scheer's vessels into the jaws of the Grand Fleet only to see the opportunity to annihilate them thrown away. Beatty had achieved a historic victory, he was the man of the hour, another Nelson. Once this legend was established, the culprit was easy to find: the overcautious, defensive-minded Commander-in-Chief, famous for his antipathy toward journalists and dislike of their visits to the fleet at Scapa Flow.

For the men in the fleet, the result of the battle had been a terrible disappointment. The enemy had appeared before their guns, they were in a position to annihilate—and then, the Germans had disappeared. Still, the faith of the fleet in the Commander-in-Chief remained unshaken. Captain William Fisher of the dreadnought *St. Vincent* wrote to Jellicoe the day after the battle, "May I go outside strict service custom and say that every officer and man in *St. Vincent* believes in you before any one." William Goodenough, commodore of Beatty's light cruisers, wrote, "God bless you, Sir. I have never felt so bound to you in affection and respect than at this moment." Many retired admirals, including the mutual antagonists Fisher and Beresford, sent congratulations. "Your deployment into battle was Nelsonic and inspired," Fisher wrote, "and in consequence you saved Beatty from destruction and in one hour—*given vision*—you would have ensured Trafalgar." From the Admiralty, Balfour consoled him: "You were robbed by physical conditions of a victory which, with a little good fortune, would have been complete and crushing and I feel deeply for your disappointment. But . . . you have gained a victory which is of the utmost value to the Allied cause." Jellicoe himself, having eaten only half a loaf, refused to be cheered up. To the First Lord, he offered to submit to an investigation: "I hope that if my actions were not considered correct, you will have no hesitation in having them enquired into," adding, "I often feel that the job is more than people over fifty-five can tackle for very long." On his way south to visit the Admiralty, he stopped at Rosyth and came on board *Lion* where, according to Beatty, Jellicoe put his head in his hands and confessed, "I missed one of the greatest opportunities a man ever had."

Beatty's behavior toward Jellicoe after the battle operated on two levels. On the surface, he was supportive and condoling. "First, I want to offer you my deepest sympathy in being baulked of your great victory which I felt was assured when you hove in sight," he wrote on June 9. "I can well understand your feelings and that of the Battle Fleet, to be so near and miss is worse than anything. The cussed weather defeats us every time. . . . Your sweep southward was splendid and I made certain we should have them at daylight. I cannot believe now that they got in the northeast of you. . . . It was perhaps unfortunate that those who sighted the enemy to the northward did not make reports. . . . I do hope you will come here in *Iron Duke* soon, it would do us from top to bottom great honour to know that we have earned your approbation. . . . We are part of the Grand Fleet and would like to see our Commander-in-Chief. . . . Please come and see us and tell us that we retain your confidence."

Beneath the surface, however, Beatty was seething. Convinced that, through excessive caution, Jellicoe had robbed him of the victory he thought he had won, he raged about his superior. Dannreuther of the *Invincible* saw Beatty at Rosyth after the battle: "I spent an hour or more alone with him in his cabin on board the *Lion,* while he walked up and down talking about the action in a very excited manner and criticising in strong terms the action of the Commander-in-Chief in not supporting him. I was a young commander at the time and still regard that hour as the most painful in my life." Six months later, when Beatty succeeded Jellicoe as Commander-in-Chief of the Grand Fleet, his feelings had not subsided. A farewell letter to Walter Cowan, captain of *Princess Royal,* contained a nasty innuendo: "As you well know, my heart will always be with the battle cruisers who can get up some speed, but I'll take good care that when they are next in it up to the neck that our Battle Fleet shall be in it too."

Some of Jellicoe's Grand Fleet supporters responded in kind. A lieutenant complained to his diary of the "arrogant, slipshod" battle cruisers. Rear Admiral Alexander Duff of the 4th Battle Squadron wrote: "There is no doubt that before May 31, the Battle Cruiser Force were swollen headed and truculent and their own idea was to annihilate the High Seas Fleet . . . with just sufficient support of battleships, all to be under the command of Beatty. The game was to be kept in their hands, we were not even to be spectators. With this end in view, Beatty persuaded the C-in-C to give him the 5th Battle Squadron. Then came May 31 when the German battle cruisers severely mauled ours and Beatty did not make use of the 5th Battle Squadron as support; in fact, he left them to their own devices."

Eventually, Beatty's feelings percolated high enough to deny Jellicoe immediate promotion to Admiral of the Fleet, the usual reward for a successful admiral.* This was due in part to a letter from retired Admiral of the Fleet Sir Hedworth Meux, a Beatty admirer, to the king's private secretary: "If Jellicoe had grasped the opportunity which Providence, assisted by Beatty, placed in his way and destroyed the German fleet, he ought to have been made an Earl. But instead . . . practically the whole of the fighting was done by the battle cruisers, and our battle fleet only fired a very few rounds. . . . Jellicoe has done splendid work as an organizer and driller of the fleet, but as yet I am sorry to say he has shown no sign of being a Nelson."

As Meux's letter indicates, naval officers began mustering in opposing Jellicoe and Beatty camps soon after the battle. The Jutland Controversy simmered during the remaining two years of the war; then, in peacetime, open hostilities broke out at the Admiralty, in the press, and in dueling books. This animosity reached a level of rancor, accusation, and epithet that no British naval officer ever directed at Admiral Scheer or Hipper.

—

Over the years, only one of the four senior admirals at Jutland, two German and two British, entirely escaped criticism. Franz von Hipper, the veteran of the Scarborough Raid and the Dogger Bank, led his battle cruisers at Jutland with confidence and skill and managed to triumph over Beatty's superior force. His ships stood up not only to the British battle cruisers but also to the 15-inch guns of battleships—although he later said, "It was nothing but the poor quality of their bursting charges that saved us from disaster." During the Run to the South, Hipper sank two British battle cruisers and led an unsuspecting Beatty to the High Seas Fleet, as well. Hipper should not be blamed for obeying Scheer's command to pursue Beatty to the north, thereby thrusting the High Seas Fleet into the arms of the Grand Fleet. The training and élan of the German battle cruiser squadron, for which Hipper was responsible, proved themselves when his battered, crippled ships, lacking their admiral, charged the enemy in order to save Scheer's battleships. Hipper

*In a letter to a friend, Ethel Beatty wrote, "Now that it is all over, there seems very little to say except to *curse* Jellicoe for not going at them as the battle cruisers did and never stopping until we had annihilated them. I hear he was frightened to death in case he *might* lose a battleship. I think the real truth [is] he was in a *deadly* funk and of course it makes one perfectly sick with the Admiralty trying to make out he is a great man and did all he could and that he is a great *leader.* He failed hopelessly. . . . It makes one so *furious.* I feel I can't bear it."

On the other hand, two other Royal Navy officers were quickly promoted. A week after the battle, Captain Thomas Jackson, Director of the Operations Division of the Admiralty, who had bungled Room 40's interception of *Friedrich der Grosse*'s call sign and failed to tell Jellicoe that Scheer was at sea, was promoted to rear admiral. Later in the summer, Lieutenant Commander Ralph Seymour, Beatty's signals officer, who had mishandled numerous critical signals at Jutland, received early promotion and was decorated with a DSO.

made no mistakes at Jutland and was the only one of the four senior admirals present to come away with his reputation enhanced.

—

Reinhard Scheer was a bold, experienced tactician, famous for his quick decisions, who had the misfortune to command the smaller fleet at Jutland. The High Seas Fleet was made up of superbly built ships with efficient officers and crews having superior training in areas such as night fighting; if the numbers of ships on each side had been equal, the outcome might easily have been different. Scheer's tactics, based on recognition that the strength of his fleet was inferior, were to blend the use of the weapons systems carried by his dreadnoughts and destroyers. The battleships would fight a gunnery duel if they encountered a weaker enemy, but Scheer himself was a torpedo specialist and believed that the torpedo could be as decisive as the gun. If his dreadnoughts encountered an enemy as strong, or stronger, they would rapidly withdraw under cover of smoke screens and massed destroyer torpedo attacks. At Jutland, Scheer's tactics and skills were sorely tested. Twice he came by accident under the guns of the British battle fleet, and on each occasion he was so completely surprised that he found the Grand Fleet crossing his T. Scheer's first turnaround escape was brilliantly executed, but his second—when he turned back toward the Grand Fleet from which he had escaped only thirty minutes before—detracts from his reputation. It was clumsily executed; but, as before, he was hugely assisted by luck and the weather. Scheer had never wanted to fight this particular battle and, from the moment he discovered that he was confronting the entire Grand Fleet, his preoccupation was to get away, if necessary sacrificing his battle cruisers and destroyers. The High Seas Fleet fought bravely and well, but in the end, Reinhard Scheer succeeded not in winning a victory but in escaping annihilation.*

—

David Beatty was an impetuous, bulldog type of fighter, courageous and impatient for action. His preferred tactic was to charge the enemy, and he ex-

*After the war, Scheer's Flag Lieutenant at Jutland, Ernst von Weizsäcker, offered an unflattering portrait of his chief during the battle: "Scheer had but the foggiest idea of what was happening during the action and . . . his movements were not in the least dictated by superior tactical considerations. On the contrary, he had only two definite ideas: to protect the *Wiesbaden* and, when that was no good, to disentangle himself and go home. Talking of the destroyer attack . . . the origin lay in Scheer saying, 'The destroyers have not done anything yet—let them have a go.' . . . Scheer's success lay in his ability to make a decision, but he knew nothing of tactics, although he was against sitting in harbor and liked to get the fleet to sea when he could. . . . In other words, Scheer was much like any other admiral and by no means the tactical genius and superman that the present day historian tries to make out."

In 1936, when Weizsäcker said this, he was acting director of the Political Department of the Foreign Ministry of Nazi Germany.

pected his captains to follow without having to be told. With men who had long been with him and understood his ways—his battle cruiser captains and the commodores of the light cruiser squadrons attached to the battle cruiser force—this simple system worked well. Unfortunately, he did not explain his tactics to men new to his command, especially the two rear admirals, Moore and Evan-Thomas, who played critical roles in his two most famous battles, the Dogger Bank and Jutland. Beatty's failure to acquaint Moore with his style of leadership led to Hipper's escape at the Dogger Bank; because of a similar failure to brief Evan-Thomas, he engaged Hipper at Jutland without the initial support of the powerful 5th Battle Squadron. In other areas, too, Beatty's leadership was flawed. Leaving initiative to subordinates was one thing; ignoring slipshod performance was another. Mistake after mistake was made by his signals staff, led by the hapless Ralph Seymour. And Beatty's effort at Jutland was marred by his continuing failure to improve the poor gunnery of his battle cruisers.

In the immediate aftermath of the battle, Beatty won huge popular praise and was proclaimed another Nelson, but the facts scarcely justify these laurels. Beatty had six battle cruisers and four of the most powerful battleships in the world, as well as fourteen light cruisers and twenty-seven destroyers; Hipper had five battle cruisers, five light cruisers, and twenty-two destroyers. Yet in spite of this preponderance, Beatty lost two battle cruisers and Hipper lost none. Scheer may not have defeated Jellicoe, as claimed by the German communiqué, but there is no doubt that Hipper defeated Beatty.

Beatty began badly at Jutland by failing to concentrate before he attacked. At 10:10 a.m., Beatty ordered the four *Queen Elizabeth*s of the 5th Battle Squadron to take station five miles northwest of *Lion.* Had the battleships been closer, or had they had been stationed on a bearing where an enemy was most likely to appear (southeast, for example), Hipper's battle cruisers would have been subjected to overwhelming fire from the beginning. Once the enemy was discovered, Beatty, determined not to let Hipper get away as he had at the Dogger Bank, turned the battle cruisers at high speed to the southeast, signaling the battleships five miles away to follow. But the signal was given by flag hoist, which could not be distinguished from *Barham,* and it was not repeated by searchlight or wireless. Minutes went by before Evan-Thomas realized that the battle cruisers had altered course and turned to follow. By then, his four giant battleships were ten miles astern.

In the artillery duel that followed, British battle cruiser gunfire inflicted little damage on German ships. Hipper later compared this shooting unfavorably to that of the 5th Battle Squadron and other British battleships while *Lützow*'s gunnery officer stated, "Neither *Lion* nor *Princess Royal* hit us once between 4.02 and 5.23 p.m.; their total hits were three in ninety-five minutes." There was also the usual confusion in fire distribution between Beatty's ships, leaving *Derfflinger* to shoot untroubled. The same mistake had been made at the Dogger Bank. Potentially, Beatty's most harmful error at Jutland was his failure to keep Jellicoe informed as to the position of the enemy battle fleet. Jellicoe had counted on Beatty to provide this vital information, but during the Run to the North, Beatty lost touch with the High Seas Fleet. As a result, he could not tell the Commander-in-Chief what Jellicoe desperately needed to know before deciding in which direction to deploy. Only at the last minute, and largely by instinct, did Jellicoe choose correctly.

The battle cruiser losses at Jutland were not Beatty's fault—ship designers, naval constructors, captains, and gunnery officers bore this responsibility. And, despite these losses and his own errors, Beatty made an important contribution to the British victory: he led Scheer and the German battle fleet to Jellicoe. This significantly mitigates Beatty's numerous errors and his defeat by Hipper. But it certainly does not make David Beatty the hero of Jutland.

—

John Jellicoe, who defeated Scheer and the German fleet at Jutland, was the most unassuming of the four principal admirals who fought the battle. A quiet, methodical man, he was a consummate professional whose success in the navy had been based on discipline, foresight, loyalty, self-confidence, and imperturbable calm at moments of crisis. In his long career afloat and ashore, he had gathered immense technical knowledge, and he commanded the fleet with a soberly realistic understanding of the material strengths and weaknesses of his ships and guns. His organizational abilities had reached a peak in the months at Scapa Flow where he had rigorously drilled the Grand Fleet in tactics and gunnery. His intended tactics were to deploy and exercise his huge margin of superior firepower by staging a massive artillery duel with the enemy fleet; at the same time, he insisted on showing suitable deference to the enemy's possible use of underwater weapons. Jellicoe's principal weakness as a commander was his inflexibility. He was a perfectionist. Everything was centralized in the flagship; he had difficulty delegating and often became immersed in detail. Wishing to leave nothing to chance, he had drawn up the Grand Fleet Battle Orders, seventy pages of detailed instructions, intended to control the fleet under every imaginable circumstance. The contrast between this style of command and Beatty's freewheeling "Follow me" was enormous.

Jellicoe had waited twenty-two months for this moment. Although during the battle, he was never fully aware of the strength or composition of the German fleet, he managed twice to cross Scheer's T, to pound the High Seas Fleet and drive it into retreat. His deployment to port, the complex, massive movement of twenty-four battleships from six columns into a single line, which enabled him to cross Scheer's T, was brilliantly conceived and executed. Jellicoe's critics maintain that by deploying away from the enemy, he surrendered 4,000 yards at a time when every yard and minute counted, but the greater weight of professional opinion supports his decision. This includes the official German naval history, which declared that had Jellicoe deployed to starboard rather than port, "he would have led his ships into a position which would have been only too welcome for the German fleet." Half a century later, Admiral of the Fleet Lord Cunningham, Britain's naval hero of the Second World War, wrote, "I hope I would have been given enough sense to make the same deployment as John Jellicoe did."

Critics also blamed Jellicoe for not plunging forward, Beatty style, in pursuit of Scheer after the first German turnaway. But this was exactly the situation Jellicoe had foreseen in October 1914, when he warned the Admiralty that, because of the danger of mines or torpedoes, he would not pursue a retreating enemy. Again, he was severely belabored for turning away from the German destroyer torpedo attack covering Scheer's second turnaway. But this tactic was standard in all navies and Hipper, Beatty, Hood, Evan-Thomas, and Sturdee all used it at Jutland. Beatty had employed it at the Dogger Bank, too, when he turned away from a supposed periscope.

The weather and the clock, as well as Hipper and Scheer, were Jellicoe's enemies. Had the battle begun three hours earlier, had the visibility been that of the Falkland Islands battle, had there been the same ample sea room given Sturdee against Spee, the outcome at Jutland would have been different. Again, a decisive result might have been possible at daybreak on June 1 had the Commander-in-Chief been better served, first by the Admiralty, which failed to pass on German signals, then by those British captains who saw German battleships passing behind them. Nothing could have saved the High Seas Fleet had Jellicoe stood between it and Horns Reef with eighteen hours of daylight ahead.

Criticism of Jellicoe for not being another Nelson and hurling himself at the enemy is unfair. Tactics are governed by strategy and Jellicoe's strategic purpose was to retain command of the sea. The destruction of the High Seas Fleet was a secondary object—highly desirable but not essential. In the words of the historian Cyril Falls, "He fought to make a German victory impossible rather than to make a British victory certain." Ultimately, Jellicoe achieved both.

—

It was Beatty, simply being Beatty, who was mostly responsible for the Jutland Controversy. Immediately after the battle, he began what became a sustained effort to impose his own version of events on the public mind and the official record. His first move, made when the guns were scarcely cold, was to lobby to have his confidential report to Jellicoe and the Admiralty released and published. Announcing to Jellicoe that "I am not particularly sensitive to criticism," he went on to complain that the handling of his reports after the

Dogger Bank had made him look like "a rotter of the worst description," and that, since Jutland, "I have already been the subject of a considerable amount of adverse criticism and I am looking to the publication of the despatch to knock it out. It is hard enough to lose my fine ships and gallant pals, but to be told I am a hare-brained maniac is not quite my idea of British fairness and justice. So I ask you to have my story published." Jellicoe did his best to accommodate his thin-skinned subordinate by releasing portions of Beatty's report to the press. Nevertheless, in private the Commander-in-Chief observed to the First Sea Lord, "I do not understand his attitude in regard to the despatch. It is surely not his business to edit or to have anything to do with the plans which it is proposed to publish. The telegram sent me yesterday in which he asks to see the new plan before publication astonished me. . . . My view would have been for the Admiralty to have told him that the plan was none of his business."

After the war, on April 3, 1919, both Jellicoe and Beatty were promoted to Admiral of the Fleet, but the subsequent distribution of national gratitude was inequitable. Beatty was elevated to an earldom and awarded a grant of £100,000 for his services; Jellicoe was given the lesser title of viscount and £50,000. In the meantime, on January 23, 1919, Admiral Rosslyn Wester Wemyss, who succeeded Jellicoe as First Sea Lord, assigned Captain J.E.T. Harper, an Admiralty navigation specialist, to write a straightforward official account of the Battle of Jutland, "based solely on documentary evidence and free from commentary or criticism." Harper's first draft, an unvarnished, matter-of-fact narrative, came back from the printers in October 1919, a few weeks before Wemyss retired as First Sea Lord. The proofs were approved by the Board of Admiralty and a copy was placed on the desk of the incoming First Sea Lord, Admiral of the Fleet Earl Beatty. Arriving on November 1 in the office he was to hold for the next eight years, Beatty read Harper's draft and found it deficient in praise for the role of the battle cruisers and their admiral at Jutland. It was a simple matter for Beatty to summon Harper and order him to make deletions, additions, and alterations; it was less simple to get Harper to comply. Told to throw out or "reinterpret" the mass of navigational, gunnery, and signals data he had gathered, simply on Beatty's word that these data were wrong, Harper, whose name was to be on the finished narrative, refused to do so without a written order from the First Sea Lord. The order did not come, but Harper understood the First Sea Lord's intentions; they had been made explicit when Ralph Seymour, who had followed his chief to the Admiralty, told Harper that "we do not wish to advertise the fact that the battle fleet was in action more than we can help." Beatty pushed hard. In one editorial clash, the embattled Harper refused to delete the statement that the battleship *Hercules* had been straddled and deluged with water as she deployed into the line of battle. Beatty, who had not wished the record to show that the Grand Fleet had actually been under shell fire, petulantly surrendered the point by saying, "Well, I suppose there is no harm in the public knowing that someone in the battle fleet got wet, as that is about all they had to do with Jutland." As the months went by, three former First Sea Lords—Jellicoe, Wemyss, and Sir Francis Bridgeman—asked that Harper's official narrative be published. It was not. Eventually Harper gave up and went off to command a battleship, and his version of the official narrative passed into limbo.

The first anti-Jellicoe book, *The Navy in Battle,* was published in November 1918, two weeks after the end of the war. Its author possessed varied credentials. Arthur Hungerford Pollen, one of ten children of a well-known Catholic artist, graduated from Oxford, began and soon gave up a career in law, ran unsuccessfully for Parliament, then supported himself writing articles on art, music, literature, and drama. A talented inventor, he attempted from 1900 to 1913 to persuade the Admiralty to adopt his naval fire-control system. One of those at the Admiralty who eventually said no was John Jellicoe. During the war, Pollen became a naval journalist and an admirer of Beatty; the frontispiece of his book is a heroic color portrait of the battle cruiser admiral. In line with this predisposition, Pollen's account of Jutland portrayed Beatty steering a timid and dull-minded Commander-in-Chief through the battle. The Grand Fleet's deployment, according to Pollen, was devised by Beatty:

> It is to be supposed that Sir David Beatty kept Admiral Jellicoe informed from time to time of the position, speed, and course of the enemy. . . . [Jellicoe's] plan of deployment . . . could not have been based upon his own judgement . . . but must have been dictated, either by some general principle of tactics applied to the information as to the enemy's position, speed and course as given by the Vice Admiral [Beatty], or it must have been part of a plan suggested by the Vice Admiral.

Pollen was soundly thrashed by Jellicoe adherents. Harper described him as "inadequately equipped" to write on the subject and as having written a book that "teems with inaccuracies." A. T. Patterson, the editor of *The Jellicoe Papers,* described Pollen's book as "full of errors, some of them ridiculous." John Winton, Jellicoe's latest biographer, dismissed Pollen's work as "almost unreadable."

The following year, 1919, an all-out, ad hominem attack on Jellicoe appeared in *The Battle of Jutland* by Carlyon Bellairs. The author, a member of Parliament and a Beatty idolator, described Jellicoe as "a man of tearful yesterdays and fearful tomorrows." Among his chapter titles were "The Grand Fleet Nibbles but Does Not Bite," "I Came, I Saw, I Turned Away," and "Eleven Destroyers Dismiss Twenty-four Battleships." *The Times* called

Bellairs's book "outrageous and intolerable"; Harper wrote: "It is, apparently, equitable, in the author's opinion, to ignore accuracy if such action is necessary to glorify Beatty at the expense of Jellicoe."

Meanwhile inside Beatty's inner circle, an unpleasant subplot was developing. The roly-poly Ralph Seymour had served for eight years as signals officer, courtier, jester, and worshiper. "I am the luckiest person on earth to be with David Beatty," he wrote in 1915. " 'Flags' is my Food Dictator and is very arbitrary," Beatty wrote to his wife about a diet imposed by Seymour. For some reason, perhaps because reports of the ineptitude of battle cruiser signaling were spreading, Beatty turned on Seymour, telling people that Flags had "lost three battles for me." Unfortunately, Seymour chose this moment to apply to marry Ethel Beatty's American niece Gwendolyn Field. Ethel, hearing this, "rose in all Hell's fury to break the engagement." Gwendolyn was bundled away and Seymour became persona non grata to the Beattys. Unable to handle these blows from his former benefactors, he had a nervous breakdown and was institutionalized for almost a year. On October 7, 1922, at the age of thirty-six, Flags threw himself over a cliff at Brighton.

Once the public controversy began, both Jellicoe and Beatty were silent in public, writing no articles or letters to newspapers, giving no interviews, and refusing to authorize others to write on their behalfs. From 1920 to 1924, Jellicoe was far from England, serving as governor-general of New Zealand. Meanwhile, Beatty, still First Sea Lord, had a new official Admiralty narrative in preparation. "The Admiralty," a friend wrote to Jellicoe, "are bent on proving that Jutland was fought by *Lion* and the battle cruisers somewhat impeded by the presence of some battleships in a moderately remote vicinity." A preface approved by Beatty was even more extreme: "On learning of the approach of the British main fleet, the Germans avoided further action and returned to base." In July 1923, a draft of this document was sent to Jellicoe in New Zealand for comment. He was incensed. "The carelessness and inaccuracies of this document are extraordinary and the charts and diagrams are even worse," Jellicoe wrote to a friend. "It is . . . of course a Battle Cruiser Fleet account, looked at through BCF eyes." Soon after, Jellicoe wrote to another friend: "If you had seen it when it first came to me you would have said that it was the work of a lunatic." Jellicoe's twenty-page response pointed out what he considered inaccuracies, mostly having to do with wrong information affecting the reputations of some of his officers, especially Evan-Thomas, who was accused of missing the first part of Beatty's battle with Hipper through his own incompetence. Jellicoe threatened to resign his post in New Zealand and come home to fight if the Admiralty published the new narrative without his corrections. Some but not all of his comments were included and in August 1924, a few months before he returned home, the narrative was published. It is an extraordinary document, notable for its omissions, its inaccuracies, and its unprecedented rudeness toward Jellicoe, a former Commander-in-Chief and First Sea Lord. There was no criticism of the Admiralty for its failure to tell Jellicoe that the High Seas Fleet was at sea or, subsequently, that Scheer was returning to base by Horns Reef. There was no criticism of Beatty. Jellicoe's attempt to correct errors was printed as an appendix, where it was "refuted" by Admiralty-produced footnotes written in a tone of long-suffering annoyance.

On returning home from New Zealand, Jellicoe was awarded an earldom, five years after Beatty's. Eight years had passed since Jutland but the controversy continued. Retired vice admiral Sir Reginald Bacon, a protégé of Fisher, the first captain of *Dreadnought,* and a staunch Jellicoe admirer, wrote a book titled *The Jutland Scandal.* Harper, whose official narrative had been scuttled by Beatty, was a rear admiral and now also retired; he brought out his own unofficial book, *The Truth About Jutland.* Between them, Bacon and Harper pilloried Beatty's performance: "A British force was worsted by a squadron half its strength . . . because our admiral in command was inexperienced and showed no tactical ability" (Bacon). "A want of tactical competence on the part of Lord Beatty led to the 5th Battle Squadron not being engaged during the . . . [early part] of the action at Jutland. Admiral Evan-Thomas has been ungenerously and unjustly blamed for this in the Admiralty *Narrative*" (Bacon). "Beatty now made a decision which was to cost us dearly. . . . He made the fatal and elementary mistake of dividing his forces. . . . It is incomprehensible why such a position was selected for this powerful force [the 5th Battle Squadron]" (Harper). "Then, full of ardor, without making certain that the 5th Battle Squadron had received the signal to alter course . . . [Beatty] raced away at high speed. . . . This was the action of an impulsive fighter but not that of an experienced admiral" (Bacon). "It is unpalatable—extremely unpalatable—but nevertheless an indisputable fact that in the first phase of the battle, a British squadron greatly superior in numbers and gun power, not only failed to defeat a weaker enemy who made no effort to avoid action, but in the space of fifty minutes suffered what can only be described as a partial defeat" (Harper).

Later, Harper, still angry, had more to say, this time about his experience with Beatty and the writing of the original official narrative:

> Lord Beatty's political power was such that he was able to sway the First Lord and the Prime Minister to countenance the publication of deliberate misstatements. . . . By insertions or omissions, attempts were made to disguise the fact that . . . Admiral Beatty had seriously neglected the first duty allotted to him, that of giving his Commander-in-Chief frequent and precise information of the position of the enemy; that he failed to inflict damage on a greatly inferior enemy owing to incorrect dispositions of his ships and faulty signaling; and that the

> shooting of his battle cruisers was far below the standard expected of the Royal Navy. . . . The mischief done, not only to Lord Jellicoe, but to the Navy . . . is incalculable. Admiral Jellicoe was belittled and criticised while his onetime subordinate was lauded by a crowd of unscrupulous scribblers. With no damage to his own reputation, Lord Beatty was in a position to stop this campaign of calumny by the utterance of one word. . . . He did not utter that word.

Not until many years later, deep in retirement, did Jellicoe make a public comment. At a naval seminar, he reported that the principal difficulty affecting his handling of the fleet in the battle was

> the absence of even approximately correct information from the battle cruiser fleet and its attendant light cruisers regarding the position, formation and strength of the High Seas Fleet. . . . Had Sir David Beatty reported the position of the German battle cruisers at 5.40 p.m. when he once more caught sight of them and re-engaged, the difficulties of the Commander-in-Chief would have been greatly lessened, but he made no report of any kind between 4.45 and 6.06, the latter report being in reply to urgent enquiries made by the Commander-in-Chief. . . . [Beatty] should have made it his principal duty to keep his Commander-in-Chief informed of the enemy's position. The Commander-in-Chief's battle orders laid the strongest emphasis on this duty.

—

The most accomplished writer involved in the Jutland Controversy was Winston Churchill. His account is interesting, not just because his description of the battle, published in the third volume of *The World Crisis,* which appeared in 1927, was written in Churchill's unique descriptive style, but because, in a strikingly un-Churchillian manner, he waffled. He had appointed both Jellicoe and Beatty to their posts and knew both intimately. As a former cavalry officer who had participated in a charge at Omdurman, he admired Beatty's headlong audacity; as a former First Lord, he understood Jellicoe's care for his immense strategic responsibilities. In the Jutland chapter of *The World Crisis,* he tried to have it both ways.

Churchill began in a way that could only have pleased Admiral Jellicoe, a thorough appreciation of "the consequences to Britain and her allies which would immediately have followed from a decisive British defeat. The trade and food supply of the British islands would have been paralyzed. Our armies on the continent would have been cut off from their base by superior naval force. . . . Starvation and invasion would have descended upon the British people. Ruin, utter and final, would have overwhelmed the Allied cause. . . . There would certainly be no excuse for a commander to take risks of this character with the British fleet at a time when the situation on sea was entirely favorable to us. . . . Command of the sea . . . that priceless sovereignty, was ours already. . . . We were under no compulsion to fight a naval battle." In this context, the former First Lord continued, "the standpoint of the Commander-in-Chief of the British Grand Fleet was unique. His responsibilities were on a different scale from all others. It might fall to him as to no other man—Sovereign, Statesman, Admiral or General—to issue orders which in the space of two or three hours might nakedly decide who won the war. The destruction of the British battle fleet was final." Then came Churchill's famous declaration that "Jellicoe was the only man on either side who could lose the war in an afternoon."

Having made the case for Jellicoe and caution, Churchill suddenly vaulted on the other side of the aisle: "The dominant school of naval thought and policy are severe critics of Sir John Jellicoe. . . . The attempt to centralise in a single hand the whole conduct in action of so vast a fleet failed. . . . Praiseworthy caution had induced a defensive habit of mind . . . which hampered the Grand Fleet." And thus, "the Royal Navy must find in other personalities and other episodes the golden links which carried forward through the Great War the audacious and conquering tradition of the past. . . . It is to Beatty . . . Keyes . . . Tyrwhitt . . . that the eyes of rising generations will turn."

Jellicoe, in other words, had preserved British naval supremacy and by so doing had won the war. Next time, however, it must be done differently.*

—

Churchill's appraisal of Jellicoe at Jutland came eleven years after the battle; it was not that of the officers and men of the Grand Fleet in 1916. In November of that year, when Lloyd George's new Cabinet decided that the gravity of the renewed U-boat menace required replacement of Sir Henry Jackson as First Sea Lord, Jellicoe was summoned from Scotland to take this post, and command of the Grand Fleet was handed to Beatty. On the day the news reached Scapa Flow, a midshipman larking on the quarterdeck of the battleship *King George V* realized that the ship's captain was looking at him. "He beckoned me over," said the young man, "and I doubled across and came to attention and said, 'Yes, Sir?' I looked at him and there were tears rolling down his cheeks. He said, 'Arthur, you may as well tell the gun room that Sir John Jellicoe has been superseded.' " This reaction was general: thou-

*Churchill's verdict provoked a tangential battle over the former First Lord's qualifications to write about command at sea. His liveliest critic, Vice Admiral Bacon, pictured "Mr. Churchill as he sits in an armchair in his well-lighted and commodious library, with all the many charts of Jutland showing the positions of the fleets spread out before him. . . . Here with pencil, compasses, protractor and eraser, he satisfies himself as to what Admiral Churchill would have done had he commanded the British fleet eleven years earlier."

sands of men in the fleet who knew him only by sight nevertheless thought of him not only as their Commander-in-Chief but also as a friend, a modest, honest, and decent man. When Jellicoe left *Iron Duke,* the crew cheered and wept and "stayed on deck watching his [departing] barge until she was lost to sight."

—

It is often said that after Jutland the German fleet never came out again, but, in fact, it did so three times. The first and most ambitious of these sorties, one in which another great battle almost occurred, came on August 18, 1916, eleven weeks after Jutland. Scheer had not yet been able to persuade the German government to break its promise to the United States on unrestricted submarine warfare; as the U-boats were not to be released, he decided to try once more with the battle fleet. This time, with *Lützow* sunk and *Seydlitz* and *Derfflinger* undergoing protracted repairs, Hipper had only two battle cruisers, *Moltke* and *Von der Tann,* available. To strengthen the Scouting Group, Scheer gave Hipper three dreadnought battleships, *Grosser Kurfürst, Markgraf,* and the newly commissioned 15-inch-gun *Bayern,* the mightiest warship yet built in Germany. The High Seas Fleet battleship force was back at full strength; including *König Albert,* which had missed Jutland, there now were fifteen dreadnought battleships at sea, not counting the three with Hipper. One lesson had been learned: Mauve's six predreadnoughts were left behind.

Scheer's plan was a revival of his original Sunderland operation. At dawn, Hipper would bombard the Yorkshire coastal town while Scheer and the battle fleet followed twenty miles behind. If Beatty came rushing south, his battle cruisers first would pass over two lines of waiting U-boats; then, those not torpedoed would fall into the arms of the High Seas Fleet. This time, Scheer insisted on the absolute necessity of extensive airship reconnaissance to be certain that he did not again find himself surprised by the full might of the Grand Fleet. Twenty-six U-boats and ten zeppelins were assigned these tasks, and Hipper and Scheer sailed from the Jade at 9:00 p.m. on August 18.

As usual, Room 40 alerted the Admiralty and again, the Grand Fleet sailed five hours before the High Seas Fleet. Jellicoe, who was resting at his father-in-law's house near Dundee, was picked up by the light cruiser *Royalist,* standing by for that purpose, and rushed to board *Iron Duke* at sea. The Commander-in-Chief had twenty-nine dreadnoughts, including the five *Queen Elizabeth*s, and Beatty brought six battle cruisers. This time, the Harwich Force of five light cruisers and twenty destroyers was sent to sea and ordered to join the Commander-in-Chief. The British preponderance was overwhelming.

On both sides, submarines drew first blood. At 5:05 a.m., the British submarine *E-23* torpedoed the battleship *Westfalen;* Scheer sent her home and with the rest of the fleet maintained course. At 6:00 a.m., *U-52* hit the light cruiser *Nottingham,* screening Beatty's battle cruisers, first with two torpedoes, then with a third. Because no torpedo tracks were seen, Goodenough, *Nottingham*'s squadron commodore, reported to Jellicoe that he was uncertain whether the ship had encountered mines or torpedoes. All Jellicoe's fears of underwater weapons were aroused; worried that the Grand Fleet might be entering into a new, uncharted German minefield, he reversed course for two hours. When Goodenough signaled assurance that *Nottingham* had been sunk by torpedoes, Jellicoe again reversed course and headed south. He had lost four hours, but remained in a position to intercept the High Seas Fleet. Then, shortly after noon, a German mistake saved the German fleet.

The zeppelins had been aloft through the morning, but their reports to Scheer had been confusing. The airships' clearest look at the water's surface came at a moment when the Grand Fleet was steaming north, away from the "minefield" and away from Scheer; they did not see or report Jellicoe's subsequent turn back to the south. Then, at 12:35 p.m., when Hipper was eighty-two miles from Whitby on the Yorkshire coast, the zeppelin *L-13* reported a new force of thirty ships including five battleships approaching the German main body from the south, seventy miles away. This was a misidentification: the five "battleships" were the five light cruisers belonging to the Harwich Force. Scheer jumped to the conclusion that this was an isolated British battle squadron, the sort of prey he had been seeking in all his North Sea operations. Immediately, he abandoned the bombardment of Sunderland and turned southeast at high speed, toward Tyrwhitt and away from Jellicoe. The Grand Fleet, meanwhile, was closing fast, with a long afternoon of clear visibility ahead. When the fleet was at action stations, the Commander-in-Chief signaled: "High Seas Fleet may be sighted at any moment. I look forward with entire confidence in the result." It was not to be. A thunderstorm about this time caused *L-13* to lose contact, but Scheer heard from a scouting U-boat that the Grand Fleet was approaching, sixty-five miles to the north. The Victor of the Skagerrak had no desire to repeat his "victory"; at 2:35 p.m., he abruptly turned southeast for home. An hour and a half later, Jellicoe, bitterly disappointed, also gave up and turned north for Scapa Flow. Along the way, the light cruiser *Falmouth* was struck by two torpedoes fired by *U-66.* Taken in tow, she suffered two more torpedo hits from another submarine and went to the bottom.

Two British light cruisers had been sunk and one German dreadnought damaged and this time Scheer made no claim to victory. He was displeased with his air reconnaissance. Only three of the ten airships aloft had sighted the British fleet; they had sent seven reports, four of which were wrong. In general, Scheer observed wryly, "Scouting by airships is somewhat negative in character, since the fleet is only informed by them that the main hostile fleet is *not* within their field of vision, whereas the important thing is to know where it actually is."

After this day in August 1916, the British Admiralty and Commander-in-Chief agreed that only in exceptional circumstances—a threat of invasion or an attack on the Thames or the Straits of Dover—should the British battle fleet be deployed south of the latitude of Horns Reef. When Room 40 warned on October 18 that Scheer intended another sortie, the Grand Fleet was ordered to raise steam but was held at anchor. And when a British submarine patrolling the Heligoland Bight fired a torpedo into the light cruiser *München* soon after the High Seas Fleet left the Jade, Scheer, fearing a trap, returned to harbor. Thereafter, the German admiral and Naval Staff decided that the chance of catching a part of the Grand Fleet alone at sea was too small to justify risking a major battle, and the dreadnoughts of the High Seas Fleet were kept in port. There they lay, rusting and crewed by mutineers, when the war ended on November 11, 1918.

CHAPTER 35

America Enters the War

Before Jutland, Reinhard Scheer's had not been the only—or even the most prominent—voice in Germany calling for resumption of unrestricted submarine warfare. In the spring of 1916, before the battle, that voice had belonged to Grand Admiral von Tirpitz, but Tirpitz's demand for ruthless use of the U-boats had been defeated by the chancellor, Bethmann-Hollweg, and the embittered navy minister had resigned in protest. Thereafter, the demand to unleash the U-boats was muffled but it did not go away. During June, July, and August, the submarines worked primarily with the High Seas Fleet and, except for a few merchantmen sunk under the old rules of stop-and-inspect, the campaign against merchant shipping lapsed. By autumn, however, more new U-boats were available and the navy was eager to try again. As before, the fateful question was whether releasing the U-boats would provoke America to war; and, as before, the primary opponent of taking this risk was the chancellor. This time, however, the navy had two powerful new allies. And, ironically, these two men had been placed in authority on the recommendation of Bethmann-Hollweg himself.

By the early autumn of 1916, the war on land was going badly. The attack on Verdun had become a bloodbath for both sides, the British were pressing hard on the Somme, and the Russian Brusilov offensive in the east had produced a near fatal Austrian collapse, drawing off German reserves. And then, on August 28, a new blow fell on Germany when Rumania with an army of 400,000 men joined the Allies. General von Falkenhayn, the Chief of the German General Staff, was summoned to a conference at Supreme Headquarters at Pless, where, despite the news from Rumania and the fact that more German troops would have to be sent to bolster the reeling Austrians, he urged resuming the offensive against Verdun. Appalled, Bethmann-Hollweg asked, "Where does incompetence end and crime begin?" and decided that the chief of staff must be replaced. The chancellor's candidate was General Paul von Hindenburg, commander of the Eastern Front, who he believed would be more malleable. Bethmann-Hollweg's wish became fact when the kaiser told Falkenhayn that he wished to have Hindenburg's advice on various military matters. Stiffly, Falkenhayn replied that the kaiser had only one military adviser: himself, the Chief of the General Staff. If the kaiser insisted upon receiving Hindenburg, then he, Falkenhayn, must go. "As you wish," William replied. Falkenhayn was gone before nightfall, on the way to the east to deal with Rumania. The new chief, the sixty-six-year-old hero of the Battle of Tannenberg, accepted office on the understanding that there would be no further attacks at Verdun. And with Hindenburg came his lieutenant, General Erich Ludendorff, who, many said, did most of the hero's thinking. The promotion of these two generals was the costliest mistake of Bethmann-Hollweg's career.

They made an odd couple. Shortly before Tannenberg, Hindenburg was a ponderous retired general living in Hanover. Because his credentials appealed to the kaiser (he was a Prussian nobleman, a Junker, descended from the Teutonic Knights) and to the Supreme Command (he had specialized in the study of the region of East Prussia through which the Russians were advancing) he was suddenly summoned to command the army opposing the invaders. His famous reply, the cornerstone of the towering Hindenburg legend, was "I am ready." At three o'clock in the morning, wearing the old blue uniform in which he had retired, he went to the railway station to await the train that was to bear him into history. Ludendorff, assigned to be Hindenburg's chief of staff, already was on the train. A man of middle-class origin whose life was the army, a brilliant General Staff officer, Ludendorff had advanced on the basis of ability, energy, and relentless determination.

The two men met in the middle of the night in the railway waiting room in Hanover. Hindenburg, his square, flat face topped by a thick brush haircut, had gained weight since his retirement, and his old tunic would no longer hook at the collar. His new chief of staff, whom he had never met, was shorter and round-headed; he wore a large mustache and had a thick, elongated trunk rising above unusually short legs. Ludendorff's uniform was the new German army field gray and on his chest sparkled the blue and gold of the country's highest military honor, the Ordre pour le Mérite, awarded for his part in the spectacular taking of the great Belgian fortress of Liège. Three weeks after this meeting came the victory at Tannenberg, which transformed Hindenburg into the military idol of the German people and established Ludendorff permanently at the titan's side, where he was content to operate in the shade as long as he could supply the ideas.

William, accustomed to the elegant, sophisticated Falkenhayn, disliked them both. They were charmless, they were always busy, and they refused even to pretend to listen to his endless stories. Hindenburg loudly and publicly professed his Junker allegiance to "my emperor, my king, my master," but Ludendorff had no time for these frivolities. The German biographer Joachim von Kurenberg described the working relationship between the monarch and the military workhorse:

> When the Quartermaster General had to appear before the Kaiser to make a report . . . he spoke fast, crisply and emphatically . . . with few gestures; he looked on . . . [these meetings] as unnecessary and a waste of time. His reports seemed to exclude all possibility of misapprehension. . . . If the Kaiser asked a question, Ludendorff would clap his monocle in his eye, bend over his map, mark off distances . . . detail the names and numbers of divisions, times of attack and the objective aimed at. He would point to the arrows marked on the maps which he had drawn to show the directions of the advance planned, then hurriedly roll up the maps and await the hint to withdraw. Then he would stand by the door with the *Pour le Mérite* on his collar, his lips pouting, as always, and await the sign of dismissal from his War Lord. . . . [William] would keep him standing there for a few seconds just to enjoy, if only for a moment, the triumph of still being able to give orders. At last would come the signal, then there was a click of spurs, an effortless about-turn . . . and the Quartermaster General returned to his work.

To the public, Ludendorff remained essentially faceless; Hindenburg, on the other hand, was a national icon.* William did not dare do without either of them. They owed their appointments to victory on the battlefield, and to prevail they had only to threaten resignation. William already had dismissed the legendary Tirpitz; for him now to dismiss the new saviors of the empire was politically impossible. As the months went by, the kaiser, nominally the Supreme War Lord, played a reduced role at Supreme Headquarters, functioning mainly as a mediator between the generals and civilian officials. Swiftly, the military pair moved to put the civilians in their place. On September 13, two weeks after his appointment, Ludendorff bluntly demanded that Bethmann-Hollweg extend the draft for military service or compulsory war production work to all men between fifteen and sixty. "Every day is important," he barked at the chancellor. "The necessary measures must be taken immediately."

*In August 1915, on the first anniversary of the Battle of Tannenberg, a wooden statue of Hindenburg, twelve feet high, was placed near the Reichstag in Berlin. A donation to a war-widows organization bought the right to hammer a nail into the hero's likeness. By the end of the first week, 10,000 silver nails and 90,000 ordinary nails had been driven into the wooden field marshal.

From the beginning, Hindenburg and Ludendorff favored immediate resumption of unrestricted submarine warfare. As generals, they knew better than most that Germany probably could not win the war on land. The human and material resources of the Central Powers were substantially inferior to those of the more populous and industrialized Allied coalition. In manpower, they were outnumbered on the battlefronts: 304 German, Austrian, and Turkish divisions opposed 405 Allied divisions. On the Western Front, 2.5 million German soldiers faced 3.9 million French, British, and Belgian troops equipped with more artillery, more ammunition, and more airplanes. To meet this challenge, Hindenburg and Ludendorff wished to employ every strategy and weapon likely to succeed, no matter what the risks. The most decisive appeared to be the submarine. For two years, Bethmann-Hollweg had resisted, not because he had reservations about torpedoing merchant ships, but because he feared that the torpedoing of American merchant ships would bring the United States into the war. Now the chancellor was under heavy pressure. A majority in the Reichstag and the press, Scheer and the admirals, and now Hindenburg and Ludendorff all favored unleashing the U-boats. If it was necessary to achieve this goal, they wanted the chancellor removed from office. So far, one man had saved Bethmann-Hollweg. Only the kaiser had the constitutional power to remove a chancellor and William, who had known and liked the tall, melancholy Bethmann-Hollweg since the monarch was eighteen, jealously guarded his own prerogative and refused to make a change. Accordingly, the chancellor, a widower whose eldest son had recently been killed on the Eastern Front, resisted his enemies, reminding them that his actions were not subject to parliamentary control or public opinion and that he was responsible only to the kaiser.

In opposing the U-boats, Bethmann-Hollweg had two principal allies in the bureaucracy: Gottfried von Jagow, the foreign minister, and Johann von Bernstorff, the German ambassador in Washington. Both men shared the chancellor's opinion that no success resulting from submarine warfare would be worth American entry into the war. This opinion had a halfhearted and private supporter in William himself. However irritated he might be by the United States, the kaiser did not want to fight the Americans. On the other hand, he shrank from the prospect of being considered weak by his own military chiefs or by the German people. His ambivalence was made plain during the *Lusitania* negotiations: in the same conversation, he told the American ambassador, James Gerard, that, as a Christian ruler, he would never have permitted the torpedoing of *Lusitania* if he had known that there were women and children on board—and then added brusquely, "America had better look out after this war. I shall stand no nonsense from America."

On August 31, two days after being elevated to command, Hindenburg and Ludendorff met Bethmann-Hollweg, Jagow, and Admiral Holtzendorff. To fend off their talk of using the submarines, the chancellor warned that unrestricted U-boat warfare might provoke the neutrals on Germany's border, Holland and Denmark, into declaring war on Germany. Holland alone, he declared, would be able to put more than 500,000 men into the field and either state could be used as a beachhead for British landings. Hindenburg, who was scrambling to assemble divisions to fight Germany's new enemy, Rumania, lacked the reserves to fight on any new fronts and agreed temporarily to postpone the submarine decision. At the same time, he insisted that, sooner rather than later, unrestricted submarine warfare must come. On September 10, Ludendorff buttressed his chief's opinion. An officer from the Naval Staff asked what the new Supreme Command wanted the navy to do. Ludendorff assured the officer that he and the field marshal intended to expand the submarine war as soon as the military position was stabilized; first, however, the army must bolster the Austrians, who were "nothing more than a sieve." Did the general think that the neutrals would come in as the chancellor feared? the officer asked. Grimly, Ludendorff replied that it was a great pity that the civil authorities had ever been allowed a say in the matter. Submarine warfare was a purely military question; in war, it must rest entirely with military and naval authorities to decide what forces to use and how to use them.

It did not take Bethmann-Hollweg long to recognize that by bringing in the new men, he had released a genie from its bottle. On October 5, Hindenburg advised the chancellor that "the decision for an unrestricted U-boat campaign fell primarily to the Supreme Command." Bethmann-Hollweg parried, saying that an order by the kaiser to begin unrestricted U-boat warfare would indeed be an expression of imperial authority, but that an unrestricted submarine campaign, directed not only against enemy ships but also against neutral vessels, "directly affects our relations with neutral states and thus represents an act of foreign policy . . . for which I have sole and untransferable responsibility." Unwilling at that moment to challenge this position, the generals backed away.

—

Across the Atlantic, two years after the outbreak of war, the predominant opinion of the American people continued to be that the struggle was a purely European affair; Woodrow Wilson's 1916 reelection campaign was based on a single, powerful claim: "He kept us out of war." Political and military neutrality, however, had not prevented the United States from enjoying an ever-growing volume of trade in war supplies, general cargo, and foodstuffs, which now firmly attached the American economy to the Allied war effort. In theory, U.S. commercial loans and trade in food and munitions were equally available to the Central Powers, but theory and actual usefulness to the German cause ran up against the implacable barrier of Allied control of the oceans.

In the formation of neutral opinion, the different methods of the belligerents in fighting economic war at sea weighed heavily against the Germans. The British blockade infringed on the freedom of the seas, but these incidents, sometimes infuriating, did not put lives at risk or even seriously retard the flow of goods. By contrast, unrestricted U-boat warfare, threatening and sometimes taking neutral ships and neutral lives, challenged the American government either to abandon use of the world's oceans or take whatever steps were necessary to ensure the safety of American lives and cargoes. Twice, acts by German submarines had forced a crisis. The sinking of *Lusitania* in May 1915 and the sinking of *Sussex* in April 1916 had led each time to prolonged negotiations in which President Wilson attempted to force Germany to acknowledge American rights without invoking the ultimate threat of a war that neither he nor the American people wanted. Both times, Wilson succeeded, and all U-boats operating in the North Sea, the Channel, the eastern Atlantic, and the Mediterranean had been ordered to surface, establish the identity of the ship they had stopped, and allow neutral ships to pass.

In the autumn of 1916, an episode much closer to home caused friction between the British and American governments. At 3:00 on the afternoon of October 7, the new German submarine *U-53,* with four of her ballast tanks altered for carrying fuel, surfaced and anchored in the harbor of Newport, Rhode Island. The captain, Hans Rose, came ashore in his dress uniform to pay his respects to the American admiral commanding a destroyer flotilla based in Newport. Then he mailed a letter to the German ambassador and picked up local newspapers, which listed vessels in port about to sail and named their destinations. Observing protocol, the American admiral returned the visit and came on board to inspect the U-boat and admire its diesel engines. He was followed—with Rose's permission—by many curious American naval officers, their wives, Newport civilians, reporters, and a photographer. At 5:30 p.m., observing all conventions limiting the stay of belligerent warships in neutral ports, Rose weighed anchor and put to sea. At dawn the next morning, *U-53* lay on the surface in international waters off the Nantucket lightship where she began sinking ships. During the day, Rose stopped, searched, and sank seven merchant vessels: five British, one Dutch, and one Norwegian. All crew members were permitted to leave their ships before they were sunk.

No person was harmed that day and *U-53*'s behavior outside American territorial waters had been conducted according to the rules of cruiser warfare and international law. Still, in Massachusetts and surrounding states, the sinking of merchant vessels so close to home inspired a sense of terrified vulnerability. In Britain, the reaction was official and public fury. Not only were the British appalled by the fact of U-boat activity at that great distance, but they were bitterly critical of the fact that sixteen American destroyers had clustered near the Nantucket lightship, had witnessed the sinkings, and, although picking up passengers and crews from their lifeboats, had done nothing to inhibit the submarine. At one point, *U-53* was so close to an American warship that the submarine had to reverse engines to avoid collision. Later in the day, another destroyer, lying near the abandoned Dutch steamer, was asked by Rose to move away so that he might sink the ship. Obligingly, the destroyer moved and *U-53* fired two torpedoes, sending the ship to the bottom. For the submarine, it was a successful voyage. *U-53* returned to Germany, having covered 7,550 miles without refueling and having stopped only once, for the two and a half hours in Newport. In her wake, she left huge newspaper sales along the Eastern Seaboard, urgent conferences at the State Department, angry cries in the House of Commons, and eventually a soothing speech by Sir Edward Grey, who explained to his countrymen that the American warships had had no legal right to intervene in the belligerent activities of *U-53*.

By mid-autumn of 1916, Woodrow Wilson believed that American relations with the Central Powers were becoming more amicable. It was true that the country still generally favored the Allies, but with Germany's *Sussex* pledge still in force, most Americans wanted simply to let Europeans kill one another however they wished without American participation. Wilson, however, was unwilling to leave it at that. Repelled by the mindless slaughter at Verdun and on the Somme, he made up his mind that it was his duty—his mission—to use his position as the leader of the one great neutral state to persuade the warring powers to call a halt. In September, the Germans and Austrians as well as the British and French were told that the president would launch a mediation effort as soon as he was reelected.

In the presidential campaign, Charles Evans Hughes, the Republican candidate, a moderate former Supreme Court Justice, was supported by the eastern, pro-Allied, interventionist wing of the electorate; Wilson had the support of most southern, midwestern, and western "stay-out-of-the-war" voters. But the election was not decided on Election Day, November 7. Hughes, accumulating early majorities in the East, surged to a lead and on November 8 *The New York Times* announced that "Charles E. Hughes Has Apparently Been Elected President." Theodore Roosevelt, who hated Wilson, happily declared that "the election of Mr. Hughes is a vindication of our national honor." Then Hughes fell back and for two days the result teetered on the returns from California. It was not until November 22 that a Hughes telegram conceding defeat finally reached Wilson—"It was a little moth-eaten when it got here," the president observed. In the end, Wilson won California by 3,806 votes. He had a nationwide popular majority of 691,385. He carried only a single northeastern state, New Hampshire, and that by fifty-six votes. In the electoral college the votes split 277 to 254.

The election was a squeaker by most people's count, but Wilson treated it as a landslide. The president had what he desired: absolute control of American foreign policy. He did not need to listen to Congress, his Cabinet, his own ambassadors, or ambassadors from anywhere else. He was acutely sensitive to public opinion, and only to public opinion. Now, reelected, Wilson was free to take up his mission. The carnage in Europe must be stopped; this could be done only by showing favoritism to neither side. Wilson recognized that "if Germany won, it would change the course of civilization and make the United States a military nation," but he was also keenly aware of the derision the French and English press had directed at him when early returns had predicted the election of Hughes. Now empowered by the American people to do what he wished, Wilson began tapping out drafts of a peace mediation offer on his typewriter. His goal was a negotiated peace, to be achieved by asking each of the warring powers to submit a statement of its war aims and where it would be willing to compromise in order to make peace. Together, he and they would discover a middle ground.

As the president typed, the belligerents' ambassadors in Washington bent their ears to pick up what they could of the message coming from his keys. As always, they could learn nothing from Wilson himself, who would not see them, but they could learn much by talking to the little man with a receding chin who was the president's best friend. Edward House was the one exception to the reclusive president's rigid policy of excluding everyone from the inner world of his work and thought. House was a wealthy Texan who, in return for his support of one of the state's governors, had been awarded the honorary title of colonel. Active and influential in Texas politics, he had gravitated toward Wilson in 1911, when the then governor of New Jersey was beginning his run for the Democratic presidential nomination. He worked effectively as an intermediary between Wilson and Bryan and, by the time of Wilson's election, he could have been appointed to almost any position he wished in the new administration. He asked for none. This was sufficient to make him an object of intense scrutiny by a press determined to fix his place in the political firmament: "He holds no office and never has held any, but he far outweighs Cabinet officers in Washington affairs. . . . He is a figure without parallel in our political history. . . . Colonel House asks nothing for himself. He hates the limelight. . . . House is one of the small wiry men who do a great deal without any noise. He is a ball bearing personality; he moves swiftly but with never a squeak."

The solution to the riddle of House was that he had made himself the closest friend Woodrow Wilson ever had. The colonel did not even live in Washington—he lived with his wife in Manhattan—but he came to Washington often, and on these visits he always stayed at the White House. At the end of an evening of intimate conversation, Wilson routinely escorted House to his room to ask whether everything was properly laid out. When the president came to New York, he was always a guest in House's small apartment on Fifty-third Street.

Wilson valued House's advice above all others'. "Mr. House is my second personality," the president explained. "He is my independent self. His thoughts and mine are one." To House himself, he said, "You are the only person in the world with whom I can discuss everything." When war broke out, Europeans as well as Americans became aware of the mysterious Colonel House, who had no office and carried no title but "personal friend of the President"—which was enough to open every door in Washington, London, and Berlin. "Instead of sending Colonel House abroad," one journalist suggested, "President Wilson should go to Europe himself to find out just what the people there think of him. Wilson could leave Colonel House here to act as president during his absence." House became the conduit through which foreign governments and their ambassadors in Washington learned what the American president was thinking.

One of these ambassadors, Great Britain's Sir Cecil Spring-Rice, was an extraordinarily poor choice. His friends, made during an earlier tour of diplomatic duty in America, were all Republicans. He wrote to Theodore Roosevelt as "My Dear Theodore," to Massachusetts senator Henry Cabot Lodge as "My Dear Cabot," and to the reclusive guru Henry Adams as "Uncle Henry." He was an anti-Semite.* As a negotiator, Spring-Rice was irritable and shrill; one ardently pro-Allied State Department official said that he always left Spring-Rice "feeling a sympathy for the Germans." In Woodrow Wilson's Washington, the ambassador uttered the wrong opinions in the wrong ears. "At one time," he complained to Colonel House, "this country was composed of pure rock, but now it is composed of mud, sand, and some rock, and no one can predict how it will shift or in what direction." House easily understood that Roosevelt and Wilson were being compared. On occasion, Spring-Rice had tantrums. "I would be glad if you would not mention Bernstorff's name in my presence again," he once hissed at House when the latter mentioned that he had just seen the German ambassador. "I do not want to talk to anyone who has just come from talking to him or to Germans." An Anglophile himself, House discreetly wrote to Sir Edward Grey at the Foreign Office, suggesting that "Sir Cecil's nervous temperament sometimes does not lend itself well to the needs of the present moment." Grey ignored the letter and the ambassador remained.

Despite Spring-Rice's nastiness, his political analysis was useful to Grey. "There is a strong sense that our sea power is exercised in a way, not so much

*He advised Adams that he was reading "a little book by a Jew-boy" and complained to Sir Edward Grey of American "Jew bankers who show a strong preference for Germany" as well as of "Jews capturing the principal newspapers and bringing them over as much as they dare to the German side."

to injure American commerce and trade, as to hurt American pride and dignity. No one could argue for a moment that our war measures have ruined this country; America has never been so rich. But the facts are that American trade is in a way under British control." Later he summarized by saying, "Our blockade measures are, not a wound, but a hair shirt." In December 1916, he tried, in a series of letters, to tell Balfour, Grey's successor at the Foreign Office, about Woodrow Wilson: "The President rarely sees anybody. He practically never sees ambassadors and when he does, exchanges no ideas with them. Mr. Lansing is treated as a clerk who receives orders which he has to obey at once without question." "I have been in Russia, Berlin, Constantinople and Persia which are all popularly supposed to be autocratic governments. But I have never known any government so autocratic as this. This does not mean that the president acts without consulting the popular will. On the contrary, his belief and practice is that he must not lead the people until he knows which way they want to go." "Here [in Washington] we regard the White House rather as Vesuvius is regarded in Naples, that is, as a mysterious source of unexpected explosions." "The president's great talents and imposing character fit him to play a great part. He feels it and knows it. He is already a mysterious, rather Olympian personage, shrouded in darkness from which issue occasional thunderbolts.* He sees nobody who could be remotely suspected of being his equal."

Spring-Rice, like Grey, knew that without American credit, food, and munitions, the Allies could not win the war. This flow must not be interrupted; therefore, Woodrow Wilson's sensitive, prickly nature must be appeased. Given time, the Germans could be counted on to make a mistake, and then events would proceed to an almost certain conclusion. Meanwhile, Britain must wait. "There was one mistake in diplomacy that, if it had been made, would have been fatal to the cause of the Allies," Grey wrote later. "It was carefully avoided. This cardinal mistake would have been a breach with the United States, not necessarily a rupture, but a state of things which would have provoked American interference with the blockade, or led to an embargo on exports of munitions from the United States." Spring-Rice's assignment was to make certain that this mistake was avoided. His task was to be patient.

*Wilson, during these critical months, was sometimes "shrouded in darkness" for personal reasons unknown beyond his inner circle. His general health was poor and he suffered frequently from severe headaches. "There would come days," said Edith Wilson, his wife since December 1915, "when he was incapacitated by blinding headaches that no medicine could relieve. He would give up everything and the only cure seemed to be sleep. We would make the room cool and dark and when at last merciful sleep would come, he would lie for hours in this way, apparently not even breathing. Sometimes this sleep would last five, six, or even eight hours. He would awake refreshed and able at once to take up work and go on with renewed energy."

Count Johann von Bernstorff, the ambassador of Imperial Germany, could not afford to wait. Elegant, aristocratic, with blue eyes and a red mustache, he was charming, candid, and adaptable, the most popular ambassador in Washington before the war. He had been born in London, where his diplomat father had been stationed, and he had served eight years in the Prussian Guards before joining the Foreign Ministry. He married an American and now had served eight years as ambassador to the United States. He spoke impeccable English and French; he waltzed, played tennis, golf, and poker, and pretended to be interested in baseball. Socially, all doors opened to him and he instructed the doormen at the German embassy on Massachusetts Avenue to show into his office any newspaperman who cared to call. Five American universities had given him an honorary degree; these included Columbia, the University of Chicago, and Woodrow Wilson's own Princeton.

Knowing America, Bernstorff understood the consequences of unleashing German submarines against American shipping. Month after month, behind his amiable façade, he struggled to keep his country off this ruinous path. Along with Bethmann-Hollweg and Jagow, he hoped that President Wilson would intervene and stop the war. Through the summer and early fall of 1916, he pleaded with the chancellor to postpone the U-boat decision until after the American election. "If Wilson wins at the polls, for which the prospect is at present favorable," Bernstorff told Bethmann-Hollweg on September 6, "the president will at once take steps towards mediation. He thinks in that case to be strong enough to compel a peace conference. Wilson regards it as in the interest of America that neither of the combatants should gain a decisive victory." Bethmann-Hollweg and Jagow waited eagerly for word from their ambassador. On September 26, the chancellor cabled Bernstorff: "The whole situation would change if President Wilson were to make an offer of mediation to the powers." Wilson remained silent. On October 14, increasingly anxious, Bethmann-Hollweg cabled the ambassador, "Demand for unrestricted submarine campaign increasing here. Spontaneous appeal for peace, towards which I again ask you to encourage him, would be gladly accepted by us. You should point out Wilson's power, and consequently his duty, to put a stop to slaughter. If he cannot make up his mind to act alone, he should get into communication with Pope, King of Spain and European neutrals." On November 16, after Wilson's election, Jagow pushed Bernstorff: "Desirable to know whether president willing to take steps towards mediation and if so which and when." On November 20, Jagow cabled again: "We are thoroughly in sympathy with the peace tendencies of President Wilson. His activity in this direction is to be strongly encouraged." Bernstorff replied, "Urge no change in submarine war until decided whether Wilson will open mediation. Consider this imminent." Still, Wilson did not act.

The German generals, however, wanted to hear no more from Bernstorff of the long-awaited mediation offer. It was clear that no peace Wilson could arrange would be acceptable to the Supreme Command. "The German people wish no peace of renunciation," stormed Ludendorff, "and I do not intend to end being pelted by stones." The U-boats must be unleashed, and those opposed to this decision removed from office. If, for the moment, Bethmann-Hollweg remained untouchable, at least the generals could rid themselves of another enemy, Foreign Minister von Jagow. On November 22, Jagow, who had never wanted the job and was almost incapacitated by its burdens, resigned and his vigorous undersecretary, Arthur Zimmermann, was appointed foreign minister. That day, the American chargé d'affaires, calling on the chancellor, found him "a man broken in spirit, his face deeply furrowed, his manner sad beyond words."

—

Affecting the internal struggles of the German government, pressing down on the chancellor and the generals alike, was the grim weight of the British blockade. The extinction of German overseas trade had not directly affected the German army, which continued to be adequately supplied with food and ammunition, but the army's well-being came at a cost to the civilian population. The third winter of the war was known in Germany as the turnip winter because turnips in many guises found their way into the people's basic diet. Most recognizable foods were scarce. Milk was available to people over six years old only with a doctor's prescription. Bread was made first from potatoes, then from turnips. Eggs, which had been limited in September to two per person per week, were doled out in December at one egg every two weeks. Pork, a staple of the traditional German diet, disappeared; in August 1914, Berlin stockyards were slaughtering 25,000 pigs every week; by September 1916, the figure was 350. Sugar and butter could be purchased only in minute quantities. The 1916 potato harvest had failed, and potato ration cards were required in hotels and restaurants. Even in June that year, three Americans had walked down Unter den Linden where every window and balcony was festooned with red, white, and black flags celebrating the "victory" at Jutland and the prospect that the blockade would soon be broken. Entering the Zollernhof restaurant, they picked up the bill of fare and for the first time read, "Boiled Crow."

By winter, the grip of the blockade had tightened. "We are all gaunt and bony now," wrote the English-born Princess Blücher. "We have dark shadows around our eyes and our thoughts are chiefly taken up with wondering what our next meal will be." Coal was scarce; in Berlin only every other street light was lit. In Munich, all public halls, theaters, art galleries, museums, and cinema houses were closed for lack of heat. Women waiting in long lines to buy food were exposed to winter rain, snow, and slush. The women returned to unheated houses, where their children, having no warm clothes, had been kept in bed all day.

These privations aroused the German people to hatred. They were bitter at their own government, which had promised a short war, brilliant victories, and a greater Germany. Their rage was far greater at their enemies, primarily Britain, which had imposed the blockade. And every day they read in their newspapers that the nation possessed a weapon that could break the blockade. Week by week, throughout Germany, the clamor rose higher: Unleash the submarines! The U-boat now became a symbol not only of revenge and victory, but also of the end of the war and peace.

—

Bethmann-Hollweg, who had reluctantly approved of Jagow's dismissal as a means of buying time, realized that he could no longer wait for Wilson. On December 9, when the American election had been over for a month and still nothing was heard from Washington, the chancellor resolved on a dramatic step: Germany herself would propose negotiations to end the war. It was a favorable moment; the German military position had temporarily improved. The British offensive on the Somme had been drowned in blood, the Russian Brusilov campaign had been checked, and Rumania had been crushed. The kaiser, seeing a new way to seize the limelight, supported the chancellor. "To propose to make peace is a moral act," William wrote. "Such an act needs a monarch whose conscience is awake and who feels himself responsible to God, who acknowledges his duty to all men—even his enemies; a monarch who feels no fear because his intentions may be misinterpreted, who has in him the will to deliver the world from its agony. I have the courage to do this and I will risk it for God's sake."

Grudgingly, the generals and admirals agreed to delay an unrestricted submarine campaign until one last demonstration could be made to the German public and to world opinion that Germany had no other choice. Their quid pro quo was that if Bethmann-Hollweg's attempt to bring about a peace conference should fail—as they fully expected—the U-boats would be unleashed. The new foreign minister, Zimmermann, had put it in a way the military men could accept. "Intensified submarine war toward America would certainly be facilitated," Zimmermann said, "if we could refer to such a peace action." Zimmermann also saw another advantage: the move would drive away an obnoxious interloper. To an off-the-record press conference, he explained that, as Germany "was threatened by a peace move by Mr. Wilson, we would fix it so this person would not have his finger in the pie." The German peace note, circulated on December 12 and announcing that the Central Powers invited the nations at war to begin negotiations for a peaceful settlement, came as a surprise to everyone. "In a deep moral and religious sense of duty towards this nation and beyond it towards humanity, the emperor now considers that the moment has come for official action towards peace," Bethmann-Hollweg explained to the Reichstag. William's announcement to the army was delivered in sterner language: "Soldiers! In agreement with the sovereigns of my allies and with consciousness of victory, I have made an offer of peace to the enemy. Whether it will be accepted is uncertain. Until that moment arrives, you will fight on."

—

By December 1916, the Asquith coalition government in Britain was coming apart, the central issue being the effectiveness of the prime minister himself. Asquith had always governed as a relaxed chairman of the board, hearing all arguments, then postponing decisions until consensus emerged.* Now, after eight years in office, he was tired and, to make matters worse, his focus was blurred by the recent death in action of his eldest son. David Lloyd George, a Liberal colleague who had served under Asquith for many years, saw his chance. Asquith's leadership had become "visibly flabbier, tardier, and more flaccid," the ambitious Welshman declared; what was needed was a new War Committee of three, chaired by himself and excluding the prime minister, who would be allowed to keep that office with diminished authority. When Asquith refused this political emasculation, his government collapsed. Lloyd George resigned; then Asquith resigned, and on December 10, a new, Lloyd George government took office with Grey out as foreign secretary and Balfour shifted from the Admiralty to the Foreign Office. Two days later, the German peace note arrived. The Allies saw clearly that the peace being offered was a conqueror's peace. Europe from the English Channel to the Black Sea was in the grip of the Central Powers; the German army occupied Belgium, Poland, Serbia, Rumania, and ten of the richest provinces of France. Now, the note suggested, the rulers of Germany would be willing to call off the war if they could keep everything they had occupied. On December 30, Lloyd George told the House of Commons that "to enter into a conference on the invitation of Germany, proclaiming herself victorious, is to put our heads in a noose." Both Britain and France rejected the German note.

—

The Allies' emphatic rejection of Bethmann-Hollweg's peace offer further weakened the chancellor in Berlin. Admiral von Holtzendorff said, "Since I do not believe in a quick effect of the beautiful peace gesture, I am totally committed to the use of our crucial weapon—unrestricted submarine

*In Cabinet meetings, "it was not unknown for the Prime Minister to be writing letters while the discussion proceeded," said Austen Chamberlain, the secretary of state for India. "The result was that complete confusion prevailed and when at last he intervened with a statement that, 'Now that is decided, we had better pass on to . . .' there would be a general cry of 'But what is decided?' and the discussion would begin all over again."

warfare." Hindenburg insisted that "diplomatic and military preparations for an unrestricted U-boat campaign begin so that it may for certain begin at end of January." But now came another complication—and a last opportunity for the chancellor. On December 18, the president of the United States finally issued his own peace note to the warring powers. Presenting himself as "the friend of all nations," Wilson asked each of the belligerents to declare its war aims so that a search for middle ground could begin. "It may be," he declared, "that peace is nearer than we know. . . . The objects which the statesmen of the belligerents on both sides have in mind in this war are virtually the same, as stated to their own peoples and to the world." Privately, House told Bernstorff that Wilson would not hesitate to use heavy economic pressure to coerce the Allies if he thought their conditions unreasonable.

Wilson's note was received unwillingly by all to whom it was addressed. The German reply arrived first, on December 26. It was a polite rebuff, declaring that Germany was willing to meet its enemies, but preferred to negotiate with them directly on neutral ground, without the assistance of the United States. Bernstorff pointed out to Berlin that Wilson wished only to be informed of the war aims of both sides so that the belligerents could identify their differences. He was ignored. Specifics were precisely what the German government did not wish to reveal, because such revelations would arouse in Germany a bitter struggle over what German war aims actually were. Nor did the German government wish Wilson to be present at the conference because, as Zimmermann told Bernstorff, "we do not want to run the risk of being robbed of our gains by neutral pressure." The kaiser's reaction was blunt: "I go to no conference. Certainly not one presided over by him."

The Allied reply came two weeks later. Despite their exhaustion, the Allies believed they were winning the war and regarded Wilson's mediation offer as an effort, witting or unwitting, to rescue their enemies from the consequences of defeat. They wanted no compromises that would leave Germany in a position to renew the struggle later. Lloyd George actively resented Wilson's effort to "butt in," as he put it. At the end of September, before becoming prime minister, he had made clear his disdain for any American mediation efforts. "There had been no such intervention when we were being hammered though the first two years, as yet untrained and ill-equipped," he told an American newspaperman. "Now the whole world—including humanitarians with the best of motives—must know that there can be no outside interference at this stage. Britain will tolerate no interference until Prussian military despotism is broken beyond repair." Wilson's phrase, equating the war aims of the opposing sides as "virtually the same" and thus seeming to exonerate Germany and ignore or cheapen the sacrifices of the Allies, appeared less neutral than mischievous. The American ambassador, Walter Page, reported that King George V had wept when the subject came up at lunch. On January 12, 1917, the governments of Britain and France firmly rejected peace talks. The sole cause of war, they declared, was the brutal, unprovoked aggression of Germany and Austria-Hungary. German misdeeds were set forth at length and specific Allied war aims were listed, including evacuation of all occupied territories and enormous reparations and indemnities. Until this was achieved and Germany so reduced that fear of another war did not hang over them, they would continue to fight. France, especially, felt that never again would she be supported by as strong a combination of powers and have as good a chance of beating Germany to her knees. In Washington, however, the negative Allied response produced exactly the reaction Spring-Rice had feared: a resentful president who decided that the two sides, equally intractable, were equally guilty. His peace initiative momentarily thwarted, Wilson decided that the other pillar of his foreign policy, American neutrality, must be buttressed. "There will be no war," he told House. "This country does not intend to become entangled in this war. It would be a crime against civilization if we entered it."

—

Wilson's peace move was of no interest to the German Supreme Command. Ludendorff already had declared *"Ich pfeife auf Amerika"* (I don't give a damn about America) and had informed the American military attaché that the United States could do no greater harm to Germany by declaring war than it already was doing by supplying the Allies. For months, stories about American war munitions and foodstuffs flowing across the Atlantic had appeared in German newspapers. "If it were not for American ammunition, the war would have been finished long ago" became a nationwide refrain. A copy of an advertisement by the Cleveland Automatic Tool Company depicting a new artillery shell and printed in *The American Machinist* was laid on every desk in the Reichstag. A drawing distributed throughout Germany depicted a freighter in an American port ready to take on a cargo of ammunition. Massed in the background were three groups of German soldiers doomed to become casualties of this single cargo: "30,000 killed, 40,000 seriously wounded, 40,000 lightly wounded." Not surprisingly, the German public supported a U-boat effort intended to cut this transatlantic supply line and preserve the lives of their husbands, sons, and brothers.

James Gerard, the American ambassador to Germany, bore the brunt of this hostility. Gerard, a former justice of the New York State Supreme Court, had come to Berlin in 1913; in May 1914, he had believed that war between Germany and the United States was unthinkable. Beginning in August 1914, however, Gerard was denied contact with the head of the state to which he was accredited. "An ambassador is supposed to have the right to demand an audience with the kaiser at any time," Gerard later wrote, "[but] on each occasion my request was refused. I was not even permitted to go to the railway station to bid him goodbye when he left for the front." Nine months later,

Gerard asked the American military attaché "to tell the kaiser that I had not seen him for so long a time that I had forgotten what he looked like." Through the attaché, the kaiser retorted, "I have nothing against Mr. Gerard personally, but I will not see the ambassador of a country which furnishes arms and ammunition to the enemies of Germany." Another five months passed, until finally, in September 1915, Gerard wrote to Bethmann-Hollweg: "Your Excellency: Some time ago I requested you to arrange an audience for me with His Majesty. Please take no further trouble about this matter. Yours sincerely." Immediately, Gerard was granted an audience.

The ambassador was summoned again six months later, after the settlement of the *Sussex* affair. This time Gerard was escorted to Supreme Headquarters in the French town of Charleville-Mézières, fifty miles behind the western battlefront. Before seeing the kaiser, he was asked condescendingly by William's staff what America could do if Germany recommenced unrestricted submarine warfare. "I said that nearly all great inventions used in war were made by Americans: barbed wire, the airplane, the telephone, the telegraph—and the submarine. I believed that if forced into it, we would come up with something else." The Germans replied, "While you might invent something and will furnish money and supplies to the Allies, the public sentiment of your country is such that you will not be able to raise an army large enough to make an impression."

On May 1, 1916, Gerard was taken to see Kaiser William, strolling in a garden. "Do you come bearing peace or war?" the kaiser asked, and then launched into a monologue: Americans, he said, had "charged Germany with barbarism in warfare, but that as emperor and head of the church, he had wished to carry on war in knightly manner. He then referred to the British blockade and said that before he allowed his family and grandchildren to starve he would blow up Windsor Castle and the whole Royal Family of England. . . . The submarine had come to stay . . . and a person traveling on an enemy merchant ship was like a man traveling in a cart behind the battle lines—he had no just cause for complaint if injured." The kaiser then asked why America had complained about the *Lusitania* but had done nothing to break the British blockade.

Gerard put his answer into metaphor: "If two men entered my house and one stepped on my flowerbeds and the other killed my sister, I should probably pursue the murderer first. [As for] those traveling on the seas in belligerent merchant ships, it was different from those traveling in a cart behind enemy lines because the travelers on land were on belligerent territory while those on the sea were on territory which, beyond the three-mile limit, was free." The kaiser argued that *Lusitania*'s passengers had been warned before the ship sailed. Gerard replied, "If the chancellor warns me not to go out on the Wilhelmsplatz, where I have a perfect right to go, the fact that he gave me the warning does not justify him in killing me if I disregarded his warning."

Gerard's meeting with the emperor did not diminish the widespread antagonism he met in Berlin. Caricatures of Uncle Sam and President Wilson appeared daily in German newspapers. At one point, Gerard was obliged to deny in print a story that his wife had pinned a German decoration he had received on the collar of the family dog. In January 1916, a large wreath with an American flag draped in mourning was placed at the base of the statue of Frederick the Great near the royal palace on Unter den Linden. A silk banner was inscribed, "Wilson and his press are not America." For four months, Gerard protested, but the police refused to act. Then Gerard announced that he would go with his own photographer and himself remove the wreath. Instantly, it disappeared. Subsequently, Gerard and his staff were in a concert box when a man in the next box began shouting that people in the hall were speaking English. Told that it was the American ambassador, the man shouted that Americans were worse than the English. Finally, in January 1917, a few weeks before the ambassador left Berlin, the heavyset Grand Duke of Mecklenburg-Schwerin planted himself in front of Gerard. " 'You are the American ambassador and I want to tell you that the conduct of America in furnishing arms and ammunition to the enemies of Germany is stamped deep on the German heart, that we will never forget it and some day we will have our revenge.' He spoke in a voice so loud and slapped his chest so hard that everyone in the room stopped their conversation in order to hear. He wore on his breast the orders of the Black Eagle, the Red Eagle, the Elephant and the Seraphim and when he struck all this menagerie, the rattle was quite loud." Gerard reminded him that American behavior was legal under the Hague Convention. "We care nothing for treaties," bellowed the nobleman, and stalked away.

—

Even as the two peace initiatives, German and American, were failing, events were moving rapidly. At the end of December, a French counterattack at Verdun recovered most of the ground lost earlier in the year. Austria told Berlin that she was near the end of her resources and could not last another winter. The Emperor Franz Joseph had died in November at the age of eighty-six and been succeeded by his thirty-year-old great-nephew Karl, who told William imploringly, "We are fighting against a new enemy which is more dangerous than the Entente—against international revolution which finds its strongest ally in general starvation." William ignored him. Hindenburg told Bethmann-Hollweg, "We must resume torpedoing armed enemy merchantmen without notice. We received a slap in the face from all their parliaments. [In August] you said I should choose the time, depending on the military situation. That moment will be the end of January." Bethmann-Hollweg reminded the field marshal that unrestricted submarine warfare affecting neutral ships and Germany's relations with neutral states both were aspects of foreign policy, "for which I alone bear the responsibility. The question must be cleared up with America [Germany's *Sussex* pledge was still in force]. Many people in neutral countries already believed that our peace offer was in bad faith and indeed only stated at all as a starting point for the unrestricted submarine campaign. We must do everything possible to avoid intensifying that impression." Hindenburg wished to waste no time on "clearing up questions" with America. "Unfortunately, our military situation makes it impossible that negotiations of any kind should be allowed to postpone military measures which have been recognized as essential, and thus paralyze the energy of our operations," the field marshal told the chancellor. "I must adhere to that view in no uncertain manner. It goes without saying that I myself shall never cease to insist with all my might and in the fullest sense of responsibility for the victorious outcome of the war, that everything of a military nature shall be done which I regard as necessary."

Meanwhile, a significant member of the military high command had changed sides. Admiral von Holtzendorff, the Chief of the Naval Staff, who in the spring of 1916 had supported Bethmann-Hollweg and opposed Tirpitz's insistence on unrestricted submarine warfare, had been told by Scheer that because the U-boats were still tethered, the fleet was losing confidence in the Naval Staff. On December 22, Holtzendorff sent Hindenburg and the Supreme Command a 200-page memorandum in which he advocated unleashing the U-boats. This document laid out figures and charts of shipping tonnage available to Great Britain, with comprehensive calculations of such factors as world grain prices, cargo space, freight rates, shipping insurance rates, and shortages in England of cotton, iron and other metals, wood, wool, and petroleum. All these numbers then marched with mathematical precision to the conclusion that the U-boats could break Britain's power to resist within six months. "A decision must be reached before the autumn of 1917," Holtzendorff wrote, "if the war is not to end in the exhaustion of all parties and consequently disastrously for us. Of our enemies, Italy and France are economically so hard hit that it is only by the energy and force of England that they are still kept on their feet. If we can break England's back, the war will immediately be decided in our favor." Holtzendorff stressed that the unrestricted submarine campaign was to be directed, not merely, or even primarily, at ships carrying munitions, but against all imports necessary to life in the British Isles; it was to strike at the general economic capacity of the British to continue the war. "The backbone of England consists in her shipping which brings to the British Isles the necessary supplies of food and materials for war industries." Success would be reflected not only in rising freight rates and insurance rates for ocean cargoes, but in higher prices of bread and other foodstuffs in the British Isles.

Holtzendorff calculated that 10.75 million tons of British and neutral shipping was required to keep Britain fed and supplied. Once unleashed, he argued, the submarines should be able to sink at least 600,000 tons of shipping every month; another million tons of neutral shipping would be frightened away. "We may reckon that in five months, shipping to and from England will be reduced by thirty-nine percent. England would not be able to stand that. I do not hesitate to assert that, as matters now stand, we can force England to make peace in five months by an unrestricted U-boat campaign. But this holds good only for a really unrestricted U-boat campaign."

The admiral's argument and the statistics supplied in the Naval Staff memorandum were not enough. As long as Bethmann-Hollweg refused to agree, the kaiser would not give permission for unrestricted warfare. On January 8, the chancellor, fighting for time, told the Chief of the Naval Staff that even if unrestricted warfare must begin, he still needed an interval to prepare the neutrals. Then, suddenly, Admiral von Müller, a Bethmann-Hollweg ally who had always supported the chancellor, defected. "After our peace feelers and their curt rejection by the Allies, circumstances warrant the use of this weapon which offers a reasonable chance of success," Müller wrote in his diary on January 8. "I told Holtzendorff he could rely on my support." Müller's entry was written at the castle of Pless in Silesia where he, the kaiser, Hindenburg, Ludendorff, and Holtzendorff had gathered. That night, Bethmann-Hollweg, suffering from severe bronchitis, boarded a train in Berlin. It would take him to Pless, and to a meeting that would seal the fate of Imperial Germany.

—

Since the day in October 1915 when impertinent French aviators dropped a bomb near the kaiser's "frontline" villa in Charleville in France, German Supreme Headquarters had been moved to the more secure and comfortable site of Prince Hans von Pless's white, 300-room castle near Breslau, in Silesia. Prince Hans, William's bosom companion, possessed one of the great fortunes in Germany, based on Silesian coal and thousands of acres of land. The prince was also married to one of the kaiser's favorite women, the beautiful English-born Daisy Cornwallis-West.* "Oh, I am most unhappy. I am always misunderstood," the unhappy emperor had said to Daisy one night before the war, dropping a tear onto his cigar. Now that war had come, Daisy stayed mostly out of sight, keeping to her own apartments at Pless and having nothing to do with that grim military pair, Hindenburg and Ludendorff.

*Curiously, Daisy of Pless was a former sister-in-law of Winston Churchill's romantically unconventional American mother, Jennie. After the death of Lord Randolph Churchill, Winston's father, Jennie married Daisy's handsome brother George Cornwallis-West, known in the family as Buzzie. The marriage was an embarrassment for Winston because George was nineteen years younger than Jennie and only two weeks older than her son. Now, while Daisy was nominal hostess to the German Supreme Command, her brother George was in the British army.

In fact, the decision was made while the chancellor was still on the train. On the evening of January 8, the military and naval leaders of Germany suddenly heard the kaiser announce that he would support unrestricted U-boat warfare, "even if the chancellor is opposed." Further, Müller wrote in his diary, "His Majesty voiced the very curious viewpoint that the U-boat war was a purely military affair which did not concern the chancellor in any way." Early the next morning, Müller met Bethmann-Hollweg at the station to warn him that everything was already settled. Driving to the castle, Müller explained his own defection and begged the "agitated and depressed" Bethmann-Hollweg to come along. "For two years," Müller contended, "I have always been for moderation, but now, in the altered circumstances, I consider unrestricted warfare to be necessary and that it has a reasonable chance of success." The chancellor remained silent. At six o'clock that evening, Bethmann-Hollweg entered the palace's red damask reception hall with tall French windows overlooking a terrace and a park set with lakes, lawns, flower gardens, and giant chestnut trees now covered with winter frost. Hindenburg, Ludendorff, Holtzendorff, Müller, and others were waiting. The kaiser, pale and fidgety, stood by a great chair, his right hand resting on the table. Next to his hand was a copy of Holtzendorff's memorandum.

The chancellor, despite knowing that the decision had been made, spoke for an hour. He cited Bernstorff's opinion that America's entrance into the war would mean Germany's defeat. He reiterated the ambassador's conviction, and his own belief, that Wilson's peace offer was genuine and should be pursued. Bernstorff had been assured that the president meant to press his mediation hard and would coerce the Allies if they resisted his diplomacy. William grunted with impatience and Bethmann-Hollweg halted; he was speaking in a vacuum. The chancellor realized that if he forced William to choose between himself and Hindenburg, the field marshal would win. He surrendered: "If the military authorities consider the U-boat war necessary, I am not in position to oppose them."

Admiral von Holtzendorff then repeated the argument in his memorandum: unrestricted warfare, "in the course of which every enemy and neutral ship found in the war zone will be sunk without warning," would allow his U-boats to sink 600,000 tons a month and thus force England to capitulate. He went further: "I pledge on my word as a naval officer that no American will set foot on continental soil." Hindenburg added, "We are in a position to meet all eventualities against America. We need the most energetic and ruthless action possible. We must begin." Defeated, Bethmann-Hollweg nodded and said, "Of course, if victory beckons, we must act."

No more was required. The kaiser signed a document already prepared: "I command that unrestricted submarine warfare shall begin on February 1 in full force." Then, followed by his generals and admirals, he left the room. The chancellor remained behind, hunched in a chair. Baron von Reischach, a court official, entered and, seeing the lonely figure, asked, "Have we lost a battle?" "No," said Bethmann-Hollweg, "but *finis Germaniae.*" "You should resign," said Reischach. Bethmann-Hollweg did not resign. Instead, wrapping himself in a traditional Prussian cloak of duty to his king, he remained, politically enfeebled, for another six months. In July 1917, when Ludendorff demanded that the kaiser choose between himself and Bethmann-Hollweg, the chancellor, who had been in office for eight years, resigned. He was replaced by Dr. Georg Michaelis, a nonentity who had been assistant state secretary in the Prussian Ministry of Food. Michaelis lasted for one hundred days.

Holtzendorff immediately forwarded the imperial command to Scheer. In order to achieve maximum psychological impact, the new campaign was not to be announced until the evening of January 31, a few hours before the first torpedoes would be fired. Thereafter, submarines would waste no warning shots and send no boarding parties to examine papers and cargo. Hospital ships were to be spared, except in the English Channel, where Ludendorff believed the Red Cross was being used to mask troop transports. Ships clearly identified as neutral steamers, Belgian relief ships, and passenger liners were to be given one week to reach port safely. Then they, too, were to be sunk without warning.

—

In Washington, neither Wilson nor Bernstorff was aware that the submarine decision had been made. Both men continued working—for peace if that was still possible; for American neutrality, if not. To the ambassador, the critical thing was to keep the talk going in Berlin; as long as that continued, he believed that Bethmann-Hollweg could hold back the submarines. To facilitate Bernstorff's contact with Zimmermann in Berlin, Wilson authorized the German foreign minister to send messages in German code to his ambassador in Washington over the State Department cable. Lansing bitterly opposed this breach of diplomatic practice, but Wilson, believing that the nobility of his ends justified these unprecedented means, overrode his secretary of state. At the president's insistence, Bernstorff had promised to use the cable only for transmitting and discussion of peace offers.

At first, the cable hummed exclusively with messages on the intended subject although they were not of a nature for which either the president or the ambassador had hoped. On January 10—the day after the decisive conference at Pless—Zimmermann informed Bernstorff that "American intervention for definite peace negotiations is entirely undesirable." Frantically, Bernstorff cabled back: "This government [the United States] must be given time. As everything is decided by Wilson, discussion with Lansing is mere formality. It is my duty to state clearly that I consider a rupture with the United States inevitable if action [releasing the submarines] is taken." On

January 19, Bernstorff was belatedly informed of the Pless decision to start the unrestricted U-boat campaign on February 1—and ordered to say nothing about it until the day before. Immediately, he cabled Zimmermann asking for a one-month grace period for neutral merchantmen and to give Wilson's peace efforts some extra time. Otherwise, he said, "war inevitable." The kaiser saw this telegram and wrote in its margin, "I do not care."

Now, only Wilson remained hopeful. Weighing the replies to his peace initiative, he had concluded that the war aims of the Allies were as grasping as those of the Germans. His approach now was so even-handed that Bernstorff reported to Berlin, "Remarkable as this may sound to German ears, Wilson is regarded here very generally as pro-German." On January 22, the president made his historic "peace without victory" speech to the Senate. "Victory would mean a victor's terms imposed upon the vanquished," he said. "It would be accepted in humiliation, under duress, at an intolerable sacrifice, and would leave a sting, a resentment, a bitter memory upon which terms of peace would rest, not permanently, but only as upon quicksand. Only a peace between equals can last." The reaction in America was mixed. Some applauded the idealism of the president's words: Theodore Roosevelt jeered, "Peace without victory is the natural ideal of the man who is too proud to fight." Bernstorff, hearing the speech and harboring the secret of a policy repugnant to him, decided not to give up. On January 27, he cabled Zimmermann:

> House suddenly invited me to visit him. . . . If only we had confidence in him, the president was convinced that he would be able to bring about peace conferences. He would be particularly pleased if Your Excellency were at the same time to declare that we are prepared to enter peace conference on the basis of his appeal. . . . If the U-boat campaign is opened now without further ado, the president will regard this as a smack in the face and war with the United States will be inevitable. . . . On the other hand, if we acquiesce in Wilson's proposal and plans come to grief on the stubbornness of our enemies, it would be very hard for the president to come into the war against us even if by that time we begin unrestricted submarine war. It is only a matter of postponing the declaration for a little while. . . . I am of the opinion that we shall obtain a better peace now by means of conferences, than we should if the United States joined the ranks of our enemies.

Bethmann-Hollweg, seeing this message, asked the navy to wait. He was told it was too late; twenty-one U-boats had already put to sea. On January 29, the chancellor cabled Bernstorff: "Please thank the president. If his offer had only reached us a few days earlier, we should have been able to postpone opening of the new U-boat war. Now, however, in spite of the best will in the world, it is, owing to technical reasons, unfortunately too late. Extensive military preparations have already been made which cannot be undone and U-boats have already sailed with new instructions." The kaiser made no apologies; the die having been cast, he returned to bluster: "Agreed, reject. . . . Now, once for all, an end to negotiations with America. If Wilson wants war, let him make it, and let him then have it!"

—

At ten minutes past four on the afternoon of January 31, 1917, a hapless Ambassador Bernstorff formally called on Secretary of State Lansing to announce that Germany would begin unrestricted submarine warfare that night at midnight. A single exception to the submarine blockade would be allowed: once a week, one U.S. passenger ship would be permitted to pass provided that it carried no contraband and docked only at Falmouth, only on Sundays. For identification, the vessel must be painted with meter-wide alternating red and white vertical stripes and must fly a large checkered white and red flag on every mast—"striped like a barber's pole and a flag like a kitchen tablecloth," fumed an indignant American historian.

After Lansing had read the German note, Bernstorff said, "I know it is very serious, very, and I deeply regret that it is necessary."

"I believe you do regret it," Lansing replied, "for you know what the result will be. But I am not blaming you personally."

"You should not," said Bernstorff. "You know how constantly I have worked for peace."

"I do know it," said Lansing and, seeing the ambassador's eyes blurred with tears, took his extended hand. Then Bernstorff bowed, Lansing said, "Good afternoon," and the meeting was over.*

To Lansing, an interventionist who believed that a German victory would be intolerable and that sooner or later the United States must enter the war to support the Allies, there was a positive side to Bernstorff's announcement. To Wilson, however, it came as a blow to the foundations of his beliefs and policy. Before Lansing could reach the White House, an Associated Press bulletin announcing the German government's decision was placed in the hands of Joseph Tumulty, the president's secretary. Tumulty entered the Oval Office. "He looked up from his writing," the secretary said. "Without

*When Bernstorff reached Berlin via Sweden several weeks later, Bethmann-Hollweg told him that he had been forced to consent to the U-boat campaign because "the German people would never have understood if we had concluded an unsatisfactory peace without attempting to win by means of our last and most effective weapon." When Bernstorff saw the kaiser, William took him for a walk in the park and affably steered clear of all political discussion. Ludendorff, however, was unforgiving. "In America you wanted to make peace. You evidently thought we were at the end of our tether," he said. "No, I did not think that," Bernstorff replied. "But I wanted to make peace before we came to the end of our tether."

comment, I laid the fateful slip of paper on his desk and silently watched the expressions that raced across his strong features: first, blank amazement, then incredulity, then gravity and sternness, a sudden grayness of color, a compression of the lips and the familiar locking of the jaw which always characterized him in moments of supreme resolution. Handing the paper back to me, he said in quiet tones: 'This means war.' "

In Berlin, Zimmermann, dry-eyed, almost cheerful, was informing Gerard. "You will see, everything will be all right," he told the ambassador. "America will do nothing, for President Wilson is for peace and nothing else. Everything will go on as before. I have arranged for you to go to General Headquarters and see the kaiser next week and everything will be all right." Gerard then cabled Washington that Germans felt "contempt and hatred for America" as "a fat, rich race without a sense of honour and ready to stand for anything in order to keep out of war." At Pless that night after dinner, the kaiser read aloud to the company a long academic essay on the eagle as an heraldic beast. The evening, Müller wrote in his diary, was "gruesome."

—

On the day following Bernstorff's visit to Lansing, Colonel House came to the White House to find Wilson pacing the floor of his library, nervously rearranging his books. Mrs. Wilson suggested golf. House said that he thought that people might consider this trivial at such a time. The president suggested a private game of pool, which the two men played. Wilson's anguish stemmed from the fact that his freedom of action had been stripped away. Repeatedly over two and a half years, he had said that the United States would not tolerate unrestricted submarine warfare. To yield now on the principle of freedom of the seas would stain American honor and make his own word meaningless. He had no choice. He must break diplomatic relations. On February 3, he ordered that Bernstorff be given his passports and that Gerard be recalled from Berlin. But even these actions did not mean that the United States intended to declare war. The president still found it unthinkable that the German government would deliberately destroy American and other neutral ships. Announcing the diplomatic rupture to Congress, he said, "I refuse to believe that it is the intention of the German authorities to do in fact what they have warned us they feel at liberty to do. . . . Only overt acts on their part can make me believe it even now." In taking this position, Wilson once again captured the high ground in American public opinion. Spring-Rice, writing to Balfour, counseled patience, warning that although the diplomatic situation was brightening for the Allies, the strongest influence in the country remained the desire to remain neutral and too much should not be expected right away. "The main point is whether and how far the United States government is willing and able to defend its rights," he said. "Many people here think that it may be willing (although that is doubtful) but that it is not able. There is no doubt that the temper of the Congress is pacific."

During the first month following the break in diplomatic relations, the nation's attitude and behavior were disjointed. The president continued to wait, partly to see what the Germans would do and partly for public opinion to crystallize. Congress debated large appropriations for the army and navy. Two American merchant ships, the *Housatonic* and the *Lyman M. Law,* were torpedoed with no loss of life. Meanwhile, the German threat to sink all merchant ships on sight had a dragging effect on the economy. Nervous American shipowners were reluctant to send their ships to sea, and harbors on the Eastern Seaboard were clogged with anchored vessels. As the ships jammed together, the paralysis spread inland along the railways; thousands of freight cars, unable to unload, the foodstuffs inside them spoiling, were parked on sidings. With the economy slumping, chambers of commerce demanded action, pacifists rallied to demand that American ships stay out of war zones, and interventionists shouted for the arming of merchant ships with orders to shoot on sight. Theodore Roosevelt, purple with indignation, shouted, "He is endeavoring to sneak out of war. He is yellow all through." On February 26, Wilson reluctantly requested Congress to authorize the arming of American merchantmen to protect them "in their legitimate and peaceful pursuits on the seas." While he was speaking, news arrived that the small Cunard liner *Laconia* had been torpedoed without warning. Twelve civilian passengers, including two Americans, both women, were dead.*

—

Arthur Zimmermann, the new foreign minister of the German empire, was "a very jolly sort of large German," said Ambassador Gerard. Zimmermann

*The circumstances of these deaths were particularly grim. *Laconia* was first torpedoed at 10:30 at night. Twenty minutes after the first torpedo struck, and as the passengers were taking to the lifeboats, the U-boat captain fired a second torpedo. The lifeboat holding the two American women and seventeen other passengers scraped down the side of ship as it was lowered, and it arrived in the water, said Wesley Frost, the American consul at Queenstown, Ireland, "leaking like a basket. It filled with water instantly but was buoyed up by air-tanks under its thwarts. . . . [It] drifted away through a chilling drizzle, coasting the twelve-foot ocean swells in the black darkness. . . . As the night wore on, two American ladies found it necessary to stand continuously on their feet, so deep had settled the water-logged boat. These ladies were Mrs. Mary Hoy of Chicago and her daughter, Miss Elizabeth Hoy . . . proceeding to London to join Mrs. Hoy's husband and son.

"At half past one o'clock . . . gray-haired Mrs. Hoy sank down and tucked her head back like a tired child and entered the last sleep. After this, Miss Elizabeth Hoy's mind seemed to be unhinged. She kept chafing the hands of the stiffening remains of her mother and pouring endearments into those deaf ears, until an hour later a merciful heaven released her overtaxed spirit in its turn. . . . When the wan dawn suffused the winter sea, the eleven survivors found themselves shipmates with eight staring corpses."

once had crossed America by train, spending two days in San Francisco and three days in New York. In Berlin, this qualified him as an expert on American affairs equivalent to Bernstorff, who had spent eight years in the United States. The former chancellor Bernhard von Bülow was unimpressed by his newly promoted countryman. Zimmermann, he said, "is filled with the best of intentions, one of those Germans who mean well, whose industry is unquestionable, whose virtues are solid and apparent, an excellent fellow who would have done very good and useful work had he stayed in the consular service. He might have done even better as a public prosecutor. People would have greeted him on all sides as he came every morning to take his aperitif at the local hotel, 'Good morning. Good health, Your Honor.' "

In Berlin, Zimmermann liked to speak bluntly. During the *Lusitania* crisis, when he was still Jagow's deputy, he reminded Gerard of the large German-American population in the United States. "The United States does not dare to do anything against Germany because we have five hundred thousand German reservists in America who will rise in arms against your government if it should dare to take any action against Germany," he said, striking the table with his fist. "I told him," the ambassador replied, "that we have five hundred and one thousand lamp posts in America and that is where the German reservists would find themselves if they tried any uprising." During the *Sussex* affair, Zimmermann said to a group of German reporters, "Gentlemen, there is no use wasting words about Mr. Wilson's shamelessness and impudence, but we have torn the mask from his face." Now, confronting another submarine crisis, Zimmermann was confident that he could handle the Americans. Germany, he assured Gerard, would not begin unrestricted submarine warfare without first reaching an understanding with America. At a grand dinner on January 6, assembled at the Hotel Adlon by the American Chamber of Commerce to honor Ambassador Gerard, the ambassador told the guests that "relations between the two countries had never been better" and that "so long as such men as . . . Hindenburg and Ludendorff . . . Müller . . . Holtzendorff and State Secretary Zimmermann are at the head of the civil, military and naval services in Germany, it will undoubtedly be possible to keep these good relations intact."

Behind his mask of bonhomie, however, the jolly Zimmermann was concocting something unpleasant for his American friend. During the weeks following the Pless decision, the foreign minister looked for ways to contribute to the coming submarine campaign. He came up with an extraordinary scheme designed to keep America occupied on her own side of the Atlantic once the U-boats began sinking American ships. On the chance that war might come between the United States and Germany, he proposed to arrange in advance a Mexican-German alliance that would pledge Mexico to invade the United States. Mexico was to be lured into this folly by the assurance that following a German victory she would be restored her lost territories of Texas, New Mexico, and Arizona. In addition, Mexico was to work diligently to persuade Japan to join the alliance. To assure rapid, secure communication with Mexico City, Zimmermann decided to make use of the State Department cable that Wilson had made available to Bernstorff for communicating American peace proposals to Berlin. Bernstorff, of course, had promised that this channel would be used only for this purpose, but Zimmermann saw no need to honor the ambassador's word. On January 16, the German foreign minister sent a coded message on the American cable through Washington to German minister Eckhardt in Mexico:

> We intend to begin unrestricted submarine warfare on the first of February. We shall endeavor in spite of this to keep the United States neutral. In the event of this not succeeding, we make Mexico a proposal of alliance on the following basis: Make war together, make peace together, generous financial support, and an understanding on our part that Mexico is to reconquer the lost territory in Texas, New Mexico and Arizona. The settlement in detail is left to you.
>
> You will inform the president [of Mexico] of the above most secretly as soon as the outbreak of war with the United States is certain and add the suggestion that he should, on his own initiative, invite Japan to immediate adherence and at the same time mediate between Japan and ourselves.
>
> Please call the [Mexican] president's attention to the fact that the unrestricted employment of our submarines now offers the prospect of compelling England to make peace within a few months. Zimmermann.

The telegram arrived at the Department of State in Washington on January 17 and was delivered, still in code, to Bernstorff at the German embassy. Bernstorff decoded and read his information copy and, having no choice, forwarded the original to Mexico. Meanwhile, the telegram, promptly decoded, was also in the hands of Room 40.

For nineteen days, the Zimmermann telegram lay in an Admiralty safe, awaiting the moment when it could be discreetly handed to the Americans. The problem was how to present the telegram without revealing to the Americans—and thereby, through leaks, perhaps informing the Germans—that Britain had broken the German code. On February 5, two days after the American diplomatic rupture with Germany, Admiral William Reginald Hall, Room 40's chief, decided he could wait no longer and took the decoded telegram to the Foreign Office. Balfour read it and knew that the Allied cause had been blessed. On February 23, the British foreign secretary formally presented the Zimmermann telegram to Walter Page, the American ambassador, who transmitted it to Washington. When Lansing, who had sensed all along that the Germans could not be trusted, told the president how the Zimmermann telegram had been sent, Wilson clutched his head and cried out, "Good Lord! Good Lord!"

The president held the telegram only a single day. On February 28, while a bill authorizing the arming of American merchant ships was being debated in the House of Representatives, he gave it to the press. Next day, March 1, *The New York Times* announced, "Germany Seeks Alliance Against U.S.: Asks Japan and Mexico to Join Her." The news that the German government was conniving to slice off and give away pieces of the United States enraged the American public and in a surge of patriotic emotion the armed merchant-ship bill passed the House, 403–13. Even so, eleven pacifist senators, led by Robert La Follette of Wisconsin, filibustered and on March 4, Congress adjourned without passing the legislation. Wilson immediately did what he could have done weeks before: he used his executive authority to issue an order to arm American merchantmen. The question of the telegram's authenticity was resolved on March 3 when Zimmermann, believing by now that it made no difference whether America was hostile, freely acknowledged authorship.

For another month, Wilson and the country awaited the "overt act." On March 12, the American steamer *Algonquin* was sunk by gunfire; the crew escaped and reached land after twenty-seven hours in open boats. On March 18, three American merchant ships, the *Illinois, City of Memphis,* and *Vigilancia,* were torpedoed without warning; fifteen members of *Vigilancia*'s crew were lost. "If he does not go to war," Theodore Roosevelt wrote privately to Henry Cabot Lodge, "I shall skin him alive." Still, for another two weeks, the president waited. At a Cabinet meeting on March 20, he went around the table, asking each member for advice. The unanimous recommendation was war, but Wilson gave no hint of his own opinion. The following day, he summoned Congress to a special session on April 2 to hear "a communication concerning grave matters of national policy."

It was raining in Washington that evening when the president drove to the Capitol. His car was surrounded by a squadron of cavalry provided at the insistence of Lansing and the Attorney General, who worried that a "fanatical pro-German, [an] anarchist or pacifist" might attempt an assassination. "I shall never forget it," wrote Ambassador Spring-Rice. "The Capitol was illuminated from below—white against a black sky. I sat on the floor of Congress. The president came in, and in a perfectly calm, deliberate voice, he recited by word and deed what Germany had said and done." "The present German submarine warfare against commerce is a warfare against mankind," Wilson said. "There is one choice we cannot make, we are incapable of making: we will not choose the path of submission." He asked formal acknowledgment that "the status of belligerent has been thrust upon us," and then went on to say, "It is a fearful thing to lead this great peaceful people into war. But the right is more precious than peace. The world must be made safe for democracy. The day has come when America is privileged to spend her blood and her might for the principles that gave her birth. God helping her, she can do no other." Congress debated and on April 4, the Senate voted for war, 82–6. On April 6, the House confirmed the decision, 373–50.

It had happened as the American president, the German chancellor, and the German ambassador to Washington had feared: the decision to begin a new unrestricted submarine campaign had brought America into the war.

CHAPTER 36

The Defeat of the U-boats

Between February and April 1917, the massacre of merchant shipping in the waters around the British Isles began in earnest and Admiral Holtzendorff's promise that Britain would be starved into surrender seemed on its way to realization. Holtzendorff had said that sinking 600,000 tons a month would suffice for the purpose. The February figure, 520,000 tons, approached Holtzendorff's goal; the March figure, 564,000 tons, was closer still. In April, the figure soared above the German admiral's most extravagant hope: 860,000 tons of shipping were destroyed. These losses, which included neutral ships, so intimidated many Norwegian, Danish, Dutch, and Swedish captains that, in February alone, 600 neutral merchantmen in British ports refused to sail.

Three great trade routes brought goods and raw materials into Great Britain. One of these came up the Irish Sea from the southwest to Liverpool and Bristol; another lay around the north of Ireland, thence down to Liverpool; a third came into the Channel and up to Southampton and other Channel ports. The focal point for most of this trade lay in what the Royal Navy called the Western Approaches: the wide expanse of waters between Lands End, the Irish coast, and the Bay of Biscay. It was here that the U-boats were creating, in Churchill's words, "a veritable cemetery of British shipping." The agents responsible for filling this cemetery were about 130 U-boats, of which fewer than half were at sea at any given moment. By now, two and a half years into the war, early submarines like the one that had sunk *Bacchante*'s three sisters were antiques. The undersea craft now operating in the Western Approaches were 240 feet long, displaced 820 tons, and carried a 4.1-inch deck gun, six torpedo tubes, and sixteen torpedoes. They could remain at sea for four to six weeks. Submarines fitted as minelayers transported from thirty-six to forty-two mines. In addition, smaller U-boats 100 feet long with a surface speed of 8 knots, carrying two tubes and four torpedoes, were based in Flanders and operated in the Channel and the North Sea. These small submarines were prefabricated in Germany and brought in sections by rail to Bruges, in Belgium, where they were assembled; from Bruges, they traveled by canal to Zeebrugge and Ostend, and from there they put to sea.

Britain's first lines of defense against these enemies were layers of mines and nets laid and strung across the Channel and in the German Bight. Once the submarines reached the high seas, the Royal Navy relied on surface ships, primarily destroyers, to defeat them. British destroyers, designed to attack enemy surface warships, could churn the water at 34 knots, far in excess of the 15 to 17 knots a surfaced submarine could make, but once submerged, the submarine was safe. A modern U-boat could travel as much as eighty miles under water before having to come up, and no destroyer—or sloop, trawler, or yacht pressed into service against the U-boats—could know where that would be.

Inability to attack a submerged enemy was only part of the problem involving British destroyers. Another complication was that there were too few of them. The British navy simply did not possess enough destroyers to screen the Grand Fleet, maintain the Harwich Force, secure the Channel crossings, and simultaneously protect merchant shipping from submarines. In April 1917, Britain had in commission about 260 destroyers, many old and badly worn after three years of service. The best 100 were assigned to the Grand Fleet, and no one wished to send the dreadnoughts into battle without their protective screen. Even so, in February 1917, Beatty reluctantly permitted eight destroyers to be borrowed from the Grand Fleet for antisubmarine work in southern waters. From every other station, the admirals or commodores in charge chorused that their flotillas could not be stripped without compromising their missions: the Harwich Force covered the southern North Sea and the Dutch coast; the Dover Patrol confronted thirty German U-boats and thirty destroyers based in Flanders; military expeditions in Greece and the Middle East required destroyers to guard their transports and supply ships. Nor was there much hope from new construction: Britain was producing destroyers at a rate of only four or five per month, a rate the shipyards said could not increase for many months.

Meanwhile, the U-boats were not only eating away the imported food stocks needed by Britain's civilian population, they also were directly sapping the lifeblood of the Royal Navy itself. The fleet's newest and most powerful dreadnoughts, its new light cruisers, and all of its destroyers burned fuel oil. The tankers bringing oil from Hampton Roads in America were large and slow, presenting fat, easy targets for submarines. So many tankers had been sunk that Britain's reserve of fuel oil had dropped alarmingly; a six-month reserve had shrunk to a supply sufficient for only eight weeks. In consequence, the Admiralty had ordered Grand Fleet battle squadrons to cruise at no more than three-fifths speed except in case of emergency.

Jellicoe had come to the Admiralty to deal with the submarine menace, but once in office and seeing its dimensions, he was shaken. "The shipping situation is by far the most serious question of the day," he wrote to Beatty at the end of December 1916. "I almost fear it is nearly too late to retrieve it. Drastic measures should have been taken months ago to stop unnecessary imports, ration the country and build ships. All is being started now, but it is nearly, if not quite, too late." Late was better than never; the effort to build merchant ships faster than the enemy was sinking them was set in motion. Merchant vessel design was standardized and 35,000 skilled workers were recalled from army service and returned to the shipyards. To provide steel for new merchant ships, the Admiralty canceled orders for five new light cruisers and three giant battle cruisers. A dragnet was set to locate and purchase neutral ships. "The world's ports were ransacked for tonnage. . . . Decrepit steamers fetched fabulous prices and even old sailing vessels, derelict or used as harbor hulks, were reconditioned and sent to sea again," wrote Ernest Fayle, the official historian of the British merchant marine in the Great War. The result was an additional 1,163,000 tons brought into the merchant fleet in 1917. Unfortunately, this addition equaled only about one-quarter of Britain's losses of 4.01 million tons of merchant shipping during that year.

Much of this work was done by ministries and departments other than the Admiralty; the navy's task was to see that once these ships were built or reconditioned and sent to sea, they survived. On December 18, 1916, Jellicoe appointed Rear Admiral Alexander Duff as head of a new Anti-Submarine Division. Duff laid out new protected trade routes for merchantmen sailing independently to Britain, frequently changing these routes to confuse U-boat commanders. Destroyers and smaller craft were deployed to patrol these ocean highways. More mines were laid and more merchantmen were armed. Still the rate of shipping losses continued to mount. "The position is exceedingly grave," Jellicoe wrote to the First Lord and the War Cabinet on February 21, 1917. Soon, he feared, the government would have "to determine how long we can continue to carry on the war if the losses of merchant shipping continue at the present rate."

—

One approach to fighting the U-boats was guile, trickery, and ambush. Former merchant ships with Royal Navy crews and hidden guns were sent to sea, in the hope that their apparent innocence and vulnerability would lure submarines to their destruction. These vessels, which fought some of the most heroic actions of the war, were known variously as Special Service ships and mystery ships. Eventually the name that stuck was Q-ships.

To the eye, a Q-ship seemed merely one of the myriad small freighters, tramp steamers, motor drifters, even sailing vessels crossing the ocean on a hundred different courses with a thousand separate purposes. At first, honest ships this size were plums ripe for picking by German U-boat commanders. The submarine rose to the surface, allowed the crew and passengers to enter lifeboats, and then, hoarding their torpedoes for more important targets, placed time bombs in the victim's hold. It did not take long, once the war against commercial shipping had begun, for the Admiralty to realize that this procedure—the U-boat abandoning the safety of the deep in order to approach the vessel it meant to sink—offered opportunity. No ship is more vulnerable than a submarine on the surface. The idea of tricking such deadly craft into presenting themselves in their condition of greatest jeopardy appealed to the inventive mind of Winston Churchill; not surprisingly, these dangerous theatricals were initiated during his administration of the Admiralty. But Churchill's few Q-ships, fitted out in the winter of 1914–15, had no success: one never saw a submarine; another caught a single glimpse of a U-boat, which dived and disappeared. In May 1915, an even more ingenious bit of trickery was conjured up and sent to sea. A lonely trawler flying the British flag was sent out to move slowly across the ocean on seemingly innocent business. From its stern, however, two lines—one a tow cable, the other a telephone wire—dropped off the stern into the depths, where both were attached to a submerged British submarine. Should a U-boat take the bait, the fact would be communicated by telephone to the friendly submarine, which would cast off the tow and maneuver underwater into position to torpedo the U-boat. In June 1915, the British submarine *C-24,* cruising off Aberdeen in tow from the trawler *Taranaki,* torpedoed and sank *U-40.* On being brought aboard the trawler, the rescued U-boat captain bitterly complained that his boat had been sunk by a "dirty trick." The following month, north of Scapa Flow, the submarine *C-27,* working with the trawler *Princess Louise,* torpedoed and sank *U-23.* By then, however, Churchill had left the Admiralty and the Q-ship–submarine tandem did not survive him long.

Nevertheless, the Q-ship concept itself survived and flourished. The idea that camouflage could lure a deadly, but fragile, submarine within range of a well-aimed 4-inch gun had a continuing, seductive attraction for the navy. The crews of the Q-ships, all volunteers, were naval officers and seamen who disguised themselves as civilians and learned to mimic the appearance and crisis behavior of a freighter's crew. In the presence of a submarine, a "panic party"—some members of the Q-ship's crew—would hurriedly abandon the ship, tumbling into lifeboats and rowing away. Those still on board would remain concealed, waiting for the submarine to surface and come within range of their hidden guns.

The concept was simple, but staging this deadly nautical theater required much delicate nuance. Q-ships were crowded, since half the men on board had to depart as the panic party when the ship was attacked. Thus, a merchant ship designed for six officers and twenty-six men now might carry eleven officers and sixty men. To deceive the captain of a surfaced U-boat staring intently through his binoculars across the water, or surveying his prey through his periscope, the Q-ship crew had to become actors. Stripped of their uniforms and clothed in rags picked up in dingy waterfront shops, they let their hair and beards grow long and their mustaches sprout and droop. One Royal Navy captain paced his Q-ship bridge wearing a long blond wig, which he thought made him look like a Dutch pilot. The regular navy's scrupulous deference to rank was laid aside: no salutes were given or returned; seamen slouched and shuffled, kept their hands in their pockets and their pipes in their mouths. Garbage was dumped carelessly over the side—anathema in a man-of-war. Yet, despite their slovenly appearance, the discipline and readiness for action of a Q-ship crew was greater than that on the flagship of the Grand Fleet.

Most important, of course, was the concealment of the guns. Some were placed behind wooden bulwarks, which, at the pull of a lever, would instantly collapse, nakedly exposing the gun to the submarine and the submarine to the gun. Later, when U-boats became more cautious, they would sail submerged around the halted "merchant ship," minutely scrutinizing its decks and sides, looking for signs such as seams or hinges in deck house bulwarks that might betray its true identity. In response, the guns were concealed in hatchways and covered by tarpaulins as if they were cargo. Sometimes guns were placed inside false lifeboats, which would suddenly fall away, giving the gun its freedom. Eventually, Q-ships carried hidden depth charges that could be rolled off the stern, and some were even equipped with submerged torpedo tubes.

The British could continue this kind of masquerade warfare only as long as the Germans delivered themselves into British hands; success, therefore, depended upon secrecy as to the existence, whereabouts, and tactics of mystery ships. Best for the British would be for the Germans to know only that some submarines did not return from sea—perhaps they had hit mines. But it was inevitable that eventually a Q-ship attack would fail and a surprised U-boat would survive to creep home and report what had happened. Once the secret was out, German newspapers described Q-ship warfare as "barbarous" and "contrary to the rules of civilized warfare." Now, to the U-boats, every British or Allied merchant vessel became a possible Q-ship. Submarines could no longer board and place bombs on ships; they were forced to stay beyond the range of a freighter's guns and sink by long-range gunfire, or remain beneath the surface and fire precious torpedoes. This was not what the U-boats wanted. And so the Q-ships improved their acting to convince their nervous prey that all was well, suspicions were groundless, and no peril lay in coming closer.

Q-ship duty was a unique blend of extreme danger and the dullest monotony. Back and forth through dangerous waters steamed the ships, hoping to meet a submarine. Success in this strange service could mean seeing the white bubbles of a torpedo approaching from the port or starboard beam. Sometimes when a torpedo struck, Q-ship men would be killed, but the ship itself was unlikely to sink quickly. This was the result of further guile: Q-ship cargo holds were crammed with wood or empty oil drums to provide the vessel with additional buoyancy.

Everything that happened from the moment a U-boat announced itself was designed to deceive the watching submarine captain. The panic party ran up and down the deck in apparent dismay and then scrambled into a lifeboat. Sometimes on lowering a boat, one end would deliberately be lowered too fast, spilling the men into the water. A seaman pretending to be the captain would be the last to board, carrying a bundle of "the ship's papers." The submarine might surface and make for these boats to collect the papers or take prisoners. Once U-boat captains became aware that they might be dealing with a Q-ship, the procedure changed. To satisfy himself, the captain would surface two or three miles away and shell the apparently abandoned merchant ship, calculating that if men had been left aboard, his shells would kill them. The Q-ship gun crews, stretched out on deck beside their guns, had to endure this bombardment without moving. Meanwhile, the Q-ship captain lay on his bridge, peeking through a hole in the canvas wall, waiting to use his voice tube to command his gunners. If the submarine was persuaded that the merchantman was abandoned, it would approach submerged to within a few hundred yards. The submarine captain would steer completely around the stricken vessel, using his periscope to study every detail. If something provoked doubt, the U-boat captain faced a decision. To surface so near a Q-ship meant the loss of his submarine. On the other hand, to leave a merchantman still afloat meant that it might be saved. If the U-boat captain decided to come up, the Q-ship captain would see the swirling water that signified a submarine was surfacing not far from the muzzles of his hidden guns. "Stand by," he would whisper through the voice tube—then, at the top of his lungs, "Let go!" The White Ensign would soar up the halyard, the false bulwarks and lifeboats would collapse, and the guns would open fire. The submarine's only chance was to submerge rapidly. Submariners were always ready to dive, even at the cost of losing those comrades on deck or in the conning tower who were unable to get below before the hatches closed. Often, however, before the boat could submerge, trained Q-boat gun crews could blow a dozen holes in its hull. When this happened, it was only minutes before the U-boat took its final plunge, leaving behind a heaving mixture of black oil, pieces of floating wood, and, sometimes, a few survivors.

—

From the beginning, the primary sphere of Q-ship operations was off the southwest coast of Ireland, where the U-boats concentrated their attacks on merchant shipping headed for the British Isles. In this region, early in the history of Q-ship operations, a dark stain was smeared across the otherwise bright pages of Allied mystery ship exploits. On August 19, 1915, 100 miles south of Queenstown, *U-27* stopped the British steamer *Nicosian* with her cargo of munitions and 250 American mules destined for the British army in France. The freighter's crew and passengers, including American mule drivers, had taken to the lifeboats and the submarine was about to sink the vessel when, from a distance, the British Q-ship *Baralong,* disguised as an American cargo vessel and flying the American flag, observed what was happening and hurried forward. The submarine at this early stage of the war accepted the Stars and Stripes as neutral and remained on the surface, permitting *Baralong* to approach. Steering carefully, *Baralong*'s captain managed to keep *Nicosian* between his ship and the U-boat so that the German captain never had a serious, long look at the oncoming Q-ship. When *Baralong* finally emerged from behind the deserted *Nicosian,* the range was only 600 yards. Thirty-five British shells quickly sank *U-27,* which left a dozen German survivors in the water swimming for the nearby *Nicosian.* Whereupon, *Baralong*'s captain, fearful—he said later—that if the swimmers were allowed to board the freighter, they would attempt to scuttle it, ordered the twelve Royal Marines on board his ship to open fire. Some of the swimmers, including the U-boat captain, were killed in the water; others were shot as they struggled up a rope ladder hanging from *Nicosian*'s side. Four German sailors managed to reach the deserted freighter's deck and vanished. A party of marines followed them on board, hunted them down, and killed them. Whether this shooting was done in cold blood or whether the Germans were, in fact, caught trying to scuttle the ship was never known; the Admiralty immediately embargoed all news of the affair. Nevertheless, the appalled American mule drivers, who had watched from their lifeboats, eventually reached home and told the American press that the Germans had been murdered and that the false American colors, supposed to have been set aside before the Q-ship went into action, had never been replaced. Outraged, the German government demanded that *Baralong*'s crew be tried for murder. The Admiralty dismissed the demand, explaining that perhaps the Q-ship's captain and crew had been on edge because eight British steamers were sunk that day on the Western Approaches, one of these being the 15,000-ton White Star liner *Arabic,* which *Baralong* had heard crying for help. The London press came up with the additional excuse that on that same day, two German destroyers had fired on the crew of a British submarine grounded on a Baltic sandbar, killing fourteen British sailors—although how this news might have reached and inflamed *Baralong*'s crew 700 miles away was left untold. The *Baralong* marine corporal who put a bullet into the head of the swimming German captain explained simply that, in his view, all Germans were "vermin."

—

During the war, Q-ships sank twelve U-boats. A quarter of these were destroyed by Gordon Campbell. When the war began, this stocky, phlegmatic Englishman was a thirty-year-old lieutenant commander in charge of an old destroyer; no one would have picked him out as a future hero. But Campbell went to Q-ships, where his icy nerves and determination to sink submarines resulted, in the words of Rear Admiral William Sims, the senior American naval officer in Europe, in "some of the most admirable achievements in the whole history of naval warfare." Jellicoe, normally laconic, went further: Campbell and his Q-ships, he said, had "a record of gallantry, endurance and discipline which has never been surpassed afloat or ashore."

Gordon Campbell sailed on his first Q-ship for nine months before sighting a U-boat. He persevered, using the time to add inventive touches to his ship. Because some merchant ship masters took their wives to sea, Campbell dressed one of his men as a woman and positioned this figure in a chair on the bridge cradling a bundle to represent a baby. His first opponent was *U-68,* which he sank on March 22, 1916. The submarine signaled its presence by firing a torpedo, which missed. Campbell's reaction was to take no apparent notice and continue his course and speed. "A tramp steamer," he explained, describing his ship as he hoped the submarine captain had seen it, "could not be expected to know what a torpedo track looked like." On deck, his crew continued to lounge about, smoking their pipes. Suddenly, the submarine surfaced astern and moved up the port side. Whereupon Campbell sank it.

After that, he had to wait almost another year. On February 17, 1917, Campbell's Q-ship, *Farnborough,* steaming 100 miles southwest of Queenstown, was struck by a torpedo. Campbell was delighted; he had instructed his ship's officers that "should the Officer of the Watch see a torpedo coming, he is to increase or decrease speed as necessary to ensure it hitting." The panic party immediately abandoned ship. Campbell's adversary, Captain Bruno Hoppe, in *U-83,* was an experienced commander; taking no chances, he remained submerged and conducted a lengthy periscope examination of his target. He first inspected the panic party in its lifeboat; his periscope came so close that one of the men in the lifeboat said to another, "Don't speak so loud. He'll hear you." Then Hoppe circled *Farnborough,* coming so near that Campbell could see the submarine's hull under the water. Apparently satisfied that the ship was harmless, Hoppe surfaced only 100 yards away. The moment he popped up in his conning tower, the first British shell arrived, decapitating him and dropping his headless body back down into the control room. *U-83,* punctured by forty-five shells, sank quickly, leaving two survivors. Fifteen members of *Farnborough*'s crew were decorated, including Campbell, who was awarded the Victoria Cross. The citation explaining the circumstances could not be made public and it became known as the mystery VC.

Campbell's third and final triumph occurred on the morning of June 7, 1917, when his Q-ship *Pargust* was struck by a torpedo off the south coast of Ireland. By then, because U-boats were wary and less willing to rise to the surface, some decoy vessels had been fitted with torpedo tubes to use against submerged submarines. *Pargust* was one of these. By now, too, the panic party had further enhanced its dramatic performance: one of Campbell's officers, playing the part of the ship's captain, went over the side wearing a bowler hat and carrying a "pet parrot" (stuffed) in a green cage. For thirty minutes, the submarine minelayer *UC-29* circled the ship, conducting a periscope reconnaissance. Campbell waited. When the submarine surfaced, it was fifty yards away. Campbell opened fire with his guns and fired his torpedo, which missed. The U-boat's engine-room hatch opened and several men came on deck as if to surrender. *Pargust* ceased fire but when the U-boat started to move again, apparently attempting to escape, the Q-ship resumed firing. The German sailors on the submarine's deck were swept off by a wave. More shots were fired and suddenly, the U-boat blew up—her own mines had exploded. After the action, when Campbell was asked to recommend honors for his men, he replied that he could not single out individuals; the crew's bravery had been collective. Accordingly, the king bestowed two Victoria Crosses on the ship to be awarded to one officer and one seaman, chosen by a secret ballot of their peers.

The summer of 1917 marked the end of this dangerous game. In August 1917, six Q-ships were lost, and thereafter no German submarine was destroyed by a mystery ship. U-boat commanders were too suspicious to come close enough for Q-ship guns to reach them. The U-boats were now equipped with fourteen to sixteen torpedoes, so it was safer for U-boat captains to torpedo merchant ships without coming to the surface.

Before the end came, however, the most extraordinary of all Q-ship battles was fought. Not surprisingly, the captain of the British ship in this action was Gordon Campbell. On the morning of August 8, 1917, his 3,000-ton Q-ship *Dunraven,* disguised as an armed merchant vessel, was quietly plowing the Bay of Biscay, offering herself to submarine attack. Besides the small gun visible on her stern—appropriate to an armed merchantman—*Dunraven* also concealed four heavier guns, two underwater torpedo tubes, and four depth charges. About eleven o'clock, a surfaced U-boat appeared on the distant horizon, saw *Dunraven,* turned in her direction, and submerged. Campbell, playing the victim, began doing an occasional indifferent zigzag and ordered heavy funnel smoke as if he were attempting to escape; at the same time, he actually reduced speed to allow his enemy to close. Forty-five minutes later, *U-61* rose from the sea less than two miles away and opened fire with her deck gun. When one of the shells landed in the water near the engine room, Campbell released a huge cloud of steam to suggest a boiler hit; this was a trick achieved with specially installed perforated pipes designed to release bursts of steam on the captain's command. *Dunraven,* playing a distressed armed merchantman, returned the U-boat's fire with her unconcealed stern gun, making certain that all shots missed. Meanwhile, on an open frequency the submarine could hear, the "merchant ship" radioed loudly for help.

At 12:25 p.m., when the U-boat was scarcely half a mile away, Campbell ordered, "Abandon ship." *Dunraven* slowly turned broadside to the submarine so that the German captain could witness the theatrical pandemonium. The panic crew tumbled into the lifeboats, one of which was purposely mishandled in lowering and left behind hanging vertically from one of its davits. Encouraged, the captain of *U-61* closed warily and continued firing. Suddenly, a shell hit *Dunraven*'s stern, landing amid a concentration of hidden guns, ammunition, depth charges, and men. A depth charge exploded, tossing the small after gun into the air. Two more German shells crashed into the stern, producing flames and clouds of black smoke. The magazine and the remaining depth charges all being in the stern, it was obvious to Campbell that a larger explosion was coming. The crew of the secret 4-inch gun placed immediately above the magazine also knew the danger but remained motionless. *U-61* passed around the stern from port to starboard less than 500 yards away, but the black smoke pouring from the Q-ship's burning stern made it impossible for the British gunners to aim. In two minutes, the U-boat would be absolutely clear, presenting a perfect target. Campbell had to choose between opening fire under difficult conditions or leaving his men immobile in grave danger until the submarine was in the clear. As Campbell saw it, it was his duty and that of his crew to wait. He waited. They waited.

As *U-61* was passing close astern of *Dunraven,* two depth charges blew up in what even the stolid Campbell described as "a terrific explosion." The concealed 4-inch gun and its gun crew were hurled along the deck, along with many unexploded shells. Remarkably, the men all lived. The U-boat, warned by the size of the explosion that it was confronting a Q-ship, performed a crash-dive and disappeared. Campbell now knew that soon he would be torpedoed. Still, with his ship crippled and stationary, the after deck a mass of flames, the magazine not yet exploded, and a torpedo certain, Campbell, intent on sinking his enemy, radioed all potential assistance to keep away.

At 1:20 p.m., a torpedo struck *Dunraven*'s starboard side. The ruse of merchant seamen abandoning ship had already been exhausted. But a roaring fire now engulfed the greater part of the vessel and there is a moment when even a Q-ship must be abandoned. Hoping that the German captain would believe that this moment had arrived, Campbell gave the order "Abandon ship" for the second time. A second panic party, organized impromptu, went over the side into rafts. Still, twenty-three men remained on board: the gun crews of the two working guns still concealed, the men at the two torpedo tubes, the ship's doctor, nine wounded men, and four men lying prone on the bridge. One of them was Campbell.

U-61 rose to the surface. Was the burning ship finally abandoned or not? Uncertain, the submarine fired a few more shells into the wreck and then submerged. For forty-five minutes, showing only its periscope, the U-boat circled its listing, burning victim. During this time, the fire on *Dunraven* grew larger and boxes of gunpowder and 4-inch shells began exploding in the flames. At 2:30 p.m., the U-boat surfaced a few hundred yards directly astern of the Q-ship, where no gun could bear on her. For twenty minutes, more shells were fired into the stricken ship. The men on board remained motionless.

At 2:50 p.m., *U-61* ceased fire, submerged, and moved past *Dunraven*'s port side at a distance of only 150 yards. Campbell, his ship burning and sinking, decided to wait no longer. Only a small part of the submarine's periscope was visible but it was enough to reveal depth and position. At 2:55 p.m., he fired a torpedo. Unfortunately, his ship was listing and his aim was spoiled. The bubbles passed just ahead of the periscope and the U-boat, unaware, came slowly around to the starboard side. Given a second chance, Campbell fired his second torpedo. This time, he and others heard a metallic clang: the torpedo had made contact, but had failed to explode. The submarine captain heard the same thing and promptly dived deep, gave up the battle, and returned to Germany. Campbell now genuinely signaled for help and an American armed yacht and two British destroyers arrived to rescue his crew. *Dunraven* was taken in tow, but that night, her White Ensign flying, she foundered. Two members of her crew, a lieutenant and a petty officer, were awarded the Victoria Cross. Gordon Campbell, in lieu of a second Victoria Cross, was given a bar to his first. This, along with his Distinguished Service Order with two bars, made him the most highly decorated man in the Royal Navy during the Great War.

—

By the time of *Dunraven*'s epic battle, help was coming from America. At the end of March 1917, Rear Admiral William S. Sims, the president of the U.S. Naval War College at Newport, Rhode Island, was ordered to report immediately and secretly to Washington. He was not to appear at the Navy Department, but to contact his superiors by telephone. In this manner, Sims learned that United States probably would soon be at war with Germany and that he was to leave at once for England, where he was to coordinate American cooperation with the Royal Navy. Sims sailed for England as "Mr. S. W. Davidson," wearing civilian clothes and carrying no uniform in his luggage. His American steamship struck a mine as it approached Liverpool; the passengers were transferred to another vessel and reached England safely on April 9. There, "Mr. Davidson" was met by a special train and hurried to London. By then, his alias was unnecessary; three days earlier, Congress had declared war on Germany.

William Sims, a tall, erect, white-haired man born in Canada, became an American, entered the navy, and made his name as a gunnery specialist. He had been Inspector of Target Practice and had commanded the battleship *Minnesota* and then a flotilla of destroyers before going to the War College. The obvious reason for sending Sims to Britain was that five years earlier he had made a speech in London that at the time seemed likely to blight his career. At the Guildhall in 1910, then Captain Sims had promised the Lord Mayor and a large audience that in the event of a war with Germany, Britain could "rely upon the last ship, the last dollar, the last man, and the last drop of blood of her kindred beyond the sea." For this bit of unauthorized, public Anglophilia, Sims had received a direct reprimand from President Taft. Now, however, when a senior officer was needed to coordinate planning with the British navy, Sims's enthusiasm was remembered favorably. Not all American officers shared his views. Before Sims left Washington, the navy's senior admiral, William S. Benson, Chief of Naval Operations, admonished him, "Don't let the British pull the wool over your eyes. It's none of our business pulling their chestnuts out of the fire. We would as soon fight the British as the Germans."

In London, Sims found the British public largely oblivious to the danger facing their country. The government had ceased to publish figures for tonnages sunk and the crowds packing the theaters every night were cheerfully ignorant of the fact that only six weeks' supply of wheat remained in the country. The truth was that the Germans had discovered a way to win the war and were on their way to accomplishing it. Unless the appalling destruction of merchant tonnage could be substantially checked, Britain's withdrawal from the war was not far off.

On the morning of April 10, Sims called on Jellicoe at the Admiralty. The two men were friends; they had met in China in 1901 and had kept in touch because of their mutual interest in naval gunnery. Sims greatly admired the British admiral. The First Sea Lord, he said, was "a small man, powerful in frame . . . indefatigable . . . profound . . . simple and direct . . . the idol of the officers and men of the Grand Fleet. . . . Success made him more quiet, soft spoken and dignified. . . . He was all courtesy, all brain . . . approachable, frank, open-minded." And Jellicoe's "smooth-shaven face when I met him that morning was, as usual, calm, smiling imperturbable."

Greeting his visitor, Jellicoe took a paper out of his drawer and handed it across the table. It was a record of the tonnage of British and neutral shipping losses of the last few months.

"I was fairly astounded," Sims wrote later,

> for I had never imagined anything so terrible. I expressed my consternation to Admiral Jellicoe.
>
> "Yes," he said, as quietly as though he were discussing the weather and not the future of the British Empire. "It is impossible for us to go on with the war if losses like this continue."
>
> "What are you going to do about it?" I asked.
>
> "Everything that we can. We are increasing our anti-submarine forces in every possible way. We are using every possible craft we can with which to fight submarines. We are building destroyers, trawlers and other like craft as fast as we can. But the situation is very serious and we shall need all the assistance we can get."
>
> "It looks as though the Germans are winning the war," I remarked.
>
> "They will win unless we can stop these losses—and stop them soon," the Admiral replied.
>
> "Is there no solution for the problem?" I asked.
>
> "Absolutely none that we can see now," Jellicoe announced.

Bad as it was, Jellicoe expected the situation to get worse. Summer was coming, which would give the submarines more daylight and milder weather. Jellicoe could calculate and apply the arithmetic as well as Holtzendorff could; it was relatively easy to determine how long the Allies could last. What the figures said was that, unless something could be done quickly, the end would come about November 1.

Jellicoe was not alone in his alarm. King George V invited Sims to spend a night at Windsor Castle and after dinner, over cigars, told him that the sinkings must be stopped or the Allies would lose the war. Only the prime minister remained optimistic. Lloyd George—"a big, exuberant boy," as Sims described him—was "always laughing and joking, constantly indulging in repartee and by-play. His face never betrayed the slightest anxiety. 'Oh, yes, things are bad,' he would say with a smile and a sweep of his hand. 'But we shall get the best of the submarines—never fear!' "

Sims told Jellicoe that no one in the United States realized that the situation was so serious and asked how America could help. The greatest need, Jellicoe stressed, was for "every available destroyer, trawler, yacht, tug and other small craft of sufficient speed to deal with submarines." He asked that America build more merchant ships to replace the losses. He also suggested that the United States might repair and put into service all German liners and cargo ships interned in American ports. Sims, listening to Jellicoe, immediately grasped the implications for the United States. If Britain and France were forced to surrender, the peace terms would include the surrender of the

British and French fleets. The U.S. Navy would then be left alone to fight a German-British-French armada.

Simms cabled Washington, describing for men separated from the war by 3,000 miles the gravity of the submarine crisis. The best way for the United States to help immediately, he said, was by sending destroyers and light surface craft to serve in the waters west of Ireland along which lay the shipping routes that meant life or death to the Allied cause. Ambassador Page wholeheartedly supported Sims and personally asked President Wilson to send thirty destroyers. On April 13, Sims was told that six U.S. destroyers were coming immediately, with more to follow. On April 14, Destroyer Division 8 of the U.S. Atlantic Fleet, based in York River, Virginia, departed for Boston to fit out for "long and distant service."

—

For the first thirty-two months of war, British and Allied merchantmen had sailed independently, setting their own courses and speeds, conforming vaguely to a system of advisory routing established by the Admiralty, but taking their chances on encountering submarines. Safety was seen to lie in large numbers of merchant vessels widely dispersed, in the cloak of night and storms, in equipping some merchantmen with deck guns, in occasional zigzagging, and, most important, in luck. As late as January 1917, an Admiralty memorandum specifically reiterated this policy and condemned any other: "Wherever possible, vessels should sail singly. . . . The system of several ships sailing in company as a convoy is not recommended in any area where submarine attack is a possibility. . . . It is evident that the larger the number of ships forming the convoy, the greater the chance of a submarine being enabled to attack successfully." "A submarine could remain at a distance and fire her torpedo into the middle of the convoy with every chance of success."

By April 1917, the ferocity of the U-boat offensive had torn these assumptions to shreds. The new solution, reluctantly accepted by the Admiralty, was the convoy system it had just condemned. Ironically, the British navy had already had substantial success with convoy. Grand Fleet battle squadrons, escorted by destroyers, steamed in close formation through waters infested with U-boats—and no dreadnought had ever been sunk by a submarine. In effect, the dreadnoughts were under convoy. Troop transports were convoyed to the Mediterranean and Gallipoli. Closer to home, the British navy successfully convoyed troops and supplies across the Channel to France every day without ever losing a man, a gun, or a horse. In addition, ships carrying coal to France were now under convoy. Coal was a major British export, essential to the economy and war production of her allies, France and Italy, as well as to the economy of neutral Norway. France alone needed to import 1.5 million tons of coal every month and cross-Channel colliers made 800 round-trips a month. In February, four convoys—which the Admiralty preferred to call controlled sailings—sailed every day under escort by armed trawlers. Between February 10, when the first convoy sailed, and the end of April, 2,600 convoyed crossings went back and forth to France and only 5 colliers were sunk; the rate of loss was 0.19 percent. From February through August, 8,900 ships were convoyed; 16 were sunk, a rate of 0.18 percent. On April 4, the decision had been made to place Scandinavian trade—British coal to Scandinavia; Scandinavian metal ores, nitrates, wood, and foodstuffs to Britain—under convoy. In the first month of this arrangement, the rate of shipping losses plummeted from 25 percent to 0.24 percent.

Why, then, did the Admiralty wait so long before extending the convoy system to the larger arena of the Western Approaches? Jellicoe's answer, in large part, was the lack of destroyers. When Sims asked whether convoys might work in this critical area, Jellicoe said the number of escorts available was "totally insufficient." It was to make up this dearth that the First Sea Lord had pressed Sims, and Sims, in turn, had pressed the Navy Department to send American destroyers to Europe. But the Admiralty had other reasons for wariness. Naval officers doubted the ability of merchant vessels steaming in columns to keep close and accurate station, especially at night; merchantmen, the navy felt, would not be able to follow signals and zigzag in unison; they varied in speed and tended to straggle, a difficulty that could be overcome only by reducing the speed of convoy to that of the slowest ship. Further, the simultaneous arrival of a large number of ships would badly congest harbors and dock facilities, thereby slowing the rate and diminishing the volume of goods imported.

The Admiralty's hesitations were matched by those of the weatherbeaten, practical men who captained British merchantmen. On February 23, 1917, three weeks after the unrestricted submarine campaign began and eleven days before America entered the war, Jellicoe invited ten captains of cargo steamers then lying in the London docks to call on him at the Admiralty. There, the First Sea Lord asked for their views on the feasibility of placing ships in convoy as protection against U-boats. He emphasized the necessity of good station keeping in close formation; ideally, vessels should travel in lines only 500 yards apart. "Absolutely impossible," the ten captains replied in chorus. "We have so few competent deck officers that the captain would have to be on the bridge the whole twenty-four hours." Also, they lacked suitable engine-room telegraphs with which fine-tune speed; their inexperienced engineers could not make the delicate adjustments required; the poor quality of coal they burned delivered varying power to the propellers, making impossible the constant slight variations in speed required to keep station. In general, their ships were undermanned and the personnel were inexperienced. They could not maneuver at night or in fogs and gales in close formation without lights. They were certain they would lose more ships to collision than submarines could sink. Emphatically, the captains declared that they did not want convoys; they would rather sail alone and take their chances.

This meeting at the Admiralty had taken place near the end of February. Between then and the end of April, the situation became much worse: within three months, almost 2 million tons of the world's merchant shipping had been sent to the bottom. Meanwhile, in the same three months, Britain had sunk only seven submarines. These grim facts were forcing the Admiralty to reconsider beginning Atlantic convoys. Duff was already monitoring the results of the coal convoys to France and Jellicoe had approved institution of convoys to Scandinavia. The obstacle to extending convoy to the Western Approaches remained the lack of escorts. Jellicoe was heavily criticized for his tardiness in authorizing ocean convoy, but for him, it was a matter of drawing conclusions from technical data; he neither pushed nor opposed convoy purely on principle. His nature was to be cautious in a new situation. Jellicoe could make a quick decision—he had done so in deploying the fleet at Jutland—but he had not done so then, and would not do so now, until he possessed all the obtainable information. This was Jellicoe's way.

Lloyd George's way was different. Watching the shipping losses soar, he roared with anger and poured contempt on the "palsied and muddle-headed Admiralty" with its "atmosphere of crouching nervousness," its "condition of utter despair," and its "paralytic documents." He had looked, he announced, into the "fear-dimmed eyes of our Mall admirals" and seen only "stunned pessimism." The "High Admirals" were "men whose caution exceeded their courage," who "go about with gloomy mien and despondent hearts," whose "reports are full of despair." During the last week of April, the prime minister staged a drama—or so he later claimed. On April 23, he raised in the War Cabinet the question of shipping losses and the possibility of convoy. Jellicoe, who was present, said that convoy was under consideration; that the obstacle was the shortage of destroyers; that American destroyers had been promised but none had yet arrived. That night at the Admiralty, Duff came to Jellicoe's office and told him that the shipping losses had convinced him that a wider system of convoy must be attempted. Jellicoe asked Duff to draw up a minute putting this recommendation in specific detail. On April 25, the War Cabinet met and again discussed the submarine crisis. According to Lord Beaverbrook, who was not there, Lloyd George "announced his intent to go himself to the Admiralty and make peremptory decisions." The visit was set for April 30. On April 26, Duff produced his minute for Jellicoe, and on April 27 the First Sea Lord approved the recommendations and authorized an experimental convoy from Gibraltar to the Channel. As a result, when Lloyd George arrived at the Admiralty three days later, Jellicoe told the prime minister that a convoy system was under trial. According to Hankey, who was present, Lloyd George was pleased "and spent the whole day there very pleasantly, lunching with Admiral Jellicoe and his wife and four little girls—Lloyd George having a great flirtation with a little girl of three." Beaverbrook's version—again, he was not there—was, "On the 30th of April, the prime minister descended on the Admiralty, seated himself in the First Lord's chair, and took over the full reins."

Seventeen years later, Lloyd George announced in his *War Memoirs* that he was responsible for the decision to adopt convoy. "Apparently the prospect of being overruled in their own sanctuary galvanised the Admiralty. Accordingly, when I arrived at the Admiralty, I found the Board in a chastened mood. . . . I insisted on their giving a trial to the Gibraltar convoy." Professor A. T. Patterson, Jellicoe's biographer and the editor of his letters, labels Lloyd George's account "a travesty of the facts." Duff's minute was of sufficient length and detail, says Patterson, as to "virtually preclude the possibility of its having been thrown together in a few hours" following the prime minister's announcement of his intended visit. In 1928, Duff wrote to Jellicoe and stated emphatically that his own convoy proposal to Jellicoe had been influenced only by the mounting shipping losses: "My impression was that he [Lloyd George] came to look into Admiralty organization generally. There is no foundation for the belief that his visit was in any way the cause of my suggestion that the time had arrived for starting convoy." Jellicoe himself later wrote that any statement that his approval of Duff's minute and the decision to begin trial convoys "was the result of pressure brought to bear on the Admiralty from the War Cabinet is quite incorrect. The views of experienced naval officers on a technical question involving the gravest responsibility could not possibly be affected by outside opinion, however high the quarter from which that opinion emanated." Sir Edward Carson, who was First Lord at the time, read Lloyd George's claim in the former prime minister's *War Memoirs* with indignation. "The little popinjay," he said of Lloyd George, had told "the biggest lie ever was told! Jellicoe did not oppose the convoy system but required time to organize it. At first there were not enough ships available for that work. But the prime minister would not listen to reason. 'Sack the lot!' was his favorite expression. 'Why don't you get fresh men with sea experience?' One day I said to him, 'I must be under a strange hallucination, Prime Minister, for I thought that Admiral Jellicoe had just come from the sea.' "*

*Lloyd George's language and behavior in this episode were wholly characteristic of this unusual, often unruly Welshman. In Parliament and in the country, he delivered speeches that were "something between incomparable drama and a high class vaudeville act," wrote the historian George Dangerfield. Buttressed by a towering ego, an unwillingness to lose any battle, and a refusal to accept that his success often came at high cost to others, Lloyd George had shouldered his way to the highest position in British politics. But the new prime minister had a dark side; no one saw this more clearly than his eldest son, Richard.

"My father," explained Richard Lloyd George, "once under the spell of the exercise of his own charm, whether it concerned an audience at a public meeting or consisted of one person, became completely carried away, without any other idea in his head, without a thought of con-

On May 10, sixteen merchant vessels, sailing in three columns and escorted by two armed merchantmen and three armed yachts, departed Gibraltar for England, traveling at 6½ knots. Eight days later, the convoy was met at the outer edge of the submarine danger zone by six destroyers from Devonport, and on May 20 the sixteen merchantmen reached Plymouth unharmed. No U-boats had been encountered and, equally important, the merchant captains had found that they could keep station, obey signals, and zigzag in unison, and furthermore that they "had enjoyed more sleep than they had had for months." This success led to another experimental convoy, this time across the North Atlantic. On May 24, twelve merchant ships left Hampton Roads for Britain, traveling at 9 knots. They were escorted most of the way by the cruiser *Roxburgh* and, on reaching the danger zone, were met by eight destroyers. Two slow steamers straggled and dropped out; one of these was torpedoed. The remaining ships arrived safely on June 7. Despite fog and heavy weather, the navy reported that their station keeping had been excellent.

The success of these two trial convoys encouraged the Admiralty to expand the effort. In June, sixty-four merchant vessels, gathered in four convoys, were escorted from Hampton Roads to Britain. Assembling safely and receiving instructions inside American harbors rather than in the open sea, North Atlantic convoys began running every fourth day. By the end of July, twenty-one convoys made up of 354 ships had crossed the Atlantic; of the convoyed ships, submarines sank two. This plunge in shipping losses demolished the "too many eggs in one basket" objection to convoy. In the first place, the presence of convoy escorts eliminated the threat of attack by gunfire and forced U-boats to use torpedoes. And to make an underwater attack now became more difficult: the submarine commander had to come within range—the ideal was about 700 yards—while somehow eluding the escorts. Against ships sailing independently, the U-boat had generally been able to maneuver into position, fire a torpedo, watch his victim sink, and then look

---

sequences. . . . My father was probably the greatest natural Don Juan in the history of British politics. . . . His entire life, including fifty-three years of marriage to my mother, was involved with a series of affairs with women. . . . My father's chief safeguard in these affairs was that he was almost never seriously involved emotionally. . . . He had no sense of loyalty to his mistresses, and could present a bold, indignant front, with flat protestations that he was being 'victimised by these vainglorious harpies who wanted to boast of their conquest of me.'. . . There was almost never any continuing association, so that at any particular time he could declare without fear of contradiction, 'Hardly know the woman. Haven't seen her for months and not the least intention of seeing her again.'

"To portray his life without taking into account this side of his personality," the son concludes, "is like failing to depict Beethoven's handicap of deafness during the composition of his greatest works."

This was the personality with which Jellicoe and the Admiralty had to contend.

around for his next target. With a convoy, the whole mass of ships swept by together and was gone. Essentially, as Sims graphically described it, convoy was managing to "establish a square mile of the surface of the ocean in which submarines could not operate and then move that square along until port was reached."

Often, the U-boats never saw the convoy or its escorts. "The size of the sea is so vast that the difference between the size of a convoy and the size of a single ship shrinks in comparison almost to insignificance," Winston Churchill later wrote. "There was in fact very nearly as good a chance of a convoy of forty ships in close order slipping unperceived between the patrolling U-boats as there was for a single ship; and each time this happened, forty ships escaped instead of one." This phenomenon was also noted by Karl Doenitz, a U-boat commander who became the commander of German submarines, the Commander-in-Chief of the German navy, and the last führer of the Third Reich in World War II. Of the effect of convoy in the Great War, he wrote:

> The oceans at once became bare and empty. For long periods at a time, the U-boats, operating individually, would see nothing at all; and then suddenly up would loom a huge concourse of ships, thirty or fifty or more of them, surrounded by a strong escort of warships of all types. The solitary U-boat, which most probably had sighted the convoy purely by chance, would then attack, thrusting again and again . . . for perhaps several days and nights until the physical exhaustion of the commander and crew called a halt. The lone U-boat might well sink one or two ships, or even several, but that was a poor percentage of the whole. The convoy would steam on. In most cases, no other German U-boat would catch sight of it and it would reach Britain, bringing a rich cargo of foodstuffs and raw materials safely to port.

The success of convoy forced naval officers fighting submarines to shift their thinking. Trained in the Royal Navy's tradition of offensive warfare, they had previously considered convoy to be a defensive tactic in which warships handed the initiative to the enemy and then plodded along beside merchant ships awaiting attack. Most officers preferred aggressive hunting for submarines. Reality turned these tactics upside down. Convoy, it turned out, concentrated surface naval forces where the submerged enemy was bound to come if he wished to do harm. The inviting presence of so many targets drew U-boats to a place where the antisubmarine craft could get at them and kill them. To make convoy work, however, there had to be sufficient escort ships. Where would Britain find them?

—

On Friday, May 4, 1917, six modern, four-stacker U.S. Navy destroyers entered the Irish harbor of Queenstown. The morning was brilliant, with the sun sparkling on smooth water and shining on the green hills rising behind the town. Ships in the harbor welcomed the newcomers by flying the American flag from a forest of masts. In the town, the Stars and Stripes floated from public buildings and private houses. Along the shore, thousands of people cheered and waved. Watching the American warships come in, British seamen noticed that they were longer and larger than British destroyers, qualities that would give them greater endurance and radius of action on the Western Approaches. The American commander was Joseph K. Taussig, who in 1900, as a twenty-one-year-old midshipman, had been wounded near Tientsin during the Boxer Rebellion campaign. Recovering, Taussig found himself lying on a cot next to a forty-year-old Royal Navy captain named John Jellicoe who had been more severely wounded the same day. Seventeen years later, when Taussig came ashore in Queenstown, the First Sea Lord welcomed him in the name of "the British nation and the British Admiralty and [with] every possible good wish from myself. We shall all have our work cut out to subdue piracy."

Taussig was also welcomed by Vice Admiral Sir Lewis Bayly, the British Commander-in-Chief in Queenstown, who was to have operational control of dozens of American destroyers over the next eighteen months. The first six American destroyer captains were invited to dinner at Admiralty House the night they arrived. "Dine in undress; no speeches," said Bayly's invitation, and four of the six were asked to sleep over, "to get a good rest." Taussig and his fellow Americans walked up the steep hill to Admiralty House overlooking the harbor and found at the top an unsmiling man with a weatherbeaten face and iron-gray hair, standing in a worn uniform with his hands behind his back. He shook hands, then turned to Taussig and asked, "When will you be ready to go to sea?"

"We are ready now, sir, as soon as we finish refueling," Taussig said.

"I will give you four days from time of arrival. Will that be sufficient?"

On May 17, six more American destroyers arrived at Queenstown; another six came a week later. These and all subsequent American vessels arriving in Queenstown were placed under Bayly's command because Sims had convinced his superiors in Washington that American warships in Europe—and the U.S. Navy as a whole—should be used as a reinforcement pool for the hard-pressed Allied navies. Sims rejected—and convinced his superiors in Washington to reject—any thought of attempting to operate an independent American fleet in Europe. The result was a remarkable suspension of national and service pride by the U.S. Navy to further the effort of winning the war. In this scheme, Bayly played his role to perfection. Soon after American destroyers arrived in Queenstown, most of Bayly's British destroyers were transferred to the Channel and the North Sea, leaving the British admiral in command of a mostly American force. "He watched over our ships and their men with the jealous eye of a father," said Sims. "He always referred to 'my destroyers' and 'my Americans' and woe to anyone who attempted to interfere with them. Once or twice a dispute arose between an American destroyer commander and a British; in such cases Admiral Bayly vigorously took the part of the American. 'You did perfectly right,' he would say to our men and then turn all his guns against the interfering Britisher." Bayly's effort to create an international force succeeded; American officers called him Uncle Lewis—sometimes to his face—and some brought him their personal problems. Bayly was a widower and his hostess was his Australian niece, Violet Voysey, who poured tea, presided over dinners, listened for hours, and made the Americans feel that Admiralty House was their temporary home.

Beyond this, a strong personal tie developed between Bayly and Sims. This had not been widely predicted. Bayly was a stern, hard-driving disciplinarian who, said one officer, "attributed his success to working a minimum of eleven hours a day on six days a week, never smoking before 10 p.m., walking at least twenty miles on Sunday, playing tennis for an hour at 6:30 a.m. on fine mornings and running around Greenwich Park at 5:30 p.m." He had few friends. Writing Taussig before the first American destroyers arrived, Sims had warned that Bayly was said to be "a peculiarly difficult man to deal with." Sims had met Bayly at the Admiralty, "and when I was introduced to him he was very rude as he was also to some very high Admiralty officials present. It was evidently one of Admiral Bayly's bad days." Soon afterward, Bayly had a good day. "I do not consider that I am in charge of two different kinds of destroyers," he wrote to Sims one week after Taussig arrived. "We are all one here. I have told the captains of your destroyers, as I tell ours, that the way to prevent misunderstandings and doubts is to come and see me. . . . I am always here and my business is to help them. Should you come here, please come to Admiralty House. I do not entertain but can make you comfortable." Three weeks later, Sims received an even more unexpected letter: "I have a suggestion," wrote Bayly. "If I should go on leave for 18 to 23 June, would you like to run the show in my absence? I should like it and you are the only man of whom I could truthfully say that. Your fellows would like it and it would have a good effect all around. . . . And if the Admiralty during my absence 'regret that you should have,' etc., I will take the blame. If they give you a DSO, keep it." Sims was delighted, Jellicoe approved, and on June 18, 1917, the dark blue flag of an American admiral ran up in front of Admiralty House in Queenstown. For five days, Sims was Commander-in-Chief of all British and American naval forces operating on the coast of Ireland.

By the end of June, Bayly commanded twenty-eight American destroyers; by July 5, thirty-four; by the end of July, thirty-seven. Ultimately, 8,000

American seamen were based at Queenstown; when the war ended, there were seventy-nine American destroyers in European waters—at Queenstown, Brest, and Gibraltar. Of these, only one was lost to enemy action. This was *Jacob Jones,* sunk by a torpedo from *U-53.* This submarine's captain was the celebrated Hans Rose, whose unexpected visit in October 1916 had astonished the citizens of Newport, Rhode Island. In May 1918, on the anniversary of the arrival of the first American destroyers in Queenstown, Bayly issued a memorandum to all U.S. naval forces under his command: "To command you is an honor, to work with you is a pleasure, and to know you is to know the best traits of the Anglo-Saxon race."

—

No matter how many American destroyers arrived in Europe, submerged U-boats could not be destroyed until new weapons were developed. One of these was the hydrophone, a listening device designed to pick up the propeller sounds of a submarine underwater. In 1915, an early version of this instrument was able, under optimum conditions, to pick up submerged U-boats two miles away. But the hydrophone was useless when operated aboard a moving ship; the noise of the vessel's own machinery and of water passing along the vessel's hull drowned out the sounds made by a U-boat propeller. And if the hunting vessel stopped to listen in silence, it became an easy target for a torpedo. As work continued, hydrophones improved. Meanwhile, however, even when a submerged submarine was pinpointed, surface vessels had no weapon to destroy it. Often, British seamen had looked down to see the long, gray cigar shape of a submerged U-boat moving beneath them and been able to do nothing. Their frustrations were addressed in 1916, when the first depth charges came aboard their ships. A metal can or barrel containing 300 pounds of TNT and rolled off the stern of a destroyer, this weapon was detonated by a pressure fuse set for a specific depth. A thousand Type D depth charges were ordered in August 1916, and on December 13, 1916, the first U-boat perished in this terrible way. Production of depth charges was slow: early in 1917 the normal allotment to an Allied antisubmarine vessel was two. By early 1918, however, most antisubmarine craft were equipped with thirty-five to forty depth charges, and in the last ten months of the war, nineteen U-boats were sunk by depth-charge attack.

The horror of dying this way can only be imagined. Sims described such an attack as seen from the surface: "First, the depth charge exploded, causing a mushroom of water. . . . Immediately afterward, a secondary explosion was heard; this was a horrible and muffled sound coming from the deep, more powerful and more terrible than any that could have been caused by the destroyer's 'ash can.' An enormous volcano of water and all kinds of debris arose from the sea. . . . As soon as the water subsided, great masses of heavy black oil began rising to the surface and completely splintered wood and other debris appeared." In this case, death came quickly, but sometimes the end was prolonged. Sims also described a U-boat, located by hydrophones and heavily depth-charged, which then fell silent beneath the waves. "Then a propeller was heard faintly turning or attempting to turn . . . a slight grating or squeaking such as might have been made by damaged machinery. This noise lasted a few seconds and then stopped. Presently it started up again and then once more it stopped. The submarine was making a little progress, but fitfully; she would go a few yards and then pause." The surface vessels dropped more depth charges and listened again. "There was a lumbering noise such as might be made by a heavy object trying to drag its hulk along the muddy bottom; this was followed by silence, showing that the wounded vessel could advance only a few yards." By now, the surface vessels had used all of their depth charges and could only wait. "All night long, the listeners reported scraping and straining noises from below but these grew fainter and fainter." They listened for hours and then, the following afternoon, heard "a sharp, piercing noise. . . . Only one thing in the world could make a sound like that . . . the crack of a revolver." More of these pistol cracks followed, counted by the listeners above. "In all, twenty-five shots came from the bottom of the sea." Then, silence.

—

Neither convoy nor depth charges made a difference quickly. In May 1917, shipping losses dropped to 616,000 tons, a dramatic decline from the slaughter of April, but this was due neither to the commencement of ocean convoy nor to the arrival of American warships; neither had yet had time to take effect. Losses declined because the U-boat fleet simply could not maintain the tremendous effort it had made in April. But the prospect before the German Naval Staff continued bright. In May, only two U-boats were sunk, while eight new U-boats were commissioned. Meanwhile, the British Admiralty desperately strained to find destroyers. On May 7, three days after the first American ships anchored at Queenstown, Beatty wrote to Jellicoe, "We have thirty-seven destroyers at Scapa and fourteen at Rosyth." In June, Beatty calculated that if the Grand Fleet were forced to put to sea, it might have only forty—instead of a hundred—destroyers available for a fleet action. Also in June, the submarines got a second wind: shipping losses rose to 696,000 tons. And then the tide gradually began to turn. In July, 555,000 tons were sunk; in August, the figure was 472,000 tons. The average was over half a million tons a month, but Admiral Holtzendorff's late summer harvest deadline for Britain's surrender was passing and Britain remained steadfastly in the war. In September, shipping losses dropped to 353,000 tons, and ten submarines were lost. That same month, eighty-three convoys crossed the Atlantic. In October, shipping losses rose to 466,000 tons, but they fell in November to 302,000 tons. By the end of that month, 90 percent of British ocean shipping was under convoy. Even though losses mounted again in December, to 414,000 tons, the worst was over. From January through April, monthly losses of merchant shipping averaged 325,000 tons; from May to the end of the war, about 230,000 tons. During the last year of the war, 92 percent of Allied shipping sailed in convoy; the loss rate in the convoys was less than .5 percent.

For the German navy, the loss curve had been in the opposite direction. Between May and July 1917, fifteen U-boats were lost, but the ratio remained favorable: fifty-three merchant ships were sunk for each U-boat lost. Moreover, twenty-four new U-boats replaced the fifteen lost. Even so, the German High Command now understood that the unrestricted campaign was not going to bring Britain to her knees within six months. Rather than give up, the Naval Staff extended its time limit. In early July, ninety-five new submarines were ordered for delivery beginning in the summer of 1918. German losses continued to be heavy: in the last five months of 1917, thirty-seven U-boats were sunk; from January to April 1918, twenty-four U-boats were lost. Beginning in April, American and British shipyards were building more merchant tonnage than was being destroyed. Through all of this, as Arthur Marder has pointed out, it was not the numbers of submarines sunk that truly counted in achieving victory over the U-boats; rather, it was the survival rate of the merchant ships that were their intended victims. Sinking submarines was a bonus, not a necessity. What mattered was that the merchant ships survive and deliver their cargoes. If they could do that—because the U-boats had been avoided or forced to keep out of the way—it did not matter how many U-boats were sent to the bottom.

CHAPTER 37

Jellicoe Leaves, Beatty Arrives, and the Americans Cross the Atlantic

John Jellicoe, slow to appreciate the value of convoy and hesitant to begin without sufficient escorts, nevertheless guided the navy in 1917 to the brink of victory over the submarines. Whereupon, on Christmas Eve, he was sacked—to use one of Lloyd George's favorite words. Jellicoe had been appointed First Sea Lord by Arthur Balfour and arrived at the Admiralty a week before Balfour left for the Foreign Office. The new First Lord was Sir Edward Carson, a Protestant Irishman whose resistance to Home Rule had won him the prewar title of "uncrowned King of Ulster." Carson did not pretend to any knowledge of the navy—"My only qualification is that I am absolutely at sea," he told an audience—but he worked hard to learn, frequently visited the fleet, and won the admirals' trust. "As long as I am at the Admiralty, the sailors will have full scope," he told a public audience. "They will not be interfered with by me and I will not let anyone interfere with them." This arrangement worked on Carson's side, but Jellicoe still could not escape from meetings where every politician insisted on having his say. "I am overwhelmed with work at present. War Councils waste half my time," he wrote to Beatty after two weeks in office. "I spent from 10.30 a.m. till 6.15 p.m. on War Council yesterday and *decided nothing*. This is the common routine," he wrote soon after. And later still: "The Imperial War Cabinet meets three times a week besides the ordinary War Cabinet daily and I find as a consequence very little time for the work of the war. The waste of time is abominable, but I cannot be away or something may get settled to which I should object."

In his first winter at the Admiralty, Jellicoe suffered from influenza and severe neuritis. In January 1917, Fisher found him in bed, "seedy but indomitable. Poor chap! His one and only terror was the German submarine menace which, as he truly says, one and a half years of Admiralty apathy has made so prodigious as to be almost beyond cure!" By May 1917, what Lloyd George perceived to be Jellicoe's unwarranted delay over the convoy decision placed the First Sea Lord high on the prime minister's list of men who must be removed. For his part, Jellicoe regarded the prime minister as dangerously frivolous. On the eve of a visit by Lloyd George to Rosyth, the First Sea Lord warned Beatty: "You will remember no doubt what an impressionable man he is and how apt to fly off at a tangent. One has to be cautious in talking to him. He is a hopeless optimist and told me seriously the other day that he knew for a fact we could feed the population even if *all* our supplies were cut off!! He gets figures from any source and believes them if they suit his views." Jellicoe knew, of course, that Lloyd George was displeased with him. "I have got myself much disliked by the Prime Minister and others," Jellicoe wrote to Beatty on June 30. "I fancy there is a scheme on foot to get rid of me. The way they are doing it is to say I am too pessimistic. . . . I expect it will be done by first discrediting me in the press."

Carson vigorously defended his First Sea Lord. "Wherever you read criticisms of my colleague, Sir John Jellicoe, try to find out what is the origin of them," he advised one audience. It did not matter. Jellicoe had no trouble identifying the source of his troubles: it was 10 Downing Street. Hankey noted early in July that "the PM is hot for getting rid of Jellicoe." King George V later said that the prime minister "had his knife into him [Jellicoe] for some time." Carson himself wrote later, "At one point, Lloyd George was so rude to Jellicoe that the First Sea Lord came to me and pressed me to accept his resignation."

> "My dear Admiral," I said, "who is your ministerial chief?" And he replied, "Why you, sir."
>
> So I said, "Have you ever found that I lacked confidence in you?" and he was good enough to reply that there were the happiest relations between us.
>
> "Then my dear Admiral," I said, "let me say to you what I should say to the youngest officer in the service—Carry on."

Nevertheless, the attack on the First Sea Lord and the Admiralty broadened. Lord Northcliffe, the owner of *The Times* and *Daily Mail* (the "reptile press," according to Vice Admiral Sir Charles Madden, Jellicoe's brother-in-law), commanded half of the London newspaper market and had trained his sights on Jellicoe. "You kill him. I'll bury him," the prime minister supposedly said to Northcliffe regarding the admiral. "No one can feel the smallest confidence in the present Admiralty," editorialized Northcliffe's *Daily Mail.* "If it does not fall soon, it will bring down our country with it." The inventor-journalist Arthur Pollen assaulted Jellicoe in the press, at London dinner parties, even by writing to leaders of the American government. In a letter written to President Wilson's press secretary and intended for the president's eyes, Pollen declared, "The British Admiralty has done nothing of a constructive character since the war began and . . . if we [Americans] act on the assumption that they have, we will face disaster." To Assistant Secretary of the Navy Franklin D. Roosevelt, Pollen spoke of the "extraordinary folly" of Jellicoe and the Admiralty.* Behind the First Sea Lord's back, a group of young naval officers used the office of the War Cabinet secretary, Maurice Hankey, to place their complaints before the prime minister. Later, Jellicoe wrote: "One can gather from some books written since the war that there were apparently certain junior officers who went to, and were received by, Mr. Lloyd George, who gave him their ideas for dealing with the submarine menace. Personally, I never heard of their proposals. It is true that Mr. Lloyd George did make one or two suggestions to me for dealing with the menace, but these were of such a nature that they could not have emanated from the brain of any naval officer."

Beatty's attitude toward Jellicoe at this time has been described as "ambivalent"; a better word would be "hypocritical." To Jellicoe's face, Beatty was supportive. On July 2, he urged the beleaguered First Sea Lord to ignore "what the intriguers set themselves to do. And you must stick at all costs to your intention of not volunteering to go, that would be fatal. Do not be goaded into any step of that kind no matter what the press or anybody else says. Keep yourself fit and damn the Papers and the Critics." And yet the previous month, Beatty had written to a woman friend that "J. J. [Jellicoe] was always a half-hearted man . . . [who] . . . dislikes men of independence and loves sycophants and toadies." Beatty assured this friend that if he wanted the Admiralty for himself, he could have it, "if J. J. departs, as he would if I started a war to the knife. . . . I am faced with a quandary. If I go the whole length of denunciation with the Admiralty and their ways and I am successful, it means that I should have to go to the Admiralty. That means leaving the Grand Fleet. It is a question of which is the most important appointment to the Nation."

Meanwhile, whatever her private feelings toward her husband, Ethel Beatty worked faithfully in London to promote his career and to undermine Jellicoe as First Sea Lord. She made a friend of Arthur Pollen and in May 1917 wrote to Beatty, "I telephoned Mr. Pollen to come and see me which he did. He tells me he has declared open warfare against Jellicoe and he is going to have him removed in a month's time." Later, at a dinner party, "I talked to Pollen and he says in another two months Jellicoe will go. . . . The American

*Jellicoe responded to Pollen's attacks by saying, "It fell to me to turn down his inventions on more than one occasion."

admiral [Sims] was there. . . . Pollen had been putting him right about the battle of Jutland."

Lloyd George, meanwhile, had decided that he himself could best run the Admiralty but that "unless I were present at the Admiralty every day to supervise every detail of administration, it would be impossible for me promptly to remove all hindrances and speed up action." As a first step, he removed Carson on July 17 and installed his own man. The new First Lord was Sir Eric Geddes, a Scot described by Sims as "a giant figure whose mighty frame, hard and supple muscles, and power of vigorous and rapid movement, would have made him one of the greatest [of] heavy-weight prize fighters." In fact, Geddes was a railway man who had worked for the Baltimore and Ohio Railway, managed a railway in India, and then risen to the top of the British North Eastern Railway. In wartime, he went to the Ministry of Munitions and then was asked to reorganize the railway system behind the British front in France. Fond of medals and titles and saying that he needed status to facilitate his work, he had been given the honorary military rank of major general. In May 1917, Lloyd George moved him to the Admiralty as controller, to supervise all shipbuilding for the navy and the merchant marine. Before going, Geddes insisted on being made a vice admiral. He was supplied with a uniform, which he wore to work with his officer's cap tilted down over one eye—in the manner of Beatty.

The navy hardly knew what to make of this "masquerading" admiral; Lord Esher, the backstage close friend of King Edward VII, Admiral Jacky Fisher, and almost everyone else of consequence in British political life, described Geddes as a figure from Gilbert and Sullivan: "a general today and an admiral tomorrow." Admiral Oliver, the Chief of Staff, was disgusted. "We have been upside down here ever since the North-Eastern Railway took over. Geddes is mad about statistics and has forty people always making graphs and issuing balance sheets full of percentages." Geddes's chief statistician, Oliver said, "used to bother me frequently for material to work on. To keep peace and to keep him away and occupy him and his staff, my staff used to make up data mixed with weather conditions and phases of the moon which kept them occupied. In a few months, wonderful graphs appeared." It fell to Jellicoe to tell Geddes that his new methods were not working:

> I said that the organisation set up by him had failed to produce better results—if as good results—as the old organisation in the hands of naval officers and Admiralty officials. I mentioned that the shipbuilders could not work with the new officials . . . that their methods caused great and avoidable delays. I also found the armament firms very dissatisfied with the new organisation which delayed matters and was much inferior to working direct with the Director of Naval Ordnance. I knew well that great pressure was constantly brought to bear on the Di-

> rector and Chief Inspector of Naval Ordnance to accept designs and munitions which were not up to the standard of efficiency required for the Navy.

Ignoring protests, Geddes pushed forward. He was accustomed to being obeyed, and senior admirals were no more to him than subordinate railway officials. At one point, disputing Jellicoe's attempt to recommend a knighthood for Admiral Duff, the First Lord withheld approval, saying that he did not like this admiral's manner. Jellicoe replied that he was recommending Duff "for his services not his manner." On Christmas Eve, 1917, Lloyd George's ax, eagerly swung by Geddes, fell on Jellicoe. The First Sea Lord was in his Admiralty room, about to go home to his pregnant wife and his four young daughters. His last appointment that day was with a group of Grand Fleet captains who had presented him with a silver model of his flagship, *Iron Duke*. The visitors were leaving when at 6:00 p.m. a special messenger delivered a blue envelope marked "Personal and strictly private." It was from the First Lord:

> After very careful consideration, I have come to the conclusion that a change is desirable in the post of First Sea Lord. I have not, I can assure you, arrived at this view hastily or without personal regret and reluctance. I have consulted the Prime Minister and with his concurrence, I am asking to see the King to make this recommendation to him.

Jellicoe replied that night:

> I have received your letter. You do not assign a reason for your action, but I assume that it is due to a want of confidence in me. Under these conditions you will realise that it is difficult for me to continue my work. I shall therefore be glad to be relieved as soon as possible.

The next morning, Christmas Day, Geddes telephoned Lloyd George and reported that the deed was done. "It's a good thing," the prime minister said. Then, addressing Jellicoe as "Dear Sir," the Welshman wrote him a single sentence: "I have the honor to inform you that His Majesty has been pleased to approve of my recommendation that the dignity of a peerage of the United Kingdom should be conferred on you. Yours faithfully, D. Lloyd George." Jellicoe pondered and then decided to accept for the sake of the navy and his children. He was made a viscount, "a title usually reserved for a moderately efficient Cabinet Minister on retirement," said Jellicoe's friend Admiral Bacon.

Geddes said later that he fired Jellicoe "in the way I thought least likely to offend his feelings," but the firing occurred at a moment when no newspapers would appear for two days. The Sea Lords—excepting Vice Admiral Sir Rosslyn Wester Wemyss, who had already agreed to succeed Jellicoe as First Sea Lord—were informed on Christmas Day. When Jellicoe told them that "the change was not of my seeking," the admirals protested to Geddes: "We had full confidence in Sir John Jellicoe's ability and fitness to perform his responsible duties and were most gravely concerned and disturbed by this sudden removal. . . . We therefore decided to request you . . . to inform us of the reasons which caused this step to be taken." Geddes agreed to see the Sea Lords two at a time and informed them that, two months earlier, he had spoken to the two previous First Lords, Carson and Balfour, in the presence of Lloyd George, and that both former First Lords had told him that they did not consider Jellicoe the best man to lead the Admiralty. Carson vehemently denied ever having said this; Balfour was vague. Geddes then reversed himself and denied that he had ever quoted Carson against Jellicoe. Carson, now enraged, declared that not only had he never declared that Jellicoe was not the best man for the post, but indeed he had said that Jellicoe "was the only man for First Sea Lord." Entangled in this briar patch, Geddes turned back on the Sea Lords and huffed, "I would remind you that the appointment and removal of Sea Lords is entirely a matter for His Majesty and His Majesty's government." Constitutionally, Geddes was correct. The Sea Lords, who had considered collective resignation, told Jellicoe that as "we have realised that we cannot possibly bring you back and we may do great harm to the country," they had decided to remain.

News of the dismissal spread quickly. Almost worse than the fact of it was the way it was done. Vice Admiral Sir Stanley Colville, Commander-in-Chief, Portsmouth, called it "disgraceful" and "a personal affront to the navy." Madden, second in command of the Grand Fleet, was "mutinous, explosive and very bitter"; Vice Admiral Sir Cecil Burney, a former Grand Fleet battle squadron commander, called it "scandalous and wicked"; Prince Louis of Battenberg declared, "I cannot find words to express my disgust and indignation"; Goodenough said, "Never a man stood higher in the estimation of his friends, his brother officers and every man and boy in the Service." Asquith wrote to Jellicoe, "No one knows better—perhaps no one as well as I—what the state and the Allied cause owe to you. When history comes to be written, you have no reason to fear the verdict." Margot Asquith declared flatly, "I look upon the Government as insane." Messages of devotion came from around the fleet. "We want you back," said the men of the 10th Submarine Flotilla. "You are our Idol and one who we would follow to the death. 'Come back!' is the message from the Lower Deck to you."

Jellicoe did not come back. Britain's senior admiral had been dismissed by a costumed railway man, acting on behalf of a prime minister whose attitude toward the "High Admirals" was "Sack the lot!" The man who had trained the Grand Fleet for battle, who had issued the crucial deployment command at Jutland and sent the German navy fleeing into harbor, whose fleet had enforced the blockade that destroyed Germany's will to fight, and who, before departing, had broken the back of the U-boat campaign, was gone. Three months later, Sir Edward Carson told the House of Commons what had happened: "The whole time that I was First Lord of the Admiralty, one of the greatest difficulties I had was the constant persecution—for I can call it nothing else—of certain high officials in the Admiralty who could not speak for themselves—constant persecution which, I have no doubt, could have [been] traced to reasons and motives of the most malignant character. Over and over again while I was at the Admiralty, I had the most constant pressure put upon me to remove officials, among them Sir John Jellicoe."

—

When Jellicoe left the Grand Fleet, David Beatty succeeded him as Commander-in-Chief. Promoted at forty-five to become the navy's youngest full admiral, he had boarded *Iron Duke,* whose crew, devoted to Jellicoe, was unhappy to see him; as Beatty arrived, it took a direct order from the ship's captain to wring a halfhearted welcoming cheer from the men. Nor did the relationship improve. Somehow, the flamboyant hero of the battle cruiser force cut a poor figure on *Iron Duke.* "At sea," explained one young torpedo man, describing the difference between the two admirals, "a figure in a duffel coat and sometimes wearing a white cap cover would come through the mess decks with an 'Excuse me' and that would be Sir John making his way to the bridge. When Beatty came on board it was 'CLEAR LOWER DECKS!' and a file of marines wearing short arms with Beatty in the middle. We never liked him." Beatty felt the antipathy and because, in addition, he wanted a newer, bigger, faster ship, he transferred his flag two months later to *Queen Elizabeth.* "There was," he wrote, "too much of Jellicoe in *Iron Duke.*"

The new Commander-in-Chief inherited an enormous, complex nautical war machine, trained by Jellicoe over twenty-eight months against the day when it would destroy the German navy. Under Beatty, the mission remained the same. The Grand Fleet, swinging on its moorings at Scapa Flow, commanded the surface of the sea, making possible both the blockade that was crippling Germany, and the effort against the U-boats. Had this massive surface sea power not existed, Germany would have won the war—without needing U-boats. Abruptly and catastrophically, Allied maritime commerce would have been disrupted and then severed by German surface ships; British soldiers and munitions would not have crossed the Channel into France; subsequently, American troops would not have embarked for Europe. Britain would have been forced to choose between starvation and surrender; either way, her participation in the war would have ended. The United States on its own would have confronted a victorious Germany able to draw on the combined resources of Europe. These facts seemed obvious, but not everyone was able to grasp them. "One of my difficulties during 1917," Jellicoe said later of his tenure as First Sea Lord, "was to make the prime minister realise that the whole of the Allied cause was dependent on the Grand Fleet holding the surface command of the sea." In any case, now that Jellicoe was gone, David Beatty became "the one man on either side who could lose the war in an afternoon."

Three weeks after taking command, Beatty led the Grand Fleet to sea to test his skill at controlling so large a body. There was a mishap that was not Beatty's fault: two destroyers collided and sank, with most of their crews. Back in Scapa Flow, Beatty began rewriting the fleet's tactical Battle Orders. Always critical of Jellicoe's rigid system, under which the Commander-in-Chief controlled every movement of the fleet, he decentralized authority. Battle squadron and division commanders were encouraged to act independently and even to anticipate the Commander-in-Chief's wishes. This loosening did not go too far: in action, the fleet was still to be concentrated in a single line of battle. If, however, enemy destroyers threatened a torpedo attack, as they had at Jutland, Beatty declared himself willing to face the risk rather than turn away. "Only by keeping the enemy fleet engaged can the initiative remain with the British fleet and a decision be obtained," he said. "The torpedo menace will be accepted and the fleet turned toward the retiring enemy."

Aside from this important change in tactics, Beatty's overall North Sea strategy became almost more cautious than Jellicoe's. Maintaining British naval supremacy now was Beatty's duty. On paper, the task seemed simple enough. Numerically, the British preponderance in dreadnoughts was even more overwhelming than it had been under Jellicoe. Three more 15-inch-gun *Resolution*-class battleships had been added to the fleet, and by March 1917, Beatty commanded thirty-two British dreadnought battleships; Scheer then had twenty-one.* Similarly, British superiority in battle cruisers was comfortable. After losing three of these ships at Jutland, where the Germans lost one, the Grand Fleet had seven battle cruisers to Germany's four. Then, in August and September 1916, the British added two more: *Renown* and *Repulse,* armed with six 15-inch guns. Not until February 1918 did Hipper receive the new battle cruiser *Hindenburg,* sister of *Derfflinger,* with eight 12-inch guns. But numbers, as Jutland had taught, were not everything. Beatty now feared what Jellicoe had feared: that British ships, particularly

*Beatty's dreadnought strength declined on the night of July 9, 1917, when the battleship *Vanguard,* lying at anchor at Scapa Flow, suddenly blew up. There were only two survivors of a crew of more than 800. The cause was assigned to a spontaneous explosion of powder in one of the magazines.

the battle cruisers, were structurally inferior to German in armor and underwater protection. Equally worrisome to Beatty was the constant draining of Grand Fleet destroyer strength for the antisubmarine campaign. Beatty asked for help; possibly some destroyers could be sent from the Mediterranean. Unfortunately, the Admiralty replied, it was impossible to spare any from anywhere. Worried that his fleet had been left too weak in screening craft to fight a battle, Beatty told an Admiralty conference on January 2, 1918, that "the correct strategy of the Grand Fleet is no longer to endeavour to bring the enemy to action at any cost, but rather to contain him in his bases until the general situation becomes more favourable to us." The Admiralty and the War Cabinet approved.

It was the Germans who provoked the first surface action during Beatty's North Sea command. Britain had promised a monthly shipment of 250,000 tons of British coal to Norway, and convoys composed largely of neutral ships were sailing daily, usually escorted by two British destroyers and several armed trawlers. U-boat success against the convoys had been minimal, so Scheer decided to try a surprise surface attack. The distance to the convoy routes from Horns Reef was between 300 and 350 miles; only twelve to fourteen hours' steaming for a 30-knot vessel. Poor weather in autumn and winter decreased the likelihood of such vessels being observed. Scheer chose the fast new minelaying light cruisers *Brummer* and *Bremse,* each armed with four 6-inch guns and—more important—possessing a speed of 34 knots. On October 17, 1917, a westbound Scandinavian convoy of twelve merchant vessels was under convoy by two British destroyers, *Strongbow* and *Mary Rose,* and two armed trawlers. At dawn, lookouts on *Strongbow* reported two strange vessels on a converging course. The destroyer, taking them for British cruisers, flashed recognition signals. There was no response until suddenly, before the crew could reach action stations, *Strongbow* was smothered by accurate 6-inch gunfire at a range of 3,000 yards. *Mary Rose* hurried up and was dealt similar punishment. Both destroyers sank, and then nine merchant vessels were hunted down and sunk. No British ship was able to send a wireless report and, although at the time of the attack, sixteen British light cruisers were at sea south of the convoy route, the German cruisers returned to port unscathed. Beatty did not learn what had happened until 4:00 p.m.; "Luck was against us," he said.

Two months later, on December 12, Scheer attacked again. The assailants this time were four modern German destroyers; the victims, an eastbound Scandinavian convoy of five neutral merchant ships escorted by two British destroyers. The attack took place twenty-five miles off the Norwegian coast in blinding rain squalls and a heavy sea that concealed all but the masts and funnel tops of the destroyers. Again, German gunnery was excellent: within forty-five minutes, all the ships in the convoy and one British destroyer were sunk. This time Beatty sent out battleships, battle cruisers, and twelve light cruisers to intercept, but the German ships escaped through the Skagerrak. "We do have the most cursed luck," Beatty complained. "I never anticipated that the Hun would use destroyers so far afield." Daily convoys to Scandinavia were terminated and larger convoys were dispatched every fourth or fifth day, now escorted by dreadnoughts of the Grand Fleet.

This offered Scheer a different, perhaps greater opportunity. Aware that the convoys were being escorted by battleships, he decided on a bold stroke. The German battle cruisers and light cruisers and a flotilla of destroyers of Hipper's Scouting Groups would attack the convoy and its escort while, with the rest of the High Seas Fleet, Scheer waited sixty miles to the southwest. If all went well and the British took the bait, he might at last be able to achieve what German admirals had sought since the beginning of the war: the destruction of an isolated dreadnought squadron of the Grand Fleet. At 5:00 a.m. on April 23, 1918, the German battle cruisers, three dreadnought battle squadrons, three light cruiser squadrons, and four flotillas of destroyers sailed from Schillig roads. Neither side had much information about the other. Scheer had restricted wireless to an absolute minimum, sharply limiting Room 40's ability to provide useful information, and a dense fog over the entire North Sea restricted air reconnaissance by zeppelins. Nevertheless, all was going well; Hipper and the attack force were forty miles off the Norwegian coast in the vicinity of Bergen, when, at 5:10 a.m. on the twenty-fourth, *Moltke* suffered a mechanical breakdown. Her starboard inner propeller dropped off and before the turbine could be stopped racing, a gear wheel flew to pieces. Metal shards from the broken wheel tore into an auxiliary condenser, the engine room flooded, and the starboard and center engines ceased to work. Hipper ordered *Moltke* to fall back on the battle fleet. *Moltke* tried to obey, but salt water in her boilers reduced her speed to a crawl. At 6:40 a.m., she broke radio silence and told Scheer that her breakdown was serious and her speed only 4 knots. At 8:45 a.m. she reported that she was "out of control." At 10:50 a.m. the battleship *Oldenburg* took *Moltke* in tow and the main fleet turned back for home. Scheer meanwhile ordered Hipper to go forward with the operation and the battle cruisers continued steering northwest at 18 knots. Hipper crossed and reconnoitered the convoy route, found nothing, and, at 2:10 p.m., turned back. In fact, there was no convoy; the Naval Staff had miscalculated its sailing date by twenty-four hours. British intelligence had been no better that day. Not until Scheer and Hipper began talking by wireless was the Admiralty even aware that a large German naval force was operating far out in the North Sea. Early that afternoon, the Grand Fleet cleared the Firth of Forth in a thick fog: thirty-one battleships, four battle cruisers, twenty-four light cruisers, and eighty-five destroyers. It was the last time during the war that the full strength of the Grand Fleet was set in motion, but once again Beatty's luck was out. The High Seas Fleet was 100 miles ahead of him and out of reach. At 6:37 p.m., Scheer reached the swept channels through the minefields and *Moltke* cast off her tow from *Oldenburg*. She was lumbering home when a torpedo from the British submarine *E-42* struck her. Eighteen hundred tons of seawater poured in, but *Moltke* still managed to reach the Jade under her own power. Considering what Scheer had hoped for, he, too, had been unlucky.

—

In the winter of 1915, when the Admiralty first moved the battle cruisers to a permanent base in the Firth of Forth, Ethel Beatty established a residence for herself and her husband on shore. The place she chose was Aberdour House, a comfortable old stone and stucco house with a tiled roof on a hill overlooking the Firth from the north, about six miles from the fleet landing at Rosyth. Beatty promptly ordered construction of a clay tennis court, where, when his ships were in harbor, he played every fair afternoon. Usually, he came ashore in his admiral's barge for lunch, being met by his automobile and driven the fifteen minutes up the hill to Aberdour House. Beatty loved tennis, "because it is exercise in concentrated form and you don't waste valuable time chasing a miserable, helpless ball over the hills." On the court, he played as if he were at war. He slapped his partner on the back, cheered good shots, and exhorted greater effort when they seemed to be losing. "Here, we can't let it stand like this!" he would cry. "It will never become us to be beaten." When it rained, Beatty and his guests—admirals or captains from the fleet—took long walks over the hills or joined the party dancing before a huge open fireplace in a large hall at nearby Aberdour Castle. Beatty seldom danced but he liked watching, enjoying the warmth, the music, and the presence of women. Reluctantly, he left to return to his ship for dinner, in obedience to his own order that all hands be back aboard by 7:30 in the evening. When he took command of the Grand Fleet and moved to Scapa Flow, this pleasant routine was interrupted, but the lease on Aberdour House and its tennis court was continued.

The truth was that most of the activities centered on Aberdour House were a charade. Beatty was miserable in his marriage. His wife and her "utterly unpredictable moods" dominated his thoughts; Beatty described some nights with Ethel as "worse than Jutland." Lady Beatty had always considered her husband selfish because he was so consumed by the navy and went off to sea, leaving her alone. As long as he commanded only the battle cruisers and they were based in the Firth of Forth, she could have him around and could play the grand hostess at Aberdour House. When he moved to Scapa Flow, in the far north, she felt herself abandoned again. Her response was renewed promiscuity, a matter that was common knowledge in the couple's intimate society, but never mentioned. Beatty, however, was constantly reminded. Once, he left Aberdour House to return to his ship and then, remembering that he had left his cigarette case behind, returned to collect it.

He found his wife in bed with one of his officers. Yet he never considered divorce. He continued to write to "Darling Tata," and signed himself "Ever your devoted David." He blamed himself for her moods and behavior. "Tata," he wrote on one occasion, "you accuse me of being cross, bad-tempered, saying cutting things which indeed were far from my thoughts or intention." A month later, he wrote again,

> You must give me a little more time to get accustomed to the new conditions and your changed feelings. You see, in the past you have spoiled me horribly and given me so much love and sympathy that it is difficult to realise that I must do without it or without so much of it. . . . Let me impress upon you that I am really tumbling to the altered conditions, that I in no way wish to monopolise your entire life, that I have no wish to be the orbit, against your will, round which everything will revolve, to be the center of your efforts to live, which, as you put it, makes me a horribly selfish, egotistical person. I truly am not that, really. . . . I realise you like to be more independent and indeed am thankful for it. All I ask is that you should do exactly as you wish at all times. All I truly care for is that you should be happy and contented.

Rejected and lonely, Beatty found consolation. During the last two years of the war, the Commander-in-Chief of the Grand Fleet was deeply involved in a love affair with Eugenie Godfrey-Faussett, a woman in her early thirties with much-praised long golden hair. Eugenie's husband, twenty-one years older than she, was Captain Bryan Godfrey-Faussett, of the Royal Navy, the intimate friend and equerry of King George V who had arranged Ethel Beatty's presentation at court. Eugenie initiated the correspondence with Beatty, writing to him in June 1916 to congratulate him on his role at Jutland. His reply, addressed to "Dear Mrs. Godfrey," noted properly that he had been glad to see her husband "looking so well" when he had visited the fleet with the king, and concluded, "Yours ever, David Beatty." Through the remainder of 1916, Eugenie kept writing. After becoming Commander-in-Chief, Beatty replied that, "exiled" to Scapa Flow, he appreciated "your letters more than ever, so will you write and tell me all the news?" Formality began to erode and Beatty wrote, "Bless you my dear (is that too familiar?) for your delightful letters, the best I ever get." In January 1917 he began calling her Eugenie—"because Godfrey told me to"—and asked her to stop calling him *Sir* David. Boldly, Eugenie sent him a new mattress for the bed in his new flagship's cabin and he replied that he would "dream all the pleasanter now that I know you tried it." When she began doing volunteer hospital work, he wrote that he was "sure you look delicious in your hospital garb. I wish I could see you. Is that asking too much?" By April 1917, it was "Eugenie, you are a darling and I love you and your letters more than ever." On April 17, he came to London for two days of Admiralty conferences and a private lunch with Eugenie. Returning to the fleet, Beatty wrote, "Eugenie, dear, was it a dream? That one perfectly divine day . . . three very short hours of intense pleasure." At the beginning of May, he told her that he read "the nicest parts" of her letters "over and over again," and, "I wish, how I wish, that it were possible for you to do all the nice things you said you would like to do."

In August 1917, Beatty brought the major part of the Grand Fleet down to the Firth of Forth and persuaded Ethel to invite Eugenie to come and stay at Aberdour House. ("Tata loves having you," Beatty assured her.) Eugenie stayed a month; Beatty later wrote, "for four weeks I was able to see you almost every day." Captain Godfrey-Faussett had remained on duty in London and Ethel was often away; as a result, says Beatty's most recent biographer, "the indications are that Bryan was well and truly cuckolded." Thereafter, Eugenie became Beatty's "dearest comrade of Dreamland." He reprimanded her when she told him that she had burned a letter written to him at midnight "because it was not respectable. There is nothing that could be 'not respectable' between us and I should have adored it and I don't like respectable things of any sort anyway. . . . I love you all over from your glorious hair to the tips of your toes."

Meanwhile, Beatty's private relationship with his wife continued unchanged. On September 4, soon after he and Eugenie left Aberdour—he for Scapa Flow, Eugenie for London—he wrote to Ethel, "You must know that I am quite unhappy when you are not with me. I know, dear heart, that I am rather an impossible person, difficult to get on with and moody and peevy at times. I know also that it has cost me some change in your feelings towards me. But you must believe me when I say that I just worship you today as I have ever done from the moment I first saw you."

After another short meeting in London in October 1917, Eugenie asked Beatty by letter, "Did anything that happened when you were here make some of your thoughts come true?" He answered, "They all came true [and] the reality was sweeter and more divine than my 'thoughts.' My visit to London was a visit to fairy land with a beautiful golden-haired Fairy Queen." In January, she sent him a collection of erotic fairy stories she had written, set in an imaginary land of the Arabian Nights. Beatty wrote back that he could "administer love potions just as successfully" as her characters. In April, when she wrote saying she wanted to see her "Comrade in Dreamland," he replied, "It would not be a case of a Comrade in Dreamland for I would never let you sleep—unless you swooned and then I would bring you to with caresses." The admiral then produced a literary effort of his own:

Here's to you and here's to Blighty,
I'm in pajamas, you in a nighty,
If we are feeling extra flighty,
Why in pajamas and Why the nighty?

Beginning in April 1918, when the entire Grand Fleet was permanently based in the Firth of Forth, Beatty and Eugenie often met in the afternoon at the North British Hotel in Edinburgh. Eugenie would take a room; Beatty would arrive and go straight up. That summer, she sent him a book about techniques of lovemaking. "What an amazing book!" he wrote to her. "To learn that all the Troubles in Domestic Life are due to the fact that the man is too quick and the lady too slow. What a tragedy! I am sure that the man should do all he could to prolong the thrills, they are so damnably short, but how is it to be done?" In his next letter, he proposed his own solution: to "kiss you from the tips of your toes upwards and take some time about it, *Adorata Mia*."

Despite his affair with Eugenie, David and Ethel continued exchanging gossip and belittling people they didn't like; it was as if they realized that denigrating common enemies brought them closer together. Beatty wrote that Lloyd George was a "dirty dog" and "a demagogue, pure and simple." Geddes was another "dirty dog," "weak as ditch water." Edwin Montagu, minister of munitions—the man who had taken Venetia Stanley away from Asquith—was "the Jew Montagu." "Yes," Beatty wrote to his wife, "he is appalling to look at with that immense conceit and self-confidence common to the Hebrew tribe." Ethel called Churchill "a dead dog" and "a disappointed blackguard." When the war ended, Beatty left the Grand Fleet and returned to London with Ethel. He now had two women in the same city. As he and Ethel were expected to present the picture of a happily married hero and his devoted wife, he and his "Golden-Haired Comrade" had to reconsider their relationship. Eugenie took the lead, asking what their future would be. Beatty replied that he was "a selfish beast," who "ought to say that I must not trouble you more and ought to retire gracefully out of your life"—the implication being that he hoped she would say that he did not have to. He explained his feelings for his wife as those of duty and gratitude, not passion: "I am truly devoted to Tata, so much so that I efface myself in my desire to see her happy. I cannot forget all that she has been to me for the last twenty years, all that she has done for me, all that she has given me." But once the war began, he said, he had "looked for love and sympathy and did not get them . . . until you came along and gave me both." Nevertheless, the signature on this letter, written in April 1919 as Beatty was leaving for France with Ethel, told Eugenie much. He had written: "Heaps of love, Ever Yours, David."*

*In 1920, when Ethel had the first of a series of nervous breakdowns, Beatty, desperate, wrote to Eugenie, asking for help. His wife's "perpetual black despair," he said, made his own "present dog's life not worth living." In 1924, at Beatty's request, Eugenie accompanied Ethel on a trip to the Riviera. Ethel became "quite impossible," telling Eugenie that she hated her, and Eugenie left her in the hands of "an interesting young man available to wait on her"; Beatty, past caring about infidelity, hoped only that Ethel would not come home.

—

In July 1917, Sims accompanied Jellicoe to Scapa Flow and, on returning to London, relayed to Washington the First Sea Lord's urgent request that the U.S. Navy send its four strongest coal-burning battleships to reinforce the Grand Fleet. The reason for Jellicoe's appeal was that the Royal Navy was short of manpower; there simply were not enough trained seamen to man the new British light cruisers, destroyers, and submarines about to be commissioned. The Admiralty's proposed solution was to take five of the Channel Fleet's predreadnought *King Edward*–class battleships out of commission and use their crews—each of these old ships carried 1,000 men—to provide officers, gunnery and torpedo ratings, and other personnel for the new warships. The *King Edwards*, whose task had been to guard the eastern approaches to the Channel, would be replaced by four *Superbs*, the oldest dreadnoughts in the Grand Fleet. The *Superbs* in turn—if the Americans agreed—would be replaced in the Grand Fleet by four U.S. Navy dreadnoughts.

Despite Sims's endorsement, the Navy Department in Washington at first rejected Jellicoe's request. One reason was doctrinal: most American admirals were disciples of Alfred Thayer Mahan, the apostle of sea power, who had decreed that a battle fleet must remain concentrated. Already, the American admirals felt that they had compromised their fleet's integrity by giving up the destroyers needed to screen their battleships; now they were resolved not to dribble away the battleships themselves. Behind this decision also lay the long-range concern that, should the Allies lose the war, the United States alone might have to face the German fleet. In addition, there was the deep American suspicion of Japan and fear of a two-ocean conflict. On top of all this, there was a practical reason for refusing to send the battleships to Europe. The fleet had been providing gun crews to scores of armed American merchant vessels, so the gunnery complement of many warships, including battleships, was sadly depleted. Until new men could be trained, the ships were not ready to fight.

No officer felt more strongly that American battleships should remain in American waters than the navy's senior admiral, Chief of Naval Operations William S. Benson. In May, a month after America entered the war, a British government mission including Foreign Secretary Arthur Balfour had tried to convince Benson and Secretary of the Navy Josephus Daniels to postpone the American 1916 dreadnought-building program in favor of building more destroyers for escort work. Their views had not changed. "The future position of the United States must in no way be jeopardized by any disintegration of our main fighting fleet," Daniels said. Benson concurred: "The U.S. believes that the strategic situation necessitates keeping the battleship force concentrated and cannot therefore consider sending part of it across." Refusing to give up, Sims replied, "I cannot see that sending a division of ships would be any disintegration of our fleet, but merely an advance force interposed between us and the enemy fleet."

At the Navy Department, Mahan's principles were sacrosanct, but views began to change when America's two most senior American admirals—Admiral Henry T. Mayo, Commander-in-Chief of the U.S. Atlantic Fleet, and then Benson himself—traveled to the British Isles. Mayo arrived in London on August 29, 1917, for discussions at the Admiralty followed by a visit to the Grand Fleet at Scapa Flow. There, Beatty was at his hospitable best, briefly hauling down his own Commander-in-Chief's flag from *Queen Elizabeth* and hoisting the four-star flag of his American guest. Beatty's private description of Mayo was less generous; to Eugenie, he characterized the American admiral as "a dear old cup of tea who never did anything wrong in his life; an impeccable old gentleman—that's no use now, is it?" Back in London, Mayo heard Jellicoe ask again for American battleships and, on the basis of what he had seen and heard, responded favorably. Now only Benson blocked the way.

On November 7, the Chief of Naval Operations arrived in London, where three days of discussions at the Admiralty produced another conversion. On November 10, Benson cabled Secretary Daniels, recommending the sending of four coal-burning American dreadnoughts to the Grand Fleet. Benson went further: if conditions warranted, he was willing in the spring to send the entire U.S. battle fleet to Europe. Benson's abrupt reversal stemmed from more than a sudden attack of Anglophilia. He could see that the presence of American battleships would give the navy a greater voice in Allied naval strategy and would enhance the prestige and morale of the U.S. fleet. He also recognized that if America's powerful battleship fleet remained idle throughout the war, it might be difficult to extract money from Congress to build future dreadnoughts. On November 25, Battleship Division 9 of the U.S. Atlantic Fleet—*New York, Wyoming, Florida,* and *Delaware*—sailed from Hampton Roads for Scapa Flow.

—

Antagonism between the American and German navies went back to June 1898, when an American naval squadron commanded by Commodore George Dewey had a potentially dangerous confrontation with a German force under Vice Admiral Otto von Diederichs in Manila Bay. In the months preceding this episode, the kaiser had announced, "I am determined, when the opportunity arises, to purchase or simply to take the Philippines from Spain." In May 1898, the German consul in Manila told Berlin that the time had come to choose a German prince to become king of the Philippines. Then war broke out between Spain and America. Dewey caught the Spanish Far Eastern Squadron at anchor, quickly annihilated it, and, lacking troops to land

and seize the Philippine capital, established a blockade of Manila. A German flotilla, larger than Dewey's force, appeared and was responsible for minor infractions of international blockade regulations. When Dewey insisted on stopping German warships crossing his blockade line, Diederichs sent his Flag Lieutenant to the American flagship *Olympia* to protest. Dewey lost his temper. "Why, I shall stop each vessel whatever may be her colors!" he said. "And if she does not stop, I shall fire at her! And that means war, do you know, Sir? And I tell you, if Germany wants war, all right, we are ready."

In the years that followed, Dewey and Diederichs each became the senior officer of his respective navy. Each was convinced that war between the two countries was possible, but German contingency planning was far more thorough. After defeating the U.S. fleet off the east coast of the United States, Norfolk, Hampton Roads, and Newport News were to be occupied, after which the Germans would move up Chesapeake Bay toward Washington and Baltimore. "Unsparing, merciless assaults" would follow against New York City and Boston. Long Island was to be the springboard for attacks on New York, and Great Gull, Gardiner, Fishers, Plum, and Block islands were given special consideration. Brooklyn would be seized and Manhattan bombarded in an operation for which "2 to 3 battalions of infantry and 1 battalion of engineers seem fully sufficient." There was no thought of penetrating farther inland; these blows to America's seaboard population centers were considered enough to bring the nation to terms.

The American war plan against Germany at the turn of the century never imagined the German army being landed on American soil. Instead, American planners expected a German naval assault in the Caribbean aimed at acquiring naval bases in the West Indies and colonies in South America. To meet this threat, the American Atlantic Fleet would concentrate in the Caribbean where the decisive battle would be fought. Given the problems a German fleet would face in crossing the Atlantic and in coaling upon arrival, the Navy Department—and especially Dewey—was confident of an American victory.

This irrelevant strategy had not been updated since the outbreak of war in Europe, and in April 1917 the U.S. Navy was wholly unprepared for the battles it was about to fight.

It was afflicted with a serious imbalance in warship types. It possessed fourteen modern dreadnought battleships, but only seventy-four destroyers. These were far too few to screen the dreadnoughts and still look after the navy's twenty-three predreadnoughts, its ten armored cruisers, and its twenty-five light cruisers. No provision whatever had been made for destroyers doing convoy duty for merchant ships. This discrepancy was not entirely the navy's fault. For years, the Navy Department had asked Congress for money to build four new destroyers to accompany the construction of each new battleship; every year Congress had appropriated money for only one or two. In

1917, the latest American destroyers were among the best in the world, but only fifty-one of the seventy-four in commission were modern. More new ships were under construction, but the same imbalance persisted: six dreadnoughts, ten light cruisers, and only ten destroyers.

The American navy's construction plans, like those of the German navy, had been victimized by the *Dreadnought* revolution. No president believed more passionately in sea power than Theodore Roosevelt, and during his eight years in office, the United States had laid down thirteen battleships. All became instantly obsolete with the commissioning of Jacky Fisher's HMS *Dreadnought.* And when, at the end of his presidency, Roosevelt painted his new predreadnoughts white and sent them around the world to parade American naval power, the Great White Fleet served mainly to advertise its own obsolescence. Immediately, the Americans, like the Germans, responded to the British dreadnought by building their own. By December 1917, when Benson sent the battleships to Scapa Flow, fourteen American dreadnoughts were in commission.

Even so, the four dreadnoughts sent to Europe were not America's most modern. They were coal burners rather than oil burners and their selection was due, not to Benson's reluctance to send his latest ships, but to the Royal Navy's candid admission that, while it had ample coal, it could not provide fuel oil for America's new oil-burning battleships. In speed and armament, the four American ships sent were the equivalent of most of Beatty's ships. *Delaware,* the oldest, was commissioned in 1910, carried ten 12-inch guns, and was capable of 21 knots. *Florida,* completed in 1911, and *Wyoming,* completed in 1912, carried twelve 12-inch. *New York,* commissioned in 1914, and her sister *Texas,* which stayed home, were the last coal-burning dreadnoughts in the U.S. Navy. The ten 14-inch guns of *New York* and *Texas* had leap-frogged the armament of the British 13.5-inch-gun battleships; they, in turn, had been leap-frogged by the British *Queen Elizabeth*s and *Resolution*s with their eight 15-inch.

—

Off the Newfoundland Grand Banks, the four American battleships bound for Europe encountered a ninety-mile-an-hour Atlantic gale. Gigantic seas battered the ships, crushed lifeboats, and sprang deck hatches. Tons of water poured into *New York,* putting her down by the bow with eight feet of water in her forward storerooms. When the storm-scarred ships entered Scapa Flow on the morning of December 7, 1917, a young American lieutenant on *New York* saw "a glorious golden dawn . . . hills blending with clouds, purple and gold. . . . When our anchors plunged into the flow, three mighty cheers went up from Beatty's *Queen Elizabeth.*" Beatty himself was watching and raised his hat in salute. A few days later, this same American officer "climbed to the crest of a little island called Flotta to look over the great land-locked harbor. Spread out below me, swinging aimlessly to the whims of the eddying currents, lay the Grand Fleet." And when his ship first sailed from Scapa Flow, "I came on deck in the morning in blazing sunrise and beheld a sight never to be forgotten. The Grand Fleet stretched before me, belching dense volumes of black smoke."

The American battleships were placed under the operational control of the Commander-in-Chief of the Grand Fleet and designated the 6th Battle Squadron. British flag signals, radio codes, tactical maneuvering orders, and fire-control methods were adopted and Royal Navy signalmen were lent to the American battleships to teach British methods. Less could be done to help American gunnery. Target practice in Pentland Firth revealed the difference between the veteran British and the novice American ships. The Americans' rate of fire and their accuracy were "distinctly poor and disappointing," Beatty told the Admiralty. Nevertheless, he said, they were "desperately keen" and he would try not to hurry them too much.

The American battleships and their crews, accustomed to the long blue swells of the Pacific, the cobalt waters of the Caribbean, and even the gray storms of the North Atlantic, were unprepared for the character of the North Sea. "It is not that it blows any harder in the North Sea than in many other parts of the world," Rear Admiral Hugh Rodman, the commander of the American battleship force, wrote to Benson, "but that it seems to be almost continually blowing, shifting rapidly from one point of the compass to another and kicking up a rough cross sea. In addition there is a great deal of snow, hail, sleet and rain, often coupled with fog and mist." In the Pentland Firth, with a strong tide running against the wind, the strong tidal currents and heavy seas pushed battleships a quarter mile out of position. The upper and main decks even of dreadnoughts were repeatedly smothered. "I have seen the largest battleships apparently sucked under until only the superstructures on the upper deck were visible when they would slowly rise from their submergence and the water pour off their decks as it might from some huge turtle . . . [coming] to the surface."

Personal relations between the British and American sailors were excellent. Rodman, a tall, blunt-spoken Kentuckian, noted for his amiability, his earthiness, and his excellent hand at bridge, had graduated sixty-first in a class of sixty-two from Annapolis, served with Admiral Dewey at Manila Bay, and earned a high reputation for seamanship. Beatty did his best to make the Americans feel welcome. When the fleet was in the Firth of Forth, Rodman and his senior captains were frequent guests at Aberdour House. At Scapa Flow, the Americans were allotted space for a baseball diamond. On the Fourth of July, Beatty gave the American battleships two days off and sent them to a separate cove in the Flow to celebrate. The Commander-in-Chief sent greetings on "this greatest of Liberty Days," and many Grand Fleet admirals boarded *New York* to help celebrate. In relays, 200 men at a time from each American ship were allowed to go ashore. Most congregated at the Temperance Hotel in Kirkwall. Privately, Americans complained that British ships were "too cold for men brought up in American homes. They are likewise poorly ventilated by our standards. They do not go in for laundries and other labor-saving devices such as motor-driven dough mixers and potato peelers." But British ships had one convenience American sailors envied: rum for the men and whiskey for the officers, both prohibited on ships of the U.S. Navy.

On February 5, Beatty wrote to Ethel, "I am sending old Rodman out on an operation of his own which pleases him and gives them an idea that they are really taking part in the war. I trust they will come to no harm." The following day, February 6, the 6th Battle Squadron took its first turn at escorting a convoy to Norway. The four American battleships left the "lavender, snow-powdered hills" of Scapa Flow with a squadron of British light cruisers and screening destroyers, all under Rodman's command. At sea, wrote the young American officer, "the atmosphere was crystal clear, seeming to magnify each star a dozen times." In the middle of the night, "the north burst into a brilliant arc of light, and moving streamers. A magnificent display of the *aurora borealis* followed, rolling its curtains of delicate fire across a surface of reflected brilliance. Against this arc, our ships stand out silhouetted sharply black." Next day, the rising mist revealed "the coast of Norway: against a wall of snow-capped mountains backing up its jagged cliffs." Having delivered the convoy's thirty merchant vessels and while waiting to pick up a return convoy, Rodman's ships were attacked by submarines—or so they believed. Three of the four battleships reported seeing periscopes and torpedo wakes. *Wyoming*'s captain was unconvinced that submarines had been present, and a British destroyer reported porpoises. Rodman, however, was certain that his ships had been attacked and officially reported two torpedoes fired at *Florida* and two at *Delaware.* After the war, German naval records revealed that no U-boat had attacked battleships that day off the Norwegian coast.

Returning to Scapa Flow, the 6th Battle Squadron was augmented by the arrival of the battleship *Texas, New York*'s sister. This addition resulted from Rodman's request for a fifth battleship so that his division could maintain a constant four-ship strength and still allow for repair and refit. *Texas,* trying her gunnery, proved inferior to the four ships that had spent two months with the Grand Fleet. Although *Texas* had won an Atlantic Fleet gunnery trophy, Rodman grumbled, "she was not ready to fire under wartime conditions."

On March 8, it was again the Americans' turn to escort the Scandinavian convoy and Rodman put to sea with four battleships, five light cruisers, and twelve destroyers. Again, the convoy was delivered and Rodman waited through the night to pick up the returning convoy. A thick fog at dawn made the rendezvous difficult to manage and several big ships narrowly escaped collision. Three of the four battleships were separated and did not rejoin until morning. Once again, *Florida* and *Delaware* reported periscopes. On April 17, the Americans sailed on their last convoy assignment. Again, they had bad luck. *Texas* reported a periscope, which no one else saw. A gale came up, pushing merchantmen and escorts here and there, and when the wind died, the scattered convoy stretched across the sea for sixty miles.

Gradually, the gunnery of the American battleships improved. By June, after six months in the North Sea, Rodman reported the firing as "exceptionally fine, much better than we have ever done previously." Beatty did not agree. Because of the American ships' poor performance and the permanent absence of one Grand Fleet battleship division off escorting the Scandinavian convoys, he never permitted release of the three *Superb*s which the American dreadnoughts had been brought over to replace. The Commander-in-Chief, according to one of his staff officers, still considered the American ships "rather as an incubus to the Grand Fleet than otherwise. They have not even yet been assimilated to a sufficient degree to be considered the equivalent to British dreadnoughts, yet for political reasons he [Beatty] does not care that the Grand Fleet should go to sea without them." At sea the 6th Battle Squadron was always stationed last in line, "where they were least likely to interfere with the movements of the fleet."

On July 29, the battleship *Arkansas,* a sister of *Wyoming,* arrived to relieve *Delaware,* which returned to Hampton Roads. In target practice, *Arkansas* was every bit as poor as the other American battleships had been when they arrived. By November 9, 1918, she was coping with another enemy: she had 259 influenza cases on board, and eleven men died.

During the summer of 1918, three more American dreadnought battleships arrived in Europe. The Admiralty and the Navy Department feared that the German Naval Staff might send one or more fast battle cruisers into the North Atlantic to attack troop transports crowded with American soldiers. If the 27-knot *Derfflinger* could place herself in the midst of a troop convoy, thousands of American soldiers would drown. To protect the convoys, the new oil-burning dreadnoughts *Nevada* and *Oklahoma,* along with the coal-burning *Utah,* were ordered to Berehaven, Ireland. The three dreadnoughts at Berehaven were under American, not British, operational control, but they had been assigned no screening destroyers. Meanwhile, thirty-four American destroyers commanded by the British admiral Lewis Bayly were based at Queenstown, 100 miles away. Before the American battleships could go to sea, therefore, their admiral had to borrow American destroyers from Bayly. For tactical, not national, reasons, Bayly was reluctant. He agreed that the battleships must be screened in submarine-infested waters, but he also feared the disruption of his finely tuned convoy assignments. He promised to do his best and managed from time to time to loan destroyers for the battleships to go to sea for gunnery practice. Only once, on October 14 when two troop convoys were entering the danger zone, was a real alert sounded for a surface raider. The three American battleships put to sea escorted by seven American destroyers. No raider appeared.

During the war, nine American dreadnoughts served in European waters; six with the Grand Fleet, three at Berehaven. Two more, *Pennsylvania* and *Arizona,* came over after the armistice.* None of these American dreadnoughts ever met the High Seas Fleet. But neither, after Jutland, did any British dreadnought.

—

Americans from the president on down wanted the war to end quickly, and they were not put off by convention, effort, or expense. One grandiose American proposal was the complete sealing off of the North Sea by a barrier from Scotland to Norway to block the passage of submarines. Some American engineers made the preposterous suggestion that this be achieved by building a massive stone breakwater 230 miles long and 300 to 900 feet deep. On May 10, 1917, the British naval mission in Washington heard another grand-scale proposal involving a vast webbing of mines and nets that would stretch across the same area. Reporting to the Admiralty, the mission said that the "United States is prepared to bear the cost and maintain the barrier with necessary small craft. . . . This scheme involves the violation of Norwegian territorial waters concerning which the Foreign Office could express opinion. A formal protest by Norwegian government is probable but there is strong feeling here that it should be overridden." The plan's strongest advocate was Franklin D. Roosevelt, the enthusiastic assistant secretary of the Navy. "It is physically quite possible to construct a thousand miles of nets two hundred feet in depth," Roosevelt urged. "It is also perfectly possible to construct 500,000 mines. The cost of manufacturing, transporting and installing 1,000 miles of net and 500,000 mines has been variously estimated at from $200,000,000 to $500,000,000. The Allied governments can well afford the expenditure if only in comparison with the value of the merchant tonnage sunk during the first five months of the present year."

The Admiralty was appalled. The distance, the depth of the water, the effect of storms and strong currents on mine anchors and tethers, the amount of material required, the impossibility of finding ships to bring these materials from America—all made the gargantuan proposal appear inconceivable. But Roosevelt and the Americans did not give up. In September 1917, dur-

***Utah, Oklahoma,* and *Arizona,* along with *West Virginia,* were sunk at Pearl Harbor, and *Pennsylvania, New Mexico, Mississippi, Colorado,* and *Tennessee* were severely damaged. *Nevada* escaped sinking only because she was able to get under way and her captain ran her aground. All of these ships except *Utah, Oklahoma,* and *Arizona* were repaired or raised and rebuilt in time to participate in the ultimate defeat of Japan.

ing his visit to London, Admiral Mayo raised the idea again. This time, the Admiralty was willing to discuss the project, although more in an effort to conciliate the Americans than because of a genuine conversion. Finally, in October, the Admiralty approved what was to be called the Northern Barrage, providing the Americans supplied the mines and most of the minelayers.

The American navy went to work. In mid-October, the Navy Department awarded a contract for 100,000 mines. Four months later, on March 3, 1918, the first mines of the Northern Barrage splashed into the North Sea. The minefield, divided into British and American zones, was 230 miles long and 30 miles wide. Over this expanse, 15 rows of mines were laid; the mines were set 100 yards apart at depths of 45, 160, and 240 feet. Through the spring, summer, and fall of 1918, minelaying continued and, although the armistice came before the Northern Barrage was complete, over 70,000 mines were laid—56,571 by the Americans, 13,546 by the British. The cost was $40 million. The problem of Norway was never solved. British and American patrols often saw U-boats using Norwegian coastal waters and Wemyss advised the War Cabinet that "U.S. naval authorities realise that the results of their exertions in production and laying a vast quantity of mines are largely reduced by the inertia of Norway." Norway, nevertheless, remained unwilling to prevent U-boats from using her territorial waters, either by mining them herself or by allowing the Allies to do so.

The Northern Barrage did not close the North Sea to U-boat passage; submarines traveled back and forth at a rate of thirty or forty a month. The toll taken by the Barrage is uncertain. Only four submarines are known to have been destroyed. One was *U-156,* a large *Deutschland*-class minelayer returning from the U.S. East Coast, where one of her mines had sunk the American cruiser *San Diego;* her fate was assumed from the fact that her captain signaled his base that he was approaching the Barrage and would signal again once he was through; he and his boat were never heard from again. Sims believed that at least four more submarines had been sunk and six seriously damaged crossing the Barrage; German naval records do not support this belief.

—

In the summer of 1918, seven large *Deutschland*-class U-boats appeared off the Eastern Seaboard of North America, assigned to mine convoy assembly points and attack unescorted shipping. Mines were laid from Newfoundland to Cape Hatteras, with particular attention paid to the entrance to Chesapeake Bay. The campaign sank 110,000 tons of merchant shipping and the obsolete American armored cruiser *San Diego.* An eleven-year-old, 14,000-ton ship with a crew of 1,250, *San Diego* had been escorting troop convoys across the Atlantic. Her value in this line of work is difficult to imagine;

against a submerged U-boat, she could do nothing; had she been asked to confront *Derfflinger* or any other German battle cruiser sent into the North Atlantic, her lot would have been martyrdom. Even so, on the morning of July 19, 1918, *San Diego* was steaming down the Long Island coast bound for New York to pick up a convoy. Off Fire Island, the ship struck a mine laid by *U-156,* sank rapidly, and left more than a thousand men bobbing in the water. Because the coast was nearby, many rescue vessels arrived quickly and only six lives were lost. *San Diego* was the only large American warship lost during the war.

—

The U.S. Navy played a major role in transporting over 2 million American soldiers to Europe. By June 1918, American troops were pouring into France at the rate of 300,000 a month. The safety of their troop convoys lay in a combination of speed and heavy escort: troopships never moved at less than 12 knots; many reached 15; and the big ocean-liner greyhounds reached 22 and more—all far beyond the speed of a submerged submarine. In addition, a convoy of four or five large troopships would be surrounded by as many as ten or twelve destroyers. Under these conditions, the U-boats were as ineffective as they had been against Grand Fleet dreadnoughts in the North Sea.

More than half of the vessels carrying the soldiers were British or—ironically—German. Before the war, Americans going abroad were accustomed to traveling on European ocean liners and few large American passenger ships had been built. The great British liners—*Aquitania, Mauretania,* and *Olympic*—became troop transports. And within hours of the declaration of war, the U.S. Coast Guard seized all North German Lloyd and Hamburg-America vessels interned in American harbors. Among these were several prewar luxury liners, including the world's largest, the giant 52,000-ton *Vaterland,* which, renamed *Leviathan,* became a U.S. Navy troop transport. By "hot bunking"—assigning one bunk to two men, each man having ownership for twelve hours—the ship's capacity was doubled and *Leviathan* carried 8,000 or 9,000 soldiers to Europe on every voyage. Other German ships were given new names and pressed into service: *Cincinnati* became *Covington, Kronprinzessin Cecilie* became *Mount Vernon, Kaiser Wilhelm II* became *Agamemnon.* The German liner *President Lincoln* kept its original name.

The U-boats' mission was to sink these British and former German ships filled with seasick young Americans. Only one was sunk carrying soldiers to France. This was the transport *Tuscania,* torpedoed on February 5, 1918, off the coast of Ireland with 2,179 American soldiers on board, mostly National Guardsmen from Michigan and Wisconsin. One hundred sixty-six soldiers drowned, along with forty-four members of the British crew. The toll of troopships returning to North America was heavier. *President Lincoln* was torpedoed, westbound from France to the United States, with 715 men on board including sick and wounded soldiers, two of them completely paralyzed. All were evacuated into lifeboats and picked up fifteen hours later by two American destroyers, which had raced 275 miles at 25 knots. Twenty-seven crewmen died; all of the soldiers were saved. The troopship *Covington,* returning home from Brest, went down with a loss of seven men. *Antilles* went down with sixty-seven men, *Moldavia* with fifty-six, and *Ticonderoga* with 215. *Mount Vernon,* the former *Kronprinzessin Cecilie,* was attacked when she was homeward bound and carrying 350 sick and wounded soldiers, 150 of whom were unable to move. Thirty-five sailors were killed by a torpedo explosion and the ship settled ten feet deeper in the water. But she did not sink. One troop transport struck back. On the night of May 12, 1918, the giant White Star liner *Olympic,* sister of *Titanic,* crammed with American soldiers, sighted *U-103* on the surface. Making 24 knots, *Olympic* rammed the submarine and cut her in half.

—

In every war, there is a last man killed in action; in naval war, a last ship sunk in battle. In the Great War, the last sinking on each side involved a submarine, first as victim, then as assailant. On October 25, 1918, two weeks before the armistice was signed, *UB-116* sailed from Heligoland carrying eleven torpedoes; Captain Hans-Joachim Emsmann's intention was to enter Scapa Flow and torpedo as many moored battleships as he could. Unfortunately, Emsmann was badly advised on two counts. Six months earlier, the Grand Fleet had moved south to the Firth of Forth. In addition, Hoxa Sound, which he had been told was unguarded, was defended by hydrophones, which picked up the sound of approaching ships; by seabed cables, which caused a galvanometer needle to flick when an electric current was induced by the magnetic field of a crossing vessel; and by mines, which could be detonated electrically from the shore. This combination of defenses was too much for Emsmann to overcome and *UB-116* was efficiently and suddenly destroyed.*

The last British warship sunk was *Britannia,* a predreadnought battleship of the 16,500-ton *King Edward VII* class. Bound for Gibraltar on the morning of November 9, 1918—two days before the armistice was signed—the ship saw and managed to avoid two torpedoes before being struck by a third. She went down slowly and her crew was taken off by escorting destroyers. Three hours later, the battleship sank. From her resting place on the ocean floor, the nearest point of land is Cape Trafalgar.

*The rest of this story is told on p. 161.

CHAPTER 38

Finis Germaniae

The German gamble to win the war with an unrestricted U-boat offensive had failed. Britain did not starve and sue for peace, America joined the Allies, the blockade continued to reap its grim toll, and Germany was on the brink of physical and psychological exhaustion. Then, unexpectedly, the German Supreme Command was given one last chance. After the fall of the tsar, the provisional government had kept Russia in the war for another eight months, but the success of the Bolshevik coup d'état in November 1917 led to Russia's surrender. A million German and Austrian troops including fifty divisions of veteran infantry were released from the Eastern Front, and Ludendorff was offered another opportunity. Through the winter, trains carrying hundreds of thousands of German soldiers and 3,000 guns rumbled west across Germany. In the spring, for the first time since August 1914, the German army would have approximate numerical parity with the Allies on the Western Front. But this equivalence would be only temporary. Once the masses of American infantry now assembling in their training camps at home were transported across the Atlantic, the advantage Germany had gained by the defeat of Russia would be eliminated. It was clear to Ludendorff that he must strike before the Americans arrived.

In January 1918, on the eve of this last great German offensive, 6.5 million men faced one another on the Western Front. Allied soldiers numbered 3.9 million: 2.6 million French, 1.2 million British and empire troops, and 100,000 Belgians. Facing them were 2.5 million Germans, but by March 1918, with the addition of the million soldiers brought from the Russian front, Ludendorff would have 3.5 million men. The date set for the attack was March 21 and the kaiser assumed a victory. "If an English delegation came to sue for peace," he told his entourage, "it must first kneel before the German imperial standard, for this is a victory of monarchy over democracy."

—

All Germans had ridiculed the idea that an unmilitary nation like America could produce a large army. In addition, Germany's admirals had promised that, even if America adopted conscription, U-boats could prevent the passage of this army across 3,000 miles of ocean. In April 1917, when the United States entered the war, it seemed the Germans were right; there was then no unit in the U.S. Army larger than a regiment. In the first three weeks after war was declared, only 32,000 American men voluntarily enlisted. Then, on May 18, Congress passed a draft law, authorizing immediate expansion of the regular army to 488,000 men and the National Guard to 470,000. Nine million draft-eligible men registered on June 5; selection among them began on July 20, and 2,810,000 were ordered to report by September to training camps still being built. Meanwhile, on May 28, Major General John J. Pershing, the newly designated commander of the American Expeditionary Force, had left New York for Liverpool. On June 28, the first elements of his force—four regular army infantry regiments and one artillery regiment, newly combined into the 1st Division of the U.S. Army—landed at St. Nazaire and on the Fourth of July paraded before cheering crowds on the Champs-Elysées. Two days later, Pershing forwarded to Washington his appraisal of what would be required. "A force of about 1,000,000 men," he cabled the secretary of war, "is the smallest unit which in modern war will be a complete, well-balanced, and independent fighting organization." This might not be enough to win the war, Pershing said, but it was the number "which may be expected to reach France in time for an offensive in 1918."

At first, the Americans came slowly. By early November 1917, there were only 87,000 American soldiers in France. By the end of December, there were 175,000, including four complete divisions. These American divisions were huge—each had 25,000 to 28,000 men, including 16,000 riflemen; in contrast, the rifle strength of many French divisions was now down to 5,000 or 6,000 men. But the American soldiers arrived poorly trained and woefully ill-equipped with modern weapons of war—"naked so to speak," said a German staff analyst. Many units actually underwent basic training in France, learning from British and French instructors how to throw hand grenades, use machine guns, fire trench mortars and field artillery, do night signaling and wire-cutting, and prepare for gas attacks. Most of the heavy military equipment the Americans possessed was supplied by the French: 3,100 pieces of field artillery, 1,200 howitzers, 4,800 airplanes. By March 1918, when the United States had been at war for almost a year, the American army in France still numbered only 318,000 men. Only one division, the 1st, which had crossed the Atlantic the preceding June, was actually on line on the Western Front and it was assigned to a quiet sector of eastern France where its presence permitted the withdrawal of veteran French troops for use in the fighting zones.

—

The newspaper *Kölnische Zeitung,* sensing that Ludendorff's offensive would be the last great battle of the war, called it the *Kaiserschlacht,* the Kaiser's Battle. It was planned as a rolling series of blows designed to fall sequentially at different points along the Western Front. The first massive stroke, code-named Michael, fell on the British army on the northern part of the front on March 18, 1918. According to Winston Churchill, who was present behind the lines, "There was no surprise about the time or general direction of the attack. The surprise consisted in its weight, scale and power. . . . There rose in less than one minute the most tremendous cannonade I shall ever hear." Ten divisions of the British Fifth Army were shattered. By March 26, Ludendorff had penetrated thirty-seven miles through the British lines and was close to rupturing the French and British fronts at their point of juncture; this done, he could choose between rolling the British back to the Channel or driving the French before him toward Paris.* With the integrity of the whole Allied front threatened, unity of command from the Alps to the Channel became an imperative. On April 3, Ferdinand Foch, Chief of the French General Staff, was asked "to coordinate the action of the British and French armies" and on April 14, he was formally appointed Supreme Commander of all Allied armies on the Western Front. In this crisis, Pershing offered his Americans: "Infantry, artillery, aviation—all that we have are yours; use them as you wish." In fact, Pershing possessed little artillery or aviation, but he did have infantry and the Allies reached for it eagerly. By the end of April, 302,000 British soldiers, more than a quarter of the British army in France, had been killed, wounded, or taken prisoner; German losses were equally heavy: between March 21 and April 10, the Germans lost 349,000 men.

In the days that followed, a glimmer of hope was provided by the arrival in April of another 119,000 Americans in France; by the end of that month, the American Expeditionary Force numbered 430,000 men. More arrived in

*On March 23, 1918, the third day of Ludendorff's offensive, a shell fired by a massive gun seventy-five miles away exploded on No. 6, Quai de Seine in Paris. This shell, which had soared twenty-four miles above the earth before descending, was the first of 367 projectiles fired at the French capital over the next four and a half months by a gun the Allies called Big Bertha and the Germans the Paris Gun. Its most spectacular success came on Good Friday, March 29, when a shell hit the Church of St. Gervais in central Paris, killing eighty-eight worshipers and wounding sixty-eight. The weapon had no military value; its purpose, like that of the zeppelin raids on Britain, was to inspire terror. Germans justified its use as retaliation for the blockade.

May; by June 1, there were 650,000 American soldiers in France. In June, another 279,000 came and in July still another 250,000, so that by July 31, more than a million American soldiers were on the continent of Europe. And millions more were on the way; the success of Ludendorff's spring offensive had inspired Wilson to authorize creation of an army of eighty divisions numbering 4 million men. The immediate question was how the American soldiers already in France were to be used. The British saw in the packed infantry of the large American divisions the replacements needed to rebuild the ten British divisions shattered by Ludendorff. Pershing, despite his impulsive gesture of March 26, was adamantly opposed to amalgamation. Unlike Sims, who was willing to use the American navy as a pool from which Allied navies could draw reinforcements, Pershing was committed to the creation of an independent American army that—once enough American divisions had been trained—would operate in its own sector of the line under his command. Field Marshal Haig, the British Commander-in-Chief in France, considered Pershing's attitude "obstinate" and "stupid," but Marshal Joseph Joffre—old "Papa Joffre," the hero of the Marne in 1914—agreed with Pershing that attempting to mesh American troops into Allied formations would be a mistake. "There would be an adverse effect," he told Pershing. "American battalions would find themselves commanded by a British general with a British staff. They would resent orders received under such circumstances, [orders] which they would accept without question under an American commander. In case of a reverse, there would be the tendency to blame the command. There must also be considered the effect on the American people." Nevertheless, as Ludendorff continued to hammer the Allied armies, and Allied generals and politicians pleaded desperately for the integration of arriving American manpower into existing veteran British and French units, Pershing gave ground, permitting American troops to be loaned to foreign commanders but only in units of at least divisional size. Always, he emphasized that once enough American divisions were trained and ready to fight, he wanted them back to fight under his command in a sector of the battlefront that would be strictly American.

Ludendorff had calculated in March that the Americans could not reach the front in sufficient numbers to make a difference until midsummer. At the beginning of May, he still believed that he had three months, May, June, and July, to win the war. On May 27, he hurled another thunderbolt, this time at the French sector of the front, advanced forty miles, and reached the Marne east of Château-Thierry. On May 31, the Germans crossed the river and seized a bridgehead fifty-six miles from Paris. Soissons fell and Amiens and Rheims were threatened; on June 1, the French government began preparing to leave Paris for Bordeaux. In this new crisis, when General Henri Philippe Pétain asked Pershing for help, two American divisions were ordered to the front. Suddenly, in Churchill's words, "the roads . . . began to be filled with endless streams of Americans . . . [an] inexhaustible flood of gleaming youth . . . crammed in their lorries . . . singing the songs of a new world at the tops of their voices . . . arriving in floods to reanimate the mangled body of a France bled white by the innumerable wounds of four years." On June 2, the American 2nd and 3rd Divisions joined in an Allied counterattack along the Marne. At Belleau Wood, an overgrown former hunting preserve, the 2nd Division, which contained a brigade of U.S. Marines, cleared a square mile of dense wilderness that seemed to have a machine gun behind every tree. The Marines suffered 5,200 casualties, but earned a compliment from a staff officer of the German Seventh Army: "The moral effect of our own gunfire cannot seriously impede the advance of the American infantry."

By the end of June, time was running out on Ludendorff. American divisions were regularly being fed into the active battle; by mid-July, six were at the front and another twelve were in the line or in reserve in quiet sectors. Seven more were in training in France and fifty-five were assembling in the United States. And given the dense mass of American infantry in these units, the twenty-five American divisions already in France equaled fifty British, French, or German divisions.

The final blow of the *Kaiserschlacht* was launched on July 15, when Ludendorff attacked between Rheims and Soissons. Six German spearheads crossed the Marne and advanced four miles, but then were stopped in their tracks. Two days later, Foch counterattacked on the western side of the Marne salient with twenty-three divisions including five double-strength American divisions. On the night of July 18, Ludendorff ordered the German troops that had crossed the Marne three days before to retreat across the river. Three weeks later, in the north, the British army, which had not been heavily engaged in three months and now was reinforced to a strength of sixty divisions, began its offensive. On August 8, a British, Canadian, and Australian attack, spearheaded by 600 tanks rolling through fields of ripening wheat, advanced seven miles the first day and captured thousands of prisoners and hundreds of guns. German morale was shattered; retreating troops shouted, "You're prolonging the war," at fresh units coming up. "August 8 was the black day of the German Army in the history of this war," Ludendorff said later. In the 120 days following March 21, the German offensive had inflicted 448,000 casualties on the British army and 490,000 on the French. The Americans had lost 9,685 dead and wounded. But the German army, which had no reserves on which to draw, had suffered 963,000 casualties. "The war," Ludendorff announced, "must be ended."

During July, the American army in France had increased by another 306,000 men, bringing the total in France to 1.3 million. On July 24, Pershing finally achieved his personal goal, command of an American army in the field, when he signed an order creating the First Army, American Expeditionary Force, which would become operational on August 10. On September 12, fifteen American divisions and five French and French colonial divisions, all under Pershing's command, attacked the Saint-Mihiel salient, a 200-square-mile protrusion jutting thirteen miles west into the Allied line south of Verdun. The Germans already were abandoning the salient and the Americans captured it within two days, along with 13,000 prisoners. On September 26, Pershing launched the largest American offensive of the war: 550,000 Americans and 110,000 French and French colonial troops plunged into the woods, ravines, streams, and gulches of the Meuse-Argonne, driving north toward Sedan. Meanwhile, in September, 257,000 more Americans arrived in France; another 180,000 were due to arrive in October. Ultimately, 2.08 million men of the AEF crossed the Atlantic.

The American army did not defeat the German army in 1918, nor was it the fighting ability of American soldiers that persuaded the German government to seek an armistice. Casualty figures best reveal who fought the Great War: 1.7 million French soldiers died, as did 1.7 million Russians, 1 million from the British empire, 460,000 Italians, 340,000 Rumanians, Belgians, and Serbs, and 116,000 Americans. And on the other side, 2 million Germans, 1.5 million from Austria-Hungary, 350,000 Turks, and 95,000 Bulgarians. Essentially, it was not important how well the new American army fought; what was decisive was that these enthusiastic, green American soldiers were pouring into Europe in a massive, endless torrent. Their arrival had the same demoralizing effect on the German Supreme Command as on the average German soldier. In four years of war, Germans had defeated the Russians and the Rumanians and had held at bay the combined armies of the French and British empires, But now they were confronted by an entirely new enemy with (for practical purposes) unlimited resources. This dire situation was a direct result of the colossal misjudgment made by Germany's military and naval leaders in authorizing unrestricted submarine warfare. Ultimately, the American army came to France, not just in spite of the U-boats, but because of them.

—

"You don't know Ludendorff, who is only great at a time of success," Bethmann-Hollweg once told a colleague. "If things go badly, he loses his nerve." This characteristic was strikingly apparent on July 18 as Foch stunned German Supreme Headquarters with his first powerful counterattack. Hindenburg proposed a maneuver to deal with the French offensive. "Then, all of a sudden, General Ludendorff joined in the conversation," said a staff officer who was present. "He declared that anything of that sort was utterly unfeasible and must therefore be forgotten as he thought he had already made abundantly clear to the field marshal. The field marshal left the table without a word of reply and General Ludendorff departed, clearly annoyed and scarlet in the face." The confrontation resumed later that day. "This is how we must direct the counterattack; that would solve the crisis at once," Hindenburg declared.

"At this General Ludendorff straightened up from the map and with an expression of rage on his face turned towards the door letting out one or two words like 'Madness!' in profound irritation. The field marshal followed and said to him, 'I should like a word with you.' "

After the "Black Day" of August 8, Ludendorff ricocheted among panic, indiscriminate rage, and cheerful, irrational optimism. Alarmed, his staff arranged for a psychiatrist to visit. At the end of his interview, Dr. Hocheimer told Ludendorff that he was "overworked" and that his "drive and creative power had been damaged." Ludendorff nodded, agreeing with this analysis. On August 14, only six days after the "Black Day," Ludendorff and Hindenburg met the kaiser, Chancellor von Hertling, the crown prince, and the thirty-year-old Austrian emperor, Karl, at the Hôtel Britannique in Spa, Belgium. Karl had come to announce that Austria could not continue the war through the winter; "We are absolutely finished," he said. But Ludendorff, overruling the idea of absolute finality, proposed, instead, "gradually paralyzing the enemy's will to fight by a strategic defensive," a policy and a phrase that, the German historian Fritz Fischer has pointed out, contain "almost incomprehensible contradictions." In essence, Ludendorff was admitting that the war could not be won, but asserting that if a defensive front could be maintained, Germany might still be able to keep Belgium and Luxembourg, and Austria might salvage her multiethnic empire. To achieve this "strategic defensive," Ludendorff demanded help to bolster the Western Front; Emperor Karl, diverted from his original purpose, found himself promising to send Austrian divisions to France. Hindenburg closed the conference by saying, "I hope that we shall be able to make a stand on French soil and thus in the end to impose our will on the enemy." A different appraisal of the situation came a few days later from army group commander Crown Prince Rupprecht of Bavaria, who wrote to Prince Max of Baden, "By the mistaken operation beyond the Marne and the series of heavy reverses which followed—absolutely fatal both materially and morally—our military situation has deteriorated so rapidly that I no longer believe we can hold out over the winter. It is even possible that a catastrophe will come earlier."

Emperor Karl returned to Vienna, and on September 10—"like lightning out of a clear sky"—reverted to his original intention and addressed an Austrian peace offer to the United States. It did no good; Secretary of State Lansing immediately rejected the note. On September 20, the Social Democrats in the German Reichstag demanded that Chancellor von Hertling ask for an immediate armistice on the basis of no annexations and the complete democratization of the German political system. On September 27, Bulgaria pleaded for an armistice, offering to demobilize her army and restore all conquered territory. Meanwhile, in the Hôtel Britannique at Spa, Ludendorff's maps were pinned to the walls of his suite one floor above Hindenburg's; there, on the afternoon of September 28, Ludendorff disintegrated. Trembling, he began to storm against the kaiser, the government, and the politicians in the Reichstag. His staff closed the door to muffle his ranting until he gradually subsided. At six that evening, still pale, Ludendorff descended to Hindenburg's suite to explain his reasons for demanding an immediate armistice. He believed that in the west Germany would have to accept Wilson's Fourteen Points, but that in the east the immense booty of the Brest-Litovsk treaty with the Soviets might still be kept. The next day, the kaiser, Chancellor von Hertling, and Foreign Minister Paul von Hintze arrived at the Britannique. Ludendorff, again in control, brusquely announced that an armistice must be concluded "at once, as early as possible"; it would be best to arrange it within twenty-four hours. The kaiser, Hertling, and Hintze were dumbfounded; the only way to end the fighting so quickly would be to surrender. Nevertheless, William agreed that Wilson should be approached about an armistice. For the seventy-five-year-old Hertling, this was too much: he resigned. On October 1, the kaiser asked his own cousin Prince Max, heir to the Grand Duchy of Baden, to become chancellor and to seek an immediate armistice. Max accepted, but said that negotiations would take time; he begged for "ten, eight, or even four days before I have to appeal to the enemy." Ludendorff, saying, "I want to save my army," bombarded Prince Max with telegrams—six on a single day—and attempted to hurry the kaiser. "I am not a magician," William testily replied. "You should have told me that fourteen days ago." On October 4, King Ferdinand of Bulgaria abdicated and fled to Vienna. On October 5, Prince Max sent a note to Wilson via Switzerland, accepting the president's Fourteen Points as a basis for negotiations. Lansing replied on Wilson's behalf on October 8, demanding prompt German evacuation of all occupied territory in France and Belgium as a preliminary to an armistice and a guarantee of good faith. On October 12, Germany pledged do this. During these days, the Allied armies rolled forward all along the line in France and the Flemish coast. On October 17, Ostend and, on October 19, Zeebrugge were evacuated by the Germans after four years of occupation, forcing the German navy to blow up four U-boats and five destroyers that could not be made ready to sail.

Meanwhile, continuing war at sea threatened to upset the momentum toward peace. On October 4, the passenger vessel *Hirano Maru* was torpedoed off the coast of Ireland with the loss of 292 lives. On October 10, a twenty-two-year-old German U-boat captain torpedoed the Irish mail steamer *Leinster* and then torpedoed her again while she was sinking. Of the 720 people on board, 176 drowned, including women and children. On October 14, Wilson, through Lansing, demanded the end of the U-boat campaign and announced that neither the United States nor its allies "will consent to consider an armistice so long as the armed forces of Germany continue their illegal and inhuman practices. . . . At the very time the German government approaches the United States with proposals of peace, its submarines are engaged in sinking passenger ships at sea—and not the ships alone, but the very boats in which the passengers and crews seek to make their way to safety." Balfour was more succinct: "Brutes they were and brutes they remain."

Command of the German navy was now in new hands. On August 11, Admiral von Holtzendorff, suffering from severe heart disease, had been replaced as Chief of the Naval Staff by Scheer, who, in turn, handed over the High Seas Fleet to Hipper. Scheer promptly moved Naval Staff headquarters from Berlin to Spa; there, he could coordinate policy more closely with Ludendorff, whom he admired. Defying the reality that the war was almost over, Scheer refused to give up on the unrestricted submarine campaign and immediately demanded a preposterous crash program to build 450 new submarines at a rate of thirty-six a month. When Wilson insisted on termination of the unrestricted submarine campaign, Scheer and Ludendorff joined in fierce opposition. "The navy does not need an armistice," Scheer declared on October 16, while Ludendorff said the next day, "To allow ourselves to be deprived of our submarine weapon would amount to capitulation." The two warriors lost this battle. Prince Max, by threatening to resign, obtained an order from the kaiser and, on October 20, Germany renounced the submarine campaign against merchant shipping. Ludendorff later complained that this "concession to Wilson was the heaviest blow to the army and especially to the navy. The cabinet had thrown in the sponge." On October 21, Scheer, angry at being overridden, recalled all submarines at sea and placed them at the disposal of the High Seas Fleet commander for action against Allied warships. After twenty-one months, Germany's unrestricted U-boat campaign was over.

On October 17, at a conference in Berlin, Ludendorff suddenly denied that he had ever demanded an armistice within twenty-four hours and declared that Germany possessed sufficient strength to keep fighting. On October 23, Wilson added a new condition for peace: the kaiser's removal. If the United States government "must deal with the military masters and monarchical autocrats of Germany," the president said, "it must demand, not peace negotiations, but surrender." Hearing this, William and his wife, Dona, approached hysteria. "The hypocritical Wilson has at last thrown off the mask," William announced. "The object of this is to bring down my House, to set the monarchy aside." The empress raged at "the audacity of the *parvenu* across the sea who thus dares to humiliate a princely house which can look back on centuries of service to people and country." Ludendorff rebelled against Wilson's military conditions, saying that they went far beyond the simple battlefield armistice he was seeking. On October 24, defying the authority of the chancellor, he issued a proclamation to the army, countersigned by Hindenburg. Wilson's proposals, he declared, are "a demand for unconditional surrender [and are] thus unacceptable to us as soldiers." Prince Max, enraged by this insubordination, again gave the kaiser a choice: Ludendorff or himself. On October 26, William summoned Hindenburg and Ludendorff to Bellevue Castle in Berlin. Speaking first to Ludendorff, William upbraided the general for countersigning a proclamation to the army that was in direct conflict with the policy of the chancellor and the government. Ludendorff immediately offered his resignation, which William accepted. Clicking his heels, the soldier who had dominated Germany for twenty-six months departed. Hindenburg subsequently offered his own resignation, but was curtly told, "You stay." Afterward, William was happy. The "Siamese twins," he declared, were now separated. Outside the castle, Ludendorff, furious that Hindenburg had not resigned with him, would not accompany the field marshal back to the General Staff building. "I refuse to drive with you," he said. When Hindenburg asked why, Ludendorff replied, "I refuse to have any more dealings with you because you treat me so shabbily."

On October 27, Germany accepted all of Wilson's conditions. On October 29, Austria-Hungary agreed to an armistice with Italy and, on November 2, with the rest of the Allied powers. On October 31, Turkey left the war. That afternoon, Prince Max, stricken with influenza, was given a massive dose of sleeping drops and slid into two days of unconsciousness.

—

With the German empire in its death throes, two groups in the German navy, first the admirals, then the seamen, took matters into their own hands. The submarine weapon had been sheathed but the High Seas Fleet remained a powerful force. Enraged by the U-boat decision, Scheer and the Naval Staff decided to use the surface ships in one last offensive thrust, a bold variation on earlier unsuccessful attempts to lure the Grand Fleet over a U-boat ambush. The difference this time was that the Germans intended to fight a battle whether or not the U-boats had managed to reduce the Grand Fleet's numerical superiority. Further, the German admirals did not care whether the High Seas Fleet won or lost; they cared only that it inflict heavy damage on the Grand Fleet. Hipper agreed with Scheer that "an honorable battle by the fleet—even if it should be a fight to the death—will sow the seed for a new German fleet of the future." Besides preserving honor, a battle that inflicted severe damage on the Grand Fleet might also influence the peace negotiations in Germany's favor.

The operation was set in motion on October 22 when Captain Magnus von Levetzow of the Naval Staff Operations Department came to Wilhelmshaven and orally gave Scheer's order to Hipper: "The High Seas Fleet is directed to attack the English fleet as soon as possible." Nothing was put in writing, for two reasons: first, Scheer wished to keep the plan secret from the British; second, knowing the impact the operation would have on armistice negotiations, he wished to hide it also from the German government in Berlin. Neither the kaiser nor the chancellor was informed. Scheer explained later that he had already mentioned to the kaiser that giving up submarine warfare meant that the surface fleet would again have "complete freedom of action." The kaiser had not reacted and Scheer seized upon William's silence as tacit approval. Subsequently, Scheer defended himself more boldly: "I did not regard it [as] necessary to obtain a repetition of the kaiser's approval. In addition, I feared that this could cause further delay and was thus prepared to act on my own responsibility." Prince Max said later that if he had known of Scheer's plan, he would have approved it, but at the time he was given no chance to approve or disapprove. "I specifically reiterate that I did not recognize the chancellor's competence over operational measures and for that reason I did not seek his approval," Scheer declared.

Hipper issued his tactical orders on October 24. The entire High Seas Fleet would leave Heligoland Bight at night and advance into the southern part of the North Sea. The force would be more powerful than that commanded by Scheer at Jutland: Hipper would bring five battle cruisers, eighteen dreadnought battleships, twelve light cruisers, and seventy-two destroyers. The purpose of the operation was to lure the Grand Fleet over freshly laid minefields and six lines of waiting U-boats into the southern North Sea, where the High Seas Fleet would be waiting to engage whatever British warships survived the passage south. To create this lure, German light cruisers and destroyers would launch provocative raids along the Belgian coast and into the Thames estuary. Specifically, one destroyer flotilla supported by three light cruisers would bombard the coast of Flanders, which had been abandoned by the German army a week before, while five destroyers and seven light cruisers attacked shipping in the Thames estuary. The Flanders bombardment would be supported by Hipper's battle fleet of eighteen dreadnought battleships escorted by forty-three destroyers, while the Thames attack was to be covered by five German battle cruisers including the new *Hindenburg*. After the raids, the retiring squadrons and flotillas would retreat to the Dutch coast, where the entire High Seas Fleet would concentrate. There, Hipper expected to meet the Grand Fleet coming down from the north and to bring it to action on the evening of the second day, October 31. If, by some mischance, the two battle fleets did not meet, all available German destroyers were to break away and sweep north toward the Firth of Forth. If the British fleet was found, the destroyers were instructed to launch their torpedoes in mass volleys, no less than three from each destroyer at a single time. The operation, for all its "death ride," Götterdämmerung appearance, was well planned and stood a chance of success—at least, as success was defined by Scheer and Hipper. Both admirals hoped that, in addition to salvaging the honor of the German navy, "a tactical success might reverse the military position and avert surrender."

On October 27, Scheer approved Hipper's plan and the operation was set for October 30. Twenty-two U-boats took positions along the Grand Fleet's probable line of advance from Scotland; one of these was *UB-116,* which would be blown up by shore-controlled mines while trying to enter Scapa Flow. The surface ships of the High Seas Fleet began to assemble in Schillig roads on the afternoon of October 29, with the sortie scheduled for dawn the next day. The admirals had not reckoned, however, on the war-weariness and defeatism of the German crews. Rumors of the impending operation and the words "suicide mission" were spreading from mouth to mouth and ship to ship. On October 27, when light cruisers of the 4th Scouting Group were ordered to load mines at Cuxhaven, forty-five stokers from *Strassburg* hid themselves in the dockyard. When the battle cruisers passed through the locks from Wilhelmshaven's inner harbor into the roadstead, 300 men from *Derfflinger* and *Von der Tann* climbed over the side and disappeared ashore.

The arrival in the anchorage of three battleship squadrons from other naval bases gave substance to the rumor that the fleet was about to go out to seek a glorious end off the coast of England. Unlike the admirals and officers, the seamen had no intention of being sacrificed for honor's sake. Not only could they see no point in defeat and meaningless death, but they regarded the operation as a deliberate attempt to sabotage negotiations to end a war already lost. When one *Markgraf* seaman jumped on a turret and called for three cheers for President Wilson, a deck crowded with men roared approval. Insubordination welled up on *König, Kronprinz Wilhelm, Kaiserin, Thüringen,* and *Helgoland.* On all these ships, seamen had no interest in "an honorable death for the glory of the fleet"; they wanted surrender, discharge, and permission to go home.

A red sunset on the evening of October 29 turned the calm waters of the anchorage crimson. About 7:00 p.m., the wind came up, bringing a series of rain squalls. Hipper summoned his admirals and captains on board his flagship, *Baden,* for a final briefing. The conference was delayed because on *Thüringen* the crew made trouble about the captain's boat leaving the ship. At first, Hipper tried to disregard news of these disturbances, but at 10:00 p.m., he changed his mind and decided that the fleet was not ready to sail. Next morning, when the destroyer crews learned of the disturbances on the battleships, they asked to continue alone with the planned operation. Hipper considered this possibility, but when he heard that the trouble had spread to *Friedrich der Grosse* and *König Albert* and that the disturbances on *Thüringen* and *Helgoland* had developed into full-scale mutinies, he decided that he had no choice but to cancel the entire operation. To prevent the spread of mutiny, he ordered the dreadnought squadrons dispersed to Kiel, Cuxhaven, and Wilhelmshaven.

Thüringen and *Helgoland* remained behind. When their crews still refused orders, Hipper ordered marines to arrest them. Two steamers carrying 250 heavily armed marines approached the battleships, while a submarine and five destroyers, their torpedo tubes loaded, cleared for action at point-blank range. The mutineers surrendered and were taken to prison in Wilhelmshaven. Meanwhile, however, Hipper's dispersal of the fleet, instead of quarantining the disloyal groups, served only to spread the infection. The 3rd Battle Squadron—*König, Kronprinz Wilhelm, Kaiserin,* and *Markgraf*—reached Kiel on November 1 with many seamen in irons. On arrival, 4,000 sailors paraded in the streets and demanded release of the prisoners. Workers' and Sailors' Councils were formed and on November 4 took control of the port. The battleship *König* had gone into dry dock with the flag of the Imperial Navy still flying. On November 5, when a sailor attempted to replace the flag with a red banner, the ship's captain shot him dead near the mast. The response was rifle fire from buildings overlooking the ship, which wounded the captain and killed two officers. Later that day a band of sailors invaded the residence in Kiel Castle of Grand Admiral Prince Henry of Prussia, the kaiser's brother and Commander-in-Chief of the Baltic Fleet. Henry fled, escaping from Kiel driving a truck that flew a red flag. By the end of the first week of November, mutiny had become revolution. Thirty-five thousand armed sailors crowded the streets of Wilhelmshaven, Workers' and Soldiers' Councils had been established in the port city, and briefly there existed a Republic of Oldenburg with Leading Stoker Bernhard Kuhnt as president. On November 9, when the red flag was hoisted on Hipper's flagship *Baden,* the Commander-in-Chief of the High Seas Fleet silently packed his bags and went ashore. Groups of sailors streamed out of Kiel and Wilhelmshaven by truck, train, and ship and raised red flags in naval harbors along the North Sea and Baltic coasts. Then came the great commercial ports of Hamburg and Bremen and, as revolution spread across Germany, interior cities such as Cologne, Hanover, Frankfurt, Dresden, Munich, and, eventually, Berlin.

—

On Friday morning, November 8, Marshal Foch, representing all Allied armies, and the First Sea Lord, Admiral Wemyss, representing the Allied navies, waited on a train parked on a siding in the forest of Compiègne for the arrival of Germany's armistice delegation. While a cold rain fell on the oak trees outside, Foch assured Wemyss that if the Germans refused to agree to Allied armistice terms, he could force the capitulation of the entire German army within three weeks. At 7:00 a.m. a train carrying the German delegates, led by the Reichstag leader, Matthias Erzberger, rolled into another siding 200 yards away. Other than the French sentries in blue-gray uniforms pacing under the trees, there was nothing in sight but rain and falling leaves.

The meeting began at 9:00 a.m. and Foch presented the Allies' terms. The naval demands included demilitarization of Heligoland, all nations to be given access to the Kaiser Wilhelm Canal, surrender of all submarines and internment of Germany's ten latest battleships, six battle cruisers, eight light cruisers, and fifty most modern destroyers. Failure to execute any of these terms would allow the Allies to resume the war within forty-eight hours. Meanwhile, until the treaty of peace was actually signed, the blockade of Germany would remain in force. The German naval representative, Captain Vanselow, protested that internment of the German fleet could not be accepted because the fleet had never been beaten. Grimly, Wemyss replied that if that was what was needed, the German fleet had only to come out. When Wemyss asked for 160 submarines, Vaneslow replied that there were not nearly 160 to be had. This gave Wemyss the chance to demand what he really wanted: *all* German submarines. The meeting was adjourned so that the German delegation could communicate these terms to Berlin.

—

On November 9, even as Foch was dictating terms to Erzberger, Admiral Scheer informed the kaiser that he could no longer rely on the navy. "My dear admiral," William replied, "I no longer have a navy." In fact, he was losing far more than that. Before the end of that day, William had abdicated, both as German emperor and as King of Prussia, and the establishment of a German republic had been proclaimed from a balcony of the Reichstag building. Early the following morning, William was persuaded to leave Spa for the Netherlands, thirty miles away, where he had been offered refuge in Kasteel Amerongen, the home of the Dutch-English Count Godard Bentinck. On the journey through a driving rain, William was silent. But when the car pulled up in the rain before the main entrance of the moated seventeenth-century château, he gave a deep sigh of relief. "Now," he said to Count Bentinck, rubbing his hands together, "you must let me have a cup of real, good, hot, strong English tea." Instead of English tea, he got a real Scots high tea: Amerongen had a Scots housekeeper, and soon a teapot and a tray of biscuits, scones, and shortbread were set before Queen Victoria's eldest grandson.

—

A week later, on November 16, Erich Ludendorff disguised himself with a false beard and a pair of blue spectacles and sneaked away to Denmark. Recognized in Copenhagen, he fled again, this time to Sweden, where he lived for three months in a country house near Stockholm before returning to Germany. He met Adolf Hitler and in 1923 marched at his side in the unsuccessful Munich Beer Hall Putsch. In 1924, Ludendorff was elected to the Reichstag as a Nazi deputy and in 1925, Hitler persuaded him to run for president of Germany. Of 24 million votes cast, Ludendorff received 280,000.

—

The German delegation returned to Compiègne on Sunday, November 10, and was received at midnight. At 5:10 a.m. on November 11—the 1,586th day of the Great War—the weary delegates finally signed the document ending hostilities that day at 11 a.m. Before signing, Erzberger looked at Foch and said, "The German people, who stood steadfast against a world of enemies for fifty months, will preserve their freedom and unity no matter how great the external pressure. A people of seventy millions may suffer but it cannot die." Steadily gazing back, Foch said, *"Très bien."*

That afternoon, in the Firth of Forth, the Grand Fleet Commander-in-Chief ordered all ships to "splice the main brace"—to serve the men an extra ration of rum. The exceptions to Beatty's order were the American ships, which were dry. At seven that night, the men in the anchorage were deafened by a continuous din of foghorns, sirens, and steam whistles. Sky rockets and colored signal bombs burst in the air, while searchlight beams swept across water and sky, finding and fixing on White Ensigns and American flags. On the big ships, bands played and sailors mobbed sacrosanct quarterdecks. *Queen Elizabeth*'s crew came in a body to the admiral's cabin where Beatty and his staff were sitting down to dinner. "For He's a Jolly Good Fellow" rose from hundreds of throats. The men invited the officers to dance, and captains, commanders, and lieutenants waltzed, fox-trotted, and did the military polka with seamen and marines until two o'clock in the morning. At one point, a picket boat from *Inflexible* came alongside *New York* to take a group of American officers to the battle cruiser where they could drink champagne.

—

It was agreed by all the Allied powers that the entire German submarine fleet would be surrendered with no possibility of return. The British and French governments also wanted the German surface fleet surrendered to the Allies. The Americans were less eager for this; they did not want the ships, but preferred that neither the British nor the French have them. Instead, the United States proposed temporary internment of the surface vessels in neutral ports until a final decision was made at the peace conference. This course was adopted and two neutral governments, Norway and Spain, were approached. Both declined to receive the German ships, now seething with mutiny. Accordingly, the Allied Naval Council accepted Wemyss's suggestion that all seventy-four surface ships be interned at Scapa Flow under the supervision of the Grand Fleet. There, German skeleton crews would remain on board because, under international law, interned ships still belonged to the German government. Little time was allowed for delivery. If the ships designated for internment were not ready to sail on November 18, the Allies said, Heligoland would be occupied. On the night of November 12, a radio message from Beatty requested that a German flag officer come to the Firth of Forth to make arrangements. The next afternoon, Hipper's representative, Rear Admiral Hugo Meurer, left Wilhelmshaven for Scotland on the new light cruiser *Königsberg.*

At seven o'clock on the evening of November 15, Meurer and four other German officers walked up the gangplank of *Queen Elizabeth.* Around them, a black night and thick fog in the Firth of Forth hid the shapes and lights of the rows of dreadnoughts near Beatty's flagship. Reaching the quarterdeck, Meurer was received in silence by two British officers assigned to escort him to the Commander-in-Chief. Powerful electric lights created a path across the quarterdeck to Beatty's quarters; outside the path everything was darkness, but along its edge stood a line of marine sentries, light gleaming off the steel of their fixed bayonets. Beatty and his officers sat at a large dining room table with their backs to a wall hung with prints of Nelson's victories. On the table was a small bronze lion, a reminder of the admiral's years with the battle cruisers. When the Germans entered, Beatty stood and, looking straight at Meurer, said, "Who are you?" "Rear Admiral Hugo Meurer," the German replied. "Have you been sent by Admiral von Hipper to arrange the details for carrying out the terms of the armistice which refer to the surrender of the German fleet?" Beatty asked. "Yes," said Meurer. "Where are your credentials?" Beatty asked. These were produced, and Beatty said, "Pray be seated." Beatty then read his prepared instructions. "They were greatly depressed," Beatty wrote afterward to Eugenie, "and I kept feeling sorry for them, but kept repeating to myself, *Lusitania,* Belgian atrocities, British prisoners of war. . . . Meurer, in a voice like lead with an ashen grey face, said, 'I do not think the Commander-in-Chief is aware of the condition of Germany,' and then began to describe the effect of the blockade. Germany was destroyed utterly. I said to myself thank God for the British navy and told them to return with their answers in the morning." Meurer then informed Beatty that three delegates of the Sailors' and Workers' Council were on board *Königsberg* and insisted on accompanying him and taking part in the discussions. "I naturally said I knew them not and did not intend to know them better," Beatty reported, telling Meurer that no one but the German admiral and his staff would be allowed to leave *Königsberg.* This "seemed a source of relief to the stricken party." At 9:00 p.m., the Germans stepped back into the darkness to begin the twelve-mile trip to their ship. Beatty went to bed "and was nearly sick."

The following morning, the Germans returned two hours late because of what Beatty described as "the thickest fog I have ever seen in the Firth of Forth." It was arranged that the U-boats would surrender to Tyrwhitt at Harwich and the surface ships to Beatty in the Firth of Forth, from where they would proceed to Scapa Flow for internment. Meurer asked for extensions of time, pleading that German seamen would not bring the ships over. "The men will not obey. . . . I have now no authority. . . . We must have food." Meurer "prated about the honor of their submarine crews being possibly assailed," Beatty told Eugenie. "It nearly lifted me out of my chair. I scathingly replied that their personal safety would be assured." It was a long day; the Germans remained on board until midnight. Finally, when it came to signing the required documents, Beatty thought Meurer "would collapse. He took two shots at it, putting his pen down twice [before he signed]." Before leaving the British flagship, the Germans were given a meal. "I saw a leg of mutton being taken in for the five officers," said Ernle Chatfield, now the captain of *Queen Elizabeth.* Afterward, a steward told him, "They left nothing but the bone, sir!" As the Germans were leaving, a marine guard saw a German officer look around nervously and then stuff something inside his greatcoat. The officer was confronted and a large piece of cheddar cheese was found in his pocket.

The first defeated German warships to appear in British waters were the U-boats. During fifty-one months of war, German submarines had sunk a total of 5,282 British, Allied, and neutral merchant ships totaling 11,153,000 tons at the cost of 178 U-boats and 511 officers and 4,576 men. Three hundred and ninety-two submarines had been built before and during the war; therefore, the loss rate was almost 50 percent. At the time of the armistice, the German navy still possessed 194 U-boats, with a further 149 under construction. Britain wanted them all destroyed. Harwich had been designated as the port of surrender and Tyrwhitt was assigned to supervise the operation. When the Harwich Force cruisers and destroyers weighed anchor on November 20 and steamed to a rendevous point off Lowestoft, all hands were at action stations; Tyrwhitt was taking no chances. Out of the morning mist, a German transport that was to take the submarine crews back to Germany appeared, followed in a single line by twenty of the latest U-boats. Tyrwhitt had instructed his men that strict silence must be maintained when passing close to a U-boat and that there must be absolutely no cheering. Nevertheless, as one officer watched "the low-lying, sinister forms of U-boats emerge from the mist," his feelings overwhelmed him. He likened the moment to being in Piccadilly and "seeing twenty man-eating tigers walk up from Hyde Park Corner and lie down in front of the Ritz to let you cut off their tails and put their leads on." Tyrwhitt's force steamed past the submarines, detaching destroyers as they went so that each five U-boats had a destroyer in front and one on each beam. About 10 a.m., this line of ships reached a second rendezvous where two destroyers waited with British prize crews to put aboard the U-boats. The submarines anchored under the guns of the British destroyers; motor launches carried the British prize crews from the destroyers to the submarines. The boarding parties, each consisting of two or three armed officers and fifteen men, hoisted the White Ensign over the German flag. The German captains then were required to sign assurances that their boats were in an efficient condition, with torpedoes on board but torpedo warheads removed, and that no booby traps or other unpleasant surprises had been left aboard. The German crews, having been told that they would be taken into a British port, concluded that they were about to be paraded through the streets. Once assured that this was not so, they became communicative and helpful, explaining the intricacies of their boats to the British officers. "In nearly every case," said Commander Stephen King-Hall, "the German officers seemed anxious to assist in every way possible and give as much information concerning the working of the boat as was feasible." As each submarine proceeded into Harwich harbor with a prize crew in control and the German crew lined up on the forward deck, it passed through a swarm of small boats, crowded with spectators. Despite this assembly, Tyrwhitt's order was obeyed and there was complete silence. At 4:00 p.m., a motor launch came alongside each U-boat, the Germans gathered their personal belongings, the German captain saluted, the salute was returned, and the Germans were taken to the transport ship waiting outside. Behind, "as the sun sank in a splendour of crimson and gold, the long line of twenty U-boats, harmlessly swinging around their buoys, reflecting the last rays of the sun from their conning towers, made a picture which will remain forever in the minds of . . . [those who saw them]."

For the next eleven days, this remarkable procession continued. On November 21, the second day, nineteen more U-boats came over; a twentieth sank or was scuttled in passage. On the third day, twenty-one submarines arrived. One German captain told a British officer that, eight months after the sinking of *Lusitania,* his submarine had been within 400 yards of *Mauretania,* the destroyed liner's sister, with all his tubes ready to fire, but, owing to the crisis involving the United States, he had not fired. And that, on his return to Germany, he had received a personal letter from the kaiser commending him for his discretion. On November 24, twenty-eight submarines came over; on the twenty-seventh, twenty-seven more arrived, including *U-9,* which had sunk *Aboukir, Hogue,* and *Cressy* four years before. On December 1, the arrival of eight more U-boats brought the total number delivered to 123. Meanwhile, another nine had been interned in neutral ports. This left Germany with sixty-two seaworthy U-boats and construction continuing on another 149. When these numbers were ascertained in December by the Allied Naval Council, an ultimatum was issued: every completed U-boat must be made seaworthy and brought to England immediately; those unable to proceed under their own power were to be towed; all boats under construction were to be destroyed. Eventually, 176 submarines were delivered to the British at Harwich. An additional eight foundered on their way across the North Sea although no crew member was lost. The operable U-boats reaching Harwich were divided up and distributed among the Allies: 105 to Britain, forty-six to France, ten to Italy, and two to Belgium. All were destroyed except ten of the forty-six allotted to France

—

Franz von Hipper refused to lead the German surface fleet to Britain and Rear Admiral Ludwig von Reuter was given the assignment. As Hipper watched his dreadnoughts leaving Schillig roads, he said, "My heart is breaking. I have nothing more to do." Across the North Sea, the Grand Fleet was waiting. Before dawn on November 21, the light cruiser *Cardiff* slipped out of the Firth of Forth to meet the German ships and guide them to the rendezvous with Beatty's fleet. Then, as the sun came up, battleships, battle cruisers, armored and light cruisers, and escorting destroyers—in all, 370 ships—manned by 90,000 men of the British, American, and French navies, left the harbor. It was a sunlit morning, with a light breeze to blow out the flags, although haze limited visibility to about five miles. British ships flew every White Ensign they possessed, as though they were going into action. The crews were at action stations, although, at Beatty's command, all main turrets were trained fore and aft. Contact was made at 9:30 a.m. about forty miles east of May Island when *Cardiff* appeared, trailing a kite balloon with observers on board. *Cardiff* was followed in sunshine and mist by the battle cruiser *Seydlitz,* then the other German battle cruisers and a long line of battleships, their huge guns trained fore and aft. All told, there were seventy German ships: nine battleships, five battle cruisers, seven light cruisers, and forty-nine destroyers. In each type of ship, there was a deficiency of one in the numbers promised by the armistice agreement: one battleship, *König,* and a light cruiser, *Dresden,* had been left behind with engine problems; the new battle cruiser *Mackensen,* still under construction, was unready for sea; one destroyer, *V-70,* had struck a mine crossing the North Sea and sunk. Nevertheless, the approaching ships were the cream of the High Seas Fleet. The Allied fleet steamed past the head of the German line, then reversed course and took station in two long columns on parallel courses, one on either side of its former enemies, about six miles apart. Speed was 12 knots. In all Allied ships, fire-control directors were trained on the German vessels, with range and bearing constantly plotted. The turrets were not trained, but ammunition hoists were loaded and shells waited at the breeches of the guns. Targets at ranges of 3,500 and 5,000 yards were assigned and then passed along from one Allied ship to the next so that each German warship was always subject to coverage. Later, it was clear that these precautions had been unnecessary. All powder and ammunition had been removed from the German ships and, in some cases, range finders, gun sights, and breech blocks as well. Passing May Island, Beatty signaled one of the German squadrons to come to 17 knots and close up. The reply came back, "We cannot do better than twelve knots. Lack lubricating oil."

The procession entered the Firth of Forth and by noon, the German ships were anchored under the guns of the Inchkeith fortifications. Hardly had the anchors been dropped when German seamen appeared at the rails with hook and line to try to catch their dinner. Boats of every description—steamers, yachts, fishing boats, and rowboats—milled about, their passengers staring up at the gray steel ships. Ethel Beatty in her yacht, *Sheelah,* passed very close to *Seydlitz,* drawing mocking laughter from the German crew, which enraged the admiral's wife. Meanwhile, the Grand Fleet steamed past the Germans, proceeding to its anchorage above and below the Forth bridge. Last of all came *Queen Elizabeth* and Beatty, who signaled, "The German flag will be hauled down at sunset today and will not be hoisted again without permission." Beatty had ordered silence in the presence of the defeated enemy, but after the Germans anchored, *Queen Elizabeth* pulled out of line and stopped. As the whole Allied fleet passed by, each vessel cheered, colors dipped, guards presented arms, and bands struck up the national anthems of Britain, France, and the United States. Then, said Ernle Chatfield, "I took the fleet flagship to her buoy above the bridge and told the commander to assemble the crew on the quarterdeck. I walked aft with the admiral and asked him to say a few words to them. 'I don't think that there is anything I can say,' he said. But as he turned to go down the ladder to his cabin with the ship's company's cheers ringing in his ears, he faced them and said with a smile, 'Didn't I tell you they would have to come out?' "

At 3:37 p.m., sunset in the Forth, a bugle sounded on *Queen Elizabeth* and the White Ensign was lowered throughout the fleet. Simultaneously at Inchkeith, the German imperial flag came down on seventy warships. At six o'clock, Beatty attended a thanksgiving service on the quarterdeck of his flagship and then sat down to dinner with thirty-two guests including Admiral Sims and a French admiral. Not present were the two greatest British admirals of that era: John Arbuthnot Fisher, who conceived and created the Grand Fleet, and John Rushworth Jellicoe, who commanded it through the greater part of the war. No one was willing to say whether these men had been slighted intentionally or whether the Admiralty simply forgot to invite them.

—

Over the next several days, the interned ships left the Firth of Forth in groups for Scapa Flow. Two German destroyer flotillas went first, on November 22, and the light cruisers and remaining destroyers followed over the next two days. The dreadnoughts started moving on the twenty-fourth, accompanied by British battleships and battle cruisers; by Wednesday, November 27, all seventy German warships were anchored at Scapa Flow. The battleship *König* arrived from Germany on December 6 along with the light cruiser *Dresden* and the destroyer *V-129,* sent as a replacement for the mined *V-30.* The seventy-fourth and last German ship interned was the new battleship *Baden.* She arrived on January 9, 1919, as a substitute for the unfinished battle cruiser *Mackensen,* which the Allies had demanded but which was never sufficiently completed to go to sea.

At Scapa Flow, all radio equipment was removed from the interned ships and the crews were reduced to maintenance size. Twenty thousand men had brought the ships across the North Sea. On December 3, 4,000 returned to Germany on two ships bringing supplies from Wilhelmshaven. Another 6,000 went home on December 6 and 5,000 more on December 12. This left behind a total of 4,815 men, scattered through the anchored fleet. Each battle cruiser kept 200 men on board, battleships 175, light cruisers 80, and each destroyer 20, enough to maintain the ships and to enable them to steam at reduced speed. This provision was important to the Germans because they still hoped that the ships might be returned to Germany on the conclusion of a peace treaty. Thereafter, the thinning out continued and an average of a hundred men went home on the supply ships every month of the internment.

Guard duty over the interned fleet was assigned to battle squadrons of the Royal Navy. After the armistice, the Grand Fleet had been split up, redistributed, and renamed. Admiral Sir Charles Madden became Commander-in-Chief of the Atlantic Fleet and it was his squadrons that did guard duty, rotating a month at a time. The permanent harbor wardens were armed trawlers, which constantly patrolled the lines of German ships. It was impressed on all British officers and sailors at Scapa Flow that until a peace treaty was signed the armistice was only a pause in the war. The sole channel of official communication permitted between the interned ships and the guard ships was from Admiral von Reuter to the British admiral commanding the guard squadron. And unless the matter was urgent, this communication had to be in writing. On occasions when Britons and Germans actually met, salutes were authorized, but handshakes barred. There is a story that, after spending a winter at Scapa Flow, a German officer said to a Briton, "If you spent four years in this place, you deserved to win the war." The story is assuredly apocryphal; none of the postwar, live-and-let-live camaraderie prerequisite to such a conversation existed between Briton and German at Scapa Flow.

For seven months, the seventy-four interned German warships became a part of the landscape of Scapa Flow. Their crews were demoralized and apathetic. Discipline was loose and unwieldy; even Reuter's orders had to be countersigned by the Soldiers' Council. Sailors got up late, did little work, and lounged on deck, smoking in the presence of officers. Cleaning was abandoned and the mess decks were so deep in filth that German officers blushed when British officers came on board. Some destroyers, infested by rats, were left unoccupied. Neither officers nor men were allowed to go ashore. To cope with monotony, sailors fished, wrote letters, played chess, gambled, sang, and danced. Food was adequate—the British insisted that all of it come from Germany and supplies were brought from Wilhelmshaven twice a month—so the catching of fish and seagulls was more for diversion than nourishment. German seamen received 300 cigarettes or seventy-five cigars per month, and a generous allotment of alcohol. There were doctors in the fleet, but no dentist, and the British refused to provide one. Men with decayed teeth or broken dentures had priority in going home. Two German chaplains, a Protestant and a Roman Catholic, served the entire fleet. Outgoing mail to Germany was censored; later, incoming also. Only British newspapers were allowed on board and these were delivered four days late. Communication between German ships was by flag or signal light only. No visiting between ships was permitted; it was prohibited even to lower a boat, at the risk of being fired upon.

On Reuter's flagship, *Friedrich der Grosse,* an especially disorderly group calling itself the Red Guard made a practice of stomping on the steel deck over the admiral's cabin when he was trying to sleep. At one point, fearing that this mutinous element might try to take over the ship, Reuter asked the British admiral to give him support if this were attempted. Prompt assistance was promised. Even so, the flagship became, in Reuter's words, a "madhouse" and on March 25, he shifted his flag to the light cruiser *Emden.* When two of the worst-behaved seamen were ordered back to Germany and refused to go, two British destroyers came alongside with crews at action stations to remove them and send them to a British prison.

Over the months, Reuter convinced his former enemies that he was a serious, trustworthy officer, doing his best to carry out the terms of the armistice. Both sides understood that the future of Reuter's ships would be decided in Paris, where the peace treaty was being negotiated and where the future of the German fleet was only one of many important items on the agenda. The subject provoked disagreement. France, which had built no warships since before the war, wanted at least one-quarter of the German ships; Italy wanted another quarter. Britain, with the largest fleet in the world—a fleet beyond her postwar ability to support—wanted the German fleet destroyed. America, creating a new fleet of modern dreadnoughts, had no interest in rusting German warships.

Neither the Allied Naval Council nor the British Admiralty nor the German government let Reuter know what was happening in Paris. The armistice had specifically forbidden the ships' destruction and Reuter had stressed to his captains that he would do nothing unless the British attempted to seize them without the German government's consent. Nevertheless, Reuter and his officers all felt themselves still bound by a standing order of the Imperial Navy that no German warship was to be allowed to fall into enemy hands. Accordingly, on June 17, Reuter drew up and distributed a detailed order for scuttling the ships. German captains were instructed that "all internal watertight doors and hatchway covers, ventilator openings and port holes are to be kept open at all times." Preparations were to be made to open valves, condenser intakes, and submerged torpedo tubes, admitting the sea. Lifeboats complete with white flags of truce would be prepared for the speedy evacuation of crews. The signal for immediate scuttling would be "Paragraph Eleven. Confirm." Reuter's task was made easier when two German supply ships arrived and on June 18 departed, carrying home another 2,700 men of the interned fleet. Now, fewer than 1,800 remained on the warships at Scapa Flow; these were men who could be depended on and whose number would not swamp the lifeboats that could be launched.

Reuter's first awareness that a crisis was approaching came from a copy of *The Times* of London dated June 17, which reported that the Allies had issued an ultimatum: unless the German government accepted their terms and signed the peace treaty by noon on Saturday, June 21, the armistice would be set aside and hostilities resumed. Reuter did not read this newspaper until the afternoon of June 20. He decided at that moment to scuttle his ships the following morning, June 21. But by the twentieth, its news was no longer accurate. In the interim, the Allies had decided to permit the Germans two additional days to make up their minds; the deadline now was 7:00 p.m. on June 23. Reuter, not having been officially informed of either the original deadline or its extension, now expected the British to attempt to seize his ships at any moment beginning on the morning of the twenty-first. On his own responsibility and without any written order from the German government, he determined to act before British sailors boarded his ships.

The guard ships at Scapa Flow included the five new *Resolution*-class battleships of the 1st Battle Squadron, commanded by Vice Admiral Sir Sydney Fremantle. Fremantle had received no instructions from the Admiralty or from the First Sea Lord, Admiral Wemyss, in Paris, as to the disposition of the interned ships at the termination of the armistice. Expecting that when the peace treaty was signed, the terms would include the surrender of the German vessels and aware that Reuter might try to scuttle them first, the Allied Naval Council on June 20 authorized seizure of the interned ships at the moment the armistice expired: 7:00 p.m. on June 23. Throughout the internment, the British battle squadrons on guard duty at Scapa Flow had been authorized to carry out training exercises at sea from time to time. On the night of June 20, Fremantle decided to take his ships to sea at 9:00 a.m. on June 21 in order to practice the battle squadron's defense against a massed destroyer attack. He planned to return to the Flow on the afternoon of the twenty-third and to seize the German fleet that night.

Saturday, June 21, 1919, was an idyllic summer day. The sun shone from a blue sky, the air was warm, and a slight swell was running in the Flow. Reuter prepared himself carefully, wearing his dress uniform with all his decorations. Emerging onto *Emden*'s quarterdeck, he watched Fremantle take the 1st Battle Squadron to sea: the five British battleships were accompanied by two light cruisers and nine destroyers. Two British destroyers, seven trawlers, and a number of drifters remained behind in the anchorage. At 10:00 a.m., Reuter sent the preparatory message that all ships be attentive to signals from the flagship. The decisive signal was hoisted at 11:20 a.m.: "Paragraph Eleven. Confirm." Sent by signal flags, the command was repeated by semaphore and searchlights.

For a while, nothing appeared unusual. The 500-ton tug and water tender *Flying Kestrel* was visiting the interned fleet that morning with an excursion party of 400 children from Orkney schools. As the little vessel passed down the lines of anchored ships, the children saw some German sailors playing mouth organs; other Germans thumbed their noses at the children. Then, as noon approached, a flurry of activity broke out. Brightly colored flags fluttered in the sunlight above *Emden*'s bridge. At the stroke of noon, all ships hoisted the colors of the Imperial Navy. Then those watching saw *Friedrich der Grosse* listing to starboard. As water poured into her hull in solid green jets, the great ship rolled farther until her masts, funnels, turrets, and guns began disappearing under water. The great red hull rose up and then plunged down in two wide whirlpools of hissing foam. The time was 12:16 p.m. Other big ships began listing and heeling at extraordinary angles. A young man on the *Flying Kestrel* remembered steam rushing out of vents "with a dreadful roaring hiss" and the "sullen rumblings . . . as the great hulls slant giddily over and slide with horrible sucking and gurgling noises under the water." The sinking continued for five hours. *Friedrich der Grosse* was the first ship to go down and *Hindenburg* the last, at 5:00 p.m. In that time, fifteen of sixteen German dreadnoughts in the Flow went to the bottom. *Baden* obstinately refused to sink and was beached in a waterlogged condition. It was possible to tow a few other ships into shallow water before they sank. Four light cruisers, *Emden, Frankfurt, Bremse,* and *Nürnberg,* were beached in this manner; four went down. Of fifty destroyers, thirty-two sank, fourteen were beached, and four remained afloat.

The small British guard ships rushed about doing what they could. Some attempted to tow sinking ships. Others, in an effort to drive German seamen back to their ships to stop them from sinking, opened rifle fire on lifeboats flying white flags; in one of these lifeboats carrying thirteen men, three were killed and four wounded. A young woman on the *Flying Kestrel* saw "a [British] drifter towing two or three lifeboats filled with German sailors. One of them got up with a knife in his hand and tried to cut his boat free of the towrope. A Royal Marine raised his rifle and shot him." British sailors boarded the battleship *Markgraf* and found the captain supervising the ship's scuttling. Seeing the British, he waved a white flag. He was shot through the head. At Scapa Flow that day, nine Germans were killed and sixteen wounded by gunfire.

At 12:20 p.m., Fremantle had received an urgent signal from one of the guard destroyers: "German battleship sinking." Rushing back at full speed, the British battleships entered the harbor at 2:30 p.m. It was too late. Everywhere, German vessels, large and small, were in various stages of sinking, belching bubbles of air, explosive waterspouts, and gigantic upsurges of oil. Tied together, the destroyers went down in pairs. By five o'clock, only a few German ships remained afloat, with parts of others rising out of the water. A vast stain of oil spread across the Flow, littered with boats, hammocks, life belts, and chests. Reuter was brought aboard *Revenge* to face Fremantle's wrath and to learn for the first time that the armistice had been extended by two days. That night, the British battleships sailed for Cromarty Firth with the 1,774 German officers and men on board forced to sleep on steel decks without blankets.

At Invergordon the next morning, Fremantle sent his prisoners ashore, but not before a final confrontation. Speaking to Reuter and his officers lined up on the quarterdeck of *Revenge,* Fremantle told the German admiral that he had "violated common honour and the honourable traditions of seamen of all nations. With an armistice in full operation, you recommenced hostilities without notice. By your conduct, you have added one more to the breaches of faith and honour of which Germany has been guilty in this war. You have proved to the few who doubted it that the word of the New Germany is no more to be trusted than that of the old. I now transfer you as prisoners of war."

Afterward, the British navy was criticized for having permitted the scuttling. The French were especially angry, having expected to incorporate some of the largest vessels into their navy. Wemyss's private reaction was good riddance: "I look upon the sinking of the German fleet as a real blessing. It disposes once for all the thorny question of the distribution of these ships." Scheer, for a different reason, also was pleased. "I rejoice. The stain of surrender has been wiped from the escutcheon of the German Fleet. The sinking of these ships has proved that the spirit of the fleet is not dead. This last act is true to the best traditions of the German navy."

The German officers and seamen killed and wounded at Scapa Flow were the last casualties of the war, and the survivors sent ashore at Invergordon became the last prisoners of war. On June 28, 1919, a week after the scuttling of the German fleet, the Treaty of Versailles was signed in the same Hall of Mirrors where, forty-eight years before, Otto von Bismarck had proclaimed the creation of the German empire. Now, the empire had melted away. The fleet was at the bottom of the sea. The Great War was over.

Notes

ABBREVIATIONS USED IN NOTES:

FGDN: *Fear God and Dread Nought: Correspondence of Admiral of the Fleet Lord Fisher,* ed. A. J. Marder, 3 vols., London: Jonathan Cape, 1952–59.

L and V: Hough, Richard. *Louis and Victoria: The Family History of the Mountbattens.* London: Weidenfeld & Nicholson, 1974.

CHAPTER 1: JULY 1914

3 "Ha ha! The mailed fist": Cowles, 242.
4 "talks with great energy": Topham, 226.
4 "If he laughs": Balfour, 138.
4 "We Hohenzollerns": Ibid., 154.
4 "our old ally": Ibid., 155.
4 "You have sworn loyalty to Me": Nichols, 130.
4 "There will be no quarter": Balfour, 226–27.
5 "not false but fickle": Bülow, II, 555.
5 "Whenever I have to go": Ibid.
5 "lumbering monstrosity": Raeder, 33.
5 "brother officers": Zedlitz, 176.
5 "I don't care for women": Topham, 230.
6 "two clean, cold sheets": Davis, 204.
6 "the damned family": Bülow, I, 544.
6 "I had a peculiar passion": William II, 229.
6 "When as a little boy": Bülow, II, 36.
6 "Heavy on the water": William II, 49.
7 "The Regatta used to be": Eckardstein, 55.
7 "Now, Rhodes, tell me": "The Widow," *Intimacies,* 193.
7 "a very nice boy": Tuchman, *Guns of August,* 2.
7 "Dearest Nicky . . . Your affectionate Willy": Massie, *Nicholas and Alexandra,* 83.
7 "the tsar is only fit to live": Newton, 199.
8 "We must seize the trident": Balfour, 206.
8 "Between 1864 and 1870": Tirpitz, I, 13, 15.
9 "a collection of experiments": Ibid., 129.
9 "Fancy wearing the same uniform": Lee, I, 654.
10 "It never even occurred": Bülow, I, 513.
10 "Without a superior fleet": E. L. Woodward, 374.
11 "dangerous little Serbian viper": Mansergh, 132.
11 "I constantly wonder": Spender, 399.
11 "The Slavs were born to serve": Ibid., 363.
11 "If His Majesty the Emperor": Ibid., 364.
11 "Terrible shock": Rose, 167.
12 "Should a war": Geiss, 77.
12 "the possibility of its acceptance": Ibid., 114.
13 "joyful duty": Cecil, II, 207.
13 "a nation in the European sense": Geiss, 183.
13 "That's a pretty strong note": Görlitz, 5.
13 "operational briefing": Ibid., 6.
13 "I received verbal orders": Goldrick, 6.
14 "I explained the latest telegram": Görlitz, 6.
14 "My fleet has orders to sail": Cecil, II, 203.
14 "A brilliant achievement": Geiss, 222.
15 Two days before: For the conversation between George V and Prince Henry, see Nicholson, 245–46.
15 "I have the word of a king": Tirpitz, I, 361.
17 "First Fleet squadrons all disperse": Goldrick, 6.
17 "the most formidable document": Mansergh, 225.
17 "Happily there seems to be no reason": Asquith, *Letters to Venetia,* 123.
17 "ministers with their weekend holidays": Hough, *L and V,* 280.
17 "I went down to the beach": Churchill, I, 197.
18 "do whatever was necessary": Ibid., 198.
18 "No ships of the First Fleet": Gilbert, I, 50.

18 "The British fleet is preparing": Churchill, I, 210.
19 "others of whom": Ibid., 211.
19 "and therefore if possible": Ibid., 200, 211–12.
19 At 5:00 that evening: Ibid., 212.
19 "We may now picture this great fleet": Ibid., 212–13.
20 "I feared": Ibid., 212.
20 "He looked at me": Churchill, *Great Contemporaries,* 123.
20 "We looked at each other": Ibid., 212–13.
20 "I told him what we had done": Ibid., 213.
20 "the movements of the fleet are free": Ibid.
21 "Many do not know much more": Bülow, I, 391.
21 "There was not much margin here": Churchill, I, 243.
23 "In view of present circumstances": Hough, *The Great Dreadnought,* 121.
23 "The Turkish battleships were vital": Churchill, I, 209.
25 "In view of our ultimatum": Ibid., 227.
25 "Commence hostilities": Ibid., 229.
25 "The collier's winches suddenly stopped": Dewar, 161.

CHAPTER 2: *GOEBEN* IS YOUR OBJECTIVE

27 "would easily be able to avoid the French": Churchill, I, 222–23.
27 "A droop-jawed, determined little man": Robert James, 9.
29 "We did not plead much": McLaughlin, 54.
30 "the African coast": Kopp, 23.
30 "like an armadillo": Marder, I, 55.
31 "Your first task": Churchill, I, 222–24.
31 "*Goeben* must be shadowed": Ibid., 223.
31 "Watch on mouth of Adriatic": Ibid., 224.
31 "Very good. Hold her": Ibid.
31 "to prevent *Goeben* leaving": McLaughlin, 49.
32 "a backstairs cad . . . a sneak": Fisher, *FGDN,* II, 360.
32 "a serpent of the lowest type": Ibid., 418.
32 "Sir Berkeley Mean": Ibid., 447.
32 "went to Balmoral": Ibid., 418.
32 "Winston has sacrificed the country": Ibid., 458.
32 "I fear this must be my last communication": Ibid., 451–52.
33 "Use Malta as if it were Toulon": Churchill, I, 229.
33 "break in upon": Ibid., 222.
33 "in quest of his colleague": Hough, *Great War,* 71.
34 "The idea of turning about": McLaughlin, 56.
34 "sowing death and panic": Ibid.
34 "Our trick succeeded brilliantly": Kopp, 24.
34 "like a giant azure bell": Ibid., 27.
35 "giant grey monsters": Ibid., 28.
35 "not French ships": McLaughlin, 60.
35 "The overheated air": Kopp, 30.
36 "*Goeben* . . . is evidently going to interfere": Churchill, I, 224.
36 "Winston with all his war paint on": Asquith, *Letters to Venetia,* 150–51.
36 "no act of war": Churchill, I, 225.
36 "the tortures of Tantalus": Ibid., 226.
36 "unable to utter a word": Ibid., 227.
36 "Sent hands to tea": McLaughlin, 59.
37 "*Goeben* out of sight": Hough, *Great War,* 74.
37 "for the last time": McLaughlin, 67.
37 "With a heavy heart": Ibid., 68.
38 "Numerous Sicilians": Ibid.
38 "At present time": Ibid., 69.
38 "It was impossible for me": Ibid.
39 "Italian government have declared neutrality": Churchill, I, 226.
40 "Had it been put to me": Ibid., 250.
40 "Certainly if . . . [Milne]": Ibid., 254.
40 "Is Austria neutral power": McLaughlin, 66.
40 "First Cruiser Squadron and *Gloucester*": Ibid.
41 "*Goeben* altering course to southward": Ibid., 71.
42 the Silver King: Ibid., 32.
42 "the handsomest officer": Ibid., 105.
42 "met Mrs. Troubridge in the Abbey": Ibid., 30.
42 "they must not be surprised": Ibid., 74.
43 For Troubridge's conversations with Wray, see Ibid., 76–77.
43 "I cannot turn away": Marder, II, 26.
43 "Being only able to meet *Goeben*": McLaughlin, 78.
44 "Why did you not continue": Ibid.
44 "With visibility at the time": Ibid.
45 "gradually . . . drop astern": Corbett, I, 66.
45 "Have engaged at long range": Hough, *Great War,* 77.
45 "Commence hostilities at once": Marder, II, 30.

46 "Negative my telegram": Hough, *Great War,* 81.
46 "Indispensable military necessity": Tuchman, *Guns of August,* 157.
47 "Enter. Demand surrender": McLaughlin, 84.
47 "Action Stations": Kopp, 66.
47 "Request pilot": Ibid., 67.
47 "Please follow me": Ibid., 68.
48 "They are to allow them to enter" and "Yes": Kannengiesser, 26.
48 "interesting," but that "as we shall insist": Asquith, *Letters to Venetia,* 168.
48 "temporarily and superficially": Tuchman, *Guns of August,* 159.
49 "I have even more terrible news for you": Morgenthau, 81.
49 "we could not afford to do without": Churchill, I, 29.
49 "insolent," "defiant," and "openly fraudulent": Ibid., 491.
50 "more slaughter, more misery and ruin": Churchill I, 252.
50 "careful examination . . . their Lordships approved": Milne, 146.
51 "Your sole duty": Churchill, I, 491.
51 "amazing misconduct": McLaughlin, 108.
51 "signally failed": Ibid., 107–8.
51 "had a very fair chance": Ibid., 111.
51 "did, from negligence": Ibid., 112.
51 "Do not be brought to action": Churchill, I, 222.
51 "fixed and unalterable opinion": McLaughlin, 110.
51 Troubridge and Milne: Marder, II, 34.
51 "he had no intention to engage": McLaughlin, 111.
52 "All I could gain": Ibid., 107.
52 "deep conviction": Ibid., 133.
52 "a desperate one": Ibid.
52 "It was at this psychological moment": Marder, II, 27.
53 "the limited ammunition of *Goeben*": Churchill, I, 251.
53 "Up to the range of sixteen thousand yards": McLaughlin, 120.
53 "superior force . . . fully and honorably": Ibid., 145.
54 "Sir Berkeley Goeben": Fisher, *FGDN,* III, 52.
54 "this most disastrous event": Ibid., 53.
54 "an amateur on shore": Milne, 16.
54 "They pay me to be an admiral": Hough, *Great War,* 84.
55 "Even if all our ships had been sunk": Pope, 197.

CHAPTER 3: JELLICOE

56 "the only man on either side": Churchill, III, 112.
56 "Jellicoe to be Admiralissimo": Fisher, *FGDN,* II, 424.
57 "If war comes before 1914": Ibid., 443.
57 "our beloved Commander-in-Chief": Marder, II, 10.
57 "really does too much": Fisher, *FGDN,* II, 418–19.
58 "one of the cleverest cadets": Winton, 12.
58 "Jellicoe was admired": Goldrick, in *The Great Admirals,* ed. Sweetman, 365.
58 "Property of Admiral Sir John Jellicoe": Bacon, *Jellicoe,* 8.
58 "swam with extraordinary vigor": Bacon, *Jellicoe,* 53.
59 "I felt the shock": *Jellicoe Papers,* I, 10.
60 "I don't think I shall ever forget": Bacon, *Jellicoe,* 113.
61 "one of the five best brains": Winton, 101.
61 "far greater protection": *Jellicoe Papers,* I, 13.
61 "I had a decided admiration": Ibid., 22.
62 "On my way to Keil": Ibid., 15.
62 "I think it shows": Ibid., 17.
63 "If one asks English naval officers": Marder, I, 410.
63 "It did not take me very long": *Jellicoe Papers,* 26–27.
63 "He thanked me": Ibid., 30.
64 "certainly one of the future leaders": Ibid.
64 "brilliant and daring": Ibid., 29.
65 "War with Germany": Bacon, *Jellicoe,* 190.
65 "in certain circumstances": Jellicoe, *Grand Fleet,* 3.
66 "I had the most profound respect": Ibid., 5.
66 "the fleet might conclude": Ibid.
67 "These are not times": Gilbert, I, 60.
67 "respectfully and most earnestly": Winton, 142.
67 "We have absolute confidence": Ibid.
67 For the messages between Churchill and Jellicoe, see *Jellicoe Papers,* I, 41–42.
68 "When I reported myself": Jellicoe, *Grand Fleet,* 4.
69 "as always, a most gallant officer": Ibid., 5.

70 "would cause unprecedented disaster": *Beatty Papers,* I, 112.
70 "We received the terrible news": *Beatty Papers,* I, 113.
70 "Your feelings do you credit": Churchill, I, 218.
70 "I hope I never have to live": *Jellicoe Papers,* I, 48.
70 "My dear Jellicoe": Bacon, *Jellicoe,* 202.
71 "Look here, old chap": Ibid., 203.

CHAPTER 4: FIRST DAYS

72 "the principal object": Marder, I, 367.
73 "a steady and serious": Ibid., 371.
73 "In a war with Germany": Ibid., II.3.
73 "Great Britain cannot help": Ibid., I, 431.
73 "Owing to recent": Ibid., 424.
73 "so long as": Ibid., II, 3.
76 "As it is": Ibid., I. 372–73.
76 "Before the war": Dewar, 152.
76 "There was only one": Scheer, 11.
76 "equalization of forces": Groos, I. 54.
77 "dropping things overboard": Patterson, *Tyrwhitt,* 46.
77 "the first British shot in the war": Keyes, *Memoirs,* I, 68.
78 "if we go up on a mine": Goldrick, 66.
78 "The foremost half of the ship": Ibid., 67.
79 "stagger out of the chart house": Keyes, *Memoirs,* I, 70.
79 "the strong odor of petroleum": Groos, I, 233.
79 "Tomorrow, Sunday,": Churchill, I, 256.
80 "In the years": Tuchman, *Guns of August,* 121.
80 "contemptible little army": Patterson, *Jellicoe,* 61.
80 "The more English": Tuchman, *Guns of August,* 121.
81 "We grudged every light cruiser": Churchill, I, 286–87.
81 "the mother country": Bean, I, 16.
82 "without the loss of a single ship": Churchill, I, 305.

CHAPTER 5: BEATTY

84 "For no apparent reason": Chalmers, 122–23.
84 "observe the private unhappiness": Barnett, 135.
86 "free ranging": Charles Beatty, 34.
87 "Some months ago": Chalmers, 75–76.
87 "So great is the joy": Ibid.
87 "Dear Arthur": Charles Beatty, 40.
87 "wilful and beautiful": Tree, 16.
87 "divorce crushed my father's spirit": Ibid., 18.
87 "Your mother has sent me": Ibid., 26.
88 "You have done a great deal of grumbling": *Beatty Papers,* I, 11.
88 "My darling Tata": Ibid., 8.
88 "Well, love": Chalmers, 118.
89 "J-aaack": Charles Beatty, 42.
89 "What? Court Martial my David": Leslie, 211.
89 "I have thought for a long time": *Beatty Papers,* 15.
89 "beautiful, opulent, ambitious": Roskill, 36.
89 "the most unhappy man": Ibid.
89 "We have eight admirals": *Beatty Papers,* 23.
89 "As you know, 'Lion' and I": Ibid., 16–17.
90 "I felt as if I was an ogre": *Beatty Papers,* 30–31.
90 "Rear Admiral Beatty": Chalmers, 105.
90 "David must have known": Charles Beatty, 57.
90 "Mum, Mum, come": Chalmers, 111.
90 "made no secret": Charles Beatty, 57.
90 "My little lady": Roskill, 45.
91 "David was threatening to leave the Navy": Ibid., 43–44.
91 "The fact is that the Admiralty": *Beatty Papers,* 34.
92 "The vessel was commanded": Churchill, *My Early Life,* 178–79.
92 "You are quite right": *Beatty Papers,* 11–12.
92 "I see in the papers": Ibid., 28.
92 "You seem very young": Morgan, 322.
92 "My first meeting": Churchill, I, 88.
92 "I had two hours solid conversation": *Beatty Papers,* 35.
92 "I hope to be able to squeeze": Ibid., 65.
93 "Oh dear, I am so tired": Ibid., 46.
93 "viewed naval strategy": Churchill, I, 88.
93 "I had no doubts": Ibid.
93 "a love of doing everything": Chalmers, 116.
93 "a nice old thing": Ibid., 124.
94 "You must not bother": *Beatty Papers,* 66.
95 "There seems to be something wrong": Chatfield, 143.
96 "I have often been asked": Goodenough, 91.

CHAPTER 6: THE BATTLE OF THE BIGHT

97 "We are still wandering": *Beatty Papers,* I, 120.
97 "What is the Navy doing" and "offensive measures": Roskill, *Beatty,* 82.
97 "When are we going to make war": Keyes, *Memoirs,* I, 76.
98 "simple and daring": Churchill, I, 308.
98 "too fully occupied": Keyes, *Memoirs,* I, 80.
98 "gave me an opportunity": Ibid., 81.
99 "damned slow": Patterson, *Tyrwhitt,* 41.
99 "from the oldest and slowest": Ibid., 54.
100 "a destroyer sweep": Chalmers, 142.
100 "Propose to cooperate": Goldrick, 85.
100 "Until I know the plan of operations": Ibid.
100 "Cooperation by battle fleet": Ibid., 86.
100 "We are to rendezvous": Chalmers, 143.
101 "Are you taking part": Ibid.
101 The German defensive arrangements in the Heligoland Bight are described in Groos, I, 131–33.
102 "Attacked by enemy cruisers": Goldrick, 88.
103 "hunt destroyers": Ibid.
104 "were in boiling water": Groos, I, 150.
105 "as a sample": Corbett, II, 109.
106 "Please chase westward": Goldrick, 97.
106 "Cruisers are our cruisers": Ibid.
106 "I was not informed": *Beatty Papers,* I, 126.
106 "I came under detailed orders": Goldrick, 98.
107 "to cut off the retreat": Groos, I, 175.
107 "We received a very severe and most accurate fire": Chalmers, 145–46.
108 "Am attacked by large cruiser": *Beatty Papers,* I, 124.
108 "a hornets' nest": Marder, II, 51.
108 "intercepting various signals": *Beatty Papers,* I, 129.
109 "What do you think we should do": Chatfield, 134.
109 "Am proceeding to your support": Goldrick, 101.
109 "heavy smoke clouds": Groos, I, 176.
109 "very wisely fled like a stag": King-Hall, 54.
109 "Even in the act": Goldrick, 102.
110 "furrowed": King-Hall, 55.
110 "The ship reared": Groos, I, 179.
110 "We closed down on her": King-Hall, 55.
110 "Mainz was incredibly brave": Chalmers, 146.
110 "The state of *Mainz*": Groos, I, 178–79.
110 "Sink the ship": Ibid., 177.
111 "A young German officer": Keyes, *Memoirs,* I, 88.
111 "I really was beginning to feel a bit blue": Marder, II, 52.
111 "Following in each other's wake": King-Hall, 57.
111 "There straight ahead of us": Chalmers, 146.
112 "As we approached": Chatfield, 125.
112 "The turrets swung around": Ibid.
113 "A small German ship": Ibid.
113 "the first salvo fell": Goldrick, 106.
113 "completely enveloped": Groos, I, 185.
113 "The Admiral told me": Chatfield, 126.
113 "drifting among corpses": Groos, I, 218.
114 "not to engage": Ibid., 193.
114 "At 8:23 p.m.": Ibid., 198.
115 "It seems your anchor": Chalmers, 152.
115 "The end justified the means": Marder, II, 52.
115 "We had a great reception": Ibid.
116 "the only action which was possible": Ibid.
116 "It was good work": *Beatty Papers,* I, 121.
116 "Poor devils": Chalmers, 152–53.
116 "I had thought I should have received": Ibid., 154.
116 "It really was awfully fine": Patterson, *Tyrwhitt,* 62–63.
116 "I think an absurd fuss": *Keyes Papers,* I, 19.
117 "I think it right to tell you": Ibid., 17–18.
118 "a greater expenditure of ammunition": Chatfield, 127.
118 "The battle was of immense": Marder, II, 54.
118 "It was no great naval feat": Chatfield, 126.
118 "Enemy battle cruiser squadron": Groos, I, 283.
119 "the long-suppressed battle ardor": Ibid., 210.
119 "However heavy the losses": Ibid., 216.
120 "the larger part": Ibid., 215.
120 "hold itself back": Bennett, *Naval Battles,* 151.
120 "in his anxiety": Goldrick, 115.
120 "August 28": Tirpitz, II, 91.
120 "on the approach of the English": Ibid., 92–93.
121 "They knew we were coming": Chalmers, 154.

121 "[We] could not go messing about": Marder, II, 55.
121 "The Germans knew nothing": Churchill, I, 309.

CHAPTER 7: SUBMARINES AND MINES: "FISHER'S TOYS"

122 "water conducts shock": Keegan, *The Price of Admiralty,* 97.
123 "Death near": Fisher, *Records,* 177–78.
123 "playthings" and "Fisher's toys": Marder, *Anatomy,* 559.
123 "un-English": Ibid., 368
123 "underhanded method of attack": Mackay, 298.
124 "I shall be very disappointed": Fisher, *FGDN,* I, 366.
124 "the cleverest officer in the navy": Marder, I, 83.
124 "exercised an extraordinary influence": Marder, *Anatomy,* 366.
125 "dressed like North Sea fishermen": Keyes, I, 47.
125 "I note by examining": Hough, *Great War,* 174.
125 "the notoriously short, steep seas": Keyes, *Memoirs,* I, 102.
126 "Under the circumstances": Goldrick, 121.
126 "We have no money to waste": Hough, *Great War,* 169.
126 "for experiments connected with submarines": Ibid., 170.
126 "her employment": Ibid.
127 "Our submarine fleet": Gray, 28.
129 "Think of . . .": Keyes, *Memoirs,* 76–77.
129 "the 'live bait' squadron": Churchill, I, 323.
130 "My dear fellow": Marder, II, 57.
130 "The *Bacchante*s ought not to continue": Churchill, I, 324.
130 "I should not have given in": Kerr, 248.
130 "Still rather rough": Goldrick, 127.
132 "Oh, no. I have only broken one arm": Hoehling, 42.
133 "three cruisers": Thomas, 18.
133 "I could see their gray-black sides": Hoehling, 48.
133 "to make my aim sure": Ibid.
133 "a dull thud": Thomas, 20.
134 "Abandon ship": Corbett, I, 175.
134 "the sun shining on pink": Hoehling, 50.
134 "a terrific crash": Ibid.
135 "This time we were so bold": Thomas, 24.
135 "*Aboukir* and *Hogue* sinking": Corbett, I, 174.
135 "a sudden explosion": Hoehling, 52.
135 "Keep cool, my lads": Ibid., 54.
136 "Knowing where they were supposed to be": Patterson, *Tyrwhitt,* 73.
136 "It was very difficult": Hoehling, 55.
136 "They looked just like rows and rows of swallows": Patterson, *Tyrwhitt,* 73.
136 "men climbed like ants": Thomas, 25.
136 "She careened far over": Gray, 36.
137 "On 22 September": Groos, II, 56.
137 "It is well-known": *The Times* (London), September 25, 1914, 8.
137 "of no great value": Churchill, I, 326.
137 "We heard *Aboukir* crying out": *Beatty Papers,* I, 136.
138 "It was pure murder": Fisher, *FGDN,* III, 61.
138 "The disaster . . . followed": Churchill, I, 326.
138 "One would expect senior officers": Ibid., 327.
138 "a cruiser patrol": Marder, II, 58.
138 "were placed in a cruel position": Ibid., 55.
138 "that most of the officers concerned": Churchill, I, 327.
138 "If one ship is torpedoed": Goldrick, 133.
140 "indiscriminate and distinctly barbarian": Marder, II, 72.
140 "cowardly weapon" and "the weapon of the weak": Ibid., 70.
143 "We can only approve": Scheer, 62.
144 "It is suicidal": *Jellicoe Papers,* I, 71.
144 "rely to a great extent": Ibid., 75.
144 "This may and probably will": Ibid., 76.
145 "full confidence in your contemplated conduct": Marder, II, 76.

CHAPTER 8: "SHALL WE BE HERE IN THE MORNING?"

146 "The Grand Fleet was uneasy": Churchill, I, 380.
148 "Don't spend another penny": Marder, *Anatomy,* 467.
148 "I got Rosyth delayed": Fisher, *Memories,* 193.
148 "I have always been 'dead on' for Cromarty": Ibid., 214.
148 "of the utmost gravity": Marder, I, 421.
149 "a great seawater lake": Hewison, 6.
150 "The great majority of the men": Ibid., 52.
151 "Having to choose between the two": Ibid., 57.

151 "The Admiralty have been so frequently charged": Ibid.
152 "I often wondered": Jellicoe, *Grand Fleet,* 29.
153 "I can only imagine": Ibid., 30–31.
153 "It appeared to me": Ibid., 30.
154 "No one, we believed": Churchill, I, 381.
154 "prepare for a torpedo attack": Hewison, 69.
154 "No trace of a submarine": Jellicoe, *Grand Fleet,* 118.
155 "the fleet could not remain at a base": Ibid.
155 "I long for a submarine defense at Scapa": *Jellicoe Papers,* I, 73.
155 "Shall we be here in the morning": Scott, 276.
155 "I think it is right that you should know": Churchill, I, 389–91.
156 "Every effort will be made": Ibid., 391–92.
157 "In pre-war days": Jellicoe, *Grand Fleet,* 79.
157 "No one seriously contemplated": Churchill, I, 381–82.
157 "Reproach has been levelled": Ibid., 383.
158 "I interpreted my duty": Ibid., 240
160 "It seems to be impossible": *FGDN,* III, 131.

CHAPTER 9: PRINCE LOUIS DEPARTS

163 "We are only playing at war": Chalmers, 161.
163 "Winston, I hear": *Beatty Papers,* I, 118.
163 "If he would either leave": Marder, II, 83.
163 "If we only had a Kitchener": *Beatty Papers,* I, 144.
164 "waving his stick": Gilbert, I, 173.
165 "undertake command": Ibid., 176.
165 "What we desire": Ibid., 197.
165 "I can't tell you": Asquith, *Letters to Venetia,* 274.
165 "such a darned fool": Marder, II, 85.
166 "a remarkably nice boy": Brough, 88.
166 "stick it out a bit longer": Hough, *L and V,* 66.
167 "My dearest Georgie": Ibid., 111.
167 "I hate the idea": Marder, I, 406.
168 "German princeling" and "court favorite": Hough, *L and V,* 161.
168 "I am sure you must miss": Ibid., 163.
168 "She hopes and expects": Ibid., 171.
168 "perhaps the outstanding officer": Chatfield, 84.
169 "There are literally hundreds": Marder, I, 407.
169 "He is the ablest officer": Randolph Churchill, II, 534.
169 "more English than the English": Fisher, *FGDN,* II, 398.
169 "if his name had been Smith": Randolph Churchill, 534.
169 "There is no one else": Hough, *L and V,* 301.
170 "All my experience at the Admiralty": Randolph Churchill, II, 630.
170 "unworthy of the royal mind": Gretton, 88.
170 "We met every day": Churchill, I, 241.
170 "It happened in a large number of cases": Ibid.
170 "I accepted full responsibility": Ibid., 240.
171 "Quite concur": Marder, II, 88.
171 "court favorite": Hough, *L and V,* 88.
171 "I heard by chance": Marder, II, 86–87.
171 "I have never known more malignant rancour": Hough, *L and V,* 196.
172 "Should a German boss our navy": Ibid., 246.
172 "to live more in England": Kerr, 126.
172 "never understood": Ibid., 335.
172 "Sir, when I joined the Royal Navy": Churchill, I, 90.
173 "whether it was true": Hough, *L and V,* 301.
173 Germhun: Ibid., 302.
173 "The latest rumor": Ibid., 300.
174 "the conversation having turned": Ibid., 303.
174 "In time of war": Ibid.
174 "Dear Lord Charles Beresford": Ibid., 304.
175 "Prince Louis was a big man": Marder, I, 407.
175 "you must not ever consider leaving": Hough, *L and V,* 305.
175 "Winston has been pouring out his woes": Ibid.
175 "grave doubt is expressed": Gilbert, I, 215.
175 "Blood is said to be thicker than water": Marder, II, 86.
175 "Winston came here": Asquith, *Letters to Venetia,* 287.
176 "Poor Louis B's resignation": Hough, *L and V,* 307.
176 "Louis behaved with great dignity": Asquith, *Letters to Venetia,* 290.

176 "I have lately been driven": Churchill, I, 435.
176 "I beg you to release me": Gilbert, I, 225.
176 "There is no more loyal man": Nicholson, 251.
176 "profound sorrow": Kerr, 258.
176 "mean and contemptible slander": Ibid.
176 "a national humiliation": Ibid., 256.
176 "It was an awful wrench": Goldrick, 155.
176 "up to the end": Marder, II, 87.
177 "On one day": Haldane, 302.
177 "before the war ended": Ibid., 306.
177 "he started and grew pale": Nicholson, 309.
177 "George Rex": Hough, *L and V,* 319.
177 "Arrived Prince Hyde": Kerr, 289.
177 "to right a great wrong": Kerr, 285.

CHAPTER 10: ADMIRAL VON SPEE'S VOYAGE

179 "to keep the native population": Hough, *Pursuit,* 29.
180 "We must take advantage": Ibid., 27.
180 "Thousands of German Christians": Balfour, 209.
181 "as if he had swallowed a broom handle": Hough, *Pursuit,* 20.
181 "The women seemed": Ibid., 32.
182 "To my shame": Ibid., 33.
183 "I do not think we were far wrong": Pochhammer, 16.
183 "Very nice place, indeed": Ibid., 22.
183 "alone of the Marianas": Ibid., 36.
184 "a glorious sight": Ibid., 42–43.
184 "Strained relations": Bennett, *Naval Battles,* 53.
185 "threatened state of war": Pochhammer, 49.
185 "The whole beautiful world": Ibid., 51.
185 "the British had elected": Ibid., 55–56.
185 "The monotonous noise": Ibid., 60.
186 "Von Spee was a cut flower": Churchill, I, 295.
187 "In event of a war against Great Britain": Bennett, *Coronel and the Falklands,* 46.
187 "It is impossible to judge from here": Ibid., 64.
190 "If coaling the whole squadron": Ibid., 62.
190 "We wish you success": Pochhammer, 68.
190 "I thank Your Excellency": Hohenzollern-Emden, 39.
190 "I shall proceed to Chile": Bennett, *Coronel and the Falklands,* 63.
191 "The seemingly limitless desert": Pochhammer, 83.
191 "In the evening": Hough, *Pursuit,* 58.
193 "If no enemy ship approaches": Hirst, 72.
194 "vastly to his astonishment": Spencer-Cooper, 46.
194 "to gaze at the outside": Hough, *Pursuit,* 78.
195 "in glorious sunlight": Pochhammer, 135.
196 "furniture removal": Hohenzollern-Emden, 78.
196 "we had five or six vessels collected": Bennett, *Naval Battles,* 55.
196 "The *Emden*'s company": Ibid., 59.
196 "the chief reason": Marder, II, 104.
197 "It is almost in our heart": Bennett, *Coronel and the Falklands,* 72–73.

CHAPTER 11: ADMIRAL CRADOCK'S VOYAGE

198 "The map of the world": Churchill, I, 296.
198 "we could not be": Ibid., 295.
198 "as the days succeeded one another": Ibid., 408.
201 "Probably *Scharnhorst, Gneisenau*": Bennett, *Coronel and the Falklands,* 54–55.
203 "She was the fastest": Chatfield, 47.
203 "the guns . . . on the main deck": Bennett, *Coronel and the Falklands,* 17.
203 "It certainly is the limit": Ibid.
203 "Sir William White": *FGDN,* II, 432.
204 "Sighted *Monmouth*": Hirst, 15.
204 "Later on, when leave could be taken": Ibid., 6.
208 "It is advisable to operate": Ibid., 57.
208 "*Gneisenau* and *Scharnhorst*": Bennett, *Coronel and the Falklands,* 80.
208 "No certain information": Ibid., 81.
209 "Few can steam well": *Jane's Fighting Ships—1914,* 53.
209 "If she did not break down": Marder, II, 106.
210 "Situation changed": Bennett, *Coronel and the Falklands,* 82.
211 "I have a feeling": Sweetman, 79.
211 "urgent importance": Ibid.
212 "it blew, snowed, hailed": Spencer-Cooper, 22–23.
212 "We finally got past caring": Ibid., 23.
212 "It seemed to both the captain": Chatterton, *Gallant Gentlemen,* 70.
213 "a good square meal": Hirst, 52.
213 "snug as a bug": Ibid., 54.
213 "She has already been condemned twice": Ibid.

213 "It appears that *Scharnhorst*": Churchill, I, 410.
213 "Does *Defence* join my command": Ibid., 411.
213 "regulations of the Panama Canal Company": Bennett, *Coronel and the Falklands,* 91.
215 "It always appeared to me": Chatterton, *Gallant Gentlemen,* 71–72.
215 "It would be best for the British ships": Churchill, I, 411.
215 "Settled": Ibid.
215 "I understand from our conversation": Ibid., 411–12.
216 "a citadel around which": Ibid., 414.
216 "entirely a contrary opinion": Hirst, 94.
217 "I trust circumstances": Ibid., 93.
217 For William Denbow, see: Hough, *Great War,* 96.
217 "It is clear that": Ibid., 412.
218 "*Good Hope* left": Bennett, *Coronel and the Falklands,* 95.
218 "shining with that special, well-groomed": Sweetman, 74.
218 "would come wandering up": Bennett, *Coronel and the Falklands,* 14.
218 "one of our very best officers": Fisher, *FGDN,* II, 101.
218 "the navy was not": Bennett, *Coronel and the Falklands,* 15.
219 "When a hammock is being used": Ibid., 14.
219 "fought hard, played hard": Hough, *Pursuit,* 86.
219 "Engage the enemy more closely": Sweetman, 74.
219 he hoped when his time came: Dreyer, 90.
219 "That ribbon": Bennett, *Coronel and the Falklands,* 26.
219 "Cradock thought his chances were small": Marder, II, 111.
219 "only in case": Ibid., 112.
219 "I will take care": Ibid., 111.
219 "The admiral was a very brave old man": Bennett, *Coronel and the Falklands,* 92.
219 "He knew what he was up against": Ibid., 95.
219 "With reference to orders": Churchill, I, 416.
220 "gravely preoccupied" and "This telegram is": Ibid.
220 "*Defence* is to remain": Ibid., 417.
221 "The words 'sufficient force' must have seared": Hirst, 96–97.
221 "tired of protesting": Ibid., 97.
221 "I am going to attack the enemy now": Ibid., 29.
221 "I am sure I should": Churchill, I, 416.
221 "Speaking of Admiral Cradock's position": Ibid., 418.
221 "Two of the lieutenant commanders": Hirst, 99.
221 "*Monmouth, Good Hope* and *Otranto* coaling": Churchill, I, 417–18.
222 "alone this time": Chatterton, *Gallant Gentlemen,* 72.
222 "that we expected to sight the enemy": Ibid.
224 "Clear the decks": Pochhammer, 138.
224 "Maneuver well executed": Hirst, 101.
224 like a haystack: Pitt, 5.

CHAPTER 12: THE BATTLE OF CORONEL

225 "in a quarter of an hour": Pitt, 57.
225 "Does my smoke": Pochhammer, 141.
225 "When the sun was sufficiently low": Ibid, 141–43.
226 "We had in sight": Chatterton, *Gallant Gentlemen,* 74.
226 "But when we saw those damned four funnels": Copplestone, 236.
227 "We all thought he would leave *Otranto*": Bennett, *Coronel and the Falklands,* 38.
227 "I cannot go down and engage": Ibid.
228 "Follow in the admiral's wake": Pitt, 8.
228 "I am going to attack": Hirst, 105.
228 "And now began the saddest": Churchill, I, 422.
229 "the most rotten show imaginable": Marder, II, 113.
229 "The waves rose high": Bennett, *Coronel and the Falklands,* 31.
230 "The enemy had the range perfectly": Hirst, 106.
230 "As the two big enemy ships": Copplestone, 143.
231 "her funnels illuminated": Hickling, 47.
231 "She looked like a splendid firework display": Copplestone, 143.
232 "The moon was rising": Chatterton, *Gallant Gentlemen,* 77.
232 "Are you all right": Hirst, 109.
233 "I want to get stern to sea": Ibid., 110.
233 "I felt that I could not help her": Chatterton, *Gallant Gentlemen,* 78.
233 "It was obvious": Hirst, 110.
233 "It was awful having to leave": Bennett, *Coronel and the Falklands,* 35.
233 "utterly dispirited": Hickling, 50–51.

234 "Both British armored cruisers": Bennett, *Coronel and the Falklands,* 36.
235 "I fired until the *Monmouth*": Sweetman, 72.
235 "It was terrible to have to fire": Bennett, *Coronel and the Falklands,* 37.
235 "Have sunk enemy cruiser": Ibid.
235 "Bravo, *Nürnberg*": Pochhammer, 154.
235 "With God's help": Ibid., 157.
236 "The creature just lay there": Copplestone, 145.
236 "*Good Hope,* though bigger than *Scharnhorst*": Pitt, 65.
236 "pretty, black-eyed women": Pochhammer, 163.
237 "When I went ashore": Pitt, 64.
237 "drunken, mindless idiot": Ibid., 66–67.
237 "I drink to the memory": Ibid.
237 "They will do nicely for my grave": Ibid.
237 "I am quite homeless": Hough, *Pursuit,* 116.
237 "*Defence* has been ordered": Churchill, I, 419.
238 "We were already talking to the void": Ibid.
238 "The Admiralty have no official confirmation": *Official Naval Dispatches,* 32.
238 "a belligerent warship": Ibid., 33.
238 "Can you imagine": Marder, II, 115.
238 "the British have allowed their old cruisers": Sweetman, 73.
238 "Poor old Kit Cradock": *Beatty Papers,* I, 159.
239 "He had no clear plan": Marder, II, 110.
239 "I fear he saw red": Chalmers, 180.
239 "let himself be caught": Marder, II, 110.
239 "I cannot accept for the Admiralty": Churchill, I, 414–16.
239 "It ought not to be necessary": Ibid., 424.
240 "we could instantly concentrate": Ibid., 414.
240 "The *Defence* had been refused him": Marder, II, 111.
240 "I will take care I do not suffer": Ibid.
241 "We are of the opinion": Churchill, I, 426.
241 "Why did . . . [Cradock] attack": Corbett, I, 356–57.
242 "by attacking the memory": Bennett, *Naval Battles,* 102.
242 "Not under control": Hirst, 124.

CHAPTER 13: "VERY WELL, LUCE, WE'LL SAIL TOMORROW"

244 "*Carnarvon, Cornwall* should join": Churchill, I, 469.
245 "But I found Lord Fisher in a bolder mood": Ibid., 465.
245 "Order *Invincible*": Ibid., 466.
245 "Sir John Jellicoe rose to the occasion": Ibid.
245 "important not to weaken the Grand Fleet": *Jellicoe Papers,* I, 82.
246 "Once ships fall into dockyard hands": Churchill, I, 473.
246 "The earliest possible date": Ibid.
246 "Friday the thirteenth": Ibid.
246 "*Invincible* and *Inflexible* are needed": Ibid., 475.
247 "to keep an eye on Charlie": Bennett, *Coronel and the Falklands,* 124.
247 "that damned fool": Bennett, *Naval Battles,* 105.
247 "one of the most brilliant": Hough, *Great War,* 105.
247 "pedantic ass": Tarrant, *Invincible,* 44.
248 "Never such utter rot": Fisher, *FGDN,* III, 77.
248 "The destruction of the German [Spee's] Squadron": Bennett, *Naval Battles,* 105.
248 "Very well, we sail": Ibid., 58.
248 "Your main and most important duty": Ibid., 59.
248 "small flocks": Tarrant, *Invincible,* 46.
250 "In some trepidation": Hickling, 66.
250 "Very well, Luce, we'll sail tomorrow": Ibid.
253 "1. Little result": The Naval Staff guidelines for Spee appear in Hirst, 156–58.
253 "proposed to put": Tirpitz, II, 83–84.
254 "to encroach in any way": Ibid., 84.
254 "What are your intentions": Hirst, 159.
254 "The cruiser squadron intends to break through": Pitt, 72.
254 "German if possible": Ibid., 73.
255 "The seas were huge": Bennett, *Coronel and the Falklands,* 134.
255 "Rain clouds hung over the jagged peak": Pochhammer, 191.

CHAPTER 14: THE BATTLE OF THE FALKLAND ISLANDS

258 "A four-funnel and a two-funnel": Hirst, 171.
258 "Enemy in sight": Ibid.

258 "Well, for God's sake, do something": Hickling, 74.
258 "Mr. Hirst, go to the masthead": Hirst, 173.
259 "Send the men to breakfast": Pitt, 103.
259 "He came at a very convenient hour": Bennett, *Coronel and the Falklands,* 140.
259 "engage the enemy": Ibid., 142.
259 "As we got near the harbor entrance": Dixon, 26.
260 "Admiral Spee arrived at daylight this morning": Churchill, I, 436.
260 "As we approached": Pochhammer, 201.
261 "Do not accept action": Bennett, *Coronel and the Falklands,* 143.
262 "The visibility of the fresh, calm atmosphere": Pochhammer, 202.
262 "It was a perfect day": Hough, *Great War,* 113.
262 "struck by the magnificent weather": Tarrant, *Invincible,* 56.
262 "No more glorious moment": Hirst, 177.
263 "Two vessels soon detached themselves": Pochhammer, 202–3.
263 "ships' companies have time": Tarrant, *Invincible,* 57.
263 "Picnic lunch": Ibid.
264 "transports or colliers": Bennett, *Coronel and the Falklands,* 144.
264 "Towards noon": Pochhammer, 203–4.
264 "to get along with the work": Bennett, *Coronel and the Falklands,* 145.
264 "Engage the enemy": Hirst, 179.
264 Fidgety Phill: Tarrant, *Invincible,* 58.
264 "the roar from the forward turret guns": Verner, 8.
265 "*Gneisenau* will accept action": Pitt, 110.
266 "The German firing was magnificent": Bennett, *Coronel and the Falklands,* 147.
266 "It is certainly damned bad shooting": Hickling, 82.
267 "we did not seem to be hitting": Tarrant, *Invincible,* 61.
267 "At this rate": Hickling, 82.
267 "With the sun still shining on them": Pitt, 112.
267 "A shell grazed": Pochhammer, 206.
268 "Every minute we gained": Ibid., 208.
268 "The thick clouds of smoke": Ibid., 209.
269 "for the first time, I experienced the luxury": Verner, 10–11.
270 "a truly lovely sight": Hough, *Pursuit,* 155.
270 "She was being torn apart": Tarrant, *Invincible,* 67.
270 "rapid independent": Pitt, 118.
270 "We were most obviously hitting": Verner, 11.
270 For the signals between Spee and Maerker, see Bennett, *Coronel and the Falklands,* 149–50.
270 "Endeavor to escape": Pitt, 128.
271 "the men with their powder-blackened faces": Pochhammer, 210.
272 "All men overboard": Ibid., 217.
273 "We cast overboard": Spencer-Cooper, 104–5.
273 "Lower all your boats": Bennett, *Coronel and the Falklands,* 154.
273 "The ship inclined": Pochhammer, 217–22.
274 "Flag to *Inflexible*": Ibid., 227.
274 "In the name of all our officers": Bennett, *Coronel and the Falklands,* 155–56.
276 "Am anxious to save life": Hirst, 191.
276 "If anyone can reach the ensign": Ibid., 194.
277 "We are a crippled old ship": Dixon, 19.
277 "Our shooting was rotten": Ibid., 22.
279 "outrageous" and "an overwhelming desire": Pochhammer, 240.
279 "emphatic and unanimous": Verner, 25.
279 "There is nothing at all to show": Copplestone, 169.
280 "Well, Beamish": Bennett, *Coronel and the Falklands,* 154.
281 "It really is a spanking victory": Ibid., 166–67.
281 "It has done us all": *Beatty Papers,* I, 174.
281 "like an armadillo": *FGDN,* III, 77.
281 "the only substantial victory": Fisher, *Records,* 221.
281 "We cannot but be overjoyed": Fisher, *FGDN,* III, 91.
281 "This was your show": Churchill, I, 452.
282 "Your letter pleasant": Ibid.
282 "criminal ineptitude": *FGDN,* III, 101.
282 "report fully reason": Bennett, *Coronel and the Falklands,* 171.
282 "Their Lordships selected me": Marder, II, 125–26.
282 "Last paragraph": Bennett, *Coronel and the Falklands,* 173.
283 "dilatory and theatrical": Tarrant, *Invincible,* 71.
283 It was "an irony": Marder, II, 124.
283 "No one in history": Bennett, *Coronel and the Falklands,* 137.

284 "at the head of some magnificent gorge": Hirst, 219.
285 "villainous-looking face" and "pendulous nose": Dixon, 60.

CHAPTER 15: FISHER RETURNS TO THE ADMIRALTY

287 "He is a wonderful creature": Asquith, *Letters to Venetia,* 266–67.
287 "We talked all day": Churchill, I, 73.
287 "fell desperately in love": Fisher, *FGDN,* II, 397.
288 "My dear Winston": Randolph Churchill, *Young Statesman,* 530.
288 "My dear Fisher": Ibid.
288 "My beloved Winston": Churchill, I, 79.
288 "I want to see you very much": Randolph Churchill, *Young Statesman,* 532.
288 "I plied him with questions": Churchill, I, 77.
288 "I began our conversations": Ibid., 78.
288 "I think Winston Churchill": Mackay, 432.
288 "betrayed the navy": Randolph Churchill, *Young Statesman,* 565.
289 "The liquid fuel problem": Churchill, I, 132–33.
289 "Contact with you": Mackay, 454.
289 "Winston is quite cross": Ibid.
289 "Tomorrow old Fisher comes down": Gilbert, I, 216.
289 "[Watching] him narrowly to judge": Churchill, I, 401–02.
289 "make our country feel": Gilbert, I, 215.
289 "that I could work": Churchill, I, 402.
290 "with some reluctance": Marder, II, 90.
290 "He seems as young as ever": Ibid.
290 "He is already a Court Favorite": Gilbert, I, 226.
290 "Undoubtedly the country will benefit": Ibid., 227.
290 "They have resurrected old Fisher": Chalmers, 160–61.
291 "horrible appointment": Wemyss, *Life and Letters,* 186.
291 "Everything began to move": Bacon, *Fisher,* II, 161–62.
292 "a genius without a doubt": Fisher, *FGDN,* II, 409.
292 "I was never in the least afraid": Churchill, I, 402.
292 "Lord Fisher was the most distinguished": Ibid., 403.
292 "the formidable energy": Ibid., 405.
292 "I can't dine out": Gilbert, I, 264.
292 "Once, I remember": Gretton, 198.
293 "extraordinary spectacle": Hough, *Great War,* 145.
293 "an almost unsleeping watch": Churchill, I, 405.
293 "we made an agreement": Ibid.
293 "Port and starboard lights": Ibid., 406.
294 "everything that can be finished": Ibid., 454.
294 "make his wife a widow": Keyes, *Memoirs,* I, 130.
295 "large light cruisers": Marder, II, 96.
295 "They were an old man's children": Churchill, I, 459.
295 "Lord Fisher hurled himself": Ibid., 456.
295 "order to his subordinates": Gilbert, I, 228.
295 "I backed him up": Churchill, I, 460.
296 "a projectile": Fisher, *FGDN,* I, 291.
296 "criminal folly": Marder, II, 192.
296 "a million Russian soldiers . . . within eighty-two miles": Bacon, *Fisher,* II, 188.
296 "on that 14 miles": *FGDN,* II, 455.
296 "convoy and land": James, *A Great Seaman,* 138.
296 "We gratefully accept": Churchill, II, 39.
297 "storm and seize": Marder, II, 186.
297 "a palpable reluctance": Churchill, II, 42.
297 "Churchill would often look in": James, *A Great Seaman,* 144.
297 "I am wholly with you": Churchill, II, 43.
297 "Although the First Sea Lord's strategic conceptions": Ibid., 41–42.
298 "how an attack on Borkum": Marder, II, 190.
298 "Welcome back": Gilbert, I, 264.
298 "We one and all": Ibid., 184.
298 "First Sea Lord to see": Churchill, II, 358.
298 "Winston has so monopolized": Fisher, *FGDN,* III, 99–100.
299 "The situation is very curious": *Beatty Papers,* I, 173.
299 "inkling that he was": Bonham Carter, 321.

CHAPTER 16: "THE REQUIREMENTS OF THE COMMANDER-IN-CHIEF WERE HARD TO MEET"

300 "weakening the Grand Fleet": Winton, 154.
300 "Is *Princess Royal* to go": Goldrick, 172.
300 "*Princess Royal*'s coal expenditure": *Jellicoe Papers,* I, 81.
301 "*Princess Royal* should have proceeded": Goldrick, 172.

301 "The *Tiger* is absolutely unfit" and "a present for the Germans": Fisher, *FGDN,* III, 68.
301 "We cannot rely": *Jellicoe Papers,* I, 97.
301 "The inferiority": Ibid., 99.
301 "I admit the force": Fisher, *FGDN,* III, 82.
303 "we must always be ready": Ibid., 443.
303 "The requirements": Churchill, I, 443.
304 "Since war began": Ibid., 445.
304 "We cannot reinforce you": Ibid., 447.
304 "I think we have to stand fast": Ibid.
304 "As A. K. Wilson observed": Ibid., 448.
305 "The coast has been so denuded": Ibid., 445.
305 "The Admiralty have in mind": Ibid.
305 "I regret to appear importunate": *Jellicoe Papers,* I, 94.
305 "as I am directed to use this base": Churchill, I, 447.
305 "I know perfectly well": Ibid.
305 "have five torpedoes each": Churchill, I, 447.
305 "You know the difficulty": *Jellicoe Papers,* I, 103.
305 "wearing": Churchill, I, 448.
305 "No one can blame": Ibid., 447–48.
306 "It is necessary to construct": Ibid., 527–28.
306 "The next day": Scott, 272.
307 "The ships could not accompany the fleet": Jellicoe, *Grand Fleet,* 173.
308 "mislead the Germans": Churchill, II, 299.
308 "astonished to see": Denham, 50.

CHAPTER 17: THE YARMOUTH RAID AND ROOM 40

310 "the battle fleet must avoid": Scheer, 68.
310 "escort the cruisers": Goldrick, 159.
310 "I don't want": Waldeyer-Hartz, 127.
311 "Two battle cruisers": Groos, II, 265.
312 "Early in the morning": Churchill, I, 440–42.
313 "I won't wear it": Waldeyer-Hartz, 129.
313 "It appeared that the risk": Groos, II, 267.
313 "One could not assume": Ibid.
314 "short, thick-set man with keen blue eyes": Beesly, 9.
314 "a mauve shirt": Ibid., 10.
315 "The fuses are lit": Kahn, *Enigma,* 19.
316 "the German light cruiser *Magdeburg*": Churchill, I, 462.
316 number 151: Beesly, 5.
317 "drying before Ewing's fire": Kahn, *Enigma,* 24.
317 "Some days earlier": Ibid.
317 "*SKM* key": Beesly, 24.
317 "No fears": Ibid.
318 "virtual certainty": Ibid.

CHAPTER 18: THE SCARBOROUGH RAID: "WITHIN OUR CLAWS"

319 Queen of Watering Places: *Daily Mail,* Dec. 17, 1914, 8.
319 "greatness, vastness of enterprise": Perrett, introduction.
320 "I could see in the mist": *Daily Mail,* Dec. 17, 1914, 6.
320 "Just before eight o'clock": Ibid.
320 "resolutely in bed": Roskill, *Beatty,* 105.
321 "was killed": *Daily Telegraph,* Dec. 19, 1914, 10.
322 "a special lookout": Ward, 7.
324 "deplorable" and "which was stationed": Keyes, *Memoirs,* 151.
324 "1,150 shells": Groos, III, 82.
324 "The Germans have come": *Daily Chronicle,* Dec. 17, 1914, 7.
325 "I must get that medal": *Daily Mail,* Dec. 18, 1914, 5.
325 "Look, there's my teddy bear": Ibid.
325 "assassin squadron" and "Scarborough bandits": Marder, II, 149.
325 "the stigma of the baby-killers": *The Times,* Dec. 21, 1914, 8.
325 "a colossal act of murder": Ibid.
325 "The bombardment . . . was": *Daily Chronicle,* Dec. 17, 1914, 8.
326 "So far as the Hartlepools": Ibid.
326 "Demonstrations of this character": Ward, 28.
326 "The best police force": Marder, II, 148.
326 "It would no doubt": *The Times,* Dec. 18, 1914, 9.
326 "The purpose of the Royal Navy": Ibid., Dec. 17, 1914, 9.
326 "We hope that the authorities": Ward, 28–29.
327 "There has been": *Daily Telegraph,* Dec. 18, 1914, 10.
327 "Cannot we use": Ibid., Dec. 19, 1914, 10.
327 "This does not, however, prevent": Scheer, 68.
329 "Have lost touch": Waldeyer-Hartz, 133.
329 "Bombardment off shore": Ibid.
330 For the conversation between Hipper and Raeder, see ibid., 134.
330 "decided in favor": Groos, III, 77.
330 "with remarkable coolness": Ibid., 78.
331 "Operation completed": Goldrick, 202.
331 "Where is the main fleet": Waldeyer-Hartz, 136.

332 "flying raid" and "insult bombardment": Marder, II, 130.
332 "They can never again": Goldrick, 191.
332 "Good information just received": Churchill, I, 465.
333 "before daylight tomorrow": Ibid.
333 "were precisely the sort": Goldrick, 192.
334 "A great deal of cruising": Churchill, I, 464.
334 "was only thirty miles south": Groos, III, 63.
335 "an imperturbability": Goodenough, 86.
335 "never spoke": Goldrick, 215.
335 "passed in the dark": Young, 90.
336 "I think raid": Ibid.

CHAPTER 19: THE SCARBOROUGH RAID: HIPPER ESCAPES

338 "fairly turned tail": Corbett, II, 28.
339 "Here at last": Marder, II, 136.
339 "Our premature turning": Scheer, 71.
339 "Never again": Goldrick, 195.
339 the one heaven-sent opportunity: Churchill, I, 472–73.
339 "On December 16": Tirpitz, II, 285.
339 "There was . . . no compulsion": Churchill, I, 473.
341 "Am keeping in touch": Young, 93.
341 "I am being chased": Ibid.
342 "if I might lead around": Chatfield, 129.
342 "The fine sunrise": Young, 92.
342 "Are you going after *Roon*": Corbett, II, 29.
342 "Have heard nothing of *Roon*": Goldrick, 197.
343 "Scarborough being shelled": Young, 94.
343 For the exchange of signals between Warrender and Beatty, see Young, 94.
343 "I was in my bath": Churchill, I, 466.
343 "The bombardment of open towns": Ibid., 467–68.
345 "Light cruisers must go in": Goldrick, 202.
345 "Enemy will in all probability": Corbett, II, 36.
345 "Enemy is probably returning": Churchill, I, 468.
345 "At eleven o'clock": Ibid., 475.
346 "Engaged with enemy cruisers": Young, 97.
347 "Tell that light cruiser": Ibid., 98.
347 "Light cruiser resume station": Corbett, II, 38.
347 "Enemy's cruisers bearing south by east": Goldrick, 206.
348 For the signals exchanged between Beatty and Goodenough, see Chalmers, 171, and Goldrick, 206.
348 "Enemy in sight": Goldrick, 207.
348 "No, not until the Vice Admiral signals": Dreyer, 103.
349 "Our golden moment": Ibid., 103–4.
349 "He never spoke to me": Ibid., 103.
349 "Enemy cruisers and destroyers in sight": Corbett, II, 40.
349 "Enemy's course east": Goldrick, 208.
350 "Relinquish chase": Ibid., 209.
351 "Am being chased": Groos, III, 256.
351 "five enemy battleships": Ibid., 257.
351 "Enemy is out of sight": Ibid.
351 "Are you in danger": Ibid., 258.
351 "No": Ibid.
352 "Telegraph and telephone": Churchill, I, 468–69.
353 "Twenty destroyers": Goldrick, 209.
353 "Certainly not advisable" and "It is too late": Ibid.
353 "I had a most trying day": Keyes, *Memoirs,* I, 145.
353 "The High Seas Fleet is at sea": Ibid.
353 In the Admiralty War Room: For the discussion, see Churchill, I, 470.
354 "We sent you a terrible message": Keyes, *Memoirs,* I, 148–49.
354 "It *was* terrible": Ibid., 149.
354 "Words fail me": Ibid., 147.
355 "The more we heard": Young, 111.
355 "nearly broke my heart": *Jellicoe Papers,* I, 111–12.
355 "The happenings of the last week": Chalmers, 175.
355 "There never was a more disappointing day": *Jellicoe Papers,* I, 110–12.
355 "He knows cruiser work": Ibid., 111.
355 "intensely unhappy": Marder, II, 144.
356 "The Commodore gives": Ibid., 145.
356 "Should an officer commanding": *Jellicoe Papers,* I, 117–18.
356 "To break off an action": Ibid., 120.
356 "Beatty [is] very severe": Ibid., 112.
356 "Goodenough was so close": Hough, *Great War,* 128.
356 "The true guilt": Ibid.
356 "He lost three battles": Marder, II, 140.
356 "They were all actually in our grasp": Ibid., 143.
357 *"a fool":* Goldrick, 213.
357 "I suppose you must": Fisher, *FGDN,* III, 185.

357 "Lord Fisher said": Hough, *Great War,* 128–29.
358 "There never was such bad luck": *Jellicoe Papers,* I, 108.
358 "Dissatisfaction was widespread": Churchill, I, 477–78.
359 "a regular bombardment": *The Times,* Dec. 18, 1914, 9.
359 "the life of a single German soldier": Ibid., Dec. 21, 1914, 8.
359 "the bombardment possibly heralds": Ibid., Dec. 18, 1914, 10.
359 "It is extremely probable": Scheer, 72.
359 "because he was afraid": Marder, II, 147.
359 "entirely as a war measure": Waldeyer-Hartz, 141.
359 "The advance of the main fleet": Groos, III, 72–73.
359 "The restrictions enforced": Scheer, 72.
359 "The effort to preserve the fleet": Groos, III, 110.

CHAPTER 20: THE CUXHAVEN RAID: "STUPID GREAT THINGS, BUT VERY BEAUTIFUL"

362 "As a naval officer": Tirpitz, I, 181.
362 "would be of no particular value": Marder, I, 336.
362 "I rated the zeppelin much lower": Churchill, I, 313.
363 "Aviation supersedes": Randolph Churchill, *Winston S. Churchill,* II, 672.
363 "for the protection": Churchill, I, 312.
363 "or seaplanes as I christened them": Ibid.
363 "I had fifty efficient": Ibid.
363 "airships on nocturnal missions": Layman, 15.
364 "our dockyards": Marder, I, 339.
364 "airplanes were the only means": Churchill, I, 314.
364 "by bombing from airplanes": Ibid., 314–15.
364 "the largest possible force": Ibid., 315.
365 "[I] arrived at 5 p.m.": Patterson, *Tyrwhitt,* 81.
366 "I got considerable butter": Ibid., 83.
366 "the enemy had a force present": Jellicoe, *Grand Fleet,* 165.
366 "to deliver to the German mainland": Layman, 61.
366 "stewards who had been landed": Patterson, *Tyrwhitt,* 95.
367 The twin-hangar structure: The information about German navy zeppelins is from Layman, 74.
368 "a thick ground fog": Ibid., 86.
370 "My method of defense": Goldrick, 223.
370 "given ordinary sea room": Ibid., 121.
370 "Zeppelins are not": Patterson, *Tyrwhitt,* 98.
370 "I wish all ships a Merry Christmas": Ibid.
371 "ship-wrecked mariners": Layman, 112.
372 "not by their exertions": Ibid., 120.
372 "They are awfully pleased": Patterson, *Tyrwhitt,* 98.
373 "information from a trustworthy source": Churchill, II, 62–63.
373 a letter to Churchill: Fisher, *FGDN,* III, 124.
373 "My dear Fisher": Churchill, II, 64.
374 "clawed down in flames": Ibid, I, 313.

CHAPTER 21: THE BATTLE OF THE DOGGER BANK: "KINGDOM COME OR TEN DAYS' LEAVE"

376 "No offensive is to be carried": Churchill, II, 61.
376 "If the weather tomorrow": Groos, III, 191–92.
377 "Scouting Forces are to reconnoiter": Ibid., 192–93.
378 "He looked at me intently": Ibid., 129.
378 "Wilson wanted a rendezvous": James, *A Great Seaman,* 145–46.
379 "Four German battle cruisers": Churchill, II, 130.
379 "Through the long hours": Ibid., 131.
379 "the morning being": Young, 172.
380 "I had the first watch": Ibid., 175–76.
382 "The same efficiency": *Beatty Papers,* I, 249.
382 "The eastern horizon": Young, 177.
383 "The day was so clear": Goodenough, 92.
383 "Am in action": Young, 178.
384 "I was anxious at all costs": Waldeyer-Hartz, 151.
384 "at least eight large ships": Ibid.
385 "The pace at which the enemy": Ibid, 152.
385 "Enemy sighted are four battle cruisers": Young, 178.
385 "As day broke": Chatfield, 131.
385 "On the horizon ahead": Hough, *Great War,* 132.
386 "Get us within range": Chatfield, 132.
386 A midshipman on *Indomitable:* Schofield, 68.
387 Beatty's signals: Young, 179–82.
387 "Well done, *Indomitable*": Ibid., 183.
387 "We were all in high spirits": Ibid., 184.

388 "*Lion* being our leading ship": Ibid., 218–19.
388 "How soon should we open fire": Chatfield, 132.
388 "We could see": Young, 183.
388 "Open fire": Ibid.
388 "to universal astonishment": Churchill, II, 136.
389 "The enemy appeared": Young, 182.
389 "a glare amid the smoke": Ibid., 183.
389 "Destroyers take station": Ibid., 184.
390 "Up to now": Ibid.
391 "to the conning tower": Chatfield, 133.
391 "It was impossible to endure the wind": Ibid., 185.
391 "The Admiral and his staff": Ibid., 190–91.
392 "Engage the corresponding ship": Marder, II, 159.
392 "the unmolested *Moltke*": Ibid., 160.
393 "Salvos of three": Goldrick, 263.
393 "At nine a.m. . . . our battle cruisers": Scheer, 80.
393 "the view . . . from the fire control": Waldeyer-Hartz, 152.
393 "The action signals": Ibid.
393 "The chances of support": Ibid.
393 "a great glowing mass of fire": Young, 187.
394 "A shell struck *Seydlitz*": Chatfield, 134.
394 "Need assistance badly": Groos, III, 285.
394 "Main fleet and flotillas": Ibid.
395 "It was wonderful to see": Bennett, *Naval Battles,* 161.
395 "cleaving the water": Schofield, 67.
395 "My range finder was useless": Goldrick, 264.
395 "Many . . . details registered": Young, 216–17.
396 "very nearly smothered": Ibid., 205.
396 "so violent": Ibid., 189.
396 "we must have been struck": Chatfield, 134.
397 "Close the enemy as rapidly": Goldrick, 271.
397 "We thought our last moment": Young, 192.
397 "Attack the enemy": Ibid., 193.
398 "At 10.54 a.m., submarines were reported": *Beatty Papers,* I, 217.
398 "*Lion* hoisted the signal": Pelly, 148–50.
399 "Good heavens, Sir": Goldrick, 273.
399 "Had he turned and steered": Bacon, *Modern Naval Strategy,* 71.
399 "The best course": Marder, II, 161.
400 "the whole spirit and direction": Churchill, II, 138.
400 "it was impossible to endure": Young, 185.
401 "What we need now": Goldrick, 275.
403 "Only when he realized": Waldeyer-Hartz, 159.
403 "I dismissed": Ibid., 153.
403 "If Hipper's leadership": Ibid., 159.
404 "in stern turret D": Ibid., 157.

CHAPTER 22: THE BATTLE OF THE DOGGER BANK: "WHY DIDN'T YOU GET THE LOT?"

406 "a kind of obsession": Young, 196.
406 "*Blücher* was under fire": Goldrick, 277, and Young, 208–9.
406 "stayed for about twenty seconds": Schofield, 67.
406 "was in a pitiable condition": Patterson, *Tyrwhitt,* 107.
406 "It was a pathetic sight": Schofield, 67.
407 "As an example": Corbett, II, 98.
407 "As we turned": Young, 207.
407 "a tremendous picture": Bennett, *Naval Battles,* 163.
408 "Reports High Seas Fleet coming out": Young, 198.
408 "Some one said, 'Moore is reporting": Churchill, II, 132.
408 "There can be few": Ibid.
409 "the horrid news": Chatfield, 134.
409 "an extraordinary spectacle": Young, 201.
409 "around him, cheering": Ibid.
409 "The *Lion* was one huge grandstand": Ralph Seymour, 67.
409 "with the admiral's flag": Young, 201.
411 "an escort of thirteen": Goldrick, 283.
411 "Germans are preparing": Ibid.
411 "It was a strange journey": Young, 204.
412 "Keep a good lookout": Ibid.
412 "The silence of the ship": Ibid., 204–5.
412 "There was a thick fog": Ibid., 219.
413 "It was a bad decision": Chatfield, 136.
413 "incredibly small and mean": Young, 232.
413 "I most heartily congratulate": Young, 211.
413 "It will be some time": Marder, II, 166.
414 "After yesterday's action": Ibid., 167.

414 "For the second time": Churchill, II, 140.
414 "The disappointment": Keyes, *Memoirs,* I, 163.
414 "I think the spectacle": Marder, II, 167.
414 "I am against all charges": *Jellicoe Papers,* I, 144.
414 "despicable" and "No signals": Marder, II, 168.
415 "if, as has since been stated": Ibid.
415 "wanted to have": *Jellicoe Papers,* I, 144.
415 "poltroon" to *"Any fool can obey orders":* Fisher, *FGDN,* III, 150–51.
415 "Pelly did very badly": *Jellicoe Papers,* I, 144–45.
415 "had done very well": Ibid., 145.
415 "Special emphasis is laid": Marder, II, 169.
415 "The future and the present": Ibid., 171.
416 "in a split second": Chalmers, 196.
416 "urgently inquiring": Young, 224.
416 "I was taken": Ibid., 225.
416 "We know from themselves": Chalmers, 197.
416 "I've quite made up": Fisher, *FGDN,* III, 150.
416 "an indecisive fight": Marder, II, 167.
416 "Well do I remember": Churchill, II, 89.
417 "My impression": Young, 205.
417 "we had no director firing": Ibid., 206.
417 "Every one of them": Ibid., 222.
418 "would immediately have been fastened upon": Ibid.
418 "The result of the engagement": Churchill, II, 143.
418 "suspicion that the gunnery": Jellicoe, *Grand Fleet,* 181.
418 "We went out to sea": Young, 233.
419 "in a marked degree": *Beatty Papers,* I, 250.
420 "Jellicoe's Battle Squadrons": Fisher, *FGDN,* III, 156.
420 "The fundamental fact": Ibid., 200.
420 "I imagine the Germans": *Jellicoe Papers,* I, 152.
421 "The dominant feeling": Marder, II, 165.
421 "Our own fire": Waldeyer-Hartz, 154.
421 "There seems no obvious": Scheer, 84.
422 "Hits on *Tiger* aft": Waldeyer-Hartz, 156.
422 "I cannot confirm": Ibid., 153.
422 "The tactical dispositions": Ibid., 163.
422 "Seeing so many": Scheer, 86.
422 "With the Dogger Bank": Waldeyer-Hartz, 157.
422 "in English waters": Ibid.
422 "All ships other": Ibid., 154.
423 "The consumption of ammunition": Ibid., 156.
423 "The working chamber": Bennett, *Naval Battles,* 164.
424 "The unexpected presence": Scheer, 86.
424 "It must be considered": Bennett, *NavalBattles,* 165.
424 "Not apparent": Ibid.
424 "The blame": Groos, III, 243.
424 "short and square built": Marder, II, 166.
425 "Apart from submarine warfare": Churchill, II, 146–47.
425 "the second navy": Marder, II, 175.

CHAPTER 23: "A DEMONSTRATION AT THE DARDANELLES"

428 "a chivalry which surely outstripped": Marder, II, 231.
428 "It now appears": Gilbert, I, 289–90.
428 "Who expected Carden": Fisher, *FGDN,* III, 166.
428 "[Your] sole duty": Churchill, I, 491.
429 "it is a good thing": Gilbert, I, 299.
430 *"You smug-faced crowds":* Siegfried Sassoon, "Suicide in the Trenches," from *Counter-attack and Other Poems* (1918).
431 "Are there not other alternatives": Churchill, II, 44.
432 "I do not see": Ibid., 94.
432 "I CONSIDER": Fisher, *FGDN,* III, 117.
433 "His Majesty's less valuable ships": James, *Gallipoli,* 26.
434 "Do you consider": Churchill, II, 97–98.
434 "I do not consider": Ibid.
434 "he seemed at this time": Ibid., 100.
434 "Your view is agreed with": Ibid., 99.
434 "until the impossibility": Gilbert, I, 333.
434 "the Dardanelles appeared": Ibid.
435 "Time required for operations": Churchill, II, 102.
435 "the plan produced a great impression": Ibid.
435 "firing all her ammunition": Marder, II, 206.
435 "any sailor who attacked a fort": Fisher, *Memories,* 81.
435 "A ship can no more stand up": Marder, II, 215.
437 "The War Council had been sitting": Hankey, I, 265–66.
437 "with all the inexorable force": Lloyd George, I, 338–39.
438 "we could leave off": Churchill, II, 110–11.

438 "That the Admiralty should prepare": Ibid., 111.
438 "The Cabinet have decided": Fisher, *FGDN,* III, 133.
438 "I just abominate": Ibid., 142.
438 "is a projectile to be fired": Fisher, *FGDN,* I, 291.
439 "I had not the same weight": Magnus, 286.
439 "All powerful": Churchill, II, 172–73.
439 "I made it a rule": James, *Gallipoli,* 32.
440 First Lord, I have no desire": Churchill, II, 154.
440 "We play into Germany's hands": Ibid., 155–56.
440 "Being already in possession": Ibid., 157.
441 "Not to use them": Ibid., 161–62.
442 "I entreat you": Gilbert, I, 364.
438 "I am not in accord": Fisher, *FGDN,* III, 147–48.
442 "undoubtedly involves risks": Magnus, 319.
442 "he had understood": Fisher, *Memories,* 71, 90, and Churchill, II, 164.
442 "in view of the Steps": Churchill, II, 163.
442 "if satisfactory progress": Hankey, I, 272.
442 "it was difficult" and "the Turks": Ibid.
442 "an obstinate": Asquith, *Letters to Venetia,* 405.
442 "long and very friendly": Churchill, II, 165.
442 "I am in no way concealing": Ibid.
442 "He always out-argues me": James, *Gallipoli,* 37.
442 "I am sure I am right": Ibid.
443 "When I finally decided": Churchill, II, 165.
443 "This I took as the point": Ibid.
443 "When the operation": James, *Gallipoli,* 37.
443 "The more I consider": Churchill, II, 301.
443 "A failure or check": Ibid., 303.
443 "You are just simply eaten up": Ibid.

CHAPTER 24: THE MINEFIELDS

447 "I do not intend": Keyes, *Memoirs,* I, 195.
448 "the number of persons": Churchill, II, 194.
448 "Our affairs in the Dardanelles": Marder, II, 240.
448 "the capsizing of one little state": James, *Gallipoli,* 50.
450 "We could not go on": Keyes, *Memoirs,* I, 207.
452 "recognised sweeping risks": Ibid., 211.
452 "When we got into the Straits": Ibid.
453 "The less said about that night": Ibid., 212.
453 "Your original instructions": Ibid., 213.
453 "fully concurred": Ibid.
453 "a minute later": Ibid.
454 "I do not understand": Ibid., 216.
454 "We have given the Carden plan": Churchill, II, 216.
455 "One gesture with a wand": Ibid., 215.
455 "was never more resolute": Ibid., 216.
455 "who had a sort of feeling": James, *Gallipoli,* 50.
456 "Everyone's blood was up": Churchill, II, 217.
455 "Everything was eagerness": Morgenthau, 222.
455 "My poor admiral": *Keyes Papers,* I, 107.
456 "I do not understand": Keyes, *Memoirs,* 216–17.
456 "a complete break down": *Keyes Papers,* I, 109.
456 "a real fine fellow": Marder, II, 245.
456 "One could not feel": Churchill, II, 220.
456 "Personal and Secret": Ibid., 221.

CHAPTER 25: THE NAVAL ATTACK ON THE NARROWS

457 "a naval attack": Moorehead, 62.
457 "no human power": Chatterton, *Dardanelles Dilemma,* 132.
460 "pulped": Verner, 65.
460 "Thank you, old chap": Ibid., 69.
460 "Fore-control out of action": Ibid., 60.
460 "For God's sake, put out the fire": Ibid.
461 "down her side and across her bottom": Chatterton, *Dardanelles Dilemma,* 140.
461 *"Sauvez-vous":* Usborne, 115.
461 "I did not think": Keyes, *Memoirs,* I, 237.
462 "Tell my people": Verner, 63.
462 "The admiral directs you": Keyes, *Memoirs,* I, 240.
462 "blazing away": Ibid., 241.
462 "If you do not propose": Ibid.
463 "Except for the searchlights": Ibid., 245.
464 "We are all getting ready": Hamilton, I, 40.
465 "continue the naval operations": Churchill, II, 231.
465 Lines from Kipling's "If" are in *The Oxford Dictionary of Quotations,* 2nd ed., 297.
466 "to be in a position": Churchill, II, 231.
466 "a disaster": Wemyss, 41.
466 "reap the fruits": Marder, II, 235.
466 "I am being most reluctantly driven": Hamilton, I, 37.

467 "You know my view": Ibid.
467 "a fine-looking man": Ibid., 21.
467 "Constantinople must surrender": Ibid., 42.
468 "I lost no time": Keyes, *Memoirs,* I, 257.
468 "I wish to place on record": Ibid., 186.
468 "It appears better": Ibid., 258.
468 "I do not hold": Ibid., 266.
468 "consternation": Churchill, II, 233.
468 "to renew the attack": Ibid., 234.
468 "insuperable resistance": Ibid., 234–35.
469 "because it was supported": Ibid., 234.
469 "What more could we want": Ibid.
469 "pressed to the very utmost": Ibid., 235.
469 "with grief": Ibid., 248–49.
469 "we had lost fewer men": Ibid., 249.
469 "Confident, commanding, magnanimous": Ibid.
469 "The whole Ottoman state": Morgenthau, 227–28.

CHAPTER 26: GALLIPOLI: THE LANDINGS

471 "The Dardanelles: futile without soldiers": Lloyd George, I, 374.
471 "If the navy required": Marder, II, 233.
471 "either to seize the Gallipoli peninsula": Magnus, 321.
472 "if the fleet cannot get through": Marder, II, 235.
472 "unless the navy are convinced": Magnus, 322.
473 "too sanguine": Ibid.
473 "very second rate": Ibid.
473 For the Kitchener-Hamilton conversations at the War Office, see Hamilton, I, 2–16.
474 "Only two sorts": Ibid., 19.
474 "thyme-scented breezes": Ibid., 18–19.
475 "of whom": Ibid., 57.
476 "it is not customary": Morgenthau, 45.
477 "scattered like frontier guards": Kannengiesser, 91.
477 "would have found resistance": Sanders, 61.
477 "If the English will only leave me alone": Kannengiesser, 96.
477 "The British allowed us": Sanders, 58.
477 "I have no roving commission": Hamilton, I, 58.
477 "The slipshod manner": Wemyss, *Life and Letters,* 210.
479 "In my mind": James, *Gallipoli,* 89.
479 "It's too wonderful": Bonham-Carter, 296.
479 Rupert Brooke's poetry is quoted by Moorehead, 110.
479 "He died at 4.46": James, *Gallipoli,* 94.
479 "Nature was so peaceful": Ibid., 95.
479 "On deck it is hardly light": Ibid., 115.
480 "Casualties?": Ibid., 210.
481 "the cross fire from the fleet": Hamilton, I, 15.
481 "From the vigour": James, *Gallipoli,* 192.
482 *"The more I consider":* Churchill, II, 301.
482 "*We cannot send*": Ibid., 303.
482 "Seriously, my friend": Ibid., 307.
482 "every officer": Ibid., 306.
482 "You are a foolish woman": Gilbert, I, 540.
483 "Although I have acquiesced": Fisher, *FGDN,* III, 216–18.
483 "I honestly feel": Ibid., 221.
483 "The sea for an area": Chatterton, *Dardanelles Dilemma,* 239.
484 "was very much relieved": Churchill, II, 346.
484 "The *Queen Elizabeth*": Ibid.,
484 "could not stand the fear": Magnus, 338–39
484 "We think that the moment": Churchill, II, 348.
484 "sulphurous": Ibid., 350.
484 "against the Dardanelles operations": Ibid., 351.
484 "This remarkable interruption": Ibid.
485 "I could see": Bacon, *Fisher,* II, 214.
485 "I must ask you": Churchill, II, 353.
485 "Well, good night, Fisher": Bacon, *Fisher,* II, 251.
485 "I send this to you": Churchill, II, 554.
485 "Fisher has resigned": Ibid., 359.
486 "First Lord: After further anxious reflection": Fisher, *FGDN,* III, 228.
486 "In the King's name": Gilbert, I, 563.
486 "A combative grimness": Lloyd George, I, 198–99.
486 "to escape from Winston": Hankey, I, 315.
487 "My dear Fisher: The only thing": Churchill, II, 360.
487 "YOU ARE BENT": Fisher, *FGDN,* III, 231.
487 "in the name of friendship": Churchill, II, 363.
487 "Dear Winston: As usual": Fisher, *FGDN,* III, 234.
487 "Stick to your post": Hough, *Fisher,* 343.
487 "I would far sooner": Fisher, *FGDN,* III, 243.

487 "would be a worse calamity": Roskill, *Beatty,* 127.
488 "Lord Fisher": Marder, II, 281.
488 "Then the situation is impossible": Beaverbrook, I, 106.
488 "No, I have thought of that": Churchill, II, 364.
488 "No, this will not do": Ibid., 366.
489 "W.C. MUST go": Fisher, *FGDN,* III, 237.
489 "What are we to do for you": Churchill, II, 366.
489 "It is not impossible": Ibid., 368.
489 "a serious view": Mackay, 502.
489 "He should have been hanged": Ibid., 503.
490 "guarantee the successful termination": Fisher, *FGDN,* III, 241.
490 "I shall have": Ibid.
490 "I am afraid": Marder, II, 290.
490 "a fit of megalomania": Asquith, *Memories and Reflections,* II, 113.
490 "Fisher's mind is somewhat unhinged": Ibid.
490 "ought to be shot": Hankey, I, 318.
490 "Dear Lord Fisher: I am commanded": Asquith, *Memories and Reflections,* II, 111.
490 "You don't care": Gilbert, I, 584.
491 "Why do you part": Ibid., 588.
491 "the letter of a maniac": Ibid., 589.
491 "My dear Winston: You must take it": Ibid., 594.
491 "horrible wound": Marder, II, 289.
491 "I gather": Gilbert, 598.
491 "to beginners in the Cabinet": Lloyd George, I, 205.
491 "He asked what": Churchill, II, 374–75.
491 "The navy breathes": *Beatty Papers,* I, 273.
491 "We owe you a debt": Mackay, 505.
491 "He is young": Gilbert, I, 600.
491 "When he left": Ibid., 605.

CHAPTER 27: "SOME CORNER OF A FOREIGN FIELD"

492 "I saw them": James, *Gallipoli,* 204.
492 "all the ships": Kannengiesser, 169.
493 "Yes, and here comes": Goodchild, 169–71.
493 "like melted glass": Hamilton, II, 53.
493 "fills me with a desperate longing": Ibid., 6.
494 "That evening, Kemal Bey": Kannengiesser, 130.
494 "I do not order you": Moorehead, 140.
494 "It will be quite impossible": Hamilton, II, 13.
494 "We bit, fisted": Keyes, *Memoirs,* I, 404, 405, and James, *Gallipoli,* 290.
495 "spread around the beaches": Churchill, II, 445.
495 "We might have the hills": Hamilton, II, 66.
495 "he had not been very fit": Ibid., 64.
495 "From bankrupt to millionaire": Ibid., 163–64.
496 "We can't feed Russia": Ibid., 203.
496 "an elaborate explanation": Ibid., 241.
496 "You would refuse to believe": Ibid., 258.
496 "The fact is": Ibid.
496 "an irresponsible statement by an ignorant man": Ibid., 259.
496 "The 10th went forward": Bean, II, 617–18.
496 "a cheery old fellow": Hankey, I, 404, 426.
496 "side-show": James, *Gallipoli,* 321.
497 "General Monro was": Churchill, II, 489.
498 "on the strength": Beaverbrook, I, 164.
498 "Well, Commodore": Keyes, *Memoirs,* I, 437.
498 "It is not often": Ibid., 449.
499 "Most secret. Decipher yourself": Ibid., 450.
499 "I have seen the place": Ibid, 461.
500 "I realised": Wemyss, 220.
500 "All indications": Ibid., 224.
500 "a disastrous mistake": Ibid., 224–25.
500 "The Navy is prepared": Ibid., 225–26.
500 "The 'unanimous military opinion' ": Wemyss, 226.
500 "responsible generals": Keyes, *Memoirs,* I, 489.
501 "As long as war exists": Wemyss, 241.
502 "Mr. Balfour was most sympathetic": Keyes, *Memoirs,* I, 520.
502 "he had always felt": Ibid., 522–23.
502 "Searching my heart": Churchill, II, 169.

CHAPTER 28: THE BLOCKADE OF GERMANY

503 "the miracle weapon": Ritter, III, 119.
504 "the nearest run thing": Longford, *Wellington,* I, 489.
504 "Mr. President": Bell, 547.
505 "in conformity": Ibid., 38.
505 "all materials useful": Guichard, 17.
506 "A close commercial blockade": Bell, 31.

507 "Finally, to further empower": Chatterton, *Big Blockade,* 30.
508 "We have only two objects": Bell, 52.
508 "conditional contraband is liable": Guichard, 23.
508 "the efficient conduct": Tuchman, *Guns of August,* 334.
509 "The surest way": Grey, II, 104.
509 "to secure the maximum": Ibid., 107.
510 "was conducted": Bell, 34.
510 "We rather feared": Chatterton, *Big Blockade,* 51.
511 "A campaign protracts itself": Bell, 194.
512 "There is nothing certain": Groos, I, 54–55.
513 "During the last week": Bell, 63.
513 Scheer's complaints about the impact of the British blockade are in Scheer, 215–17.
515 "From a purely military point of view": Tarrant, *U-boat Offensive,* 12.
516 "The gravity of the situation": Scheer, 223.
516 "Viewed from the standpoint": Bell, 206.
517 "Gentlemen, always realize": Cecil, II, 221.
517 On December 21: The Tirpitz-Wiegand interview is in Bell, 210–11.
517 "he wished to sound": Görlitz, 51.
518 "eminent financiers": Bell, 211.
518 "The waters surrounding": Ibid., 217.
519 "It was disloyal": Tirpitz, II, 146–47.
519 "Pohl, by his vanity": Görlitz, 296.
519 "Instead of which": Ibid.
519 "We are not in a position": Bell, 208.
520 "England would be forced": Tirpitz, II, 150.
520 "a silly question": Ibid.
520 "For urgent political reasons": Scheer, 230.
520 "This order makes success impossible": Ibid.
520 "H.M. the Emperor has commanded": Ibid.
521 "if, in spite of the exercise": Tarrant, *U-boat Offensive,* 14.
521 "a handful of naval officers": Bell, 219.
521 "The question that really troubles me": Simpson, 31.
521 "war has no amenities": Bacon, *Fisher,* I, 121.
521 "one flag": Simpson, 31.
521 "There were a few points": Churchill, II, 280.
521 "losses will no doubt": Bell, 221.
522 "an indefensible violation": Charles Seymour, *Neutrality,* 33.
522 *"une chose énorme":* Bell, 217.
523 "in the interest": Görlitz, 68.
523 "absolutely crazy": Ibid., 65.
523 "when they are recognizable": Jarausch, 274.
526 "with the avowed object": Bell, 233.
526 "I think we may say": Ibid., 241.
527 "an atrocious act of lawlessness": Dos Passos, 123.
527 "wanton and indiscriminate": Simpson, 120.
527 "the growing number": Jarausch, 275.
527 "could not be responsible": Bell, 424.

CHAPTER 29: *LUSITANIA* AND THE AMERICAN REACTION

528 "Just now": Preston, 49.
529 "NOTICE": Ibid., 91.
529 "Madam, your secret is safe": Ibid., 96. This story and many others describing the passengers and the last voyage of the doomed ship are presented by Diana Preston in her recent, detailed book *Lusitania.*
530 "The American people": Simpson, 83.
530 "This afternoon": Charles Seymour, *House Papers,* I, 361.
530 "bloody monkeys": Preston, 108.
531 "Royal Navy Reserved Merchant Cruiser": Preston, 386.
531 "Either the *Lusitania*": Simpson, 151.
532 "Yes, by God": Preston, 216.
532 "trying to put life jackets": Ibid., 233.
532 "soon gave it away": Ibid., 204.
534 "faces registered": Frost, 235–36.
534 "and the Emperor and Government": Preston, 294.
534 "My highest appreciation": Ibid., 308.
534 "With joyful pride": Simpson, 9.
535 "My life would not": Heckscher, 23.
535 "stern, absolute": Ibid., 24.
536 "I shall not aid": Dos Passos, 10.
536 "political suicide": Heckscher, 269.
536 "talking to Mr. Bryan": Spring-Rice, II, 202.
536 "by self-inflicted degrees": Heckscher, 295.
536 "Everything that I love": Bell, 48.
537 "the example of America": Ibid., 425.
537 "I do not know": Heckscher, 365.
537 "The government of the United States": Bell, 428.
538 "a strict accountability": Charles Seymour, *Neutrality,* 16.
538 "has permitted in silence": Bell, 247.

538 "Are you sure the American": Gerard, 258.
538 "as safe as if": Bell, 425.
538 "traveling on a volcano": Ibid.
538 "for the immediate future": Ibid., 426.
538 "the most definite instructions": Ibid.
539 "In a comparatively short": Ibid., 423.
539 "I am myself positive": Ibid., 431.
540 "stubbornly repeated that": Ibid., 433.
540 "Whatever may be the facts": Ibid., 435.
540 "The United States cannot admit": Ibid., 436.
541 "You people are not neutral": Preston, 341.
541 "steely glitter": Charles Seymour, *House Papers,* II, 6.
541 "Mr. Bryan, you are not warranted": Ibid.
541 "it must be taken": Bell, 438.
541 "there would appear": Ibid.
541 "arrogant": This and the following are from ibid., 439.
542 "The events of the past": Ibid., 441.
542 "ghastly": Tirpitz, II, 233.
542 "servile": Ibid., 282.
542 "a contemptible little man": Ibid., 339.
542 "kowtowing": Ibid., 172.
542 "America is so shamelessly": Ibid., 351.
542 "as I had been shot at": Bell, 442.
543 "I cannot continue to walk": Jarausch, 278.
546 "ineffective, illegal and indefensible": Bell, 545.
546 "There is no parallel": Ibid., 446.
547 "if all restrictions were removed": Tirpitz, II, 172.
548 "His Majesty took": Görlitz, 126.
548 "mad dog": Ibid.
548 "A desperate situation": Ibid., 136.
549 "smoked cigarette after cigarette": Ibid., 140.
549 "His Majesty's nerves": Ibid., 145.
549 "The grave anxiety": Ibid., 146.
549 "indescribable": Blücher, 120.
551 "utterly incompatible": Bell, 594.
551 "If it is still": Ibid.
551 "impertinence:" Heckscher, 386.
551 "until further orders": Tarrant, *U-boat Offensive,* 30.
552 "to escape": Ibid.
552 "the cessation": Ibid.

CHAPTER 30: THE EVE OF JUTLAND

554 "We knew that Scheer": Weizsäcker, 30.
555 "was of cheerful disposition": Ibid., 31.
555 "One could not find": Marder, III, 42.
557 "terrible pain": Philbin, 123.
557 "You know I am very fond": Waldeyer-Hartz, 192–93.
558 "Vice Admiral Hipper no longer possesses": Philbin, 124.
558 "coming forward": Ibid.
558 "I agree": Ibid.
559 "another raid": Marder, II, 433.
563 "hammer and tongs": Waldeyer-Hartz, 203.
565 "covering the sea": Hase, 69.
566 "I heard rumors": *Beatty Papers,* I, 274.
566 "The horrid Forth": Chalmers, 207.
566 "I wish we could entice them": *Jellicoe Papers,* I, 184.
566 "Until the High Seas Fleet": Ibid., 203.
567 "a horrible crunching": Tarrant, *Battleship Warspite,* 20.
567 "the stronger I make Beatty": Ibid., 225.
567 "terrible disappointment": *Jellicoe Papers,* I, 188.
567 "collectively and separately": Gordon, 46.
568 "This is a great mistake": Marder, III, 41.
568 "shockingly unprofessional": Gordon, 56–57.
569 "I'm glad to say": *Jellicoe Papers,* I, 175.
571 "coaling, sleeping": Gordon, 30.
571 "I should not select it": King-Hall, 36–37.
571 "as smooth": Ibid., 36.
571 "it was, I suppose": Copplestone, *Silent Watchers,* 2.
572 "Jellicoe . . . worked": Marder, II, 443.
572 "Every night": Dreyer, 96.
572 "It's splendid": Winton, 160–61.
572 "Look here, Jack": Bacon, *Jellicoe,* 235.
573 "of a particularly lurid description": Bacon, *Jellicoe,* 245.
573 "five French" and "United States press": Jellicoe, *Grand Fleet,* 245.
573 "I am not at all well": Winton, 161.
573 "You must take": Ibid.
573 "I am laid": *Jellicoe Papers,* I, 132.
573 "My beloved Jellicoe": Bacon, *Jellicoe,* 228.
573 "feeling really fit": Ibid., 146.
573 "Please don't overdo": *Beatty Papers,* I, 281.
574 "a totally different being": *Jellicoe Papers,* I, 185.
574 "I expect you will know": Bacon, *Jellicoe,* 239.
574 "At ease": Gordon, 18.
574 "smiling, clapped his hands": Winton, 167.
574 "I am being pressed": *Beatty Papers,* I, 301–2.
574 "You ask me": Ibid., 303.
575 "Germans intend": *Jellicoe Papers,* I, 254.
576 "After a thoroughly": Bingham, 133.

576 "blazing red": Brown and Meehan, 95.
576 "Inside the ships": Gibson and Harper, 102.
578 "If there is no news": *Jellicoe Papers,* 259.

CHAPTER 31: JUTLAND: BEATTY VS. HIPPER

579 "about a thousand bare-headed sailors": Gordon, 71.
579 "We did not appear": Ibid., 73.
580 "In the Jade": Irving, 36.
580 "No definite news": Gordon, 73.
580 "a party of very clever fellows": Marder, III, 47.
580 "Those chaps": Ibid.
582 "Ridiculous," "angry": Gordon, 72–73.
582 "buffoon": Ibid., 416.
583 "Ship ahead blowing off steam": Oakeshott, 36.
583 "Green two five": Ibid., 37.
583 "Enemy in sight": *Official Despatches,* 443.
583 "Two cruisers, probably hostile": Ibid.
584 "Nearly everyone agreed": Hase, 73.
584 "Clear for action": Ibid., 77.
584 "When we turn north": *Official Despatches,* 443.
585 "The only way": Bacon, *Jutland Scandal,* 178.
586 "putting on as many clothes": King-Hall, 130.
586 "All the cups": Gordon, 105.
586 "urinal buckets": Costello and Hughes, 127.
587 "Have sighted": *Official Despatches,* 444.
587 "Smoke seems to be": Ibid., 445.
587 "Sea suitable for getting off": Ibid., 433.
589 "it was one": Chalmers, 229.
589 "Suddenly my periscope": Hase, 80.
589 "how splendid": Oakeshott, 42.
590 "The enemy battle cruisers": Chatfield, 140–41.
590 "a moment of supreme tension": Raeder, 66.
590 "The six ships": Hase, 81.
590 "dense masses of smoke": Ibid., 83–84.
591 "The Zeiss lenses": Ibid., 86.
591 "His unruffled calm": Waldeyer-Hartz, 204.
591 "could not be separated": Ibid., 205.
591 "Hipper left his telescope": Ibid.
591 "from this time on": Fawcett and Hooper, 62.
592 "With each salvo fired": Hase, 85.
592 "His curiosity": Ibid.
593 "Q turret has gone": Chatfield, 143.
593 "No further confirmation": Chalmers, 231–32.
593 "We were altering course": Fawcett and Hooper, 17.
594 "with their huge bow waves": Chalmers, 233.
593 "It happened so suddenly": Fawcett and Hooper, 18.
594 "Behind the battle cruiser line": Hase, 93.
594 "Although out in the open sea": Tarrant, *Warspite,* 23.
595 "quivered and reverberated": Gibson and Harper, 133.
595 "The *Queen Mary* was firing less rapidly": Hase, 89.
595 "I saw one salvo": Fawcett and Hooper, 19–20.
596 "We disappeared": Ibid., 18–19.
596 "*Princess Royal* blown up, sir": Churchill, III, 129.
596 "There seems to be something wrong": Chatfield, 143.
598 "Those of us": Goodenough, 95.
598 "We saw ahead of us": Ibid.
598 "If you're going to make": Ibid.
598 "URGENT": *Official Despatches,* 453.
599 "the weather was extremely clear": Scheer, 147.
599 "Course of enemy's battle fleet": *Official Despatches,* 453.
599 "I can truthfully say": Marder, III, 71.
599 "Simply by steering": Chalmers, 243.
599 "Alter course": *Official Despatches,* 453.
600 "I suddenly saw": Fawcett and Hooper, 67–68.
601 "The turning point": Ibid., 60–61.
601 "the securing of arteries": Ibid., 49.
601 "a lull in the action": Ibid., 14–15.
602 "When we turned": Ibid., 61.
602 "until swelling from burns": Gordon, 410.
602 "did his best": Ibid.
602 "Six, eight, nine salvos": Ibid., 411.
602 "Everything was dark chaos": Fawcett and Hooper, 64.
602 "The effect was agonizing": Tarrant, *Warspite,* 35–36.
602 "restless agony": Ibid., 36.
603 "On its way": Fawcett and Hooper, 72.
603 "three stokers dead": Gordon, 413.
604 "Give chase": Scheer, 149.
604 "Prepare to renew": *Official Despatches,* 455.

CHAPTER 32: JUTLAND: JELLICOE VS. SCHEER

606 "large amount of smoke": *Official Despatches,* 444.
606 "Smoke seems to be": Ibid., 445.
607 "several ships were flying": Fawcett and Hooper, 98.
607 "Am engaging enemy": *Official Despatches,* 450.
607 "Proceed immediately": Ibid., 451.
608 "under fire from enemy battleships": Tarrant, *Jutland,* 281.
608 "a great cloud": Bennett, *Jutland,* 103.
608 "Look after yourself": Ibid., 104.
609 "a shell took off": Ibid.
609 "Yes, I am engaging": *Official Despatches,* 451.
609 "Have sighted enemy": Ibid., 452.
609 "Enemy's battle fleet": Ibid., 453.
609 "every face radiant": Schoultz, 118.
609 "Urgent. Fleet action": *Official Despatches,* 453.
609 "in a state of very great excitement": Marder, III, 94.
609 "Balfour stayed": James, *A Great Seaman,* 155.
610 "You must steer": *Official Despatches,* 450.
610 "Keep just clear": Ibid., 452.
610 "Can you pass": Ibid., 454.
610 "What can you see": Ibid., 457.
610 "our battle cruisers": Ibid.
610 "I wish somebody": Bacon, *Jellicoe,* 265.
611 "suddenly burst": Gordon, 433.
611 "Where is enemy's battle fleet": *Official Despatches,* 457.
611 "Enemy's battle cruisers bearing southeast": Ibid., 458.
611 "Enemy battle fleet in sight": Ibid., 459.
612 "I therefore decided": Jellicoe, *Grand Fleet,* 350.
612 "One must agree": Tarrant, *Jutland,* 123.
612 "I heard the signalman": Dreyer, 146–47.
613 "Dreyer, commence": Ibid., 147.
613 "the supreme moment": Corbett, III, 361.
613 "the peak moment": Marder, III, 101.
613 "Dreyer, I think it is time": Dreyer, 149.
613 "as thick as the traffic": Marder, III, 112.
614 "fired a salvo over us": Fawcett and Hooper, 81.
614 "a light cruiser squadron": Marder, III, 117.
614 "dressed in all her glory": Tarrant, *Warspite,* 31.
615 "Twenty-four hours earlier": Gibson and Harper, 176.
615 "berserk": Marder, III, 113.
615 "while center stage": Gordon, 443.
616 "got a bit rattled": Ibid., 447.
617 "highly satisfactory": Tarrant, *Invincible,* 97.
617 "The gunnery": Hayward, 118.
618 "Your firing is very good": *Official Despatches,* 168.
618 "At 6.29 p.m., the veil of mist": Hase, 102–3.
618 "I have never seen anything": Fawcett and Hooper, 130.
618 "My gun layer": Ibid.
618 "Pick up survivors": *Official Despatches,* 460.
618 "had not a scratch": Fawcett and Hooper, 136.
618 "Is wreck": *Official Despatches,* 462.
619 "a kind of paralysis": Waldeyer-Hartz, 208.
619 Hipper's conversations with Raeder and Harder are in ibid.
619 "a hole as big": Ibid., 210.
620 "breaking into a ripple": Gordon, 440.
621 "had but the foggiest idea": Marder, III, 225.
621 "It was now obvious": Scheer, 152.
621 "in the vicinity": Tarrant, *Jutland,* 281.
622 "While the battle is progressing": Frost, *Battle of Jutland,* 328.
622 "I could not see": Marder, III, 123.
623 "Can you see": *Official Despatches,* 461.
623 "a heavy shock": Ibid., 67.
624 "all sense of danger": Wheeler-Bennett, 97.
625 "If the enemy followed": Scheer, 155.
625 "It was as yet too early": Tarrant, *Jutland,* 151.
625 "The fact is": Weizsäcker, 33.
626 "if I'd done it": Marder, III, 128.
626 "bunched together": Irving, 163.
627 "an almost continuous flickering": Ibid., 157.
627 "Splinters penetrated": *Official Despatches,* 80.
627 *"Schlachtkreuzer ran":* Groos, V, 319.
628 "We were steaming": Hase, 110–13.
628 "Operate against": Tarrant, *Jutland,* 283.
629 "altered course to starboard": Fawcett and Hooper, 121–22.
630 "following exactly in our course": Ibid., 117.
630 "torpedo was either deflected": Ibid.
631 "eight or even more": Irving, 173.

632 "full confidence": Marder, II, 76.
633 "Submit van": *Official Despatches,* 466.
633 "posturing": Gordon, 467.
633 "To tell the truth": Marder, III, 145.
633 "Follow our battle cruisers": *Official Despatches,* 468.

CHAPTER 33: JUTLAND: NIGHT AND MORNING

635 "I went back": Dreyer, 151.
636 "must have inevitably led": Jellicoe, *Grand Fleet,* 372.
636 "It was known to me": Ibid., 373.
636 "Nothing would make me fight": *Jellicoe Papers,* I, 271.
637 "to steer south": *Official Despatches,* 21.
637 "fulfill three conditions": Jellicoe, *Grand Fleet,* 374.
637 "No night intentions": Bennett, *Battle of Jutland,* 128.
637 "made from dark slabs" Costello and Hughes, 206.
638 "Please give me challenge": *Official Despatches,* 473.
639 "First sign of enemy challenge": Tarrant, *Jutland,* 286.
639 "the 'V' became an 'X' ": Gibson and Harper, 220.
639 "I can't help who it is": Goodenough, 96.
639 "Those who have not": Marder, III, 162–63.
640 "A signalman suddenly": King-Hall, 149–53.
641 "Three [German] destroyer flotillas": *Official Despatches,* 474.
641 "I should not for a moment": *Admiralty Narrative,* 108.
641 "German battle fleet ordered home": *Official Despatches,* 475.
641 "The lamentable part": Marder, III, 174.
642 "Of course, if the Admiralty" Bennett, *Jutland,* 135.
642 "criminal neglect": Marder, III, 176.
642 "had left the War Room": Bennett, *Jutland,* 135.
643 "and all the time": Fawcett and Hooper, 179.
643 "A blaze of searchlights": Ibid., 173.
644 "four big ships": Ibid., 193–94.
645 "At 11.40": *Official Despatches,* 219–20.
646 "constant attacks by torpedo craft": Ibid., 201.
646 "At 11.35 p.m., we observed": Ibid., 271.
646 "which I surmised": Ibid., 195–96.
646 "whether the various observations": Gordon, 487.
647 "that the crew": Scheer, 161–62.
647 "a grand but terrible": Ibid., 162.
647 "URGENT. PRIORITY. Enemy's battle fleet": Marder, III, 166.
648 "URGENT. I am attacking": Ibid.
648 "Amidships on the waterline": Fawcett and Hooper, 208.
648 "Every now and then": Legg, 122.
648 "A cruiser on fire": Fawcett and Hooper, 202–3.
648 "violent action flared up": Bennett, *Jutland,* 127.
649 "Owing to the bad visibility": *Official Despatches,* 598.
651 "I did not challenge her": Ibid., 93.
651 "I missed the chance": Marder, III, 184.
652 "It was inadvisable": *Official Despatches,* 376.
653 "These difficulties rendered it undesirable": Jellicoe, *Grand Fleet,* 385.
653 "the double purpose": Marder, III, 188.
653 "lifted its nose": Fawcett and Hooper, 213.
654 "Damage yesterday": *Official Despatches,* 488.
654 "Enemy fleet has returned": Ibid.
654 "None appeared to suffer": Fawcett and Hooper, 196.
654 "I want to ascertain": *Official Despatches,* 506.
654 "wreck of *Queen Mary*": Ibid.
654 "When did *Queen Mary*": Ibid., 509.
654 "Was cause of sinking": Ibid., 511.
654 "Do not think it was mines": Ibid., 514.
656 "bobbing about": Fawcett and Hooper, 93.
656 "triumph of organization": Ibid., 94.
656 "sat down on the settee": Chalmers, 262.
656 "[It was] an awful sight": Gordon, 470.
656 "The wounded who could speak": King-Hall, 156.
657 "Very rapidly": Gordon, 477–78.
657 "how he had found": Marder, III, 495.
657 "poor charred bodies": Bennett, *Jutland,* 153.
657 "poor, unrecognisable scraps": Gordon, 496.
657 "an awful smell": Hayward, 146–47.

CHAPTER 34: JUTLAND: AFTERMATH

658 "not yet returned": Marder, III, 234.
658 "intoxicated with its victory": Ibid.

658 The German newspaper headlines I quote appear in Tarrant, *Jutland,* 247.
658 "Trafalgar Is Wiped Out": Gibson and Harper, 256.
659 "annihilation": Ibid.
659 "the arrogant presumption": Ibid., 256–57.
659 "almost hysterical": Marder, III, 234.
659 "The journey": Tarrant, *Jutland,* 274.
659 "cock-crowing": Marder, III, 235.
659 "Nevertheless": Ibid., 253.
660 "prompt contradiction": Irving, 9.
660 London newsboys: Gibson and Harper, 258.
661 "On the afternoon": Newbolt, IV, 3.
661 "I desired": Marder, III, 243.
661 The quotations from the *Daily Telegraph* and *Daily News* are taken from ibid., 241.
661 "They've failed me": Gordon, 498.
662 "having driven the enemy": Newbolt, IV, 6.
662 "substantial victory": This and the following quotations are from Marder, III, 243–44.
662 "Will the shouting": Tarrant, *Jutland,* 250.
663 "It is not customary": Gordon, 504.
663 "The German fleet has assaulted": Tarrant, *Jutland,* 250.
663 "talked twaddle": Beaverbrook, 71.
663 One night over dinner: Dugdale, 115–16.
663 "Rightly or wrongly": Magnus, 372.
664 "the dirtiest night": Gordon, 503.
664 "a timetable": Jellicoe, *Grand Fleet,* 423.
664 "I feel in a measure": Marder, III, 237.
666 "the superiority": Ibid., 198.
666 "the supreme quality": Tirpitz, I, 173.
666 "Hit first": Marder, III, 203.
668 "laughable" and "broken to pieces": Chatfield, 153.
668 green boys: Marder, III, 263.
669 "May I go outside": *Jellicoe Papers,* I, 268.
669 "God bless you, Sir": Ibid., 270.
669 "Your deployment into battle": Fisher, *FGDN,* III, 358.
669 "You were robbed": Marder, III, 236–37.
669 "I hope that": Ibid., 237.
670 "I often feel": Ibid.
670 "I missed": Ibid.
670 "First, I want to offer you": *Jellicoe Papers,* I, 277.
670 "I spent an hour": Marder, III, 238.
670 "As you well know": Ibid.
670 "arrogant, slipshod": Ibid., 246.
670 "There is no doubt": Ibid.
671 "If Jellicoe had grasped": Ibid., 245.
671 "Now that it is all over": *Beatty Papers,* I, 369.
671 "It was nothing": Marder, III, 81.
672 "Scheer had but": Ibid., 226.
673 "Neither *Lion* nor *Princess Royal*": Harper, *Truth,* 157.
675 "he would have led": Marder, III, 105.
675 "I hope I would": Ibid.
675 "He fought to make": Ibid., 226.
675 "I am not particularly sensitive": *Jellicoe Papers,* I, 288.
676 "I do not understand": *Beatty Papers,* I, 280.
676 "based solely:" Harper, *Truth,* 5.
676 "we do not wish": *Jellicoe Papers,* II, 465.
677 "Well, I suppose": Ibid., 471.
677 "It is to be supposed": Pollen, *The Navy in Battle,* 338–39.
677 Harper described Pollen: Harper, *Truth,* 146.
677 "full of errors": *Jellicoe Papers,* II, 412.
677 "almost unreadable": Winton, 287.
677 "a man of tearful yesterdays": Bellairs, 80.
678 "outrageous and intolerable": Harper, *Truth,* 170.
678 "It is, apparently": Ibid., 169.
678 "I am the luckiest person": Ralph Seymour, 71.
678 " 'Flags' is my Food Dictator": *Beatty Papers,* I, 408.
678 "lost three battles": Marder, II, 140.
678 "rose in all Hell's fury": Roskill, *Beatty,* 316.
678 "The Admiralty are bent": Bacon, *Jellicoe,* 438.
678 "On learning of the approach": Patterson, *Jellicoe,* 233.
678 "The carelessness": *Jellicoe Papers,* II, 417–18.
678 "It is . . . of course": Ibid.
678 "If you had seen": Bacon, *Jellicoe,* 440.
679 "A British squadron was worsted": Bacon, *Scandal,* 97.
679 "A want of tactical competence": Ibid., xv.
679 "Beatty now made a decision": Harper, *Truth,* 50–51.
679 "Then, full of ardor": Bacon, *Scandal,* 90.
679 "It is unpalatable": Harper, *Truth,* 69–70.
679 "Lord Beatty's political power": *Jellicoe Papers,* II, 462.

680 "the absence of even approximately": Marder, III, 90, 93.
680 "the consequences to Britain": Churchill, III, 110.
681 "the standpoint": Ibid., 112.
681 "The dominant school": Ibid., 111.
681 "The attempt to centralise": Ibid., 169.
681 "the Royal Navy must find": Ibid., 169–70.
681 "Mr. Churchill as he sits": Bacon, *Scandal,* 194.
682 "He beckoned me over": Gordon, 519.
682 "stayed on deck": Ibid., 521.
683 "High Seas Fleet may be sighted": Marder, III, 292.
683 "Scouting by airships": Ibid., 298.

CHAPTER 35: AMERICA ENTERS THE WAR

686 "Where does incompetence": Jarausch, 294.
686 "As you wish": Görlitz, 199.
686 "I am ready": Hindenburg, 81.
687 "When the Quartermaster General": Kürenburg, 325.
687 "Every day is important": Jarausch, 344.
688 "America had better": Gerard, *Four Years,* 252.
688 "nothing more than a sieve": Ludendorff, *General Staff,* 278.
689 "the decision for an unrestricted": Ibid., 281.
689 "directly affects our relations": Ibid.
689 "He kept us out of war": Ritter, III, 301.
691 "Charles E. Hughes": Heckscher, 415.
691 "the election of Mr. Hughes": Baker, VI, 296.
691 "It was a little moth-eaten": Heckscher, 415.
692 "if Germany won": Charles Seymour, *House Papers,* I, 293.
692 "He holds no office": Ibid., II, 113.
693 "Mr. House is my second personality": Ibid., I, 115.
693 "You are the only person": Ibid., 116.
693 "personal friend of the President": Ibid., 247.
693 "Instead of sending": Ibid., II, 113.
693 "My Dear Theodore": Spring-Rice, II, 252.
693 "My Dear Cabot": Ibid., 291.
693 "Uncle Henry": Ibid., 180.
693 "a little book by a Jew-boy": Ibid., 170.
693 "Jew bankers": Ibid., 248.
693 "Jews capturing": Ibid., 245.
693 "feeling a sympathy": Charles Seymour, *House Papers,* II, 99.
693 "At one time": Ibid., 76.
693 "I would be glad": Ibid.
693 "Sir Cecil's nervous temperment": Ibid., 57.
693 "There is a strong sense": Spring-Rice, II, 343.
694 "Our blockade measures": Ibid., 354.
694 "The President rarely": Ibid., 366.
694 "I have been in Russia": Ibid., 372.
694 "Here [in Washington]": Ibid., 368.
694 "The president's great talents": Ibid., 374.
694 "There would come days": Wilson, 116.
694 "There was one mistake": Grey, II, 160.
695 "If Wilson wins": Bernstorff, 244.
695 "The whole situation": Ibid., 246.
695 "Demand for unrestricted": Ibid., 254–55.
695 "Desirable to know": Ibid., 260.
695 "We are thoroughly": Ibid., 266.
695 "Urge no change": Ibid., 260.
696 "The German people wish": Tuchman, *Zimmermann Telegram,* 126.
696 "a man broken": Ibid., 121.
696 "Boiled Crow": Curtain, 152.
696 "We are all gaunt": Blücher, 158.
697 "To propose to make peace": Cecil, II, 242.
697 "Intensified submarine war": Jarausch, 297.
697 "was threatened by a peace move": Tuchman, *Zimmermann Telegram,* 127.
697 "In a deep moral": Gerard, *Four Years,* 353–54.
698 "Soldiers!": Ibid., 354.
698 "it was not unknown": Chamberlain, 111.
698 "visibly flabbier": Lloyd George, II, 411.
698 "to enter into a conference": Cowles, 375.
698 "Since I do not believe": Jarausch, 297.
699 "diplomatic and military preparations": Ludendorff, *General Staff,* 294.
699 "It may be": Charles Seymour, *House Papers,* II, 404.
699 "we do not want": Bernstorff, 275.
699 "I go to no conference": Balfour, 371.
699 "butt in": Lloyd George, II, 280.
699 "There had been": Ibid.
700 "There will be no war": Charles Seymour, *House Papers,* II, 412.
700 *"Ich pfeife":* Herwig, *Politics of Frustration,* 121.
700 "If it were not for": Curtain, 120.
700 "30,000 killed": Ibid., 121.

700 "An ambassador is supposed": Gerard, *Four Years,* 219.
701 "to tell the kaiser": Ibid.
701 "I have nothing": Ibid.
701 "Your Excellency": Ibid., 250.
701 "I said that": Ibid., 366.
701 "While you might invent": Ibid.
701 "Do you come": Ibid., 339.
701 "charged Germany": Ibid., 340.
701 "If two men": Ibid., 341.
701 "If the chancellor": Ibid., 342–43.
702 "Wilson and his press": Ibid., 313.
702 " 'You are the American' ": Ibid., 226–27.
702 "We are fighting": Balfour, 375.
702 "We must resume": Ludendorff, *General Staff,* 293–94.
703 "for which I alone": Ibid., 295–96.
703 "Unfortunately, our military situation": Ibid., 298–99.
703 "A decision must be reached": Scheer, 248.
703 "The backbone of England": Ibid.
704 "We may reckon": Ibid., 249–50.
704 "After our peace feelers": Görlitz, 229.
704 "Oh, I am most unhappy": Daisy of Pless, 256.
704 Buzzie: Ibid., 31.
705 "even if the chancellor": Görlitz, 299.
705 "agitated and depressed": Ibid.
705 "For two years": Ibid.
705 "If the military authorities": Ludendorff, *General Staff,* 340.
705 "in the course": Tuchman, *Zimmermann Telegram,* 139.
705 "I pledge on my word": Reischach, 261.
705 "We are in a position": Ludendorff, *General Staff,* 305.
705 "Of course, if": Ibid., 306.
705 "I command": Ibid.
706 "Have we lost": Reischach, 260.
706 "American intervention": Bernstorff, 281.
706 "This government": Ibid., 280.
707 "war inevitable": Ibid., 306.
707 "I do not care": Görlitz, 232.
707 "Remarkable as this may sound": Bernstorff, 302.
707 "Victory would mean": Ibid., 310–14.
707 "Peace without victory": Knock, 113.
707 "House suddenly": Bernstorff, 319–20.
707 "Please thank the president": Ibid.,7320–22.
708 "Agreed, reject": Charles Seymour, *American Neutrality,* 24.
708 "striped like a barber's pole: Tuchman, *Practicing History,* 168.
708 Handing the note: The Lansing-Bernstorff conversation is reported in Lansing, 211–12.
708 "the German people": Bernstorff, 344.
708 "In America you wanted": Ibid., 352.
708 "He looked up": Tumulty, 254–55.
709 "You will see": Gerard, *Four Years,* 376.
709 "contempt and hatred": Herwig, *Politics of Frustration,* 124.
709 "a fat, rich, race": Trask, 44.
709 "gruesome": Görlitz, 237.
709 "I refuse to believe": Charles Seymour, *House Papers,* II, 442.
709 "The main point": Spring-Rice, 377–78.
710 "He is endeavoring": Tuchman, *Zimmermann Telegram,* 162.
710 "leaking like a basket": Wesley Frost, 88–91.
710 "a very jolly": Charles Seymour, *House Papers,* I, 186.
711 "is filled with the best of intentions": Bülow, III, 178.
711 "The United States does not dare": Gerard, *Four Years,* 237.
711 "I told him": Ibid.
711 "Gentlemen, there is": Tuchman, *Zimmermann Telegram,* 113.
711 "relations between": Gerard, *Four Years,* 363.
711 "so long as such men": Bülow, III, 301.
712 "We intend": The text of the Zimmermann telegram appears in Hendrick, III, 333.
713 "Good Lord": Lansing, 228.
713 "Germany Seeks Alliance": *New York Times,* March 1, 1917.
713 "If he does not go to war": Heckscher, 435.
713 "a communication": Ibid., 437.
713 "fanatical pro-German": Lansing, 239.
713 "I shall never forget it": Spring-Rice, 389.
713 "The present German": Baker, VI, 510–14.

CHAPTER 36: THE DEFEAT OF THE U-BOATS

715 "a veritable cemetery": Churchill, IV, 362.
717 "The shipping situation": *Jellicoe Papers,* II, 125.
717 "The world's ports": Fayle, quoted by Marder, IV, 65.
717 "The position is exceedingly grave": *Jellicoe Papers,* II, 146.
718 "dirty trick": Kemp, 13.

719 "barbarous" and "contrary to the rules": Sims, 144.
720 "Stand by": Ibid., 185.
722 "vermin": Chatterton, *Gallant Gentlemen,* 175.
722 "some of the most admirable": Sims, 170.
722 "a record of gallantry": Jellicoe, *The Crisis of the Naval War,* 73.
722 "A tramp steamer": Campbell, 108.
722 "should the Officer": Chatterton, *Q-Ships,* 193–94.
722 "Don't speak": Campbell, 187.
724 "a terrific explosion": Ibid., 271.
726 "Mr. S. W. Davidson": Sims, 4.
726 "rely upon the last ship": Ibid., 79.
726 "Don't let the British": Klachko and Trask, 58.
726 "a small man": Sims, 7–8.
726 Greeting his visitor: The Sims-Jellicoe conversation is reported in ibid., 9.
727 "a big, exuberant boy": Ibid., 15–16.
728 "long and distant service": Taffrail, 327.
728 "Wherever possible": Marder, IV, 121.
728 "A submarine could remain": Terraine, 53.
728 controlled sailings: Marder, IV, 138.
729 "totally insufficient": Ibid., 122.
729 "Absolutely impossible": Sims, 107.
730 "palsied and muddle-headed Admiralty": Lloyd George, III, 95.
730 "atmosphere of crouching": Ibid., 83.
730 "condition of utter despair": Ibid., 81.
730 "paralytic documents": Ibid., 80.
730 "fear-dimmed eyes": Ibid., 85.
730 "stunned pessimism": Ibid., 86.
730 "High Admirals": Ibid., 108.
730 "men whose caution": Ibid., 81, 95.
730 "announced his intent": Ibid., 106.
730 "and spent": Hankey, II, 650.
731 "On the 30th": Beaverbrook, 155.
731 "Apparently the prospect": Lloyd George, III, 107.
731 "a travesty": Patterson, *Jellicoe,* 174.
731 "virtually preclude": *Jellicoe Papers,* II, 114.
731 "My impression": Marder, IV, 162.
731 "was the result": Jellicoe, *The Submarine Peril,* 130–31.
731 "The little popinjay": Bacon, *Jellicoe,* 388.
731 "something between": Dangerfield, 22.
731 "My father": Richard Lloyd George's remarks are on pages 42 and 63 of his book, *My Father, Lloyd George.*
732 "had enjoyed more sleep": Marder, IV, 186.
732 "too many eggs": Ibid., 131.
733 "establish a square mile": Sims, 111.
733 "The size of the sea": Churchill, IV, 364.
733 "The oceans at once": Doenitz, 4.
734 "the British nation": Sims, 55.
734 "Dine in undress": Ibid., 56.
734 "When will you be ready": Ibid., 58.
735 "He watched over": Ibid., 65.
735 Uncle Lewis: Ibid., 75.
735 "attributed his success": Marder, II, 12–13.
735 "a peculiarly difficult man": *Anglo-American Naval Relations,* 213.
735 "I do not consider": Ibid., 219.
735 "I have a suggestion": Ibid., 225.
736 "To command you": Bayly, 249.
736 "First, the depth charge": Sims, 153–54.
737 "Then a propeller": Ibid., 225.
737 "There was a lumbering noise": Ibid., 226.
737 "All night long": Ibid., 227.
737 "a sharp, piercing noise": Ibid.
737 "In all, twenty-five shots": Ibid.
737 "We have thirty-seven destroyers": *Jellicoe Papers,* II, 163.

CHAPTER 37: JELLICOE LEAVES, BEATTY ARRIVES, AND THE AMERICANS CROSS THE ATLANTIC

739 "uncrowned King": Marder, IV, 54.
739 "My only qualification": Ibid., 55.
739 "As long as I am": Beaverbrook, 151.
739 "I am overwhelmed": *Jellicoe Papers,* II, 123.
739 "I spent from 10.30 a.m.": Ibid., 127.
739 "The Imperial War Cabinet meets": Ibid., 154.
739 "seedy but indomitable": *Jellicoe Papers,* II, 139.
740 "You will remember": Ibid., 156.
740 "I have got myself": Ibid., 173.
740 "Wherever you read": Beaverbrook, 162.
740 "the PM is hot": Roskill, *Hankey,* 406.
740 "had his knife": Marder, IV, 327.
740 "At one point": The Carson-Jellicoe conversation is reported in Bacon, *Jellicoe,* 390.
740 "reptile press": Marder, IV, 110.
740 "You kill him": Ibid., 327.
740 "No one can feel": Ibid., 323.

741 "The British Admiralty has done": *Anglo-American Naval Relations,* 71.
741 "extraordinary folly": Ibid., 107.
741 "It fell to me": Marder, IV, 110.
741 "One can gather": Jellicoe, *Submarine Peril,* 36.
741 "ambivalent": Marder, IV, 327.
741 "what the intriguers set": *Beatty Papers,* II, 174.
741 "J. J. was always": Ibid., I, 426.
741 "I telephoned Mr. Pollen": Ibid., 422.
741 "I talked to Pollen": Ibid., 429.
742 "unless I were present": Lloyd George, III, 113.
742 "a giant figure": Sims, 258.
742 "masquerading": Marder, IV, 213.
742 "a general today": Ibid., 176.
742 "We have been upside down": James, *A Great Seaman,* 159–60.
742 "used to bother me": Ibid., 159.
742 "I said that the organisation": *Jellicoe Papers,* II, 240–41.
743 "for his services": Ibid., 243.
743 "After very careful": Ibid., 246.
743 "I have received": Ibid., 246–47.
743 "It's a good thing": Marder, IV, 341.
743 "Dear Sir": *Jellicoe Papers,* II, 247.
743 "a title usually reserved": Bacon, *Jellicoe,* 386.
743 "in the way I thought": *Jellicoe Papers,* II, 246.
744 "the change was not": Ibid., 245.
744 "We had full confidence": Ibid., 248.
744 "was the only man": Ibid., 249.
744 "I would remind you": Ibid., 250.
744 "we have realised": Ibid., 254.
744 "disgraceful": Ibid.
744 "mutinous": Ibid., 255.
744 "scandalous": Ibid.
744 "I cannot find words": Ibid., 256.
744 "Never a man": Ibid., 257.
744 "No one knows better": Ibid., 260.
744 "I look upon": Ibid.
744 "We want you back": Ibid., 263.
744 "Sack the lot!": Bacon, *Jellicoe,* 389.
745 "The whole time": Beaverbrook, 181–82.
745 "At sea, a figure": Gordon, 523.
745 "There was too much": Roskill, *Beatty,* 206.
746 "One of my difficulties": Jellicoe, *Submarine Peril,* 159.
746 "Only by keeping": *Beatty Papers,* I, 462.
746 "The torpedo menace": Ibid., 460.
747 "the correct strategy of the Grand Fleet": Marder, V, 134.
747 "Luck was against us": Ibid., IV, 298.
748 "We do have": Ibid., 314.
748 "out of control": Ibid., V, 151.
749 "because it is exercise": Hunter, 17.
749 "Here, we can't let it stand": Ibid., 21.
749 "utterly unpredictable": Marder, IV, 26.
749 "worse than Jutland": Ibid.
750 "Darling Tata": Roskill, *Beatty,* 203.
750 "You accuse me": Chalmers, 216–17.
750 "You must give me": Ibid.
750 His reply: These letters from Beatty to Eugenie appear on pages 204, 205, 209, 211, 217, 221, 223, 226, 230, and 231 of Stephen Roskill's biography, *Earl Beatty: The Last Naval Hero.* Roskill, a former Royal Navy captain, was the official historian of the Royal Navy in World War II.
751 "You must know": *Beatty Papers,* I, 449.
751 Eugenie asked Beatty: The letters that follow (including Beatty's verse) appear on pages 235, 254, 255, 263, and 266 of Roskill, *Beatty.*
752 "dirty dog": *Beatty Papers,* I, 386.
752 "a demagogue": Ibid., 431.
752 Geddes a "dirty dog" and "weak as ditch water": Ibid., 452.
752 "The Jew Montagu": Ibid., 451.
752 Churchill "a dead dog" and "a disappointed blackguard": Ibid., 445.
752 "a selfish beast": Roskill, *Beatty,* 281.
752 "I am truly devoted": Ibid., 265.
752 "Heaps of love": *Beatty Papers,* II, 35.
752 "perpetual black despair" and "present dog's life": Roskill, *Beatty,* 304.
752 "quite impossible" and "an interesting young man": Ibid., 341.
753 "The future position of the United States": Jones, 6.
753 "The U.S. believes": *Anglo-American Naval Relations,* 331.
754 "I cannot see": Ibid., 332.
754 "a dear old cup of tea": Roskill, *Beatty,* 230.
754 "I am determined": Herwig, *The Politics of Frustration,* 25.
755 "Why, I shall stop": Ibid., 31.
755 "Unsparing, merciless assaults": Ibid., 52.
755 "2 to 3 battalions": Herwig and Trask, 44.
756 "a glorious golden dawn": Hunter, 13–14.
756 "climbed to the crest": Ibid., 94.
757 "I came on deck": Ibid., 95.
757 "distinctly poor": Jones, 44.

757 "desperately keen": Roskill, *Beatty,* 243.
757 "It is not that it blows": *Anglo-American Naval Relations,* 342.
757 "I have seen": Rodman, 283–84.
757 "this greatest": Jones, 58.
758 "too cold for men": *Anglo-American Naval Relations,* 361.
758 "I am sending": *Beatty Papers,* I, 508.
758 "lavender, snow-powdered hills": Hunter, 99.
758 "the atmosphere was crystal": Ibid., 103.
758 "the north burst": Ibid.
758 "the coast of Norway": Ibid.
758 "she was not ready": Jones, 43.
759 "exceptionally fine": Ibid., 55.
759 "rather as an incubus": *Anglo-American Naval Relations,* 327.
759 "where they were least likely": Jones, 44.
760 "United States is prepared": *Anglo-American Naval Relations,* 374.
760 "It is physically": Ibid., 376–77.
761 "U.S. naval authorities": Ibid., 391.

CHAPTER 38: FINIS GERMANIAE

764 "If an English delegation": Görlitz, 245.
765 "A force of about": Vandiver, II, 728.
765 "naked so to speak": Herwig, *First World War,* 422.
766 *Kaiserschlacht:* Görlitz, 346.
766 "There was no surprise": Churchill, IV, 411–13.
766 the Paris Gun: Moyer, 245.
766 "to coordinate the action": Vandiver, II, 875.
767 "Infantry, artillery, aviation": Ibid., 876.
767 "obstinate" and "stupid": Herwig, *First World War,* 407.
767 "There would be": Vandiver, II, 849.
767 "the roads . . . began": Churchill, IV, 454.
768 "The moral effect": Vandiver, II, 898.
768 "You're prolonging": Ludendorff, II, 683.
768 "August 8": Ibid., 679.
768 "The war must be ended": Ibid., 684.
769 "You don't know Ludendorff": Görlitz, 406.
769 "Then, all of a sudden": Barnett, 340.
770 "overworked" and "drive": Goodspeed, 260.
770 "We are absolutely finished": Fischer, 630.
770 "gradually paralyzing": Ibid., 627.
770 "almost incomprehensible": Ibid.
770 "I hope that": Ibid., 628.
770 "By the mistaken operation": Geis, 255.
770 "like lightning": Fischer, 630.
771 "at once": Ibid., 634.
771 "ten, eight": Goodspeed, 268.
771 "I want to save my army": Ibid.
771 "I am not a magician": Cecil, II, 278.
771 "will consent to consider": Max of Baden, II, 88.
772 "Brutes they were": Gibson and Prendergast, 323.
772 "The navy does not need": Herwig, *German Naval Officer Corps,* 240.
772 "To allow ourselves to be": Ludendorff, II, 748.
772 "concession to Wilson": Ibid., 756.
772 "must deal with": Balfour, 397.
772 "The hypocritical Wilson": Ibid., 398.
772 "the audacity": Ibid.
773 "a demand": Ludendorff, II, 761.
773 "You stay": Cecil, II, 285.
773 "Siamese twins": Ibid.
773 "I refuse": Görlitz, 413.
773 "an honorable battle": Marder, V, 173.
773 "The High Seas Fleet is directed": David Woodward, 114.
774 "complete freedom of action": Scheer, 353.
774 "I did not regard it": Horn, 209–10.
774 "I specifically reiterate": Ibid., 210.
775 "a tactical success": Marder, V, 173.
775 "suicide mission": Philbin, 160.
775 "an honorable death": Horn, 221.
777 "My dear admiral": Herwig, *German Naval Officer Corps,* 261.
777 "Now you must let me": Bülow, III, 329–30.
778 "The German people" and *"Très bien":* Moyer, 297.
778 "For He's a Jolly Good Fellow": Ralph Seymour, 118.
779 At seven o'clock on the evening: Beatty's two meetings with Admiral Meurer are related in Beatty's letter to Eugenie, *Beatty Papers,* I, 572–74, and in Ralph Seymour, 120–21.
780 "I saw a leg of mutton": Chatfield, 175.
780 "the low-lying, sinister forms": King-Hall, 231.
781 "In nearly every case": Ibid., 232.
781 "as the sun sank": Ibid., 236.
782 "My heart is breaking": Herwig, *German Naval Officer Corps,* 266.
782 "We cannot do better": Hunter, 177.
783 "The German flag": Marder, V, 191.

783 "I took the fleet flagship": Chatfield, 176–77.
785 "madhouse": Van Der Vat, *The Grand Scuttle,* 147.
785 "all internal watertight doors": Marder, V, 279.
786 "Paragraph Eleven": Ibid.
787 "with a dreadful": Van Der Vat, *The Grand Scuttle,* 173.
787 "a drifter towing": Ibid., 176.
788 "German battleship sinking": Marder, V, 281.
788 "violated common honor": Ibid., 283–84.
788 "I look upon the sinking": Wemyss, *Life and Letters,* 432.
788 "I rejoice": Woodward, 184–85.

Bibliography

Admiralty. *Battle of Jutland, Official Despatches with Appendices,* 2 vols. Vol. 1, text; Vol. 2, maps. London: His Majesty's Stationery Office, n.d.

———. *Narrative of the Battle of Jutland.* London: His Majesty's Stationery Office, 1924.

Anglo-American Naval Relations, 1917–1919. Michael Simpson, ed. Navy Records Society, 1991.

Ashmead-Bartlett, E. *Despatches from the Dardanelles.* London: George Newnes, 1915.

———. *The Uncensored Dardanelles.* London: Hutchinson, 1928.

Aspinall-Oglander, Brig. Gen. C. F. *Military Operations: Gallipoli. The Official History of the Great War.* 2 vols. London: Heinemann, 1929, 1932.

Asquith, H. H. (Earl of Oxford). *Memories and Reflections, 1852–1927.* 2 vols. Boston: Little, Brown, 1928.

———. *Letters to Venetia Stanley.* Michael and Eleanor Brock, eds. Oxford: Oxford University Press, 1982.

Audoin-Rouzeau, Stephane and Annette Becker. *14–18: Understanding the Great War.* New York: Hill and Wang, 2002.

Auten, Harold. *Q-boat Adventures.* London: Herbert Jenkins, 1919.

Bacon, Admiral Sir Reginald. *The Dover Patrol, 1915–1917.* 2 vols. New York: Doran, 1919.

———. *The Life of Lord Fisher of Kilverstone.* 2 vols. London: Hodder and Stoughton, 1929.

———. *The Jutland Scandal.* New and revised edition. London: Hutchinson, 1933.

———. *The Life of Earl Jellicoe.* London: Cassell, 1936.

———. *From 1900 Onward.* London: Hutchinson, 1940.

Bacon, Admiral Sir Reginald, and Francis E. McMurtrie. *Modern Naval Strategy.* London: Frederick Muller Ltd., 1940.

Bailey, Thomas A., and Paul B. Ryan. *The Lusitania Disaster.* New York: Free Press, 1975.

Baker, Ray Stannard. *Woodrow Wilson: Life and Letters.* Vols. 5 and 6. New York: Doubleday, Doran, 1935.

Balfour, Michael. *The Kaiser and His Times.* Boston: Houghton Mifflin, 1964.

Banks, Arthur. *A Military Atlas of the First World War.* Barnsley, South Yorkshire: Leo Cooper, 1997.

Barker, Dudley. *Prominent Edwardians.* New York: Atheneum, 1969.

Barnett, Correlli. *The Sword Bearers.* New York: William Morrow, 1964.

Bassett, Ronald. *Battle Cruisers: A History, 1908–1948.* London: Macmillan, 1981.

Bauer, Hermann. *Als Führer der U-Boot im Weltkrieg.* Leipzig: Koehler & Amelang, 1943.

Bayly, Admiral Sir Lewis. *"Pull Together!"* London: Harrap & Co., 1939.

Bean, C.E.W. *Official History of Australia in the War of 1914–18: The Story of Anzac.* 2 vols. Sydney: Angus & Robinson, 1921, 1934.

Beatty, Charles. *Our Admiral.* London: W. H. Allen, 1980.

Beatty, David. *The Beatty Papers.* 2 vols. B. McL. Ranft, ed. Navy Records Society, 1989–1993.

Beaverbrook, Lord. *Politicians and the War, 1914–1916.* London: Collins, 1960.

Beesly, Patrick. *Very Special Admiral: The Life of Admiral J. H. Godfrey.* London: Hamish Hamilton, 1980.

———. *Room 40: British Naval Intelligence, 1914–1918.* London: Hamish Hamilton, 1982.

Bell, A. C. *A History of the Blockade of Germany, 1914–1918.* London: Her Majesty's Stationery Office, 1961.

Bellairs, Commander Carlyon. *The Battle of Jutland: The Sowing and the Reaping.* London: Hodder and Stoughton, 1920.

Bennett, Geoffrey. *Coronel and the Falklands.* London, Pan Books, 1962.

———. *The Battle of Jutland.* London: B. T. Batsford, 1964.

———. *Naval Battles of the First World War.* London: Batsford, 1968.

Berghahn, V. R. *Germany and the Approach of War in 1914.* New York: St. Martin's Press, 1973.

Bernstorff, Count Johann. *My Three Years in America.* London: Skeffington and Son, n.d. (German original pub. 1920).

Bethmann-Hollweg, Theobald. *Reflections on the World War.* London: Butterworth, 1920.

Bingham, Barry. *Falklands, Jutland, and the Bight.* London: John Murray, 1919.

Birnbaum, Karl E. *Peace Moves and U-boat Warfare.* Archon Books, 1970.

Blücher, Princess Evelyn. *An English Wife in Berlin.* New York: E. P. Dutton, 1920.

Bonham Carter, Violet. *Winston Churchill: An Intimate Portrait.* New York: Harcourt, Brace, 1965.

Breyer, Siegfried. *Battleships and Battle Cruisers, 1905–1970.* New York: Doubleday, 1973.

Brough, James. *The Prince and the Lily.* New York: Coward-McCann, 1975.

Brown, Malcolm. *The Imperial War Museum Book of the First World War.* Norman, Okla.: University of Oklahoma Press, 1993.

Brown, Malcolm, and Patricia Meehan. *Scapa Flow.* London: Penguin, 1968.

Bülow, Prince Bernhard von. *Memoirs.* 4 vols. Boston: Little, Brown, 1932.

Burt, R. A. *British Battleships of World War I.* Annapolis: Naval Institute Press, 1986.

Buttlar Brandenfels, Treusch von. *Zeppelins over England.* New York: Harcourt Brace, 1932.

Bywater, Hector C., and H. C. Ferraby. *Strange Intelligence: Memoirs of the Naval Secret Service.* London: Constable, 1931.

Campbell, Rear Admiral Gordon. *My Mystery Ships.* New York: Doubleday, 1929.

Campbell, N.J.M. *Jutland: An Analysis of the Fighting.* Annapolis: Naval Institute Press, 1986.

Carnegie Endowment for International Peace. *Official German Documents Relating to the World War.* 2 vols. Oxford University Press, 1923.

Cecil, Algernon. *British Foreign Secretaries, 1807–1916.* London: G. Bell, 1927.

Cecil, Lamar. *Wilhelm II.* 2 vols. Chapel Hill: University of North Carolina Press, 1996.

Chalmers, Rear Admiral W. S. *The Life and Letters of David Earl Beatty.* London: Hodder and Stoughton, 1951.

Chamberlain, Austen. *Down the Years.* London: Cassell, 1935.

Chatfield, Lord Ernle. *The Navy and Defence: An Autobiography.* London: William Heinemann, 1942.

Chatterton, E. Keble. *Q-ships and Their Story.* London: Sidgwick & Jackson, 1922.

———. *The Big Blockade.* London: Hurst & Blackett, 1932.

———. *Gallant Gentlemen.* London: Hurst & Blackett, 1931.

———. *Dardanelles Dilemma.* London: Rich & Cowan, 1935.

Chickering, Roger. *Imperial Germany and the Great War, 1914–1918.* Cambridge, Eng.: Cambridge University Press, 1998.

Churchill, Randolph S. *Winston S. Churchill.* Volume II: *Young Statesman, 1901–1914.* Boston: Houghton Mifflin, 1967.

Churchill, Winston S. *The World Crisis.* 4 vols. London: Thornton Butterworth, Ltd., 1923–1927.

———. *Great Contemporaries.* New York: Putnam, 1937.

———. *My Early Life.* London: Odmans Press, 1958.

Compton-Hall, Richard. *Submarines and the War at Sea, 1914–1918.* London: Macmillan, 1991.

Copplestone, Bennett. *The Silent Watchers.* New York: Dutton, 1918.

Corbett, Sir Julian S., and Henry Newbolt. *History of the Great War: Naval Operations.* 5 vols. London: Longmans, Green, 1928.

Costello, John, and Terry Hughes. *Jutland 1916.* London: Weidenfeld & Nicholson, 1976.

Cousins, Geoffrey. *The Story of Scapa Flow.* London: Frederick Muller, 1965.

Cowles, Virginia. *The Kaiser.* New York: Harper & Row, 1963.

Cunningham, Admiral of the Fleet Viscount. *A Sailor's Odyssey.* London: Hutchinson, 1951.

Curtain, D. Thomas. *The Land of Deepening Shadow.* New York: Doran, 1917.

Davies, Richard Bell. *Sailor in the Air.* London: Peter Davies, 1967.

Davis, Arthur N. *The Kaiser as I Knew Him.* New York: Harper and Brothers, 1918.

Dawson, Lionel. *Flotillas: A Hard-Lying Story.* London: Rich & Cowan, 1933.

———. *Sound of the Guns: Sir Walter Cowan.* Oxford, Eng.: Pen-in-Hand, 1949.

Denham, H. M. *Dardanelles: A Midshipman's Diary.* London: John Murray, 1981.

Dewar, Vice Admiral K.G.B. *The Navy from Within.* London: Gollancz, 1939.

Diary of H.M.S. Queen Elizabeth: January to May 1915. Printed by permission of the Admiralty, 1919. No further publication information given.

Dixon, T. B. *The Enemy Fought Splendidly.* Poole, Dorset: Blandford Press, 1983.

Doenitz, Grand Admiral Karl. *Memoirs: Ten Years and Twenty Days.* Annapolis: U.S. Naval Institute Press, 1959.

Domelier, Henri. *Behind the Scenes at German Headquarters.* London: Hurst and Blackett, 1919.

Dos Passos, John. *Mr. Wilson's War.* New York: Doubleday, 1962.

Dreyer, Admiral Sir Frederic. *The Sea Heritage.* London, Museum Press, 1955.

Dugdale, Blanche E. C. *Arthur James Balfour, 1906–1930.* London: Hutchinson, 1939.

Eckardstein, Baron Hermann von. *Ten Years at the Court of St. James, 1895–1905.* London: Butterworth, 1921.

Edwards, Bernard. *Salvo!: Classic Naval Gun Actions.* London: Arms and Armour, 1995.

Farwell, Byron. *Over There: The United States in the Great War.* New York: Norton, 1999.

Fawcett, H. W., and G.W.W. Hooper. *The Fighting at Jutland: The Personal Experiences of Forty-five Officers and Men of the British Fleet.* London: Macmillan, 1921.

Fayle, C. Ernest. *Seaborne Trade.* 3 vols. London: John Murray, 1920–1923.

Feldman, Gerald D. *Army, Industry and Labor in Germany, 1914–1918.* Princeton, N.J.: Princeton University Press, 1966.

Feuer, A. B. *The U.S. Navy in World War I.* London: Praeger, 1999.

Fischer, Fritz. *Germany's Aims in the First World War.* New York: Norton, 1967.

Fisher, John Arbuthnot. *Memories and Records.* 2 vols. New York: Doran, 1920.

———. *Fear God and Dread Nought: The Correspondence of Admiral of the Fleet Lord Fisher of Kilverstone.* Arthur Marder, ed. 3 vols. London: Cape, 1952–59.

Freiwald, Ludwig. *Last Days of the German Fleet.* London: Constable, 1932.

Frost, Holloway H. *The Battle of Jutland.* Annapolis: U.S. Naval Institute Press, 1936.

Frost, Wesley. *German Submarine Warfare.* London and New York: Appleton, 1918.

Geiss, Imanuel. *July 1914: The Outbreak of the First World War: Selected Documents.* New York: Norton, 1974.

Gerard, James W. *My Four Years in Germany.* New York: Doran, 1917.

———. *Face to Face with Kaiserism.* London: Hodder & Stoughton, 1918.

Gibson, Langhorne, and Vice Admiral J.E.T. Harper. *The Riddle of Jutland.* New York: Coward-McCann, 1934.

Gibson, R. H., and Maurice Prendergast. *The German Submarine War, 1914–1918.* London: Constable, 1931.

Gies, Joseph. *Crisis 1918.* New York: Norton, 1974.

Gilbert, Martin. *Winston S. Churchill: The Challenge of War, 1914–1916.* 2 vols. Boston: Houghton Mifflin, 1971.

Gill, C. C. *Naval Power in the War, 1914–1918.* New York: Doran, 1919.

Goldrick, James. *The King's Ships Were at Sea.* Annapolis: Naval Institute Press, 1984.

———. "John Jellicoe: Technology's Victim." In *The Great Admirals.* Jack Sweetman, ed. Annapolis: Naval Institute Press, 1997.

Gooch, G. P. *Recent Revelations of European Diplomacy.* London: Longmans, Green, 1928.

Goodchild, George. *The Last Cruise of the Majestic.* London: Simpkin, Marshall, 1917.

Goodenough, Admiral Sir William. *A Rough Record.* London and New York: Hutchinson, 1943.

Goodspeed, D. J. *Ludendorff.* Boston: Houghton Mifflin, 1966.

Gordon, Andrew. *The Rules of the Game: Jutland and British Naval Command.* Annapolis: Naval Institute Press, 1996.

Görlitz, Walter, ed. *The Kaiser and His Court: The Diaries, Notebooks and Letters of Admiral Georg von Müller.* New York: Harcourt, Brace, 1964.

Grant, Robert M. *U-boats Destroyed.* London: Putnam, 1964.

———. *U-boat Intelligence, 1914–1918.* Hamden, Conn.: Archon Books, 1969.

Gretton, Vice Admiral Sir Peter. *Winston Churchill and the Royal Navy.* New York: Coward-McCann, 1968.

Grey of Fallodon (Viscount Edward Grey). *Twenty-five Years, 1892–1916.* 2 vols. New York: Frederick A. Stokes, 1925.

Groner, Erich. *German Warships, 1815–1945.* Vol. 1: *Major Surface Vessels.* Vol. 2: *U-boats and Mine Warfare Vessels.* London: Conway Maritime Press, 1990.

Groos, Captain Otto, and Admiral Walther Gladisch. *Der Krieg in der Nordsee.* 7 vols. Berlin: Ernst Mittler und Sohn, 1920–65.

Guichard, Louis. *The Naval Blockade, 1914–1918.* London: Philip Allen, 1930.

Haldane, Richard Burdon. *An Autobiography.* New York: Doubleday, Doran, 1929.

Halpern, Paul G. *The Naval War in the Mediterranean, 1914–1918.* Annapolis: Naval Institute Press, 1987.

———. *A Naval History of the First World War.* Annapolis: Naval Institute Press, 1994.

Hamilton, General Sir Ian. *Gallipoli Diary.* 2 vols. New York: Doran, 1920.

Hankey, Maurice. *The Supreme Command, 1914–1918.* 2 vols. London: Allen & Unwin, 1961.

Hanssen, Hans Peter. *Diary of a Dying Empire.* Bloomington: Indiana University Press, 1955.

Harper, Rear Admiral J.E.T. *The Truth About Jutland.* London: John Murray, 1927.

Harries, Meirion, and Susie Harries. *The Last Days of Innocence: America at War, 1917–1918.* New York: Random House, 1997.

Hase, Commander Georg von. *Kiel and Jutland.* London: Skeffington, 1921.

Haythornthwaite, Philip J. *Gallipoli, 1915.* London: Osprey, 1991.

Hayward, Victor. *H.M.S. Tiger at Bay.* London: William Kimber, 1977.

Heckscher, August. *Woodrow Wilson: A Biography.* New York: Scribners, 1991.

Hendrick, Burton J. *The Life and Letters of Walter H. Page.* 3 vols. New York: Doubleday, Page, 1922.

Herwig, Holgar H. *The German Naval Officer Corps.* Oxford, Eng.: Clarendon Press, 1973.

———. *Politics of Frustration: The United States in German Naval Planning, 1889–1914.* Boston: Little, Brown, 1976.

———. *Luxury Fleet: The Imperial German Navy, 1888–1918.* London: Allen & Unwin, 1980.

———. *The First World War: Germany and Austria-Hungary, 1914–1918.* New York: Arnold, 1997.

Herwig, Holgar H., and David F. Trask. "Naval Operations Plans Between Germany and the USA, 1898–1913." In *The War Plans of the Great Powers, 1880–1914.* Paul Kennedy, ed. London: Allen & Unwin, 1979.

Hewison, W. S. *This Great Harbor: Scapa Flow.* Kirkwall, Scotland: Orkney Press, 1990.

Hickling, Vice Admiral Harold. *Sailor at Sea.* London: William Kimber, 1965.

Higgins, Trumbull. *Winston Churchill and the Dardanelles.* New York: Macmillan, 1963.

Hilditch, A. Neville. *Coronel and the Falkland Islands.* London and New York: Oxford University Press, 1915.

Hindenburg, Paul von. *Out of My Life.* London and New York: Cassell, 1921.

Hirst, Lloyd. *Coronel and After.* London: Peter Davies, 1934.

Hoehling, A. A. *The Great War at Sea.* New York: Galahad Books, 1965.

Hohenzollern-Emden, Franz Joseph. *Emden: The Last Cruise of the Chivalrous Raider.* Brighton: Lion Press, 1989.

Horn, Daniel. *The German Naval Mutinies of World War I.* New Brunswick, N.J.: Rutgers University Press, 1969.

———. *The Private War of Seaman Stumpf: The Unique Diaries of a Young German in the Great War.* London: Leslie Frewin, 1969.

Hough, Richard. *The Great Dreadnought: The Strange Story of H.M.S. Agincourt.* New York: Harper & Row, 1966.

———. *First Sea Lord: Admiral Lord Fisher.* London: Allen & Unwin, 1969.

———. *The Pursuit of Admiral von Spee.* London: Allen & Unwin, 1969.
———. *Louis and Victoria: The Family History of the Mountbattens.* London: Weidenfeld & Nicholson, 1974.
———. *The Great War at Sea, 1914–1918.* New York: Oxford University Press, 1983.
Howard, Michael. *The First World War.* New York: Oxford University Press, 2002.
Hubatsch, Walther. *Die Ära Tirpitz: Studien zur Deutschen Marinepolitik 1890–1918.* Göttingen, West Germany: Musterschmidt Verlag, 1955.
Hull, Isabel. *The Entourage of Kaiser Wilhelm II, 1888–1918.* Cambridge, Eng.: Cambridge University Press, 1982.
Hunter, Francis T. *Beatty, Jellicoe, Sims and Rodman.* New York: Doubleday, Page, 1919.
Hurd, Archibald, and Henry Castle. *German Sea Power: Its Rise, Progress and Economic Basis.* New York: Scribners, 1913.
Irving, John. *Coronel and the Falklands.* London: Philpot, 1927.
———. *The Smoke Screen of Jutland.* London: William Kimber, 1966.
James, Robert Rhodes. *Gallipoli.* New York: Macmillan, 1965.
———. *Churchill: A Study in Failure.* New York: World, 1970.
James, Admiral Sir William. *A Great Seaman: The Life of Admiral of the Fleet Sir Henry Oliver.* London: H. F. & G. Witherby, 1956.
Jameson, Rear Admiral Sir William. *The Fleet That Jack Built: Nine Men Who Made a Modern Navy.* New York: Harcourt, Brace, 1962.
Jane's Fighting Ships, 1914. New York: Arco, 1969.
Jane's Fighting Ships of World War I. London: Random House, 1990.
Jarausch, Konrad H. *The Enigmatic Chancellor: Bethmann-Hollweg and the Hubris of Imperial Germany.* New Haven: Yale University Press, 1973.
Jellicoe, Admiral Viscount John. *The Grand Fleet, 1914–1916.* London: Cassell, 1919.
———. *The Crisis of the Naval War.* London: Cassell, 1920.
———. *The Submarine Peril.* London: Cassell, 1934.
———. *The Jellicoe Papers.* A. Temple Patterson, ed. 2 vols. Navy Records Society, 1966.
Jenkins, Roy. *Asquith.* New York: Chilmark Press, 1964.
———. *Churchill: A Biography.* New York: Farrar, Straus & Giroux, 2001.
Jensen, Jurgen. *Kiel im Kaiserreich 1871–1918.* Karl Wachholtz Verlag, 1978.
Jones, Jerry W. *U.S. Battleship Operations in World War I.* Annapolis: Naval Institute Press, 1998.
Jose, Arthur W. *Official History of Australia in the War.* Vol. IX, *The Royal Australian Navy.* Sydney: Angus & Robinson, 1928.
Kahn, David. *The Codebreakers.* New York: Macmillan, 1967.
———. *Seizing the Enigma.* Boston: Houghton Mifflin, 1991.
Kannengiesser, Hans. *The Campaign in Gallipoli.* London: Hutchinson, 1927.
Keegan, John. *The Price of Admiralty.* New York: Viking, 1989.
———. *The First World War.* New York: Knopf, 1999.
Kemp, Paul. *U-boats Destroyed.* Annapolis: Naval Institute Press, 1997.
Kennedy, Paul. *The Rise and Fall of British Naval Mastery.* Malabar, Fla.: Robert E. Krieger, 1982.
———. *The Rise of the Anglo-German Antagonism.* London: Allen & Unwin, 1982.
———. *Strategy and Diplomacy, 1870–1945.* London: Fontana, 1984.
Kerr, Admiral Mark. *Prince Louis of Battenberg.* New York: Longmans, Green, 1934.
Keyes, Sir Roger. *Naval Memoirs.* 2 vols. London: Thornton Butterworth, 1934.
———. *The Fight for Gallipoli.* London: Eyre & Spottiswoode, 1941.
———. *Keyes Papers.* Paul G. Halpern, ed. Navy Records Society, 1979.
King-Hall, Stephen. *A North Sea Diary, 1914–1918.* London: Newnes, 1936.
———. *My Naval Life.* London: Faber & Faber, 1952.
Klachko, Mary, and David Trask. *Admiral William Shepherd Bennett, First Chief of Naval Operations.* Annapolis: Naval Institute Press, 1987.
Knight, E. F. *The Harwich Naval Forces.* London and New York: Hodder and Stoughton, 1919.
Knock, Thomas J. *To End All Wars.* New York: Oxford University Press, 1992.

Koop, Gerhard, and Erich Mulitze. *Die Marine in Wilhelmshaven.* Koblenz: Bernard & Graefe Verlag, 1987.

Kopp, Georg. *Two Lone Ships.* London: Hutchinson, 1931.

Kürenberg, Joachim von. *The Kaiser.* New York: Simon & Schuster, 1955.

Lansing, Robert. *War Memoirs.* New York: Bobbs-Merrill, 1935.

Layman, R. D. *The Cuxhaven Raid.* London: Conway Maritime Press, 1985.

———. *Naval Aviation in the First World War.* Annapolis: Naval Institute Press, 1996.

Lee, Sir Sydney. *King Edward VII: A Biography.* 2 vols. London: Macmillan, 1927.

Legg, Stuart. *Jutland.* New York: John Day, 1966.

Leslie, Shane. *Long Shadows.* London: John Murray, 1966.

Liddell Hart, B. H. *The War in Outline, 1914–1918.* London: Faber & Faber, 1936.

———. *Through the Fog of War.* London: Faber & Faber, 1938.

Lloyd George, David. *War Memoirs.* 5 vols. Boston: Little, Brown, 1933.

Lloyd George, Richard. *Lloyd George, My Father.* New York: Crown, 1961.

London, Charles. *Jutland 1916.* Oxford, Eng.: Osprey Publishing, 2000.

Lorey, Rear Admiral Hermann. *Der Krieg in den türkischen Gewässern.* 2 vols. Berlin: Ernst Mittler und Sohn, 1928–1938.

Ludendorff, General Erich. *My War Memories.* 2 vols. London: Hutchinson, 1919.

———. *The General Staff and Its Problems: The History of the Relations Between the High Command and the German Imperial Government.* Vol. 1. London: Hutchinson, 1920.

Macintyre, Captain Donald. *Jutland.* London: Evans Brothers, 1957.

Mackay, Ruddock. *Fisher of Kilverstone.* Oxford, Eng.: Clarendon Press, 1973.

Magnus, Philip. *Kitchener: Portrait of an Imperialist.* London: John Murray, 1958.

Mahan, Alfred T. *The Influence of Sea Power upon History.* London: Sampson, Low, Marston, 1890.

———. *On Naval Warfare: Selected Writings.* Boston: Little, Brown, 1942.

Manchester, William. *The Last Lion: Winston Spencer Churchill.* Vol. 1. Boston: Little, Brown, 1983.

Mansergh, Nicholas. *The Coming of the First World War.* London: Longmans, Green, 1949.

Marder, Arthur J. *From the Dreadnought to Scapa Flow.* 5 vols. London: Oxford University Press, 1961–1970.

———. *The Anatomy of British Sea Power.* New York: Octagon Books, 1976.

Marshall, S.L.A. *World War I.* Boston: Houghton Mifflin, 1987.

Masefield, John. *Gallipoli.* New York: Macmillan, 1917.

Max of Baden, *Memoirs.* 2 vols. New York: Scribners, 1928.

McCormick, Donald. *The Mystery of Lord Kitchener's Death.* London: Putnam, 1959.

McLaughlin, Redmond. *The Escape of the Goeben.* New York: Scribners, 1974.

Messimer, Dwight R. *Find and Destroy: Antisubmarine Warfare in World War I.* Annapolis: Naval Institute Press, 2001.

Miller, Frederick. *Under German Shellfire: The Hartlepools, Scarborough and Whitby.* West Hartlepool: Robert Martin, 1915.

Milne, Admiral Sir A. Berkeley. *The Flight of the Goeben and the Breslau.* London: Everleigh Nash, 1921.

Morgan, Ted. *Churchill: Young Man in a Hurry, 1874–1915.* New York: Simon & Schuster, 1982.

Morgenthau, Henry. *Ambassador Morgenthau's Story.* New York: Doubleday, 1919.

Moorehead, Alan. *Gallipoli.* New York: Ballantine Books, 1996.

Morris, Joseph. *The German Air Raids on Great Britain, 1914–1918.* London: Sampson Low, Marston & Co., n.d.

Moyer, Laurence V. *Victory Must Be Ours: Germany in the Great War, 1914–1918.* New York: Hippocrene, 1995.

Muir, Surgeon Rear Admiral John R. *Years of Endurance.* London: Philip Allan, 1936.

Murfett, Malcolm H. *The First Sea Lords: From Fisher to Mountbatten.* Westport, Conn.: Praeger, 1995.

Newton, Lord. *Lord Lansdowne: A Biography.* London: Macmillan, 1929.

Nichols, J. Alden. *Germany After Bismarck.* Cambridge, Mass.: Harvard University Press, 1958.

Nicolson, Harold. *King George V: His Life and Reign.* London: Constable, 1952.

Oakeshott, Ewart. *The Blindfold Game: "The Day" at Jutland.* London and New York: Pergamon Press, 1969.

Official Naval Despatches: The Admiralty's Reports, August–December 1914. Dewsbury, Eng.: Fernmoor Publications, n.d.

Padfield, Peter. *Aim Straight: A Biography of Sir Percy Scott.* London: Hodder and Stoughton, 1966.

———. *The Battleship Era.* London: Rupert Hart-Davis, 1972.

———. *The Great Naval Race: Anglo-German Naval Rivalry, 1900–1914.* New York: David McKay, 1974.

Parkes, Dr. Oscar. *British Battleships.* London: Seeley Service, 1973.

Parmelee, Maurice. *Blockade and Sea Power.* London: Hutchinson, 1924.

Paschall, Rod. *The Defeat of Imperial Germany.* Chapel Hill, N.C.: Algonquin Books, 1989.

Patterson, A. Temple. *Jellicoe: A Biography.* London: Macmillan, 1969.

———. *Tyrwhitt of the Harwich Force.* London: MacDonald, 1973.

Pelly, Admiral Sir Henry. *300,000 Sea Miles: An Autobiography.* London: Chatto & Windus, 1938.

Penn, Geoffrey. *Fisher, Churchill and the Dardanelles.* Barnsley, S. Yorkshire: Pen & Sword Books, 1999.

Perrett, Bryan. *A Sense of Style: The Grand Hotel, Scarborough.* Merseyside: Mitchell and Wright, 1991.

Phillbin, Tobias R. *Admiral von Hipper: The Inconvenient Hero.* Amsterdam: B. R. Gruner, 1982.

Pitt, Barrie. *Zeebrugge.* London: Cassell, 1958.

———. *Coronel and Falkland.* London: Cassell, 1960.

Pless, Princess Daisy of. *Princess Daisy of Pless.* New York: Dutton, 1929.

Pochhammer, Captain Hans. *Before Jutland: Admiral von Spee's Last Voyage.* London: Jarrolds, 1931.

Pollen, Anthony. *The Great Gunnery Scandal: The Mystery of Jutland.* London: Collins, 1980.

Pollen, Arthur H. *The Navy in Battle.* London: Chatto & Windus, 1919.

———. *The Pollen Papers.* Jon Tetsuro Sumida, ed. Navy Records Society, 1984.

Pope, Dudley. *The Battle of the River Plate.* Annapolis: Naval Institute Press, 1956.

Preston, Diana. *Lusitania: An Epic Tragedy.* New York: Walker, 2002.

Puleston, W. D. *Mahan: The Life and Work.* New Haven: Yale University Press, 1939.

Raeder, Erich. *My Life.* Annapolis: Naval Institute Press, 1960.

Raeder, Erich, and Eberhard von Mantey. *Der Kreuzerkrieg in den ausländischen Gewässern.* 3 vols. Berlin: Ernst Mittler und Sohn, 1922–1937.

Raleigh, Walter. *The War in the Air.* Vol. 1. Oxford, Eng.: Clarendon Press, 1922.

Reischach, Hugo von. *Under Three Emperors.* London: Constable, 1927.

Repington, Lt. Col. C. *The First World War.* 2 vols. Boston: Houghton Mifflin, 1920.

Reuter, Vice Admiral Ludwig von. *Scapa Flow: An Account of the Scuttling.* London: Hurst and Blackett, 1940.

Ritter, Gerhard. *The Sword and the Scepter: The Problem of Militarism in Germany.* 4 vols. Coral Gables: University of Miami Press, 1972.

Roberts, J. M. *A History of Europe.* New York: Penguin, 1997.

Rodger, N.A.M., ed. *The Naval Miscellany.* Vol. 5. Navy Records Society, 1984.

Rodham, Rear Admiral Hugh. *Yarns of a Kentucky Admiral.* Indianapolis: Bobbs-Merrill, 1928.

Rohl, John C. G., and Nicolaus Sombert. *Kaiser Wilhelm II: New Interpretations.* Cambridge, Eng.: Cambridge University Press, 1982.

Rose, Kenneth. *King George V.* London: Macmillan, 1983.

Roskill, Captain S. W. *Hankey: Man of Secrets.* Vol. 1. London: Collins, 1970.

———. *Churchill and the Admirals.* London: Collins, 1977.

———. *Earl Beatty: The Last Naval Hero.* New York: Atheneum, 1981.

———, ed. *Documents Relating to the Naval Air Service.* Vol. 1, 1908–1918. Navy Records Society, 1969.

Ruge, Vice Admiral Friedrich. *Scapa Flow 1919: The End of the German Fleet.* London: Ian Allen, 1973.

Sanders, Otto Liman von. *Five Years in Turkey.* Annapolis: Naval Institute Press, 1927.

Scheer, Admiral Reinhard. *Germany's High Sea Fleet in the World War.* New York: Peter Smith, 1934.

Schofield, Vice Admiral Brian. "Jacky Fisher, HMS *Indomitable* and the Dogger Bank Action: A Personal Memoir." In *Naval Warfare in the Twentieth Century.* Gerald J. Jordan, ed. London: Croom Helm, 1977.

Schoultz, Commodore Georg von. *With the British Battle Fleet: War Recollections of a Russian Naval Officer.* London: Hutchinson, 1925.

Schubert, Paul, and Langhorne Gibson. *Death of a Fleet, 1917–1919.* New York: Coward, McCann, 1933.

Scott, Admiral Sir Percy. *Fifty Years in the Royal Navy.* New York: Doran, 1919.

Seymour, Charles. *The Intimate Papers of Colonel House.* Boston: Houghton Mifflin, 1926.

———. *American Neutrality, 1914–1917.* New Haven: Yale University Press, 1935.

Seymour, Lady. *Commander Ralph Seymour, R.N.* Glasgow: Printed for private circulation by Robert MacLehose and Company Ltd. at The University Press, 1926.

Sidman, Charles F. *The German Collapse in 1918.* Lawrence, Kan.: Coronado Press, 1972.

Simpson, Colin. *The Lusitania.* Boston: Little, Brown, 1972.

Sims, Rear Admiral William S. *The Victory at Sea.* New York: Doubleday, Page, 1920.

Smith, Gene. *When the Cheering Stopped: The Last Years of Woodrow Wilson.* New York: Morrow, 1964.

Smith, Peter. *Hard-Lying: The Birth of the Destroyer.* London: William Kimber, 1971.

Smith, Stephen John. *The Samoa Expeditionary Force, 1914–1915.* Wellington, N.Z.: Ferguson & Osborn, 1924.

Spector, Ronald H. *At War at Sea: Sailors and Naval Combat in the Twentieth Century.* New York: Viking, 2001.

Spencer-Cooper, H. *The Battle of the Falkland Islands.* London: Cassell, 1919.

Spender, J. A. *Fifty Years of Europe: A Study in Pre-War Documents.* London: Cassell, 1925.

Spindler, Rear Admiral Arno. *Der Handelskrieg mit U-Booten.* 5 vols. Berlin: Ernst Mittler und Sohn, 1932–66.

Spring-Rice, Sir Cecil. *Letters and Friendships.* 2 vols. Boston: Houghton Mifflin, 1929.

Strachan, Hew, ed. *World War I: A History.* New York: Oxford University Press, 1998.

Sumida, Jon Tetsuro. *In Defence of Naval Supremacy.* Boston: Unwin Hyman, 1989.

———. "A Matter of Timing: The Royal Navy and the Tactics of Decisive Battle, 1912–1915," in *The Journal of Military History,* vol. 67, no. 1 (January 2003).

Sweetman, Jack. "Coronel: Anatomy of a Disaster." In *Naval Warfare in the Twentieth Century, 1900–1945.* Gerald Jordan, ed. London: Croom Helm, 1977.

Sydenham of Combe, et al. *The World Crisis by Winston Churchill: A Criticism.* London: Kennikat Press, 1927.

"Taffrail" (Captain Taprell Dorling). *Endless Story.* London: Hodder & Stoughton, 1931.

Tarrant, V. E. *Battlecruiser Invincible.* Annapolis: Naval Institute Press, 1986.

———. *The U-boat Offensive, 1914–1945.* Annapolis: Naval Institute Press, 1989.

———. *Battleship Warspite.* Annapolis: Naval Institute Press, 1990.

———. *Jutland: The German Perspective.* Annapolis: Naval Institute Press, 1995.

Taylor, J. C. *German Warships of World War I.* London: Ian Allen, 1969.

Terraine, John. *The U-boat Wars, 1916–1945.* New York: Putnam, 1989.

Thomas, Lowell. *Raiders of the Deep.* London: Heinemann, 1929.

Tirpitz, Grand Admiral Alfred von. *My Memoirs.* 2 vols. New York: Dodd, Mead, 1919.

Topham, Anne. *Memories of the Kaiser's Court.* London: Methuen, 1914.

Trask, David F. *Captains and Cabinets.* Columbia, Mo.: University of Missouri Press, 1972.

Tree, Ronald. *When the Moon Was High.* London: Macmillan, 1975.

Tuchman, Barbara W. *The Zimmermann Telegram.* New York: Viking, 1958.

———. *The Guns of August.* New York: Macmillan, 1962.

———. *Practicing History.* New York: Knopf, 1981.

Tumulty, Joseph P. *Woodrow Wilson as I Know Him.* Garden City, N.Y.: Doubleday, Page, 1921.

Usborne, Vice Admiral C. V. *Smoke on the Horizon: Mediterranean Fighting, 1914–1918.* London: Hodder & Stoughton, 1933.

———. *Blast and Counterblast: A Naval Impression of the War.* London: John Murray, 1935.

Van Der Vat, Dan. *The Grand Scuttle.* Annapolis: Naval Institute Press, 1986.

———. *The Ship That Changed the World.* Bethesda: Adler & Adler, 1986.

Vandiver, Frank E. *Black Jack: The Life and Times of John J. Pershing.* 2 vols. College Station, Tex.: Texas A & M University Press, 1977.

Verner, Rudolf. *The Battle Cruisers at the Action of the Falklands.* London: John Bale Sons & Danielson, 1920.

Vincent, C. Paul. *The Politics of Hunger: The Allied Blockade of Germany, 1915–1919.* Athens, Ohio: Ohio University Press, 1985.

Waldeyer-Hartz, Captain Hugo von. *Admiral von Hipper.* London: Rich & Cowan, 1933.

Ward, J. M. *Dawn Raid: The Bombardment of the Hartlepools, December 16, 1914.* Hartlepool: Atkinson Print, 1989.

Wegner, Vice Admiral Wolfgang. *The Naval Strategy of the World War.* London: Rich & Cowan, 1933.

Weizsäcker, Ernst von. *Memoirs.* Chicago: Regnery, 1951.

Wemyss, Lady. *The Life and Letters of Lord Wester Wemyss.* London: Eyre & Spottiswoode, 1935.

Wemyss, Lord Rosslyn Wester. *The Navy in the Dardanelles Campaign.* London: Hodder & Stoughton, 1924.

Wheeler-Bennett, John W. *King George VI: His Life and Reign.* New York: St. Martin's Press, 1958.

Weir, Gary. "Reinhard Scheer: Intuition Under Fire." In *The Great Admirals.* Jack Sweetman, ed. Annapolis: Naval Institute Press, 1997.

"The Widow of an American Diplomat." In *Intimacies of Court and Society.* New York: Dodd, Mead, 1912.

Wile, Frederick W. *Men Around the Kaiser.* Indianapolis: Bobbs-Merrill, 1914.

William II. *My Memoirs, 1878–1918.* London: Cassell, 1922.

Williams, John. *The Other Battleground. The Home Fronts: Britain, France and Germany, 1914–1918.* Chicago: Regnery, 1972.

Wilson, Edith Bolling. *My Memoir.* Indianapolis: Bobbs-Merrill, 1938.

Winton, John. *Jellicoe.* London: Michael Joseph, 1981.

Woodward, David. *The Collapse of Power.* London: Arthur Barker, 1973.

Woodward, E. L. *Great Britain and the German Navy.* New York: Oxford University Press, 1935.

Yates, Keith. *Graf Spee's Raiders.* Annapolis: Naval Institute Press, 1995.

———. *Flawed Victory: Jutland, 1916.* Annapolis: Naval Institute Press, 2000.

Ybarra, Thomas R. *Hindenburg: The Man with Three Lives.* New York: Duffield and Green, 1932.

Young, Filson. *With the Battle Cruisers.* London: Cassell, 1921.

Zedlitz-Trutzschler, Count Robert von. *Twelve Years at the Imperial German Court.* New York: Doran, 1924.

Acknowledgments

Fifty years ago at Oxford, reading and writing tutorial essays about European diplomacy in the period 1871–1914, I first had a sense of the implacable chain of events that moved like a Greek tragedy toward the ultimate catastrophe of the Great War. All the nations involved, I learned, were motivated by the desire to achieve national security—either in hegemony, in alliance systems, or by accumulating weapons, or in combinations of these. The particular competition that most interested me was the Anglo-German dreadnought-building race, in which, for many years, two racially kindred and economically linked European states devoted staggering portions of their national wealth to building battleships—then the ultimate embodiment of sea power. The result, of course, was the opposite of that intended. Rather than achieving security, Britain believed herself ever-increasingly threatened; rather than earning England's respect and partnership, Germany's construction of a massive fleet propelled Great Britain into near alliances with Germany's enemies, France and Russia. In 1914, the search for security led to war.

Years later, in the 1970s, with both the United States and the Soviet Union seeking security by acquiring tens of thousands of nuclear weapons, each state holding over the other the threat of M.A.D.—Mutually Assured Destruction—I thought often of the earlier arms race between Britain and Germany. This parallel provided the genesis of my book *Dreadnought: Great Britain, Germany, and the Coming of the Great War.* Originally, I had intended *Dreadnought* to include the war itself, but that book carried the story only up to the night Britain and Germany went to war. It is at this point that *Castles of Steel* begins.

This personal history will explain why I first want to thank Christopher Seton-Watson, my tutor at Oriel College, Oxford, who introduced me to the drama as well as the details of great power diplomacy in the years before the Great War. The hours spent with him led me into the world described in these two books. Five of my friends at Oxford, the late Charles Till Davis, Edmund and Mary Keeley, Michael McGuiness, and Michael Jaffrey, have always known of this interest and have never stinted in their comradeship and support.

My oldest friend, my brother, Kim Massie, and my equally dear friend Jack May have kept me going though the years. Sometimes, in writing, when I reach a stone wall, a phone call to one of them, or to Lorna Massie or Lynn May, shows me the way. Hours of conversation about history and the law with these two men and with Gilbert Merritt, and the late Herbert Shayne, and Henry Walker, while walking the Cotswolds or traveling down the Mississippi, the Potomac, and the Florida Keys, have helped me sharpen my thinking.

For their friendship and constant support I thank James Marlas and Marie Nugent-Head, Tom and Annick Mesko, Peter and Masha Sarandinaki, Jeremy Nussbaum and Charline Spektor, Roger and Carolyn Horchow, Richard and Kris Hart, Jon and Stephanie Levi,

Janet Byrne and Ivan Solotaroff, Eve and Dennis Mykytyn, Leonard and Pamela Gallin Yablons, Charles and Deborah Flock, Warren and Jan Adelson, Jan and Carl Ramirez, Ingrid Roberg and John Clark, Jeff Seroy and Douglas Stumpf, William F. Buckley, Erica Jong and Kenneth Burrows, Theresa Boyd and Ruth Nisco. For performing what seems to me a medical miracle on behalf of one of my children I thank Dr. William E. Hellenbrand and Dr. Welton M. Gersony.

A number of writers, editors, agents, and artists have given me continuing encouragement and good advice. I think particularly of Art Spiegelman and Françoise Mouly, Robert and Aline Crumb, the late Joseph Heller, Thomas Pynchon and Melanie Jackson, Edmund and Sylvia Morris, Robert and Ina Caro, David Remnick and Esther B. Fein, Dan Franklin, Gillon Aitken, Eric Vigne, François Samuelson, Georgina Capel and Antony Cheetham, Peter Prescott, J. Robert Moskin, Matt Clark, Sidney and Avida Offit, and Helen Fisher.

Over the twenty-two years I have been working on these two books, many people have given me professional help. Robert Gottlieb, Robert Bernstein, and Katherine Hourigan were supportive when the project was coming to life. Along the way, Joni Evans, Harry Evans, Ann Godoff, and Gina Centrello have given me their enthusiastic support. David Stewardson and Carol Schwartz have assisted in making it possible for me to visit Scapa Flow, Scarborough and Hartlepool, Wilhelmshaven and Kiel, Malta, Istanbul and the Dardanelles, the Straits of Magellan, Valparaíso, the Falkland Islands, and Tsingtao.

I have worked in and drawn material from the Yale University libraries and am particularly grateful to Lorrie Klein of Sterling Memorial Library for helping me to spend many days in the stacks. Robin Lima helped me obtain books and transcripts from the U.S. Naval War College Library in Newport, Rhode Island. Pamela Bernstein and Pamela Strachan of the Irvington, New York, Public Library traced and borrowed books for me through the interlibrary loan system. I have also used the New York Public Library, the Public Record Office in London, the British Ministry of Defence Libraries, and the British Library Newspaper Library. I am grateful to the staffs of all these institutions for their efficient and cheerful help. Jack Faber, a remarkable private military book dealer, found many rare and useful volumes for me.

A manuscript passes through many experienced and expert hands on its way to becoming a book. Among those who have helped me are Benjamin Dreyer, Evan Camfield, Jolanta Benal, Dominique Troiano, Casey Reivich, James Lambert, Pei Loi Koay, Ann Weinerman, Erich Schoeneweiss, Tom Perry, and Sally Marvin. Overseeing everyone and everything in this process has been one of the great editors of our time, Robert Loomis. If there is something good to be said about a paragraph, a page, or a chapter, Bob will say it and leave the writer exuberant. If there is a misstep, a gentle nudge—backed, if necessary, by steel—moves the writer onto a firmer path. I think Bob cares as much about my books as I do.

Most important, my family has supported me with an enduring affection and patience. This includes Dolores Karl, whose professional skill saved me from dozens of actual or potential computer disasters, Fred Karl, Rebecca Karl, Judith Karl and John Ennis, Dotte Kaufman, and Patricia and Vincent Civale. My children, Christopher, Sophia, Nora, Bob, Elizabeth, and Susanna—some near, some far—have given me encouragement and love. Not only has Deborah Karl done this, but because she knows the English language better than I do, whenever she has touched the manuscript, it has improved.

Index

Page numbers in *italics* refer to maps.